LEGAL OFFICE PROCEDURES

SEVENTH EDITION

Tina Kamakaris, BA, BEd

Jane Kamakaris

Louis Kamakaris

Foreword by Gordon A. Ullman, BA, LLB

OWL PUBLISHING *o/b* TIKAM PUBLISHING INC.
Copyright © 2017 Owl Publishing.
63 Cheeseman Drive, Markham, Ontario L3R 3G3.

LEGAL OFFICE PROCEDURES, SEVENTH EDITION
by Tina Kamakaris, Jane Kamakaris, Louis Kamakaris.

Copyright © 2017 Owl Publishing o/b Tikam Publishing Inc.

Printed and bound in Canada.

Interior Design and Composition: Greg Devitt Design; Sharon Lucas Creative.

Library and Archives Canada Cataloguing in Publication

Kamakaris, Tina, author
        Legal office procedures / Tina Kamakaris, Jane
Kamakaris, Louis Kamakaris. -- Seventh edition.

Includes index.
ISBN: 978-1-896512-56-3

        1. Procedure (Law)--Ontario--Textbooks. I. Kamakaris, Jane,
author II. Kamakaris, Louis, author III. Title.

KEO167.K34 2017   347.713'05   C2017-904298-7
KF319.K34 2017

NOTE: The substantive law in this book provides the background, or the rationale, for the procedures which this book covers. This is, therefore, not a definitive book on law on any subject. For such matters, one should rely on statutes or on formal texts on law or on professional legal advice.

Also available:

Legal Office Procedures Workbook (interfacing files)
Legal Office Transcription (audio files; grammar)
Instructor support

Owl Publishing
 o/b Tikam Publishing Inc.
63 Cheeseman Drive
Markham, Ontario L3R 3G3

Visit us at: http://www.owlpublishing.ca

To Dimitra, for all the times you took me by the hand, and still do. I miss you, Mom.

Tina Kamakaris

To Michael, for your never-ending love, support, and commitment to family, and to Emmanuel and Ava, for filling our home with laughter and joy.

Jane Kamakaris

To my family, thank you for your love and support.

Louis Kamakaris

Table of Contents

Foreword xiii

Preface xiv

Acknowledgments xvi

PRACTICE MANAGEMENT

CHAPTER 1
THE LEGAL OFFICE ENVIRONMENT 1

The Legal Office 1
Lawyers 1
Law Societies 3
Law Associations. 3
Law Clerks, Legal Assistants, and Paralegals 3
Practical Skills 3
Soft Skills - Professionality 5
Licensed Paralegals 6
Getting Started in Legal Office Procedures 7
Chapter Summary 8
Review Questions 8
Precedents 9

CHAPTER 2
LEGAL OFFICE RECORDS MANAGEMENT 11

Handling the Telephone 11
Handling Mail 12
Conflict of Interest 12
Opening a New Client File 14
New Client Identification and Verification 17
Alphabetical Filing System 18
Closing Files 20
Reminder Systems 20
Chapter Summary 23
Review Questions 23
Precedents 24

CHAPTER 3
LEGAL OFFICE DOCKETS AND ACCOUNTS 27

Bank Accounts. 27
Accounting 27
Fees 28
Disbursements 28
Retainer Letter or Agreement 29

Dockets 29
Activity List 29
Docket Preparation 30
Accounts 31
Trust Statement 32
Legal Aid Accounts 32
Chapter Summary 33
Review Questions 33
Precedents 34

CHAPTER 4
EFFECTIVE LEGAL WRITING AND ORAL PRESENTATIONS 41

Basic Principles of Legal Writing 41
Guide to Effective Legal Writing 43
Guide to Effective Oral Presentations 45
Simplified Guide to Legal Punctuation 48
Comma 48
Semicolon, Colon, Apostrophe 51
Quotation Marks 52
Numbers 52
Legal Capitalization 53
Chapter Summary 54
Review Questions 54

CHAPTER 5
LEGAL OFFICE CORRESPONDENCE 55

Letter Styles 55
Parts of Legal Letters 56
Envelopes 59
Guide to Addressing Government and
    Judicial Officials 60
Chapter Summary 61
Review Questions 61
Precedents 62

CHAPTER 6
LEGAL RESEARCH AND MEMORANDUMS OF LAW 65

Interoffice Memorandums 65
Legal Memorandums 65
Quotations 65
Electronic Legal Research 67
Sources of Law 68
Federal and Provincial Statutes 68
Canadian Statute Citations 68
Canadian Law Reports 70

Case Citations 70
Neutral Citations 72
Canadian Law Report Series 73
English Law Report Series 75
Chapter Summary 75
Review Questions 75
Precedents .76

LITIGATION

CHAPTER 7

THE COURT SYSTEM OF CANADA 79

Supreme Court of Canada 80
Federal Court 80
Provincial and Territorial Courts 80
The Ontario Court System 80
Superior Court of Justice 80
Small Claims Court 80
Family Court of the Superior Court of Justice
    (Family Court) 81
Ontario Court of Justice 81
Appeal Courts 82
Divisional Court 82
Court of Appeal for Ontario 83
Court Offices 83
Criminal and Civil Law 83
Criminal Law 84
Provincial Offences 85
Prosecution of Provincial Offences 85
Summary Conviction Offences—Steps to Trial 87
Indictable Offences—Steps to Trial 88
Civil Law 90
Small Claims Court—Steps to Trial 90
Chapter Summary 92
Review Questions 93
Precedents .94

CHAPTER 8

PREPARING AND SERVING COURT DOCUMENTS 99

Preparing Court Documents 99
Court Forms 102
Issuing Documents 103
Serving Documents 103
Filing Documents 103
Delivery of Documents 103
Lawyer of Record 103
Calculating Time For Service 103
Proof of Service 104
Methods of Service 105
Personal Service 105
Alternatives to Personal Service 105
Ordinary Service on a Lawyer of Record 107
Substituted Service and Dispensing with Service 109
Chapter Summary 110
Review Questions 110
Precedents .111

CHAPTER 9

INTRODUCTION TO CIVIL LITIGATION 119

Rules of Civil Procedure 119
Types of Civil Litigation Procedures 120
Ordinary Procedure 120
Simplified Procedure 121
Steps in Simplified Procedure Actions 121
Mandatory Mediation 124
Case Management 124
Practice Directions 125
Class Actions 125
Chapter Summary 126
Review Questions 127
Precedents .128

CHAPTER 10

COMMENCING THE CIVIL LITIGATION ACTION 135

The Civil Litigation Action 135
Starting the Civil Litigation Action 136
Preliminary Considerations 137
Is It Too Late 137
Is Title of Proceeding Correct 137
Title of Proceeding 137
Drafting the Statement Of Claim 140
Statement of Claim (For Money Only), Form 14A 141
Statement of Claim (General), Form 14A 141
Basic Claims in Statements of Claim 141
Preparation and Distribution of Statement of
    Claim (General), Form 14A 142
Information for Court Use, Form 14F 143
Notice of Action, Form 14C 143
Preparation and Distribution of Statement of Claim
    (Action Commenced by Notice of Action),
    Form 14D 143
Chapter Summary 144
Review Questions 144
Precedents .145

CHAPTER 11

DEFENDING THE CIVIL LITIGATION ACTION 157

Pleadings 158
Notice of Intent to Defend, Form 18B 159
Statement of Defence, Form 18A 159

Drafting the Statement of Defence 159
Reply, Form 25A 160
Jury Notice, Form 47A 160
Close of Pleadings 160
Chapter Summary 161
Review Questions 161
Precedents 162

CHAPTER 12
COUNTERCLAIMS AND THIRD PARTY CLAIMS   169

Counterclaims 169
Statement of Defence and Counterclaim
   (Against Parties to Main Action Only), Form 27A 169
Statement of Defence and Counterclaim (Against
   Plaintiff and Person not Already Party to
   Main Action), Form 27B 169
Defence to Counterclaim, Form 27C 170
Reply to Defence to Counterclaim, Form 27D 171
Crossclaims 171
Third Party Claims 171
Chapter Summary 172
Review Questions 172
Precedents 173

CHAPTER 13
DISCOVERIES   187

Discoveries 187
Discovery Plan 187
Discovery of Documents 188
Affidavit of Documents, Form 30A 189
Preparation and Distribution of Affidavit of Documents
   (Individual), Form 30A 190
Request to Inspect Documents 190
Examination for Discovery 191
Notice of Examination 192
Preparation and Distribution of Notice of Examination,
   Form 34A 192
Examination for Discovery by Written Questions 193
Inspection of Property 193
Medical Examination 193
Chapter Summary 194
Review Questions 194
Precedents 195

CHAPTER 14
PRE-TRIAL   203

Pre-Trial 203
Mandatory Mediation 204
Setting Action Down for Trial 204
Preparation and Distribution of the Trial Record 204
Placing Action on Trial List 205
Pre-Trial Conference 205

Expert Witnesses 206
Summons to Witness (At Hearing), Form 53A 206
Offers to Settle 207
Chapter Summary 208
Review Questions 208
Precedents 209

CHAPTER 15
TRIAL   223

Trial Stage 223
Trial Brief 223
Brief of Authorities 224
Trial 224
Judgment 224
Preparation and Distribution of Judgment, Form 59B . . 224
Costs 225
Bill of Costs 227
Preparation and Distribution of Bill of Costs, Form 57A . . 227
Assessment of Costs 228
Chapter Summary 228
Review Questions 228
Precedents 229

CHAPTER 16
APPLICATIONS   235

Applications 236
Notice of Application 237
Preparation and Distribution of Notice of Application,
   (Form 14E) 238
Notice of Appearance 238
Affidavits in Opposition and Affidavits in Reply 238
Examination of Witness 239
Cross-Examination on Affidavit 239
Transcripts 239
Applicant's Application Record and Factum 240
Respondent's Application Record and Factum 241
Confirmation of Application 241
Hearing 241
Judgment 241
Costs and Assessment of Costs 242
Chapter Summary 242
Review Questions 242
Precedents 243

CHAPTER 17
MOTIONS   257

Motions 258
Types of Motions 258
Preliminary Considerations 259
Notice of Motion 260
Preparation and Distribution of Notice of
   Motion (Form 37A) 260
Moving Party's Motion Record 261

Responding Party's Motion Record. 261
Factums 262
Confirmation of Motion 262
Motion Costs. 262
Motion Hearing. 263
Order. 263
Preparation and Distribution of Order (Form 59A). 263
Chapter Summary 264
Review Questions 264
Precedents 265

CHAPTER 18
DISPOSITION WITHOUT TRIAL AND ENFORCEMENT OF ORDERS 279

Default Judgment 279
Default Judgment in Liquidated Damages 280
Preparation and Distribution of Requisition for Default
    Judgment (Form 19D) 280
Preparation and Distribution of Default Judgment
    (Form 19A). 281
Preparation and Distribution of Bill of Costs
    (Form 57A). 281
Default Judgment in Unliquidated Damages 281
Discontinuance by Plaintiff 282
Summary Judgment 282
Enforcement of Orders 283
Writ of Seizure and Sale 283
Preparation and Distribution of Writ of Seizure and
    Sale (Form 60A) 284
Requisition for Writ of Seizure and Sale. 284
Direction to Enforce Writ of Seizure and Sale 284
Garnishments 285
Chapter Summary 286
Review Questions 286
Precedents 287

FAMILY LAW

CHAPTER 19
MARRIAGE AND DOMESTIC CONTRACTS 299

Marriage 299
Marriage and the Change of Name Act. 301
Annulment of Marriage 301
Domestic Contracts 301
Marriage Contracts. 302
Cohabitation Agreements 304
Separation Agreements 304
Preparation and Distribution of Domestic Contracts . . . 305
Paternity Agreements 306
Chapter Summary 306

Review Questions 306
Precedents 307

CHAPTER 20
INTRODUCTION TO FAMILY LAW 319

Major Influences on Family Law Reform 319
Historical Background of Family Law 320
Ontario Family Law Act 320
Net Family Property 321
Equalization of Net Family Property. 323
Calculating Net Family Property (NFP) 323
Ontario Children's Law Reform Act 327
Children and Child Support. 328
Child Support Guidelines 328
Family Responsibility Office. 331
Chapter Summary 331
Review Questions 331
Precedents 333

CHAPTER 21
FAMILY LAW RULES AND PROCEDURES 337

The Family Law Rules 337
Courts Handling Family Law Cases. 337
Family Court of the Superior Court of Justice. 337
Statutes to which the Family Law Rules Apply 338
Procedural Stages in Family Law 339
Mandatory Information Program 339
Case Management 340
Starting the Family Law Case 340
Service of Family Law Documents 341
Financial Statements 343
Net Family Property Statements 344
Preparation and Distribution of Financial Statement
    (Support Claims), Form 13 344
Family Law Motions 346
Types of Family Law Motions. 346
Family Law Motions For Temporary Orders. 346
Family Law Motions to Change Final Orders 347
Chapter Summary 348
Review Questions 348
Precedents 349

CHAPTER 22
COMMENCING A DIVORCE CASE 365

Courts Hearing Divorce and Other Family Issues 366
Divorce. 366
Grounds for Divorce 366
Claims Under Different Statutes 367
Custody 367

Access 369
Preliminary Considerations in a Divorce Case 369
Starting the Divorce Case 370
Application (General) 371
Preparation and Distribution of Application (General),
    Form 8. 371
Financial Statement 372
Preparation and Distribution of Financial Statement
    (Property and Support Claims), Form 13.1 372
Form 35.1: Affidavit In Support of Claim for Custody
    or Access 374
Preparation and Distribution of Affidavit in Support of
    Claim for Custody or Access (Form 35.1) 375
Affidavit of Service 376
Continuing Record 377
Chapter Summary 378
Review Questions 379
Precedents 380

CHAPTER 23

CONTESTING A DIVORCE 409

Contested Divorce 409
Answer 409
Reply 410
Case Conference 410
Settlement Conference 411
Net Family Property Statement 412
Preparation and Distribution of Net Family Property
    Statement (Form 13B) 412
Trial Management Conference 412
Trial Record 413
Trial 413
Divorce Order 413
Certificate of Divorce 413
Simple/Sole and Joint Divorces 414
Chapter Summary 415
Review Questions 415
Precedents 416

CORPORATE AND COMMERCIAL LAW

CHAPTER 24

UNINCORPORATED BUSINESSES 437

Sole Proprietorships 437
Partnerships 437
Liability and Other Obligations of Sole Proprietorships
    and General Partnerships 439
Licensing 440
The Business Name 441
Partnership Agreements 442

Preparation and Distribution of Partnership
    Agreements 442
Other Forms of Unincorporated Businesses 443
Chapter Summary 444
Review Questions 444
Precedents 445

CHAPTER 25

CORPORATE LAW 451

Basic Concepts 451
Intermediate Concepts 454
Advantages and Disadvantages of Incorporating 457
Chapter Summary 458
Review Questions 458

CHAPTER 26

INCORPORATING A BUSINESS CORPORATION 459

Incorporating an Ontario Business Corporation 459
Preliminary Considerations 459
Name of Corporation 460
Professional Corporations 461
Articles of Incorporation 461
Preparation and Distribution of Articles of
    Incorporation, Form 1 462
Certificate of Incorporation 466
Chapter Summary 466
Review Questions 467
Precedents 468

CHAPTER 27

ORGANIZING THE BUSINESS CORPORATION 477

Keeping Corporate Records 477
Corporate Supplies 478
By-Laws and Resolutions 478
By-Laws 478
Resolutions 479
Initial Organization 479
Statutory Requirements 480
Resolutions of Directors 480
Share Certificates 481
Minute Book Registers 481
Resolutions of Shareholders 482
Special Resolutions of Shareholders 482
Making Notarial and Certified Copies 482
Initial Return 482
Preparation and Distribution of Initial Return, Form 1 . . . 482
Law Firm Personnel as First Directors and
    Incorporators 483
Reporting Letter and Account 483
Chapter Summary 484

Review Questions 484
Precedents 485

CHAPTER 28
POST-INCORPORATION MATTERS
509

Formal Meetings 509
OBCA Requirements for Meetings of Directors 510
OBCA Requirements for Meetings of Shareholders. . . . 511
Annual Meetings and Resolutions 512
Preparation and Distribution of Minutes of Meetings . . . 513
Special Resolutions 513
Ordinary Resolutions 514
Preparation and Distribution of Resolutions in Writing . 514
Notice of Change 514
Preparation and Distribution of Notice of Change,
    Form 1. 515
Changes by Notice of Change 515
Changes by Articles of Amendment 516
Changes by Articles of Amalgamation 516
Chapter Summary 518
Review Questions 518
Precedents 519

CHAPTER 29
CORPORATE AND COMMERCIAL LAW
549

Corporate and Commercial Law 549
Financing Personal Property 550
Basic Principles of Contract Law 550
Contractual Relationships 550
Commercial Contracts 551
Security Agreements 551
Personal Property Security Registration (PPSR)
    System 552
Electronic Registration 553
Financing Statement/Claim for Lien, Form 1C 553
Financing Statement, Form 1C. 554
Claim for Lien 554
Claim for Lien, Form 1C 555
Financing Change Statement/Change Statement,
    Form 2C 555
Changes Under the PPSA 555
Changes Under the RSLA 555
PPSA Enquiries (Searches). 556
Chapter Summary 557
Review Questions 557
Precedents 558

CHAPTER 30
INTRODUCTION TO REAL ESTATE
563

Real Property. 563
Types of Land Ownership 563
Title 564
Other Interests in Land 565
Agreements of Purchase and Sale 566
Chapter Summary 567
Review Questions 567
Precedents 568

CHAPTER 31
LAND REGISTRATION SYSTEMS
571

Land Registration Systems 571
Registry System 571
Land Titles System 572
Land Registry Offices and Divisions 572
Electronic Registration 572
Legal Description of Land 573
Chapter Summary 574
Review Questions 574
Precedents 576

CHAPTER 32
TRANSFERS
581

What is a Transfer 581
Electronic Transfer 581
Preparing the Electronic Transfer 581
Transferors 584
Transferees. 586
Land Transfer Tax Statements 587
Over to the Other Side 588
Transfer/Deed, Form 1 588
Chapter Summary 589
Review Questions 589
Precedents 590

CHAPTER 33
CHARGES/MORTGAGES AND REMEDIES
593

What is a Charge. 593
Types of Charges/Mortgages. 593
Types of Charge/Mortgage Repayments 594
Preparing the E-Reg Charge/Mortgage. 596
Charge/Mortgage, Form 2 601
Remedies Under Charges/Mortgages 601

Power of Sale 601
Possession. 601
Foreclosure. 601
Judicial Sale 602
Chapter Summary 602
Review Questions 603
Precedents 604

CHAPTER 34
DISCHARGES AND RELATED DOCUMENTS 609

Discharge of Charge 609
The E-Reg Discharge of Charge 610
The Discharge of Charge/Mortgage, Form 3 612
The E-Reg Transfer of Charge 613
The E-Reg Postponement of Interest. . . . 613
Chapter Summary 614
Review Questions 614
Precedents 615

CHAPTER 35
SALE TRANSACTIONS 621

Standard Documents Prepared in Sale Transactions . . . 621
The Sale Transaction 622
Statement of Adjustments 624
Preparation and Distribution of Statement of Adjustments 624
Getting Ready for Closing 628
After Closing 629
Chapter Summary 630
Review Questions 630
Precedents 631

CHAPTER 36
PURCHASE TRANSACTIONS 641

Standard Documents Prepared in Purchase Transactions. 641
The Purchase Transaction 642
Land Transfer Tax 647
Land Transfer Tax Statements/Affidavit 648
Getting Ready for Closing 651
The E-Reg Closing 652
After Closing 653
Title Insurance 653
Chapter Summary 654
Review Questions 654
Precedents 655

CHAPTER 37
CONDOMINIUMS 681

Condominiums 681
The Unit 681
Common Elements. 682
Condominium Corporations 682
Occupancy Agreements 683
Condominium Residential Resale Transactions 684
Chapter Summary 685
Review Questions 685
Precedents 686

CHAPTER 38
TITLE SEARCHING — A NEW PERSPECTIVE 687

Title Searching 687
Automated Titles in Registry System 688
Automated Titles in Land Titles System 688
Title Searching—Registry System 688
Title Searching—Land Titles System 689
The Planning Act 690
Searching under the Planning Act 691
Planning Act Exceptions, Exemptions and Restrictions 693
Title Searching Using Teraview 694
Chapter Summary 698
Review Questions 698
Precedents 700

ESTATES

CHAPTER 39
WILLS AND POWERS OF ATTORNEY 709

The Will 709
Preparation and Distribution of Will 712
Affidavit of Execution of Will, Form 74.8 712
Preparation and Distribution of Affidavit of Execution of Will, Form 74.8 712
Holograph Will 713
Multiple Wills 713
Codicil 714
Powers of Attorney. 714
Chapter Summary 716
Review Questions 716
Precedents 717

CHAPTER 40
INHERITANCE 725

The Succession Law Reform Act 725
The Family Law Act 726
Chapter Summary 727
Review Questions 727

CHAPTER 41

APPLICATION FOR CERTIFICATE WITH A WILL

729

Application for Certificate of Appointment of Estate
Trustee with a Will (Individual Applicant),
Form 74.4 729
Will 729
Value of Estate 730
Personal Property 730
Real Estate 731
Preparation and Distribution of Application for
Certificate of Appointment of Estate Trustee
with a Will (Individual Applicant), Form 74.4 733
Notice of an Application for a Certificate of
Appointment of Estate Trustee with a Will,
Form 74.7 734
Affidavit of Service of Notice (with a Will),
Form 74.6 734
Certificate of Appointment of Estate Trustee
with a Will, Form 74.13 734
Renunciation of Right to a Certificate of Appointment
of Estate Trustee with a Will (or Succeeding Estate
Trustee), Form 74.11 734
Consent to Applicant's Appointment as Estate Trustee
with a Will, Form 74.12 735
Application for Certificate of Appointment As
Succeeding Estate Trustee with a Will,
Form 74.21 736
Mediation 736
Estate Information Return 736
Chapter Summary 737
Review Questions 737
Precedents 738

CHAPTER 42

APPLICATION FOR CERTIFICATE WITHOUT A WILL

759

Application for Certificate of Appointment of Estate
Trustee without a Will (Individual Applicant),
Form 74.14 759
Preparation and Distribution of Application for
Certificate of Appointment of Estate Trustee
without a Will (Individual Applicant) Form 74.14 760
Notice of an Application for a Certificate of
Appointment of Estate Trustee without a Will,
Form 74.17 760
Affidavit of Service of Notice (without a Will),
Form 74.16 760
Certificate of Appointment of Estate Trustee
without a Will, Form 74.20 761

Renunciation of Prior Right to a Certificate of
Appointment of Estate Trustee without a Will,
Form 74.18 761
Consent to Applicant's Appointment as Estate Trustee
without a Will, Form 74.19 762
Bond, Form 74.33 762
Preparation and Distribution of Bond, Form 74.33 762
Application for Certificate of Appointment as
Succeeding Estate Trustee without a Will,
Form 74.24 763
Mediation 763
Estate Information Return 763
Chapter Summary 764
Review Questions 764
Precedents 765

CHAPTER 43

DISTRIBUTION OF ESTATES

775

Distribution of Estates 775
Notarial Copies 776
Notice to Creditors 776
Final Income Tax Returns 776
Distribution of Real Estate 776
Distribution of Personal Property 779
Release of Estate Trustee (with or without a Will) 780
Winding Up the Estate 780
Passing of Accounts 780
Reporting Letter and Account 781
Chapter Summary 782
Review Questions 782
Precedents 783

Glossary 791

Index to Precedents 799

Index 802

Foreword

In reviewing this edition of *Legal Office Procedures*, I am reminded of how important law clerks' and legal assistants' contributions are to the knowledge and efficiency of the legal team and how critical they are to the implementation of proper legal services.

The practice of law has changed significantly over the recent past. Technology has made a huge impact. I welcome the knowledge, organization and dedication of the author in providing a current, comprehensive manual, providing the reader with all the basic information needed to understand the structure and concepts of a law practice. These materials are successfully designed in a readable and digestible format to enable you to grasp concepts, starting with the set up of a law firm to the more complex real estate title search.

The content is smartly chronicled and intelligent. Using this text will provide you with the confidence and foundation you will need to work in a legal environment of any size. The experience, diligence and pride of the author are evident throughout the materials.

My law practice has extended over decades, and I have been exposed to many law clerks and legal assistants who have learned from these materials. We know those persons are always prepared and properly educated. These materials will serve you and the rest of us in the legal profession very well.

Gordon A. Ullman
Black Sutherland LLP

Preface

This edition of *Legal Office Procedures* is your most up-to-date legal educational textbook for law clerks, legal assistants, legal administrative assistants, and paralegals. This edition includes the statutory amendments that have come into force since the previous edition, and it also includes the new Office Administration-Legal Program Standard of the Ministry of Advanced Education and Skills Development. The new co-authors who are graduates from law clerk and legal administration programs and are also employed in the legal field bring to this edition a real inside view of the legal office environment and a firsthand perspective on the skills and professionalism that legal students require for a successful legal career.

The hallmarks and mainstays which *Legal Office Procedures* has originated and is renowned for continue in this edition, including:

- Start-to-finish files with ongoing full life cycle scenarios, to Aristotle's, "The whole is greater than the sum of its parts." Like a big puzzle that is difficult to put all the pieces together without seeing the overall big picture on the front cover, the start-to-finish files of *Legal Office Procedures* allow you to see the big picture and to understand the relevance and significance of each procedural part. This effective, holistic method of learning lends meaning to your legal work by eliminating mechanical performance and also provides you with a good level of independence in the workplace by enabling you to anticipate and act with initiative on the next procedural step.

- Step-by-step practice and procedure aptly exemplified by substantive law, case law, and completed precedents, including chapter summaries and review questions.

- Straight forward student-centered language that presumes no prior legal knowledge, to Benjamin Franklin's, "Tell me, I will forget. Teach me, I may remember. Involve me, I will understand."

- Concise, comprehensive coverage of the most commonly practised areas of law — practice management, civil litigation, criminal litigation, family, corporate and commercial, real estate, and estates — all under a single cover, as opposed to seven costly, individually priced books. *Legal Office Procedures* covers your entire legal curriculum and renders you at once employable in any and all of these areas of practice.

Legal Office Procedures is your affordable, highly respected, and handy practical legal resource, carrying you from your legal classroom, to your legal field placement, to your legal workplace.

Also available:
Legal Office Procedures Workbook (interfacing files and practical exercises)
Legal Office Transcription (audio files, legal terminology, and grammar exercises)
Instructor support

About the Authors

Tina Kamakaris is a professor emeritus of Seneca College. She has a Bachelor of Arts in English Literature from the University of Toronto. Professor Kamakaris is also a certified teacher under the *Education Act* of the Province of Ontario, having graduated from the Ontario Institute for Studies in Education (OISE) of the University of Toronto. Professor Kamakaris combines her extensive experience as a college instructor with her legal office knowledge to create the high-quality *Legal Office Procedures* collection of works that is respected throughout professional and educational communities, setting a high bar that others aim to reach. The author uses a heuristic and intuitive writing style that is concise, easy to follow, and ideal for students new to the subject. The author is the reputed doyenne of law clerk, legal assistant, legal office administration, and paralegal educators.

Jane Kamakaris is a working legal assistant/law clerk with over 20 years of experience. She is an Honour Roll graduate of the Office Administration – Legal program at Humber College and the Law Clerk program of the Institute of Law Clerks of Ontario through George Brown College. With this exceptional combination of legal education and legal experience, Jane brings unique insights to the student of *Legal Office Procedures*, including firsthand knowledge of the types of skills and professionalism that legal students require for success in their legal career. Jane also provided valuable work to the previous edition of *Legal Office Procedures*. At work, Jane admires new hires arriving on their first day of work with their *Legal Office Procedures* textbook tucked under their arm, striking a confident, ready-to-work image, to the delight of their new legal employer.

Louis Kamakaris is a working risk management adviser, quality control analyst, and real estate appraisal reviewer in the mortgage industry. He has over 15 years of experience working in law-related departments of medium and large financial firms. Louis is a graduate of the Law Clerk program at Seneca College. Louis has a unique perspective on the *Legal Office Procedures* collection of works in that he has worked for Owl Publishing during the production of previous editions of these works as well as used the *Legal Office Procedures* text and *Legal Office Procedures Workbook* as prescribed books in the Law Clerk program at Seneca College during his law clerk studies at Seneca College. Louis brings these exceptional firsthand insights to the *Legal Office Procedures* collection of works and to the student of *Legal Office Procedures*.

Acknowledgments

To Gordon A. Ullman and Robert S. Sutherland of the Ontario Bar, and Pamela Briggs.

To long-time colleagues and supporters and new ones: Lynn Berry, Algonquin College; Norlanda Joseph, College Boreal; Suzanne Louiseize, Canadore College; Mary Liidemann CDI College; Janet Bradley, Conestoga College; Peggy Hinan, Durham College; Lesley Wagner, Durham College; Daniel Basquill, Eastern College; Teresa Stork, George Brown College; Lynne Johnson-Murphy, Georgian College; Amanda MacDonald, Holland College; Anita John, Humber College, Carolyn Smith, Humber College; Veronica Robinson, KLC College; Jane Clarke, Mohawk College; Nancy Bellantino, Niagara College; Patricia Drozdoski, Niagara College; Denise Swyers, College of the North Atlantic; Voula Zafiris, Northern College; Janet Ashton, Robertson College; Melissa Pavlica, St. Clair College; Fulvio Valentinis, St. Clair College; Cathy Sheehan, St. Lawrence College; Katherine Willis, St. Lawrence College; Christine Spinosa, Seneca College; Christine Gigler, Sheridan College; Lisa Mendez, Sheridan College; Henry Lowi, triOS College.

To Paul Gribilas, William Alexiou, Doug Thomson, Greg Devitt, Sharon Lucas.

To Anthony Rezek, Kevin Smulan, Rosalind Wright, Marina Salvatore, Jenna Willliams at Emond Publishing.

Thank you.

Items reprinted with the kind permission of the following copyright holders:

CONVEYANCER®, FASTCOMPANY™, WILL BUILDER™, and ESTATE-A-BASE™ are all trade-marks of Do Process Software Ltd. and are used with permission.
CourtSide EDX
Cyberbahn Group
DIVORCEmate Software Inc.
Government of Canada, Department of Justice
KorbitecInc. (ACL Software)
Law Society of Upper Canada
LexisNexis Canada Inc. LexisNexis is a registered trademark of Reed Elsevier Properties Inc., used under licence. PCLaw™ is a trademark of LexisNexis Practice Management Systems Inc.
Ministry of the Attorney General
Ministry of Government and Consumer Services
OnCorp Direct
Ontario Bar Association
Ontario Real Estate Association
Queen's Printer for Ontario
Teranet Inc. (Teraview®Software)
Thomson Reuters Canada Limited

CHAPTER 1

THE LEGAL OFFICE ENVIRONMENT

Laws should be like clothes; they should be tailored to fit the people they are meant to serve. And when the laws do not fit the people, or the people do not fit the laws, legal wars break out and land on the doorstep of the legal profession — happily, the *second* oldest profession.

This chapter covers an overview of the legal office environment and the role of lawyers, law clerks, legal assistants (also referred to as legal administrative assistants), and paralegals. At points of the gavel, you will read decided court cases that will reinforce the substantive law discussed and also help you see how our courts interpret our laws when people sue.

THE LEGAL OFFICE

The legal office, or law firm, is the place where lawyers carry on the business of law. Most law firms practise as **L**imited **L**iability **P**artnerships, identified by the abbreviation **LLP** following the partnership name, which basically means that the law partners are not personally liable for any negligent acts of other partners or employees who are directly supervised by other partners. Law firms vary in size, ranging from one lawyer to over two hundred lawyers. Figure 1.1 shows the organizational structure of the small law firm of Michael, Eliad & Redford LLP. The law firm consists of the three partners whose surnames make up the name of the law firm. The law firm employs one associate (hired lawyer), who is Margaret Nesh, and one articling student (student lawyer). Both Ms. Nesh and the articling student report to the partners. The law firm also employs legal assistants, law clerks, a paralegal, a receptionist, and a bookkeeper.

Note from Figure 1.1 that you are a **law clerk/assistant** to Mr. Robert B. Redford. You report directly to Mr. Redford and, by extension, to the remaining partners. Whenever the need arises, you are also expected to do work for the associate and the articling student. The same applies to the remaining legal support staff. This reporting structure is typical of many small law firms. Figure 1.2 is an organizational chart of a large law firm. It features a sophisticated organizational hierarchy with numerous departments, services, and career positions typical of many large law firms.

LAWYERS

Education   Generally, Ontario lawyers must obtain a university degree; pass a Law School Admission Test (LSAT); obtain from a law school a Bachelor of Laws degree (LLB) or its equivalent Juris Doctor (JD) degree; write a barrister and a solicitor licensing examination; complete either (a) an articling period during which they work under the supervision of a lawyer, or (b) a Law Practice Program consisting of a training course and a work placement; and comply with the

Figure 1.1 Organizational Chart of Michael, Eliad & Redford LLP, Small Law Firm

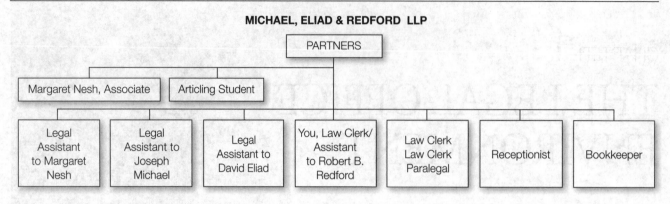

Figure 1.2 Organizational Chart, Large Law Firm

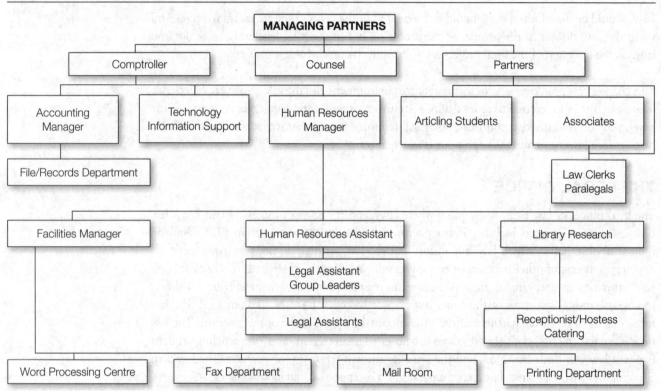

terms of the good character requirement under Part VI of the Lawyer Licensing Process Policies. Lawyers are then said to be "called to the bar," which is basically a graduation ceremony for lawyers; they are issued a class L1 licence and can practise law in Ontario as barristers and solicitors.

Barristers and solicitors   The terms come from early English usage. Originally in England, the section of the court where only the lawyers for the parties involved in a law suit were permitted to enter was physically divided from the area of the spectators by a **bar**; hence, **bar**rister. In England, barristers are trial, or litigation, lawyers, and solicitors are lawyers who work in all non-litigation areas of law, e.g. real estate. Canadian lawyers perform both functions and are referred to as barristers and solicitors.

Lawyers   Litigation lawyers in Ontario are known as **lawyers**. The *Rules of Civil Procedure* have been amended to replace the terms solicitor and counsel with the term lawyer. The change

Legal Office Procedures

was made in the interest of plain language and consistency as all three terms: solicitor, counsel, and lawyer, had been inconsistently used in the *Rules of Civil Procedure*. The *Courts of Justice Act*, the *Family Law Rules*, and the *Rules of Small Claims Court* also use only the term lawyer.

LAW SOCIETIES

The Canadian legal profession governs itself through a law society in each province, Figure 1.3. In Ontario, it is the Law Society of Upper Canada. All Ontario lawyers must become members of the Law Society of Upper Canada in order to practise law. Lawyers in practice must comply with the Law Society's *Rules of Professional Conduct*. Here are two sample rules from the *Rules of Professional Conduct*:

Rule 3.2-7 A lawyer shall not knowingly assist in or encourage any dishonesty, fraud, crime, or illegal conduct or instruct a client or any other person on how to violate the law and avoid punishment.

Rule 3.3-1 A lawyer at all times shall hold in strict confidence all information concerning the business and affairs of the client acquired in the course of the professional relationship and shall not divulge any such information unless (a) expressly or impliedly authorized by the client; (b) required by law or by order of a tribunal of competent jurisdiction to do so; (c) required to provide the information to the Law Society; or (d) otherwise permitted by rules 3.3-2 to 3.3-6.

LAW ASSOCIATIONS

Canadian lawyers may voluntarily become members of the Canadian Bar Association, which has branches in each province. The Ontario branch is called Ontario Bar Association. There are also county and district law associations. Law associations are to be distinguished from law societies in that law associations aim to represent the interests of lawyers, whereas law societies aim to protect the interests of the public against unscrupulous lawyers.

LAW CLERKS, LEGAL ASSISTANTS, AND PARALEGALS

There is a wide variety of careers in today's law office. The ones working closest with the lawyer and the client are **law clerks**, **legal assistants** (also referred to as **legal administrative assistants**), and lawyer-supervised **paralegals**. The legal work among these legal careers often overlaps, in that all require knowledge of procedural law, i.e. practical "how to" knowledge, as well as substantive law, i.e. knowledge of the theory of law. A general distinction is that law clerks and lawyer-supervised paralegals require a greater knowledge of substantive law. For facility, we refer to law clerks, legal assistants, and lawyer-supervised paralegals, collectively, as **law clerks/assistants.** Law clerks/assistants may work in any area of law in which the supervising lawyer practises.

PRACTICAL SKILLS

Proficient keying, computer literacy, competency in language craftsmanship, spelling, proofreading, checking for exactness, sense, and coherence, and questioning when in doubt are crucial skills in all aspects of legal work. As important is knowledge of legal software that is commonly used in practice, some of which includes: Elite Enterprise and PCLaw for legal accounting, DIVORCEmate for family law, ACL for civil litigation, Fast Company for corporate, Conveyancer for real estate, Teraview for real estate electronic registration, and Estate-A-Base for wills and estates, almost all of which are used in this manual.

Legal TIP

Law Clerks/Assistants must never give legal advice and must always keep client matters confidential.

Figure 1.3 Provincial/Territorial Law Societies and Courts in Canada

Law Society and Code of Conduct	Highest Court of First Instance
The Law Society of Alberta http://www.lawsociety.ab.ca • *Code of Conduct*	Court of Queen's Bench https://albertacourts.ca
The Law Society of British Columbia http://www.lawsociety.bc.ca • *Code of Professional Conduct for British Columbia*	Supreme Court of British Columbia http://www.courts.gov.bc.ca
The Law Society of Manitoba http://www.lawsociety.mb.ca • *Code of Professional Conduct*	Court of Queen's Bench for Manitoba http://www.manitobacourts.mb.ca
The Law Society of New Brunswick http://lawsociety-barreau.nb.ca/en • *Code of Professional Conduct*	Court of Queen's Bench http://www.gnb.ca/cour/index-e.asp
Law Society of Newfoundland & Labrador http://www.lawsociety.nf.ca • *Code of Professional Conduct*	The Supreme Court of Newfoundland and Labrador http://www.court.nl.ca
Law Society of the Northwest Territories http://www.lawsociety.nt.ca • *Code of Professional Conduct*	Supreme Court of the Northwest Territories http://www.nwtcourts.ca
Nova Scotia Barristers' Society http://www.nsbs.org • *Code of Professional Conduct*	The Supreme Court http://www.courts.ns.ca
Law Society of Nunavut http://lawsociety.nu.ca • *The Canadian Bar Association Code of Professional Conduct*	Nunavut Court of Justice http://www.nunavutcourts.ca
The Law Society of Upper Canada https://www.lsuc.on.ca • *Rules of Professional Conduct* (Lawyers) • *Paralegal Rules of Conduct* (Licensed Paralegals)	Superior Court of Justice http://www.ontariocourts.on.ca
The Law Society of Prince Edward Island http://lawsocietypei.ca • *Code of Professional Conduct*	Supreme Court of Prince Edward Island http://www.gov.pe.ca/courts
Barreau due Québec http://www.barreau.qc.ca/en • *Code of Professional Conduct of Lawyers*	Superior Court of Quebec http://www.tribunaux.qc.ca
The Law Society of Saskatchewan http://www.lawsociety.sk.ca • *Code of Professional Conduct*	Court of Queen's Bench http://www.sasklawcourts.ca
The Law Society of Yukon http://www.lawsocietyyukon.com • *Code of Professional Conduct*	Supreme Court of Yukon http://www.yukoncourts.ca

Legal terminology Legal terms have legal meanings and require thorough knowledge for correct placement and usage. Here, for your amusement, are excerpts from law firm letters which reveal an embarrassing lack of language skills and legal terminology:

> The thought of what her husband will do next is making my client all erotic and depressed.
> (The word erotic should be erratic.)

> He died undusted and without a shoe. Should read: He died intestate and without issue.
> (**Intestate** means **without having made a will**; **issue** means **children**.)

Practice and procedure Work in the legal office consists almost entirely of **practice** (tasks routinely done) and **procedure** (tasks requiring specific legal steps). In practical terms, this means carrying a client file from start to finish. Typical practice and procedure tasks include: meeting with clients; scheduling appointments; opening client files; maintaining dockets and reminder systems; drafting pleadings; preparing correspondence and accounts; researching legal questions and preparing memorandums of law; issuing and filing court documents; preparing incorporation documents; preparing wills; and preparing real estate documents, all of which are covered in this manual.

Substantive law Substantive law means the substance, or theory, of law. Substantive knowledge gives meaning to your work because it tells you why a particular task needs to be done. Lack of knowledge of substantive law results in a mechanical performance and limits the use of initiative and good judgment so necessary in legal work. If, for example, the law clerk/assistant understands why a statement of defence must be served and filed within the applicable time limit, the law clerk/assistant could ensure that the lawyer is alerted to the deadline and thus avoid the serious consequences which could ensue if the deadline were to be missed.

Confidentiality The very nature and business of law involves individuals who are on either the positive or the negative side of the law. Whatever the client's business, be it a minor civil matter, such as a dispute with a neighbour over the exact proximity of a mutual fence, or a serious criminal offence, such as rape or murder, it must be regarded at all times as privileged and confidential information. Discussions of clients' business outside of the law firm are an indefensible breach of duties and ethics. Law firms routinely have law clerks/assistants sign confidentiality agreements, Precedent 1.1, to this effect. Jeopardy to the client, the lawyer, or the law firm must never be chanced. Consider the case situation of a young law clerk/assistant who, in her enthusiasm, leaked to her friends the fact that a well-known celebrity would be visiting her law firm the following morning. Youthful eagerness could not be contained, and overnight, a throng of fans gathered at the law firm to catch a glimpse of their idol and, at the same time, embarrass our law clerk/assistant upon arrival at the office.

SOFT SKILLS — PROFESSIONALITY

In all law-related capacities, soft skills such as the ability to get along with people and to communicate effectively are personal qualities which almost always triumph over naked skill proficiencies. Ample are the theories of behavioural scientists such as McGregor, Maslow, and Herzberg about the need for understanding what motivates positive and negative human behaviour and how soft skills such as a positive attitude and the ability to communicate effectively are necessary for a successful legal career. We refer to these important soft skills as **professionality** (professionalism and personality).

Positive attitude   Attitude concerns itself with a physical behaviour as well as with a way of thinking and feeling. Whether in positive or negative terms, this state of body and mind ultimately reveals itself. Consider the following guidelines in evaluating your own attitude and understanding that of others:

- Know yourself and how others see you; assess objectively your personal strengths and weaknesses, your disposition, grooming, and attire.
- Understand what motivates a particular behaviour in others; consider the individual as a whole, reserve judgment, and empathize.
- Avoid impulsive speech or action. To regret what has been left unsaid or undone is to be still in control, but to grieve over that which has been said or done is to openly submit to lack of self-control.
- Admit to an error, apologize, and offer to rectify the problem. It takes more nobility to swallow pride than to wave it on a banner.
- Perceive merit in everyone and praise liberally but meaningfully.
- Use humour to soothe, delight, and relieve. A good sense of humour begins with the ability to laugh at oneself.
- Employ tact and talent; the difference is that talent has the natural strength of knowing what to do, whereas tact has the virtue of knowing how and when to do it.

Ability to communicate effectively   Human interaction is not only unavoidable but also difficult because to be effective, it must be performed at various levels. Consider, for example, the variety of ways in which the same message would be delivered to a child, a friend, an acquaintance, a business associate, or an employer. In business, the levels of communication usually consist of superiors, subordinates, colleagues, business acquaintances, and business friends. Applying appropriate regard and discretion when communicating within the hierarchy of your workplace is key to effective communication. Following are guidelines for effective communication, both on and off the job:

- Listen attentively to a speaker instead of concerning yourself with what you intend to say next.
- Participate and share in the responsibility of effective communication. It takes at least two to communicate, and it might only sometimes be the other at fault.
- Take care to avoid misconstruing or distorting messages and meanings.
- Beware of the proverbial "grapevine." It takes greater strength to dissuade gossip than to nourish it.
- Present a difference of opinion rationally and objectively.
- Attempt to resolve a personality conflict or, at least, to make a difficult situation tolerable. Not everyone with whom we meet or work becomes a close or intimate friend.
- Regard another's statements without belligerence, without eagerness for personal victory, without contempt, and without any airs of superiority.

LICENSED PARALEGALS

Legal TIP

The law forbids licensed paralegals to hold themselves out as lawyers.

Licensed paralegals are legal professionals who are licensed and regulated by the Law Society of Upper Canada. Licensed paralegals may work with lawyer supervision in a law firm or without lawyer supervision in a business enterprise of their own. To become licensed, paralegals must complete a college paralegal course that is accredited by the Law Society; write a paralegal licensing examination; be of good character, e.g. must not have been in any legal trouble or fired for cause; apply to the Law Society for a P1 (Paralegal) licence; and abide by the *Paralegal Rules of Conduct* which the Law Society prescribes. Licensed paralegals may provide legal services in a limited scope of practice: Small Claims Court, tribunals, provincial offences, and minor summary conviction offences. It is anticipated that the paralegal scope of practice may be expanded to include certain family law matters where not only **paralegals**, but also **law clerks** and **law students** may be permitted to provide legal services. See how the following well-known case paved the way for the licensing of paralegals. It is the 1987 case between the Law Society of Upper Canada and Mr. Brian Lawrie and his paralegal firm POINTTS.

The Law Society of Upper Canada prosecuted Mr. Brian Lawrie and POINTTS (Provincial Offences Information and Traffic Ticket Service) for doing work that only lawyers are permitted to do. Mr. Brian Lawrie, a Toronto paralegal and former police constable, operated POINTTS, a business franchise. A lower court ruled against Mr. Lawrie. Mr. Lawrie then appealed to the Ontario Court of Appeal, and the Court of Appeal ruled that POINTTS may practise in such areas as minor traffic violations, landlord and tenant disputes, small claims, labour board hearings, and some summary convictions.

GETTING STARTED IN LEGAL OFFICE PROCEDURES

Welcome to the law firm of Michael, Eliad & Redford LLP. You will be working as a law clerk/assistant to Mr. Robert Bret Redford. You will find step-by-step guidance and completed precedents throughout this *Legal Office Procedures* manual to help you gain thorough knowledge and understanding of the type of work you will encounter in the legal office.

Working with precedents   Much of the work in the law office is generated from **precedents**. Precedents are examples of previously completed legal documents. The rich selection of precedents in this *Legal Office Procedures* manual is located at the end of each chapter and will not only assist you during your legal studies, but also serve as your trusty practical reference tool in your legal career.

A *Legal Office Procedures* student workbook is available to help you build practical skill proficiencies. Also available are *Legal Office Transcription* audio files to help you develop legal office transcription skills.

CHAPTER SUMMARY

The law office is also referred to as a law firm. Many law firms operate as limited liability partnerships where lawyers are not liable for the negligent acts of other partners. The Law Society of Upper Canada regulates the legal profession, and all lawyers must become members of it in order to practise law.

There are many careers in the law office, including **law clerks** and **legal assistants** (also referred to as **legal administrative assistants**). Their duties are similar and often overlap, the main difference being that law clerks require more extensive knowledge of substantive law. Legal assistants and law clerks can work in all of the areas of law in which a supervising lawyer practises. **Paralegals** are licensed professionals who may work with or without lawyer-supervision and may run independent businesses to provide only those legal services that the law permits them to provide. For facility, this manual refers to law clerks, legal assistants, and lawyer-supervised paralegals, collectively, as **law clerks/assistants.** Law clerks/assistants must never give legal advice and must always keep client matters confidential.

Among the important skills which successful law clerks/assistants must possess are those relating to language mastery and effective communication as well as such personal attributes as a positive attitude, conscientiousness, flexibility, and a good sense of humour.

REVIEW QUESTIONS

1. What is the name of the law society which governs Ontario lawyers?
2. What is the difference between substantive law and procedural law?
3. What is a precedent?
4. What are your strongest personal and business skills?
5. Paralegals are medical workers who drive ambulances to scenes of emergency.
   Yes___ No___

MICHAEL, ELIAD & REDFORD LLP

Name of Employee:_____

Position___Law Clerk/Legal Assistant_____   Date:_____

In consideration of my employment by Michael, Eliad & Redford LLP, a law firm (Firm), I agree with Michael, Eliad & Redford LLP as follows:

1. Definitions

(a) Personal information   As used in this agreement, **personal information** means any information about an identifiable individual or that permits an individual to be identified. It includes information which is voluntarily provided by an individual. Personal information includes information to which I may have access in connection with my employment.

(b) Proprietary information   As used in this agreement, **proprietary information** includes, by way of example and without limitation, trade secrets, software, data, and copyrightable materials, and financial data of the Firm's clients. Proprietary information includes information to which I may have access in connection with my employment.

(c) Third party information   As used in this agreement, **third party information** means confidential personal and/or proprietary information I have received and/or may in the future receive from third parties. Third party information includes information to which I may have access in connection with my employment.

2. Confidentiality

I understand and agree that my employment creates a relationship of confidence and trust between me and the Firm with respect to (a) all personal information, (b) all proprietary information, and (c) all third party information, all of which is referred to in this agreement, collectively, as **confidential information. At all times, both during my employment with the Firm and after its termination, I will keep in confidence and trust all such confidential information and will not use or disclose any such confidential information except as may be necessary in the ordinary course of performing my duties in the Firm.** The restrictions set forth in this section 2 will not apply to information which is generally known now or in the future to the public, unless such knowledge results from an unauthorized disclosure by me, but this exception will not affect the application of any other provision of this agreement to such information in accordance with the terms of such provision.

3. Materials

All documents, disks, hard drives, computers or other equipment, records, apparatus, equipment and other physical property, whether or not pertaining to personal information, proprietary information, and/or third party information, which are furnished to me by the Firm or are produced by me in connection with my employment will be and remain the sole property of the Firm. I will return to the Firm all such materials and property as and when requested by the Firm. In any event, I will return all such materials and property immediately upon termination of my employment for any reason. I will not take with me any such material or property or any copies thereof upon such termination.

4. Injunction

I agree that it would be difficult to measure any damages caused to the Firm which might result from any breach by me of the promises set forth in this agreement, and that in any event, money damages would be an inadequate remedy for any such breach. Accordingly, I agree that if I breach, or propose to breach, any portion of this agreement, the Firm shall be entitled, in addition to all other remedies that it may have, to an injunction or other appropriate equitable relief to restrain any such breach without showing or proving any actual damage to the Firm.

I understand that this agreement affects important rights. I have read it carefully and am satisfied that I understand it.

Accepted and agreed to by:

MICHAEL, ELIAD & REDFORD LLP

By:_____   _____
                                                 Signature of Employee

CHAPTER 2
LEGAL OFFICE RECORDS MANAGEMENT

Business is like fire -- nothing happens unless you build one. This chapter covers the day-to-day practices that keep the engine of an effective legal office practice running smoothly.

HANDLING THE TELEPHONE

Answering machines and voice mail systems are capable of automatically taking and printing a caller's message. Following are some basic guidelines for handling person-to-person calls:

Handling all calls   Make the first impression a favourable one by answering on the first or second ring. Identify the office and yourself, "Mr. Redford's office, Jane Smith speaking." Be tactful and accommodating and maintain your composure. Remember, good will takes years to create, but only seconds to destroy.

Handling urgent calls   The very nature of the business of law often involves clients with urgent calls. It is prudent to take the caller at his or her word and put the call through without much ado, even if it means interrupting a meeting, "I am sorry to interrupt, Mr. Redford, but Mr. Brown is on the line and says it is urgent." If the lawyer is out of the office and out of reach, "I am sorry, Mr. Brown, but Mr. Redford is out of the office today; could Mr. Michael or Mr. Eliad be of help?"

Taking messages   When the lawyer wishes no calls, say "I am sorry, Mr. Brown, but Mr. Redford is unable to take your call at the moment; may I take a message, or would you like his voice mail?" When taking a message, write it down clearly on a telephone message slip, Figure 2.1, or as is often the practice, email the message to the lawyer.

Figure 2.1

To	Robert B. Redford
Date	Nov. 11/-- Time 11:30 a.m.

WHILE YOU WERE OUT

M r. John Smith

Of   Smith & Associates

Phone (416) 491-1111   2203

Area code Number   Extension

Telephoned ✔	Please call ✔
Returned your call___	Will call again___
Called to see you_____	Wants to see you_

Message   Meeting on Friday is on.

Taken by___yi_____Urgent___

HANDLING MAIL

Voice mail   Check your voice mail messages regularly, and act on them promptly. Determine the ones that you can handle yourself. Transcribe detailed voice mail messages and bring them to the lawyer's attention. Make a note of any action you took with regard to any voice mail, and place it in both the paper file and the online file to enable others who may be working on the same file to view what has been done. Lawyers usually retrieve and handle their own voice mail messages.

Email   Save the email in the client's file electronically and print it out and hand it to the lawyer for action.

Paper mail   In some law firms, the receptionist opens and date-stamps the firm's incoming paper mail and distributes it to the law clerks/assistants of the respective lawyers; in other law firms, the law clerk/assistant opens and date-stamps the paper mail for the lawyer. In either case, the law clerk/assistant usually scans the paper mail to the respective directory before handing it to the lawyer for action. Once the lawyer reviews the mail, he or she will instruct you with any action to be taken or to file it away.

CONFLICT OF INTEREST

Before you open a new client file, check that no conflict of interest exists. A conflict of interest would occur where the same lawyer or the same law firm acts for both sides in a case, e.g. for both the plaintiff as well as the defendant in a litigation action. The *Rules of Professional Conduct* prohibit lawyers from acting for both sides as doing so may compromise the lawyer's ability to protect the interests of each side. Lawyers may, however, act in conflict in certain non-litigation matters (e.g. real estate) if both sides consent in writing to having the same lawyer act. If in doubt, you should consult the lawyer or the *Rules of Professional Conduct* to confirm when a lawyer can act for both sides.

When checking for conflict of interest, be sure to run a check on your client as well as on any opposite party in the matter because if it turns out that your firm has, at any time in the past or present, acted for the opposite party, the firm must turn down acting for the client in the new matter. Many law firms perform their conflict of interest searches through such software as PCLaw's "Conflict Search" feature, which is capable of searching by options such as last name or address. The law clerk/assistant keys in the desired search option, e.g. last name, and the system will bring up any files opened containing that last name or any dockets entered that may contain that last name. Here is a sample of a PCLaw conflict of interest search, followed by the corresponding printout indicating clearance:

Figure 2.2 Conflict Search, Nicholas Romano

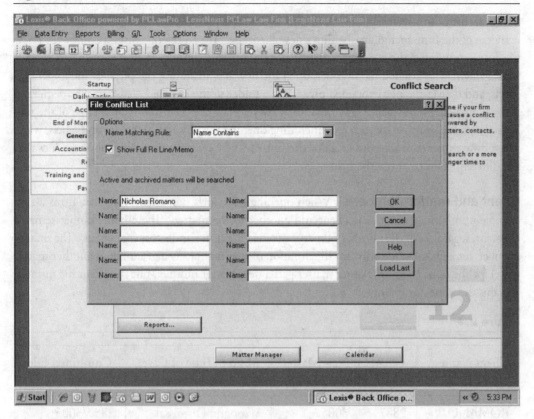

Figure 2.3 Conflict Search Results, Nicholas Romano

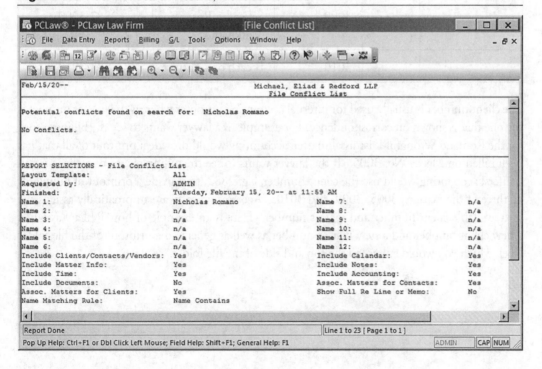

OPENING A NEW CLIENT FILE

Large law firms usually have a file/records management department handling all of the file-related activities of the firm, including opening a new client file. The law clerk/assistant completes a new file form containing the necessary client information and submits it electronically to records management who assign a file number, open the new file, including the physical file folder and labels, and deliver the newly opened physical file folder to the law clerk/assistant who requested it to be opened. With smaller law firms, each lawyer's law clerk/assistant is in charge of the file-related activities for that lawyer's files, including opening the physical file folder and labels, while the software maintains a record of all of the firm's files by centrally recording all of the files that the different lawyers within the firm open.

Client and matter numbers When opening a file for a new client, most law firms assign two file numbers — one to the client and another to the matter. The **client** number remains constant, regardless of the number of matters (cases) the firm handles for that client. The **matter** number remains the same only for the duration of that matter. When acting on another matter (case) for the same client, the other matter gets a new matter number, but the client file number remains the same, for example:

Figure 2.4

Client Name	Client No.	New Matter No.	Matter (Type of Case)	Combined File No.
ROMANO, Nicholas	2887	3005	Wrongful Dismissal	2887/3005
		3009	Sale of 5 Roses Road Markham	2887/3009
		3010	Breach of Contract	2887/3010

The client number is usually used for internal accounting purposes whereas the matter number is the one that is shown on correspondence. For example, if a lawyer wants to see the billing record for the Romano Wrongful Dismissal matter, accounting would provide a printout of all that has been billed on Matter No. 3005. If the lawyer wants to see the billing record of a client for all matters, accounting would use the client number, e.g. 2887, to provide a printout of billing for all three of the matters, 3005, 3009, and 3010. Accounting software automatically assigns the next available client number and matter number. Here is an example of how PCLaw assigned a new client number and a new matter number as well as generated a printout of the file folder label, which you would adhere to the top and side of the file folder.

Figure 2.5 New Client and Matter Numbers, Nicholas Romano

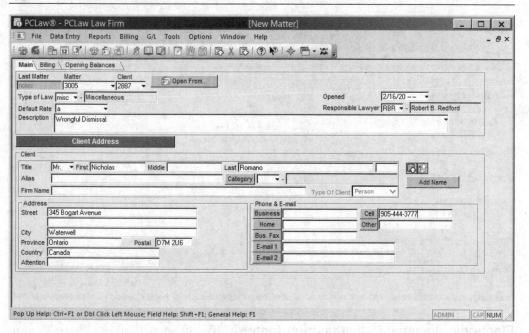

Figure 2.6 File Opening Label, Nicholas Romano

ROMANO, Nicholas 3005 Re: Wrongful Dismissal Client No. 2887 345 Bogart Avenue Waterwell, Ontario D7M 2U6 Tel: 905-444-3777 Date Opened: February 16, 20--	**ROMANO, Nicholas** 3005 Re: Wrongful Dismissal Client No. 2887 345 Bogart Avenue Waterwell, Ontario D7M 2U6 Tel: 905-444-3777 Date Opened: February 16, 20--

Paper files   Law firms usually use the traditional legal size (8 ½ x 14") paper folders when opening new files. The computer-generated label is adhered to the front and side of the folder. Different colour folders are usually used as sub-files, e.g. green for real estate documents, blue for pleadings, yellow for expert reports, red for original signed documents, etc. A correspondence brad is also usually kept at the front of the file, and the correspondence is kept in chronological order, with most recent on top. Most lawyers keep their physical files, usually in alphabetical order, in filing cabinets assigned to them near their offices, with the most recent files being stored in their offices. The files that the law clerk/assistant is working on are kept on the desk of the law clerk/ assistant.

Electronic files   Electronic files are usually organized and managed through Microsoft Word. A new folder or directory is usually opened for a client and subfolders are created for each matter of the same client. Here is an example of the files which Robert B. Redford is handling, including the subfolders for the various matters of Mr. Romano:

Figure 2.7 Directory, Nicholas Romano

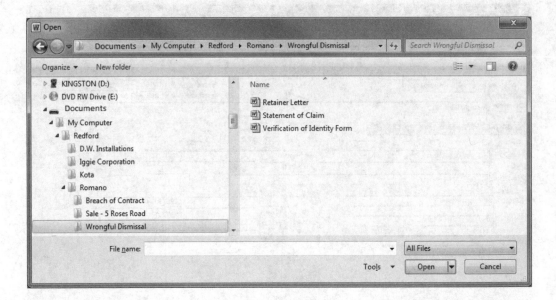

Electronic document identification footers   Identify each document clearly so as to make retrieval easy for all who might be involved in working on a particular document. Here are the steps for creating your footer.

Creating Document Identification Footer – Windows 7/8/10 Versions:

1. Save your document in the client directory, giving it a clearly identifiable name (and date/ reference initials, if helpful).
2. While still within your document, cursor to the top of the first page of your document.
3. Click Insert; click Footer; click Blank.
4. While still on the Insert Ribbon, click Quick Parts; click Field. Under Categories, click Document Information, and under Field Names, click File Name. Under Field Options, click Add path to file name, then click Ok. Your footer should appear at the foot of your document.
5. Highlight footer and make font smaller.
6. Click Close Header and Footer.

Your footer should appear at the foot of each page of your document, e.g.:

> C:\Documents\My Computer\Redford\Romano\Wrongful Dismissal\Statement of Claim.docx

Creating Document Identification Footer – Windows 7/8/10 Versions:

Follow the steps on the following Windows 7/8/10 screen display to create a document identification footer; the sample footer at the foot of the screen was created using the steps on the screen.

Figure 2.8 Creating Document Identification Footer, Windows 7/8/10

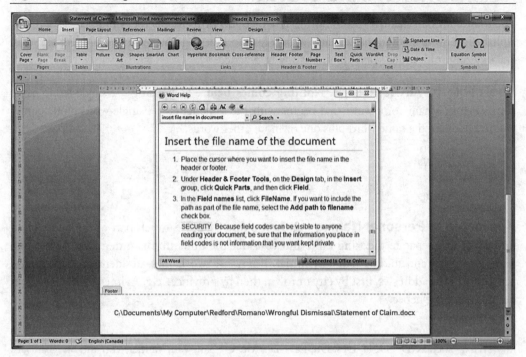

Client list   When the system assigns the next available client number to a new client, the system also automatically adds that client's name to an alphabetical list of all of the clients of the firm. The client list feature of PCLaw, for example, prints out a list by client name, file number, or matter number, as you require. Print the client list often to keep it updated as it changes with each new entry of new clients. See Precedent 2.1 for a sample PCLaw printout of Robert B. Redford's client list and Precedent 2.2 for a sample PCLaw client list of our firm, Michael, Eliad & Redford LLP.

NEW CLIENT IDENTIFICATION AND VERIFICATION

Client identification and verification requirements, referred to as KYC (know your client), are in effect in Ontario. These measures are intended to enhance public protection by preventing fraudulent or criminal activities. Identifying the client means obtaining certain information from your client such as the name, address, and occupation of your client and any third party directing or instructing your client: for example, your client is a corporation and the third party providing instructions is the president. Verifying the identity of the client means looking at an original identifying document (photo identification) to ensure that your client and any third parties are who they say they are. You are only required to verify the identity of your client and such third parties if you are involved in a funds transfer activity, e.g. a real estate transaction. Client identification applies to clients who are individuals, Precedent 2.3, and those who are corporations, Precedent 2.4. The Law Society of Upper Canada requires lawyers and self-employed licensed paralegals to retain a record of the client identification form and also a copy of the documents received to verify the identity of a client, e.g. copy of driver's licence, passport, etc.

ALPHABETICAL FILING SYSTEM

The most common manual method of filing which law firms use is the simplified "as written" alphabetical filing method, particularly with regard to indexing business names. Here are some key indexing rules which you will find handy in practice:

Applicable to All Names   **1. Nothing comes before something**   A single-letter name comes before a name of a word that begins with the same letter. A single-word name comes before a name of the same word plus one or more other words, etc.

As Written	As Filed
A	A
A. Aaron	Aaron, A.

Applicable to Personal Names   **2. Last name first**   Treat each part of the name of an individual as a separate indexing unit, and consider the units in this order: last name, first name or initial, and middle name or initial, if any. If two names are identical, alphabetize according to the addresses, first by city or town, then by province: e.g. Aylmer, Ontario, comes before Aylmer, Quebec.

Note:
(a) Prefixes such as De, De la, Des, Du, La, Mac, Mc, O', San, Van, Vander, Von and St. (Saint), as well as apostrophes and hyphens, are written as part of the surname and are indexed as one unit.
(b) Titles such as Mrs., Miss, Dr., Professor, Captain, and Reverend are placed at the end of the name, usually enclosed in parentheses.
(c) Academic degrees such as LL.B., B.Sc., Ph.D., and CPA are not included unless needed as identifying elements where two or more names are otherwise identical.

As Written	As Filed
Anne-Marie J. Blake	Blake, Anne-Marie J.
Anne Marie J. Blake	Blake, Anne Marie J.
Anne Marie J. Blake-Andrews	Blake-Andrews, Anne Marie J.
Elwin D'Angelo	D'Angelo, Elwin
Elizabeth MacDonald	MacDonald, Elizabeth
Allan McDonald	McDonald, Allan
Dr. R. P. St. Denis	Saint Denis, R. P. (Dr.)

Applicable to Business Names   **3. First word first**   Business names are filed as written, e.g. first word of the name first, then second, etc. When the name of a business includes a person's surname, plus one or more given names, index the name either in the same way as a personal name or as written, but be consistent. Acronyms are also filed as written with the acronym representing one word (often with the full name spelled out in parentheses).

Note:
Articles: a, an, the; prepositions: from, to, by, in, of, on, at; conjunctions: and, &; hyphens and apostrophes are included.

As Written	As Filed
CBC	CBC
IBM	IBM
Nelson Dairy	Nelson Dairy
The Neuman Corporation	Neuman Corporation (The)
Cynthia Neuman Boutiques	Neuman, Cynthia, Boutiques*
Toronto-Hamilton Courier Service	Toronto-Hamilton Courier Service
Walsh Bros. Ltd.	Walsh Bros. Ltd.
Wool & Lace Shop of Shops	Wool & Lace Shop of Shops

*or Cynthia Neuman Boutiques (filed behind "C")

Applicable to Number Names   **4. Numbers in names** Names beginning with numbers are indexed as written in numerical sequence and before the alphabetically arranged names. If the numbers appearing at the beginning of the name are spelled out, they are considered as one filing unit, e.g. "Five Hundred," and are indexed and filed alphabetically.

As Written	As Filed
24 Hour Shop	24 Hour Shop
500 Lounge	318 Tavern (The)
The 318 Tavern	500 Lounge
Two Bells Ltd.	Baskerville 2000 Club
Baskerville 2000 Club	Baskerville 5000 Club
Baskerville 5000 Club	Five Hundred Club
Five Hundred Club	Two Bells Ltd.

Applicable to Educational Institution Names   **5. Distinctive name first** Consider the distinctive name first, but transpose personal names, or file them as written, but be consistent. If the non-distinctive words, e.g. university, college, appear at the beginning of the name, consider them as the last indexing unit.

As Written	As Filed
George Brown College of Applied Arts and Technology	Brown, George, College of Applied Arts and Technology*
University of Calgary	Calgary, University (of)
York University	York University

*or George Brown College of Applied Arts and Technology (filed behind "G")

CLOSING FILES

Files are closed when all work has been completed on them, and the client owes no money to the firm. A client ledger is printed from the firm's accounting software to confirm that there are no active dockets, disbursements, trust monies, or receivables owing on the file. Once it is confirmed that there is nothing outstanding on the file, the law clerk/assistant files the client ledger on the correspondence brad in the paper file. The lawyer then writes a memo to the accounting department, giving instructions to close the file in the accounting software. Some law firms scan the entire closed file and store it online for easy retrieval, if necessary. Other law firms physically store closed files at off-site storage management facilities with the use of a password. The law clerk/assistant logs on the facility's website and enters such information as the file number of the closed file, client name, matter, and the box number that the off-site storage facility has assigned to the firm for the storage of the closed files. Lawyers must keep closed files usually for a minimum of six years. Once closed, the law clerk/assistant purges the file before storage to reduce its bulk. When purging the file, keep the following guide in mind:

Discard: Extra draft copies and duplicates of documents and correspondence and other papers that are not likely to be useful in the future.

Keep everything else, and deliver to the client any documents that belong to the client. Some of these include:
- documents the lawyer prepared for the benefit of the client, and for which, the client has paid.
- documents which the client sent to the lawyer before the retainer or which a third party sent to the lawyer during the retainer.
- client's original documents and any other documents not already provided to the client in the course of the retainer, e.g. pleadings, affidavits, transfers, charges, or similar documents.

REMINDER SYSTEMS

The *Rules of Professional Conduct* require lawyers to maintain a reminder system of limitation periods and due dates. Limitation periods are dates by which the lawyer must **begin** a court action or the client loses his or her right to do so. Due dates are deadlines by which the lawyer must prepare, serve, or file documents. Unheeded limitation and due dates may place the client in default and result in malpractice action against the lawyer. The legal reminder system is often referred to as a "tickler" because it "tickles" the lawyer's memory about approaching limitation and due dates.

Automated reminder systems This system is called **task manager** because it stores reminders as **tasks** in the online calendar through such software as Microsoft Outlook which is the email program that most law firms use.

Online calendars The online calendar is where the tasks (reminders) are saved so others can access the online calendar. The lawyer and the law clerk/assistant have access to each other's online calendars as well as to the calendars of other lawyers, law clerks, legal assistants, and paralegals with whom they may be working. Many lawyers make their own task entries in the online calendar, although either the lawyer or the law clerk/assistant may do so. Usually, at the beginning of each week, the law clerk/assistant checks the calendar for what tasks are due for that week and prints out copies of the list of tasks for the lawyer and for the law clerk/assistant. The law clerk/assistant is responsible for keeping track of the tasks, that is, making sure that the calendared task is done and the due date met.

How task managers work   The lawyer or the law clerk/assistant, but usually the lawyer, determines the due date, e.g. March 31, by which a task must be done, e.g. a statement of claim. The law clerk/assistant then sets the task in the online calendar for March 31, entering the file name, number, and task, e.g. statement of claim. The law clerk/assistant also sets a reminder, usually about one or two days before the due date, e.g. March 29. On that day, the system will automatically bring up a reminder message about the due date of March 31. Once the law clerk/assistant completes the task, i.e. prepares the statement of claim, the law clerk/assistant notes it in the online calendar as having been 100 percent completed, and that cancels out the reminder. Here is an example of the reminder in the Romano file about the preparation of a statement of claim:

Figure 2.9   Task Reminder, Nicholas Romano

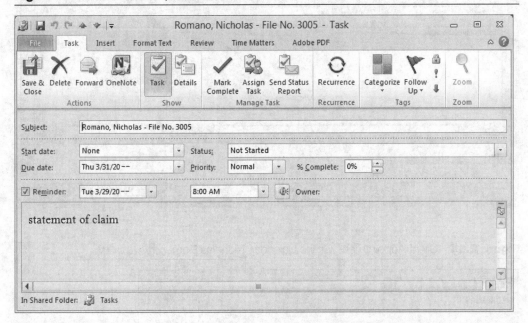

Online appointments   Either the lawyer or the law clerk/assistant may enter appointments such as meetings with clients, court attendances, etc. in the same online calendar as that in which tasks are entered, so that any number of lawyers, legal assistants, law clerks, and paralegals may access it for checking or booking appointments. To book an appointment, open the calendar of the particular lawyer to see what dates and times are available, book the appointment, and save it to the lawyer's calendar. The lawyer may at any time check his or her online calendar from his or her computer to see the appointments for the day. A few lawyers may use the paper calendars and diaries in which either the lawyer or the law clerk/assistant books appointments manually. Here is an example of how to save the date and time of an appointment in the online calendar, followed by an example of the block of time, e.g. 10 a.m. to 12 p.m. booked on the online calendar in the Romano file:

Figure 2.10   Online Client Appointment, Nicholas Romano

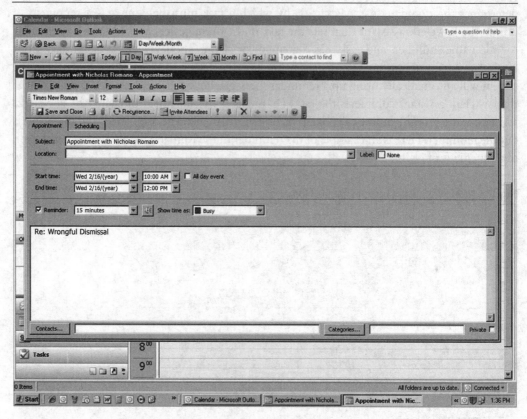

Figure 2.11   Client Appointment, Online Calendar, Nicholas Romano

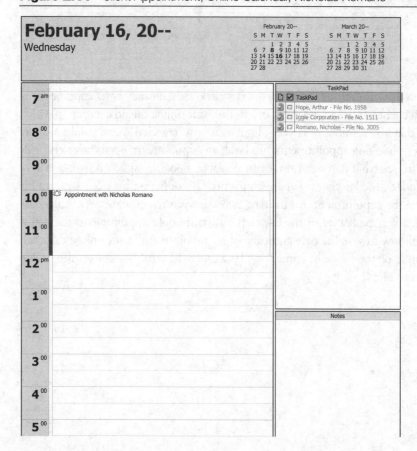

CHAPTER SUMMARY

There are day-to-day activities that are critical to the smooth running of the law firm. These include handling the telephone, voice mail, and paper mail; opening new client files, booking client appointments, maintaining reminder systems, and managing electronic files and client records. When opening new client files, it is necessary for law firms to run a conflict of interest search and also identify and/or verify the identity of each new client.

REVIEW QUESTIONS

1. What is a conflict of interest?
2. What does KYC mean?
3. What is involved in establishing a new client identification and verification?
4. What is a reminder system?
5. A "tickler" is a person who makes people laugh. Explain.
6. What is the difference between a client number and a matter file number?

Precedent 2.1   Electronic Client List of Lawyer, Excerpt, PCLaw

Michael, Eliad & Redford LLP
List of Clients - Billing Address

Client	Billing Name / Billing Address / Billing City, Province, Postal		Maj	Clnt	Intro	Lwyer	Business / Fax / Home
	Matter	**Description**	**Law Type**	**Rate**	**Resp.**	**Assg.** **Oth.Stf**	**Open Date**
1017	Havisham, Maria 333 GST Drive Newmarket, Ontario L2K 2D1						905-859-1268
	3560	Divorce	mat	A	RBR	RBR	Feb 15/20–
1486	Jones, Herbert 146 Camelot Avenue Toronto, Ontario M6K 2W2						416-768-5867
	2347	Sale of 146 Camelot Avenue	re	A	RBR	RBR	Feb 18/20–
0102	Mandamo Properties Ltd. 1750 Finch Avenue East, Room 3244 Toronto, Ontario M2V 2X5						416-250-5800
	2773	Incorporation	corp	A	RBR	RBR	Feb 18/20–
1316	Murphy, James 46 Original Street Aurora, Ontario L2C 4T4						905-738-3831
	2653	Estate of Arthur William Gold	est.	A	RBR	RBR	Sep 10/20–
2887	Romano, Nicholas 345 Bogart Avenue Waterwell, Ontario D7M 2U6					**RBR**	905-444-3777
	3005	Wrongful Dismissal	misc	A	RBR	RBR	Feb 16/20–

Precedent 2.2   Electronic Client List of Law Firm, Excerpt, PCLaw

Michael, Eliad & Redford LLP
List of Clients - Billing Address

Client	Billing Name / Billing Address / Billing City, Province, Postal		Maj	Clnt	Intro	Lwyer	Business / Fax / Home
	Matter	**Description**	**Law Type**	**Rate**	**Resp.**	**Assg.** **Oth.Stf**	**Open Date**
1331	Bear, Edward 879 Merton Road Toronto, Ontario M7W 2W6					**JAM**	416-719-1752
	2649	Copyright Infringement	lit	A	JAM	JAM	Mar 25/20–
1288	Dixon, Wendy 2 Stetson Street Waterwell, Ontario D4L 6N4						
	2513	Postponement of Interest	re	A	JAM	JAM	Jan 20/20--
0065	Eyre, Jane 99 Rochester Boulevard Waterwell, Ontario D4R 5Q3						905-923-9263
	1427	Injury	lit	A	DWE	DWE	Feb 19/20–
1017	Havisham, Maria 333 GST Drive Newmarket, Ontario L2K 2D1						905-859-1268
	3560	Divorce	mat	A	RBR	RBR	Feb 15/20–
0922	Mason, Jennifer 88 Golden Gate Road Hamilton, Ontario L2A 2W6						1-905-522-2255
	1777	Negligence	lit	A	JAM	JAM	Apr 10/20--

MICHAEL, ELIAD & REDFORD LLP

CLIENT IDENTIFICATION FORM
INDIVIDUAL CLIENTS
Please Print

Section 1

Last Name:	First Name:	Middle Name(s):
Romano	Nicholas	

Home Address:
345 Bogart Avenue, Waterwell, Ontario, D7M 2U6

Home Phone Number:	Business Phone Number (if applicable):
905-444-3777	

Occupation or Occupation(s):
Executive marketing supervisor

Section 2

Is individual client representing a third party?

Yes   No

		If yes, please request and complete a new form for each corporate entity or individual represented

Section 3 – IDENTIFICATION REQUIRED, copy attached:

ALSO FOR USE IN VERIFYING IDENTITY PURSUANT TO LAW SOCIETY RULES

Client to provide an original government issued identification that is valid and <u>has not</u> <u>expired</u>:

	Yes			Yes
Driver's licence		OR	Birth certificate	
Provincial/Territorial health card		OR	Passport	
Citizenship card		OR	Other similar record	

Section 4 – VERIFICATION OF IDENTITY, if required

Identity verified by (print name	Date verified
Robert B. Redford	February 16, 20--

_____
Responsible Lawyer signature

MICHAEL, ELIAD & REDFORD LLP
Barristers and Solicitors

VERIFICATION OF IDENTITY
(For use where the client or the third party is an organization)

Name: _____ Watergate Nixon Corp. _____

Business Address: _____ 435 Woodward Road, Courtice, Ontario   L8K 9Y3 __

Business Phone No.: _____ 905-495-2011 _____

Incorporation or Business Identification No.: _____ 002223874 _____

Place of Issue: _____ Ontario _____

Type of Business or Activity: _____ Surveillance _____

Person Authorized to Instruct

Name: _____ Richard Playfoot _____

Position: _____ President _____

Phone No.: _____ 905-239-3939 _____

Original Documents Reviewed - Copy Attached

 ❏ Driver's Licence
 ❏ Birth Certificate
 ❏ Passport
 ❏ Other_____

Name and Occupation(s) of Director (Maximum of 500 characters)

_____ Richard Playfoot, President of Corporation _____

Names, Addresses and Occupation(s) of Owners or Shareholders owning a 25% interest or more of the organization or shares in the organization (maximum of 500 characters)

Richard Playfoot, 3859 Lakeshore Blvd. W., Miss., Ontario, L8K 2M7 – 100% shareholder ____

Original Document Reviewed - Copy Attached

 ❏ Certificate of Corporate Status
 ❏ Annual Filings of the Organization(specify type)_____
 ❏ Partnership Agreement
 ❏ Trust Agreement
 ❏ Articles of Association
 ❏ Other (specify type)_____

Meeting Date Identity Verified:_____ September 5, 20– _____

Identity Verified By: _____ Robert B. Redford _____

Date File Reviewed by Lawyer:_____

Name of Lawyer:_____

CHAPTER 3

LEGAL OFFICE DOCKETS AND ACCOUNTS

This chapter discusses the essential aspects of effective practice management, including time management, legal banking, and billing practices.

BANK ACCOUNTS

The Law Society of Upper Canada requires law firms to operate two separate bank accounts: a **general** account and a **trust** account.

General bank account This account is the firm's business bank account out of which lawyers transact the firm's business. Lawyers must deposit in this account only money belonging to the firm and received from clients in payment of services **already** rendered (completed).

Trust bank account This account is the firm's bank account in which lawyers must deposit money **in trust** for the client, i.e. money that belongs to the client. Technically, all money that a client pays to the firm belongs to the client until the firm completes the services to the client. Examples of money that lawyers hold in trust for their clients include retainer money and real estate purchase money. Here is an excerpt from relevant sections of the Law Society's by-laws respecting trust money:

> Every licensee who receives money in trust for a client shall immediately pay the money into an account at a chartered bank...to be kept in the name of the licensee, or in the name of the firm of licensees of which the licensee is a partner, through which the licensee practises law or provides legal services or by which the licensee is employed, and designated as a trust account... [A] licensee receives money in trust for a client if the licensee receives from a person...money that belongs in whole or in part to a client...

Legal TIP
Unless otherwise instructed, write cheques for client disbursements (expenses) on the firm's general account. Lawyers may reimburse themselves right away by writing trust account cheques to the firm in the amount of the disbursements already paid out on behalf of the client.

ACCOUNTING

The firm's accounting department or office manager is usually in charge of posting the deposit of trust or general accounts from clients, usually through billing and accounting software which keeps track of the balances in the trust and general accounts. The accounting staff makes all bank entries through such accounting software as, for example, PCLaw, which then automatically tallies up the total and prints out a deposit slip. Accounting then takes the deposit slip to the bank to make the trust or general account deposit.

FEES

Fees are monies lawyers charge for providing legal services to their clients. Lawyers charge fees on the basis of an hourly rate. The hourly rate is usually based on a lawyer's length of experience — the longer the length of experience, the higher the hourly rate. In some areas of law, such as real estate, lawyers may charge a flat fee instead of an hourly fee.

Law clerk and paralegal fees   Under the *Rules of Civil Procedure,* lawyers may, in addition to their own fees, also include in their accounts to their clients fees for services which law clerks and paralegals provide.

Contingency fees   Contingency fees are legal fees that lawyers can charge only if they win the case. Lawyers may take on cases on a contingency fee basis in class actions and other litigation cases, except family law or criminal or quasi-criminal matters.

DISBURSEMENTS

Disbursements are a firm's out-of-pocket expenses which lawyers pay in a client's matter. Examples of disbursements include court fees, fees of other government agencies, and costs for photocopying, couriers, cab fares, and parking. Lawyers pay for such disbursements out of their firm's general account and get reimbursed when billing the client by charging the disbursements back to the client. For basic, internal disbursements such as photocopying, many law firms use software that is attached to the photocopier and to the printer of the law clerk/assistant. The software requires the entering of the client's file number and automatically posts the disbursement to the client's file. Postage and long distance telephone calls are similarly set up to require the client's file number for automatic posting.

For disbursements from outside sources such as, for example, couriers, the law clerk/assistant when ordering a courier online provides the client's file number as a reference number, and the courier sends its invoice to the firm's accounting department electronically who then posts the disbursement to the client's file for billing. In the case of a lawyer's personal out-of-pocket expenses, the lawyer usually completes an expense sheet template, Precedent 3.1, equivalent to a paper petty cash requisition, and submits a paper copy to accounting, usually once a month. Accounting processes the expense by posting it to the file number of the respective clients and reimburses the lawyer via a firm cheque.

Cheque requisitions   Cheque requisitions for payment of disbursements are usually done online through accounting software and are charged to the client by file number. The law clerk/assistant completes the requisition online and sends it to accounting who will then print out the cheque through PCLaw and have it signed and returned to the law clerk/assistant who requested it. Here is an example of a PCLaw cheque requisition in the Romano case for the filing fee of a statement of claim:

Figure 3.1   PCLaw Cheque Requisition, Romano

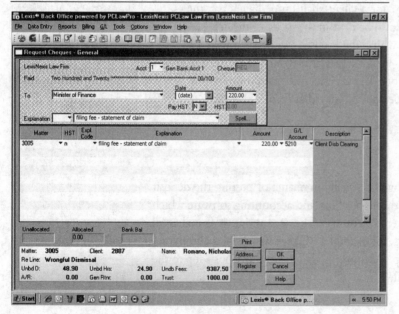

RETAINER LETTER OR AGREEMENT

A retainer letter or agreement, Precedent 3.2, is a document which outlines the legal services to be provided to the client and the terms of payment of the legal fees. Along with the retainer letter or agreement, lawyers usually request clients to provide a deposit which will be applied toward the payment of legal expenses. The firm's accounting staff deposits the retainer money in the firm's trust account as it is money that belongs to the client until the lawyers complete some or all of the legal services, at which time, the lawyers may render an invoice to the client, then transfer the retainer money from the trust account to the firm's general account as money earned for services rendered and belonging to the firm. Here is an example of a PCLaw retainer deposit in the Romano case:

Figure 3.2   PCLaw Retainer, Romano

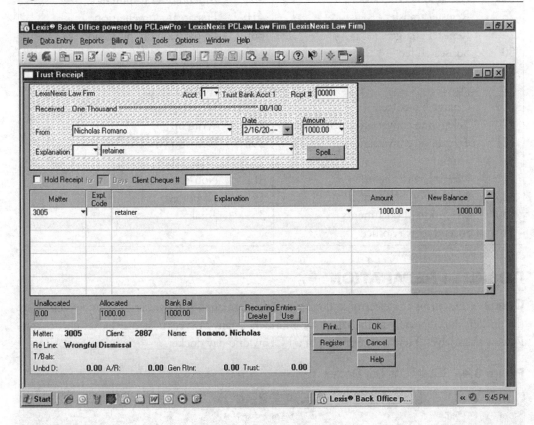

DOCKETS

Dockets are lawyers' records of time spent on a client matter. Time is the basis on which lawyers usually bill their clients. There is billable and non-billable time. Billable is time spent on a client matter, and non-billable is time spent on other activities, e.g. administrative activities. Lawyers multiply the docketed time by their hourly rate, e.g. $400/hr. x 0.5 = $200. Lawyers usually docket time in tenths of an hour, on six-minute intervals, as follows:

0.1 = 6 min	0.2 = 12 min	0.3 = 18 min	0.4 = 24 min	0.5 = 30 min
0.6 = 36 min	0.7 = 42 min	0.8 = 48 min	0.9 = 54 min	1.0 = 60 min

ACTIVITY LIST

An activity list is a list of short forms of legal services intended for speed and convenience in preparing dockets. There is no standard activity list as each law firm creates its own, and thus the short forms vary among law firms according to preference. Following is a sample activity list:

Figure 3.3

ACTIVITY LIST			
1	Client disbursements recovered	200	Incorporation and organization costs
2	Photocopying charges		
3	Long distance telephone calls	300	Receive discharge documents
10	Filing of documents	310	Register discharge of charge
11	Transportation costs	315	Forward release of interest
20	Land transfer tax	320	Report to client
21	Search fee(s)	400	Attend negotiations with
22	Execution certificate	401	Amend offer to purchase
23	Register transfer	410	Prepare documentation
24	Register charge	600	Preparation of application
50	Subsearch fee	601	Prepare appeal
91	Long distance telephone charges	602	Attend meeting at
92	Postage	650	Attend closing
100	Charge block fee	651	Meeting/consultation with client
120	Telephone conversation with client	880	Write up
121	Telephone conversation on behalf of you	890	Write down
		21	Chargeable
122	Meeting with client	0	Non-chargeable
123	Meeting on behalf of client	14	Disbursed
130	Execution of documents	35	Total
140	Attend registry office		

DOCKET PREPARATION

Online Law firms use electronic docketing through such software as PCLaw, which posts the dockets automatically to the client file number. Many lawyers post the docket entries into PCLaw themselves. Here is an example of a PCLaw one-day docket.

Figure 3.4 PCLaw One-Day Docket

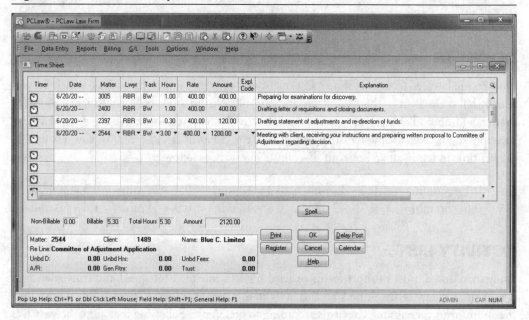

Legal Office Procedures

By timer   Legal software, such as PCLaw, allows the lawyer or the law clerk to engage a timer while making phone calls, reviewing work, or doing anything else that is docketable for an indication of precise time spent. Then, the lawyer or the law clerk enters in the date, file number, and description of the timed activity, and saves the docket when completed in PCLaw where the time spent is charged to the client's file number at billing time.

Figure 3.5 PCLaw Timer

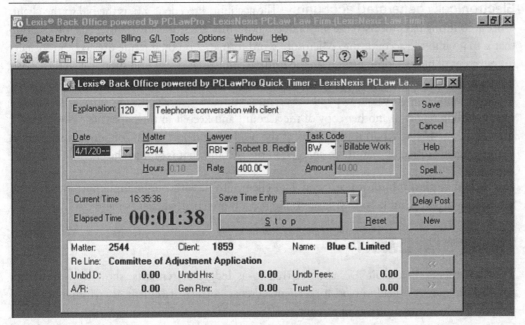

By computer template   With this method of docketing, Precedents 3.3 and 3.4, the lawyer accesses the computer template and keys in the docket tasks and prints out the template docket, or prints out the template in blank and handwrites the docket tasks. The lawyer then hands the paper copy to the law clerk/assistant who enters the docket into the accounting system to be charged to the client's file number at billing time.

ACCOUNTS

An account is a lawyer's bill to the client. It outlines the lawyer's fees and disbursements for work done on a file. The information which goes in accounts is generated from the dockets which the law clerk/assistant has entered, together with the disbursements which accounting has posted to the client file number. Be sure, therefore, that the file numbers and spelling of the file are correct when posting dockets and when generating accounts so that the right charges are made to the right client. Lawyers prepare an account at the completion of every file. That is how lawyers get paid for the services they provide. In cases which take a long time to complete, lawyers usually issue **interim accounts**; that is, they bill their clients intermittently, e.g. monthly or quarterly, throughout the life of the case. This ensures that lawyers receive most or all of their money by the time a case is over.

Harmonized sales tax (HST)   Computer accounting software is capable of automatically tracking and calculating the HST. Law firms are a service industry, and HST applies to the services they provide. HST is, therefore, payable on all legal fees, and it is usually shown in the accounts which lawyers send out to their clients at the time of billing. Computer software is usually programmed to determine those disbursements which are subject to HST and those which are not. In general, any government-imposed fee that a lawyer pays as an agent for the client, e.g. issuing a statement of claim, registering a transfer, is not subject to HST.

Legal TIP

If your firm has been charged HST on a client disbursement, include the disbursement in the account as subject to HST.

Pre-billing reports   Generally, law firms generate accounts once a month, usually at the end of each month. Once all of the dockets and disbursements for the month have been posted, the lawyer gives you a list of client files for which the lawyer requires a pre-billing report, Precedent 3.5. You would then generate the pre-billing report (referred to as pre-bill) through your accounting software and give it to the lawyer who will assign the fee he or she wishes to charge. You would then photocopy the pre-billing report and submit it to the accounting department for processing.

Electronically generated accounts   The account, Precedent 3.6, is the bill to the client. Once accounting has processed the pre-billing report, they electronically transfer the information that is to go into the account into Microsoft Word format. You then refine the account, usually for purposes of presentation, print it on the firm's accounts stationery, and submit it to the lawyer for approval. The lawyer approves the original which you forward to the client. Attach a copy of the pre-billing report to one copy of the account and give it to accounting; attach one copy of the pre-billing report to another copy of the account and keep it in the paper file. Never send a copy of the pre-billing report to the client, as the pre-billing report might contain adjustments in charges that are different than those charged in the account that is sent to the client.

Number of copies, minimum 3: Send 1 to client; give 1, with pre-billing report attached, to accounting department; keep 1, with pre-billing report attached, in client's file.

TRUST STATEMENT

Trust statements, Precedent 3.7, also referred to as **ledger statements**, show how your firm handled the money it held in trust for a client. Prepare a trust statement, therefore, only when your firm held money in trust for a client.

Manually prepared accounts   There is no prescribed form for accounts, electronic or manual. See Precedent 3.7 for a style commonly used in practice. Another less frequently used style is to use the left two-thirds of the sheet for the description of services and the right one-third for the fees and disbursements columns. Key points include: Use the firm's accounts stationery. Begin each account with: TO PROFESSIONAL SERVICES RENDERED: or TO SERVICES RENDERED: End all accounts with THIS IS OUR ACCOUNT. Include the interest statement as a standard statement in all accounts, whether or not fully paid. E.& O.E. stands for "Errors and Omissions Excepted." Prepare a trust statement (only if your firm holds client money in its trust account) on a separate sheet or at the foot of the account.

Number of copies, minimum 3: Send 1 to client; give 1 to accounting department; keep 1 in client's file.

LEGAL AID ACCOUNTS

Legal Aid Ontario   Legal Aid Ontario is a corporation created under the *Legal Aid Services Act*. The mandate of Legal Aid Ontario is to provide less costly legal services to people who are unable to afford private lawyers. It is responsible to the Attorney General because the Ontario government is funding it. Legal Aid Ontario has offices in many areas across the province, each administered by an area director.

Legal Aid Panel   Lawyers who wish to act for Legal Aid clients submit an application to Legal Aid. Legal Aid assigns a number to each lawyer who applies, which number the lawyer must use in his or her communications with Legal Aid. Legal Aid then places the lawyer's name on a list of lawyers known as the "Legal Aid Panel." From this list, a Legal Aid applicant may choose any lawyer he or she wishes to retain. When lawyers place their names on the Legal Aid panel, they agree to:

- Provide legal services to Legal Aid clients on a lower fee structure.
- Provide legal services equal to the quality provided to other clients.
- Treat confidentially the fact that the client is a legal aid recipient.

Legal Aid Ontario also operates a **duty counsel panel** which consists of lawyers appointed to assist any person appearing in court without having retained a lawyer.

Legal Aid Tariff The tariff prescribes the maximum annual number of hours for which lawyers may bill Legal Aid on behalf of Legal Aid clients. The hourly rate is based on a three-tier level of experience, with the longer the experience, the higher the hourly rate. In addition, Legal Aid also pays hourly rates for work which law clerks or students-at-law have done on a case.

Basic procedure Legal Aid Ontario issues a certificate to an eligible Legal Aid applicant. The applicant completes and sends or hand-delivers the certificate to a lawyer of choice from the Legal Aid panel. The lawyer signs and submits the certificate to Legal Aid to indicate his or her acceptance of the case. At the completion of the case, or intermittently, the lawyer bills Legal Aid Ontario for services rendered. The **Legal Accounts Department** of Legal Aid Ontario handles all of the bills which lawyers submit and pays the lawyers on behalf of the Legal Aid clients; Legal Aid Ontario then collects all or part of the money from any Legal Aid client who is able to pay it back.

Legal Aid Online Legal Aid Ontario has established a Legal Aid Online billing system where a lawyer can invoice Legal Aid Ontario through a dedicated, secured website by keying in his or her lawyer number and password, entering the billing details, and submitting the bill electronically. The system provides immediate confirmation of the account.

CHAPTER SUMMARY

Law Society regulations require all lawyers to maintain two bank accounts–a general account and a trust account. The general account is the account out of which the law firm pays its bills and operates its business. The trust account is the account in which lawyers deposit money that belongs to clients, i.e. money held in trust for a client.

Generally, lawyers bill their clients on the basis of the amount of time they spend on their clients' cases. The forms on which lawyers and often law clerks record the time they spend on a client's file are called dockets. Legal accounting software automatically generates pre-billing reports and accounts based on docketed entries. Accounts are lawyers' bills to the clients. Legal Aid Ontario offers fee-for-service legal aid to people who need lawyers and who cannot afford private lawyers.

REVIEW QUESTIONS

1. What is the difference between a general account and a trust account?
2. What is a docket?
3. What is an account?
4. In what situation would you prepare a trust statement?
5. Disbursements are items scattered about in law offices. Explain.

EXPENSES FOR ROBERT REDFORD

Date	File #	Client Name	Paid To	Description	Net	HST	Amount
CLIENT FILE CHARGES:							
Jul 25/--	2544	Blue C. Limited	T.P.A. Carpark	Parking - Meeting at Committee of Adjustment	$ 10.00	$ 1.30	$ 11.30
Jul 19/--	2544	Blue C. Limited	Print Three	Photocopies of plans	$ 28.00	$ 3.64	$ 31.64
Sep 6/--	2544	Blue C. Limited	Metro Taxi	Taxi cab ride to Ontario Municipal Board	$ 15.00	$ 1.95	$ 16.95
					$ -	$ -	$ -
					$ -	$ -	$ -
					$ 53.00	$ 6.89	
					$ 6.89		$ 59.89
					$ 59.89		
OTHER EXPENSE:							

RETAINER

1. Scope of Retainer

I, NICHOLAS ROMANO, the undersigned, hereby retain and employ MICHAEL, ELIAD & REDFORD LLP, Barristers and Solicitors, the "Firm," as my lawyers and authorize the Firm to represent me in the Wrongful Dismissal action and to take such actions, conduct such proceedings, perform such services, make such disbursements and employ such lawyers, agents and other experts as the Firm considers necessary or proper for the conduct of such matters on my behalf.

2. Deposit

I agree that the fee will not be less than $25,000.00. I also agree that I will be requested to provide an advance on my account of legal fees and disbursements from time to time. I agree to deposit with you the sum of $5,000.00 as an initial retainer, $1,000.00 of which I have already provided you with, and to deposit from time to time such interim retainer monies as the Firm may require to meet anticipated fees and disbursements in connection with this matter. This money will be held in the Firm's trust account to my credit to be applied toward such disbursements and legal fees when incurred. I understand that work will not be performed unless sufficient advances are paid to cover the work to be performed.

3. Fees, Disbursements, HST and Interest

(a)   I agree that the legal fees for this matter will be based on an hourly rate, which is presently $400.00 per hour.

(b)   I understand that in addition to the legal fees, my bill will include reasonable and necessary disbursements of money paid by the Firm on my behalf.

(c)   I understand that lawyers are required to charge HST on legal services and must further remit HST following issue of an invoice to a client. In addition to fees and disbursements, I agree to promptly pay any HST chargeable for legal services.

(d)   I agree that all accounts, including interim accounts, are payable upon receipt, and I agree to pay interest on any amounts outstanding for more than thirty (30) days in accordance with the *Solicitor's Act*.

4. Appropriation of Client's Trust Funds Received from Third Parties

I understand that in the course of this matter, the Firm may receive monies in trust from third parties to my credit. I authorize the Firm to deduct from such monies legal fees, disbursements, and interest on outstanding bills or taxes. I also agree that any settlement funds which are obtained on my behalf with respect to the matter herein shall be made payable to MICHAEL, ELIAD & REDFORD LLP, in Trust, and this shall serve as my irrevocable and sufficient authority for doing so. I also agree that any settlement funds or proceeds, which are paid on my behalf to MICHAEL, ELIAD & REDFORD LLP, in Trust, shall be used to pay any accounts owing by me to the Firm for services rendered.

5. Disclosure

I understand that subject to my legal requirements to disclose information, all communications with the Firm will be kept confidential. I acknowledge and agree that the Firm may disclose information regarding my file to such of the Firm's partners, associates or staff as may be reasonably necessary, and I understand that they will be bound by the same duty of confidentiality.

6. Termination of Our Services

I agree that in the Firm's discretion, it may withdraw from acting on my behalf upon delivery of notice to my last known address, and I agree to execute a consent to this effect if an application to the Court is required. Without limiting the generality of this paragraph, I agree that an instruction to the Firm to take action, which the Firm considers to be unprofessional or illegal, will be grounds for termination of the retainer. I further agree that non-payment of any account will be grounds for immediate termination by the Firm of this retainer.

_____   _____
Date   Signature

Precedent 3.3 One-Day Template Docket

<u>Robert B. Redford</u>		<u>RBR</u>	<u>June 20/--</u>	DOCKETS READY FOR ASSISTANT
Name		**No.**	**Date**	

Total Billable Hours for this date: **6.5**

DATE	FILE #	FILE NAME	TIME	COMMENTS
June 20/--	2544	Blue C. Limited	3.0	Meeting with client, receiving your instructions and preparing written proposal to Committee of Adjustment regarding decision.
June 20/--	3005	Romano, Nicholas	1.0	Preparing for examinations for discovery.
June 20/--	2400	Brown, John	1.0	Drafting letter of requisitions and closing documents.
June 20/--	2397	Jones, Herbert	0.3	Drafting statement of adjustments and re-direction of funds.
June 20/--	1863	Younger, Robert	0.5	Telephone conversation with client regarding debt collection.
June 20/--	2773	Mandamo Properties	0.7	Preparing articles of incorporation and reviewing NUANS name search.

Precedent 3.4 One-Client Template Docket

<u>Robert B. Redford</u>	<u>RBR</u>	DOCKETS READY FOR ASSISTANT
Name	**No.**	

Total Billable Hours for this date: **17.0**

DATE	FILE #	FILE NAME	TIME	COMMENTS
June 20/--	2544	Blue C. Limited	3.0	Meeting with client, receiving your instructions and preparing written proposal to Committee of Adjustment regarding decision.
July 15/--	2544	Blue C. Limited	1.7	Meeting on behalf of client, discussions with Paul Lindsay, land surveyor, and with Committee of Adjustment regarding variation of reference plan.
July 17/--	2544	Blue C. Limited	1.0	Preparation of application for severance of property.
July 19/--	2544	Blue C. Limited	2.5	Preparation of appeal to Ontario Municipal Board.
July 25/--	2544	Blue C. Limited	0.3	Attending meeting at Committee of Adjustment to serve notice of appeal.
Aug 15/--	2544	Blue C. Limited	2.0	Attending meeting at Committee of Adjustment for severance.
Aug 26/--	2544	Blue C. Limited	1.5	Meeting/consultation with client to review application before Committee of Adjustment and potential problems.
Sept 4/--	2544	Blue C. Limited	2.0	Preparation of appeal from second decision of Committee of Adjustment.
Sept 6/--	2544	Blue C. Limited	3.0	Attending meeting at Ontario Municipal Board for hearing.

Precedent 3.5 Pre-Billing Report

Blue C. Limited

			File #:	2544
Attention:	Mr. I.C. Blue, President		Inv #:	

RE: Committee of Adjustment Application

DATE	DESCRIPTION	TASK	HOURS	AMOUNT	LWYR
Jun 20/--	Meeting with client, receiving instructions and preparing written proposal to Committee of Adjustment regarding decision.	BW	3.00	1,200.00	RBR
Jul 15/--	Meeting on behalf of client, discussions with Paul Lindsay, land surveyor, and with Committee of Adjustment regarding variation of reference plan.	BW	1.70	680.00	RBR
Jul 17/--	Preparation of application for severance of property.	BW	1.00	400.00	RBR
Jul 19/--	Preparation of appeal to Ontario Municipal Board.	BW	2.50	1,000.00	RBR
Jul 25/--	Attending meeting at Committee of Adjustment to serve notice of appeal.	BW	0.30	120.00	RBR
Aug 15/--	Attending meeting at Committee of Adjustment for severance.	BW	2.00	800.00	RBR
Aug 26/--	Meeting/consultation with client to review application before Committee of Adjustment and potential problems.	BW	1.50	600.00	RBR
Sep 04/--	Preparation of appeal from second decision of Committee of Adjustment.	BW	2.00	800.00	RBR
Sep 06/--	Attending meeting at Ontario Municipal Board for hearing.	BW	3.00	1,200.00	RBR
	Totals		17.00	$6,800.00	
	Total HST on Fees			$884.00	

FEE SUMMARY:

Lawyer	Hours	Effective Rate	Amount
Robert B. Redford	17.00	$400.00	$6,800.00

DISBURSEMENTS		Disbursements	Receipts
Jun 30/--	Photocopying charges	38.00	
	Application fee for consent to severance*	160.00	
Jul 15/--	Surveys/Plans	141.59	
Jul 20/--	Photocopying charges	30.00	
	Totals	$369.59	$0.00
	Total HST on Disbursements	$27.25	
	Total Fees & Disbursements		**$8,080.84**
	Previous Balance		$0.00
	Previous Payments		$0.00
	Balance Due Now		**$8,080.84**
	AMOUNT QUOTED:		**$0.00**

Michael, Eliad & Redford LLP

863 Seneca Lane

Toronto, Ontario M4J 1P6

Telephone No. (416) 363-1079   Facsimile No.   (416) 363-2628

Blue C. Limited   November 11/--

1090 Desert Road

Toronto, Ontario M5G 1B3

File #:	2544

Attention: Mr. I.C. Blue, President   Inv #:   1

RE: Committee of Adjustment Application

TO ALL PROFESSIONAL SERVICES RENDERED in this matter to date, including:

Jun-20-xx   RBR   Meeting with client, receiving instructions and preparing written proposal to Committee of Adjustment regarding decision.

Jul-15-xx   RBR   Meeting on behalf of client, discussions with Paul Lindsay, land surveyor, and with Committee of Adjustment regarding variation of reference plan.

Jul-17-xx   RBR   Preparation of application for severance of property.

Jul-19-xx   RBR   Preparation of appeal to Ontario Municipal Board.

Jul-25-xx   RBR   Attending meeting at Committee of Adjustment to serve notice of appeal.

Aug-15-xx   RBR   Attending meeting at Committee of Adjustment for severance.

Aug-26-xx   RBR   Meeting/consultation with client to review application before Committee of Adjustment and potential problems.

Sep-04-xx   RBR   Preparation of appeal from second decision of Committee of Adjustment.

Sep-06-xx   RBR   Attending meeting at Ontario Municipal Board for hearing.

Totals	$6,800.00
HST on Fees	$884. 00

Disbursements

Photocopying charges	68.00
Application fee for consent to severance*	160.00
Surveys/Plans	141.59

Totals	$369.59
HST on Disbursements	$27.25

Total Fees, Disbursements & HST	**$8,080.84**

Balance Due Now	**$8,080.84**

* tax-exempt

Interest runs on this account at the rate of 0.5% per annum on unpaid fees, disbursements or other charges, calculated from a date that is one (1) month after the date the account is delivered, pursuant to the provisions of the Solicitor's Act, RSO 1990, as amended.

November 11, 20--

Ms. Amanda Lupino
420 Kamel Road
Toronto, Ontario M6N 3P4

OUR REFERENCE NO. ___888___

IN ACCOUNT WITH: **MICHAEL, ELIAD & REDFORD LLP**
BARRISTERS AND SOLICITORS   HST REGISTRATION NO. 987654321
863 Seneca Lane
Toronto, Ontario   M4J 1P6

Telephone No. (416) 363-1079 Facsimile No. (416) 363-2628 www.mer.ca E-mail rbrdfrd@mer.com

Re: Lupino purchase from Morden
          420 Kamel Road, Toronto

TO PROFESSIONAL SERVICES RENDERED:
To receiving and considering the agreement of purchase and sale; to arranging for search of title
and considering it; to preparing the preliminary correspondence to the vendor's lawyers and to
the public utilities and tax, building, and zoning departments and considering the replies; to
preparing the letter of requisitions and considering the replies to it; to receiving charge/mortgage
documentation from Tender Trust, preparing documents, and providing drafts to Tender Trust; to
arranging for execution of documents; to arranging for charge/mortgage funds; to numerous
telephone conversations with vendor's lawyers and with you; to closing the transaction and
registering documents; to reporting to you and to Tender Trust.

OUR FEE	$950.00
HST	123.50

Disbursements

Subject to HST

Paid for photocopies and fax	$ 25.25
Paid courier	20.00
Paid to search title	149.49
Paid to Teraview for registration fee - transfer	10.55
Paid to Teraview for registration fee - charge	10.55
Paid to MLTT administration fee	75.00
Paid for searches	44.00
	$334.84
HST	43.53
	$378.37

	$378.37	378.37
Carried forward		$1,451.87

Precedent 3.7 Account and Trust Statement, Manually Prepared, page 2

Ms. Amanda Lupino   - 2 -   November 11, 20--

Brought forward $1,451.87

Not Subject to HST
Paid to register transfer $ 63.35
Paid to register charge   63.35
Paid for tax certificate   65.00
Paid for building compliance letter   194.24
Paid to search executions   56.50   442.44

TOTAL FEES AND DISBURSEMENTS $1,894.31
Transferred from trust for payment of our account   1,894.31

BALANCE DUE   Nil

                                    THIS IS OUR ACCOUNT
                                    MICHAEL, ELIAD & REDFORD LLP
                                    Per:
RBR/yi
                                    Robert B. Redford
E. & O. E.

According to the *Solicitors Act,*   % interest per year will be charged, one month after this statement is sent.

Precedent 3.7 Account and Trust Statement, Manually Prepared, page 3

Ms. Amanda Lupino   - 3 -   November 11, 20--

TRUST STATEMENT

Received from you $ 44,900.00
Received from Tender Trust   200,000.00
Paid on closing $239,280.68
Paid brokerage fee   1,755.00
Paid land transfer tax   1,675.00
Paid title insurance premium   280.00
Transferred for payment of our account   1,894.31
Cheque to you (enclosed)   15.01
                                           $244,900.00 $244,900.00

RBR/yi

CHAPTER 4

EFFECTIVE LEGAL WRITING AND ORAL PRESENTATIONS

This chapter covers the basic principles and mechanics of effective legal writing and oral presentations with exclusive examples by Manitoba's Justice John A. Scollin and Ontario's Justice Thomas G. Zuber.

BASIC PRINCIPLES OF LEGAL WRITING

At some point in your legal career, you will find yourself writing legal correspondence, drafting legal documents, and presenting a case in court. Following are the basic principles of writing which, when applied correctly, will enable you to write competently.

1. **Use correct grammar and avoid misplaced modifiers**   Adjectives, adverbs, or modifying phrases must accompany, or go as close as possible to, the thing they are modifying. If they do not, a misplaced modifier occurs. Here are two examples:

> Sitting in the cage, he saw the monkey scratch his head. (**He** appears to be in the cage.)
> Compare: Sitting in the cage, the monkey scratched his head.

> She borrowed an egg from a neighbour that was rotten. (**Neighbour** appears to be rotten.)
> Compare: She borrowed a rotten egg from a neighbour.

2. **If one will do, do not use two--words**   Get to the point. Your message should have no unnecessary words for the same reason that "a drawing should have no unnecessary lines and a machine no unnecessary parts." (*The Elements of Style*, William Strunk, Jr. & E. B. White).

> In regard to your letter, please be advised that the first case herein was settled in the amount of $2,000, and the second piece of litigation was disposed of out-of-court in the sum of $3,000, while the amount of the accord reached amicably in the third suit herein was $5,000.

> Compare: We settled the first case for $2,000; the second, for $3,000; the third, for $5,000.

3. **Use the active voice as opposed to the passive voice**   The active voice makes the subject do the action and tells directly who did it; the passive voice torments the fact.

> Active voice: John sent the letter.
> Passive voice: The letter was sent by John; or the letter was sent.

4. **Use specific words as opposed to general words**   Specific words call up pictures in your message and remove vagueness.

> General words: An interval of unfavourable weather accumulated.
> Specific words: It rained every day for a month.

5. **Use parallel construction**   Express items of the same importance in the same grammatical form: that is, if you begin a series with a noun, use nouns throughout the series; do the same with other parts of speech.

> Incorrect: She likes reading, swimming, to skate, and to ride.
> Correct: She likes **reading, swimming, skating,** and **riding.**
> or She likes **to read**, swim, skate, and **ride**.

Incorrect:	**Correct:**
This part will discuss:	This part will discuss how to:
-what we must do to deal effectively with corporate politics	-**deal** with corporate politics
-stressful situations	-**cope** with stressful situations
-managing people is a difficult task	-**function** as effective managers

6. **Make statements reader-centred**   A reader-centred, as opposed to a writer-centred, message emphasizes the reader, or at least achieves a good "we-you" balance.

> <u>We</u> sent the documents some time ago, and <u>we</u> requested that they be returned to <u>us</u> as soon as possible, but <u>we</u> have not received them to date.

> Compare: Would <u>you</u> please promptly return the documents <u>we</u> sent <u>you</u> last July 20.

7. **Put statements in positive form**   This principle conveys tact and professionalism. When used correctly, it enables you to convert a negative message into a positive one or frame a negative or "bad news" message in positive terms. One of the simpler ways of applying this principle is to avoid the use of negative words such as **not** and **cannot** and other accusatory, antagonizing, or contemptuous words. Think of this principle like you do of Robin Hood — "He is bad news but in a good way" (from a former student).

> Negative: We regret that we cannot send the documents until after November 8.
> Positive: We will send the documents to you after November 8.

> Negative: You do not appear to understand that the separation agreement is a binding contract.
> Positive: Please note that the separation agreement is a binding contract.

> Negative: He did not think that studying English was very important.
> Positive: He thought the study of English unimportant.

GUIDE TO EFFECTIVE LEGAL WRITING

All writing, including legal writing, follows a time-honoured three-part structure. The Greek philosopher Aristotle taught the three-part structure in many of his works, including the *Rhetoric*, which deals with legal logic. You know it well today by the following three parts: **introduction**, **body**, and **conclusion**. The purpose of the three-part structure is to enable the busy reader to immediately get the most important points of the message by reading only the introduction and the conclusion. The details in the body can wait until later. Always check your own writing to ensure that the introduction and the conclusion facilitate the reader in this important way.

Legal TIP

In very short writings, the entire piece may consist of a single two- or three-line paragraph. Still, organize the **order** of your ideas in the three-part structure.

Getting ready to write
1. Identify the reason for writing.
2. Jot down the main points you wish to make.
3. Write a draft, applying three-part structure and the above principles of legal writing.
4. Revise, revise, and revise.
5. Polish and proofread for correct grammar, word usage, spelling, and punctuation.

Writing legal correspondence (letters and memos) The three-part structure is easy to apply. Just answer the question posed for each part, and the three-part structure will take its shape.

Figure 4.1

INTRODUCTION:	What is your reason for writing? (Keep the introduction short – one to four sentences.)
BODY:	What are your **back-up details**? (Provide as many concise paragraphs as are necessary to make your case about the reason for writing.)
CONCLUSION:	What specific **action** do you require from, or offer to, the reader? (Keep the conclusion short – one to four sentences.)

Example of a letter in three-part structure using the above formula:

Figure 4.2

Dear Mr. Edison:

We are concerned about the delay in the Smith v. Jones action. (Reason for writing.)

On February 26, you informed us that you had resolved the delay; however, we have received no word from you since that date. A check at the court office indicates no further action from you, and our clients are anxious to proceed to trial as quickly as possible...(Back-up details about the reason for writing.)

Please let us hear of your intentions by Friday the 15th. (Action.)

Yours very truly,

Writing legal reports and presentations The three-part structure for writing legal reports and presentations is as follows:

Figure 4.3

INTRODUCTION:	Announce the **scope** of your discussion (i.e. state the specific points you will cover.)
BODY:	Discuss the **back-up details** for each point you announced, providing headings for each such point.
CONCLUSION:	**Summarize** your discussion, and state any action you require from, or offer to, the reader.

Example of a judge's report in three-part structure using the above formula:

Figure 4.4   (From *Report of the Ontario Courts Inquiry*, Justice T. G. Zuber, by permission)

INTRODUCTION **reason/purpose** → Scope →	As long as there have been courts, there have been complaints that they are not functioning properly....**[W]hen the complaints become persistent and when they focus on the same issues time after time, then perhaps there are matters which need to be addressed and problems which need to be corrected.** This (report) will set out some of the problems and complaints which have been raised concerning the administration of justice, and about which there appears to be some consensus.

B
 	
O
 	
D
 	
Y
	COSTS
	   The most common complaint about the justice system is that the cost of litigation is prohibitive.
	
	   It is generally conceded that only the very wealthy, or the poor on legal aid, can afford to go to court....Even minor criminal matters can be expensive to defend....The cost of litigating property division disputes in matrimonial cases has been known to exceed the value of all the assets accumulated by the divorcing couple....
	
	THE PUBLIC
	   ...The complaints the general public makes about the administration of justice stem largely from the impression given by the courts that they are designed by, and run exclusively for the benefit of, lawyers....
	
	THE CRIMINAL JUSTICE SYSTEM
	   The criminal justice system, in particular, comes under attack. A common refrain is that criminal law protects the accused, but ignores the needs of the victims and witnesses...
	<div align="center">***</div> It is not possible, or even likely, that this Inquiry can address every complaint made with respect to the administration of justice....[C]omplaints such as those respecting the insensitivity of the criminal law to the plight of the victim stem from the state of the substantive law....However, many of the complaints addressed to the Inquiry are well founded and the problems contained therein are susceptible of solution.

CONCLUSION Summary → Action →	

GUIDE TO EFFECTIVE ORAL PRESENTATIONS

It is like death–it could strike at any point in your life. It could strike in the classroom, it could strike in the boardroom, it could strike in the PTA room, it could strike in the courtroom; but it *will* strike, and when it does, your degree of public speaking skill will determine to a great extent how seriously people take what you have to say. In your career as a law clerk/assistant, you may be called upon from time to time to attend court for a variety of reasons such as seeking adjournments or pleading cases in Small Claims Court. Such activities require skills in public speaking, and such skills are acquired by training in giving oral presentations.

Dealing with nervousness   Even severe nervousness lasts only the first few seconds of your presentation. Studies show, however, that people experience very little nervousness or anxiety when they have a well-prepared presentation, know their material well, and have practised presenting it. The use of visuals is also known to reduce nervousness because it deflects the spotlight from the speaker. Be well prepared, speak clearly and sincerely, with poise and spontaneity, and you will succeed. Remember, nervousness is naturally invisible. No one in the audience can see it, no matter how intense it might be.

Types of presentations   Two frequently used types are the **informative** and the **persuasive**. The purpose of an informative presentation is, of course, to inform. The audience will acquire greater knowledge, skill, or understanding of a particular topic, e.g. the audience will be able to change a flat tire:

Informative: Today, I will speak to you about chinchillas. I will tell you about their grooming habits, their social habits, and their mating habits.

A far more difficult task falls on the persuasive presentation, the purpose of which is to persuade the audience to accept your point of view.

Persuasive: According to the Ministry of Labour, speech is essential for about eight out of ten jobs. Off the job, speech is even more important. In fact, we use speech three times more than writing. Clearly, we cannot afford to either work or play without public speaking skills.

Reasoning techniques   There are many. The most useful ones in the legal field, however, are the **inductive** and the **deductive** reasoning techniques. As a general rule, use **inductive** reasoning when your audience is likely to be unreceptive to your point of view and **deductive** when your audience is likely to agree with you.

Inductive reasoning   In this technique, you start with information that is specific, e.g. statistics, so as to arrive at a desired generalization, as in the persuasive example above. This is the renowned Aristotelian logic, so named after the Greek philosopher Aristotle (384-322 B.C.). It is the technique lawyers usually use today to persuade judges and juries to see things their way.

Deductive reasoning   The deductive reasoning technique, on the other hand, starts with a general principle or idea and moves to establish a specific one. The deductive technique also comes to us from Aristotle. A classic example of this Aristotelian logic goes like this:

> All men are mortal.
> Socrates is a man.
> Therefore, Socrates is mortal.

Legal TIP

To hold the attention of your audience during your presentation, try this: Place an object, any object, e.g. an apple, a toy, conspicuously on your lectern. Everyone will be attentive awaiting your mention of the object.

Legal TIP

If you are expected to field questions at the end of your presentation, plant a question, i.e. pick a question in advance, and give it to a friend to raise in the event of a lull in the questions from your audience. This will get the ball rolling.

Methods of delivery   There are four methods of delivering a speech or presentation:

1. **Impromptu** This is the unexpected, on-the-spot method of delivery. You do this in class when answering your instructor's questions; in meetings when asked to comment on an issue; in court when the judge addresses you in a particular case. When you are called upon to speak on the spot, the most effective way to arrange your thoughts in a hurry is chronological: past, present, future.

2. **Extemporaneous** This method requires a fully prepared speech or presentation delivered by occasionally referring to brief, usually highlighted, notes or cue cards. It is neither read verbatim nor presented from memory. Next to the impromptu method, it impresses as being the most natural and spontaneous. Use the extemporaneous method of delivery in all of your speeches or presentations.

3. **Manuscript** This method requires a fully prepared speech or presentation that is read word for word. It is used when very exact wording is required as in political policy speeches, presidential inaugural speeches, and speeches from the throne. Set this one aside until you are called upon to deliver the speech from the throne.

4. **Memorized** This method requires a fully prepared speech or presentation entirely committed to memory. Unless you are Laurence Olivier, leave it alone because memory is unreliable – it fails us best when we need it most. A memorized speech or presentation is also difficult to deliver with a feeling of sincerity and spontaneity, two extremely important characteristics in delivery of speeches and presentations.

Presenting with a bang   As discussed earlier in this chapter, successful presentations are always ones which are well-written and well-practised. To give your presentation an extra "bang," however, follow the outline set out in Figure 4.5.

Figure 4.5

INTRODUCTION:	*Begin with an attention-getting opening of your topic. This may include an anecdote, a quotation, a historical event, or your own refreshingly worded statement. Give a preview of the main points you will cover. Following are some examples of attention-getting openings:*
	"Take a look around you; every third person in this room will die in the next ten years." (Will Rogers speaking on heart disease).
	"My job is to speak to you today. As I see it, your job is to listen. If by any chance you should finish before I do, will you please raise your hand." (A lawyer at a Canadian Bar Association conference).
BODY:	*Put the opening and the closing as close together as possible so that the length of your speech does not outlast the attention span of your audience.*
	Present your topic clearly and concisely. Reinforce your argument with statistics, testimonies, examples, metaphors, quotations, and visuals.
CONCLUSION:	*Summarize the main points to insure your audience gets your message. Make your closing statement a memorable one. Following are examples of memorable closings:*
	"Let us therefore brace ourselves to our duties, and so bear ourselves that, if the British Empire and its Commonwealth last for a thousand years, men will still say, 'This was their finest hour.'" (Sir Winston Churchill, House of Commons Speech, June 18, 1940).
	"Stay Hungry. Stay Foolish. ...I have always wished that for myself. And now, as you graduate to begin anew, I wish that for you. Stay Hungry. Stay Foolish." (Steve Jobs, Apple Computer CEO, Commencement Speech, June 12, 2005, Stanford University).

A judge's speech on presentations   Figure 4.6 contains excerpts from a speech which one of our country's most prolific and colourful judges, the Honourable Justice John A. Scollin, gave to lawyers who were newly called to the Bar of the Province of Manitoba. Note how clearly Justice Scollin's speech demonstrates the three-part structure and how well His Honour outlines the content of each part: the introduction, the body, and the conclusion.

Figure 4.6

The first task of any speaker is to tell you what he is going to talk about. First I am going to show you – by two examples – the benefit of a brief, direct and compact style of presentation. This, of course, is useful in any field, whatever the subject, but it is essential in law. Second, I am going to give you an example, in what I hope will also be a brief, direct and compact style, of the way in which judges reason. Third and lastly, I am going to end with some observations, a few serious, a few not, on our much vaunted *Charter of Rights*.

...I will emphasize the one virtue that all lawyers <u>should</u> have and that the litigation lawyer <u>must</u> have. Those of you who plan a life in court have to learn only the three-letter alphabet of the advocate: ABC. A is for acuity, the acumen to see, analyze and judge the issues; B is for brevity, and C is for clarity...

First, the general rule of twenty: put your pen down at twenty pages or your posterior down at twenty minutes... Mark Twain said: "Few sinners are saved after the first twenty minutes of a sermon."

Second, if the weather permits, dress your prose in shorts or a miniskirt. If a short word fits, use it. Long words are as depressing as long faces; inevitable sometimes, but you should try to use them only as often as you go to funerals.

Third, do the same with sentences. An overloaded sentence risks sinking like an overloaded tanker. So with paragraphs.

Fourth, get your best argument out first, whether you privately think it is Goliath rather than David. And, just in case the judge or tribunal didn't follow you the first time, summarize your best argument at the end.

Fifth. ...Use the active form rather than the passive. Instead of "It has been suggested by counsel for the plaintiff," write or say, "Plaintiff's counsel has suggested." Avoid jargon.

Sixth, read written argument over to yourself to see how it's likely to appeal to the judicial eye. But don't ever plant your feet and read your written argument word for word in court. That is an invitation to either active impatience or passive boredom. Simply highlight your points, expand briefly if you have to, and sit down.

So there is the advocate's ABC...and so the second and final mnemonic I commend to you is this: your degree of LL.B. Think of the two L's as standing for only two cases on the issue, the Leading and the Latest. Generally that is enough. And think of the B as standing for Backup, the 30 or so other cases that you must know just in case you are called on to distinguish them.

In summary, both words and cases are the lawyer's employees. Don't employ more of them than you need and choose them with care. That way they will serve you loyally and well and, best of all, they won't expose you to vicarious liability.

(Justice John A. Scollin, from a speech to lawyers newly called to the Bar of Manitoba, by permission).

SIMPLIFIED GUIDE TO LEGAL PUNCTUATION

Punctuation is to writing what traffic signs or signals are to driving: for example, the period is parallel to the stop sign; the semicolon, to the yellow signal; the colon, to the one-way sign; and the comma, to the yield sign or to slowing down where necessary. Misuse can be misleading or deadly. Consider, for amusement, these simple examples:

> I want to eat Grandma.
> Compare: I want to eat, Grandma.

> I am not getting any; better come home right away. (Benny Hill, British television performer.)
> Compare: I am not getting any better; come home right away.

COMMA (,)

Legal TIP

Where none of the following rules applies, omit the comma or the pair of commas.

Generally, the most frequently used and misused punctuation mark is the comma. The difficulty in learning and applying it correctly lies, no doubt, in the many grammatical technicalities that govern its use. Yet, no other field demands more precision in the use of the comma than does the legal field because legal meanings cannot be open to variable interpretations or misinterpretations. Master the following simplified comma rules and tips, and you will be able to handle the comma correctly in nearly all legal applications.

Comma Rule 1	Example
Place a comma before any one of these seven coordinating conjunctions (connecting words) when they form a compound sentence (i.e. two complete sentences): *and, but, or, nor, for, so,* and *yet.* A complete sentence has a <u>subject</u> and a <u>verb.</u>	<u>Susan</u> <u>is</u> an excellent lawyer, and <u>she</u> <u>expects</u> to win the case. Compare: <u>Susan</u> <u>is</u> an excellent lawyer and <u>expects</u> to win the case. *(No subject in second part; not a compound sentence; no comma.)*

Understanding the correct application of Comma Rule 1 enables you to recognize correct grammatical sentences and, therefore, avoid such serious grammatical errors in writing as run-on sentences and comma splices:

Example of a run-on sentence: (a) Susan is an excellent lawyer she expects to win the case.
Example of a comma splice: (b) Susan is an excellent lawyer, she expects to win the case.

To correct a run-on sentence or a comma splice, use (a) a **comma** and a **conjunction**, (b) a period, or (c) a **semicolon**.

(a) Susan is an excellent lawyer**, and** she expects to win the case. (Corrected by a comma and a conjunction.)

(b) Susan is an excellent lawyer**. S**he expects to win the case. (Corrected by a period and a capital "S.")

(c) Susan is an excellent lawyer**; s**he expects to win the case. (Corrected by a semicolon and a small "s.")

Comma Rule 2	Example
Place a comma after a *dependent clause* that introduces an <u>independent clause</u> (a complete sentence). (A dependent clause may contain a subject and a verb, but it depends for its meaning on the complete sentence following it.)	*Having heard the verdict,* <u>they decided to let the matter go.</u> *If you become hopelessly mired in a sentence,* <u>it is best to start fresh.</u>

Comma Rule 3	Example
Enclose the following information in a pair of commas: a. <u>Nonessential information</u>	a. The defendant, <u>who was very handsome,</u> entered the courtroom last. Compare: The man **who entered the courtroom last** was the defendant. *(No commas; bolded information is essential--identifies which of an implied number of men was the defendant.)*
b. <u>Interrupting information</u>	b. The shareholders met yesterday and, <u>after lengthy discussions,</u> decided to scrap the agreement.
c. <u>Appositives</u> *(one noun modifying another noun)*	c. Jill Smith, <u>president of ABC Limited,</u> attended the conference. The defendant, <u>George Clark Pirkko,</u> denies the allegations.

Comma Rule 4	Examples
Use a comma to separate two or more items in a series. (Take care about omitting the comma before the conjunction in the last item of a series, which is often done in common practice.)	1. We need an <u>intelligent</u>, <u>enterprising</u> person for the job. *(Two adjectives, both describing person.)* 2. There is a <u>red</u> brick building on the property. *(One adjective, no comma; red describes brick, not building.)* *To test, read the sentence with the coordinating conjunction **and** between the adjectives:* We need an intelligent **and** enterprising person for the job. But: There is a red **and** brick building on the property. 3. In the courtroom sat a sheriff, a police officer, a lawyer eating a hamburger**, and** a parakeet. Compare: In the courtroom sat a sheriff, a police officer, a lawyer eating a hamburger and a parakeet. *(Without the comma before the conjunction **and** in the last item in the series, the lawyer appears to be eating the hamburger **and** the parakeet.)*
Dates	The certificate was dated Thursday, January 27, 20--, and was registered on the 28th day of January, 20--. *(Use ordinals, i.e. 1st, 2nd, 3rd, etc. only when the day comes before the month.)* Compare: A certificate dating back to January 20-- is on file. *(No comma when the date consists of only the month and the year.)*
Addresses	My client works at 77 Sunset Boulevard, Oshawa, Ontario, and plays in Hamilton, Ontario.

Comma Rule 5	Examples
Use a comma for clarity, omission, or sudden turn of thought.	You know, nothing is accomplished without hard work. Compare: You know nothing... Hard work leads to success; wit, to greatness. *(Omission —"leads to" has been omitted after "wit.")* Not charity, but simple justice. *(Sudden turn of thought.)*

SEMICOLON (;)	
1. Use a semicolon to separate two closely related sentences.	She made extraordinary demands on the plaintiff; he persevered. Compare: She made extraordinary demands on the plaintiff, but he persevered.
2. Use a semicolon before transitional words, such as *accordingly, consequently, furthermore, however, namely, nevertheless,* when they come between two complete sentences.	(a) Tracy is an excellent law clerk/assistant; however, she is very inexperienced. Compare: (b) Tracy, however, is very inexperienced.
3. Use a semicolon to separate a series of phrases containing commas.	To preparing, serving, and filing application; to meeting with you; to preparing, serving, and filing record;...

Legal TIP

If the transitional comes in the middle of two complete sentences, as in (a), it is **always** preceded by a semicolon and followed by a comma. If it comes in the middle of one complete sentence, as in (b), it is **always** enclosed in a **pair** of commas.

COLON (:)	
1. Use a colon to introduce matter that follows.	There are three kinds of lies: lies, damned lies, and statistics. (*The Canadian Style*, Department of the Secretary of State of Canada.)

APOSTROPHE (')	
Use the apostrophe to show possession, or ownership, of one noun (person, place, or thing) by another noun. To indicate the possessive form, follow these rules:	
1. Add an apostrophe and "s" to singular or plural nouns that do not already end in "s" and to singular nouns that do end in "s."	A month's interest; children's toys; witness's testimony. Chris's books; *Jones'/Jones's pet. (*Some personal names that end in "s" may be written with either an apostrophe or an apostrophe and an "s.")
2. Add an apostrophe to a plural noun that ends in "s."	The two witnesses' testimonies; the two Chrises' books; three months' interest; the Joneses' pet.

Legal TIP

To distinguish the difference in usage between its and it's, remember this: "Its" is a possessive pronoun; it **never** takes an apostrophe; "it's" is a contraction of *it is* or *it has*.

QUOTATION MARKS (" ")

Use quotation marks to indicate the exact words someone spoke or wrote.   Place punctuation marks inside the closing quotation mark if the punctuation marks are part of the quotation, and outside the closing quotation mark if they are not. This applies when quoting matter from a written source. When forming quotations in your own composition,

• Always place commas and periods inside the closing quotation mark, and semicolons and colons outside the closing quotation mark:

> He said, "yes," "no," and "maybe"; nevertheless, he decided to stay with the firm.
> Mr. Redford said, "We'll close early on Friday."

• Always place question marks (?) and exclamation marks (!) inside the closing quotation mark if you are forming a quotation which is itself a question or exclamation, and outside if the quotation is not itself a question or exclamation:

> Nancy asked, "Who said we'll close early on Friday?" (Quotation is a question.)
> Why did Mr. Redford say, "We'll close early on Friday"? (Entire statement is a question.)

NUMBERS

1. **In general, use figures for emphasis and words for formality.**

2. **Use words with o'clock and figures with a.m. and p.m.** Use lower case a.m. and p.m. since capitals may be mistaken for other standard abbreviations, e.g. amplitude modulation (A.M.)

> 9 a.m., or 9:00 a.m., 3:30 p.m. (figures for emphasis.)
> ten o'clock in the morning; half past one o'clock in the afternoon (words for formality.)

3. **Use figures to express distance, mass, dimension, size, temperature, and interest rates.**

> 45 km   5 kg   3 m   size 7   22 C   10 ½ percent

> (Always write out **percent**, instead of **%**, when it is not in a table or in economic, financial, and statistical documents; use no periods after metric abbreviations.)

4. **In correspondence and court documents, use figures to express amounts of money (amounts are considered readily verifiable). In most other legal documents, e.g. real estate, use words and figures, one to verify the other.**

> 25c, $0.25, or 25 cents; $1,500.00, $1,500, 1500; $215,000.00, $215,000.

> Five Hundred Forty-Nine Thousand Seven Hundred Dollars and Ten Cents ($549,700.10).

LEGAL CAPITALIZATION

1. Capitalization of common nouns.

Modern legal usage employs increasingly fewer capitals as it strives for simplicity and ease of reading. This is reflected in the style guides of the federal and provincial governments and in almost all formal legal writings, including the *Rules of Civil Procedure*, the *Family Law Rules*, and the *Courts of Justice Act*. Note, for example, the use of the lower case in all common nouns in the following excerpts from the *Rules of Civil Procedure*, i.e. names of documents (statement of claim), party titles (plaintiff), titles of public officers (sheriff), and other common nouns (court):

"Where a notice of action is used, the plaintiff shall file a statement of claim...and no statement of claim shall be filed thereafter except with the written consent of the defendant or with leave of the court obtained on notice to the defendant." (*Rules of Civil Procedure*, subrule 14.03(3)).

"[D]isbursements paid to a sheriff, registrar, official examiner, court reporter or other public officer and to which the party is entitled...on filing with the sheriff or registrar a copy of a receipt for each disbursement." (*Rules of Civil Procedure*, subrule 60.19(2)(b)).

Capitalization of common nouns, however, varies widely in practice. With the use of legal software, some of which may be set to the capitalization preferences of each law firm, there is a general tendency to capitalize common nouns in documents and correspondence, e.g. Statement of Claim, Plaintiff, Corporation, Agreement, etc. Thus, the precedents in this manual generally reflect this style of capitalization; the textual discussion in this manual, however, generally follows the lower case style as illustrated above in the excerpts from the *Rules of Civil Procedure*. Follow the capitalization preferences of your law firm.

2. Capitalize proper nouns (proper names of persons, places, and things).

> John Smith, City of Toronto, Town of Waterwell, Superior Court of Justice, Ministry of the Attorney General, ABC Corporation, XYZ Pets.

3. Capitalize only the common noun which immediately precedes a letter/s or a number/s; if the term number/s precedes a figure, express it as No. or Nos.

By-law No. 1	Chapter 24
Account No. 25691	Exhibit A or Exhibit 1, Exhibit Nos. 1 to 5
Policy No. 36127	Schedule A
Lot 75, Plan 7431	Grade 6
Charge/Mortgage No. 32751	*Rule 10

Minor subdivisions: page 2, (p. = page; pp. = pages), line 6, note 2, paragraph 14, size 7, *rule 10.12, subsection ii, section 5, or s. 5. (When **section** refers to statutes, regulations, or citations, use the abbreviated form, and do not capitalize it, e.g. s 5. Do capitalize it, and write it out in full when it refers to other documents, e.g. Section 5.)

*The *Rules of Civil Procedure* require that when referring to the rule itself as a whole, e.g. Rule 14, the initial R be capitalized, but not when referring to rule 14.03 or subrule 1.01(2)(a).

CHAPTER SUMMARY

Legal writing should use grammatically correct sentences and plain language. It should be concise and precise, and it should use the active voice, which makes the subject do the action. The focus of the message should be on the reader rather than the writer, and the message should be set in a positive tone to demonstrate tact and professionalism.

Always organize legal letters and memos in a three-part structure, which consists of an introduction, a body, and a conclusion. Announce the reason for writing in your introduction, provide the back-up details in the body, and conclude with an action line.

At some point in your career, you will be called upon to speak in court, or in a meeting, or to give a presentation. Studies show that when giving a presentation, you can greatly minimize any nervousness by being well prepared and using visuals effectively. When writing your speech or presentation, provide an attention-getting opening, close it with a summary and a memorable final statement, and make your argument in the middle clear and concise, using concrete evidence, statistics, quotations, and examples to substantiate your argument. Whether your speech or presentation is informative or persuasive, in the inductive or the deductive mode, the method of delivery should be the extemporaneous method.

REVIEW QUESTIONS

1. Write this sentence in a positive tone, and apply correct punctuation where necessary:
   Since your client has not filed the documents we cannot proceed with the case.
2. Write the following sentence in the active voice:
   It has been suggested by counsel for the plaintiff...
3. Parallel construction is when a company builds buildings side-by-side. Explain.
4. In which part of a three-part structure should you state the reason for writing?
5. In which part of a three-part structure do you place the action line?
6. What is an extemporaneous speech or presentation?
7. Which reasoning technique would you use with an unreceptive audience: inductive___ deductive___?
8. What should be the first item in the opening of your speech or presentation?
9. Apply correct punctuation and apostrophes where necessary in the following sentences:
   (a) The judge listened to the argument but he ordered the defendant to pay.
   (b) Although the judge listened to the argument he ordered the defendant to pay.
   (c) The judge however ordered the defendant to pay.
   (d) The court closed its doors and the judge said its time to adjourn but one lawyers questions kept coming.

CHAPTER 5
LEGAL OFFICE CORRESPONDENCE

This chapter covers legal correspondence and letter styles as used in practice and also includes a guide to addressing government and judicial officials.

LETTER STYLES

Letters are like shoes—they deliver the message in a variety of styles. A letter style is the form in which the information in a letter is arranged on paper. Legal correspondence follows the same letter styles as those used in non-legal businesses. Three commonly used letter styles are:

> Full block (also referred to as block), **Precedent 5.1**
> Block (also known as modified block), **Precedent 5.2**
> Semiblock (also known as modified block with indented paragraphs), **Precedent 5.3**

For guidelines on how to write, or compose, effective legal letters, memos, reports, and presentations as well as how to punctuate your composition, see Chapter 4.

About letters   The salutation and complimentary closing of letters are punctuated in one of these styles:

> **Mixed punctuation** which requires a colon following the salutation (Dear Sir:) and a comma following the complimentary closing (Yours truly,).

> **Open punctuation** which requires no punctuation at these two points.

Set-up of letters   Letters are usually keyed on 8 ½ × 11" law firm letterhead, as shown in Precedents 5.1 to 5.3. Computer software pre-sets letter styles to law firm preferences. In the absence of it, follow these guidelines for all letter styles:

1. Set a minimum of 25 mm (one inch) left and right margins.
2. Key in the date as many or as few line spaces below your firm's letterhead as are necessary to place the letter attractively on the firm's letterhead.
3. Leave a double space between the date and the inside address, three or four line spaces in the signature block, and a double space between all other letter parts and paragraphs.

> **Legal TIP**
>
> Mixed and open punctuation are styles that apply **only** to salutations and complimentary closings. The body of letters follows standard punctuation rules (set out in Chapter 4).

PARTS OF LEGAL LETTERS

The parts of legal letters are the same as those of standard business letters, but the information in legal letters might differ slightly, as follows.

Date line   Not to be taken mischievously – this is just a day on the calendar on which you prepare the letter. Key the date thus: August 15, 20--, or 15 August 20--. Avoid use of numeric dates, e.g. 20-- 02 04, as they may cause confusion. The letter style you use determines the placement of the date line. See the precedents at the back of this chapter.

Delivery and special notations in legal letters   Key delivery and special notations a double space after the date. They include, in block capitals: REGISTERED MAIL, BY COURIER, BY DOCUMENT EXCHANGE, BY FAX, DELIVERED BY HAND, PERSONAL, WITHOUT PREJUDICE (means contents of letter cannot be used in evidence). See Figure 5.1 for examples of the correct placement of delivery and special notations in letters.

Barristers and Solicitors   This traditional professional description usually follows the name of the law firm in the inside address. Although the default description is barristers and solicitors, use the description that is on the letterhead of incoming correspondence as some law firms use **Lawyers**, instead of barristers and solicitors, for their professional description on their letterhead; in the alternative, the description may be omitted, as is increasingly done. Follow the practice in your law firm.

Inside address   This is the receiver's address, the party to whom you are writing. Use the receiver's firm name and address exactly as it appears on the letterhead of incoming correspondence. If this is your initial writing, call up the firm or look it up on the internet. Following are examples of the various forms of inside addresses used in practice:

Figure 5.1

Addressed to Firm	Addressed to Individual	Addressed to Someone's Attention
REGISTERED MAIL	PERSONAL	WITHOUT PREJUDICE
Jones, Smith & Brown LLP Barristers and Solicitors Suite 1234 5 Fifth Avenue Churchill, ON L7M 1B1	Mr. Tom Jones Jones, Smith & Brown LLP Barristers and Solicitors Suite 1234 5 Fifth Avenue Churchill, ON L7M 1B1	Jones, Smith & Brown LLP Barristers and Solicitors Suite 1234 5 Fifth Avenue Churchill, ON L7M 1B1
Dear Counsel: (or Dear Sirs and Madams:)	Dear Mr. Jones:	Attention: Ms. Mary Smith
Re: David v. Goliath	Re: David v. Goliath	Dear Counsel: (or Dear Ms. Smith: or Dear Sirs and Madams:) Re: David v. Goliath

Attention line   This line, example in Figure 5.1, directs the letter to the person handling the matter; technically, however, since the inside address is to the firm, others within the firm may open and act on the letter if necessary. Although the salutation usually greets the law firm, lawyers may instead greet the individual named in the attention line. For automated printing of envelopes or labels, it is acceptable to include the attention line in the inside address as shown in Figure 5.2.

Figure 5.2

Jones, Smith & Brown LLP
Barristers and Solicitors
Attention: Ms. Mary Smith
Suite 1234
5 Fifth Avenue
Churchill, ON L7M 1B1

Salutation   The salutation greets, or "salutes," the law firm; hence, salutation. Use the salutation that your law firm prefers, e.g. Dear Counsel, Dear Sirs and Madams, or Ladies and Gentlemen.

Subject line   The word **Re** (Latin *in re*, in the matter of) or **Subject** usually begins the subject line, with or without the use of a colon or underline. Always key your own client's name first. Compare the following examples of subject lines as they would appear in your firm's letters and in the letters of the opposite lawyers:

OUR CORRESPONDENCE	THEIR CORRESPONDENCE

1. Re: Smith ats. Brown
          Motor Vehicle Accident
	1. Re: Brown v. Smith
	          Motor Vehicle Accident

2. Re: Green v. Jones and others
          Dissolution of Partnership
	2. Re: Jones and others ats. Green
	          Dissolution of Partnership

or Re: Green v. Jones, *et al*
          Dissolution of Partnership
	or Re: Jones, *et al* ats. Green
	          Dissolution of Partnership

3. Re: Brown purchase from Smith
          14 Tempest Avenue, Toronto
	3. Re: Smith sale to Brown
	          14 Tempest Avenue, Toronto

Notes: In the first example, we act for Smith whom Brown is suing; hence, Smith is at the suit of (ats.) Brown. In the second example, we act for Green who is suing (v. = versus) Jones and others (Latin *et al*). In the third example, we act for Brown, the purchaser.	

Letter endings   Unless otherwise instructed, end letters in one of the following ways, as applicable:

Figure 5.3

Writer is a Partner or Sole Practitioner	Writer is a Partner or an Associate	Writer is an Employee
Yours very truly,	Yours very truly,	Yours very truly,
	MICHAEL, ELIAD & REDFORD LLP	MICHAEL, ELIAD & REDFORD LLP
*Robert B. Redford		Per:
RBR/yi	*Robert B. Redford	*Jay Lo Law Clerk
Enclosure/Enc./enc.	RBR/yi	JL/yi
c: Mr. Tim Bitts		

*Omit degrees, distinctions such as Q.C. (Queen's Counsel), and personal titles after the writer's name. Include a preferred personal title for women to help the reader address a reply, e.g. (Mrs.) Jane Smith. Include (Mr.) Brooke O'Leary only if the name's gender is unclear.

Complimentary closing, signature block, and reference initials   Key in Yours truly, Yours very truly, or Sincerely, as your lawyer prefers, a double space after the final paragraph. The firm name and the word **Per** (see Figure 5.3) mean the writer writes on behalf of the firm. Always include the word "Per" and the position of writers who are employees, e.g. Law Clerk, Legal Assistant, Paralegal, or Student-at-Law. The reference initials are usually those of the writer of the letter and the law clerk/assistant who keyed the letter (yi = your initials).

Enclosure notations   Key an enclosure notation when you are enclosing correspondence or documents in the envelope, in addition to the letter. See Figure 5.3.

Copy notations   Sometimes it is necessary to send a copy of a letter to someone other than the addressee, e.g. to our client, Mr. Tim Bitts. Key **Copy to:**, **c**, **c:**, or **cc:** (= copies, usually to a list of individuals), with or without the colon, on the original and on all copies.

Blind copy notations   This is a secret. Occasionally, it is necessary to send a copy of a letter to someone other than the addressee without the addressee's knowledge; hence, "blind copy" (bc:). Key this notation only on the bc recipient's copy and on your file copy for later reference, but **not** on the original. Place it, usually two line spaces after the last keyed item in the letter.

Postscript   A writer uses this notation to emphasize a thought or add an afterthought. Key it a double space after the last keyed item in the letter, and run the lines full length across; read the following examples:

P.S. This postscript is in **block** style because the paragraphs in the letter are also in block style.	P.S. This postscript is in **indented** style because the paragraphs in the letter are also in indented style.

Second and subsequent page headings   Examples of second and subsequent page headings follow. Although the block second page heading is usually used only in full block letter styles, many writers prefer the use of the horizontal second page heading for all letter styles, including the full block letter style.

HORIZONTAL SECOND PAGE HEADINGS

Jones, Smith & Brown LLP	-2-	November 11, 20--
Mr. Tom Jones Jones, Smith & Brown LLP	-2-	November 11, 20--
Jones, Smith & Brown LLP Attention: Ms. Mary Smith	-2-	November 11, 20--

BLOCK SECOND PAGE HEADINGS

Jones, Smith & Brown LLP	Mr. Tom Jones	Jones, Smith & Brown LLP
Page 2	Jones, Smith & Brown LLP	Attention: Ms. Mary Smith
November 11, 20--	Page 2	Page 2
	November 11, 20--	November 11, 20--

ENVELOPES

Prepare an envelope for each letter you write. Follow the illustrations in Figures 5.4 and 5.5:

Figure 5.4

MICHAEL, ELIAD & REDFORD LLP 1 Barristers and Solicitors 863 Seneca Lane Toronto, Ontario M4J 1P6	2
REGISTERED MAIL Attention: Mr. Raymond G. Castles 3	
Castles & Sands LLP 4 Barristers and Solicitors Suite 900 205 Portage Street Markham, ON L3R 3G3	
5	

1. This section is for your return address. Post office stickers (e.g. Registered Mail) shall appear approximately 7 mm below the return address and within sections 1 and 3.
2. This section is for postage stamps or postal meter impressions.
3. The address, including attention instructions, may be keyed anywhere in sections 3 & 4.
4. The postal code must appear in section 4, either as the last line of the address or on the same line as the last line with at least two character spaces after the name of the province.
5. Leave this space entirely blank. It's the machine sorting code band.

From the Canada Post Guide, by Permission of the Minister of Public Services and Procurements

Microsoft Word includes features that automatically allow you to create and print envelopes directly from the inside address contained in your letter or utilizing the contact addresses from your Microsoft Outlook address book.

Figure 5.5

MICHAEL, ELIAD & REDFORD LLP   1
Barristers and Solicitors
863 Seneca Lane
Toronto, Ontario   M4J 1P6

2

REGISTERED MAIL   Castles & Sands LLP   3
                         Barristers and Solicitors   4
                         Attention: Mr. Raymond G. Castles
                         Suite 900
                         205 Portage Street
                         Markham, Ontario
                         L3R 3G3

5

GUIDE TO ADDRESSING GOVERNMENT AND JUDICIAL OFFICIALS

FEDERAL GOVERNMENT

Governor General	His/Her Excellency The Right Honourable (*Full Name*)	Excellency:
Prime Minister	The Right Honourable (*Full Name*), *P.C., M.P. Prime Minister of Canada	Dear Prime Minister:
Cabinet Minister	The Honourable (*Full Name*), P.C., M.P. Minister of (*Department*)	Dear Minister:
Chief Justice	The Right Honourable (*Full Name*) Chief Justice of Canada	Sir: or Madam:

*Privy Councillor, Member of Parliament

PROVINCIAL GOVERNMENT

Premier	The Honourable (*Full Name*) Premier of the Province of--	Dear Premier:
Member of Parliament	Mr./Ms. (*Full Name*), M.P.P. Government of (*Name of Province*)	Dear Sir: or Dear Madam: or Dear Mr./Ms. (*Surname*):
Chief Justice	The Honourable (*Full Name*) Chief Justice of (*Name of Province*)	Dear Chief Justice (*Surname*):
Attorney General	The Honourable (*Full Name*) Attorney General of (*Name of Province*)	Dear Sir: or Dear Madam:

Superior Court Judge	The Honourable Mr./Madam Justice *(Full Name)* Superior Court of Justice	Your Honour: or Dear Mr./ Madam Justice *(Surname)*:
Provincial Court Judge	The Honourable Mr./Madam Justice *(Full Name)* Ontario Court of Justice	Your Honour: or Dear Mr./ Madam Justice *(Surname)*:
Justice of the Peace	His/Her Worship *(Full Name)* Justice of the Peace (Name of Court)	Your Worship:

MUNICIPAL GOVERNMENT

Mayor	His/Her Worship *(Full Name)* Mayor City/Town of *(Name)*	Dear Mayor *(Surname)*:

All correspondence may close with "Yours respectfully."

CHAPTER SUMMARY

Three letter styles are in common use among the legal profession: full block, block, and semi-block. The most frequently used letter style, however, is the full block letter style. All letter styles have standard parts which are the same in all letter styles. When you write letters on behalf of the law firm, use the letter style that the firm prefers. When writing to other law firms, remember to name your own client first in the subject line.

There are three different signature block styles that law firms customarily use, depending on the position of the writer within the law firm.

Prepare an envelope for each letter. Remember never to show the notation "without prejudice" on an envelope and never to show a blind copy notation on the original of a letter.

REVIEW QUESTIONS

1. What information does the date line of a letter consist of?
2. What is an inside address?
3. Write the correct complimentary closing for a letter which you are writing on behalf of Michael, Eliad & Redford LLP.
4. Where on the envelope would you key the "Without Prejudice" notation?
5. What is a blind copy notation?

TELEPHONE NO. (416) 363-1079
FACSIMILE NO. (416) 363-2628
www.mer.ca
E-mail rbrdfrd@mer.com

Letterhead ➤

MICHAEL, ELIAD & REDFORD LLP
BARRISTERS AND SOLICITORS
863 SENECA LANE
TORONTO, ONTARIO M4J 1P6

Date line ➤ February 26, 20--

Delivery notation ➤ DELIVERED BY COURIER

Inside address or ➤ Castles & Sands LLP
Address of receiver Barristers and Solicitors
Suite 900
205 Portage Street
Markham, Ontario
L3R 3G3

Attention line ➤ Attention: Mr. Raymond G. Castles

Salutation ➤ Dear Counsel:

Subject line ➤ Re: The Full Block Letter Style

B

This is the full block letter style that you asked us about with a view to adopting it for use in your firm.

O

The full block letter style is called so because all of its lines begin flush with the left margin, with no indentations. Many law firms use the full block style, sample enclosed, for its simplicity. That is one of the reasons why Canada's Treasury Board recommends the use of the full block letter style for their administrative correspondence.

D ➤

For your reference, we have shown in the left margin the names of the various parts of the full block letter style. You will be happy to know that these letter parts are standard and are the same for all other letter styles, including the block and the semi-block letter styles. The full block letter style is as easy to set up as it is attractive. You may wish to adopt it for use in your firm for its time-saving practicality and simple good looks.

Y

Complimentary ➤ Yours very truly,
closing
MICHAEL, ELIAD & REDFORD LLP

Signature block ➤

Robert B. Redford

Reference initials ➤ RBR/yi
(yi=your initials)

Enclosure ➤ Enc.

Copy notation ➤ c: Margaret T. Nesh

TELEPHONE NO. (416) 363-1079
FACSIMILE NO. (416) 363-2628
www.mer.ca
E-mail rbrdfrd@mer.com

MICHAEL, ELIAD & REDFORD LLP
BARRISTERS AND SOLICITORS
863 SENECA LANE
TORONTO, ONTARIO   M4J 1P6

February 26, 20--

Mr. Raymond G. Castles
Castles & Sands LLP
Barristers and Solicitors
Suite 900
205 Portage Street
Markham, Ontario
L3R 3G3

Dear Mr. Castles:

Re: The Block Letter Style

Here is an example of the block letter style which you thought you might like to compare with the full block letter style before deciding on which one to adopt for use in your law firm.

Many law firms use the block letter style because it combines some of the attractive features of the full block and semi-block letter styles: for example, the block letter style features the date, the complimentary closing, and the signature block all starting at the centre of the letter moving to the right of centre. Of course, no political connotations are to be read into this right-of-centre movement. Note that the paragraphs contain no indentations.

In this example, we have shown you a personal salutation and a signature block that some law firms prefer to use where the writer is a partner or a sole practitioner. We enclose a copy of the full block letter style for your convenience in comparing the two before you make your decision.

You may like the well-balanced look of the block letter style and adopt it for use in your law firm to convey a well-balanced business image.

Yours truly,

Robert B. Redford

RBR/yi

Enc.

TELEPHONE NO. (416) 363-1079
FACSIMILE NO. (416) 363-2628
www.mer.ca
E-mail rbrdfrd@mer.com

MICHAEL, ELIAD & REDFORD LLP
BARRISTERS AND SOLICITORS
863 SENECA LANE
TORONTO, ONTARIO M4J 1P6

February 26, 20--

Castles & Sands LLP
Barristers and Solicitors
Suite 900
205 Portage Street
Markham, ON   L3R 3G3

Attention: Mr. Raymond G. Castles

Dear Sirs and Madams:

Re: The Semiblock Letter Style

You asked us to show you the semiblock letter style so that you may compare it to the full block and block letter styles before deciding on the one that will be the ambassador of your firm's correspondence.

The semiblock letter style is the same as the block style, except that its paragraphs are indented, usually by five or ten spaces, and the subject line is centred.   The semiblock letter style is the most traditional of all three commonly used letter styles that we have shown you, and many law firms prefer to use it because of its traditional standing.

In this example, we once again take the liberty to show you an alternative signature block to the one that we showed you in the full block and block letter styles. Here, we have included the name of the law firm followed by the word "Per." This form of signature block means that the writer is writing on the authority of the law firm and not personally. Many law firms use this form of signature block, particularly where the writer is an employee.

Should you decide to adopt this traditional letter style for your firm's use, it is sure to deliver your correspondence like a proven, reliable friend.

Yours very truly,

MICHAEL, ELIAD & REDFORD LLP

Per:

Jay Lo
Law Clerk

JL/yi

(or where the writer himself/herself keyed the letter)

/jl

LEGAL RESEARCH AND MEMORANDUMS OF LAW

The legal research discussion in this chapter includes a detailed breakdown of how to construct legal citations that provide a cross-Canada, and beyond, road map that directs the reader to where to locate the law.

INTEROFFICE MEMORANDUMS

Interoffice memorandums, or "memos," are standard in all businesses, including the business of law. They are written messages between people within the office; hence, interoffice. For that reason, memos are not usually mailed out and do not require mailing envelopes. Memos are usually written on 8 ½ x 11" memo letterhead. The discussion in Chapter 5 about reference initials, enclosures, copy (c:), and blind copy (bc:) notations applies equally to memos. Writers may sign their memos either above the reference initials (yi = your initials) or initial their memos right beside their keyed name in the **From** line; see Precedent 6.2. In the law office, memos have two purposes:

1. To conduct day-to-day interoffice communication among law office staff; Precedent 6.2.
2. To report legal research, Precedent 6.3.

LEGAL MEMORANDUMS

Remember your high school research essay on tadpoles? Legal memorandums are research "essays" on law. Frequently, a senior lawyer writes a regular interoffice memo, Precedent 6.2, asking a junior lawyer or a law clerk to research the written law and the case law (court decisions) that would support and help prove a case at hand. The junior lawyer or law clerk then reports the findings back to the senior lawyer in a **legal memorandum**, or **memo of law**, Precedent 6.3. There is no prescribed format for memos of law. The format may include the facts, issue, short conclusion, discussion, summary, and recommendation. The first part of a legal memorandum usually contains statute research, and the second part usually contains case law research. If judges have in the past ruled in favour of people in the same situation as that of the client, the lawyer may use the findings to support his or her arguments in court. For real-life examples of court rulings, follow the gavel 🔨 throughout this manual.

QUOTATIONS

A quotation is text copied word for word from other sources. It is called a quotation because it is usually identified by opening and closing quotation marks (" "). Quoted matter is the most important feature in legal research, but knowing how to present it in a legal memorandum can

Chapter 6 Legal Research and Memorandums of Law

be tricky. The following guidelines will help you handle quotations correctly when preparing legal memorandums.

Long quotations   Quotations of more than three or four lines are generally considered to be long quotations and are referred to as **block**, or **set off**, quotations. In memos of law, handle block quotations as follows:

1. Indent block quotations from both the left and right margins, and use single spacing.
2. Do not place quotation marks either at the beginning or at the end of block quotations. The indentation replaces the quotation marks.
3. If there is quoted matter within a block quotation, enclose the quoted matter in regular quotation marks (as opposed to single quotation marks).
4. Do not indent the first line of a long quotation unless that line is the first indented line in the original.

Here is a correctly indented long quotation from the Dominion Law Reports which relates to a well-known murder case:

Figure 6.1

> The terms of reference of the Royal Commission required the commission to inquire into, report and make recommendations concerning the investigation of the death, the charge and the prosecution of M., the subsequent conviction and sentencing of M. for the murder for which he was subsequently found to be not guilty and such other related matters which the commission considered relevant to the inquiry. In the course of its hearings the commission sought to compel the five members of Court of Appeal who had sat on the reference to attend and testify concerning certain aspects of the reference. The three matters on which it sought to compel testimony were the inclusion of the former Attorney-General on the panel hearing the reference, the composition of the record that was in fact before the Court of Appeal and what factors in the opinion of the Court of Appeal constituted a miscarriage of justice. The judges of the Court of Appeal refused to attend and applied to the Nova Scotia Supreme Court for a declaration that the commission had no authority to compel their attendance by virtue of judicial immunity.
>
> 61 Dominion Law Reports (4th) p. 688

Short quotations   Quotations of fewer than three or four lines are considered to be short quotations and are not set off. They are incorporated in the writer's text and are, therefore, known as **run-in** quotations. Place quotation marks around short quotations to distinguish them from the writer's text. Refer to Precedent 6.3 for examples of run-in quotations. If there is a quotation within the quoted matter, use single quotation marks (' ') to distinguish the quotation within the quotation.

Omissions and additions with long and short quotations

1. Use the ellipsis (...) (Greek, meaning omission) to indicate wording omitted from the original. A fourth dot indicates the wording ended in a period.
2. Where there is an error or a confusing expression in the original, indicate it immediately following the error or confusing expression thus: [*sic*] (Latin, means the error was in the original).

3. For special emphasis, <u>underline</u> or **bold face** quoted wording, but indicate the emphasis is yours thus: [Emphasis added].
4. Enclose in square brackets any other insertions that are not part of the original wording.
5. The following quotation is an example of the correct use of omissions and additions and is taken from the original long quotation in Figure 6.1. To see the full effect (and identify the mysterious M.), compare the two quoted passages.

Figure 6.2

[T]he Royal Commission [was] required...to inquire into...the subsequent conviction and sentencing of M. [Donald Marshall] for the murder for which he was subsequently found to be not guilty.... In the course of its hearings the commission sought to compel the five members of [the] Court of Appeal who had sat on the reference to attend and testify.... The judges of the Court of Appeal <u>refused to attend</u> [emphasis added]...by virtue of judicial immunity.

6l Dominion Law Reports (4th) p. 688

ELECTRONIC LEGAL RESEARCH

Nearly all of the information that goes in a memo of law comes from legal research. Whether lawyers conduct their legal research in an off-site law library, in their firm's library, or at their desktops, chances are they use some form of electronic method. Electronic research enables the researcher to access the most current cases even before they are available in paper copy. Online research offers statutes, regulations, court decisions, law reports, and legal commentary from across Canada and around the world with links to related cases.

Electronic research is available through such databases as LexisNexis Quicklaw, CanLII, and WestlawNext Canada. Law firms may open an account with these services where they pay an hourly rate or a flat rate. Online systems are capable of searching for a legal concept, e.g. "wrong-ful dismissal," as well as for a legal component, e.g. "radio announcer," and will access only those cases which contain a combination of the two components. In addition, the internet has become a most widely used research tool, but users can be traced back to the firm who has visited the website, which might sometimes be an undesirable side effect.

Style of legal citations   The style of the legal citations in this chapter requires no periods in the citation abbreviations (see the *Canadian Guide to Uniform Legal Citation*, 8 ed., Carswell), whereas the traditional style of legal citations requires the periods in the citation abbreviations. You may come across citations in the traditional style either in your legal research of older cases, as in Precedent 6.1, or as a preference in practice. Note, however, that even where the traditional style is preferred, the neutral citations, which the courts assign to their decisions, must be written without the periods in the court abbreviations, as shown in the *Mustapha* case below. If you are instructed to write statute and case citations in the traditional style, follow these examples:

Access to Information Act, R.S.C. 1985, c. A-1
Employment Standards Act, R.S.O. 1990, c. E.14, as am. by S.O. 1919, c. 16 and S.O. 1991, c. 43, s. 2
Dawson v. Helicopter Exploration Co., [l955] 3 D.L.R. 404 (S.C.C.)
Mustapha v. Culligan of Canada Ltd., 2008 SCC 27, [2008] 2 S.C.R. 114

SOURCES OF LAW

The primary sources of law are as follows:

Statutes   Statutes are also referred to as **acts** or **laws** and are the written laws of the federal or provincial government. Generally, the difference between acts and statutes is that **acts** are the individual acts themselves, and **statutes** are the volumes which contain a collection of individual acts. The purpose of statute research is to see what the written laws are in the case at hand: for example, the two indented paragraphs in the memo of law in Precedent 6.3 are quoted from Section 52 of the *Bills of Exchange Act* because they are deemed to be relevant in the case at hand.

Law reports   Law reports are books which publish notable court decisions. These decisions are called **case law** or **common law**, as opposed to written law, because they are not statute law; they are court interpretations of the written law in cases that come before the courts. The purpose of case law research is to see how the courts have interpreted the written laws in the decisions they render in cases similar to the case at hand: for example, the *Fairchild v Ferguson* case in Precedent 6.3 was reported in a law report series called *Supreme Court Reports* (SCR). This case has been cited because it has been deemed to be favourably relevant in the case at hand.

FEDERAL AND PROVINCIAL STATUTES

Statutes and revised statutes   Federal and provincial statutes are volumes which contain a collection of federal and provincial acts. Generally, statutes are published sessionally. The sessional volumes are then updated from time to time and consolidated into new volumes. These consolidations usually contain all of the existing federal or provincial laws which were valid at the time of the consolidation and are identified by the word "revised" or by the letter "R." Following are examples of federal and provincial statutes and revised statutes:

Figure 6.3

Federal Statutes	Provincial Statutes
Statutes of Canada (SC) *Canada Elections* Act, SC 2000, c 9	Statutes of Ontario (SO) *Residential Tenancies Act,* 2006, SO 2006, c 17
Federal Revised Statutes	**Provincial Revised Statutes**
Revised Statutes of Canada (RSC) *Access to Information Act,* RSC 1985, c A-1	Revised Statutes of Ontario (RSO) *Children's Law Reform Act,* RSO 1990, c C.12

Note that the last time the federal government issued traditional periodic revised statutes was 1985, and the last time the Ontario government issued traditional periodic revised statutes was 1990. That is why you will always see the years 1985 and 1990, respectively, when referring to the last revision dates of federal and provincial statutes. Generally, after these dates, the federal government and the Ontario government have not undertaken a traditional periodic revision because they revise (consolidate) their respective statutes on an ongoing basis online where they also indicate the consolidation period, i.e. the date to which a statute (act) is current. A similar statute revision process also applies to other provinces/territories.

Canadian statute citations   A citation is a written reference to the proper name of a statute/act similar to that of a book title in a footnote, endnote, or bibliography of an essay or report. As with footnotes, endnotes, or bibliographies, the purpose of a citation (reference) is to enable readers, e.g. judges, to confirm the source and authenticity of a quotation. The following citation is an example of how the name of the act would be cited (referenced) in a memo of law and in court documents:

Access to Information Act, RSC 1985, c A-1.

The above citation tells readers that they will find the *Access to Information Act* in Chapter A-1 (the A is for Access, the first initial of the name of the act) in a volume entitled *Revised Statutes of Canada*, abbreviated as RSC, which volume was published in 1985. Since all acts are published by either the federal or provincial government, in this case, the federal government (from the "C" for Canada in the abbreviation RSC), there is no private publisher to be referenced as would be the case when referencing a textbook title.

Preparing statute citations   Following are some examples of federal and provincial acts as they should be cited (referenced) in legal memos and court documents. Statute citations may consist of five or more parts, each separated by a comma. Follow along in the following breakdown to help you understand and prepare correct statute citations:

Employment Standards Act, RSO 1990, c E.14, as amended by SO 1919, c 16 and SO 1991, c 43, s 2
Business Corporations Act, RSO 1990, c B-16
Canada Business Corporations Act, RSC 1985, c C-44
Criminal Code, RSC 1985, c C-46, s 745 (QL)

Figure 6.4

1	2	3	4	5
Proper Name of Act	**Statute Abbreviation and Year Published**	**Chapter No. & First Initial of Name of Act**	**Amending Statute Year and Chapter No.**	**Section Number & Electronic Service**
Employment Standards Act	RSO 1990	c E.14	as amended by SO 1991, c 16 and SO 1991, c 43	s 2
Business Corporations Act	RSO 1990	c B-16		
Canada Business Corporations Act	RSC 1985	c C-44		
Criminal Code	RSC 1985	c C-46		s 745 *(QL)
*Quicklaw				

Notes:

1. Key the name of the act in italics, or underline, followed by a comma:
   Employment Standards Act,   Employment Standards Act,

2. Key the statute abbreviation, usually without spaces between the letters, and the year in which the statute was published, followed by a comma: **RSO 1990,** (Do not enclose the year in either square or round brackets as these apply only to years in case citations.)

3. Use the abbreviation for chapter, and key the chapter number, followed by a comma: **c E.14,** (The E is a reference to the first initial of the name of the act, Employment.)

4. Key any amending statute, followed by a comma: **as amended by SO 1991, c 16 and SO 1991, c 43,** (This statute was amended twice in 1991.)

5. Key the section number and any electronic service: **s 2; s 745 (QL).** Use only abbreviations, e.g. s (section), ss (sections), subs (subsections), Supp (supplement).

How to cite English statutes English statutes are usually used only for analogy as they carry little legal influence because they are of no effect outside of England. English statutes follow a different method of revision and consolidation from Canadian statutes, and some use regnal years. Following are examples of English statute citations as they should appear in legal memos and court documents:

> *Guardianship Act l973* (UK), l973, c 29.
> *Punishment of Incest Act, l908* (UK), *8 Edw 7, c 46.
>
> *In the 8th year of reign of King Edward VII. He was crowned king on January 22, l90l; the statute was passed in 1908, the 8th year.

English statutes are cited in the same way as Canadian statutes, except:

1. Use the regnal year for statutes passed before January 1, 1963, and the calendar year for those passed after January 1, 1963. (During 1963, the method of revision and consolidation was converted to calendar years.)
2. Identify English statutes with "(UK)" (United Kingdom) either after the name of the statute or, where the year is part of the proper name, after the year, e.g. 1973 (UK). If the year is part of the proper name and is prior to 1963, place a comma before the year, e.g. Act, 1908. If the year is repeated, as in the *Guardianship Act*, the first instance means it is part of the proper name of the statute, and the second, the year in which the statute was published.

CANADIAN LAW REPORTS

Research is also necessary for the kinds of decisions which the courts have made in cases similar to the one at hand. That research comes from law reports. The law reports are small books which contain court rulings on **cases** and are therefore referred to as **case law** or **common law** (as opposed to written law). Lawyers may present favourable case law to judges to help get a favourable decision in the case at hand.

Case citations Case citations are the proper referencing of cases, similar to referencing books in footnotes, endnotes, or bibliographies. The purpose of case citations is to enable readers, e.g. judges, to confirm the source and the authenticity of the court rulings cited.

See Precedent 6.1 for an excerpt from the *Dominion Law Reports* series. It is the landmark abortion case of Chantal Daigle. Here, for your interest, is the background in that case: Ms. Daigle's boyfriend, Tremblay, who fathered the child while they were living together, obtained a court injunction when, after the two split up, Ms. Daigle indicated to him her intention to have an abortion. The court stopped Ms. Daigle, ruling the fetus was a "human being" and needed protection. Ms. Daigle appealed to the Quebec Court of Appeal claiming the right to have the abortion, and lost. She then appealed to the Supreme Court of Canada. While the Supreme Court of Canada was arriving at its decision, however, Ms. Daigle, now twenty-two weeks into the pregnancy, had the abortion performed in Boston, Massachusetts. The Supreme Court of Canada ruled in her favour after the event.

Abbreviations   Some frequently used abbreviations in law reports include:

Figure 6.5

JUDGES IN CASE RULINGS	NAMES OF COURTS IN CASE CITATIONS	
J (Justice, Judge)	(BCCA)	British Columbia Court of Appeal
	(MBCA)	Manitoba Court of Appeal
JA (Justice of Appeal, Judge of Appeals Court)	(NLCA)	Supreme Court of Newfoundland and Labrador, Court of Appeal
	(NSCA)	Nova Scotia Court of Appeal
	(ONCA)	Ontario Court of Appeal
JJ (Justices, Judges)	(ONSC)	Ontario Superior Court
	(QCCA)	Quebec Court of Appeal
JJA (Justices of Appeal, Judges of Appeals Court)	(SCC)	Supreme Court of Canada

How to cite Canadian cases   Here are examples of correct Canadian case citations as they should appear in legal memos and court documents:

> *Tremblay v Daigle* (1989), 59 DLR (4th) 609 (QCA)
> *Dawson v Helicopter Exploration Co,* [1955] 3 DLR 404 (SCC)

Square and round brackets   Square and round brackets play a significant role only in case citations, not in statute citations. Here is how they work:

Square brackets [ ] and the year   The square brackets give the following message to the legal reader: "If the year is in square brackets, look for the law report by **year**, and then consider the volume number, if any." Generally, the year in square brackets is the year in which the law report was **published**. In the *Dawson v Helicopter Exploration Co*, the volumes would be stacked chronologically by year, e.g. 1955, Volumes 1, 2, 3...; 1956, Volumes 1, 2, 3.... If you ignored the year, you might pick up Volume 3 of a year other than 1955 and not find the *Dawson* case.

Round brackets ( ) and the year   The round brackets give the following message to the legal reader: "If the year is in round brackets, look for the law report by **volume number** only." The year in round brackets is the year in which the case was **heard** and is, therefore, no indication of the source in which the case was reported. The round brackets indicate that the year is parenthetical information, i.e. unnecessary to finding the case. Thus, in the *Tremblay v Daigle* case, Volume 59 would be stacked next to Volume 58, regardless of the year in which the volumes were published, and to find the *Daigle* case, you must look in Volume 59.

Reading case citations   Note that case citations are divided in two main parts by a comma — the **case** itself and the **source** in which the case was reported. The following table will help you read and understand case citations:

Legal TIP

Always place a comma **before** the square brackets because the year belongs with the name of the **law report** and **after** the round brackets because the year belongs with the name of the **case**.

Legal TIP

Reporter series numbers, if any, should be placed in round brackets and abbreviated as (2d), (3d), (4th), **not** (2nd), (3rd), and **not** in superscript (2nd) (3^{d}) (4th).

Figure 6.6

CASE	SOURCE				
Case Name (and Year Heard)	Placement of Comma	Volume No. or Year Case Published	Law Report Series (if any) and Page No.	Court Rendering Decision	How to Find It
Tremblay v Daigle (1989)	after (year)	Vol 59	*DLR (4th) 609	(QCA)	By volume (Volume 59)
Dawson v Helicopter Exploration Co	before [year]	[1955]	3 DLR 404	(SCC)	By year [1955]
Notes: *Use lower case "v" no period (v = versus) *Dominion Law Reports,* 4th series, page 609					

NEUTRAL CITATIONS

Neutral citations are court-assigned citations which identify hot-off-the bench judgments that courts publish directly on the internet before such judgments are reported in any privately-owned law report publishers. Neutral citations are referred to as such because they make no reference to any series of law reports. Neutral citations cite only the **case name** (also referred to as style of cause), **year of the judgment** (decision), **name of court**, and **case number**, separated only by a comma after the case name, for example:

Atec Marketing Limited v Heart and Stroke Foundation of Canada, 2007 ONCA 1
(The neutral citation indicates that the judgment was rendered in the year 2007 by the Court of Appeal for Ontario (ONCA) which was the court's 1st judgment in 2007. In fact, this was this court's first judgment *ever* using neutral citations.)

R v Andrew Del Riccio, 2010 ONSC 1
(The neutral citation indicates that the judgment was rendered in the year 2010 by the Ontario Superior Court of Justice (ONSC) which was the court's 1st judgment in 2010. In fact, this was this court's first judgment *ever* using neutral citations.)

Neutral citations are legal citations which are database-friendly, usually doing away with the use of periods between the letters of the acronyms which electronic databases also usually do away with. Neutral citations are designed for electronic database and internet retrieval and are intended to be referred to first, followed by parallel citations from reporter series or electronic databases, as in the following examples:

Mustapha v Culligan of Canada Ltd, 2008 SCC 27, [2008] 2 SCR 114
(The neutral citation indicates that the judgment was rendered in the year 2008 by the Supreme Court of Canada which was the court's 27th judgment in 2008. The case was subsequently reported in Volume 2 of the Supreme Court Reports (SCR) beginning at page 114.)

R v Andrew Del Ricchio, 2010 ONSC 1 (CanLII)
(The neutral citation is as described above. The case was subsequently reported in CanLII (Canadian Legal Information Institute), a non-profit database organization managed by the Federation of Law Societies of Canada.)

Pinpoint references   Pinpoint references are used when citing to a particular paragraph or page number in a judgment. Pinpoint references apply to neutral citations as well as traditional citations. A pinpoint reference to a page number is usually cited as shown in the *Mustapha v Culligan of Canada Ltd* case. A pinpoint reference to a paragraph is usually preceded by the phrase "at para" or "at paras" as follows:

Sansalone v Wawanesa Mutual Insurance Co, 2000 SCC 25 at para18
(The neutral citation indicates that the judgment was rendered in the year 2000 by the Supreme Court of Canada which was the court's 25th judgment in 2000; the pinpoint reference is to paragraph 18.)

How to cite English cases   Although English law reports vary in manner and frequency of publishing, case citations involving English law reports are written in the same way as Canadian cases:

Lane v Holloway, [1967] 3 All ER 129 (CA)

CANADIAN LAW REPORT SERIES

Canadian law reports are published weekly, monthly, or annually. There are many series, but the ones most commonly used fall into the following categories:

Federal:	Dominion Law Reports - DLR
	Supreme Court Reports - SCR
Provincial:	Ontario Reports - OR
	New Brunswick Reports - NBR
Regional:	Western Weekly Reports - WWR
	Maritime Provinces Reports - MPR

Following is an alphabetical list of commonly used Canadian law reports. The years are shown in either square or round brackets as they should appear in citations. Refer to these when preparing legal memos. You may find complete lists of law reports in many legal publications and dictionaries.

Figure 6.7

NAME OF REPORT SERIES	YEAR	ABBREVIATION
Alberta Law Reports	(1977-)	Alta. LR (2d)
All Canada Weekly Summaries	[1977-1979] (1980-)	ACWS ACWS (2d)
British Columbia Law Reports	(1977-1988) (1988-)	BCLR BCLR (2d)
Canadian Cases on the Law of Torts	(1976-)	CCLT
Dominion Law Reports	(1912-1922) [1923-1955] (1956-1968) (1969-1984) (1984 -)	DLR DLR DLR (2d) DLR (3d) DLR (4th)
Dominion Tax Cases	(1920-)	DTC
Exchequer Court Reports of Canada	[1923-1971]	Ex CR
Federal Court Reports (Canada)	[1971-]	FC or Fed R
Manitoba Reports	(1979-)	MR (2d)
New Brunswick Reports	(1825-1929) (1969-)	NBR NBR (2d)
Newfoundland & Prince Edward Island Reports	(1971-)	Nfld & PEIR
Nova Scotia Reports	(1970-)	NSR (2d)
Ontario Appeal Reports	(1876-1900)	OAR
Ontario Law Reports	(1901-1931)	OLR
Ontario Reports	(1882-1900) [1931-1973] (1974 -)	OR OR OR (2d)
Ontario Weekly Notes	[1933-1962]	OWN
Saskatchewan Reports	(1979-)	SR
Supreme Court Reports (Canada)	(1876-1922) [1923-]	SCR SCR
Western Weekly Reports	(1912-1916) [1917-1950 and 1971-]	WWR WWR

ENGLISH LAW REPORT SERIES

Square bracket and round bracket requirements vary. Generally, years before 1891 require round brackets:

NAME OF REPORT SERIES	YEAR	ABBREVIATION
All England Law Reports	[Mainly]	All ER
Appeal Cases	[1891-]	AC
Chancery Division	[1891-]	Ch
King's Bench	[1891-]	KB
Queen's Bench	[1891-]	QB

CHAPTER SUMMARY

Interoffice memorandums are used for communicating within the law firm. Legal memorandums, or memos of law, are memos of legal research on a question of law for a case at hand. The first part of a memo of law usually contains statute research, and the second part contains case law research. Most law firms use some type of electronic research, including online systems where lawyers pay for the services they use.

A legal memo may contain long quotations (of more than three or four lines) which you should indent on both sides of the margin and use single spacing. With long quotations, you use quotation marks (" ") only if there is a quotation within the long quotation. Short quotations are shorter than three or four lines, and you incorporate them in the writer's paragraph. Legal memos must also contain statute and case citations.

Special rules apply to the correct citation of statutes and cases: for example, in case citations, a year enclosed in square brackets [ ] is essential in locating the law report, whereas a year enclosed in round brackets ( ) is not needed in locating the law report. Also, a comma always precedes square brackets and follows round brackets.

REVIEW QUESTIONS

1. What is a statute citation?
2. What is a case citation?
3. Does a comma go before or after square brackets?
4. How are past court rulings useful to the case at hand in court?
5. Explain how a statute is a legal commemorative monument.
6. Correctly cite the following:
   (a) Anti-Terrorism Act Statutes of Canada 2001 Chapter 41.
   (b) Children's Law Reform Act Revised Statutes of Ontario 1990 Chapter C-12
   (c) Smith v. Wanded 1972 3 Ontario Reports 101 (Ont. C.A.)
   (d) Brown versus Dickens 1967 62 Dominion Law Reports (2d) 167 (Ont. S.C.J.)

609

Tremblay v. Daigle

Quebec Court of Appeal, Bernier, Nichols, Chouinard, LeBel and Tourigny JJ.A
July 26, 1989

Constitutional law – Charter of Rights – Right to life, liberty and security – Father obtaining interlocutory injunction to restrain mother from having abortion – No denial of woman's right to liberty or security in circumstances – Canadian Charter of Rights and Freedoms, s. 7

Constitutional law – Provincial Bills of Rights – Right to life – Legislation guaranteeing human being right to life – Whether human being includes foetus – Charter of Human Rights and Freedoms, R.S.Q. 1977, c. C-12, s. 1.

Injunctions – Interlocutory relief – Balance of convenience – Father obtaining interlocutory injunction to restrain mother from having abortion – Considerations in granting injunctions – Canadian Charter of Rights and Freedoms, s. 7 – Charter of Human Rights and Freedoms, R.S.Q. 1977, c. C-12, s. 1 – Civil Code of Lower Canada, arts. 338, 345.

The respondent brought an application for an interlocutory injunction to restrain the appellant from having an abortion around her 18th week of pregnancy. The child had been conceived while the parties cohabited. On the breakup of their relationship, the appellant sought an abortion. The trial judge granted the interlocutory injunction.

On appeal, held, Chouinard and Tourigny JJ.A. dissenting, the appeal should be dismissed.

Per Bernier J.A.: A child conceived, but not yet born, regardless of the stage of the pregnancy, possesses a civil status. He cannot be deprived of his natural right to life without cause which is just, sufficient and acceptable in a free and democratic society. When the interests of the mother are contrary to those of the unborn child, the father has the right, on serious and reasonable grounds not contrary to the interests of the unborn child, to oppose an abortion. The grounds invoked by the appellant were not sufficiently serious to deprive the unborn child of the right to be carried to term and to be born. The birth was desired, the foetus was normal, and the appellant's health excellent. The fact that she broke off her living arrangements did not constitute sufficient grounds for terminating, despite the opposition of the father, a pregnancy so far advanced.

Per Nichols J.A.: The preponderance of the evidence was to the effect that neither the life nor health of the mother was in danger. Therefore, the appellant's right to the security of her person was not in issue. The provisions of the *Civil Code of Lower Canada* permitting the appointment of a curator to the unborn child and granting patrimonial rights to him indicate an essential premise that the unborn child has the right to life. The mother's right to liberty does not exclude the right to life of the foetus, and it does not include an unrestricted right to abortion. The appellant's right to liberty in s. 7 of the Canadian Charter of Rights and Freedoms could not include a right to

---

610   DOMINION LAW REPORTS   59 D.L.R. (4th)

terminate her pregnancy freely at this stage in light of the fact that it was a desired pregnancy, that the life and health of the mother were not in danger, and that the evidence indicated the child was normal. When it is a question of resolving a conflict between the free control by a woman of her body and the right to life of the being she carries, the balance is tipped in favour of the foetus, both because of the rights to which it is entitled and because of the balance of inconvenience.

Per LeBel J.A.: Within the meaning of the Quebec *Charter of Human Rights and Freedoms,* R.S.Q. 1977, c. C-12, the foetus was a human being. Section 1 states that every human being has a right to life and to personal security, inviolability and freedom and possesses juridical personality. This interpretation is in harmony with the rules established by the *Civil Code of Lower Canada* recognizing rights in the foetus to take part in a succession. These rules of law, particularly those in the *Civil Code of Lower Canada,* recognize and structure a juridical personality. The foetus has rights distinct from the pregnant woman, and these rights must be balanced against and compared to the mother's rights to security and liberty in s. 7 of the *Canadian Charter of Rights and Freedoms,* which are not unlimited. Protection of the foetus would constitute a reasonable limit, at its stage of development and on the facts established. At this stage, when it is close to the threshold of viability, the balance of inconvenience favours the foetus.

Per Tourigny J. A., dissenting: A "human being" within s. 1 of the Quebec Charter cannot be anything other than a physical person. The foetus is not a person and cannot enjoy rights accorded to persons by the Quebec Charter. The *Civil Code of Lower Canada* does not give rights to the unborn child. It provides rights which a child, when born alive and viable, may enjoy. They are essentially conservatory measures which, pending birth, protect the interests of the child born alive and viable. Articles 338 and 345 do not confer substantive rights. They only provide mechanisms for protecting incapable persons in the exercise of rights otherwise granted to them at law. The interpretation of these general legal provisions cannot infringe the rights guaranteed to pregnant women by s. 7 of the Canadian Charter or deny their existence.

Per Chouinard J.A., dissenting: Section 752 of the *Code of Civil Procedure,* R.S.Q. 1977, c. C-25, permits an interlocutory injunction when the applicant appears entitled to it and it is considered necessary in order to avoid serious and irreparable injury to him. There was no serious issue of law in favour of the respondent in the present state of the Quebec Charter nor the recognition of certain rights which are mostly patrimonial in nature in the unborn child (conditional upon his birth and viability). In addition, a serious issue of law does not appear to exist in light of the fundamental right of the appellant to deal with her body as defined in the *Morgentaler* decision.

R. v. Morgentaler (1988), 44 D.L.R. (4th) 385, 37 C.C.C. (3d) 449, [1988] I S.C.R. 30, 62 C.R. (3d) 1, 31 C.R.R. 1, 26 O.A.C. 1, 82 N.R. 1, consd...

MICHAEL, ELIAD & REDFORD LLP

MEMORANDUM

DATE:　　　October 25, 20--

TO:　　　　Margaret Nesh

FROM:　　　Robert B. Redford *RBR*

RE:　　　　Ilche McCann Limited and Hollow Products Limited

In this file, we have a promissory note made by Hollow Products Limited to our client and signed by its two officers. Because the two signatures appear above the corporate name, there seems to be some question as to whether this obligates the two directors personally rather than the corporation itself.

Please read the law and see if you can also find any case support.

Robert B. Redford

RBR/yi

*Alternative ways of signing

MICHAEL, ELIAD & REDFORD LLP

MEMORANDUM

DATE: October 27, 20–

TO: Robert B. Redford

FROM: Margaret Nesh

RE: Ilche McCann Limited and Hollow Products Limited

There seems to be nothing in any of the literature I checked or in the *Bills of Exchange Act* or the *Business Corporations Act* that relates directly to any difference between officers of a corporation signing above or below the corporate name.

The *Business Corporations Act* does, however, hold that when a note or security is signed by an agent or officer of a corporation, there may be personal liability if there is no mention of the corporate name in "legible characters." In this case, the corporate name is clearly shown.

Section 52 of the *Bills of Exchange Act* states:

> 52(1) Where a person signs a bill as drawer, endorser or acceptor and adds words to a signature indicating he signs for or on behalf of his principal, or in a representative character, he is not personally liable; but the mere addition to a signature of words describing him as agent, or as filling a representative character, does not exempt him from personal liability.

> (2) In determining whether a signature on a bill is that of a principal or that of the agent by whose hand it is written, the construction most favourable to the validity of the instrument shall be adopted.

I was able to find the following two case supports:

1. In *Fairchild v Ferguson* (1892), 21 SCR 484, the manager of a company gave a promissory note in payment of goods purchased by him in the capacity of manager of the company. The note stated: "Sixty days after date we promise to pay..." and it was signed by the manager thus: "R., Manager, O.L. Company." It was held that the intention of both R. and the payees was to make the company liable, that the note was given on behalf of the company and not by R. personally.

2. The case of *Chapman v Smethurst*, [1909] 1 KB 927 (CA) indicates a tendency to look at the intent rather than the form of the document. The note in that case stated: "I promise to pay..." and was signed "J. H. S. Laundry and Die Works Limited, J. H. S., Managing Director." Action was brought against J. H. S. personally. Although the note did not purport to be signed for, or on behalf of, the company, the stamped name of the company over the written signature of the defendant was held sufficient to show that it was the company's note and not the defendant's.

This case appears to support the provisions of the present *Business Corporations Acts* throughout Canada, which limit the personal liability of agents or officers of corporations when signing securities or notes where the name of the corporation is legibly set out.

MN/yi

CHAPTER 7

THE COURT SYSTEM OF CANADA

This chapter looks at the court system of Canada, including the provincial and territorial courts, the fundamental principles of criminal and civil law, and the criminal and civil court process.

Figure 7.0   Court System of Canada

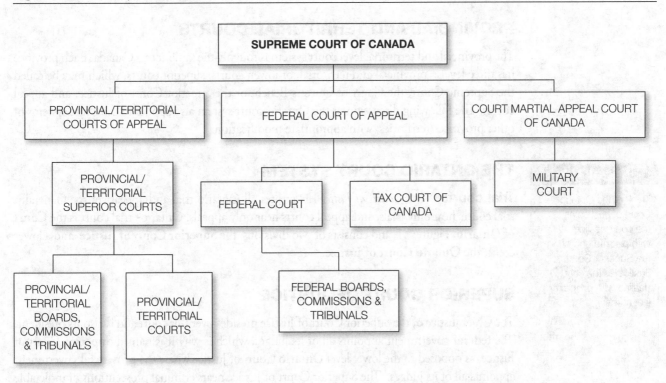

The organization of Canada's judicial system is a function of Canada's Constitution and particularly of the *Constitution Act*, 1867. By virtue of the *Constitution Act*, authority for the judicial system in Canada is divided between the federal government and the provincial governments. The *Constitution Act*, 1867, empowers each province to establish its own court system. Section 92 reads:

> In each Province the Legislature may exclusively make Laws in relation to....[t]he Administration of Justice in the Province, including the Constitution, Maintenance, and Organization of Provincial Courts, both of Civil and of Criminal Jurisdiction, and including Procedure in Civil Matters in those Courts.

SUPREME COURT OF CANADA

This is the highest and final court of appeal in Canada. It sits in the main courtroom of the Supreme Court of Canada building in Ottawa. The Chief Justice of Canada presides over it, and it consists of the Chief Justice of Canada and eight other justices. The Supreme Court of Canada hears criminal and civil appeals from the courts of appeal of all provinces and gives advisory opinions to the federal government, if requested, on the interpretation of the Canadian *Constitution*. In some cases, the Supreme Court of Canada must grant leave (permission) to an appellant before hearing the appellant's appeal. Normally, the issue or legal point must be of some public importance before the Supreme Court of Canada would grant such a leave.

FEDERAL COURT

The Federal Court specializes in areas such as intellectual property, maritime law, federal-provincial disputes, and civil cases related to terrorism. The Tax Court specializes in hearing appeals from tax assessments. The Federal Court of Appeal reviews the decisions of both the Federal Court and Tax Court. Administrative boards and tribunals are not part of the court system. They deal with disputes over interpretation and application of laws and regulations such as entitlement to employment insurance or disability benefits, refugee claims, and human rights.

PROVINCIAL AND TERRITORIAL COURTS

The provincial and territorial level court system is roughly the same across Canada. Each province has three levels: provincial and territorial, or lower, courts; superior courts, which may be called the Supreme Court, the Court of Queen's Bench, or the Superior Court of Justice; and appeal courts. The following discussion of the Ontario court system also applies to the court systems of other provinces/territories, with appropriate modification.

THE ONTARIO COURT SYSTEM

Trial courts The *Courts of Justice Act* creates all Ontario trial and appeal courts. Generally, trial courts hear only trials, and appeal courts hear only appeals. Ontario's trial court is the **Court of Ontario,** Figure 7.1, and consists of two divisions: the **Superior Court of Justice** and a lower court, the **Ontario Court of Justice**.

Legal TIP

Think of the Ontario Court of Justice as the court dealing with **people** and of the Superior Court of Justice as the court dealing with **property** (i.e. money).

SUPERIOR COURT OF JUSTICE

The Chief Justice of the Superior Court of Justice presides over this court and is also its president. The **federal** government appoints all of its judges, which is why it is named **Superior** Court of Justice, as opposed to the lower level **Ontario** Court of Justice where the **provincial** government appoints all of its judges. The Superior Court of Justice hears criminal prosecutions of indictable offences and all civil suits. In criminal jury trials, the jury consists of twelve individuals, all of whom must agree on the verdict. In civil jury trials, the jury consists of six individuals, five of whom must agree on the verdict. The Superior Court of Justice has three branches: the Small Claims Court, the Family Court, and the Divisional Court.

SMALL CLAIMS COURT

This is a court for claims under $25,000, excluding interest and costs. The Chief Justice of the Superior Court of Justice heads the Small Claims Court and is also its president. It is a same level court as the Superior Court of Justice, but it is specifically designated as an informal court

Figure 7.1 Court of Ontario

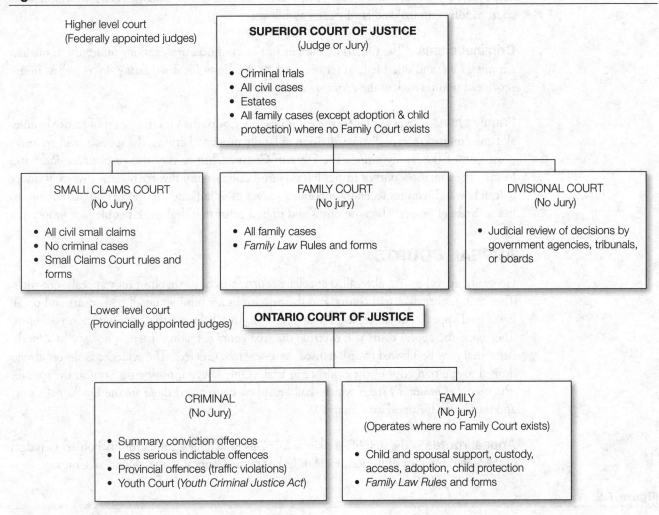

Higher level court
(Federally appointed judges)

SUPERIOR COURT OF JUSTICE
(Judge or Jury)

- Criminal trials
- All civil cases
- Estates
- All family cases (except adoption & child protection) where no Family Court exists

SMALL CLAIMS COURT
(No Jury)

- All civil small claims
- No criminal cases
- Small Claims Court rules and forms

FAMILY COURT
(No jury)

- All family cases
- *Family Law* Rules and forms

DIVISIONAL COURT
(No Jury)

- Judicial review of decisions by government agencies, tribunals, or boards

Lower level court
(Provincially appointed judges)

ONTARIO COURT OF JUSTICE

CRIMINAL
(No Jury)

- Summary conviction offences
- Less serious indictable offences
- Provincial offences (traffic violations)
- Youth Court (*Youth Criminal Justice Act*)

FAMILY
(No jury)
(Operates where no Family Court exists)

- Child and spousal support, custody, access, adoption, child protection
- *Family Law Rules* and forms

intended for people to represent themselves in court. One judge hears trials. The judge may be a Superior Court of Justice judge, or to expedite cases, the regional senior judge may appoint lawyers to act as deputy judges (part-time judges) of the Small Claims Court.

FAMILY COURT OF THE SUPERIOR COURT OF JUSTICE (FAMILY COURT)

The Family Court of the Superior Court of Justice (Family Court) is a same level court as the Superior Court of Justice. The Chief Justice of the Superior Court of Justice heads the Family Court and is also its president. The mandate of the Family Court is to deal exclusively with all family matters arising from both provincial and federal laws. Judges of the Superior Court of Justice hear all Family Court cases. The Family Court operates in numerous municipalities across the province and is expected to gradually expand throughout the province. The *Family Law Rules* and forms apply to the Family Court and to all other courts having jurisdiction to hear family cases.

ONTARIO COURT OF JUSTICE

The provincial, as opposed to the federal, government appoints the judges of the Ontario Court of Justice; this is why this court is a lower level court than the Superior Court of Justice. The

Chief Justice of the Ontario Court of Justice is president of the Ontario Court of Justice. This court handles criminal and family cases as follows:

Criminal cases   The Ontario Court of Justice conducts prosecutions under the Canadian *Criminal Code* and other federal statutes such as the *Youth Criminal Justice Act* as well as under provincial statutes such as the *Highway Traffic Act*.

Family cases   In places where there is no Family Court, the Ontario Court of Justice handles all family matters, except divorce, division of family property between the spouses, and exclusive possession of the family home. The Ontario Court of Justice uses the *Family Law Rules* and forms. The Ontario Court of Justice has no jurisdiction to hear divorce because divorce is under federal law and requires federally appointed judges to adjudicate. It also has no jurisdiction to hear matters of property because this is said to be a court that deals with **people**, not property.

APPEAL COURTS

Generally, appeal courts, also called appellate courts, are courts that hear only appeals, not trials. They rank higher than trial courts, and their decisions are binding on all trial courts and on all lower level appeal courts. People go to appeal when they believe a trial court's decision is unjust. They hope the appeal court will overrule the trial court decision. There is no jury in appeals. An appeal may be allowed (won), refused, or a new trial ordered. The evidence is almost always limited to the transcript of the evidence at trial. Only lawyers, not parties, appear on appeals. The *Courts of Justice Act* states which shall be appeal courts, and these are the Divisional Court and the Court of Appeal for Ontario.

Appeal routes   The simplified chart below illustrates appeal routes for final orders of judges of the Superior Court of Justice. Final orders of masters appeal to the Divisional Court.

Figure 7.2

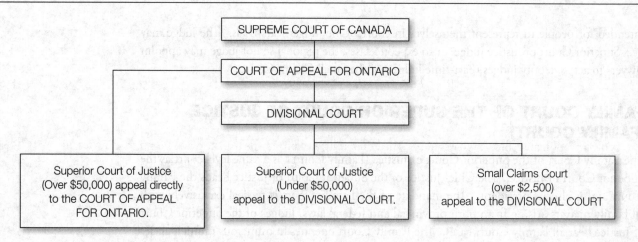

DIVISIONAL COURT

No one knows why this court is named so. The Divisional Court is an appeal court ranking lower than the Court of Appeal for Ontario and hears only civil appeals. It sits in each region, giving the region local appeal jurisdiction to help expedite appeals of less serious cases. Generally, three judges of the Superior Court of Justice sit together in the Divisional Court. As with all branches of the Superior Court of Justice, the Chief Justice of the Superior Court of Justice is its head and president.

COURT OF APPEAL FOR ONTARIO

The Court of Appeal for Ontario is Ontario's highest appellate court. It consists of the Chief Justice of Ontario, the Associate Chief Justice of Ontario, and fourteen or more other judges called justices of appeal. The Court of Appeal sits mainly at Osgoode Hall, Toronto, in panels of one or three judges. Appeals to the Court of Appeal for Ontario are, therefore, usually heard in Toronto. In very important appeals, more than three judges may sit, but the number of judges must be an uneven number to avoid deadlock decisions. The decisions of the Court of Appeal are binding on all lower courts, but may be overturned by the Supreme Court of Canada.

The Court of Appeal for Ontario hears civil appeals of more than $50,000 (excluding costs) and almost all criminal appeals. Appeals from trial courts going directly to the Court of Appeal for Ontario are said to be appeals of **first instance** or **first appeals**. Appeals from lower appeal courts are known as **second** appeals. To discourage frivolous appeals, the Court of Appeal for Ontario must give its permission (leave) before it hears second appeals.

COURT OFFICES

Generally, the province of Ontario is divided into counties, districts, and regional municipalities. There is usually a court house in each county, district, or regional municipality. Each court house operates through an administrative office, commonly referred to as the **court office**. It is this office that you deal with when starting a law suit, and this is where you file all subsequent documents relating to the law suit, usually until it is finished.

Administrative officers The court office of the Superior Court of Justice is administered by a **local registrar**. The local registrar acts on behalf of the **registrar** who is the supervisor of all local registrars. The administrative officer of the Small Claims Court and that of the Family Court is a **clerk**.

CRIMINAL AND CIVIL LAW

The following two historical cases will help you understand the basic difference between criminal and civil law; the first is a criminal case, the second is civil:

R v Dudley and Stephens. In this historic 1884 English case, Dudley and Stephens were shipwrecked for twenty days without food. As a result, they killed seventeen-year old Parker, who was also on board, and fed on his remains until the two were picked up by a passing ship. Dudley and Stephens reasoned that Parker was the most dispensable since he suffered most from the effects of starvation and since, as the youngest, had no family to come home to. The court found Dudley and Stephens guilty of murder and sentenced them to death. (Later, the Queen granted them mercy, and their death sentence was commuted to life imprisonment. Then, with the help of various legal efforts, they were both released after serving six months in prison.)

McErlean v Sarel and the City of Brampton. In this notable 1985 Canadian case, the court made one of the largest negligence awards in Canadian legal history. Fourteen-year old McErlean fell off his trail bike after colliding head-on with the bike which thirteen-year old Neil Sarel was riding. The two boys had been biking in an abandoned area belonging to the City of Brampton, Ontario, which area the City had clearly marked with a "No Trespassing" sign. McErlean suffered permanent brain damage, was left a quadriplegic, and sued Sarel and the City. The court found the City of Brampton and Sarel both to blame and ordered them to pay over $7 million to McErlean for his injuries. (In 1987, the City of Brampton appealed, and the court overturned the money award and set aside the award and the finding of negligence for re-examination.)

Legal TIP

Criminal cases are between the State and individuals. Civil cases are between individuals. In criminal cases, the purpose is to punish the guilty, usually by a fine or imprisonment. In civil cases, the purpose is to compensate the person who was wronged, usually by an award of money known as **damages**.

Canada's court system enforces two different bodies of law:

(1) criminal law, which punishes individuals for conduct that is in violation of the law as set out in the *Criminal Code* of Canada, and

(2) civil law, which involves one party seeking compensation from another party for a wrongful act done to the first party by the second party.

CRIMINAL LAW

Safeguards In Canada, we are fortunate to have constitutional safeguards to prevent innocent persons from being convicted of crimes. We are presumed to be innocent until proven guilty. We must be proven guilty beyond a reasonable doubt. We have the right to remain silent. In indictable offences (serious offences e.g. murder), we are entitled to be tried by a jury of twelve citizens chosen at random, and if even one juror has a doubt about our guilt, we cannot be convicted. We are entitled to have a lawyer represent us and cross-examine our accusers. The lawyer who practises criminal litigation is known as a criminal lawyer (an unfortunate description which should not be taken too literally).

The *Criminal Code* Canada's criminal law is set out in the *Criminal Code*. The *Criminal Code* applies to all Canadian provinces and territories. In criminal law, it is the Crown, i.e. the government, acting on behalf of all members of society through a lawyer known as a Crown prosecutor, or Crown attorney, who prosecutes individuals who commit criminal offences, i.e. acts that are harmful to an individual and society.

Mens rea *Mens rea* refers to a "guilty mind" or the intention or knowledge of criminal wrongdoings. *Mens rea* offences are offences under the *Criminal Code*. A *mens rea* offence usually contains words such as "willfully," "knowingly," or "intentionally" in the law creating the offence. *Mens rea* applies only to criminal offences; it does not apply to civil wrongdoings.

Beyond a reasonable doubt This is the standard of proof in criminal offences, and it applies only to criminal offences and not to civil wrongdoings. Basically, it means there is sufficient evidence to convince a reasonable person beyond doubt of the guilt of the accused. Guilt in criminal offences must be proved beyond a reasonable doubt by two elements:

(a) that the accused committed the crime, and

(b) that the accused had a guilty mind, i.e. intended, or planned, to commit the crime.

Summary conviction offences Summary conviction offences are less serious criminal offences under the *Criminal Code*. Examples include causing a disturbance in a public place and trespassing at night. Under s.787 of the *Criminal Code*, the punishment for summary conviction offences is a maximum fine of $5,000, or imprisonment of up to six months, or both. Summary conviction offences are named so because they are tried summarily, i.e. by way of a short trial without a jury.

Indictable offences These are more serious criminal offences under the *Criminal Code* such as murder or sexual assault. Indictable offences carry longer maximum jail sentences and higher fines than summary conviction offences. Also, indictable offences are subject to more complex court proceedings. Generally, the accused has the option to be tried in the Ontario Court of Justice without a preliminary hearing or a jury, or in the Superior Court of Justice with a preliminary hearing and by a judge alone or by a judge and jury.

Hybrid offences A hybrid offence, also referred to as a "dual procedure offence," is a criminal offence which may be tried by a summary conviction procedure or by indictment at the option of the prosecutor; hence, "dual procedure offence." Examples of hybrid offences include impaired driving, theft under $5,000, and sexual assault. If the nature of the hybrid offence is serious (for example, sexual assault can include either touching or full intercourse) or the offender has a serious prior criminal record, the Crown prosecutor may decide to prosecute by indictment (instead of by summary conviction) so that there are more serious sentencing options available to the judge.

Where tried All criminal cases, whether summary or indictable, begin in the Ontario Court of Justice where there are no jury trials. The Ontario Court of Justice gives final decisions in all summary conviction offences. It also gives final decisions in those indictable offences where the accused chooses to be tried by a judge of the Ontario Court of Justice. The Ontario Court of Justice also holds preliminary hearings in those indictable offences where the accused chooses to be tried by a judge of the Superior Court of Justice and gives final decisions in the weaker ones of these and sends the ones with sufficient evidence to the Superior Court of Justice for a full trial where the accused may choose trial by a judge alone or by a judge and jury.

Jury The jury in criminal trials consists of twelve jurors, and the verdict of the twelve jurors must be unanimous.

PROVINCIAL OFFENCES

The Ontario Court of Justice is Ontario's provincial court. This court hears virtually all provincial offences as well as offences against municipal by-laws, usually before a justice of the peace. Provincial offences are summary conviction offences and include non-criminal and quasi-criminal offences. The *Provincial Offences Act* (POA) sets out procedures for the prosecution of offences under other provincial statutes and regulations and municipal by-laws, examples of which include:

- Speeding, careless driving, or not wearing your seat belt (*Highway Traffic Act*)
- Failing to surrender your insurance card or possessing a false or invalid insurance card (*Compulsory Automobile Insurance Act*)
- Being intoxicated in a public place or selling alcohol to a minor (*Liquor Licence Act*)
- Trespassing or failing to leave premises after being directed to do so (*Trespass to Property Act*)
- *Occupational Health and Safety Ac*t and Ministry of Environment violations
- Noise, taxi, and animal care (city by-laws).

Here is an example of a careless driving offence as set out under the Ontario *Highway Traffic Act*:

> 130. Every person is guilty of the offence of driving carelessly who drives a vehicle or street car on a highway without due care and attention or without reasonable consideration for other persons using the highway and on conviction is liable to a fine of not less than $400 and not more than $2,000 or to imprisonment for a term of not more than six months, or to both, and in addition his or her licence or permit may be suspended for a period of not more than two years.

PROSECUTION OF PROVINCIAL OFFENCES

The procedure for the prosecution of provincial offences is set out in Part I, Part II, and Part III of the *Provincial Offences Act*. Precedents 7.3 and 7.4 are examples of provincial offence notices:

Part I   Part I begins with an offence notice which is usually a **ticket** (other than a parking ticket): for example, a speeding ticket is a Part I offence notice. Part I offence notices are usually used for less serious provincial offences such as failure to carry a driver's licence while driving or the consumption of alcohol in a public place. Note, however, that while Part I offences are less serious offences, it is up to the provincial offences officer or police officer to elect to proceed by Part I, a less formal ticketing process, than by Part III which compels the offender to appear in court. Part I offence notices usually include a set fine; no imprisonment. Under Part I, the offender has the following options:

(a) plead guilty and pay the total amount of the fine shown on the ticket,

(b) choose early resolution meeting with the prosecutor, which the court will then schedule and notify the offender, and at which, the offender may obtain disclosure (evidence) of the charges from, and discuss the charges with, the prosecutor, possibly resulting in a reduced fine or a lesser charge, either of which would mean a guilty plea; (a not guilty plea is not part of this option), or

(c) choose to go to trial to challenge the ticket in court.

Part II   Part II begins with a parking infraction notice (parking **ticket**). Part II applies exclusively to parking infractions which are primarily created by municipal by-laws. Parking infractions include a set fine; no imprisonment. The offender may choose to:

(a) voluntarily pay the fine indicated on the parking ticket (which means a guilty plea), or

(b) request a trial to challenge the ticket in court.

Part III   Part III begins with a **summons** (not a ticket) and includes a first court appearance date. A summons is used for more serious offences. These offences cannot be resolved like tickets through the payment of a set fine; they require a court attendance. That is why there is no dollar amount shown on the summons. Some of these offences can be prosecuted under Part I or Part III at the option of the police officer or provincial offences officer. The decision to charge under Part III, instead of under Part I, may depend on the circumstances or consequences of the commission of the offence: for example, an employer may be charged under the *Occupational Health and Safety Act* for failure to provide its employees with appropriate protective devices under a Part I offence notice; however, if the failure to provide such protective devices resulted in a serious injury or death to an employee, the employer may be charged under the Part III offence instead. With Part III offences, the court may impose much higher fines than those applicable to Part I offences, and imprisonment is also a sentencing option.

Statute of limitations   Think of a statute of limitations as a law of expiry dates within which one can sue or be sued: for example, section 76 (1) of the *Provincial Offences Act* has a statute that prohibits persons from being charged six months after the date on which an offence was committed. Similarly, section 786 of the *Criminal Code* of Canada has a statute that prohibits persons from being tried for a summary conviction offence more than six months after the criminal offence was committed. There is no time limit under the *Criminal Code* to when charges can be laid in indictable offences, and an accused can be charged many years after a criminal act has occurred.

Paralegal representation The Law Society permits licensed paralegals to provide legal services within a permitted scope of practice, including represent someone:

- in Small Claims Court
- in the Ontario Court of Justice under the *Provincial Offences Act*
- on summary conviction offences under the *Criminal Code* where the maximum penalty does not exceed **six months** imprisonment. These may include minor criminal offences under the *Criminal Code* of Canada (which are federal as opposed to provincial offences) such as causing a disturbance or harassing phone calls. They may also include theft under $5,000, assault, and mischief to private property, provided the Crown elects to proceed by way of summary conviction
- before administrative tribunals.

SUMMARY CONVICTION OFFENCES—STEPS TO TRIAL

Figure 7.3 Summary Conviction Offences

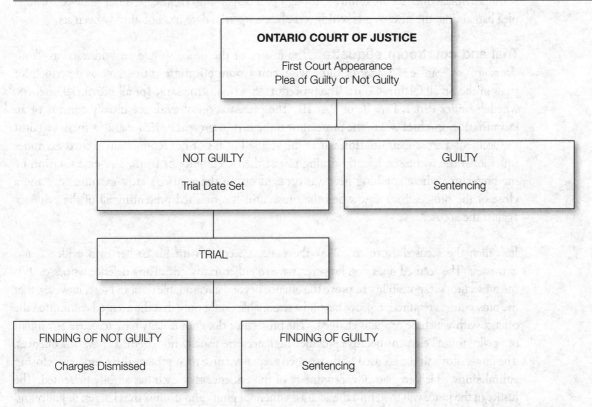

All summary conviction offences are usually tried in the provincial court, which is the Ontario Court of Justice, usually before a justice of the peace. Summary conviction offences usually carry a maximum of six months in jail. Following are the basic steps to trial in summary conviction offences:

First court appearance   This is not a trial date. Note that a first court appearance usually occurs where the offence notice is a **summons** under Part III, not a ticket. Either the accused or his or her representative must appear at the first court appearance. The first court appearance is procedural and is for the purpose of disclosure. This is where the accused is likely to receive the prosecutor's sentencing position and a summary of the case against the accused. Disclosure is the evidence that the prosecutor has in his or her possession for use in prosecuting the accused. The disclosure documents may consist of the investigating officer's notes, witness statements, photographs, and diagrams. The accused is entitled to receive from the prosecutor copies of the disclosure documents, usually free of charge.

Plea bargaining   Plea bargaining may occur in Part I, Part II, and Part III offences. This is usually when the accused or his or her representative negotiates with the prosecutor for the purpose of having the charges against the accused reduced or dismissed. Generally, plea bargaining occurs by arranging resolution meetings with the prosecutor and may begin as soon as the accused receives an offence notice, or on or before a first court appearance, or before a trial. Most provincial offences are resolved through plea bargaining. If the case is not resolved through plea bargaining, the next step is setting a trial date if a trial date has not already been set.

Trial and courtroom etiquette   The justice of the peace should be addressed as "Your Worship," or "Sir," or "Madam." Otherwise, **courtroom etiquette** is the same as described for trials in the Small Claims Court. The procedure at a trial is the same for all provincial offences, whether under Part I, Part II, or Part III. The presentation of evidence usually consists of an **examination-in-chief** where the prosecutor is the first to present evidence and witnesses against the accused; a **cross-examination** where the accused or his or her representative cross-examines (questions) the witnesses, usually aiming to test their credibility or truth; a **re-examination** by the prosecutor where anything new was brought out in the accused's cross-examination; and a **close** of the prosecution's case when the prosecutor has finished presenting all of the evidence against the accused.

It is then the accused's turn to follow the same procedure with his or her own evidence and witnesses. The accused does not, however, have to either testify or call any defence witnesses. It is the prosecutor's responsibility to prove the offence beyond a reasonable doubt. Note, however, that the prosecutor is required to prove beyond a reasonable doubt only that the accused committed the offence with which he or she is charged. The prosecutor does not usually have to prove any intent or "guilty mind" element because provincial offences are usually not deemed *mens rea* offences. The prosecutor and the accused or the accused's representative then present their respective **closing submissions** which are basically a summary of the evidence that each has already presented. The justice of the peace will then find the accused either not guilty and dismiss the charges, or guilty and either immediately, or at a later date, give his or her judgment and sentencing. Generally, sentences for provincial offences may include a fine, probation, jail, or other orders.

INDICTABLE OFFENCES - STEPS TO TRIAL

Plea bargaining is also routinely conducted in indictable offences; it is done through resolution meetings with the Crown at any time in advance of the trial. At trial, the judge, whether in the Ontario Court of Justice or the Superior Court of Justice, is addressed as "Your Honour," or "Sir," or "Madam." The evidence at trial is usually presented in the same manner as that described for summary conviction offences, including an examination-in-chief, a cross-examination, a re-examination, and a closing. With indictable offences, the Crown must prove the accused's guilt beyond a reasonable doubt. Upon a finding of guilty, the judge will pronounce his or her sentence either at the end of the trial or at a later date. Upon a finding of not guilty, the accused will be acquitted, i.e. cleared of all charges. Here is a basic overview of the steps to trial in indictable offences:

Figure 7.4 Indictable Offences

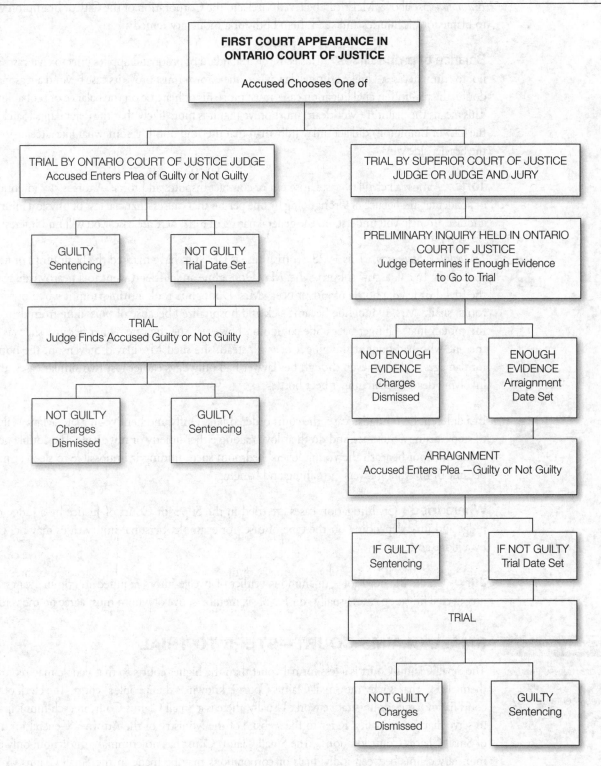

CIVIL LAW

In civil litigation, people sue other people. The state is not involved. Generally, all cases that do not arise from violations to federal criminal laws and provincial quasi-criminal laws are civil litigation cases. Civil litigation cases involve private disputes and wrongdoings between citizens, including businesses and corporations: for example, in the *McErlean v Sarel and the City of Brampton* case above, McErlean believed Sarel and the Corporation of the City of Brampton were to blame for his injuries and sued them both for a monetary remedy.

Balance of probabilities   This is the civil standard of proof and applies only to civil cases and not to criminal cases. Unlike criminal law where the Crown must prove its case beyond a reasonable doubt, the plaintiff in civil litigation cases must prove his or her case on the balance of probabilities. This means the plaintiff (McErlean) must prove that it is more likely that the defendants (Sarel and the City of Brampton) did act unlawfully than that they did not. It is somewhat like a teeter-totter; the heavier side wins.

Torts   Almost all civil law cases arise out of contract disputes and torts. A tort is any intentional or accidental negligence or wrongdoing by one person that causes financial loss or physical injury to another. To help you understand the general nature of torts, here are cases you will find interesting:

Donoghue v Stevenson. This 1928 Scottish case is fabled to have marked the beginnings of negligence law. In a Glasgow suburb, Mrs. May Donoghue and a friend went to a nearby café where the friend ordered a bottle of ginger beer. Mrs. Donoghue took a drink from it when out fell a rotten snail. Mrs. Donoghue became sick and hospitalized because of poisoning from drinking the contaminated ginger beer. She could not, however, sue the café owner because she was not the one who had bought the ginger beer. Instead, she sued Mr. David Stevenson, the bottler, for damages and won, even though her lawyer had only days earlier lost two similar cases, these involving dead mice in ginger beer bottles.

In a different 1990 English case, the court ordered Jane Duffy and her live-in mate, Mark Wilson, to stop causing a nuisance and do their lovemaking either quietly or not at all. The couple occupying the floor beneath the young lovers' bedroom sued, finding it impossible to sleep at night because of the young lovers' "groaning and banging."

Where tried   Civil litigation cases are tried in the Superior Court of Justice by a judge or a judge and jury, depending on the type of case: for example, personal injury cases may be tried by a judge and jury.

Jury   Unlike the need for a unanimous verdict of twelve jurors required in criminal cases, the jury in civil litigation cases usually consists of six members, five of whom must agree on the verdict.

SMALL CLAIMS COURT—STEPS TO TRIAL

Legal TIP

If you are represented by a lawyer or a paralegal, your representative may complete the necessary forms for you.

The Small Claims Court is a less formal court than the higher courts so that people may represent themselves. That is why the Small Claims Court is known as the "people's" court. The **clerk** of this court handles the administrative work. Usually, there is a Small Claims Court in each municipality to serve that municipality. Refer to the website of the Ministry of the Attorney General for a list of Small Claims Court locations. The Small Claims Court has no criminal jurisdiction; only civil monetary claims between individuals or corporations may be made in the Small Claims Court, and this court will order only monetary compensation (known as **damages**) or recovery of personal property. Examples of the types of claims that one can sue for in the Small Claims Court include damages in automobile accidents, property damages, some landlord and tenant disputes, broken verbal or written contracts, bad cheques, unpaid wages, or the collection of personal debts. All claims must be within the permitted Small Claims Court monetary limit, and the party suing must prove his or her case on the **balance of probabilities**. This means the judge finds it more likely than not that the other party is at fault and should compensate the party suing.

Courtroom etiquette   At trial, dress neatly and stand each time you speak to the judge, and address the judge as "Your Honour." Stand when the judge addresses you and also when you question your own or the opposing witnesses. Cell phones must be turned off. No food or beverages are allowed. Following are the basic procedural steps to trial in the Small Claims Court:

Complete a plaintiff's claim, Form 7A, Precedent 7.1   The form is available through legal software and also on the website of the Ministry of the Attorney General through the Small Claims Court link, as are all other Small Claims Court forms. You may view and print a blank form to fill out by hand, or you may complete it online and print it out. You are the plaintiff. Make sure that the name of the defendant (the party you are suing) is correct and that it is spelled correctly. Key or write clearly, in your own words, the amount you claim and the party you claim it from, e.g. the defendant; give reasons why you are entitled to your claim, and include a claim for interest and costs. The court cannot award you interest and costs unless you claim them. Make a minimum of three copies of your claim: original for the court file, one copy to serve on the defendant, one copy for your records. Attach to the original and to each copy of your claim a **copy** of any documents that help prove your case, but keep the originals as you might need to hand them to the judge if you proceed to trial.

File the plaintiff's claim, Form 7A   If your claim is for a fixed amount of money, e.g. NSF cheque or overdue rent, you may pay the fee and file your claim online, and the court clerk will email you a court-stamped copy of your claim. Otherwise, you may file your claim, fixed amount or not, in person or by mail. In person, take the original and two copies of your claim to the Small Claims Court that is nearest to where the defendant lives or carries on business or where the event took place. Pay the court fee. The court clerk will stamp the original and the copies of your claim and assign a court file number to your claim, and that court file number must appear on all copies of your claim and on every subsequent document that relates to your case. The court clerk will keep the stamped **original** claim (with supporting documents) in the court file and return the stamped copies to you. This is what is referred to as **filing** your claim in court. The next step is serving your claim.

Serve the plaintiff's claim, Form 7A   After filing your claim with the court, you must either yourself serve (give) a stamped copy of the claim and supporting documents on the defendant (party being sued) or arrange for a friend or a representative to serve it. This is how the defendant learns that you are suing him or her. Whoever serves the claim must prepare, but not file until the time for filing a defence has passed, an **affidavit of service, Form 8A**, proving that the defendant received a copy of the filed claim. Note that you must serve the claim within six months after the date you filed it in court. Also note that the court will automatically dismiss your case within two years after it was commenced if it has not been disposed of in some way, e.g. by settlement or trial.

Serve and file a defence, Form 9A, Precedent 7.2 The defence form contains the defendant's side of the story, and the court file number on the original and on all copies of the defence form must be the same as that which appears on the plaintiff's claim. Within the prescribed time, **twenty days**, the defendant must serve a copy of the defence form, together with copies of any documents that support the defendant's claim, on the plaintiff in person or by mail, courier, fax, or having someone serve it. The person who served the defence must complete an **affidavit of service, Form 8A**, as proof that the plaintiff was served with the defence (and supporting documents). The defendant must then either mail or take the **original** defence, Form 9A, (and copies of any supporting documents) and the **original** affidavit of service, Form 8A, to the court office where the plaintiff's claim was filed, pay the court fee, and file these documents in that court office. This is how the court learns that the defendant will be defending the case. Note that if the defendant fails to file a defence within the prescribed time, the plaintiff may take steps to have judgment, referred to as "default judgment," signed against the defendant, which usually means that the plaintiff will have won his or her case.

Settlement conference   After the defendant files a defence, the next step is a settlement conference. The court will send a **notice of settlement conference** to all parties, notifying the parties to attend the settlement conference. The settlement conference is an informal meeting with a judge who will not be the same judge as the trial judge so that that judge's decision would not be influenced by the settlement discussions. The purpose of the settlement conference is to reach a settlement. The parties must attend the settlement conference, with or without representatives (but no witnesses). If the parties agree to a final settlement, the judge will usually make an order to this effect and the case is ended without the necessity to go to trial. If settlement fails, the judge will give the clerk a memorandum listing any issues settled and those remaining in dispute, and the clerk will provide the memorandum to the trial judge. One of the parties, usually the plaintiff, must request a trial date and pay the fee for setting the action down for trial, and once that is done, the clerk fixes the date for the trial and sends a **notice of trial** to all parties.

Trial   Bring to the trial the evidence and any witnesses that help prove your claim, and be sure to have a list of questions that you wish to ask your own witnesses and the opposing witnesses. The procedure in civil trials is the same as that described for summary conviction offences trials, i.e. it consists of an **examination-in-chief** by you (the plaintiff); a **cross-examination** of your witnesses by the defendant; a **re-examination**; and a **close**, followed by the defendant's turn to do the same with his or her evidence and witnesses, if any, followed by the respective **closing submissions.** On the **balance of probabilities**, the judge then gives his or her decision called a **judgment**. If you (the plaintiff) win, the judge will order the loser to pay you a certain amount of money (known as **damages**). If you win, the judge may also order the loser to pay you some of your court costs. If you lose, the judge may dismiss your case and may order you to pay to the defendant some of the defendant's court costs, which would be in addition to paying your own court costs.

Collecting on the judgment   Note that winning does not mean the court makes the loser pay the judgment you so justly won. There is no imprisonment for a debt in Ontario, and the court does not force the losing party to pay your judgment. In fact, the judgment is only the first of a number of new steps that you must take in order to collect. You may, for example, garnishee the losing party's wages or file a lien against his or her property to get your money. You must initiate these new steps yourself.

CHAPTER SUMMARY

By virtue of the *Constitution Act*, 1867, authority for the judicial system in Canada is divided between the federal government and the provincial governments. The provincial/territorial level court system is roughly the same across Canada.

The Court of Ontario consists of two divisions--the Superior Court of Justice and the Ontario Court of Justice. The Superior Court of Justice has three branches: Small Claims Court, Family Court, and Divisional Court. The Ontario Court of Justice consists of two branches: criminal and family. The federal government appoints all the judges of the Superior Court of Justice, whereas the provincial government appoints all the judges of the Ontario Court of Justice. This is why the **Superior** Court of Justice ranks higher than the **Ontario** Court of Justice. There are two appellate courts in Ontario: the lower, Divisional Court, and the Court of Appeal for Ontario, which is the highest court of appeal in Ontario. The Supreme Court of Canada is the highest court of appeal in Canada.

In criminal law, the Crown prosecutes individuals who have committed acts that are in violation of the laws set out in the *Criminal Code* of Canada. All criminal cases begin in the Ontario Court of Justice where there are no jury trials. In that court, the judge gives final judgment (1) in all summary offences, which are less serious offences, and (2) in those indictable offences where the judge finds insufficient evidence to warrant a trial in the Superior Court of Justice. Where the evidence warrants a trial in the Superior Court of Justice, the accused has a choice of a trial by a judge or a judge and jury. A jury in criminal trials consists of twelve jurors, all of whom must agree on the verdict of guilt or innocence beyond a reasonable doubt. Provincial offences are summary conviction offences and include non-criminal and quasi-criminal offences. The *Provincial Offences Act* sets out the procedures for the prosecution of provincial offences.

In civil law, one party sues another party who has committed a wrongful act against the first party, causing the first party to suffer a financial loss or injury. Generally, civil cases are tried in the Superior Court of Justice by a judge or a judge and jury. A jury in civil litigation cases consists of six jurors, five of whom must agree on the verdict. To get a basic sense of civil litigation procedures, a good place to start is in the Small Claims Court where the steps are fairly similar to those in the higher courts, but shorter and simpler.

REVIEW QUESTIONS

1. Name the two divisions of the Court of Ontario.
2. Does the Small Claims Court deal with criminal cases or civil, or both?
3. What makes the Superior Court of Justice a higher ranking court than the Ontario Court of Justice?
4. What is the difference between trial courts and appeal courts?
5. What is the distinction between criminal and civil litigation?
6. Why are summary offences tried only in the summer?
7. Do torts give rise to criminal or civil litigation?
8. What two elements prove guilt in criminal cases?
9. What does "balance of probabilities" mean?
10. What is the name of the document that begins a law suit in the Small Claims Court?
11. What is a summary conviction offence?
12. What is an indictable offence?
13. What does *mens rea* mean?
14. The provincial/territorial level court system is roughly the same across Canada. No___Yes___
15. What is the *Criminal Code*?
16. Guilt in criminal offences must be proved beyond a reasonable doubt by which two elements?
17. What is an examination-in-chief in a Small Claims Court trial?
18. Name the case cited in the text that is said to have marked the beginning of negligence law.
19. Name the historic case cited in the text that effectively illustrates criminal law.
20. Name the notable case cited in the text that effectively illustrates civil law.

ONTARIO

Superior Court of Justice

Plaintiff's Claim

Form 7A Ont. Reg. No.: 258/98

Seal

Toronto

Small Claims Court
**444 Yonge Street, 2nd
Floor College Park
Toronto, Ontario M5B 2H4**

Address

416-325-8994

Phone number

Claim No.

Plaintiff No. 1

☐ Additional plaintiff(s) listed on attached Form 1A.   ☐ Under 18 years of age.

Last name, or name of company		
Sean Sanali, trading as Kennedy Apartments		
First name	Second name	Also known as

Address (street number, apt., unit)		
99 Laser Street		
City/Town	Province	Phone no.
Toronto	**Ontario**	**416-499-9998**
Postal code		Fax no.
M1K 3R5		**416-499-9999**
Representative		LSUC #

Address (street number, apt., unit)		
City/Town	Province	Phone no.
Postal code		Fax no.

Defendant No. 1

☐ Additional defendant(s) listed on attached Form 1A.   ☐ Under 18 years of age.

Last name, or name of company		
Winters		
First name	Second name	Also known as
Agnes		

Address (street number, apt., unit)		
145 Victoria Street		
City/Town	Province	Phone no.
Toronto	**Ontario**	**419-493-3333**
Postal code		Fax no.
M4K 3Y5		
Representative		LSUC #

Address (street number, apt., unit)		
City/Town	Province	Phone no.
Postal code		Fax no.

Les formules des tribunaux sont affichées en anglais et en français sur le site www.ontariocourtforms.on.ca. Visitez ce site pour des renseignements sur des formats accessibles.

SCR 7.01-7A (February 12, 2015) CSD

Continued on next page

FORM 7A   PAGE 2   Claim No. _____

REASONS FOR CLAIM AND DETAILS

Explain what happened, including where and when. Then explain how much money you are claiming or what goods you want returned.

If you are relying on any documents, you **MUST** attach copies to the claim. If evidence is lost or unavailable, you **MUST** explain why it is not attached.

What happened?
Where?
When?

The plaintiff's claim is under a guarantee which the defendant signed. The defendant guaranteed the payment of rent for James Smith and Julie Smith who are tenants of Apartment 1407, 20 Kennedy Road, Toronto, Ontario. The tenants breached their contract with the landlord by moving out before the lease had expired. A copy of the defendant's guarantee is attached. Also attached is a copy of a letter from the tenants and the landlord's reply.

The plaintiff cliams from the defendant:
1.   Rent for the month of November in the amount of $2,957.00.
2.   Prejudgment interest.
3.   Postjudgment interest.
4.   Costs of this action.

SCR 7.01-7A (February 12, 2015) CSD   Continued on next page

FORM 7A   PAGE 3   Claim No. _____

How much? $ **$2,957.00**
                                     (Principal amount claimed)

☐ ADDITIONAL PAGES ARE ATTACHED BECAUSE MORE ROOM WAS NEEDED.

The plaintiff also claims pre-judgment interest from   November 1, 20—   under:
                                                              (Date)

(Check only one box)
☒ the *Courts of Justice Act*
☐ an agreement at the rate of _____ % per year
and post-judgment interest, and court costs.

Prepared on: _____   December 1 , 20 --
                                                              (Signature of plaintiff or representative)

Issued on: _____   December 1 , 20 --
                                                              (Signature of clerk)

CAUTION TO DEFENDANT: IF YOU DO NOT FILE A DEFENCE (Form 9A) and an Affidavit of Service (Form 8A) with the court within twenty (20) calendar days after you have been served with this Plaintiff's Claim, judgment may be obtained without notice and enforced against you. Forms and self-help materials are available at the Small Claims Court and on the following website: www.ontariocourtforms.on.ca.

CAUTION TO PARTIES: Unless the court orders or the rules provide otherwise, **THIS ACTION WILL BE AUTOMATICALLY DISMISSED** if it has not been disposed of by order or otherwise two (2) years after it was commenced and a trial date or assessment under subrule 11.03(2) has not been requested.

For information on accessibility of court services for people with disability-related needs, contact:
Telephone: 416-326-2220 / 1-800-518-7901   TTY: 416-326-4012 / 1-877-425-0575

SCR 7.01-7A (February 12, 2015) CSD

FORM 9A   PAGE 2   SC.-**-29350-83

Claim No.

THIS DEFENCE IS BEING FILED ON BEHALF OF: (Name(s) of defendant(s))

Agnes Winters

and I/we: (Check as many as apply)

☒ Dispute the claim made against me/us.

☐ Admit the full claim and propose the following terms of payment:

$ _____ per _____ commencing _____ , 20 ____ .
  (Amount)   (Week/month)

and propose the following terms of payment:

☐ Admit part of the claim in the amount of $ _____

$ _____ per _____ commencing _____ , 20 ____ .
  (Amount)   (Week/month)

REASONS FOR DISPUTING THE CLAIM AND DETAILS:

Explain what happened, including where and when. Explain why you do not agree with the claim made against you.

If you are relying on any documents, you **MUST** attach copies to the Defence. If evidence is lost or unavailable, you **MUST** explain why it is not attached.

What happened?   1.   **The defendant denies that any rent is due or owing on Apartment 1407, 20**
Where?   **Kennedy Road, Toronto, Ontario, for the month of November 20— because the**
When?   **plaintiff has applied the tenants' security deposit to that month's rent.**

         2.   **If the plaintiff cliams damages as a result of breach of contract, then the plaintiff**
              has failed in his obligation to mitigate his damages. The defendant, therefore,
              submits that this action be dismissed with costs.

Continued on next page

SCR 9.01-10 03-9A (January 23, 2014) CSD

ONTARIO

Superior Court of Justice   **Defence**

Form 9A Ont. Reg. No.: 258/98

Toronto   SC.-**-29350-83
Small Claims Court   Claim No.
444 Yonge Street, 2ⁿᵈ Floor
College Park
Toronto, Ontario M5B 2H4
Address

416-325-8994
Phone number

Plaintiff No. 1   ☐ Additional plaintiff(s) listed on attached Form 1A.   ☐ Under 18 years of age.

Last name, or name of company		
Sean Sanali, trading as Kennedy Apartments		
First name	Second name	Also known as
Address (street number, apt., unit)		
99 Laser Street		
City/Town	Province	Phone no.
Toronto	**Ontario**	**416-499-9998**
Postal code		Fax no.
M1K 3R5		**416-499-9999**
Representative		LSUC #

Defendant No. 1   ☐ Additional defendant(s) listed on attached Form 1A.   ☐ Under 18 years of age.

Last name, or name of company		
Winters		
First name	Second name	Also known as
Agnes		
Address (street number, apt., unit)		
145 Victoria Street		
City/Town	Province	Phone no.
Toronto	**Ontario**	**416-493-3333**
Postal code		Fax no.
M4K 3Y5		
Representative		LSUC #

Les formules des tribunaux sont affichées en anglais et en français sur le site www.ontariocourtforms.on.ca. Visitez ce site pour des renseignements sur formats accessibles.

SCR 9.01-10 03-9A (January 23, 2014) CSD

     Legal Office Procedures

ICON Location Code
Code d'emplacement du RIII

Form 7, *Provincial Offences Act*, Ontario Court of Justice
Formulaire 7, Loi sur les infractions provinciales, Cour de justice de l'Ontario

Summons
Assignation

(print name / nom en lettres moulées)

believes and certifies that on the day of | Y / A | 2 | 0 | M / M | D / J | Time / heure | M
croit et atteste que le

Name (given / prénom) (initials / initiales)
Nom (family / nom de famille)

Address (number and street / numéro et nom de la rue)
Adresse

(municipality / municipalité) (P.O. / C.P.) (province) (postal code / code postal)

Driver's licence no. / N° de permis de conduire | Juris / Aut. Lég.

Birth date / Date de naissance | Sex / | Motor vehicle involved / | Commercial | Collision involved / | Witnesses /
Y / A | M / M | D / J | Sexe | Véhicule impliqué | Utilitaire | Collision | Témoins
| | | | □ N / N | □ Y / O | □ Y / O | □ Y / O

At (municipality / municipalité)
À

Did commit the offence of
A commis l'infraction de

contrary to sect.
contrairement à l'art.

| | Juris | Commercial | CVOR | NSC | Code
| | Aut. Lég. | Utilitaire | IUVU | CNS
Plate no. | | □ Y / O | □ Y / O | □ Y / O
N° de la plaque d'immatriculation

CVOR No. - NSC No. / N° de l'IUVU - N° du CNS

This is therefore to command you in Her
Majesty's name to appear before the Ontario
Court of Justice. / Pour ces motifs, il vous est
enjoint, au nom de Sa Majesté, de comparaître
devant la Cour de justice de l'Ontario.

Officer No. | Platoon | Unit
N° de l'agent | Peloton | Unité

| Y / A | 2 | 0 | M / M | D / J | Time / heure | M
Ct. room / Salle d'audience | at the Ontario Court of Justice POA Office at / à la Cour
de justice de l'Ontario, Bureau des infractions provinciales au

And to attend thereafter as required by the court in order to be dealt with according to
law, this summons is served under Part I of the *Provincial Offences Act*.
Et d'être présent(e) par la suite selon les exigences du tribunal, afin d'être traité(e) selon
la loi. La présente assignation vous est signifiée conformément à la Partie I de la Loi sur
les infractions provinciales.

Signature of Provincial Offences Officer / Signature de l'agent des infractions provinciales

POA 0861 (March 17, 2011 / 17 mars 2011) CSD

FORM 9A   **PAGE 3**   SC-**-29350-83
Claim No.

**Why I/we disagree
with all or part of
the claim:**

☐ **ADDITIONAL PAGES ARE ATTACHED BECAUSE MORE ROOM WAS NEEDED.**

Prepared on: **December 11** , 20 --

(Signature of defendant or representative)

NOTE: Within seven (7) calendar days of changing your address for service, notify the court and all
other parties in writing.

**CAUTION TO
PLAINTIFF(S):** If this Defence contains a proposal of terms of payment, you are deemed to have accepted the
terms **unless** you file with the clerk and serve on the defendant(s) a Request to Clerk (Form 9B)
for a terms of payment hearing **WITHIN TWENTY (20) CALENDAR DAYS** of service of this
Defence [R. 9.03(3)].

SCR 9.01-10.03-9A (January 23, 2014) CSD

Important – If you do not exercise one of the following options within 15 days of receiving this notice, you will be deemed not to dispute the charge and a justice may enter a conviction against you. Upon conviction, additional costs will be added to the total payable. If the fine goes into default, an administrative fee will be added and steps will be taken to enforce your defaulted fine. For example, information may be provided to a consumer reporting agency and for certain offences, including speeding, your driver's licence may be suspended.

OPTION 1 – Plea of Guilty – Voluntary Payment of Total Payable: I plead guilty and payment of the total payable is enclosed (follow the instructions on the "payment notice").

OPTION 2 – Early Resolution – Meet with Prosecutor (by choosing this option you **do not** forego the right to a trial):

☐ **I request a meeting with a prosecutor to discuss the possible resolution of the charge.** I understand that if I fail to attend the scheduled meeting, I will be deemed not to dispute the charge and may be convicted in my absence.

I request a _____ language interpreter.
          (Leave blank if inapplicable)

☐ I live more than *[Court to insert distance of not more than 75 km]* from the courthouse listed below and I would like to meet the prosecutor by *[Court to insert electronic method(s) available locally]*.

You must send this notice to the Ontario Court of Justice, Provincial Offences Office address below. You will be sent a meeting notice to the address on the file. Notify the court if your address changes.

OPTION 3 – Trial Option – DO NOT MAIL – I intend to appear in court to plead not guilty and have an English language trial. You or your representative MUST attend in person at the court office shown below within the times and days shown to file a notice of intention to appear in court. Bring this notice with you.

Important – Si vous n'exercez pas une des options suivantes dans un délai de 15 jours à compter de la réception du présent avis, vous serez réputé(e) ne pas contester l'accusation et un juge pourra inscrire une déclaration de culpabilité contre vous. Sur déclaration de culpabilité, des frais additionnels s'ajouteront au montant total exigible. En cas de défaut de paiement de l'amende, des frais administratifs s'ajouteront et des mesures seront prises pour faire exécuter le paiement de votre amende. Par exemple, l'information peut être transmise à une agence de renseignements sur le consommateur, et dans le cas de certaines infractions, dont l'excès de vitesse, votre permis de conduire peut être suspendu.

OPTION 1 – Plaidoyer de culpabilité – Paiement volontaire du montant total exigible : Je plaide coupable et le montant total exigible est joint à la présente (suivre les instructions figurant au « l'avis de paiement »).

OPTION 2 – Résolution rapide – Rencontre avec le poursuivant (si vous choisissez l'option suivante, **vous ne renoncez pas** au droit d'obtenir un procès) :

☐ **Je désire une rencontre avec le poursuivant pour discuter du règlement relatif à l'infraction.** Je comprends que si je n'assiste pas à la rencontre, je serai réputé(e) ne pas contester l'accusation et un juge pourra inscrire une déclaration de culpabilité contre moi en mon absence.

Je demande l'aide d'un interprète de langue _____
                                          (À remplir s'il y a lieu)

☐ J'habite à plus de [ajouter la distance désirée jusqu'à concurrence de 75 km] du palais de justice mentionné ci-dessous et j'aimerais que la rencontre avec le poursuivant ait lieu par [ajouter la méthode électronique offerte].

Vous devez envoyer cet avis au Bureau des infractions provinciales de la Cour de justice de l'Ontario à l'adresse indiquée ci-dessous. Vous recevrez un avis de rencontre à l'adresse figurant au dossier. Vous devez aviser le tribunal si vous changez d'adresse.

OPTION 3 – Procès – NE PAS ENVOYER PAR LA POSTE – Je désire comparaître devant un juge pour inscrire un plaidoyer de non-culpabilité et subir un procès en français. Vous ou votre représentant DEVEZ vous présenter au greffe du tribunal aux dates et aux heures indiquées pour déposer un avis d'intention de comparaître devant le tribunal. Apportez le présent avis au greffe du tribunal.

Ontario Court of Justice / Cour de justice de l'Ontario
Provincial Offences Office / Bureau des infractions provinciales
[Court to insert Address, Hours of Operation] / [ajouter l'adresse et les heures d'ouverture]

FOR INFORMATION ON ACCESS TO ONTARIO COURTS FOR PERSONS WITH DISABILITIES: [Court to insert information]
POUR PLUS DE RENSEIGNEMENTS SUR L'ACCÈS DES PERSONNES HANDICAPÉES AUX TRIBUNAUX DE L'ONTARIO : [ajouter l'information]

ICON Location Code
Code d'emplacement du RII

Offence number
Numéro d'infraction

Form 4, Provincial Offences Act, Ontario Court of Justice, O. Reg. 108/11
Formulaire 4, Loi sur les infractions provinciales, Cour de justice de l'Ontario, Règl. de l'Ont. 108/11

Offence Notice
Avis d'infraction

(print name / nom en lettres moulées)

believes and certifies that on the day of
croit et atteste que le

Y / A M / M D / J Time / heure M
2 0

Name
Nom
(family / nom de famille) (initials / initiales)

(given / prénom)

Address
Adresse
(number and street / numéro et nom de la rue)

(municipality / municipalité) (P.O. / C.P.) (postal code / code postal) (province)

Driver's licence no. / Nᵒ de permis de conduire Juris / Aut. Lég.

Birth date / Date de naissance Sex Motor vehicle involved Collision involved Witnesses
Y / A M / M D / J Sexe Véhicule impliqué Collision Témoins
☐ N / N ☐ Y / O ☐ Y / O

At
À
(municipality / municipalité)

Did commit the offence of
A commis l'infraction de

contrary to
contrairement à
sect.
l'art.

Plate no. Juris Commercial CVOR NSC Code
Nᵒ de la plaque d'immatriculation Aut. Lég. Utilitaire IUVU CNS
☐ Y / O ☐ Y / O ☐ Y / O

CVOR No. – NSC No. / Nᵒ de l'IUVU - Nᵒ du CNS

And I further certify that I served an offence notice personally upon the person charged on the offence date.
J'atteste également qu'à la date de l'infraction, j'ai signifié, en mains propres, un avis d'infraction à la personne accusée.

☐ Or other service date of:
Autre date de signification, le :

Signature of issuing Provincial Offences Officer
Signature de l'agent des infractions provinciales

Officer No. Platoon Unit
Nᵒ de l'agent Peloton Unité

Set fine of Total payable
Amende fixée de Montant total exigible
$ $ $ $

Total payable includes set fine, applicable victim fine surcharge and costs. / Le montant total exigible comprend l'amende fixée, la suramende compensatoire pour l'aide aux victimes applicable et les frais.

Important:
You have 15 days from the day you receive this notice to choose one of the options on the back of the notice.

Important :
À compter de la réception du présent avis, vous avez 15 jours pour choisir une des options décrites au verso de l'avis.

Legal Office Procedures

CHAPTER 8

PREPARING AND SERVING COURT DOCUMENTS

Court documents play by the rules. This chapter provides detailed guidance on preparing court documents and effecting service under the rules.

PREPARING COURT DOCUMENTS

Court documents must always wear the name of the court. The *Rules of Civil Procedure* prescribe the forms to be used and identify each form by the rule number which prescribes it: for example, Rule 4 requires that an affidavit be in Form 4D. Under Rule 4, the basic format of court documents consists of three parts and a backsheet:

HEADING	Includes the title of proceeding (name of plaintiff and defendant)
BODY	Includes the title of the document (statement of claim)
ENDING	In Precedent 8.1, begins at the date, which is the date of preparing the document In Precedent 8.2, begins at the jurat (Sworn before me...)
BACKSHEET	Required for nearly all court documents, Precedents 8.1 and 8.2

Figure 8.1 Heading

Heading

Court File No. CV-**-2345

ONTARIO
SUPERIOR COURT OF JUSTICE

BETWEEN:

GEORGE J. SMITH and THOMAS JONES
↓2

Plaintiffs
↓2

Title of Proceeding →   and
↓2

JANE AUSTEN
↓2

Defendant
↓2

Heading   Figure 8.1 is an example of a heading of a court document. For a full view of this document, see Precedent 8.1 at the back of this chapter.

The heading of all court documents includes the court file number, the name of the court, the word BETWEEN, and the **title of proceeding**, which consists of the name of the plaintiff (the party suing) and the name of the defendant (the party being sued). Once the plaintiff and the defendant have been named in the title of proceeding, they are usually referred to as the parties.

Key the names of the parties in block capital letters. If individuals, key at least one given name and the surname of each individual. A middle name, if any, may be expressed in full or by an initial, e.g. GEORGE J. SMITH. The heading in Figure 8.1 indicates that the action has been brought in the Superior Court of Justice under Court File No. CV-**-2345 (CV = civil action; ** = last two digits of the year in which the action was commenced), that George J. Smith and Thomas Jones are the plaintiffs, and that they are suing Jane Austen, the defendant.

Figure 8.2 Body

Body
(double space)
↓

STATEMENT OF DEFENCE

1. The Defendant admits the allegations contained in paragraph 1 of the

Statement of Claim.

2. The Defendant denies the allegations contained in paragraphs 2 and 4

of the Statement of Claim.

3. The Defendant has no knowledge of the allegations contained in

paragraphs 3, 5, 6, and 7 of the Statement of Claim...

Body   The body of a court document gives the details of the law suit and includes the title of the document, e.g. STATEMENT OF DEFENCE. The body of a court document is usually double spaced, with or without additional line spacing between paragraphs. Figure 8.2 is an excerpt of a body of a court document.

Legal Office Procedures

Figure 8.3 Ending

Ending
↓

Date: November 11, 20--

Michael, Eliad & Redford LLP
Barristers and Solicitors
863 Seneca Lane
Toronto, Ontario   M4J 1P6

Robert B. Redford
Tel: (416) 363-1079
Fax: (416) 363-2628

Lawyers for the Defendant

TO: Castles & Sands
        Suite 900
        205 Portage Street
        Markham, ON   L3R 3G3

        Barry F. Sands
        Tel: (905) 495-2222
        Fax: (905) 495-2223

        Lawyers for the Plaintiffs

Ending   The ending of a court document may vary, depending on the type of court document. The ending in Figure 8.3 applies to nearly all court documents that are not affidavits.

The ending of most court documents begins with the date of preparation of the document. The first law firm shown is almost always the firm who prepared the document on behalf of the party for whom the firm acts. Being able to "read" endings of court documents will prove of value to you in your legal work. For example, we can "read" from the ending in Figure 8.3 that Michael, Eliad & Redford is the firm acting for the defendant and that Robert B. Redford is the lawyer who is handling the defendant's case. The "TO" refers to the party who is to be served, e.g. Castles & Sands who are acting for the plaintiffs. Mr. Barry F. Sands is the lawyer handling the plaintiffs' case. If we look at the heading of this document in Figure 8.1, we can further see that the plaintiffs are George J. Smith and Thomas Jones and that our client, the defendant, is Jane Austen.

Figure 8.4 Ending of Affidavits

(Jurat)

SWORN BEFORE ME at the   )

City of Toronto, in the Province of   )

Ontario,   )
                                                  _____
                                                  Frederick Flintstone
on May   , 20--.   )

)

Commissioner for Taking Affidavits

Ending of affidavits Figure 8.4 is an example of an ending which applies to nearly all affidavits. For a full view of an affidavit, see Precedent 8.2 at the back of this chapter.

The affidavit ending is known as a **jurat**. Every affidavit has a jurat. A person making an affidavit is called a **deponent**. The deponent must swear before a commissioner to the truth of an affidavit. A commissioner is a person authorized by law to take such affidavits. By "reading" this ending, we can get the following information:

1. Mr. Frederick Flintstone is our client and is the deponent of the affidavit. Mr. Flintstone will be signing the affidavit "at the City of Toronto, in the Province of Ontario," which is a general reference to the location of our law firm where Mr. Flintstone will attend to sign the affidavit on the line drawn for his signature.

2. A commissioner, usually the lawyer in the capacity of a commissioner, will sign in the space above "Commissioner for Taking Affidavits" and will also fill in the day of the month of May in the space provided, which would be the day on which Mr. Flintstone signs the affidavit.

Backsheet The *Rules of Civil Procedure* require that nearly all court documents have a backsheet. The backsheet, Precedents 8.1 and 8.2, is a back coversheet that identifies the document when it is faced down. That is why the backsheet repeats much of the information that is on the first page of the document to which it relates. Prepare a backsheet, usually on a separate plain sheet of paper in landscape position. Legal software automatically prints out a backsheet for each court document you prepare.

The title of proceeding on backsheets may be a short title, showing the name of the first of several parties, followed by the phrase **and others**, e.g. GEORGE J. SMITH, and others v. JANE AUSTEN, and others, if any. Some lawyers might still use the Latin *et al* for "and others." The *Rules of Civil Procedure* (see subrule 4.02(1)(b)) and most other law-related writings, however, discourage the use of Latin terms in the interest of lay readers. The backsheet also indicates the place where the proceeding was commenced, the title of the document, along with the name and address of your law firm, the name of the lawyer handling the action and the lawyer's Law Society of Upper Canada (LSUC) registration number, the firm's telephone and fax numbers, and the party for whom the firm is acting.

Place the backsheet, facing out, behind the document to which it belongs, and staple the document on the top left corner so that, when you turn the document over, the staple is on the top right corner of the document and the keyed side of the backsheet facing up.

COURT FORMS

The forms which the *Rules of Civil Procedure* prescribe are available in PDF and Word files on the website of the Ministry of the Attorney General, under "Forms under *Rules of Civil Procedure*." Many law firms use computerized forms through commercially available legal software such as the Automated Civil Litigation (ACL) software by Korbitec Inc. which is the software used in this manual.

Note that some law firms have their legal software set up so as to have it automatically print the firm name in bolded solid capital letters. Other law firms prefer the standard lower case style. Also, some law firms have their legal software set up so as to have it automatically print the name of the plaintiff or defendant following "lawyers for the plaintiff/defendant" even where there is only one plaintiff or defendant. Having the name of an only plaintiff or defendant printed on this line, however, is not considered to be good practice because it implies that there is more than one plaintiff or defendant and that the law firm is acting for only one of the plaintiffs or defendants. Expect, therefore, variations in practice, and use the style which your law firm prefers.

ISSUING DOCUMENTS

All documents that start a proceeding are known as an **originating process** and must be **issued** to be official. To issue an originating process, e.g. a statement of claim, submit the original and one copy to the court office, and pay the required court fee. The local registrar assigns a court file number and affixes the court seal and dates and signs the original. The originating process is now issued. The local registrar returns the issued original to you and keeps the copy for the court file. The court file number identifies the proceeding and must, therefore, appear on all subsequent court documents that relate to the same proceeding. Keep the issued original in the client's file. Serve a copy, usually a photocopy of the issued original, on the defendant.

SERVING DOCUMENTS

Serving means **giving** a court document to a person named in the title of proceeding. Serving court documents is how one party learns what the other party is doing in the proceeding: for example, the defendant discovers he or she is being sued when the plaintiff serves the defendant with a statement of claim. The plaintiff, on the other hand, learns that the defendant will defend the action when the defendant serves the plaintiff with a statement of defence.

FILING DOCUMENTS

Filing means submitting a copy of a document to the court for the court's records. Usually, a party who has served a document must file a copy of that document with proof of service in the court office where the proceeding was started. Filing is usually done either by mail or by attending in person at the court office and leaving a copy with court staff. If filed by mail and the court office has no record of the receipt of the document, the document is deemed not to have been filed.

DELIVERY OF DOCUMENTS

Under the *Rules of Civil Procedure* the terms "deliver" and "delivery" mean the serving **and** filing with proof of service of a court document: for example, a statement of defence is deemed to have been delivered when the lawyer for the defendant has served the statement of defence on the lawyer for the plaintiff and has filed a copy of it, together with proof of service, in the court office.

LAWYER OF RECORD

Generally, a lawyer of record is a lawyer who has been named in a court document as being the lawyer who is representing the plaintiff or the defendant in a court proceeding. A lawyer of record (formerly, solicitor of record) is also referred to as a "lawyer with carriage."

CALCULATING TIME FOR SERVICE

Rule 3 of the *Rules of Civil Procedure* provides the following:

1. Where a period of seven days or less is prescribed, holidays are not to be counted. Holidays include Saturdays, Sundays, and statutory holidays.

2. Where there is a reference to a number of days between two events, the days are counted by excluding the day on which the first event happens and including the day on which the second event happens.

3. Where service of a document, other than an originating process, is made after 4 p.m. on a business day, or at any time on a holiday, service is deemed to have been made on the next day that is not a holiday.

Seven days or less   Say an event were to happen on Tuesday the 23rd, and seven days were required between service and the event; service would happen on Friday, the 12th. If, however, you were to serve the document after 4 p.m. on Friday the 12th, you would have lost the seven-day time requirement because service after 4 p.m. is deemed to have been made on the next day that is not a holiday, e.g. Monday the 15th, which, in effect, would end up to be a day short of the seven-day requirement. Here is a calendar example:

Figure 8.5

Sunday	Monday	Tuesday	Wednesday	Thursday	Friday	Saturday
7	8	9	10	11	12 day of service (excluded day)	13 holiday (not included)
14 holiday (not included)	15	16	17	18	19	20 holiday (not included)
21 holiday (not included)	22	23 day of event (included day)	24	25	26	27

Seven days or more   If there is a reference to time of more than seven days, then weekends and holidays are included. If an event were to happen, say, on March 21, and twenty days were required between the service and the event, then the service would happen on March 1. The twenty-day count is as follows: March 1 is excluded and March 21 is included = 20 days.

PROOF OF SERVICE

To protect the rights of all parties, the court requires written proof that a document has been properly served on the other party, or on the party's lawyer, before accepting such a document for filing in court.

Matching the proof   The kind of service you effect usually determines the kind of proof of service you require, e.g. if you effect service by mail, the proof of service is your affidavit of service by mail. Rule 16 of the *Rules of Civil Procedure* provides that proof of service may also be printed, stamped, or "stuck" on the backsheet of a copy of the document served. See the precedents at the back of this chapter for samples of service stamps that are commonly used in practice.

METHODS OF SERVICE

Rule 16 of the *Rules of Civil Procedure* states that the originating process may be served either by **personal service** or by an **alternative to personal service**.

PERSONAL SERVICE

Personal service usually means attending in person and handing the document to the party who is to be served personally. This ensures that the party sued receives it and becomes aware of the law suit. Personal service is required only for an originating process, e.g. a statement of claim. A process server (a private business for serving documents), the sheriff, or a member of your firm may effect personal service. Generally, firms use a process server for serving an originating process. Personal service is accomplished as follows:

In person   The process server, or other server, attends at the party's residence or place of business, as the case may be, and personally hands a copy of the issued originating process to the party to be served. The process server, or other server, need not produce the original document or have it in his or her possession at the time of service.

Proof of service: The affidavit of service of the person effecting personal service, Precedent 8.3, or where service was effected by a sheriff, the sheriff's certificate of service.

Effective date of service: The day on which the document was served.

Figure 8.6

PERSONAL SERVICE OF ORIGINATING PROCESS ON VARIOUS PARTIES	
Individual	Serve the individual.
Corporation	Serve an officer, director, agent, or manager of the corporation.
Partnership	Serve any one of the partners or a manager of the partnership.
Sole Proprietorship	Serve the sole proprietor (owner) or a manager.
Minor (under the age of 18)	Serve the litigation guardian, if any. • If no litigation guardian, serve the minor with one copy, and leave another copy with his or her parent or guardian who resides with the minor. • If the proceeding is about a minor's interest in an estate or trust, serve the minor by leaving a copy of the document with the Children's Lawyer.
Mentally Incapable Person	Serve the guardian or attorney (i.e. person holding a power of attorney). • If no guardian or attorney, serve one copy on the Public Guardian and Trustee and another copy on the mentally incapable person.

ALTERNATIVES TO PERSONAL SERVICE

An alternative to personal service applies only to an originating process and means the originating process could not be served by personal service, e.g. the party might be evading service. The originating process must, therefore, be served by an alternative to personal service, as follows:

1. **Leaving a copy with an adult person in the same household**   This method requires at least one unsuccessful attempt at personal service. If, on the second or subsequent attempts,

the party is not at home, the server may leave a copy of the document, in a sealed envelope addressed to the party, with an adult who lives in the same household. On the same day, or the next day, the server must mail another copy of the document to the party at the same address.

Proof of service: Server's affidavit of service by leaving a copy with an adult, Precedent 8.3 (at notes).

Effective date of service: Five days after mailing the copy of the document.

2. Mailing an acknowledgment of receipt card   This method requires no attempt at personal service. You may simply mail, by regular lettermail or registered mail, a copy of the document, together with an **acknowledgment of receipt card** (similar to a postcard), to the party at his or her address. Use this method where the party is expected to accept service because it is only effective as of the date the sender receives back the acknowledgment of receipt card.

Proof of service: Your affidavit of service by mail, Precedent 8.3 (at notes).

Effective date of service: The date you received back the acknowledgment of receipt card.

3. Obtaining acceptance of service   This method applies where a party has hired a lawyer, but the lawyer might not yet be on record as being the party's lawyer. This method is effected by leaving a copy with the lawyer and obtaining an endorsement of acceptance of service from the lawyer personally. Basically, the lawyer's acceptance of service confirms that the lawyer has become the lawyer of record for that party.

Proof of service: The lawyer's acceptance of service endorsement. The endorsement may be keyed or stamped, Precedent 8.8.

Effective date of service: The date of the acceptance of service.

Here is a summary of the methods of personal service and alternatives to personal service:

Figure 8.7

PERSONAL SERVICE Applies Only to Originating Process				
Who Serves It	**How Service Effected**	**Proof of Service**	**Effective Date of Service**	**Precedent**
process server law firm sheriff	in person	affidavit of service	day of service	Precedent 8.3
ALTERNATIVES TO PERSONAL SERVICE Apply Only to Originating Process				
process server law firm sheriff	leaving a copy with an adult in same household, plus mailing a copy on same or next day	affidavit of service	5 days after mailing	Precedent 8.3 (at notes)
lawyer for plaintiff	mailing acknowledgment of receipt card	affidavit of service (with acknowledgment of receipt card attached)	date of receipt of acknowledgment of receipt card	Precedent 8.3 (at notes)
lawyer for plaintiff	obtaining acceptance of service	acceptance of service endorsement	date of acceptance	Precedent 8.8

Legal Office Procedures

ORDINARY SERVICE ON A LAWYER OF RECORD

A lawyer of record is usually served by ordinary service. Ordinary service usually applies to all documents that come after the originating process. When you serve documents on a lawyer of record, it means that the party being served has retained a lawyer. Service on a lawyer of record may be effected by any one of the following methods of ordinary service:

1. ADMISSION OF SERVICE

(a) Deliver by hand two copies of the document to the office of the opposite lawyer, after having stamped or keyed on the backsheet of one copy an admission of service endorsement (Figure 8.8). Leave the plain copy with the opposite lawyer, and request that the opposite lawyer, or another authorized person in that lawyer's office, admit service by completing the admission of service endorsement. Instead of hand delivering, you may mail the two copies to the opposite lawyers, instructing them to keep one copy and admit service on the other copy and return that copy to you. This is not a favoured method among the profession because the opposite lawyers may delay admitting service for tactical reasons.

Proof of service: The completed admission of service endorsement, Figure 8.8 and Precedent 8.7.
Effective date of service: The date of admission of service.

Figure 8.8 Backsheet with Completed Admission of Service Endorsement, Keyed or Stamped

GEORGE J. SMITH and THOMAS JONES v. JANE AUSTEN		
Plaintiffs	Defendant	Court File No. CV-**- 2345
		ONTARIO SUPERIOR COURT OF JUSTICE
		Proceeding commenced at Toronto
		STATEMENT OF DEFENCE
Service of a copy of this document admitted on.. *November 11, ...(year).....* *Castles & Sands*............................ Lawyer(s) for *the Plaintiffs*		Michael, Eliad & Redford LLP Barristers and Solicitors 863 Seneca Lane Toronto, Ontario M4J 1P6 Robert B. Redford (48000R) Tel: (416) 363-1079 Fax: (416) 363-2628 rbrdfrd@mer.com Lawyers for the Defendant

(b) Sometimes the opposite lawyers might refuse to admit service, usually because no one authorized to admit service is available to do so. If so, leave a copy of the document with an employee, e.g. the receptionist. Get that employee's name, and make a note of the date and time you left the copy with the employee.

Proof of service: Your affidavit of service, Precedent 8.4 (at notes).
Effective date of service: The date you left the copy with the employee.

2. SERVICE BY MAIL

Mail a copy of the document by regular lettermail or registered mail to the opposite lawyers.

Proof of service: Your affidavit of service by mail on a lawyer, Precedent 8.4. See also Precedent 8.5.

Effective date of service: Five days after mailing.

3. SERVICE BY FACSIMILE

Fax the document, but prepare a cover page indicating: your firm's name, address, and telephone number; the name of the lawyer to be served; the date and time of transmission; the total number of pages transmitted, including the cover page; your firm's fax number, and the name and telephone number of a person in your firm to contact in the event of transmission problems. Where service is made by faxing between 4 p.m. and midnight, it is deemed to have been made on the following day. Under subrule 16.05(3.2), a motion record, application record, trial record, appeal book and compendium, or book of authorities may **not** be served by fax **at any time**, unless the party to be served gives prior consent.

Proof of service: Your affidavit of service by fax, Precedent 8.4 (at notes). See also Precedent 8.6.

Effective date of service: The date of faxing.

4. SERVICE BY COURIER

Send a copy to the lawyer's office by courier.

Proof of service: Your affidavit of service by courier, Precedent 8.4 (at notes).

Effective date of service: The second day following the day on which you gave the courier the document; if that second day is a holiday, on the next business day after that day.

5. SERVICE BY E-MAIL

Service by e-mail may be made either on consent of the parties or by court order. The affidavit of service must indicate whether service was on consent or by court order. Where e-mail service is made between 4 p.m. and midnight, it is deemed to have been made on the following day. Attach a copy of the document to your e-mail, and e-mail it to the opposing lawyer. Be sure your e-mail includes your firm's name, address, telephone number, fax number, e-mail address, date and time of transmission, and the name and telephone number of a person to contact in the event of transmission problems.

Proof of service: Affidavit of service (by e-mail), Precedent 8.4 (at notes).

Effective date of service: The date of e-mailing.

6. SERVICE BY DOCUMENT EXCHANGE

If the firm being served is a subscriber to a document exchange (a central service set up for the purpose of exchanging documents among lawyers), take two copies of the document to the document exchange. The document exchange date-stamps both copies in front of you. Deposit one date-stamped copy in the document exchange service for the lawyer being served to pick up; keep the other date-stamped copy for your records.

Proof of service: Date stamped on document; see also Precedent 8.4 (at notes).
Effective date of service: The day after the date stamped by the document exchange, and if that day is a holiday, on the next day that is not a holiday.

7. SERVICE BY ELECTRONIC DOCUMENT EXCHANGE

An electronic document exchange is a web-based service. To use it, lawyers must be subscribers or members of the service. The service automatically generates a **record of service** as required by subrule 16.09(4.1) which may be printed out and filed in court as proof of service, requiring no affidavit of service. Where service is made between 4 p.m. and midnight, it is deemed to have been made on the following day.

Proof of service: A record of service, Precedent 8.9.
Effective date of service: The date of service.

Here is a summary of ordinary service on a lawyer of record:

Figure 8.9

ORDINARY SERVICE ON A LAWYER OF RECORD Applies to All Documents After the Originating Process			
Method of Service	**Proof of Service**	**Effective Date of Service**	**Precedent No.**
admission of service	admission of service endorsement, stamped or keyed	date of admission of service	Precedent 8.7
service refused	affidavit of service	date of leaving copy with employee	Precedent 8.4 (at notes)
mail	affidavit of service by mail	5 days after mailing	Precedent 8.4 Precedent 8.5
facsimile	affidavit of service by fax	date of faxing (if after 4 p.m., next day)	Precedent 8.4 (at notes) Precedent 8.6
courier	affidavit of service by courier	second business day following day document given to courier	Precedent 8.4 (at notes)
e-mail	affidavit of service by e-mail	date of e-mailing (if after 4 p.m., next day)	Precedent 8.4 (at notes) Precedent 8.8
document exchange	document exchange date stamp	day following date stamped (if a holiday, on next day that is not a holiday)	Precedent 8.4 (at notes)
electronic document exchange	record of service	date of service	Precedent 8.9

SUBSTITUTED SERVICE AND DISPENSING WITH SERVICE

If the lawyer is unable to serve the originating process, or any other document, by personal service or by an alternative to personal service, the lawyer may obtain a court order to allow service of the document by a different method, e.g. by registered mail or by publishing a notice of the law suit in a newspaper where the party is believed to be residing. This is known as substituted service.

Proof of service varies, depending on the kind of substituted service made, e.g. if by notice in a newspaper, the newspaper's affidavit of publishing the notice, together with a copy of the newspaper clipping. In an order for substituted service, the court usually specifies the effective date of service. In the alternative, where the court deems it necessary in the interest of justice, the court may make an order dispensing with service. In that case, the document is deemed to have been served on the date of the order.

CHAPTER SUMMARY

The *Rules of Civil Procedure* prescribe all court forms. Every court document must have a title of proceeding and usually also a backsheet.

A court document that starts a law suit is known as an **originating process**. The court must issue all originating process documents. Almost all court documents must be served. Serving a court document means giving a copy of the document to the parties involved in the law suit. There are two methods of serving an originating process: by personal service, which basically means serving the party personally at his or her home, or by an alternative to personal service, which involves leaving a copy of the document, in a sealed envelope addressed to the party, with an adult who lives in the same household, and on the same day, mailing another copy of the document to the party at the place of residence.

Documents other than an originating process may be served on the lawyer of record by ordinary service which includes service by admission of service, mail, fax, courier, e-mail, electronic document exchange, or document exchange. Regardless of the method of service used, a party must file the document in court, with proof of service, for the court's records.

REVIEW QUESTIONS

1. What is an originating process?
2. What information is included in a title of proceeding?
3. Which document requires service either by personal or an alternative to personal service?
4. Explain the process involved in issuing an originating process.
5. Where on a court document would you usually place an admission of service endorsement?
6. When is service effective if done by an admission of service?
7. What is a lawyer of record?
8. What does the term "delivered" mean when it refers to a court document?
9. What is a backsheet?
10. A jurat is the place where a jury sits in a courtroom. Explain.

Heading ↓6 lines

Court File No. CV-**-2345
↓2

ONTARIO
SUPERIOR COURT OF JUSTICE
↓2

BETWEEN:
↓2

GEORGE J. SMITH and THOMAS JONES
↓2

Plaintiffs

Title of Proceeding →   and   ↓2
↓2

JANE AUSTEN
↓2

Defendant
↓2

Body
(double space)
↓

STATEMENT OF DEFENCE

1. The Defendant admits the allegations contained in paragraph 1 of the Statement of Claim.

2. The Defendant denies the allegations contained in paragraphs 2 and 4 of the Statement of Claim.

3. The Defendant has no knowledge of the allegations contained in paragraphs 3, 5, 6, and 7 of the Statement of Claim...

Ending
↓

Date: November 11, 20–

Michael, Eliad & Redford LLP
Barristers and Solicitors
863 Seneca Lane
Toronto, Ontario M4J 1P6

Robert B. Redford
Tel: (416) 363-1079
Fax: (416) 363-2628

Lawyers for the Defendant

TO: Castles & Sands
         Suite 900
         205 Portage Street
         Markham, ON L3R 3G3

         Barry F. Sands
         Tel: (905) 495-2222
         Fax: (905) 495-2223

         Lawyers for the Plaintiffs

Court File No. CV-**-2345

ONTARIO
SUPERIOR COURT OF JUSTICE

Proceeding commenced at Toronto

STATEMENT OF DEFENCE

Michael, Eliad & Redford LLP
Barristers and Solicitors
863 Seneca Lane
Toronto, Ontario
M4J 1P6

Robert B. Redford (48000R)
Tel: (416) 363-1079
Fax: (416) 363-2628
rbrdfrd@mer.com

Lawyers for the Defendant

GEORGE J. SMITH and THOMAS JONES   v.   JANE AUSTEN
Plaintiffs   Defendant

Court File No. **CV-**-1234**

ONTARIO
SUPERIOR COURT OF JUSTICE

B E T W E E N:

FREDERICK FLINTSTONE

Plaintiff

- and -

BERNARD RUBBLE

Defendant

AFFIDAVIT

I, FREDERICK FLINTSTONE, of the City of Bedrock, in the County of Boulder, the Plaintiff in this action, MAKE OATH AND SAY:

1.   I commenced this action against the Defendant on January 27, (year). At that time, my lawyer advised me…

2.   I never attended at the Defendant's place of residence, although we did meet at a club to discuss the situation…

3.   I make this Affidavit for no improper purpose.

SWORN BEFORE ME at the City of
Toronto, in the Province of Ontario this
.... day of May, (year)

}

_____
Commissioner for Taking Affidavits
(or as may be)

_____
Frederick Flintstone

Court File No. CV-**-1234

ONTARIO
SUPERIOR COURT OF JUSTICE

PROCEEDING COMMENCED AT
TORONTO

AFFIDAVIT

MICHAEL, ELIAD & REDFORD LLP
Barristers and Solicitors
863 Seneca Lane
Toronto, Ontario
M4J 1P6

Robert B. Redford (48000R)
Tel: 416-363-1079
Fax: 416-363-2628
rbrdfrd@mer.com

Lawyers for the Plaintiff

FREDERICK FLINTSTONE
Plaintiff

-and-

BERNARD RUBBLE
Defendant

Court File No. CV-**-1234

ONTARIO
SUPERIOR COURT OF JUSTICE

BETWEEN:

FREDERICK FLINTSTONE

Plaintiff

and

BERNARD RUBBLE

Defendant

AFFIDAVIT OF SERVICE

I, JANE JONES, of the City of Toronto, in the Province of Ontario,   MAKE OATH

AND SAY:

[1] 1. On November 11, (year), I served the Defendant, Bernard Rubble, with the Statement of

Claim by leaving a copy with him at 6 Blue Street, Waterwell, Ontario.

2. I was able to identify the person by means of inquiring if his name was Bernard Rubble,

which he confirmed it was.

SWORN BEFORE ME at the City of	)
Toronto, in the Province of Ontario,	) _____
on December , (year) .	) Jane Jones
	)
Commissioner for Taking Affidavits	
(or as may be)	

Notes:
[1] *If served by mail as an alternative to personal service, substitute:*
1. On November 11, (year), I sent to the Defendant, Bernard Rubble, by registered mail a copy of the Statement of Claim.

2. On November 29, (year), I received the attached Acknowledgment of Receipt Card bearing a signature that purports to be the signature of Bernard Rubble.

[1] *If served by leaving a copy with an adult person in the same household as an alternative to personal service, substitute:*
1. I served the Defendant, Bernard Rubble, with the Statement of Claim by leaving a copy on November 11, (year), at 2:30 p.m. with a person, Mary Levec, who appeared to be an adult member of the same household in which Bernard Rubble is residing, at 6 Blue Street, Waterwell, Ontario, D7T 5Y2, and by sending a copy by regular lettermail (*or registered mail*) on November 11, (year), to Bernard Rubble at the same address.

2. I ascertained that the person was an adult member of the household by means of observing the person and by asking if she lived at that address, to which she answered she did.

3. Before serving the documents in this way, I made an unsuccessful attempt to serve the Defendant personally at the same address on November 10, (year). (*If more than one attempt has been made, add:* and again on *date*.)

Court File No. CV-**-1234

ONTARIO
SUPERIOR COURT OF JUSTICE

BETWEEN:

FREDERICK FLINTSTONE

Plaintiff

and

BERNARD RUBBLE

Defendant

AFFIDAVIT OF SERVICE

     I, JANE JONES, of the City of Toronto, in the Province of Ontario, MAKE OATH
AND SAY:

[1] 1. I served the Defendant with the Affidavit of Documents by sending a copy by regular
lettermail on April 15, (year), to Castles & Sands, the lawyers for the Defendant, at Suite
900, 205 Portage Street, Markham, Ontario, L3R 3G3.

SWORN BEFORE ME at the City of)	
Toronto, in the Province of Ontario,)	_____
on May , (year) .)	Jane Jones

Commissioner for Taking Affidavits
    (or as may be)

Notes:

[1]*If served by fax, substitute:*

1. I served the Defendant with the Affidavit of Documents by sending a copy by fax to Fax No. 905-495-2223 on April 15, (year), to Castles & Sands, the lawyers for the Defendant.

[1]*If service by courier, substitute:*

1. I served the Defendant with the Affidavit of Documents by sending a copy by (*name of courier*), a courier, to Castles & Sands, the lawyers for the Defendant, at Suite 900, 205 Portage Street, Markham, Ontario, L3R 3G3.

2. The copy was given to the courier on April 15, (year).

[1]*If served by e-mail, substitute:*

1. I served the Defendant with the Affidavit of Documents on April 15, (year), by e-mailing a copy to Castles & Sands, the lawyers for the Defendant, in accordance with subrule 16.06.1(1) and on consent of the parties.

    Legal Office Procedures

Precedent 8.4   Affidavit of Service by Mail (on Lawyer of Record) — Notes continued

¹If service refused, substitute:
1. On May 1, (year), I personally attempted to serve Castles & Sands, lawyers for the Defendant (*or* Plaintiff), with a copy of the Affidavit of Documents. Castles & Sands refused to accept service, and I left a copy of the Affidavit of Documents with their receptionist, Miss Mary Smith. These steps constitute good and sufficient service.

¹If served by document exchange, substitute:
1. On May 1, (year), I served a copy of the Affidavit of Documents on Castles & Sands, a member or subscriber of Z Document Exchange Limited, Box No. 52, lawyers for the Defendant (*or* Plaintiff). I deposited the copy of the Affidavit of Documents at Z Document Exchange Limited at Toronto, Ontario, where a representative of Z Document Exchange Limited date-stamped the original and a copy in my presence.

Precedent 8.5   Affidavit of Service by Mail Stamp

I...
of the..........................of..
in the..........................of..
make oath and say/affirm:
On...
I served this document by sending a copy by regular lettermail
to..
lawyer(s) for the...
at..
....

Sworn/Affirmed before me at the)
...............of.............................)
in the..)   _____
....)   Deponent's signature
on..)

Commissioner for Taking Affidavits

Precedent 8.6   Affidavit of Service by Facsimile Stamp

I...
of the..........................of..
in the..........................of..
make oath and say/affirm:
On...
I served this document by telephone transmission of a facsimile copy to the office of the lawyer(s) for the
....
at Fax No...

Sworn/Affirmed before me at the)
...............of.............................)
in the..)   _____
....)   Deponent's signature
on..)

Commissioner for Taking Affidavits

Precedent 8.7   Admission of Service Endorsement

Service of a copy of this document admitted

on..*November 11,* ....*(year)*.....

Michael, Eliad & Redford LLP..............
Lawyer(s) for *Defendant*

Precedent 8.8   Acceptance of Service Endorsement

Service of a copy of this document accepted

on..

....
Lawyer(s) for

 **RECORD OF SERVICE**

Court File No.: ZC-0000000

ONTARIO
SUPERIOR COURT OF JUSTICE

BETWEEN:

ACME CO. LTD.

Plaintiff(s)

-and-

XYZ CORP.

Defendant(s)

Document Served: Factum of the Plaintiff

Number of Pages Served: 36

Served by: Benjamin Harpers, lawyer for Acme Co. Ltd., benjamin@harpers.com

Served on: Nigel Watkins

Date and Time of Service: March 31, 20xx @ 12:06 AM

This Record of Service was generated by Courtside EDX, an electronic document exchange under Rule 16 of the *Rules of Civil Procedure* and Rule 6 of the *Family Law Rules*.

The recipient of the above documents has consented to service by electronic document exchange pursuant to Rule 6(2)(c.1) of the Family Law Rules when registering for CourtSide EDX.

 This QR code contains a link to an online copy of this Courtside EDX Record of Service.

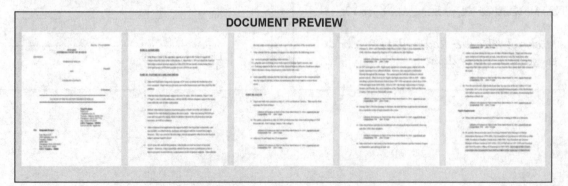

DOCUMENT PREVIEW

The complete document served can be accessed online by clicking here.

CHAPTER 9

INTRODUCTION TO CIVIL LITIGATION

This chapter discusses civil litigation as an adversarial system of justice and provides details of the procedural stages through which civil litigation actions must proceed in reaching trial.

Civil litigation (from the Latin *litigatio*, a dispute) involves law suits between private citizens, where a **plaintiff** (the party who begins a law suit) sues a **defendant** (the party who is being sued), usually for monetary compensation because the defendant did something wrong or was negligent in some way.

RULES OF CIVIL PROCEDURE

Regardless of the type of civil litigation dispute, the civil litigation action is adversarial and resembles that of a tennis match. The ball, which starts on the plaintiff's side of the court, goes over to the defendant's side, and back and forth between the two players, until they are both at trial, at which time, the court gives its judgment (decision) in favour of one of the parties, based on the facts and the law.

It would be difficult to conduct an adversarial dispute without rules. The *Rules of Civil Procedure* set out all of the rules to be followed in civil disputes, including all of the court forms to be used. This ensures province-wide uniformity in procedures (steps) and documents (court forms). Following is an example of how Rule 14 tells all lawyers how to begin an action and what court forms to use in doing so. Note that the court forms are correlated with the rule numbers that prescribe them, e.g. Form 14A is a statement of claim (general) under Rule 14:

HOW PROCEEDINGS COMMENCED

By Issuing Originating Process
14.01(1) A proceeding shall be commenced by the issuing of an originating process...

ACTIONS--BY STATEMENT OF CLAIM OR NOTICE OF ACTION

Statement of Claim
14.03(1) The originating process for the commencement of an action is a statement of claim (Form 14A (general) or 14B (mortgage actions)), except as provided by,

   (a) subrule (2) (notice of action)...

TYPES OF CIVIL LITIGATION PROCEDURES

Generally, there are two main types of procedures in civil litigation — **ordinary procedure** and **simplified procedure**.

ORDINARY PROCEDURE

All ordinary procedure actions proceed to trial in these five stages: (1) claim, (2) pleadings, (3) discoveries, (4) pre-trial, and (5) trial, as shown in Figure 9.1. Note that all actions that reach trial begin with a document called **statement of claim** and end with a judgment. The steps may vary only in the **pleadings** stage where defendants may **defend**, **counterclaim**, **crossclaim**, or commence a **third party proceeding**, depending on which route would be appropriate in the case at hand. The remaining stages of discoveries, pre-trial, and trial are the same in all ordinary procedure actions, regardless of which route the defendant might have taken in the pleadings stage.

Figure 9.1   STEPS IN TRIAL — ORDINARY PROCEDURE

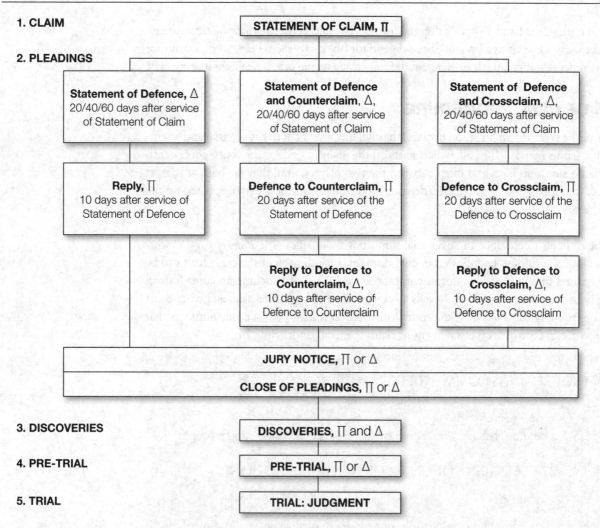

Greek pi ∏ = Plaintiff   Greek delta Δ = Defendant
20/40/60 = 20 days within Ontario; 40 days elsewhere in Canada or USA; 60 days anywhere else.

SIMPLIFIED PROCEDURE

Rule 76 of the *Rules of Civil Procedure* sets out the simplified procedure. It is called a simplified procedure basically because the procedural steps tend to be shorter than those in ordinary procedure actions. The simplified procedure applies to all actions for claims over the Small Claims Court amount and up to $100,000, exclusive of interest and legal costs. The simplified procedure also applies to actions where there are multiple plaintiffs or defendants with each plaintiff's or defendant's claim being for $100,000 or less, exclusive of interest and legal costs.

The plaintiff may use the simplified procedure for claims over the monetary jurisdiction of $100,000, provided the parties agree. There are, however, costs consequences if the simplified procedure is not used when it should have been: for example, if the plaintiff did not use the simplified procedure and at trial it is shown that the action met the criteria for using the simplified procedure, a plaintiff who wins judgment will usually not recover any legal costs.

STEPS IN SIMPLIFIED PROCEDURE ACTIONS

1. Statement of claim	7. Mandatory mediation (only in Ottawa, Toronto, and Windsor)
2. Statement of defence	8. Setting action down for trial
3. Close of pleadings	9. Pre-trial conference
4. Affidavit of documents	10. Placing action on trial list
5. Oral examinations for discovery	11. Trial record
6. Settlement discussions	12. Summary or ordinary trial

Statement of claim   The statement of claim (Form 14A), Precedent 9.1, is the same form as that used in ordinary procedure actions, except that it includes immediately above the heading "CLAIM" a note to the effect that the action is under the simplified procedure. The plaintiff prepares the statement of claim under the simplified procedure and has it issued (sealed by the court). The plaintiff serves an issued copy on the defendant and files a copy in court with proof of service. Subrule 14.03(4.1) requires that an **information for court use, Form 14F** (see Chapter 10) be filed in court when an originating process is issued. Form 14F is only filed in court; it is not issued or served since it is for court use only.

Statement of defence   The statement of defence and the entire pleadings stage (counterclaims, crossclaims, third party claims, and replies) are the same in the simplified procedure as they are in the regular procedure, shown in Figure 9.1. The defendant has **twenty days** if served within Ontario, **forty days** if served in another province or in the United States of America, and **sixty days** if served anywhere else to serve a statement of defence.

Close of pleadings   Once the time for serving and filing the applicable pleadings has ended, the pleadings are said to be closed.

Affidavit of documents   Rule 76.03 provides for affidavits of documents. Within **ten days** after the close of pleadings, and at the party's own expense, a party must serve an affidavit of documents (Form 30A or 30B), together with copies of the documents listed in Schedule A of the affidavit of documents. The affidavit of documents is the same form as that used in ordinary procedure actions, except that when used under the simplified procedure, it must list the names and addresses of any potential witnesses. A lawyer will not be permitted to call a witness who is not listed in the affidavit of documents, unless the court orders otherwise.

Oral examinations for discovery   Rule 76.04 provides for limited oral examinations for discovery. Oral examinations for discovery are limited to up to two hours in total per party, i.e. per side, regardless of the number of parties or other persons to be examined. Lawyers may choose to use the oral examination for discovery process to obtain information from the other party that would help determine the strength of the other side's case. Oral examinations for discovery are like mini trials where lawyers ask questions of the opposing party. Oral examinations are held outside of the court in offices of private businesses known as special examiners.

Settlement discussion and documentary disclosure   Rule 76.08 provides for settlement discussion and documentary disclosure. Within **60 days** after the filing of the first statement of defence or notice of intent to defend, the parties must conduct settlement discussions, either by way of a meeting or a telephone call, and consider whether (a) all documents relevant to the action have been disclosed, and (b) settlement of any or all issues is possible.

Mandatory mediation   Rule 24.1 applies to mandatory mediation. Mandatory mediation in simplified procedure actions applies to actions which are commenced in Ottawa, Toronto, or Windsor. A mediation session must be held within **180 days** after the first defence or notice of intent to defend has been filed, unless the court orders otherwise. In effect, a mediation session should be held at the latest by the date of setting the action down for trial, or at least a **notice of name of mediator and date of session (Form 24.1A)** must be filed with the mediation co-ordinator by one of the parties by the time of setting the action down for trial. **Seven days** before the mediation session, the parties must provide the mediator with a **statement of issues (Form 24.1C)**, Precedent 9.2. The mediator must provide a mediator's report within **ten days** of completion of the mediation session.

Setting action down for trial   Rule 76.09 applies to setting down for trial. Within **180 days** after the first statement of defence or notice of intent to defend is filed, the plaintiff must set the action down for trial by serving a **notice of readiness for pre-trial conference (Form 76C)**, Precedent 9.3, on every party to the action, and filing it forthwith with proof of service. If the plaintiff does not act, then any other party must serve and file the notice of readiness for pre-trial conference (Form 76C).

In Toronto, under practice direction, the party filing a notice of readiness for pre-trial conference, Form 76C, must also file a **certificate of lawyer** (see Chapter 14), indicating proof that a **notice of name of mediator and date of session (Form 24.1A)** has been filed with the mediation co-ordinator (in practice lawyers also file a copy of Form 24.1A with the certificate of lawyer; see Chapter 14), or that the mediator has filed a report with the mediation co-ordinator, or that the mediation issue has been otherwise dealt with.

Pre-trial conference   Rule 76.10 provides for a pre-trial conference. Once the notice of readiness for pre-trial conference (Form 76C) has been filed in court, the registrar shall serve notice of a pre-trial conference on the parties at least **45 days** before the scheduled date of the pre-trial conference. A pre-trial conference is **mandatory** in simplified procedure actions. A pre-trial conference is a hearing before a judge or a master. The reason for the pre-trial conference is to determine the current issues and the positions of each party. At least **five days** before the date of the pre-trial conference, each party must:

(a) file,

    (i) a copy of the party's affidavit of documents and copies of the documents relied on for the party's claim or defence,

    (ii) a copy of any expert reports, and

    (iii) any other material necessary for the pre-trial conference; and

(b) deliver,

    (i) a two-page statement setting out the issues and the party's position with respect to them, and

    (ii) a trial management checklist (Form 76D), Precedent 9.4.

Placing the simplified procedure action on trial list   Under rule 76.11, the registrar shall place the action on the appropriate trial list immediately after the pre-trial conference. At the end of the pre-trial conference, if the parties fail to settle the case, they may agree to proceed either by way of an ordinary trial or a summary trial, and if they cannot agree, the pre-trial conference judge will decide. Once the mode of trial has been determined, the pre-trial conference judge will fix a date for trial.

Trial record   At least **ten days** before the date fixed for trial, the party who set the action down for trial shall serve a trial record on every party to the action and file the record with proof of service. If the parties have opted for an ordinary trial, the contents of the trial record are as set out in Rule 48.03, as follows:

The trial record in ordinary trial shall contain:

(a) a table of contents, describing each document by its nature and date;

(b) a copy of any jury notice;

(c) a copy of the pleadings, including those relating to any counterclaim or crossclaim;

(d) a copy of any demand or order for particulars of a pleading and the particulars in response;

(e) a copy of any notice of amounts and particulars of special damages;

(f) a copy of any order respecting the trial; and

(g) a certificate signed by the lawyer setting the action down, basically stating that the record contains all of the required documents.

The trial record in summary trial shall contain the following, as set out in subrule 76.11(4):

(a) a table of contents describing each document, including each exhibit, by its nature and date and, in the case of an exhibit, by exhibit number or letter;

(b) a copy of the pleadings, including those relating to any counterclaim, crossclaim, or third party claim;

(c) a copy of any demand or order for particulars of a pleading and the particulars delivered in response;

(d) a copy of any order respecting the trial;

(e) a copy of all the affidavits served by all the parties for use on the summary trial; and

(f) a certificate signed by the lawyer of the party filing the trial record, stating that it contains the documents described in clauses (a) to (e).

Summary trial or ordinary trial   Rule 76.12 provides for a summary trial. A summary trial is a shorter trial than an ordinary trial basically because it consists of affidavit evidence and time-limited examinations on affidavit evidence, generally as follows:

- The evidence of the parties is presented by way of affidavits.
- Examinations in chief are limited to 10 minutes. Examinations in chief basically means the plaintiff or defendant may examine their own deponents of any affidavits for not more than 10 minutes.
- Cross-examinations are limited to 50 minutes per party.
- Re-examination of a deponent who is cross-examined is limited to 10 minutes.
- After the presentation of evidence, oral arguments are limited to 45 minutes per party.

MANDATORY MEDIATION

Rule 24.1 provides for mandatory mediation. Mediation is mandatory in simplified procedure actions as well as ordinary procedure actions in Ottawa, Toronto, and Windsor. Basically, mandatory mediation is a settlement session required by the Rules. The parties must come before an objective party outside of the court, called a mediator, to discuss the possibilities of settlement or to narrow any issues in dispute so as to save court time and expense. The mediation session may be held at the mediator's office, the office of one of the parties or one of the lawyers, or at the court facilities. The parties and their lawyers must attend the mediation session, unless the court orders otherwise. A lawyer may not attend in the place of a party. If there is an agreement resolving some or all of the issues in dispute, the parties or their lawyers must sign it. If the agreement settles the entire action, the defendant must file a notice with the court to that effect. If there is no settlement reached, the action continues to court.

How mediation is administered   A mediation co-ordinator for each municipality maintains a list of approved mediators and handles the administration of the mediation for that municipality. There are also mediators who are independent of the approved list; all, however, are bound by the same mediation rules. The fees of approved mediators are regulated. The fees of independent mediators are not regulated. The parties may pick a mediator from either list.

Failure to select a mediator   If within **180 days** of the filing of the first defence or notice of intent to defend the court has received no indication that the parties have selected a mediator, or that they have conducted a mediation session, or that they have otherwise dealt with the issue of mediation, the court will assign a mediator and notify the parties. The assigned mediator will then advise the parties of the date of the mediation session at least **twenty days** before the date of the mediation session.

CASE MANAGEMENT

Rule 77 of the *Rules of Civil Procedure* provides for case management. Case management involves a judge or a case management master assigned to oversee cases and promote resolution of disputes or bring cases to trial in a timely manner. Rule 77 provides for case management only in cases where the court determines there is a need; therefore, a case is not automatically subject to case management.

Application of rule Rule 77 applies only to ordinary procedure actions and applications commenced in Ottawa, Toronto, and Windsor, and **only by court order**. Case management does not apply to any simplified procedure actions (including any commenced in Ottawa, Toronto, and Windsor). (There are no applications in simplified procedure.) Here is a summary of mandatory mediation, case management, and discoveries, and their respective applications in simplified procedure and ordinary procedure actions:

Figure 9.2

SIMPLIFIED PROCEDURE				
Location	**Mandatory Mediation** (Rule 24.1)	**Case Management** (Rule 77)	**Oral Examinations for Discovery**	**Written Questions Cross-Examination on Affidavits Examination of Witness on Motion**
Ottawa Toronto Windsor	within 180 days of filing of first defence (actions)	not applicable	total of 2 hours per party	not permitted
other Regions	not applicable	not applicable	total of 2 hours per party	not permitted
ORDINARY PROCEDURE				
Ottawa Toronto Windsor	within 180 days of filing of first defence (actions)	only by court order (actions and applications)	total of 7 hours per party	permitted
other Regions	not applicable	not applicable	total of 7 hours per party	permitted

PRACTICE DIRECTIONS

Practice directions are usually a supervising judge's "memo" to the legal profession of changes in practice. Practice directions do not change the *Rules of Civil Procedure*; they vary or refine the rules. The rules apply to all regions in the province. The practice directions usually apply only to the issuing region to suit the needs of that region. Expect, therefore, practice variations among court offices across the province.

CLASS ACTIONS

Class actions are law suits that a group of individuals or corporations collectively starts against a corporation, an individual, or a group of corporations or individuals. An example of a well known class action was the case involving the victims of Hepatitis C suing the Red Cross as a result of the victims having received blood that was tainted with the Hepatitis C virus. The class members must have common interests and issues and can have one person represent them, and that person is referred to as the **representative plaintiff** or the **representative defendant**, as the case may be.

Class action procedure   Generally, the steps in ordinary procedure actions apply equally to class actions; however, the *Class Proceedings Act* prescribes additional procedures to supplement those that the *Rules of Civil Procedure* prescribe. Here are some of the more significant additional steps in class actions:

1. The representative plaintiff must seek a certification order from the court, certifying (approving) the proceeding as a class proceeding and appointing the person as a representative plaintiff.

2. The representative plaintiff prepares the statement of claim using the ordinary procedure statement of claim form, except for the wording **Proceeding under the *Class Proceedings Act*** being keyed one blank line above the title of the document.

3. The representative plaintiff must give notice of the action to the class members. The members of the class are presumed to be in the action and bound by the court's decision, unless they opt out within a time limit that the court would set. Those who opt out will not share in any judgment or settlement obtained in the class action, but they are free to start separate proceedings.

Contingency fees   Contingency fees are available in civil litigation cases, including class actions. A contingency fee is an agreement in writing where the client pays no fees unless and until there is recovery in the lawsuit. Contingency fees are based on a percentage of the amount of money that a client wins in an action. Lawyers are prohibited from getting paid more than the client recovers. Since contingency fees are **contingent** upon winning the case, it is only **winnable** class action cases, or other civil litigation cases, that are usually considered for prosecution.

CHAPTER SUMMARY

The *Rules of Civil Procedure* set out the steps which actions must follow in trials and prescribe the court forms which lawyers must use in each step. The rules apply to all actions across the province. This ensures province-wide uniformity in procedures (steps) and documents (forms). There are two types of actions – ordinary procedure actions and simplified procedure actions. The major difference between ordinary procedure and simplified procedure actions is that the steps in simplified procedure actions are somewhat shorter. There are also class actions under the *Class Proceedings Act* which are law suits that a group of individuals or corporations collectively start.

Practice may vary among different regions across the province because of practice directions, which are judges' memos to lawyers to carry out certain procedural steps that are designed to serve the needs of a particular region.

Legal Office Procedures

REVIEW QUESTIONS

1. List the procedural steps in simplified procedure actions and give a brief explanation of each step.
2. Name the procedural stages that ordinary actions go through to reach trial.
3. Name the document which begins an ordinary procedure action and a simplified procedure action.
4. Name the document to be filed when setting a simplified procedure action down for trial.
5. What is the purpose of mandatory mediation?
6. What is the basic difference between an ordinary trial and a summary trial?
7. Practice directions are directions which require one to practise a particular task to perfection. Explain.
8. Name the rule number that governs simplified procedure actions.
9. Which rule number of the *Rules of Civil Procedure* prescribes Form 14A?

Court File No.

ONTARIO
SUPERIOR COURT OF JUSTICE

B E T W E E N :

(Court Seal)

LUCILLE PLASKA

Plaintiff

and

LANDLORD PROPERTY MANAGEMENT INC.
and HERMAN SHERMAN

Defendants

STATEMENT OF CLAIM

TO THE DEFENDANT(S):

    A LEGAL PROCEEDING HAS BEEN COMMENCED AGAINST YOU by the Plaintiff. The Claim made against you is set out in the following pages.

    IF YOU WISH TO DEFEND THIS PROCEEDING, you or an Ontario lawyer acting for you must prepare a Statement of Defence in Form 18A prescribed by the *Rules of Civil Procedure*, serve it on the Plaintiff's lawyer or, where the Plaintiff does not have a lawyer, serve it on the Plaintiff, and file it, with proof of service, in this court office, **WITHIN TWENTY DAYS** after this Statement of Claim is served on you, if you are served in Ontario.

    If you are served in another province or territory of Canada or in the United States of America, the period for serving and filing your Statement of Defence is forty days. If you are served outside Canada and the United States of America, the period is sixty days.

    Instead of serving and filing a Statement of Defence, you may serve and file a Notice of Intent to Defend in Form 18B prescribed by the *Rules of Civil Procedure*. This will entitle you to ten more days within which to serve and file your Statement of Defence.

    IF YOU FAIL TO DEFEND THIS PROCEEDING, JUDGMENT MAY BE GIVEN AGAINST YOU IN YOUR ABSENCE AND WITHOUT FURTHER NOTICE TO YOU. IF YOU WISH TO DEFEND THIS PROCEEDING BUT ARE UNABLE TO PAY LEGAL FEES, LEGAL AID MAY BE AVAILABLE TO YOU BY CONTACTING A LOCAL LEGAL AID OFFICE.

    TAKE NOTICE THIS ACTION WILL AUTOMATICALLY BE DISMISSED if it has not been set down for trial or terminated by any means within five years after the action was commenced unless otherwise ordered by the court.

Date   _September , (year)_   Issued by   _____
                                                                             Local Registrar

Address of court   393 University Avenue, 10th Floor
office: Toronto, Ontario M5G 1E6

TO: **LANDLORD PROPERTY MANAGEMENT INC.**
               132 Fairdown Avenue
               Toronto, Ontario M3K 4B2

AND TO: **HERMAN SHERMAN**
               54 Saber Boulevard
               Toronto, Ontario M7B 1WN

-2-

(In an action under the simplified procedure provided in Rule 76, add:)

THIS ACTION IS BROUGHT AGAINST YOU UNDER THE SIMPLIFIED PROCEDURE PROVIDED IN RULE 76 OF THE RULES OF CIVIL PROCEDURE.

CLAIM

1.   The Plaintiff claims:

    (a) the sum of $100,000.00 as damages for breach of contract;

    (b) in the alternative, the sum of $100,000.00 as damages for negligence;

    (c) payment by the Defendants of all sums that the Plaintiff paid for moving costs;

    (d) interest on the above sums pursuant to sections 128 and 129 of the *Courts of Justice Act*, RSO 1990, c C.43, as amended;

    (e) the costs of this action, plus harmonized sales tax;

    (f) such further and other relief as this Honourable Court may deem just.

2.   The Plaintiff is a resident of the City of Toronto, and was at all material times a tenant in a property municipally known as 99 Barn Street, Toronto, Ontario, that the Defendant Herman Sherman owned and the Defendant Landlord Property Management Inc. managed as landlord.

3.   The Plaintiff states that subsequent to the expiry of a written lease, the Plaintiff continued her tenancy as a month-to-month tenant.

4.   The Plaintiff states that the Defendants were under a duty to the Plaintiff to reasonably, capably, and competently provide accommodations in compliance with all applicable contractual and statutory standards as defined by her lease, *the Residential Tenancies Act*, as well as the provisions of the Toronto Municipal Code.

5.   On or about the evening of January 11, (year), the Plaintiff's son found his bed and the floor in his upstairs bedroom flooded and the ceiling in his room had broken from the weight of water leaking through the roof.

6.   The Plaintiff also discovered that water had seeped into the basement, flooding the basement floor which the Defendants had repaired after a similar flooding the previous summer.

7.   The Plaintiff contacted the property manager that the Defendants employed, who inspected the premises, but no action was taken, and the Plaintiff then contacted the Building Department, Inspection Section.

8.   The ceiling in one of the bedrooms was sagging and in danger of collapsing. Despite constant efforts to bail out the water on a constant basis, the water was accumulating faster than the Plaintiff could remove it, seriously damaging the Plaintiff's personal effects and furnishings. In an attempt to mitigate her damages, the Plaintiff kept moving her furniture from room to room, ultimately running out of any area free from water leaks or flooding.

9.   The building inspector arrived, and upon inspecting the property, immediately telephoned the corporate Defendant and advised the Defendants that they would be charged for violations of property standards and that work orders would be issued immediately requiring the Defendants to implement repairs.

-3-

10.   On that day, the Plaintiff hired movers to remove her furnishings and put them into storage. The Defendants offered no alternate accommodations to the Plaintiff and her son, and the only offer of monetary compensation was a $500.00 payment to cover the Plaintiff's personal insurance deductible and as partial reimbursement for the Plaintiff's rent payments for two months.

11.   Three days later, while the repair work was going on, the superintendent telephoned the Plaintiff and asked what the Plaintiff intended to do about the premises which the Plaintiff had vacated. The Plaintiff advised that she would consider her options once the Defendants had indicated when the repairs would be done.

12.   In order to ensure that there could be no complaint by the Defendants that the Plaintiff had been uncooperative or had somehow prevented access to the premises so that repairs could be carried out, the Plaintiff provided a set of keys to the premises to the superintendent.

13.   The Plaintiff's ex-husband, who was making enquiries on the Plaintiff's behalf as to the progress of the repairs, was advised by the Defendants' lawyer that the Defendants were taking the position that the Plaintiff, by providing the keys to her unit and abandoning the premises, had terminated her tenancy.

14.   A week later, the building inspector inspected the premises and advised the Plaintiff that the repairs to the premises were still incomplete and that the deadline for compliance had been extended for ten days.

15.   The building inspector also advised the Plaintiff that the Defendants had rented the premises to new tenants.

16.   The Plaintiff has also discovered that the Defendants have, in fact, rented out the premises to the new tenants for $1,150.00 per month, which is higher than the rent paid by the Plaintiff to the Defendants, which was $950.00 per month. The Plaintiff therefore states that the Defendants are profiting from their breaches of contract as set out above, all to the continued financial and personal detriment of the Plaintiff.

The Plaintiff proposes that this action be tried at: Toronto

   September   , 20--
(Date of issue)

                           MICHAEL, ELIAD & REDFORD LLP
                           Barristers and Solicitors
                           863 Seneca Lane
                           Toronto, Ontario   M4J 1P6

                           Robert B. Redford
                           Tel: 416-363-1079
                           Fax: 416-363-2628

                           Lawyers for the Plaintiff

Court File No.

ONTARIO
SUPERIOR COURT OF JUSTICE

PROCEEDING COMMENCED AT
TORONTO

STATEMENT OF CLAIM

MICHAEL, ELIAD & REDFORD LLP
Barristers and Solicitors
863 Seneca Lane
Toronto, Ontario
M4J 1P6

Robert B. Redford (48000R)
Tel: 416-363-1079
Fax: 416-363-2628
rbrdfrd@mer.com

Lawyers for the Plaintiff

LANDLORD PROPERTY MANAGEMENT INC. and **HERMAN SHERMAN**
Defendants

-and-

LUCILLE PLASKA
Plaintiff

Court File No. **CV-**-1111**

ONTARIO
SUPERIOR COURT OF JUSTICE

B E T W E E N:

LUCILLE PLASKA

Plaintiff

and

LANDLORD PROPERTY MANAGEMENT INC.
and HERMAN SHERMAN

Defendants

STATEMENT OF ISSUES

(To be provided to mediator and parties at least seven days before the mediation session)

1.   <u>Factual and legal issues in dispute</u>

The Plaintiff (or Defendant) states that the following factual and legal issues are in dispute and remain to be resolved *(Issues should be stated briefly and numbered consecutively)*.

1.   The Defendants' obligation to the Plaintiff under the terms of the contract dated November 28, (year).

2.   <u>Party's position and interests (what the party hopes to achieve)</u>

1.   The Plaintiff would like full compensation for the extensive damages to her personal property.

3.   <u>Attached documents</u>

Attached to this form are the following documents that the Plaintiff (*or* defendant) considers of central importance in the action:

1.   Statement of Claim
2.   Statement of Defence
3.   Contract dated November 28, (year)

October 20, 20--

_____
(party's signature)
*(Name, address, telephone number and fax number of
lawyer of party filing statement of issues, or of party)*

MICHAEL, ELIAD & REDFORD LLP
Barristers and Solicitors
863 Seneca Lane
Toronto, Ontario   M4J 1P6

Robert B. Redford
Tel: 416-363-1079
Fax: 416-363-2628

Lawyers for the plaintiff

NOTE: When the Plaintiff provides a copy of this form to the mediator, a copy of the pleadings shall also be included.

NOTE: Rule 24.14 provides as follows:

All communications at a mediation session and the mediator's notes and records shall be deemed to be without prejudice settlement discussions.

(Needs no backsheet)

132   *Legal Office Procedures*

LUCILLE PLASKA
Plaintiff

-and-

LANDLORD PROPERTY MANAGEMENT INC. and **HERMAN SHERMAN**
Defendants

Court File No. CV-**-1111

ONTARIO
SUPERIOR COURT OF JUSTICE

PROCEEDING COMMENCED AT
TORONTO

**NOTICE OF READINESS FOR
PRE-TRIAL CONFERENCE**

MICHAEL, ELIAD & REDFORD LLP
Barristers and Solicitors
863 Seneca Lane
Toronto, Ontario
M4J 1P6

Robert B. Redford (48000R)
Tel: 416-363-1079
Fax: 416-363-2628
rbrdfrd@mer.com

Lawyers for the Plaintiff

Court File No. **CV-**-1111**

ONTARIO
SUPERIOR COURT OF JUSTICE

B E T W E E N:

LUCILLE PLASKA

Plaintiff

and

LANDLORD PROPERTY MANAGEMENT INC.
and HERMAN SHERMAN

Defendants

NOTICE OF READINESS FOR PRE-TRIAL CONFERENCE

The Plaintiff is ready for a pre-trial conference and is setting this action down for trial. A pre-trial conference in the action will proceed as scheduled and the trial will proceed when the action is reached on the trial list, unless the court orders otherwise.

CERTIFICATE

I CERTIFY that there was a settlement discussion under rule 76.08.

November   , 20--

_____
(Signature of solicitor)
MICHAEL, ELIAD & REDFORD LLP
Barristers and Solicitors
863 Seneca Lane
Toronto, Ontario
M4J 1P6

Robert B. Redford
Tel: 416-363-1079
Fax: 416-363-2628

Lawyers for the Plaintiff

TO: **CASTLES & SANDS**
Suite 900-205 Portage Street
Markham, Ontario L3R 3G3

Raymond G. Castles
Tel: 905-495-2222
Fax: 905-495-2223

Lawyers for the Defendants

4. Admissions

Are the parties prepared to admit any facts for the purposes of the trial or summary trial?

Yes [X] no [ ]

5. Document brief

Will there be a document brief? yes [ ] no [X]

6. Request to admit

Will there be a request to admit? yes [ ] no [X]

If so, have the parties agreed to a timetable? yes [ ] no [ ]

7. Expert's reports

Are any expert's reports anticipated? yes [ ] no [X]

8. Amendments to pleadings

Are any amendments likely to be sought? yes [ ] no [X]

9. Mode of trial

Have the parties agreed to a summary trial? yes [ ] no [X]

Have the parties agreed to an ordinary trial? yes [ ] no [X]

If the parties have not agreed about the mode of trial, what mode of trial is being requested by the party filing this checklist?

ordinary trial

10. Factum of Law

Will the parties be submitting Factums of Law? yes [ ] no [X]

(Needs no backsheet)

Court File No. CV-**-1111

ONTARIO
SUPERIOR COURT OF JUSTICE

B E T W E E N:

LUCILLE PLASKA

Plaintiff

and

LANDLORD PROPERTY MANAGEMENT INC.
and HERMAN SHERMAN

Defendants

(Insert name of party filing this form): Lucille Plaska, Plaintiff

TRIAL MANAGEMENT CHECKLIST

Trial Lawyer - Plaintiff(s): Robert B. Redford
Michael, Eliad & Redford LLP, 863 Seneca Lane, Toronto, Ontario, M4J 1P6

Trial Lawyer - Defendant(s): Raymond G. Castles
Castles & Sands, 900 – 205 Portage Street, Markham, Ontario, L3R 3G3

Filed by Plaintiff
Filed by Defendant
Filed by subsequent party

1. Issues Outstanding

(a) liability: breach of contract by Defendants

(b) damages: full compensation for damages to personal property

(c) other: damages as per Statement of Claim

2. Names of Plaintiff's witnesses

n/a

3. Names of Defendant's witnesses

Legal Office Procedures

CHAPTER 10

COMMENCING THE CIVIL LITIGATION ACTION

This chapter begins the civil litigation action and provides some practical points to consider when litigation becomes a reality.

COMMENCING THE CIVIL LITIGATION ACTION Rule 14, *Rules of Civil Procedure*	
Statement of claim, ∏ • issued, served within six months of date of issue, and filed with proof of service	or **Notice of action**, ∏ • issued (served **later** with statement of claim) **Information for court use**, ∏ • not issued or served • filed with notice of action **Statement of claim**, ∏ • filed (not issued) within 30 days of date of issue of notice of action • served, together with notice of action, within six months of date of issue of **notice of action**, and filed with proof of service
Information for court use, ∏ • not issued or served • filed with statement of claim	
∏ (Greek pi) = **P**laintiff	

THE CIVIL LITIGATION ACTION

In civil litigation actions, the plaintiff and defendant are adversaries in the full sense of the word. Each fights hard to win the case. They do not make any admissions or concede anything to the other party unless the law requires them to do so, or it is to their advantage to do so.

The step-by-step progression to trial resembles that of a tennis match. The ball, which starts on the plaintiff's side of the court, goes to the defendant's side, and back and forth between the two players. The plaintiff hopes to prove his or her case in court on the basis of the facts and the law and to obtain compensation from the court. The most frequent form of compensation is an award of money and is known as **damages**. Unless the parties settle out of court, all actions for damages begin with a **statement of claim** and end with a **judgment**.

The court office and court fees   Much of your work involves either written or personal contact with the local court office, which provides services relating to civil litigation actions. The court office charges a fee for each service it provides. The amount of the court fees is set out in a schedule of fees under the *Administration of Justice Act*. The court fees schedule is available on the website of the Ministry of the Attorney General. Make cheques payable to the **Minister of Finance**.

STARTING THE CIVIL LITIGATION ACTION

Rule 14 of the *Rules of Civil Procedure* governs how civil litigation actions are to be started. Subrule 14.03(1) requires that actions be started by a statement of claim or a notice of action. Since these documents originate the civil litigation action, they are collectively referred to as an **originating process**. When you prepare a statement of claim or a notice of action, your firm acts for the **plaintiff** in the action. Prior to preparing the statement of claim or the notice of action, however, much preliminary work is usually carried out, some of which includes:

Opening a new file, making reminders/ticklers, checking for conflict of interest, conducting new client identification and verification, preparing a retainer and preparing any medical authorizations, Precedent 10.6. (Medical authorizations are usually required in cases involving personal injury so that doctors and hospitals who treated a client would release the medical information.) All of these tasks (except for the medical authorization which is inapplicable in the case at hand) have already been completed in Chapters 2 and 3, complete with screen prints and precedents, for our new client NICHOLAS ROMANO, as follows:

NICHOLAS ROMANO — NEW FILE SUMMARY	
New client: Nicholas Romano **Address:** 345 Bogart Avenue Waterwell, Ontario D7M 2U6 **Telephone:** 905-444-3777 Re: Wrongful Dismissal	**Defendant:** Eastern Cast Iron Corporation 9 Cloud Street Waterwell, ON D3K 4B2
Tasks Completed in Chapter 2	Tasks Completed in Chapter 3
1. New Client No. 2887 2. New Matter No. 3005 3. File label 4. Online appointment and online calendar 5. Conflict search 6. Identity verification 7. Online reminder	1. Retainer 2. Online retainer deposit - $1,000 trust account 3. Online cheque requisition re filing of statement of claim
ROMANO v. EASTERN CAST IRON CORPORATION <u>Re: Wrongful Dismissal</u> Mr. Nicholas Romano was fired from his job. We begin his wrongful dismissal case in this chapter. The story unfolds in subsequent chapters as we carry the action to trial. As you will note from the statement of claim (general), Precedent 10.1, Mr. Romano is suing Eastern Cast Iron Corporation for firing him as executive marketing supervisor. We have also prepared the information for court use, Precedent 10.2, which we must file in court when we issue the statement of claim. The notice of action in Precedent 10.3 and the corresponding statement of claim in Precedent 10.4 show you the alternative procedure which would apply if we needed more time to prepare Mr. Romano's statement of claim. See how Eastern Cast Iron Corporation defends in the next chapter.	

PRELIMINARY CONSIDERATIONS

Prior to preparing the statement of claim, the lawyer considers many preliminary items and asks you to do many related tasks, often without telling you why you are doing what you are doing. Lawyers do this. To help you avoid working mechanically, here are some common preliminary considerations and the reasons for them.

IS IT TOO LATE

Limitation periods are time limits within which the plaintiff must **begin** the action or lose the right to do so. Limitation periods range from a few months to, in most cases, two years from the date the problem originally arose. To do an effective job in the law office, you need to have a very strong awareness of the general effects of missed limitation periods. Here is a case in point:

On August 3, a law clerk of a Kenora, Ontario, firm left the statement of claim, together with the court fee, at the court office in Kenora, requesting court staff to issue it. The personal injury case involved a two-year limitation period, expiring on August 5. The court office did not process the statement of claim until August 9, four days after the limitation period had expired, and the defendants Ralph and Bernice Proury moved for summary judgment to dismiss Mr. Rocco Tummillo's action. (Judge L.C. Kozak ruled, however, that the limitation be extended since it was not the plaintiff's fault for missing the limitation period.)

In some court offices, it is common practice to leave documents at the court office counter for issuing, which the court office issues the same day, or at the very latest, the next day. According to the rules, only documents other than an originating process may be **filed** by leaving them at, or mailing them to, the court office. The Kenora case exemplifies the potential danger of missing limitation dates and also the practice variations that may exist among court offices.

IS TITLE OF PROCEEDING CORRECT

Use the legal name of all parties and spell it correctly. Incorrectly named parties do not invalidate the action, but correcting the name after you begin the action is costly and time-consuming as the court may order it done. Lawyers must also ensure that the right party is named plaintiff or defendant. Here is a case in point:

In a Toronto case, *Elia v Kvistbo*, the plaintiff thought he was suing the person who rear-ended him, but found he had no action at all when Mr. Elia's original lawyers, Battiston and Assoc., mistakenly named the driver of the car in **front** of the plaintiff's car as defendant. Mr. Justice Paul T. Matlow dismissed a motion by Mr. Elia's new lawyer, Mr. Harold Rosenberg, to add the correct defendants. Justice Matlow found the original lawyer negligent in suing the wrong party and said the plaintiff "must look other than to the proposed defendants for relief." In addition, the limitation period for adding the right defendant had expired since the original lawyer had started the action only six days before the period expired. The only action available to Mr. Elia would be to sue the original lawyer for damages.

TITLE OF PROCEEDING

The title of proceeding consists of the names of the plaintiff and the defendant, referred to as the parties. The parties in the title of proceeding may include individuals, corporations, partnerships, and sole proprietorships. Follow along on how each of these should be expressed in the title of proceeding and why.

Individuals not under disability Individuals not under disability are adults who are capable of conducting their own affairs. These individuals may represent themselves in law suits, or they may hire a lawyer to represent them. Key at least one given name and the surname (middle name, if any, may be an initial or written out in full) of each adult, usually in block capital letters, thus:

ROBERT YOUNGER	
	Plaintiff
and	
STEPHEN WONDER	
	Defendant

Individuals under disability Individuals under disability are people who are minors (under the age of majority, i.e. under 18), or are mentally incapable, or are otherwise incapable of managing their own affairs. Another person, usually a relative, must stand along with them in the title of proceeding. That person is known as a **litigation guardian**, and all court documents must be served on the litigation guardian. The **Children's Lawyer**, in the case of a minor, or the **Public Guardian and Trustee**, in the case of a mentally incapable adult, may act as litigation guardian if no relative exists or is willing. To ensure individuals under disability are fairly represented in court, they **must** have a lawyer represent them, in addition to being represented by a litigation guardian.

Plaintiff under disability If the party under disability is the plaintiff (or applicant), a litigation guardian, who is not the Children's Lawyer or the Public Guardian and Trustee, may act without court appointment but must consent to so act by filing an affidavit with the court. If the plaintiff under disability has a guardian or an attorney under a power of attorney with authority to act as litigation guardian, then that guardian or attorney has the right to act as litigation guardian before any other individual.

Defendant under disability If the party under disability is the defendant (or respondent), no individual may act as litigation guardian without court approval. This is to ensure the litigation guardian will act in the best interest of the defendant and not of himself or herself. If the defendant under disability has a guardian or an attorney under a power of attorney with authority to act as litigation guardian, then that guardian or attorney has a right to so act before any other individual, but must file an affidavit with the court before acting as litigation guardian. If there is no private individual willing to act, the court appoints the Children's Lawyer for minors and the Public Guardian and Trustee for adults who are mentally incapable (formerly, mentally incompetent) or are otherwise incapable of managing their affairs. The title of proceeding would be thus:

TIMOTHY LITTLE, a minor, by his Litigation Guardian, HAROLD LITTLE	
	Plaintiff
and	
NANCY JONES, a minor, by her Litigation Guardian, the CHILDREN'S LAWYER	
	Defendant

If the litigation guardian acts for a plaintiff or a defendant under disability, as well as for himself or herself personally, e.g. both were injured in the same accident, the title of proceeding would be thus (with parallel wording in the case of defendants):

> TIMOTHY LITTLE, a minor, by his Litigation Guardian, HAROLD LITTLE, and HAROLD LITTLE, personally
>
> Plaintiffs

Corporations   Corporations cannot represent themselves, either as plaintiffs or defendants. A lawyer must represent them, unless the court grants permission otherwise. Since a corporation is not an individual, the law requires a lawyer to represent the corporation so as to limit who can appear on behalf of the corporation and to avoid, for example, a junior employee appearing. A corporation can, however, apply to have a senior executive, e.g. the president, represent it, instead of a lawyer. Use only the registered name of the corporation. To ensure you have the registered name, conduct a name search through the Ministry of Government and Consumer Services. The title of proceeding involving corporations is thus:

> ABC LETTERS LIMITED
>
> Plaintiff
>
> and
>
> 123 NUMBERS INC.
>
> Defendant

Where the corporation operates under a different business name, the title of proceeding would be thus:

> ABC LETTERS LIMITED carrying on business *(or* c.o.b.*)* as THE BOOK CELLAR
>
> Plaintiff
>
> and
>
> 123 NUMBERS INC.
>
> Defendant

Partnerships   Partnerships may sue and be sued in the partnership name, not in the personal names of the partners, unless the partners are suing each other.   If you serve the statement of claim on the partnership (this is accomplished by serving a partner or a person in charge of the business), the judgment binds the partnership property only, not the personal property of the partners. If the lawyer wants the judgment to bind the partnership property as well as the personal property of any or all partners, the lawyer must serve the partnership as well as every partner whom the lawyer wishes to make personally liable. In that case, prepare a **notice to alleged partner, Form 8A**, and serve it, together with the statement of claim, on the partnership and on the particular partner/s. Then, when judgment is obtained, the lawyer can enforce personally against the partner/s, not just against the partnership assets. You may distinguish partnerships from corporations by the absence of the words corporation, limited, or incorporated, or their respective abbreviations, from partnership names. Conduct a partnership name search as in corporations above. The title of proceeding involving partnerships may be styled in one of the following ways:

FAST PAINTING PARTNERS	or JASON DAVID JONES and HENRY BAKER carrying on business (*or* c.o.b.) as FAST PAINTING PARTNERS

Sole proprietorships The information for partnerships applies equally to sole proprietorships, with appropriate modifications. The sole proprietor may sue and be sued in the sole proprietorship's name, and the title of proceeding may be styled in either of the following ways:

BO BOUTIQUE	or BO DEREK carrying on business (*or* c.o.b.) as BO BOUTIQUE

Estate trustee (formerly, executor or administrator)   A deceased's estate may sue or be sued through a **personal representative**. A personal representative is a collective legal description of an **estate trustee with a will** (formerly, executor) and an **estate trustee without a will** (formerly, administrator). If the action is against an estate that has no personal representative, the plaintiff's lawyer must make a motion to the court to have the court appoint a **litigation administrator** to represent the deceased's estate in this litigation only; hence, **litigation** administrator. The following title of proceeding indicates that the estate of the plaintiff has a personal representative and may be styled in either of the ways shown; the estate of the defendant has no personal representative, but rather, has a court appointed litigation administrator:

JEROME SINK, Personal Representative of the Estate of NICOLAS DeBACK

or

JEROME SINK, Estate Trustee with a Will (or without a Will)
of the Estate of NICOLAS DeBACK

Plaintiff

and

THOMAS McPHERSON, Litigation Administrator
of the Estate of CLARKE JAMES GABLE

Defendant

DRAFTING THE STATEMENT OF CLAIM

In drafting the statement of claim, show your firm's respect for the judge by writing plainly, concisely, and without unnecessary use of legalese. See the chapter on "Effective Legal Writing and Oral Presentations." The statement of claim is the first document the defendant receives to tell him or her of the law suit. The statement of claim originates the action and is why it is referred to as an **originating process**. The statement of claim sets out everything the plaintiff claims. Note that if you neglect to include a claim in the statement of claim, your client will lose it because the judge cannot award that which has not been claimed.

Issuing and serving the statement of claim   You must issue the statement of claim and serve an issued copy on the defendant within six months of the date of issuing.

Statement of claim forms   There are two types of statement of claim forms: one is a **statement of claim (for money only)** and the other is a **statement of claim (general)**. Note, however, that both of these types of statements of claim are represented by the same form, Form 14A, which provides for the applicable adjustment. Sometimes, it is difficult to understand why the one form is used and not the other form. Following is some information to help you see which form is used when and why.

STATEMENT OF CLAIM (FOR MONEY ONLY), FORM 14A

Liquidated damages   Read "exact" for "liquidated" damages. If the plaintiff has a bill, invoice, IOU, or some other piece of paper that proves the defendant owes an **exact** amount of **money** to the plaintiff, the claim is for liquidated damages. The form to use is a statement of claim (for money only), Precedent 10.5.

STATEMENT OF CLAIM (GENERAL), FORM 14A

Unliquidated damages   Read "estimated" for "unliquidated" damages. If the plaintiff sues the matchmaker for making the wrong match, the claim is for unliquidated damages, and the form to use is a statement of claim (general), Precedent 10.1. This is so because the amount the plaintiff claims is estimated on the basis of how much suffering the matchmaker caused to the plaintiff; it is, therefore, a general amount.

BASIC CLAIMS IN STATEMENTS OF CLAIM

The following claims are usually included in all statements of claim, whether the statements of claim are for money only or general:

General and special damages   The statement of claim may include both general damages and special damages. General damages is the amount of money the plaintiff claims for loss or injury as a result of the wrongful act of the defendant; special damages are any out-of-pocket expenses the plaintiff was forced to incur as a result of the wrongful act of the defendant, e.g. loss of salary, medical expenses, etc. Include the amount of the general damages claimed and the amount of any special damages known at the time of preparing the statement of claim; notify the defendant in writing before trial of any additional amounts of special damages since special damages may accumulate while the action is in process.

Prejudgment interest   A statement of claim usually includes a claim for prejudgment interest. Prejudgment interest runs from the date the event giving rise to the law suit occurred to the date the court gives the judgment. Prejudgment interest is payable on the amount of damages which the judge orders to be paid. The losing party pays the prejudgment interest as well as the amount of damages ordered payable.

Legal TIP

If the last paragraph on page 1 of a statement of claim, Form 14A, contains a space ($.......) for costs, the statement of claim is for money only.

Legal TIP

Use a for money only form whenever the plaintiff sues to collect on a money debt. Use the general form in all other cases.

Postjudgment interest   A statement of claim usually includes a claim for postjudgment interest. Postjudgment interest is payable on the amount of damages ordered payable and runs from the date the judge gives the judgment to the date the losing party pays the amount of damages ordered payable.

Legal TIP

Always include a claim for prejudgment and postjudgment interest in the statement of claim if there is a dollar figure in the claim. An example of a case without a dollar figure is one when the client wants the neighbour to stop mowing the lawn at four in the morning, i.e. an injunction.

How is prejudgment interest claimed   If the claim is for liquidated damages, the rate of interest is often specified in the original debt, e.g. *IOU this amount at 13 percent interest*. If so, claim "prejudgment interest of 13 percent pursuant to the IOU." If the original debt was silent on the rate of interest, or the claim is for unliquidated damages, claim prejudgment interest under the *Courts of Justice Act* by specifically mentioning the act and the section number, without specifying any percentage rate.

Claiming prejudgment interest under the *Courts of Justice Act* entitles your client to the bank rate of interest that was applicable at the time the event for the action arose. You may obtain the rate of prejudgment interest from the website of the Ministry of the Attorney General; however, at the time of preparing the statement of claim, you need not show the actual rate of interest or any calculation of it in the statement of claim. The lawyer usually needs the actual rate just before the trial to make some kind of pre-calculation of interest so that if the client wins, the lawyer may submit the pre-calculation to the judge for inclusion in the judgment.

How is postjudgment interest claimed   Claim postjudgment interest under the *Courts of Justice Act* by specifically mentioning the act and the section number, without specifying the percentage rate. This entitles your client to claim the interest rate applicable at the time the court gives the judgment. You may obtain the rate of postjudgment interest from the website of the Ministry of the Attorney General.

Costs   Costs are the plaintiff's legal costs. You must claim them to get them if your firm wins. The amount of costs claimed is seldom specified because the legal costs accumulate until the end of the action.

PREPARATION AND DISTRIBUTION OF STATEMENT OF CLAIM (GENERAL), FORM 14A

You require: The lawyer's interview notes; your preliminary consideration notes; any name searches. Follow along in Precedents 10.1 and 10.5. The wording guides completion. Key points include:

Leave the following information blank for the local registrar, or his or her designate, to complete when you issue the statement of claim: court file number, **day** in dates, local registrar's signature. Once the court assigns the court file number, that number must appear on every subsequent court document that relates to the same action. If using the **for money only** form, obtain your firm's policy on what amount to include for costs. Key the court address, usually the one nearest your firm. Write the address of the court office in your area:_____

_____

At **TO:** (means to whom served), key the name and the complete address of the defendant. If there is more than one defendant, leave one blank line and key:
AND TO: for each additional defendant, followed by his or her name and complete address.
The place of trial is the plaintiff's choice and is usually the same court where you issue the statement of claim. Any party to the action may make a motion to the court to change the originally named place of trial. The court may make the change if it finds the change results in a greater overall convenience and if a fair trial cannot be had at the originally named place.

Backsheet: Use a separate sheet of paper for the backsheet. For **proceeding commenced**, key the name of the city where the court in which you will issue the statement of claim is located. For such considerations as fair trial or travel convenience, actions may be **commenced** at one city and **tried** at another. Unless the action is transferred to another city, however, all documents are filed in the court where the action was commenced, and the name of the city on the backsheet indicates which court that is.

Number of copies, minimum 5: Issue the original and keep it in your client's file; file 1 issued copy in the court office; leave 2 issued copies with a process server for service on the defendant; keep 1 issued copy in client's file.

INFORMATION FOR COURT USE, FORM 14F

Subrule 14.03(4.1) requires that an **information for court use, Form 14F**, Precedent 10.2, be filed together with the statement of claim, Form 14A, or notice of action, Form 14C, at the time of issuing Form 14A or Form 14C. Note that the information for court use, Form 14F, is filed in court; it is not issued or served since it is for court use only.

NOTICE OF ACTION, FORM 14C

If the limitation period is close to expiring and there is insufficient time for the lawyer to gather all of the information necessary to prepare a full statement of claim, the lawyer may prepare and have the court issue a **notice of action**, Form 14C, Precedent 10.3, briefly outlining the claim. The notice of action serves two purposes: one, it technically begins the action within the limitation period; and two, it gives the lawyer an additional thirty days to prepare and file the statement of claim in the action.

What happens to the notice of action, Form 14C Have the notice of action, Form 14C, issued but do not serve it yet. File one issued copy of the notice of action, Form 14C, in court, together with an information for court use, Form 14F. Keep the issued original notice of action in the file.

Prepare the statement of claim (action commenced by notice of action), Form 14D, and file (not issue) a copy of it in court within thirty days from the date of issue of the notice of action. Serve a copy of the issued notice of action, Form 14C, together with a copy of the statement of claim (action commenced by notice of action), Form 14D, on the defendant within six months of issuing the notice of action. The statement of claim, Form 14D, is only **filed** instead of **issued** because the notice of action has already been issued, and the court opened its file in the action at that time. The lawyer may change or extend the claim in the statement of claim, (action commenced by notice of action). The instructions for preparing a statement of claim (general) apply to preparing a notice of action, with appropriate modifications.

PREPARATION AND DISTRIBUTION OF STATEMENT OF CLAIM (ACTION COMMENCED BY NOTICE OF ACTION), FORM 14D

You require: The notice of action. Follow along in Precedent 10.4. The wording guides completion. Key points include:

Obtain the court file number and title of proceeding from the issued notice of action. Beneath the title, key the date on which the notice of action was issued; obtain the date of issue from the notice of action. This connects the statement of claim to the notice of action and, therefore, makes issuing the statement of claim unnecessary. The instructions for preparing a regular statement of claim apply, with necessary modifications.

Number of copies, minimum 4: File 1 in the same court office that issued the notice of action; attach 1 each to a copy of the notice of action for a total of 2 sets, and arrange for these to be served together on the defendant; keep 1 in client's file.

CHAPTER SUMMARY

A civil litigation action begins with a statement of claim and, if carried all the way to trial, ends with a judgment. The form of the statement of claim can be for money only, which you would use when the party you are suing owes an exact amount of money, or general, when the amount of money is an estimated amount.

When preparing a statement of claim, be sure that you are within the statutory limitation period for starting the law suit and that the name of the party/ies you are suing is correct. The title of proceeding may also include a litigation guardian and/or the Children's Lawyer as in the case of individuals under disability, or a personal representative (i.e. estate trustee), or a litigation administrator as in the case of deceased individuals. Also, if the law suit involves a claim for money, be sure to also claim prejudgment and postjudgment interest and any special damages (out-of-pocket expenses) that your client incurred, including a claim for costs.

If the limitation period is close to expiring and there is insufficient time for the lawyer to gather all of the information necessary to prepare a statement of claim, the lawyer may prepare and have the court issue a notice of action (instead of a statement of claim). The notice of action begins the action within the limitation period and allows an extra thirty days for the preparation and filing of the statement of claim.

REVIEW QUESTIONS

1. What is a statement of claim?
2. What happens to a statement of claim after it is prepared?
3. What name is given to a person who acts for a plaintiff or a defendant under disability?
4. Which statement of claim form would you use in claims for unliquidated damages?
5. What is the purpose of a notice of action?
6. What details do you obtain from a notice of action when preparing the related statement of claim?
7. What is the difference between liquidated damages and unliquidated damages.
8. What is prejudgment interest?
9. What is postjudgment interest?
10. Explain why in civil litigation a claim for damages means asking to buy damaged goods.

Court File No.

ONTARIO
SUPERIOR COURT OF JUSTICE

B E T W E E N:

(Court Seal)

NICHOLAS ROMANO

Plaintiff

and

EASTERN CAST IRON CORPORATION

Defendant

STATEMENT OF CLAIM

TO THE DEFENDANT(S):

A LEGAL PROCEEDING HAS BEEN COMMENCED AGAINST YOU by the Plaintiff. The Claim made against you is set out in the following pages.

IF YOU WISH TO DEFEND THIS PROCEEDING, you or an Ontario lawyer acting for you must prepare a Statement of Defence in Form 18A prescribed by the *Rules of Civil Procedure*, serve it on the Plaintiff's lawyer or, where the Plaintiff does not have a lawyer, serve it on the Plaintiff, and file it, with proof of service, in this court office, WITHIN TWENTY DAYS after this Statement of Claim is served on you, if you are served in Ontario.

If you are served in another province or territory of Canada or in the United States of America, the period for serving and filing your Statement of Defence is forty days. If you are served outside Canada and the United States of America, the period is sixty days.

Instead of serving and filing a Statement of Defence, you may serve and file a Notice of Intent to Defend in Form 18B prescribed by the *Rules of Civil Procedure*. This will entitle you to ten more days within which to serve and file your Statement of Defence.

IF YOU FAIL TO DEFEND THIS PROCEEDING, JUDGMENT MAY BE GIVEN AGAINST YOU IN YOUR ABSENCE AND WITHOUT FURTHER NOTICE TO YOU. IF YOU WISH TO DEFEND THIS PROCEEDING BUT ARE UNABLE TO PAY LEGAL FEES, LEGAL AID MAY BE AVAILABLE TO YOU BY CONTACTING A LOCAL LEGAL AID OFFICE.

TAKE NOTICE THIS ACTION WILL AUTOMATICALLY BE DISMISSED if it has not been set down for trial or terminated by any means within five years after the action was commenced unless otherwise ordered by the court.

Date _____November_____, (year)   Issued by _____

Local Registrar

Address of court   393 University Avenue, 10th Floor
office: Toronto, Ontario M5G 1E6

TO: **EASTERN CAST IRON CORPORATION**
           9 Cloud Street
           Waterwell, ON D3K 4B2

-2-

CLAIM

1.   THE PLAINTIFF CLAIMS:

   (a) damages in the amount of $190,000 for wrongful dismissal with respect to his employment with the Defendant or, in the alternative, damages in the amount of $190,000 for breach of contract of employment by the Defendant;

   (b)   prejudgment interest from October 14, 20--, to the date of judgment, pursuant to section 128 of the *Courts of Justice Act,* RSO 1990, c C.43, as amended;

   (c) his costs of this action, plus harmonized sales tax;

   (d) postjudgment interest on the amounts described in paragraphs (a), (b), and (c) from the date of judgment to the date of payment, pursuant to section 129 of the *Courts of Justice Act,* RSO 1990, c C.43, as amended;

   (e) such further and other relief as to this Honourable Court may seem just.

2.   The Plaintiff is a resident of the City of Waterwell and until on or about the 14th day of October, 20--, held the position of executive marketing supervisor with the Defendant.

3.   The Defendant is a corporation incorporated pursuant to the laws of the Province of Ontario and at all material times carried on business in Ontario as a cast iron retailer.

4.   On or about the 14th day of October, 20--, and effective the 18th day of October, 20--, the Plaintiff was suddenly and without warning dismissed from his employment as executive marketing supervisor of the Defendant without just cause and without any or adequate notice or remuneration in lieu of notice.

Legal Office Procedures

-3-

5.   As a result of the Defendant's breach of contract, the Plaintiff has sustained damages, including such remuneration as he would otherwise have enjoyed during any reasonable period of notice and the value of bonus payments and the value of all other benefits attached to his contract of employment.

6.   The Plaintiff has suffered and is continuing to suffer loss of income and loss of other benefits as a result of his wrongful dismissal by the Defendant or, in the alternative, as a result of the Defendant's breach of contract.   In addition, the Plaintiff has incurred expenses in his attempts to obtain employment, particulars of which will be provided prior to trial.

The Plaintiff proposes that this action be tried at: Toronto

  November   , 20--   **MICHAEL, ELIAD & REDFORD LLP**
(Date of issue)   Barristers and Solicitors
                                        863 Seneca Lane
                                        Toronto, Ontario
                                        M4J 1P6

                                        Robert B. Redford
                                        Tel: 416-363-1079
                                        Fax: 416-363-2628

                                        Lawyers for the Plaintiff

NICHOLAS ROMANO
Plaintiff

-and- EASTERN CAST IRON CORPORATION
Defendant

Court File No.

ONTARIO
SUPERIOR COURT OF JUSTICE

PROCEEDING COMMENCED AT
TORONTO

STATEMENT OF CLAIM

MICHAEL, ELIAD & REDFORD LLP
Barristers and Solicitors
863 Seneca Lane
Toronto, Ontario
M4J 1P6

Robert B. Redford (48000R)
Tel: 416-363-1079
Fax: 416-363-2628
rbrdfrd@mer.com

Lawyers for the Plaintiff

Court File No.

ONTARIO
SUPERIOR COURT OF JUSTICE

B E T W E E N :

NICHOLAS ROMANO

Plaintiff

and

EASTERN CAST IRON CORPORATION

Defendant

INFORMATION FOR COURT USE

1. This proceeding is an: [X] action [ ] application
2. Has it been commenced under the *Class Proceedings Act*, 1992?   [ ] yes   [X] no

3. If the proceeding is an action, does Rule 76 (Simplified Procedure) [ ] yes [X] no apply?
NOTE: Subject to the exceptions found in subrule 76.01(1), it is MANDATORY to proceed under Rule 76 for all cases in which the money amount claimed or the value of real or personal property claimed is $100,000 or less.

4. The Claim in this proceeding (action or application) is in respect of:

(Select the __one__ item that __best__ describes the nature of the main claim in the proceeding.)

Bankruptcy or insolvency law	[ ]	Motor vehicle accident	[ ]
Collection of liquidated debt	[ ]	Municipal law	[ ]
Constitutional law	[ ]	Partnership law	[ ]
Construction law (other than construction lien)	[ ]	Personal property security	[ ]
Construction lien	[ ]	Product liability	[ ]
Contract law	[X]	Professional malpractice (other than medical)	[ ]
Corporate law	[ ]	Real property (including leases; excluding mortgage or charge)	[ ]
Defamation	[ ]	Tort: economic injury (other than from medical or professional malpractice)	[ ]
Employment or labour law	[ ]		
Intellectual property law	[ ]	Tort: personal injury (other than from motor vehicle accident)	[ ]
Judicial review	[ ]	Trusts, fiduciary duty	[ ]
Medical malpractice	[ ]	Wills, estates	[ ]
Mortgage or charge	[ ]		

CERTIFICATION

I certify that the above information is correct, to the best of my knowledge.

Date: _____   _____
Signature of lawyer
(if no lawyer, party must sign)

(Needs no backsheet)

Court File No.

ONTARIO
SUPERIOR COURT OF JUSTICE

B E T W E E N:

(Court Seal)

NICHOLAS ROMANO

Plaintiff

and

EASTERN CAST IRON CORPORATION

Defendant

NOTICE OF ACTION

TO THE DEFENDANT(S)

    A LEGAL PROCEEDING HAS BEEN COMMENCED AGAINST YOU by the Plaintiff. The Claim made against you is set out in the Statement of Claim served with this Notice of Action.

    IF YOU WISH TO DEFEND THIS PROCEEDING, you or an Ontario lawyer acting for you must prepare a Statement of Defence in Form 18A prescribed by the *Rules of Civil Procedure*, serve it on the Plaintiff's lawyer or, where the Plaintiff does not have a lawyer, serve it on the Plaintiff, and file it, with proof of service, in this court office, WITHIN TWENTY DAYS after this Notice of Action is served on you, if you are served in Ontario.

    If you are served in another province or territory of Canada or in the United States of America, the period for serving and filing your Statement of Defence is forty days. If you are served outside Canada and the United States of America, the period is sixty days.

    Instead of serving and filing a Statement of Defence, you may serve and file a Notice of Intent to Defend in Form 18B prescribed by the *Rules of Civil Procedure*. This will entitle you to ten more days within which to serve and file your Statement of Defence.

    IF YOU FAIL TO DEFEND THIS PROCEEDING, JUDGMENT MAY BE GIVEN AGAINST YOU IN YOUR ABSENCE AND WITHOUT FURTHER NOTICE TO YOU. IF YOU WISH TO DEFEND THIS PROCEEDING BUT ARE UNABLE TO PAY LEGAL FEES, LEGAL AID MAY BE AVAILABLE TO YOU BY CONTACTING A LOCAL LEGAL AID OFFICE.

    TAKE NOTICE THIS ACTION WILL AUTOMATICALLY BE DISMISSED if it has not been set down for trial or terminated by any means within five years after the action was commenced unless otherwise ordered by the court.

Date   November 3   , (year)   Issued by   _____

    Local Registrar

Address of court
office: 393 University Avenue
    10th Floor
    Toronto, Ontario
    M5G 1E6

TO: **EASTERN CAST IRON CORPORATION**
    9 Cloud Street
    Waterwell, ON D3K 4B2

NICHOLAS ROMANO
Plaintiff

-and-   EASTERN CAST IRON CORPORATION
Defendant

Court File No.

ONTARIO
SUPERIOR COURT OF JUSTICE

PROCEEDING COMMENCED AT
TORONTO

NOTICE OF ACTION

MICHAEL, ELIAD & REDFORD LLP
Barristers and Solicitors
863 Seneca Lane
Toronto, Ontario
M4J 1P6

Robert B. Redford (48000R)
Tel: 416-363-1079
Fax: 416-363-2628
rbrdfrd@mer.com

Lawyers for the Plaintiff

-2-

CLAIM

1.   The Plaintiff's claim is for

(a)   damages in the amount of $190,000 for wrongful dismissal or, in the

alternative, for breach of contract of employment by the Defendant;

(b)   prejudgment and postjudgment interest pursuant to sections 128 and 129

of the *Courts of Justice Act*, RSO 1990, c C.43, as amended;

(c)   his costs of this action, plus harmonized sales tax;

(d)   such further and other relief as to this Honourable Court may seem just.

Date of issue

MICHAEL, ELIAD & REDFORD LLP
Barristers and Solicitors
863 Seneca Lane
Toronto, Ontario
M4J 1P6

Robert B. Redford
Tel: 416-363-1079
Fax: 416-363-2628

Lawyers for the Plaintiff

Court File No.   CV-**-76542

ONTARIO
SUPERIOR COURT OF JUSTICE

B E T W E E N :

NICHOLAS ROMANO

Plaintiff

and

EASTERN CAST IRON CORPORATION

Defendant

STATEMENT OF CLAIM
Notice of Action issued on November 3, (year)

1.   The Plaintiff claims:

(a)   damages in the amount of $190,000 for wrongful dismissal with respect to

his employment with the Defendant or, in the alternative, damages in the amount

of $190,000 for breach of contract of employment by the Defendant;

(b)   prejudgment interest from October 14, 20--, to the date of

judgment, pursuant to section 128 of the *Courts of Justice Act*, RSO

1990, c C.43, as amended;

(c)   his costs of this action, plus harmonized sales tax;

(d)   postjudgment interest on the amounts described in paragraphs (a),

(b), and (c) from the date of judgment to the date of payment, pursuant to

section 129 of the *Courts of Justice Act*, RSO 1990, c C.43, as amended;

(e)   such further and other relief as to this Honourable Court may seem just.

-2-

2.   The Plaintiff is a resident of the City of Waterwell and until on or about the 14th day of October, 20--, held the position of executive marketing supervisor with Eastern Cast Iron Corporation.

3.   The Defendant is a corporation incorporated pursuant to the laws of the Province of Ontario and at all material times carried on business in Ontario as a cast iron retailer.

4.   On or about the 14th day of October, 20--, and effective the 18th day of October, 20--, the Plaintiff was suddenly and without warning dismissed from his employment as executive marketing supervisor of the Defendant without just cause and without any or adequate notice or remuneration in lieu of notice...

Date: November 11, 20--

MICHAEL, ELIAD & REDFORD LLP
Barristers and Solicitors
863 Seneca Lane
Toronto, Ontario
M4J 1P6

Robert B. Redford
Tel: 416-363-1079
Fax: 416-363-2628

Lawyers for the Plaintiff

(prepare backsheet)

Court File No.

ONTARIO
SUPERIOR COURT OF JUSTICE

B E T W E E N :

(Court Seal)

ROBERT YOUNGER

Plaintiff

and

STEPHEN WONDER

Defendant

STATEMENT OF CLAIM

TO THE DEFENDANT(S):

A LEGAL PROCEEDING HAS BEEN COMMENCED AGAINST YOU by the Plaintiff. The Claim made against you is set out in the following pages.

IF YOU WISH TO DEFEND THIS PROCEEDING, you or an Ontario lawyer acting for you must prepare a Statement of Defence in Form 18A prescribed by the *Rules of Civil Procedure*, serve it on the Plaintiff's lawyer or, where the Plaintiff does not have a lawyer, serve it on the Plaintiff, and file it, with proof of service, in this court office, WITHIN TWENTY DAYS after this Statement of Claim is served on you, if you are served in Ontario.

If you are served in another province or territory of Canada or in the United States of America, the period for serving and filing your Statement of Defence is forty days. If you are served outside Canada and the United States of America, the period is sixty days.

Instead of serving and filing a Statement of Defence, you may serve and file a Notice of Intent to Defend in Form 18B prescribed by the *Rules of Civil Procedure*. This will entitle you to ten more days within which to serve and file your Statement of Defence.

IF YOU FAIL TO DEFEND THIS PROCEEDING, JUDGMENT MAY BE GIVEN AGAINST YOU IN YOUR ABSENCE AND WITHOUT FURTHER NOTICE TO YOU. IF YOU WISH TO DEFEND THIS PROCEEDING BUT ARE UNABLE TO PAY LEGAL FEES, LEGAL AID MAY BE AVAILABLE TO YOU BY CONTACTING A LOCAL LEGAL AID OFFICE.

IF YOU PAY THE PLAINTIFF'S CLAIM, and $750.00 for costs, within the time for serving and filing your Statement of Defence, you may move to have this proceeding dismissed by the Court. If you believe the amount claimed for costs is excessive, you may pay the Plaintiff's Claim and $400.00 for costs and have the costs assessed by the Court.

TAKE NOTICE THIS ACTION WILL AUTOMATICALLY BE DISMISSED if it has not been set down for trial or terminated by any means within five years after the action was commenced unless otherwise ordered by the court.

Date ___September_____ , (year)   Issued by _____

Local Registrar

Address of court   393 University Avenue, 10th Floor
office: Toronto, Ontario
                            M5G 1E6

TO: **STEPHEN WONDER**
             132 Fairmeadow Avenue
             Waterwell, ON D3K 4B2

Legal Office Procedures

-2-

CLAIM

1.   The Plaintiff claims:

(a)   the amount of $187,498.43;

(b)   prejudgment interest on this amount in accordance with section 128 of the *Courts of Justice Act*, RSO 1990, c C.43, as amended, from March 1, 20--, to the date of judgment;

(c)   his costs of this action, plus harmonized sales tax;

(d)   postjudgment interest in accordance with sections 129 of the *Courts of Justice Act*, RSO 1990, c C.43, as amended, from the date of judgment to the date of payment;

(e)   such further and other relief as to this Honourable Court may seem just.

2.   The Plaintiff resides in the City of Waterwell, in the Province of Ontario, and is engaged in the business of renovating and repairing buildings.

3.   The Defendant resides in the City of Waterwell, in the Province of Ontario.

4.   In or about the month of March 20--, the Defendant hired the Plaintiff to do alterations to the property known municipally as 13 Ralph Road, Waterwell, Ontario.

5.   By letter dated September 8, 20--, the Defendant informed the Plaintiff that these premises were owned by R. B. Head Limited and that all future billings were to be amended accordingly.

6.   The Plaintiff billed the Defendant a total of $199,499.50. Of this amount, the Defendant has paid the sum of $12,001.07, with $187,498.43 remaining outstanding.

7.   Despite the Plaintiff's repeated requests, the Defendant has refused or neglected to pay this amount.

The Plaintiff proposes that this action be tried at: Toronto

September   , 20--
(Date of issue)

MICHAEL, ELIAD & REDFORD LLP
Barristers and Solicitors
863 Seneca Lane
Toronto, Ontario M4J 1P6

Robert B. Redford
Tel: 416-363-1079
Fax: 416-363-2628

Lawyers for the Plaintiff

(prepare backsheet)

AUTHORIZATION

TO: *(Name and address of doctor/hospital)*

Re: **John James Smith** (*client*)
               Date of Loss:
               Date of Birth:
               OHIP No.:
               Our File No.:

THIS IS YOUR AUTHORIZATION AND DIRECTION to release to:

MICHAEL, ELIAD & REDFORD LLP
Barristers and Solicitors
863 Seneca Lane
Toronto, Ontario
M4J 1P6

Telephone No. (416) 363-1079

my complete file, including but not limited to: all clinical notes and records, reports, charts, consultation reports, original radiographs, tests, photographs, and copies of same in your possession, and this shall be your good and sufficient authority for so doing.

DATED at Toronto, Ontario, this _____ day November, 20--.

_____   _____
Witness   John James Smith

CHAPTER 11

DEFENDING THE CIVIL LITIGATION ACTION

This chapter covers the pleadings stage of the civil litigation action where the defendant gets to tell his or her side of the story.

THE PLEADINGS STAGE	
Statement of defence, Δ • delivered within 20/40/60 days after service of statement of claim **Reply**, ⊓ • delivered within 10 days after service of statement of defence **Jury notice**, ⊓ or Δ • delivered at any time before close of pleadings ⊓ (Greek pi) = Plaintiff Δ (Greek delta) = Defendant	or **Notice of intent to defend**, Δ • delivered within 20/40/60 days after service of statement of claim **Statement of defence**, Δ • delivered within 30 days after service of statement of claim
CLOSE OF PLEADINGS	

ROMANO v. EASTERN CAST IRON CORPORATION
Re: Wrongful Dismissal

We continue with Mr. Romano's file. Castles & Sands, the lawyers for Eastern Cast Iron Corporation, have now served us with a notice of intent to defend, Precedent 11.1, and a statement of defence, Precedent 11.2. According to the defendant's statement of defence, Mr. Romano's performance as executive marketing supervisor was unsatisfactory; furthermore, Mr. Romano apparently agreed with the performance assessment and also agreed to go down a level and take the position of an office manager, which he accepted and then voluntarily left the company.

In response to Eastern's statement of defence, we served Castles & Sands with Mr. Romano's reply, Precedent 11.3. In his reply, Mr. Romano states that he rejected Eastern's offer of the position of office manager because Eastern offered him a salary that was $10,000 less than what he was making when the defendant fired him. Mr. Romano also states in the reply that the defendant praised Mr. Romano's performance as executive marketing supervisor as being exemplary.

We will now leave it up to a jury to decide, and we have served Castles & Sands with a jury notice, Precedent 11.4. The pleadings are now closed in this action; the next stage is discoveries.

PLEADINGS

Pleadings are called so because they provide an opportunity for the parties to plead, or tell, their side of the story. Pleadings include such documents as statements of defence, replies, and counterclaims. The pleadings stage usually begins when a defendant is served with a statement of claim and retains a lawyer to defend the action. Usually, the lawyer interviews the defendant, checks for conflict of interest, checks the client's identity, obtains a retainer, and begins to act for the defendant by preparing the statement of defence on behalf of the defendant.

Time is of the essence   Pleadings must be delivered (served and filed with proof of service) within the time limits specified in the *Rules of Civil Procedure*. The time limits follow a **20/40/60** rule. If the defendant misses the prescribed time limit, the plaintiff may note the defendant in default and win the case automatically, without carrying the action to trial. Lawyers will often extend the time periods specified in the rules, but this is always subject to the client's instructions.

THE 20/40/60 RULE	
PRESCRIBED TIME FOR DELIVERY OF STATEMENT OF DEFENCE	PLACE OF SERVICE
20 days after statement of claim	If claim served in Ontario
40 days after statement of claim	If claim served elsewhere in Canada or USA
60 days after statement of claim	Anywhere else
Add 10 days to each time frame noted above	If notice of intent to defend is filed within the prescribed time

Dismissal of action for delay   Under rule 48.14, the registrar will dismiss an action for delay if the action has not been set down for trial or terminated by any means within five years of the commencement of the action. The registrar will serve on the parties an order dismissing the action, and the lawyer who was served with such an order must promptly give a copy of the order to his or her client.

Amendment to pleadings   Rule 26 permits amendments to pleadings, provided the amendments do not add or remove a party in the action. Generally, a party may make a change in his or her pleading, e.g. withdraw something he or she has admitted to, **before** the close of pleadings, i.e. before all the pleadings have been served and filed. If a party wishes to make amendments to a pleading **after** the close of pleadings, or if the amendment adds or removes a party in the action, the party requiring the amendment must obtain the court's permission.

How amendments to pleadings are distinguished   The lawyer making amendments to a pleading distinguishes the amended part by underlining it in black once for the first amendment, twice for a second, and three times for a third. If the amendments are extensive, the lawyer must file a fresh copy, date it the same date as the original pleading, and entitle it "amended statement of defence" (or claim, or other). The local registrar approves the amended pleading by checking the rule number, or other authority under which the amendment is authorized, signing the amended pleading, and keeping a copy of it. The lawyer making the change serves the amended pleading on all parties.

NOTICE OF INTENT TO DEFEND, FORM 18B

The notice of intent to defend, Form 18B, buys time--ten more days than the time allowed--in which to deliver (serve and file with proof) the statement of defence. Deliver the notice of intent to defend, Form 18B, Precedent 11.1, within **twenty days** of the date of service of the statement of claim. Use it only when there is insufficient time within the twenty-day time limit to prepare the statement of defence; otherwise, skip it and deliver only the statement of defence. If preparing a notice of intent to defend, key the court file number and the title of proceeding as they appear in the statement of claim.

Number of copies, minimum 3:   Serve 1 on plaintiff's lawyer; file 1, with proof of service, in court office where action was commenced; keep 1 in client's file.

STATEMENT OF DEFENCE, FORM 18A

The statement of defence, Form 18A, Precedent 11.2, is the defendant's side of the story. Deliver it (serve and file with proof) within **twenty days** of the date of service of the statement of claim, or within **thirty days** of the date of service of the statement of claim if you have delivered a notice of intent to defend.

Drafting the statement of defence   Show your firm's respect for the judge by writing plainly, concisely, and with no unnecessary legalese. See the chapter on "Effective Legal Writing and Oral Presentations" in this manual. Address every paragraph or allegation contained in the plaintiff's statement of claim as follows:

By admission, e.g. The defendant admits the allegation contained in paragraph 2 of the statement of claim.
By denial, e.g. The defendant denies the allegation contained in paragraph 3 of the statement of claim.
By statement of no knowledge, e.g. The defendant has no knowledge of the allegations contained in paragraphs 4 and 7 of the statement of claim.

Silence about an allegation may be deemed an admission, with one exception: the amount of damages claimed is deemed to be denied, unless the defendant specifically admits it. In preparing the statement of defence, Form 18A, key the court file number and the title of proceeding as they appear in the statement of claim.

Number of copies, minimum 3: Serve 1 on plaintiff's lawyer; file 1, with proof of service, in court office where action was commenced; keep 1 in client's file.

REPLY, FORM 25A

A reply, Form 25A, Precedent 11.3, is the plaintiff's reply, or response, to the defendant's statement of defence. Deliver a reply, if any, within **ten days** of service of the statement of defence. The court deems the plaintiff to automatically **deny** the allegations made in the defendant's statement of defence; therefore, deliver a reply only if:

1. the plaintiff intends to prove a version of the facts that is different from the version that the defendant claims in the statement of defence, which version the plaintiff has not already pleaded in the statement of claim, or
2. the plaintiff's allegations, when not pleaded, would take the defendant by surprise at trial.

Number of copies, minimum 3: Serve 1 copy of the reply on defendant's lawyers; file 1, with proof of service, in court where the action was commenced; keep 1 in client's file.

JURY NOTICE, FORM 47A

The plaintiff or the defendant may request a trial by jury by delivering a jury notice, Form 47A, Precedent 11.4, at any time before the close of pleadings. The *Courts of Justice Act* states which trials may be tried with or without a jury. Generally, liquidated damages cases are heard without a jury because the amount claimed is usually clear cut; hence, there is little on which a jury could deliberate. Unliquidated claims, on the other hand, usually those resulting from torts, e.g. personal injury, may be heard by a jury if either party so chooses. The jury in these cases deliberates on establishing fault or blame in the wrongful act and decides on the appropriate amount of damages. Generally, electing trial by jury is based on how likely it is for the party electing it to sway the jury's sympathy in that party's favour.

Number of copies, minimum 3: Serve 1 copy on opposite lawyer; file 1, with proof of service, in court where action was commenced; keep 1 in client's file.

CLOSE OF PLEADINGS

The close of pleadings **closes** the pleadings stage. This means all parties who should have delivered a pleading (a defence or counterclaim) either have already done so, or have been noted in default for not doing so. Generally, noting in default means the parties who have not delivered a pleading can no longer do so because the time for doing so has elapsed. Once the pleadings are noted closed, a party can neither deliver a pleading nor receive notice of any steps in the action, unless the court orders otherwise.

Legal Office Procedures

CHAPTER SUMMARY

The pleadings stage is where the opposing side gets to tell his or her side of the story. The deadline for delivering a statement of defence is twenty days after service of the statement of claim. A defendant can deliver a notice of intent to defend, which gives the defendant an extra ten days to prepare and deliver a statement of defence. When the statement of defence raises a new point which requires a response, the plaintiff responds by delivering a reply. All pleadings must be served on the opposing parties and filed in court, with proof of service, for the court's records. A jury notice is served and filed when a party chooses a trial by jury. A **close of pleadings** generally means the deadline for serving and filing pleadings has passed, and any parties who have failed to file a pleading can no longer do so, unless the court orders otherwise.

REVIEW QUESTIONS

1. What is a statement of defence?
2. In what situation is a notice of intent to defend used?
3. What types of actions are usually tried without a jury?
4. What does "close of pleadings" mean?
5. A statement of defence is prepared and served by the plaintiff. Explain.
6. In what situation would the delivery of a reply be necessary?

Court File No.   CV-**-76542

ONTARIO
SUPERIOR COURT OF JUSTICE

B E T W E E N:

NICHOLAS ROMANO

Plaintiff

and

EASTERN CAST IRON CORPORATION

Defendant

NOTICE OF INTENT TO DEFEND

The Defendant, Eastern Cast Iron Corporation, intends to defend this action.

Date: November 5, 20--

         CASTLES & SANDS
         Suite 900-205 Portage Street
         Markham, Ontario   L3R 3G3

         Raymond G. Castles
         Tel: 905-495-2222
         Fax: 905-495-2223

         Lawyers for the Defendant

TO: **MICHAEL, ELIAD & REDFORD LLP**
         Barristers and Solicitors
         863 Seneca Lane
         Toronto, Ontario
         M4J 1P6

         Robert B. Redford
         Tel: 416-363-1079
         Fax: 416-363-2628

         Lawyers for the Plaintiff

(prepare backsheet)

Court File No.   CV-**-76542

ONTARIO
SUPERIOR COURT OF JUSTICE

B E T W E E N:

NICHOLAS ROMANO

Plaintiff

and

EASTERN CAST IRON CORPORATION

Defendant

STATEMENT OF DEFENCE

1.   The Defendant, Eastern Cast Iron Corporation, admits the allegations contained in paragraphs 2 and 3 of the Statement of Claim.

2.   The Defendant denies the allegations contained in paragraphs 4 and 5 of the Statement of Claim.

3.   The Defendant has no knowledge in respect of the allegations contained in paragraph 6 of the Statement of Claim and puts the Plaintiff to the strict proof of them.

4.   The Defendant pleads that on October 14, 20--, a representative of the Defendant discussed with the Plaintiff the Plaintiff's performance as executive marketing supervisor of the Defendant.   The Defendant's representative pointed out to the Plaintiff that the Plaintiff's performance as an executive marketing supervisor had not been satisfactory.   The Plaintiff agreed with the assessment and further agreed that he should return to being an office manager, which position he had held prior to being an executive marketing supervisor.

-2-

5.   The Defendant pleads that the Plaintiff, after having accepted the position of office manager, voluntarily left the employment of the Defendant and is not entitled to any damages for wrongful dismissal or otherwise.

6.   Further, and in the alternative, the Defendant pleads that if the Plaintiff is entitled to any damages for wrongful dismissal, then such damages should be reduced by reason of the failure of the Plaintiff to perform his services as executive marketing supervisor in a satisfactory fashion.

Date: November 15, 20--

CASTLES & SANDS
Suite 900-205 Portage Street
Markham, Ontario   L3R 3G3

Raymond G. Castles
Tel: 905-495-2222
Fax: 905-495-2223

Lawyers for the Defendant

TO: **MICHAEL, ELIAD & REDFORD LLP**
Barristers and Solicitors
863 Seneca Lane
Toronto, Ontario
M4J 1P6

Robert B. Redford
Tel: 416-363-1079
Fax: 416-363-2628

Lawyers for the Plaintiff

Legal Office Procedures

Court File No. CV-**-76542

NICHOLAS ROMANO
Plaintiff

-and-

EASTERN CAST IRON CORPORATION
Defendant

ONTARIO
SUPERIOR COURT OF JUSTICE

PROCEEDING COMMENCED AT
TORONTO

STATEMENT OF DEFENCE

CASTLES & SANDS
Suite 900–205 Portage Street
Markham, Ontario L3R 3G3

Raymond G. Castles (36996F)
Tel: 905-495-2222
Fax: 905-495-2223
raymond@castlessands.ca

Lawyers for the Defendant

Court File No.   CV-**-76542

ONTARIO
SUPERIOR COURT OF JUSTICE

B E T W E E N:

NICHOLAS ROMANO

Plaintiff

and

EASTERN CAST IRON CORPORATION

Defendant

REPLY

1.   The Plaintiff, Nicholas Romano, admits the allegations contained in paragraph 1 of the Statement of Defence.

2.   The Plaintiff denies the allegations contained in paragraphs 3 to 6, inclusive, of the Statement of Defence.

3.   The Plaintiff rejected the Defendant's offer of a position as an office manager on or about the 16th day of October, 20--, as the Defendant offered a salary in the amount of $40,000 per year, $10,000 lower than the Plaintiff's rate of salary at the time of his dismissal.

4.   The Defendant failed to offer an alternative position to the Plaintiff commensurate with the Plaintiff's experience and responsibilities and the remuneration and benefits that the Plaintiff enjoyed as at the date of his termination.

5.   At no time prior to October 14, 20--, did the Defendant express any dissatisfaction whatsoever with the Plaintiff's performance as an executive marketing supervisor.   The

-2-

Defendant, in fact, had informed the Plaintiff on a number of occasions prior to October 14, 20--,

that the Plaintiff's performance of his duties as executive marketing supervisor was exemplary.

Date: November 23, 20--

MICHAEL, ELIAD & REDFORD LLP
Barristers and Solicitors
863 Seneca Lane
Toronto, Ontario
M4J 1P6

Robert B. Redford
Tel: 416-363-1079
Fax: 416-363-2628

Lawyers for the Plaintiff

TO: **CASTLES & SANDS**
Suite 900-205 Portage Street
Markham, Ontario   L3R 3G3

Raymond G. Castles
Tel: 905-495-2222
Fax: 905-495-2223

Lawyers for the Defendant

(prepare backsheet)

Court File No.   CV-**-76542

ONTARIO
SUPERIOR COURT OF JUSTICE

B E T W E E N:

NICHOLAS ROMANO

Plaintiff

and

EASTERN CAST IRON CORPORATION

Defendant

JURY NOTICE

THE PLAINTIFF, NICHOLAS ROMANO, REQUIRES that this action be tried by a

jury.

Date: November 27, 20--

MICHAEL, ELIAD & REDFORD LLP
Barristers and Solicitors
863 Seneca Lane
Toronto, Ontario
M4J 1P6

Robert B. Redford
Tel: 416-363-1079
Fax: 416-363-2628

Lawyers for the Plaintiff

TO: **CASTLES & SANDS**
Suite 900-205 Portage Street
Markham, Ontario   L3R 3G3

Raymond G. Castles
Tel: 905-495-2222
Fax: 905-495-2223

Lawyers for the Defendant

(prepare backsheet)

CHAPTER 12

COUNTERCLAIMS AND THIRD PARTY CLAIMS

This chapter covers that part of the pleadings stage that tells everybody's side of the story through pleadings that are collectively referred to as counterclaims.

COUNTERCLAIMS

Counterclaims are pleadings where parties to actions can make claims against each other as well as against new parties. The pleadings involved in counterclaims include the following:

Statement of Defence and Counterclaim (Against Parties to Main Action Only), Form 27A	Statement of Defence and Counterclaim (Against Plaintiff and Person Not Already Party to Main Action), Form 27B

Defence to Counterclaim, Form 27C Reply to Defence to Counterclaim, Form 27D

STATEMENT OF DEFENCE AND COUNTERCLAIM (AGAINST PARTIES TO MAIN ACTION ONLY), FORM 27A

In this counterclaim, the defendant basically states, "Not only do I not owe the plaintiff any money, but the plaintiff owes me money." The first part of the pleading is the defence to the plaintiff's statement of claim, and the second part is the counterclaim against the plaintiff; hence, statement of defence **and** counterclaim. The lawyer for the defendant must serve the statement of defence and counterclaim (against parties to main action only), Form 27A, Precedent 12.1, on all parties to the action within **20/40/60 days** after service of the statement of claim and file it, with proof of service, in the court office where the action was commenced.

STATEMENT OF DEFENCE AND COUNTERCLAIM (AGAINST PLAINTIFF AND PERSON NOT ALREADY PARTY TO MAIN ACTION), FORM 27B

In this counterclaim, the defendant, Fred, defends the action against the plaintiff, Barnie, and counterclaims against the plaintiff Barnie **and** against a new person, George. The statement of defence and counterclaim (against plaintiff and person not already party to main action), Form 27B, Precedent 12.2, differs from the one where the counterclaim is against the parties to the main action, as follows:

1. The heading of the statement of defence and counterclaim (Form 27B) contains a second title of proceeding, which must also appear on all subsequent documents, e.g:

First title of proceeding:	Barnie is plaintiff and Fred is defendant
Second title of proceeding:	Fred is plaintiff by counterclaim and Barnie and George are defendants to the counterclaim

STATEMENT OF DEFENCE AND COUNTERCLAIM

2. Form 27B must be issued because it constitutes an originating process against the new party (George) being brought in.

3. Rule 27.04 requires that where a new party is being brought in, Form 27B be served, after it has been issued, on the parties to the main action and, together with all the pleadings previously delivered in the main action, on a defendant to the counterclaim who is not already a party to the main action, and be filed with proof of service within **thirty days** after the statement of defence and counterclaim is issued, or at anytime before the defendant is noted in default.

DEFENCE TO COUNTERCLAIM, FORM 27C

Under Rule 27.05, the defence to counterclaim, Form 27C, Precedent 12.3, is delivered as follows:

(1) The plaintiff and any other defendant to a counterclaim who is already a party to the main action shall deliver a defence to counterclaim, Form 27C, within 20 days after service of the statement of defence and counterclaim.

(2) Where the plaintiff delivers a reply in the main action, the defence to counterclaim shall be included in the same document as the reply and the document shall be entitled a reply and defence to counterclaim.

(3) A defendant to a counterclaim who is not already a party to the main action shall deliver a defence to counterclaim, Form 27C, within 20/40/60 days after service of the statement of defence and counterclaim.

For example:

After being served with the statement of defence and counterclaim (against plaintiff and person not already party to main action), Form 27B, the following would apply:

Defence to counterclaim, Form 27C, by Barnie
Defence to counterclaim, Form 27C, by George

Where the plaintiff, Barnie, delivers a reply to Form 27B, however, the following would apply:

> Reply and defence to counterclaim, Form 27C, by Barnie
> Defence to counterclaim, Form 27C, by George

Note that only Barnie, not George, may deliver a reply because Barnie, in the role of the original plaintiff, would be replying to the statement of defence part of the statement of defence and counterclaim (against plaintiff and person not already party to main action), Form 27B.

REPLY TO DEFENCE TO COUNTERCLAIM, FORM 27D

A reply to defence to counterclaim, Form 27D, is not required unless the previous pleading raises an issue that had not been previously raised in any other pleading. Where prepared, the defendant to the main action (Fred) delivers this pleading within **ten days** after service of the defence to counterclaim.

CROSSCLAIMS

Crossclaims are battles between defendants, usually over who is liable to the plaintiff for the plaintiff's claim. Crossclaims do not add new parties, and the title of proceeding remains the same throughout the action.

Statement of defence and crossclaim (Form 28A)   See Precedent 12.4. In this pleading, one defendant, A, defends the action against the plaintiff, X, and crossclaims against a co-defendant, B. Prepare it for the crossclaiming defendant A. Use the same title of proceeding as that in the the statement of claim. Serve it on all parties to the action within **20/40/60 days** after service of the statement of claim, and file it with proof of service in the court where the action was commenced.

Defence to crossclaim (Form 28B)   Where defendant B disputes defendant A's crossclaim, serve a defence to crossclaim, Form 28B, on all parties, within **twenty days** after service of the statement of defence and crossclaim, and file it with proof of service.

Reply to defence to crossclaim (Form 28C)   If delivered, prepare it usually for the crossclaiming defendant A. Serve it on all other parties, and file it with proof of service within **ten days** after service of the defence to crossclaim.

THIRD PARTY CLAIMS

Third party claims involve the defendant disputing the plaintiff's statement of claim and bringing a new claim against a new person, known as a third party. The defendant's claim is neither against the plaintiff nor against a defendant within the main action; it is against the third party. Essentially, the defendant says, "If I am responsible to the plaintiff, so are you, the third party." Often, the defendant is blaming the third party entirely: for example, Peter, the plaintiff, sues Paul, the defendant, because the house Peter bought was found to be substandard. Paul, the defendant, sues Mary, the third party, saying that Paul only followed Mary's plans, so it was really all Mary's fault.

Distinguish a third party claim from a statement of defence and counterclaim (against plaintiff and person not already party to main action) where the defendant in that pleading makes a counter-

Legal TIP

All document names which include the word "reply" are prepared only if the previous document raises an issue that had not been previously raised in any other pleading.

claim against a new person **as well as against the plaintiff**; whereas in a third party claim, the defendant claims only against the third party. If the defendant in a third party claim wins, he or she automatically **loses** his or her claim against the third party because having won means the defendant in a third party claim was not liable to the plaintiff as the plaintiff had claimed, and therefore, the third party was also not liable to the plaintiff as the defendant in a third party claim had claimed.

Third party claim file number   The *Rules of Civil Procedure* require that the court assign to third and subsequent party claims the same court file number as the court file number in the main action followed by a suffix letter: for example, where the court file number in the main action is 1234, the court file number in the third party claim would be 1234A, that in the fourth party claim would be 1234B, etc. This enables the court to identify third and subsequent party claims relating to the same main action and place them on the trial list immediately after the main action.

Third party claim (Form 29A)   Prepare the third party claim, Precedent 12.5, for the defendant who claims against a third party. The third party claim is an originating process as far as the third party is concerned and must be issued. Issue it, usually within **ten days** of service of the statement of defence, in the court office where the action was commenced. Serve it on the third party, together with all of the pleadings delivered to date, within **thirty days** after issuing.

Third party defence (Form 29B)   Prepare and serve Form 29B within **20/40/60 days** of service of the third party claim. Key the general heading as it appears in the third party claim.

Reply to third party defence (Form 29C)   If delivered, prepare it usually for the defendant who served the third party claim. Serve it within **ten days** of service of the third party defence, and file it with proof of service.

CHAPTER SUMMARY

All of the pleadings in this chapter involve situations in which the **defendant** in an action can make a **counterclaim** against the plaintiff, a **counterclaim** against the plaintiff and a new person, a **crossclaim** against a co-defendant, or a **third party claim**.

Where the defendant adds a new party to the action, as in the case of a statement of defence and counterclaim (against plaintiff and person not already party to main action) or a third party claim, the defendant must have those documents issued before serving them because they represent an originating process concerning the new parties. In addition, a statement of defence and counterclaim (against plaintiff and person not already party to main action) must show a second title of proceeding to represent the role reversal between the original parties and the claim against the new person; all subsequent documents must show both titles of proceeding.

REVIEW QUESTIONS

1. In what situation does a counterclaim contain a second title of proceeding?
2. Who claims against whom in a crossclaim?
3. Who claims against whom in a third party claim?
4. Explain why 20/40/60 is used to refer to the defendant's age.
5. How many days does an Ontario defendant have in order to respond to a statement of claim?
6. A is plaintiff, B is defendant, and C is new person:
   (a) Write out the correct title of proceeding.
   (b) Explain who is counterclaiming against whom?

Court File No. CV-**-47987

ONTARIO
SUPERIOR COURT OF JUSTICE

B E T W E E N:

VIYELLA CONTRACTING CO. LIMITED

Plaintiff

- and -

WALTER RALPH RICHMAN

Defendant

STATEMENT OF DEFENCE AND COUNTERCLAIM

1.   The Defendant admits the allegations contained in paragraphs 2, 3, 4, and 5 of the Statement of Claim.

2.   The Defendant denies the allegations contained in paragraphs 1, 6, 7, 10, and 12 of the Statement of Claim.

3.   The Defendant has no knowledge in respect of the allegations contained in paragraph 11 of the Statement of Claim.

4.   The Plaintiff and the Defendant entered into a written agreement dated June 28, 20--, pursuant to which the Plaintiff was to construct and deliver a bar to the Wonderbar Restaurant in the City of Waterwell. The delivery date agreed to was July 27, 20--, and time was of the essence. The price agreed upon was $125,000.00, which sum the Defendant paid to the Plaintiff.

5.   The Defendant states that the Plaintiff was in breach of the agreement referred to in the Statement of Claim because the Plaintiff never completed the work by the delivery date, despite repeated calls and requests to the Plaintiff after the delivery date to come and complete the work. As time was of the essence, the Defendant was forced to complete the work that the Plaintiff left unfinished, at additional cost to the Defendant...

12.   The Defendant asks that this action be dismissed with costs.

-2-

COUNTERCLAIM

13.   The Plaintiff by Counterclaim, Walter Ralph Richman, claims:

(a)   special damages of $17,500.00;

(b)   general damages for $75,000.00 for the breach of agreement described in paragraph 6(b) of the statement of defence;

(c)   interest on the amount of $75,000.00 at the prevailing statutory rate from the date this cause of action arose;

(d)   prejudgment interest in accordance with section 128 of the *Courts of Justice Act*, RSO 1990, c C.43, as amended;

(e)   postjudgment interest in accordance with section 129 of the *Courts of Justice Act*, RSO 1990, c C.43, as amended;

(f)   the costs of this proceeding, plus harmonized sales tax; and,

(g)   such further and other relief as this Honourable Court may deem just.

14.   The Plaintiff by Counterclaim, Walter Ralph Richman, repeats and relies upon the allegations in the Statement of Defence in support of the Counterclaim.

November 3, 20--

MICHAEL, ELIAD & REDFORD LLP
Barristers and Solicitors
863 Seneca Lane
Toronto, Ontario   M4J 1P6

Robert B. Redford
Tel: 416-363-1079
Fax: 416-363-2628

Lawyers for the Defendant

TO: **CASTLES & SANDS**
Suite 900-205 Portage Street
Markham, Ontario L3R 3G3

Raymond G. Castles
Tel: 905-495-2222
Fax: 905-495-2223

Lawyers for the Plaintiff

(prepare backsheet)

Legal Office Procedures

Court File No. **CV-**-5678**

ONTARIO
SUPERIOR COURT OF JUSTICE

BETWEEN:

(Court Seal)

WELLING LIMITED

Plaintiff

- and -

ERIC ADVERTISING OF CANADA LTD.

Defendant

AND BETWEEN:

ERIC ADVERTISING OF CANADA LTD.

Plaintiff by Counterclaim

- and -

WELLING LIMITED and MINT INCORPORATED

Defendants to the Counterclaim

STATEMENT OF DEFENCE AND COUNTERCLAIM

TO THE DEFENDANT(S) TO THE COUNTERCLAIM

A LEGAL PROCEEDING has been commenced against you by way of a Counterclaim in an action in this Court. The Claim made against you is set out in the following pages.

IF YOU WISH TO DEFEND THIS COUNTERCLAIM, you or an Ontario lawyer acting for you must prepare a Defence to Counterclaim in Form 27C prescribed by the *Rules of Civil Procedure*, serve it on the Plaintiff by counterclaim's lawyer or, where the Plaintiff by Counterclaim does not have a lawyer, serve it on the Plaintiff by Counterclaim, and file it, with proof of service, in this Court, WITHIN TWENTY DAYS after this Statement of Defence and Counterclaim is served on you.

If you are not already a party to the main action and you are served in another province or territory of Canada or in the United States of America, the period for serving and filing your defence is forty days. If you are served outside Canada and the United States of America, the period is sixty days.

-2-

If you are not already a party to the main action, instead of serving and filing a Defence to Counterclaim, you may serve and file a Notice of Intent to Defend in Form 18B prescribed by the *Rules of Civil Procedure*. This will entitle you to ten more days within which to serve and file your Defence to Counterclaim.

IF YOU FAIL TO DEFEND THIS COUNTERCLAIM, JUDGMENT MAY BE GIVEN AGAINST YOU IN YOUR ABSENCE AND WITHOUT FURTHER NOTICE TO YOU. IF YOU WISH TO DEFEND THIS PROCEEDING BUT ARE UNABLE TO PAY LEGAL FEES, LEGAL AID MAY BE AVAILABLE TO YOU BY CONTACTING A LOCAL LEGAL AID OFFICE.

IF YOU PAY THE AMOUNT OF THE COUNTERCLAIM AGAINST YOU, and $750.00 for costs, within the time for serving and filing your Defence to Counterclaim, you may move to have the Counterclaim against you dismissed by the Court. If you believe the amount claimed for costs is excessive, you may pay the amount of the Counterclaim and $400.00 for costs and have the costs assessed by the Court.

Date   August   , (year)   Issued by _____
                                                                      Local Registrar

                                          Address of
                                          court office: 393 University Avenue
                                                          10th Floor
                                                          Toronto, Ontario
                                                          M5G 1E6

TO: **MINT INCORPORATED**
           432 King Street West
           Toronto , Ontario
           M6K 7Y3

AND TO: **CASTLES & SANDS**
           Suite 900-205 Portage Street
           Markham, Ontario
           L3R 3G3

           Raymond G. Castles
           Tel: (905) 495-2222
           Fax: (905) 495-2223

           Lawyers for the Defendant to the Counterclaim, Welling Limited

-3-

STATEMENT OF DEFENCE

1.   The Defendant admits the allegations contained in paragraph 2 of the fresh amended Statement of Claim.

2.   The Defendant denies the allegations contained in paragraphs 1, 3, 7, and 9 of the Statement of Claim.

3.   The Defendant has no knowledge in respect of the allegations contained in paragraph 8 of the Statement of Claim.

4.   The Plaintiff and Mint Incorporated retained the Defendant to provide general advertising services, including a study of their marketing requirements, advising on advertising and promotion of their products, and acting on their instructions to purchase various media space requirements and other promotional material or services. Mint Incorporated carries on business as a manufacturer and supplier of medals and is the sole owner of the Plaintiff, Welling Limited.

COUNTERCLAIM

5.   The Plaintiff by Counterclaim claims:

    (a)   the sum of $115,349.35;

    (b)   interest on the said sum of $115,349.35 at the rate of five percent per year from June 13, 20--, to the date of payment or judgment;

    (c)   prejudgment interest in accordance with section 128 of the *Courts of Justice Act*, RSO 1990, c C.43, as amended;

    (d)   postjudgment interest in accordance with section 129 of the *Courts of Justice Act,* RSO 1990, c C.43, as amended;

    (e)   the costs of this proceeding, plus harmonized sales tax;

    (f)   such further and other relief as this Honourable Court may deem just.

6.   The Defendant to the Counterclaim, Mint Incorporated, requested Eric Advertising of Canada Ltd. to provide general advertising services and services with regard to the Kings and Queens series of medals to the Defendants to the Counterclaim pursuant to instructions issued from time to time by Mint Incorporated and Welling Limited. Eric Advertising of Canada Ltd. sent all estimates pertaining to its advertising services to Mint Incorporated in connection with such advertising services. Mint Incorporated and Welling Limited owe Eric Advertising of Canada Ltd. for all of the advertising services which it provided and which are more particularly referred to below.

7.   Between January and June 20--, the Plaintiff by Counterclaim provided general advertising services to Mint Incorporated and Welling Limited…

August   , 20--

    MICHAEL, ELIAD & REDFORD LLP
    Barristers and Solicitors
    863 Seneca Lane
    Toronto, Ontario   M4J 1P6

    Robert B. Redford
    Tel: 416-363-1079
    Fax: 416-363-2628

    Lawyers for the Plaintiff by Counterclaim,
    Eric Advertising of Canada Ltd.

Court File No. CV-**-5678

WELLING LIMITED and MINT INCORPORATED
Defendants to the Counterclaim

ERIC ADVERTISING OF CANADA LTD.
Defendant

-and-

ONTARIO
SUPERIOR COURT OF JUSTICE

PROCEEDING COMMENCED AT
TORONTO

STATEMENT OF DEFENCE AND COUNTERCLAIM

MICHAEL, ELIAD & REDFORD LLP
Barristers and Solicitors
863 Seneca Lane
Toronto, Ontario
M4J 1P6

Robert B. Redford (48000R)
Tel: 416-363-1079
Fax: 416-363-2628
rbrdfrd@mer.com

Lawyers for the Plaintiff by Counterclaim,
Eric Advertising of Canada Ltd.

WELLING LIMITED
Plaintiff
ERIC ADVERTISING OF CANADA LTD.
Plaintiff by Counterclaim

-and-

Court File No. CV-**-5678

ONTARIO
SUPERIOR COURT OF JUSTICE

BETWEEN:

WELLING LIMITED

Plaintiff

- and -

ERIC ADVERTISING OF CANADA LTD.

Defendant

AND BETWEEN:

ERIC ADVERTISING OF CANADA LTD.

Plaintiff by Counterclaim

- and -

WELLING LIMITED and MINT INCORPORATED

Defendants to the Counterclaim

DEFENCE TO COUNTERCLAIM
OF MINT INCORPORATED

1.   The Defendant to the Counterclaim, Mint Incorporated, admits the allegations contained in paragraph 1 of the Counterclaim.

2.   The Defendant to the Counterclaim, Mint Incorporated, denies all other allegations contained in the Counterclaim.

3.   At no time did Mint Incorporated instruct Eric Advertising of Canada Ltd. to purchase media space requirements or any other promotional material or services.

4.   Mint Incorporated specifically denies any debt or obligation that Eric Advertising of Canada Ltd. incurred as a result of the services alleged to have been rendered with regard to the

-2-

Kings and Queens series of medals. If such work or services were rendered, then they were made nugatory by the resulting default of Eric Advertising of Canada Ltd.

5.   Mint Incorporated denies a right on the part of Eric Advertising of Canada Ltd. to claim interest prior to the delivery of the Statement of Defence and Counterclaim to this action. At no time did the Defendant expressly or impliedly indicate that interest would be claimed on any outstanding amounts prior to the delivery of the Statement of Defence and Counterclaim in this action.

6.   The Defendant to the Counterclaim, Mint Incorporated, asks that the Counterclaim be dismissed with costs.

September 22, 20--

CASTLES & SANDS
Suite 900 – 205 Portage Street
Markham, Ontario
L3R 3G3

Raymond G. Castles
Tel: (905) 495-2222
Fax: (905) 495-2223

Lawyers for the Defendants to the Counterclaim,
Mint Incorporated and Welling Limited

TO: **MICHAEL, ELIAD & REDFORD LLP**
Barristers and Solicitors
863 Seneca Lane
Toronto, Ontario
M4J 1P6

Robert B. Redford
Tel: 416-363-1079
Fax: 416-363-2628

Lawyers for the Plaintiff by Counterclaim,
Eric Advertising of Canada Ltd.

Court File No. CV-**-5678

ERIC ADVERTISING OF CANADA LTD.

Defendant

WELLING LIMITED and MINT INCORPORATED

Defendants to the Counterclaim

-and-

WELLING LIMITED

Plaintiff

ERIC ADVERTISING OF CANADA LTD.

Plaintiff by Counterclaim

ONTARIO
SUPERIOR COURT OF JUSTICE

PROCEEDING COMMENCED AT
TORONTO

**DEFENCE TO COUNTERCLAIM OF
MINT INCORPORATED**

CASTLES & SANDS
Suite 900-205 Portage Street
Markham, Ontario L3R 3G3

Raymond G. Castles (36996F)
Tel: 905-495-2222
Fax: 905-495-2223
raymond@castlessands.ca

Lawyers for the Defendants to the Counterclaim,
Mint Incorporated and Welling Limited

Court File No. CV-**-03704

ONTARIO
SUPERIOR COURT OF JUSTICE

B E T W E E N:

DONALD DUCK and JANE DUCK

Plaintiffs

- and -

QUALITY CERAMICS CORPORATION and
PAR CONSTRUCTION LIMITED

Defendants

STATEMENT OF DEFENCE AND CROSSCLAIM
OF THE DEFENDANT QUALITY CERAMICS CORPORATION

1.   The Defendant, Quality Ceramics Corporation, admits the allegations contained in paragraphs 4, 5, and 7 of the Statement of Claim.

2.   The Defendant, Quality Ceramics Corporation, denies the allegations contained in paragraphs 1, 8, and 9 of the Statement of Claim.

3.   The Defendant, Quality Ceramics Corporation, has no knowledge in respect of the allegations contained in paragraphs 2, 3, 6, and 11 of the Statement of Claim.

4.   There is no contract between the Plaintiffs and the Defendant, Quality Ceramics Corporation…

15.   The Defendant, Quality Ceramics Corporation, pleads that this action be dismissed against it with costs.

CROSSCLAIM

16.   The Defendant, Quality Ceramics Corporation, claims against the Defendant, Par Construction Limited:

(a)   contribution and indemnity under sections 2 and 3 of the *Negligence Act*, RSO 1990, c N.1, as amended, for any amounts which the Defendant, Quality Ceramics Corporation, may be found to be responsible to the Plaintiffs;

-2-

(b)   contribution and indemnity under the common law and equity for any amounts which the Defendant, Quality Ceramics Corporation, may be found to be responsible to the Plaintiffs;

(c)   the costs of the main action, plus harmonized sales tax;

(d)   the costs of this Crossclaim, plus harmonized sales tax;

(e)   such further and other relief as this Honourable Court may deem just.

17.   The Defendant, Quality Ceramics Corporation, states that if the Plaintiffs have suffered damage, which is not admitted, such damage was caused by the negligence of the Defendant, Par Construction Limited, and did not result from any act or omission of the Defendant, Quality Ceramics Corporation.

Date September 7, 20--

MICHAEL, ELIAD & REDFORD LLP
Barristers and Solicitors
863 Seneca Lane
Toronto, Ontario   M4J 1P6

Robert B. Redford
Tel: 416-363-1079
Fax: 416-363-2628

Lawyers for the Defendant,
Quality Ceramics Corporation

TO: **SMITH & JONES**
15 Martin Street
Toronto, Ontario M9T 3R2

Peter Smith
Tel: (416) 491-0001
Fax: (416) 491-0002

Lawyers for the Defendant,
Par Construction Limited

AND TO: **CASTLES & SANDS**
Suite 900-205 Portage Street
Markham, Ontario L3R 3G3

Raymond G. Castles
Tel: 905-495-2222
Fax: 905-495-2223

Lawyers for the Plaintiffs   (prepare backsheet)

-2-

Instead of serving and filing a third party defence, you may serve and file a Notice of Intent to Defend in Form 18B prescribed by the *Rules of Civil Procedure*. This will entitle you to ten more days within which to serve and file your third party defence.

YOU MAY ALSO DEFEND the action by the Plaintiff against the Defendant by serving and filing a Statement of Defence within the time for serving and filing your third party defence.

IF YOU FAIL TO DEFEND THIS THIRD PARTY CLAIM, JUDGMENT MAY BE GIVEN AGAINST YOU IN YOUR ABSENCE AND WITHOUT FURTHER NOTICE TO YOU. IF YOU WISH TO DEFEND THIS PROCEEDING BUT ARE UNABLE TO PAY LEGAL FEES, LEGAL AID MAY BE AVAILABLE TO YOU BY CONTACTING A LOCAL LEGAL AID OFFICE.

IF YOU PAY THE AMOUNT OF THE THIRD PARTY CLAIM AGAINST YOU, and \$1,000.00 for costs, within the time for serving and filing your third party defence, you may move to have the third party claim against you dismissed by the Court. If you believe the amount claimed for costs is excessive, you may pay the amount of the third party claim and \$400.00 for costs and have the costs assessed by the Court.

Date	Issued by _____
	Local Registrar
Address of court office:	393 University Avenue
	10th Floor
	Toronto, Ontario
	M5G 1E6

TO: **TRUSTY INSURANCE BROKERS LTD.**
25 Nipigon Street
Mississauga, Ontario L7W 9Q2

AND TO: **JOHN SMITH**
25 Nipigon Street
Mississauga, Ontario L7W 9Q2

Court File No. CV-**-2222

ONTARIO
SUPERIOR COURT OF JUSTICE

B E T W E E N:

(Court Seal)

NICOLE CACCINI

Plaintiff

- and -

SAFEST INSURANCE COMPANY

Defendant

- and -

TRUSTY INSURANCE BROKERS LTD. and JOHN SMITH

Third Party

THIRD PARTY CLAIM

TO THE THIRD PARTY

A LEGAL PROCEEDING HAS BEEN COMMENCED AGAINST YOU by way of a Third Party Claim in an action in this Court.

The action was commenced by the Plaintiff against the Defendant for the relief claimed in the Statement of Claim served with this Third Party Claim. The Defendant has defended the action on the grounds set out in the Statement of Defence served with this Third Party Claim. The Defendant's Claim against you is set out in the following pages.

IF YOU WISH TO DEFEND THIS THIRD PARTY CLAIM, you or an Ontario lawyer acting for you must prepare a defence in Form 29B prescribed by the *Rules of Civil Procedure*, serve it on the lawyers for the other parties or, where a party does not have a lawyer, serve it on the party, and file it, with proof of service, WITHIN TWENTY DAYS after this Third Party Claim is served on you, if you are served in Ontario.

If you are served in another province or territory of Canada or in the United States of America, the period for serving and filing your third party defence is forty days. If you are served outside Canada and the United States of America, the period is sixty days.

Legal Office Procedures

-3-

CLAIM

1.   The Defendant claims against the Third Party:

    (a)   a declaration that the third parties are liable to the Defendant for all or part of the

          Plaintiff's Claim which the Defendant may be ordered by this Honourable Court to

          satisfy;

    (b)   contribution and indemnity under sections 2 and 3 of the *Negligence Act*, RSO

          1990, c N.1, as amended, for any amounts which the Defendant may be found to

          be responsible to the Plaintiff;

    (c)   contribution and indemnity under common law and equity for any amounts which

          the Defendant may be found to be responsible to the Plaintiff;

    (d)   the costs of the main action, plus harmonized sales tax;

    (e)   the costs of this Third Party Claim, plus harmonized tax;

    (f)   such further and other relief as this Honourable Court may deem just.

2.   The Plaintiff in the main action alleges that she was the owner and operator of a motor

vehicle which was subject to a policy of insurance with the Defendant.

3.   The Plaintiff in the main action alleges that her motor vehicle was involved in a motor

vehicle accident causing damages totalling $40,530.83, together with interest and costs, pursuant

to the alleged contract of insurance with the Defendant.

4.   The Defendant in its Statement of Defence denies the said policy of insurance and denies

any liability to the Plaintiff for the said sum of $40,530.83.

-4-

5.   The Defendant has further pleaded in its Statement of Defence that an application for a standard automobile policy of insurance which purported to be signed on behalf of the Plaintiff was submitted to the Defendant, which application contained misrepresentations that were made by the Plaintiff or her agents, Trusty Insurance Brokers Ltd., or John Smith, or both of them.

6.   The Defendant has further pleaded in its Statement of Defence that it relied upon the truthfulness of the statements in the application for a standard automobile policy, and if a policy of automobile insurance was issued by the Defendant, which is not admitted but denied, the Defendant would not have issued such policy of insurance had it known of the misrepresentations contained in the application.

7.   If the Defendant is found at trial to be liable for the Plaintiff's claim, or any part of it, then the Defendant is entitled to contribution, indemnity, or relief over from the third parties to the full extent of the damages so found and the costs of the main and Third Party actions.

September   , 20--

MICHAEL, ELIAD & REDFORD LLP
Barristers and Solicitors
863 Seneca Lane
Toronto, Ontario
M4J 1P6

Robert B. Redford
Tel: 416-363-1079
Fax: 416-363-2628

Lawyers for the Defendant

(prepare backsheet)

CHAPTER 13
DISCOVERIES

This chapter discusses the "show and tell" stage in the civil litigation action which is the discoveries stage.

THE DISCOVERIES STAGE
Discovery Plan, Π & Δ • 60 days after pleadings close • not served; not filed
Affidavit of Documents, Π & Δ • before examination for discovery • served; not filed
Examinations for Discovery, Π or Δ • maximum 7 hours per party • before setting action down for trial Π (Greek pi) = Plaintiff Δ (Greek delta) = Defendant

DISCOVERIES

Going to trial is much like going into an open book examination--no surprises, no histrionics; all evidence to be used at trial must be discovered in this, the discoveries, stage.

The discoveries stage comes after the close of pleadings when all parties' pleadings are in and the parties can determine from the pleadings what other evidence, if any, they will require from each other. The discoveries stage is a sorting out "show and tell" process. Each party's lawyer sorts out the relevant documents he or she will use as evidence at trial and tells the other about them; hence, **discovery**. The purpose is to get a sense of the strength of the other side's case and settle or eliminate as many issues as possible out of court to cut back on court time and expense.

Methods of discovery   Include: discovery of documents, examination for discovery, examination by written questions, inspection of property, and medical examination. Of these, the **discovery of documents** and the **examination for discovery** are automatic and are rarely omitted, except in the simplest and most straight forward cases. The other methods of discovery, inspection of property and medical examination, require **leave** (the court's permission).

DISCOVERY PLAN

The first step in the discovery process is a discovery plan. Rule 29.1 of the *Rules of Civil Procedure* requires the parties to consult with each other and work out a discovery plan if they intend to obtain evidence from each other by any method of discovery.

Evidence must be relevant In preparing the discovery plan, the parties must consider what evidence they would disclose, and they must select for disclosure only evidence that is **relevant** to any matter in issue in the action, instead of evidence that **relates** to any matter in issue in the action. In the case of electronic evidence, referred to as e-discovery, the parties should be prepared to disclose all relevant electronic evidence and must consider the relevance, the cost, and the format in which electronic information, such as e-mails, websites, databases, and computer documents, will be produced, given the large volume that is often involved.

Time and content of discovery plan The parties must agree on a discovery plan the earlier of **sixty days** after pleadings close, or longer if the parties agree, and must keep the discovery plan updated as to any changes in the information contained in it. The discovery plan must be in writing and must set out the following:

- the scope of discovery
- dates for serving of affidavits of documents
- how and when documents will be produced
- who will be examined and when
- the duration of the examination for discovery
- any other information that is appropriate to the importance and complexity of the action

Form of discovery plan The rules do not prescribe a form for a discovery plan; hence, the discovery plan could take any form, provided it complies with the requirements of the rule. In practice, lawyers prepare the discovery plan in the format of a court document, Precedent 13.1. In some cases, such as those involving a limited number of documents or a small dollar value, the discovery plan may take the form of a letter. The discovery plan is not served or filed in court. It is a document agreed upon between the parties. If the parties fail to agree to a discovery plan, the court may refuse to grant any relief or to award any costs on any motions relating to discovery.

ROMANO v. EASTERN CAST IRON CORPORATION
Re: Wrongful Dismissal
_____

We continue with Mr. Romano's action. We have consulted with the defendant's lawyers and were able to work out a discovery plan, Precedent 13.1. We have also prepared the affidavit of documents, Precedent 13.2, which we will serve on Eastern's lawyers, Castles & Sands. Castles & Sands must serve us with their client's affidavit of documents as well, so that we, too, may see the list of documents which they intend to use as evidence at the trial. Precedent 13.3 is the notice of examination which we have prepared for service on Castles & Sands. It notifies them that we have scheduled an examination for discovery where we would like to ask questions of their client based on the documents in their client's affidavit of documents. In the next chapter, we prepare for trial.

DISCOVERY OF DOCUMENTS

In this method of discovery, lawyers on both sides must tell each other what documents they each will use as evidence at trial. The discovery of documents is made by preparing and serving an **affidavit of documents** in which lawyers disclose all of the relevant documents so that the other side can **discover** what these documents are; hence, **discovery of documents**. The *Rules of Civil Procedure* define **document** to include a sound recording, videotape, film, photograph, chart, graph, map, plan, survey, book of account, and data and information in electronic format.

AFFIDAVIT OF DOCUMENTS, FORM 30A

The affidavit of documents, Form 30A, Precedent 13.2, must list only those documents that the parties determine to be **relevant**. At any time after the discovery plan, each lawyer must prepare and serve the affidavit of documents on the opposing lawyer. The affidavit of documents is **not** filed in court and does not require the parties to actually attach the documents themselves to the affidavit, but only to indicate what the documents are. The actual production of the non-privileged documents occurs at the next step, the **examination for discovery**, at which time, the parties must bring the non-privileged documents for the other side to see and examine.

The affidavit of documents requires the disclosure of relevant non-privileged, as well as relevant privileged (confidential), documents. Privileged documents may neither be shown to the opposite lawyer nor used in evidence at trial, except to discredit a witness, unless the court orders otherwise. The reason for listing the privileged documents in the affidavit of documents is to enable the opposing lawyer, or the court, to determine from the types of documents mentioned if privilege has been, in fact, properly claimed. Here are some guidelines on what may constitute grounds for privilege.

Grounds for privilege   Judges vary in their interpretations of privileged (confidential) documents. One test in claiming privilege is whether or not the opposite side is likely to successfully challenge the claim. Generally, however, lawyers may claim privilege on the following three grounds:

1. That the documents are between **lawyer and client** and are prepared for the purpose of giving or receiving **legal advice**. This ground is known as a **lawyer-client** privilege. If a lawyer claims it, the lawyer must use wording to that effect in the affidavit of documents to identify that ground for privilege.
2. That the documents are prepared **in contemplation of litigation**, also referred to as **litigation privilege**. Such documents may be prepared by the client, by the lawyer, or by third parties. This ground for privilege would appear to include all documents in the case. Distinguish, however, that only those documents which contain **opinions, predictions, or analyses as to who is or is not liable** in the case may be claimed as privileged documents; the rest are non-privileged documents, regardless of when or by whom prepared. Generally, if the privileged documents were prepared before starting the law suit, lawyers use the phrase **in contemplation of litigation** to identify that ground for privilege in the affidavit of documents. If the privileged documents were prepared during the progress of the case, lawyers use the phrase **for use in this litigation** or **litigation privilege**.
3. That the documents are prepared **without prejudice**. These usually include documents for the purpose of settling the case. Lawyers use the phrase **without prejudice** or **without prejudice communication privilege** to identify that ground for privilege in the affidavit of documents.

To avoid tactical manoeuvring, the affidavit of documents basically works like this: If the lawyer wants to use a document at trial, he or she must mention it in the affidavit of documents. If the lawyer does not want to use a document because it is not in his or her favour and does not mention it, or improperly claims privilege, the court may order the lawyer to produce the document. If a non-party has a document, the interested lawyer may obtain it by court order. If either side's lawyer receives additional documents, he or she must serve on the opposing lawyer a supplemental affidavit of documents to update the first affidavit.

You require: A list of the relevant documents sorted into categories to suit Schedules A, B, and C of the affidavit. See Precedent 13.2. Wording guides completion. Key points include:

Prepare a separate affidavit of documents for each plaintiff or defendant for whom you act in the action. If a corporation or a partnership, the form is Form 30B, and the person authorized to sign on behalf of the corporation or partnership swears the affidavit.

Schedule A: List all relevant non-privileged documents, i.e. only those documents which the lawyer intends to use as evidence at trial. Examples of non-privileged documents include: hospital records, medical reports, insurance policies, employment contracts or other contracts or agreements, invoices, receipts, electronic information, photographs, or video tapes showing injuries or sites relevant to the case.

Schedule B: List all privileged documents, i.e. documents that the lawyer objects to having the other side see, mainly because they contain opinions, predictions, or analyses of who is or is not to blame in the case. See Precedent 13.2 for standard entries used in practice; note the absence of individual itemization. Example entries of privileged documents:

1. Letters, memos, notes of telephone conversations, reports, and other documents **between lawyer and client for the purpose of giving or receiving legal advice** on the case.
2. Litigation privilege: correspondence and reports of medical experts, insurance investigators, environmental analysts, including plans, sketches, photographs, or statements; clients' or lawyers' memos to employees (e.g. to law office staff) about the case, and memos to file (i.e. memos "for the record" of the file) prepared in contemplation of litigation and during the progress of this action for use in this litigation.
3. Letters and documents marked **without prejudice**.

Schedule C: This schedule basically asks: "If you are using originals as evidence, where are the copies; if you are using copies, where are the originals?" For example, in the case of out-going letters, your firm does not have the originals because the recipients of the letters have them. For the purposes of Schedule C, therefore, your firm **was** in possession of the originals before sending them out, but not any more; similarly, if your firm sent copies of original documents or copies of copies to various parties, your firm **was** in possession of such copies before sending them out, but not any more because the recipients now have those copies or duplicates. See the precedent for a standard entry used in practice.

Number of copies, minimum 2: Serve 1 on all opposite lawyers; keep 1 in client's file (not filed in court).

REQUEST TO INSPECT DOCUMENTS

Either side's lawyer may serve on the other a **request to inspect documents, Form 30C**. The purpose is to take an advance look at a particular non-privileged document that is mentioned in the opposite side's affidavit of documents or in any pleading so as to prepare for the examination for discovery. The lawyer served with the request must make an appointment, within **five business days** of service of the request, for the requesting lawyer to see the required document. The requesting lawyer is entitled to make a copy of the document at his or her own expense.

Number of copies, minimum 2: Serve 1 on lawyers to whom you direct the request; keep 1 in client's file (not filed in court).

EXAMINATION FOR DISCOVERY

The examination for discovery is the follow up to the affidavit of documents. The examination for discovery is for the purpose of verbally questioning the opposite party on the documents listed in that party's affidavit of documents and on other things.

Duration of oral examinations for discovery   Pursuant to Rule 31.05.1, the duration of oral examinations for discovery is limited to a total of **seven hours** per party (i.e. per side). The seven-hour maximum per party applies regardless of how many parties or other persons are to be examined: for example, if there are ten defendants to be examined, the lawyer for the plaintiff has a maximum of seven hours in which to examine all ten of the defendants, and vice versa for the lawyer for the defendant. Each party may be examined only **once**, or more than once with the court's permission. The lawyers for each party must set out the expected duration of their respective oral examinations for discovery in the agreed upon discovery plan. Where more than seven hours are required, the parties can consent to more time or seek a court order for more time. The purpose of the seven-hour time limit is to minimize the costs often associated with lengthy oral examinations for discovery.

What takes place at examinations for discovery   The **examination for discovery** method of discovery involves **oral** (verbal) evidence. It is like a mini trial where the examining lawyer asks questions of the opposite party, referred to as an **adverse party**, and the adverse party's lawyer is present to ensure no improper questions are asked of the adverse party. A recorder is also present to record the questions and answers and to produce a keyed transcript. Both sides' lawyers must conduct an oral examination for discovery of each other's clients, either in one sitting, if all cooperate, or separately. Unless the court orders otherwise, only lawyers and their clients may appear at examinations for discovery. The private, informal setting is to enable parties to answer questions more freely. An examination for discovery may also be videotaped, either on consent of the parties or by court order; a transcript must be produced, nevertheless. The lawyers may use the videotape and transcript as evidence at trial.

Where and before whom held   Unless all parties' lawyers agree otherwise, a party must be examined in the county where that party lives. The examination for discovery may be held in an official examiner's office or in a reporting service office, both of which are private businesses. The examination is held before an official examiner, or before a person that an official examiner assigns, or before a person that a reporting service names. This means that the person before whom the examination takes place might **not** be an official examiner. Under the rules, the person to be examined is deemed to have agreed on the "unofficial" examiner (and on the time and place of the examination), unless the person to be examined makes a motion showing that the person (or the time or place) is unsuitable for the proper conduct of the examination.

Making the appointment for examination for discovery   Either side's lawyer may initiate the appointment for the examination for discovery, but it is usually the plaintiff's lawyer who does so. Book the appointment with the official examiner or the reporting service that your firm normally uses. If the party being examined requires an interpreter, that party's lawyer must arrange for the interpreter.

What to bring   Unless the examining lawyer indicates otherwise, the lawyer for the party being examined must bring to the examination for discovery copies of all of the non-privileged documents listed in that party's affidavit of documents.

Examination of non-parties   Either lawyer may examine a non-party, but only with permission of the court, and only after that lawyer has completed the examination for discovery. This ensures that lawyers examine only such non-parties as the examinations for discovery revealed to be necessary, and not for the purpose of delaying. If the lawyer is examining a non-party who lives in Ontario, prepare, issue, and serve, by personal service only, a **summons to witness (examination out of court), Form 34B**. Attach attendance money to compensate the non-party for attending. Do the same for a non-party who lives outside Ontario, except use a **summons to a witness outside Ontario, Form 53C**.

Transcripts   At the conclusion of the examination for discovery, all lawyers usually order a transcript of the examination for discovery to refer to at trial in the event the parties give testimony that is contradictory to what they gave at the examination for discovery. The official examiner also provides a court copy of the transcript. At trial, when a lawyer checks a party's contradiction, the lawyer hands the court copy of the transcript to the judge to read the part proving the contradiction; otherwise, the trial judge must have no prior access to the transcript, so as not to influence his or her trial decision.

NOTICE OF EXAMINATION

After serving the affidavit of documents and setting up the appointment for the examination for discovery, prepare a **notice of examination, Form 34A**, Precedent 13.3, before going on with the examination for discovery. The notice of examination **notifies** the opposite lawyers of the appointment you have set up for the examination for discovery and also asks them to bring all of the non-privileged documents which they disclosed in their affidavit of documents. Although preparing and serving the notice of examination is not always necessary, particularly if the opposite side cooperates, many lawyers prepare and serve it as a precaution for non-attendance. If you serve it, do so at least **two days** before the date of the appointment. Parties are not entitled to attendance money since they caused the action. This is why you do not include attendance money with the notice of examination, whereas you do with a summons to witness (examination out of court) for non-parties.

Tactical use of notice of examination   Lawyers may make tactical use of the notice of examination in that the lawyer who first serves it is entitled to examine first and therefore discover the other side's evidence first; however, it may be of equal advantage to hear the other side's examining approach first. Another advantage of serving the notice of examination is that if anyone who is served with it fails to attend, it gives the lawyer who served it an automatic right to obtain a **certificate of non-attendance** from the official examiner as proof in obtaining a court order to compel the party to attend and be examined.

PREPARATION AND DISTRIBUTION OF NOTICE OF EXAMINATION, FORM 34A

You require: The appointment details. See Precedent 13.3. You may also use an appointment form that the official examiner's office usually supplies. The wording guides completion. Key points include:

If the party to be examined is a corporation, key the name of the person who will take the examination on behalf of the corporation, and key **on behalf of XYZ Corporation**. The rules require the party to be examined to bring to the examination for discovery all of the non-privileged documents that the party has disclosed in the affidavit of documents; therefore, you usually need not set out any other documents in the notice of examination unless you require the party to bring a "thing" that a document refers to, e.g. "a sample of a 10 mm drill bit." The "other examinations" paragraph refers to examinations other than oral examinations for discovery.

Number of copies, minimum 3: Serve 1 on opposite lawyers; keep 1, with proof of service, in file for possible use on motion for non-attendance; keep 1 in client's file (not filed in court).

EXAMINATION FOR DISCOVERY BY WRITTEN QUESTIONS

Rule 35.01 of the *Rules of Civil Procedure* provides for examinations for discovery by written questions and answers. Lawyers may use an examination for discovery either by written questions or by oral examination, but not both, because an adverse party may be examined **only once**. The written questions method is suitable for long-distance adverse parties with only a few straight forward questions to answer. However, if more than one lawyer is entitled to examine an adverse party, e.g. where there are two or more plaintiffs or defendants, each with separate lawyers, the examination must be by way of an **oral** examination for discovery, and there must be only **one** oral examination for discovery. This requires all lawyers entitled to examine to be present and to examine the adverse party in one sitting, since an adverse party may be examined only once. This is done to minimize costs. The same grounds of relevancy and privilege apply in written questions as they do in oral examinations for discovery.

If written questions are used, serve the opposite lawyers with **questions on written examination for discovery, Form 35A**, Precedent 13.4. The opposite lawyers must provide the answers in **answers on written examination for discovery, Form 35B**, Precedent 13.5, within **fifteen days** of service of the questions. If the lawyer needs more answers, he or she may, within **ten days** after receipt of the first answers, serve a further list of questions to which the opposite lawyers must provide further answers within **fifteen days**. If the answers are evasive, the court may order the party to answer them properly either by swearing an affidavit or by undergoing an oral examination. Either party's lawyer may use all or part of the written answers as evidence at trial.

INSPECTION OF PROPERTY

Lawyers may use this method only with permission of the court because it constitutes an extraordinary step. It is usually required when the case involves real property, e.g. land or a house: for example, if one party claims the property is insulated with urea-formaldehyde and the other disputes it, an inspection of the property would prove or disprove the claim.

MEDICAL EXAMINATION

Lawyers may use this method only with permission of the court because it constitutes an extraordinary step. It is usually required when the mental or physical condition of a party is in question, and the court must order an objective health practitioner to examine the party.

CHAPTER SUMMARY

Discoveries are for the purpose of discovering what relevant evidence all sides have on which they will base their case and whether the evidence is strong enough to continue on to trial or settle out of court.

The parties must agree to a discovery plan before they can obtain any evidence from each other. The two methods of discovery that are usually conducted are the discovery of documents and the examination for discovery. The discovery of documents consists of an affidavit of documents in which the parties list all of the documents they intend to use at the trial. Parties may not use any documents at trial that they have omitted from the affidavit of documents. The examination for discovery consists of oral questioning of the parties on the documents which they each have listed in their respective affidavits of documents. The duration of an examination for discovery is limited to a maximum of seven hours per party, regardless of the number of parties or other persons to be examined, unless the parties consent or seek a court order for more time. Lawyers may use the method of written questions instead of an oral examination for discovery, but not both. Other methods of discovery include inspection of property and medical examinations. These methods, however, require court permission before a party may conduct them.

REVIEW QUESTIONS

1. What is the purpose of discoveries?
2. What is a discovery plan?
3. What is the difference between a discovery of documents and an examination for discovery?
4. Which documents do you use to notify parties and non-parties of an examination for discovery?
5. In an examination for discovery, do lawyers examine adverse parties or their own clients?
6. How many oral examinations for discovery may an adverse party undergo?
7. What is the total duration for examinations for discovery?
8. Which methods of discovery require leave?
9. What is attendance money?
10. The word "privileged" in discoveries refers to an affluent class of people. Explain.

Court File No. CV-**-76542

ONTARIO
SUPERIOR COURT OF JUSTICE

BETWEEN:

NICHOLAS ROMANO

Plaintiff

and

EASTERN CAST IRON CORPORATION

Defendant

DISCOVERY PLAN

LAWYERS FOR THE PLAINTIFF(S):   MICHAEL, ELIAD & REDFORD LLP
Barristers and Solicitors
863 Seneca Lane
Toronto, Ontario   M4J 1P6

Robert B. Redford
Tel: 416-363-1079
Fax: 416-363-2628

LAWYERS FOR THE DEFENDANT(S):   CASTLES & SANDS
Suite 900-205 Portage Street
Markham, Ontario   L3R 3G3

Raymond G. Castles
Tel: 905-495-2222
Fax: 905-495-2223

A.   INTENDED SCOPE OF DOCUMENTARY DISCOVERY:

1.   Documentary discovery on behalf of the Plaintiff will include the following:

• Agreement dated March 1, 20--, between Nicholas Romano and Eastern Cast Iron Corporation.
• Letter dated October 14, 20--, from Eastern Cast Iron Corporation to Nicholas Romano.
• Letter dated October 16, 20--, from Nicholas Romano to Eastern Cast Iron Corporation.
• Any documents that are relevant to the proceedings and which may come to light in the course of the examinations.

2.   Documentary discovery on behalf of the Defendant will include the following:

-2-

In preparing its Affidavit of Documents, the Defendant will review the hard copy files, emails, and other electronic files in its possession, control, or power.

B.   DATES FOR SERVICE OF AFFIDAVIT OF DOCUMENTS:

PLAINTIFF(S):

The Plaintiff delivered his Affidavit of Documents in November 20–. Subject to any undertakings given at his examination for discovery for the production of further documents, and subject to the continuing disclosure obligation set out in rule 30.07 of the *Rules of Civil Procedure*, the Plaintiff has satisfied his obligations pursuant to Rule 30 of the *Rules of Civil Procedure* to produce documents.

DEFENDANT(S):

The Defendant shall deliver its Affidavit of Documents by December 1, 20–.

C.   INFORMATION RESPECTING THE TIMING, COSTS AND MANNER OF THE PRODUCTION OF DOCUMENTS BY THE PARTIES AND ANY OTHER PERSONS

1.   The productions from each party's Affidavit of Documents shall be delivered in hard copy, on request, at a cost not exceeding $0.25 per page.

D.   NAMES OF PERSONS INTENDED TO BE PRODUCED FOR ORAL EXAMINATION AND INFORMATION RESPECTING TIMING AND LENGTH OF EXAMINATIONS

Plaintiff(s):

Name of person to be examined: Nicholas Romano
Date and Time: January 5, 20–, at 10 a.m.
Length of examination: will not exceed 7 hours.

Defendant(s):

Name of person to be examined: John Hungate, representative for the Defendant.
Date and time: January 30, 20–, at 10:30 a.m.
Length of examination: will not exceed 7 hours.

-3-

E.   **ANY OTHER INFORMATION INTENDED TO RESULT IN THE EXPEDITIOUS AND COST EFFECTIVE COMPLETION OF THE DISCOVERY PROCESS**

1.   The productions from each party's Affidavit of Documents shall be delivered in hard copy on request at a cost not exceeding $0.25 per page.

2.   Answers to any undertakings given at any of the above-noted Examinations for Discovery shall be delivered by February 15, 20--.

3.   All refusals motions shall be booked by February 25, 20--.

4.   There shall be no inspections of property per Rule 32 of the *Rules of Civil Procedure.*

5.   There shall be no physical or mental examinations of any party, nor any medical reports filed per Rule 33 of the *Rules of Civil Procedure.*

6.   Unless otherwise agreed to by the parties in writing, there shall be no Examinations for Discovery by written questions per Rule 35 of the *Rules of Civil Procedure.*

As agreed upon by the parties.

DATED AT Toronto, Ontario, this   day of   , 20--.

MICHAEL, ELIAD & REDFORD LLP
Per:

_____
Robert B. Redford

Lawyers for the Plaintiff

DATED AT Markham, Ontario, this   day of   , 20--.

CASTLES & SANDS
Per:

_____
Raymond G. Castles

Lawyers for the Defendant

(prepare backsheet)

Court File No.   CV-**-76542

ONTARIO
SUPERIOR COURT OF JUSTICE

B E T W E E N:

NICHOLAS ROMANO

Plaintiff

and

EASTERN CAST IRON CORPORATION

Defendant

AFFIDAVIT OF DOCUMENTS

I, Nicholas Romano, of the City of Waterwell, in the County of Mandolee, MAKE OATH AND SAY:

1.   I have conducted a diligent search of records and made appropriate enquiries of others to inform myself in order to make this affidavit. This affidavit discloses, to the full extent of my knowledge, information and belief, all documents relevant to any matter in issue in this action that are or have been in my possession, control or power.

2.   I have listed in Schedule A those documents that are in my possession, control or power and that I do not object to producing for inspection.

3.   I have listed in Schedule B those documents that are or were in my possession, control or power and that I object to producing because I claim they are privileged, and I have stated in Schedule B the grounds for each such Claim.

4.   I have listed in Schedule C those documents that were formerly in my possession, control or power but are no longer in my possession, control or power, and I have stated in Schedule C when and how I lost possession or control of or power over them and their present location.

5.   I never had in my possession, control or power any document relevant to any matter in issue in this action other than those listed in Schedules A, B and C.

6.~~   I have listed in Schedule D the names and addresses of persons who might reasonably be expected to have knowledge of transactions or occurrences in issue.~~ *(Strike out this paragraph if the action is not being brought under the simplified procedure.)*

      Legal Office Procedures

-2-

SWORN BEFORE ME at the City of
Toronto, in the Province of Ontario
this .... day of   , 20--

}

_____
Commissioner for Taking Affidavits
(or as may be)

_____
Nicholas Romano

LAWYER'S CERTIFICATE

I CERTIFY that I have explained to the deponent,

(a)   the necessity of making full disclosure of all documents relevant to any matter in issue in the action;

(b)   what kinds of documents are likely to be relevant to the allegations made in the pleadings; and

(c)   if the action is brought under the simplified procedure, the necessity of providing the list required under rule 76.03.

Date: , 20--

_____
Robert B. Redford

-3-

SCHEDULE A

Documents in my possession, control or power that I do not object to producing for inspection. *(Number each document consecutively. Set out the nature and date of the document and other particulars sufficient to identify it.)*

1. Agreement dated March 1, 20--, between Nicholas Romano and Eastern Cast Iron Corporation.
2. Letter dated October 14, 20--, from Eastern Cast Iron Corporation to Nicholas Romano.
3. Letter dated October 16, 20--, from Nicholas Romano to Eastern Cast Iron Corporation.

SCHEDULE B

Documents that are or were in my possession, control or power that I object to producing on the grounds of privilege. *(Number each document consecutively. Set out the nature and date of the document and other particulars sufficient to identify it. State the grounds for claiming privilege for each document)*

(a) **Lawyer-Client Privilege:** Documents containing confidential professional communications passing between the deponent, or the deponent's agent and the deponent's legal advisers directly related to the seeking or receiving of legal advice or legal assistance.

(b) **Litigation Privilege:** Documents comprised of notes, memoranda, reports, confidential correspondence, and copies thereof, prepared for the purposes of obtaining or providing advice concerning this litigation, of obtaining or providing information and evidence to be used in this litigation and preparing for and prosecuting this litigation.

(c) **Without Prejudice Communication Privilege:** Documents containing or reflecting communications of a without prejudice nature concerning the matters in issue in this litigation.

SCHEDULE C

Documents that were formerly in my possession, control or power but are no longer in my possession, control or power. *(Number each document consecutively. Set out the nature and date of the document and other particulars sufficient to identify it. State when and how possession or control of or power over each document was lost, and give the present location of each document.)*

The originals of out-going correspondence and duplicates of other documents referred to in Schedule A, which should be in the possession of the respective recipients.

SCHEDULE D

*(To be filled in only if the action is being brought under the simplified procedure.)*Names and addresses of persons who might reasonably be expected to have knowledge of transactions or occurrences in issue.

(prepare backsheet)

Legal Office Procedures

-2-

Date   , 20--

MICHAEL, ELIAD & REDFORD LLP
Barristers and Solicitors
863 Seneca Lane
Toronto, Ontario
M4J 1P6

Robert B. Redford
Tel: 416-363-1079
Fax: 416-363-2628

Lawyers for the Plaintiff

TO: **CASTLES & SANDS**
Suite 900-205 Portage Street
Markham, Ontario L3R 3G3

Raymond G. Castles
Tel: 905-495-2222
Fax: 905-495-2223

Lawyers for the Defendant

(prepare backsheet)

Court File No. CV-**-76542

ONTARIO
SUPERIOR COURT OF JUSTICE

B E T W E E N:

NICHOLAS ROMANO

Plaintiff

and

EASTERN CAST IRON CORPORATION

Defendant

NOTICE OF EXAMINATION

TO: John Hungate

YOU ARE REQUIRED TO ATTEND, on Tuesday, January 30, 20--, at 10:30 a.m. at the office of E. R. Burger, Suite 305, 65 Queen Street West, Toronto, Ontario, M7T 9R2, Telephone No. (416) 967-3456, *(name, address and telephone number of examiner)* for *(choose one of the following)*:

[ ]   Cross-examination on your affidavit dated *(date)*
[ ]   Examination for discovery
[X]   Examination for discovery on behalf of or in place of Eastern Cast Iron Corporation
[ ]   Examination in aid of execution
[ ]   Examination in aid of execution on behalf of or in place of *(identify party)*

YOU ARE REQUIRED TO BRING WITH YOU and produce at the examination the documents mentioned in subrule 30.04(4) of the *Rules of Civil Procedure*, and the following documents and things: *(Set out the nature and date of each document and give particulars sufficient to identify each document and thing)*

1.   All original documents including any sound recording, videotape, film, photograph, chart, graph, map, plan, survey, book of account and information recorded or stored by means on any device in your possession, control or power which are relevant to any matters in issue in this proceeding and a list of all documents over which you claim privilege.

Court File No. CV-**-4355

ONTARIO
SUPERIOR COURT OF JUSTICE

B E T W E E N:

EDWARD BEAR

Plaintiff

and

JOHN DENNVER

Defendant

ANSWERS ON WRITTEN EXAMINATION FOR DISCOVERY

I, John Dennver, of the City of Waterwell, in the County of Mandolee, Defendant in this action, MAKE OATH AND SAY that the following answers to the questions dated November 8, 20--, submitted by the Plaintiff, are true, to the best of my knowledge, information and belief:

1. *(Number each answer to correspond with the question. Where the deponent objects to answering a question, state: I object to answering this question on the ground that it is irrelevant to the matters in issue or that the information sought is privileged because (specify) or as may be.)*

SWORN BEFORE ME at the City of
Markham, in the Regional Municipality of
York this .... day of ...., 20--

_____
Commissioner for Taking Affidavits
(or as may be)

_____
JOHN DENNVER

(prepare backsheet)

Court File No. CV-**-4355

ONTARIO
SUPERIOR COURT OF JUSTICE

B E T W E E N:

EDWARD BEAR

Plaintiff

and

JOHN DENNVER

Defendant

QUESTIONS ON WRITTEN EXAMINATION FOR DISCOVERY

The Plaintiff has chosen to examine the Defendant for discovery by written questions and requires that the following questions be answered by affidavit in Form 35B prescribed by the Rules of Civil Procedure, served within fifteen days after service of these questions.

1. *(Number each question)*

November 8, 20--

MICHAEL, ELIAD & REDFORD LLP
Barristers and Solicitors
863 Seneca Lane
Toronto, Ontario
M4J 1P6

Robert B. Redford
Tel: 416-363-1079
Fax: 416-363-2628

Lawyers for the Plaintiff

TO: **CASTLES & SANDS**
Suite 900-205 Portage Street
Markham, Ontario L3R 3G3

Raymond G. Castles
Tel: 905-495-2222
Fax: 905-495-2223

Lawyers for the Defendant

(prepare backsheet)

CHAPTER 14
PRE-TRIAL

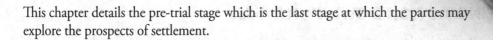

This chapter details the pre-trial stage which is the last stage at which the parties may explore the prospects of settlement.

THE PRE-TRIAL STAGE
Mandatory Mediation (only in Ottawa, Toronto, Windsor) • before setting down for trial
Setting Down for Trial, ∏ or ∆ • after close of pleadings
Placing action on Trial List, by Registrar • 60 days after action is set down for trial, or earlier on consent
Scheduling Pre-trial Conference, ∏ or ∆; if not, Registrar • within 180 days of setting action down for trial • pre-trial conference brief delivered 5 days before pre-trial conference
Pre-Trial Conference, ∏ and ∆ ∏ (Greek pi) = Plaintiff. ∆ (Greek delta) = Defendant

PRE-TRIAL

In the pre-trial stage, the action is set down for trial, and a pre-trial conference is held where the parties may try to settle the action. The threat or reality of the impending trial makes this an appropriate time to bring the parties to serious settlement negotiations.

> ### ROMANO v. EASTERN CAST IRON CORPORATION
> Re: Wrongful Dismissal
>
> We continue with Mr. Romano's action. We have set the action down for trial and served and filed the trial record, Precedent 14.1. We have also prepared the summons to witness, Precedent 14.5, summoning Mr. Irving Wallace to testify on behalf of Mr. Romano.   Mr. Wallace is the new office manager Eastern hired at a salary of $50,000 per year, which is what Mr. Romano was making at the time of his dismissal, and which is $10,000 per year more than Eastern had offered Mr. Romano for the position of office manager.   Next, the judge and jury will speak.

MANDATORY MEDIATION

Rule 24.1 applies to mandatory mediation. Mandatory mediation applies only to actions which are commenced in Ottawa, Toronto, or Windsor. A mediation session must be held within **180 days** after the first defence or notice of intent to defend has been filed, unless the court orders otherwise. In effect, a mediation session should be held at the latest by the date of setting the action down for trial, or at least a **notice of name of mediator and date of session (Form 24.1A)**, Precedent 14.3, must be filed with the mediation co-ordinator by one of the parties by the time of setting the action down for trial. **Seven days** before the mediation session, the parties must provide the mediator with a **statement of issues (Form 24.1C)** (see Chapter 9). The mediator must provide a mediator's report within **ten days** of completion of the mediation session.

SETTING ACTION DOWN FOR TRIAL

At any time after the close of pleadings, any party who is ready may set the action down for trial. Usually, however, it is the plaintiff's lawyer who sets it down. Setting down involves the serving on every other party and filing with proof of service of a **trial record**.

Trial record   The trial record is for the judge to use at trial and contains the documents which the rules require to be included. Subrule 48.03(1) of the *Rules of Civil Procedure* requires that the trial record, Precedent 14.1, contain the following, as applicable:

1. Table of contents, describing each document by name and date.
2. Copy of any jury notice.
3. Copy of the statement of claim.
4. Copy of the pleadings, including those relating to any counterclaim or crossclaim.
5. Copy of any demand or order for particulars of a pleading and the particulars delivered in response.
6. Copy of any notice of amounts and particulars of special damages delivered.
7. Copy of any order respecting the trial.
8. Certificate of lawyer.

In addition (where mediation is mandatory):

9. Copy of **certificate of lawyer** regarding mediation, Precedent 14.2. This certificate is filed with the trial record under practice direction for the Toronto Region. It is basically for the purpose of indicating to the court that mediation has been dealt with. Follow the practice in your region.

10. Copy of **notice of name of mediator and date of session, Form 24.1A**, Precedent 14.3, with proof of service. Although the rules do not require it, it is common practice for lawyers in the Toronto Region to file a copy of this form with the trial record as proof that a mediation session has been scheduled.

PREPARATION AND DISTRIBUTION OF THE TRIAL RECORD

You require: Copies of the applicable documents listed above, in order listed. There is no prescribed form for a trial record. Legal software generates a trial record, Precedent 14.1. Key points include:

Include all of the applicable documents in the order listed above, excluding backsheets, and place a numeric or alphabetic tab between each document. Re-number the existing pages sequentially, by hand or numbering machine, at the top right corner of each page, e.g. first page of the first document is **1**, next page of the same document is **2**, first page of the next document is **3**, etc. Note that a jury notice, if any, is the first document in the table of contents.

Backsheet: The rules require that the backsheet for records be keyed on light blue cover stock paper, which legal stationers supply. This is the back cover page of the trial record. The judge usually uses it to write his or her reasons for judgment.

Assembly of trial record: Assemble the trial record contents in the same sequence as listed above, including the divider tabs, with the light blue trial record backsheet at back. Staple along the left margin at top, middle, and bottom so as to form a booklet. If the trial record is very bulky, many law firms use spiral binding done within or outside the firm.

Number of copies, minimum 3: Serve 1 on the opposite lawyer; file 1, with proof of service, in the court where the action was commenced; keep 1 in client's file.

Supplemental trial record: If any of the following documents become available after filing the trial record, the rules require the lawyer who filed the trial record to add these to the trial record prior to trial. This ensures the judge has all of the facts at the trial. Prepare it in the same way as the trial record and entitle it **supplemental trial record**:

1. Copy of any notice of amounts and particulars of special damages delivered after the filing of the trial record.
2. Copy of any order respecting trial made after the filing of the trial record.
3. Copy of any memorandum signed by the lawyer or of any court order, following a pre-trial conference.
4. In an undefended action, copy of any affidavit to be used as evidence at trial.

PLACING ACTION ON TRIAL LIST

Under subrule 48.06(1), **sixty days**, or earlier if all parties consent, after the action is set down for trial, the local registrar automatically places a defended action on the trial list. There are two trial lists, jury and non-jury. If the trial record contains a jury notice, the action will be placed on the list of trials by jury; if not, by non-jury. Once the action is placed on the trial list, the parties are deemed to be ready for trial, and the trial will proceed when the action is reached on the trial list, unless a judge orders otherwise.

PRE-TRIAL CONFERENCE

A pre-trial conference is required in all actions, unless the court orders otherwise. Within **180 days** after the parties set the action down for trial, the parties must schedule with the registrar a date and time for the pre-trial conference. If the parties do not schedule a pre-trial conference within 180 days of setting down the action for trial, the registrar will schedule a pre-trial conference date and give notice to the parties to appear.

Pre-trial conference brief **Five days** before the pre-trial conference, the parties must deliver a **pre-trial conference brief** under rule 50.04 which must include a concise statement, without argument, of the following matters:

1. The nature of the proceeding.
2. The issues raised and the party's position.
3. The names of the witnesses that the party is likely to call at the trial and the length of time that the evidence of each of those witnesses is estimated to take.
4. The steps that need to be completed before the action is ready for trial and the length of time that it is estimated that the completion of those steps will take.

Form of pre-trial conference brief   The rules do not prescribe a form for a pre-trial conference brief. The form of a pre-trial conference brief, therefore, varies and may be styled in the form of a court document or a memorandum: for example, under practice direction in the Toronto Region, the pre-trial conference brief is styled in a **pre-trial conference memorandum/ brief**, Precedent 14.4, and includes a list of witnesses. Follow the practice in your region.

Who attends the pre-trial conference   Lawyers must attend the pre-trial conference, and parties must participate either by personal attendance or via telephone or video conference if undue travel time or expense would be required for a personal attendance.

What happens at a pre-trial conference   The pre-trial judge meets with the lawyers and their parties in an informal setting and reviews, in a general way, the evidence and the strengths and weaknesses of each party's case. The pre-trial judge may often indicate how he or she would decide the case as a way of encouraging a settlement based on these comments. The pre-trial conference judge must not be the same judge as the trial judge, and communication of the pre-trial conference discussions must not be made to the trial judge so as not to influence the decision of the trial judge. Where no settlement is reached at the pre-trial conference, the pre-trial conference judge sets the date for trial and completes a pre-trial conference report which sets out what steps are needed to be completed before the action is ready for trial and the expected time to complete those steps and the anticipated length of trial.

EXPERT WITNESSES

Expert witnesses are witnesses such as doctors, engineers, accountants, and sociologists. The expert witnesses provide reports which may be helpful in achieving settlement at the pre-trial conference and will be also used at trial. Within **sixty days** of an action being set down for trial, the parties must agree to a schedule setting out the dates for service of expert reports. In practice, however, most lawyers agree simply to be governed by the timelines set out in the rules for delivery of expert reports, which timelines are as follows:

1. A party who wishes to call an expert at trial must serve a copy of the expert's report at least ninety days before the pre-trial conference. The expert's report must be signed by the expert and must include the expert's name and address, qualifications, a summary of his or her opinion, and an acknowledgment of the expert's duty to be fair, objective, and non-partisan. Without this, the expert may not testify.

2. The responding expert report must be served at least sixty days before the pre-trial conference.

SUMMONS TO WITNESS (AT HEARING), FORM 53A

In general, serve a **summons to witness (at hearing), Form 53A**, Precedent 14.5, on every witness. You may, after paying a fee, obtain a pre-signed summons to witness (at hearing) form from the court office. Serving the witness with a summons to witness, Form 53A, ensures that a witness attends trial and that a judge would not interpret any non-attendance as a tactical delay. Thus, if a witness who is served with a summons to witness (at hearing) fails to attend without good reason, the judge may issue a warrant for the arrest of that witness. Once arrested, the witness can be jailed until he or she testifies. Also, if a witness cannot attend because of some unexpected problem such as a serious illness or family emergency, the trial judge is far more likely to adjourn the trial until the witness is available. Prepare the summons to witness (at hearing), issue it, and serve it, together with attendance money, by personal service only, and not by an alternative to personal service. The rules do not prescribe a time limit for service of a summons to witness (at hearing).

Attendance money and travel allowance   Attendance money compensates a witness for time spent **attending** and testifying in court. Travel allowance is also paid to a witness on a flat rate per day if the witness lives in the same place as the place of trial, and if elsewhere, on a per kilometre basis. As well, overnight accommodation and meal allowance is paid to an out-of-town witness who is required to remain overnight. The amount of money paid for these allowances is set out in the tariff in the *Rules of Civil Procedure*.

Number of copies, minimum 2: Issue and serve 1 on the witness; keep 1, with proof of service, in client's file.

OFFERS TO SETTLE

The *Rules of Civil Procedure* encourage parties to settle before reaching trial. The parties may conduct settlement negotiations using the offer to settle mechanism that the rules prescribe. Offers to settle work on this general principle: "If you make a reasonable offer which the other side rejects and you win in the same amount as the offer or more, the court will reward you by ordering the losing party to pay your legal costs." Either side's lawyer may make an **offer to settle, Form 49A,** Precedent 14.6, at any time before trial, but if the offering lawyer wants to win legal costs, he or she must serve the offer to settle at least **seven days** before the trial. If the other lawyer accepts, he or she must serve an **acceptance of offer to settle, Form 49C**, Precedent 14.7. The judge must have no knowledge of any rejected offer until the judge delivers the judgment so as not to influence his or her decision. The party to whom an offer is made has the right, even after counteroffering or rejecting the offer, to reconsider and accept the original offer at any time until the offering party serves a **notice of withdrawal of offer, Form 49B.**

Plaintiff's offer   If the plaintiff offers, and the defendant rejects, and the plaintiff wins in the same amount or **more** at trial, the plaintiff is usually entitled to **partial indemnity** costs (lower scale) to the date of service of the offer and **substantial indemnity** costs (higher scale) from that date on. This encourages the **plaintiff** to initiate settlement.

Defendant's offer   If the defendant offers, and the plaintiff rejects, and the plaintiff wins in the same amount or **less**, the plaintiff is usually entitled to **partial indemnity** costs to the date the offer was served, and the defendant is usually entitled to **partial indemnity** costs from that date. This encourages the **defendant** to make a reasonable offer as early as possible because even if the defendant loses, he or she still wins some costs from the date of serving the offer.

Number of copies, minimum 2: Serve 1 on opposing lawyers; keep 1 in client's file.

CHAPTER SUMMARY

In the pre-trial stage, whichever side is ready for trial sets the action down for trial. This is done by serving and filing, with proof of service, a trial record. The *Rules of Civil Procedure* prescribe the contents of the trial record, which is like a booklet for the judge to refer to at trial. Sixty days after a party files the trial record, the local registrar places the action on the trial list. Where either party will call witnesses to testify at the trial, that party must serve each witness with a summons to witness. A pre-trial conference is mandatory in all actions, and everybody and their lawyer must attend to discuss settlement and weigh the strengths and weaknesses of each party's case. If the parties reach no settlement, the pre-trial conference judge sets a date for trial. The judge who conducts the pre-trial conference may not be the same judge as the judge who presides at the trial. The parties may make offers to settle without having to reveal any offers to the trial judge so as not to influence his or her decision at trial.

REVIEW QUESTIONS

1. What is the purpose of a pre-trial conference?
2. What is the difference between setting the action down for trial and placing it on the trial list?
3. What is the purpose of a trial record?
4. Which document ensures that a witness will attend trial?
5. Which party to the action may make an offer to settle?
6. Explain why attendance money is paid to everyone who attends a trial.

Court File No. CV-**-76542

ONTARIO
SUPERIOR COURT OF JUSTICE

B E T W E E N:

NICHOLAS ROMANO

Plaintiff

and

EASTERN CAST IRON CORPORATION

Defendant

TRIAL RECORD

(date prepared)

MICHAEL, ELIAD & REDFORD LLP
Barristers and Solicitors
863 Seneca Lane
Toronto, Ontario
M4J 1P6

Robert B. Redford
Tel: 416-363-1079
Fax: 416-363-2628

Lawyers for the Plaintiff

TO: **CASTLES & SANDS**
Suite 900-205 Portage Street
Markham, Ontario L3R 3G3

Raymond G. Castles
Tel: 905-495-2222
Fax: 905-495-2223

Lawyers for the Defendant

-2-

Court File No. CV-**-76542

ONTARIO
SUPERIOR COURT OF JUSTICE

B E T W E E N:

NICHOLAS ROMANO

Plaintiff

and

EASTERN CAST IRON CORPORATION

Defendant

TRIAL RECORD

TABLE OF CONTENTS

Tab   **Page No.**

1.   Jury Notice dated November 27, 20--…………………………..................................1

2.   Statement of Claim dated November 2, 20-- 2

3.   Statement of Defence dated November 15, 20--...4

4.   Reply dated November 23, 20--..5

5.   Certificate of Lawyer dated March 26, 20--..6

Court File No. CV-**-76542

ONTARIO
SUPERIOR COURT OF JUSTICE

B E T W E E N :

NICHOLAS ROMANO

Plaintiff

and

EASTERN CAST IRON CORPORATION

Defendant

CERTIFICATE OF LAWYER

I, ROBERT BRET REDFORD, lawyer for the plaintiff, Nicholas Romano, certify that the trial record contains the documents indicated below in the following order as required by Rule 48.03(1) (a) to (g) of the *Rules of Civil Procedure*:

(a)   a table of contents, describing each document by its nature and date;

(b)   a copy of any jury notice;

(c)   a copy of the pleadings, including those relating to any counterclaim or crossclaim;

(d)   ~~a copy of any demand or order for particulars of a pleading and the particulars delivered in response;~~

(e)   ~~a copy of any notice of amounts and particulars of special damages delivered under clause 25.06(9)(b);~~

-2-

(f)   a copy of any order respecting the trial;

I ALSO CERTIFY THAT.

(g)   the time for delivery of pleadings has expired;

(h)   the defendant has failed to deliver a statement of defence has been noted in default;

(i)   judgment has been obtained against the defendant, ; and

(j)   the action has been:

(i)   discontinued as against the defendant, ; and

(ii)   dismissed as against the defendant, .

THE APPROXIMATE LENGTH OF TRIAL ____3____ DAYS

March   , 20--

_____
                                    Robert B. Redford

Court File No. CV-**-76542

ONTARIO
SUPERIOR COURT OF JUSTICE

PROCEEDING COMMENCED AT
TORONTO

TRIAL RECORD

MICHAEL, ELIAD & REDFORD LLP
Barristers and Solicitors
863 Seneca Lane
Toronto, Ontario
M4J 1P6

Robert B. Redford (48000R)
Tel: 416-363-1079
Fax: 416-363-2628
rbrdfrd@mer.com

Lawyers for the Plaintiff

(light blue)

NICHOLAS ROMANO
Plaintiff

-and-

EASTERN CAST IRON CORPORATION
Defendant

**SUPERIOR COURT OF JUSTICE
(TORONTO REGION)
CERTIFICATE**

Court File No. CV-**-76542

ONTARIO
SUPERIOR COURT OF JUSTICE

B E T W E E N :

NICHOLAS ROMANO

Plaintiff

and

EASTERN CAST IRON CORPORATION

Defendant

I, Robert B. Redford, lawyer for the Plaintiff, Nicholas Romano, certify that:

☒ a form 24.1A (notice of name of mediator and date of session) has been filed with the mediation co-ordinator;

☐ the report by mediator indicating that the mediation has been concluded has been filed with the mediation co-ordinator;

☐ an order has been obtained from a judge or case management master exempting the action from mediation; or,

☐ an order has been obtained from a judge or case management master extending the deadline for mediation until after the action is set down for trial.

☐ this action is exempt from Mandatory Mediation pursuant to Rule 24.1.04(2.1)

This certification applies even where the parties have agreed to postpone a mediation session to a date more than 180 days after the first defence has been filed as permitted by Rule 24.1.

Dated at Toronto, Ontario, this   day of March, 20--.

_____
Signature of Lawyer/Party

MICHAEL, ELIAD & REDFORD LLP
Barristers and Solicitors
863 Seneca Lane
Toronto, Ontario M4J 1P6

Robert B. Redford
Tel: 416-363-1079
Fax: 416-363-2628

Lawyers for the Plaintiff (needs no backsheet)

Court File No. CV-**-76542

ONTARIO
SUPERIOR COURT OF JUSTICE

B E T W E E N:

NICHOLAS ROMANO

Plaintiff

and

EASTERN CAST IRON CORPORATION

Defendant

NOTICE OF NAME OF MEDIATOR & DATE OF SESSION

TO: MEDIATION CO-ORDINATOR

1.   I certify that I have consulted with the parties and that the parties have chosen the

following mediator for the mediation session required by Rule 24.1: Christine Spinosa.

2.   The mediator is named in the list of mediators for Toronto *(name county)*.

3.   The mediation session will take place on March 20, 20--.

February   , 20--   **MICHAEL, ELIAD & REDFORD LLP**
                                       Barristers and Solicitors
                                       863 Seneca Lane
                                       Toronto, Ontario   M4J 1P6

                                       Robert B. Redford
                                       Tel: 416-363-1079
                                       Fax: 416-363-2628

                                       Lawyers for the Plaintiff

                                                        (prepare backsheet)

Court File No. CV-**-1750

ONTARIO
SUPERIOR COURT OF JUSTICE
(Toronto Region)

PRE-TRIAL MEMORANDUM

Please return this form to the **Civil Trial Office**, 7th Floor, 330 University Avenue, Toronto, Ontario M5G 1R7. **Faxes or e-mails will not be accepted.**

SHORT TITLE:

Hepburn Renovations Ltd. v. Spencer Ricardo Tracy and Lillian Amanda Tracy

Jury ☐   Non-Jury ☒

Date of Pre-trial Conference: <u>November 8, 20--</u>   Time: 10:30 a.m.

COMPANION ACTION(S) *(include short title, court file # and any third party action to be tried with this one)*:

PRE-TRIAL CONFERENCE MEMORANDUM
OF THE PLAINTIFFS

Party Name(s):   Hepburn Renovations Ltd.

Lawyer: Robert B. Redford
MICHAEL, ELIAD & REDFORD LLP

This party acknowledges that:

Pleadings are in order	X
Motions are complete	X
Documents and/or other productions are complete	X
Oral examinations are complete	X
Transcripts are available	☐
Notices to admit and responses are complete	☐
Mediation has taken place	☐
Experts' reports have been exchanged	☐

Page 1 of 4

Legal Office Procedures

Court File No. CV-**-1750

Lawyers attending for the party submitting this   X
Pre-trial brief is lawyer with carriage

I will be representing myself at the trial   ☐

List Lawyers for all the parties:

Party	Represented by:
Spencer Ricardo Tracy and Lillian Amanda Tracy	CASTLES & SANDS

List Lawyers for all the parties in companion action(s):

Party	Represented by:

PART I – SETTLEMENT BRIEF

(a)   Concise statement of the material facts, clearly specifying which facts are controversial and which are not:

1.   The Plaintiff is a supplier of wholesale fruits and vegetables. The Plaintiff supplied the Defendant with apples totalling a value of $15,000.00. The Defendant refused to pay the invoice.

2.   The Defendant admits purchasing the apples from the Plaintiff, but alleges they were unfit and not of merchantable quality.

(b)   Concise statement of the legal issues, if any, and overview *without argument* of the parties' positions on the legal issues:

1.   Was there a binding contract between the Plaintiff and Defendant?

2.   What is the value of the goods sold to the Defendant by the Plaintiff?

3.   Is the Defendant entitled to any set-off for goods supplied which were allegedly not of merchantable quality and unfit for their intended purpose?

(c)   Concise summary of the evidence to be called *(Complete Appendix A - list of every witness that may be called, including estimated length.)*

1.   Steven Cohen - 2 hours.

(d)   Attach **relevant portions ONLY** of transcripts, experts' reports and any documents central to understanding the issues.

1.   The Plaintiff will be producing its ordinary business records, being invoices and associated documents.

Page 2 of 4

Court File No. CV-**-1750

PART II – TRIAL MANAGEMENT BRIEF

(a)   What, if any, steps remain to be taken before trial?

1.   Mediation session.

(b)   How much time is needed to complete any remaining steps?

1.   It is estimated the mediation session will take half a day.

(c)   Agreed estimated length of time for trial: One day

(d)   Have lawyers, witnesses and experts confirmed their availability for trial?

Yes   X   No   ☐

(e)   Please provide any other information relevant to fixing a date for trial:

_____   _____
Date   Robert B. Redford

MICHAEL, ELIAD & REDFORD LLP
Barristers and Solicitors
863 Seneca Lane
Toronto, Ontario   M4J 1P6

Robert B. Redford
Tel: 416-363-1079
Fax: 416-363-2628

Lawyers for the Plaintiff

Page 3 of 4

APPENDIX A:

List of Witnesses That May be Called

Name of Witness	Party to be Called By	Estimated Length
Steven Cohen	Plaintiff	2 hours

Court File No. CV-**-1750

SPENCER RICARDO TRACY AND LILLIAN AMANDA TRACY

Defendants

-and-

HEPBURN RENOVATIONS LTD.

Plaintiff

ONTARIO
SUPERIOR COURT OF JUSTICE

PROCEEDING COMMENCED AT
TORONTO

**PRE-TRIAL MEMORANDUM
(TORONTO REGION)**

MICHAEL, ELIAD & REDFORD LLP
Barristers and Solicitors
863 Seneca Lane
Toronto, Ontario
M4J 1P6

Robert B. Redford (48000R)
Tel: 416-363-1079
Fax: 416-363-2628
rbrdfrd@mer.com

Lawyers for the Plaintiff

Court File No. CV-**-76542

ONTARIO
SUPERIOR COURT OF JUSTICE

B E T W E E N :

NICHOLAS ROMANO

Plaintiff

and

EASTERN CAST IRON CORPORATION

Defendant

SUMMONS TO WITNESS

TO: Irving Wallace
       1 Second Lady Street
       Toronto, Ontario M2R 8Q3 *(Name and address of witness)*

YOU ARE REQUIRED TO ATTEND TO GIVE EVIDENCE IN COURT at the hearing of this proceeding on Monday, April 30, (year), at 10:00 a.m. at the Court House, 393 University Avenue, 10th Floor, Toronto, Ontario, M5G 1E6 and to remain until your attendance is no longer required.

YOU ARE REQUIRED TO BRING WITH YOU and produce at the hearing the following documents and things: *(Set out the nature and date of each document and give particulars sufficient to identify each document and thing).*

ATTENDANCE MONEY for one (1) day(s) of attendance is served with this summons, calculated in accordance with Tariff A of the *Rules of Civil Procedure*, as follows:

Attendance allowance of $50.00 daily	$50.00
Travel allowance	$3.00
Overnight accommodation and meal allowance	N/A
TOTAL:	$53.00

If further attendance is required, you will be entitled to additional attendance money.

IF YOU FAIL TO ATTEND OR REMAIN IN ATTENDANCE AS REQUIRED BY THIS SUMMONS, A WARRANT MAY BE ISSUED FOR YOUR ARREST.

Date   March   , 20--   Issued by
                                                                     Local Registrar

                               Address of court
                               office: 393 University Avenue
                                          10th Floor
                                          Toronto, Ontario M5G 1E6

This summons was issued at the request of, and inquiries may be directed to:

MICHAEL, ELIAD & REDFORD LLP
Barristers and Solicitors
863 Seneca Lane
Toronto, Ontario   M4J 1P6

Robert B. Redford
Tel: 416-363-1079
Fax: 416-363-2628

Lawyers for the Plaintiff   (prepare backsheet)

Court File No. CV-**- 4234

ONTARIO
SUPERIOR COURT OF JUSTICE

BETWEEN:

JANE EYRE

Plaintiff

and

MANFRED MARK O'DONNELL

Defendant

OFFER TO SETTLE

The Defendant offers to settle this proceeding on the following terms:

1.   If the Plaintiff accepts this Offer before June 15, 20--, the Defendant shall pay to the Plaintiff the amount of $10,000 as a once and for all lump sum.

2.   If the Plaintiff does not accept this Offer before June 15, 20--, then the Defendant offers to pay to the Plaintiff the amount of $5,000 as a once and for all lump sum.

3.   Each party is to bear his or her own costs.

4.   The Plaintiff shall provide to the Defendant a release from any and all claims pleaded in this action.

5.   The Plaintiff will file a Notice of Discontinuance dismissing this action.

6.   This Offer expires on June 22, 20--, at 6 p.m.

Date   March 10, 20–

TO: **BEST AND BUNGLE**
39 Park Avenue
Toronto, ON M6E 1A2

Roger Best
Tel: (416) 363-5467
Fax: (416) 363-5466

Lawyers for the Plaintiff

MICHAEL, ELIAD & REDFORD LLP
Barristers and Solicitors
863 Seneca Lane
Toronto, Ontario M4J 1P6

Robert B. Redford
Tel: (416) 363-1079
Fax: (416) 363-2628

Lawyers for the Defendant

(prepare backsheet)

JANE EYRE v. MANFRED MARK O'DONNELL
Plaintiff   Defendant

Court File No. CV-**-4234

ONTARIO
SUPERIOR COURT OF JUSTICE

Proceeding commenced at Toronto

ACCEPTANCE OF OFFER TO SETTLE

BEST AND BUNGLE
Barristers and Solicitors
39 Park Avenue
Toronto, Ontario
M6E 1A2

Roger Best (12345W)
Tel: (416) 363-5467
Fax: (416) 363-5466
rogerbest@bestbungle.com

Lawyers for the Plaintiff

Court File No. CV-**- 4234

ONTARIO
SUPERIOR COURT OF JUSTICE

BETWEEN:

JANE EYRE

Plaintiff

and

MANFRED MARK O'DONNELL

Defendant

ACCEPTANCE OF OFFER TO SETTLE

The Plaintiff accepts your Offer to Settle dated March 10, 20--.

Date March 25, 20--

BEST AND BUNGLE
Barristers and Solicitors
39 Park Avenue
Toronto, Ontario M6E 1A2

Roger Best
Tel: (416) 363-5467
Fax: (416) 363-5466

Lawyers for the Plaintiff

TO: **MICHAEL, ELIAD & REDFORD LLP**
Barristers and Solicitors
863 Seneca Lane
Toronto, Ontario M4J 1P6

Robert B. Redford
Tel: (416) 363-1079
Fax: (416) 363-2628

Lawyers for the Defendant

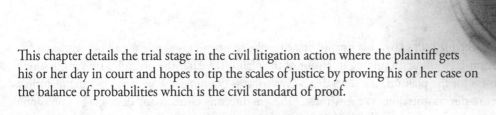

CHAPTER 15
TRIAL

This chapter details the trial stage in the civil litigation action where the plaintiff gets his or her day in court and hopes to tip the scales of justice by proving his or her case on the balance of probabilities which is the civil standard of proof.

THE TRIAL STAGE
Trial
Judgment
Bill of Costs

ROMANO v. EASTERN CAST IRON CORPORATION
Re: Wrongful Dismissal

We have reached the final step in Mr. Romano's action. As you will note from the judgment, Precedent 15.3, Justice Pinsent found that although Eastern was justified in dismissing Mr. Romano who was discovered at trial to have had a very poor disposition, Eastern had not paid him the bonuses that he had rightfully earned while in their employ. The bonuses amounted to $45,000, and Justice Pinsent ordered Eastern to pay that amount to Mr. Romano, plus his costs on a partial indemnity basis, but awarded no other claim. We prepared the bill of costs, Precedent 15.4, which Justice Pinsent considered and awarded to Mr. Romano. We have now come to the end of the Romano case.

TRIAL STAGE

The litigation action is now at trial. This means the parties did not settle at the pre-trial conference.

TRIAL BRIEF

The trial brief, Precedent 15.1, is for the lawyer's use at trial and contains all of the documents the lawyer will refer to at trial. Distinguish this from the trial record which is for the judge's use and which includes only those documents which the *Rules of Civil Procedure* require to be included. The trial brief is usually bulky and is, therefore, often placed in three-ring binders or is spiral-bound. There is no prescribed form in the rules for trial briefs. Lawyers have personal preferences in organizing the trial brief. Generally, however, the trial brief is organized chronologically by category of documents with corresponding tabs.

BRIEF OF AUTHORITIES

A brief of authorities, Precedent 15.2, contains copies of decided cases and statutes that support the case at hand. Lawyers prepare a brief of authorities in nearly every trial and provide the trial judge with a copy. The purpose is to argue on the basis of the case law and the statutes contained in the brief, and thus favourably influence the judge's decision. There is no prescribed form in the rules for briefs of authorities. Lawyers prepare them according to preference following proper rules of case and statute citations. For examples of reported cases and details on how to key case and statute citations, refer to Chapter 6.

TRIAL

At trial, the plaintiff's lawyer is usually first to make an opening statement and call witnesses for the plaintiff (witnesses testifying in favour of the plaintiff). After the plaintiff's lawyer questions a witness for the plaintiff, the defendant's lawyer cross-examines the witness, and the plaintiff's lawyer re-directs questions to the witness. The re-directing corrects any damaging impressions or testimony that the defendant's lawyer was able to extract from the witness. After the plaintiff's lawyer has introduced all of his or her evidence and presented all of his or her witnesses, it is then the turn of the defendant's lawyer to follow in the same procedure with witnesses for the defendant. Both sides end by making a closing statement.

JUDGMENT

At the conclusion of the trial, the judge (or judge and jury) gives the decision known as **judgment**. The judge usually writes the **reasons for judgment** on the back of the trial record or on a separate "reasons for decision" document. After trial, usually the winning lawyer incorporates the judge's decision into a formal judgment document, Form 59B, Precedent 15.3. The winning lawyer then sends two copies of the judgment to the losing lawyer for **approval as to form and content**. If the losing lawyer agrees that the judgment correctly reflects the decision of the judge, he or she keeps one copy and writes "approved as to form and content" on the other copy and returns the "approved as to form and content" copy to the winning lawyer. This is proof to the court that the losing lawyer has examined the judgment for accuracy.

Issuing and entering judgment To make the judgment official, the winning lawyer must take the original judgment, together with the approved as to form and content copy, to the court where the proceeding was commenced to have the judgment issued, entered, and filed. The judgment is **issued** by the registrar signing and sealing the original judgment. It is **entered** pursuant to subrule 59.05(2) by the registrar either inserting a copy of the issued judgment in an entry book or microfilming it, and it is **filed** by the registrar filing a copy of the issued judgment in the court file. The issued and entered original is returned to the winning lawyer.

PREPARATION AND DISTRIBUTION OF JUDGMENT, FORM 59B

You require: Usually the lawyer's notes of the judge's decision taken at trial or a photocopy of the judge's written decision. Follow along in Precedent 15.3. Litigation software presets the form so that only the variable information need be keyed.

The name of the judge and the date on which the judge gave the judgment is keyed thus:

THE HONOURABLE	)	FRIDAY, THE 3RD DAY OF
MR. JUSTICE SURNAME	)	MARCH, (YEAR)
OR		
THE HONOURABLE	)	FRIDAY, MARCH 3, (YEAR)
MADAM JUSTICE SURNAME	)	

The preamble indicates the judgment is the result of an ACTION (instead of an application), that the trial lasted three days, that everybody's lawyers and the parties were present at the trial, and that the judge arrived at the judgment after **reading** the pleadings and **hearing** the evidence at trial. Each new judgment point begins with the words THIS COURT ORDERS.

In the first numbered paragraph, insert the amount of damages awarded. This figure usually includes prejudgment interest. In the second numbered paragraph, insert the amount of costs awarded, if specified; otherwise, the paragraph usually ends by indicating the costs scale, e.g. partial indemnity scale. In the final unnumbered paragraph, obtain the postjudgment interest rate from the website of the Ministry of the Attorney General and insert it. The judgment ends with a signature line. The judgment is usually signed by either the judge who gave the judgment or by the local registrar on behalf of the judge.

Number of copies, minimum 6: Issue and enter 1; send 2 to losing lawyers; they return 1 approved as to form and content; 1 for court's entry book; 1 for court file; keep 1 in the client's file.

COSTS

Costs are the legal fees and disbursements lawyers charge for representing their clients in the action. Judges usually use costs as a tool to indicate which party had a more just case. Lawyers know amongst themselves that the measure of their success at trial is often reflected in the way in which the judge awards costs. When a judge awards costs to the plaintiff, it means the defendant pays a specified amount of the plaintiff's legal costs (as well as his or her own legal costs), and vice versa when costs are to the defendant. Note that an award of costs rarely indemnifies parties in the full amount of the legal costs which lawyers charge their clients. In awarding costs, judges are required to **fix** the amount of costs on the basis of either a partial indemnity or a substantial indemnity scale:

Partial indemnity This is the scale on which the court most frequently awards costs. Partial indemnity usually covers only about half of the total costs that the lawyer charges the client. That is because the partial indemnity scale allows lower hourly rates than lawyers charge their clients and only those disbursements which are permitted under the tariff, e.g. fees paid to court.

Substantial indemnity This scale covers almost all of a party's legal costs. The substantial indemnity scale imposes the same tariff restrictions on fees and disbursements as the partial indemnity scale but is a higher scale by about 1.5 times the partial indemnity costs. The substantial indemnity scale, however, is rarely awarded, except in exceptional cases such as when the losing party has failed to abide by the *Rules of Civil Procedure*.

Disbursements   For the purpose of costs submissions, lawyers must claim only such disbursements as are permitted under Part II, Tariff A.   To give you an idea of the types of disbursements allowed, here is an excerpt from Part II, Tariff A:

PART II - DISBURSEMENTS

21. Attendance money actually paid to a witness who is entitled to attendance money, to be calculated as follows:
    1. Attendance allowance for each day of necessary attendance.........................$50
    2. Travel allowance, where the hearing or examination is held,
        (a) in a city or town in which the witness resides, $3.00 for each day of necessary attendance...
22. Fees or expenses actually paid to a court, court reporter, official examiner or sheriff under the regulations under the *Administration of Justice Act*.
23. For service or attempted service of a document,
    (a) in Ontario, the amount actually paid, not exceeding the fee payable to a sheriff under the regulations under the *Administration of Justice Act*;
    (b) outside Ontario, a reasonable amount...
23.2 Fees actually paid to a mediator in accordance with Ontario Regulation 291/99 made under the *Administration of Justice Act*...

Hourly rates   For purposes of costs submissions, the Costs Sub-Committee of the Civil Rules Committee has provided the legal profession with the following guidelines on hourly rates for lawyers, law clerks, and students-at-law.   Note that these are maximum rates; lawyers usually submit hourly rates that come within these maximums:

MAXIMUM PARTIAL INDEMNITY HOURLY RATES	
PROVIDER OF LEGAL SERVICES	MAXIMUM HOURLY FEE
Law clerks	Maximum of $80.00 per hour
Student-at-law	Maximum of $60.00 per hour
Lawyer (less than 10 years)	Maximum of $225.00 per hour
Lawyer (10 years or more but less than 20 years)	Maximum of $300.00 per hour
Lawyer (20 years and over)	Maximum of $350.00 per hour

MAXIMUM SUBSTANTIAL INDEMNITY HOURLY RATES (Partial Indemnity × 1.5)	
PROVIDER OF LEGAL SERVICES	MAXIMUM HOURLY FEE
Law clerks	Maximum of $120.00 per hour
Student-at-law	Maximum of $90.00 per hour
Lawyer (less than 10 years)	Maximum of $337.50 per hour
Lawyer (10 years or more but less than 20 years)	Maximum of $450.00 per hour
Lawyer (20 years and over)	Maximum of $525.00 per hour

Costs to be paid forthwith or in the cause   Ontario has what is known as a "loser pays" costs system. Generally, costs ordered payable "forthwith" means that the losing party must pay the costs without delay. Where costs are ordered payable "in the cause" they tend to be interim costs, e.g. costs on motions, and are payable to the party to whom the costs were awarded only if the party ultimately wins at the trial. However payable, the recovered costs usually reimburse the client for only part of the total amount of the lawyer's fees that the client has paid over the duration of the action. The client remains responsible for paying the balance of the legal costs to his or her lawyer.

BILL OF COSTS

At the end of the trial, the judge usually makes a decision as to which party is entitled to costs and whether on the scale of partial or substantial indemnity. Subrule 57.01(5) requires the party who is awarded costs to serve a bill of costs (Form 57A), Precedent 15.4, on the other parties and file it with proof of service. In practice, however, at the end of the trial, the lawyer who won costs often submits his or her bill of costs to the judge, along with written (or oral) submissions, and sends a copy of the bill of costs to the losing lawyer who may argue against the figure being requested. The judge will then make his or her decision on the amount of the costs. The bill of costs helps the judge arrive at the figure of the costs award. Note that the bill of costs is not the same as an account which lawyers send out when billing their clients.

PREPARATION AND DISTRIBUTION OF BILL OF COSTS, FORM 57A

You require: Pre-billing report. Commercial legal accounting software is capable of producing the amounts of fees and disbursements which apply to bills of costs. Follow along in Precedent 15.4. Key points include:

Group the legal services according to the sequence of steps in trial. Indicate the name of the lawyer, law clerk, or student-at-law who provided the legal services, the number of hours, and the hourly rate charged under either the partial indemnity scale or the substantial indemnity scale. Double check your calculations. Attach copies of the dockets that relate to the claim for fees. Attach copies of invoices that relate to the claim for disbursements.

Number of copies, minimum 3: Serve 1 on unsuccessful lawyer; file 1 in court with proof of service; keep 1 in client's file.

ASSESSMENT OF COSTS

Under subrule 57.01(3.1) the court may only in exceptional cases refer costs for assessment. Generally, an assessment of costs is done when a client challenges an account. An assessment of costs means that an assessment officer of the court will review the lawyer's bill of costs and decide on what the final amount of costs should be. The assessment process is as follows:

1. A copy of the bill of costs and the judgment that ordered costs to be assessed is filed in the court where the action was commenced and an appointment is made with the assessment officer.
2. The court gives a **notice of appointment for assessment of costs** which the party making the appointment must serve, together with a copy of the bill of costs, on the opposite lawyers, at least **seven days** before the appointment. This enables the opposite lawyers to attend and speak to the assessment.
3. At the conclusion of the assessment of costs, the assessment officer specifies in a **certificate of assessment of costs** (pre-completed by the lawyer who initiated the assessment of costs) the amount of costs as assessed and allowed.

CHAPTER SUMMARY

At the trial stage, the parties prepare their respective trial briefs and briefs of authorities for their respective use at trial. The trial brief, usually in a three-ring binder, is the lawyer's personal reference book which contains all of the documents to which the lawyer will refer in arguing the case. The brief of authorities, on the other hand, contains only such statutes and case law which are helpful in proving the client's case, and the lawyer must provide the judge with a copy of it for the judge's reference.

At trial, the plaintiff's lawyer makes the opening statement and calls any witnesses for the plaintiff, and the defendant's lawyer cross-examines. Then, it is the turn of the defendant's lawyer to do the same with any witnesses for the defendant. Both sides end by making a closing argument, at the end of which, the judge delivers the court's decision, which is called a judgment. The winning lawyer puts the terms of the judgment in a formal judgment document, sends the judgment to the other side to approve, and issues and enters the approved judgment in court.

When a judge awards costs to a party, he or she fixes the costs on the basis of either a partial indemnity or substantial indemnity scale. Costs on a partial indemnity scale cover only part of the winning party's legal costs, and the winning party is responsible for paying the balance of the costs to his or her lawyer. The losing party is responsible for paying the winning party's costs award as well as the entire legal costs of the losing party's own lawyer.

REVIEW QUESTIONS

1. Who uses a trial brief?
2. What is a brief of authorities?
3. What is a judgment?
4. What are partial indemnity costs?
5. Explain how a bill of costs is the same as an account which the lawyer sends when billing the client.

Court File No. 789/--

ONTARIO

SUPERIOR COURT OF JUSTICE

BETWEEN:

COPPOLA CONSTRUCTION LIMITED

Plaintiff

and

LIZI BORDEN and ANNA KARENINA

Defendants

TRIAL BRIEF

TABLE OF CONTENTS

VOLUME I

DESCRIPTION	TAB NO.
Statement of Claim dated June *(day)*, *(year)*	1
Statement of Defence dated June *(day)*, *(year)*	2
Reply dated June *(day)*, *(year)*	3
Transcript of the examination for discovery of Frank Coppola dated August *(day)*, *(year)*	4
Answers to undertakings of the examination for discovery of Frank Coppola dated August *(day)*, *(year)*	5
Transcript of the examination for discovery of Lizi Borden dated August *(day)*, *(year)*	6
Answers to undertakings of the examination for discovery of Lizi Borden dated August *(day)*, *(year)*	7

i

Court File No. 789/--

ONTARIO

SUPERIOR COURT OF JUSTICE

BETWEEN:

COPPOLA CONSTRUCTION LIMITED

Plaintiff

and

LIZI BORDEN and ANNA KARENINA

Defendants

TRIAL BRIEF

MICHAEL, ELIAD & REDFORD LLP
Barristers and Solicitors
863 Seneca Lane
Toronto, Ontario M4J 1P6

Robert B. Redford
Tel: (416) 363-1079
Fax: (416) 363-2628

Lawyers for the Defendants

ONTARIO

SUPERIOR COURT OF JUSTICE

BETWEEN:

COPPOLA CONSTRUCTION LIMITED

Plaintiff

and

LIZI BORDEN and ANNA KARENINA

Defendants

BRIEF OF AUTHORITIES

DESCRIPTION | TAB NO.

J R Building Company v Financial Frontier Ltd (1871), 7 Ch App 161 1

Acre Land Company, Re, [1896] 2 Ch 743 2

Brown v Ace Developers (1962), 33 DLR (2d) 317 (NBCA); affirmed, [1963] SCR 312 3

March v Dimes, [1976] 2 SCR 200, [1975] 6 WWR 673, 75 CLLC 14,286, 5 NR 523, 25 CCC (2d) 186, 62 DLR (3d) 68 4

Searle v Peter, [1963] 3 All ER 770 5

MICHAEL, ELIAD & REDFORD LLP
Barristers and Solicitors
863 Seneca Lane
Toronto, Ontario M4J 1P6

Robert B. Redford
Tel: (416) 363-1079
Fax: (416) 363-2628

Lawyers for the Defendants

VOLUME II*

DESCRIPTION | TAB NO.

CHRONOLOGY OF EVENTS - December (year) to August (year)

CORRESPONDENCE

Letter from Coppola Construction to Lindberg Company dated December (day),(year). 8

Letter from Lindberg Company to Anna Karenina dated December (day), (year) 9

Letter from Lindberg Company to Anna Karenina dated January (day), (year) 10

Letter from Anna Karenina to Coppola Construction dated February (day), (year) ... 11

Letter from Coppola Construction to Lizi Borden dated March (day), (year) 12

Memorandum from Anna Karenina to Lizi Borden dated April (day), (year) 13

AGREEMENTS

Agreement between Anna Karenina and Lizi Borden dated January (day), (year) 14

Agreement between Coppola Construction and Anna Karenina and Lizi Borden dated February (day), (year) 15

Agreement between Anna Karenina and Lizi Borden dated March (day), (year) 16

LEASES

Lease between Anna Karenina and Lindberg Company dated February (day), (year) . 17

REPORTS

Report of Omega Real Estate Appraising Company dated August (day), (year) 18

*On the first page of Volume II of the trial brief, repeat the heading and the title. Do the same for any subsequent volumes.

ii

Court File No. CV-**-76542

ONTARIO
SUPERIOR COURT OF JUSTICE

THE HONOURABLE	)	FRIDAY, THE 30th
	)	
MR. JUSTICE PINSENT	)	DAY OF APRIL, 20--

B E T W E E N :

(Court Seal)

NICHOLAS ROMANO

Plaintiff

and

EASTERN CAST IRON CORPORATION

Defendant

JUDGMENT

THIS ACTION was heard this 28th, 29th and 30th day of April, 20--, with a Jury at the Court House, 393 University Avenue, 10th Floor, Toronto, Ontario, M5G 1E6, in the presence of the lawyers for all parties, the Plaintiff and the Defendant appearing in person,

ON READING THE PLEADINGS AND HEARING THE EVIDENCE and the submissions of the lawyers for the parties,

1.   THIS COURT ORDERS that the Plaintiff recover from the Defendant the sum of $45,000.00.

2.   THIS COURT ORDERS that the Defendant pay to the Plaintiff his costs of this action forthwith fixed on a partial indemnity scale in the amount of $35,449.69.

THIS JUDGMENT bears post judgment interest at the rate of 4% per annum effective from the date of this Judgment. Where there is default in payment, the payment in default shall bear interest only from the date of default.

_____
(Signature of Judge)

Court File No. CV-**-76542

NICHOLAS ROMANO
Plaintiff

-and-

EASTERN CAST IRON CORPORATION
Defendant

ONTARIO
SUPERIOR COURT OF JUSTICE

PROCEEDING COMMENCED AT
TORONTO

JUDGMENT

MICHAEL, ELIAD & REDFORD LLP
Barristers and Solicitors
863 Seneca Lane
Toronto, Ontario
M4J 1P6

Robert B. Redford (48000R)
Tel: 416-363-1079
Fax: 416-363-2628
rbrdfrd@mer.com

Lawyers for the Plaintiff

Court File No. CV-**-76542

ONTARIO
SUPERIOR COURT OF JUSTICE

B E T W E E N :

NICHOLAS ROMANO

Plaintiff

and

EASTERN CAST IRON CORPORATION

Defendant

BILL OF COSTS

AMOUNTS CLAIMED FOR FEES AND DISBURSEMENTS

(Following the items set out in Tariff A, itemize the claim for fees and disbursements. Indicate the names of the lawyers, students-at-law and law clerks who provided services in connection with each item. In support of the claim for fees, attach copies of the dockets or other evidence. In support of the claim for disbursements, attach copies of invoices or other evidence.)

Partial Indemnity

PLEADINGS
Drafting Statement of Claim, receipt and review of Statement
of Defence, draft Reply.

Robert B. Redford – 3.9 hours @ $250.00/hr.	$975.00
Jill Doe – 2.2 hours @ $60.00/hr.	132.00

PRODUCTION OF DOCUMENTS
Receive and assemble client documents, prepare and deliver
Affidavit of Documents.

Robert B. Redford – 3.5 hours @ $250.00/hr.	875.00
Jill Doe – 2.5 hours @ $60.00/hr.	150.00

EXAMINATIONS FOR DISCOVERY
Prepare for and attend upon Examinations for Discovery of all parties.

Robert B. Redford – 4 hours @ $250.00/hr.	1,000.00

MEDIATION
Prepare and deliver Mediation Brief, receipt and review of opposing
Mediation Brief to prepare for and attend upon mediation.

Robert B. Redford – 4.9 hours @ $250.00/hr.	1,225.00
Jill Doe – 3.1 hours @ $60.00/hr.	186.00

PRE-TRIAL CONFERENCE
Prepare Pre-Trial Conference Memorandum, prepare and attend
upon pre-trial conference.

Robert B. Redford – 2.4 hours @ $250.00/hr.	600.00
Jill Doe – 1.1 hours @ $60.00/hr.	66.00

-2-

PREPARATION FOR TRIAL
Reviewing transcripts and exhibits, compiling document briefs,
obtaining and organizing evidence, preparing evidentiary documents
for trial.

Robert B. Redford – 60.5 hours @ $250.00/hr.	15,125.00
Jill Doe – 10.2 hours @ $60.00/hr.	612.00
Robert B. Redford – at trial: 3 days @ $2,300.00/day	6,900.00

JUDGMENT
Preparation of Bill of Costs.
Preparation of Writ of Seizure and Sale.

Robert B. Redford – 3 hours @ $250.00/hr.	750.00
Jill Doe – 2 hours @ $60.00/hr.	120.00
TOTAL FEES	$28,716.00
HST	3,733.08
	$32,449.08

DISBURSEMENTS

Paid fee to court to issue Statement of Claim*	$ 220.00	
Paid fee to service of Statement of Claim	200.00	
Paid fee to court to pass Trial Record*	405.00	
Paid fee to mediator	600.00	
Paid for transcripts for Examination for Discovery	165.00	
Paid for photocopying	600.00	
Paid for Quicklaw research	500.00	
Paid for corporate search	37.31	
	$ 2,727.31	
HST on disbursements amount of $2,102.31	273.30	
Total disbursements	$ 3,000.61	3,000.61
TOTAL FEES AND DISBURSEMENTS		$35,449.69

*Not subject to HST

STATEMENT OF EXPERIENCE

A claim for fees is being made with respect to the following lawyers:

Name of Lawyer	Years of Experience
Robert B. Redford	10 years or more
Jill Doe (law clerk)	

TO: **CASTLES & SANDS**
            Suite 900 - 205 Portage Street
            Markham, Ontario L3R 3G3

            Raymond G. Castles
            Tel: 905-495-2222
            Fax: 905-495-2223

            Lawyers for the Defendant

(prepare backsheet)

CHAPTER 16
APPLICATIONS

This chapter details the steps in proceedings commenced by applications and also looks at how applications differ from actions.

Figure 16.1 Steps in Applications

Notice of Application and Supporting Affidavit, A
- issued and served at least 10 days before hearing date (20 days if outside Ontario)
- filed at least 7 days before hearing date
- information for court use, not issued or served; filed at time of issuing notice of application

Notice of Appearance, R
- served and filed forthwith

Affidavits in Opposition, R, **and Affidavits in Reply,** A
- served and filed at least 4 days before hearing date

Examination of Witness, A or R
- summons to witness (examination out of court)
- served at least 2 days before examination date

Cross-examination on Affidavit, A or R
- notice of examination
- served at least 2 days before examination date

Applicant's Application Record and Factum, A
- served and filed at least 7 days before hearing date

Respondent's Factum
- served and filed a least 4 days before hearing

Respondent's Application Record, if any, R
- served and filed at least 4 days before hearing

Confirmation of Application, A
- sent not later than 2 p.m., 3 days before hearing date

Hearing

Judgment, A or R

A = Applicant
R = Respondent

APPLICATIONS

There are two ways to start a law suit. One is by action; the other is by application. Rule 38 of the *Rules of Civil Procedure* applies to applications. Applications are law suits parallel to actions, except that applications rarely claim **money**, although they can be about money. Applications are quicker than actions because they rely mainly on affidavit evidence (referred to as **documentary evidence**) and because application hearings are shorter than trials. The originating process in applications is a **notice of application** which the lawyer for the applicant must issue and serve in the same way as a statement of claim in actions. The parties in applications are called **applicant** and **respondent** and are parallel to plaintiff and defendant in actions.

When used Applications are used where either a statute (act) or rule authorizes their use. That is why you will always see in their title of proceeding the name of the statute or rule under which they are brought. Rule 14.05 of the *Rules of Civil Procedure* specifically states when applications are to be used. Excerpts follow:

> *Application under Statute*
> 14.05(2) A proceeding may be commenced by an application to the Superior Court of Justice or to a judge of that court, if a statute so authorizes.
>
> *Application under Rules*
> (3) A proceeding may be brought by application where these rules authorize the commencement of a proceeding by application or where the relief claimed is,
>
> (a) the opinion, advice or direction of the court on a question affecting the rights of a person in respect of the administration of the estate of a deceased person or the execution of a trust...

Legal TIP

Generally, use actions where the claim is for money; use applications everywhere else.

Applications on notice Applications **on notice** are applications which the lawyer must serve on the respondent. The application gives notice of the law suit to the respondent; hence, "on notice."

Application without notice Applications without notice are ones which the lawyer does not serve on the respondent, usually because the application is urgent and there is no time to serve it, which is often the case where a lawyer is applying for an injunction. Usually, injunctions are orders stopping a party from doing something, e.g. removing goods or money from Canada to another country.

Legal TIP

The title of proceeding in all application documents must always include the statute and/or the rule under which the application is authorized.

Who hears applications Judges hear all applications.

Where commenced and heard The applicant names the place of commencement, which is usually the place where the applicant lives. Under the rules, an application is heard in the county where the proceeding was commenced or to which it has been transferred, unless the court orders otherwise.

Short and long applications Short applications are those whose length of hearing lasts for two hours or less. To schedule a hearing for short applications, or urgent ones, you may choose any date on which a judge is scheduled to hear applications. To schedule a hearing for long applications, i.e. applications of more than two hours, you must obtain a hearing date from the court office before preparing the notice of application. When obtaining the hearing date, have this information on hand:

- What the application is about and the names of all parties and their lawyers.
- The rule or act under which the application is made.
- Whether the application is without notice or is on consent (approved by all parties).

Practice directions Judges in various regions, including Toronto, issue practice directions which require the scheduling of short and long application (and motion) hearings to be done in a way that best suits the needs of that specific region. Follow the procedure under practice direction in your region. For details on scheduling requirements for applications (and motions) under practice direction in the Toronto Region, see Chapter 17.

CONSTANTINE v. OUMBRIE
Re: Dissolution of Partnership

We act for Mr. Constantine who wants to dissolve the business partnership he has been carrying on with Ms. Maria Oumbrie under the name of Ghoul Sales and Service, which is a subsidiary of Lucifer Dies Limited. According to our client, Ms. Oumbrie has been secretly dealing with Lucifer Dies Limited to push our client out of the partnership. We have prepared the notice of application, Precedent 16.1, for an order to dissolve the partnership. We have also prepared the supporting affidavit of our client, Precedent 16.2.

Ms. Oumbrie has filed a notice of appearance, Precedent 16.3. In preparation for the application hearing, we have prepared the application record, Precedent 16.4, the applicant's factum, Precedent 16.5, and the confirmation of application, Precedent 16.6. Note from the factum that some of the facts in dispute are whether or not a partnership exists since it was only an oral partnership agreement, and Ms. Oumbrie maintains that there never was any such agreement.

The application hearing came before Justice Right who ruled in our client's favour in the judgment, Precedent 16.7. The Constantine v. Oumbrie application is now completed.

NOTICE OF APPLICATION

Applications begin with a **notice of application (Form 14E)**. Prepare the notice of application on behalf of the applicant, issue it (usually with a supporting affidavit attached to it), and arrange for a process server, or other, to serve it (together with the supporting affidavit), by personal service or an alternative to personal service, on the respondent at least **ten days** before the date of hearing or **twenty days** before the date of hearing if served outside of Ontario. File it, with proof of service, in the court office where the application is to be heard at least **seven days** before the date of hearing. Note that since the authority for applications derives from either a statute or a rule, the title of proceeding in the notice of application and in every subsequent document that relates to the same application must include the name of the statute or rule under which the lawyer is bringing the application.

Legal TIP

Applications are governed by Rule 38, but because the notice of application is an originating process, it is prescribed by Rule 14, which is the originating process rule; that is why the notice of application form is described by that rule number, i.e. Form 14E (instead of being described as a form under Rule 38).

You require: The lawyer's interview notes; rule or act which authorizes the application. Follow along in Precedent 16.1. Legal software prompts you at places where insertions are to be made. Notes on items not self-explanatory follow:

Leave the court file number, date, and local registrar lines blank for the court to insert when issuing. In the title of proceeding, key the name of the statute or rule under which the application is authorized. Applications are usually heard at the court house where they are commenced. The time of hearing usually starts at 10 a.m., and lawyers await their turn. If the application is without notice, address it "To" the Local Registrar of this Honourable Court.

Number of copies, minimum 5: Issue 1 and retain it in the file; file 1 in court office at time of issuing; give 2 to the process server, 1 to serve on the respondent (with supporting affidavit), 1 to return to your office, with proof of service; keep 1 in client's file.

Supporting affidavit Since a supporting affidavit (Form 4D), Precedent 16.2, contains evidence that **supports** the grounds for the application, it is almost always prepared, served, and filed together with the notice of application. The title of proceeding must be exactly the same as that in the notice of application. The supporting affidavit must be clear and credible; otherwise, the opposite side may attack it in a cross-examination on affidavit. The supporting affidavit must not be made in the name of the lawyer who will argue the application at the hearing. It is best to have the affidavit made in the name of your client. Prepare the supporting affidavit using the standard affidavit form (Form 4D) and backsheet (Form 4C). Serve it, together with the notice of application, on the respondent at least **ten days** before the date of hearing. File it, with proof of service, at least **seven days** before the hearing.

NOTICE OF APPEARANCE

Once served with the notice of application and supporting affidavit, the respondent must serve forthwith a **notice of appearance (Form 38A)**, Precedent 16.3, on the lawyers for the applicant, and file it, forthwith, with proof of service, in the court office where the application is to be heard. The notice of appearance is referred to as such because it **notifies** the applicant that the respondent intends to appear (attend) at the hearing to speak to the application. Unless the respondent serves and files a notice of appearance, he or she may not file any other documents or take any other steps in the application. In preparing the notice of appearance, key in the court file number and the title of proceeding exactly as they appear in the issued notice of application.

Number of copies, minimum 3: Serve 1 on lawyer for applicant; file 1, with proof of service, in court where application is to be heard; keep 1 in client's file.

AFFIDAVITS IN OPPOSITION AND AFFIDAVITS IN REPLY

Rule 39 provides for evidence on motions and applications. The respondent may tell his or her side of the story by serving and filing an **affidavit in opposition (Form 4D)**. The applicant may "comment" on the affidavit in opposition by serving and filing an **affidavit in reply (Form 4D)**. If any of these affidavits are not clear or credible, the opposite lawyer may put your client under cross-examination on affidavit to clarify the doubts. The respective lawyers must serve and file these affidavits in the court where the application is to be heard, not later than **four days** before the hearing. Preparation and distribution are the same as for the supporting affidavit, with appropriate modifications.

EXAMINATION OF WITNESS

Rule 39.03 provides for evidence by examination of a witness before the hearing. This examination usually involves adverse witnesses who are non-parties. It usually applies in an application where the person who has the best evidence, or some valuable evidence, is unable or unwilling to give an affidavit. In this situation, the lawyer can compel an examination of this witness so that the lawyer can put a transcript of that examination before the judge at the hearing in place of an affidavit. The lawyer for either the applicant or respondent may examine such witnesses to obtain transcripts to refer to at the application hearing. The examination of such witnesses is done in the same manner as an oral examination for discovery.

The lawyer wishing to examine such a witness must do so **after** delivering all of the affidavits that he or she intends to rely on at the hearing and **before** cross-examining on affidavits. The first restriction ensures the examining lawyer does not have the tactical advantage of proceeding without first revealing his or her own client's affidavit evidence. The second restriction puts a limit on any delay tactics that lawyers might use, since if lawyers do delay the examination of witness until after the cross-examination on affidavit, they must obtain court permission in order to conduct the examination of witness. If an examination of a witness is necessary, serve the witness with a **summons to witness (examination out of court) (Form 34B)**, together with attendance money, usually at least two days before the examination. Use personal service only.

CROSS-EXAMINATION ON AFFIDAVIT

Rule 39 provides for evidence by cross-examination on affidavit. If any of the affidavits filed in the application are not clear or credible, the doubting lawyer may cross-examine the opposite party who swore the affidavit so as to clarify the problems. This is why the cross-examination is held after all of the affidavits are served. It is referred to as a cross-examination on affidavit because the initial testimony is represented in the affidavit itself, parallel to the testimony a party gives to his or her own lawyer on a witness stand; the cross-examination on affidavit is parallel to the **opposite** lawyer's cross-examining (questioning) of the witness on the stand; hence, **cross-examination** on affidavit. To notify the opposite lawyer of your firm's intention to cross-examine their client, serve them with a **notice of examination (Form 34A)** at least **two days** before the examination. If done, the examination is almost the same as an oral examination for discovery and is arranged in the same manner, with appropriate modifications.

TRANSCRIPTS

The oral evidence of a witness at an examination of witness and that of a deponent at a cross-examination on an affidavit are transcribed in hard copy by the facility where the examination was held. Under Rule 34.18, the party who intends to refer to a transcript of evidence at the hearing of an application must file a copy of the transcript in court where the application is to be heard at least **four days** before the hearing. Transcripts of evidence are bound in the same way as application records, including a cover page and table of contents and a **light grey** (subrule 4.07(2)) backsheet in cover stock paper.

APPLICANT'S APPLICATION RECORD AND FACTUM

Rule 38.09 provides for an application record and factum. The applicant's lawyer must serve and file an application record and a factum in every application.

Applicant's application record   Prepare the application record, Precedent 16.4, and serve it on all opposite lawyers at least **seven days** before the date of hearing. File it, with proof of service, in the court office where the application is to be heard at least **seven days** before the hearing. Subrule 38.09(2) requires an applicant's application record to contain the following:

1. Table of contents by name and date of document and, if there are any exhibits, by exhibit number or letter.
2. Copy of notice of application.
3. Copy of all affidavits and other documents served by any party for use at the application hearing.
4. List of all relevant transcripts of evidence in chronological order, but not necessarily the transcripts themselves.
5. Copy of any other material that is in the court file and that the lawyer believes is necessary for the hearing of the application.
6. Factum consisting of a concise argument stating the facts and law relied on by the applicant. (Separate book).

In preparing the application record, you need not include backsheets, unless they contain proof of service. Any material served by a party for use on an application may be filed, together with proof of service, as part of the party's application record and need not be filed separately if the record is filed within the time prescribed for filing the notice or other material. Subrule 4.07(a) requires that backsheets for application records be prepared on **light blue** cover stock paper.

Number of copies, minimum 3: Serve 1 (with factum) on the opposite lawyer; file 1 (with factum), with proof of service; keep 1 (with factum) in client's file.

Factum   The rules require a factum to accompany every application record, although the judge may, very rarely, order that factums are not needed. A factum, Precedent 16.5, gives a summary of the facts in the case and sets out statutes and cases favourable to the case at hand. Serve it, with the application record, on all opposite lawyers at least **seven days** before the date of hearing. File it, with the application record and with proof of service, in the court office where the application is to be heard at least **seven days** before the hearing. The factum is for the judge's reference at the hearing. The lawyer uses his or her own separate copy of it to argue before the judge.

Factum form   There is no prescribed form for factums. Factums are parallel to briefs of authorities in actions, except factums are mandatory. For details on how to prepare statute and case citations in factums, refer to Chapter 6. The applicant's factum must be bound front and back in **white** covers. Here is a summary of the binding and colour requirements for applications, as prescribed by Rule 4.07:

SUMMARY OF COLOUR REQUIREMENTS IN APPLICATIONS	
DOCUMENT	COLOUR
Applicant's record	Backsheet in light blue cover.
Respondent's record	Backsheet in light blue cover.
Applicant's factum	Bound front and back in white covers.
Respondent's factum	Bound front and back in green covers.
Transcripts	Backsheet in light grey cover.

RESPONDENT'S APPLICATION RECORD AND FACTUM

Rule 38.09 requires that the respondent serve and file a factum. The respondent need not, however, serve and file a respondent's application record, unless the respondent determines that the applicant should have included relevant documents in the applicant's record but did not, or unless the respondent intends to refer to new documents at the hearing that the respondent has not already served on the applicant and that are, therefore, not already included in the applicant's application record. The respondent's factum must be bound front and back in **green** covers. Serve the factum and any respondent's application record on all parties' lawyers, and file these, with proof of service, in the court office where the application is to be heard at least **four days** before the hearing.

CONFIRMATION OF APPLICATION

The applicant's lawyer must check with the opposite lawyer to make sure that the application hearing will go on as scheduled and must send to the registrar of the court where the application is to be heard a **confirmation of application (Form 38B)**, Precedent 16.6, by fax or email, or by leaving it at the court office no later than 2 p.m. at least **three days** before the hearing date. The lawyer for the applicant must also send a copy of the confirmation of application to the respondent by fax or email. If the applicant's lawyer fails to give confirmation, the application will not be heard, unless the court orders otherwise.

HEARING

The **hearing** is referred to as such in applications to distinguish it from a **trial** in actions. Usually, only the lawyers for the parties (without their clients) attend the hearing of an application, at which time, they present their arguments, and the judge gives his or her judgment.

JUDGMENT

Usually, the lawyer for the successful party prepares the formal judgment document, Precedent 16.7, has the opposite lawyers **approve** it as to **form and content**, and has it issued and entered in the same manner as a trial judgment. Prepare the judgment, Form 59B, in the same manner as a judgment at trial. Include the "Application under" line as it appears on the notice of application. Judgments in applications begin with THIS APPLICATION to distinguish them from judgments in actions, which begin with THIS ACTION.

Number of copies, minimum 6: Issue and enter 1; send 2 to losing lawyers; they return 1 approved as to form and content; submit 1 to local registrar for order/judgment book and 1 for court file; keep 1 in client's file.

COSTS AND ASSESSMENT OF COSTS

Rule 57 requires that when the court awards costs, it shall fix such costs, using the same criteria as in actions; that is, on the basis of the same tariffs and costs submissions. Generally, only in an exceptional case would the court refer costs for assessment. In such cases, follow the procedure described for costs and assessment of costs in actions, as it applies equally to costs and assessment of costs in applications.

CHAPTER SUMMARY

Applications differ from actions in that applications rarely claim money for damages, although they may often be about money. There are two types of applications—on notice and without notice—and both begin with the same document called **notice of application**, which is an originating process. An application on notice is one where the notice of application must be issued and served on the respondent. An application without notice is one where either there is no respondent to be served or where the application is urgent. Applications are quicker than actions because the evidence is mainly in the form of affidavits. Factums are required in all applications. At the hearing of applications, only the lawyers for the parties attend (not their clients) to argue the case before a judge, at the end of which hearing, the judge pronounces his or her judgment.

REVIEW QUESTIONS

1. What makes applications quicker than actions?
2. What is the purpose of a supporting affidavit?
3. When is a cross-examination on affidavit necessary?
4. What is a factum?
5. When is the filing of a respondent's application record necessary?
6. Is a factum required of the applicant as well as the respondent?
7. What is documentary evidence?
8. "Hearing" in applications means listening very, very intently. Explain.

Court File No.

ONTARIO
SUPERIOR COURT OF JUSTICE

B E T W E E N :

(Court Seal)

GUS CONSTANTINE

Applicant

- and -

MARIA OUMBRIE

Respondent

APPLICATION UNDER THE *Partnerships Act*, RSO 1990, c P.5, s 35, as amended. *(insert statutory provision or rule under which the application is made.)*

NOTICE OF APPLICATION

TO THE RESPONDENT(S)

A LEGAL PROCEEDING HAS BEEN COMMENCED by the Applicant. The Claim made by the Applicant appears on the following page.

THIS APPLICATION will come on for a hearing on Friday, August 25, 20--, at 10:00 a.m. at 393 University Avenue, 10th Floor, Toronto, Ontario, M5G 1E6.

IF YOU WISH TO OPPOSE THIS APPLICATION, to receive notice of any step in the Application or to be served with any documents in the Application you or an Ontario lawyer acting for you must forthwith prepare a Notice of Appearance in Form 38A prescribed by the *Rules of Civil Procedure*, serve it on the Applicant's lawyer or, where the Applicant does not have a lawyer, serve it on the Applicant, and file it, with proof of service, in this court office, and you or your lawyer must appear at the hearing.

IF YOU WISH TO PRESENT AFFIDAVIT OR OTHER DOCUMENTARY EVIDENCE TO THE COURT OR TO EXAMINE OR CROSS-EXAMINE WITNESSES ON THE APPLICATION, you or your lawyer must, in addition to serving your Notice of Appearance, serve a copy of the evidence on the Applicant's lawyer or, where the Applicant does not have a lawyer, serve it on the Applicant, and file it, with proof of service, in the court office where the Application is to be heard as soon as possible, but at least four days before the hearing.

IF YOU FAIL TO APPEAR AT THE HEARING, JUDGMENT MAY BE GIVEN IN YOUR ABSENCE AND WITHOUT FURTHER NOTICE TO YOU. IF YOU WISH TO OPPOSE THIS APPLICATION BUT ARE UNABLE TO PAY LEGAL FEES, LEGAL AID MAY BE AVAILABLE TO YOU BY CONTACTING A LOCAL LEGAL AID OFFICE.

Date   July   , 20--   Issued by
                                                           Local Registrar

Address of court
office: 393 University Avenue
                   10th Floor
                   Toronto, Ontario   M5G 1E6

TO: **MARIA OUMBRIE**
      66 Charon Boulevard
      Toronto, Ontario   M5G 1T2

-2-

APPLICATION

1.   The Applicant makes Application for: *(State here the precise relief claimed.)*

(a)   an order dissolving the Partnership between the Applicant and the Respondent, Maria Oumbrie (Oumbrie), carrying on business under the firm name and style of Ghoul Sales and Service;

(b)   directing an accounting of those monies paid or payable by Ghoul Sales and Service (Ghoul) to the Respondent, any person, corporation, association, firm or undertaking in which the Respondent is involved or controls on behalf of the Respondent, the Applicant, or the Partnership.

2.   The grounds for the Application are: *(Specify the grounds to be argued, including a reference to any statutory provision or rule to be relied on.)*

(a)   the Respondent has been guilty of such conduct which is calculated to prejudice the carrying on of the Partnership business;

(b)   the Applicant relies upon the provisions of the *Partnerships Act*, RSO 1990, c P.5, s 35, as amended.

3.   The following documentary evidence will be used at the hearing of the Application: *(List the affidavits or other documentary evidence to be relied on.)*

(a)   the Affidavit of Gus Constantine and the exhibits referred to in the Affidavit, sworn July 20, 20--, filed in court;

(b)   such further and other evidence as the lawyers may advise and this Honourable Court may permit.

July   , 20--   **MICHAEL, ELIAD & REDFORD LLP**
                                         Barristers and Solicitors
                                         863 Seneca Lane
                                         Toronto, Ontario   M4J 1P6

                                         Robert B. Redford
                                         Tel: 416-363-1079
                                         Fax: 416-363-2628

                                         Lawyers for the Applicant

Court File No.

ONTARIO
SUPERIOR COURT OF JUSTICE

PROCEEDING COMMENCED AT
TORONTO

NOTICE OF APPLICATION

MICHAEL, ELIAD & REDFORD LLP
Barristers and Solicitors
863 Seneca Lane
Toronto, Ontario
M4J 1P6

Robert B. Redford (48000R)
Tel: 416-363-1079
Fax: 416-363-2628
rbrdfrd@mer.com

Lawyers for the Applicant

MARIA OUMBRIE
Respondent

-and-

GUS CONSTANTINE
Applicant

Court File No.

ONTARIO
SUPERIOR COURT OF JUSTICE

B E T W E E N:

GUS CONSTANTINE

Applicant

- and -

MARIA OUMBRIE

Respondent

APPLICATION UNDER *Partnerships Act*, RSO 1990, c P.5, s 35, as amended. *(insert statutory provision or rule under which the application is made.)*

AFFIDAVIT

I, GUS CONSTANTINE, of the City of Ottawa, in the Regional Municipality of Ottawa-Carleton, MAKE OATH AND SAY:

1. I am the Applicant and, as such, have knowledge of the matters contained in this Affidavit.

2. The Respondent, Maria Oumbrie (Oumbrie), resides in the City of Toronto, in the Province of Ontario.

3. On June 26, 20--, by oral agreement, Oumbrie and I established an equal Partnership under the firm name of Ghoul Sales and Service (Ghoul), at 35 Medusa Street, Toronto, Ontario. Ghoul is a subsidiary of Lucifer Dies Limited headquartered in Vancouver, British Columbia.

4. Oumbrie and I shared in all the profits and expenses attendant to this business on an equal basis.

5. In August 20--, Oumbrie presented me with a cheque for $50,000 for my share of the Partnership and informed me that Lucifer Dies Limited had declared Oumbrie its exclusive representative and that unless I accepted the money I would end up with nothing. I refused the offer.

-2-

6.   The approximate present value of the contracts which I have secured or which I anticipate will be secured for Lucifer Dies Limited by our Partnership is $1,853,250.25. Annexed to this my Affidavit and marked as Exhibit A is a sales summary.

7.   I have concluded that there is owing by Lucifer Dies Limited to our Partnership by way of commission the sum of approximately $396,203.75. I am not aware of what portion, if any, of this commission has been paid by Lucifer Dies Limited to Oumbrie. However, Oumbrie has not accounted to me for same.

8.   Under the circumstances, Oumbrie, with the cooperation of Lucifer Dies Limited, has closed me out of all future dealings with our Partnership business, has retained all of our Partnership profits solely for herself, and has made it impossible for me to continue in the Partnership with Oumbrie.

9.   I make this Affidavit for no improper purpose.

SWORN BEFORE ME at the City of Toronto,
in the Province of Ontario this .... day of July,
20--

}

_____   _____
   Commissioner for Taking Affidavits   Gus Constantine
          (or as may be)

(prepare backsheet)

Court File No. CV-**-66228

ONTARIO
SUPERIOR COURT OF JUSTICE

B E T W E E N:

GUS CONSTANTINE

Applicant

- and -

MARIA OUMBRIE

Respondent

APPLICATION UNDER *Partnerships Act*, RSO 1990, c P.5, s 35, as amended. *(insert statutory provision or rule under which the application is made.)*

NOTICE OF APPEARANCE

The Respondent intends to respond to this Application.

Date: July 5, 20--

CASTLES & SANDS
Suite 900-205 Portage Street
Markham, Ontario   L3R 3G3

Raymond G. Castles
Tel: 905-495-2222
Fax: 905-495-2223

Lawyers for the Respondent

TO: **MICHAEL, ELIAD & REDFORD LLP**
Barristers and Solicitors
863 Seneca Lane
Toronto, Ontario
M4J 1P6

Robert B. Redford
Tel: 416-363-1079
Fax: 416-363-2628

Lawyers for the Applicant

(prepare backsheet)

Precedent 16.4 Application Record, page 2

Court File No. CV-**-66228

ONTARIO
SUPERIOR COURT OF JUSTICE

B E T W E E N :

GUS CONSTANTINE

Applicant

- and -

MARIA OUMBRIE

Respondent

APPLICATION UNDER *Partnerships Act*, RSO 1990, c P.5, s 35, as amended. *(insert statutory provision or rule under which the application is made.)*

APPLICATION RECORD

TABLE OF CONTENTS

Tab		Page No.
1.	Notice of Application dated July 1, 20--	1
2.	Affidavit of Gus Constantine sworn July 1, 20--	3
3.	Exhibit A referred to in Affidavit of Gus Constantine sworn July 1, 20--	4
4.	Affidavit of Maria Oumbrie sworn August 2, 20--	5
5.	Transcript of cross-examination on affidavit held August 10, 20--	10

(prepare backsheet - light blue)

Precedent 16.4 Application Record, page 1

Court File No. CV-**-66228

ONTARIO
SUPERIOR COURT OF JUSTICE

B E T W E E N :

GUS CONSTANTINE

Applicant

- and -

MARIA OUMBRIE

Respondent

APPLICATION UNDER *Partnerships Act*, RSO 1990, c P.5, s 35, as amended. *(insert statutory provision or rule under which the application is made.)*

APPLICATION RECORD

MICHAEL, ELIAD & REDFORD LLP
Barristers and Solicitors
863 Seneca Lane
Toronto, Ontario
M4J 1P6

Robert B. Redford
Tel: 416-363-1079
Fax: 416-363-2628

Lawyers for the Applicant

TO: **CASTLES & SANDS**
Suite 900-205 Portage Street
Markham, Ontario L3R 3G3

Raymond G. Castles
Tel: 905-495-2222
Fax: 905-495-2223

Lawyers for the Respondent

Court File No. CV-**-66228

ONTARIO
SUPERIOR COURT OF JUSTICE

B E T W E E N:

GUS CONSTANTINE

Applicant

- and -

MARIA OUMBRIE

Respondent

APPLICATION UNDER *Partnerships Act*, RSO 1990, c P.5, s 35, as amended. *(insert statutory provision or rule under which the application is made.)*

APPLICANT'S FACTUM

MICHAEL, ELIAD & REDFORD LLP
Barristers and Solicitors
863 Seneca Lane
Toronto, Ontario
M4J 1P6

Robert B. Redford
Tel: 416-363-1079
Fax: 416-363-2628

Lawyers for the Applicant

TO: **CASTLES & SANDS**
Suite 900-205 Portage Street
Markham, Ontario   L3R 3G3

Raymond G. Castles
Tel: 905-495-2222
Fax: 905-495-2223

Lawyers for the Respondent

-2-

Court File No. CV-**-66228

ONTARIO
SUPERIOR COURT OF JUSTICE

B E T W E E N :

GUS CONSTANTINE

Applicant

- and -

MARIA OUMBRIE

Respondent

APPLICATION UNDER *Partnerships Act*, RSO 1990, c P.5, s 35, as amended. *(insert statutory provision or rule under which the application is made.)*

APPLICANT'S FACTUM

PART I - INTRODUCTION

1.   The Applicant, Gus Constantine (Constantine), claims:

(a)   a dissolution of his business partnership with Maria Oumbrie (Oumbrie) carried on under the name and style of Ghoul Sales and Service;

(b)   the Respondent has been guilty of such conduct which is calculated to prejudice the carrying on of the partnership business;

(c)   an accounting.

PART II - SUMMARY OF FACTS

2.   Constantine has sworn that he and Oumbrie entered into an oral partnership agreement by which they became equal partners with respect to the Ghoul Sales and Service (Ghoul) products.

3.   Oumbrie says that she and Constantine were not and never have been partners in the Ghoul business.

4.   Oumbrie admitted on cross-examination that Constantine always did 50 percent of the work associated with the business and received 50 percent of the profits and that Constantine and Oumbrie each paid one-half of the expenses associated with the business.

5.   Constantine was forced out of the partnership with no equitable compensation.

-3-

PART III - STATEMENT OF ISSUES, LAW & AUTHORITIES

6.   Section 2 of the *Partnerships Act*, RSO 1990, c P.5, as amended, provides that a "partnership is

the relation that subsists between persons carrying on a business in common with a view to profit."

7.   Section 1.(1) of the *Partnerships Act* defines business to include "every trade, occupation and

profession."

8.   While an agreement, express or implied, between the parties to carry on business together is

essential to the existence of a partnership, it is not necessary that the parties should have intended to

create the partnership relationship if by their conduct they have in fact created one. Even if any or all of

the parties to the transaction assert there is no partnership between them, the court must still examine the

transaction and determine on a point of law whether a partnership exists.

>   Botham v Keefer (1878), 2 OAR 595
>   Beattie v Dickson (1909), OWR 565
>   Schmidt v Schmidt, [1986] 4 WWR (Alta CA)

9.   Section 35 of the *Partnerships Act* provides

>   35   On application by a partner, the court may order dissolution of the
>   partnership,
>
>   (d)   when a partner, other than the partner suing, wilfully or persistently
>   commits a breach of the partnership agreement, or otherwise so conducts
>   himself in matters relating to the partnership business that is not
>   reasonably practicable for the other partner or partners to carry on the
>   business in partnership with him.

10.   On the dissolution of a partnership, the partners have the right to have the partnership accounts

taken and the business wound-up and adjusted accordingly. In determining matters which should be

referred on the accounting, where a partner who continues in the business to the exclusion of the other

partners and makes use of either the former partnership's assets or the business connection derived

therefrom, that partner is accountable to the former partner for the profits attributable thereto.

>   Lindley on Partnership 14th ed (1979) pp 438 and 639

-4-

11.   In determining the value of the assets of a partnership, the goodwill of the business must be

included in the absence of express agreement to the contrary.

       Hibben v Collister (1900), 30 SCR 459

PART IV - ORDER REQUESTED

Order dissolving the partnership

Order directing an accounting of monies

ALL OF WHICH IS RESPECTFULLY SUBMITTED this   day of August, 20--.

_____
                 Robert B. Redford

MICHAEL, ELIAD & REDFORD LLP
Barristers and Solicitors
863 Seneca Lane
Toronto, Ontario M4J 1P6

Robert B. Redford
Tel: 416-363-1079
Fax: 416-363-2628

Lawyers for the Applicant

SCHEDULE A

LIST OF AUTHORITIES

1.

SCHEDULE B

TEXT OF STATUTES, REGULATIONS & BY - LAWS

1.

(prepare front and back covers in white)

-2-

Date: August   , 20—

TO: **SUPERIOR COURT OF JUSTICE**
        393 University Avenue
        10th Floor
        Toronto, Ontario
        M5G 1E6
        FAX:

TO: **CASTLES & SANDS**
        Suite 900-205 Portage Street
        Markham, Ontario L3R 3G3

        Raymond G. Castles
        Tel: 905-495-2222
        Fax: 905-495-2223

        Lawyers for the Respondent

MICHAEL, ELIAD & REDFORD LLP
Barristers and Solicitors
863 Seneca Lane
Toronto, Ontario
M4J 1P6

Robert B. Redford
Tel: 416-363-1079
Fax: 416-363-2628

Lawyers for the Applicant

(prepare backsheet)

Court File No. CV-**-66228

ONTARIO
SUPERIOR COURT OF JUSTICE

B E T W E E N:

GUS CONSTANTINE

Applicant

- and -

MARIA OUMBRIE

Respondent

APPLICATION UNDER the *Partnerships Act*, RSO 1990, c P.5, s 35, as amended *(Insert statutory provision or rule under which the application is made.)*

CONFIRMATION OF APPLICATION

I, ROBERT B. REDFORD, with the law firm of Michael, Eliad & Redford LLP, lawyer for the Applicant, confirm that the Application to be heard on August 25, 20--, at 10:00 a.m. will proceed on the following basis:

[ ]   for an adjournment on consent to ....(date).

[ ]   for a contested adjournment to ....(date), for the following reason:

(specify who is requesting the adjournment and why, and who is opposing it and why)

[ ]   for a consent order

[X]   for hearing of all the issues

[ ]   for hearing of the following issues only (specify)

I estimate that the time required for the Application will be: 60 minutes for the Applicant and 60 minutes for the Respondent for a total of 120 minutes.

Court File No. CV-**-66228

ONTARIO
SUPERIOR COURT OF JUSTICE

THE HONOURABLE)   FRIDAY, THE 25th
)
MR. JUSTICE RIGHT)   DAY OF AUGUST, 20--

B E T W E E N:

(Court Seal)

GUS CONSTANTINE

Applicant

- and -

MARIA OUMBRIE

Respondent

APPLICATION UNDER *Partnerships Act*, RSO 1990, c P.5, s 35, as amended. *(insert statutory provision or rule under which the application is made.)*

JUDGMENT

THIS APPLICATION was heard this day without a jury at the court house, 393 University Avenue, 10th Floor, Toronto, Ontario, M5G 1E6, in the presence of the lawyers for all parties,

ON READING THE NOTICE OF APPLICATION AND THE EVIDENCE FILED BY THE PARTIES, and on hearing the submissions of the lawyers for the parties,

1.   THIS COURT ORDERS AND ADJUDGES that the partnership between the Applicant and the Respondent, carrying on business under the firm name and style of Ghoul Sales and Service be and the same is hereby dissolved.

2.   THIS COURT ORDERS AND ADJUDGES that the Respondent account for those monies paid or to be paid by Ghoul Sales and Service to the Respondent, to any other person on the Respondent's behalf and to any corporation, association, firm or undertaking with which the respondent is involved or controls.

_____
(Signature of Judge)

Court File No. CV-**-66228

MARIA OUMBRIE
Respondent

-and-

GUS CONSTANTINE
Applicant

ONTARIO
SUPERIOR COURT OF JUSTICE

PROCEEDING COMMENCED AT
TORONTO

JUDGMENT

MICHAEL, ELIAD & REDFORD LLP
Barristers and Solicitors
863 Seneca Lane
Toronto, Ontario
M4J 1P6

Robert B. Redford (48000R)
Tel: 416-363-1079
Fax: 416-363-2628
rbrdfrd@mer.com

Lawyers for the Applicant

CHAPTER 17
MOTIONS

This chapter discusses motions and their use as a temporary detour from the main steps of actions and applications.

Figure 17.1 Steps in Motions

Moving Party's Motion Record, MP
- notice of motion
- supporting affidavit
- factum (if any)
- affidavit of service
- served and filed at least 7 days before motion hearing

Examination of Witness, MP or RP
- summons to witness (examination out of court)
- served at least 2 days before examination date

Cross-examination on affidavit, MP or RP
- notice of examination (on affidavit)
- served at least 2 days before examination date

Responding Party's Motion Record, RP
- affidavit in opposition
- factum (if any)
- affidavit of service
- served and filed at least 4 days before motion hearing

Confirmation of Motion, MP
- sent not later than 2 p.m., 3 days before hearing

Hearing: Order

MP = Moving Party (party who makes the motion)   RP = Responding Party

MOTIONS

Motions are a legal mechanism by which lawyers can request the courts to solve problems that arise while a proceeding is in progress. Motions are governed by Rule 37 of the *Rules of Civil Procedure* and apply in both actions and applications. Motions do not usually decide a case; they decide only a particular issue within a case; therefore, motions are seldom independent proceedings, but rather, incidental steps within proceedings: for example, if a defendant were to file a jury notice where a trial by jury were inapplicable, the plaintiff could file a motion seeking a court order to strike out the jury notice. Once the court grants the order, the jury notice is struck out, and the action returns to its regular steps, e.g. close of pleadings, discoveries, etc., to be tried without a jury. Here is a visual example of the motion as an incidental step within an action:

Figure 17.2

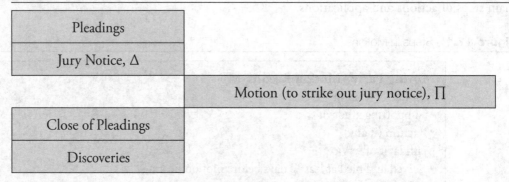

Difference between motions and applications The steps in motions are almost identical to those in applications because, like applications, motions are quick and rely on affidavit evidence. One of the major differences, however, is that an application (like a statement of claim) is an **originating process** which begins a proceeding, whereas a motion is usually an incidental step within an application. Once the court solves the incidental problem, the application resumes its regular path toward the hearing of the application.

How are motions made Motions are made by a document known as a **notice of motion, Form 37A**. The party who makes the motion is commonly referred to as the **moving party** and the party responding to the motion as the **responding party**. Note, however, that in all motion documents, the parties retain their **original** titles of plaintiff and defendant, where the motion is brought in an action, and applicant and respondent, where the motion is brought in an application. That is because a motion is not an originating process and, therefore, the parties must carry their respective original titles.

TYPES OF MOTIONS

Motions on notice Motions on notice are motions that lawyers must serve on all opposite parties.

Motions without notice Motions without notice (sometimes referred to as *ex parte* motions) are motions where there is no other party involved, or the other party, if any, does not have to be served, either because all parties have consented to the bringing of the motion, in which case, the motion is referred to as a **motion on consent**, or because the motion is urgent, and time is of the essence.

Motions in writing   Motions in writing are motions which may be heard and determined by a judge or a master solely on written evidence, usually without the attendance of the parties to present oral arguments unless the court orders otherwise. Motions in writing tend to be motions on consent or motions where the issues of fact and law are not complex.

PRELIMINARY CONSIDERATIONS

Where heard   All motions are brought and heard in the county where the proceeding was commenced or to which it has been transferred unless the court orders otherwise.

Who hears motions   Judges, masters, and the registrar. Under rule 37.02 the registrar has jurisdiction to hear motions on consent and other matters such as motions to amend pleadings. A judge has jurisdiction to hear all motions; a master has jurisdiction to hear any motion, except a motion which only a judge can hear; some motions which only a judge can hear include:

- Motions requesting changes to an order that a judge has previously made.
- Motions for judgment on consent involving a party under disability.
- Motions that an act or rule states a judge must hear.
- Motions in an appeal.

Who attends motion hearings   The lawyers, usually without their respective parties.

Short and long motions   A short motion is one of two hours or less in length, and a long motion is one of more than two hours.

Practice directions   Judges in various regions, including Toronto, issue practice directions which require the scheduling of short and long motion (and application) hearings to be done in a way that best suits the needs of that specific region.   Follow the procedure under practice direction in your region. For example, under practice direction, the scheduling of most motions (and applications) in the Toronto Region is done through the Civil Practice Court/Civil Scheduling Unit.

Legal TIP

Motions within the jurisdiction of a master or the registrar are made to the **court**. Motions within the jurisdiction of a judge are made to a **judge**.

Legal TIP

Motions usually result in court **orders** which solve temporary issues within a proceeding; actions and applications result in court **judgments** which solve the entire proceeding.

We act for Mr. and Mrs. Rubicon in this motion. The Rubicons are plaintiffs in an action where their previous lawyer, Mr. Stanley Footloose, failed to produce some medical records that the Rubicons at their examinations for discovery undertook to produce; this failure ultimately resulted in an order by Justice Fedor dismissing the action. The Rubicons have retained our firm to resurrect the action.

We prepared the notice of motion, Precedent 17.1, and a supporting affidavit, Precedent 17.2, by Mr. Footloose and attached to the affidavit as Exhibit C a copy of Justice Fedor's order, Precedent 17.3. We prepared the motion record, Precedent 17.4, and the confirmation of motion, Precedent 17.5; we also prepared a costs outline, Precedent 17.6, in anticipation of winning the motion.

The motion came before Justice Fare. In his order, Precedent 17.7, Justice Fare denied our motion. As a result, the Rubicons lost their action, although they could, if they wish, sue Mr. Footloose for damages. To avoid this, Mr. Footloose offered to pay the Rubicons $60,000 out of the lawyers' liability insurance fund. We have prepared the full and final release, Precedent 17.8, for the Rubicons to sign, fully releasing Mr. Footloose from any liability and thus ending the entire action.

NOTICE OF MOTION

A motion begins with a notice of motion (Form 37A). A notice of motion is usually not an originating process; that is why it is not issued. A notice of motion notifies the opposite lawyers that you are requesting the court to solve an interim problem within an action or application. Serve the notice of motion, together with a supporting affidavit, on all opposite lawyers at least **seven days** before the hearing date of the motion. File the notice of motion and supporting affidavit, with proof of service, in the court office where the motion is to be heard at least **seven days** before the hearing date.

PREPARATION AND DISTRIBUTION OF NOTICE OF MOTION (FORM 37A)

You require: The file. Follow along in Precedent 17.1. Legal software provides prompts at places requiring variable information. Notes on items not self-explanatory follow:

Key the title of proceeding as it appears in the originating process. Key **to the court** for all motions, except motions that a judge must hear. Key **to a judge** for all motions that only a judge can hear. (If the motion is without notice, address it to the Local Registrar of this Honourable Court.) Motions are usually heard starting at 10 a.m., and lawyers await their turn. That is why the notice of motion reads "at 10 a.m. **or as soon after that time as the motion can be heard**." Method of hearing:

- if the motion is on consent, unopposed, or made without notice, mark "in writing under subrule...";
- if the motion contains a factum, mark "in writing as an opposed motion under subrule...";
- in all other cases, mark "orally."

Number of copies, minimum 4: Serve 1 (with supporting affidavit) on responding lawyer; file 1 with proof of service; 1 for motion record; keep 1 in client's file.

Supporting affidavit Since a **supporting affidavit**, Precedent 17.2, contains evidence that **supports** the grounds for the motion, it is almost always served together with the notice of motion.

Affidavit in opposition, affidavit in reply, examination of witness, and cross-examination on affidavit The description of these documents given under applications applies equally to motions, with appropriate modifications.

MOVING PARTY'S MOTION RECORD

Prepare a motion record for all motions on notice. Motions without notice do not usually require a motion record and are made by filing only the notice of motion and the affidavit in support. The lawyer for the moving party must serve the motion record on all opposite parties and file it with proof of service at least **seven days** before the motion is to be heard. Subrule 37.10(2) requires that a motion record include:

1. Table of contents of all documents by name and date and of all exhibits by name, date, and exhibit number.
2. Copy of the notice of motion.
3. Copy of all affidavits and other materials served by any and all parties for use on the motion.
4. List of the transcripts that the moving party's lawyer intends to refer to, in chronological order, but not the transcripts themselves since these are filed in court separately.
5. Copy of any other document that the moving party's lawyer intends to refer to at the hearing.

In preparing the motion record, the title is MOTION RECORD to distinguish it from a trial or application record. Instead of filing the motion documents separately, a party may include all of the documents **with proof of service** in the motion record. The backsheet of motion records is prepared on **light blue** cover stock paper.

Number of copies, minimum 4: Serve 1 on opposite lawyers; file 1, with proof of service; 1 for the lawyer to use at hearing; keep 1 in client's file.

RESPONDING PARTY'S MOTION RECORD

Subrule 37.10(3) requires a responding party's motion record only if the moving party's motion record is incomplete. A responding party's motion record, if any, includes:

1. A table of contents describing each document, including each exhibit, by its nature and date and, in the case of an exhibit, by exhibit number or letter; and
2. A copy of any material to be used by the responding party on the motion and not included in the motion record.

Serve the responding party's motion record, if any, on all parties and file it with proof of service in the court office of the place of hearing at least **four days** before the hearing.

FACTUMS

Subrule 37.10(6) provides for factums. Factums are usually not required in motions, except in special cases such as motions for summary judgment, motions for appeal, and motions on a question of law. If they wish, however, the parties may serve factums in any motion. If so, the moving party must serve the factum and file it with proof of service at least **seven days** before the motion hearing, and the responding party must serve and file it with proof of service at least **four days** before the motion hearing. The moving party's factum must be bound front and back in **white** covers, and the responding party's factum must be bound front and back in **green** covers.

CONFIRMATION OF MOTION

Rule 37.10.1 requires a confirmation of motion in all motions. The moving party's lawyer must check with the opposing lawyer to make sure that the motion hearing will go on as scheduled and must send to the registrar a **confirmation of motion (Form 37B)**, Precedent 17.5, by fax or e-mail or by leaving it at the court office no later than 2 p.m. at least **three days** before the hearing date. The lawyer for the moving party must also send a copy of the confirmation of motion to the other party by fax or e-mail. Failure to send a confirmation motion means the motion will not be heard.

MOTION COSTS

Rule 57.03 provides for costs on a motion. The court fixes the motion costs and usually orders the losing party to pay the costs within **thirty days** of the motion. If the party ordered to pay the motion costs fails to pay the costs within **thirty days**, the court may dismiss or stay the party's proceeding, strike out the party's defence, or make such other order as is just.

Costs outline (Form 57B)   To help the court fix the motion costs, each party must prepare and exchange with the other a **costs outline (Form 57B)**, Precedent 17.6, and bring the costs outline to the motion hearing in anticipation of winning the motion. Here is subrule 57.01(6):

> Unless the parties have agreed on the costs that it would be appropriate
> to award for a step in a proceeding, every party who intends to seek costs
> for that step shall give to every other party involved in the same step,
> and bring to the hearing, a costs outline (Form 57B) not exceeding three
> pages in length.

Note from subrule 57.01(6), above, that a costs outline is not to be confused with a bill of costs. Unless the judge orders otherwise, a costs outline is to be submitted to the judge at the hearing of an interlocutory **step**, e.g. a motion, by both parties who intend to seek costs for that particular step in the event they are successful on the motion. A bill of costs, on the other hand, is to be prepared **after trial** by the party who has **already won** costs. In practice, however, you may find that the costs outline and the bill of costs are sometimes used interchangeably.

MOTION HEARING

Usually, only lawyers, and not their clients or witnesses, attend the motion hearing and present oral arguments on the motion. At the conclusion of the hearing, the judge or master gives the order. The losing party must abide by the order, and the proceeding resumes in its regular steps in the action or application, as the case may be. Any party may obtain an appointment from the judge or the master hearing the motion to have the motion heard, in whole or in part, by way of a telephone or a video conference; all necessary documents must be, nevertheless, prepared as usual.

ORDER

Orders in opposed motions   An order (instead of a judgment) is usually the court's decision in motions. Once the judge or master gives the order, the successful party prepares it in a formal document, (Form 59A), sends it to the opposite lawyer for approval as to form, and leaves the order, together with an approved as to form copy, with the registrar for the signature of the judge, officer or registrar. The successful party then has the signed order issued and entered in the court where the proceeding was commenced in the same manner as a trial judgment.

Orders in motions in writing   With motions in writing, which are usually motions on consent or motions where the issues of fact and law are not complex, a **draft** order (Form 59A) is usually filed with the motion documents so that the judge or master may sign it upon arriving at a decision. It is referred to as a "draft" order because the judge or master may change it, usually by handwriting and initialling the changes before signing it, dismiss it altogether, or write up a completely new order, often on the backsheet of the motion record. The signed draft order is issued and entered in the court where the proceeding was commenced in the same manner as a trial judgment.

PREPARATION AND DISTRIBUTION OF ORDER (FORM 59A)

You require: The notice of motion; the supporting affidavit. Almost all of the information in the order comes from these documents. Follow along in Precedent 17.7. Key points include:

If the motion is made **to a judge**, key:

THE HONOURABLE MR./MADAM JUSTICE	)	DAY, APRIL	, (year)
	)		
	)or	DAY, THE	DAY OF APRIL, (year)

If the motion is made **to the court**, key:

MASTER	)	DAY, APRIL	, (year)
	)		
	)or	DAY, THE	DAY OF APRIL, (year)

The judge or the master usually fills in his or her name and the date when signing the order. (If you prepare the order in advance, you do not usually know the name of the judge or master who will hear the motion). The title is ORDER to distinguish it from a judgment. The preamble indicates the order is a result of a MOTION. Begin each paragraph with THIS COURT ORDERS. If the order includes payment of money, key the standard interest clause as of the date of the order. Key a signature line for the signature of the judge or master.

Number of copies, minimum 6: send 2 to losing party; they return 1 approved as to form; issue and enter 1; 1 for the order book; 1 for court file; keep 1 in client's file.

CHAPTER SUMMARY

A motion is an interim proceeding within an action or application. There are motions on notice, which the moving party must serve on the responding party, and without notice, which, usually in the interest of urgency, need not be served on any party. Motions begin with a document called a **notice of motion (Form 37A)**, and all supporting evidence is in the form of an affidavit. The moving party sets down the motion for hearing by serving and filing a motion record. The court fixes the motion costs and usually orders the losing party of the motion to pay them. The parties to a motion must exchange costs outlines and bring them to the motion hearing to enable the court to fix the amount of the costs. The court's decision in motions is usually an order, as opposed to a judgment.

REVIEW QUESTIONS

1. Are there motions in actions as well as in applications?
2. Do motions begin a proceeding or do they come during a proceeding?
3. What are motions?
4. Who may hear motions?
5. Which document begins a motion?
6. What is the court's decision on a motion called?
7. What type of supporting evidence must accompany a notice of motion?
8. Explain why a notice of motion is always an originating process.

Court File No. CV-**-4721

ONTARIO
SUPERIOR COURT OF JUSTICE

B E T W E E N :

EDNA RUBICON and ALI RUBICON

Plaintiffs

- and -

WENDY MING, LORNA TERESA BAILY, ALPHA INSURANCE COMPANY
OF CANADA and BETA ASSURANCE COMPANY OF CANADA

Defendants

NOTICE OF MOTION

The Plaintiffs will make a Motion to a Judge on Monday, April 30, 20--, at

10:00 a.m., or as soon after that time as the Motion can be heard at the Court House, 393

University Avenue, 10th Floor, Toronto, Ontario M5G 1E6.

PROPOSED METHOD OF HEARING: The Motion is to be heard *(choose appropriate*

option)

[ ] in writing under subrule 37.12.1(1) because it is *(insert one of on consent,*

unopposed or made without notice);

[ ] in writing as an opposed motion under subrule 37.12.1(4);

[X] orally.

-2-

THE MOTION IS FOR *(State here the precise relief sought)*

(a)   An Order setting aside the Order of the Honourable Mr. Justice Fedor, dismissing the Plaintiffs' action for failure to fulfill undertakings given at their Examinations for Discovery and for failure to comply with the Order of the Honourable Mr. Justice Pascal;

(b)   the costs of this Motion payable by the Defendants, Wendy Ming and Lorna Teresa Baily; and

(c)   such further and other relief as this Honourable Court may deem just.

THE GROUNDS FOR THE MOTION ARE *(Specify the grounds to be argued, including a reference to any statutory provision or rule to be relied on)*

(a)   Rules 1.04 and 37.14 of the Rules of Civil Procedure.

(b)   The Order dismissing the Plaintiffs' action was obtained on a Motion brought without notice to the Plaintiffs.

(c)   The Order of the Honourable Mr. Justice Pascal permitting the Defendant to move, without notice, for a dismissal of the Plaintiffs' action was unnecessarily Draconian given the fact that there is no meaningful liability issue to be tried in this action.

(d)   Such further and other grounds as the lawyers may advise.

THE FOLLOWING DOCUMENTARY EVIDENCE will be used at the hearing of the

motion: *(List the affidavits or other documentary evidence to be relied on)*

-3-

(a)   The Affidavit of Stanley Footloose.

(b)   The pleadings and proceedings in this action.

(c)   The transcripts from the Examinations for Discovery of Edna Rubicon and Ali Rubicon.

(d)   The Orders of the Honourable Mr. Justice Fedor and the Honourable Mr. Justice Pascal.

(e)   Such further and other evidence as the lawyers may advise and this Honourable Court may permit.

April 2, 20--

MICHAEL, ELIAD & REDFORD LLP
Barristers and Solicitors
863 Seneca Lane
Toronto, Ontario
M4J 1P6

Robert B. Redford
Tel: 416-363-1079
Fax: 416-363-2628

Lawyers for the Plaintiffs

TO: **CASTLES & SANDS**
Suite 900-205 Portage Street
Markham, Ontario L3R 3G3

Raymond G. Castles
Tel: 905-495-2222
Fax: 905-495-2223

Lawyers for the Defendants

Court File No.CV-**-4721

EDNA RUBICON and ALI RUBICON
Plaintiffs

-and-

WENDY MING et. al.
Defendants

ONTARIO
SUPERIOR COURT OF JUSTICE

PROCEEDING COMMENCED AT
TORONTO

NOTICE OF MOTION

MICHAEL, ELIAD & REDFORD LLP
Barristers and Solicitors
863 Seneca Lane
Toronto, Ontario
M4J 1P6

Robert B. Redford (48000R)
Tel: 416-363-1079
Fax: 416-363-2628
rbrdfrd@mer.com

Lawyers for the Plaintiffs

Court File No. CV-**-4721

ONTARIO
SUPERIOR COURT OF JUSTICE

B E T W E E N:

EDNA RUBICON and ALI RUBICON

Plaintiffs

- and -

WENDY MING, LORNA TERESA BAILY, ALPHA INSURANCE COMPANY
OF CANADA and BETA ASSURANCE COMPANY OF CANADA

Defendants

AFFIDAVIT OF STANLEY FOOTLOOSE

I, Stanley Footloose, of the City of Toronto, in the Province of Ontario, MAKE OATH

AND SAY:

1.   I was originally retained by the Plaintiffs to commence an action for damages arising out
of a motor vehicle accident.

2.   At the Examinations for Discovery of both the Plaintiffs held on March 10, 20--, the
Plaintiffs gave undertakings to obtain medical records.

3.   On June 2, 20--, the Defendants brought a motion for an order dismissing the Plaintiffs'
claim for failure to fulfill undertakings given at their Examinations for Discovery. The
Honourable Mr. Justice Pascal ordered the Plaintiffs to comply with the undertakings within
sixty days of the date of the motion, failing which the Defendants would be at liberty to bring a
motion, without notice, to dismiss the Plaintiffs' claims. Attached to my affidavit and marked as
Exhibit A is a true copy of the Order of the Honourable Mr. Justice Pascal.

4.   By letter dated June 30, 20--, I forwarded to the lawyers for the Defendants all of the
information I had obtained, in compliance with a substantial number of undertakings. Attached
to my Affidavit and marked as Exhibit B is a true copy of my letter.

-2-

5.   Due to a lack of communication between myself and my associate, Mr. Allan Curley, to whom I had passed the Plaintiffs' file, a misunderstanding arose as to who had responsibility for insuring that the balance of the undertakings would be complied with.

6.   On September 28, 20--, the Defendants brought a successful motion, without notice, to dismiss the Plaintiffs' action for failure to comply with undertakings pursuant to the Order of the Honourable Mr. Justice Pascal. Attached to my Affidavit and marked as Exhibit C is a true copy of the Order of the Honourable Mr. Justice Fedor dismissing the Plaintiffs' action.

7.   The Order of the Honourable Mr. Justice Fedor was not served by the Defendants. The Order first came to my attention in November 20-- when I attempted to arrange completion of the outstanding undertakings.

8.   In April 20--, the Plaintiffs retained new lawyers, the firm of Michael, Eliad & Redford LLP.

9.   I verily believe that at all times the Plaintiffs have intended to proceed with this action.

10.   I verily believe that the Defendants would not suffer any prejudice that could not be compensated for by costs or an adjournment if the order dismissing the Plaintiffs' action were to be set aside.

11.   I verily believe that this is a fit and proper circumstance for an Order setting aside the Order of the Honourable Mr. Justice Fedor dismissing the Plaintiffs' action for failure to comply with undertakings and failure to comply with the Order of the Honourable Mr. Justice Pascal.

12.   I make this Affidavit in support of a motion to have the order of the Honourable Mr. Justice Fedor set aside and for no improper purpose.

SWORN BEFORE ME at the City of
Toronto, in the Province of Ontario this
.... day of ....April.............., 20--

}

_____   _____
       Commissioner for Taking Affidavits   *(Signature of deponent)*
              (or as may be)

(prepare backsheet)

ONTARIO
SUPERIOR COURT OF JUSTICE

Court File No. CV-**- 4721

ONTARIO
SUPERIOR COURT OF JUSTICE

THE HONOURABLE MR. JUSTICE LEE FEDOR   )   THURSDAY, SEPTEMBER 28, (year)
)

BETWEEN:

EDNA RUBICON and ALI RUBICON

Plaintiffs

and

WENDY MING, LORNA TERESA BAILY, ALPHA INSURANCE COMPANY OF CANADA
and BETA ASSURANCE COMPANY OF CANADA

Defendants

ORDER

THIS MOTION made by the defendants for an order dismissing the plaintiffs' claim for failure to fulfill undertakings given at their examination for discovery and for the plaintiffs' failure to comply with the order of the Honourable Justice Pascal was read this day at the Court House, 393 University Ave., 10th Floor, Toronto, Ontario.

ON READING the affidavit of Raymond G. Castles, sworn and filed, and the exhibits thereto,

1. THIS COURT ORDERS that the plaintiffs' claim be dismissed for failure to fulfill undertakings given at their examination for discovery and for the plaintiffs' failure to comply with the order of the Honourable Mr. Justice Pascal.

_____
Lee Fedor

*This is Exhibit C referred to in the affidavit
of Stanley Footloose sworn before me this
     day of   April   , (year)*

Robert B. Redford
A Commissioner, etc.

ENTERED AT TORONTO
In Book No. 77
as Document No. 101
on Sept. 28, (year)
by   *C.J. Smith*

Court File No. CV-**-4721

ONTARIO
SUPERIOR COURT OF JUSTICE

B E T W E E N:

EDNA RUBICON and ALI RUBICON

Plaintiffs

- and -

WENDY MING, LORNA TERESA BAILY, ALPHA INSURANCE COMPANY
OF CANADA and BETA ASSURANCE COMPANY OF CANADA

Defendants

MOTION RECORD

(Date prepared)

MICHAEL, ELIAD & REDFORD LLP
Barristers and Solicitors
863 Seneca Lane
Toronto, Ontario
M4J 1P6

Robert B. Redford
Tel: 416-363-1079
Fax: 416-363-2628

Lawyers for the Plaintiffs

TO: **CASTLES & SANDS**
Suite 900-205 Portage Street
Markham, Ontario L3R 3G3

Raymond G. Castles
Tel: 905-495-2222
Fax: 905-495-2223

Lawyers for the Defendants

EDNA RUBICON and ALI RUBICON   -and-   WENDY MING et. al.
Plaintiffs   Defendants

Court File No.CV-**-4721

ONTARIO
SUPERIOR COURT OF JUSTICE

PROCEEDING COMMENCED AT
TORONTO

MOTION RECORD

MICHAEL, ELIAD & REDFORD LLP
Barristers and Solicitors
863 Seneca Lane
Toronto, Ontario
M4J 1P6

Robert B. Redford (48000R)
Tel: 416-363-1079
Fax: 416-363-2628
rbrdfrd@mer.com

Lawyers for the Plaintiffs

(light blue)

Court File No. CV-**-4721

ONTARIO
SUPERIOR COURT OF JUSTICE

B E T W E E N :

EDNA RUBICON and ALI RUBICON

Plaintiffs

- and -

WENDY MING, LORNA TERESA BAILY, ALPHA INSURANCE COMPANY
OF CANADA and BETA ASSURANCE COMPANY OF CANADA

Defendants

MOTION RECORD
TABLE OF CONTENTS

Page No.

Notice of Motion dated April 2, 20— 1

Affidavit of Stanley Footloose sworn April 2, 20— 2

Exhibit A, Order of the Honourable Justice Pascal dated June 2, 20— 4

Exhibit B, Letter to Castles & Sands dated June 30, 20— 5

Exhibit C, Order of the Honourable Justice Fedor dated September 28, 20— 6

-2-

(c)   The transcripts from the Examinations for Discovery of Edna Rubicon and Ali Rubicon.

(d)   The Orders of the Honourable Mr. Justice Fedor and the Honourable Mr. Justice Pascal.

(e)   Such further and other evidence as the lawyers may advise and this Honourable Court may permit.

I estimate that the time required for the motion, including costs submissions, will be 60 minutes for the moving party and 60 minutes for the responding party for a total of 120 minutes.

April 25, 20--

MICHAEL, ELIAD & REDFORD LLP
Barristers and Solicitors
863 Seneca Lane
Toronto, Ontario
M4J 1P6

Robert B. Redford
Tel: 416-363-1079
Fax: 416-363-2628

Lawyers for the Plaintiffs

TO: **SUPERIOR COURT OF JUSTICE**
393 University Avenue
10th Floor
Toronto, Ontario
M5G 1E6

TO: **CASTLES & SANDS**
Suite 900-205 Portage Street
Markham, Ontario L3R 3G3

Raymond G. Castles
Tel: 905-495-2222
Fax: 905-495-2223

Lawyers for the Defendants

(prepare backsheet)

Court File No. CV-**-4721

SUPERIOR COURT OF JUSTICE

B E T W E E N:

EDNA RUBICON and ALI RUBICON

Plaintiffs

- and -

WENDY MING, LORNA TERESA BAILY, ALPHA INSURANCE COMPANY OF CANADA and BETA ASSURANCE COMPANY OF CANADA

Defendants

CONFIRMATION OF MOTION

I, Robert B. Redford, with the law firm of Michael, Eliad & Redford LLP, lawyer for the moving party, confirm that the moving party has conferred or attempted to confer with the other party and that the motion to be heard on April 30, 20--, will proceed on the following basis:

[ ]   for an adjournment on consent to .... (date).

[ ]   for a contested adjournment to .... (date), for the following reason:

(specify who is requesting the adjournment and why, and who is opposing it and why)

[ ]   for a consent order

[X]   for hearing of all the issues

[ ]   for hearing of the following issues only (specify)

The presiding Judge will be referred to the following materials: (please be specific)

(a)   The Affidavit of Stanley Footloose.

(b)   The pleadings and proceedings in this action.

Court File No. CV-**-4721

ONTARIO
SUPERIOR COURT OF JUSTICE

B E T W E E N :

EDNA RUBICON and ALI RUBICON

Plaintiffs

- and -

WENDY MING, LORNA TERESA BAILY, ALPHA INSURANCE COMPANY
OF CANADA and BETA ASSURANCE COMPANY OF CANADA

Defendants

COSTS OUTLINE

The Plaintiff provides the following outline of the submissions to be made at the hearing in support of the costs the party will seek if successful:

Fees (as detailed below)	$	1,830.00
Estimated lawyer's fee for appearance	$	500.00
Disbursements (as detailed in the attached appendix)	$	500.00
Total	$	2,830.00

The following points are made in support of the costs sought with reference to the factors set out in subrule 57.01(1):

- the amount claimed and the amount recovered in the proceeding

$275,000.00 claimed.

- the complexity of the proceeding

Relatively complex; original action dismissed on motion without notice.

- the importance of the issues

Of general importance to the public.

- the conduct of any party that tended to shorten or to lengthen unnecessarily the duration of the proceeding

Lack of communication between the Plaintiffs' former lawyers.

- whether any step in the proceeding was improper, vexatious or unnecessary or taken through negligence, mistake or excessive caution

Order of Justice Fedor dismissing the Plaintiffs' action was never served on the Plaintiffs.

- a party's denial of or refusal to admit anything that should have been admitted

n/a

- the experience of the party's lawyer

10 years or more

-2-

- the hours spent, the rates sought for costs and the rate actually charged by the party's lawyer

FEE ITEM *(e.g. pleadings, affidavits, cross-examinations, preparation, hearing, etc)*	PERSONS *(identify the lawyers, students and law clerks who provided services in connection with each item together with their year of call, if applicable)*	HOURS *(specify the hours claimed for each person identified in column 2)*	PARTIAL INDEMNITY RATE *(specify the rate being sought for each person identified in column 2)*	ACTUAL RATE*
Preparation of Notice of Motion, supporting Affidavit, and Factum, including case law research	Jill Doe, law clerk	4.0 hours	$60/hr	$100/hr
Review of Plaintiffs' file from previous lawyers	Robert B. Redford Year of call 20--	2.5 hours	$300/hr	$400/hr
Prepare for motion hearing	Robert B. Redford Year of call 20--	2.8 hours	$300/hr	$400/hr

* *Specify the rate being charged to the client for each person identified in column 2. If there is a contingency fee arrangement, state the rate that would have been charged absent such arrangement.*

- any other matter relevant to the question of costs

n/a

LAWYER'S CERTIFICATE

I CERTIFY that the hours claimed have been spent, that the rates shown are correct and that each disbursement has been incurred as claimed.

Date: _____   _____

(Date prepared)   Signature of lawyer

MICHAEL, ELIAD & REDFORD LLP
Barristers and Solicitors
863 Seneca Lane
Toronto, Ontario   M4J 1P6

Robert B. Redford
Tel: 416-363-1079
Fax: 416-363-2628

Lawyers for the Plaintiffs

TO: **CASTLES & SANDS**
             Suite 900-205 Portage Street
             Markham, Ontario L3R 3G3

             Raymond G. Castles
             Tel: 905-495-2222
             Fax: 905-495-2223

             Lawyers for the Defendants   (prepare backsheet)

Legal Office Procedures

Court File No. CV-**-4721

ONTARIO
SUPERIOR COURT OF JUSTICE

THE HONOURABLE	)	MONDAY, THE 30TH
	)	
MR. JUSTICE A. B. FARE	)	DAY OF APRIL, 20--

B E T W E E N :

(Court Seal)

EDNA RUBICON and ALI RUBICON

Plaintiffs

- and -

WENDY MING, LORNA TERESA BAILY, ALPHA INSURANCE COMPANY
OF CANADA and BETA ASSURANCE COMPANY OF CANADA

Defendants

ORDER

THIS MOTION, made by the Defendants for an order to set aside the Order of the

Honourable Mr. Justice Fedor which Order dismissed the Plaintiffs' action for failure to fulfill

undertakings they were required to fulfil by a prior Order of the Court was heard this day at the

Court House, 393 University Avenue, 10th Floor, Toronto, Ontario.

ON READING the Affidavit of Stanley Footloose, sworn and filed, and the exhibits

thereto, and on hearing the submissions of lawyers for all parties,

1.   THIS COURT ORDERS that the Plaintiffs' motion for an order to set aside the order of

the Honourable Mr. Justice Fedor be denied.

2.   THIS COURT ORDERS that there be no Order as to costs.

_____
Signature of Court Officer

(prepare backsheet)

FULL AND FINAL RELEASE

IN CONSIDERATION of the payment of the sum of Sixty Thousand Dollars ($60,000.00) inclusive of interest, costs and disbursements, we, the undersigned, Edna Rubicon and Ali Rubicon, on our own behalf and on behalf of our heirs, executors, administrators and assigns do hereby release and forever discharge STANLEY FOOTLOOSE and the LAWYERS' PROFESSIONAL INDEMNITY COMPANY, including their insurers, principals, executors, administrators, successors and assigns, from any and all actions, causes of action, claims and demands, for damages, loss or injury, howsoever arising, which heretofore may have been or may hereafter be sustained by us in consequence of a motor vehicle collision and the subsequent involvement and activities of Stanley Footloose arising out of the retainer by the undersigned, and any resulting lawyer-client contract and relationship, express or implied, between Stanley Footloose, the Lawyers' Professional Indemnity Company, and Edna Rubicon and Ali Rubicon, which more particularly gave rise to an action in the Ontario Superior Court of Justice, Court File No. CV-**-4721, including all damages, loss and injury not now known or anticipated but which may arise in the future and all effects and consequences thereof.

AND FOR THE SAID CONSIDERATION, WE further agree not to make any claim or take any proceedings against any other person, persons or corporation who might claim contribution or indemnity under the provisions of the *Negligence Act* and the amendments thereto from the person, persons and corporations discharged by this release.

IT IS UNDERSTOOD AND AGREED that the said payment or promise of payment is deemed to be no admission whatsoever of liability on the part of the said Stanley Footloose or the Lawyers' Professional Indemnity Company.

IN ENTERING into this release we hereby represent and warrant that we have had the advice of counsel, who is counsel of our choice, and that counsel has explained the terms of this release to us and that these terms are fully understood and voluntarily accepted by us.

WE DO HEREBY AUTHORIZE AND DIRECT you to make all settlement funds payable to our lawyer, Mr. Robert B. Redford, Michael, Eliad & Redford, in trust.

IN WITNESS WHEREOF WE have hereunto set our hands and seal this   day of   , 20--.

SIGNED, SEALED & DELIVERED   )
In the presence of   )
)

_____   _____
                Witness   Edna Rubicon

_____   _____
                Witness   Ali Rubicon

I am a lawyer and I hereby represent and declare that I have fully explained the foregoing Release to the signing party and it was acknowledged to me that the signing party understands the Release and the legal effect thereof. The signature which appears at the end of the Release is that of my client.

DATED at _____, this _____ day of _____, 20--.

(needs no backsheet)

_____
        Robert B. Redford
MICHAEL, ELIAD & REDFORD LLP
Lawyers for the Plaintiffs

CHAPTER 18

DISPOSITION WITHOUT TRIAL AND ENFORCEMENT OF ORDERS

This chapter details the procedural steps in situations where a defendant fails to defend an action or a judgment debtor fails to pay the damages ordered.

DEFAULT JUDGMENT

Rule 19 of the *Rules of Civil Procedure* provides for default proceedings. Obtaining a default judgment is one way of ending an action without going to trial. If a defendant fails to serve and file a statement of defence or a notice of intent to defend within the required time limit or at all, the plaintiff may automatically sign judgment against the defendant. Such a judgment is known as a **default judgment** because the defendant **defaulted** in responding to the plaintiff's statement of claim. Obtaining a default judgment, then, means the plaintiff won the action without going to trial. Figure 18.1 shows the steps in obtaining a default judgment in actions for **liquidated** and **unliquidated** damages. In either case, obtaining default judgment ends the action.

> ### Legal TIP
>
> A statement of claim **for money only** involves an action for liquidated damages; a statement of claim **general** involves an action for unliquidated damages.

Figure 18.1

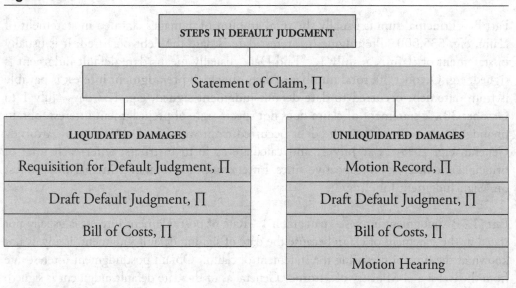

∏ (*Greek pi*) = Plaintiff

DEFAULT JUDGMENT IN LIQUIDATED DAMAGES

Obtaining default judgment in liquidated damages is automatic because liquidated damages usually represent a clear cut debt that the defendant owes to the plaintiff and that the plaintiff claimed in the statement of claim, e.g. the defendant failed to pay back a money loan. In a claim for liquidated damages, the plaintiff can obtain default judgment from the local registrar upon filing the following documents:

1. Proof of service of the statement of claim.
2. A requisition for default judgment (Form 19D). This requisition instructs the local registrar to note the defendant in default (basically, make a note in the court file that the defendant has not filed a statement of defence) and to sign the default judgment against the defendant. Under subrule 19.01(4), if a party is under disability, the party may be noted in default only with leave by a judge obtained on motion under rule 7.07.
3. A draft default judgment (Form 19A). This is the default judgment you are requesting the local registrar to sign.
4. A bill of costs (Form 57A). The bill of costs itemizes the lawyer's legal fees and disbursements to date, usually according to the tariff. The defendant must pay these costs since he or she is deemed to have lost the case.
5. Applicable court fees.

Typically, the local registrar checks the court file to confirm that the defendant has, in fact, failed to file a statement of defence and, if that is so, signs the default judgment which the plaintiff enters in the same manner as a trial judgment. Once the default judgment is signed, it means the plaintiff won the case in the amount of damages claimed in the statement of claim as well as legal costs, usually in the amount set out in the bill of costs.

PREPARATION AND DISTRIBUTION OF REQUISITION FOR DEFAULT JUDGMENT (FORM 19D)

You require: The statement of claim with proof of service. Follow along in Precedent 18.1. Notes on items not self-explanatory follow:

Key same title of proceeding and court file number as shown in statement of claim.

Part B - Principal sum is usually the total amount of damages claimed in statement of claim, e.g. $35,000. Prejudgment interest date is date the debt occurred; it is usually in statement of claim, e.g. July 1. "End Date" usually means date default judgment is signed, e.g. October 30; total number of days on which prejudgment interest is payable is from date debt occurred to date default judgment signed, e.g. 122 days (July 1 to October 30). If statement of claim does not specify rate of prejudgment interest, obtain prejudgment rate as of date the debt occurred from website of Ministry of Attorney General, e.g. 10% as at July 1, and calculate as form instructs; enter each total of principal and interest on respective lines. Enter combined total of principal and interest on "Sign Judgment for" line.

Part C - Postjudgment interest - paragraph 1 - Rate of postjudgment interest is usually not stated in the statement of claim because the date of signing default judgment, if any, is not known at the time of preparing the statement of claim. Obtain postjudgment interest rate from the website of Ministry of Attorney General as of the date default judgment is signed, e.g. October 30, 10%, and enter it in paragraph 1. When rate of postjudgment interest is not stated in the statement of claim it is claimed under the *Courts of Justice Act*; check that box in paragraph 1. You cannot calculate the total amount of postjudgment interest at this time because the interest continues to run until defendant pays the judgment.

Paragraph 2 - Costs - Indicate fixed or assessed costs, usually **fixed** unless you are claiming costs beyond those which the tariff allows.

Number of copies, minimum 2: File 1 in court where action was commenced; keep 1 in client's file.

PREPARATION AND DISTRIBUTION OF DEFAULT JUDGMENT (FORM 19A)

You require: The statement of claim, the completed requisition for default judgment, the bill of costs. Follow along in Precedent 18.3. Notes on items not self-explanatory follow:

The title is JUDGMENT. (It is only commonly referred to as default judgment.) Note that it is the local registrar who gives and signs a default judgment in liquidated damages (instead of a judge). The amount of the judgment is usually the amount claimed in statement of claim combined with prejudgment interest; obtain amount of judgment from Part B, "sign judgment for" line of requisition for default judgment. Leave amount of costs blank for local registrar to fix and insert based on bill of costs. Obtain postjudgment interest rate from Part C, paragraph 1, of requisition for default judgment or from website of Ministry of Attorney General and insert in judgment.

Number of copies, minimum 4: Local registrar signs, enters, and returns 1 to you; inserts 1 in court's order/judgment book; puts 1 in court file; keep 1 in client's file.

PREPARATION AND DISTRIBUTION OF BILL OF COSTS (FORM 57A)

You require: Client's docket; copy of tariff. See Precedent 18.2. Key points include:

Unless otherwise instructed, obtain the amounts of fees and disbursements from the tariff. Obtain the amount for service of the statement of claim usually from the process server's bill in the client's file.

Number of copies, minimum 2: File 1 in court; keep 1 in client's file.

DEFAULT JUDGMENT IN UNLIQUIDATED DAMAGES

Where the plaintiff's claim is for unliquidated damages, e.g. damages for injuries the plaintiff suffered in an accident, obtaining default judgment is not automatic. Instead, the plaintiff's lawyer makes a motion and argues for default judgment before a judge who may either give a default judgment or, in complex cases, refer the action to trial. The reason for proceeding with a motion instead of having the local registrar automatically sign a default judgment, as is the case in liquidated damages, is that the amount of money the plaintiff claimed in the statement of claim was for unliquidated damages, which is not as clear cut an amount as that in liquidated damages; therefore, it requires a judge to determine how much money would sufficiently compensate the plaintiff. To sign default judgment in unliquidated damages:

1. Pay the applicable court fees.
2. File proof of service of the statement of claim.
3. File a motion record containing:
   - a notice of motion (without notice) and supporting affidavit;
   - a copy of the statement of claim;
   - any other documents the lawyer will use as evidence at the motion hearing.
4. Attach to the motion record the bill of costs and the draft default judgment, both prepared as discussed above for signing default judgment in liquidated damages.

Motion hearing The lawyer who files the motion for default judgment appears at the hearing to argue the motion. If the lawyer argues successfully, the judge signs the draft default judgment either as is or makes handwritten changes. This is why, prior to the judge signing it, it is referred to as a draft default judgment. Once signed, issue and enter the default judgment in the same manner as an ordinary judgment. In complex cases, the judge may order a trial. If so, set the action down for trial in the usual manner. The defendant is not notified. At the trial, your client must testify personally to prove his or her damages, and the judge will then award what he or she determines to be an appropriate amount of damages.

DISCONTINUANCE BY PLAINTIFF

Discontinuance is another way of ending an action without going to trial. If the action is settled or the plaintiff, for whatever reason, does not wish to continue the action, the plaintiff may discontinue all or part of the action by serving all parties, before the close of pleadings, with a **notice of discontinuance Form 23A** and filing it, with proof of service, in the court office where the action was commenced. This notifies everybody that the action has ended. If the plaintiff discontinues after the close of pleadings, the parties can file a consent with the court agreeing that the case is discontinued, or the plaintiff must instead serve on all parties a notice of motion and supporting affidavit to let those parties who may have filed pleadings know of the discontinuance and to give all parties the opportunity to attend the motion hearing. This is because anyone who filed a statement of defence in the lawsuit would want compensation for his or her legal costs in defending the lawsuit. If the plaintiff is unwilling to pay the defendant's costs, the defendant is entitled to ask the judge at the hearing of the motion to order the plaintiff to pay all or at least some of the defendant's costs. If a party to an action is under disability, the action may be discontinued by or against the party only with leave of a judge under rule 7.07.1.

Effects of discontinuance on counterclaims, crossclaims, and third party claims If a defendant has counterclaimed and the plaintiff discontinues the action, the counterclaim is deemed to be discontinued, but the defendant may, within thirty days after the plaintiff files the notice of discontinuance, deliver a **notice of election to proceed with counterclaim.** Crossclaims and third party claims are usually deemed to be dismissed.

SUMMARY JUDGMENT

Rule 20 of the *Rules of Civil Procedure* provides for summary judgments. A summary judgment is a "quick" judgment on grounds that there is insufficient evidence or cause in the pleadings to warrant continuing on in the action. The plaintiff or defendant, whichever one believes the other's pleading contains insufficient evidence to continue, may serve and file a **notice of motion** and a **supporting affidavit** to obtain a summary judgment against the opposite party. The motion may be in respect of all or part of the claim. Each party must serve and file a factum.

Factum   The moving party's factum must be served and filed with proof of service in the court office where the motion is to be heard at least **seven days** before the hearing. The responding party's factum must be served and filed with proof of service in the court office where the motion is to be heard at least **four days** before the hearing.

Judgment   At the end of the motion hearing, the judge gives his or her decision in a **judgment**. This is one of only a few motions in which the decision resulting from a motion is referred to as a **judgment** instead of an order. That is because the judgment has the effect of a trial judgment since it finalizes either part of the action or the entire action. In the alternative, where the judge finds insufficient grounds for granting a summary judgment, the judge may order that the action proceed with an ordinary trial.

ENFORCEMENT OF ORDERS

Rule 60 of the *Rules of Civil Procedure* provides for the enforcement of orders (and judgments). A major misconception is that obtaining a court order (or judgment) means making the loser pay. In fact, the order is only legal proof that the court ordered the losing party to pay. In civil actions, the court can neither force the losing party to pay the order nor jail him or her for not paying it. Collecting on the order is, therefore, yet another completely new action. The various ways available to make the losing party pay the amount ordered are referred to as **enforcement of orders**. Enforcement of orders includes enforcement of judgments. Two common ways of enforcing an order or a judgment are: writs of seizure and sale and garnishments.

WRIT OF SEIZURE AND SALE

Rule 60.07 provides for enforcement of orders and judgments by way of a writ of seizure and sale. Basically, a writ of seizure and sale, also referred to as an execution, or writ of execution, gives public notice of an unpaid judgment or order against the defendant's personal and real estate property. Once the writ of seizure and sale has been issued, the **creditor** (party who won judgment) may instruct the sheriff to seize and sell any property the **debtor** (party ordered to pay) owns so as to satisfy the amount owing on the judgment or order. To begin the writ of seizure and sale procedure, the lawyer issues a **writ of seizure and sale (Form 60A)**, Precedent 18.4, usually in the court that gave the judgment. To issue the writ of seizure and sale, take these main documents to the court office:

- Writ of seizure and sale
- Requisition for writ of seizure and sale
- Copy of judgment or order, as entered
- Court fees

The local registrar issues the writ of seizure and sale, files a copy of the writ and of the requisition in the court office file, and returns the issued original writ of seizure and sale to you.

Filing writ of seizure and sale with sheriff   Once the local registrar issues the writ of seizure and sale, file a copy of it in the sheriff's office. Generally, when a writ of seizure and sale is delivered to the sheriff, it binds all of the real and personal property of the debtor within the jurisdiction (judicial district or county) of the sheriff. The creditor must, therefore, file a writ of seizure and sale with the sheriff and with the Land Titles office in each jurisdiction where the debtor may have real and personal property. Basically, the writ of seizure and sale places a lien on the personal and real property of the debtor. Generally, if the debtor attempts to sell any such property, the sale money must go first toward paying off the judgment or order. If the writ of seizure and sale is to remain in force, the creditor must renew it every **six years** by filing with the sheriff a **request to renew**, which may be filed electronically.

PREPARATION AND DISTRIBUTION OF WRIT OF SEIZURE AND SALE (FORM 60A)

You require: The judgment or order; the bill of costs. Follow along in Precedent 18.4. Notes on items not self-explanatory follow:

The court file number is usually the same as that shown on the judgment or order. The writ of seizure and sale is directed to the sheriff of the place where the debtor is believed to own property.

Paragraph (a) - obtain amount and postjudgment interest rate from default judgment or from paragraph (a) of requisition for writ of seizure and sale.
Paragraph (c) - obtain costs from bill of costs and postjudgment interest from default judgment or from paragraph (c) of requisition for writ of seizure and sale.

If set up to do so, legal software such as ACL automatically inserts the amount of court fees on the backsheet.

Number of copies, minimum 3: File 1 in court; file 1 in sheriff's office; keep 1 in client's file.

Electronic filing   Under subrule 60.07(1.1), the creditor may file the requisition for writ of seizure and sale electronically, in which case, neither a copy of the order as entered nor any other evidence is required to be filed with the requisition, and the writ of seizure and sale shall be issued electronically.

REQUISITION FOR WRIT OF SEIZURE AND SALE

This requisition, Precedent 18.5, is your instructions to the local registrar to issue the writ of seizure and sale. It is otherwise almost the same as the writ of seizure and sale. Note that this requisition is provided for under subrule 60.07(1) but there is no prescribed form. A standard form, as shown in Precedent 18.5, is provided through the ACL software program.

DIRECTION TO ENFORCE WRIT OF SEIZURE AND SALE

Instead of waiting for payment until the debtor sells any of his or her property on which the creditor has placed a writ of seizure and sale through the sheriff's office, the creditor may collect on the judgment or order sooner by directing the sheriff to sell the debtor's personal or real property. To do this, at any time after filing the writ of seizure and sale

Legal Office Procedures

with the sheriff, the creditor may file, usually with the same sheriff, a copy of the judgment or order as entered and a **direction to enforce the writ of seizure and sale (Form 60F)**, Precedent 18.6. This document gives the sheriff authorization to act on seizing and selling the debtor's property in payment of the amount owing on the judgment or order. Under subrule 60.07(13.0.1), the creditor may file the direction to enforce the writ of seizure and sale (Form 60F) electronically, in which case, it is not necessary to also file with it a copy of the judgment or order as entered.

GARNISHMENTS

Rule 60.08 of the *Rules of Civil Procedure* provides for the payment or recovery of money by way of garnishments. Garnishments are another method of collecting on a judgment or order. The creditor may collect on the judgment or order from anyone who owes money to the debtor, e.g. individual, employer, bank, or trust company.

A garnishment proceeding begins with the issuing and serving of a **notice of garnishment (Form 60H)** on the garnishee. The most common garnishee is the debtor's employer. The employer garnishee, for example, must deduct from the debtor's (employee's) salary a certain amount toward payment of the employee's debt, less a small amount for the garnishee's administrative costs for processing the employee's debt payments. A notice of garnishment remains in force for **six years** from the date of its issue and may be renewed every six years before the existing notice of garnishment expires by filing with the registrar where the proceeding was commenced a requisition for renewal of garnishment, together with an affidavit setting out the particulars of the amount owing, required by subrule 60.08(4).

Examinations in aid of execution Frequently in garnishment proceedings, lawyers conduct examinations in aid of execution, similar to examinations for discovery, to discover how much money the debtor can afford to pay and, therefore, how much the garnishee should deduct from the debtor's salary. Once the debtor pays off the judgment in full, the creditor's lawyer must serve on the garnishee and on the sheriff a notice of termination of garnishment to end the garnishment.

Documents required To begin garnishment proceedings, the following documents are required:

1. Requisition for garnishment (Form 60G), Precedent 18.7.
2. Copy of the judgment or order, as entered.
3. Affidavit setting out particulars of the amount owing and other particulars such as address of debtor and name and address of each person to whom a notice of garnishment is to be directed.
4. Notice of garnishment (Form 60H).
5. Garnishee's statement (Form 60I).

Once you file the requisition for garnishment and the affidavit setting out the particulars of the amount owing, the registrar shall issue the notice of garnishment (Form 60H) naming as garnishees the persons named in the affidavit and shall send a copy of the notice of garnishment to the sheriff of the county in which the debtor lives or, if the debtor lives outside Ontario, to the sheriff of the county in which the proceeding was commenced. In addition, the creditor's lawyer must serve, using any of the prescribed methods of service, the following:

On the debtor: A copy of the notice of garnishment and a copy of the affidavit setting out the particulars of the amount owing.

On the garnishee: A copy of the notice of garnishment and a blank copy of the garnishee's statement.

CHAPTER SUMMARY

There are a number of ways in which actions can end without reaching trial, including obtaining a default judgment, which may be done if the defendant fails to respond to the statement of claim. If the action is for liquidated damages, the local registrar has authority to automatically sign default judgment against the defendant. If the action is for unliquidated damages, the plaintiff must make a motion to a judge who will determine the amount of money that would be fair to award to the plaintiff for damages. Another way to end an action is by way of a summary judgment. Either a plaintiff or a defendant, whichever one believes there is insufficient evidence in the pleadings to continue to trial, may make a motion for summary judgment against the opposite party which, if granted, would end the action.

Enforcement of an order or a judgment means taking steps to make the losing party pay the amount of money awarded to the winning party in an order or judgment. Two ways of collecting on orders and judgments are writs of seizure and sale and garnishments. A writ of seizure and sale is like a lien or debt on the personal or real property of the person who owes money on a judgment or order. A garnishment, on the other hand, allows the winner to collect on the judgment or order from anyone who owes money to the losing party, including the losing party's employer so as to garnish the losing party's wages.

REVIEW QUESTIONS

1. When do you use a requisition for default judgment?
2. What is the difference in procedure between a default judgment in liquidated and unliquidated damages?
3. What is the purpose of a writ of seizure and sale?
4. When is a direction to enforce writ of seizure and sale used?
5. What is a default judgment?
6. The difference between liquidated damages and unliquidated damages is that liquidated damages refers to damages caused by the spilling of liquids. Explain.

Court File No. CV-**-863

ONTARIO
SUPERIOR COURT OF JUSTICE

B E T W E E N :

D. W. INSTALLATIONS INC.

Plaintiff

- and -

MILLAR BOND ROBERT

Defendant

REQUISITION FOR DEFAULT JUDGMENT

TO THE LOCAL REGISTRAR at Toronto (393 University Avenue)

I REQUIRE you to note the Defendant, Millar Bond Robert, in default in this action on the ground that the Defendant has failed to deliver a Statement of Defence within the time required by the *Rules of Civil Procedure*, although duly served on October 5, 20--.

I REQUIRE Default Judgment to be signed against the Defendant Millar Bond Robert.

Default Judgment may properly be signed in this action because the Claim is for

[X]   a debt or liquidated demand in money

[　]   recovery of possession of land

[　]   recovery of possession of personal property

[　]   foreclosure, sale or redemption of a mortgage

(Debt or liquidated demand)

[X]   There has been no payment on account of the Claim since the Statement of Claim was issued. *(Complete Parts B and C.)*

OR

[　]   The following payments have been made on account of the Claim since the Statement of Claim was issued. *(Complete Parts A and C.)*

-2-

PART A - PAYMENT(S) RECEIVED BY PLAINTIFF

(Complete this part only where part payment of the claim has been received. Where no payment has been received on account of the claim, omit this part and complete Part B.)

1.   Principal

Principal sum claimed in Statement of Claim (without interest) $ _____

Date of Payment	Amount of Payment	Payment Amount Principal	Applied to Interest	Principal Sum Owing
TOTAL	$	$	$	A $

2.   Prejudgment interest

(Under section 128 of the Courts of Justice Act, judgment may be obtained for prejudgment interest from the date the cause of action arose, if claimed in the statement of claim.)

Date on which Statement of Claim was issued...

Date from which prejudgment interest is claimed ....

The Plaintiff is entitled to prejudgment interest on the Claim, calculated as follows:

(Calculate simple interest only unless an agreement relied on in the statement of claim specifies otherwise. Calculate interest on the principal sum owing from the date of last payment To calculate the interest amount, count the number of days since the last payment, multiply that number by the annual rate of interest, multiply the result by the principal sum owing and divide by 365.)

Principal Sum Owing	Start Date	End Date (Date of Payment)	Number of Days	Rate	Interest Amount

The last End Date should be the date judgment is signed.

                                                            TOTAL B $ _____

Principal Sum Owing (Total A above) $ _____

Total Interest Amount (Total B above) $ _____

SIGN JUDGMENT FOR .... $ _____

-3-

PART B - NO PAYMENT RECEIVED BY PLAINTIFF

(Complete this part only where no payment of the claim has been received.)

1.   Principal

Principal sum claimed in Statement of Claim (without interest)   A $35,000.00

2.   Prejudgment interest

(Under section 128 of the Courts of Justice Act, judgment may be obtained for prejudgment interest from the date the cause of action arose, if claimed in the statement of claim.)

Date on which Statement of Claim was issued...October 1, 20--

Date from which prejudgment interest is claimed ....July 1, 20--

The Plaintiff is entitled to prejudgment interest on the Claim, calculated as follows:

(Calculate simple interest only unless an agreement relied on in the statement of claim specifies otherwise. To calculate the interest amount, count the number of days and multiply that number by the annual rate of interest, multiply the result by the principal sum owing and divide by 365.)

Principal Sum Owing	Start Date	End Date (Date of Payment)	Number of Days	Rate	Interest Amount
$35,000.00	Jul. 1/--	Oct. 30/--	122	10%	$1,169.86

The last End Date should be the date judgment is signed.

TOTAL B $	$1,169.86
Principal Sum Owing (Total A above) $	$35,000.00
Total Interest Amount (Total B above) $	$1,169.86
SIGN JUDGMENT FOR .... $	$36,169.86

PART C – POSTJUDGMENT INTEREST AND COSTS

1.   Postjudgment interest

        The Plaintiff is entitled to postjudgment interest at the rate of 10 per cent per year,

        [X]   under the *Courts of Justice Act,* as claimed in the Statement of Claim.
        OR

-4-

[ ]   in accordance with the Claim made in the Statement of Claim.

2.   Costs

The Plaintiff wishes costs to be,

[X]   fixed by the local registrar.
OR
[ ]   assessed by an Assessment Officer.

October   , 20--

_____
(signature of plaintiff's lawyer or plaintiff)

MICHAEL, ELIAD & REDFORD LLP
Barristers and Solicitors
863 Seneca Lane
Toronto, Ontario
M4J 1P6

Robert B. Redford
Tel: 416-363-1079
Fax: 416-363-2628

Lawyers for the Plaintiff

(prepare backsheet)

Court File No. CV-**-863

ONTARIO
SUPERIOR COURT OF JUSTICE

B E T W E E N :

D. W. INSTALLATIONS INC.

Plaintiff

- and -

MILLAR BOND ROBERT

Defendant

BILL OF COSTS

AMOUNTS CLAIMED FOR FEES AND DISBURSEMENTS

(Following the items set out in Tariff A, itemize the claim for fees and disbursements. Indicate the names of the lawyers, students-at-law and law clerks who provided services in connection with each item. In support of the claim for fees, attach copies of the dockets or other evidence. In support of the claim for disbursements, attach copies of invoices or other evidence.)

Partial Indemnity

Pleadings
Drafting Statement of Claim
Robert B. Redford – 4 hours @ $300.00/hr. $1,200.00
Jill Doe – 3 hours @ $80.00/hr.   240.00

Default Judgment
Robert B. Redford – 2.8 hours @ $300.00/hr.   840.00
Jill Doe – 2 hours @ $80.00/hr.   160.00

TOTAL FEES $2,440.00
HST   317.20
     $2,757.20

DISBURSEMENTS

Paid fee to court to issue Statement of Claim* $ 220.00
Paid for service of Statement of Claim   46.28
Paid for Requisition for Default Judgment*   160.00
     $ 426.28
HST on disbursements amount of $46.28   6.02
Total disbursements $ 432.30 $ 432.30

TOTAL FEES AND DISBURSEMENTS $3,189.50

*Not subject to HST

STATEMENT OF EXPERIENCE

A claim for fees is being made with respect to the following lawyers:

Name of Lawyer   Years of Experience

Robert R. Redford   10 years
Jill Doe (law clerk)

TO: (prepare backsheet)

Court File No. CV-**-863

ONTARIO
SUPERIOR COURT OF JUSTICE

B E T W E E N :

(Court Seal)

D. W. INSTALLATIONS INC.

Plaintiff

- and -

MILLAR BOND ROBERT

Defendant

JUDGMENT

On reading the Statement of Claim in this action and the proof of service of the Statement

of Claim on the Defendant, filed, and the Defendant having been noted in default,

1.   IT IS ORDERED AND ADJUDGED that the Defendant pay to the Plaintiff the sum of

$36,169.86 and the sum of $ for the costs of this action.

This Judgment bears interest at the rate of   10   per cent per year from its date.

Date   October   20--   Signed by   _____

Local Registrar

Address of
court office: 393 University Avenue
10th Floor
Toronto, Ontario
M5G 1E6

RCP-E 19A (prepare backsheet)

Court File No. CV-**-863

ONTARIO
SUPERIOR COURT OF JUSTICE

B E T W E E N :

D. W. INSTALLATIONS INC.

Plaintiff

- and -

MILLAR BOND ROBERT

Defendant

WRIT OF SEIZURE AND SALE

TO: The Sheriff of the City of Toronto

Under an Order of this Court made on October 30, 20--, in favour of D. W. Installations Inc.

YOU ARE DIRECTED to seize and sell the real and personal property within your county or district of

Surname of individual or name of corporation/firm, etc.
Robert

First given name *(individual only)*	*Second given name* *(individual only)(if applicable)*	*Third given name* *(individual only)(if applicable)*
Millar	Bond	

and to realize from the seizure and sale the following sums:

    (a) $36,169.86 and interest at 10 per cent per year commencing on October 30, 20--;

-2-

(Where the writ is for two or more periodic or instalment payments, substitute:)

Amount of Payment: $_____   Due Date: _____

(b) $_____ and interest at _____ per cent per year on the payments in

default commencing on the date of default;

(c) $3,189.50 for costs together with interest at 10 per cent per year commencing on

October 30, 20--; and

(d)   your fees and expenses in enforcing this Writ.

YOU ARE DIRECTED to pay out the proceeds according to law and to report on the execution

of this Writ if required by the party or lawyer who filed it.

Dated at Toronto _____   Issued by _____
                                                                                                         Registrar

on _____   Address of Court office

393 University Avenue
10th Floor
Toronto, Ontario
M5G 1E6

Legal Office Procedures

Court File No. CV-**-863

D. W. INSTALLATIONS INC.
Plaintiff

-and-

MILLAR BOND ROBERT
Defendant

ONTARIO
SUPERIOR COURT OF JUSTICE
PROCEEDING COMMENCED AT
TORONTO

WRIT OF SEIZURE AND SALE

Creditor's Name: ....D. W. Installations Inc.
Creditor's Address: ....79 Bayview Avenue
Toronto, Ontario M3Y 9E3

Lawyer's name: Robert B. Redford

Lawyer's address and telephone no.:

MICHAEL, ELIAD & REDFORD LLP
Barristers and Solicitors
863 Seneca Lane
Toronto, Ontario
M4J 1P6

Robert B. Redford (48000R)
Tel: 416-363-1079
Fax: 416-363-2628
rbrdfrd@mer.com

Lawyers for the Plaintiff

FEES		
Fee	Item	Officer
$	Paid for this Writ	
$	Lawyer's fee for issuing Writ	
	First Renewal	
	Second Renewal	
	Third Renewal	

RENEWAL		
Date	Officer	

-2-

(b) $ _____ and interest at _____ per cent per year on the payments in
default commencing on the date of default;

(c) $3,189.50 for costs together with interest at 10 per cent per year commencing on
October 30, 20--; and

(d) your fees and expenses in enforcing this Writ.

Order made on October 30, 20--

_____
Robert B. Redford

October _____ , 20--

MICHAEL, ELIAD & REDFORD LLP
Barristers and Solicitors
863 Seneca Lane
Toronto, Ontario
M4J 1P6

Robert B. Redford
Tel: 416-363-1079
Fax: 416-363-2628

Lawyers for the Plaintiff

(prepare backsheet)

Court File No. CV-**-863

ONTARIO
SUPERIOR COURT OF JUSTICE

B E T W E E N:

D. W. INSTALLATIONS INC.

Plaintiff

- and -

MILLAR BOND ROBERT

Defendant

REQUISITION FOR WRIT OF SEIZURE AND SALE

TO THE LOCAL REGISTRAR at Toronto

I REQUIRE a Writ of Seizure and Sale in favour of D. W. Installations Inc. directed to
the Sheriff of the City of Toronto against the real and personal property of

Surname of individual or name of corporation/firm, etc.		
Robert		

First given name (individual only)	Second given name (individual only)(if applicable)	Third given name (individual only)(if applicable)
Millar	Bond	

and to realize from the seizure and sale the following sums:

(a) $36,169.86 and interest at 10 per cent per year commencing on October 30, 20--;

(Where the writ is for two or more periodic or instalment payments, substitute:)

Amount of Payment: $ _____   Due Date: _____

Precedent 18.6   Direction to Enforce Writ, page 1

Sheriff's File No.

ONTARIO
SUPERIOR COURT OF JUSTICE

B E T W E E N:

D. W. INSTALLATIONS INC.

Creditor

and

MILLAR BOND ROBERT

Debtor

DIRECTION TO ENFORCE WRIT

TO: The Sheriff of the City of Toronto

Under an Order of this Court in favour of D. W. Installations Inc. made on October 30, (year), Millar Bond Robert was ordered to pay the sum of $36,169.86 with interest at the rate of 10 per cent per year commencing on October 30, (year) and costs of $3,189.50 *(as fixed or assessed)* with interest at the rate of 10 per cent per year commencing on October 30, (year). Since the Order was made, the creditor has received the following payments:

Date of payment   Amount of Payment

Under rule 60.19 of the *Rules of Civil Procedure*, the creditor is entitled to costs in the amount of,

(a) $275.00 for the preparation of documents in connection with issuing, renewing and filing with the Sheriff the Writ of Execution or Notice of Garnishment;

-2-

(b) $185.00 for disbursements paid to a Sheriff, registrar, official examiner, court reporter or other public officer and to which the creditor is entitled under subrule 60.19(1); *(Attach copy of all receipts)*

(c) $ _____ for an amount determined in accordance with Tariff A for conducting an examination in aid of execution; *(Attach affidavit confirming that examination was conducted, and a bill of costs.)*

(d) $ _____ for any other costs to which the creditor is entitled under subrule 60.19(1). *(Attach certificate of assessment)*

YOU ARE DIRECTED to enforce the Writ of Seizure and Sale issued on October 30, (year) and filed in your office for a sum sufficient to satisfy the total of the amounts set out above, together with subsequent interest, and your fees and expenses.

October 30, (year)

_____
Robert B. Redford

MICHAEL, ELIAD & REDFORD LLP
Barristers and Solicitors
863 Seneca Lane
Toronto, Ontario
M4J 1P6

Robert B. Redford (48000R)
Tel: 416-363-1079
Fax: 416-363-2628

Lawyers for the Plaintiff

(prepare backsheet)

-2-

4. $270.00 for disbursements paid to a Sheriff, registrar, official examiner, court reporter or other public officer and to which the creditor is entitled under subrule 60.19(1). *(Attach copies of all receipts.)*

5. $ _____ for an amount determined in accordance with Tariff A for conducting an examination in aid of execution. *(Attach affidavit confirming that examination was conducted, and a bill of costs.)*

6. $35.00 for any other costs to which the creditor is entitled under subrule 60.19(1). *(Attach certificate of assessment.)*

7. $163.00 for postjudgment interest to today's date. *(Calculate by counting the number of days that the principal sum has been owing, multiplying that number by the annual rate of interest, then multiplying by the principal sum owing and dividing by 365.)*

Date: _____

_____
(Signature of creditor or creditor's lawyer)
(Name, address and telephone number of creditor or creditor's lawyer)

MICHAEL, ELIAD & REDFORD LLP
Barristers and Solicitors
863 Seneca Lane
Toronto, Ontario
M4J 1P6

Robert B. Redford
Tel: 416-363-1079
Fax: 416-363-2628

Lawyers for the Creditor

(prepare backsheet)

Court File No. CV-**-2345

ONTARIO
SUPERIOR COURT OF JUSTICE

B E T W E E N:

JENNY LEE

Creditor

and

GEORGE JUGGLE

Debtor

and

KRAFT AUTO BODY SHOP

Garnishee

REQUISITION FOR GARNISHMENT

TO: The Local Registrar at Toronto

I REQUIRE a Notice of Garnishment to be issued in this proceeding, in accordance with the attached draft Form 60H. The total amount to be shown in the Notice of Garnishment is $44,115.00, made up as follows:

1. $42,397.00 for principal owing under the Judgment or Order, including prejudgment interest.

2. $975.00 for the costs of the action.

3. $275.00 for the preparation of documents in connection with issuing, renewing and filing with the Sheriff a Writ of Execution or Notice of Garnishment.

CHAPTER 19
MARRIAGE AND DOMESTIC CONTRACTS

This chapter discusses the requirements for getting married and the role that domestic contracts play in issues arising when couples live together, marry, or separate.

MARRIAGE

Under the Canadian *Constitution*, the federal government is authorized to make marriage laws. This enables the federal government to ensure that marriage laws are the same in all provinces. People who wish to get married in Canada must meet certain federal legal requirements which are known as **essential requirements**. The Canadian *Constitution* also permits each province to make its own laws relating to the steps which people must follow in order to get married, and such provincial legal requirements are known as **formal requirements**.

What is marriage   Under Canada's *Civil Marriage Act*, "marriage, for civil purposes, is the lawful union of two persons to the exclusion of all others." Marriage is a legal contract between two people who may be of the same, or opposite, sex. Same-sex marriages (marriages between two men or two women) became legal in Canada on July 20, 2005, with the passing of the *Civil Marriage Act*. Many provinces permit same-sex marriages, including Ontario.

Essential requirements   To be eligible for marriage, people must meet the following essential requirements:

> **Unmarried status**   Neither party may marry if such party is already married. If either party does so, the guilty party will have committed the crime of **bigamy** (from the Greek, *two concurrent marriages*), and the second marriage would be invalid because Canada fosters a monogamous society (one spouse at one time).
>
> **Mental capacity**   At the time of marriage, both parties must be able to understand the duties and responsibilities of the marriage they are entering into; in addition, neither must be under the influence of drugs or alcohol. If mental capacity exists at the time of marriage but ceases to exist afterward, the marriage remains valid.
>
> **Close relationships**   Under Canada's *Marriage (Prohibited Degrees) Act*, persons **cannot** marry if they are lineally related, i.e. closely related by blood or adoption. For example, a person cannot marry his or her parent, grandparent, child,

> **Legal TIP**
>
> The engagement ring — in Ontario, you cannot sue for breach of promise of marriage. The general rule is the party who broke off the engagement forfeits the ring.

grandchild, great grandchild, brother, sister, half-brother, or half-sister. Persons not too closely related by blood, e.g. uncles and nephews, or by affinity (i.e. by marriage) or adoption are not prohibited from marrying each other by reason only of their relationship.

Free consent Neither party must be coerced into the marriage, and there must be no fraud or misrepresentation. An unrevealed pregnancy, for example, constitutes misrepresentation.

Sexual capacity Each party must be able to perform sexual intercourse. To be valid, a marriage must be consummated. A marriage is consummated on the first occasion when the spouses engage in post-marital sexual intercourse. If either party is unable to perform sexual intercourse, as for example, through impotence, the marriage is said to be non-consummated and may be annulled. A spouse's refusal to have sex, however, is not in itself a ground for annulment on the basis of non-consummation.

Age (as established by each province) The provinces establish the age required for marrying, and the age varies among the provinces. In Ontario, the age is eighteen without parental consent and sixteen or seventeen with the consent in writing of both parents. In Ontario, persons under the age of sixteen cannot marry, even with permission from their parents.

Formal requirements Formal requirements are established by each province and include such things as getting a marriage licence, being married by someone qualified to perform a marriage ceremony, and making sure that the event is witnessed and registered. Under Ontario's *Marriage Act*, the formal requirements for getting married in Ontario include:

Marriage licence You may download the marriage licence application from the ServiceOntario website. Once you have filled out the application for marriage licence, you must apply for the marriage licence in person, usually at the local city hall or municipal office. Both of you must bring valid identification, such as a birth certificate (along with any change of name certificate), current passport, record of immigrant landing or Canadian citizenship card, along with photo identification, when applying for the marriage licence. If both of you have signed the application for marriage certificate, then only one of you must attend in person and bring for both of you the required identification. There is a fee for purchasing a marriage licence. The marriage licence is usually issued on the same day, provided all documentation is correct. The marriage licence is valid for three months from the date of purchase. This means you must get married before the marriage licence expires because if it does expire you must purchase another one.

The ceremony You can have a civil or a religious ceremony. In either case, you require a marriage licence. If you wish a civil ceremony (e.g. being married at the city hall instead of having a church wedding), you must book an appointment for it at your local city hall or municipal office. Civil ceremonies are performed by a judge or a justice of the peace. Religious ceremonies must be performed by a religious official, e.g. a priest or, for some religions, a publication of banns. (Usually, you do not need a marriage licence if you are having your banns read in a church, provided the banns are being registered with the Ontario government.) In either case, both of you must physically stand before the person who is solemnizing the marriage in the presence of two witnesses. At the conclusion of the marriage ceremony, the spouses, the solemnizer, and the witnesses must sign the marriage licence. The person who performed the marriage will forward the signed marriage licence to the Office of the Registrar General for registration.

Marriage certificate   The marriage certificate (see Chapter 22 for a precedent) is proof that the marriage took place and that it was registered with the government. After your marriage, apply for a marriage certificate through the Office of the Registrar General by completing a request for marriage certificate. You may complete a request for marriage certificate form online through the ServiceOntario website, or you may download the form in PDF format from the same website.

MARRIAGE AND THE CHANGE OF NAME ACT

Ontario law does not require spouses to change their last name upon marriage. You may continue to use your pre-marriage last name (surname), or you may simply assume your spouse's last name (surname), or a combination of your last name and your spouse's last name as a hyphenated surname, e.g. Wendy Smith-Jones. You may proceed to change all your identification (health card, driver's licence, passport, banking information, etc.) with the use of your marriage certificate. No formal name change is required because this name change does not change your legal name, that is, the name on your birth certificate, whereas if you go the route of legally changing your name, usually done by completing an **election to change surname** form, your last name (surname) as it appears on your birth certificate will change. Your birth certificate, in that case, will show your new last name and your previous last name.

ANNULMENT OF MARRIAGE

If it can be proven that one of the essential requirements for marriage is missing, then the marriage is annulled and is considered never to have happened. Examples include: where a spouse is already married or is related lineally or by adoption, where a spouse was threatened into marriage, or where a spouse was mislead as to the nature of the ceremony because the ceremony was held in a language not understood by one of the parties, or where the marriage was not consummated by sexual intercourse. Note here that it is the party who is not responsible for the non-consummation who could claim non-consummation. Generally, marriages of males below the age of 15 and girls below the age of 12 may be annulled. Also, under the *Declarations of Death Act, 2002*, if one of the spouses goes missing in circumstances of peril for seven years, or more, without contact, that spouse is presumed legally dead, and the marriage is deemed to be over.

DOMESTIC CONTRACTS

Domestic contracts are agreements that deal with family-related matters. The act that permits the creation of domestic contracts in Ontario is the *Family Law Act*. The act provides for: **marriage contracts, cohabitation agreements**, and **separation agreements**. Domestic contracts that are drawn on reason and fairness overrule almost all provisions of the *Family Law Act*. The intent is to allow couples ample flexibility to settle their own affairs without resorting to the courts.

It is only in the absence of a domestic contract that the spouses must resort to the *Family Law Act* for settling their disputes. Hence, the *Family Law Act* protects couples who do not have domestic contracts; those who do, are protected by the terms of the domestic contract itself because they have, in effect, opted out of the provisions of the *Family Law Act*. Domestic contracts must be in writing, and they must be signed by the parties to the contract and witnessed.

Preliminary considerations in preparing domestic contracts Lawyers must draw domestic contracts so that the terms are enforceable, not only at the present time, but also years later when the parties might challenge the terms. This involves the lawyer checking the law and obtaining complete financial and property information between the parties as well as personal background information about the parties and their children. The lawyer usually obtains this information at the initial client interview, often by completing self-designed checklists and by also having the client fill out financial statement forms.

Validity of domestic contracts Under the *Family Law Act*, to be valid, a domestic contract must be in writing, signed, and witnessed. Section 56 of the *Family Law Act* sets out the most common grounds upon which a domestic contract can be challenged; these pertain mainly to failure to disclose assets and failure to understand the contract. Part III of the *Family Law Act* pertains mainly to unconscionable support provisions on which a domestic contract can be challenged. In effect, the court can overrule domestic contracts on the following grounds, even where the parties have agreed to the contrary, if:

- either party failed to disclose significant assets, debts, or liabilities when the domestic contract was made;
- either party did not understand the consequences of the contract or signed it under duress or misrepresentation;
- the contract is clearly unfair;
- the contract is not in the best interest of the children (for example, if the amount of the child support the contract provides for is too low).

Independent legal advice Independent legal advice is not a formal requirement for a domestic contract to be valid, but it is good practice to prevent challenges to the contract. Independent legal advice means each party should see a separate lawyer for advice on how the domestic contract affects him or her. Even where the parties feel it unnecessary, this is a must since either party may later claim he or she did not understand the contract or that he or she was the victim of duress, misrepresentation, or mistake. Each party's lawyer includes proof of independent legal advice by signing a **certificate of independent legal advice**, Precedent 19.3, and attaching it to the domestic contract. A clause that the client acknowledges receiving independent legal advice and is signing the contract voluntarily usually forms part of every domestic contract.

MARRIAGE CONTRACTS

A marriage contract, Precedent 19.1, is an agreement between parties who are married or intend to marry. If entered into prior to marriage, a marriage contract is commonly referred to as a pre-nuptial agreement. In the agreement, the couple outlines the rights and obligations during marriage and how the couple would handle their affairs in the event of separation, divorce, or death.

Property   In a marriage contract, you may exclude property which you own and which you do not wish to be shared with your spouse in the event of divorce. This is because in the event of divorce, the *Family Law Act* provides that the value of nearly all family property must be shared equally between the spouses, regardless of who owns or paid for such property. This right also extends to the home you live in during your marriage, referred to as the matrimonial home, no matter who owns it or who paid for it, even if one of you brought it into the marriage. In effect, a marriage contract is the only way to exclude the matrimonial home and other property from being shared because the terms of a marriage contract override the provisions made under the *Family Law Act*.

Careful what you sign away   The law permits marriage contracts to state that the value of the matrimonial home or other property is not to be shared equally or at all, or that your share of any property is to be in an amount that is less than it should be, as well as state what your spousal support obligations will be. Note that if you were to sign away these rights in your marriage contract you will find the courts reluctant to make changes to your marriage contract unless you could prove to the court that the other party was dishonest about his or her financial affairs at the time you signed the contract, or that you did not understand the nature or consequences of the contract, or for general reasons of contract law, such as undue influence, mistake, etc. Some key provisions normally made in marriage contracts include:

- **Ownership in, or division of, property**   Read through Precedent 19.1 for an example situation. See also the list of **assets and liabilities** which lawyers usually attach to the marriage contract. Since the value of property brought into the marriage is not "shareable," the list of assets and liabilities establishes the pre-marriage property value in the event of separation or divorce.
- **Support obligations**   The *Family Law Act* makes it an obligation for **spouses** to financially support each other. The marriage contract may spell out who would pay to whom and how much. This is usually spousal, as opposed to child, support.
- **Education and moral training of children**   The spouses may agree on which spouse will have the right to direct the education and moral training of their children, but not the right to custody of, or access to, their children.
- **Other**   The spouses may agree on any other matter that will settle their affairs.
- **Exceptions**   Under the *Family Law Act*, the spouses may **not** include in a marriage contract the following provisions:

1. They may **not** name the spouse who will have custody of, or access to, the children.
2. They may **not** include child support (as opposed to spousal support). The issues of custody, access, and child support can only be decided after the spouses separate.
3. The owner spouse of the matrimonial home may **not** require the non-owner spouse to give up his or her right to **live** in it. This is known as the **right of possession** of the matrimonial home.

The first two exceptions aim to protect the children in that it is impossible to determine in advance which of the two spouses would be the better parent or how much child support would be fair and adequate. The third exception aims to ensure that the spouse who is not the registered owner of the matrimonial home is not left without shelter. Even if included, the court could disregard these provisions if it is in the best interest of the children to do so.

COHABITATION AGREEMENTS

A cohabitation agreement, Precedent 19.2, is a contract entered into by parties who are living together or intend to live together in a conjugal relationship and who are not married to each other. Cohabitation means "living together" and is referred to as a common-law relationship. Roughly, "conjugal" means living together as a married couple with sexual relations that are the same as those between a married couple. A cohabitation agreement is essentially the same as a marriage contract and may include:

- ownership in, or division of, property
- support obligations
- the right to direct the education and moral training of their children, but not the right to custody of, or access to, their children
- any other matter in the settlement of their affairs

Note that the *Family Law Act* provisions about equal sharing of family property, such as the matrimonial home, do not apply to common-law couples; those rights apply only to married couples. When a common-law couple separates, the home that they lived in belongs to the person whose name is on the title to the property. It is, therefore, very important that cohabitation agreements spell out how the parties wish to divide their property in the event of separation because the courts usually do not change domestic contracts unless you prove to the court that the other party was dishonest about his or her financial affairs at the time you signed the contract, or that you did not understand the nature or consequences of the contract, or for general reasons of contract law, such as undue influence, mistake, etc.

Cohabitation agreements cannot provide for custody, access, or child support (as opposed to spousal support). Custody, access, and child support can only be decided after the parties separate. If the parties get married, the co-habitation agreement becomes the parties' marriage contract.

SEPARATION AGREEMENTS

A separation agreement, Precedent 19.3, is a contract entered into by married couples or common-law couples who have separated, that is, they are living separate and apart, usually no longer in the same residence. Couples who continue to live under the same roof, however, may still be found to be living separate and apart based on the fact that they are living independent lives. A separation agreement deals with many of the same matters that a marriage contract deals with, except it recognizes that the marriage or the common-law relationship has ended. A separation agreement may include the following:

- ownership in, or division of, property
- support obligations (spousal and child support)
- the right to direct the education and moral training of their children
- the right to custody of, or access to, their children, and
- any other matter in the settlement of their affairs

Note that a separation agreement is the only domestic contract which may include the following provisions:

- The spouses may name the spouse who will have custody of, or access to, the children.
- The non-owner spouse may release his or her right to possession of the matrimonial home.

Once signed, the separation agreement is binding upon both spouses. Should the spouses later divorce, the separation agreement may be filed in court as evidence. Note that with respect to the inclusion of custody, access, and the release of a spouse's right to possession of the matrimonial home, the court may disregard these provisions where it is in the best interest of the children to do so. Note also that the court has power to set aside support provisions or waivers of support if such provisions result in unconscionable circumstances or mean that the prospective recipient of the support must instead depend on public assistance. The court does not otherwise change the terms of a separation agreement unless you prove to the court that the other party was dishonest about his or her financial affairs at the time you signed the contract, or that you did not understand the nature or consequences of the contract, or for general reasons of contract law, such as undue influence, mistake, etc.

PREPARATION AND DISTRIBUTION OF DOMESTIC CONTRACTS

You require: The lawyer's interview notes; draft contract, if any. Follow along in Precedent 19.1, marriage contract, traditional style; in Precedent 19.2, cohabitation agreement, modern style; and in Precedent 19.3, separation agreement, modern style. Follow the style preference of your firm. Key points include:

Heading Use standard margins. If preferred, use legal size paper. The traditional or the modern style may be used for any domestic contract. Unless the lawyer indicates otherwise, however, use the modern style to avoid outmoded terms such as "hereinafter." Leave the **day** blank for the lawyer to fill in when the client signs.

Body Except for the variable information, e.g. names, dates, almost all of the information comes from software or computerized precedents. Double space.

Ending In the traditional style, wording such as "the parties hereto have hereunto set their hands and seals the day, month, and year first above written" means the parties signed on the date shown in the heading of the document. The phrase "Signed, Sealed and Delivered," basically means the parties signed the document before a witness, sealed it, and delivered a copy to each party. Two separate witnesses, usually each party's lawyer, sign opposite their respective client's signature to indicate independent witnessing. This is why there are two separate lines for witnesses.

Prepare a **certificate of independent legal advice** for all domestic contracts, and be sure there are two certificates of independent legal advice attached to each contract, the second by the other party's lawyer. Prepare a **certificate of independent legal advice** *and* a **list of assets and liabilities** only for marriage contracts and cohabitation agreements.

Backsheet   Many law firms use templates for preparing backsheets. Backsheets are usually prepared on standard size paper in landscape position and usually use about the centre 1/3 of the sheet for the keyed information, Precedent 19.3. Backsheets prepared on legal size paper in landscape position usually use about the second quarter from the left margin of the sheet for the keyed information.

Legal TIP

Domestic contracts are not court documents. That is why the name of a court is not in the heading.

Number of copies, minimum 5: The parties execute 4: 1 for each party; 1 in the file; 1 to other lawyer; 1 unsigned in file.

PATERNITY AGREEMENTS

The *Family Law Act* provides that if a man and a woman who are not spouses enter into an agreement for the payment of the expenses of a child's prenatal care and birth, support of a child, or funeral expenses of the child or the mother, such an agreement is known as a paternity agreement. Generally, it means that the father has acknowledged paternity of the child and that he is willing to take responsibility for the support of the child.

CHAPTER SUMMARY

Domestic contracts are agreements married and not married couples make about family-related matters. The most common domestic contracts include marriage contracts, cohabitation agreements, and separation agreements.   Each of these contracts requires independent legal advice to insure that each party understands the terms of the contract. Marriage contracts may not include provisions about which spouse will have custody of, or access to, any children, nor may the owner spouse of the matrimonial home require the non-owner spouse to give up his or her right to live in it (referred to as a right of possession). A separation agreement is the only domestic contract which may name the spouse who will have custody of, or access to, any children and also the only domestic contract in which the non-owner spouse may release his or her right of possession to the matrimonial home.

REVIEW QUESTIONS

1. How can spouses opt out of the *Family Law Act*?
2. List three provisions which may not be included in a marriage contract.
3. What is a cohabitation agreement?
4. What types of provisions may be included in a cohabitation agreement?
5. List three of the provisions which may be included in a separation agreement?
6. Explain why a right of possession is a law which permits people to have illegal drugs in their possession.

THIS IS A MARRIAGE CONTRACT made on December , 20--.

BETWEEN:

RHETT BUTLER, of the City of Toronto, in the Province of Ontario
(hereinafter referred to as "Rhett")

and

SCARLET O'HARA, of the Town of Tara, in the Province of Ontario
(hereinafter referred to as "Scarlet")

WHEREAS Rhett and Scarlet intend to marry on March 25, (year);

AND WHEREAS Rhett is a medical doctor and Scarlet is a lawyer, and they intend to pursue their separate careers after marriage on a full-time basis, both before and after they have children;

AND WHEREAS Rhett and Scarlet wish to enter into this Agreement to govern their respective property interests and their rights and obligations to each other during their marriage and upon termination of their marriage or upon death or otherwise.

NOW THEREFORE in consideration of mutual love and affection and in consideration of the premises and mutual covenants herein, and their intended marriage, the parties hereto agree as follows:

DEFINITIONS

1. In this Agreement, unless the context otherwise requires:

(a) "Act" means the *Family Law Act*, RSO 1990, or any successor legislation thereto;

(b) "Property" shall have the meaning set out in Part I of the Act.

SEPARATION OF PROPERTY

2. All Property owned by Rhett or by Scarlet, whether acquired before or after the date of this Agreement, shall be and remain the separate and exclusive Property of the owner. Scarlet will not make any claim to any Property which is Rhett's, and Rhett will not make any claim to any Property which is Scarlet's. Without limiting the generality of the foregoing, no Property of either party shall be included in determining "net family property" within the meaning of the Act; and neither party will make any claim against the other or the estate of the other pursuant to section 5 of the Act; and neither party will claim any interest in or right to the Property of the other pursuant to any principle of trust law or other law.

NO WAIVER OF PART II RIGHTS

3. Nothing in this Agreement shall limit either party's rights under Part II of the Act.

-2-

FINANCIAL DISCLOSURE

4. Rhett and Scarlet each warrant that full disclosure has been made by each to the other of his or her financial means and circumstances.

SUPPORT

5. Rhett and Scarlet each acknowledge that each of them is able to provide adequately for his or her own support. Neither shall be obliged to support the other, either during their marriage, upon their separation, or upon the annulment or the dissolution of their marriage. Scarlet agrees that she will not make any claim against Rhett for support, and Rhett agrees that he will make no claim against Scarlet for support.

RELEASE OF RIGHTS IN EACH OTHER'S ESTATE

6. Rhett and Scarlet release each other from all claims and rights that he or she may have in the estate of the other upon the other dying intestate, or to act as an estate trustee of the other's will or estate, whether by way of statutory allowance or right under laws of any jurisdiction in force from time to time in the Province of Ontario.

EXECUTION OF OTHER DOCUMENTS

7. Rhett and Scarlet shall, at any time and from time to time, execute and deliver to the other any document or documents that the other reasonably requires to give effect to the terms of this agreement.

INDEPENDENT LEGAL ADVICE

8. Each of the parties acknowledges that he or she

      (a) has received independent legal advice;

      (b) understands his or her rights and obligations under this Agreement;

      (c) has made full and complete disclosure to the other of significant assets, debts, and liabilities as set out in Schedule A attached hereto;

      (d) is signing this Agreement voluntarily.

      IN WITNESS WHEREOF each of the parties has signed this Agreement under seal before a witness.

SIGNED, SEALED AND DELIVERED
   in the presence of

_____	_____
Witness as to the signature of Rhett Butler	Rhett Butler
_____	_____
Witness as to the signature of Scarlet O'Hara	Scarlet O'Hara

(Prepare backsheet; prepare certificate of independent legal advice.)

SCHEDULE "A"

RHETT'S Statement of Income, Assets and Liabilities.

INCOME:	$80,000.00
ASSETS:	
Mercedes Benz automobile	$ 30,000.00
Current bank account	2,500.00
Trusty guaranteed investment certificates	50,000.00
Personal and household effects	15,000.00
Interest in Rhett Butler M.D. practice	90,000.00
Total Assets	$267,500.00
LIABILITIES:	
Loan from mother, Elizabeth Butler	
non-interest bearing, due on demand	$100,000.00
Total Liabilities	$100,000.00
NET WORTH:	$167,500.00

SCHEDULE "B"

SCARLET'S Statement of Income, Assets and Liabilities.

INCOME:	$ 75,000.00
ASSETS:	
Residence at 9 Gable Street, Tara, Ontario	$190,000.00
Current bank account	1,000.00
Jewellery, personal, and household effects	27,000.00
Total Assets	$293,000.00
LIABILITIES:	
Charge on 9 Gable Street, Tara, Ontario	$150,000.00
(due March 25, (year), at interest of 11% per year)	
Total Liabilities	$150,000.00
NET WORTH:	$143,000.00

THIS IS A COHABITATION AGREEMENT DATED   February   , (year).

BETWEEN:

HERBERT DONALD THATCHER

and   (HERBERT)

ANNE GREENGABLES

(ANNE)

1.   Background

1.1   Herbert and Anne are cohabiting and have cohabited since in or about the month of January, (year).

1.2   They have not married but contemplate the possibility of marriage at some time in the future. If they do marry, they will negotiate a new agreement to settle their rights and obligations under the marriage.

1.3   Neither of them has any children.

1.4   They have agreed to purchase a house and lot to use as their Common Residence.

1.5   Anne owns the household furniture and furnishings which will be used in the Common Residence.

1.6   Herbert and Anne each desire by this Agreement to settle their rights and obligations with respect to support and Property, as these rights and obligations may apply during their cohabitation, upon separation, and upon death.

2.   Definitions

2.1   In this Agreement:

   (a)   "Herbert" means Herbert Donald Thatcher;

   (b)   "Anne" means Anne Greengables;

   (c)   "Property" means real or personal property or any interest in such property;

   (d)   "Common Residence" and "Residence" mean the house and lot at 49 Avonlea Avenue, Toronto, Ontario.

3.   Agreement

3.1   Herbert and Anne each agree to be bound by the terms of this Agreement.

4.   Effective Date of Agreement

4.1   This Agreement takes effect on the day it is executed.

5.   Purchase of Common Residence

5.1   Herbert and Anne have agreed to purchase a house and lot to use as their Common Residence with the purchase being made on the terms set out in the agreement of purchase and sale according to the copy attached as a schedule to this Agreement. The purchase will be financed by Herbert and Anne assuming the existing first and second charges and paying the balance for the deposit and the amount due on closing totalling One Hundred Fifty-Three Thousand Eight Hundred Dollars ($153,800.00) out of the separate Property of Herbert and the separate Property of Anne. Herbert will contribute from his separate Property the amount of Fifty-Three

-2-

Thousand Eight Hundred Dollars ($53,800.00), and Anne will contribute from her separate Property the amount of One Hundred Thousand Dollars ($100,000.00).

5.2   The Common Residence may be sold at any time at the request of either of the parties and will be sold if the parties separate or one of them dies.

5.3   Out of the proceeds of the sale after discharging the charges or other encumbrances, if any, and the costs of sale, Herbert will have returned to him the Fifty-Three Thousand Eight Hundred Dollars ($53,800.00) contributed to the purchase before and on closing, without interest, and Anne will have returned to her the One Hundred Thousand Dollars ($100,000.00) contributed to the purchase before and on closing, without interest, subject only to the sale resulting in a deficit, in which case, the deficit will be borne by Herbert and Anne in equal shares. If there is no deficit, the balance of the proceeds, if any, will be divided equally between Herbert and Anne.

6.   Expenses Related to Common Residence

6.1   Herbert and Anne will share equally in the payment of all expenses related to their Common Residence, including all expenses for upkeep and repair, and all payments due under or for any charge, insurance, and taxes with respect to the residence.

7.   Ownership of Property Other Than Common Residence

7.1   Where Property is registered or recorded in the name of a party, whether for public purposes, as in the case of real property, or private purposes, as in the case of a bank account, the ownership of that Property will be determined according to the registered or recorded ownership.

8.   Contents of Home

8.1   If a separation of the parties should occur, the contents of the family residence or any successor residence will be distributed between the parties by each of Herbert and Anne retaining his or her own furnishings and any personal items or clothing, and any items owned by either of them as of the date that they commenced cohabiting, and thereafter by an equal division of the value of the remaining contents, or by the equal division of the contents, as the parties may agree.

9.   Excluded Property

9.1   Herbert and Anne agree that for the purposes of this Agreement, all excluded property shall mean:

    (a)   all assets and contingent assets owned by either of them as of the date that the parties commence cohabitation;

    (b)   all those assets specifically set out elsewhere in this Agreement;

    (c)   all property inherited by either of them after the parties commence cohabitation; and

    (d)   all chattels, personal or real property, causes of action or accounts receivable as set out in Schedules A and B attached to this Agreement.

-3-

10.   Release of Support

10.1   Each party releases the other from all claims and obligations for support during their cohabitation and upon separation arising under the *Family Law Act* or its successor.

11.   Financial Provision

11.1   Should any children be born to Herbert and Anne, the responsibility for making financial provision for the family during cohabitation will be assumed jointly by the parties in proportion to their respective financial abilities as may be agreed upon from time to time.

12.   Independent Legal Advice

12.1   Each of the parties acknowledges that he or she has had independent legal advice or the opportunity to obtain independent legal advice, understands his or her respective rights and obligations under this Agreement, and is signing this Agreement voluntarily.

13.   Effective Date

13.1   The effective date of this Agreement is the date on which the latter party signs it.

TO EVIDENCE THEIR AGREEMENT HERBERT AND ANNE HAVE SIGNED THIS AGREEMENT BEFORE A WITNESS.

DATE:

_____   _____
Witness   Herbert Donald Thatcher

DATE:

_____   _____
Witness   Anne Greengables

   (Prepare backsheet)   *(Prepare list of assets and liabilities; prepare certificate of independent legal advice.)*

THIS IS A SEPARATION AGREEMENT DATED   (date)

Between

SHIRLEY TEMPLE

(SHIRLEY)

AND

ROBERT MICHAEL TEMPLE

(ROBERT)

1.   Background

1.1   SHIRLEY and ROBERT were married on September 17, 20--.

1.2   They separated on August 19, 20-- . The parties will continue living separate and apart.

1.3   They have one child, Bonnie Amelia Temple, born November 8, 20-- ("Bonnie").

1.4   This Agreement replaces all oral or written agreements made between the parties.

2.   Definitions

2.1   In this Agreement:

(a)   "child" means Bonnie,

(b)   "cohabit" means to live with another person in a relationship resembling marriage,

(c)   "company" means [name of company],

(d)   "cottage" means the property at [address] in [place],

(e)   "equalization payment" means the payment referred to in s. 5(1) of the *Family Law Act*,

(f)   "CRA" means Canada Revenue Agency,

(g)   "FRO" means the Family Responsibility Office described in the *Family Responsibility and Support Arrears Enforcement Act*, or any successor support enforcement agency,

DIVORCEmate Software Inc. www.divorcemate.com 2009.06

(h)   "Guidelines" means the Child Support Guidelines, as defined in s. 2(1) of the *Divorce Act*,

(i)   "indexing factor" means the percentage change for a given month in the Consumer Price Index for Toronto for prices of All-Items (as published by Statistics Canada) from the same month of the previous year,

(j)   "matrimonial home" means the property at 1939 Goodship Drive in Toronto,

(k)   "net family property" means net family property as defined in the *Family Law Act*, and

(l)   "property" means property as defined in the *Family Law Act*.

3.   Freedom From The Other

3.1   SHIRLEY and ROBERT will not harass or speak ill of each other.

4.   Parenting

4.1   SHIRLEY will have custody of Bonnie.

5.   Child Support

5.1   The parties each support Bonnie without contribution from the other. Any application of the Guidelines would result in an amount of child support that is inappropriate. The parties' present child support arrangements are reasonable and meet the objectives of the Guidelines.

6.   Releases

6.1   This Agreement is a full and final settlement of all issues between SHIRLEY and ROBERT and all rights and obligations arising out of their relationship.

6.2   Except as otherwise provided in this Agreement, SHIRLEY and ROBERT release each other from all claims at common law, in equity or by statute against each other, including claims under the *Divorce Act*, the *Family Law Act*, and the *Succession Law Reform Act*.

7.   General Terms

7.1

(a)   SHIRLEY and ROBERT have both had independent legal advice, SHIRLEY from Robert B. Redford and ROBERT from Raymond G. Castles.

(b)   SHIRLEY and ROBERT:

   (i)   understand his or her rights and obligations under this Agreement and its nature and consequences,

   (ii)   acknowledge that this Agreement is fair and reasonable,

   (iii)   acknowledge that they are not under any undue influence or duress, and

   (iv)   acknowledge that both are signing this Agreement voluntarily.

TO EVIDENCE THEIR AGREEMENT SHIRLEY AND ROBERT HAVE SIGNED THIS AGREEMENT BEFORE A WITNESS.

DATE:

_____   _____

Witness   SHIRLEY TEMPLE

DATE:

_____   _____

Witness   ROBERT MICHAEL TEMPLE

CERTIFICATE OF INDEPENDENT LEGAL ADVICE

I, Robert B. Redford, of the City of Toronto, in the Province of Ontario, lawyer, certify that I was consulted by SHIRLEY TEMPLE, one of the parties to the attached Separation Agreement, with respect to her rights and obligations under this Agreement.

I acted only for SHIRLEY TEMPLE and fully explained to her the nature and effect of the Agreement. SHIRLEY TEMPLE acknowledged that she completely understood the nature and effect of the Agreement. SHIRLEY TEMPLE executed the Agreement in front of me and confirmed that she was entering into the Agreement of her own volition without any fear, threats, compulsion or influence by ROBERT MICHAEL TEMPLE or any other person.

Dated at Toronto this   [date]:

_____
Robert B. Redford

CERTIFICATE OF INDEPENDENT LEGAL ADVICE

I, Raymond G. Castles, of the City of Markham, in the Regional Municipality of York, lawyer, certify that I was consulted by ROBERT MICHAEL TEMPLE, one of the parties to the attached Separation Agreement, with respect to his rights and obligations under this Agreement.

I acted only for ROBERT MICHAEL TEMPLE and fully explained to him the nature and effect of the Agreement. ROBERT MICHAEL TEMPLE acknowledged that he completely understood the nature and effect of the Agreement. ROBERT MICHAEL TEMPLE executed the Agreement in front of me and confirmed that he was entering into the Agreement of his own volition without any fear, threats, compulsion or influence by SHIRLEY TEMPLE or any other person.

Dated at Markham this   [date]:

_____
Raymond G. Castles

DATED:

Between:

SHIRLEY TEMPLE

and

ROBERT MICHAEL TEMPLE

SEPARATION AGREEMENT

Robert B. Redford
Michael, Eliad & Redford LLP
863 Seneca Lane
Toronto, ON M4J 1P6
Tel: (416) 363-1079
Fax: (416) 363-2628
rbrdfrd@mer.com

CHAPTER 20

INTRODUCTION TO FAMILY LAW

The road to family equity is paved with inequity. This chapter covers the major influences on family law reform, including an introduction to the *Family Law Act* and the *Children's Law Reform Act* where today we find most of Ontario's family law.

MAJOR INFLUENCES ON FAMILY LAW REFORM

One case that is considered to have largely contributed to family law reform is the 1973 divorce case of Irene Murdoch, a Saskatchewan ranch wife whose marriage broke down after twenty-five years, and who claimed part ownership in the ranch that her husband owned. The Murdochs ranched together, and Mrs. Murdoch did all of the work on the ranch that her husband did. Mr. Murdoch never paid Mrs. Murdoch wages for her work contribution, and the *Income Tax Act* did not then recognize interspousal work as work that should be salaried. Mr. Murdoch did not dispute Mrs. Murdoch's testimony about the work she had put into the ranch over their twenty-five years of marriage. The divorce court, however, awarded her maintenance (support) only, and denied her claim to part ownership in the ranch, mainly because the ranch was registered on title in Mr. Murdoch's name only.

The case went to the Supreme Court of Canada, and that court also concluded that Mrs. Murdoch had no legal claim to the ranch. Under the laws of the day, Mrs. Murdoch could make no legal claim to the ranch unless she could prove that Mr. Murdoch was holding part of the land in trust for her; Mr. Murdoch, on the other hand, among other things, could only hold such land in trust for Mrs. Murdoch if Mrs. Murdoch had made some financial contribution to Mr. Murdoch for the purchase of the land.

Had Mrs. Murdoch contributed money toward the purchase of the farm, the court would have given her part ownership on the basis of the then legal remedy known as **constructive trust.** Basically, constructive trust meant that when a non-owner spouse made a financial contribution toward property that the other spouse owned, the non-owner spouse could rely on the doctrine of **trust** to be considered part owner of the property. Mr. Justice Bora Laskin, the only dissenter in the Murdoch decision, thought Mrs. Murdoch should have been entitled to the constructive trust remedy because of her contribution of physical labour as mother and farm wife over the twenty-five years of the marriage.

In 1980, the Supreme Court of Canada, this time in majority with Mr. Justice Bora Laskin, applied the constructive trust remedy in the Ontario case of *Pettkus v Becker*. Rosa Becker and Lothar Pettkus lived together for 19 years in common law. Ms. Becker paid all the bills for rent, food, clothing, and other living expenses from her salary, and Mr. Pettkus saved his salary and bought, in his name alone, a bee-keeping farm which they both operated.

Ms. Becker moved out permanently, claiming Mr. Pettkus was mistreating her. She claimed one-half the value of the $300,000 bee-keeping operation and other businesses Mr. Pettkus bought while the couple lived together. Instead, the judge awarded Ms. Becker forty beehives, without the bees, and $1,500 in cash. The judge determined that Ms. Becker's financial and labour contributions to the business were an investment in the "hope of seducing a young man into marriage." (She was 29 when they met; he, 24). Ms. Becker appealed to the Ontario Court of Appeal and won $150,000, half of the value of the businesses. Mr. Pettkus appealed to the Supreme Court of Canada, and that court upheld Ms. Becker's award of $150,000. Six years after her Supreme Court of Canada victory, however, Ms. Becker committed suicide in protest of the legal system because she never received a penny of her $150,000 award. The court had ordered two pieces of land sold in 1984 to enable her to collect on the judgment; however, Ms. Becker's lawyer, Mr. Gerald E. Langlois, took the entire amount of $68,000 from the sale of the land for his legal fees.

 In another landmark decision, the 1986 case of *Sorochan v Sorochan*, the Supreme Court of Canada again applied the constructive trust remedy, this time with property Mr. Sorochan owned **before** Mrs. Sorochan moved in with him. Mr. and Mrs. Sorochan lived together for forty-two years on a farm and had six children, but never married. The court awarded Mrs. Mary Sorochan one-third of her husband's farm property, ruling that Mrs. Sorochan's forty-two years of domestic labour, farm chores, and caring for the children contributed toward the preserving and maintaining of the property, thus preventing its loss or deterioration.

HISTORICAL BACKGROUND OF FAMILY LAW

Much of the inequity in Irene Murdoch's divorce decision was the result of a combination of inadequate provincial laws and other inherited doctrines. For example, in the past, interspousal rights in family property were determined on the doctrine of **unity of legal personality**. This was much a doctrine of "What's mine is mine and what's yours is also mine." The husband and wife were treated as one legal entity upon marriage, with the husband becoming the absolute owner of all personal and real property the wife owned before marriage. The wife lost all autonomy and could not legally hold or manage property.

Next, family law saw a completely opposite doctrine, that of **separate property**. This was a law of "What's mine is mine, what's yours is yours, and what's ours is also mine, unless you prove financial contribution." Each spouse owned the property each brought into the marriage or bought with his or her own money during the marriage. Both owned the property they bought together during marriage, but only according to how much money each contributed toward the purchase. As a result, the courts regularly found the homemaker to have contributed none or the spouse with the lower salary to have contributed less. This was the law under which Irene Murdoch sought justice and lost. Her case did, however, pave the way to family law changes. In Ontario, it gave way to the *Family Law Act*, 1986.

ONTARIO FAMILY LAW ACT

Ontario's *Family Law Act* (FLA) aims to bring equality between the spouses in person and in property. The FLA recognizes marriage as an equal partnership in that it gives a 50/50 split of the property the spouses acquire during marriage, no matter which spouse owns it. Note, however, that this law of a 50/50 split does not extend to common-law spouses; it applies only to spouses who are legally married. A common-law spouse seeking a share of the property accumulated between the spouses while living together has to make a claim on the doctrine of **constructive trust,** typically, the Becker and Sorochan remedy, above.

Note, however, that in February 2011, two unanimous Supreme Court of Canada rulings applied remedies to common-law spouses that are similar to those covering married couples in provincial law. One of the rulings involved the Vancouver case of common-law spouses Margaret Patricia Kerr and Nelson Dennis Baranow where a lower court awarded Kerr a share of the house they shared which was in Baranow's name. Although that decision was overturned on appeal, the Supreme Court of Canada ordered a new trial in the case. The other ruling involved the Ottawa case of common-law spouses Michele Vanasse and David Sequin. The Supreme Court of Canada restored a lower court ruling, which had been overturned on appeal, that gave Vanasse half the value of the wealth Sequin accumulated during the 3 1/2 year period when she was home looking after the children, enabling him to travel and devote more time to the company which Sequin had developed. Thus, as long as the property claimant can show a contribution to the asset or the growth of the assets, he or she will be entitled to share by way of a monetary award.

Division of family property   The FLA basically says: "During marriage, what's mine is mine, and what's yours is yours. On separation, however, your property and my property become our property to share equally, except for what we each brought into the marriage." In effect, it is the growth in property value during the marriage that the spouses share equally, and that property value is known as **net family property**.

Valuation date   Net family property is calculated as of the **valuation date**, that being the date of separation, the date of divorce, or the date of annulment, whichever is the earliest.

Limitation periods   To begin proceedings for division of property, spouses have up to two years after the final divorce order or up to six years after the date the parties separate.

NET FAMILY PROPERTY

Subsection 4(1) of the *Family Law Act* defines net family property as the value of all the property, except property described in subsection (2) [excluded property], that a spouse owns on the valuation date, after deducting,

> (a) the spouse's debts and other liabilities, and

> (b) the value of property, other than a matrimonial home, that the spouse owned on the date of the marriage, after deducting the spouse's debts and other liabilities, other than debts or liabilities related directly to the acquisition or significant improvement of a matrimonial home, calculated as of the date of the marriage.

> ...The liabilities referred to in clauses (a) and (b) of the definition of "net family property" in subsection (1) include any applicable contingent tax liabilities in respect of the property.

What is included in net family property   Included in the net family property is any property that the *Family Law Act* defines as "property." Under Part I of the *Family Law Act*, "property" means any interest, present or future, vested or contingent in real or personal property and includes,

(a) property over which a spouse has, alone or in conjunction with another person, a power of appointment exercisable in favour of himself or herself,

(b) property disposed of by a spouse but over which the spouse has, alone or in conjunction with another person, a power to revoke the disposition or a power to consume or dispose of the property, and

(c) in the case of a spouse's rights under a pension plan, the imputed value, for family law purposes, of the spouse's interest in the plan, as determined in accordance with section 10.1, for the period beginning with the date of the marriage and ending on the valuation date.

Matrimonial home   The matrimonial home is any property the spouses live in and use for their family enjoyment; hence, there can be more than one matrimonial home, e.g. the house in Hamilton for the fall, the condominium in Florida for the winter, and the cottage in Muskoka for the summer. The FLA gives special status to the matrimonial home in that the non-owner spouse has as much right to **live** in the matrimonial home as does the owner spouse. The owner spouse is the one in whose name the matrimonial home is registered on title. The non-owner's right to live in the matrimonial home is referred to as a **right of possession** (not ownership). The law protects the non-owner's right of possession in that the owner spouse cannot sell or charge/mortgage the matrimonial home without the non-owner's signature.

Matrimonial home is included   Under Part II of the *Family Law Act*, the matrimonial home must be included in the net family property, no matter when or how acquired (even if by gift or inheritance or if brought into the marriage). The only way to exclude the matrimonial home from the net family property is by a domestic contract. The court may, nevertheless, make an order giving exclusive possession of the matrimonial home to one spouse, regardless of which spouse owns it, particularly where the court deems this to be in the best interest of any children.

No pre-marriage deductions for matrimonial home   The spouse who brought the matrimonial home into the marriage cannot deduct the pre-marriage value from the net family property, nor can any date-of-marriage deductions be made for debts or liabilities related to the acquisition or significant improvement of the matrimonial home.

Jointly owned property   Jointly owned property is owned equally by the spouses because it is registered in both their names on title. Include in the net family property of each spouse one-half the value after deducting one-half the debt. Do this also for the matrimonial home if it is jointly owned. If the value of any jointly owned property increases or decreases from the valuation date to the date of the court decision, settlement, or sale, each joint owner is entitled to one-half the increase or decrease. The value and debts of jointly owned property, therefore, are established as of the date of final resolution, regardless of the net value on the valuation date. Contrast this with the value of individually owned property which value remains as established on the valuation date, regardless of any subsequent increase or decrease, unless the court rules otherwise.

Legal Office Procedures

What is excluded from net family property   Under subsection 4(2) of Part I of the *Family Law Act*, the following property is excluded from the calculation of net family property:

1. Property, other than a matrimonial home, that was acquired by gift or inheritance from a third person after the date of the marriage.
2. Income from property referred to in paragraph 1, if the donor or testator has expressly stated that it is to be excluded from the spouse's net family property.
3. Damages or a right to damages for personal injuries, nervous shock, mental distress or loss of guidance, care and companionship, or the part of a settlement that represents those damages.
4. Proceeds or a right to proceeds of a policy of life insurance, as defined under the *Insurance Act*, that are payable on the death of the life insured.
5. Property, other than a matrimonial home, into which property referred to in paragraphs 1 to 4 can be traced.

   Example: Mary inherited $5,000 after marriage and used the money to buy a painting that was worth $10,000 on the date of separation. Mary can exclude the entire $10,000 from her net family property. However, if Mary were to use the $5,000 to pay down the mortgage on the family home or to renovate it, Mary will have lost her right to exclude the $5,000 from her net family property. Once money is put into the family home, it must be shared, even if the money came from a gift or an inheritance or other property that the law says does not have to be shared with the other spouse.

6. Property that the spouses have agreed by a domestic contract is not to be included in the spouse's net family property.
7. Unadjusted pensionable earnings under the Canada Pension Plan.

EQUALIZATION OF NET FAMILY PROPERTY

Subsection 5(1) of the *Family Law Act* provides that when a divorce is granted, the spouse whose net family property is the lesser of the two net family properties is entitled to one-half the difference between them. For example, if the husband's net family property is $60,000 and the wife's net family property is $40,000, the difference in net family property is $20,000. The **equalization of net family property** is accomplished by the husband paying the wife $10,000, i.e. one-half the difference of the net family property of $20,000.

CALCULATING NET FAMILY PROPERTY (NFP)

Following is a handy formula for calculating the net family property. Note that in arriving at the NFP, excluded property is included and then subtracted so as to cancel it out. This inclusion/exclusion process is done basically for purposes of disclosure as a party's failure to disclose property could result in the courts dismissing the party's case.

Figure 20.1

CALCULATION FORMULA FOR NET FAMILY PROPERTY	JACK	JILL
1. Add up value of all property at date of separation (including excluded property and matrimonial home)	600,000	580,000
2. Add up and subtract value of all debts at date of separation	(21,000)	(20,000)
3. Add up and subtract value of total excluded property at date of separation	(0)	(100,000)
4. Net worth at date of separation	579,000	460,000
5. Add up value of all assets (other than matrimonial home) at date of marriage	2,000	240,000
6. Add up and subtract value of all debts at date of marriage	(1,000)	(2,000)
7. Net worth at date of marriage	1,000	238,000
8. Subtract step 7 from step 4 = NFP	578,000	222,000
9. Subtract lower NFP from higher NFP: 578,000 minus 222,000 = 356,000		
10. Equalization payment is one half the NFP difference: 356,000 ÷ 2 = 178,000		

Figure 20.2

NET FAMILY PROPERTY (NFP)	
NFP - Jack	$578,000
NFP - Jill	-$222,000
NFP Difference	$356,000
NFP Difference ÷ 2 = equalization payment	$178,000
EQUALIZATION PAYMENT	
Jack pays Jill $178,000	

Applying the NFP calculation formula   The formula for calculating the net family property of Jack and Jill in Figure 20.1 reflects the following assets and liabilities of Jack and Jill. To help you understand how the amounts in Figure 20.1 were arrived at, see also Figure 20.3, which shows the detailed calculation of the net family property of Jack and Jill on the basis of the following assets and liabilities:

JACK'S ASSETS AND LIABILITIES
(Married on December 13; separated on February 14 (5 years later))

Assets at date of marriage:
House valued at $100,000 - used as the couple's matrimonial home after marriage; Term deposit $2,000.

Debts at date of marriage: Student loan $1,000

Assets at date of separation:
House which Jack owned before marriage and became the matrimonial home after marriage valued at $490,000. Term deposit $10,000.
Cottage bought during marriage as joint tenants valued at $200,000.

Debts at date of separation:
Charge/Mortgage owing on jointly owned cottage in total of $40,000; Credit card $1,000.

JILL'S ASSETS AND LIABILITIES
(Married on December 13; separated on February 14 (5 years later)

Assets at date of marriage:
House valued at $200,000, sold it before marriage as the couple decided to live in Jack's house. Jill invested the money in savings bonds. XYZ shares inherited from grandmother $40,000.

Debts at date of marriage:
Credit card $2,000.

Assets at date of separation:
Car valued at $20,000. Savings bonds purchased using the $200,000 from selling her house before marriage, now worth $300,000. ABC shares inherited from grandfather worth $100,000. XYZ shares inherited from grandmother before marriage now worth $60,000. Cottage jointly owned with Jack worth $200,000.

Debts at date of separation:
Charge/Mortgage on jointly owned cottage total of $40,000

Debts Subsection 4(5) of the *Family Law Act* provides that if a spouse's net family property is less than zero, then it is deemed to be equal to zero. This provision might often result in an unequal split of the family property. Here are examples in point.

1.

	Husband	Wife
Assets	$11,000	$ 4,000
Debts	19,000	24,000
Net Family Property	0	0
Equalization payment	0	0

Example 1 - both spouses separate with a significant debt. In this example, the husband has a negative net family property of -$8,000 ($19,000 minus $11,000), and the wife has a negative net family property of -$20,000 ($24,000 minus $4,000). NFP is zero. This situation results in each person being individually liable for the debts held in his or her name alone.

2.

	Husband	Wife
Assets	$ 10,000	$230,000
Debts	180,000	0
Net Family Property	0	$230,000

Equalization payment: wife pays to husband $115,000

Example 2 - one spouse holds assets - other spouse holds debts. In this example, the husband has a negative net family property of -$170,000 ($180,000 minus $10,000), which is deemed to be zero. In effect, after accounting for the husband's negative net

Figure 20.3

APPLYING THE NFP CALCULATION FORMULA		
ASSETS AT SEPARATION	**JACK**	**JILL**
House [1]	$490,000	$0.00
Term deposit	10,000	0.00
Cottage (held jointly) 1/2	100,000	100,000
Car	0.00	20,000
Savings bonds	0.00	300,000
XYZ shares from grandmother		60,000
ABC shares from grandfather		100,000
TOTAL ASSETS	600,000	580,000
(LESS) DEBTS		
Charge/Mortgage on cottage held jointly 1/2	(20,000)	(20,000)
Credit card	(1,000)	0.00
(LESS) EXCLUDED PROPERTY		
ABC shares from grandfather [2]	0.00	(100,000)
ASSETS LESS DEBTS AT SEPARATION	579,000	460,000
ASSETS AT MARRIAGE		
Term deposit	2,000	0.00
House (sold)		200,000
XYZ shares from grandmother [3]		40,000
(LESS) DEBTS AT MARRIAGE		
Student loan	(1,000)	0.00
Credit card	0.00	(2,000)
ASSETS LESS DEBTS AT MARRIAGE	1,000	238,000
NET FAMILY PROPERTY	578,000	222,000

Notes:

[1] House Jack owned at date of marriage - there is no deduction of any pre-marriage value of the house because the house became the couple's matrimonial home. The matrimonial home is always included in the net family property, regardless of when purchased or by which spouse owned. (In effect, if the house were the only family asset at the date of separation, Jill could walk away with $245,000 – half of the value of $490,000 as at the date of separation.)

[2] Shares inherited from grandfather are excluded property - inherited **after** marriage.

[3] Shares inherited from grandmother do not qualify as excluded property because Jill got them **before** marriage. Their value at date of marriage ($40,000) is deducted from the value at date of separation ($60,000), and the increase during marriage ($20,000) is subject to sharing.

family property of -$170,000, the husband would leave the marriage with a debt of only $55,000. The wife, on the other hand, would end up with assets of only $115,000.

How is the equalization payment made   Generally, one spouse pays off the other either in cash or by transferring property over to the name of the other spouse. Physical division of some property, e.g. a house, is impractical. This is why the net family property is calculated on the basis of **value,** or worth, rather than on who gets which piece of property. In cases of extensive real estate property, businesses, etc., expert valuators, e.g. real estate appraisers or chartered business valuators, are hired to do the valuations. In simpler cases, however, the cost of expert valuators may outweigh the worth of the property, and the client and the lawyer may simply estimate the value.

The court may see it differently   Subsection 5(6) provides for a variation of share. Although the formula for a 50/50 split is to be followed, the court retains the discretion to deem such a split unfair in circumstances such as the following:

1. Where a spouse fails to disclose debts or other liabilities existing as of the date of marriage (this would inflate the spouse's pre-marriage property value).
2. Where the equalization payment is disproportionately large in relation to a marriage that is of less than a five-year duration.
3. Where a spouse intentionally depletes his or her net family property.

ONTARIO CHILDREN'S LAW REFORM ACT

The *Children's Law Reform Act* (CLRA) gives all children an equal legal status, whether born in or out of marriage. The act gives all children the right to financial support from their parents, whether or not the parents are married, and provides for custody and access.

Presumption of paternity   To ensure fathers do not evade their support responsibilities, subsection 8(1) of the CLRA makes the following presumptions of paternity. The man is deemed to be the father if:

1. he was married to the mother of the child when the child was born.
2. he was married to the mother of the child within 300 days before the child was born.
3. he was married to the mother of the child after the child was born and has acknowledged he is the father.
4. he was living with the mother in a common-law relationship of some permanence when the child was born or the child was born within 300 days after they ceased living together.
5. he and the mother have agreed, under the *Vital Statistics Act*, to have the man registered as the father.
6. he has been found in previous court proceedings to be the father.

Paternity tests   Section 10 of the CLRA provides a mechanism for establishing paternity. One situation where establishing paternity might be necessary is where a former girlfriend is suing a former boyfriend for child support for a child he had no idea he had fathered. A paternity test would reveal if the former boyfriend is or is not the biological father; if the former boyfriend is not the biological father, he would not be required to pay support.

A father wrongly accused of paternity may prove that he is not the father by submitting to a blood test or a DNA test. Blood testing, however, proves only that a man is not the father and is meaningful only where it is possible to compare the blood samples of the mother, the child, and the alleged father. DNA testing is less intrusive than blood testing as it requires a much smaller blood sample, or it can be done with the use of a small saliva sample from the child and the alleged father, providing a 99.9 percent accuracy, and the mother need not be tested.

In either case, the taking of blood samples or DNA samples requires the consent of the person tested, unless the court orders otherwise. If a person refuses to submit to a court's request for a blood test, however, the court may draw its own conclusions: for example, if a man refuses to provide a blood sample, the court may infer that the man is the father. If a woman refuses to provide a blood sample or refuses to allow the child to undergo blood testing, the court may infer that the woman knows the man is not her child's father.

CHILDREN AND CHILD SUPPORT

Under the *Divorce Act* (federal), parents must support "any child of the marriage" who is under the age of majority or has reached the age of majority but is not independent, e.g. is attending college or is ill. Under the Ontario *Family Law Act* (provincial), a parent must support a child who is under the age of 18 or is over the age of 18 and is in a full-time program of education.

CHILD SUPPORT GUIDELINES

The child support guidelines are tables which set out the amount of child support payable on the basis of a parent's annual income before taxes. The *Federal Child Support Guidelines* contain separate tables for all provinces/territories, including the province of Ontario, and apply to nearly all provinces/territories, usually only in divorce cases because divorce is under federal jurisdiction. For non-divorce cases, e.g. where the parties are not married to each other or are married to each other and have separated but neither of them has applied for divorce, each province/territory follows its own provincially devised child support guidelines. In Ontario, the *Federal Child Support Guidelines* for Ontario, simplified tables, Precedent 20.1, apply regardless of whether the child support orders or agreements are made under federal (*Divorce Act*) or provincial (*Family Law Act*) jurisdiction because Ontario made changes to its *Family Law Act* adopting the federal support guidelines. Generally, if the paying party lives in Ontario, the federal tables for Ontario apply. If the paying party lives elsewhere in Canada, the federal tables for the province in which the paying party lives apply.

Sole custody The simplified tables set out incomes rounded to the nearest $100: for example, if in a sole custody case Jack's annual income before taxes were $35,438, the rounded annual income would be $35,400. You would look for $35,400 in the income column of the simplified tables and at the number of children column, e.g. two, to determine the monthly amount of child support payable, which in this case would be $514. Jack would pay Jill (assuming that Jill had sole custody of the two children) $514 child support per month.

The *Federal Child Support Guidelines* also provide an official version of tables which set out incomes in $1000 increments and provide a percentage for calculating child support amounts between income increments. Here is an excerpt from the official version tables showing support payable for two children:

Figure 20.4

From	To	Basic amount	Plus %	of income over
35000	35999	508	1.38	35000
36000	36999	522	1.22	36000
37000	37999	534	1.20	37000

Under the official version tables, Jack's income of $35,438 would be rounded to the nearest $1000 which would be $35,000. Look for $35,000 in the income column of the official version tables, on the page for two children. The basic child support amount is $508 and the percentage on the $438 (of the $35,438) is 1.38. Multiply $438 x 1.38% ÷100 = $6.04. Jack would pay Jill (assuming that Jill had sole custody of the two children) $514.04 ($508 + $6.04) child support per month.

> The formula: 508 + [1.38% x 438 ÷ 100] ($30,438 minus $30,000)
> 508 + [1.38/100 x 438]
> 508 + [0.0138 x 438]
> 508 + $6.04 = $514.04

Both federal and provincial support guidelines run to a maximum annual gross income of $150,000. The following table applies in both federal and provincial support guidelines for incomes over $150,000:

Figure 20.5

Income/ Revenu ($)	Monthly Award /Paiement mensuel			
	One Child/ Un enfant	**Two Children/ Deux enfants**	**Three Children/ Trois enfants**	**Four Children/ Quatre enfants**
For Income over $150,000	1263 plus 0.74% of income over $150,000	2012 plus 1.14% of income over $150,000	2611 plus 1.44% of income over $150,000	3120 plus 1.78% of income over $150,000
Pour revenu dépassant 150 000$	1263 plus 0.74% du revenu dépassant 150 000$	2012 plus 1.14% du revenu dépassant 150 000$	2611 plus 1.44% du revenu dépassant 150 000$	3120 plus 1.78% du revenu dépassant 150 000$

Split custody   Generally, split custody is where there are two or more children and one or more children live with one parent more than 60 percent of the time over the course of a year, and one or more children live with the other parent more than 60 percent of the time over the course of a year. Under s.8 of the Regulations of the Ontario *Child Support Guidelines*, where each parent or spouse has custody of one or more children, the amount of an order for the support of a child is the difference between the amount that each parent or spouse would otherwise pay if such an order were sought against each of the parents or spouses. Here is a simplified example for determining the amount of child support in split custody cases, using the simplified tables for Ontario:

Chapter 20 *Introduction to Family Law*

Suppose Jack and Jill have a split custody arrangement where two of the children will live with Jill and one child will live with Jack. Typically, calculation in split custody situations is based on figuring out the amount of support Jack would pay Jill for the two children in Jill's care, and the amount of support that Jill would pay Jack for the one child in Jack's care, and subtracting the lesser amount from the higher amount on the basis of total income of, for example, $50,000 for Jack and $40,000 for Jill.

Jack would pay a monthly amount (for two children in Jill's custody)	$743
Jill would pay a monthly amount (for one child in Jack's custody)	-360
Jack would pay monthly support to Jill (the difference)	$383

Shared custody   Under section 9 of the *Federal Child Support Guidelines*, where a parent exercises a right of access to, or has physical custody of, a child for not less than 40 percent of the time over the course of a year, the amount of the order for the support of a child must be determined by taking into account,

(a) the amounts set out in the applicable tables for each of the parents;
(b) the increased costs of shared custody arrangements; and
(c) the condition, means, needs, and other circumstances of each parent and of any child for whom support is sought.

For example, the amount of support in shared custody cases for, say, two children would be determined by looking at the tables to find out the amount each of the parents would pay to the other if the other had sole custody of both children. According to the table, George who earns $40,000 per year would pay $579; Julia who earns $35,000 per year would pay $508; the difference is $71 which George would pay to Julia. Assuming that Julia's increased costs of shared custody were $20 per month more than George's costs, the parents may agree that George would pay $91 ($71 + $20) per month for child support to Julia because he earns more.

Special circumstances   The court has the power to order an amount for special expenses that is in addition to the basic support payments set out in the *Child Support Guidelines*. Special expenses include the cost of child care needed for the parent with custody to work or go to school; health-related expenses for the child, such as orthodontic, prescription drug, therapy, or hearing aid costs; expenses for post-secondary education for the child, as well as circumstances that may cause undue hardship.

Arranging child support online   The Province of Ontario provides an online service for calculating and recalculating child support obligations without going to court. Under amendments made to the *Family Law Act*, parents may use this service if they do not already have a court order or a domestic contract setting out the amount of child support payable. Once both parents agree with the use of the online service, they provide the ministry with the income information required. The ministry then calculates the amount of child support payable based on the *Federal Child Support Guidelines* for Ontario and also provides the parents with a **notice of calculation or recalculation** which includes the amount of support payable and is treated like a court order for purposes of enforcement by the Family Responsibility Office. Generally, this online service is available where one parent lives with the child or children 60 percent of the time, the parents do not currently live together, and both parents and the child or children live in Ontario. At the federal level, Justice Canada offers an online look-up only service where a parent in any province/territory can look up the amount of child support payable by entering the paying parent's annual gross income, the number of children entitled to support, and the province/territory in which the paying parent lives.

FAMILY RESPONSIBILITY OFFICE

The *Family Responsibility and Support Arrears Enforcement Act* requires that nearly all support orders be automatically filed with the government's Family Responsibility Office (FRO) which has authority to collect support payments from the payor (the spouse ordered to pay) and forward the support payments to the recipient spouse either by direct deposit to the bank account of the recipient spouse or by cheque mailed to the recipient spouse. If the payor fails to make the support payment/s, the FRO has the authority to take various measures to enforce payment on behalf of the recipient spouse, including suspend a payor's driver's licence or passport, garnishee a payor's wages or bank account, collect from the payor's income tax refund or employment insurance benefits, if any, and issue a writ of seizure and sale against a payor's property or assets.

For every court order that awards support, the court also, at the same time, makes, signs, and enters a **support deduction order**, Precedent 20.2, and files it, together with a **support deduction order information form**, Precedent 20.3, with the FRO. Generally, the lawyer who wins the support order for the client prepares the support deduction order and the support deduction order information form and submits them to the court for processing. Note that a party who wins may be a payor applicant who, for example, motions for and wins an order for paying a reduced amount of support.

> **Legal TIP**
>
> The support deduction order is the order to the FRO to pursue collection of the support payments. It is an order in addition to the court order which awarded the support to the spouse.

CHAPTER SUMMARY

Family law has seen a lot of changes through the struggles of spouses who have had to turn to the courts for justice. The 1973 Irene Murdoch case helped put family law on the road to family equality reform. In 1986, Ontario introduced the *Ontario Family Law Act* which aims to bring equality between the spouses. It recognizes marriage as an equal partnership in that it gives a 50/50 split of the property the spouses acquire during marriage, regardless of which spouse owns the property. Included in the calculation of the net family property is the matrimonial home, regardless of which spouse brought it into the marriage and without deducting any pre-marriage value or liabilities. The only way to exclude the matrimonial home from the net family property is by a domestic contract.

The *Children's Law Reform Act* gives children the right to financial support from their parents, whether or not the parents are married and also provides for custody and access. The act also provides a mechanism for establishing paternity and parentage. The amount of child support in Ontario is based on the *Federal Child Support Guidelines* which provide tables for Ontario and other provinces/territories.

REVIEW QUESTIONS

1. What may substitute for financial contribution when courts apply the remedy of constructive trust?
2. How does the Ontario *Family Law Act* divide property during marriage and at separation?
3. How can one exclude the matrimonial home from the net family property?
4. What portion of jointly owned property is included in net family property?

5. An equalization payment means splitting the dinner bill in half when dining out with your spouse. Explain.
6. What types of claims may be made under the Ontario *Family Law Act*?
7. What types of claims may be made under the Ontario *Children's Law Reform Act*?
8. What are *Child Support Guidelines*?
9. What are child support payments based on when calculated under the federal and provincial *Child Support Guidelines*?
10. If Jack earned $40,000 per year and Jill earned $50,000 per year, and they had split custody of their three children (two children with Jack; one child with Jill):
    (a) what would be the amount of the child support payments?
    (b) who would pay support to whom?
11. If Jack earned $70,325 per year and was ordered to pay child support for all three of the children who are in the custody of Jill, what would be the total amount of child support payable?
12. Suppose there were only two children, both in the custody of Jack, and Jill was ordered to pay child support on the basis of her salary of $69,100 per year. What would be the amount of the support payments which Jill would make to Jack?

Precedent 20.1 Ontario Child Support Guidelines, page 1

Ontario

Federal Child Support Amounts: Simplified Tables
Montants fédéraux de pensions alimentaires pour enfants: Tables simplifiées

Income/ Revenu ($)	Monthly Award/ Paiement mensuel ($) No. of Children/ N^bre d'enfants				Income/ Revenu ($)	Monthly Award/ Paiement mensuel ($) No. of Children/ N^bre d'enfants				Income/ Revenu ($)	Monthly Award/ Paiement mensuel ($) No. of Children/ N^bre d'enfants				Income/ Revenu ($)	Monthly Award/ Paiement mensuel ($) No. of Children/ N^bre d'enfants			
	1	2	3	4		1	2	3	4		1	2	3	4		1	2	3	4
32400	274	473	637	774	37800	334	544	731	885	43200	390	633	821	988	48600	438	723	931	1100
32500	275	474	639	776	37900	335	545	732	887	43300	391	635	823	990	48700	438	724	933	1102
32600	276	475	641	778	38000	336	546	734	889	43400	392	637	825	992	48800	439	726	934	1104
32700	277	477	643	780	38100	337	548	736	891	43500	393	638	827	993	48900	440	727	936	1106
32800	278	478	645	782	38200	338	549	737	893	43600	394	640	829	995	49000	441	728	938	1108
32900	280	480	647	784	38300	339	551	739	895	43700	395	642	831	997	49100	442	730	940	1110
33000	281	481	649	786	38400	341	553	740	896	43800	395	643	833	999	49200	443	731	942	1113
33100	282	482	651	788	38500	342	554	742	898	43900	396	645	835	1001	49300	444	733	944	1115
33200	283	484	653	790	38600	343	556	743	900	44000	397	647	837	1003	49400	445	734	947	1118
33300	284	485	654	793	38700	344	558	745	902	44100	398	649	839	1005	49500	446	736	949	1120
33400	285	487	656	795	38800	345	559	746	904	44200	399	650	841	1007	49600	447	737	951	1123
33500	287	488	658	797	38900	346	561	748	906	44300	400	652	843	1009	49700	448	739	953	1125
33600	288	489	660	799	39000	348	563	749	907	44400	401	654	845	1011	49800	449	740	955	1128
33700	289	491	662	801	39100	349	565	751	909	44500	402	656	847	1012	49900	449	742	957	1130
33800	290	492	663	803	39200	350	566	752	911	44600	403	657	849	1014	50000	450	743	959	1133
33900	291	494	665	806	39300	352	568	754	913	44700	404	659	852	1016	50100	451	745	961	1135
34000	292	495	667	808	39400	353	570	755	915	44800	404	661	854	1018	50200	452	746	963	1138
34100	293	496	669	810	39500	354	571	757	917	44900	405	662	856	1020	50300	453	748	966	1140
34200	294	498	671	812	39600	355	573	758	918	45000	406	664	858	1022	50400	454	749	968	1143
34300	295	499	672	815	39700	356	575	760	920	45100	407	666	860	1024	50500	455	751	970	1145
34400	296	500	674	817	39800	357	576	761	922	45200	408	667	862	1026	50600	456	752	972	1148
34500	297	502	676	819	39900	359	578	763	924	45300	409	669	864	1028	50700	457	754	974	1150
34600	299	503	678	821	40000	360	579	764	926	45400	410	671	866	1030	50800	458	755	976	1153
34700	300	504	680	823	40100	361	581	766	928	45500	411	672	868	1031	50900	459	757	979	1155
34800	301	506	681	826	40200	362	583	767	930	45600	412	674	870	1033	51000	460	758	981	1158
34900	302	507	683	828	40300	363	584	769	932	45700	413	675	872	1035	51100	461	760	983	1160
35000	303	508	685	830	40400	364	586	771	934	45800	413	677	874	1037	51200	462	761	985	1163
35100	304	509	687	832	40500	365	588	772	936	45900	414	679	876	1039	51300	463	763	988	1165
35200	305	511	689	834	40600	366	590	774	938	46000	415	680	878	1041	51400	464	764	990	1168
35300	306	512	690	836	40700	367	591	776	941	46100	416	682	880	1043	51500	465	766	992	1170
35400	308	514	692	839	40800	368	593	777	943	46200	417	683	882	1046	51600	466	767	994	1173
35500	309	515	694	841	40900	369	595	779	945	46300	418	685	884	1048	51700	466	769	996	1175
35600	310	516	696	843	41000	370	597	781	947	46400	419	687	886	1050	51800	467	770	999	1178
35700	311	518	698	845	41100	371	599	783	949	46500	420	688	888	1052	51900	468	772	1001	1180
35800	312	519	699	847	41200	372	600	784	951	46600	421	690	890	1055	52000	469	773	1003	1183
35900	313	520	701	849	41300	373	602	786	953	46700	422	692	893	1057	52100	470	774	1005	1186
36000	315	522	703	851	41400	374	604	787	955	46800	422	693	895	1059	52200	471	776	1007	1188
36100	316	523	705	853	41500	374	605	789	957	46900	423	695	897	1061	52300	472	777	1009	1191
36200	317	524	706	855	41600	375	607	790	958	47000	424	697	899	1064	52400	473	779	1012	1193
36300	318	526	708	857	41700	376	609	792	960	47100	425	699	901	1066	52500	474	780	1014	1196
36400	319	527	709	859	41800	377	610	793	962	47200	426	701	903	1069	52600	475	782	1016	1198
36500	320	528	711	861	41900	378	612	795	964	47300	427	702	905	1071	52700	476	783	1018	1201
36600	321	529	713	863	42000	379	614	797	966	47400	428	704	908	1074	52800	477	785	1020	1203
36700	322	531	714	865	42100	380	616	799	968	47500	429	706	910	1076	52900	478	786	1022	1206
36800	323	532	716	867	42200	381	617	801	970	47600	430	708	912	1079	53000	479	787	1024	1208
36900	324	533	717	869	42300	382	619	803	972	47700	431	709	914	1081	53100	480	788	1026	1211
37000	325	534	719	871	42400	383	621	805	973	47800	431	711	916	1084	53200	481	790	1028	1213
37100	326	535	720	873	42500	384	622	807	975	47900	432	713	918	1086	53300	482	791	1031	1216
37200	327	536	722	875	42600	384	624	809	977	48000	433	715	920	1088	53400	483	793	1033	1218
37300	328	538	723	876	42700	385	625	811	979	48100	434	716	922	1090	53500	484	794	1035	1221
37400	329	539	725	878	42800	386	627	813	981	48200	435	718	924	1092	53600	484	796	1037	1223
37500	330	540	726	880	42900	387	629	815	983	48300	435	719	925	1094	53700	485	797	1039	1226
37600	331	541	728	882	43000	388	630	817	984	48400	436	720	927	1096	53800	486	799	1041	1228
37700	333	542	729	884	43100	389	632	819	986	48500	437	722	929	1098	53900	487	800	1044	1231

Precedent 20.1 Ontario Child Support Guidelines, page 2

Ontario

Federal Child Support Amounts: Simplified Tables
Montants fédéraux de pensions alimentaires pour enfants: Tables simplifiées

Income/ Revenu ($)	Monthly Award/ Paiement mensuel ($) No. of Children/ N^bre d'enfants				Income/ Revenu ($)	Monthly Award/ Paiement mensuel ($) No. of Children/ N^bre d'enfants				Income/ Revenu ($)	Monthly Award/ Paiement mensuel ($) No. of Children/ N^bre d'enfants				Income/ Revenu ($)	Monthly Award/ Paiement mensuel ($) No. of Children/ N^bre d'enfants			
	1	2	3	4		1	2	3	4		1	2	3	4		1	2	3	4
54000	488	802	1046	1233	59400	540	883	1157	1367	64800	592	963	1261	1502	70200	641	1040	1360	1621
54100	489	803	1048	1236	59500	541	885	1159	1369	64900	593	964	1262	1505	70300	641	1041	1361	1624
54200	490	805	1050	1238	59600	542	886	1160	1372	65000	594	966	1264	1507	70400	642	1042	1363	1626
54300	491	806	1053	1241	59700	543	888	1162	1374	65100	595	968	1266	1509	70500	643	1044	1365	1628
54400	492	808	1055	1243	59800	544	889	1164	1377	65200	596	969	1268	1512	70600	644	1045	1367	1630
54500	493	809	1057	1246	59900	545	891	1166	1379	65300	597	971	1270	1514	70700	645	1047	1368	1632
54600	494	811	1059	1248	60000	546	892	1168	1382	65400	598	972	1272	1516	70800	646	1048	1370	1634
54700	495	812	1061	1251	60100	547	893	1170	1384	65500	599	974	1274	1519	70900	646	1049	1372	1637
54800	496	814	1064	1253	60200	548	895	1172	1387	65600	600	975	1276	1521	71000	647	1051	1374	1639
54900	497	815	1066	1256	60300	549	896	1174	1389	65700	601	977	1277	1523	71100	648	1052	1376	1641
55000	498	817	1068	1258	60400	550	898	1176	1392	65800	602	978	1279	1526	71200	649	1054	1378	1643
55100	499	818	1070	1261	60500	551	899	1177	1394	65900	602	980	1281	1528	71300	650	1055	1380	1646
55200	500	820	1072	1263	60600	552	901	1179	1397	66000	603	981	1283	1530	71400	651	1057	1381	1648
55300	501	821	1074	1266	60700	552	902	1181	1399	66100	604	983	1285	1532	71500	652	1058	1383	1650
55400	502	823	1077	1268	60800	553	904	1183	1402	66200	605	984	1287	1535	71600	653	1060	1385	1652
55500	503	824	1079	1271	60900	554	905	1185	1404	66300	606	986	1289	1537	71700	654	1061	1387	1655
55600	504	826	1081	1273	61000	555	906	1187	1407	66400	607	987	1291	1539	71800	655	1063	1389	1657
55700	505	827	1083	1276	61100	556	907	1189	1409	66500	608	989	1293	1541	71900	656	1064	1391	1659
55800	506	829	1085	1278	61200	557	909	1191	1412	66600	609	990	1294	1544	72000	657	1066	1393	1661
55900	507	830	1087	1281	61300	558	910	1193	1414	66700	610	992	1296	1546	72100	658	1067	1394	1663
56000	508	832	1089	1283	61400	559	912	1195	1417	66800	611	993	1298	1548	72200	658	1068	1396	1664
56100	509	833	1091	1286	61500	560	913	1196	1419	66900	612	995	1300	1551	72300	659	1069	1397	1666
56200	510	835	1093	1288	61600	561	915	1198	1422	67000	613	996	1302	1553	72400	660	1071	1399	1668
56300	511	836	1096	1291	61700	562	916	1200	1424	67100	614	997	1304	1555	72500	661	1072	1400	1670
56400	512	838	1098	1293	61800	563	918	1202	1427	67200	615	999	1306	1557	72600	661	1073	1401	1671
56500	513	839	1100	1296	61900	564	919	1204	1429	67300	615	1000	1307	1559	72700	662	1074	1403	1673
56600	514	841	1102	1298	62000	565	921	1206	1432	67400	616	1002	1309	1562	72800	663	1075	1404	1675
56700	515	842	1104	1301	62100	566	922	1208	1434	67500	617	1003	1311	1564	72900	664	1076	1406	1677
56800	516	844	1106	1303	62200	567	924	1210	1437	67600	618	1005	1313	1566	73000	664	1077	1407	1678
56900	516	845	1109	1306	62300	568	925	1212	1439	67700	619	1006	1315	1568	73100	665	1078	1409	1680
57000	517	847	1111	1308	62400	569	927	1213	1442	67800	620	1008	1316	1570	73200	666	1080	1411	1682
57100	518	849	1113	1310	62500	570	928	1215	1444	67900	620	1009	1318	1572	73300	667	1081	1413	1685
57200	519	850	1115	1313	62600	570	930	1217	1447	68000	621	1010	1320	1574	73400	668	1083	1414	1687
57300	520	852	1117	1315	62700	571	931	1219	1449	68100	622	1011	1322	1576	73500	669	1084	1416	1689
57400	521	853	1119	1318	62800	572	933	1221	1452	68200	623	1013	1324	1578	73600	669	1085	1418	1691
57500	522	855	1121	1320	62900	573	934	1223	1454	68300	624	1014	1325	1581	73700	670	1087	1420	1694
57600	523	856	1123	1323	63000	574	936	1225	1457	68400	624	1015	1327	1583	73800	671	1088	1422	1696
57700	524	858	1124	1325	63100	575	937	1227	1460	68500	625	1017	1329	1585	73900	672	1090	1424	1698
57800	525	859	1126	1328	63200	576	939	1229	1462	68600	626	1018	1331	1587	74000	673	1091	1426	1700
57900	526	861	1128	1330	63300	577	940	1231	1465	68700	627	1019	1333	1589	74100	674	1092	1428	1702
58000	527	862	1130	1332	63400	578	942	1233	1467	68800	628	1021	1334	1592	74200	675	1094	1430	1704
58100	528	864	1132	1334	63500	579	943	1235	1470	68900	629	1022	1336	1594	74300	676	1095	1431	1706
58200	529	865	1134	1337	63600	580	945	1237	1472	69000	630	1023	1338	1596	74400	677	1096	1433	1709
58300	530	867	1136	1339	63700	581	946	1239	1475	69100	631	1024	1340	1598	74500	677	1098	1435	1711
58400	531	868	1138	1342	63800	582	948	1241	1477	69200	632	1026	1342	1600	74600	678	1099	1437	1713
58500	532	870	1140	1344	63900	583	949	1243	1480	69300	633	1027	1343	1602	74700	679	1101	1439	1715
58600	533	871	1141	1347	64000	584	951	1245	1482	69400	634	1028	1345	1605	74800	680	1102	1440	1717
58700	534	873	1143	1349	64100	585	952	1247	1485	69500	634	1030	1347	1607	74900	681	1103	1442	1719
58800	534	874	1145	1352	64200	586	954	1249	1487	69600	635	1031	1349	1609	75000	682	1105	1444	1721
58900	535	876	1147	1354	64300	587	955	1251	1490	69700	636	1032	1350	1611	75100	683	1106	1446	1723
59000	536	877	1149	1357	64400	588	957	1253	1492	69800	637	1034	1352	1613	75200	684	1108	1448	1725
59100	537	879	1151	1359	64500	589	958	1255	1495	69900	638	1035	1354	1615	75300	685	1109	1449	1727
59200	538	880	1153	1362	64600	590	960	1257	1497	70000	639	1037	1356	1617	75400	686	1110	1451	1729
59300	539	882	1155	1364	64700	591	961	1259	1500	70100	640	1038	1358	1619	75500	686	1112	1453	1731

Ⓨ Ontario

SUPPORT DEDUCTION ORDER
Family Responsibility and Support Arrears Enforcement Act, 1996

Form 1

Court File No.

**FL28263

Ontario Family Court of the Superior Court of Justice
Name of Court

50 Eagle Street West, Newmarket, Ontario L3Y 6B1
Location

Judge

Date

Between

MARK RONALD TWAIN

Applicant / Petitioner / Plaintiff

and

MARISSA FIONA TWAIN

Respondent / Defendant

SUPPORT DEDUCTION ORDER

Upon making an order this day which provides for the payment of support and on making the necessary inquires required by section 11 of the *Family Responsibility and Support Arrears Enforcement Act, 1996:*

1. **THIS COURT ORDERS THAT**

   MARK RONALD TWAIN
   (Name of Payor)

   pay support as set out in the attached information form.

2. **THIS COURT ORDERS THAT** any income source that receives notice of this support deduction order make payments to the Director of the Family Responsibility Office in respect of the payor out of money owed to or paid by the income source to the payor.

_____
Signature of Judge, Registrar or Clerk of the Court

www.DIVORCEmate.com

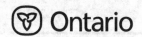 **Ontario**

SUPPORT DEDUCTION ORDER
INFORMATION FORM
Family Responsibility and Support Arrears Enforcement Act, 1996

Form 2

Court File No.
**FL28263

Name of Court **Ontario Family Court of the Superior Court of Justice**

Location **50 Eagle Street West, Newmarket, Ontario L3Y 6B1**

NOTE: Please Print. Complete Parts A and B ONLY. Leave Parts C, D, E and F blank to be completed by court.

A.   INFORMATION FOR THE FAMILY RESPONSIBILITY OFFICE

INFORMATION ON PARTIES   Family Responsibility Office Case Number *(if known)*

Payor

Payor Name	Birthdate (dd/mm/yyyy)	Sex
MARK RONALD TWAIN	06/06/(year)	[x] M [ ] F

Street Number	Unit/Suite/Apt.	Street Name
75		Deep Road

City/Town	Province	Postal Code
Waterwell	Ontario	D4G 5P2

Social Insurance Number	Mother's Maiden Name	Language Preference
345 678 910	Samuel	English

Home Telephone Number	Work/Business Telephone Number	Cell Phone Number
905-455-1586	905-926-1191	

Recipient

Recipient Name	Birthdate (dd/mm/yyyy)	Sex
MARISSA FIONA TWAIN	30/06/(year)	[ ] M [x] F

Street Number	Unit/Suite/Apt.	Street Name
492		Clemens Crescent

City/Town	Province	Postal Code
Waterwell	Ontario	D7R 6D6

Social Insurance Number	Mother's Maiden Name	Language Preference
910 876 543	Charo	English

Home Telephone Number	Work/Business Telephone Number	Cell Phone Number
905-455-7878	905-367-7986	

PAYOR'S EMPLOYMENT

Employer/Income Source Name

Payroll Office Address

Street Number	Unit/Suite/Apt.	Street Name
43		Rosemarie Drive

City/Town	Province	Postal Code
Waterwell	Ontario	D4U 1W6

[X] Self employed *(provide legal name of business and address)*
      Mark Twain Family Physician

[ ] Unemployed

[ ] Receiving welfare, family benefits or other form of social assistance

[ ] Receiving employment insurance benefits

[ ] Other *(i.e., workers' compensation, pension, etc.)*

[ ] Recipient does not know

SUPPORT ORDER INFORMATION

Is the support order a variation of a previous support order?   [ ] Yes [X] No   If "Yes", date of previous order

www.DIVORCEmate.com

Form 2: Support Deduction Order Information Form (page 2) Court File Number ****FL28263**

C, D, E and F to be COMPLETED BY COURT

B. The attached support deduction order relates to a support order which says that:

C.

TYPE OF SUPPORT ORDER
☐ Temporary ☐ Final

MARK RONALD TWAIN _____ is required to pay support
Payor Name

for the following persons:

Name	Birthdate (dd/mm/yyyy)	Amount Payable	Frequency	Start Date (dd/mm/yyyy)	End Date (if any) (dd/mm/yyyy)
Spouse: a.		$			
Other Dependants b. Amanda May Twain	06/02/(year)	$			
c.		$			
d.		$			
e.		$			
f.		$			

D. SPECIAL EXPENSES

Name of Child / Children	Birthdate (dd/mm/yyyy)	Amount	Frequency	Start Date (dd/mm/yyyy)	End Date (if any) (dd/mm/yyyy)
		$			
		$			
		$			
		$			
		$			
		$			

E. COST OF LIVING ADJUSTMENTS (DOES NOT APPLY TO CHILD SUPPORT)

Support is indexed in accordance with s. 34(5) of the _Family Law Act_ ☐ Yes ☐ No

If other indexing, explain method of calculation:

F. ARREARS – If the order is retroactive, if the order is a variation order or if the order provides for an arrears payment

schedule, are arrears owing as of the date of the order? ☐ No ☐ Yes If "Yes" the amount of arrears = $

and the arrears are to be paid as follows (if applicable)

PARTS A AND B COMPLETED BY: (please print)

Name	Title (if solicitor for a party, identify which party)	Telephone Number
Robert B. Redford	Lawyer for the applicant.	(416) 363-1079

CHAPTER 21

FAMILY LAW RULES AND PROCEDURES

This chapter provides some practical preliminary points to consider prior to starting a family law case.

THE FAMILY LAW RULES

The *Family Law Rules* prescribe the procedural steps to be followed when family cases proceed to court, and the *Family Law Act* covers much of the substantive law that applies to family issues.

Family law forms   The *Family Law Rules* prescribe all of the forms to be used in all family law cases, including divorce cases, regardless of the court in which family law cases are tried. All family law forms are identified by the rule number which prescribes them: for example, Rule 8 states that to start a case, a person shall file a **Form 8: Application (General)**. All family law forms under the *Family Law Rules* are available on the website of the Ministry of the Attorney General. The ministry has **Family Guides** on its site with instructions on how to fill out the forms online. Many law firms use commercial family law software, such as DIVORCEmate, which is the family law software used in this manual.

Court fees   The courts charge fees for their services according to a schedule of fees under the *Family Law Rules*.

COURTS HANDLING FAMILY LAW CASES

Three courts handle family law cases: the Family Court of the Superior Court of Justice, the Superior Court of Justice, and the Ontario Court of Justice. The forms and procedures are the same in all three courts because the *Family Law Rules* apply to all family law cases in all three courts.

FAMILY COURT OF THE SUPERIOR COURT OF JUSTICE

The Family Court of the Superior Court of Justice, referred to as the **Family Court**, exists in the following locations and may eventually expand to other locations in the province:

Barrie Bracebridge Brockville Cobourg Cornwall	Durham Region Hamilton Kingston Lindsay	London L'Orignal Napanee Newmarket	Ottawa Perth Peterborough St. Catharines
(The Family Court also sits regularly in Huntsville, Collingwood, Midland, and Orillia.)			

The Family Court's administrator is the **clerk**. The Family Court is the only court in Ontario which can hear all family law cases. In all other sites across Ontario, family law matters are divided between the Superior Court of Justice and the Ontario Court of Justice. Here is a summary of the three courts and the types of claims each court can hear:

Figure 21.1

COURTS WITH FAMILY LAW JURISDICTION	
Name of Court	**Types of Claims**
Family Court of the Superior Court of Justice (Family Court) (Where Family Court exists)	Divorce, child support, spousal support, custody of children, access to children, division of family property, exclusive possession of matrimonial home, adoption, and child protection.
Superior Court of Justice (Where no Family Court exists)	Divorce, child support, spousal support, custody of children, access to children, division of family property, exclusive possession of matrimonial home. **Cannot hear adoption and child protection**.
Ontario Court of Justice (Where no Family Court exists)	Child support, spousal support, custody of children, access to children, adoption, and child protection. **Cannot hear divorce, division of property, and exclusive possession of matrimonial home**.

STATUTES TO WHICH THE FAMILY LAW RULES APPLY

(i) the *Change of Name Act*

(ii) Parts III, VI and VII of the *Child and Family Services Act*

(iii) the *Children's Law Reform Act*, except sections 59 and 60

(iv) the *Divorce Act* (Canada)

(v) the *Family Law Act*, except Part V

(vi) the *Family Responsibility and Support Arrears Enforcement Act*

(vii) sections 6 and 9 of the *Marriage Act*

(viii) the *Interjurisdictional Support Orders Act*

The federal and provincial statutes under which most family law claims are made are the following:

The Ontario *Family Law Act* (FLA) -- provides for most family law claims, except divorce, custody, and access. Basically, the FLA provides for money-related and property-related claims such as support and division of family property.

The Ontario *Children's Law Reform Act* (CLRA) – provides for non-monetary claims and deals exclusively with matters relating to the welfare of children, e.g. custody and access. It does not provide for divorce.

The *Divorce Act* of Canada (federal act) — provides for divorce, support, custody, and access.

Family law cases may make claims under all three of these acts simultaneously as well as any other applicable acts. Family law cases do not always include a claim for divorce. When a family law case makes no claim for divorce, it is usually because the spouses are seeking to settle other family disputes, such as child support during separation, because the courts will not grant a divorce until the courts are satisfied that the parties have made adequate arrangements for child support.

PROCEDURAL STAGES IN FAMILY LAW

Family law cases proceed to trial in the following three stages:

Figure 21.2

(1) DEFINE THE ISSUES IN DISPUTE	(2) NARROW AND SETTLE THE ISSUES	(3) TRIAL
1. Application (Financial Statement) 2. Answer 3. First Court Date (First court date is given in fast track cases in the Family Court and in all cases in the Ontario Court of Justice)	4. Case Conference 5. Settlement Conference 6. Trial Management Conference	7. Trial
This stage in the case involves: -preparing court forms -serving the other party -filing with the court	**This stage in the case involves:** Attending conferences before a judge to: -establish time frames -make full disclosure -obtain early orders, if any -narrow and settle issues -plan for a trial, if necessary	**This stage in the case involves:** A trial where the trial judge makes a final order as to any unresolved issues
MOTIONS Under Rule 14 of the *Family Law Rules*, no motions can be heard before a case conference is held, except for urgent or procedural motions.		

MANDATORY INFORMATION PROGRAM

The Mandatory Information Program (MIP) is under Rule 8.1 of the *Family Law Rules* and applies to contested issues relating to separation and divorce, including issues relating to custody, access, child/spousal support, the matrimonial home, or net family property. It does not apply where the claim is only for divorce or joint divorce. The MIP is usually held at family court locations across the province, and it is usually the first step in a court case. The program uses a triage approach at the start of a case to identify issues the parties need help resolving and includes a mandatory information session which both parties must attend separately. Typically, at the time the applicant files his or her application, the court clerk provides the applicant with an **applicant's notice**, Precedent 21.5, setting out the date on which the applicant must attend an information session and also includes a **respondent's notice**, setting out a separate date on which the respondent must attend an information session. The form of the respondent's notice is identical to the applicant's notice except that it is directed to the respondent instead of the applicant. The applicant must serve the respondent's notice together with the application. Both parties must bring their notices when they attend their respective information sessions. The person who conducts the information session must complete each party's **certificate of attendance**, Precedent 21.5, which certificate forms part of each party's notice. Each party must file the notice with the completed certificate of attendance in court before proceeding with any further steps in the case, except a respondent may serve and file an answer and either party may schedule a case conference.

CASE MANAGEMENT

Nearly all family law cases are under case management. Case management means that the court assigns a judge to each family law case to manage the case. The job of the case management judge is to meet with the parties in a number of case conferences with a view to helping the parties resolve their issues as quickly as possible without having to resort to trial, if possible.

First court date and case tracks There are two tracks in family cases: fast track and standard track. Fast track cases are all cases that do not include claims for divorce and/ or claims involving property. Standard track cases are all cases in which there are claims for divorce and/or claims involving property. Fast track cases are given the first court date as soon as the application is filed and the first court date is written on the application. The first court date is for the purpose of ensuring that all the necessary documents have been served and filed. If they have been, the next step is a case conference. In standard track cases there is no first court date. Rather, the first step in the court process will be a case conference, scheduled at the request of one of the parties. There are tracks only in the Family Court and the Ontario Court of Justice:

> **Family Court** All cases are placed on the fast track, except cases claiming divorce and/or property, which are placed on the standard track.

> **Ontario Court of Justice** All cases are placed on the fast track. (The Ontario Court of Justice has no jurisdiction over claims for divorce and/or property; these would require the standard track.)

> **Superior Court of Justice** There are no tracks in this court. A case shall come before the court when a case conference or a motion is scheduled, whichever comes first, and the clerk shall schedule a case conference on any party's request.

STARTING THE FAMILY LAW CASE

Under Rule 8 of the *Family Law Rules*, all family law cases begin by filing in court a form called **application**. This applies in all courts that deal with family law cases. The party starting the application is the **applicant** and is the party suing. The party responding to the application is the **respondent** and is the party being sued. The court seals the application by placing the court seal on the top left corner of the first page of the application, assigns a court file number for the case, and returns the sealed application to you, a copy of which must be served by special service on the respondent.

Where started and heard   Rule 5 of the *Family Law Rules* provides that family law cases be started in the municipality where a party, e.g. the applicant, resides or, if the case deals with custody of, or access to, a child, in the municipality where the child ordinarily resides, unless the court orders otherwise. All steps in the case must also take place in the municipality where the case is started or transferred. If it is substantially more convenient to deal with a case or any step in the case in another municipality, the court may order that the case or step be transferred to that municipality.

Legal TIP

Generally, there are only orders in family law cases; no judgments.

SERVICE OF FAMILY LAW DOCUMENTS

Rule 6 of the *Family Law Rules* provides for service of documents. There are two methods of serving documents: special service and regular service. Generally, all applications must be served by special service to ensure that the opposite party learns that he or she is being sued. Documents subsequent to the application may be served by regular service. Following is a summary of the methods of service permitted in family law cases:

Figure 21.3

SUMMARY OF SERVICE	
Persons effecting any type of service must be at least 18 years of age.	
SPECIAL SERVICE	
Special service must be carried out by a person other than the applicant.	
ON WHOM MADE	HOW MADE
Person to be served	1. Leaving a copy with that person or that person's lawyer. 2. Leaving a copy in an envelope addressed to the person with an adult at the person's residence and, on the same day or the next day, mailing another copy at that address. 3. Mailing a copy with an acknowledgment of service prepaid return postcard.
Mentally incapable person	Leaving a copy with that person and with the guardian of that person's property and, if none, with the Public Guardian and Trustee.
Child under 18	Leaving a copy with the child and with the child's lawyer, if any.
Children's Aid Society	Leaving a copy with an officer, director, or employee of the society.
REGULAR SERVICE	
Person to be served or person's lawyer	Mail, courier, fax, email, document exchange, or electronic document exchange. If by fax, maximum length of document, including the cover page, must be not more than 20 pages, unless by consent or court order. (Trial records, appeal records, factums, or books of authorities may not be served by fax at any time, unless the person to be served consents.) If by document exchange, deposit at lawyer's document exchange. If by email or electronic document exchange, only by consent or court order.
SUBSTITUTED SERVICE	
Person to be served	If the whereabouts of the person are unknown, the lawyer may bring a motion for substituted service using a method which the court would choose.

Following is a summary of effective dates of service and their corresponding proof of service:

Figure 21.4

EFFECTIVE DATE OF SERVICE						
Leaving a Copy	**Mail**	**Fax/Email**	**Courier**	**Document Exchange**	**Electronic Document Exchange**	**Acknowledgment Card**
On the day copy was left	On fifth day after mailing	On date shown on first page of fax or in email message; if after 4 p.m., on following day	On day after courier picks up document, if same-day service; two days after, if next-day service	On day after the date stamped on document	On date shown on record of service; if after 4 p.m., on following day	On day of receipt of acknowledgment card
PROOF OF SERVICE						
Affidavit of service, acceptance or admission of service	Affidavit of service, acceptance or admission of service	Affidavit of service, acceptance or admission of service	Affidavit of service, acceptance or admission of service	Date stamped on the document served	Record of service	Return of signed acknowledgment card

Legal TIP

With any method of service, if made on a day when court offices are closed, service is effective on the next day on which they are open.

Time   For purposes of calculating time for service between two events under the *Family Law Rules*, exclude the day of the first event and include the day of the second event. If a rule or order provides a period of less than seven days for something to be done, do not count Saturdays, Sundays and any other days when court offices are closed.   Subrule 3(4) of the *Family Law Rules* provides the following examples of how time is to be counted:

1. Notice of motion must be served not later than **four days** before the motion date (see subrule 14(11)). Saturday and Sunday are not counted, because the notice period is less than seven days....   Service on the day set out in the left column below is in time for the motion to be heard on the day set out in the right column below.

Service on	Motion may be heard on the following
Monday	Friday
Tuesday	Monday
Wednesday	Tuesday
Thursday	Wednesday
Friday	Thursday
Saturday	Friday
Sunday	Friday

Legal Office Procedures

2. A respondent who is served with an application in Canada has 30 days to serve an answer... A respondent who is served with an application on October 1 is in time if the answer is served on or before October 31. A respondent served on November 1 is in time if the answer is served on or before December 1.

3. If the last day for doing something under these rules or an order is New Year's Day, January 1, which is a day when court offices are closed, the time expires on January 2. If January 2 is a Saturday, Sunday or other day when court offices are closed, the time expires on January 3. If January 3 is a day when court offices are closed, the time expires on January 4.

FINANCIAL STATEMENTS

Rule 13 of the *Family Law Rules* prescribes two financial statement forms: **Form 13: financial statement (support claims)** and **Form 13.1: financial statement (property and support claims).** Form 13 is to be used where support (child and/or spousal) is the only claim made. Form 13.1 is to be used where the claim includes property, property and child and/or spousal support, or exclusive possession of the matrimonial home and its contents. The forms, as applicable, must be served and filed together with the application. Once served on the respondent, the respondent must then also serve and file the applicable form of financial statement, even if the respondent will not be filing an answer to the application. The court needs this information to enable it to make a fair decision as to who should pay how much to whom. A **certificate of financial disclosure, Form 13A**, Precedent 21.0, which is a checklist for all of the income and property disclosure documents provided, must be served with the respective form of financial statement. Attach to Form 13 or Form 13.1, as the case may be, the following proof of current income:

- Income tax returns for each of the past three taxation years,
- Copy of the party`s notices of assessment and any notices of reassessment for each of the past three taxation years, and if these are unavailable for any of the past three taxation years,
- An Income Deductions printout from the Canada Revenue Agency for each of those years.

If the claim includes property, serve the required property disclosure documents, along with a Form 13A, within 30 days of service of Form 13.1. The longer time for service of the property disclosure documents intends to enable a party to obtain the required, often complicated, property information.

Exceptions to filing financial statements   A party need not file any financial statements where:

(a) the claim is for spousal, as opposed to child, support under the *Divorce Act* (Canada) **and** the   parties file a consent agreeing not to serve and file financial statements.

(b) the claim is only for child support in the amount specified in the child support guidelines.

(c) the claim is only for custody and access (without claiming support, property division, or exclusive possession of the matrimonial home and its contents).

(d) the parties to a consent motion to change a temporary support order file a consent agreeing not to serve and file financial statements.

Obligation to update financial statements   Subrule 13(12) requires that if any financial statements are more than 30 days old, each party must serve and file a new financial statement or an affidavit either stating that the information in the last financial statement has not changed or, if the changes are minor, giving details of the changes. In the case of an applicant or a moving party, the updated documents must be served and

Legal TIP

It is the *Family Law Act*, not the *Divorce Act*, that requires financial statements and net family property statements.

Legal TIP

Money-related claims, e.g. support and division of property, require completion of money-related documents such as financial statements and net family property statements.

filed at least **seven days** before (a) a case conference, (b) a settlement conference, or (c) a trial; and in the case of a respondent or a responding party, the updated documents must be served and filed at least **four days** before the same events.

NET FAMILY PROPERTY STATEMENTS

Subrule 13(14) of the *Family Law Rules* requires that each party to a property claim under Part I of the *Family Law Act* (i.e. equalization of net family property) must serve and file a **net family property statement (Form 13B)** or, if the party has already served and filed a net family property statement, an affidavit stating that the information in that statement has not changed, (a) not less than **30 days** before a settlement conference and (b) not more than 30 days and not less than **seven days** before a trial. Form 13B summarizes the contents of Form 13.1 of both spouses and shows the amount of their net family property (NFP) and the amount of the equalization payment which the spouse with the higher NFP must pay to the spouse with the lower NFP.

Here is a summary of the various financial statements and the types of claims for which they are required:

Figure 21.5

FINANCIAL STATEMENTS AND NET FAMILY PROPERTY STATEMENTS		
Form 13: Financial Statement (Support Claims)	**Form 13.1: Financial Statement (Property and Support Claims)**	**Form 13B: Net Family Property Statement**
<u>Types of Claims:</u> Spousal and/or child support or change in support (Not property)	<u>Types of Claims:</u> Property division, equalization payment, or exclusive possession of matrimonial home & its contents (with or without a claim for support)	<u>Types of Claims:</u> Property under Part I of the *Family Law Act* (i.e. equalization of net family property)
<u>Served and Filed:</u> When making or responding to an application or motion (whether or not contesting the case).	<u>Served and Filed:</u> When making or responding to an application or motion (whether or not contesting the case).	<u>Served and Filed:</u> By each party, not less than 30 days before a settlement conference and not more than 30 days and not less than 7 days before a trial.

PREPARATION AND DISTRIBUTION OF FINANCIAL STATEMENT (SUPPORT CLAIMS), FORM 13

You require: Interview notes or hand-completed draft of financial statement (support claims) by client. Follow along in Precedent 21.1. The wording guides completion. Notes on items not self-explanatory follow:

(In the interest of proceeding from simpler to more challenging tasks, which is the learning objective throughout this manual, we discuss the preparation of the simpler and shorter Form 13 here so as to lay the groundwork for preparing Form 13.1 (next chapter) which is longer.)

Use Form 13 where your client is claiming only spousal and/or child support. To get a monthly figure, multiply any weekly income by 4.33 or divide any yearly income by 12. Period of 12 months may be from any month in a year, e.g. July (last year) to June (this year); January (this year) to December (this year). If you are using DIVORCEmate software, the software has an automated conversion of numbers feature: for example, if you input w, b, or y (weekly, bi-weekly, yearly) after the number, the program will convert it to a monthly number once you click the "calculate" button, e.g. $2000y will calculate to $166.67 monthly; $10w will calculate to $43.30 monthly. DIVORCEmate automatically calculates all numbers inserted in Form 13 (and Form 13.1), including automatically deducting the debts and liabilities from the assets.

Generally, the client provides the lawyer with an estimated value of most items. Law firms have lists of accredited appraisers of household items, business evaluators, and real estate appraisers which they provide to the client for items that require professional opinions such as works of art or antiques. For pre-owned cars, the value would be as listed in the Canadian Black Book (commonly referred to as the "black book").

Part 1: Income and Part 2: Expenses: Show income and expenses on a monthly basis. Income from employment should be gross income, i.e. before any deductions for income tax, pension, employment insurance, etc. Other Benefits column - include any benefits that a client has received but has not had to pay for, e.g meal allowances, company car, health plans, etc.

Part 3: Assets: Show the present value of all of your client's assets that are in the client's name alone; if owned jointly, show half the value in the "Value" column and make a note of the entire value in the "Details" column.

Part 4: Debts: For all debts, note whether the debt is in the client's name alone, or if owned jointly, put only the client's portion of the debt in the "Full Amount Now Owing" column and show the entire debt owed under the "Creditor" column.

> Part 2: Expenses - Proposed budget: DIVORCEmate provides this form at the end of Form 13. It is a DIVORCEmate form and is optional. It is not part of the prescribed Form 13. It is identical to that provided at the end of Form 13.1 (sample in Form 13.1, Chapter 22). If your client is aware of any material changes, either up or down, in the near future, you should complete this form in order to disclose any material change in circumstances; otherwise, this form may be omitted.

Schedule A - Additional sources of income: If your client receives income from any of the sources listed on Schedule A, you must complete Schedule A and attach it to the financial statement Form 13. Include the annual amount of these additional sources of income on line 11 of "Part 1 Income Source" in Form 13, divide the amount by 12 and enter the monthly amount in the "Amount Received/Month" column.

Schedule B - Other income earners in the home: Complete Schedule B only if the client claims spousal support or undue hardship and attach it to the financial statement.

Schedule C - Special or extraordinary expenses for the child(ren): Complete Schedule C only if the client claims special or extraordinary expenses for the child and attach it to the financial statement Form 13. The types of special expenses for which your client can make a claim are listed on Schedule C, e.g. childcare expenses, etc. Show the net annual amount, divide the annual amount by 12 and also show the net monthly amount. Also attach proof of the expenses claimed.

Number of copies, minimum 3: 1 attach to application (general), original in continuing record, 1 in file.

Financial statement brief   Many law firms maintain a financial statement brief correlated by tab to each part in the financial statement, with a table of contents listing the date of the document and the tab behind which the document may be found. The financial statement brief contains documents which prove, or substantiate, the figures in the financial statement, e.g. appraisals, valuations, investment statements, insurance policies, in the event the client is cross-examined on the financial statement.

FAMILY LAW MOTIONS

Rules 14 and 15 of the *Family Law Rules* provide for motions. A motion is a formal request to the court to grant an order on a family issue. All family law motions begin with a document called **notice of motion**. The party making the family law motion is referred to as the moving party, and the party responding to the motion is referred to as the responding party. Note, however, that in the family law motion documents, the parties retain their original titles of **applicant** and **respondent**. A family law motion can be with notice or without notice; motions without notice are also referred to as *ex parte* motions. A family law motion with notice is one which is served on the opposing party. A family law motion without notice is one which is not served on the opposing party and is usually used where there is an emergency, e.g. family violence or child abduction.

No motions before a case conference   Generally, motions in family law cases cannot be made before a case conference has been held, basically because hopes are that the case conference will help the parties sort out their issues enough so as to eliminate the need for any motions. Family law motions can, however, be made before the holding of a case conference, or at any time during a case, in situations of emergency, e.g. family violence or child abduction.

TYPES OF FAMILY LAW MOTIONS

The *Family Law Rules* provide for two types of motions — motions for a temporary order, which are motions brought during the progress of the present case, and motions to change a final order, which are motions seeking to change a final order from a past case, i.e. a case that has already been completed.

Where are motions started and heard   Family law motions for temporary orders are usually started and heard in the court where the family law application to which they relate was started. Family law motions to change final orders may be started and heard in the municipality where the party making the motion lives or, if they are motions for custody or access, in the municipality where the child lives. Parties may make arrangements with the clerk to have the motion heard by telephone or video conference.

FAMILY LAW MOTIONS FOR TEMPORARY ORDERS

Rule 14 of the *Family Law Rules* provides for motions for temporary orders. When family law motions are brought during the progress of a present case, they are referred to as motions for temporary orders because they usually seek an order on a "for the time being" basis, e.g. for temporary custody, until the issues are permanently settled between the spouses or finally determined by a judge at a trial. The following case is an example of a motion for a temporary order for custody:

TOPHLER, Alvin
Re: Motion

We act for Mr. Alvin Tophler on a motion to get his five-year old son John back from Mrs. Tophler. Note from Mr. Tophler's affidavit, Precedent 21.3, that Mr. Tophler is separated from his wife and has interim (temporary) custody of the little boy and that Mrs. Tophler, along with her boyfriend, took the young boy for a visit and never returned him to our client. In the notice of motion, Precedent 21.2, Mr. Tophler is asking the court to order Mrs. Tophler to return little John to him and, if Mrs. Tophler refuses, to authorize the sheriff to bring back the little boy to the temporary custody of Mr. Tophler until the trial when the court will give its final decision as to which of the parents will have permanent custody. The decision of the judge is in the order, Precedent 21.4.

Steps in family law motions for temporary orders The documents to be prepared include:

- Notice of motion, Form 14, Precedent 21.2
- Supporting affidavit, Form 14A, Precedent 21.3
- Financial statement (support claims), Form 13, Precedent 21.1, or
- Financial statement (property and support claims), Form 13.1, as the case may be
- Affidavit of service, Form 6B
- Confirmation, Form 14C
- Table of contents for continuing record (listing the documents being served)

1. Obtain from the court a date for the hearing of the motion.
2. Serve a copy of the notice of motion and the supporting affidavit, including any financial statements, usually if the motion is for support, and a copy of the table of contents for the continuing record on the respondent at least **four days** before the motion hearing.
3. File the documents, with proof of service, at least **two days** before the motion hearing.
4. File the confirmation no later than 2 p.m. **two days** before the date of the motion hearing.

FAMILY LAW MOTIONS TO CHANGE FINAL ORDERS

Rule 15 of the *Family Law Rules* provides for motions to change final orders or agreements. When family law motions are brought seeking to change a final ruling which the courts have already made in a case that is finished, such motions are referred to as motions to change final orders. Motions to change final orders may also seek to change the terms of a separation agreement which the spouses have already signed. Motions to change final orders cannot be made without notice, and they must be served by special service and not by regular service because they constitute new starts against old orders or agreements: for example, the court can change the original custody or support provisions of a final order or agreement if the court is satisfied that a change in circumstances justifies the change.

Steps in family law motions to change final orders Typical steps in bringing family law motions to change final orders include the following:

1. Prepare and take the following documents, as applicable, to the court for the clerk to issue the motion to change:
   - Motion to change, Form 15
   - Change information form, Form 15A
   - Financial statement, Form 13 or 13.1, if required
   - Blank response to motion to change, Form 15B
   - Blank consent to motion to change, Form 15C
   - Blank financial statement, Form 13 or 13.1, if required
   - Affidavit of service, Form 6B

2. Serve on the respondent the above documents, along with a copy of the final order or separation agreement attached to the change information form, Form 15A, and file the documents with proof of service. The responding party has **30 days** (60 days if served outside Canada or USA) to either respond, usually by serving and filing a **response to motion to change, Form 15B**, and a financial statement, Form 13 or 13.1, as applicable (these are the blank documents which the moving party included with service), or sign the **consent to motion to change, Form 15C**, (the blank Form 15C included with service).

CHAPTER SUMMARY

The *Family Law Rules* govern all family law cases throughout the Province of Ontario whether the family law cases are brought in the Family Court of the Superior Court of Justice (Family Court), the Superior Court of Justice, or the Ontario Court of Justice. All family law cases are under a family case management system. Documents that begin family law cases are usually served by special service, and all subsequent documents are served by regular service.

The *Family Law Rules* prescribe the forms and procedures to be used in all family law cases. Family law cases begin with an application, and the parties are referred to as applicant and respondent. Family law applications carry the family law case all the way to trial if not settled prior to trial. A party claiming support or property must file a financial statement, and the respondent must also file a financial statement, whether or not the respondent intends to contest the case. Family law motions are usually brought by a notice of motion. There are motions for a temporary order which are usually brought during the progress of the present case, and there are motions to change a final order from a past case.

REVIEW QUESTIONS

1. Name the three courts with jurisdiction to hear family law cases.
2. Name one method of special service and its corresponding effective date of service.
3. Explain the types of claims provided for under the *Family Law Act* and the *Children's Law Reform Act*.
4. What is the name of the document that begins all family law cases?
5. What is the name of the document that begins all family law motions?
6. Name the three stages through which family law cases proceed to trial.
7. Explain why a fast track is the speediest track to the finish line in amateur drag racing.
8. Name the day on which a motion would be heard if service were made last Tuesday and four days were required between service and the date of hearing.
9. Explain the basic differences in use between a financial statement, Form 13, a Form 13.1, and a net family property statement, Form 13B.
10. Explain the difference between a motion for temporary order and a motion to change a final order.

x

x

ONTARIO

Ontario Family Court of the Superior Court of Justice
(Name of Court)

at **50 Eagle Street West, Newmarket, Ontario L3Y 6B1**
(Court office address)

Court File Number
**FL28263

**Form 13A:
Certificate of Financial
Disclosure**

Applicant(s)

Full legal name & address for service — street & number, municipality, postal code, telephone & fax numbers and e-mail address (if any).	Lawyer's name & address — street & number, municipality, postal code, telephone & fax numbers and e-mail address (if any).
Mark Ronald Twain **75 Deep Road** **Waterwell, Ontario** **D4G 5P2** **Tel: (905) 455-1586**	**Robert B. Redford** **Michael, Eliad & Redford LLP** **863 Seneca Lane** **Toronto, Ontario M4J 1P6** **Tel: (416) 363-1079** **Fax: (416) 363-2628** **rbrdfrd@mer.com**

Respondent(s)

Full legal name & address for service — street & number, municipality, postal code, telephone & fax numbers and e-mail address (if any).	Lawyer's name & address — street & number, municipality, postal code, telephone & fax numbers and e-mail address (if any).
Marissa Fiona Twain **492 Clemens Crescent** **Waterwell, Ontario** **D7R 6D6** **Tel: (905) 455-7878**	**Raymond G. Castles** **Castles & Sands** **Suite 900 - 205 Portage Street** **Markham, Ontario L3R 3G3** **Tel: (905) 495-2222** **Fax: (905) 495-2223** **raymond@castlessands.ca**

TO THE PARTIES

You must provide complete financial disclosure to the other party in your case. A list of the documents you must provide to the other party is set out in Rule 13 of the Family Law Rules. You must list in this form all of the documents that you are providing to the other party in support of the information set out in your financial statement.

Once you have completed this form:

- if your case includes support with or without special expenses but does not include a claim for division of property, you must:

    o attach all required documentation to the completed certificate

    o serve this certificate (with attached documentation) on the other party with your completed Financial Statement

- if your case includes a claim for division of property with or without a claim for support, you must:

    o attach all required documentation to the completed certificate

    o serve this certificate (with attached documentation) on the other party within 30 days of the day that your Financial Statement was due to be served

- If you have served any additional or updated financial disclosure before the settlement conference, you must prepare, serve and file an updated Certificate of Financial Disclosure

If you do not provide financial disclosure as required, a court may make an order against you.

You must file a copy of this certificate with the court. If you are the applicant or the moving party in your case, you must file this certificate seven days before the case conference. If you are the respondent, you must serve it four days before the case conference.

FLR 13A (January 6, 2015) CSD

DivorceMate.com

**Form 13A: Certificate of
Financial Disclosure (page 2)**

	Court File Number	**FL28263

Document Number	Document Description	Date of Document *(yyyy/mm/dd)*
Part A: Sources of Income		
Personal Income Tax Returns *(Complete with Schedules)*		
1.	Income tax return - Year 1	(year)/04/30
2.	Income tax return - Year 2	(year)/04/30
3.	Income tax return - Year 3	(year)/04/30
Notices of Assessment and Reassessment		
4.	Notice of Assessment – Year 1	(year)/06/15
5.	Notice of Assessment – Year 2	(year)/06/15
6.	Notice of Assessment – Year 3	(year)/06/15
Employment Income		
Self-Employment Income		
7.	Financial statements for Mark Twain Family Physician - Year 1	(year)/12/31
8.	Financial statements for Mark Twain Family Physician - Year 2	(year)/12/31
9.	Financial statements for Mark Twain Family Physician - Year 3	(year)/12/31
Partnership Income and Interests in a Partnership		
Income from a Privately Held Corporation		
Beneficial Income from, and Interest in, a Trust		
Income from Employment Insurance or Social Assistance		

Precedent 21.0 Certificate of Financial Disclosure, pages 4

Form 13A: Certificate of
Financial Disclosure (page 4)

Part C: Claim for Equalization of Net Family Property

Assets and Liabilities at Valuation Date *(Provide the statement issued closest to the date of separation)*

Real Estate

Savings and Investments

Pensions

Life Insurance Policies

Interest in a Sole Proprietorship

Interest in a Partnership

Interest in a Publicly Held Corporation

Interest in a Privately Held Corporation

Precedent 21.0 Certificate of Financial Disclosure, pages 3

Form 13A: Certificate of
Financial Disclosure (page 3)

Pensions and Annuities

Income From Spousal Support

Tax Benefits or Rebates

Investment and Interest Income

Rental Income

Other Income

Part B: Special and Extraordinary Expenses

Precedent 21.0 Certificate of Financial Disclosure, pages 5

Form 13A: Certificate of
Financial Disclosure (page 5)

Court File Number   **FL28263

Trust Interests

Property I own which does not belong in any of the other categories

Liabilities

Assets and Liabilities at Marriage Date

Assets

Liabilities

Excluded Property

I am the ___Applicant___ in this case. I certify that I have provided the opposing party with all of the documents that I have identified in this checklist.

Certified at ___Toronto___ _(City)_ on ___ _(Date)_

Precedent 21.0 Certificate of Financial Disclosure, pages 6

Form 13A: Certificate of
Financial Disclosure (page 6)

Court File Number   **FL28263

_____
(Signature of Party)

ONTARIO

Ontario Family Court of the Superior Court of Justice

(Name of Court)

	Court File Number
	**FL28263

at   **50 Eagle Street West, Newmarket, Ontario L3Y 6B1**

Court office address

**Form 13: Financial Statement
(Support Claims)
sworn/affirmed**

....

Applicant(s)

Full legal name & address for service — street & number, municipality, postal code, telephone & fax numbers and e-mail address (if any).	Lawyer's name & address — street & number, municipality, postal code, telephone & fax numbers and e-mail address (if any).
Mark Ronald Twain **75 Deep Road** **Waterwell, Ontario** **D4G 5P2** **Tel: (905) 455-1586**	**Robert B. Redford** **Michael, Eliad & Redford LLP** **863 Seneca Lane** **Toronto, Ontario M4J 1P6** **Tel: (416) 363-1079** **Fax: (416) 363-2628** **rbrdfrd@mer.com**

Respondent(s)

Full legal name & address for service — street & number, municipality, postal code, telephone & fax numbers and e-mail address (if any).	Lawyer's name & address — street & number, municipality, postal code, telephone & fax numbers and e-mail address (if any).
Marissa Fiona Twain **492 Clemens Crescent** **Waterwell, Ontario** **D7R 6D6** **Tel: (905) 455-7878**	**Raymond G. Castles** **Castles & Sands** **Suite 900 – 205 Portage Street** **Markham, Ontario L3R 3G3** **Tel: (905) 495-2222** **Fax: (905) 495-2223** **raymond@castlessands.ca**

INSTRUCTIONS

You must complete this form if you are making or responding to a claim for child or spousal support or a claim to change support, unless your only claim for support is a claim for child support in the table amount under the *Child Support Guidelines*.

You may also be required to complete and attach additional schedules based on the claims that have been made in your case or your financial circumstances:

- If you have income that is not shown in Part I of the financial statement (for example, partnership income dividends, rental income, capital gains or RRSP income), you must also complete **Schedule A**.

- If you have made or responded to a claim for child support that involves undue hardship or a claim for spousal support, you must also complete **Schedule B**.

- If you or the other party has sought a contribution towards special or extraordinary expenses for the child(ren) you must also complete **Schedule C**.

NOTES:

*You must **fully and truthfully** complete this financial statement, including any applicable schedules. You must also provide the other party with documents relating to support and property and a Certificate of Financial Disclosure (Form 13A) as required by Rule 13 of the Family Law Rules.*

If you are making or responding to a claim for property, an equalization payment or the matrimonial home, you must complete Form 13.1: Financial Statement (Property and Support Claims) instead of this form.

1. **My name is** *(full legal name)*   Mark Ronald Twain

   I live in *(municipality & province)*   Waterwell, Ontario

FLR 13 (January 6, 2015)   www.DivorceMate.com

Form 13:	**Financial Statement**	**(page 2)**	Court File Number:	****FL28263**
	(Support Claims)			

and I swear/affirm that the following is true:

PART 1: INCOME

2. I am currently

☐ employed by *(name and address of employer)*

☒ self-employed, carrying on business under the name of *(name and address of business)*
Mark Twain Family Physician, 43 Rosemarie Drive, Waterwell, Ontario D4U 1W6

☐ unemployed since *(date when last employed)*

3. I attach proof of my year-to-date income from all sources, including my most recent *(attach all that are applicable)*:

☐ pay cheque stub ☐ social assistance stub ☐ pension stub ☐ workers' compensation stub

☐ employment insurance stub and last Record of Employment

☒ statement of income and expenses/ professional activities (for self-employed individuals)

☐ other (e.g. a letter from your employer confirming all income received to date this year)

4. Last year, my gross income from all sources was $ 150,000.00 *(do not subtract any taxes that have been deducted from this income)*.

5. ☒ I am attaching the following required documents to this financial statement as proof of my income over the past three years, if they have not already been provided:

- a copy of my personal income tax returns for each of the past three taxation years, including any materials that were filed with the returns. *(Income tax returns must be served but should NOT be filed in the continuing record, unless they are filed with a motion to refrain a driver's license suspension.)*

- a copy of my notices of assessment and any notices of reassessment for each of the past three taxation years;

- where my notices of assessment and reassessment are unavailable for any of the past three taxation years or where I have not filed a return for any of the past three taxation years, an Income and Deductions printout from the Canada Revenue Agency for each of those years, whether or not I filed an income tax return.

  Note: An Income and Deductions printout is available from Canada Revenue Agency. Please call customer service at 1-800-959-8281.

OR

☐ I am an Indian within the meaning of the *Indian Act* (Canada) and I have chosen not to file income tax returns for the past three years. I am attaching the following proof of income for the last three years *(list documents you have provided)*:

(In this table you must show all of the income that you are currently receiving whether taxable or not.)

	Income Source	**Amount Received/Month**
1.	Employment income (before deductions)	
2.	Commissions, tips and bonuses	
3.	Self-employment income (Monthly amount before expenses: $12,500.00)	$12,500.00
4.	Employment Insurance benefits	
5.	Workers' compensation benefits	
6.	Social assistance income (including ODSP payments)	
7.	Interest and investment income	

Form 13:	**Financial Statement**	(page 3)	Court File Number:	**FL28263
	(Support Claims)			

8.	Pension income (including CPP and OAS)	
9.	Spousal support received from a former spouse/partner	
10.	Child Tax Benefits or Tax Rebates (e.g. GST)	
11.	Other sources of income (e.g. RRSP withdrawals, capital gains) (*attach Schedule A and divide annual amount by 12)	
12.	**Total monthly income from all sources:**	**$12,500.00**
13.	**Total monthly income X 12 = Total annual income:**	**$150,000.00**

14.   Other Benefits

Provide details of any non-cash benefits that your employer provides to you or are paid for by your business such as medical insurance coverage, the use of a company car, or room and board.

Item	Details	Yearly Market Value
	Total	**$0.00**

PART 2: EXPENSES

EXPENSE	Monthly Amount
Automatic Deductions	
CPP contributions	
EI premiums	
Income taxes	
Employee pension contributions	
Union dues	
SUBTOTAL	**$0.00**
Housing	
Rent or mortgage	$800.00
Property taxes	$250.00
Property insurance	$150.00
Condominium fees	
Repairs and maintenance	$200.00
SUBTOTAL	**$1,400.00**
Utilities	
Water	$50.00
Heat	$110.00
Electricity	$100.00
Telephone	$71.36
Cell phone	
Cable	$85.00
Internet	
SUBTOTAL	**$416.36**
Household Expenses	
Groceries	$480.00

EXPENSE	Monthly Amount
Household supplies	$100.00
Meals outside the home	$240.00
Pet care	
Laundry and Dry Cleaning	$60.00
SUBTOTAL	**$880.00**
Childcare Costs	
Daycare expense	
Babysitting costs	
SUBTOTAL	**$0.00**
Transportation	
Public transit, taxis	
Gas and oil	$400.00
Car insurance and license	$300.00
Repairs and maintenance	$100.00
Parking	$50.00
Car Loan or Lease Payments	
SUBTOTAL	**$850.00**
Health	
Health insurance premiums	$50.00
Dental expenses	$150.00
Medicine and drugs	$50.00
Eye care	$80.00
SUBTOTAL	**$330.00**
Personal	
Clothing	$150.00
Hair care and beauty	$50.00

Form 13:   **Financial Statement**   (page 4)   Court File Number: ****FL28263**
             (Support Claims)

Alcohol and tobacco		Clothing for children	
Education *(specify)*		Children's activities	$200.00
Entertainment/recreation (including children)	$150.00	Summer camp expenses	$100.00
		Debt payments	$150.00
Gifts	$100.00	Support paid for other children	
		Other expenses not shown above *(specify)*	
SUBTOTAL	**$450.00**	(books/charities)	$100.00
Other expenses		**SUBTOTAL**	**$1,300.00**
Life insurance premiums			
RRSP/RESP withdrawals	$500.00	**Total Amount of Monthly Expenses**	**5,626.36**
Vacations	$250.00	**Total Amount of Yearly Expenses**	**$67,516.32**
School fees and supplies			

PART 3: ASSETS

Type		Details	Value or Amount
		State Address of Each Property and Nature of Ownership	
Real Estate	1	492 Clemens Crescent, Waterwell, ON D7R 6D6 Full value $360,000; joint 50%	$180,000.00
	2		
	3		
		SUBTOTAL	**$180,000.00**
		Year and Make	
Cars, Boats, Vehicles	1	(year) Mercedes 380 SL	$20,000.00
	2	(year) Evinrude 65 HP boat	$4,500.00
	3		
		SUBTOTAL	**$24,500.00**
		Address Where Located	
Other Possessions of Value (e.g. computers, jewellery, collections)	1	Furnishings and appliances at matrimonial home	$17,500.00
	2	Paintings located at matrimonial home	$6,750.00
	3		
		SUBTOTAL	**$24,250.00**
		Type – Issuer – Due Date – Number of Shares	
Investments (e.g. bonds, shares, term deposits and mutual funds)	1	Pref. Shares, Pitt Steele, Jan. 1 (year), 47 shares	$75,000.00
	2	Canada Savings Bonds, Nov. 2 (year)	$10,000.00
	3		
		SUBTOTAL	**$85,000.00**
		Name and Address of Institution - Account Number	
Bank Accounts	1	Regal Bank, 2 Bay St., Waterwell, ON 83444	$1,860.90
	2	Regal Bank, 2 Bay St., Waterwell, ON 965789	$345.98
	3		
		SUBTOTAL	**$2,206.88**
		Type and Issuer - Account Number	
Savings Plans R.R.S.P.s Pension Plans R.E.S.P.s	1	Regal Trust RRSP- Account No. 09571	$9,947.29
	2	Regal Trust RRSP - Account No. 08945	$9,398.33
	3		
		SUBTOTAL	**$19,345.62**
		Type – Beneficiary – Face Amount	*Cash Surrender Value*
Life Insurance	1	London Life, Applicant, $100,000 (Policy No. 4768910)	$400,000.00

| Form 13: | Financial Statement
(Support Claims) | (page 5) | Court File Number: | **FL28263 |

		2		
		3		
			SUBTOTAL	**$400,000.00**
	Name and Address of Business			
Interest in Business (*attach separate year-end statement for each business*)	1	Mark Twain Family Physician 43 Rosemarie Dr., Waterwell, ON D4U 1W6		$50,000.00
	2			
	3			
			SUBTOTAL	**$50,000.00**
	Name and Address of Debtors			
Money Owed to You (*for example, any court judgments in your favour, estate money and income tax refunds*)	1	Ontario Health Insurance Plan (in any one month for services rendered)		$10,000.00
	2			
	3			
			SUBTOTAL	**$10,000.00**
	Description			
Other Assets	1			
	2			
	3			
			SUBTOTAL	**$0.00**

| Total Value of All Property | **$795,302.50** |

PART 4: DEBTS

Type of Debt	Creditor (name and address)	Full Amount Now Owing	Monthly Payments	Are Payments Being Made? (Yes/No)
Mortgages, Lines of Credits or other Loans from a Bank, Trust or Finance Company	Bank of Nova Scotia 4 Third St., Toronto, ON M2U 2W6 Mortgage on house, joint 50% Full amount $220,000	$110,000.00	$1,500.00	Yes
	CIBC, 5 May St. Toronto, ON M2W 2F6 (new car)	$26,000.00	$500.00	Yes
Outstanding Credit Card Balances	MasterCard 8 Kay St., Toronto, ON M6W 3F3	$2,500.00		
	American Express 9 Jay St., Toronto, ON M6W 3F3	$500.00		
	VISA 7 Elm St., Toronto, ON M3F 2U9	$978.15		
Unpaid Support Amounts				

Form 13:	**Financial Statement** (page 6) **(Support Claims)**	Court File Number:	****FL28263**

Other Debts	Mary Twain 4 King St., Hamilton, ON L3W 6F6 Mother (Promissory Note)	$100,000.00		**No**

Total Amount of Debts Outstanding	**$239,978.15**

PART 5: SUMMARY OF ASSETS AND LIABILITIES

Total Assets	**$795,302.50**
Subtract Total Debts	**$239,978.15**
Net Worth	**$555,324.35**

NOTE: *This financial statement must be updated no more than 30 days before any court event by either completing and filing:*
- *a new financial statement with updated information, or*
- *an affidavit in Form 14A setting out the details of any minor changes or confirming that the information contained in this statement remains correct.*

Sworn/Affirmed before me at
City of Toronto

                    (municipality)

  in Province of Ontario

                 (province, state or country)

  on

           (date)

                     Commissioner for taking affidavits
          (Type or print name below if signature is illegible.)

Signature
(This form is to be signed in front of a lawyer, justice of the peace, notary public or commissioner for taking affidavits.)

Schedule C
Special or Extraordinary Expenses for the Child(ren)

Child's Name	Expense	Amount/yr.	Available Tax Credits or Deductions*
1.			
2.			
3.			
4.			
5.			
6.			
7.			
8.			
9.			
10.			
Total Net Annual Amount			**$0.00**
Total Net Monthly Amount			**$0.00**

* Some of these expenses can be claimed in a parent's income tax return in relation to a tax credit or deduction (for example childcare costs). These credits or deductions must be shown in the above chart.

I earn $ _____ per year which should be used to determine my share of the above expenses.

NOTE:

Pursuant to the Child Support Guidelines, a court can order that the parents of a child share the costs of the following expenses for the child:

- Necessary childcare expenses;
- Medical insurance premiums and certain health-related expenses for the child that cost more than $100 annually;
- Extraordinary expenses for the child's education;
- Post-secondary school expenses; and,
- Extraordinary expenses for extracurricular activities.

Schedule A
Additional Sources of Income

Line	Income Source	Annual Amount
1.	Net partnership income	
2.	Net rental income (Gross annual rental income of $ ___)	
3.	Total amount of dividends received from taxable Canadian corporations	
4.	Total capital gains ($ ___) less capital losses ($ ___)	
5.	Registered retirement savings plan withdrawals	
6.	Income from a Registered Retirement Income Fund or Annuity	
7.	Any other income (specify source)	
	Subtotal	

Schedule B
Other Income Earners in the Home

Complete this part only if you are making or responding to a claim for undue hardship or spousal support. Check and complete all sections that apply to your circumstances.

1. ☐ I live alone.
2. ☐ I am living with (full legal name of person you are married to or cohabiting with)
3. ☐ I/we live with the following other adult(s):
4. ☐ I/we have (give number) _____ of child(ren) who live(s) in the home.
5. ☐ My spouse/partner works at (place of work or business)
   ☐ does not work outside the home.
6. ☐ My spouse/partner earns (give amount) $ _____ per _____
   ☐ does not earn any income.
7. ☐ My spouse/partner or other adult residing in the home contributes about $ _____ per _____ towards the household expenses.

ONTARIO

Ontario Family Court of the Superior Court of Justice
(Name of Court)

Court File Number
FL12234

at **50 Eagle Street West, Newmarket, Ontario L3Y 6B1**
(Court office address)

Form 14: Notice of Motion

Applicant(s)

Full legal name & address for service — street & number, municipality, postal code, telephone & fax numbers and e-mail address (if any).	Lawyer's name & address — street & number, municipality, postal code, telephone & fax numbers and e-mail address (if any).
Alvin Tophler **45 Adler Avenue** **Waterwell, Ontario** **D2K 2D1** **Tel: (905) 436-3632**	**Robert B. Redford** **Michael, Eliad & Redford LLP** **863 Seneca Lane** **Toronto, Ontario M4J 1P6** **Tel: (416) 363-1079** **Fax: (416) 363-2628** **rbrdfrd@mer.com**

Respondent(s)

Full legal name & address for service — street & number, municipality, postal code, telephone & fax numbers and e-mail address (if any).	Lawyer's name & address — street & number, municipality, postal code, telephone & fax numbers and e-mail address (if any).
Virginia Annie Tophler **99 Crimson Road** **Broda, Ontario** **D3B 1W8** **Tel: (905) 892-6323**	

The person making this motion or the person's lawyer must contact the clerk of the court by telephone or otherwise to choose a time and date when the court could hear this motion.

TO THE PARTIES:

THE COURT WILL HEAR A MOTION on *(date)* November 24, 20--

at *(time)* 10 a.m. **, or as soon as possible after that time at:** *(place of hearing)*

50 Eagle Street West, Newmarket, Ontario L3Y 6B1

This motion will be made by *(name of person making motion)* Alvin Tophler
who will be asking the court for an order for the item(s) listed on page 2 of this notice

[X] A copy of the affidavit(s) in support of this motion is served with this notice.

[ ] A notice of a case conference is served with this notice to change an order.

If this material is missing, you should talk to the court office immediately.

The person making this motion is also relying on the following documents in the continuing record: *(List documents)*
Copy of separation agreement.

If you want to oppose this motion or to give your own views, you should talk to your own lawyer and prepare your own affidavit, serve it on all other parties not later than 4 days before the date above and file it at the court office not later than 2 days before that date. Only written and affidavit evidence will be allowed at a motion unless the court gives permission for oral testimony. You may bring your lawyer to the motion.

IF YOU DO NOT COME TO THE MOTION, THE COURT MAY MAKE AN ORDER WITHOUT YOU AND ENFORCE IT AGAINST YOU.

_____ *Date of signature* _____ *Signature of person making this motion or of person's lawyer*	**Robert B. Redford** **Michael, Eliad & Redford LLP** **863 Seneca Lane** **Toronto, Ontario M4J 1P6** **Tel: (416) 363-1079** **Fax: (416) 363-2628** **rbrdfrd@mer.com** *Typed or printed name of person or of person's lawyer, address for service, telephone & fax number & e-mail address (if any)*

FLR 14 (June 15, 2007)

www.DIVORCEmate.com

Form 14: Notice of Motion (page 2)   Court File Number   ****FL12234**

NOTE TO PERSON MAKING THIS MOTION: *You MUST file a Confirmation (Form 14C) not later than 2:00 p.m. two days before the date set out above.*

If this is a motion to change past and future support payments under an order that has been assigned to a government agency, you must also serve this notice on that agency. If you do not, the agency can ask the court to set aside any order that you may get in this motion and can ask for court costs against you.

State the order or orders requested on this motion.

1. An Order compelling the Respondent to return John Tophler, born June 10, (5 years ago), to the interim custody of the Applicant until such time as a final order of custody is made.

2. An Order authorizing the Applicant to apprehend John Tophler, born June 10, (5 years ago), and authorizing the Sheriff to apprehend the said child and deliver him to the Applicant who was awarded interim custody of the said child, subject to access by the Respondent.

3. An Interim Order restraining the Respondent, her servants and agents, and any person acting on her behalf, from removing or causing the removal of the said child from the care of the Applicant and from interfering in any manner whatsoever with the Applicant's interim custody, care, or control of the said child.

4. Costs of this Motion.

ONTARIO

Ontario Family Court of the Superior Court of Justice	Court File Number
(Name of Court)	****FL12234**

at   50 Eagle Street West, Newmarket, Ontario L3Y 6B1

         (Court office address)

Form 14A: Affidavit (General)

dated ....

Applicant(s)

Full legal name & address for service — street & number, municipality, postal code, telephone & fax numbers and e-mail address (if any).	Lawyer's name & address — street & number, municipality, postal code, telephone & fax numbers and e-mail address (if any).
Alvin Tophler **45 Adler Avenue** **Waterwell, Ontario** **D2K 2D1** **Tel: (905) 436-3632**	**Robert B. Redford** **Michael, Eliad & Redford LLP** **863 Seneca Lane** **Toronto, Ontario M4J 1P6** **Tel: (416) 363-1079** **Fax: (416) 363-2628** **rbrdfrd@mer.com**

Respondent(s)

Full legal name & address for service — street & number, municipality, postal code, telephone & fax numbers and e-mail address (if any).	Lawyer's name & address — street & number, municipality, postal code, telephone & fax numbers and e-mail address (if any).
Virginia Annie Tophler **99 Crimson Road** **Broda, Ontario D3B 1W8** **Tel: (905) 892-6323**	

My name is

(Full legal name)   **Alvin Tophler**

I live in

(municipality and province)   **Waterwell, Ontario**

and I swear/affirm that the following is true:

Set out the statements of fact in consecutively numbered paragraphs. Where possible, each numbered paragraph should consist of one complete sentence and be limited to a particular statement of fact. If you learned a fact from someone else, you must give that person's name and state that you believe that fact to be true.

1. I am the father of John Tophler who was born on June 10, (5 years ago), and who is the child of my marriage to the Respondent.

2. The Respondent is the mother of the child.

3. The Respondent and I entered into a Separation Agreement on September 28, 20--, whereby I was awarded interim custody of the child, subject to access by the Respondent.

4. On or about the 30th day of September, (year), the Respondent moved out of the matrimonial home to live with Mr. Anthony Queen in the City of Broda, in the Province of Ontario. From the conversations I have had with the Respondent, I believe that she and Mr. Queen have lived together since September 30, 20--.

5. On or about the 15th day of December, 20--, the Respondent and Mr. Queen took my son, John Tophler, to Broda, Ontario, for a visit, and the Respondent telephoned me later on that date stating that she intended to keep my son there with her and Mr. Queen. The Respondent has not returned my son, John Tophler, to me to date.

6. I request that this Honourable Court order the Respondent to return my son, John Tophler, to me at once as I am the lawful interim custodial parent as per the Separation Agreement dated September 28, 20--.

.Put a line through any blank space on this page.

Sworn/Affirmed before me at:

City of Toronto

                       (municipality)

in   Province of Ontario

                  (province, state or country)

on ....

           (date)

Commissioner for taking affidavits

(Type or print name below if signature illegible.)

Signature

(This form to be signed in front of a lawyer, justice of the peace, notary public or commissioner for taking affidavits.)

FLR 14A (September 1, 2005)

	ONTARIO	Court File Number
SEAL	**Ontario Family Court of the Superior Court of Justice** *(Name of Court)*	****FL12234**
	at **50 Eagle Street West, Newmarket, Ontario L3Y 6B1** *(Court office address)*	**Form 25: Order (General)** [X] **Temporary** [ ] **Final**

Applicant(s)

(Full legal name & address for service: street, number, municipality, postal code telephone & fax numbers & e-mail address (if any).)*	*Lawyer's name & address: street, number, municipality, postal code, telephone & fax numbers & e-mail address (if any).*
Alvin Tophler **45 Adler Avenue** **Waterwell, Ontario** **D2K 2D1** **Tel: (905) 436-3632**	**Robert B. Redford** **Michael, Eliad & Redford LLP** **863 Seneca Lane** **Toronto, Ontario M4J 1P6** **Tel: (416) 363-1079** **Fax: (416) 363-2628** **rbrdfrd@mer.com**

The Honourable

Justice Rumpleson

Judge (Print or type name)

November 24, (year)

Date of order

Respondent(s)

Full legal name & address for service: street, number, municipality, postal code telephone & fax numbers & e-mail address (if any).	*Lawyer's name & address: street, number, municipality, postal code, telephone & fax numbers & e-mail address (if any).*
Virginia Annie Tophler **99 Crimson Road** **Broda, Ontario** **D3B 1W8** **Tel: (905) 892-6323**	

The court heard an application/motion made by *(name of person or persons)*

Alvin Tophler

The following persons were in court *(names of parties and lawyers in court)*

Robert B. Redford, lawyer for Alvin Tophler

The court received evidence and heard submissions on behalf of *(name or names)*

Alvin Tophler

THE COURT ORDERS THAT:

1. The Respondent forthwith delivers up to the Applicant the interim custody, care, and control of John Tophler, born June 10, (5 years ago).

2. The Sheriff or any law enforcement officer in the Province of Ontario be and is hereby directed to deliver John Tophler, born June 10, (5 years ago), into the care of the Applicant.

3. The Respondent, her servants and agents, and any person acting on her behalf, be and is hereby restrained from removing or causing the removal of the said child from the care of the Applicant and from interfering in any manner whatsoever with the Applicant's interim custody, care, or control of the said child.

4. There be no Order as to costs.

Put a line through any blank space left on this page.

Date of signature	*Signature of judge or clerk of the court*

FLR 25 (September 1, 2005)

www.DIVORCEmate.com

demande dans votre cause ou la date de la conférence relative à la cause dans l'Avis de conférence relative à la cause.

You must bring your copy of this form to the Mandatory Information Program. The certificate of attendance at the end of the form will be stamped and returned to you at the end of the session. You are required to file the stamped form with the court before you can take any further steps in your case, except a respondent may serve and file an answer and a party may schedule a case conference.

Vous devez apporter avec vous une copie du présent formulaire à la séance du Programme d'information obligatoire. Le certificat de participation qui figure au bas du formulaire sera estampillé. Vous devrez récupérer celui-ci à la fin de la séance. Vous devez déposer le formulaire dûment estampillé auprès du tribunal avant de pouvoir poursuivre votre affaire, à deux exceptions près : l'intimé pourra signifier et déposer sa réponse et une partie pourra inscrire au rôle une conférence relative à la cause.

Note to the applicant: You are required to serve a copy of the respondent's notice with your application and other documents that may have been filed to start your case.

Remarque à l'attention des requérants : Vous devez joindre une copie de l'avis de l'intimé à votre requête ou à tout autre document que vous avez déposé avec le dossier d'introduction de la cause.

Note to the parties: If you need to reschedule your attendance at the Mandatory Information Program, please call

Avis aux parties: Si vous avez besoin de reprogrammer votre présence à la séance du Programme d'information obligatoire, s'il vous plaît appelez

---

CERTIFICATE OF ATTENDANCE

THIS IS TO CERTIFY THAT ON _____ THE APPLICANT ATTENDED:

[ ] Session 1 Only

[ ] Sessions 1 and 2

OF THE MANDATORY INFORMATION PROGRAM.

(Presenters: Please check the applicable box and sign where indicated)

_____
Signature of Presenter

CERTIFICAT DE PARTICIPATION

PAR LA PRÉSENTE, IL EST CONFIRMÉ QUE, LE _____, LE REQUÉRANT OU LA REQUÉRANTE A PARTICIPÉ À:

[ ] *Seulement séance 1*

[ ] *Séances 1 et 2*

UNE SÉANCE DU PROGRAMME D'INFORMATION OBLIGATOIRE.

(Présentateurs : S'il vous plaît cocher la case appropriée et signer à l'endroit indiqué.)

_____
Signature du présentateur

Applicant's Notice / *Avis du requérant*

Ontario Court of Justice
Cour de Justice de l'Ontario

at / situé(e) au 50 Eagle Street West
Newmarket, Ontario L3Y 6B1

Court File Number / *Numéro de dossier du greffe*

APPLICANT'S MIP NOTICE /
AVIS DU REQUÉRANT - PIO
Mandatory Information Program /
Programme d'information obligatoire

Applicant(s) / *Requérant(e)(s)*

Full legal name and address for service — street and number, municipality, postal code, telephone and fax numbers and e-mail address (if any).
Nom et prénom officiels et adresse aux fins de signification — numéro et rue, municipalité, code postal, numéros de téléphone et de télécopieur et adresse électronique (le cas échéant).

Maria Shelley Havisham
333 GST Drive
Newmarket, Ontario
L2K 2D1

Lawyer's name and address — street and number, municipality, postal code, telephone and fax numbers and e-mail address (if any).
Nom et adresse de l'avocat(e) — numéro et rue, municipalité, code postal, numéros de téléphone et de télécopieur et adresse électronique (le cas échéant).

Robert B. Redford
Michael, Eliad & Redford LLP
863 Seneca Lane
Toronto, Ontario M4J 1P6
Tel: (416) 363-1079 / Fax: (416) 363-2628
rbredford@amer.com

Respondent(s) / *Intimé(e)(s)*

Full legal name and address for service — street and number, municipality, postal code, telephone and fax numbers and e-mail address —
Nom et prénom officiels et adresse aux fins de signification — numéro et rue, municipalité, code postal, numéros de téléphone et de télécopieur et adresse électronique (le cas échéant).

Lawyer's name and address for service — street and number, municipality, postal code, telephone and fax numbers and e-mail address (if any).
Nom et adresse de l'avocat(e) — numéro et rue, municipalité, code postal, numéros de téléphone et de télécopieur et adresse électronique (le cas échéant).

Brian Havisham
111 Sussex Drive
Ottawa, Ontario
K3B 1W8

TO THE APPLICANT: / *A L'ATTENTION DU REQUÉRANT OU DE LA REQUÉRANTE :*

You are required to attend a **two-hour** Mandatory Information Program (MIP) on:
Vous devez participer à une séance de deux heures du Programme d'information obligatoire (PIO) le

10-APR-20— at 10:00 AM
at/à/au *à*

50 Eagle Street West, Newmarket, Ontario L3Y 6B1

Latecomers will not be admitted.
Les personnes qui arrivent en retard ne seront pas acceptées.

The session will provide you with information about separation, the legal process, and options for resolving differences, including alternatives to going to court. This session will include some general legal information, but not any legal advice or legal services specific to your situation.

Au cours de la séance d'information, plusieurs sujets seront abordés : la séparation, le processus juridique et les divers modes de règlement des différends, y compris les modes de règlement extrajudiciaires. Cette séance comprendra des informations juridiques générales, mais pas tout conseil ou de services juridiques spécifiques à votre situation.

This MIP session does not replace any other court events in your case. You are still required to attend all other scheduled court events, including a first court date or case conference. Check the front page of the application in your case for your first court date or the Case Conference Notice for your case conference date.

La séance du Programme d'information obligatoire ne remplace pas d'autres comparutions devant le tribunal dans le cadre de votre dossier. Vous devez assister à toutes les audiences prévues, y compris la première comparution ou la conférence relative à la cause. Vous trouverez la date de la première comparution sur la première page de la

---

Legal Office Procedures

CHAPTER 22

COMMENCING A DIVORCE CASE

This chapter covers the steps in starting a divorce case. The following is a summary of the usual steps in which family law cases, including divorce, proceed to trial.

Figure 22.1 Family Law Cases (Including Divorce)

A
- Application (served immediately by special service only)
- Financial Statement, if any
- Affidavit in Support of Claim for Custody or Access, if any

R
- Answer
- Financial Statement, if any
- Affidavit in Support of Claim for Custody or Access, if any
- **30 days** after service of application; 60 days if outside Canada or United States

A
- Reply, if any - (10 days after service of Answer)

MOTIONS, A or R; at any time, but motion may **not** be heard before a case conference is held, unless urgent.
- Notice of Motion and supporting Affidavit, served **4 days** before motion date, filed **2 days** before motion date.
- Confirmation, A and R; served and filed by **2 p.m. 2 days** before motion date.

CASE CONFERENCE, A or R; at any time; exploring chances of settling; setting date for next step in case.
- Case Conference Notice, party who scheduled case conference.
- Case Conference Brief, A and R; served and filed **7 days** before conference date by A; **4 days** before by R.
- Confirmation, A and R; served and filed by **2 p.m. 2 days** before conference date.

SETTLEMENT CONFERENCE, court schedules it at any time; if no settlement, court schedules case for trial.
- Settlement Conference Brief, A and R; served and filed **7 days** before conference date by A; **4 days** before by R.
- Confirmation, A and R; served and filed by **2 p.m. 2 days** before conference date.

TRIAL MANAGEMENT CONFERENCE, A or R; deciding how trial will proceed.
- Trial Management Brief, A and R; served and filed **7 days** before conference date by A; **4 days** before by R.
- Confirmation, A and R; served and filed by **2 p.m. 2 days** before conference date.

Trial Record, A, served and filed **30 days** before trial
TRIAL - conducted as in civil actions

A=Applicant   R=Respondent

COURTS HEARING DIVORCE AND OTHER FAMILY ISSUES

The following courts have jurisdiction to hear divorce cases: the Family Court where it exists and the Superior Court of Justice where a Family Court does not exist. The Ontario Court of Justice has no jurisdiction to hear divorce cases, mainly because divorce is under federal jurisdiction (under the *Divorce Act* of Canada), and the judges in the Ontario Court of Justice are provincially, as opposed to federally, appointed and have only provincial jurisdiction.

DIVORCE

It is obvious but sometimes overlooked that only married spouses may be divorced. Divorce is a legal termination of a marriage. Upon obtaining a certificate of divorce, the former spouses are free to remarry each other or others if they wish. The provision for divorce is under federal jurisdiction and is provided for under the *Divorce Act* of Canada, whereas the procedural steps for obtaining a divorce are under provincial jurisdiction and are prescribed by the Ontario *Family Law Rules*. The procedure for obtaining a divorce is, therefore, the same throughout the province of Ontario.

GROUNDS FOR DIVORCE

The *Divorce Act* (Canada) permits divorce on the following grounds: (1) separation of one year, (2) adultery, or (3) physical or mental cruelty.

> **Legal TIP**
>
> If the relationship has ended but both spouses are still living under the same roof, they may still be considered to be living separate and apart if they are no longer behaving as though they were married.

Separation of one year   Generally, separation means living in separate places. Regardless of which spouse separated from the other, either spouse may claim separation of one year as a ground for divorce. Either spouse may file for divorce before a full year of separation has occurred, but the divorce cannot be granted until a separation of one year has elapsed. To encourage the spouses to reconcile or to try to make the marriage work again, the spouses may, at any time during their separation, resume living together for 90 days or less. If the reconciliation does not work out, the spouses can continue to count the one-year period starting from the date of the original separation. If, however, the spouses stay together for more than the 90 days, they have to start counting the one year again.

Adultery   Adultery happens when the husband or the wife willingly has sexual intercourse with someone else -- even if this happens after the husband and wife have separated. Adultery must be proved. Typically, it may be proved by having the spouse who committed it admit that fact, usually by way of an affidavit. If the adulterous spouse will not admit to the adultery, then the spouse claiming adultery as the ground must prove it some other way, e.g by having witnesses testify that they actually know the adultery happened. Only the spouse who did not commit adultery may claim adultery as a ground for divorce. Thus, the adulterous spouse cannot benefit from his or her own act of adultery. If the ground for divorce is adultery, the applicant may, usually for purposes of exposure, name the person with whom adultery is alleged to have been committed. In that case, the applicant must serve the named person with the application, usually without the financial statement, if any. That person then has all of the rights of a respondent in the case. There is no waiting period where the ground for divorce is adultery, except for the time it takes to process the case.

Physical or mental cruelty   Only the spouse who has suffered physical or mental cruelty may use it as a ground for divorce. This, too, is intended not to benefit the spouse who has inflicted cruelty. Physical or mental cruelty must be proved; mental cruelty is more

Legal Office Procedures

difficult to prove than physical cruelty. The spouse claiming physical or mental cruelty must prove that the behaviour of the offending spouse made it unbearable or intolerable for the non-offending spouse to go on living together. There is no waiting period where the ground for divorce is physical or mental cruelty, except for the time it takes to process the case.

No collusion, connivance, or condonation It is important to note that the *Divorce Act* requires that there be no collusion, connivance, or condonation involved between the spouses when seeking divorce. Generally, collusion means the spouses have made an arrangement or agreement to fabricate a ground for divorce, e.g. adultery that never happened, to speed up the divorce (instead of having to wait until a year of separation has passed). Connivance, albeit rare, is when one spouse encourages the other one to commit a marital offence, e.g. adultery or cruelty, for the purpose of obtaining a divorce. Condonation is when, for example, a husband learns his wife has committed adultery but decides to forgive it and continues to have sexual relations with her. In effect, this means that he may have forgiven her in a legal sense and be unable to get a divorce based on that adultery.

CLAIMS UNDER DIFFERENT STATUTES

In the interest of resolving all family-related issues in a single case, the applicant may combine the claims provided under the *Divorce Act* (Canada) as well as those provided under provincial laws, namely, the Ontario *Family Law Act* (FLA) and the Ontario *Children's Law Reform Act* (CLRA).

Claims under *Divorce Act* (Canada) The *Divorce Act* (Canada), which is a federal act, provides for the following claims: divorce, support, custody, and access (the last three are referred to as "corollary relief"). The applicant may make a claim only for divorce, provided financial support arrangements have been put in place for any children, or all of the claims under the *Divorce Act*.

Claims under provincial acts The FLA provides for such **money-related** claims as spousal and child support and for division of family property which is why there is a requirement for the serving and filing of financial statements. The FLA does not provide for custody or access. The CLRA provides for custody and access, which are **people-related** claims special to children. The applicant may make claims under any one or both of these acts, or under all three acts, to cover rights under both federal as well as provincial jurisdictions.

Overlapping claims While claims for support, custody, and access between federal and provincial statutes overlap, it is important to note that the basic claims which are provided under the *Divorce Act* (Canada), i.e. divorce, custody, child support, and spousal support, aim to be uniformly available to spouses and children throughout Canada and that the powers granted under the *Divorce Act* supersede powers granted under corresponding provincial statutes. The provincial statutes duplicate and expand on these claims (minus divorce) mainly to ensure and protect the welfare of any children involved and to ensure that spouses look to each other for spousal and child support and not to the provincial government.

CUSTODY

Generally, under the *Divorce Act*, **custody** means the legal ability and responsibility to make major decisions for a child's care and upbringing such as where the child will live, where the child will go to school, what medical treatment the child will receive, and what religion the child will follow. Thus, custody is about which parent has the decision-making authority about the child's care and upbringing rather than about which parent the child lives with or how much time the child spends with each parent. Generally, however, the type of custody ordered e.g. sole custody or joint custody, usually also determines which parent the child will live with or how much time the child will spend with each parent. There are different types of custody, and understanding them will help you in your work in family cases.

Sole custody This type of custody means one parent has the unshared, hence, **sole**, responsibility and authority to make major decisions about the child's care and how the child will be raised. Typically, the child lives primarily with the parent who has sole custody, and the other parent has the right to access. The parent having sole custody is referred to as the **custodial parent** and the other parent as the **non-custodial, or access, parent**. The non-custodial parent usually has the right to know about the decisions the custodial parent makes and express an opinion, but the custodial parent has the right to make all final decisions. Under the *Divorce Act*, custodial parents must, nevertheless, act in a way that encourages the child in his or her relationship with the other parent.

Joint custody This means both parents equally share the responsibility for making important decisions for a child, e.g. where the child goes to school, medical treatment, religious upbringing, no matter which parent the child lives with. Joint custody is more about who can make decisions concerning the child than it is about the time the child spends with each parent. The child might live half the time with each parent or most of the time with one parent. Either way, both parents have the right to make decisions about important matters concerning their child. The courts are usually reluctant to make joint custody orders unless the parents are able to cooperate on matters involving the care and upbringing of their child.

Shared custody Generally, this means both parents have joint custody of the child, e.g. making major decisions about the child as well as both parents spend fairly equal time with the child, e.g. the child lives one week with one parent and the following week with the other parent; in effect, the child has two homes. Under the *Federal Child Support Guidelines*, shared custody is where a child lives at least 40 percent of the time with each parent over the course of a year. Note that under the *Federal Child Support Guidelines*, the amount of time a child spends with each parent is usually linked to the amount of child support to be paid by the parent ordered to pay: for example, where the child spends at least 40 percent of the time with each parent, the amount of child support to be paid by the parent ordered to pay may be lowered because the expenses associated with taking care of the child would be more or less equal between both parents.

Split custody Generally, split custody is where, under the *Federal Child Support Guidelines*, some of the children live with one parent more than 60 percent of the time over the course of a year, and the remaining children live with the other parent more than 60 percent of the time over the course of a year. Each parent has sole custody in terms of making decisions for the care and upbringing of the children who live with that parent. Often, this arrangement is that the children are together on weekends alternating between their parents' homes, but they live separately during the week. Courts are reluctant to make split custody orders as it means splitting the children up. The courts may consider making split custody orders, however, where the children are old enough to express an opinion about which parent they wish to live with.

ACCESS

Generally, access means the right of the non-custodial parent to have contact with the child, e.g. visit and spend time with the child, usually on specified days, and to receive information about the child's health, education, and general situation. If the court is worried about the child's safety with the access parent, or if the access parent and the child have not spent much time together, the court can order supervised access. The person who supervises the visits can be a member of the family or someone else. Supervised visits can also occur at supervised access centres where staff monitor the visits. In the case where the custodial parent does not allow access of the child to the non-custodial parent as ordered to do so, the non-custodial parent can ask the court to transfer custody of the child over to the non-custodial parent.

PRELIMINARY CONSIDERATIONS IN A DIVORCE CASE

Who may file for divorce   If the ground for divorce is separation of one year, either spouse may file for divorce as soon as the spouses separate; however, the court will grant the divorce only after one full year's separation has elapsed. If the ground for divorce is adultery, the adulterous spouse cannot file for divorce. Similarly, if the ground for divorce is physical or mental cruelty, the spouse who inflicted the cruelty cannot file for divorce.

Central Registry of Divorce Proceedings   Whenever a party applies for a divorce anywhere in Canada, the Central Registry of Divorce Proceedings at the federal Department of Justice is notified. The purpose of the registry is to prevent spouses from knowingly or unknowingly starting two separate divorce cases. For this to work, the lawyer prepares a **registration of divorce proceeding form** which the court clerk sends to the Central Registry of Divorce Proceedings, and the Central Registry of Divorce Proceedings issues a clearance certificate to the court where the divorce case was commenced. Where the spouses have each commenced separate divorce proceedings, the spouse who first registered a registration of divorce proceeding form with the Central Registry of Divorce Proceedings is deemed to be the first to have initiated the divorce, and that spouse receives a clearance certificate to proceed. The court will not grant a divorce until a clearance certificate has been filed.

Office of the Children's Lawyer   If the application for divorce includes a claim for custody or access, either spouse or the court may ask the Office of the Children's Lawyer to investigate both spouses and prepare a report making recommendations as to what parenting arrangements would be best for the children. The Office of the Children's Lawyer files the report with the court and sends copies to the lawyers for the parties. Either spouse may dispute any statement in the report by sending a formal dispute of the report to the court and to the Office of the Children's Lawyer.

Limitation period   Once divorced, if the spouses have not resolved other issues, e.g. property division, the spouse wishing to make a claim must do so within two years of the effective date of the divorce or lose the right to do so. Here is a case in point:

In *Iafrate v Iafrate*, a Hamilton, Ontario, case, Judge Patricia Wallace rejected Mr. Anzelmo Iafrate's bid to have his wife's support and property division action dismissed because it was out of time. The divorce judgment was given on November 27, 1986. Mrs. Iafrate started the action on December 20, 1988. Judge Wallace ruled that the limitation period had not expired since the two-year limitation period runs from the date the divorce takes **effect**, which according to the certificate of divorce was December 28, 1988. This put Mrs. Iafrate's claim within the limitation period by eight days.

Marriage certificate   Contact your client to bring in the marriage certificate, Precedent 22.1. Clients sometimes hear you in disbelief that this would be the occasion for which they need their marriage certificate. You must file the original marriage certificate in court, usually at the time of sealing the application. The judge needs to see the marriage certificate as proof of marriage before granting the divorce.

Obtaining a copy of the marriage certificate   Sometimes the client cannot provide the marriage certificate, either because he or she has lost it, or the other spouse has it and will not release it. To obtain a copy of the marriage certificate, and if the marriage took place in Ontario, you may apply online to the Office of the Registrar General and send in your application for marriage certificate electronically, and you may charge the applicable fee on your credit card. Be sure to print and retain a copy of the payment receipt for purposes of tracking the progress of your application, which you are able to do using the ministry's Online Status inquiry. The application requires information about the bride and groom, date and place of marriage, etc. In certain cases, such as when the applicant is not paying by credit card or supporting documentation is required to be attached to the application, you may print and complete a hard copy of the request/application for marriage certificate and mail it to the Office of the Registrar General instead of submitting it online.

STARTING THE DIVORCE CASE

A divorce case may be started in the municipality where the applicant lives. If, in addition to divorce, the applicant also claims custody or access and the children live with the other spouse, the place to start the divorce case must be where the children live. This minimizes disruption to the children who might be required to testify at trial. Following is an outline of the basic steps involved in starting a divorce case:

Step 1 Have the following   • Application, including any attachments
documents ready: • Registration of divorce proceeding form
• Marriage certificate
• Court fees.

Step 2 Take the above documents to the court office. The court clerk assigns a file number, puts the court seal on the application, and returns the sealed application to you. The court clerk may give the applicant two notices — one for the applicant with a date to attend the mandatory information program, and another, with a different date, which the applicant must provide to the respondent, for the respondent to attend the mandatory information program. See Chapter 21.

Step 3 Serve one sealed copy of the application, including any attachments, on the respondent by special service.

Step 4 File in court an affidavit of service by the person who effected service.

Step 5 Wait for the respondent to serve and file an answer.

> HAVISHAM, Maria Shelley
> Re: Divorce
>
> We act for Mrs. Havisham who is filing for divorce from her husband, Mr. Brian Havisham. In her application (general), Form 8, Precedent 22.3, Mrs. Havisham's claim includes divorce, custody, support, and division of property. Mrs. Havisham wants custody of the four children: John, Paul, George, and Ryan, who are presently living with her. According to Mrs. Havisham, Mr. Havisham earns more than enough to enable him to support Mrs. Havisham and their four children. Mrs. Havisham is unable to work because she is managing the children's music careers. We have prepared the financial statement, Form 13.1, Precedent 22.4, and the affidavit in support of claim for custody or access, Form 35.1, Precedent 22.5, and have served all of the documents, together with the continuing record, Precedent 22.2. Note that Mrs. Havisham must attend the mandatory information program; see the applicant's notice in Chapter 21. Watch for Mr. Havisham's answer in the next chapter.

APPLICATION (GENERAL)

Under Rule 8 of the *Family Law Rules*, most cases, including divorce cases, begin with a **Form 8: application (general)**, Precedent 22.3. The party suing is the **applicant**, and the party being sued is the **respondent**. An application (general) may be used where the applicant is asking for divorce as well as custody, support, or division of property. The court clerk seals (issues) the application by placing the court seal on it and gives the case a court file number. That court file number must appear on all subsequent documents in the case.

PREPARATION AND DISTRIBUTION OF APPLICATION (GENERAL), FORM 8

You require: Interview notes or draft of application general as hand-completed by client. Follow along in Precedent 22.3. The wording guides completion. Notes on items not self-explanatory follow:

No first court date — first court date applies only to fast track cases; divorce is standard track. Check the standard track box. Check the "includes a claim for property..." box.
Family history - provide details as required.

Claims under the *Divorce Act* — Check the appropriate claim boxes, e.g. if application includes a claim for divorce, check the 00 divorce box, if spousal support, check the 01 support for me box; if support for children according to *Child Support Guidelines*, check the 02, if not, check 03 box; if custody, check 04 box, etc.

Claims under the *Family Act* or *Children's Law Reform Act* — Generally, if you have checked any boxes from 01 to 05, you usually also check the same claim boxes (boxes 10 to 14) under the *Family Law Act* or *Children's Law Reform Act* column; if a claim for restraining order, check box 15, etc.

Claims relating to property — Check boxes 20 to 24 as applicable. Always check the costs box.

Give details of order sought in narrative form. Check the applicable grounds for divorce box, and give details under **important facts supporting my other claims**, if any.

> **Legal TIP**
>
> Checking box 20 usually means the case requires a **net family property statement**.

Number of copies, minimum 3: original in continuing record, 1 served on respondent, 1 in client file.

FINANCIAL STATEMENT

Rule 13 of the *Family Law Rules* provides for the requirement of financial statements. For a detailed discussion on financial statements, refer to Chapter 21. If the applicant is claiming support or a division of property, the applicant must serve and file a **Form 13.1: financial statement (property and support claims)**. The respondent must also serve and file a Form 13.1: financial statement (property and support claims) whether or not the respondent intends to file an answer in the case. Attach to Form 13.1 proof of current income as follows:

- Income tax returns for each of the past three taxation years,
- Copy of the party`s notices of assessment and any notices of reassessment for each of the past three taxation years, and if these are unavailable for any of the past three taxation years, an
- Income deductions printout from the Canada Revenue Agency for each of those years.

Serve Form 13.1 and the proof of **income** documents with the application, along with a certificate of financial disclosure, Form 13A, which is a checklist for all of the income and property disclosure documents provided. Serve the disclosure of **property** documents, along with a Form 13A, within 30 days after service of the financial statement Form 13.1.

PREPARATION AND DISTRIBUTION OF FINANCIAL STATEMENT (PROPERTY AND SUPPORT CLAIMS), FORM 13.1

You require: Interview notes or draft of Form 13.1 as hand-completed by client. Follow along in Precedent 22.4. The wording guides completion. Notes on items not self-explanatory follow:

Use this form where the applicant is claiming property or exclusive possession of matrimonial home and its contents, whether or not a claim for support is also included. To get a monthly figure, you must multiply any weekly income by 4.33 or divide any yearly income by 12. Period of 12 months may be from any month in a year, e.g. July (last year) to June (this year); January (this year) to December (this year). If you are using DIVORCEmate software, the software has an automated conversion of numbers feature. If you input w, b, or y (weekly, bi-weekly, yearly) after the number, the program will convert it to a monthly number once you click the "calculate" button, e.g. $2000y will calculate to $166.67 monthly; $10w will calculate to $43.30 monthly. DIVORCEmate automatically calculates all numbers inserted in Form 13.1 (and Form 13), including automatically deducting the debts and liabilities from the assets.

Generally, the client estimates the value of most items, but firms have lists of accredited appraisers of household items, business evaluators, and real estate appraisers which they provide to the client for items that require professional opinions such as works of art or antiques. For pre-owned cars, the value would be as listed in the Canadian Black Book (commonly referred to as the "black book").

Part 1: Income, Part 2: Expenses – These parts are identical to those in Form 13. See Chapter 21 for details.

Part 3: Other income earners in the home - This part is identical to **Schedule B** in Form 13. See Chapter 21 for details.

Part 4: Assets In and Out of Ontario – Part 4 (a): List all real property the client owned and the respective estimated market value on the --
"date of marriage" if the client owned the property at the date of marriage.
"valuation date," i.e. date of separation. If your client is the non-owner spouse of the matrimonial home, do not include the matrimonial home. (The estimated market value on the matrimonial home will come up in the financial statement that the **owner** spouse must file.) Unless otherwise specified in the title document, e.g. transfer/deed, the percentage share in joint tenancy or tenancy in common is usually 50 percent. If your client is a joint owner in the matrimonial home or other land, put half the estimated market value here and show the full value in the "Address of Property" column. (Do not deduct any charge/mortgage here as it will be deducted under "Debts and Other Liabilities.")
"today" put the value of the property as of the date you prepare Form 13.1 but only if your client still has an interest in that property.

Part 4 (b): General Household Items and Vehicles – Note the following in this category: "Household goods & furniture" the value should be that which the client would get if he or she were to sell the item/s, not the replacement value. Cars, etc. - value should be that of obtaining a comparable car or "black book" value. Jewellery, etc. - value should be what a jeweller or private buyer would pay if the jewellery was placed for sale. Put private buyer value for other items as well, except works of art or antiques - these may require value of professional appraisers.

Part 4 (c): Bank Accounts, Savings, Securities and Pensions etc. – For bank accounts as at the date of marriage, list only if the client still has those bank accounts in the amounts as at the date of marriage according to bank records or client records. Securities includes shares, stocks, bonds, GICs. Pensions means private pensions with the client's employer (in addition to any registered pension plans).

Part 4 (d) to (g) same procedure as for 4 (a) to 4 (c).

Part 5: Debts and Other Liabilities – List all of your client's debts on the date of marriage, valuation date, and today. Include your client's share of any charges/mortgages on the matrimonial home only if your client is listed as owner under "Land." If your client is jointly liable for any charge/mortgage or other debt, indicate the total debt owed in the "details" column and half the debt in the "valuation date" column, "date of marriage" column and "today" column, as the case may be.

Part 6: Property, Debts and Other Liabilities on Date of Marriage – This is a summary of all assets and liabilities (debts) **on the date of marriage**, excluding the matrimonial home. (The owner spouse of the matrimonial home does not get credit for the value of it on the date of marriage if that property was the matrimonial home on the date of separation.) Enter in the "assets" column the total assets for each category listed (the amounts come from the totals of the respective categories in Form 13.1). Enter in the "liabilities" column the total liabilities from the "date of marriage" column of Part 5: Debts and Other Liabilities, excluding any date of marriage charges/mortgages on the matrimonial home.

Part 7: Excluded Property – This part lists the categories of properties that are excluded from net family property. If your client has property in any of these categories, enter the value on valuation date (including any growth during marriage) and provide the applicable details. (To qualify for exclusion, any property in these categories must have been received **after** marriage.) Remember, however, that any excluded property you list in this part, e.g. painting $2,000, you must also have already listed the value of that property, e.g. painting $2,000, under the applicable category in "Part 4(b) General Household Items and Vehicles" so as to cancel it out and therefore not include it in the calculation of the net family property. See Chapter 20 for details on excluded property.

> Part 2: Expenses – Proposed Budget and Financial Statement Summary, Budget: Net Family Property: DIVORCEmate provides these forms at the end of Form 13.1. They are DIVORCEmate forms and are optional. They are not part of the prescribed Form 13.1. If your client is aware of any material changes, either up or down, in the near future, you should complete these pages in order to disclose any material change in circumstances; otherwise, these forms may be omitted.

Schedule A – Additional sources of income: If your client receives income from any of the sources listed on Schedule A, you must complete Schedule A and attach it to the financial statement Form 13.1. Include the annual amount of these additional sources of income on line 11 of "Part 1 Income Source" in Form 13.1, divide the amount by 12 and enter the monthly amount in the "Amount Received/Month" column.

Schedule B – Special or extraordinary expenses for the child(ren): Complete Schedule B only if the client claims special or extraordinary expenses for the child and attach it to the financial statement Form 13.1. The types of special expenses for which your client can make a claim are listed on Schedule B, e.g. childcare expenses, etc. Show the net annual amount, divide the annual amount by 12 and also show the net monthly amount. Also attach to the financial statement proof of the expenses claimed. Note that this schedule is identical to Schedule C in Form 13. Here are the parallel schedules in Forms 13 and 13.1:

Form 13.1	Form 13
Part 3 - Other Income Earners in the Home	Schedule B - Other Income Earners in the Home
Schedule A - Additional Sources of Income	Schedule A - Additional Sources of Income
Schedule B - Special or Extraordinary Expenses for the Child(ren)	Schedule C - Special or Extraordinary Expenses for the Child(ren)

Number of copies, minimum 3: original in continuing record; 1 served (with attachments), 1 in client file.

FORM 35.1: AFFIDAVIT IN SUPPORT OF CLAIM FOR CUSTODY OR ACCESS

Under Rule 35.1 of the *Family Law Rules*, whenever an application or an answer contains a claim for custody or access, the applicant or the respondent, as the case may be, must complete

Legal Office Procedures

a **Form 35.1: affidavit in support of claim for custody or access**, Precedent 22.5. This affidavit is an outline of a parenting plan for the court to consider when making a decision about custody or access. The affidavit requires police records checks for non-parents who may be seeking a custody order and also requires information about any child protection cases in which any person seeking custody or access may have been involved. A child protection case is usually one where a child is or has been at risk of suffering physical, emotional and/or sexual abuse or has not been taken for proper medical care and the Children's Aid Society (CAS) has had to remove the child from the family so as to protect the child.

Part A of the affidavit requires a judge to consider, when assessing a person's ability to act as a parent for a child, whether the person who is asking for custody of or access to a child has committed violence or abuse against the person's spouse or the child. Part B of the affidavit is to be completed only by a non-parent seeking a custody order, and among the information required of a non-parent is a police records check to be attached to Form 35.1.

PREPARATION AND DISTRIBUTION OF AFFIDAVIT IN SUPPORT OF CLAIM FOR CUSTODY OR ACCESS (FORM 35.1)

You require: Interview notes or a draft of Form 35.1 as hand-completed by your client. Follow along in Precedent 22.5. The wording guides completion. Notes on items not self-explanatory follow:

PART A: To be completed by all persons seeking custody or access.
1. If the party has legally changed his or her name or used any other names during his or her life, including when he or she married or remarried, include those names.
2. Full legal name of children means first, middle, if any, and last names.
3. "Acted as a parent." If there are children, other than those already listed in paragraph 2, include information about the applicant's biological children, adopted children, step-children, children who have been in the applicant's legal custody, and children for whom the applicant was named a legal guardian.

4. Include if possible any copies of any child protection, custody or access orders that were made in other family court cases involving the applicant or the children, including copies of any temporary and final orders.
5. If the applicant was the applicant or respondent in a child protection case, then he or she was a party in the child protection court case. If a court placed a child in the applicant's care as part of a child protection case but did not make the applicant a party, then the applicant would be a "person responsible for the care of a child."

6, 7, and 8. State if the applicant or any other party has committed violence or abuse against his or her spouse, a parent of the child in the application, a member of the applicant's household, or any child.
9. Include names of any caregivers of the child. A caregiver includes a parent, legal guardian or CAS. If the child was in the care of CAS, do not include the names of the foster parents; include only the name of the CAS and the approximate dates the child was with that CAS.

10(b). If the applicant is living with another person (other than the child in the application) and does not know if that person has a criminal record, or if any of that person's children were in the care of a CAS, the applicant must ask the person for this information and include it here.
10(f). Outline the plans for the child to have contact or access with his or her parents and with other family or community members if those people are important to the child.

If the applicant has worked out an access schedule with the respondent, include that information here, e.g. Every Friday from 5 p.m. to 8 p.m. and every other weekend from Friday after school to Sunday at 5 p.m.

10(g). Include any special needs, e.g. a medical condition requiring ongoing attention from doctors or visits to a clinic or hospital, or learning difficulties that require placement in a specific class, school, or program.

10(h). Include any family or other members who will help out with babysitting or be available to help in times of emergency. If there is no one, say "not applicable."

PART B: To be completed only by an applicant who is asking for custody of the child and who is not the parent of the child. Parents are not required to complete Part B. The applicant is deemed to be the child's parent if the applicant is the child's biological or adoptive parent. A man is presumed to be a child's father if:

- the man was married to the child's mother at the time the child was born or was married to the child's mother 300 days before the child was born;
- the man was married to the child's mother after the child was born and acknowledged that he was the child's biological father;
- the man was living with the child's mother 300 days before the child was born;
- the man certified on the statement of live birth that he was the child's father, or
- a court has found the man to be the child's father.

12. Indicate if the child for which the applicant is seeking custody has been involved in any custody or access or child protection court cases.

13. Indicate if attaching a police records check to the affidavit and if the applicant has been found guilty of, or charged with, any offences.

15. List any and all CAS in which the applicant has lived since turning 18 or becoming a parent, whichever came first, and whether any CAS has or had any protection records files, open or closed and dates opened or closed, in the name of the applicant. The respective CAS will send a report to the applicant and the court which would include information as to whether the CAS has investigated the applicant on allegations of abuse or neglect of the child, or if the CAS has started a court application involving one or more of the applicant's children, or if one or more of the applicant's children were or are in the care of the CAS.

Number of copies, minimum 3: original in continuing record, 1 served with application, 1 in client file.

AFFIDAVIT OF SERVICE

Rule 6 of the *Family Law Rules* provides for service of documents. Anyone serving documents under the *Family Law Rules* must be at least 18 years old and must complete an affidavit of service (Form 6B), Precedent 22.6. Someone other than the party must effect service of any originating documents or any documents for a proceeding that may lead to the imprisonment of a person, e.g. summons to witness, application, or motion. A process server or a friend or a family member of the party may effect service.

Number of copies, minimum 3: original in continuing record; 1 for process server, if any; 1 in client file.

CONTINUING RECORD

Rule 9 of the *Family Law Rules* provides for a continuing record, Precedent 22.2, to be started, usually with each new application or motion to change a final order. (For purposes of illustrating a cumulative table of contents, the continuing record in Precedent 22.2 lists entries beyond those which would be made at the beginning of the case.) The formal requirements for the continuing record are set out by the Family Rules Committee and are available on the Ontario Court Forms website. The formal requirements basically require that a continuing record be in the form of a three-ring binder containing all of the documents which have been served and filed in court in a case. All documents filed in the continuing record must be punched in standard three-hole format. Law firms usually keep an office copy of the continuing record. The continuing record includes a table of contents which initially the applicant's lawyer starts, serves, and files in court. Once the table of contents has been started, it must be copied and updated whenever a party serves a new document, for example:

Table of contents by applicant:　　　Application
　　　　　　　　　　　　　　　　　Financial Statement

Once the applicant serves these documents on the respondent, along with the table of contents, the respondent will update the table of contents by adding the document which the respondent must file, e.g. answer. The respondent will then serve a copy of the updated table of contents, along with the answer, on the applicant, e.g.

Table of contents by respondent:　　　Application
　　　　　　　　　　　　　　　　　Financial Statement
　　　　　　　　　　　　　　　　　Answer

Order of documents The documents in the continuing record must be filed in chronological order, with the most recently filed document at the back, e.g. documents dated June 1 first, followed by those dated June 2, then June 3, etc. A numbered tab must identify each document filed. Tabs must be in sequential order, e.g Tab 1, Tab 2, etc. A new volume must start with a new tab sequence starting with Tab 1, e.g. Volume 1, Tab 1, Tab 2, etc. Volume 2, Tab 1, Tab 2, etc.

The continuing record consists of two volumes: an endorsements volume basically containing decisions of judges in the case and a documents volume containing all of the documents filed in the case, as follows:

Figure 22.2

SINGLE CONTINUING RECORD
Endorsements Volume - Yellow Cover
1. Cumulative table of contents, listing all documents filed, in the order filed. 2. Endorsements section, containing reasons for judgment and minutes of settlement, including at least three blank sheets on which a judge dealing with any step in the case will note the disposition of that step and the date. 3. Orders section, containing the court's file copy of each order made in the case.
Documents Volume - Red Cover
Contains all documents filed in the case (There is only one cumulative table of contents located in the endorsements volume.) Documents include: applications, answers, replies, affidavits of service, financial statements, motions, affidavits, and trial management conference briefs. Each document is under a separate tab number, except affidavits of service which must be filed within the tab of the document to which they relate, behind the document, and if an affidavit of service relates to more than one document, behind the first, or main, document. (Case conference and settlement conference briefs (and income tax returns) are not filed in the continuing record.)

Separate continuing records   The court may order, or a party may request, that a separate continuing record of the parties be kept, in which case, there would be an applicant's continuing record and a respondent's continuing record. The applicant's continuing record consists of an endorsements volume (to serve both parties, yellow cover) and a documents volume (red cover), whereas the respondent's continuing record consists only of a documents volume (blue cover). Each party files their own documents in their respective documents volume and maintains their own cumulative table of contents and continuing record updated. In all other respects, e.g. volume and tab number, etc. the separate continuing records are the same as the single continuing record.

CHAPTER SUMMARY

Divorce is the legal termination of a marriage, and it is provided for under the *Divorce Act* which is a federal act. The *Divorce Act* permits the following grounds for divorce: (1) separation of one year, (2) adultery, and (3) physical or mental cruelty. Either spouse may file for divorce on the ground of separation; however, a spouse who has committed adultery or has inflicted physical or mental cruelty on the other spouse may **not** file for divorce claiming any of these as a ground for divorce.

The *Divorce Act* also provides for claims for custody, access, and support. The Ontario *Family Law Act* (FLA) provides for support and division of family property. The Ontario *Children's Law Reform Act* (CLRA) provides for claims for custody and access. A person filing for divorce may make claims under all three of these acts.

Most divorce cases begin with an **application (general)**. The *Family Law Rules* govern the court steps to be followed, regardless of the court in which the divorce cases proceed. All divorce cases are under case management. Where a claim for divorce includes support or division of family property, the applicant must serve and file a **Form 13.1 financial statement (property and support claims)**, together with income tax information for the past three years. The opposing spouse must also serve and file the parallel financial statement and income tax information, whether or not the opposing spouse intends to file an answer.

REVIEW QUESTIONS

1. Name all of the grounds for divorce.
2. What is meant by collusion in a claim for divorce?
3. What types of claims under the *Family Law Act* may a spouse include in a divorce proceeding?
4. What types of claims under the *Children's Law Reform Act* may a spouse include in a divorce proceeding?
5. What types of claims require a financial statement?
6. Name the document which begins nearly all divorce cases.
7. Explain how a continuing record is a long police record of offences which an individual has committed.
8. What is a claim for custody?
9. What is a claim for access?
10. What is the purpose of a Form 35.1 affidavit in support of claim for custody or access?

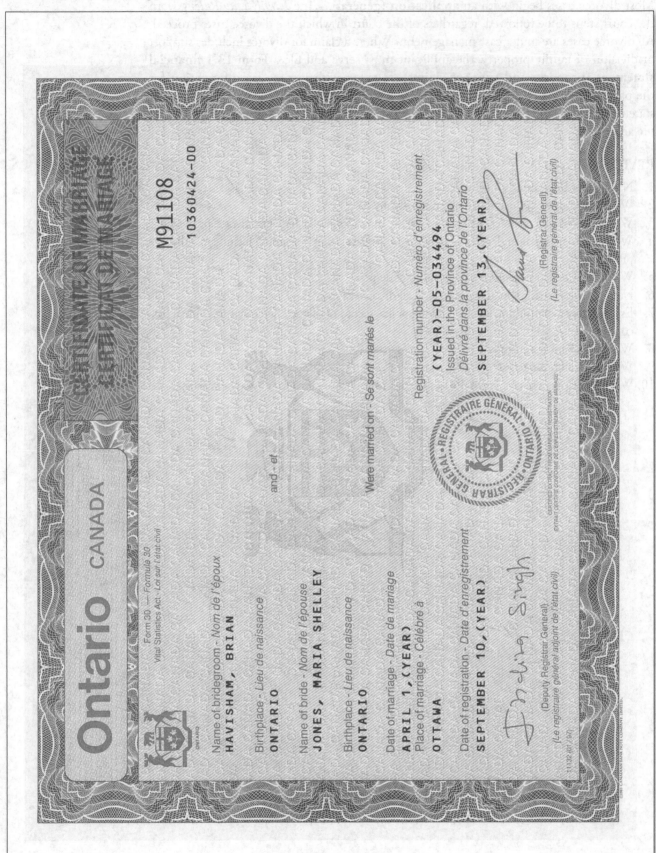

Legal Office Procedures

ONTARIO

Ontario Family Court of the Superior Court of Justice
(Name of Court)

Court File Number

at   **50 Eagle Street West, Newmarket, Ontario L3Y 6B1**
(Court office address)

Volume: .... **1** ....

Applicant(s)

Full legal name & address for service — street & number, municipality, postal code, telephone & fax numbers and e-mail address (if any).	*Lawyer's name & address — street & number, municipality, postal code, telephone & fax numbers and e-mail address (if any).*
Maria Shelley Havisham **333 GST Drive** **Newmarket, Ontario** **L2K 2D1** **Tel: (905) 859-1268**	**Robert B. Redford** **Michael, Eliad & Redford LLP** **863 Seneca Lane** **Toronto, Ontario M4J 1P6** **Tel: (416) 363-1079** **Fax: (416) 363-2628** **rbrdfrd@mer.com**

Respondent(s)

Full legal name & address for service — street & number, municipality, postal code, telephone & fax numbers and e-mail address (if any).	*Lawyer's name & address — street & number, municipality, postal code, telephone & fax numbers and e-mail address (if any).*
Brian Havisham **111 Sussex Drive** **Ottawa, Ontario** **K3B 1W8** **Tel: (613) 580-9334**	

Children's Lawyer

Name & address of Children's Lawyer's agent for service (street & number, municipality, postal code, telephone & fax numbers and e-mail address (if any)) and name of person represented.

Continuing Record

www.DIVORCEmate.com [2007.01.01]

ONTARIO

	Court File Number

Ontario Family Court of the Superior Court of Justice
(Name of Court)

at   **50 Eagle Street West, Newmarket, Ontario L3Y 6B1**
(Court office address)

Cumulative Table of Contents
Continuing Record

Applicant(s)

Full legal name & address for service — street & number, municipality, postal code, telephone & fax numbers and e-mail address (if any).	*Lawyer's name & address — street & number, municipality, postal code, telephone & fax numbers and e-mail address (if any).*
Maria Shelley Havisham **333 GST Drive** **Newmarket, Ontario** **L2K 2D1** **Tel: (905) 859-1268**	**Robert B. Redford** **Michael, Eliad & Redford LLP** **863 Seneca Lane** **Toronto, Ontario M4J 1P6** **Tel: (416) 363-1079** **Fax: (416) 363-2628** **rbrdfrd@mer.com**

Respondent(s)

Full legal name & address for service — street & number, municipality, postal code, telephone & fax numbers and e-mail address (if any).	*Lawyer's name & address — street & number, municipality, postal code, telephone & fax numbers and e-mail address (if any).*
Brian Havisham **111 Sussex Drive** **Ottawa, Ontario** **K3B 1W8** **Tel: (613) 580-9334**	

Document *(For an affidavit or transcript of evidence, include the name of the person who gave the affidavit or the evidence.)*	**Filed by** *(A = applicant or R = respondent)*	**Date of Document** *(d, m, y)*	**Date of Filing** *(d, m, y)*	**Volume/Tab**
Application	A	01/04/--	03/04/--	Volume 1, Tab 1
Affidavit of Service of Application on Respondent	A	02/04/--	03/04/--	Volume 1, Tab 1
Financial Statement	A	01/04/--	03/04/--	Volume 1, Tab 2
Affidavit in Support of Claim for Custody or Access	A	01/04/--	03/04/--	Volume 1, Tab 3
Answer	R	21/04/--	23/04/--	Volume 1, Tab 4
Affidavit of Service of Answer on Applicant	R	22/04/--	23/04/--	Volume 1, Tab 4

    $\boxed{\text{X}}$ *Continued on next sheet*

Precedent 22.2 Continuing Record, page 3

Cumulative Table of Contents (continuing record) (page 2) Court File Number

Document *(For an affidavit or transcript of evidence, include the name of the person who gave the affidavit or the evidence.)*	**Filed by** *(A = applicant or R = respondent)*	**Date of Document** *(d, m, y)*	**Date of Filing** *(d, m, y)*	**Volume/Tab**
Financial Statement	R	21/04/--	23/04/--	Volume 1, Tab 5
Affidavit in Support of Claim for Custody or Access	R	21/04/--	23/04/--	Volume 1, Tab 6
Reply	A	26/04/--	27/04/--	Volume 2, Tab 1
Affidavit of Service of Reply on Respondent	A	27/04/--	27/04/--	Volume 2, Tab 1

☐ ***Continued on next sheet***

ONTARIO

Ontario Family Court of the Superior Court of Justice

(Name of Court)

SEAL

at 50 Eagle Street West, Newmarket, Ontario L3Y 6B1

(Court office address)

Court File Number

Form 8: Application (General)

Applicant(s)

Full legal name & address for service — street & number, municipality, postal code, telephone & fax numbers and e-mail address (if any).	Lawyer's name & address — street & number, municipality, postal code, telephone & fax numbers and e-mail address (if any).
Maria Shelley Havisham **333 GST Drive** **Newmarket, Ontario** **L2K 2D1** **Tel: (905) 859-1268**	**Robert B. Redford** **Michael, Eliad & Redford LLP** **863 Seneca Lane** **Toronto, Ontario M4J 1P6** **Tel: (416) 363-1079** **Fax: (416) 363-2628** **rbrdfrd@mer.com**

Respondent(s)

Full legal name & address for service — street & number, municipality, postal code, telephone & fax numbers and e-mail address (if any).	Lawyer's name & address — street & number, municipality, postal code, telephone & fax numbers and e-mail address (if any).
Brian Havisham **111 Sussex Drive** **Ottawa, Ontario** **K3B 1W8** **Tel: (613) 580-9334**	

TO THE RESPONDENT(S):

A COURT CASE HAS BEEN STARTED AGAINST YOU IN THIS COURT. THE DETAILS ARE SET OUT ON THE ATTACHED PAGES.

☐ **THE FIRST COURT DATE IS** *(date)* _____ **AT** _____ ☐ **a.m.** ☐ **p.m.** or as soon as possible after that time, at: *(address)*

NOTE: If this is a divorce case, no date will be set unless an Answer is filed. If you have also been served with a notice of motion, there may be an earlier court date and you or your lawyer should come to court for the motion.

☐ **THIS CASE IS ON THE FAST TRACK OF THE CASE MANAGEMENT SYSTEM.** A case management judge will be assigned by the time this case first comes before a judge.

☒ **THIS CASE IS ON THE STANDARD TRACK OF THE CASE MANAGEMENT SYSTEM. No court date has been set for this case** but, if you have been served with a notice of motion, it has a court date and you or your lawyer should come to court for the motion. A case management judge will not be assigned until one of the parties asks the clerk of the court to schedule a case conference or until a motion is scheduled, whichever comes first.

IF, AFTER 365 DAYS, THE CASE HAS NOT BEEN SCHEDULED FOR TRIAL, the clerk of the court will send out a warning that the case will be dismissed within 60 days unless the parties file proof that the case has been settled or one of the parties asks for a case or a settlement conference.

IF YOU WANT TO OPPOSE ANY CLAIM IN THIS CASE, you or your lawyer must prepare an Answer (Form 10 — a blank copy should be attached), serve a copy on the applicant(s) and file a copy in the court office with an Affidavit of Service (Form 6B). **YOU HAVE ONLY 30 DAYS AFTER THIS APPLICATION IS SERVED ON YOU (60 DAYS IF THIS APPLICATION IS SERVED ON YOU OUTSIDE CANADA OR THE UNITED STATES) TO SERVE AND FILE AN**

Form 8: Application (General) (page 2)   Court File Number _____

ANSWER. IF YOU DO NOT, THE CASE WILL GO AHEAD WITHOUT YOU AND THE COURT MAY MAKE AN ORDER AND ENFORCE IT AGAINST YOU.

Check the box of the paragraph that applies to your case

☐ This case includes a claim for support. It does not include a claim for property or exclusive possession of the matrimonial home and its contents. You **MUST** fill out a Financial Statement (Form 13 – a blank copy attached), serve a copy on the applicant(s) and file a copy in the court office with an Affidavit of Service even if you do not answer this case.

☒ This case includes a claim for property or exclusive possession of the matrimonial home and its contents. You **MUST** fill out a Financial Statement (Form 13.1 – a blank copy attached), serve a copy on the applicant(s) and file a copy in the court office with an Affidavit of Service even if you do not answer this case.

IF YOU WANT TO MAKE A CLAIM OF YOUR OWN, you or your lawyer must fill out the claim portion in the Answer, serve a copy on the applicant(s) and file a copy in the court office with an Affidavit of Service.

- If you want to make a claim for support but do not want to make a claim for property or exclusive possession of the matrimonial home and its contents, you **MUST** fill out a Financial Statement (Form 13), serve a copy on the applicant(s) and file a copy in the court office.
- However, if your only claim for support is for child support in the table amount specified under the Child Support Guidelines, you do not need to fill out, serve or file a Financial Statement.
- If you want to make a claim for property or exclusive possession of the matrimonial home and its contents, whether or not it includes a claim for support, you **MUST** fill out a Financial Statement (Form 13.1, not Form 13), serve a copy on the applicant(s), and file a copy in the court office.

YOU SHOULD GET LEGAL ADVICE ABOUT THIS CASE RIGHT AWAY. If you cannot afford a lawyer, you may be able to get help from your local Legal Aid Ontario office. *(See your telephone directory under LEGAL AID.)*

_____   _____
Date of issue   *Clerk of the court*

Form 8: Application (General) (page 3)   Court File Number _____

FAMILY HISTORY

APPLICANT: Age: 45   Birthdate: *(d, m, y)* 26 February (year)

Resident in *(municipality & province)* Newmarket, Ontario

since *(date)* April 1, (last year)

Surname at birth: Smith

Surname just before marriage: Jones

Divorced before? [ ] No   [X] Yes *(Place and date of previous divorce)*
Las Vegas, (year); Paris, (year); Cuba, (year); Toronto, (year)

RESPONDENT: Age: 58   Birthdate: *(d, m, y)* 1 April (year)

Resident in *(municipality & province)* Ottawa, Ontario

since *(date)* November 1, (year)

Surname at birth: Havisham

Surname just before marriage: Havisham

Divorced before? [X] No   [ ] Yes *(Place and date of previous divorce)*

RELATIONSHIP DATES:

[X] Married on *(date)* April 1, (12 years ago)   [ ] Started living together on *(date)* _____

[X] Separated on *(date)* April 1, (last year)   [X] Never lived together   [ ] Still living together

---

THE CHILD(REN): *List all children involved in this case, even if no claim is made for these children.*

Full legal name	Age	Birthdate *(d, m, y)*	Resident in *(municipality & province)*	Now Living with *(name of person and relationship to child)*
John Havisham	11	11/04/--	Newmarket, Ontario	Maria Shelley Havisham Mother
Paul Havisham	10	10/04/--	Newmarket, Ontario	Mother
George Havisham	9	09/04/--	Newmarket, Ontario	Mother
Ryan Havisham	8	08/04/--	Newmarket, Ontario	Mother

PREVIOUS CASES OR AGREEMENTS

Have the parties or the children been in a court case before?
[X] No   [ ] Yes

Have the parties made a written agreement dealing with any matter involved in this case?
[X] No   [ ] Yes *(Give date of agreement. Indicate which of its items are in dispute.)*

Form 8: Application (General) (page 4)   Court File Number _____

Has a Notice of Calculation and/or a Notice of Recalculation been issued by the online Child Support Service in this case'

[x] No   [ ] Yes *(Give date(s) of Notice(s) of Calculation or Recalculation.)*

If yes, are you asking the court to make an order for a child support that is different from the amount set out in the Notice?

[ ] No   [ ] Yes *(Provide an explanation.)*

Have the parties arbitrated or agreed to arbitrate any matter involved in this case?

[x] No   [ ] Yes *(Give date of agreement and family arbitration award, if any.)*

CLAIM BY APPLICANT

I ASK THE COURT FOR THE FOLLOWING: *(Claims below include claims for temporary orders.)*

Claims under the *Divorce Act* *(Check boxes in this column only if you are asking for a divorce and your case is in the Superior Court of Justice or Family Court of the Superior Court of Justice.)*	Claims under the *Family Law Act* or *Children's Law Reform Act*	Claims relating to property *(Check boxes in this column only if your case is in the Superior Court of Justice or Family Court of the Superior Court of Justice.)*
00 [x] a divorce	10 [x] support for me	20 [x] equalization of net family properties
01 [x] support for me	11 [x] support for child(ren) – table amount	21 [ ] exclusive possession of matrimonial home
02 [x] support for child(ren) – table amount	12 [ ] support for child(ren) – other than table amount	22 [ ] exclusive possession of contents of matrimonial home
03 [ ] support for child(ren) – other than table amount	13 [x] custody of child(ren)	23 [x] freezing assets
04 [x] custody of child(ren)	14 [ ] access to child(ren)	24 [x] sale of family property
05 [ ] access to child(ren)	15 [x] restraining/non - harassment order	
	16 [x] indexing spousal support	
	17 [ ] declaration of parentage	
	18 [ ] guardianship over child's property	
Other claims 30 [x] costs 31 [ ] annulment of marriage 32 [x] prejudgment interest 33 [ ] claims relating to a family arbitration	50 [ ] Other *(Specify.)* _____	

Give details of the order that you want the court to make. *(Include any amounts of support (if known) and the names of the children for whom support, custody or access is claimed.)*

Form 8: Application (General) (page 5) Court File Number _____

1. I am asking for an Order for custody of the four children of the marriage, namely, John Havisham, born April 11, (11 years ago), Paul Havisham, born April 10, (10 years ago), George Havisham, born April 9, (9 years ago), and Ryan Havisham, born April 8, (8 years ago), and for support for them based on the Child Support Guidelines.

2. I am also seeking an Order for support for myself in the amount of $1,000 per month as I am unable to manage the promising music careers of the children and work in any other capacity.

3. Due to the children's talent for music and the many concerts in which they perform, my focus on their success prevents me from doing anything else, and I therefore need support.

4. The Respondent, who has become increasingly bitter since being defeated in the elections a few years ago, has the capacity to pay support for me as he is now a successful businessman.

IMPORTANT FACTS SUPPORTING MY CLAIM FOR DIVORCE

[x] **Separation:** The spouses have lived separate and apart since *(date)* April 1, (last year)   and

   [x] have not lived together again since that date in an unsuccessful attempt to reconcile.

   [ ] have lived together again during the following period(s) in an unsuccessful attempt to reconcile:
   (Give dates.) _____

[ ] **Adultery:** The respondent has committed adultery. *(Give details. It is not necessary to name any other person but, if you do name the other person, then you must serve this application on the other person.)*

[ ] **Cruelty:** The respondent has treated the applicant with physical or mental cruelty of such a kind as to make continued cohabitation intolerable. *(Give details.)*

IMPORTANT FACTS SUPPORTING MY OTHER CLAIM(S)

(Set out below the facts that form the legal basis for your other claim(s).)

1. I also seek an Order for a division of our family properties based on the assets which we acquired during the marriage.

2. Due to my concerns the assets may be dissipated, I also ask for an Order freezing the Respondent's property until the settlement of the property issues.

Put a line through any blank space left on this page.

_____   _____
Date of signature   *Signature of applicant*

LAWYER'S CERTIFICATE

For divorce cases only

My name is: Robert B. Redford

and I am the applicant's lawyer in this divorce case. I certify that I have complied with the requirements of section 9 of the *Divorce Act*.

_____   _____
Date   *Signature of Lawyer*

For information on accessibility of court services for people with disability-related needs, contact:
Telephone: 416-326-2220 / 1-800-518-7901   TTY: 416-326-4012 / 1-877-425-0575

ONTARIO

Court File Number

Ontario Family Court of the Superior Court of Justice
(Name of court)

Form 13.1: Financial Statement (Property and Support Claims) sworn/affirmed

at **50 Eagle Street West, Newmarket, Ontario, L3Y 6B1**
(Court office address)

Applicant(s)

Full legal name & address for service — street & number, municipality, postal code, telephone & fax numbers and e-mail address (if any).	*Lawyer's name & address — street & number, municipality, postal code, telephone & fax numbers and e-mail address (if any).*
Maria Shelley Havisham **333 GST Drive** **Newmarket, Ontario** **L2K 2D1** **Tel: (905) 859-1268**	**Robert B. Redford** **Michael, Eliad & Redford LLP** **863 Seneca Lane** **Toronto, Ontario M4J 1P6** **Tel: (416) 363-1079** **Fax: (416) 363-2628** **rbrdfrd@mer.com**

Respondent(s)

Full legal name & address for service — street & number, municipality, postal code, telephone & fax numbers and e-mail address (if any).	*Lawyer's name & address — street & number, municipality, postal code, telephone & fax numbers and e-mail address (if any).*
Brian Havisham **111 Sussex Drive** **Ottawa, Ontario** **K3B 1W8** **Tel: (613) 580-9334**	

INSTRUCTIONS

1. USE THIS FORM IF:
   - you are making or responding to a claim for property or exclusive possession of the matrimonial home and its contents; or
   - you are making or responding to a claim for property or exclusive possession of the matrimonial home and its contents together with other claims for relief.

2. USE FORM 13 INSTEAD OF THIS FORM IF:
   - you are making or responding to a claim for support but NOT making or responding to a claim for property or exclusive possession of the matrimonial home and its contents.

3. If you have income that is not shown in Part I of the financial statement (for example, partnership income, dividends, rental income, capital gains or RRSP income), you must also complete **Schedule A**.

4. If you or the other party has sought a contribution towards special or extraordinary expenses for the child(ren), you must also complete **Schedule B**.

*NOTE: You must **fully and truthfully** complete this financial statement, including any applicable schedules. You must also provide the other party with documents relating to support and property and a Certificate of Financial Disclosure (Form 13A) as required by Rule 13 of the Family Law Rules.*

1. **My name is** *(full legal name)*   Maria Shelley Havisham

   I live in *(municipality & province)*   Newmarket, Ontario

   and I swear/affirm that the following is true:

FLR 13 (January 6, 2015)

www.DivorceMate.cc

Form 13.1: **Financial Statement (Property and** (page 2) Court File Number: ....
Support Claims)

PART I: INCOME

2. I am currently

   [ ] employed by *(name and address of employer)*

   [ ] self-employed, carrying on business under the name of *(name and address of business)*

   [x] unemployed since *(date when last employed)*
   The date of my marriage to the Respondent.

3. I attach proof of my year-to-date income from all sources, including my most recent *(attach all that are applicable)*:

   [ ] pay cheque stub   [ ] social assistance stub   [ ] pension stub   [ ] workers' compensation stub

   [ ] employment insurance stub and last Record of Employment

   [ ] statement of income and expenses/ professional activities (for self-employed individuals)

   [ ] other (e.g. a letter from your employer confirming all income received to date this year)

4. Last year, my gross income from all sources was $ 240,000.00 *(do not subtract any taxes that have been deducted from this income)*.

5. [x] I am attaching all of the following required documents to this financial statement as proof of my income over the past three years, if they have not already been provided:

   • a copy of my personal income tax returns for each of the past three taxation years, including any materials that were filed with the returns. *(Income tax returns must be served but should NOT be filed in the continuing record, unless they are filed with a motion to refrain a driver's license suspension.)*

   • a copy of my notices of assessment and any notices of reassessment for each of the past three taxation years;

   • where my notices of assessment and reassessment are unavailable for any of the past three taxation years or where I have not filed a return for any of the past three taxation years, an Income and Deductions printout from the Canada Revenue Agency for each of those years, whether or not I filed an income tax return.

   Note: An Income and Deductions printout is available from Canada Revenue Agency. Please call customer service at 1-800-959-8281.

   OR

   [ ] I am an Indian within the meaning of the *Indian Act* (Canada) and I have chosen not to file income tax returns for the past three years. I am attaching the following proof of income for the last three years *(list documents you have provided)*:

(In this table you must show all of the income that you are currently receiving whether taxable or not.)

	Income Source	Amount Received/Month
1.	Employment income (before deductions)	
2.	Commissions, tips and bonuses	
3.	Self-employment income (Monthly amount before expenses: $)	
4.	Employment Insurance benefits	
5.	Workers' compensation benefits	
6.	Social assistance income (including ODSP payments)	

Form 13.1: **Financial Statement (Property and**   **(page 3)**   Court File Number: ....
            Support Claims)

7.	Interest and investment income	$20,000.00
8.	Pension income (including CPP and OAS)	
9.	Spousal support received from a former spouse/partner	
10.	Child Tax Benefits or Tax Rebates (e.g. GST)	
11.	Other sources of income (e.g. RRSP withdrawals, capital gains) (*attach Schedule A and divide annual amount by 12*)	
12.	**Total monthly income from all sources:**	**$20,000.00**
13.	**Total monthly income X 12 = Total annual income:**	**$240,000.00**

14.   **Other Benefits**

Provide details of any non-cash benefits that your employer provides to you or are paid for by your business such as medical insurance coverage, the use of a company car, or room and board.

Item	Details	Yearly Market Value
	Total	**$0.00**

PART 2: EXPENSES

EXPENSE	Monthly Amount		SUBTOTAL	$1,150.00
Automatic Deductions			**Household Expenses**	
CPP contributions			Groceries	$800.00
EI premiums			Household supplies	
Income taxes			Meals outside the home	$200.00
Employee pension contributions			Pet care	
Union dues			Laundry and Dry Cleaning	$200.00
SUBTOTAL	**$0.00**		**SUBTOTAL**	**$1,200.00**
Housing			**Childcare Costs**	
Rent or mortgage			Daycare expense	
Property taxes	$1,000.00		Babysitting costs	
Property insurance	$500.00			
Condominium fees			**SUBTOTAL**	**$0.00**
Repairs and maintenance			**Transportation**	
			Public transit, taxis	
SUBTOTAL	**$1,500.00**		Gas and oil	$400.00
Utilities			Car insurance and license	$300.00
Water	$150.00		Repairs and maintenance	$100.00
Heat	$350.00		Parking	$50.00
Electricity	$300.00		Car Loan or Lease Payments	
Telephone	$150.00			
Cell phone			**SUBTOTAL**	**$850.00**
Cable	$200.00		**Health**	
Internet			Health insurance premiums	
			Dental expenses	$3,200.00

Form 13.1: **Financial Statement (Property and** **(page 4)** Court File Number: ....
Support Claims)

Medicine and drugs	$150.00	RRSP/RESP withdrawals	
Eye care	$100.00	Vacations	$600.00
		School fees and supplies	$5,000.00
SUBTOTAL	**$3,450.00**	Clothing for children	
Personal		Children's activities	$4,200.00
Clothing	$1,300.00	Summer camp expenses	$1,000.00
Hair care and beauty	$200.00	Debt payments	
Alcohol and tobacco	$100.00	Support paid for other children	
Education *(specify)*		Other expenses not shown above (books, charities and allowance)	$400.00
Entertainment/recreation (including children)	$500.00		
Gifts	$200.00	**SUBTOTAL**	**$11,200.00**
SUBTOTAL	**$2,300.00**	**Total Amount of Monthly Expenses**	**$21,650.00**
Other expenses		**Total Amount of Yearly Expenses**	**$259,800.00**
Life insurance premiums			

PART 3: OTHER INCOME EARNERS IN THE HOME

Complete this part only if you are making or responding to a claim for undue hardship or spousal support. Check and complete all sections that apply to your circumstances.

1. [x] I live alone.

2. [ ] I am living with *(full legal name of person you are married to or cohabiting with)*

3. [ ] I/we live with the following other adult(s):

4. [x] I/we have *(give number)* four of child(ren) who live(s) in the home.

5. My spouse/partner [x] works at *(place of work or business)*
   Phoenix Software Ltd.

   [ ] does not work outside the home.

6. My spouse/partner [x] earns *(give amount)* $ 120,000.00 per year .

   [ ] does not earn any income.

7. [ ] My spouse/partner or other adult residing in the home contributes about $ ....
   per .... towards the household expenses.

PART 4: ASSETS IN AND OUT OF ONTARIO

If any sections of Parts 4 to 9 do not apply, do not leave blank, print "NONE" in the section.

The date of marriage is: *(give date)* April 1, (12 years ago)

The valuation date is: *(give date)* April 1, (last year)

The date of commencement of cohabitation is (if different from date of marriage): *(give date)* ....

Form 13.1: **Financial Statement (Property and** **(page 5)** Court File Number: _____
Support Claims)

PART 4(a): LAND

*Include any interest in land **owned** on the dates in each of the columns below, including leasehold interests and mortgages. Show estimated market value of your interest, but do not deduct encumbrances or costs of disposition; these encumbrances and costs should be shown under Part 5 "Debts and Other Liabilities".*

Nature & Type of Ownership *(Give your percentage interest where relevant.)*	Address of Property	Estimated Market value of YOUR interest		
		on date of marriage	on valuation date	today
Matrimonial Home Joint 50%	111 Sussex Dr., Ottawa, ON K3B 1W8 Full value $500,000.00		$250,000.00	$250,000.00
15. TOTAL VALUE OF LAND		$0.00	**$250,000.00**	$250,000.00

PART 4(b): GENERAL HOUSEHOLD ITEMS AND VEHICLES

Show estimated market value, not the cost of replacement for these items owned on the dates in each of the columns below. Do not deduct encumbrances or costs of disposition; these encumbrances and costs should be shown under Part 5, "Debts and Other Liabilities".

Item	Description	Indicate if NOT in your possession	Estimated Market value of YOUR interest		
			on date of marriage	on valuation date	today
Household goods & furniture	One-half of matrimonial home contents. Total value $100,000	Not in my possession		$50,000.00	$50,000.00
Cars, boats, Vehicles	Car (year) Volvo 740		$30,000.00	$4,000.00	$4,000.00
Jewellery, art, electronics, tools, sports & hobby, equipment	Jewellery and electronics	Not in my possession		$15,000.00	$15,000.00
Other special items					
16. TOTAL VALUE OF GENERAL HOUSEHOLD ITEMS AND VEHICLES			$30,000.00	**$69,000.00**	$69,000.00

PART 4(c): BANK ACCOUNTS, SAVINGS, SECURITIES AND PENSIONS

Show the items owned on the dates in each of the columns below by category, for example, cash, accounts in financial institutions, pensions, registered retirement or other savings plans, deposit receipts, any other savings, bonds, warrants, options, notes and other securities. Give your best estimate of the market value of the securities if the items were to be sold on the open market.

Category	INSTITUTION *(including location)/* DESCRIPTION *(including issuer and date)*	Account number	Amount / Estimated Market Value		
			on date of marriage	on valuation date	today
Savings	Great Money Bank, 4 May Road, Ottawa, ON	12345	$4,000.00	$25,000.00	$25,000.00
RRSP	Great Money Bank, 4 May Road, Ottawa, ON	678910		$10,000.00	$10,000.00
17. TOTAL VALUE OF ACCOUNTS, SAVINGS, SECURITIES AND PENSIONS			$4,000.00	**$35,000.00**	$35,000.00

Form 13.1:	Financial Statement (Property and Support Claims)	(page 6)	Court File Number:

PART 4(d): LIFE & DISABILITY INSURANCE

List all policies in existence on the dates in each of the columns below.

Company, Type & Policy No.	Owner	Beneficiary	Face Amount	Cash Surrender Value		
				on date of marriage	on valuation date	today
18. TOTAL CASH SURRENDER VALUE OF INSURANCE POLICIES				$0.00	$0.00	$0.00

PART 4(e): BUSINESS INTERESTS

Show any interest in an unincorporated business owned on the dates in each of the columns below. An interest in an incorporated business may be shown here or under "BANK ACCOUNTS, SAVINGS, SECURITIES AND PENSIONS" in Part 4(c). Give your best estimate of market value of your interest.

Name of Firm or Company	Interest	Estimated Market value of YOUR interest		
		on date of marriage	on valuation date	today
19. TOTAL VALUE OF BUSINESS INTERESTS		$0.00	$0.00	$0.00

PART 4(f): MONEY OWED TO YOU

Give details of all money that other persons owe to you on the dates in each of the columns below, whether because of business or from personal dealings. Include any court judgments in your favour, any estate money and any income tax refunds owed to you.

Details	Amount Owed to You		
	on date of marriage	on valuation date	today
20. TOTAL OF MONEY OWED TO YOU	$0.00	$0.00	$0.00

PART 4(g): OTHER PROPERTY

Show other property or assets owned on the dates in each of the columns below. Include property of any kind not listed above. Give your best estimate of market value.

Category	Details	Estimated Market Value of YOUR interest		
		on date of marriage	on valuation date	today
21. TOTAL OF OTHER PROPERTY		$0.00	$0.00	$0.00

22. VALUE OF ALL PROPERTY OWNED ON THE VALUATION DATE (Add items [15] to [21].)	$0.00	$354,000.00	$0.00

Form 13.1:   **Financial Statement (Property and**   **(page 7)**   Court File Number: _____
                Support Claims)

PART 5: DEBTS AND OTHER LIABILITIES

Show your debts and other liabilities on the dates in each of the columns below. List them by category such as mortgages, charges, liens, notes, credit cards, and accounts payable. Don't forget to include:
- *any money owed to the Canada Revenue Agency;*
- *contingent liabilities such as guarantees or warranties given by you (but indicate that they are contingent); and*
- *any unpaid legal or professional bills as result of this case.*

Category	Details	Amount owing		
		on date of marriage	on valuation date	today
Charge/Mortgage	On matrimonial home Total $40,000; joint 50%		$20,000.00	$19,000.00
Loan	Loan re Car (year) Volvo 740 Great Money Bank	$25,000.00		
23. TOTAL OF DEBTS AND OTHER LIABILITIES		$25,000.00	**$20,000.00**	$19,000.00

PART 6: PROPERTY, DEBTS AND OTHER LIABILITIES ON DATE OF MARRIAGE

Show by category the value of your property, debts and other liabilities, calculated as of the date of your marriage. (In this part, do not include the value of a matrimonial home or debts or other liabilities directly related to its purchase or significant improvement, if you and your spouse ordinarily occupied this property as your family residence at the time of separation.)

Category and details	Value on date of marriage	
	Assets	Liabilities
Land	$0.00	
General household items & vehicles	$30,000.00	
Bank accounts, savings, securities, pensions	$4,000.00	
Life & disability insurance	$0.00	
Business interests	$0.00	
Money owed to you	$0.00	
Other property *(Specify.)*	$0.00	
Debts and other liabilities *(Specify.)* Loan re Car (year) Volvo 740, Great Money Bank		$25,000.00
TOTALS	$34,000.00	$25,000.00
24. NET VALUE OF PROPERTY OWNED ON DATE OF MARRIAGE *(From the total of the "Assets" column, subtract the total of the "Liabilities" column.)*	**$9,000.00**	
25. VALUE OF ALL DEDUCTIONS (Add items [23] and [24].)	**$29,000.00**	

PART 7: EXCLUDED PROPERTY

Show by category the value of property owned on the valuation date that is excluded from the definition of "net family property" (such as gifts or inheritances received after marriage).

Category	Details	Value on valuation date
Gift or inheritance from third person Income from property expressly excluded by donor/testator Damages and settlements for personal injuries, etc. Life insurance proceeds		

Form 13.1: **Financial Statement (Property and**   **(page 8)**   Court File Number: _____
            Support Claims)

Traced property Excluded property by spousal agreement Other Excluded Property		
26. TOTAL VALUE OF EXCLUDED PROPERTY		**$0.00**

PART 8: DISPOSED-OF PROPERTY

Show by category the value of all property that you disposed of during the two years immediately preceding the making of this statement, or during the marriage, whichever period is shorter.

Category	Details	Value
27. TOTAL VALUE OF DISPOSED-OF PROPERTY		**$0.00**

PART 9: CALCULATION OF NET FAMILY PROPERTY

	Deductions	BALANCE
Value of all property owned on valuation date *(from item [22] above)*		**$354,000.00**
Subtract value of all deductions *(from item [25] above)*	**$29,000.00**	**$325,000.00**
Subtract total value of all excluded property *(from item [26] above)*	**$0.00**	**$0.00**
28. NET FAMILY PROPERTY		**$325,000.00**

NOTE: *This financial statement must be updated no more than 30 days before any court event by either completing and filing:*
- *a new financial statement with updated information, or*
- *an affidavit in Form 14A setting out the details of any minor changes or confirming that the information contained in this statement remains correct.*

Sworn/Affirmed before me at

City of Toronto

(municipality)

in Province of Ontario

(province, state or country)

on _____

(date)

Commissioner for taking affidavits
(Type or print name below if signature is illegible.)

Signature
(This form to be signed in front of a lawyer, justice of the peace, notary public or commissioner for taking affidavits.)

Form 13.1: **Financial Statement (Property and Support Claims)** (page 9)

Court File Number: _____

PART 2: EXPENSES
PROPOSED BUDGET

EXPENSE	Monthly Amount
Automatic Deductions	
CPP contributions	
Ei premiums	
Income taxes	
Employee pension contributions	
Union dues	
SUBTOTAL	**$0.00**
Housing	
Rent or mortgage	
Property taxes	
Property insurance	
Condominium fees	
Repairs and maintenance	
SUBTOTAL	**$0.00**
Utilities	
Water	
Heat	
Electricity	
Telephone	
Cell phone	
Cable	
Internet	
SUBTOTAL	**$0.00**
Household Expenses	
Groceries	
Household supplies	
Meals outside the home	
Pet care	
Laundry and Dry Cleaning	
SUBTOTAL	**$0.00**
Childcare Costs	
Daycare expense	
Babysitting costs	
SUBTOTAL	**$0.00**
Transportation	
Public transit, taxis	
Gas and oil	
Car insurance and license	
Repairs and maintenance	
Parking	
Car Loan or Lease Payments	
SUBTOTAL	**$0.00**
Health	
Health insurance premiums	
Dental expenses	
Medicine and drugs	
Eye care	
SUBTOTAL	**$0.00**
Personal	
Clothing	
Hair care and beauty	
Alcohol and tobacco	
Education (specify)	
Entertainment/recreation (including children)	
Gifts	
SUBTOTAL	**$0.00**
Other expenses	
Life insurance premiums	
RRSP/RESP withdrawals	
Vacations	
School fees and supplies	
Clothing for children	
Children's activities	
Summer camp expenses	
Debt payments	
Support paid for other children	
Other expenses not shown above (specify)	
SUBTOTAL	**$0.00**
Total Amount of Monthly Expenses:	**$0.00**
Total Amount of Yearly Expenses:	**$0.00**

Form 13.1: **Financial Statement (Property and Support Claims)** (page 10)

Court File Number: _____

FINANCIAL STATEMENT SUMMARY PAGE

BUDGET

Income

	Monthly
Income From All Sources	$0.00
Other Benefits	$0.00
Total Monthly Income and Benefits	**$0.00**

Expenses

	Actual	Proposed
Automatic Deductions	$0.00	$0.00
Housing	$0.00	$0.00
Utilities	$0.00	$0.00
Household	$0.00	$0.00
Childcare Costs	$0.00	$0.00
Transportation	$0.00	$0.00
Health	$0.00	$0.00
Personal	$0.00	$0.00
Other	$0.00	$0.00
Total Expenses		**$0.00**
Monthly Surplus / (Deficit)		**$0.00**

NET FAMILY PROPERTY

Assets

	Valuation Date
Land	[15] $0.00
General Household Items and Vehicles	[16] $0.00
Bank Accounts, Savings, Securities and Pensions	[17] $0.00
Life and Disability Insurance	[18] $0.00
Business Interests	[19] $0.00
Money Owed to You	[20] $0.00
Other Property	[21] $0.00
Total Assets [22]	**$0.00**

Deductions

Debts and Other Liabilities on Valuation Date	[23] $0.00
Net Value of Property Owned on Date of Marriage	[24] $0.00
Total Deductions [25]	**$0.00**

Exclusions

Excluded Property owned on Valuation Date	[26] $0.00
Net Family Property	**$0.00**
(Assets] minus [Deductions] minus [Exclusions])	

Notes:

Schedule A
Additional Sources of Income

Line	Income Source	Annual Amount
1.	Net partnership income	
2.	Net rental income (Gross annual rental income of $)	
3.	Total amount of dividends received from taxable Canadian corporations	
4.	Total capital gains ($) less capital losses ($)	
5.	Registered retirement savings plan withdrawals	
6.	Income from a Registered Retirement Income Fund or Annuity	
7.	Any other income (specify source)	

	Subtotal	$0.00

Schedule B
Special or Extraordinary Expenses for the Child(ren)

	Child's Name	Expense	Amount/yr.	Available Tax Credits or Deductions*
1.				
2.				
3.				
4.				
5.				
6.				
7.				
8.				
9.				
10.				

Total Net Annual Amount	$0.00
Total Net Monthly Amount	$0.00

* Some of these expenses can be claimed in a parent's income tax return in relation to a tax credit or deduction (for example childcare costs). These credits or deductions must be shown in the above chart.

☐ I earn $ per year which should be used to determine my share of the above expenses.

NOTE:

Pursuant to the Child Support Guidelines, a court can order that the parents of a child share the costs of the following expenses for the child:

- Necessary childcare expenses;
- Medical insurance premiums and certain health-related expenses for the child that cost more than $100 annually;
- Extraordinary expenses for the child's education;
- Post-secondary school expenses; and,
- Extraordinary expenses for extracurricular activities.

ONTARIO

Ontario Family Court of the Superior Court of Justice
(Name of court)

Court File Number

at **50 Eagle Street West, Newmarket, Ontario L3Y 6B1**
(Court office address)

Form 35.1: Affidavit in Support of Claim for Custody or Access, dated

Applicant(s)

Full legal name & address for service — street & number, municipality, postal code, telephone & fax numbers and e-mail address (if any).	Lawyer's name & address — street & number, municipality, postal code, telephone & fax numbers and e-mail address (if any).
Maria Shelley Havisham **333 GST Drive** **Newmarket, Ontario** **L2K 2D1** **Tel: (905) 859-1268**	**Robert B. Redford** **Michael, Eliad & Redford LLP** **863 Seneca Lane** **Toronto, Ontario M4J 1P6** **Tel: (416) 363-1079** **Fax: (416) 363-2628** **rbrdfrd@mer.com**

Respondent(s)

Full legal name & address for service — street & number, municipality, postal code, telephone & fax numbers and e-mail address (if any).	Lawyer's name & address — street & number, municipality, postal code, telephone & fax numbers and e-mail address (if any).
Brian Havisham **111 Sussex Drive** **Ottawa, Ontario** **K3B 1W8** **Tel: (613) 580-9334**	

Affidavit in Support of Claim for Custody or Access
(If you need more space, attach extra pages.)

My name is *(full legal name)*   Maria Shelley Havisham

My date of birth is *(d, m, y)*   26/02/(year)

I live in: *(name of city, town or municipality and province, state or country if outside of Ontario)*

Newmarket, Ontario

I swear/affirm that the following is true:

PART A:
TO BE COMPLETED BY ALL PERSONS SEEKING CUSTODY OR ACCESS
(Write "N/A" if any of the paragraphs do not apply to you or the child(ren).)

1.   During my life, I have also used or been known by the following names:
Maria Shelley Jones
Maria Shelley Smith

2.   The child(ren) in this case is/are:

Child's full legal name	Birthdate *(d, m, y)*	Age	Full legal name(s) of parent(s)	Name(s) of all people the child lives with now *(include address if the child does not live with you)*	My relationship to the child *(specify if parent, grandparent, family friend, etc.)*
John Havisham	11/04/--	11	Maria Shelley Havisham and Brian Havisham	Maria Shelley Havisham	Parent
Paul Havisham	10/04/--	10	Maria Shelley Havisham and Brian Havisham	Maria Shelley Havisham	Parent
George Havisham	09/04/--	9	Maria Shelley Havisham and Brian Havisham	Maria Shelley Havisham	Parent

FLR 35.1 (November 15, 2009)

Form 35.1: Affidavit in Support of Claim for Custody or Access   **(page 2)**   Court file number _____

Ryan Havisham	08/04/--	8	Maria Shelley Havisham and Brian Havisham	Maria Shelley Havisham	Parent

3.   **I am also the parent of or have acted as a parent (for example, as a step-parent, legal guardian etc.) to the following child(ren):** *(include the full legal names and birthdates of any child(ren) not already listed in paragraph 2)*

Child's full legal name	Birthdate *(d, m, y)*	My relationship to the child *(specify if parent, step-parent, grandparent, etc.)*	Name(s) of the person(s) with whom the child lives now *(if the child is under 18 years old)*

4.   **I am or have been a party in the following court case(s) involving custody of or access to any child:** *(Including the child(ren) in this case or any other child(ren). Do not include cases involving a children's aid society in this section. Attach a copy of any custody or access court order(s) or endorsement(s) you have.)*

Court location	Names of parties in the case	Name(s) of child(ren)	Court orders made *(include dates of orders)*
N/A			

5.   **I have been a party or person responsible for the care of a child in the following child protection court case(s):** *(attach a copy of any relevant court order(s) or endorsement(s) you have)*

Court location	Names of people involved in the case	Name of children's aid society	Court orders made *(include dates of orders)*
N/A			

6.   **I have been found guilty of the following criminal offence(s) for which I have not received a pardon:**

Charge	Approximate date of finding of guilt	Sentence received
N/A		

7.   **I am now charged with the following criminal offence(s):**

Charge	Date of next court appearance	Terms of release while waiting for trial *(attach copy of bail or other release conditions, if any)*
N/A		

Page 2 of 7

Form 35.1: **Affidavit in Support of Claim for**   **(page 3)**   Court file number
            Custody or Access

8.   When the court is assessing a person's ability to act as a parent, s. 24 (4) of the *Children's Law Reform Act* requires the court to consider whether the person has at any time committed violence or abuse against:

- his or her spouse;
- a parent of the child to whom the claim for custody or access relates;
- a member of the person's household; or
- any child.

I am aware of the following violence or abuse the court should consider under s. 24 (4) of the *Children's Law Reform Act:* *(describe incident(s) or episode(s) and provide information about the nature of the violence or abuse, who committed the violence and who the victim(s) was/were)*

N/A

9.   To the best of my knowledge, since birth, the child(ren) in this case has/have lived with the following caregiver(s): *(including a parent, legal guardian, children's aid society etc.)*

Child's Name	Name(s) of Caregiver(s) *(if the child was in the care of a children's aid society, give the name of that children's aid society)*	Period(s) of Time with Caregiver(s) *(d,m,y to d,m,y)*
John Havisham	Maria Shelley Havisham	11/04/-- to (present)
Paul Havisham	Maria Shelley Havisham	10/04/-- to (present)
George Havisham	Maria Shelley Havisham	09/04/-- to (present)
Ryan Havisham	Maria Shelley Havisham	08/04/-- to (present)

10.   My plan for the care and upbringing of the child(ren) is as follows:

a)   I plan to live at the following address: 333 GST Drive, Newmarket, Ontario   L2K 2D1

b)   The following people (other than the child(ren) involved in this case) will be living with me:

Full legal name and other names this person has used	Birthdate *(d, m, y)*	Relationship to you	Has a child of this person ever been in the care of a children's aid society? *(if yes, give details)*	Has this person been found guilty of a criminal offence (for which he/she has not received a pardon) or is he/she currently facing criminal charges? *(if yes, give details)*
None				

c)   Decisions for the child(ren) (including education, medical care, religious upbringing, extra-curricular activities, etc.) will be made as follows:

☐   jointly by me and *(name(s) of person(s))*

☒   by me

☐   by *(name(s) of person(s))*

(If necessary, provide additional details below.)

d) ☒   I am a stay-at-home parent.

☐   I work: ☐   full time.   ☐   part time.

Page 3 of 7

Form 35.1:	**Affidavit in Support of Claim for Custody or Access**	**(page 4)**	Court file number

☐ **I attend school:** ☐ **full time.** ☐ **part time.**

at: *(name of your place of work or school)*

☐ **I anticipate that my plans for work and/or school may change as follows:** *(complete if you know or expect that you will be doing something different from what you are doing now)*

e) **The child(ren) will attend school, daycare or be cared for by others on a regular basis as follows:**

The children will attend school.

f) **My plan for the child(ren) to have regular contact with others, including the child(ren)'s parent(s) and family members, is as follows:**

Reasonable access by the children's father.

Flexible contact with extended family members, depending on the children's schedule and what will work best for the children.

g) Check the appropriate box:

☒ **The child(ren) does not/do not have any special medical, educational, mental health or developmental needs.**

☐ **The child or one or more of the children has/have the following special needs and will receive support and services for those needs as follows:** *(if a child does not have special needs, you do not have to include information about that child below)*

Name of child	Special need(s)	Description of child's needs	Support or service child will be receiving *(include the names of any doctors, counsellors, treatment centres, etc. that are or will be providing support or services to the child)*
	☐ medical ☐ educational ☐ mental health ☐ developmental ☐ other		
	☐ medical ☐ educational ☐ mental health ☐ developmental ☐ other		
	☐ medical ☐ educational ☐ mental health ☐ developmental ☐ other		

Page 4 of 7

Form 35.1: **Affidavit in Support of Claim for**   **(page 5)**   Court file number
Custody or Access

	☐ medical		
	☐ educational		
	☐ mental health		
	☐ developmental		
	☐ other		
	☐ medical		
	☐ educational		
	☐ mental health		
	☐ developmental		
	☐ other		

h) **I will have support from the following relatives, friends or community services in caring for the child(ren):**
My mother has agreed to look after the children when needed.

11.   **I acknowledge that the court needs up-to-date and accurate information about my plan in order to make a custody or access order in the best interests of the child(ren) (subrule 35.1 (7)). If, at any time before a final order is made in this case,**

a)   there are any changes in my life or circumstances that affect the information provided in this affidavit; or

b)   I discover that the information in this affidavit is incorrect or incomplete,

I will immediately serve and file either:

a)   an updated affidavit in support of claim for custody or access (Form 35.1); or,

b)   if the correction or change is minor, an affidavit in Form 14A describing the correction or change and indicating any effect it has on my plan for the care and upbringing of the child(ren).
_____ *(Initial here to show you have read this paragraph and you understand it.)*

NOTE: If you are not the parent of the child for whom you are seeking an order of custody, you must complete Part B of this affidavit.

You are a parent of a child if:

a)   you are the biological parent of the child;

b)   you are the adoptive parent of the child;

c)   a court has declared that you are the child's parent under the *Children's Law Reform Act;* or

d)   you are presumed to be a father under section 8 of the *Children's Law Reform Act*.

If you are completing Part B, you do not have to swear/affirm the affidavit at this point. You will swear/affirm at the end of Part B.

Sworn/Affirmed before me at:	
City of Toronto	
(municipality)	
in Province of Ontario	
(province, state or country)	
on	
(Date)	
Commissioner for taking affidavits	Signature
(Type or print below if signature is illegible.)	*(This form to be signed in front of a lawyer, justice of the peace, notary public or commissioner for taking affidavits.)*

Page 5 of 7

Form 35.1:	**Affidavit in Support of Claim for**	**(page 6)**	Court file number
	Custody or Access		

PART B
TO BE COMPLETED ONLY BY A NON-PARENT SEEKING A CUSTODY ORDER

You are not a parent of a child unless:

a) you are the biological parent of the child;

b) you are the adoptive parent of the child;

c) a court has declared that you are the child's parent under the *Children's Law Reform Act;* or

d) you are presumed to be a father under section 8 of the *Children's Law Reform Act.*

NOTICE: If you are a non-parent claiming custody of a child, court staff will conduct a search of the databases maintained by the Ontario courts to identify previous or current family court cases in which you or the child(ren) may have been or may be involved and provide you with a list of those cases. This information will be shared with the court and you must provide a copy to any other party.

If the list contains information about someone other than you, you may swear or affirm an affidavit indicating that you are not the same person as the person named in the list.

In addition to the information in Part A, I swear/affirm that the following is true:

12.   **To the best of my knowledge, the child(ren) in this case has/have been involved in the following custody/ access or child protection court cases:** *(do NOT include cases in which the child was charged under the* Youth Criminal Justice Act (Canada)*)*

Child(ren)'s name(s)	Type of Case	Details of Case

13.   You must file a police records check with the court. Choose the option below that applies to you:

☐   **I have attached to this affidavit a copy of my police records check, dated** *(date of report from local police force)* _____ **. Since the date that the attached police records check was completed,**

I have been found guilty of or charged with the following offence(s):

_____

☐   **On** *(date)* _____ **, I sent a request to** *(name of local police force)* _____ **for a police records check.**

I agree to serve and file the police records check with the court within 10 days after the day I receive it. I understand that the court may not make an order for custody of the child(ren) until I have filed the police records check.

14.   **Since I turned 18 years old or became a parent, whichever was earlier, I have lived in the following places:**

Approximate dates *(month/year to month/year)*	City, town or municipality where you lived *(if outside of Ontario, give name of province, state or country)*

Page 6 of 7

Form 35.1: **Affidavit in Support of Claim for**   **(page 7)**   Court file number
                Custody or Access

15.   **I have provided a signed consent form to the court, which authorizes each of the children's aid societies listed below to send a report to me and to the court indicating:**

   •   **whether the society has any records within the meaning of the *Children's Law Reform Act* regulations relating to me; and**

   •   **the date(s) on which any files were opened and/or closed (if applicable).**

   i)   Name of children's aid society:

   ii)   Name of children's aid society:

   iii)   Name of children's aid society:

   iv)   Name of children's aid society:

   v)   Name of children's aid society:

   vi)   Name of children's aid society:

16.   I understand that if any report from a children's aid society indicates that the children's aid society has records related to me, then, unless the court orders otherwise, that report will be shared with:

   a)   the court;
   b)   any other parties in this case; and
   c)   the child(ren)'s lawyer, if there is one in this case.

   If I wish to bring a motion asking the court not to release all or part of this report, I understand that I must file my motion with the court no later than **20 days** from the day that the last report is received by the court.

   I also understand that any report indicating that a children's aid society has no records relating to me will not be shared with the court, any other party or the child(ren)'s lawyer.

   _____ *(Initial here to show you have read this paragraph and you understand it.)*

Sworn/Affirmed before me at:

_____
                    (municipality)

in   _____
                    (province, state or country)

on   _____
          (Date)

          _____
          Commissioner for taking affidavits
          (Type or print below if signature is illegible.)

                                        _____
                                                    Signature
                                        (This form to be signed in front of a lawyer,
                                        justice of the peace, notary public or commissioner for
                                        taking affidavits.)

ONTARIO

Ontario Family Court of the Superior Court of Justice
(Name of court)

Court File Number
**FL6666

at **50 Eagle Street West, Newmarket, Ontario L3Y 6B1**
(Court office address)

**Form 6B: Affidavit of Service
sworn/affirmed**

Applicant(s)

Full legal name & address for service — street & number, municipality, postal code, telephone & fax numbers and e-mail address (if any).	Lawyer's name & address — street & number, municipality, postal code, telephone & fax numbers and e-mail address (if any).
Maria Shelley Havisham **333 GST Drive** **Newmarket, Ontario** **L2K 2D1** **Tel: (905) 859-1268**	**Robert B. Redford** **Michael, Eliad & Redford LLP** **863 Seneca Lane** **Toronto, Ontario M4J 1P6** **Tel: (416) 363-1079** **Fax: (416) 363-2628** **rbrdfrd@mer.com**

Respondent(s)

Full legal name & address for service — street & number, municipality, postal code, telephone & fax numbers and e-mail address (if any).	Lawyer's name & address — street & number, municipality, postal code, telephone & fax numbers and e-mail address (if any).
Brian Havisham **111 Sussex Drive** **Ottawa, Ontario** **K3B 1W8** **Tel: (613) 580-9334**	

My name is
(full legal name)   **Thomas Jefferson**

I live in
(municipality and province)   **City of Ottawa, Province of Ontario**

and I swear/affirm that the following is true:

1. On *(date)* April 2, 20--   , at *(time)* 4:47 p.m.   , I served *(name of person to be served)*
    Brian Havisham

    with the following document(s) in this case: *(List the documents served.)*

Name of document	Author (if applicable)	Date when document signed, issued, sworn, etc.
Application (general)	Applicant	April 1, 20--
Financial Statement (Property and Support Claims)	Applicant	April 1, 20--
Affidavit in Support of Claim for Custody or Access	Applicant	April 1, 20--

NOTE: *You can leave out any part of this form that is not applicable.*

2. I served the document(s) mentioned in paragraph 1 by:

Check one box only and go to indicated paragraph.

- [X] special service. *(Go to paragraph 3 below if you used special service.)*
- [ ] mail. *(Go to paragraph 4 if you used mailed service.)*
- [ ] same day courier. *(Go to paragraph 5 if you used courier.)*
- [ ] next day courier. *(Go to paragraph 5 if you used courier.)*
- [ ] deposit at a document exchange. *(Go to paragraph 6 if you used a document exchange.)*
- [ ] an electronic document exchange. *(Go to paragraph 7 if you used an electronic document exchange).*
- [ ] fax. *(Go to paragraph 8 if you used fax.)*
- [ ] email. *(Go to paragraph 9 if you used email.)*

FLR 6B (April 12, 2016)

www.DivorceMate.com

Legal Office Procedures

Form 6B: Affidavit of Service (page 2)
sworn/affirmed

Court File Number   ****FL6666**

[ ] substituted service or advertisement. *(Go to paragraph 10 if you used substituted service or advertisement.)*

3. I carried out special service of the document(s) on the person named in paragraph 1 at *(place or address)*
   111 Sussex Drive, Ottawa, Ontario K3B 1W8
   by:

   [X] leaving a copy with the person.

   [ ] leaving a copy with *(name)*

   Check one box only. Strike out paragraphs 4 to 10 and go to paragraph 11.

        [ ] who is a lawyer who accepted service in writing on a copy of the document.

        [ ] who is the person's lawyer of record.

        [ ] who is the *(office or position)*
        of the corporation named in paragraph 1.

   [ ] mailing a copy to the person together with a prepaid return postcard in Form 6 in an envelope bearing the sender's return address. This postcard, in which receipt of the document(s) is acknowledged, was returned and is attached to this affidavit.

   [ ] leaving a copy in a sealed envelope addressed to the person at the person's place of residence with *(name)*
   who provided me with identification to show that he/she was an adult person residing at the same address and by mailing another copy of the same document(s) on the same or following day to the person named in paragraph 1 at that place of residence.

   [ ] other *(Specify. See rule 6 for details.)*

4. ~~I mailed the document(s) to be served by addressing the covering envelope to the person named in paragraph 1 at: *(set out address.)*~~

   ~~which is the address~~

        [ ] ~~of the person's place of business.~~

        [ ] ~~of a lawyer who accepted service on the person's behalf.~~

   ~~Check appropriate paragraph and strike out paragraphs 3, 5, 6, 7, 8, 9 and 10.~~

        [ ] ~~of the person's lawyer of record.~~

        [ ] ~~of the person's home.~~

        [ ] ~~on the document most recently filed in court by the person.~~

        [ ] ~~other *(Specify.)*~~

5. ~~The document(s) to be served was/were placed in an envelope that was picked up at~~ ~~a.m./p.m.~~
   ~~on *(date)*~~ ~~by *(name of courier service)*~~
   ~~a private courier service, a copy of whose receipt is attached to this affidavit.~~
   ~~The envelope was addressed to the person named in paragraph 1 at: *(Set out address.)*~~

   ~~which is the address~~

        [ ] ~~of the person's place of business.~~

        [ ] ~~of a lawyer who accepted service on the person's behalf.~~

   ~~Check appropriate paragraph and strike out paragraphs 3, 4, 6, 7, 8, 9 and 10.~~

        [ ] ~~of the person's lawyer of record.~~

        [ ] ~~of the person's home.~~

        [ ] ~~on the document most recently filed in court by the person.~~

        [ ] ~~other *(Specify.)*~~

Form 6B: Affidavit of Service (page 3)   **Court File Number**   ****FL6666**
sworn/affirmed

6. ~~The document(s) was/were deposited at a document exchange. The exchange's date stamp on the attached copy shows the date of the deposit. *(Strike out paragraphs 3, 4, 5, 7, 8, 9, 10 and 13.)*~~

7. ~~The document(s) were served through an electronic document exchange. The record of service from the exchange is attached to this affidavit. *(Strike out paragraphs 3, 4, 5, 6, 8, 9, 10 and 13.)*~~

8. ~~The document(s) to be served was/were faxed. The fax confirmation is attached to this affidavit. *(Strike out paragraphs 3, 4, 5, 6, 7, 9, 10 and 13.)*~~

9. ~~The document(s) were served by email. Attached to this Affidavit is a copy of the email that the document was attached to. *(Strike out paragraphs 3, 4, 5, 6, 7, 8, 10 and 13.)*~~

10. ~~An order of this court made on *(date)*~~   ~~allowed~~

    ☐ ~~substituted service.~~

    ☐ ~~service by advertisement. *(Attach advertisement.)*~~

    ~~The order was carried out as follows: *(Give details. Then go to paragraph 13 if you had to travel to serve substitutionally or by advertisement.)*~~

11. My relationship to, or affiliation with, any party in this case is as follows:
    None

12. I am at least 18 years of age.

13. To serve the document(s), I had to travel   25   kilometres. My fee for service of the document(s) is
    $ 47.00   , including travel.

Sworn/Affirmed before me at:

City of Ottawa
                              (municipality)

in   Province of Ontario
                              (province, state or country)

on
                                                                    _____
         (date)   *Signature*
                                                          (This form is to be signed in front of a lawyer,
         _____   *justice of the peace, notary public or*
         Commissioner for taking affidavits   *commissioner for taking affidavits.)*
    (Type or print name below if signature is illegible.)

CHAPTER 23
CONTESTING A DIVORCE

This chapter completes a contested divorce case and also offers an overview of steps in simple/sole and joint divorces.

CONTESTED DIVORCE

A typical contested divorce proceeds to trial in these steps:

1. Answer
2. Reply
3. Case conference
4. Settlement conference
5. Trial management conference
6. Trial record
7. Trial
8. Divorce order
9. Certificate of divorce

> HAVISHAM, Maria Shelley
> Re: Divorce
> _____
>
> In his answer, Precedent 23.1, Mr. Havisham is asking for joint custody of the kids and claims that Mrs. Havisham refuses to look for a job and is, therefore, not entitled to spousal support. He also wants tickets to all music performances of the kids. In her reply, Precedent 23.2, Mrs. Havisham states that it is impossible for her to manage the kids' music careers and also hold down a job. We scheduled a case conference and served and filed a case conference brief, Precedent 23.4, in the hopes that the Havishams would find common ground and settle; however, nothing much was achieved at the case conference, and the court scheduled a settlement conference at which they were finally able to hammer out all of the outstanding issues. In the divorce order, Precedent 23.7, Mr. Justice Mandamus awarded joint custody of the kids but no support for Mrs. Havisham. (Mr. Havisham offered to buy his own tickets to the kids' concerts, although the kids offered to supply him with freebies whenever possible.) We obtained Mrs. Havisham's certificate of divorce, Precedent 23.8. The Havisham divorce case has now ended.

ANSWER

Rule 10 of the *Family Law Rules* provides for answering a case using **Form 10 answer**, Precedent 23.1. The answer is parallel to a statement of defence in regular actions, in that it tells the respondent's side of the story and permits the respondent to make a claim, if any, of his or her own. Form 10 is simple to complete. If you are using the DIVORCEmate software, the program automatically inputs information from the initial database into pages 1A and 1B which are generated for user convenience only and, unless otherwise instructed, may be omitted as they are not part of the prescribed Form 10.

Within **thirty days** after service of the application and attachments on the respondent,

1. Prepare the following documents:

   - Form 10 answer
   - Financial statement mirroring the type which the applicant served on the respondent, together with the respondent's income tax returns and notices of assessment for the past three years, or an income and deduction printout from the Canada Revenue Agency
   - Form 35.1, affidavit in support of claim for custody or access, if applicable
   - Updated continuing record table of contents, adding the above documents, as applicable

2. Serve the above documents on the applicant and file the originals in the continuing record in the court office, together with an affidavit of service (Form 6B), except file only the notices of assessment for the past three years, not the income tax returns.

REPLY

Subrule 10(6) of the *Family Law Rules* provides for replying in a case using **Form 10A reply**, Precedent 23.2. The reply is the applicant's response to the respondent's answer. The applicant must serve and file a reply usually only where the respondent's answer raises a new issue that is not already in the applicant's application. Within **ten days** after service of the answer, the applicant must serve a reply, if any, on the respondent with an updated continuing record table of contents, and file the original in the continuing record, together with an affidavit of service of the reply.

CASE CONFERENCE

Under Rule 17 of the *Family Law Rules*, at least one case conference must be scheduled in every family law case, including a divorce case, for the purpose of exploring the possibility of settlement, narrowing any outstanding issues, and setting a date for the next step. The parties and their lawyers are expected to attend all conferences, unless the court orders otherwise. Either party may request a case conference, but it is usually the applicant who requests it. In preparation for the case conference, prepare the following documents:

1. Form 17 conference notice, Precedent 23.3.
2. Form 17A case conference brief, Precedent 23.4.
3. (a) A new financial statement (if the first financial statement is older than 30 days), or
   (b) An affidavit either stating no changes in the first financial statement or giving details of any minor changes.
4. Form 14C confirmation, Precedent 23.6.
5. An updated copy of the continuing record table of contents, adding the above documents, as applicable.
6. Form 6B affidavit of service.

The applicant must serve a copy of the above documents on the respondent and file the originals of the above documents in the continuing record at least **seven days** before the date of the case conference. The respondent must also serve and file the same documents as those listed above (minus the conference notice, since the applicant will have served and filed it) at least **four days** before the case conference, except for the confirmation, Form 14C, which each party must file no later than 2 p.m., **two days** before the case conference. Note that the case conference brief is not **filed** in the continuing record but that it is temporarily **placed** in the continuing record for the case conference judge to review. After the case conference, it is either returned to the respective parties or destroyed by the clerk so as to avoid exposing any settlement discussions or offers to settle to the trial judge that might influence that judge's decision should the case proceed to trial.

SETTLEMENT CONFERENCE

A settlement conference is held for the same purpose as that of a case conference, i.e. to explore the possibility of settling the case, and the two conferences may be combined, except that in a settlement conference, the settlement conference judge is expected to be more definite in rendering an opinion about the strengths and weaknesses of each party's case. The documents required in preparation for a settlement conference are the same as those set out for a case conference. Additional documents required for settlement conferences, include:

Form 17C settlement conference brief, general (which is similar to Form 17A case conference brief, general). Each party, but usually the applicant, must serve and file a Form 17C at least **seven days** before the settlement conference, and the respondent must serve and file a Form 17C at least **four days** before the settlement conference. The settlement conference brief is not filed in the continuing record, but it is temporarily placed in the continuing record for the settlement conference judge to review. After the settlement conference, it is either returned to the respective parties or destroyed by the clerk so as to avoid exposing any settlement discussions or offers to settle to the trial judge that might influence that judge's decision should the case proceed to trial.

Form 13A certificate of financial disclosure. Under subrule 13(13.1), a party who has served a corrected, updated, or new version of the financial statement (Form 13 or 13.1) must serve and file an updated Form 13A no later than **seven days** before the settlement conference, in the case of the party requesting the conference, and no later than **four days** before the settlement conference in the case of the other party.

Form 13B net family property statement, Precedent 23.5. Under subrule 13(14), if the claim includes property under Part I of the *Family Law Act*, each party must serve and file a Form 13B not less than **30 days** before a settlement conference and not more than 30 days and not less than **seven days** before a trial.

Form 13C Comparison of net family property. Under subrule 13(14.2), after serving and filing a Form 13B, the parties must also serve and file a joint Form 13C, which is basically a combined summary of the valuation date totals contained in each party's financial statement (Form 13.1). If Form 13C is completed jointly, only the party who requested the settlement conference must serve it and file it **seven days** before the settlement conference. If the parties cannot agree on a joint Form 13C, they must each serve and file a Form 13C, with the party who requested the settlement conference filing it **seven days** before the settlement conference, and the other party filing it **four days** before the settlement conference.

> **Legal TIP**
>
> You can tell the family law conferences apart by the first word in their name, e.g. a **case** conference reviews the **case**; a **settlement** conference aims to **settle** the case; a **trial** management conference prepares the case for **trial**.

NET FAMILY PROPERTY STATEMENT

Subrule 13(14) provides for the requirement of a **Form 13B net family property statement**, Precedent 23.5. Typically, this form is used where your client's claim includes a claim for an equalization of net family property. All of the amounts in Form 13B come from each party's Form 13.1 financial statement (property and support claims). Each party must serve and file a Form 13B net family property statement not less than **30 days** before a settlement conference and not more than 30 days and not less than **seven days** before a trial. Form 13B is for the purpose of calculating the net family property (NFP) of the spouses and arriving at the equalization payment payable. The lower NFP is subtracted from the higher NFP and divided by two. The result is the amount which the spouse with the higher NFP must pay to the spouse with the lower NFP.

PREPARATION AND DISTRIBUTION OF NET FAMILY PROPERTY STATEMENT (FORM 13B)

You require: Completed Form 13.1 financial statement (property and support claims) of both spouses. Follow along in Precedent 23.5. The wording guides completion. Notes on items not self-explanatory follow:

Table 1: value of assets owned on valuation date -- input by category all assets of the applicant from **on valuation date** columns of Form 13.1, starting with "Land."

Table 2: value of debts and liabilities on valuation date - input the debts from the **on valuation date** column of Form 13.1 Part 5: debts and other liabilities.

Table 3: net value of property on date of marriage -- This part excludes the matrimonial home or any charges/mortgages on the matrimonial home. Input by category all "property items" of the applicant from **date of marriage** columns of Form 13.1, Part 6. Do the same for any "debit items." Follow the same procedure for completing the respondent's columns. Obtain the figures from the respondent's Form 13.1. Final total is the net family property (NFP) and shows the amount of the equalization payment which the spouse with the higher NFP pays to the spouse with the lower NFP.

Number of copies, minimum 3: 1 served on opposing party, original filed in continuing record, 1 in file.

TRIAL MANAGEMENT CONFERENCE

Trial management conferences are provided for under Rule 17 of the *Family Law Rules*. A trial management conference was unnecessary in the Havisham divorce case since all issues in that case were settled at the settlement conference, which is usually the case in the majority of divorce cases. Where there are issues still outstanding, however, the settlement conference judge may require the parties to attend a trial management conference. The trial management conference is a last ditch attempt to settle the case, and if not, to review the evidence that will be presented at trial and estimate the length of time that the trial will require.

Either party, but usually the applicant, must serve and file a **Form 17E: trial management conference brief** at least **seven days** before the trial management conference, and the respondent must do so at least **four days** before the trial management conference. The briefs in Forms 17A, 17C and 17E are similar. Form 17E: trial management conference brief is the only conference brief which is filed in the continuing record, but with any offers to settle or sections containing settlement information being removed so as not to influence the decision of the trial judge.

TRIAL RECORD

Rule 23 of the *Family Law Rules* provides for evidence at trial and trial record. A trial record was unnecessary in the Havisham divorce case as it settled before reaching trial. Subrule 23(1) requires that when a divorce case, or any other family law case, proceeds to trial, the applicant must serve and file at least **thirty days** before the start of the trial, a trial record containing the following documents, as applicable. At least **seven days** before the trial, the respondent may serve, file, and add to the trial record any document that is not already in the trial record:

- Table of contents.
- Application, answer, and any reply.
- Any statement of facts.
- Financial statements and net family property statements by all parties, completed not more than 30 days before the record is served.
- Any affidavit in support of claim for custody or access, Form 35.1.
- Any assessment report ordered by the court or obtained by consent of the parties.
- Any temporary order relating to a matter still in dispute.
- Any order relating to the trial.
- Any transcript on which the party intends to rely at trial.
- Any expert report on which the party intends to rely at trial.

TRIAL

When a divorce case, or any other family law case, proceeds to trial, the procedure at trial is the same as in regular civil litigation trials. Following the trial, the trial judge grants the divorce order.

DIVORCE ORDER

Orders are provided for under Rule 25 of the *Family Law Rules*. The **divorce order (Form 25A)**, Precedent 23.7, contains the final terms of the divorce. Generally, the party who wins usually prepares it, serves it on the opposite lawyer and has the opposite lawyer approve it as to form and content. The party who won submits it to the court for the signature of the judge who made the order or the clerk of the court. Divorce orders do **not** finalize a divorce or end a marriage. Divorce orders are documents that formalize the **final terms** of the divorce.

Number of copies, minimum 4: 2 served on opposing party (1 to keep, the other to approve as to form and content and return), 1 filed in continuing record, 1 in client file.

CERTIFICATE OF DIVORCE

Subrule 36(8) of the *Family Law Rules* provides for a certificate of divorce which is the document which legally ends the marriage. Subsection 12(1) of the *Divorce Act* provides that a divorce takes effect on the thirty-first day after the day on which the order granting the divorce is given, unless the court orders otherwise. After that time period has passed, either party, but usually the applicant, prepares a **certificate of divorce (Form 36B)**,

Legal TIP

Generally, all court decisions in family law cases are **orders** (not judgments).

Precedent 23.8, and presents it to the clerk, along with a copy of the divorce order. The clerk checks the continuing record to verify that the required time has passed and that no appeal has been made on the divorce order and issues the certificate of divorce. Once the clerk issues the certificate of divorce, the divorce becomes final, and the spouses are free to remarry others if they wish.

SIMPLE/SOLE AND JOINT DIVORCES

Rule 36 of the *Family Law Rules* provides for a divorce based on affidavit evidence. Such a divorce may be a simple/sole divorce or joint divorce, and the form to be used in either situation is **Form 8A: application (divorce)**, Precedent 23.9. The evidence upon which the court gives a divorce order is **Form 36: affidavit for divorce**, Precedent 23.10.

Simple/sole divorce   A simple divorce, also referred to as sole divorce, deals only with a claim for divorce and no other claims, and the ground for divorce must be separation of one year. The spouses must have resolved all other issues, e.g. custody, access, support, property, through a separation agreement or court order. Once the application is served and the respondent fails to serve and file an answer, the divorce becomes an uncontested divorce and proceeds with the filing of affidavit evidence.

Joint divorce   A joint application is brought by both spouses jointly, and must be on consent of both parties. The ground for divorce must be separation of one year. A joint application may deal with claims in addition to divorce, e.g. support, custody, access, or family property, as long as both parties consent to all of the claims by both signing all of the papers. The joint divorce documents are not served on either party as both parties are the applicants.

Here is a summary of the basic steps and documents required in a simple/sole or joint divorce:

Figure 23.1

STEP 1 STARTING A SIMPLE/SOLE OR JOINT DIVORCE	
SIMPLE/SOLE DIVORCE	JOINT DIVORCE
Form 8A: Application(divorce) □ joint or ☒ simple Precedent 23.9	Form 8A: Application (divorce) ☒ joint or □ simple Precedent 23.9
• Includes divorce claim only. (All other claims must be either settled or undisputed.)	• May include divorce and other claims as long as both parties consent to all claims. Documents **not** served since both spouses are **applicants**.
• No financial statement.	• Financial statement, as applicable.
• If no answer, proceed to step 2.	• Step 2 documents filed at same time as application.

Figure 23.2

STEP 2 OBTAINING DIVORCE ORDER AND CERTIFICATE OF DIVORCE IN SIMPLE/SOLE OR JOINT DIVORCE

Applicant/s file the following documents to obtain a divorce order:

- Affidavit for divorce (Form 36), Precedent 23.10.
- Draft divorce order (Form 25A), usually 4 copies, Precedent 23.7.
- Two stamped envelopes, one addressed to one party and the other to the other party.
- Court fees.

* Under subrule 36 (6) (c), if the divorce order is to contain a support order, also prepare and file:

- an extra copy of the draft divorce order for the clerk to file with the Director of the Family Responsibility Office,
- two copies of a draft support deduction order,
- two copies of a draft support deduction order information form.

1. Once the judge grants the divorce order, the clerk mails it in the stamped envelopes to the parties.
2. Thirty-one days after the divorce order, prepare a **certificate of divorce (Form 36B)**, Precedent 23.8, and submit it to the court, together with a copy of the divorce order. The court issues the certificate of divorce and mails it to the parties, unless the court orders otherwise; the certificate of divorce is the document which legally ends the marriage.

CHAPTER SUMMARY

An answer is the document which the respondent serves and files in response to being served with an application. The steps to trial follow with a reply, a case conference, a settlement conference, a trial management conference, and a trial. The case management judge can grant a divorce order at any time during the case, provided all of the issues are resolved, or at the trial. With simple/sole or joint divorces, the judge may grant a divorce order on the basis of the applicant's affidavit evidence. In all divorce cases, whether contested or not, the divorce takes effect thirty-one days after the date of the divorce order. At that point, either party, but usually the applicant, may ask the court clerk to issue a certificate of divorce. The certificate of divorce finalizes the divorce and legally ends the marriage.

REVIEW QUESTIONS

1. Which party in a divorce case serves and files an answer?
2. When does a divorce become final?
3. Which spouse may obtain a certificate of divorce?
4. What is a case conference brief?
5. What is the difference between a divorce order and a certificate of divorce?
6. Who calls a settlement conference?
7. What is the purpose of a trial management conference?
8. List the grounds for divorce in a simple/sole divorce.
9. What is a net family property statement and when is it required?
10. In what way does a divorce order legally finalize a marriage?
11. In a divorce case, begin with an answer and list the major steps in trial and the reason/s for each step.

ONTARIO

Ontario Family Court of the Superior Court of Justice
(Name of Court)

Court File Number
**FL6666

at **50 Eagle Street West, Newmarket, Ontario L3Y 6B1**
(Court office address)

Form 10: Answer

Applicant(s)

Full legal name & address for service — street & number, municipality, postal code, telephone & fax numbers and e-mail address (if any).	Lawyer's name & address — street & number, municipality, postal code, telephone & fax numbers and e-mail address (if any).
Maria Shelley Havisham **333 GST Drive** **Newmarket, Ontario** **L2K 2D1** **Tel: (905) 859-1268**	**Robert B. Redford** **Michael, Eliad & Redford LLP** **863 Seneca Lane** **Toronto, Ontario M4J 1P6** **Tel: (416) 363-1079** **Fax: (416) 363-2628** **rbrdfrd@mer.com**

Respondent(s)

Full legal name & address for service — street & number, municipality, postal code, telephone & fax numbers and e-mail address (if any).	Lawyer's name & address — street & number, municipality, postal code, telephone & fax numbers and e-mail address (if any).
Brian Havisham **111 Sussex Drive** **Ottawa, Ontario** **K3B 1W8** **Tel: (613) 580-9334**	**Raymond G. Castles** **Castles & Sands** **Suite 900 – 205 Portage Street** **Markham, Ontario L3R 3G3** **Tel: (905) 495-2222** **Fax: (905) 495-2223** **raymond@castlessands.ca**

INSTRUCTIONS: Financial Statement

COMPLETE A FINANCIAL STATEMENT (Form 13) IF:
- you are making or responding to a claim for spousal support; or
- you are responding to a claim for child support; or
- you are making a claim for child support in an amount different from the table amount specified under the Child Support Guidelines.

You must complete all parts of the form **UNLESS** you are **ONLY** responding to a claim for child support in the table amount specified under the Child Support Guidelines **AND** you agree with the claim. In that case, only complete Parts 1, 2 and 3.

COMPLETE A FINANCIAL STATEMENT (Form 13.1) IF:
- you are making or responding to a claim for property or exclusive possession of the matrimonial home and its contents; or
- you are making or responding to a claim for property or exclusive possession of the matrimonial home and its contents together with other claims for relief.

TO THE APPLICANTS:

If you are making a claim against someone who is not an applicant, insert the person's name and address here.

AND TO: *(full legal name)* **an added respondent,**

of *(address of added party)*

My name is *(full legal name)* Brian Havisham

1. I agree with the following claim(s) made by the applicant: *(Refer to the numbers alongside the boxes on page 4 of the application form.)*
   Paragraphs 00, 02, 11, 15, 20 and 24.

2. I do not agree with the following claim(s) made by the applicant: *(Again, refer to the numbers alongside the boxes on page 4 of the application form.)*
   Paragraphs 01, 04, 10, 13, 16, 23, 30 and 32

3. [X] I am asking that the applicant's claim (except for the parts with which I agree) be dismissed with costs.

FLR 10 (October 1, 2012)

www.DIVORCEmate.com

Form 10: Answer (page 2)   Court File Number   **FL6666

---

4. [X] I am making a claim of my own. *(Attach a "Claim by Respondent" page. Otherwise do not attach it.)*

5. [X] The FAMILY HISTORY, as set out in the application,

[X] is correct   [ ] is not correct

(If it is not correct, attach your own FAMILY HISTORY page and underline those parts that are different from the applicant's version.)

6. The important facts that form the legal basis for my position in paragraph 2 are as follows: *(In numbered paragraphs, set out the facts for your position.)*

1. The Applicant, as noted in her Application, has been divorced four previous times.

2. Based on the Applicant's record of instability, I am asking for an Order for joint custody to ensure that the children have a stable home life.

3. The Applicant is obsessed with the possibility that the children may have a successful career as musicians, to the detriment of their home life and education.

4. Due to this overwhelming focus, the Applicant, although fully capable of obtaining employment as a nuclear physicist, has refused to seek employment.

5. I therefore do not believe that the Applicant should be entitled to spousal support at all.

Put a line through any blank space left on this page

Date of signature   Respondent's signature

Form 10: Answer (page 3)   Court File Number **FL6666

CLAIM BY RESPONDENT

Fill out a separate claim page for each person against whom you are making your claim(s).

7.   THIS CLAIM IS MADE AGAINST

[X] THE APPLICANT

[ ] AN ADDED PARTY, whose name is *(full legal name)*

(If your claim is against an added party, make sure that the person's name appears on page 1 of this form.)

8.   I ASK THE COURT FOR THE FOLLOWING:
(Claims below include claims for temporary orders.)

Claims under the *Divorce Act* *(Check boxes in this column only if you are asking for a divorce and your case is in the Superior Court of Justice or Family Court of the Superior Court of Justice.)*	Claims relating to property *(Check boxes in this column only if your case is in the Superior Court of Justice or Family Court of the Superior Court of Justice.)*	Claims relating to child protection
00 [X] a divorce	20 [X] equalization of net family properties	40 [ ] access
01 [ ] support for me	21 [ ] exclusive possession of matrimonial home	41 [ ] lesser protection order
02 [ ] support for child(ren) - table amount	22 [ ] exclusive possession of contents of matrimonial home	42 [ ] return of chid(ren) to my care
03 [ ] support for child(ren) - other than table amount	23 [ ] freezing assets	43 [ ] place child(ren) into care of *(name)*
04 [X] custody of child(ren)	24 [X] sale of family property	
05 [X] access to child(ren)		44 [ ] children's aid society wardship for ____ months
		45 [ ] society supervision of my child(ren)

Claims under the *Family Law Act or Children's Law Reform Act*	Other claims	
10 [ ] support for me	30 [X] costs	
11 [ ] support for child(ren) – table amount	31 [ ] annulment of marriage	
12 [ ] support for child(ren) – other than table amount	32 [X] prejudgment interest	
13 [X] custody of child(ren)	33 [ ] claims relating to a family arbitration	
14 [X] access to child(ren)		
15 [X] restraining/non-harassment order		
16 [ ] indexing spousal support		
17 [ ] declaration of parentage		
18 [X] guardianship over child's property		
50 [ ] other (*Specify.*)		

Form 10: Answer (page 4)

Court File Number   ****FL6666**

Give details of the order that you want the court to make. *(Include any amounts of support (if known) and the names of the children for whom support, custody or access is claimed.)*

1. Joint custody of the children of the marriage, namely, John Havisham, Paul Havisham, George Havisham, and Ryan Havisham.

2. Reasonable and generous access on reasonable notice.

3. Tickets to all performances by the children.

IMPORTANT FACTS SUPPORTING MY CLAIM(S)

(In numbered paragraphs, set out the facts that form the legal basis for your other claim(s).)

1. As set out above.

Put a line through any blank space left on this page

_____   _____
Date of signature   Respondent's signature

LAWYER'S CERTIFICATE

For divorce cases only

My name is: Raymond G. Castles

and I am the lawyer for *(name)*   Brian Havisham

in this divorce case. I certify that I have complied with the requirements of section 9 of the *Divorce Act.*

_____   _____
Date of signature   Signature of Lawyer

 For information on accessibility of court services for people with disability-related needs, contact:
Telephone: 416-326-2220 / 1-800-518-7901   TTY: 416-326-4012 / 1-877-425-0575

ONTARIO	Court File Number
Ontario Family Court of the Superior Court of Justice	****FL6666**
(Name of Court)	

at **50 Eagle Street West, Newmarket, Ontario L3Y 6B1**   **Form 10A: Reply by**
(Court office address)

[X] applicant

[ ] added respondent

Applicant(s)

Full legal name & address for service — street & number, municipality, postal code, telephone & fax numbers and e-mail address (if any).	Lawyer's name & address — street & number, municipality, postal code, telephone & fax numbers and e-mail address (if any).
Maria Shelley Havisham **333 GST Drive** **Newmarket, Ontario** **L2K 2D1** **Tel: (905) 859-1268**	**Robert B. Redford** **Michael, Eliad & Redford LLP** **863 Seneca Lane** **Toronto, Ontario M4J 1P6** **Tel: (416) 363-1079** **Fax: (416) 363-2628** **rbrdfrd@mer.com**

Respondent(s)

Full legal name & address for service — street & number, municipality, postal code, telephone & fax numbers and e-mail address (if any).	Lawyer's name & address — street & number, municipality, postal code, telephone & fax numbers and e-mail address (if any).
Brian Havisham **111 Sussex Drive** **Ottawa, Ontario** **K3B 1W8** **Tel: (613) 580-9334**	**Raymond G. Castles** **Castles & Sands** **Suite 900 – 205 Portage Street** **Markham, Ontario L3R 3G3** **Tel: (905) 495-2222** **Fax: (905) 495-2223** **raymond@castlessands.ca**

Name & address of Children's Lawyer's agent (street & number, municipality, postal code, telephone & fax numbers and e-mail address (if any)) and name of person represented.

INSTRUCTIONS: Financial Statement

COMPLETE A FINANCIAL STATEMENT (Form 13) IF:
- you are responding to a claim for spousal support; or
- you are responding to a claim for child support.

You must complete all parts of the form **UNLESS** you are **ONLY** responding to a claim for child support in the table amount specified under the Child Support Guidelines **AND** you agree with the claim. In that case, only complete Parts 1, 2 and 3.

COMPLETE A FINANCIAL STATEMENT (Form 13.1) IF:
- you are responding to a claim for property or exclusive possession of the matrimonial home and its contents; or
- you are responding to a claim for property or exclusive possession of the matrimonial home and its contents together with other claims for relief.

TO ALL PARTIES:

1. My name is *(full legal name)* Maria Shelley Havisham

2. I agree with the following claim(s) made by the respondent in his/her answer: *(Refer to the numbers alongside the boxes in the Answer, Form 10.)*
   Paragraphs 00, 05, 14, 15, 20 and 24.

3. I do not agree with the following claim(s) made by the respondent: *(Again, refer to the numbers alongside the boxes in the Answer, Form 10.)*
   Paragraphs 04, 13, 18, 30, and 32.

4. [X] I am asking that the respondent's claim (except for the parts with which I agree) be dismissed with costs.

5.   The important facts supporting my position in paragraph 3 are as follows: *(In numbered paragraphs, set out the reasons for your position.)*

> 1.   The Respondent, having no musical ability of his own, fails to appreciate the children's talents for music.
>
> 2.   In addition, the Respondent, still bitter at losing the elections and his position of power and influence, wishes to continue to control the lives of his children and my life as well.
>
> 3.   Based on the above, the Respondent should not be entitled to joint custody, nor should he have any control over the property of the children.
>
> 4.   As to my claim for spousal support, the Respondent ignores the fact that I am unable to manage both the music careers of the children and a nuclear reactor.

Put a line through any blank space left on this page

_____   _____
Date of signature   *Signature*

ONTARIO

Ontario Family Court of the Superior Court of Justice

(Name of Court)

Court File Number
**FL6666

at **50 Eagle Street West, Newmarket, Ontario L3Y 6B1**

(Court office address)

**Form 17:
Conference
Notice**

Applicant(s)

Full legal name & address for service — street & number, municipality, postal code, telephone & fax numbers and e-mail address (if any).	Lawyer's name & address — street & number, municipality, postal code, telephone & fax numbers and e-mail address (if any).
Maria Shelley Havisham **333 GST Drive** **Newmarket, Ontario** **L2K 2D1** **Tel: (905) 859-1268**	**Robert B. Redford** **Michael, Eliad & Redford LLP** **863 Seneca Lane** **Toronto, Ontario M4J 1P6** **Tel: (416) 363-1079** **Fax: (416-363-2628** **rbrdfrd@mer.com**

Respondent(s)

Full legal name & address for service — street & number, municipality, postal code, telephone & fax numbers and e-mail address (if any).	Lawyer's name & address — street & number, municipality, postal code, telephone & fax numbers and e-mail address (if any).
Brian Havisham **111 Sussex Drive** **Ottawa, Ontario** **K3B 1W8** **Tel: (613) 580-9334**	**Raymond G. Castles** **Castles & Sands** **Suite 900 - 205 Portage Street** **Markham, Ontario L3R 3G3** **Tel: (905) 495-2222** **Fax: (905) 495-2223** **raymond@castlessands.ca**

Name & address of Children's Lawyer's agent (street & number, municipality, postal code, telephone & fax numbers and e-mail address (if any)) and name of person represented.

TO: *(name of party or parties or lawyer(s))* Castles & Sands

A [x] **CASE CONFERENCE**   [ ] **SETTLEMENT CONFERENCE**   [ ] **TRIAL MANAGEMENT**

WILL BE HELD AT *(place of conference)*

50 Eagle Street West, Newmarket, Ontario

at *(time)* 10 a.m. **on** *(date)* November 14, (year)

The conference has been arranged at the request of   [x] the applicant   [ ] the respondent

[ ] the case management judge   [ ] *(Other; specify.)*

to deal with the following issues:

All of the issues.

You must participate at that time and date by   [x] coming to court at the address set out above.

[ ] video-conference or telephone at *(location of video terminal or telephone)*

as agreed under arrangements already made by *(name of person)*

for video/telephone conferencing.

IF YOU DO NOT PARTICIPATE AS SET OUT ABOVE, THE CASE MAY GO ON WITHOUT YOU OR THE COURT MAY DISMISS THE CASE.

_____   _____
Date of signature   *Signature of clerk of the court*

NOTE: *The party requesting the conference (or, if the conference is not requested by a party, the applicant) must serve and file a Case Conference Brief (Form 17A or 17B), Settlement Conference Brief (Form 17C or 17D) or Trial Management Conference Brief (Form 17E) not later than 7 days before the date scheduled for the conference. The other party must serve and file a brief not later than four days before the conference date. Each party must also file a Confirmation (Form 14C) not later than 2 p.m. two days before the conference.*

FLR 17 (September 1, 2005)   www.DIVORCEmate.com

ONTARIO

Ontario Family Court of the Superior Court of Justice

(Name of court)

Court File Number
**FL6666

at **50 Eagle Street West, Newmarket, Ontario L3Y 6B1**

(Court office address)

**Form 17A:
Case Conference Brief -
General**

Name of party filing this brief	Date of case conference
Maria Shelley Havisham	**November 14, (year)**

Applicant(s)

Full legal name & address for service — street & number, municipality, postal code, telephone & fax numbers and e-mail address (if any).	Lawyer's name & address — street & number, municipality, postal code, telephone & fax numbers and e-mail address (if any).
Maria Shelley Havisham **333 GST Drive** **Newmarket, Ontario** **L2K 2D1** **Tel: (905) 859-1268**	**Robert B. Redford** **Michael, Eliad & Redford LLP** **863 Seneca Lane** **Toronto, Ontario M4J 1P6** **Tel: (416) 363-1079** **Fax: (416) 363-2628** **rbrdfrd@mer.com**

Respondent(s)

Full legal name & address for service — street & number, municipality, postal code, telephone & fax numbers and e-mail address (if any).	Lawyer's name & address — street & number, municipality, postal code, telephone & fax numbers and e-mail address (if any).
Brian Havisham **111 Sussex Drive** **Ottawa, Ontario** **K3B 1W8** **Tel: (613) 580-9334**	**Raymond G. Castles** **Castles & Sands** **Suite 900 – 205 Portage Street** **Markham, Ontario L3R 3G3** **Tel: (905) 495-2222** **Fax: (905) 495-2223** **raymond@castlessands.ca**

Name & address of Children's Lawyer's agent (street & number, municipality, postal code, telephone & fax numbers and e-mail address (if any)) and name of person represented.

PART 1: FAMILY FACTS

1. **APPLICANT:**   Age: 45   Birthdate: *(d, m, y)* 26, February, (year)

2. **RESPONDENT:**   Age: 58   Birthdate: *(d, m, y)* 1, April, (year)

3. **RELATIONSHIP DATES:**

    [X] Married on *(date)*   April 1, (12 years ago)

    [X] Separated on *(date)*   April 1, (last year)

    [ ] Started living together on *(date)*

    [ ] Never lived together

    [ ] Other *(Explain.)*

4. The basic information about the child(ren) is as follows:

Child's full legal name	Age	Birthdate *(d, m, y)*	Grade/Year and School	Now living with
John Havisham	11	11/04/--	Grade 6, Millwood Boys	Mother
Paul Havisham	10	10/04/--	Grade 5, Millwood Boys	Mother
George Havisham	9	09/04/--	Grade 4, Millwood Boys	Mother
Ryan Havisham	8	08/04/--	Grade 3, Millwood Boys	Mother

FLR 17A (November 15, 2009)   www.DIVORCEmate.com

Form 17A: Case Conference Brief (General) (page 2)   Court File Number   ****FL6666**

PART 2: THE ISSUES

5. What are the issues in this case that **HAVE** been settled:

☐ child custody   ☐ spousal support   ☐ possession of home

☐ access   ☐ child support   ☐ equalization of net family property

☐ restraining order   ☒ ownership of property

☐ other *(Specify.)*

6. What are the issues in this case that have **NOT** yet been settled:

☒ child custody   ☒ spousal support   ☐ possession of home

☒ access   ☒ child support   ☒ equalization of net family property
(Attach Net Family Property Statement, Form 13B)

☒ restraining order   ☐ ownership of property

☐ other *(Specify.)*

7. If child or spousal support is an issue, give the income of the parties:

Applicant: $240,000.00   per year for the year (year)

Respondent: $120,000.00   per year for the year (year)

8. Have you explored any ways to settle the issues that are still in dispute in this case?

☒ No.   ☐ Yes. *(Give details.)*

9. Have any of the issues that have been settled turned into a court order or a written agreement?

☒ No.

☐ Yes.   ☐ an order dated

          ☐ a written agreement that is attached.

10. Have the parents attended a family law or parenting education session?

☒ No. *(Should they attend one?)*

☐ Yes. *(Give details.)*

PART 3: ISSUES FOR THIS CASE CONFERENCE

11. What are the issues for this case conference? What are the important facts for this case conference?

All of the issues indicated in paragraph 6. The children are living with their mother, and they are happy and should continue to live with their mother. The Applicant requires the Respondent to pay spousal support because she manages the children's music careers on a full-time basis and is unable to take another job to support herself.

12. What is your proposal to resolve these issues?

A court order in favour of the Applicant.

13. Do you want the court to make a temporary or final order at the case conference about any of these issues?

☒ No.   ☐ Yes. *(Give details.)*

PART 4: FINANCIAL INFORMATION

NOTE: - *If a claim for support has been made in this case, you must serve and file a new Financial Statement (Form 13 or 13.1), if it is different from the one filed in the continuing record or if the one in the continuing record is more than 30 days old. If there are minor changes but no major changes in your financial statement, you can serve and file an affidavit with details of the changes instead of a new financial statement. If you have not yet filed a financial statement in the continuing record, you must do it now. The page/tab number of the financial statement in the continuing record is*   *Volume 1, Tab 2*

Form 17A: Case Conference Brief (General) (page 3)   Court File Number   **FL6666**

14. If a claim is being made for child support and a claim is made for special expenses under the Child Support Guidelines, give details of those expenses or attach additional information.

15. If a claim is made for child support and you claim that the Child Support Guidelines table amount should not be ordered, briefly outline the reasons here or attach an additional page.

PART 5: PROCEDURAL ISSUES

16. If custody or access issues are not yet settled:

    (a) Is a custody or access assessment needed?

    [X] No.   [ ] Yes. *(Give names of possible assessors.)*

    (b) Does a child or a parent under 18 years of age need legal representation from the Office of the Children's Lawyer?

    [X] No.   [ ] Yes. *(Give details and reasons.)*

17. Does any party need an order for the disclosure of documents, the questioning of witnesses, a property valuation or any other matter in this case?

    [X] No.   [ ] Yes. *(Give details.)*

18. Are any other procedural orders needed?

    [X] No.   [ ] Yes. *(Give details.)*

19. Have all the persons who should be parties in this case been added as parties?

    [X] Yes.   [ ] No. *(Who needs to be added?)*

20. Are there issues that may require expert evidence or a report?

    [X] No.   [ ] Yes. *(If yes, provide details such as: the type of expert evidence; whether the parties will be retaining a joint expert; who the expert will be; who will be paying the expert; how long it will take to obtain a report, etc.)*

21. Are there any other issues that should be reviewed at the case conference?

    [X] No.   [ ] Yes. *(Give details.)*

_____   _____
Date of party's signature   *Signature of party*

_____   _____
Date of lawyer's signature   *Signature of party's lawyer*

ONTARIO

Ontario Family Court of the Superior Court of Justice	Court File Number ****FL6666**
(Name of Court)	

at   **50 Eagle Street West, Newmarket, Ontario L3Y 6B1**

(Court office address)

Form 13B: Net Family Property Statement

Applicant(s)

Full legal name & address for service — street & number, municipality, postal code, telephone & fax numbers and e-mail address (if any).	Lawyer's name & address — street & number, municipality, postal code, telephone & fax numbers and e-mail address (if any).
Maria Shelley Havisham **333 GST Drive** **Newmarket, Ontario** **L2K 2D1** **Tel: (905) 859-1268**	**Robert B. Redford** **Michael, Eliad & Redford LLP** **863 Seneca Lane** **Toronto, Ontario M4J 1P6** **Tel: (416) 363-1079** **Fax: (416) 363-2628** **rbrdfrd@mer.com**

Respondent(s)

Full legal name & address for service — street & number, municipality, postal code, telephone & fax numbers and e-mail address (if any).	Lawyer's name & address — street & number, municipality, postal code, telephone & fax numbers and e-mail address (if any).
Brian Havisham **111 Sussex Drive** **Ottawa, Ontario** **K3B 1W8** **Tel: (613) 580-9334**	**Raymond G. Castles** **Castles & Sands** **Suite 900 – 205 Portage Street** **Markham, Ontario L3R 3G3** **Tel: (905) 495-2222** **Fax: (905) 495-2223** **raymond@castlessands.ca**

My name is *(full legal name)*   Maria Shelley Havisham

The valuation date for the following material is *(date)*   April 1, (last year)

The date of marriage is *(date)*   April 1, (12 years ago)

(Complete the tables by filling in the columns for both parties, showing your assets, debts, etc. and those of your spouse)

Table 1: Value Of Assets Owned on Valuation Date *(List in the order of the categories in the financial statement)*			
PART 4(a): LAND			
Nature & Type of Ownership *(State percentage interest)*	**Address of Property**	**APPLICANT**	**RESPONDENT**
Matrimonial Home Joint tenancy 50%	111 Sussex Drive, Ottawa, ON K3B 1W8	$250,000.00	$250,000.00
	15. Totals: Value of Land	**$250,000.00**	**$250,000.00**

PART 4(b): GENERAL HOUSEHOLD ITEMS AND VEHICLES			
Item	**Description**	**APPLICANT**	**RESPONDENT**
Household goods & furniture	One-half of matrimonial home contents	$50,000.00	$50,000.00
Cars, boats, Vehicles	Car (year) Volvo 740 Motor boat, Lund	$4,000.00	$50,000.00
Jewellery, art, electronics, tools, sports & hobby, Equipment	Jewellery and electronics	$15,000.00	$20,000.00

FLR 13B (May 15, 2009)

www.DIVORCEmate.com

Form 13B: Net Family Property Statement (page 2)   Court File Number   **FL6666

Other special Items				
16. Totals: Value of General Household Items and Vehicles			69,000.00	$120,000.00

PART 4(c): BANK ACCOUNTS AND SAVINGS, SECURITIES AND PENSIONS

Category *(Savings, Checking, GIC, RRSP, Pensions, etc.)*	Institution	Account Number	APPLICANT	RESPONDENT
Savings	Great Money Bank	12345	$25,000.00	
RRSP	Great Money Bank	678910	$10,000.00	
GIC	CIBC			$100,000.00
17. Totals: Value of Accounts And Savings			$35,000.00	$100,000.00

PART 4(d): LIFE AND DISABILITY INSURANCE

Company, Type & Policy No.	Owner	Beneficiary	Face Amount ($)	APPLICANT	RESPONDENT
18. Totals: Cash Surrender Value Of Insurance Policies				$0.00	$0.00

PART 4(e): BUSINESS INTERESTS

Name of Firm or Company	Interests	APPLICANT	RESPONDENT
19. Totals: Value Of Business Interests		$0.00	$0.00

PART 4(f): MONEY OWED TO YOU

Details	APPLICANT	RESPONDENT
20. Totals: Money Owed To You	$0.00	$0.00

PART 4(g): OTHER PROPERTY

Category	Details	APPLICANT	RESPONDENT
21. Totals: Value Of Other Property		$0.00	$0.00

22. VALUE OF PROPERTY OWNED ON THE VALUATION DATE, (TOTAL 1) *(Add: items [15] to [21])*	$354,000.00	$470,000.00

Form 13B: Net Family Property Statement (page 3) Court File Number ****FL6666**

Table 2: Value Of Debts and Liabilities on Valuation Date

PART 5: DEBTS AND OTHER LIABILITIES

Category	Details	APPLICANT	RESPONDENT
Charge/Mortgage, joint 50%	Matrimonial Home, Great Money Bank	$20,000.00	$20,000.00
Credit Card	Visa		$15,000.00
23. Totals: Debts And Other Liabilities, (TOTAL 2)		**$20,000.00**	**$35,000.00**

Table 3: Net value on date of marriage of property (other than a matrimonial home) after deducting debts or other liabilities on date of marriage (other than those relating directly to the purchase or significant improvement of a matrimonial home)

PART 6: PROPERTY, DEBTS AND OTHER LIABILITIES ON DATE OF MARRIAGE

Category and Details	APPLICANT	RESPONDENT
Land *(exclude matrimonial home owned on the date of marriage, unless sold before date of separation).*		
General household items and vehicles	$30,000.00	$20,000.00
Bank accounts and savings	$4,000.00	$10,000.00
Life and disability insurance		
Business interests		
Money owed to you		
Other property		
3(a) TOTAL OF PROPERTY ITEMS	**$34,000.00**	**$30,000.00**
Debts and other liabilities *(Specify)*	$25,000.00	$20,000.00
3(b) TOTAL OF DEBTS ITEMS	**$25,000.00**	**$20,000.00**
24. NET VALUE OF PROPERTY OWNED ON DATE OF MARRIAGE, (NET TOTAL 3)	**$9,000.00**	**$10,000.00**

Table 4: PART 7: VALUE OF PROPERTY EXCLUDED UNDER SUBS. 4(2) OF "FAMILY LAW ACT"

Item	APPLICANT	RESPONDENT
Gift or inheritance from third person		$30,000.00
Income from property expressly excluded by donor/testator		
Damages and settlements for personal injuries, etc.		
Life insurance proceeds		
Traced property		
Excluded property by spousal agreement		
Other Excluded Property		
26. TOTALS: VALUE OF EXCLUDED PROPERTY, (TOTAL 4)	**$0.00**	**$30,000.00**

	APPLICANT	RESPONDENT
TOTAL 2: Debts and Other Liabilities *(item 23)*	$20,000.00	$35,000.00
TOTAL 3: Value of Property Owned on the Date of Marriage *(item 24)*	$9,0000.00	$10,000.00
TOTAL 4: Value of Excluded Property *(item 26)*	$0.00	$30,000.00
TOTAL 5: *(TOTAL 2 + TOTAL 3 + TOTAL 4)*	**$29,000.00**	**$75,000.00**

Form 13B: Net Family Property Statement (page 4) Court File Number ****FL6666**

	APPLICANT	RESPONDENT
TOTAL 1: Value of Property Owned on Valuation Date *(item 22)*	$354,000.00	$470,000.00
TOTAL 5: *(from above)*	$29,000.00	$75,000.00
TOTAL 6: NET FAMILY PROPERTY *(Subtract: TOTAL 1 minus TOTAL 5)*	**$325,000.00**	**$395,000.00**

EQUALIZATION PAYMENTS	Applicant Pays Respondent	Respondent Pays Applicant
		$35,000.00

_____ _____
Signature *Date of signature*

ONTARIO

Ontario Family Court of the Superior Court of Justice

(Name of Court)

Court File Number
**FL6666

at   **50 Eagle Street West, Newmarket, Ontario L3Y 6B1**

(Court office address)

Form 14C: Confirmation

Applicant(s)

Full legal name & address for service — street & number, municipality, postal code, telephone & fax numbers and e-mail address (if any).	Lawyer's name & address — street & number, municipality, postal code, telephone & fax numbers and e-mail address (if any).
Maria Shelley Havisham **333 GST Drive** **Newmarket, Ontario** **L2K 2D1** **Tel: (905) 859-1268**	**Robert B. Redford** **Michael, Eliad & Redford LLP** **863 Seneca Lane** **Toronto, Ontario M4J 1P6** **Tel: (416) 363-1079** **Fax: (416) 363-2628** **rbrdfrd@mer.com**

Respondent(s)

Full legal name & address for service — street & number, municipality, postal code, telephone & fax numbers and e-mail address (if any).	Lawyer's name & address — street & number, municipality, postal code, telephone & fax numbers and e-mail address (if any).
Brian Havisham **111 Sussex Drive** **Ottawa, Ontario** **K3B 1W8** **Tel: (613) 580-9334**	**Raymond G. Castles** **Castles & Sands** **Suite 900 – 205 Portage Street** **Markham, Ontario L3R 3G3** **Tel: (905) 495-2222** **Fax: (905) 495-2223** **raymond@castlessands.ca**

Name & address of Children's Lawyer's agent (street & number, municipality, postal code, telephone & fax numbers and e-mail address (if any)) and name of person represented.

1. My name is *(full legal name)*   Robert B. Redford

    and I am   [x]   the lawyer for *(name)*   Maria Shelley Havisham

             [ ]   *(Other; Specify.)*

2. I have   [ ]   not been able to contact the opposing lawyer or party in this case to confirm the matters set out in paragraphs 3 to 7 below because: *(Give reason for inability to contact other side.)*

      [X]   contacted the opposing lawyer or party and confirmed the matters set out in paragraphs 3 to 7 below.

3. The scheduled date and time for this   [ ] motion   [x] case conference   [ ] settlement conference

    [ ] trial management conference, is *(date)*   **November 14, (year)**   at *(time)*   **10 a.m.**

Complete only if motion is being confirmed.   [ ] A case conference was held on the issues in this motion before Justice

                  [ ] A case conference has not been held on the issues in this motion.

4. This matter is going ahead   [X] on all the issues.   [ ] on only the following issues: *(Specify.)*

    [ ] for a consent order regarding: *(Specify.)*

    [ ] for an adjournment on consent to *(date)*   because *(Give reason for adjournment.)*

    [ ] for a contested adjournment to *(date)*   asked for by

    because *(Give reason.)*

5. The judge should read pages/tabs   Tabs 1, 4, and 6   of the continuing record.

6. Total time estimate: applicant   30   minutes; respondent   30   minutes;   for a total of   60   minutes.

7. The case management judge for this case is *(Justice)*   Justice Grave

_____	_____
Date of signature	*Lawyer's or party's signature*

FLR 14C (September 1, 2005)

SEAL

ONTARIO
Ontario Family Court of the Superior Court of Justice
(Name of Court)

at   50 Eagle Street West, Newmarket, Ontario L3Y 6B1
(Court office address)

Court File Number
**FL6666

Form 25A: Divorce
Order

Applicant(s)

Full legal name & address for service – street & number, municipality, postal code, telephone & fax numbers & email address (if any).	*Lawyer's name & address - street & number, municipality, postal code, telephone & fax numbers & e-mail address (if any).*
Maria Shelley Havisham **333 GST Drive** **Newmarket, Ontario** **L2K 2D1** **Tel: (905) 859-1268**	**Robert B. Redford** **Michael, Eliad & Redford LLP** **863 Seneca Lane** **Toronto, Ontario M4J 1P6** **Tel: (416) 363-1079** **Fax: (416) 363-2628** **rbrdfrd@mer.com**

The Honourable

Justice Mandamus
Judge (print or type name)

February 26, (year)
Date of order

Respondent(s)

Full legal name & address for service – street & number, municipality, postal code, telephone & fax numbers & email address (if any).	*Lawyer's name & address - street & number, municipality, postal code, telephone & fax numbers & e-mail address (if any).*
Brian Havisham **111 Sussex Drive** **Ottawa, Ontario** **K3B 1W8** **Tel: (613) 580-9334**	**Raymond G. Castles** **Castles & Sands** **Suite 900 – 205 Portage Street** **Markham, Ontario L3R 3G3** **Tel: (905) 495-2222** **Fax: (905) 495-2223** **raymond@castlessands.ca**

The court heard an application of *(name)*   Maria Shelley Havisham

on *(date)*   February 26, (year)

The following persons were in court *(Give name of parties and lawyers in court. This paragraph may be struck out if the divorce is uncontested.)*

Maria Shelley Havisham, Brian Havisham, and lawyer for each of the parties.

This court received evidence and considered submissions on behalf of *(name or names)*

Maria Shelley Havisham and Brian Havisham.

THIS COURT ORDERS THAT:

1. *If the court decides that the divorce shall take effect earlier, replace "31" with the smaller number.*

   (full legal names of spouses)   Maria Shelley Havisham and Brian Havisham

   who were married at *(place)*   Ottawa

   on *(date)*   April 1, (12 yrs. ago)

   be divorced and that the divorce take effect   31   days after the date of this order.

(Add further paragraphs where the court orders other relief.)

2. The Applicant and the Respondent shall have joint custody of the children of the marriage, namely, John Havisham, born April 11, (11 years ago), Paul Havisham, born April 10, (10 years ago), George Havisham, born April 9, (9 years ago), Ryan Havisham, born April 8, (8 years ago).

3. The Respondent shall pay child support in accordance with the Child Support Guidelines in the amount of $2,536.00 per month.

4. The Respondent shall be entitled to reasonable access to the children on reasonable notice.

5. The Respondent shall pay to the Applicant as an equalization of net family property the sum of $35,000.00.

FLR 25A (September 1, 2005)

www.DIVORCEmate.com

Precedent 23.7

Form 25A: Divorce
Order, page 2

Form 25A: Divorce Order (page 2)   Court File Number   ****FL6666**

6. There will be no Order as to spousal support.

7. There will be no costs of this proceeding.

_____   _____
Date of signature   *Signature of judge or clerk of the court*

NOTE: *Neither spouse is free to remarry until this order takes effect, at which time you can get a **Certificate of Divorce** from the court office.*

ONTARIO

Ontario Family Court of the Superior Court of Justice
(Name of Court)

SEAL at **50 Eagle Street West, Newmarket, Ontario L3Y 6B1**
(Court office address)

Court File Number
**FL6666

Form 36B: Certificate of Divorce

Applicant

Full legal name & address for service — street & number, municipality, postal code, telephone & fax numbers and e-mail address (if any).	Lawyer's name & address — street & number, municipality, postal code, telephone & fax numbers and e-mail address (if any).
Maria Shelley Havisham **333 GST Drive** **Newmarket, Ontario** **L2K 2D1** **Tel: (905) 859-1268**	**Robert B. Redford** **Michael, Eliad & Redford LLP** **863 Seneca Lane** **Toronto, Ontario M4J 1P6** **Tel: (416) 363-1079** **Fax: (416) 363-2628** **rbrdfrd@mer.com**

Respondent(s)

Full legal name & address for service — street & number, municipality, postal code, telephone & fax numbers and e-mail address (if any).	Lawyer's name & address — street & number, municipality, postal code, telephone & fax numbers and e-mail address (if any).
Brian Havisham **111 Sussex Drive** **Ottawa, Ontario** **K3B 1W8** **Tel: (613) 580-9334**	**Raymond G. Castles** **Castles & Sands** **Suite 900 – 205 Portage Street** **Markham, Ontario L3R 3G3** **Tel: (905) 495-2222** **Fax: (905) 495-2223** **raymond@castlessands.ca**

I CERTIFY THAT the marriage of *(full legal name of spouses)*

Maria Shelley Havisham

and

Brian Havisham

which was solemnized at *(place of marriage)*

Ottawa, Ontario

on *(date of marriage)*   April 1, (12 years ago)

was dissolved by an order of this court made on *(date of divorce order)*   February 26, 20--

The divorce took effect on *(date when order took effect)*   March 29, 20--

_____
Signature of clerk of the court

_____
Date of signature

NOTE: *This certificate can only be issued on or after the date on which the divorce takes effect.*

FLR 36B (September 1, 2005)   www.DIVORCEmate.com

<table>
<tr>
<td rowspan="2">SEAL</td>
<td colspan="2" align="center">*ONTARIO*
Ontario Family Court of the Superior Court of Justice
(Name of Court)</td>
<td>Court File Number</td>
</tr>
<tr>
<td colspan="2">**at** 50 Eagle Street West, Newmarket, Ontario L3Y 6B1
(Court office address)</td>
<td>**Form 8A: Application
(Divorce)**
[x] **Simple (divorce only)**
[ ] **Joint**</td>
</tr>
</table>

Applicant(s)

Full legal name & address for service — street & number, municipality, postal code, telephone & fax numbers and e-mail address (if any).	Lawyer's name & address — street & number, municipality, postal code, telephone & fax numbers and e-mail address (if any).
Charles Long **78 Jane Street** **Newmarket, Ontario** **L2K 2D1** **Tel: (905) 859-1397**	**Robert B. Redford** **Michael, Eliad & Redford LLP** **863 Seneca Lane** **Toronto, Ontario M4J 1P6** **Tel: (416) 363-1079** **Fax: (416) 363-2628** **rbrdfrd@mer.com**

Respondent(s)

Full legal name & address for service — street & number, municipality, postal code, telephone & fax numbers and e-mail address (if any).	Lawyer's name & address — street & number, municipality, postal code, telephone & fax numbers and e-mail address (if any).
Wendy Long **11 Mannix Drive** **Watertown, Ontario** **K3B 1W8** **Tel: (705) 745-7458**	

[X]   IN THIS CASE, THE APPLICANT IS CLAIMING DIVORCE ONLY.

TO THE RESPONDENT(S):   A COURT CASE FOR DIVORCE HAS BEEN STARTED AGAINST YOU IN THIS COURT. THE DETAILS ARE SET OUT ON THE ATTACHED PAGES.

THIS CASE IS ON THE STANDARD TRACK OF THE CASE MANAGEMENT SYSTEM. No court date has been set for this case but, if you have been served with a notice of motion, it has a court date and you or your lawyer should come to court for the motion. A case management judge will not be assigned until one of the parties asks the clerk of the court to schedule a case conference or until a motion is scheduled, whichever comes first.

IF, AFTER 365 DAYS, THE CASE HAS NOT BEEN SCHEDULED FOR TRIAL, the clerk of the court will send out a warning that the case will be dismissed within 60 days unless the parties file proof that the case has been settled or one of the parties asks for a case or a settlement conference.

IF YOU WANT TO OPPOSE ANY CLAIM IN THIS CASE, you or your lawyer must prepare an *Answer* (Form 10 — a blank copy should be attached), serve a copy on the applicant and file a copy in the court office with an *Affidavit of Service* (Form 6B).
YOU HAVE ONLY 30 DAYS AFTER THIS APPLICATION IS SERVED ON YOU (60 DAYS IF THIS APPLICATION IS SERVED ON YOU OUTSIDE CANADA OR THE UNITED STATES) TO SERVE AND FILE AN ANSWER. IF YOU DO NOT, THE CASE WILL GO AHEAD WITHOUT YOU AND THE COURT MAY MAKE AN ORDER AND ENFORCE IT AGAINST YOU.

IF YOU WANT TO MAKE A CLAIM OF YOUR OWN, you or your lawyer must fill out the claim portion in the Answer, serve a copy on the applicant(s) and file a copy in the court office with an Affidavit of Service.
- If you want to make a claim for support but do not want to make a claim for property or exclusive possession of the matrimonial home and its contents, you **MUST** fill out a Financial Statement (Form 13), serve a copy on the applicant(s) and file a copy in the court office.
- However, if your only claim for support is for child support in the table amount specified under the Child Support Guidelines, you do not need to fill out, serve or file a Financial Statement.
- If you want to make a claim for property or exclusive possession of the matrimonial home and its contents, whether or not it includes a claim for support, you **MUST** fill out a Financial Statement (Form 13.1, not Form 13), serve a copy on the applicant(s), and file a copy in the court office.

YOU SHOULD GET LEGAL ADVICE ABOUT THIS CASE RIGHT AWAY. If you cannot afford a lawyer, you may be able to get help from your local Legal Aid office. *(See your telephone directory under LEGAL AID.)*

FLR 8A (April 12, 2016)   www.DIVORCEmate.com

Form 8A: Application (Divorce) (page 3)　　　　Court File Number _____

FAMILY HISTORY

APPLICANT:　　Age: 45　　Birthdate: (d, m, y) 16 March (year)

Resident in (municipality & province) Newmarket, Ontario

since (date) April 30, (year)

Surname at birth: Long

Surname just before marriage: Long

Divorced before? [X] No [ ] Yes (Place and date of previous divorce)

RESPONDENT/JOINT APPLICANT:　　Age: 42　　Birthdate: (d, m, y) 1 July (year)

Resident in (municipality & province) Watertown, Ontario

since (date) January 4, (year)

Surname at birth: Short

Surname just before marriage: Short

Divorced before? [X] No [ ] Yes (Place and date of previous divorce)

RELATIONSHIP DATES

[x] Married on (date) March 1, (year)　　　[ ] Started living together on (date)

[x] Separated on (date) April 15, (year)　　[X] Never lived together

THE CHILDREN)
List all children involved in this case, even if no claim is made for these children.

Full legal name	Age	Birthday (d, m, y)	Resident in (municipality & province)	Now Living with (name of person and relationship to child)

PREVIOUS CASES OR AGREEMENTS

Have the parties or the children been in a court case before?

[X] No [ ] Yes

Have the parties made a written agreement dealing with any matter involved in this case?

[x] No [ ] Yes (Give date of agreement. Indicate which of its items are in dispute.)

Form 8A: Application (Divorce) (page 2)　　　　Court File Number _____

[ ] **THIS CASE IS A JOINT APPLICATION FOR DIVORCE. THE DETAILS ARE SET OUT ON THE ATTACHED PAGES.** The application and affidavits in support of the application will be presented to a judge when the materials have been checked for completeness.

If you are requesting anything other than a simple divorce, such as support or property or exclusive possession of the matrimonial home and its contents, then refer to page 1 for instructions regarding the Financial Statement you should file.

_____　　　　_____
Date of issue　　　　　　　　　　　Clerk of the court

Precedent 23.9   Form 8A: Application (Divorce), Simple, page 5

Form 8A: Application (Divorce) (page 5)   Court File Number _____

☐ **Cruelty:** *(Name of spouse)* _____

has treated *(name of spouse)* _____

with physical or mental cruelty of such a kind as to make continued cohabitation intolerable.   *(Give details.)*

USE THIS FRAME ONLY IF THIS CASE IS A JOINT APPLICATION FOR DIVORCE.

The details of the other order(s) that we jointly ask the court to make are as follows: *(Include any amounts of support and the names of the children for whom support, custody or access is to be ordered.)*

IMPORTANT FACTS SUPPORTING OUR CLAIM(S)

(Set out the facts that form the legal basis for your claim(s).)

Put a line through any blank space left on this page.

Complete this section of your claim is for a divorce. Your lawyer, if you are represented, must complete the Lawyer's Certificate below.

_____
Date of signature

_____
Signature of applicant

Complete this section if you are making a joint application for divorce. Your lawyer, if you are represented, must complete the Lawyer's Certificate below.

_____
Date of signature

_____
Signature of joint applicant

_____
Date of signature

_____
Signature of joint applicant

LAWYER'S CERTIFICATE

My name is: Robert B. Redford _____   Charles Long _____

and I am the lawyer for *(name)* _____

in this divorce case. I certify that I have complied with the requirements of section 9 of the *Divorce Act.*

_____
Date of signature

_____
Signature of Lawyer

My name is: _____

and I am the lawyer for *(name)* _____

in this divorce case. I certify that I have complied with the requirements of section 9 of the *Divorce Act.*

_____
Date of signature

_____
Signature of Lawyer

Precedent 23.9   Form 8A: Application (Divorce), Simple, page 4

Form 8A: Application (Divorce) (page 4)   Court File Number _____

Has a Notice of Calculation and/or a Notice of Recalculation been issued by the online Child Support Service in this case?

☒ No   ☐ Yes   *(Give date(s) of Notice(s) of Calculation or Recalculation.)*

If yes, are you asking the court to make an order for a child support that is different from the amount set out in the Notice?

☐ No   ☐ Yes   *(Provide an explanation.)*

CLAIMS

USE THIS FRAME ONLY IF THIS CASE IS A JOINT APPLICATION FOR DIVORCE.

WE JOINTLY ASK THE COURT FOR THE FOLLOWING:

Claims under the *Divorce Act*	Claims under the *Family Law Act* or *Children's Law Reform Act*	Claims relating to property
00 ☐ a divorce	10 ☐ spousal support	20 ☐ equalization of net family properties
01 ☐ spousal support	11 ☐ support for child(ren) – table amount	21 ☐ exclusive possession of matrimonial home
02 ☐ support for child(ren) – table amount	12 ☐ support for child(ren) – other than table amount	22 ☐ exclusive possession of contents of matrimonial home
03 ☐ support for child(ren) - other than table amount	13 ☐ custody of child(ren)	23 ☐ freezing assets
04 ☐ custody of child(ren)	14 ☐ access to child(ren)	24 ☐ sale of family property
05 ☐ access to child(ren)	15 ☐ restraining/non-harassment order	**Other Claims**
	16 ☐ indexing spousal support	30 ☐ costs
	17 ☐ declaration of parentage	31 ☐ annulment of marriage
	18 ☐ guardianship over child's property	32 ☐ prejudgment interest
		50 ☐ other *(Specify.)*

USE THIS FRAME ONLY IF THE APPLICANT'S ONLY CLAIM IN THIS CASE IS FOR DIVORCE.

I ASK THE COURT FOR:
(Check if applicable.)

00 ☒ a divorce   30 ☐ costs

IMPORTANT FACTS SUPPORTING THE CLAIM FOR DIVORCE

☒ **Separation:** The spouses have lived separate and apart since *(date)*   April 15, (year) _____   and

☐ have not lived together again since that date in an unsuccessful attempt to reconcile.

☒ have lived together again during the following period(s) in an unsuccessful attempt to reconcile:
(Give dates.)

☐ **Adultery:** *(Name of spouse)* _____

has committed adultery.   *(Give details. It is not necessary to name any other person involved but if you do name the other person, then you must serve this application on the other person.)*

 Court File Number

ONTARIO

Ontario Family Court of the Superior Court of Justice
(Name of Court)

Court File Number

**FL81720

at **50 Eagle Street West, Newmarket, Ontario L3Y 6B1**
(Court office address)

Form 36: Affidavit for Divorce

Applicant(s)

Full legal name & address for service — street & number, municipality, postal code, telephone & fax numbers and e-mail address (if any).	*Lawyer's name & address — street & number, municipality, postal code, telephone & fax numbers and e-mail address (if any).*
Charles Long **78 Jane Street** **Newmarket, Ontario** **L2K 2D1** **Tel: (905) 859-1397**	**Robert B. Redford** **Michael, Eliad & Redford LLP** **863 Seneca Lane** **Toronto, Ontario M4J 1P6** **Tel: (416) 363-1079** **Fax: (416) 363-2628** **rbrdfrd@mer.com**

Respondent(s)

Full legal name & address for service — street & number, municipality, postal code, telephone & fax numbers and e-mail address (if any).	*Lawyer's name & address — street & number, municipality, postal code, telephone & fax numbers and e-mail address (if any).*
Wendy Long **11 Mannix Drive** **Watertown, Ontario** **K3B 1W8** **Tel: (705) 745-7458**	

My name is *(full legal name)* **Charles Long**

I live in *(municipality & province)* **Newmarket, Ontario**

And I swear/affirm that the following is true:

1. I am the applicant in this divorce case.

2. There is no chance of reconciliation between the respondent and me.

3. All information in the application in this case is correct, except: *(State any corrections or changes to the information in the application. Write "NONE" if there are no corrections or changes.)*

    None

4. [X] The certificate or registration of my marriage to the respondent has been signed and sealed by the Registrar of Ontario and

    [X] has been filed with the application.

    [ ] is attached to this affidavit.

    [ ] The certificate of my marriage to the respondent was issued outside Ontario. It is called *(title of certificate)*

    It was issued at *(place of issue)*

    on *(date)* _____ by *(name and title of person who issued the certificate)*

    and the information in it about my marriage is correct.

    [ ] I have not been able to get a certificate or registration of my marriage. I was married to the respondent

    on *(date)* _____

    at *(place of marriage)*

FLR 36 (September 1, 2005)

www.DIVORCEmate.com

Form 36: Affidavit for Divorce (page 3)   Court File Number   **FL 81720

(iii) ☐ a court order or written agreement dated *(date)* _____ made after the guidelines came into effect that has some direct or indirect benefits for the child(ren). I attach a copy.

(iv) ☐ a written consent between the parties dated *(date)* _____ agreeing to the payment of an amount different from that set out in the guidelines.

(b) The child support clauses of this order or agreement require payment of ($) _____ per _____ in child support.

(c) These child support clauses
☐ are not indexed for any automatic cost-of-living increases.
☐ are indexed according to *(Give indexing formula)*

(d) These child support clauses
☐ have not been changed since the day the order or agreement was made.
☐ have been changed on *(Give dates and details of changes)*

Date(s) _____   Detail(s) _____

(e) *(If you ticked off box (i), you can go to paragraph 12. If you ticked off boxes (ii), (iii) or (iv) above, then fill out the information after box of the corresponding number below. For example, if you ticked off box (iii) above, you would fill out the information alongside box (iii) below.)*

(ii) ☐ The amount being paid under this agreement is a fair and reasonable arrangement for the support of the child(ren) because: *(Give reasons.)*

(iii) ☐ The order or agreement directly or indirectly benefits the child(ren) because: *(Give details of benefits.)*

(iv) ☐ The amount to which the parties have consented is reasonable for the support of the child(ren) because: *(Give reasons.)*

12. I am claiming costs in this case. The details of this claim are as follows: *(Give details.)*

13. The respondent's address last known to me is: *(Give address.)*
11 Mannix Drive, Watertown, Ontario K3B 1W8

Put a line through any blank space on this page.

Sworn/Affirmed before me at:
City of Toronto _____ *(municipality)*
in Province of Ontario _____ *(province, state or country)*
on _____ *(date)*

_____ Signature
(This form is to be signed in front of a lawyer, justice of the peace, notary public or commissioner for taking affidavits.)

_____ Commissioner for taking affidavits
(Type or print name below if signature is illegible)

Form 36: Affidavit for Divorce (page 2)   Court File Number   **FL 81720

The marriage was performed by *(name and title)* _____ who had the authority to perform marriages in that place.

5. The legal basis for the divorce is:
☒ that the respondent and I have been separated for at least one year.
We separated on *(date)* _____ April 15, (year) _____
☐ *(Other. Specify.)*

6. I do not know about and I am not involved in any arrangement to make up or to hide evidence or to deceive the court in this divorce case.

Strike out the following paragraphs if they do not apply.

7. I do not want to make a claim for a division of property in this divorce case, even though I know that it may be legally impossible to make such a claim after the divorce.

8. ~~I want the divorce order to include the following paragraph numbers of the attached consent, settlement, separation agreement or previous court order:~~ *(List the numbers of the paragraphs that you want included in the divorce order.)*

9. ~~There are *(number)* _____ children of the marriage. They are:~~

Full legal name of child	Birthdate *(d, m, y)*

10. ~~The custody and access arrangements for the child(ren) are as follows: *(Give summary.)*~~

11. ~~These are the arrangements that have been made for the support of the child(ren) of the marriage:~~
~~(a) The income of the party paying child support is ($) _____ per year.~~
~~(b) The number of children for whom support is supposed to be paid is *(number)* _____~~
~~(c) The amount of support that should be paid according to the applicable table in the child support guidelines is _____ per month.~~
~~(d) The amount of child support actually being paid is ($) _____ per month.~~

(NOTE: - Where the dollar amounts in clauses [c] and [d] are different, you must fill out the frame on the next page. If the amounts in clauses [c] and [d] are the same, skip the frame and go directly to paragraph 12.)

Fill out the information in this frame only if amounts in 11(c) & 11(d) are different. If they are the same, go to paragraph 12.

(a) Child support is already covered by:
(i) ☐ a court order dated *(date)* _____ that was made before the child support guidelines came into effect *(before May 1st, 1997)*. I attach a copy of the order.
(ii) ☐ a domestic contract order dated *(date)* _____ that was made before the guidelines came into effect *(before May 1st, 1997)*. I attach a copy of the contract.

CHAPTER 24

UNINCORPORATED BUSINESSES

This chapter covers the various types of unincorporated businesses and how they are created and operated.

SOLE PROPRIETORSHIPS

A sole proprietorship is a business that one person owns and operates. The sole proprietorship is a form of ownership used commonly in the retail and service trades. If you set up shop selling dreams and run it yourself responsibly for profit, you have created a business known as a sole proprietorship. Almost anyone can start a business in the form of a sole proprietorship doing anything that is legal. The sole proprietor usually owns and manages the business activities and is legally responsible for all its debts and other legal obligations. The sole proprietor may employ others in his or her business. A sole proprietorship is not regulated by special laws and requires little in the way of legal assistance in its formation.

PARTNERSHIPS

A partnership, commonly referred to as a firm, is a business that **two** or more people own and operate. The *Partnerships Act* provides various rules for the partnership structure. For example, the basic criteria for forming partnerships are: there must be a business. Business means "every trade, occupation or profession." Next, the object of the business activity must be profit. If the object of the activity is social, cultural, religious, charitable, etc., the activity is not a partnership, and it is not a business. Finally, there must be a written or a verbal partnership agreement to carry on business collectively and to share in the profits. Generally, there are general partnerships, limited partnerships, and limited liability partnerships.

General partnerships General partnerships consist of two or more partners who may be individuals, unincorporated businesses, or corporations. Most partnerships are general partnerships in which each partner has a right to participate in the management of the partnership business, each partner is responsible for all debts of the partnership, regardless of his or her share of investment or portion of ownership in the partnership, and each partner is entitled to a share of any profit on the basis agreed upon among the partners. The *Partnerships Act* and a contract, if any, entered into among the partners determine the exact legal relationship among the partners. This contract is known as a partnership agreement. Although a partnership agreement is not needed in the legal formation of a partnership, a partnership agreement is almost always necessary in order that the partnership will function as the partners intend.

Limited partnerships (LP)   The *Limited Partnerships Act* governs limited partnerships. Limited partnerships consist of at least one general partner and at least one limited partner. The partners may be individuals, unincorporated businesses, or corporations. If X invests $50,000 in the partnership and says he is willing to lose only that amount towards the partnership's debts, even if the total partnership debts amount to $100,000, X is a limited partner. His liability is "limited" to the amount of money invested, e.g. $50,000. In return for this protection, however, the law prohibits a limited partner from participating in the management of the business. This is why a limited partner is sometimes referred to as a **silent partner**. The *Limited Partnerships Act* requires the limited partnership to have a written partnership agreement, Precedent 24.1, stating the amount of investment of the limited partner. A limited partner does, nevertheless, have the right, as does a general partner, to inspect the records of the partnership and to receive full disclosure of the affairs of the partnership. While the liability of the limited partner is limited to the amount which that partner contributed to the partnership, the liability of the general partner is unlimited. Limited partnerships are created by filing a **partnership declaration** under the *Limited Partnerships Act*. It is anticipated that the *Limited Partnerships Act* may see amendments that would reduce the potential for limited partner liability by permitting limited partners to take a more active role in the business.

Limited liability partnerships (LLP)   Limited liability partnerships, commonly referred to as firms, are available only to specific professions, including lawyers, paralegal licensees, accountants, health professionals, and others. The *Partnerships Act* provides for the establishment of limited liability partnerships. Limited liability partnerships offer protection to the partners against nearly all debts and liabilities. Under s. 10 (2) of the *Partnerships Act*, a partner in a limited liability partnership is not liable, by means of indemnification, contribution or otherwise, for:

(a) the debts, liabilities or obligations of the partnership or any partner arising from the negligent or wrongful acts or omissions that another partner or an employee, agent, or representative of the partnership commits in the course of the partnership business while the partnership is a limited liability partnership; or

(b) any other debts or obligations of the partnership that are incurred while the partnership is a limited liability partnership.

Limited liability partnerships do not, however, exempt a partner from personal liability for:

(a) the partner's own negligent or wrongful act or omission;

(b) the negligent or wrongful act or omission of a person under the partner's direct supervision; or

(c) the negligent or wrongful act or omission of another partner or an employee of the partnership not under the partner's direct supervision, if,

(i) the act or omission was criminal or constituted fraud, even if there was no criminal act or omission, or

(ii) the partner knew or ought to have known of the act or omission and did not take the actions that a reasonable person would have taken to prevent it.

The name of a limited liability partnership must contain as the last words or letters of its firm name the words "limited liability partnership" or the abbreviation LLP, or the French equivalents. A limited liability partnership must register its business name even if the partnership name is in the partners' exact personal names, and the partnership cannot carry on business under any other name than the registered partnership name. In most other respects, the *Partnerships Act* applies to limited liability partnerships as it does to general partnerships.

Limited liability partnerships and paralegal licensees   Subsection 61.1(1) of the *Law Society Act* provides that two or more persons who are licensed to provide legal services in Ontario (i.e. paralegal licensees) may form a limited liability partnership. Generally, the *Partnerships Act* permits professionals, such as lawyers and paralegal licensees, to practice in limited liability partnerships, provided that the act which governs the profession permits it, in this case, the *Law Society Act*, and the profession is required by that act to maintain a minimum amount of liability insurance, which the *Law Society Act* provides for both conditions.

LIABILITY AND OTHER OBLIGATIONS OF SOLE PROPRIETORSHIPS AND GENERAL PARTNERSHIPS

Self and employee obligations   A sole proprietor or a partner in a general partnership is self-employed. As such, a sole proprietor or a partner in a general partnership is not protected by employment insurance and neither contributes to employment insurance nor is entitled to collect any. The main reason for this is that a sole proprietor or a partner in a general partnership is considered not vulnerable to losing his or her job. A sole proprietor or a partner in a general partnership must, however, make the standard payroll deductions from the pay of any employees, including income tax, Canada pension, employment insurance, etc., and submit the amounts deducted to the appropriate federal and provincial government agencies.

Liability - sole proprietorships   The sole proprietor may be personally sued for any wrongful acts that the sole proprietor or his or her employees commit, and the sole proprietor must personally pay for any business debts that the business is unable to cover: for example, assume that the business goes out of business and its debts amount to $100,000. Suppose that the assets and/or inventory of the business amount to $50,000. This $50,000 would be applied toward the $100,000 debt. To satisfy the remaining $50,000 debt, creditors have the right to seize the sole proprietor's personal property, e.g. a car/s and or real estate, e.g. a house, to get their money.

Liability - general partnerships   A partnership is not a separate legal entity from the partners who compose it. This means that a person cannot be both a partner and an employee of the partnership because the partnership form of business is based on either a written contract or verbal agreement, and no person can enter into a contract with himself or herself. This ultimately means that each partner's personal assets are exposed to creditors for all debts and obligations of the partnership that are incurred while he or she is a partner.

Each partner may be personally sued for any debts, wrongful acts, or omissions that the partner or his or her employees commit while acting in the ordinary course of the partnership's business. To protect the public from one partner claiming the other responsible, each partner is deemed **jointly and severally** (together and individually) liable for the partnership's debts and wrongdoings. Generally, this means that during the course of business, if one partner causes a business debt to occur or commits a wrongful act, all of the partners are responsible and liable. If debts extend beyond the partnership's ability to pay, creditors may seize the personal assets of any one or all of the partners, based on which partner can best pay the debt. By contrast, a wrongful act by one partner is the same as if all partners committed it, and **all** may be sued.

Here is a simple example of the effects of joint and several liability:

Suppose that you and John borrowed $6,000 from the bank to buy a special piece of machinery for your partnership business. The machinery is the property of the partnership, as is all property contributed by the partners to the partnership or purchased in the course of the partnership business, and is not divisible among the partners, except when the partnership is dissolved. Thus, a partnership is viewed as a unit for some purposes but not for any debts or liabilities to creditors.

As business partners, you and John are deemed to be jointly and severally (together and individually) responsible for the repayment of the $6,000 to the bank. The bank would usually require that you and John personally guarantee the partnership's indebtedness to the bank. If the partnership cannot and does not pay back the $6,000 to the bank when required to do so, the bank can call upon you and John to pay back the loan from your personal assets.

The joint and several guarantee which you and John provided to the bank means the bank can choose to go after either you alone, or John alone, or both of you; hence, jointly and severally, to collect the entire $6,000 which the partnership owes. The bank does not have to proceed against you for $3,000 and against John for the remaining $3,000. If the bank proceeded against John alone and collected its entire $6,000, John would have to go after you to get the $3,000 that you should have paid to the bank, and vice versa. A several guarantee (as opposed to a joint and several guarantee), on the other hand, would mean that the bank would have to proceed against each of you separately -- you for $3,000 and John for the remaining $3,000.

Income and taxation   The income that a sole proprietorship or a general partnership earns is the income of the sole proprietorship or general partnership. Certain expenses for operating the business are subtracted from the income of the sole proprietorship or the general partnership to determine whether the sole proprietorship or the general partnership has a net income or a loss. In the case of a sole proprietorship, that income or loss is the income or loss of the sole proprietor, and the sole proprietor is taxed on it at the same income tax rate as that for salaried individuals. In the case of a general partnership, the partnership's net income or loss is divided among the partners in proportion to their share in the partnership. If the partners are individuals (corporations may also be partners), they are each taxed on their respective shares at the same income tax rate as are salaried individuals.

LICENSING

Certain types of businesses, **regardless of business form**, may require two types of licences—one from the provincial government to prove skill qualification; the other from the municipal government to prove the municipality (city/town) has authorized the business to operate in that municipality. Generally, provincial licences proving skill qualification are required for professional trades e.g. lawyers, doctors, dentists, architects, etc., and semi-professional trades, e.g. plumbers, mechanics, barbers, hairdressers, etc. Municipal licences are required for operating many types of businesses, including adult entertainment parlours, convenience and variety stores, laundromats, movie theatres, grocery shops, restaurants, barber and hairdressing shops, taxi cabs, parking lots, bake shops, hotels, motels, renovators, tourist resorts, butcher shops, etc. Check with the municipal licensing board, commission, or by-law officer of the municipality in which the business is to operate and with any zoning authorities to ensure that the particular business activity is permitted to operate in that municipality.

THE BUSINESS NAME

The business name of sole proprietorships and partnerships (including limited partnerships and limited liability partnerships) may be any name that does **not** end in the words Limited, Incorporated, Corporation, their respective abbreviations: Ltd., Inc., Corp., or their French equivalent, as these words and abbreviations are used only in names of businesses that are incorporated. There are other restrictions on business names: for example, words that imply the business is not a sole proprietorship but a partnership; words such as college, institute, or university cannot be used except with government permission; or words that imply the business is connected with any level of government. Names of individuals, other than individuals registering the business, may not be used. The business name must be registered in the English language. The business may, however, use a language other than English, e.g. Chinese characters, on the business letterhead or on any signs at the place of business, as long as the English name is also displayed.

Public record The Ministry of Government and Consumer Services maintains a registry of business names of sole proprietorships, general partnerships, and limited liability partnerships, among others, on public record. Anyone may search the public record, for a fee, to find the owners or principals behind a business name.

Business name search The purpose of conducting a business name search when starting a business is to find out if anyone else has registered a business name that is the same as the business name which has been selected for the business. Searching the business names public record will tell you if someone is already using a business name that is **identical** to the one selected for the business and where that business is located. It will not, however, show names that are **similar** to the name selected for the business. Note that a business name search for this purpose is not mandatory, but good practice. The *Business Names Act* does not prohibit a registration of an identical or confusingly similar business name to one already on the public record. It is the responsibility of the business, not the responsibility of the ministry, to make sure the business name is neither identical nor confusingly similar to an already registered name, because if it is, the business could be sued.

Business name registration A registration of a business name is made under the *Business Names Act*. If the business name is in the owner's exact personal name, e.g. Donald Crane, in the case of a sole proprietorship, or Jill Jones and Tom Jones, in the case of a partnership, the name need not be registered. The business name must, however, be registered before the business starts using it if the business name is other than the exact personal name, or if any other word is attached to the exact personal name, e.g. Donald Crane Music, in the case of a sole proprietorship, or Jill Jones and Tom Jones Fashions, in the case of a partnership.

How to search and register a business name   Upon payment of the applicable fees, you may conduct a business name search as well as register a business name through the following channels:

- ServiceOntario's website at www.ServiceOntario.ca.
- Self-help workstations located at ServiceOntario service locations across the province.
- Private service providers under contract with the ministry (information about service providers is available at ServiceOntario.ca).
- By mail - registrations only (not name searches) to the:

Ministry of Government and Consumer Services
Central Production and Verification Services Branch
393 University Ave., Suite 200
Toronto, ON M5G 2M2

Business name registration forms   All of the forms required to register a business name under the *Business Names Act* are available online on the ServiceOntario website. Two frequently used forms are the following:

Form 1 - Registration, Sole Proprietorship/Partnership, Precedent 24.3
Form 6 - Registration, Ontario Limited Liability Partnership, Precedent 24.5

Master business licence (MBL)   When you register a business name, you will be issued a master business licence (MBL), Precedent 24.4. The MBL contains a business name registration number, which is your business identification number (BIN), and also shows the date of registration and the five-year expiry date of your registration. The MBL is your proof of business name registration for such purposes as opening a business bank account, etc.

Registration expiry/renewal   The business name registration is valid for five years. You must renew your business name registration every five years. The five-year expiry date is usually shown on your master business licence (MBL). The ministry does not issue reminders of business name registration expiry dates.

PARTNERSHIP AGREEMENTS

Partnership agreements are contracts between the partners which spell out the rules about how the partnership business is to be run. A partnership agreement is optional in general partnerships, required in limited partnerships, and almost always prepared in limited liability partnerships. Contents vary, depending on the needs and wishes of the partners. Read through the partnership agreement precedents in this manual for examples of typical clauses that are usually included in partnership agreements. Partnership agreements are not registered since they are private contracts between the business partners.

PREPARATION AND DISTRIBUTION OF PARTNERSHIP AGREEMENTS

You require: The lawyer's instructions. There is no prescribed format for partnership agreements; follow along in Precedent 24.1, traditional style, and Precedent 24.2, modern style, which represent two commonly used styles in practice. Key points include:

Leave the **day** blank for the lawyer to fill in when the clients sign. Double or single space the body, according to lawyer preference. Use standard or legal size paper. Partnership agreements do not generally require seals or witnesses because they are private contracts; see Precedent 24.2, modern style. Traditional style agreements, however, Precedent 24.1, may contain endings that refer to signatures under seal and witness (usually the lawyer). The letters L.S. (legal seal) may be used at places of signature for individuals to represent a seal, or they may be left out. Corporate signatures usually require no seal or witness in either traditional or modern style agreements because the signatures of the corporation's signing officers are sufficient to bind the corporation.

Computerized clauses   Many of the clauses in partnership agreements are standard. In practice, many lawyers usually save the standard clauses in the computer, identify them by number, as in the modern style partnership agreement in Precedent 24.2, and select by number the required clauses to be included in each new partnership agreement.

Backsheet   On a separate sheet of paper, prepare a backsheet, Precedent 24.2, for each modern or traditional style partnership agreement. In practice, law firms usually prepare backsheets from templates. Key, in landscape format, using the centre 1/3 of the page, so that when the agreement is folded in three, the keyed 1/3 part faces up for easy identification. Do the same if using legal size paper, except use the second 1/4 from the left of the landscape sheet. Many law firms use the backsheet of **court documents** modified as a backsheet for agreements, or as is increasingly more frequently done in practice, use no backsheet.

Number of copies, minimum 3:   Give l to each partner; keep l in client's file.

Dissolution of partnership   Dissolution of partnership means the partnership has folded. This may occur when a partner wants out, and there are no partners left who want to continue; when a partner wants out and the majority will not buy him or her out; on the death of a partner; or where there is an irreconcilable difference of opinion of a partner. Under the provisions of the *Partnerships Act*, even in the absence of such a provision in a partnership agreement, a partner may dissolve a partnership by giving written notice to the other partner/s of his or her intention to dissolve the partnership. A partner may also apply to the court to dissolve the partnership on the grounds of mental incompetence of another partner, or conduct of another partner, that makes it impossible to continue the partnership. When a partnership is dissolved or discontinues the use of the partnership name, the partners must file with the ministry the same form as that in Precedent 24.3, except check the "Cancellation" box.

OTHER FORMS OF UNINCORPORATED BUSINESSES

Joint ventures   This usually involves two separate businesses working together on one project only until the project is finished. Registration is not required. The entrepreneurs could, however, enter into a written agreement to set out at least major points such as the rules by which the venture will be governed, financial and work contribution, and share in profits and losses.

Franchises   Examples of franchises include chains such as McDonald's and Tim Hortons. A franchise business begins usually with a written contract in which the franchisor (original business owner), in return for some form of compensation, grants the right to the franchisee (person who buys the franchise) to use the franchisor's distinguishing trade mark, or trade name, and requires the franchisee to conduct its business using the franchisor's methods and procedures. The franchisee pays the franchisor a certain amount of money from the profit of the franchise. Franchises may be entered into as sole proprietorships or partnerships (or corporations) and are registered in the same way as sole proprietorships or partnerships (or corporations).

CHAPTER SUMMARY

Unincorporated businesses include sole proprietorships and partnerships. Sole proprietorships are businesses that one person owns and operates. Partnerships are businesses that two or more people own and operate.

Partnerships can be general partnerships or limited partnerships. With general partnerships, all partners are responsible for the partnership's debts. With limited partnerships, a limited partner can only lose as much as the limited partner invested in the partnership and cannot participate in the management of the business. With limited partnerships, there must be at least one general partner in the partnership. A partnership agreement is optional in general partnerships and required in limited partnerships. There are also limited liability partnerships that enable professionals such as lawyers, licensed paralegals, and accountants to enter into so as to limit their liability against any wrongful acts of the other partners in the limited liability partnership. Sole proprietors and business partners are personally responsible for any business debts and are taxed at the same tax rate that applies to salaried individuals. Generally, sole proprietorships and partnerships must register their business names with the Ministry of Government and Consumer Services.

Other forms of business ownership include joint ventures where two separate businesses join forces to do a job, and franchises, commonly referred to as chains, where individuals may contract to operate a business under a well-known trade mark, or trade name, using the franchisor's methods and procedures.

REVIEW QUESTIONS

1. Who is responsible for the business debts of sole proprietorships and partnerships?
2. What is a general partnership?
3. What is a limited partnership?
4. Who may enter into a limited liability partnership?
5. Which abbreviation distinguishes a limited liability partnership?
6. How is a sole proprietorship or general partnership registered?
7. How is a limited liability partnership registered?
8. What is a master business licence?
9. Under which type of partnership may licensed paralegals operate?
10. Every how often do sole proprietorships and partnerships, who have no employees, pay employment insurance premiums?
11. Why are sole proprietors and partners in partnerships not entitled to collect employment insurance?
12. Which type of partnership requires a written partnership agreement?

THIS AGREEMENT MADE this   day of November, 20--.

BETWEEN:

THOMAS CREWSE, of the City of Waterwell,
in the County of Mandolee,

hereinafter referred to as "Crewse"

-and-

GOLDRUSH LIMITED, a Corporation incorporated under
the laws of the Province of Ontario, having its registered
office in the City of Waterwell, in the County of Mandolee,

hereinafter referred to as "Goldrush"

WHEREAS Crewse and Goldrush (the "Partners") have been carrying on a Partnership under the name of A-One Investments;

AND WHEREAS the Partners wish to set down in writing their respective rights with respect to the aforementioned Partnership;

NOW THEREFORE THIS AGREEMENT WITNESSETH that in consideration of the mutual covenants and agreements herein contained, the parties hereto agree as follows:

1.   The name of the Partnership shall continue to be A-One Investments, the business of the Partnership shall be investment consultants, and the place of business shall be 57 Milos Road, Waterwell, Ontario, D4P 9S9.

2.   The term of the Partnership shall commence on the 28th day of November, 20--, and shall continue until one month after one Partner has notified the other Partner in writing of the Partner's intention to withdraw from the Partnership.

3.   (a) The capital of the firm shall be $150,000.00 to be contributed in equal cash amounts of $75,000.00 each on the signing of the Agreement.

(b) Neither party's contribution to the Partnership shall bear interest.

4.   The Partnership capital and all other Partnership monies shall be deposited in the King Arthur and Camelot branch of the Big Bucks Bank from which all withdrawals shall be only by cheques signed jointly by Crewse and the Secretary of Goldrush.

5.   (a) Books of accounts shall be kept in accordance with standard accounting procedures.

(b) These books shall be kept on the premises and shall be open to the inspection of either Partner.

6.   Each Partner shall be entitled to draw $700.00 per week from the funds of the Partnership on account of his profits.

7.   (a) At the end of November of every year, an inventory shall be taken and the assets, liabilities, and gross and net income of the business ascertained.

(b) The net profit or net loss shall be divided equally between the Partners and the account of each shall be credited or debited accordingly.

-2-

8.   Neither Partner shall, without the written consent of the other, draw, accept, sign, or endorse any bill of exchange, promissory note, or cheque, or contract any debt on account of, or in the name of the Partnership, except in the normal course of business and up to the amount of $500.00.

9.   Crewse shall devote his whole time and attention to the Partnership business and shall not, during the term of the Partnership, engage in any other business. Goldrush shall take no part in the management of the Partnership.

10.   Should Crewse die, his estate trustees shall be entitled to receive the value of his share of the Partnership property at the time of his death, together with 8 percent interest, in lieu of profit, from that day until final settlement of the property.

11.   On termination or dissolution of the Partnership, other than by the death of Crewse, an audit shall immediately be made of the firm's assets and liabilities and the balance divided equally between the Partners, provided that the liability of Goldrush be limited to $75,000.00.

12.   (a) In the event of a disagreement between the Partners as to the conduct of the business, as to its dissolution, or as to any other matter concerning the business, the same shall be referred to arbitration within ten days of one Partner serving written notice on the other.

(b) Each Partner shall appoint one arbitrator who shall, in turn, appoint a third arbitrator.

(c) The matter referred to arbitration shall be decided by a simple majority of the arbitrators.

[1] **IN WITNESS WHEREOF** the party of the first part has hereunto set his hand and seal, and the party of the second part has hereto affixed its corporate seal attested by the hands of its proper officers duly authorized in that behalf.

SIGNED, SEALED AND DELIVERED
   in the presence of

_____ L.S.
Thomas Crewse

GOLDRUSH LIMITED

Per:_____
                President

Per: _____
                Secretary

[1] *When both parties signing are corporations, substitute:*

IN WITNESS WHEREOF the parties hereto have hereunto affixed their corporate seals attested by the hands of their proper officers duly authorized in that behalf.

A.B.C. LETTERS CORPORATION

Per:_____
              President

Per: _____
           Secretary-Treasurer

X.Y.Z. NUMBERS LIMITED

Per:_____
              President

Per: _____
            Vice-President

DATED   NOVEMBER   , (year)

RANDOLPH HEARST WARREN

and

ARTHUR L. JAMES LTD.

PARTNERSHIP AGREEMENT

Michael, Eliad & Redford LLP
Barristers and Solicitors
863 Seneca Lane
Toronto, Ontario
M4J 1P6

Robert B. Redford

↔ Use about the centre 1/3 of the landscape
    sheet

Precedent 24.2   Partnership Agreement, Modern Style

THIS PARTNERSHIP AGREEMENT is made on November   , 20--,
and is between:

1.   **PARTIES**

1.1   RANDOLPH HEARST WARREN ("Warren") and

1.2   ARTHUR L. JAMES LTD. ("James")

1.3   Warren and James are sometimes referred to in this Agreement as "Partner"
      or "Partners" as the context requires.

2.   **FORMATION OF PARTNERSHIP**

2.1   The Partners by this Agreement form a partnership (the "Partnership").

2.2   The name of the Partnership shall be PARTNERSHIP BLUES.

2.3   The Partnership shall carry on business as music publishers and
      distributors.

3.   **CONSIDERATION**

3.1   The consideration is the mutual promises in this Agreement.

4.   **MANAGEMENT**

4.1   All decisions relating to the business of the Partnership shall require the
      unanimous consent of the Partners.

5.   **CAPITAL**

5.1   The initial capital shall be One Hundred Thousand Dollars ($100,000.00).
      Each Partner shall advance one-half of the initial capital, namely, Fifty
      Thousand Dollars ($50,000.00), on the execution of this Agreement.

6.   **PROFITS**

6.1   The Partnership profits shall be divided between the Partners as in Section
      5.1 above....

20.   **GENERAL**

20.1   This Agreement shall be binding upon and shall enure to the benefit of the
       Partners and their respective heirs, executors, administrators, legal
       representatives, assigns, and successors.

21.   **EXECUTION**

21.1   As evidence of their agreement, the Partners have executed this Agreement
       in duplicate on the date shown in the heading.

       _____
       Randolph Hearst Warren

       ARTHUR L. JAMES LTD.
       Per: _____
                        President

> Ontario
>
> Ministry of Government and
> Consumer Services
>
> Ministère des Services gouvernementaux et
> des Services aux consommateurs
>
> **Registration   Form 1**
> under the *Business Names Act* - Sole Proprietorship / Partnership
>
> **Enregistrement   Formule 1**
> en vertu de la *Loi sur les noms commerciaux* -
> Entreprise personnelle / société en nom collectif

Print clearly in CAPITAL LETTERS / Écrivez clairement en LETTRES MAJUSCULES

1.   Registration Type /
     Type d'enregistrement

If B, C, or D enter "Business Identification Number" /
En cas de B, C ou D, inscrivez le n° d'identification de l'entreprise.

Page   **1**   of / de   **1**

A ☑ New   B ☐ Renewal   C ☐ Amendment   D ☐ Cancellation
     Nouvel   Renouvellement   Modification   Révocation

BIN   Business Identification No./
NIE   le n° d'identification de l'entreprise

2.
Business
Name /
Nom com-
mercial

T H E   W O R L D   A R O U N D

3.
Mailing
Address of
Registrant/
L'Adresse
postale de
Registrant

Street No./ N° de rue	Suite No. / Bureau n°	Street Name / Nom de la rue
21		**RICKLES STREET**

City / Town / Ville	Province / Province	Postal Code / Code postal
TORONTO	**ONTARIO**	**M9P 3K3**

Country / Pays
CANADA

4.   Address of principal place of business in Ontario *(PO Box not acceptable)* /
     Adresse de l'établissement principal en Ontario *(Case postale non acceptée)*   ☑ Same as above / comme ci-dessus

Street No. / N° de rue	Street Name / Nom de la rue	Suite No. / Bureau n°	City / Town / Ville
21	**RICKLES STREET**		**TORONTO**

Province / Province	Country / Pays	Postal Code / Code postal
ONTARIO	**CANADA**	**M9P 3K3**

5.   Give a brief description of the ACTIVITY being carried out under the business name./
     Résumez brièvement le genre d'ACTIVITÉ exercée sous le nom commercial.

G I F T W A R E   R E T A I L E R S

6.   Type of Registrant /
     Type de personne enregistrée

A ☐ Sole proprietorship /   B ☑ Partnership /   ☐ More than 10 Partners:
     Entreprise personnelle   Société en nom collectif   records at business address /
                                                                                         Plus de 10 associés /
                                                                                         dossiers à l'adresse d'affaires

7.   Registrant Information /
     Renseignements sur la personne enregistrée

Last Name / Nom de famille	First Name / Prénom	Middle Initial / initiale 2ᵉ prénom
COOK	**WALTER**	**A**

8.

Street No. / N° de rue	Street Name / Nom de la rue	Suite No. / Bureau n°	City / Town / Ville
48	**DUKE STREET**		**TORONTO**

Province / Province	Country / Pays	Postal Code / Code postal
ONTARIO	**CANADA**	**M1V 3Z2**

Additional Information. Only complete if the registrant is not an individual. See instructions 7/8 on the form. /
Renseignements supplémentaires. À remplir uniquement si la personne enregistrée n'est pas un particulier.
Voir les instructions 7 et 8 sur le formulaire.

Ont. Corporation No. / *(For Corporate Partners Only)*
N° matricule de la personne morale en Ontario *Pour les personnes morales associées seulement*

7.

Last Name / Nom de famille	First Name / Prénom	Middle Initial / initiale 2ᵉ prénom
PEARSON	**PIRKO**	**B**

8.

Street No. / N° de rue	Street Name / Nom de la rue	Suite No. / Bureau n°	City / Town / Ville
51	**NORTHERN DANCER CIRCLE**		**HAMLET**

Province / Province	Country / Pays	Postal Code / Code postal
ONTARIO	**CANADA**	**M6D 4Y6**

Additional Information. Only complete if the registrant is not an individual. See instructions 7/8 on the form. /
Renseignements supplémentaires. À remplir uniquement si la personne enregistrée n'est pas un particulier.
Voir les instructions 7 et 8 sur le formulaire.

Ont. Corporation No. / *(For Corporate Partners Only)*
N° matricule de la personne morale en Ontario *Pour les personnes morales associées seulement*

9.   Print name of person authorizing this registration / *(either the sole proprietor, a partner or a person acting under a power of attorney)*
If the person is a corporation, complete **additional information** below only. /
Indiquez en lettres majuscules le nom de la personne autorisant l'enregistrement / *(propriétaire unique, associé, ou personne habilitée en vertu d'une procuration).* (Si c'est une personne morale qui autorise l'enregistrement, compléter les **renseignements supplémentaires** ci-dessous).

Last Name / Nom de famille	First Name / Prénom	Middle Initial / initiale 2ᵉ prénom
COOK	**WALTER**	**A**

If person authorizing the registration is not an individual (eg. corporation, trust, syndicate), print name below and do not complete last, first and middle names above. / Si la personne qui autorise l'enregistrement n'est pas un individu (c'est-à-dire une personne morale, un trust ou syndicat) ne pas remlir le nom de famille, prénom et 2ᵉ prénom.

Additional Information / Renseignements supplémentaires

MINISTRY USE ONLY - RÉSERVÉ AU MINISTÈRE

It is the responsibility of the applicant(s) to ensure the accuracy of the information submitted.
It is an offence under section 10 of the *Business Names Act* to submit false or misleading information. / Il incombe aux demandeurs de veiller à l'exactitude des renseignements présentés. Le demandeur qui fait une déclaration fausse ou trompeuse commet une infraction en vertu de l'article 10 de la *Loi sur les noms commerciaux.*

07219 (2014/11)   © Queen's Printer for Ontario, 2014 / © Imprimeur de la Reine pour l'Ontario, 2014

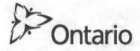 Ontario

Master Business Licence

Date Issued: 20yy-06-04
(yyyy-mm-dd)

Business Number:

Business Name and Mailing Address:
THE WORLD AROUND
21 RICKLES STREET
TORONTO, ON CA M9P 3K3

**Business
Address:**   SAME AS ABOVE

Telephone: **Ext:**   **Fax:**

Email:

**Legal
Name(s):**   THE WORLD AROUND

**Type of
Legal Entity:**   PARTNERSHIP

**Business
Activity:**   GIFTWARE RETAILERS

Business Information	Number	Effective Date (yyyy-mm-dd)	Expiry Date (yyyy-mm-dd)
BUSINESS NAME REGISTRATION	923456781	20yy-06-04	20yy-06-03

Page 1 of 1

To the Client: When the Master Business Licence is presented to any Ontario business program, you are not required to repeat information contained on this licence. Each Ontario business program is required to accept this licence when presented as part of its registration process.
If you have any questions about this Master Business Licence call the ServiceOntario Contact Centre at 1-800-565-1921 or 1-416-314-9151 or TTY 1-416-326-8566.
For more information, or access to other business-related services, call the Business Info Line, a collaboration between ServiceOntario and Industry Canada, at 1-888-745-8888 or 1-416-212-8888 or TTY 800-268-7095.
A business name registration is effective for 5 years from the date that it is accepted for registration. It is the registrant's responsibility to renew the business name prior to the expiry date and to pay the required fee.

To the Ontario business program: A client is not required to repeat any information contained in this licence in any other form used in your registration process.

SPCYBP1 20yy-06-04

Ontario

Ministry of
Government Services

Ministère des
Services gouvernementaux

Registration Form 6
under the *Business Names Act* -
Ontario Limited Liability Partnership
Extra-Provincial Limited Liability Partnership
Extra-Provincial Limited Liability Company

Enregistrement Formule 6
en vertu de la *Loi sur les noms commerciaux*
Société à responsabilité limitée de l'Ontario
Société à responsabilité limitée extraprovinciale
Société de capitaux extraprovinciale

Print clearly in CAPITAL LETTERS
Écrivez clairement en LETTRES MAJUSCULES

1. Registration Type
Type d'enregistrement

If B, C, or D enter "Business Identification Number"
En cas de B, C ou D, inscrivez le n° d'identification de l'entreprise.

Page __1__ of / de __1__

A [X] New
Nouveau

B [ ] Renewal
Renouvellement

C [ ] Amendment
Modification

D [ ] Cancellation
Révocation

BIN Business Identification No.
NIE N° d'identification de l'entreprise

2. Business Name
Nom commercial

L E G A L   B E A G L E   W O R K S   L L P

3. Mailing Address of Registrant
Adresse postale de Registrant

Street No. / N° de rue: **100**
Street Name / Nom de la rue: **BAY STREET**
Suite No. / Bureau n°: **101**

City / Town / Ville: **TORONTO**
Province / Province: **ONTARIO**
Postal Code / Code postal: **M5X 7A7**

Country / Pays: **CANADA**

4. Address of principal place of business in Ontario *(P.O. Box not acceptable)*
Adresse de l'établissement principal en Ontario *(Case postale non acceptée)*

[X] Same as above
comme ci-dessus

Street No. / N° de rue   Street Name / Nom de la rue   Suite No. / Bureau n°   City / Town / Ville

Province / Province   Postal Code / Code postal   Country / Pays

5. Give a brief description of the ACTIVITY being carried out under the business name.
Résumez brièvement le genre d'ACTIVITÉ exercée sous le nom commercial.

P A R A L E G A L   S E R V I C E S

6. Type of Registrant
Type d'entité enregistrée

[ ] More than 10 Partners: records at business address / Plus de 10 associés : dossiers à l'adresse d'affaires

A [X] Ontario Limited Liability Partnership
Société à responsabilité limitée de l'Ontario

OR
OU

B [ ] Extra-Provincial Limited Liability Partnership
Société à responsabilité limitée extraprovinciale

OR
OU

C [ ] Extra-Provincial Limited Liability Company
Société de capitaux extraprovinciale

7. Jurisdiction of Formation / Territoire d'origine
ONTARIO

8. Registrant Information *(P.O. Box not acceptable)*
Renseignements sur la personne enregistrée *(Case postale non acceptée)*

Last Name / Nom de famille: **COWELL**
First Name / Prénom: **JESSICA**
Middle Initial / Initiale 2e prénom: **J**

9. Street No. / N° de rue: **77**   Street Name / Nom de la rue: **GARLAND STREET**
Suite No. / Bureau n°   City / Town / Ville: **TORONTO**

Province / Province: **ONTARIO**
Postal Code / Code postal: **M6T 4S2**
Country / Pays: **CANADA**

Additional Information. Only complete if the registrant is not an individual. See instructions 8/9 on the form.
Renseignements supplémentaires. À remplir uniquement si la personne enregistrée n'est pas un particulier.
(Voir Instructions, art. 8 /9)

Ont. Corporation No.
N° matricule de la personne morale en Ontario

8. Last Name / Nom de famille: **MENDELSON**
First Name / Prénom: **JOSEPH**
Middle Initial / Initiale 2e prénom: **S**

9. Street No. / N° de rue: **39**   Street Name / Nom de la rue: **BENNY ROAD**
Suite No. / Bureau n°   City / Town / Ville: **WATERWELL**

Province / Province: **ONTARIO**
Postal Code / Code postal: **D4W 2S3**
Country / Pays: **CANADA**

Additional Information. Only complete if the registrant is not an individual. See instructions 8/9 on the form.
Renseignements supplémentaires. À remplir uniquement si la personne enregistrée n'est pas un particulier.
(Voir Instructions, art. 8 /9)

Ont. Corporation No.
N° matricule de la personne morale en Ontario

10. Print name of person authorizing this registration *(either a partner (for LLP), a general manager/representative (for LLC) or a person acting under power of attorney).*
Indiquez en lettres majuscules le nom de la personne autorisant l'enregistrement *(associé (s.r.l.), directeur général / représentant (s.c.), ou personne habilitée en vertu d'une procuration).*

Last Name / Nom de famille: **COWELL**
First Name / Prénom: **JESSICA**
Middle Initial / Initiale 2e prénom: **J**

Additional Information: If the person authorizing the registration is not an individual, (e.g. corporation, trust, syndicate), **set out the name, together with the name of the individual authorized to sign on that person's behalf,** in "Additional Information", and do not complete the space above **(see Instructions, number 10).** / Renseignements supplémentaires : Si l'enregistrement est autorisé par une entreprise (personne morale, société de fiducie, consortium, etc.), **indiquez ci-dessous la raison sociale de l'entité et le nom de la personne habilitée à signer (voir Instructions, art. 10).**

MINISTRY USE ONLY - *RÉSERVÉ AU MINISTÈRE*

Additional Information *(name)* / Renseignements supplémentaires *(raison sociale)*

Authorized to Sign / Signataire autorisé

Last Name / Nom de famille   First Name / Prénom

It is the responsibility of the applicant(s) to ensure the accuracy of the information submitted. It is an offence under section 10 of the *Business Names Act* to submit false or misleading information. / Il incombe aux demandeurs de veiller à l'exactitude des renseignements présentés. Le demandeur qui fait une déclaration fausse ou trompeuse commet une infraction en vertu de l'article 10 de la *Loi sur les noms commerciaux.*

CHAPTER 25
CORPORATE LAW

This chapter deals with the fundamentals of corporate law as they relate to corporations as legal entities established to conduct business.

BASIC CONCEPTS

What is a corporation   A corporation is a legal **person** created by law as a substitute for a real person. Under the law, a corporation is a legal entity, separate and apart from its owners who are the shareholders and who are protected against financial loss by a concept known as **limited liability**. In effect, a corporation is a legal creation, tangible enough to be within the reach of the law, yet protected enough to promote economic growth in a free enterprise system. As a legal substitute for a real person, a corporation can do everything that a real person can do in operating a successful business, e.g. borrow money, make contracts, operate a bank account, sue and be sued, and be held responsible for its actions in the same way as a real person would be held responsible. Since corporations are not human persons but have rights and obligations that are similar, the shareholders of a corporation elect directors who are authorized to act on the corporation's behalf.

Limited liability   This means, if the corporation is in financial trouble, the shareholders (owners) would lose only the amount of money they invested in the corporation–their **liability** toward any debts of the corporation is, therefore, **limited** to the amount invested. Except in exceptional circumstances, the shareholders cannot lose property that belongs to them personally, e.g. their houses or their cars. This gives the shareholders freedom to invest in a corporation without fearing loss of personal assets. For a simple example, assume that Homer created a corporation and bought one share of the corporation at $1. Homer's investment in the corporation is $1; if the corporation were to fail and become bankrupt, the maximum that Homer would lose would be the one share, which would be equivalent to whatever dollar value Homer originally paid for it, e.g. $1. The creditors of the corporation are not allowed to seize any of Homer's other possessions. Thus, we say that Homer's liability is limited to his shareholdings in the corporation. This is the meaning of limited liability.

Effects of limited liability   Assume that you and John have one million dollars between the two of you. You both decide you want to market "iggies" because you think they are the coming fad; nevertheless, you are not willing to risk investing your full one million dollars, but only $100,000. If you were to set up a general partnership, your creditors would seize your entire million, even though you invested only $100,000 in the general partnership. If, however, you were to set up a corporation, Iggie Corporation, you would limit your liability to the $100,000 you invested. The creditors of Iggie could seize the $100,000 but not your remaining $900,000 because that is your personal property, not Iggie's. This is the effect of limited liability.

In fact, both of you may further limit your liability to less than $100,000 if you were to each buy one share from Iggie Corporation at $1. (This is one reason why lawyers often use $1 as the purchase price of shares at the initial organization of the corporation.) The $2 (yours and John's) are your total investment and form part of Iggie's assets, and that is all you and John would lose. For the remaining $99,998, you would draw up a loan agreement between yourselves as the lenders and Iggie Corporation as the borrower. In this way, Iggie will be gradually paying you back the loan from its earnings. If Iggie were to go bankrupt, you would automatically lose the $2, but for the remaining $99,998 you would be considered a creditor of Iggie. Iggie would be obliged to pay you as much of it back as Iggie would be able to pay out of its remaining assets, provided there were no other creditors.

Jurisdiction of corporations   Corporations may be incorporated federally under the Canada *Business Corporations Act* or provincially under the Ontario *Business Corporations Act*. A federally incorporated corporation may conduct business anywhere in Canada as long as it is also registered in the province where it conducts business. Generally, a federal incorporation is usually used for corporations that conduct business in several provinces in Canada. A corporation incorporated under the laws of Ontario may conduct business in another province upon applying to that province for registration as an extra-provincial corporation.

Types of corporations   There are Crown (government owned) corporations, non-profit corporations (which must have no share capital, e.g. religious bodies or charities), and business corporations which **must** have share capital. The Ontario *Business Corporations Act* (OBCA) governs business, profit-oriented corporations; hence, the word **business** in the name of the OBCA. Under the OBCA, there are two types of business corporations: offering and non-offering, or private. Although this discussion deals with Ontario business corporations, it also applies, with appropriate modification, to business corporations in other provinces/territories as the provincial and territorial business corporation statutes are roughly the same across Canada.

Offering corporations   An offering corporation is one which offers its shares for sale to the general public on the stock market. The OBCA states that any corporation may offer its shares to the public if it files a prospectus with the Ontario Securities Commission. A prospectus is a document that fully discloses the financial status of the corporation. The prospectus is available to the general public to inspect before buying any shares of that corporation.

Non-offering/private corporations   This type of corporation does not offer its shares to the general public on the stock market. It instead selects its shareholders. A non-offering corporation does not file a prospectus. Because non-offering corporations do not offer their shares for sale to the public, they are referred to as **private** corporations; similarly, because non-offering corporations tend to be family-owned, they are also commonly referred to as **closely held** corporations. Non-offering corporations may convert into offering corporations if they file a prospectus. This manual covers only non-offering corporations since they are the ones most frequently incorporated in the law office and also since the incorporation procedure is generally the same for both offering and non-offering corporations.

How created   In Ontario, the law which permits the creation of corporations is the Ontario *Business Corporations Act* (OBCA). The OBCA requires people who wish to create a corporation to file a document known as **articles of incorporation** with the Companies and Personal Property Security Branch of the Ontario Ministry of Government and Consumer Services. The corporation is created on the date the ministry approves the articles of incorporation.

How a corporation acts   A corporation acts through its shareholders, directors, and officers. Here is a basic structure of a corporation:

Figure 25.1

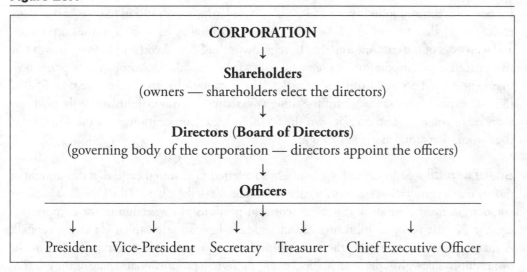

Shareholders   Basically, the shareholders own the corporation in proportion of the number of shares they own or hold. The shareholders vote annually to elect the decision-making body of the corporation which is the directors, also known as the **board of directors**, who are authorized to act on the shareholders' and corporation's behalf. Shareholders may be individuals or corporations. Although the shareholders are the owners of the corporation, they are not the corporation because the corporation is a separate entity, i.e. a separate person created by law.

Directors   The directors (also referred to as **board of directors**) manage the corporation on behalf of the shareholders who elect them. Subject to any unanimous shareholder agreement which takes back control from the directors, the directors make almost all decisions about the business of the corporation and are legally obligated to manage the corporation in the best interests of the shareholders. As soon as the shareholders elect the board of directors, they place the board of directors in complete charge, without direct shareholder supervision. The directors need not be shareholders. This option enables the corporation to hire the best people, such as specialists or others, for the job of managing. A corporation may not be a director since it lacks the physical and mental capacity to make decisions.

Officers   The directors appoint the officers to do the actual work of implementing the decisions of the directors. The officers are called so because they hold the offices of the president, secretary, etc. One person may hold two offices to accommodate one-shareholder corporations. A corporation may not be an officer because it is unable to do the physical work that officers must do.

More than one hat   Under the OBCA, it is possible for the same person to be a shareholder, a director, and an officer at the same time, or any combination of these. This enables non-offering corporations to have complete control of the corporation, and for its owners to themselves do the work if the corporation cannot afford to hire outside help: for example, if John is both the director and the president of the corporation, John would wear two hats by carrying out the duties of a director as well as those of the president as if John were two different individuals.

INTERMEDIATE CONCEPTS

Assets of a corporation   Assets are the cash and property that a corporation owns: for example, you and John invested $1 each in Iggie Corporation and in return got one share each. The $1 that each of you invested in Iggie for a total of $2 is cash to the corporation and is an asset of the corporation; that is, Iggie owns the $2, and you and John each own one share because the corporation is a separate entity from you, the shareholders. Suppose now that Iggie earned $5,000 from selling iggies. The corporation's total assets are now $5,002 ($5,000 earned from sales; $2 from issuing two shares). You and John still only own one share each; you and John do not own the $5,002. Iggie Corporation owns the $5,002, i.e. the corporation's total assets are $5,002.

Share capital   Share capital, sometimes also referred to as **stated capital**, is the amount of money that a corporation receives for each share it issues (sells). Under the OBCA, a business corporation must have share capital to represent portions of ownership in the corporation, e.g. the $2 that you and John invested in Iggie are Iggie's share capital (or stated capital). A share is a fractional part of the ownership of a corporation. As a fractional part of the ownership, a share gives the shareholder certain rights to a proportionate share of the assets of the corporation. A share, however, does not give direct ownership of the corporation's assets to the shareholder. The assets are owned by the corporation itself. The rights that a shareholder has include the right to vote at meetings, receive a dividend from the corporation's profits, and receive a proportionate share of the corporation's assets if the corporation were to fold. Remember, however, that a share does not give the shareholder direct ownership rights to the assets of the corporation. The corporation's assets are the property of the corporation, and the issued shares of the corporation are the property of the shareholders.

Proportion of ownership   The proportion of each shareholder's ownership in a corporation is determined thus: the number of shares the shareholder owns divided by the total number of shares issued (sold): for example, you own one-half, or 50 percent, of Iggie Corporation because you own one of the two shares issued (one each to you and John). You and John represent a 50/50 ownership. At a meeting of shareholders, you and John would be each able to cast one-half, or 50 percent, of the votes because you each own one-half, or 50 percent, of the issued shares.

If instead you alone owned 500 shares of Iggie Corporation and the total number of shares that all of the shareholders owned was 2,000, then you would own 500/2,000, which is one-quarter, or 25 percent of the corporation. At a meeting of the shareholders, you would be able to cast one-quarter of the votes as you have 500 votes of a total of 2,000. Your voting interest is in the same proportion as your share ownership, and the voting interest of all of the other shareholders is in the same proportion as their respective share holdings. These examples are oversimplified because they assume there is only one class of voting shares.

Net worth   Net worth is the value of assets after the corporation's debts have been paid: for example, assuming Iggie has no debts, Iggie's net worth is $5,002 ($5,000 from selling iggies and $2 from issuing the two shares to you and John). Had Iggie not sold any iggies, Iggie's net worth would have been the $2 from issuing the shares to you and John.

Assume now that Iggie Corporation borrowed $10,000 from the bank. The $10,000 borrowed is cash to the corporation and is owned by the corporation. So, Iggie Corporation now has a total of $15,002 in cash, which constitutes its total assets. If Iggie Corporation were dissolved immediately following these transactions, and assuming no other debts or liabilities occurred, and the bank did not insist upon the payment of any interest on its $10,000, the bank would receive its $10,000. The shareholders, you and John, would then share equally the equity, or net worth, of Iggie which is $5,002, i.e. $2,501 each. This represents one of the rights conferred upon the shareholders, in this case, the right to receive the proportionate share of the assets of the corporation upon dissolution, or winding up, of the corporation; therefore, as shareholders, you and John were entitled to get your money back only to the extent that the money was available; that is, after the corporation had paid back the $10,000 to the bank. If Iggie continues to be in business, the total equity, or net worth, of $5,002 could be dealt with in many ways, including the following: declare it a dividend to be paid to the shareholders, pay it in the form of salary or bonus to you and John, or keep it in the corporation to be used for the corporation's business.

Value of shares   The value of a share of a corporation is often the net worth (the value of assets after the corporation's debts have been paid) of the corporation, divided by the number of issued shares (shares that shareholders own, also referred to as outstanding shares). You may have paid only $1 to buy your share of Iggie Corporation, but the actual value of your share is $2,501 (net worth $5,002 divided by total number of shares issued, 2 = $2,501).

If the net worth of Iggie Corporation were $100,000 and you alone owned 500 shares out of a total number of 2,000 issued shares, then each of your shares would be worth $50 ($100,000 net worth divided by 2,000 issued shares). The value of your total number of shares would then be $25,000 (500 x $50). If the net worth of Iggie were $250,002 ($250,000 from sales of iggies plus $2 from the issued shares to you and John), the value of your one share would be $125,001, and the value of John's share would be $125,001 ($250,002 net worth divided by 2 shares = $125,001).

Remember that a share does not give to the shareholder direct ownership rights to the assets of the corporation. The corporation's assets are the property of the corporation. The shareholder instead owns a proportionate interest in the equity, or **net worth**, of the corporation.

Effects of limited liability on borrowing   Limited liability does not normally extend to a non-offering corporation when borrowing, and the advantage of limited liability is often lost because a bank would usually require that the main shareholders personally guarantee the corporation's indebtedness to the bank.

Suppose, for example, Iggie borrows $250,000 from the bank to buy special machinery. Since Iggie is a separate legal entity, it is considered to own this special machinery itself; you and John do not own that special machinery yourselves. You do not have a 50 percent interest in that asset; you have a 50 percent interest in the equity, or net worth, of Iggie Corporation.

One of the advantages of incorporating a corporation is to ensure that the shareholders' liability would be limited to the amount of money that the shareholders invested in the corporation. In our example, you and John each paid $1 and received one common share. In addition, the corporation earned a profit of $5,000 from selling iggies, and the corporation now has a total equity, or net worth, of $5,002. Usually, however, Iggie's bank would not be prepared to lend $250,000 to Iggie when the equity, or net worth, of the corporation is insufficient to secure the loan.

When borrowing, therefore, the advantage of limited liability is often eliminated in private corporations because the bank would require that the main shareholders personally guarantee the corporation's indebtedness to the bank (usually by way of promissory note). You and John would each jointly and severally guarantee the repayment of the $250,000 loan to the bank. A guarantee means that if Iggie Corporation cannot and does not pay back the $250,000 loan to the bank when required to do so, the bank can call upon you and John to pay back the loan from your personal assets. Trade creditors (other businesses that the corporation conducts business with on credit basis) do not generally require similar personal guarantees from the main shareholders of the corporation.

Note that you and John have jointly and severally guaranteed the loan. This means the bank can choose to go after either you alone, or John alone, or both of you to collect the full $250,000 owing by Iggie Corporation. The bank does not have to proceed against you for $125,000 and against John for the remaining $125,000. If the bank proceeded against John alone and collected the full $250,000, John would have to go after you to get $125,000. A several guarantee (as opposed to a joint and several guarantee) would mean that the bank would have to proceed against you for $125,000 and John for the remaining $125,000.

If we assume the bank did not ask for the guarantees from the shareholders (which would not normally occur in practice) and Iggie Corporation was not successful, the shareholders' liability would be limited to the amount of money that they invested in the corporation, namely, $2, which would be used to satisfy the debts of Iggie Corporation, including the bank loan, but obviously to a virtually zero extent.

The concept behind limited liability then is that Iggie Corporation is a separate entity, and the loan by the bank (assuming without personal guarantees from the principal shareholders) was made to Iggie Corporation and not to its shareholders, and accordingly, the bank would be limited to recovery of its loan from the entity with which it contracted, that being Iggie Corporation. As mentioned earlier, however, when a corporation wishes to borrow money from a bank (or other lending institution), it is standard practice for the bank (or other lending institution) to require personal guarantees from the principal shareholders.

Income and taxation   Because a corporation is a legal entity, separate from its shareholders, a corporation's income is determined and taxed separately from that of its owners, the shareholders. The federal government taxes a corporation on its net income, which is its profit. Shareholders cannot treat the net income or any loss of a corporation in which they own shares as their own income or loss. The income and loss of a corporation is taxed only as being that of the corporation. In addition to federal income tax, a corporation also pays provincial tax on its taxable income.

ADVANTAGES AND DISADVANTAGES OF INCORPORATING

Some of the more significant advantages and disadvantages between corporations and partnerships or sole proprietorships include:

Limited liability   Sole proprietors or partners in a general partnership are liable to the creditors to the full extent of their personal assets for the liabilities of their businesses and could potentially lose personal assets beyond those invested in their businesses, whereas a shareholder's liability to the creditors of the corporation is limited to the amount of his or her investment in the corporation, unless the shareholder gives personal guarantees.

Taxation   Generally, corporations pay lower rates of taxes than do sole proprietorships or partnerships because sole proprietorships or partnerships are taxed at personal rates of taxes which are higher than those of corporations. Also, being a separate legal entity, a corporation pays corporate income tax which is calculated completely separately from the shareholders' personal income tax, which is why a corporation has to file its own corporate tax return separately from the personal tax return that the individual shareholders must each file. A sole proprietor or a partner files only one tax return which is his or her personal tax return because any partnership or sole proprietorship income or loss is taxed directly to the partner or the sole proprietor personally.

Losses   A shareholder cannot add the net income or loss of the corporation to his or her own income or loss from all other sources in order to determine his or her taxable income. By contrast, each partner must include, for tax purposes, his or her share of the partnership's profit or loss. If the partnership has losses, each partner may deduct his or her share of the losses of the partnership to reduce his or her own personal income from other sources.

Borrowing   If money is to be raised from arm's length lenders (from strangers, not relatives) or from the general public, shares issued by a corporation will usually be more marketable and may offer more flexibility than the sale of a unit in a partnership.

Perpetual existence   This means that shareholders, officers, and directors can come and go without affecting the distinct legal entity of the corporation; that is, the death or withdrawal of a shareholder or director does not affect the continuity of the corporation. The remaining directors carry on the business, whereas the death of a sole proprietor may result in the proprietorship to fold, or a minor difference of opinion of a partner in a partnership may result in the permanent dissolution of the partnership.

Legal costs of creating and maintaining a corporation   Start-up costs of incorporating a business are higher than those of starting a sole proprietorship or a partnership. In addition, after incorporation, corporations must keep records specified by statute and comply with certain formalities respecting maintenance of records, including on-going costs associated with annual filings and record keeping requirements.

CHAPTER SUMMARY

A corporation is a legal person created by law having all of the rights and responsibilities that a real person has. Limited liability means that the law protects the shareholders of a corporation by limiting their financial losses to the amount of money which they have invested in the corporation. The Ontario *Business Corporations Act* governs all business corporations, and a document known as articles of incorporation creates all business corporations. Corporations may be offering corporations if they trade their shares on the stock market or non-offering, or private, if they do not.

The shareholders are the owners of a corporation; a corporation's directors manage the corporation on behalf of the shareholders; a corporation's officers, whom the directors appoint, do the actual day-to-day work.

Ownership in a corporation is represented usually by the number of voting shares that each shareholder owns, and each share represents one vote. The value of a share is not the amount of money that a shareholder paid for the share, but rather, the net worth of a corporation divided by the number of shares all shareholders own. Share capital, sometimes also referred to as stated capital, is the amount of money that a corporation receives for each share it issues (sells). Net worth is the value of assets after the corporation's debts have been paid.

REVIEW QUESTIONS

1. What is a corporation?
2. What does limited liability accomplish?
3. What is the main distinction between offering and non-offering corporations?
4. What is the role of the board of directors?
5. Are directors required to be also shareholders?
6. Which of these must be individuals as opposed to corporations: shareholders, directors, officers?
7. What is the effect of limited liability on borrowing by non-offering corporations?
8. If you owned 5 shares of Iggie Corporation, and there were 20 shares issued, what proportion of the corporation would you own?
9. If you owned 5 shares of Iggie Corporation for a total of $5, and assuming there were no other shares issued and no other assets of the corporation:
   (a) what is the share capital of Iggie Corporation?
   (b) what are the total assets of Iggie Corporation?
10. If iggie sold iggies in the amount of $1,000, and you owned the only 5 shares issued of Iggie Corporation at $1 each, and there were no debts or liabilities of the corporation,
   (a) what would be the net worth of Iggie Corporation?
   (b) what would be the value of your 5 shares?
11. Explain why the shareholders own all of the assets of a corporation.

CHAPTER 26

INCORPORATING A BUSINESS CORPORATION

The provincial and territorial business corporation statutes are roughly the same across Canada. In most Canadian jurisdictions, business corporations are created by filing articles of incorporation with the appropriate government agency; therefore, the discussion in this chapter on creating an Ontario business corporation also applies to other provinces/territories, with appropriate modification.

INCORPORATING AN ONTARIO BUSINESS CORPORATION

Ontario business corporations are incorporated under the Ontario *Business Corporations Act*. The Companies and Personal Property Security Branch of the Ontario Ministry of Government and Consumer Services administers all incorporations. Ontario business corporations are created by completing and filing a form known as **articles of incorporation**. Each part of the form is referred to as an **article**; hence, articles of incorporation. Once the ministry approves the articles of incorporation, it issues a **certificate of incorporation**. The certificate of incorporation creates the business corporation, and the approved articles of incorporation become the corporation's permanent foundation.

MANDAMO PROPERTIES LTD.
Re: Incorporation

Since sixth grade, Tom and Steve Brown have dreamed of conquering both land and water. When they would grow up, they would buy or lease land on which they would build parks and amusement resorts, and they would also charter steam vessels to carry passengers and freight on lakes, rivers, and other navigable waters. They would be rich. They would call their company Mandamo Properties Ltd.
We begin the incorporation of Mandamo Properties Ltd. with the preparation of the articles of incorporation, Precedent 26.1. We have also conducted a NUANS search, Precedent 26.3.

PRELIMINARY CONSIDERATIONS

Jurisdiction   If the corporation will operate only within Ontario, incorporation would be under the Ontario *Business Corporations Act* (OBCA). If the corporation intends to also operate in another province, the corporation must, after incorporating in Ontario, make an extra-provincial registration in the province in which it intends to do business, e.g. Nova Scotia. If the corporation will operate in every province, the corporation would be incorporated under the Canada *Business Corporations Act*.

Incorporating a new or existing business   A client may want to start a brand new corporation or convert his or her existing sole proprietorship or partnership into a corporation. In either case, the incorporation process begins with preparing and filing an articles of incorporation.

NAME OF CORPORATION

A corporation may use any name that is not likely to deceive or confuse the public. The responsibility for ensuring that the name neither deceives nor confuses rests with the lawyer (not the ministry). Whether incorporating an existing business or a new one, the proposed name of the corporation should consist of three elements: distinctive, descriptive, and legal, e.g. Telfax Communications Limited, respectively. The legal elements and their French equivalents are as follows: Limited, Limitée, Incorporated, Incorporée, or Corporation, or the corresponding abbreviations: Ltd., Ltée., Inc., or Corp. The legal element is a must; it readily distinguishes a corporation from an unincorporated business:

Unincorporated Business	Incorporated Corporations
Telfax Communications	Telfax Communications Limited
Paper Plates Company	Paper Plates Company Inc.

The name of a corporation must not be **identical** to the name of another corporation, partnership, sole proprietorship, association, or individual. Also, it must not contain words that imply the corporation is not a business corporation, e.g. a club, or words that suggest the corporation is connected with the federal or provincial government, or words such as college, institute, or university that suggest the corporation is a post-secondary educational institution, except with the written consent of the government. Generally, the proposed name may be in English only, French only, or English and French, with the use of letters from the Roman alphabet or Arabic numerals or a combination of them.

Number name   When a distinctive name of the corporation is not a priority, the corporation may use a number name such as 123456789 Ontario Inc. The ministry assigns the number upon receipt of the articles of incorporation. Note, however, that this is a **name** number and is not the same as a **corporation** number. The corporation number is the one which the ministry endorses on the corporation's certificate of incorporation.

Trade name   Corporations may incorporate under one name and carry on business under a trade name. The trade name may belong to an incorporated or unincorporated business and must be related or affiliated to the user corporation. The law allows the use of trade names to minimize business losses that may occur if the name is changed: for example, if Iggie Corporation were to buy a Tim Hortons shop, Iggie would want to continue the business under that trade name because the business is already well known by that name. To ensure the user corporation does not evade responsibility through the use of a trade name, the law deems the user corporation, e.g. Iggie Corporation, responsible for the business it trades as. The user corporation must register the trade name with the ministry. When a corporation incorporates under one name but does business under "a better known as" name, it is said to be trading as (t/a) the trade name, e.g. Iggie Corporation t/a Tim Hortons, and the business is said to be operated by (o/b) the name of the corporation, e.g. Tim Hortons o/b Iggie Corporation.

NUANS name search The ministry requires a NUANS (newly up-dated automated name search system) search, Precedent 26.3, as proof that the proposed name is sufficiently dissimilar so as not to deceive or confuse the public. NUANS searches are processed through private service providers (PSPs) known as search houses. The NUANS search must be Ontario **biased**. To order an Ontario biased NUANS search, contact the PSP your firm normally uses, giving them the proposed name of the corporation which you wish searched. If the corporation's name is in both English and French, you require a NUANS search for both versions of the name. Submit the original NUANS search, which must show the proposed name of the corporation and which must not be older than **ninety days**, to the ministry, together with the articles of incorporation. A NUANS search is not required for number names.

Legal TIP

An Ontario biased search is one which searches business names registered in Ontario only as opposed to business names registered in other provinces.

PROFESSIONAL CORPORATIONS

Section 3.1 of the Ontario *Business Corporations Act* (OBCA) permits members of numerous regulated professions such as accountants, architects, physicians, dentists, veterinarians, engineers, lawyers and licensed paralegals to operate as professional corporations. Professional corporations are governed by the OBCA as well as the by-laws of the respective profession's governing body, e.g. the Law Society. In addition to obtaining articles of incorporation under the OBCA, the professional corporation must also receive approval, usually by way of a **certificate of authorization**, from the relevant governing body of the profession before the professional can begin practising in the professional corporation. Liability and other requirements for operating as a professional corporation under the *Law Society Act*, for example, include:

- a shareholder of a professional corporation has no limit on professional liability;
- all shareholders of the professional corporation must be entitled to provide legal services in Ontario;
- the name of the professional corporation must include the words "Professional Corporation" in full;
- the professional corporation must not have a number name; and
- the professional corporation may not carry on a business other than the practice of the profession.

ARTICLES OF INCORPORATION

The articles of incorporation establish the foundation of the corporation's structure. The articles of incorporation are designed to provide ample flexibility for corporations to tailor each article to their specific needs. Thus a corporation may choose to have narrow and restricted articles, or broad and flexible ones, or a combination of these.

Paper form of articles of incorporation The paper articles of incorporation, Form 1, Precedent 26.1, is available through the ministry's ServiceOntario website. You may fill out and print a paper copy of the articles of incorporation through ServiceOntario. Many law firms use commercially available legal software such as Fast Company by Do Process Software Ltd. to prepare the paper form which is the software program used in this manual.

Electronic form of articles of incorporation With electronic filing, the articles of incorporation form differs slightly to accommodate the electronic data entry. Note, however, that the article-by-article information is the same as that on the paper articles of incorporation, minus the graphs, Precedent 26.2.

You require: Initial client interview notes or checklist. Follow along in Precedents 26.1 (paper form) and 26.2 (electronic sample). Key points include:

1. Name of corporation Key the name exactly as it appears in the NUANS report. If it is to be a number name, leave nine blank spaces (or as many blank spaces as may be required at the time you prepare the articles of incorporation) for the number, e.g. ☐☐☐☐☐☐☐☐☐ ONTARIO INC.

2. Address of the registered office Key the complete address of the registered office, which is usually the head office of the corporation; include room or suite number, if any, street name and number, or R. R. #, city, province, and postal code. The address may not be a post office box number because it gives no physical location for reaching the corporation.

3. Number of directors Directors must be individuals, not corporations. The number of directors may be fixed, e.g. one, or flexible, referred to as a floating board, e.g. a minimum of one and a maximum of ten. The OBCA requires every private (non-offering) corporation to have a minimum of one director; there is no fixed maximum as to the number of directors that a private (non-offering) corporation must have at any given time.

4. The first directors Key the first name, middle names, and surname of each first director and his or her complete residence address. The first directors organize the corporation immediately upon incorporation. Anyone over the age of eighteen and of sound mind can be a director and need not be an incorporator. At least 25 percent of the directors must be Canadian residents. If the corporation has only one director, that director must be a Canadian resident; if four, or fewer than four, one must be a Canadian resident. The Ontario *Business Corporations Act* defines a Canadian resident as "an individual who is a Canadian citizen ordinarily resident in Canada." It is anticipated that amendments to the OBCA may see the Canadian residency requirement for directors eliminated.

5. Restrictions Key None – the OBCA permits a corporation to carry on any business that a natural person is permitted to carry on. In the case of a professional corporation, however, you must specify the business which the professional corporation is permitted to carry on.

6. Classes Describe the types of shares the corporation will have. This clause of the articles of incorporation is known as the **capital clause**, and the stated classes of shares are known as the corporation's **authorized capital** because the corporation can issue shares from the authorized capital to raise **capital** (money). The OBCA permits corporations to have a maximum number or an unlimited number of any or all of the classes of shares that corporations decide to designate. Most corporations opt for the unlimited number option because if a corporation were to specify the number of shares, the corporation may issue only that number of shares and no more. The OBCA also permits corporations to tailor their shares to the specific needs of a corporation and to give the shares any name. Two standard classes of shares which are used in practice are **common** shares and **preference**, also referred to as **special**, shares.

Common shares The common shares are named so because the OBCA requires corporations to have at least **one** class of shares which would give shareholders the following common rights:

> (a) the right to vote at all meetings of shareholders, and
> (b) the right to receive the remaining property of the corporation upon dissolution.

The corporation need not give these rights to the same class of shares, but when it does, the shares are usually referred to as common shares because of their common or automatic rights.

Preference/Special shares In addition to common shares, a corporation may also have preference/special shares, which may be divided into a series or classes of shares and given any name. Typical clauses follow:

> 1. The corporation is authorized to issue an unlimited number of common shares.

This clause indicates that the corporation has designated only one class of shares, which by law must offer the holder the two common rights discussed above.

> 2. The corporation is authorized to issue an unlimited number of Class A shares.

This clause indicates the identical intent as Clause 1, but this corporation has decided to call its shares Class A rather than common shares.

> 3. The corporation is authorized to issue an unlimited number of common shares and an unlimited number of preference shares.

> 4. The corporation is authorized to issue an unlimited number of Class A shares and an unlimited number of Class B shares.

Clauses 3 and 4 indicate the identical intent, except for naming the shares as Class A and Class B, respectively, in Clause 4.

> 5. The corporation is authorized to issue an unlimited number of common shares, an unlimited number of Class A shares, and an unlimited number of Class B shares, and 100,000 Class C shares.

This clause reflects a more complex structure. In this structure, while the number of common shares, Class A shares, and Class B shares is unlimited, the corporation has placed a limit on the number of Class C shares, which means the corporation may issue up to a maximum of 100,000 Class C shares.

Identical classes of shares Subsection 22(7) of the OBCA permits two or more classes (or series within a class) of shares to be issued which may be identical, or virtually identical, to shares in another class or series in terms of their rights, privileges, and restrictions: for example, two classes of shares, Class A and Class B, can be identical in all respects except for their names. Previously, lawyers had to invent artificial distinctions between share classes to ensure that the shares would be legally recognized as separate classes.

No par value   Under s. 22 of the OBCA, Ontario corporations are not permitted to issue par value shares. All shares are, therefore, usually without par value, i.e. no share should have a face value printed on the share certificate. Generally, this means the corporation may sell shares from its treasury at whatever price the directors set. (By contrast, if a share had a par value of, say, $100, the board of directors is prohibited from selling it for less, although the board may sell it for more.)

7. Rights, privileges, restrictions   Describe the rights, privileges, and restrictions the corporation will give to each class of shares. The description is necessary to let shareholders know what they are getting in return for investing in the corporation. If the corporation has designated only common shares, the rights and restrictions of such shares are already implicit, i.e. the right to vote and to receive the remaining property of the corporation upon dissolution, and this section may be marked with Nil.

Where the corporation has designated more than one class of shares, the special rights, privileges, or restrictions for each class or series of shares must be clearly set out: for example, to attract investors without giving them the right to participate in the decision-making process of the corporation, the corporation may have a category of shares which would pay the holder dividends, but which would give no voting rights and call this category Class A shares. Class B shares could give only voting rights but pay only limited dividends, and this would attract investors who wish to take part in the operation of the corporation as owners rather than mere investors. Some common types of shares that would usually require full description in this part of the articles, include:

- Preference as to payment of dividends -- this means that the dividend is a preferential dividend, entitling a holder to be paid a dividend before a holder of another type of dividend-paying share.
- Cumulative dividend shares – cumulative dividends are dividends that, if not paid in any particular year, accumulate and must be paid, and if also preferential, must be paid before any dividends can be paid on other shares.
- Preference as to repayment of capital upon dissolution – this type of share would, upon dissolution of the corporation, give preference to the holder in repaying the capital the holder invested in the corporation before such repayment to any other holder.
- Redemption of shares at the option of the corporation -- this type of share provides that, in certain circumstances, the corporation will be entitled to require the shareholder to sell his or her shares back to the corporation.
- Right to convert into shares of another class – These are usually referred to as convertible shares.

8. The issue, transfer   Describe the special rules that the corporation must follow when it issues or transfers shares. Any restrictions usually distinguish the non-offering corporation from an offering one: for example, non-offering corporations cannot sell their shares without the approval of the directors, and that restriction is usually set out here.

9. Other provisions   Key any other clauses that are special to the corporation. The usual clauses for a private corporation are to the effect that a private corporation must not offer its shares for sale to the public and that the number of its shareholders is limited to not more than fifty. Use of corporate name in another language may also be provided for in this article.

10. Names and addresses of incorporators   Key the first name, middle names, and surname, and complete residence address of each incorporator. The law requires a minimum of one incorporator, who may be an individual or a corporation. The number of incorporators need not be the same as the number of first directors, although it usually is. Also, the incorporators are usually the same people as the first directors, although they need not be.

These articles are signed in duplicate   Key the names of the incorporators who will be signing the articles of incorporation. Where an incorporator is a corporation, key the name of the corporation, followed by the name of the officer who will be signing on behalf of the corporation, followed by the title of the officer:

<u>ABC Letters Limited, Ellen George, President</u>

Number of copies, minimum 3:   keep 1 in client's file; have incorporators sign two copies (there must be original signatures on both).

Filing the paper articles of incorporation
The paper articles of incorporation bearing original signatures on two copies, together with an Ontario biased NUANS search for the proposed name, a covering letter, and the required fee payable to the Minister of Finance may be filed as follows:

In person at the Companies and Personal Property Security Branch at the Toronto office, or at a Land Registry/ServiceOntario office in Ontario which the ministry has set up for this purpose. The locations are available on the ServiceOntario website.

By mail to the Companies and Personal Property Security Branch, Ministry of Government and Consumer Services, 393 University Ave., Suite 200, Toronto, ON   M5G 2M2.

Filing the electronic articles of incorporation
The electronic articles of incorporation are filed via the internet through a private service provider (PSP) under contract with the ministry. For this service, your firm must have an e-filing account with the PSP. A list of the PSPs is available on the ministry's ServiceOntario website. The electronic articles of incorporation require no handwritten signatures. The lawyer signs the articles of incorporation electronically as the authorized agent for the incorporators. The NUANS search is not submitted but is kept on file; only information extracted from the NUANS search, e.g. reference number, date of search, etc. is submitted; a covering letter is usually completed online through the PSPs. The PSPs charge a fee in addition to that which the ministry charges for the incorporation.

Consent to act as first director
If a person is named in the articles of incorporation as a first director but is not signing the articles as an **incorporator**, e.g. there are three people named as directors, only two of whom sign the articles as incorporators, prepare a **consent to act as first director**, Precedent 26.4, for the person not signing the articles. The paper consent to act as first director form is on the ministry's website, and you can fill and print it online. Legal software prints it out automatically when generating the articles of incorporation. Where the articles of incorporation are filed electronically, prepare a consent to act as first director for each first director who is not an incorporator and also for each first director who is an incorporator. The ministry does not require any of the consents to act as first director to be filed with the ministry. Keep them on file in the event the ministry requests copies of them at some later point.

CERTIFICATE OF INCORPORATION

With electronically filed articles of incorporation, the ministry issues the certificate of incorporation on a page by itself, Precedent 26.5. With paper articles of incorporation, the ministry endorses the articles of incorporation by stamping the certificate of incorporation, Figure 26.1, in the "For Ministry Use Only" space at the top of the first page of the articles of incorporation and returns an endorsed copy of the articles of incorporation to your firm. The corporation number which the ministry assigns is the corporation's identification number. The corporation is in existence as of the date set out on the certificate of incorporation.

Figure 26.1

For Ministry Use Only *Á l'usage exclusif du ministére*	Ontario Corporation No. *Numéro de la société en Ontario* 002345678
Ministry of Government Services	Ministère des Services gouvernementaux
CERTIFICATE This is to certify that these articles are effective on	CERTIFICAT Ceci certifie que les présents status entrent en vigueur le
JULY 18	JUILLET, 20--

"S Director
Director/Directrice
Business Corporations Act/Loi sur les sociétés par actions

CHAPTER SUMMARY

The Ontario *Business Corporations Act* governs all business corporations. The filing of an articles of incorporation creates a business corporation. Before preparing the articles of incorporation, you must conduct a NUANS name search to ensure that the proposed name of the corporation is not identical to the registered name of any other corporation. The name of every corporation should contain three elements: distinctive, descriptive, and legal, e.g. Telfax Communications Limited. The articles of incorporation name the incorporators and the first directors who will be the first managers of the corporation. The articles also set out the number of directors that the corporation will have and the types of shares and any restrictions on the issue and transfer of the shares. After submitting the articles to the ministry, either in paper or electronic format, the ministry issues a certificate of incorporation. The corporation is in existence as of the date on the certificate of incorporation.

REVIEW QUESTIONS

1. Name the document used to incorporate an Ontario business corporation.
2. A "floating" board of directors is a board used on water surfaces. Explain.
3. What is a certificate of incorporation?
4. Is the issue and transfer of shares restricted or not restricted in non-offering corporations?
5. What happens to the articles of incorporation after you prepare them?
6. If you held common shares in a corporation which offered no other classes of shares, what rights would such shares offer you as a shareholder?
7. What type of information is set out in the capital clause of the articles of incorporation?

1

Form 1
Business
Corporations
Act

Formule 1
Loi sur les
sociétés par
actions

For Ministry Use Only
À l'usage exclusif du ministère

Ontario Corporation Number
Numéro de la société en Ontario

ARTICLES OF INCORPORATION
STATUTS CONSTITUTIFS

1. The name of the corporation is: (Set out in BLOCK CAPITAL LETTERS)
   Dénomination sociale de la société : (Écrire en LETTRES MAJUSCULES SEULEMENT)

M	A	N	D	A	M	O		P	R	O	P	E	R	T	I	E	S		L	T	D	.			

2. The address of the registered office is:
   Adresse du siège social :

1750 Finch Avenue East, Room 3244

(Street & Number or R.R. Number & if Multi-Office Building give Room No.)
(Rue et numéro ou numéro de la R.R. et, s'il s'agit d'un édifice à bureaux, numéro du bureau)

Toronto

(Name of Municipality or Post Office)
(Nom de la municipalité ou du bureau de poste)

ONTARIO | M | 2 | V | 2 | X | 5 |

(Postal Code)
(Code postal)

3. Number of directors is/are:
   Nombre d'administrateurs :

   Fixed number | | **OR** minimum and maximum
   Nombre fixe | | **OU** minimum et maximum | **one (1)** | **ten (10)** |

4. The first director(s) is/are:
   Premier(s) administrateur(s) :

First name, middle names and surname *Prénom, autres Prénoms et nom de famille*	Address for service, giving Street & No. or R.R. No., Municipality, Province, Country and Postal Code *Domicile élu, y compris la rue et le numéro, le numéro de la R.R. ou le nom de la municipalité, la province, le pays et le code postal*	Resident Canadian? Yes or No *Résident canadien?* *Oui/Non*
Thomas David Brown	**61 Jasper Drive** **Aurora, Ontario L4G 3C1**	**Yes**
Stephen Thomas Brown	**61 Jasper Drive** **Aurora, Ontario L4G 3C1**	**Yes**

Document prepared
using *Fast Company,* by
Do Process Software Ltd.,
Toronto, Ontario
416.322.6111
866.367.7648

07116E (06/2007)

5. Restrictions, if any, on business the corporation may carry on or on powers the corporation may exercise.
   Limites, s'il y a lieu, imposées aux activités commerciales ou aux pouvoirs de la société.

2

There are no such restrictions on the business the Corporation may carry on or on the powers the Corporation may exercise.

6. The classes and any maximum number of shares that the corporation is authorized to issue:
   Catégories et nombre maximal, s'il y a lieu, d'actions que la société est autorisée à émettre :

The Corporation is authorized to issue an unlimited number of common shares and an unlimited number of preference shares.

Document prepared
using *Fast Company,* by
Do Process Software Ltd.,
Toronto, Ontario
416.322.6111
866.367.7648

07116E (06/2007)

3

7. Rights, privileges, restrictions and conditions (if any) attaching to each class of shares and directors authority
with respect to any class of shares which may be issued in series:
*Droits, privilèges, restrictions et conditions, s'il y a lieu, rattachés à chaque catégorie d'actions et pouvoirs des
administrateurs relatifs à chaque catégorie d'actions qui peut être émise en série :*

1. The preference shares may be issued in one or more series.

2. The directors are authorized to fix the number of shares and to determine the designation, rights, privileges, restrictions, and conditions attaching to the shares of each series, except for the first series of such shares, in respect of which, the number, designation, rights, privileges, restrictions, and conditions are set out in paragraph 4 below.

3. The preference shares of each series shall, with respect to priority in payment of dividends and in the return of capital in the event of the liquidation, dissolution, or winding up of the Corporation, be entitled to a preference over the common shares of the Corporation and over any other shares ranking junior to the preference shares.

4. The first series of preference shares shall consist of 50,000 shares designated as Series A preference shares and, in addition to the preferences attaching to the preference shares as a class set out in paragraph 3 above, shall have attached to them the following rights, privileges, restrictions and conditions:

   (a) the holder of each Series A preference share shall be entitled to receive, as and when the directors declare, out of the monies properly applicable to the payment of dividends, preferential non-cumulative cash dividends at the rate of eight percent per share per year of the amount paid to the Corporation for such share, and no more;

   (b) the holder of each Series A preference share shall not have any voting rights for the election of directors or for any other purpose;

   (c) in the event of the liquidation, dissolution or winding up of the Corporation, the holder of each Series A preference share shall be entitled to receive the amount paid to the Corporation for such share, together with all declared unpaid dividends.

5. The holder of each common share has the right to one vote for such common share at all meetings of shareholders, other than meetings of the holders of another class of shares, and to receive the remaining property of the Corporation upon dissolution.

Document prepared
using *Fast Company,* by
Do Process Software Ltd.,
Toronto, Ontario
416.322.6111
866.367.7648

07116E (06/2007)

Legal Office Procedures

4

8.   The issue, transfer or ownership of shares is/is not restricted and the restrictions (if any) are as follows:
     L'émission, le transfert ou la propriété d'actions est/n'est pas restreint. Les restrictions, s'il y a lieu, sont les suivantes :

The transfer of shares of the Corporation shall be restricted in that no shareholder shall be entitled to transfer any share or shares without either:

(a)   The approval of the directors of the Corporation expressed by a resolution passed at a meeting of the board of directors or by an instrument or instruments in writing signed by a majority of the directors; or

(b)   The approval of the holders of at least a majority of the shares of the Corporation entitling the holders thereof to vote in all circumstances (other than a separate class vote of the holders of another class of shares of the Corporation) for the time being outstanding expressed by a resolution passed at a meeting of the holders of such shares or by an instrument or instruments in writing signed by the holders of a majority of such shares.

Document prepared
using *Fast Company,* by
Do Process Software Ltd.,
Toronto, Ontario
416.322.6111
866.367.7648

07116E (06/2007)

5

9. Other provisions if any:
Autres dispositions, s'il y a lieu :

(a)   That the board of directors may from time to time, in such amounts and on such terms as it deems expedient:

(i)   borrow money on the credit of the Corporation;

(ii)   issue, reissue, sell or pledge debt obligations (including bonds, debentures, notes or other evidences of indebtedness or guarantee, secured or unsecured) of the Corporation;

(iii)   to the extent permitted by the Business Corporations Act (as from time to time amended) give directly or indirectly financial assistance to any person by means of a loan, a guarantee or otherwise on behalf of the Corporation to secure performance of any present or future indebtedness, liability or obligation of any person; and

(iv)   charge, mortgage, hypothecate, pledge or otherwise create a security interest in all or any of the currently owned or subsequently acquired real or personal, movable or immovable property of the Corporation, franchises and undertaking, to secure any debt obligations or any money borrowed, or other debt or liability of the Corporation.

(b)   To the extent permitted by the Business Corporations Act (as from time to time amended), that the board of directors may from time to time delegate to such one or more of the directors and officers of the Corporation as may be designated by the board all or any of the powers conferred on the board above to such extent and in such manner as the board shall determine at the time of each such delegation.

(c)   That the outstanding securities of the Corporation are beneficially owned, directly or indirectly, by not more than fifty persons or companies, exclusive of:

(i)   persons or companies that are, or at the time they last acquired securities of the Corporation were, accredited investors (as defined under applicable Ontario securities laws, as may be amended from time to time); and

(ii)   current or former directors, officers or employees of the Corporation or a corporation, company, syndicate, partnership, trust or unincorporated organization (each, an "Entity") affiliated (as defined under applicable Ontario securities laws, as may be amended from time to time) with the Corporation, or current or former consultants (as defined under applicable Ontario securities laws, as may be amended from time to time), who in each case beneficially own only securities of the Corporation that were issued as compensation by, or under an incentive plan of, the Corporation or an Entity affiliated with the Corporation; provided that:

(A)   two or more persons who are the joint registered holders of one or more securities of the Corporation shall be counted as one beneficial owner of those securities; and

(B)   an Entity shall be counted as one beneficial owner of the securities of the Corporation unless such Entity has been created or is being used primarily for the purpose of acquiring or holding securities of the Corporation, in which event each beneficial owner of an equity interest in the Entity or each beneficiary of the Entity, as the case may be, shall be counted as a separate beneficial owner of those securities of the Corporation.

(d)   That subject to the provisions of the Business Corporations Act, the Corporation shall have a lien on the shares registered in the name of a shareholder who is indebted to the Corporation to the extent of such debt.

(e)   That subject to the provisions of the Business Corporations Act, the Corporation may purchase any of its issued shares.

Document prepared
using *Fast Company,* by
Do Process Software Ltd.,
Toronto, Ontario
416.322.6111
866.367.7648

07116E (06/2007)

10. The names and addresses of the incorporators are:
    Noms et adresses des fondateurs :

6

First name, middle names and surname or corporate name *Prénom, autres prénoms et nom de famille ou dénomination sociale*	Full address for service or if a corporation, the address of the registered or head office giving street & No. or R.R. No., municipality, province, country and postal code *Domicile élu au complet ou, dans le cas d'une société, adresse du siège social ou adresse de l'établissement principal, y compris la rue et le numéro ou le numéro de la R.R., la municipalité, la province, le pays et le code postal*
Thomas David Brown	**61 Jasper Drive** **Aurora, Ontario L4G 3C1**
Stephen Thomas Brown	**61 Jasper Drive** **Aurora, Ontario L4G 3C1**

These articles are signed in duplicate.
Les présents statuts sont signés en double exemplaire.

Full name(s) and signature(s) of incorporator(s). In the case of a corporation set out the name of the corporation and the name and office of the person signing on behalf of the corporation
Nom(s) au complet et signature(s) du ou des fondateurs. Si le fondateur est une société, indiquer la dénomination sociale et le nom et le titre de la personne signant au nom de la société

Signature / *signature*

Thomas David Brown
Name of incorporator (or corporation name & signatories name and office)
Nom du fondateur (ou dénomination sociale et nom et titre du signataire)

Signature / *signature*

Stephen Thomas Brown
Name of incorporator (or corporation name & signatories name and office)
Nom du fondateur (ou dénomination sociale et nom et titre du signataire)

Signature / *signature*

Name of incorporator (or corporation name & signatories name and office)
Nom du fondateur (ou dénomination sociale et nom et titre du signataire)

Signature / *signature*

Name of incorporator (or corporation name & signatories name and office)
Nom du fondateur (ou dénomination sociale et nom et titre du signataire)

Document prepared using *Fast Company,* by Do Process Software Ltd., Toronto, Ontario
416.322.6111
866.367.7648

07116E (06/2007)

Page: 1

Request ID / *Demande no*

11731830

Ontario Corporation Number
Numero de la compagnie en Ontario

2345678

FORM 1

BUSINESS CORPORATIONS ACT   /

FORMULE NUMÉRO 1

LOI SUR LES COMPAGNIES

ARTICLES OF INCORPORATION
STATUTS CONSTITUTIFS

1. The name of the corporation is:

   Denomination *sociale* de la compagnie:

   MANDAMO PROPERTIES LTD.

2. The address of the registered office is:

   Adresse du *siège social:*

   1750 Finch Avenue East, Room 3244
   Toronto, Ontario M2V 2X5

   (Street & Number, or R.R. Number & if Multi-Office Building give Room No.)
   (*Rue* et numéro, ou numéro de la *R.R.* et, *s'il_ s'agit* édifice à *bureau*, numéro du *bureau*)

   TORONTO   **ONTARIO**
   CANADA   **M2V 2X5**
   (Name of Municipality or Post Office)   (Postal Code/ *Code postal*)
   (*Nom* de la *municipalité* ou du *bureau* de *poste*)

3. Number (or minimum and maximum number) of directors is:
   Minimum   1

   Nombre (ou nombres minimal et *maximal)* d'administrateurs:
   Maximum   10

4. The first director(s) is/are:

   Premieres) *administrateur(s):*

   First name, initials and surname
   Prénom, *initiales* et nom de famile

   Address for service, giving Street & No. or R.R. No., Municipality and Postal Code

   Resident Canadian   State Yes or No
   Résident *Canadien*   *Oui/Non*

   Domicile élu, y *compris* la rue et le numéro, le numéro de la *R.R.,* ou le nom de la *municipalité* et le code *postal*

   THOMAS DAVID   YES
   BROWN

   61 JASPER DRIVE

   AURORA, ONTARIO
   CANADA   L4G 3C1

Precedent 26.3 NUANS Search, page 1 only

 Ontario Reservation Report / Rapport pour réservation en Ontario

MANDAMO PROPERTIES LTD.
99857821 =MANDAMO=   Page 1 of/de 7   20--Jn29

COMPANY NAME / NOM DE L'ENTREPRISE						
JUR. | NO. | DATE | CITY / VILLE BUS. / ACT.			| EP	| TYPE	| STATUS / STATUT	| STAT. DATE / DATE EFF.
MANDAMO PROPERTIES LTD						
ON | 99857821	| 20--Jn29	|	|	|	| Prop.ESCCORP	|
MANDALA CUSTOM HOMES INC						
BC | 0000695067	| 2004Ma14	| NELSON	|	| Corp	| Active	|
MANDALA GROUP PROPERTY MANAGEMENT INC						
ON | 0001475491	| 2001Ma09	| TORONTO	|	| Bus_Corp	| Active	|
MANDALIN INVESTMENTS LTD						
ON | 0001279110	| 1998Mr16	| MINDEN	|	| Bus_Corp	| Active	|
MANDAMUS ENTERPRISES INC						
ON | 0001377824	| 1999Oc01	| ETOBICOKE	|	| Bus_Corp	| Active	|
MANDALENA INVESTMENTS INC						
ON | 0000563670	| 1983Se20	| CHATHAM	|	| Bus_Corp	| Active	| 1992Jn27
MANDALAY HOMES INC						
ON | 0002111054	| 2006Au18	| CAMPBELLVILLE	|	| Bus_Corp	| Active	|
DI MANNO ENTERPRISES LTD						
ON | 0001130699	| 1995Ma10	| CONCORD	|	| Bus_Corp	| Active	|
MANDALAY ESTATES INC						
ON | 0000470345	| 1981Fe16	| NORTH YORK	|	| Bus_Corp	| Active	| 1992Jn27
MANOTA ENTERPRISES INC						
ON | 0002001934	| 2001Mr13	| MISSISSAUGA	|	| Bus_Corp	| Active	|
MANDALE HOLDINGS LTD						
BC | 0000056404	| 1963Al19	| VICTORIA	|	| Corp	| Active	| 2003Jn11
MANDALA HOLDINGS LTD						
BC | 0000398702	| 1990De21	| VANCOUVER	|	| Corp	| Active	| 2004Fe11
DYNAMO MAINTENANCE SERVICES INC						
ON | 0002042076	| 2004Mr02	| TORONTO	|	| Bus_Corp	| Active	|
MANDALA HOLDINGS LIMITED						
CD | 0000529699	| 1974Mr07	| MONTREAL	|	| CBCA	| Active	| 1984No20
MIDANO ENTERPRISES INC						
BC | 0000670325	| 2003Ma28	| WEST VANCOUVER	|	| Corp	| Active	| 2003Jn25
MANDALA FLORAL INC						
AB | 2014093658	| 2008Jn20	| CALGARY	|	| Bus_Corp	| Active	|
MANDAMUS INC						
AB | 0203833082	| 1988Al28	| EDMONTON	|	| Bus_Corp	| Active	| 2004Au16

The Provision of the information contained in this report is subject to the Terms and Conditions contained on the last page here of. The use of this report is the sole responsiblity of the applicant. / Les renseignements contenus dans le présent rapport sont sujets aux conditions générales énoncées à la dernière page du document. La responsabilité quant à l'usage du présent rapport incombe entièrement au demandeur.

Valid until / Valide jusqu'au 20--Se27   **NUANS® Name Search System**   ESCCORP   AVN538892 V=36
                                                      Système de Recherche de Nom NUANS^MD

Request 10: 012381712
Demande n°:
Transaction 10: 039892214
Transaction n°:
Category ID: CT
Catégorie:

Date Report Produced: (year)/07/18
Document produit le:
Time Report Produced: 09:55:17
Imprimé a:

Province of Ontario
Province de l'Ontario
Ministry of Government Services
Ministère des Services gouvernementaux

Certificate of Incorporation
Certificat de constitution

This is to certify that

Ceci certifie que

MANDAMO PROPERTIES LTD.

Ontario Corporation No.

Numéro matricule de la personne morale en Ontario

00 2 3 4 5 6 7 8

is a corporation incorporated,
under the laws of the Province of Ontario.

est une société constituée aux termes
des lois de la province de l'Ontario.

These articles of incorporation
are effective on

Les présents statuts constitutifs
entrent en vigueur le

JULY 18 JU ILLE T, 20—

Director/Directrice

Business Corporations Act/Loi sur les sociétés par actions

Form 2
Business
Corporations
Act

Formule 2
Loi sur les
sociétés par
actions

CONSENT TO ACT AS A FIRST DIRECTOR
CONSENTEMENT DU PREMIER ADMINISTRATEUR

I,/Je soussigné(e)

ROBERT W. GARVEY

(First name, middle names and surname)
(Prénom, autres Prénoms et nom de famille)

address for service
domicile élu

R. R. #6, Queensville, Ontario L3O 1P2

(Street & No. or R.R. No., Municipality, Province, Country & Postal Code)
(Rue et numéro, ou numéro de la R.R., nom de la municipalité, province, pays et code postal)

hereby consent to act as a first director of
accepte par la présente de devenir premier administrateur de

HIRAM WALKER WATER WELLS INC.

(Name of Corporation)
(Dénomination sociale de la société)

(Signature of Consenting Person)
(Signature de l'acceptant)

Legal Office Procedures

CHAPTER 27

ORGANIZING THE BUSINESS CORPORATION

This chapter covers the initial organization of a newly incorporated business corporation, including organizing its structure and documenting the organization in the corporate minute book.

KEEPING CORPORATE RECORDS

The Ontario *Business Corporations Act* (OBCA) sets out the types of records that business corporations must keep:

> 140.(1) **Records**.--A corporation shall prepare and maintain, at its registered office or at such other place in Ontario designated by the directors,
>
> (a) the articles and the by-laws and all amendments thereto, and a copy of any unanimous shareholder agreement known to the directors;
>
> (b) minutes of meetings and resolutions of shareholders;
>
> (c) a register of directors in which are set out the names and residence addresses, while directors, including the street and number, if any, of all persons who are or have been directors of the corporation with the several dates on which each became or ceased to be a director;
>
> (d) a securities register complying with section 141; and
>
> (e) a register of ownership interests in land complying with section 140.1.

Business corporations keep the above records in a binder-like book known as a minute book, which is the official record book of business corporations. The directors (directors and board of directors used interchangeably) must make the minute book available to shareholders and creditors at the corporation's registered office during regular business hours. In practice, however, many non-offering corporations keep their minute books in the offices of their respective lawyers who maintain them on an ongoing basis.

CORPORATE SUPPLIES

You require the following supplies, available from legal stationers, to complete the initial organization of the newly incorporated corporation. The client usually reimburses your firm for the cost of these supplies when your firm bills the client for the incorporation services.

Minute book   There are various styles, most being loose-leaf variations of three-ring type binders. Order the type your firm usually orders or as the client instructs; see Precedent 27.1 for a sample.

By-laws 1 and 2   These by-laws may be purchased as part of the minute book package, or they may be generated from computerized firm precedents or from legal software programs.

Seal   There are various types; see Precedent 27.1. A corporate seal is an impression of the corporation's name made by a mechanical device, usually at places of corporate signatures. The OBCA does not require corporations to have a seal since the signature of the authorized officers is sufficient to bind the corporation. Nevertheless, it is common practice for corporations to obtain a seal.

Share certificates   Firms usually purchase share certificates in blank and legal software fills in the content and the types of shares they represent. Share certificates, in blank or pre-printed, are available from legal suppliers. The share certificates are said to be "with restrictions" because they usually contain restriction clauses printed on the face of them, which restriction clauses refer to the fact that non-offering corporations cannot sell shares without director approval.

BY-LAWS AND RESOLUTIONS

By-laws and resolutions are minute book records which represent the formal business activities of the corporation. Following is an overview of by-laws and resolutions to help you understand their role in the initial organization of a newly incorporated business corporation and beyond.

BY-LAWS

What are by-laws   Basically, by-laws are the permanent business rules of a corporation. By-laws are adaptations of the OBCA. Thus, while the OBCA applies to all corporations in general, by-laws are adaptations of the OBCA which apply to the specific corporation which enacts them.

Who enacts and confirms by-laws   The directors enact most of the corporation's by-laws and submit them to the shareholders for confirmation at the next meeting of shareholders, at which, the shareholders may confirm, amend, or reject the by-laws. If the shareholders confirm them at the next meeting of shareholders, the by-laws continue in effect and become permanent. If the shareholders reject a by-law, or if the directors fail to submit a by-law to the shareholders for confirmation, the by-law ceases to be effective as of the date of the next meeting of shareholders. In effect, the effective date of a by-law is the date it is enacted (passed), not the date confirmed (approved) by the shareholders. Any by-laws which the shareholders enact are effective on the date the shareholders enact them and require no further confirmation since the shareholders are the owners of the corporation.

Methods of enacting and confirming by-laws   The directors may enact by-laws either at a meeting of directors or in writing, i.e. by the signatures of all of the directors instead of at a meeting of directors. Similarly, the shareholders may confirm by-laws either at a meeting of shareholders or in writing, i.e. by the signatures of all of the shareholders instead of at a meeting of shareholders. Here is a summary of how by-laws may be enacted and confirmed:

ENACTING AND CONFIRMING BY-LAWS		
ENACTED	**CONFIRMED**	**EFFECTIVE DATE**
By directors at meetings of directors or In writing (signed by all of the directors, instead of a meeting)	By shareholders at next meeting of shareholders or In writing (signed by all of the shareholders, instead of a meeting)	From date enacted by directors until confirmed by shareholders at next meeting of shareholders, after which, by-laws become permanent or From date enacted by directors until confirmed in writing (signed by all of the shareholders, instead of a meeting), after which, by-laws become permanent

RESOLUTIONS

What are resolutions   Resolutions are formal business decisions which are recorded in the minute book of the business corporation. They are decisions **before** and resolutions **after** they are passed.

Who makes resolutions   The directors and the shareholders may make resolutions. The OBCA prescribes the matters which may be done by resolutions of directors and those which may be done by resolutions of shareholders: for example, the OBCA requires that a corporation elect officers by resolutions of directors and appoint auditors by resolutions of shareholders. Generally, shareholders make resolutions relating to the structural and financial matters of the corporation, and directors make all other resolutions. If the directors and the shareholders are the same people, they do the job of the directors and that of the shareholders as if they were two separate individuals.

Methods of passing resolutions   Resolutions of directors or resolutions of shareholders may be passed either at a meeting or in writing, i.e. by the signatures of all of the directors instead of at a meeting of directors, or by the signatures of all of the shareholders instead of at a meeting of shareholders.

INITIAL ORGANIZATION

A newly incorporated business corporation is in existence as of the date set out in the certificate of incorporation; however, the corporation is merely a shell at this point. It is necessary to organize the corporation to enable it to do business. The procedure for organizing the newly incorporated business corporation is referred to as **initial organization**. All documents in the initial organization are prepared as of the date of incorporation. The initial organization documents are required by statute and are, therefore, standard in nearly all non-offering business corporations.

Legal TIP

A general difference between by-laws and resolutions is that by-laws are rules, whereas resolutions are decisions.

Legal TIP

Resolutions of directors or shareholders require no confirmation.

STATUTORY REQUIREMENTS

To accomplish the initial organization of a business corporation, the first directors are required to complete the following activities under the OBCA:

> 117.(1) First directors meeting – After incorporation, a meeting of the directors of a corporation shall be held at which the directors may,
>
> (a) make by-laws;
> (b) adopt forms of security certificates and corporate records;
> (c) authorize the issue of securities;
> (d) appoint officers;
> (e) appoint one or more auditors to hold office until the first annual or special meeting of shareholders;
> (f) make banking arrangements; and
> (g) transact any other business.

Although the OBCA in subsection 117.(1), above, makes reference to a first directors' **meeting**, subsections 117.(2) and 129.(1) authorize the use of resolutions in writing instead of a meeting:

> **Resolution in writing**
>
> (2) Any matter referred to in subsection (1) may be dealt with by the directors by a resolution in writing in accordance with subsection 129.(1).
>
> ***
>
> **Resolution in writing**
>
> 129.(1) A resolution in writing, signed by all the directors entitled to vote on that resolution at a meeting of directors or a committee of directors, is as valid as if it had been passed at a meeting of directors or a committee of directors.

RESOLUTIONS OF DIRECTORS

Legal TIP

There is no prescribed format for any of the initial organization documents.

To complete the initial organization of Mandamo Properties Ltd., we have prepared the resolutions of directors in writing, instead of at a meeting, that being the method most commonly used in practice for non-offering business corporations. Following are the initial organization documents as per the above statutory requirements of the OBCA:

By-law 1, Precedent 27.2
By-law 2, Precedent 27.3
Resolutions of directors, Precedent 27.4
Subscriptions for shares, Precedent 27.5
Resolution of the directors re allotment and issue of shares, Precedent 27.6
Share certificates, Precedents 27.7 and 27.8
Directors' register, Precedent 27.9
Shareholders' register, Precedent 27.10
Officers' register, Precedent 27.11
Shareholders' ledgers, Precedents 27.12 and 27.13.

Number of copies, minimum 2: Insert l in minute book; keep 1 in client's file.

SHARE CERTIFICATES

Share certificates are a shareholder's proof of his or her share holdings in the corporation. Prepare a share certificate, Precedents 27.7 and 27.8, of the applicable class of shares, usually for every person who has subscribed for shares. Number the share certificates sequentially, e.g. 1, for the first certificate, 2 for the next, etc. Some firms use "C" for common shares, e.g. C-l. Start numbering at 1 for each different class of shares.

Note that under section 54 of the OBCA, a corporation may issue shares that may be certificated, i.e. represented by a share certificate, or uncertificated where no share certificates are issued. The directors of the corporation may provide for uncertificated shares by resolution, in which case, the completed shareholder's ledger or register in the minute book would replace the requirement for a share certificate. In practice, however, share certificates are usually prepared for any issued shares.

Number of copies, minimum 2: Original to the shareholder or retained in the minute book; if mailing the original, use registered mail or send by courier, and keep 1 photocopy in minute book.

Transferring shares When a shareholder sells all of the shares he or she holds, complete the part on the back of the share certificate which begins with "For value received..." Cancel the original certificate by stamping or writing CANCELLED across the face, and retain it in the minute book. Prepare a new share certificate for the new shareholder. If the shareholder transfers only some of his or her shares, follow the same procedure. Then, issue two new share certificates: one for the number of shares still held by the original shareholder and another for the new shareholder for the number of shares he or she acquired by the transfer.

MINUTE BOOK REGISTERS

The following registers are completed as part of the initial organization of the corporation and inserted in the corporation's minute book.

Directors' register This register, Precedent 27.9, is a record of all of the directors of the corporation and includes the dates on which they were elected, usually the date of incorporation, and the date on which they resigned, if applicable.

Shareholders' register This register, Precedent 27.10, is a record of all of the shareholders of the corporation and the number and types of shares they each hold.

Shareholder's ledger This ledger is a record of the shareholdings of each individual shareholder, Precedents 27.12 and 27.13.

Stock transfer register This register records shares which have been transferred from one person to another. Where prepared, assign transfer numbers in numerical order, e.g. first transfer is 1, next is 2, etc. in order of occurrence. See Chapter 28.

Interests in land in Ontario register Section 140.1 of the OBCA requires a register showing the address of any land that the corporation owns in Ontario, the date the corporation acquired the property and, if applicable, the date the corporation disposed of it. The register must also contain a copy of any deed/transfer, or similar document, showing the municipal address, if any, the registry or land titles division and property identifier number, the legal description, and the assessment roll number, if any.

RESOLUTIONS OF SHAREHOLDERS

Typically, the shareholders make resolutions relating to the structure and financial affairs of the corporation (directors make all other resolutions). We have prepared the following resolutions of shareholders, in writing, for Mandamo Properties Ltd.

Resolutions of shareholders, Precedent 27.14   The contents of these resolutions are standard in the initial organization of nearly all non-offering business corporations.

Resolutions of shareholders re exemption from audit, Precedent 27.15   The OBCA permits audit exemption when (a) a corporation is not an offering corporation, and (b) all of the shareholders consent to the audit exemption in writing for that particular year. Many small non-offering corporations are exempt and can thus legally avoid the expense of an audit.

Number of copies, minimum 2: Insert l in minute book; keep l in client's file.

SPECIAL RESOLUTIONS OF SHAREHOLDERS

Special resolutions of shareholders re number and election of directors, Precedent 27.16   Where the articles indicate a minimum and maximum number of directors, the shareholders must fix (set) the actual number of directors which the corporation's board of directors will consist of. In addition, the shareholders may, and they usually do, empower the directors to fix the number of directors in the future, if necessary. This type of structural change can only be done by a special resolution of the shareholders. A consent to act as director, Precedents 27.17 and 27.18, is required of the newly elected directors.

MAKING NOTARIAL AND CERTIFIED COPIES

The corporation needs to open a corporate bank account. For this to be done, the bank usually requires a copy of the articles of incorporation; some banks require a notarial copy, Precedent 27.19. To prepare a notarial copy of a corporate document, make a photocopy of the original and attach the notarial certificate to the top of it. To prepare a certified copy of a corporate document, e.g. special resolution, make or print a copy of the particular document and add the certificate to the foot of the document, Precedent 27.20.

INITIAL RETURN

Once the initial organization is completed, the *Corporations Information Act* requires that an initial return be filed with the ministry. The information contained in the initial return is recorded in the Ontario public record for Ontario business corporations. Prepare and file the initial return, in person or by mail, with the ministry within **sixty days** of the date of incorporation. You may also file the initial return electronically if your firm has an e-filing account with a private service provider who is under contract with the ministry for this purpose.

PREPARATION AND DISTRIBUTION OF INITIAL RETURN, FORM 1

You require: The file, the articles of incorporation, the directors' and shareholders' resolutions. Follow along in Precedent 27.21. Notes on items not self-explanatory follow:

Form The paper form is available in PDF format on the ministry's ServiceOntario website. Unless filing electronically, access the PDF initial return form through the ministry's company forms, fill it out, and print it out.

Mark the **initial return** box. The same form is used to report subsequent changes in the corporation and is then referred to as a notice of change. In practice, the name of the director who signs the form is usually entered in the c/o line. A director, an officer, or a lawyer may file the initial return. If a lawyer files it, mark the "other individual" box.

At least one completed Schedule A, Precedent 27.21, must accompany the initial return. In completing Schedule A, report all of the directors of the corporation. Only five of the most senior officer positions must be recorded for officers. If one individual is both the president and secretary of the corporation, for example, it counts as two officers, and two separate officer positions must be reported on the form. Information concerning any officers other than the five most senior officers reported on the form must be kept at the registered or head office address. The date elected, ceased (resigned), or appointed is usually the date of incorporation, which appears on the certificate of incorporation.

Number of copies, minimum 3: File 1 with ministry; insert 1 in minute book; keep 1 in client's file.

MANDAMO PROPERTIES LTD.
Re: Incorporation

All of the documents which we have prepared in this chapter complete the initial organization of Mandamo. We have also prepared the initial return, Precedent 27.21, to let the ministry know who is who in the corporation. Mandamo is now open for cruising business in the majestic vastness of the Great Lakes. But angry waters are acoming for Mandamo – in the next chapter.

LAW FIRM PERSONNEL AS FIRST DIRECTORS AND INCORPORATORS

Occasionally, for various reasons (e.g. clients would like to get started on the incorporation process but would not be available to sign the articles), law firm personnel such as lawyers or law clerks/assistants may be named in the articles of incorporation as first directors and incorporators. The law firm personnel are temporary directors only. They usually complete the initial organization in the usual manner and resign, in writing, to be replaced by the new directors who would be the permanent directors of the corporation.

REPORTING LETTER AND ACCOUNT

When the initial organization is completed, write a reporting letter to the corporation summarizing the incorporation services. Legal software automatically generates a reporting letter from the data entry you have made in the incorporation process. Also prepare the account to send with the reporting letter.

CHAPTER SUMMARY

The *Business Corporations Act* requires corporations to keep a minute book containing minutes of meetings, resolutions, and records of securities. This record-keeping begins with what is known as the initial organization which consists of all of the documents which the OBCA requires to be prepared.

Since the OBCA prescribes the business activities that the first directors and shareholders must conduct at the initial organization of a corporation, the documents prepared are usually standard for all newly incorporated corporations. Corporations act through by-laws and resolutions. Generally, shareholders make resolutions relating to the structure and financial affairs of the corporation, while directors make all other resolutions.

Upon completion of the initial organization, the corporation must prepare and file with the ministry an initial return. That return informs the ministry of the names and addresses of the directors and officers who are in charge of the corporation.

REVIEW QUESTIONS

1. What is the name of the book in which corporate records are usually kept?
2. List the activities which the OBCA prescribes for the first directors to complete in the initial organization.
3. What is meant by the phrase resolutions in writing?
4. Who can make resolutions relating to the structure and financial affairs of the corporation?
5. What is an initial return?
6. What type of information is in a shareholders' register?
7. What is the difference between a by-law and a resolution?
8. A special resolution is one which only the directors may pass. Yes___ No___
9. In which situation would you prepare a special resolution fixing the number of the board of directors?
10. In which situation would a corporation be eligible for an exemption from audit?

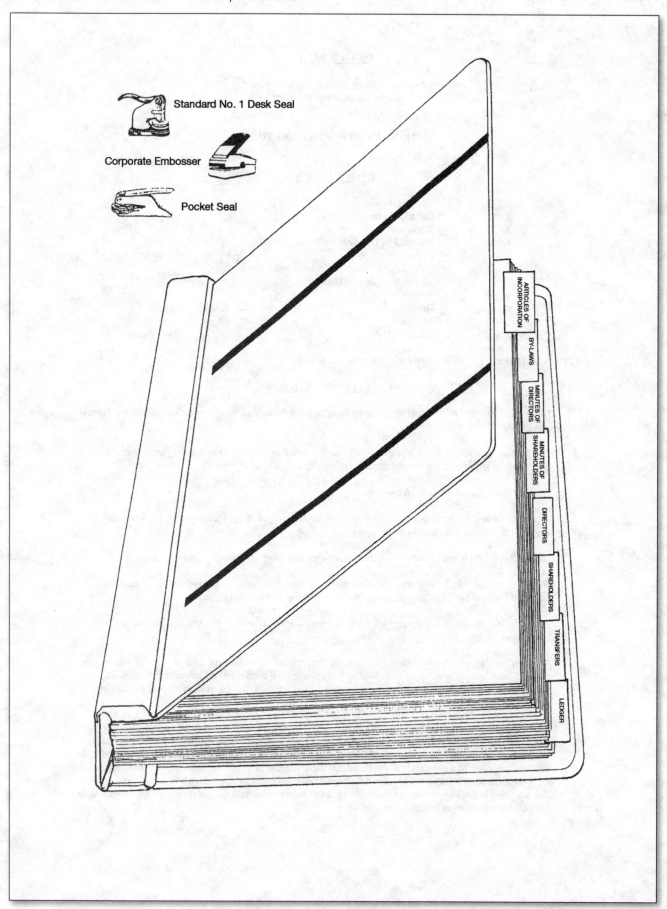

Standard No. 1 Desk Seal

Corporate Embosser

Pocket Seal

ARTICLES OF INCORPORATION

BY-LAWS

MINUTES OF DIRECTORS

MINUTES OF SHAREHOLDERS

DIRECTORS

SHAREHOLDERS

TRANSFERS

LEDGER

<u>**BY-LAW NO. 1**</u>

A by-law relating generally to the conduct
of the business and affairs of

MANDAMO PROPERTIES LTD.

C O N T E N T S

1.	-	Interpretation
2.	-	General Business Matters
3.	-	Directors
4.	-	Meetings of Directors
5.	-	Officers
6.	-	Protection of Directors, Officers and Others
7.	-	Meetings of Shareholders
8.	-	Shares
9.	-	Dividends
10.	-	Notices
11.	-	Effective Date

BE IT ENACTED as a by-law of Mandamo Properties Ltd. as follows:

1.   INTERPRETATION

1.1   <u>Definitions</u> - In this by-law and all other by-laws and resolutions of the Corporation, unless the context otherwise requires:

"Act" means the *Business Corporations Act (Ontario)*, including the Regulations made pursuant thereto, and any statute or regulations substituted therefor, as amended from time to time;

"appoint" includes "elect", and *vice versa*;

"articles" means the Articles of Incorporation and/or other constating documents of the Corporation as amended or restated from time to time;

"board" means the board of directors of the Corporation and *"director"* means a member of the board;

"by-laws" means this by-law and all other by-laws, including special by-laws, of the Corporation as amended from time to time and which are, from time to time, in force and effect;

"Corporation" means this Corporation, being the corporation to which the Articles pertain, and named "Mandamo Properties Ltd.";

"meeting of shareholders" includes an annual meeting of shareholders and a special meeting of shareholders; *"special meeting of shareholders"* means a special meeting of all shareholders entitled to vote at an annual meeting of shareholders and a meeting of any class or classes of shareholders entitled to vote on the question at issue;

"recorded address" means, in the case of a shareholder, his address as recorded in the shareholders' register; and in the case of joint shareholders, the address appearing in the shareholders' register in respect of such joint holding or the first address so appearing if there is more than one; in the case of a director, officer, auditor or member of a committee of the board, his latest address as shown in the records of the Corporation or in the most recent notice filed under the *Corporations Information Act*, whichever is the more current. The secretary may change or cause to be changed the recorded address of any person in accordance with any information believed by him to be reliable.

1.2   Rules - In the interpretation of this by-law, unless the context otherwise requires, the following rules shall apply:

a)   Except where specifically defined herein, words, terms and expressions appearing in this by-law, including the terms "resident Canadian" and "unanimous shareholder agreement" shall have the meaning ascribed to them under the Act;

b)   Words importing the singular include the plural and *vice versa*;

c)   Words importing gender include the masculine, feminine and neuter genders;

d)   Words importing a person include an individual, sole proprietorship, partnership, unincorporated association, unincorporated syndicate, unincorporated organization, trust, body corporate, and a natural person in his capacity as trustee, executor, administrator, or other legal representative.

2.   GENERAL BUSINESS MATTERS

2.1   Registered Office - The shareholders may, by special resolution, from time to time change the municipality or geographic township within Ontario in which the registered office of the Corporation shall be located, but unless and until such special resolution has been passed, the registered office shall be where initially specified in the articles.   The directors shall from time to time fix the location of the registered office within such municipality or geographic township.

2.2   Corporate Seal - The Corporation may, but need not, have a corporate seal; if adopted, such seal shall be in the form approved from time to time by the board.

2.3   Fiscal Year - Unless and until another date has been effectively determined, the fiscal year or financial year of the Corporation shall end on October 31st in each year.

2.4   Execution of Documents - Deeds, transfers, assignments, contracts, obligations and other instruments in writing requiring execution by the Corporation may be signed by the President and the Secretary together. Notwithstanding the foregoing, the board may from time to time direct the manner in which and the person or persons by whom a particular document or class of documents shall be executed. Any person authorized to sign any document may affix the corporate seal thereto.

2.5   Banking - All matters pertaining to the banking of the Corporation shall be transacted with such banks, trust companies or other financial organizations as the board may designate or authorize from time to time. All such banking business shall be transacted on behalf of the Corporation pursuant to such agreements, instructions and delegations of powers as may, from time to time, be prescribed by the board.

3.   DIRECTORS

3.1   Powers - Subject to the express provisions of a unanimous shareholder agreement, the directors shall manage or supervise the management of the business and affairs of the Corporation.

3.2   Transaction of Business - Business may be transacted by resolutions passed at meetings of directors or committees of directors at which a quorum is present or by resolution in writing, signed by all the directors entitled to vote on that resolution at a meeting of directors or a committee of directors. A copy of every such resolution in writing shall be kept with the minutes of the proceedings of the directors or committee of directors.

3.3   Number - Until changed in accordance with the Act, the board shall consist of that number of directors, being a minimum of one (1) and a maximum of ten (10), as determined from time to time by special resolution or, if the special resolution empowers the directors to determine the number, by resolution of the board.

3.4   Resident Canadians - If the board consists of only one director, that director shall be a resident Canadian. If the board consists of two directors, at least one of the two directors shall be a resident Canadian. Except as aforesaid, a majority of the directors of the Corporation shall be resident Canadians.

10.3   <u>Notices Given to Predecessors</u> - Every person who by transfer, death of a shareholder, operation of law or otherwise becomes entitled to shares, is bound by every notice in respect of such shares which was duly given to the registered holder of such shares from whom his title is derived prior to entry of his name and address in the records of the Corporation and prior to his providing to the Corporation the proof of authority or evidence of his entitlement as prescribed by the Act.

10.4   <u>Computation of Time</u> - In computing the date when notice must be given under any provision requiring a specified number of days' notice of any meeting or other event, reference shall be made to the definition given to the word "day" in the Act.

10.5   <u>Omissions and Errors</u> - The accidental omission to give any notice to any shareholder, director, officer, member of a committee of the board or auditor, or the non-receipt of any notice by any such person or any error in any notice not affecting its substance shall not invalidate any action taken at any meeting to which the notice pertained or otherwise founded on such notice.

10.6   <u>Waiver of Notice</u> - Any shareholder, proxyholder, director, officer, member of a committee of the board or auditor may waive or abridge the time for any notice required to be given him, and such waiver or abridgement, whether given before or after the meeting or other event of which notice is required to be given shall cure any default in the giving or in the time of such notice, as the case may be. Any such waiver or abridgement shall be in writing except a waiver of notice of a meeting of shareholders or of the board or of a committee of the board, which may be given in any manner.

11. EFFECTIVE DATE

11.1   <u>Effective Date</u> - Subject to its being confirmed by the shareholders, this by-law shall come into force when enacted by the board, subject to the provisions of the Act.

ENACTED by the board this 18th day of July, 20--.

_____
President

_____
Secretary   c/s

The foregoing by-law is hereby enacted by the directors of the Corporation as evidenced by the respective signatures hereto of all of the directors of the Corporation in accordance with the provisions of section 129(1) of the *Business Corporations Act* (Ontario).

DATED the 18th day of July, 20--.

_____   _____
Thomas David Brown   Stephen Thomas Brown

In lieu of confirmation at a general meeting of the shareholders, the foregoing by-law is hereby confirmed by all of the shareholders of the Corporation entitled to vote at a meeting of shareholders in accordance with the provisions of section 104(1) of the *Business Corporations Act* (Ontario), this 18th day of July, 20--.

DATED the 18th day of July, 20--.

_____   _____
Thomas David Brown   Stephen Thomas Brown

BY-LAW NO. 2

A by-law respecting the borrowing of money,
the issuing of securities and the securing of liabilities by

MANDAMO PROPERTIES LTD.
(herein called the "Corporation")

BE IT ENACTED as a by-law of the Corporation as follows:

1.   <u>Borrowing Powers</u> - Without limiting the borrowing powers of the Corporation as set forth in the Act, the board may, subject to the articles and any unanimous shareholder agreement, from time to time, on behalf of the Corporation, without the authorization of the shareholders:

   a)   borrow money on the credit of the Corporation;

   b)   issue, re-issue, sell or pledge debt obligations of the Corporation, whether secured or unsecured;

   c)   subject to the Act, give a guarantee on behalf of the Corporation to secure performance of an obligation of any person; and

   d)   mortgage, hypothecate, pledge or otherwise create a security interest in all or any property of the Corporation, owned or subsequently acquired, to secure any obligation of the Corporation.

2.   <u>Delegation of Powers</u> - Subject to the Act, the articles, the by-laws and any unanimous shareholder agreement, the board may, from time to time, delegate any or all of the powers hereinbefore specified, to a director, a committee of directors or one or more officers of the Corporation.

ENACTED by the board this 18th day of July, 20--.

_____
President

_____
Secretary   c/s

The foregoing by-law is hereby enacted by the directors of the Corporation as evidenced by the respective signatures hereto of all of the directors of the Corporation in accordance with the provisions of section 129(1) of the *Business Corporations Act* (Ontario).

DATED the 18th day of July, 20--.

_____   _____
Thomas David Brown   Stephen Thomas Brown

In lieu of confirmation at a general meeting of the shareholders, the foregoing by-law is hereby confirmed by all of the shareholders of the Corporation entitled to vote at a meeting of shareholders in accordance with the provisions of section 104(1) of the *Business Corporations Act* (Ontario), this 18th day of July, 20--.

DATED the 18th day of July, 20--.

_____   _____
Thomas David Brown   Stephen Thomas Brown

RESOLUTIONS OF THE DIRECTORS

OF

MANDAMO PROPERTIES LTD.

1.   ARTICLES OF INCORPORATION

BE IT RESOLVED THAT:

the directors acknowledge that the Corporation has been incorporated by Articles of Incorporation issued under the *Business Corporations Act* (Ontario), bearing date the 18th day of July, 20--, and they hereby direct that a copy of such Articles of Incorporation be inserted and retained in the minute book of the Corporation.

2.   BY-LAW NO. 1

BE IT RESOLVED THAT:

the directors of the Corporation do hereby approve and adopt By-Law No. 1, being a by-law relating generally to the conduct of the business and affairs of the Corporation, and the President and the Secretary be and they are hereby authorized and directed to sign and to affix the seal of the Corporation thereto.

3.   BY-LAW NO. 2

BE IT RESOLVED THAT:

the directors of the Corporation do hereby approve and adopt By-Law No. 2, being a by-law respecting the borrowing of money and the issuing of securities by the Corporation, and the President and the Secretary be and they are hereby authorized and directed to sign and to affix the seal of the Corporation thereto.

4.   APPOINTMENT OF OFFICERS

BE IT RESOLVED THAT:

the following persons be and they are hereby elected or appointed officers of the Corporation to hold office during the pleasure of the board:

THOMAS DAVID BROWN   President
STEPHEN THOMAS BROWN   Secretary

5.   APPROVAL OF SHARE CERTIFICATES

BE IT RESOLVED THAT:

the forms of share certificates annexed to these resolutions, and initialled for identification by the President, be and the same are hereby approved and adopted as the forms of share certificates of the Corporation to be issued in respect of the:

unlimited number of Common shares;
unlimited number of Preference shares;

as indicated on the said certificates.

-2-

6. CORPORATE SEAL

BE IT RESOLVED THAT:

the form of corporate seal, an impression of which is affixed beside this resolution, be and the same is hereby adopted as the corporate seal of the Corporation.

7. LOCATION OF REGISTERED OFFICE

BE IT RESOLVED THAT:

the location of the registered office of the Corporation be and the same is hereby fixed at:

> 1750 Finch Avenue East
> Room 3244
> Toronto, Ontario M2V 2X5

> in the City of Toronto

8. FISCAL YEAR END

BE IT RESOLVED THAT:

the fiscal year end of the Corporation shall terminate on October 31st in each year.

9. LOCATION OF MINUTE BOOK

BE IT RESOLVED THAT:

a) the office of: Michael, Eliad & Redford LLP
Barristers and Solicitors
863 Seneca Lane
Toronto, Ontario M4J 1P6

is hereby designated as a location at which the minute book, including the registers and corporate records of the Corporation, may be prepared, maintained and kept; and

b) the certificate of incorporation be placed and retained in the minute book.

10. CORPORATE SOLICITORS

BE IT RESOLVED THAT:

Michael, Eliad & Redford LLP, Barristers and Solicitors, be and they are hereby retained as the Corporation's solicitors and be and they are hereby authorized to accept and carry out such instructions as the directors, officers, and authorized agents of the Corporation may give them from time to time.

EACH AND EVERY OF THE FOREGOING RESOLUTIONS is hereby consented to by all of the directors of the Corporation, as evidenced by their respective signatures hereto in accordance with the provisions of section 129(1) of the *Business Corporations Act* (Ontario), this 18th day of July, 20--.

_____   _____
Thomas David Brown   Stephen Thomas Brown

SUBSCRIPTION FOR COMMON SHARE

TO: **MANDAMO PROPERTIES LTD.**

AND TO: **The Directors thereof**

I, **THOMAS DAVID BROWN**, hereby subscribe for one (1) Common share of the above Corporation at the price of $1.00 per share, and agree to pay for such share at such time and in such instalments as your board of directors may require.

DATED the 18th day of July, 20--.

_____
Thomas David Brown

SUBSCRIPTION FOR COMMON SHARE

TO: **MANDAMO PROPERTIES LTD.**

AND TO: **The Directors thereof**

I, **STEPHEN THOMAS BROWN**, hereby subscribe for one (1) Common share of the above Corporation at the price of $1.00 per share, and agree to pay for such share at such time and in such instalments as your board of directors may require.

DATED the 18th day of July, 20--.

_____
Stephen Thomas Brown

RESOLUTION OF THE DIRECTORS

OF

MANDAMO PROPERTIES LTD.

1.   ALLOTMENT AND ISSUE OF COMMON SHARES FOR CASH

BE IT RESOLVED THAT:

a)   the subscriptions from Thomas David Brown and Stephen Thomas Brown for two (2) Common shares in the capital of the Corporation be and the same are hereby accepted;

b)   the board of directors of the Corporation, acting in good faith and in the best interests of the Corporation, hereby fixes the sum of $2.00 as the aggregate consideration for the allotment and issue of the said two (2) Common shares;

c)   two Common shares in the capital of the Corporation be and they are hereby allotted and issued, subject to payment therefor, to the following persons in the numbers and at the subscription prices set opposite their respective names:

SUBSCRIPTION OF	NO. OF SHARES	PRICE PER SHARE
THOMAS DAVID BROWN	1	$1.00
STEPHEN THOMAS BROWN	1	$1.00

d)   upon receipt by the Corporation of the sum of $2.00 in respect of the consideration for the allotment and issue of the said two (2) Common shares, the said Common shares be allotted and issued to Thomas David Brown and Stephen Thomas Brown as fully paid and non-assessable, and certificates therefor be issued to them or as they may in writing direct.

THE FOREGOING RESOLUTION is hereby consented to by all of the directors of the Corporation, as evidenced by their respective signatures hereto in accordance with the provisions of section 129(1) of the *Business Corporations Act* (Ontario), this 18th day of July, 20--.

_____   _____
Thomas David Brown   Stephen Thomas Brown

Precedent 27.7   Share Certificate (Thomas David Brown), front

CERT. NO.	C-1		FROM WHOM TRANSFERRED	
FOR	1 SHARE		**TREASURY**	
ISSUED TO		Dated		
		No. Original Cert.		
THOMAS DAVID BROWN		No. Original Shares		
DATED	July 18th, 20--	No. of Shares Transferred	1	

NO. **C-1**

INCORPORATED UNDER THE LAWS OF THE PROVINCE OF ONTARIO
Subject to the Business Corporations Act(Ontario)

1 SHARE

MANDAMO PROPERTIES LTD.

This is to Certify that   THOMAS DAVID BROWN

**is the registered holder of one
Common Share in the capital of
MANDAMO PROPERTIES LTD.**

The class or series of shares represented by this Certificate has rights, privileges, restrictions or conditions attached thereto and the Corporation will furnish to a shareholder, on demand and without charge, a full copy of the text of:

(i)   the rights, privileges, restrictions and conditions attached to the shares represented by this certificate and to each class authorized to be issued and to each series insofar as the same have been fixed by the directors; and

(ii)   the authority of the directors to fix the rights, privileges, restrictions and conditions of subsequent series, if applicable.

The Corporation has a lien on the shares represented by this Certificate for the indebtedness of the shareholder to the Corporation.

The right of the shareholder to transfer the shares represented by this Certificate is subject to restrictions.

IN WITNESS WHEREOF this Corporation has caused this Certificate to be signed by its duly authorized officers.
DATED this 18th day of July

President (Thomas David Brown)   Secretary (Stephen Thomas Brown)

Precedent 27.7   Share Certificate (Thomas David Brown), back

CERTIFICATE FOR
one
Common Share of

MANDAMO PROPERTIES LTD.

Issued to: **THOMAS DAVID BROWN**
Date: **July 18th, 20--**
Certificate: **C-1**

****

For Value I received, I hereby assign and transfer unto

_____

_____ **Common Share**

represented by the within Certificate

DATED _____

In the presence of

_____   _____

CERT. NO.	C-2	FROM WHOM TRANSFERRED	
FOR	1 SHARE	**TREASURY**	
ISSUED TO		Dated	
STEPHEN THOMAS BROWN		No. Original Cert.	
		No. Original Shares	
DATED	July 18th, 20--	No. of Shares Transferred	1

NO. **C-2**

INCORPORATED UNDER THE LAWS OF THE PROVINCE OF ONTARIO
Subject to the Business Corporations Act(Ontario)

1 SHARE

MANDAMO PROPERTIES LTD.

This is to Certify that

STEPHEN THOMAS BROWN
is the registered holder of one
Common Share in the capital of
MANDAMO PROPERTIES LTD.

The class or series of shares represented by this Certificate has rights, privileges, restrictions or conditions attached thereto and the Corporation will furnish to a shareholder, on demand and without charge, a full copy of the text of:

(i) the rights, privileges, restrictions and conditions attached to the shares represented by this certificate and to each class authorized to be issued and to each series insofar as the same have been fixed by the directors; and

(ii) the authority of the directors to fix the rights, privileges, restrictions and conditions of subsequent series, if applicable.

The Corporation has a lien on the shares represented by this Certificate for the indebtedness of the shareholder to the Corporation.

The right of the shareholder to transfer the shares represented by this Certificate is subject to restrictions.

IN WITNESS WHEREOF this Corporation has caused this Certificate to be signed by its duly authorized officers.
DATED this 18th day of July

President (Thomas David Brown)   Secretary (Stephen Thomas Brown)

CERTIFICATE FOR
one
Common Share of

MANDAMO PROPERTIES LTD.

Issued to: **STEPHEN THOMAS BROWN**
Date: **July 18th, 20--**
Certificate: **C-2**

****

For Value I received, I hereby assign and transfer unto

_____

_____ Common Share

represented by the within Certificate

DATED _____

In the presence of

_____   _____

Mandamo Properties Ltd.
DIRECTORS' REGISTER

Name of Director	Date Elected	Date Resigned
THOMAS DAVID BROWN 61 Jasper Drive Aurora, Ontario L4G 3C1	Jul 18, (year)	
STEPHEN THOMAS BROWN 61 Jasper Drive Aurora, Ontario L4G 3C1	Jul 18, (year)	

Document prepared using *Fast Company* by Do Process Software Ltd.

Effective date: Jul 18, 20--

Mandamo Properties Ltd.
SHAREHOLDERS' REGISTER

Date	Name	No. of Shares	Class Of Shares Held
Jul 18, (year)	**Thomas David Brown** 61 Jasper Drive Aurora, Ontario L4G 3C1	1	Common
Jul 18, (year)	**Stephen Thomas Brown** 61 Jasper Drive Aurora, Ontario L4G 3C1	1	Common

Document prepared using **Fast Company** by Do Process Software Ltd.

Mandamo Properties Ltd.
OFFICERS' REGISTER

Name of Officer	Office Held	Date Elected	Date Resigned
THOMAS DAVID BROWN 61 Jasper Drive Aurora, Ontario L4G 3C1	President	Jul 18, (year)	
STEPHEN THOMAS BROWN 61 Jasper Drive Aurora, Ontario L4G 3C1	Secretary	Jul 18, (year)	

Document prepared using **Fast Company** by Do Process Software Ltd.

Mandamo Properties Ltd.

SHAREHOLDER'S LEDGER

THOMAS DAVID BROWN

61 Jasper Drive
Aurora, Ontario
L4G 3C1

Share Class: Common

Date	Certif. No.	Transfer No.	Transferred From/To	Sold	Bought	Balance
Jul 18, (year)	C-1	1	FROM: TREASURY		1	1

Document prepared using *Fast Company* by Do Process Software Ltd.

Mandamo Properties Ltd.

SHAREHOLDER'S LEDGER

STEPHEN THOMAS BROWN

61 Jasper Drive
Aurora, Ontario
L4G 3C1

Share Class: Common

Date	Certif. No.	Transfer No.	Transferred From/To	Sold	Bought	Balance
Jul 18, (year)	C-2	2	FROM: TREASURY		1	1

Document prepared using *Fast Company* by Do Process Software Ltd.

RESOLUTIONS OF THE SHAREHOLDERS

OF

MANDAMO PROPERTIES LTD.

1.   BY-LAW NO. 1

BE IT RESOLVED THAT:

By-Law No. 1, being a by-law relating generally to the conduct of the business and affairs of the Corporation, in the form enacted by the board of directors be and the same is hereby confirmed.

2.   BY-LAW NO. 2

BE IT RESOLVED THAT:

By-Law No. 2, being a by-law respecting the borrowing of money and the issuing of securities by the Corporation, in the form enacted by the board of directors be and the same is hereby confirmed.

3.   APPOINTMENT OF ACCOUNTANTS

BE IT RESOLVED THAT:

Hugh and Cry be appointed the accountants of the Corporation to hold office until the completion of the first annual meeting of the shareholders of the Corporation, or until a successor is appointed, at such remuneration as may be fixed by the board of directors and the board of directors is hereby authorized to fix such remuneration.

4.   INDEMNIFICATION OF DIRECTORS AND OFFICERS

BE IT RESOLVED THAT:

the Corporation indemnify and save harmless each director and officer of the Corporation and his or her heirs, executors, administrators and estates and other legal personal representatives from and against any and all liabilities, costs, charges and expenses to the extent specified in section 136 of the *Business Corporations Act* (Ontario), subject to the by-laws of the Corporation.

EACH AND EVERY OF THE FOREGOING RESOLUTIONS is hereby consented to by all of the shareholders of the Corporation entitled to vote thereon at a meeting of shareholders, as evidenced by their respective signatures hereto in accordance with the provisions of section 104(1) of the *Business Corporations Act* (Ontario), this 18th day of July, 20--.

_____   _____
Thomas David Brown   Stephen Thomas Brown

RESOLUTION OF THE SHAREHOLDERS

OF

MANDAMO PROPERTIES LTD.

1.   EXEMPTION FROM AUDIT PROVISIONS

BE IT RESOLVED THAT:

pursuant to section 148 of the *Business Corporations Act* (Ontario), all of the shareholders of the Corporation hereby consent to the exemption of the Corporation from the requirements of Part XII of the *Business Corporations Act* (Ontario) regarding the appointment and duties of an auditor in respect of the first fiscal year of the Corporation, and in respect of each fiscal year thereafter until this consent is revoked.

THE FOREGOING RESOLUTION is hereby consented to by all of the shareholders of the Corporation, as evidenced by their respective signatures hereto in accordance with the provisions of section 104(1) of the *Business Corporations Act* (Ontario), this 18th day of July, 20--.

_____   _____
Thomas David Brown   Stephen Thomas Brown

SPECIAL RESOLUTION

OF

MANDAMO PROPERTIES LTD.

1.   **NUMBER AND ELECTION OF DIRECTORS**

WHEREAS the Articles of the Corporation provide that the number of directors for the Corporation is a range with a minimum of one (1) and a maximum of ten (10);

NOW THEREFORE BE IT RESOLVED AS A SPECIAL RESOLUTION OF THE CORPORATION THAT:

i)   the number of directors comprising the board of directors of the Corporation shall be fixed at two (2), being a number within the prescribed range;

ii)   the following persons be and they are hereby elected directors of the Corporation to hold office until the first annual meeting or annual resolutions of the shareholders of the Corporation or until their respective successors are duly elected, subject to the provisions of the by-laws of the Corporation and the provisions of the *Business Corporations Act* (Ontario):

   THOMAS DAVID BROWN
   STEPHEN THOMAS BROWN

iii)   the directors of the Corporation are hereby empowered to determine the number of directors of the Corporation hereafter from time to time by resolution of the board.

THE FOREGOING SPECIAL RESOLUTION is hereby consented to and passed by all of the shareholders of the Corporation entitled to vote thereon at a meeting of shareholders, as evidenced by their respective signatures hereto in accordance with the provisions of section 104(1) of the *Business Corporations Act* (Ontario), this 18th day of July, 20--.

_____   _____
Thomas David Brown   Stephen Thomas Brown

CONSENT TO ACT AS DIRECTOR

TO: **Mandamo Properties Ltd.**

AND TO: **The Shareholders thereof**

I, THE UNDERSIGNED, hereby:

i)   consent to being elected and to acting as director of the above Corporation, such consent to take effect immediately and to continue in effect until I give written notice to the Corporation revoking such consent or until I otherwise cease to be a director of the Corporation;

ii)   consent to the holding of meetings of directors or of committees of directors by means of such telephone, electronic or other communication facilities as permit all persons participating in the meetings to communicate with each other simultaneously and instantaneously; and

iii)   certify that I am a resident Canadian within the meaning of the *Business Corporations Act* (Ontario) and that I shall notify the Corporation forthwith in the event of a change in such status.

DATED the 18th day of July, 20--.

_____
Thomas David Brown

61 Jasper Drive
Aurora, Ontario
L4G 3C1

****

"Resident Canadian" is defined under the *Business Corporations Act* (Ontario) as an individual who is:

(a)   a Canadian citizen ordinarily resident in Canada;

(b)   a Canadian citizen not ordinarily resident in Canada who is a member of a prescribed class of persons; or

(c)   a permanent resident within the meaning of the *Immigration Act (Canada)* and ordinarily resident in Canada.

CONSENT TO ACT AS DIRECTOR

TO: **Mandamo Properties Ltd.**

AND TO: **The Shareholders thereof**

I, THE UNDERSIGNED, hereby:

i)   consent to being elected and to acting as director of the above Corporation, such consent to take effect immediately and to continue in effect until I give written notice to the Corporation revoking such consent or until I otherwise cease to be a director of the Corporation;

ii)   consent to the holding of meetings of directors or of committees of directors by means of such telephone, electronic or other communication facilities as permit all persons participating in the meetings to communicate with each other simultaneously and instantaneously; and

iii)   certify that I am a resident Canadian within the meaning of the *Business Corporations Act* (Ontario) and that I shall notify the Corporation forthwith in the event of a change in such status.

DATED the 18th day of July, 20--.

_____
                                        Stephen Thomas Brown

61 Jasper Drive
Aurora, Ontario
L4G 3C1

****

"Resident Canadian" is defined under the *Business Corporations Act* (Ontario) as an individual who is:

(a)   a Canadian citizen ordinarily resident in Canada;

(b)   a Canadian citizen not ordinarily resident in Canada who is a member of a prescribed class of persons; or

(c)   a permanent resident within the meaning of the *Immigration Act (Canada)* and ordinarily resident in Canada.

C A N A D A   )   **To all whom these Presents**
)
Province of Ontario   )   **may come, be seen or known**
)
To Wit   )

I, **ROBERT B. REDFORD,** a Notary Public, in and for the Province of Ontario, by Royal Authority duly appointed, residing at the City of Toronto, in said Province, do certify and attest that the paper-writing hereto annexed is a true copy of a document produced and purporting to be the Articles of Incorporation of Mandamo Properties Ltd., dated July 18, 20--, the said copy having been compared by me with the said original document, an act whereof being requested, I have granted under my Notarial Form and Seal of Office to serve and avail as occasion shall or may require.

IN TESTIMONY WHEREOF I have hereto subscribed my name and affixed my Notarial Seal of Office at Toronto, this {Date of Notarization}.

_____
ROBERT B. REDFORD

A Notary Public in and for the Province of Ontario

CERTIFIED COPY OF A
SPECIAL RESOLUTION

OF

MANDAMO PROPERTIES LTD.

1.   NUMBER AND ELECTION OF DIRECTORS

WHEREAS the Articles of the Corporation provide that the number of directors for the Corporation is a range with a minimum of one (1) and a maximum of ten (10);

NOW THEREFORE BE IT RESOLVED AS A SPECIAL RESOLUTION OF THE CORPORATION THAT:

i)   the number of directors comprising the board of directors of the Corporation shall be fixed at two (2), being a number within the prescribed range;

ii)   the following persons be and they are hereby elected directors of the Corporation to hold office until the first annual meeting or annual resolutions of the shareholders of the Corporation or until their respective successors are duly elected, subject to the provisions of the by-laws of the Corporation and the provisions of the *Business Corporations Act* (Ontario):

THOMAS DAVID BROWN
STEPHEN THOMAS BROWN

iii)   the directors of the Corporation are hereby empowered to determine the number of directors of the Corporation hereafter from time to time by resolution of the board.

****

CERTIFICATE

CERTIFIED to be a true copy of a special resolution of MANDAMO PROPERTIES LTD. consented to by the signatures of all of the voting shareholders of the Corporation and dated the 18th day of July, 20--, as set forth in the minute book of the Corporation, which said special resolution has not been amended and is now in full force and effect.

DATED at Toronto on July 18, 20--.

_____   (c/s)
Secretary

Ontario

Ministry of Government Services	Ministère des Services gouvernementaux	
Central Production and Verification Services Branch 393 University Avenue, Suite 200 Toronto ON M5G 2M2	Direction des services centraux de production et de vérification 393, avenue University, bureau 200 Toronto ON M5G 2M2	For Ministry Use Only À l'usage du ministère seulement Page/Page **1** of/de _____

Form 1 – Ontario Corporation Initial Return / Notice of Change
Formule 1 – Personnes morales de l'Ontario Rapport initial / Avis de modification
Corporations Information Act / Loi sur les renseignements exigés des personnes morales

Please type or print all information in block capital letters using black ink.
Prière de dactylographier les renseignements ou de les écrire en caractères d'imprimerie à l'encre noire.

1. Business Corporation/ Société par actions — Notice of Change — Initial Return / Rapport initial [X]   Avis de modification [ ]
   Not-For-Profit Corporation/ Personne morale sans but lucratif [ ] [ ]

2. Ontario Corporation Number
   Numéro matricule de la personne morale en Ontario
   2345678

3. Date of Incorporation or Amalgamation/ Date de constitution ou fusion
   Year/Année **(Year)**   Month/Mois **07**   Day/Jour **18**

For Ministry Use Only À l'usage du ministère seulement

4. Corporation Name Including Punctuation/Raison sociale de la personne morale, y compris la ponctuation
   MANDAMO PROPERTIES LTD.

5. Address of Registered or Head Office/Adresse du siège social
   c/o / a/s   **THOMAS DAVID BROWN**
   Street No./N° civique **1750**   Street Name/Nom de la rue **FINCH AVENUE EAST**   Suite/Bureau
   Street Name (cont'd)/Nom de la rue (suite) **ROOM 3244**
   City/Town/Ville **TORONTO**   **ONTARIO, CANADA**
   Postal Code/Code postal **M2V 2X5**

For Ministry Use Only/ À l'usage du ministère seulement

6. Mailing Address/Adresse postale
   Street No./N° civique
   Street Name/Nom de la rue   Suite/Bureau
   Street Name (cont'd)/Nom de la rue (suite)
   City/Town/Ville
   Province, State/Province, État   Country/Pays   Postal Code/Code postal

[X] Same as Registered or Head Office/ Même que siège social
[ ] Not Applicable/ Ne s'applique pas

7. Language of Preference/Langue préférée   English - Anglais [X]   French - Français [ ]

8. **Information on Directors/Officers must be completed on Schedule A as requested.** If additional space is required, photocopy Schedule A./**Les renseignements sur les administrateurs ou les dirigeants doivent être fournis dans l'Annexe A, tel que demandé.** Si vous avez besoin de plus d'espace, vous pouvez photocopier l'Annexe A.

   Number of Schedule A(s) submitted/Nombre d'Annexes A présentées   **1**   (At least one Schedule A must be submitted/Au moins une Annexe A doit être présentée)

9. (Print or type name in full of the person authorizing filing / Dactylographier ou inscrire le prénom et le nom en caractères d'imprimerie de la personne qui autorise l'enregistrement)

   I/Je   **THOMAS DAVID BROWN**

   certify that the information set out herein, is true and correct.
   atteste que les renseignements précités sont véridiques et exacts.

   Check appropriate box
   Cocher la case pertinente
   D) [X] Director/Administrateur
   O) [X] Officer/Dirigeant
   P) [ ] Other individual having knowledge of the affairs of the Corporation/Autre personne ayant connaissance des activités de la personne morale

   NOTE/REMARQUE: Sections 13 and 14 of the **Corporations Information Act** provide penalties for making false or misleading statements or omissions. Les articles 13 et 14 de la *Loi sur les renseignements exigés des personnes morales* prévoient des peines en cas de déclaration fausse ou trompeuse, ou d'omission.

Form 1 – Ontario Corporation/Formule 1 – Personnes morales de l'Ontario
Schedule A/Annexe A

For Ministry Use Only
À l'usage du ministère seulement
Page/Page _____ of/de _____

Please type or print all information in block capital letters using black ink. Prière de dactylographier les renseignements ou de les écrire en caractères d'imprimerie à l'encre noire.	Ontario Corporation Number Numéro matricule de la personne morale en Ontario **2345678**	Date of Incorporation or Amalgamation Date de constitution ou fusion Year/Année **(Year)** Month/Mois **07** Day/Jour **18**

DIRECTOR / OFFICER INFORMATION – RENSEIGNEMENTS RELATIFS AUX ADMINISTRATEURS/DIRIGEANTS

Full Name and Address for Service/Nom et domicile élu

Last Name/Nom de famille	First Name/Prénom	Middle Names/Autres prénoms
BROWN	**THOMAS**	**DAVID**

Street Number/Numéro civique **61** Suite/Bureau

Street Name/Nom de la rue **JASPER DRIVE**

Street Name (cont'd)/Nom de la rue (suite)

City/Town/Ville **AURORA**

Province, State/Province, État	Country/Pays	Postal Code/Code postal
ONTARIO	**CANADA**	**L4G 3C1**

Director Information/Renseignements relatifs aux administrateurs

Resident Canadian/Résident canadien **X** YES/OUI ☐ NO/NON (Resident Canadian applies to directors of business corporations only.)/ (Résident canadien ne s'applique qu'aux administrateurs de sociétés par actions)

Date Elected/Date d'élection Year/Année **(Year)** Month/Mois **07** Day/Jour **18**
Date Ceased/Date de cessation Year/Année Month/Mois Day/Jour

Officer Information/Renseignements relatifs aux dirigeants

	PRESIDENT/PRÉSIDENT Year/Année Month/Mois Day/Jour	SECRETARY/SECRÉTAIRE Year/Année Month/Mois Day/Jour	TREASURER/TRÉSORIER Year/Année Month/Mois Day/Jour	GENERAL MANAGER/ DIRECTEUR GÉNÉRAL Year/Année Month/Mois Day/Jour	*OTHER/AUTRE Year/Année Month/Mois Day/Jour
Date Appointed/Date de nomination	**(Year) 07 18**				
Date Ceased/Date de cessation					

*OTHER TITLES (Please Specify)
*AUTRES TITRES (Veuillez préciser)

- Chair / Président du conseil
- Chair Person / Président du conseil
- Chairman / Président du conseil
- Chairwoman / Présidente du conseil
- Vice-Chair / Vice-président du conseil
- Vice-President / Vice-président
- Assistant Secretary / Secrétaire adjoint
- Assistant Treasurer / Trésorier adjoint
- Chief Manager / Directeur exécutif
- Executive Director / Directeur administratif
- Managing Director / Administrateur délégué
- Chief Executive Officer / Directeur général
- Chief Financial Officer / Agent en chef des finances
- Chief Information Officer / Directeur général de l'information
- Chief Operating Officer / Administrateur en chef des opérations
- Chief Administrative Officer / Directeur général de l'administration
- Comptroller / Contrôleur
- Authorized Signing Officer / Signataire autorisé
- Other (Untitled) / Autre (sans titre)

DIRECTOR / OFFICER INFORMATION – RENSEIGNEMENTS RELATIFS AUX ADMINISTRATEURS/DIRIGEANTS

Full Name and Address for Service/Nom et domicile élu

Last Name/Nom de famille	First Name/Prénom	Middle Names/Autres prénoms
BROWN	**STEPHEN**	**THOMAS**

Street Number/Numéro civique **61** Suite/Bureau

Street Name/Nom de la rue **JASPER DRIVE**

Street Name (cont'd)/Nom de la rue (suite)

City/Town/Ville **AURORA**

Province, State/Province, État	Country/Pays	Postal Code/Code postal
ONTARIO	**CANADA**	**L4G 3C1**

Director Information/Renseignements relatifs aux administrateurs

Resident Canadian/Résident canadien **X** YES/OUI ☐ NO/NON (Resident Canadian applies to directors of business corporations only.)/ (Résident canadien ne s'applique qu'aux administrateurs de sociétés par actions)

Date Elected/Date d'élection Year/Année **(Year)** Month/Mois **07** Day/Jour **18**
Date Ceased/Date de cessation Year/Année Month/Mois Day/Jour

Officer Information/Renseignements relatifs aux dirigeants

	PRESIDENT/PRÉSIDENT Year/Année Month/Mois Day/Jour	SECRETARY/SECRÉTAIRE Year/Année Month/Mois Day/Jour	TREASURER/TRÉSORIER Year/Année Month/Mois Day/Jour	GENERAL MANAGER/ DIRECTEUR GÉNÉRAL Year/Année Month/Mois Day/Jour	*OTHER/AUTRE Year/Année Month/Mois Day/Jour
Date Appointed/Date de nomination		**(Year) 07 18**			
Date Ceased/Date de cessation					

*OTHER TITLES (Please Specify)
*AUTRES TITRES (Veuillez préciser)

- Chair / Président du conseil
- Chair Person / Président du conseil
- Chairman / Président du conseil
- Chairwoman / Présidente du conseil
- Vice-Chair / Vice-président du conseil
- Vice-President / Vice-président
- Assistant Secretary / Secrétaire adjoint
- Assistant Treasurer / Trésorier adjoint
- Chief Manager / Directeur exécutif
- Executive Director / Directeur administratif
- Managing Director / Administrateur délégué
- Chief Executive Officer / Directeur général
- Chief Financial Officer / Agent en chef des finances
- Chief Information Officer / Directeur général de l'information
- Chief Operating Officer / Administrateur en chef des opérations
- Chief Administrative Officer / Directeur général de l'administration
- Comptroller / Contrôleur
- Authorized Signing Officer / Signataire autorisé
- Other (Untitled) / Autre (sans titre)

CHAPTER 28

POST– INCORPORATION MATTERS

This chapter covers post-incorporation maintenance requirements under the Ontario *Business Corporations Act* (OBCA) and also includes a look at changes which may occur during the life of a business corporation.

FORMAL MEETINGS

The OBCA requires that the shareholders hold actual annual meetings. Formal meetings are practical for corporations consisting of many directors and shareholders because meetings permit everyone to orderly speak and vote on an issue. Following is an overview of the procedure that is followed in formal meetings:

The chair of the meeting is in charge of the meeting, and the secretary of the meeting takes down notes which will become the minutes of the meeting. Formal meetings follow standard parliamentary procedure in that a person makes a motion (suggestion), and another person who believes the motion is worth discussing, seconds it. A discussion of the motion ensues, usually by way of a speakers' list (a list, in order of hand-raising priority, of people who wish to speak to the motion) until someone "calls the question." This means there has been sufficient discussion on the motion to permit everyone to determine which way to vote.

The chair or another individual reads the motion to ensure everyone understands it, and asks for "all those in favour of the motion" to vote by a show of hands. The chair takes a count of the vote, asks for a show of hands against the motion, and takes a count of that vote. If the motion receives the required number of votes, the motion is said to be carried. (Some motions require a majority vote (50 percent plus 1 vote); others require a two-thirds majority, etc. to carry.) If the motion does not receive the required number of votes, it is defeated. When carried, a motion becomes a resolution that is included in the minutes of the meeting.

The number of votes for or against the motion, or the fact that it was a vote by a show of hands (instead of a ballot), need not be recorded. Defeated motions are not normally included in the minutes. When the meeting concludes, it is either adjourned or terminated. If adjourned, it means certain matters on the agenda were not reached, and the meeting will reconvene on a later date. If the meeting is terminated, it is completed.

In serious or contentious issues, a shareholder has the right to demand a vote by a secret ballot instead of a show of hands. A secret ballot involves privately marking the vote on paper; it is how we vote at elections. In that case, the minutes would indicate that the vote was made by ballot.

Preparation and confirmation of minutes   When the meeting is over, the corporation's secretary of the meeting usually instructs your firm to have the minutes prepared in proper form for the chair's signature. Before they become the permanent record of the corporation, however, the minutes are read at the next meeting for confirmation to ensure that the final version of the minutes accurately reflects the original. The directors and shareholders each confirm their own minutes because the other would have no direct knowledge of the events.

OBCA REQUIREMENTS FOR MEETINGS OF DIRECTORS

The OBCA sets out certain requirements for the conducting of meetings of directors, the more notable of which follow:

Who calls the meetings   The board of directors, in its role as the managing body of the corporation, calls all meetings of directors as well as all meetings of shareholders. The directors must have a quorum to call a meeting. The sole director of a corporation constitutes a meeting.

Place of meetings   The board of directors usually holds directors' meetings at the corporation's registered office. The board may, if the by-laws provide, also hold meetings in or outside Ontario or Canada, as long as the majority of the meetings are within Canada. The directors may hold a meeting by teleconferencing, and if the majority of the teleconferencing directors are in Canada, the meeting is deemed to have been held in Canada.

Chair and secretary   Unless the by-laws provide otherwise, the president or, in his or her absence, a vice-president who is also a director, acts as chair of the meeting, and the secretary of the corporation usually acts as secretary of the meeting.

Notice of meeting of directors   Unless the by-laws of the corporation provide otherwise, and they usually do, e.g. they usually require shorter notice, the directors must send a written notice of the date, time, and place of the meeting to every director listed in the directors' register in the minute book at least **ten days** before the date of the meeting; however, the by-laws of a corporation generally provide that no notice of a meeting shall be necessary if all directors or shareholders are in attendance and do not object to the holding of the meeting.

Quorum of directors   A quorum is the minimum number of directors who must be present at the meeting in order to conduct a valid meeting. Each corporation's quorum is usually set in its by-laws. The quorum must be no less than **two-fifths** of the total number of the board of directors. If a corporation has fewer than three directors, all directors must be present to constitute a quorum. The quorum may exercise all of the powers of the board.

Conflict of interest   The OBCA requires directors to notify the corporation of any conflict of interest. Consequently, directors having a conflict of interest regarding a contract or transaction of the corporation must not attend any part of a meeting of directors during which such a contract or transaction is discussed and must not vote on any resolution to approve such a contract or transaction. If no quorum exists for the purpose of voting on a resolution to approve a contract or transaction only because a director is not permitted to be present at the meeting, the remaining directors are deemed to constitute a quorum for the purpose of voting on the resolution.

Voting rights and manner of voting of directors   Normally, each director is entitled to one vote. The directors usually vote by a show of hands. Most matters, or matters other than fundamental changes, are decided by a simple majority vote, usually 50 percent plus 1 vote. Unless the by-laws provide otherwise, the chair of the meeting has no second (or casting) vote to break a tie.

OBCA REQUIREMENTS FOR MEETINGS OF SHAREHOLDERS

The OBCA sets out certain requirements for the conducting of meetings of shareholders, the more notable of which follow:

Who calls shareholders' meetings   Generally, the directors call all the meetings on behalf of the shareholders.

Who chairs the shareholders' meetings   Unless the by-laws provide otherwise, the president or, in his or her absence, a vice-president who is also a director, acts as chair of the meeting, or if neither of them is present within fifteen minutes after the time appointed for the meeting, the shareholders may choose a chair from those shareholders who are present. The chair presiding at the meeting shall not have a second, or casting, vote to break a tie vote. The sole shareholder of a corporation constitutes a meeting. The OBCA may see amendments where, unless a corporation's by-laws provide otherwise, only a shareholder chosen from those present at a meeting of shareholders may act as chair of a meeting of shareholders.

Place of shareholders' meetings   Subject to the articles and any unanimous shareholder agreement, the directors determine the place of the shareholders' meetings, which may be in or outside Ontario. Unless the directors determine otherwise, the shareholders' meetings are usually held at the registered office of the corporation. Where the shareholders' meeting is held electronically, the meeting is deemed to have been held at the registered office of the corporation.

Annual meetings (of shareholders)   To protect the shareholders who, unlike directors, do not hold meetings regularly, the act requires the directors to call an annual shareholders' meeting, at which meeting, the directors must present to the shareholders the financial situation of the corporation. The directors must call the very first annual shareholders' meeting not later than **eighteen months** after incorporation. They must call all other annual meetings not later than **fifteen months** after the last annual meeting.

Special meetings (of shareholders)   In addition to the annual meetings, the directors may call special meetings of the **shareholders** whenever they require the shareholders to pass special resolutions. There are special meetings only of shareholders (not directors) because only the shareholders are empowered to pass special resolutions. According to subsection 96(5) of the OBCA, all business is deemed to be special business requiring special meetings of shareholders, except the following:

- Consideration of the minutes of an earlier meeting
- Financial statements and auditor's report
- Election of directors, and
- Reappointment of the incumbent auditor

Notice of annual meeting (of shareholders)   The directors must send written notice of meeting (of shareholders), Precedent 28.2, at least **ten days**, but not more than fifty days, before the date of the meeting, to the auditor and to each shareholder entitled to vote, and to each director on record in the minute book registers. In the case of an annual meeting, the directors must, along with the notice of meeting, mail to the shareholders the financial statements and the auditors' report, if any, for the preceding financial (fiscal) year. These materials enable the shareholders to review the financial situation of the corporation prior to attending the meeting.

Quorum of shareholders   A quorum is the minimum number of shareholders that must be present in order to conduct a valid meeting. Normally, shareholders who hold the majority of the shares and are either personally present or represented by proxy constitute a quorum. Usually, a quorum is necessary only to begin the meeting: that is, a member of the quorum may leave part way through the meeting without affecting the validity of the meeting.

Voting rights and manner of voting of shareholders   Usually, each voting share entitles the holder to one vote. The shareholders usually vote by a show of hands, except where a shareholder or a proxyholder demands a secret ballot. Except for matters that require a two-thirds vote, all other matters are usually decided by a simple majority of 50 percent plus 1 vote.

Proxy   A shareholder may, by means of a **proxy**, Precedent 28.3, appoint another person (proxyholder), who need not be a shareholder, to attend, act, and vote at the meeting as the shareholder would do if present.

ANNUAL MEETINGS AND RESOLUTIONS

Annual meetings are **shareholders'** meetings. Annual meetings give the shareholders a chance to review the annual performance of the directors and the financial progress of the corporation and to elect new directors. Annual meetings are general, as opposed to special, because the shareholders decide on the annual business by a simple majority vote. There are usually three meetings, one after the other. For facility, we will call them (pre-annual) meeting of directors, annual meeting of shareholders, and (post-annual) meeting of directors. Smaller corporations deal with the annual issues usually by signing three parallel annual resolutions instead of holding annual meetings, as follows:

Annual Minutes of Meetings	Annual Resolutions in Writing
Precedent 28.1, Minutes of Meeting of Directors (pre-annual), Camelot	Precedent 28.6, Resolutions of Directors (pre-annual), Camelot
Precedent 28.4, Minutes of Annual Meeting of Shareholders, Camelot	Precedent 28.7 Resolutions of Shareholders (annual), Camelot
Precedent 28.5, Minutes of Meeting of Directors (post-annual), Camelot	Precedent 28.8 Resolutions of Directors (post-annual), Camelot

Meeting of directors (pre-annual)   The corporation's accountants must prepare the financial statements of the corporation for the year past and supply the directors with a copy. At this meeting, the directors usually approve the financial statements and call the annual meeting of shareholders so as to present the corporation's financial statements to the shareholders.

Meeting of shareholders (annual)   This meeting is the annual shareholders' meeting which the directors called in their pre-annual meeting and which the shareholders must hold annually. Subsection 96(5) of the OBCA prescribes the following regular business to be transacted at each annual meeting of shareholders:

- Consideration of the minutes of an earlier meeting
- Approval of the financial statements and auditor's report
- Election of new directors or re-election of the same directors
- Reappointment of the auditor (or consent to exemption from audit)

Meeting of directors (post-annual)   This is the first meeting of the newly elected board of directors who, if re-elected, may be the same people as the previous directors. The main matter of business for the newly elected directors is usually appointing officers.

PREPARATION AND DISTRIBUTION OF MINUTES OF MEETINGS

You require: Instructions from the corporation or its accountants about the meetings. There is no prescribed form or style for minutes. See Precedents 28.1, 28.4, and 28.5 for styles commonly used in practice.

Number of copies, minimum 3: Insert 1 in minute book; give 1 to accountant; keep 1 in client's file.

SPECIAL RESOLUTIONS

There are two types of special resolutions: special resolutions requiring a two-thirds favourable vote; unanimous approval resolutions requiring a 100 percent favourable vote:

Special resolutions   Special resolutions require shareholder approval by either a **two-thirds** majority vote or by the signatures of all of the shareholders before they are effective. Generally, the directors draft these resolutions and present them to the shareholders for their signatures. Where too many signatures are involved, the directors may call a shareholders' meeting, known as a "special meeting," so as to obtain the two-thirds vote approval (instead of the signatures of all of the shareholders). The OBCA prescribes the matters which require special resolutions. Some of these include changing the articles of incorporation, amalgamation, or sale of the corporation. Special resolutions aim to limit the decision-making freedom of the directors on matters that affect the structure and life of the corporation. This is why only the **shareholders** are empowered to pass special resolutions. Special resolutions are, therefore, shareholders' resolutions only--there are no special resolutions of directors.

Unanimous approval resolutions   In order to pass, these resolutions require either all shareholders to vote alike or all to sign, and they usually concern matters relating to the financial affairs of the corporation, e.g. dispensing with audits. Unanimous approval is necessary to protect the interests of every shareholder, instead of only the majority, as would be the case in a majority vote. Usually, the directors draft the resolutions and present them to the shareholders for their approval in writing by way of signatures or at a meeting by way of a unanimous vote.

Legal TIP

Shareholders' resolutions, special or otherwise, never require the approval of the directors, since the shareholders are the owners.

ORDINARY RESOLUTIONS

All resolutions that are not special or unanimous resolutions are ordinary resolutions. They are called so because they require an ordinary 50 percent plus 1 vote majority to pass. The resolutions of directors and shareholders prepared for the initial organization of a corporation are examples of ordinary resolutions. The directors, as well as the shareholders, may make ordinary resolutions. All ordinary resolutions, be they resolutions of directors or shareholders, are effective as soon as they are passed, and unless they have the effect of by-laws, require no further approval or confirmation. This allows freedom in conducting the day-to-day business of the corporation.

PREPARATION AND DISTRIBUTION OF RESOLUTIONS IN WRITING

You require: Instructions from the corporation or its accountants that the corporation's financial statements are ready. There is no prescribed form for resolutions in writing. The form and style in Precedents 28.6, 28.7, and 28.8 are commonly used in practice.

Number of copies, minimum 3: Insert 1 in minute book; give 1 to accountant; keep 1 in client's file.

MANDAMO PROPERTIES LTD.
Re: Incorporation

Troubled waters hit Mandamo after the initial organization. Tom fell in love with a voluptuous American young lady whom he met on the Mandamo steam cruiser. Gradually, she lured him away to the glamour of New York's Fifth Avenue. On October 24, Tom resigned as director and president. Mr. Robert Roberts replaced him on the same date. Steve Brown remains the original shareholder, director, and secretary of Mandamo. The notice of change to the ministry, Precedent 28.15, shows the happenings. Wealthy Mr. Roberts bought out Tom, taking over not only Tom's two posts of director and president, but also Tom's 101 common shares, which Tom had by this time acquired.

If you check the directors' register in Precedent 28.9, you will see that Tom is out and Robert Roberts is in as director. In the shareholders' register, Precedent 28.10, you will see that all of the 101 shares that Tom held are now held by Mr. Roberts. The stock transfer register in Precedent 28.11 shows how Tom's 101 shares have been transferred over to Robert Roberts under Share Certificate No. C-4. Tom's individual shareholder's ledger, Precedent 28.12, shows Tom with zero holdings. A new shareholder's ledger, Precedent 28.13, shows that Tom's 101 shares are now firmly in the hands of Robert Roberts, giving Mr. Roberts complete control of Tom's and Steve's beloved Mandamo.

We have now completed the Mandamo file until any other changes occur.

NOTICE OF CHANGE

The *Corporations Information Act* requires that a **notice of change**, Precedent 28.15, be filed with the ministry. The information on the notice of change is recorded on the Ontario public record for Ontario business corporations. Once prepared, file the notice of change, in person or by mail, with the ministry within **fifteen days** of any changes. You may also file the notice of change electronically if your firm has an e-filing account with any of the private service providers (PSPs) under ministry contract for this purpose. The ministry requires no filing fee for the notice of change. There are penalties for failure to report changes, including fines, court orders to dissolve the corporation, and inability to sue or defend a law suit.

Form The form is called **Form 1 initial return/notice of change** because it is designed to be used as a notice of change as well as an initial return. The form is available in PDF format on the ministry's ServiceOntario website.

PREPARATION AND DISTRIBUTION OF NOTICE OF CHANGE, FORM 1

You require: The file, the articles of incorporation, the directors' resolution accepting the resignation; shareholders' resolution electing the new director. Follow along in Precedent 28.15. Note that whether you are filing manually or electronically, the information required for the preparation of the notice of change is the same. The instructions for completing the notice of change are the same as those provided in Chapter 27 for the preparation of the initial notice, except as follows:

Mark the "notice of change" box (instead of the "initial return" box). In practice, the name of the director who signs the form is usually entered in the c/o line. In completing Schedule A, report all of the directors and officers who currently hold office; also report all of the directors and officers who have resigned since the previous filing.

Data Extract Note that the names of any directors and officers who are already on file with the ministry must be entered exactly as shown on previous filings, e.g Norma Jean Baker, not Norma J. Baker. If the name does not match exactly, the system will create a new director or officer for the same person. To avoid this mix-up, prior to filing, order, for a fee, an electronic data extraction report, commonly referred to as a data extract. The data extract will show you the most current information on file with the ministry, so that when making changes to the existing information, you will know whether or not Norma Jean Baker was previously filed as Norma J. Baker and use the name exactly as on the data extract.

Number of copies, minimum 3: File 1 with the ministry; insert 1 in minute book; keep 1 in client's file.

CHANGES BY NOTICE OF CHANGE

Changes in corporate information such as the following are usually reported to the ministry by a notice of change within fifteen days of the change:

Change of address within municipality or geographic township If the corporation moves its registered office to a new address within the same county, district, or regional municipality, e.g. from downtown Toronto to the west end of Toronto, the documents to prepare include:

1. A resolution of directors fixing the new address (within municipality), Precedent 28.16.
2. A notice of change, Precedent 28.15.

Change of address to different municipality or geographic township The OBCA protects the shareholders and creditors by requiring the directors to seek approval from the shareholders before moving the registered office to a new county, district, or regional municipality, e.g. from Toronto to North Bay. The documents to prepare include:

1. Special resolution of shareholders approving change of address to new municipality, Precedent 28.17.
2. Resolution of directors fixing new address (new municipality), Precedent 28.18.
3. Notice of change, Precedent 28.15.

CHANGES BY ARTICLES OF AMENDMENT

From time to time, it may become necessary for a corporation to make changes to its articles of incorporation; some such changes include changing the name of the corporation, changing the number of directors, or changing the share structure of the corporation. These types of fundamental changes must be done by filing articles of amendment.

Changing the name of the corporation　　If the name of the corporation is being changed, the documents to be prepared usually include:

1. Special resolution of the shareholders approving the change of the corporation's name, Precedent 28.19.
2. NUANS search of the new name, not older than 90 days.
3. Articles of amendment, in duplicate, Precedent 28.20.
4. Resolution of directors to adopt the new seal and share certificate in the new name of the corporation.

File with the ministry the NUANS search, two manually signed copies of the articles of amendment, and a covering letter giving a contact name, address, and telephone number and enclosing the applicable fee. The ministry endorses the articles of amendment with a certificate of amendment and returns the endorsed articles of amendment to you.

CHANGES BY ARTICLES OF AMALGAMATION

The long and the short of it　　Amalgamation is the legal term for the common term **merger**. There are two types of amalgamations--a long-form amalgamation and a short-form amalgamation.

Long-form amalgamation　　This type of amalgamation involves the joining together of two or more Ontario business corporations to form one corporation. A well known analogy is the combination of two streams which join and continue along as a larger river. To effect a long-form amalgamation, the Ontario *Business Corporations Act* requires the amalgamating corporations to enter into an amalgamation agreement which, in effect, sets out all of the provisions that would ordinarily be included in the articles of incorporation of the amalgamated corporation. Typical documents prepared in long-form amalgamations include the following:

1. Special resolution of shareholders of each of the amalgamating corporations authorizing amalgamation, Precedent 28.21.

2. Amalgamation agreement, Precedent 28.22. The directors of each amalgamating corporation must approve the amalgamation agreement, and they must then submit it to the shareholders of each amalgamating corporation for approval by a special resolution of the shareholders.

3. Schedule A— statement of director or officer of each of the amalgamating corporations regarding liability, Precedent 28.23.

4. Articles of amalgamation, Precedent 28.24.

Short-form amalgamation   Generally, a short-form amalgamation involves the joining of a holding corporation, i.e. a corporation which holds all of the issued shares of its subsidiary, referred to as the parent corporation, and one or more of its subsidiary corporations. Generally, with short-form amalgamations, the directors must approve the amalgamation, but shareholder approval and an amalgamation agreement are not usually required.

In all amalgamations (long-form or short-form), the typical documents to be submitted to the ministry include:

1. Articles of amalgamation in duplicate, bearing original signatures on both copies. (Mark Box A for long-form amalgamations; mark Box B for short-form amalgamations.)

2. Schedule A — statement of director or officer of each of the amalgamating corporations regarding liability, as required under subsection 178(2) of the *Business Corporations Act*, in duplicate.

3. Schedule B — amalgamation agreement as adopted by a special resolution under s. 176 of the *Business Corporations Act* (for long-form amalgamations only), in duplicate.

OR

Schedule B — directors' resolutions, in duplicate, from each subsidiary, approved under s. 177 of the *Business Corporations Act* (for short-form amalgamations), in duplicate.

4. NUANS name search (dated not more than 90 days prior to the delivery of the articles of amalgamation) where the amalgamated corporation will use a name other than a name of one of the amalgamating corporations. Amalgamated corporations cannot keep a number name; the ministry assigns a new number name.

5. Covering letter giving a contact name, address, and telephone number and enclosing the applicable fee.

Once you receive the certificate of amalgamation, you must organize the newly amalgamated corporation as if it were a newly incorporated corporation.

CHAPTER SUMMARY

The OBCA requires corporations to keep records in the form of minutes of meetings or, in the absence of meetings, resolutions in writing. The directors call all of the meetings, and the president of the corporation usually chairs all meetings. The secretary of the corporation usually acts as secretary of the meetings.

While the directors are likely to hold meetings regularly in conducting the corporation's business, they must call at least one annual meeting of shareholders. At that meeting, the shareholders approve the financial statements of the corporation and elect new directors or re-elect the old ones. The very first annual meeting of shareholders must be held not later than 18 months after incorporation, with subsequent annual meetings not later than 15 months after the last annual meeting.

There are three kinds of resolutions: (1) special resolutions which only the shareholders can make and require either a 2/3 majority vote or the signatures of all of the shareholders before they take effect; (2) unanimous approval resolutions which also only the shareholders can make and require a 100 percent majority vote or the signatures of all of the shareholders; and (3) ordinary resolutions which the directors or the shareholders can make and require a simple majority of 50 percent plus 1 vote.

The corporation must report to the ministry any ordinary changes, such as change of directors, by filing a notice of change. Where the changes affect the structure or the name of the corporation, such changes must be made by filing articles of amendment. Other changes in corporations include amalgamations which are made by filing articles of amalgamation.

REVIEW QUESTIONS

1. Who calls shareholders' meetings?
2. What is a quorum?
3. What is the main purpose of annual meetings?
4. Are special resolutions passed by the directors or the shareholders?
5. In what way, other than holding meetings, can small corporations conduct their annual business?
6. What is a notice of change?
7. What types of changes require articles of amendment?
8. The chair of a meeting can always vote to break a tie vote. Yes____ No___
9. What are articles of amalgamation?

**MINUTES OF A MEETING OF THE BOARD OF DIRECTORS OF
CAMELOT LIMITED**
held at 55 Burlington Street, Oakville, Ontario
on the 5th day of June, 20--

PRESENT:

A quorum of directors was present, namely, Arthur King, Guinevere Queen, Lancelot Prince and Malory Thomas.

CONSTITUTION OF MEETING

The President, Arthur King, acted as Chairman and the Secretary-Treasurer, Malory Thomas, acted as Secretary of the meeting.

A quorum of the directors being present, and all the directors of the Corporation having waived notice of the meeting, the Chairman declared the meeting to be duly constituted.

MINUTES OF THE LAST MEETING OF DIRECTORS

The minutes of the last meeting of directors were unanimously taken as read and confirmed.

FINANCIAL STATEMENTS

On motion duly made, seconded and unanimously carried, the following resolution was passed:

BE IT RESOLVED THAT:

The financial statements of the corporation for the year ended on January 31, 20--, be approved and any two directors be authorized to sign the financial statements on behalf of the board of directors to evidence such approval.

ANNUAL MEETING OF THE SHAREHOLDERS

On motion duly made, seconded and unanimously carried, the following resolution was passed:

BE IT RESOLVED THAT:

Subject to such meeting being duly constituted, the annual meeting of the shareholders of the corporation be held at 55 Burlington Street, Oakville, Ontario, on Monday, the 9th day of July, 20--, at the hour of 10:00 o'clock in the morning (local time).

TERMINATION

There being no further business, the meeting was terminated.

_____   _____
Chairman   Secretary

NOTICE OF ANNUAL MEETING OF SHAREHOLDERS OF
CAMELOT LIMITED

NOTICE is hereby given that the annual meeting of the shareholders of Camelot Limited (the "Corporation") will be held at 55 Burlington Street, Oakville, Ontario, on Monday, the 9th day of July, 20--, at the hour of 10:00 a.m.:

1.   To receive and consider the report of the directors and the financial statements of the Corporation for the year ended January 31, 20--, and the report of the auditors thereon.

2.   To elect directors.

3.   To appoint auditors.

4.   To transact such other business as may properly come before the meeting.

DATED the   day of June, 20--.

BY ORDER OF THE BOARD OF DIRECTORS

_____
President

Directors of the Corporation who do not hold shares of the Corporation are entitled to receive this notice and to attend at the meeting but are not entitled to vote threat.

Shareholders who are unable to attend the meeting are to complete the attached proxy and have same brought to the meeting by the person attending as proxy. Corporate shareholders are required to complete the attached proxy and have same brought to the meeting by the person attending on behalf of such shareholder.

CAMELOT LIMITED
(the "Corporation")

PROXY

**FOR MEETING OF SHAREHOLDERS
TO BE HELD ON**

July 9, 20--

The undersigned shareholder of the Corporation hereby appoints _____ (name of proxyholder) _____ as proxy of the undersigned to represent the undersigned at the meeting of shareholders to be held at 55 Burlington Street, Oakville, Ontario, on Monday, July 9, 20--, at 10:00 a.m., or at any adjournment or adjournments of said meeting, and at such meeting to vote for the undersigned upon any and all matters which may come before the meeting, and to do any and all acts and things which the undersigned might or could do if personally present. The undersigned hereby undertakes to ratify and confirm all that the said attorney and proxy of the undersigned may do or cause to be done by virtue hereof.

IN WITNESS WHEREOF the undersigned has executed this Proxy, the   day of   20--.

_____
Name of Shareholder
(please print)

_____
(Signature)

MINUTES OF THE ANNUAL MEETING OF THE SHAREHOLDERS OF
CAMELOT LIMITED
held at 55 Burlington Street, Oakville, Ontario
on the 9th day of July, 20--, at the hour of 10:00 o'clock in the forenoon.

PRESENT IN PERSON:

The following shareholders were present at the meeting: Arthur King, Guinevere Queen and Malory Thomas.

The following shareholder was represented by proxy: Lancelot Prince

The President, Mr. Arthur King, acted as Chairman and Mr. Malory Thomas acted as Secretary of the meeting.

A quorum of shareholders being present either personally or by proxy, the Chairman declared the meeting to be duly constituted.

1.   MINUTES OF LAST MEETING

The minutes of the last meeting of shareholders were unanimously taken as read and confirmed.

2.   APPROVAL OF FINANCIAL STATEMENTS

The Chairman presented to the meeting the unaudited financial statements of the Corporation for the fiscal period ended January 31, 20--, together with the auditors' comments thereon.

On motion duly made, seconded and unanimously carried, the following resolution was passed:

BE IT RESOLVED THAT:

the unaudited financial statements of the Corporation for the fiscal period ended January 31, 20--, be and the same are hereby accepted by the shareholders of the Corporation.

3.   CONFIRMATION OF PROCEEDINGS

On motion duly made, seconded and unanimously carried, the following resolution was passed:

BE IT RESOLVED THAT:

all acts, by-laws, resolutions, contracts, proceedings, elections, appointments and payments enacted, passed, made, done or taken by the directors and officers of the Corporation since the date of the last annual meeting of shareholders of the Corporation be and the same are hereby approved, ratified and confirmed.

-2-

4. ELECTION OF DIRECTORS

The Chairman then stated that it was in order to proceed with the election of directors and called for nominations. The following persons were nominated:

Arthur King	Malory Thomas
Guinevere Queen	Lancelot Prince

There being no further nominations, the Chairman declared nominations closed.

On motion duly made, seconded and unanimously carried, the following resolution was passed:

BE IT RESOLVED THAT:

the following persons be and they are hereby elected directors of the Corporation to hold office until their respective successors are duly elected, subject to the provisions of the by-laws of the Corporation and the provisions of the *Business Corporations Act* (Ontario).

Arthur King	Malory Thomas
Guinevere Queen	Lancelot Prince

5. APPOINTMENT OF AUDITORS

BE IT RESOLVED THAT:

Table & Round be and they are hereby appointed the auditors of the Corporation to hold office until a successor is appointed, at such remuneration as may be fixed by the board of directors and the board of directors is hereby authorized to fix such remuneration.

There being no further business, the meeting was terminated.

_____   _____
Chairman   Secretary

MINUTES OF THE MEETING OF THE BOARD OF DIRECTORS OF
CAMELOT LIMITED
held at 55 Burlington Street, Oakville, Ontario
on the 9th day of July, 20--, at the hour of 11:00 o'clock in the forenoon.

PRESENT IN PERSON:

A quorum of directors was present, namely, Arthur King, Guinevere Queen, Malory Thomas and Lancelot Prince.

The President, Mr. Arthur King, acted as Chairman and Mr. Malory Thomas acted as Secretary of the meeting.

A quorum of the directors being present in person, a majority of whom were Canadian residents, and pursuant to the corporation's by-laws, no notice being required for the first meeting of a newly elected board held immediately following the annual meeting of shareholders at which it was elected, the Chair declared the meeting to be duly constituted.

1.   MINUTES OF LAST MEETING

The minutes of the last meeting of directors were unanimously taken as read and confirmed.

2.   APPOINTMENT OF OFFICERS

On motion duly made, seconded and unanimously carried, the following resolution was passed:

BE IT RESOLVED THAT:

the following persons be and they are hereby elected and appointed officers of the Corporation to hold the office referred to opposite their respective names until their respective successors shall be elected and appointed:

Arthur King	President
Malory Thomas	Secretary-Treasurer

There being no further business, the meeting was terminated.

_____   _____
Chairman   Secretary

RESOLUTIONS OF THE DIRECTORS

OF

CAMELOT LIMITED

1. APPROVAL OF FINANCIAL STATEMENTS

BE IT RESOLVED THAT:

the unaudited financial statements of the Corporation for the fiscal period ended January 31, 20--, which have been prepared by the accountants of the Corporation, consisting of a Statement of Profit and Loss for the period ended January 31, 20--, and a Balance Sheet as of the end of such period, together with a draft of the accountants' comments thereon be and the same are hereby approved, and the directors are hereby authorized to sign the Balance Sheet to evidence such approval, and be it further resolved that the said financial statements be submitted to the shareholders of the Corporation.

2. TRANSACTION OF ANNUAL BUSINESS

BE IT RESOLVED THAT:

the shareholders of the Corporation be and they are hereby requested to transact the annual business of the Corporation.

EACH AND EVERY OF THE FOREGOING RESOLUTIONS is hereby consented to by all of the directors of the Corporation, as evidenced by their respective signatures hereto in accordance with the provisions of section 129(1) of the *Business Corporations Act* (Ontario), this 5th day of June, 20--.

_____
Arthur King

_____
Guinevere Queen

_____
Lancelot Prince

_____
Malory Thomas

RESOLUTIONS OF THE SHAREHOLDERS

OF

CAMELOT LIMITED

### 1.	FINANCIAL STATEMENTS

BE IT RESOLVED THAT:

the financial statements of the Corporation for the fiscal period ended January 31, 20--, which have been prepared by the accountants of the Corporation, consisting of a Statement of Profit and Loss for the period ended January 31, 20--, and a Balance Sheet as of the end of such period, together with the accountants' comments thereon be and the same are hereby accepted by the shareholders of the Corporation.

### 2.	CONFIRMATION OF PROCEEDINGS

BE IT RESOLVED THAT:

a)	all by-laws, resolutions, contracts, proceedings, elections and appointments, enacted, passed, made or taken by the shareholders, directors or officers of the Corporation, at any time since the incorporation of the Corporation (hereinafter collectively called "the corporate proceedings") as the same are set forth or referred to in the minutes of the shareholders and directors for the Corporation and in the other records of the corporate proceedings, and all acts and proceedings taken by the directors, officers, agents or employees of the Corporation under the authority of or pursuant to any of the corporate proceedings be and the same are hereby ratified and confirmed with the effect stated in such corporate proceedings; and

b)	insofar as any such corporate proceeding shall not have been validly enacted, passed, sanctioned, confirmed, authorized or made, the same is hereby for greater certainty enacted, passed, sanctioned, confirmed, authorized or made, with retroactive effect, and in all other respects with the effect stated in the minutes and records of the Corporation.

### 3.	ELECTION OF DIRECTORS

BE IT RESOLVED THAT:

the following people be and they are hereby elected directors of the Corporation to hold office until the completion of the next annual meeting of the shareholders of the Corporation or until successors are duly elected, subject to the provisions of the by-laws of the Corporation and the provisions of the *Business Corporations Act* (Ontario):

Arthur King	Guinevere Queen
Lancelot Prince	Malory Thomas

-2-

4.   APPOINTMENT OF ACCOUNTANTS

BE IT RESOLVED THAT:

Table and Round be and they are hereby appointed the accountants of the Corporation to hold office until the completion of the next annual meeting of the shareholders of the Corporation, or until a successor is appointed, at such remuneration as may be fixed by the board of directors and the board of directors is hereby authorized to fix such remuneration.

EACH AND EVERY OF THE FOREGOING RESOLUTIONS is hereby consented to by all of the shareholders of the Corporation entitled to vote thereon at a meeting of shareholders, as evidenced by their respective signatures hereto in accordance with the provisions of section 104(1) of the *Business Corporations Act* (Ontario), this 5th day of June, 20--.

_____	_____
Arthur King	Guinevere Queen
_____	_____
Lancelot Prince	Malory Thomas

CONSENT OF SHAREHOLDERS TO EXEMPTION FROM AUDIT

CAMELOT LIMITED

The undersigned, being all of the shareholders of CAMELOT LIMITED (the "Corporation"), hereby declare that the Corporation is not offering its securities to the public.

Pursuant to section 148 of the *Business Corporations Act* (Ontario), we hereby consent to the exemption of the Corporation from the audit provisions set out in Part XII of the said Act in respect of the next ensuing fiscal year of the Corporation, and in respect of each fiscal year thereafter until this consent is revoked.

DATED the 5th day of June, 20--.

_____	_____
Arthur King	Guinevere Queen
_____	_____
Lancelot Prince	Malory Thomas

RESOLUTION OF THE DIRECTORS

OF

CAMELOT LIMITED

1.   **APPOINTMENT OF OFFICERS**

BE IT RESOLVED THAT:

the following persons be and they are hereby elected or appointed officers of the Corporation to hold office during the pleasure of the board:

Arthur King	President
Malory Thomas	Secretary-Treasurer

THE FOREGOING RESOLUTION is hereby consented to by all of the directors of the Corporation, as evidenced by their respective signatures hereto in accordance with the provisions of section 129(1) of the *Business Corporations Act* (Ontario), this 5th day of June, 20--.

_____	_____
Arthur King	Guinevere Queen
_____	_____
Lancelot Prince	Malory Thomas

Mandamo Properties Ltd.
DIRECTORS' REGISTER

Name of Director	Date Elected	Date Resigned
THOMAS DAVID BROWN	Jul 18, (year)	Oct 24, (year)
STEPHEN THOMAS BROWN 61 Jasper Drive Aurora, Ontario L4G 3C1	Jul 18, (year)	
ROBERT R. ROBERTS 13 Lucky Street Toronto, Ontario M3R 1P4	Oct 24, (year)	

Mandamo Properties Ltd.
SHAREHOLDERS' REGISTER

Date	Name	No. of Shares	Class Of Shares Held
Jul 18, (year)	**Stephen Thomas Brown** 61 Jasper Drive Aurora, Ontario L4G 3C1	1	Common
Oct 24, (year)	**Robert R. Roberts** 13 Lucky Street Toronto, Ontario M3R 1P4	101	Common

Document prepared using *Fast Company* by Do Process Software Ltd.

Effective date: Oct 24, 20--

Precedent 28.11   Stock Transfer Register

Mandamo Properties Ltd.
STOCK TRANSFER REGISTER

| Trnsf. No. | Date | Share Class | SURRENDERED | | | Transferred From | Transferred To | ISSUED | | |
			Cert. No.	No. of Shares				Share Class	Cert. No.	No. of Shares
1	Jul 18, (year)					TREASURY	Thomas David Brown	C-	1	1
2	Jul 18, (year)					TREASURY	Stephen Thomas Brown	C-	2	1
3	Jan 3, (year)					TREASURY	Thomas David Brown	C-	3	100
4	Oct 24, (year)	C-	1	1		Thomas David Brown	Robert R. Roberts	C-	4	1
5	Oct 24, (year)	C-	3	100		Thomas David Brown	Robert R. Roberts	C-	4	100

Precedent 28.12   Shareholder's Ledger

Mandamo Properties Ltd.
SHAREHOLDER'S LEDGER

THOMAS DAVID BROWN

61 Jasper Drive
Aurora, Ontario
L4G 3C1

Share Class: Common

Date	Certif. No.	Transfer No.	Transferred From/To	Sold	Bought	Balance
Jul 18, (year)	C-1	1	FROM: TREASURY		1	1
Jan 3, (year)	C-3	3	FROM: TREASURY		100	101
Oct 24, (year)	C-1	4	TO: Robert R. Roberts	1		100
Oct 24, (year)	C-3	5	TO: Robert R. Roberts	100		0

Precedent 28.13   Shareholder's Ledger

Mandamo Properties Ltd.
SHAREHOLDER'S LEDGER

ROBERT R. ROBERTS

13 Lucky Street
Toronto, Ontario
M3R 1P4

Share Class: Common

Date	Certif. No.	Transfer No.	Transferred From/To	Sold	Bought	Balance
Oct 24 (year)	C-4	4	FROM: Thomas David Brown		1	1
Oct 24 (year)	C-4	5	FROM: Thomas David Brown		100	101

Effective date: Oct 24, 20--

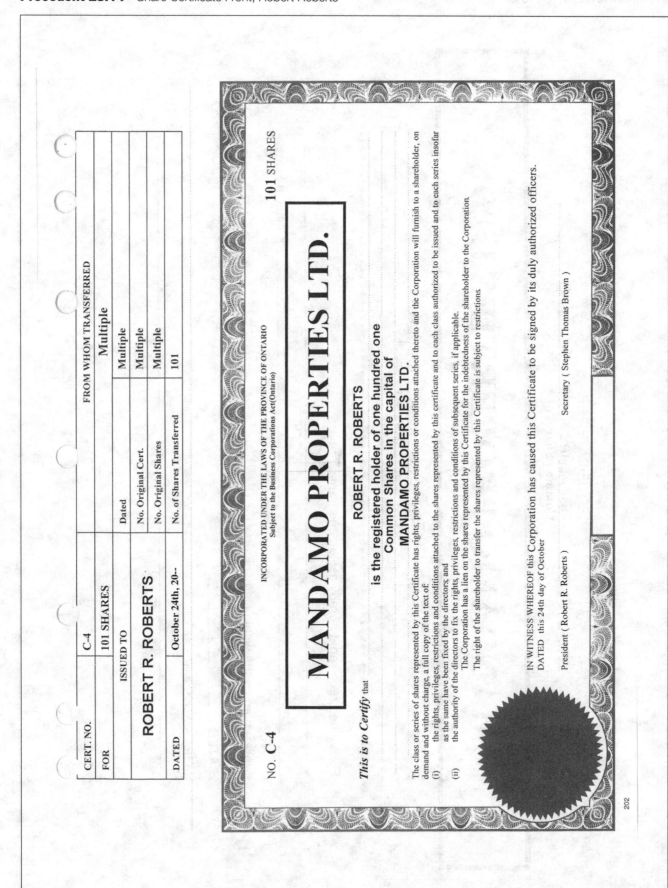

CERTIFICATE FOR
one hundred one
Common Shares of

MANDAMO PROPERTIES LTD.

Issued to: **ROBERT R. ROBERTS**
Date: October 24th, 20--
Certificate: C-4

****

For Value I received, I hereby assign and transfer unto

_____   **Common Shares**

represented by the within Certificate

DATED _____

In the presence of _____

Ontario

Ministry of **Government Services**	**Ministère des** **Services gouvernementaux**
Central Production and Verification Services Branch 393 University Avenue, Suite 200 Toronto ON M5G 2M2	Direction des services centraux de production et de vérification 393, avenue University, bureau 200 Toronto ON M5G 2M2

For Ministry Use Only
À l'usage du ministère seulement
Page/Page **1** of/de _____

Form 1 – Ontario Corporation Initial Return / Notice of Change
Formule 1 – Personnes morales de l'Ontario Rapport initial / Avis de modification
Corporations Information Act / Loi sur les renseignements exigés des personnes morales

Please type or print all information in block capital letters using black ink.
Prière de dactylographier les renseignements ou de les écrire en caractères d'imprimerie à l'encre noire.

1.
Notice of Change
Initial Return / Rapport initial
Avis de modification
Business Corporation/ Société par actions — [X]
Not-For-Profit Corporation/ Personne morale sans but lucratif

2.
Ontario Corporation Number
Numéro matricule de la personne morale en Ontario
2345678

3.
Date of Incorporation or Amalgamation/
Date de constitution ou fusion
Year/Année Month/Mois Day/Jour
(Year) **07** **18**

For Ministry Use Only
À l'usage du ministère seulement

4. Corporation Name Including Punctuation/Raison sociale de la personne morale, y compris la ponctuation
MANDAMO PROPERTIES LTD.

5. Address of Registered or Head Office/Adresse du siège social
c/o / a/s
ROBERT R. ROBERTS
Street No./N° civique Street Name/Nom de la rue   Suite/Bureau
1750 **FINCH AVENUE EAST**
Street Name (cont'd)/Nom de la rue (suite)
ROOM 3244
City/Town/Ville
TORONTO   ONTARIO, CANADA
Postal Code/Code postal
M2V 2X5

For Ministry Use Only/
À l'usage du ministère seulement

6. Mailing Address/Adresse postale

[X] Same as Registered or Head Office/ Même que siège social

[ ] Not Applicable/ Ne s'applique pas

Street No./N° civique
Street Name/Nom de la rue   Suite/Bureau
Street Name (cont'd)/Nom de la rue (suite)
City/Town/Ville
Province, State/Province, État Country/Pays Postal Code/Code postal

7. Language of Preference/Langue préférée   English - Anglais [X]   French - Français [ ]

8. **Information on Directors/Officers must be completed on Schedule A as requested.** If additional space is required, photocopy Schedule A./**Les renseignements sur les administrateurs ou les dirigeants doivent être fournis dans l'Annexe A, tel que demandé.** Si vous avez besoin de plus d'espace, vous pouvez photocopier l'Annexe A.

Number of Schedule A(s) submitted/Nombre d'Annexes A présentées **2** (At least one Schedule A must be submitted/Au moins une Annexe A doit être présentée)

9.
(Print or type name in full of the person authorizing filing / Dactylographier ou inscrire le prénom et le nom en caractères d'imprimerie de la personne qui autorise l'enregistrement)

I/Je **ROBERT R. ROBERTS**

certify that the information set out herein, is true and correct.
atteste que les renseignements précités sont véridiques et exacts.

Check appropriate box
Cocher la case pertinente

D) [X] Director/Administrateur

O) [X] Officer/Dirigeant

P) [ ] Other individual having knowledge of the affairs of the Corporation/Autre personne ayant connaissance des activités de la personne morale

NOTE/REMARQUE: Sections 13 and 14 of the **Corporations Information Act** provide penalties for making false or misleading statements or omissions. Les articles 13 et 14 de la *Loi sur les renseignements exigés des personnes morales* prévoient des peines en cas de déclaration fausse ou trompeuse, ou d'omission.

**Form 1 ¯ Ontario Corporation/Formule 1 ¯ Personnes morales de l'Ontario
Schedule A/Annexe A**

For Ministry Use Only
À l'usage du ministère seulement
Page/Page _____ of/de _____

Please type or print all information in block capital letters using black ink. Prière de dactylographier les renseignements ou de les écrire en caractères d'imprimerie à l'encre noire.	Ontario Corporation Number Numéro matricule de la personne morale en Ontario **2345678**	Date of Incorporation or Amalgamation Date de constitution ou fusion Year/Année **(Year)** Month/Mois **07** Day/Jour **18**

DIRECTOR / OFFICER INFORMATION ¯ RENSEIGNEMENTS RELATIFS AUX ADMINISTRATEURS/DIRIGEANTS
Full Name and Address for Service/Nom et domicile élu

Last Name/Nom de famille
BROWN

First Name/Prénom
THOMAS

Middle Names/Autres prénoms
DAVID

Street Number/Numéro civique
61

Suite/Bureau

*OTHER TITLES (Please Specify)
*AUTRES TITRES (Veuillez préciser)
Chair / Président du conseil
Chair Person / Président du conseil
Chairman / Président du conseil
Chairwoman / Présidente du conseil
Vice-Chair / Vice-président du conseil
Vice-President / Vice-président
Assistant Secretary / Secrétaire adjoint
Assistant Treasurer / Trésorier adjoint
Chief Manager / Directeur exécutif
Executive Director / Directeur administratif
Managing Director / Administrateur délégué
Chief Executive Officer / Directeur général
Chief Financial Officer /
Agent en chef des finances
Chief Information Officer /
Directeur général de l'information
Chief Operating Officer /
Administrateur en chef des opérations
Chief Administrative Officer /
Directeur général de l'administration
Comptroller / Contrôleur
Authorized Signing Officer /
Signataire autorisé
Other (Untitled) / Autre (sans titre)

Street Name/Nom de la rue
JASPER DRIVE

Street Name (cont'd)/Nom de la rue (suite)

City/Town/Ville
AURORA

Province, State/Province, État
ONTARIO

Country/Pays
CANADA

Postal Code/Code postal
L4G 3C1

Director Information/Renseignements relatifs aux administrateurs

Resident Canadian/ Résident canadien
X YES/OUI ☐ NO/NON

(Resident Canadian applies to directors of business corporations only.)/
(Résident canadien ne s'applique qu'aux administrateurs de sociétés par actions)

	Year/Année Month/Mois Day/Jour		Year/Année Month/Mois Day/Jour
Date Elected/ Date d'élection	**(Year)** 07 18	Date Ceased/ Date de cessation	**(Year)** 10 24

Officer Information/Renseignements relatifs aux dirigeants

	PRESIDENT/PRÉSIDENT Year/Année Month/Mois Day/Jour	SECRETARY/SECRÉTAIRE Year/Année Month/Mois Day/Jour	TREASURER/TRÉSORIER Year/Année Month/Mois Day/Jour	GENERAL MANAGER/ DIRECTEUR GÉNÉRAL Year/Année Month/Mois Day/Jour	*OTHER/AUTRE Year/Année Month/Mois Day/Jour
Date Appointed/ Date de nomination	**(Year)** 07 18				
Date Ceased/ Date de cessation	**(Year)** 10 24				

DIRECTOR / OFFICER INFORMATION ¯ RENSEIGNEMENTS RELATIFS AUX ADMINISTRATEURS/DIRIGEANTS
Full Name and Address for Service/Nom et domicile élu

Last Name/Nom de famille
BROWN

First Name/Prénom
STEPHEN

Middle Names/Autres prénoms
THOMAS

Street Number/Numéro civique
61

Suite/Bureau

*OTHER TITLES (Please Specify)
*AUTRES TITRES (Veuillez préciser)
Chair / Président du conseil
Chair Person / Président du conseil
Chairman / Président du conseil
Chairwoman / Présidente du conseil
Vice-Chair / Vice-président du conseil
Vice-President / Vice-président
Assistant Secretary / Secrétaire adjoint
Assistant Treasurer / Trésorier adjoint
Chief Manager / Directeur exécutif
Executive Director / Directeur administratif
Managing Director / Administrateur délégué
Chief Executive Officer / Directeur général
Chief Financial Officer /
Agent en chef des finances
Chief Information Officer /
Directeur général de l'information
Chief Operating Officer /
Administrateur en chef des opérations
Chief Administrative Officer /
Directeur général de l'administration
Comptroller / Contrôleur
Authorized Signing Officer /
Signataire autorisé
Other (Untitled) / Autre (sans titre)

Street Name/Nom de la rue
JASPER DRIVE

Street Name (cont'd)/Nom de la rue (suite)

City/Town/Ville
AURORA

Province, State/Province, État
ONTARIO

Country/Pays
CANADA

Postal Code/Code postal
L4G 3C1

Director Information/Renseignements relatifs aux administrateurs

Resident Canadian/ Résident canadien
X YES/OUI ☐ NO/NON

(Resident Canadian applies to directors of business corporations only.)/
(Résident canadien ne s'applique qu'aux administrateurs de sociétés par actions)

	Year/Année Month/Mois Day/Jour		Year/Année Month/Mois Day/Jour
Date Elected/ Date d'élection	**(Year)** 07 18	Date Ceased/ Date de cessation	

Officer Information/Renseignements relatifs aux dirigeants

	PRESIDENT/PRÉSIDENT Year/Année Month/Mois Day/Jour	SECRETARY/SECRÉTAIRE Year/Année Month/Mois Day/Jour	TREASURER/TRÉSORIER Year/Année Month/Mois Day/Jour	GENERAL MANAGER/ DIRECTEUR GÉNÉRAL Year/Année Month/Mois Day/Jour	*OTHER/AUTRE Year/Année Month/Mois Day/Jour
Date Appointed/ Date de nomination		**(Year)** 07 18			
Date Ceased/ Date de cessation					

Form 1 ˉ Ontario Corporation/Formule 1 ˉ Personnes morales de l'Ontario
Schedule A/Annexe A

| For Ministry Use Only |
| À l'usage du ministère seulement |
| Page/Page ____ of/de _____ |

Please type or print all information in block capital letters using black ink.
Prière de dactylographier les renseignements ou de les écrire en caractères d'imprimerie à l'encre noire.

Ontario Corporation Number Numéro matricule de la personne morale en Ontario	Date of Incorporation or Amalgamation Date de constitution ou fusion
2345678	Year/Année **(Year)** Month/Mois **07** Day/Jour **18**

DIRECTOR / OFFICER INFORMATION ˉ RENSEIGNEMENTS RELATIFS AUX ADMINISTRATEURS/DIRIGEANTS
Full Name and Address for Service/Nom et domicile élu

Last Name/Nom de famille	First Name/Prénom	Middle Names/Autres prénoms
ROBERTS	**ROBERT**	**R.**

Street Number/Numéro civique **13** Suite/Bureau

Street Name/Nom de la rue **LUCKY STREET**

Street Name (cont'd)/Nom de la rue (suite)

City/Town/Ville **TORONTO**

Province, State/Province, État	Country/Pays	Postal Code/Code postal
ONTARIO	**CANADA**	**M3R 1P4**

*OTHER TITLES (Please Specify)
*AUTRES TITRES (Veuillez préciser)
Chair / Président du conseil
Chair Person / Président du conseil
Chairman / Président du conseil
Chairwoman / Présidente du conseil
Vice-Chair / Vice-président du conseil
Vice-President / Vice-président
Assistant Secretary / Secrétaire adjoint
Assistant Treasurer / Trésorier adjoint
Chief Manager / Directeur exécutif
Executive Director / Directeur administratif
Managing Director / Administrateur délégué
Chief Executive Officer / Directeur général
Chief Financial Officer / Agent en chef des finances
Chief Information Officer / Directeur général de l'information
Chief Operating Officer / Administrateur en chef des opérations
Chief Administrative Officer / Directeur général de l'administration
Comptroller / Contrôleur
Authorized Signing Officer / Signataire autorisé
Other (Untitled) / Autre (sans titre)

*OTHER/AUTRE

Director Information/Renseignements relatifs aux administrateurs

Resident Canadian/ Résident canadien   **X** YES/OUI   NO/NON   (Resident Canadian applies to directors of business corporations only.)/ (Résident canadien ne s'applique qu'aux administrateurs de sociétés par actions)

Date Elected/ Date d'élection   Year/Année **(Year)** Month/Mois **10** Day/Jour **24**   Date Ceased/ Date de cessation   Year/Année Month/Mois Day/Jour

Officer Information/Renseignements relatifs aux dirigeants

	PRESIDENT/PRÉSIDENT Year/Année Month/Mois Day/Jour	SECRETARY/SECRÉTAIRE Year/Année Month/Mois Day/Jour	TREASURER/TRÉSORIER Year/Année Month/Mois Day/Jour	GENERAL MANAGER/ DIRECTEUR GÉNÉRAL Year/Année Month/Mois Day/Jour	*OTHER/AUTRE Year/Année Month/Mois Day/Jour
Date Appointed/ Date de nomination	**(Year)** **10** **24**				
Date Ceased/ Date de cessation					

DIRECTOR / OFFICER INFORMATION ˉ RENSEIGNEMENTS RELATIFS AUX ADMINISTRATEURS/DIRIGEANTS
Full Name and Address for Service/Nom et domicile élu

Last Name/Nom de famille	First Name/Prénom	Middle Names/Autres prénoms

Street Number/Numéro civique   Suite/Bureau

Street Name/Nom de la rue

Street Name (cont'd)/Nom de la rue (suite)

City/Town/Ville

Province, State/Province, État	Country/Pays	Postal Code/Code postal

*OTHER TITLES (Please Specify)
*AUTRES TITRES (Veuillez préciser)
Chair / Président du conseil
Chair Person / Président du conseil
Chairman / Président du conseil
Chairwoman / Présidente du conseil
Vice-Chair / Vice-président du conseil
Vice-President / Vice-président
Assistant Secretary / Secrétaire adjoint
Assistant Treasurer / Trésorier adjoint
Chief Manager / Directeur exécutif
Executive Director / Directeur administratif
Managing Director / Administrateur délégué
Chief Executive Officer / Directeur général
Chief Financial Officer / Agent en chef des finances
Chief Information Officer / Directeur général de l'information
Chief Operating Officer / Administrateur en chef des opérations
Chief Administrative Officer / Directeur général de l'administration
Comptroller / Contrôleur
Authorized Signing Officer / Signataire autorisé
Other (Untitled) / Autre (sans titre)

*OTHER/AUTRE

Director Information/Renseignements relatifs aux administrateurs

Resident Canadian/ Résident canadien   YES/OUI   NO/NON   (Resident Canadian applies to directors of business corporations only.)/ (Résident canadien ne s'applique qu'aux administrateurs de sociétés par actions)

Date Elected/ Date d'élection   Year/Année Month/Mois Day/Jour   Date Ceased/ Date de cessation   Year/Année Month/Mois Day/Jour

Officer Information/Renseignements relatifs aux dirigeants

	PRESIDENT/PRÉSIDENT Year/Année Month/Mois Day/Jour	SECRETARY/SECRÉTAIRE Year/Année Month/Mois Day/Jour	TREASURER/TRÉSORIER Year/Année Month/Mois Day/Jour	GENERAL MANAGER/ DIRECTEUR GÉNÉRAL Year/Année Month/Mois Day/Jour	*OTHER/AUTRE Year/Année Month/Mois Day/Jour
Date Appointed/ Date de nomination					
Date Ceased/ Date de cessation					

RESOLUTION OF THE DIRECTORS

OF

IGGIE CORPORATION

1.   **LOCATION OF REGISTERED OFFICE**

BE IT RESOLVED THAT:

the location of the registered office of the Corporation be and the same is hereby changed to:

    68 Charger Road
    Toronto, Ontario
    M3K 4K6

    in the City of Toronto

THE FOREGOING RESOLUTION is hereby consented to by all of the directors of the Corporation, as evidenced by their respective signatures hereto in accordance with the provisions of section 129(1) of the *Business Corporations Act* (Ontario), this   day of November, 20--.

_____   _____
Nikky Sixx   Gene Symmons

SPECIAL RESOLUTION

OF

A.B.C. LETTERS LIMITED

1. CHANGE IN LOCATION OF REGISTERED OFFICE

BE IT RESOLVED AS A SPECIAL RESOLUTION OF THE CORPORATION THAT:

the geographic township or municipality within Ontario in which the registered office of the Corporation is located be and the same is hereby changed from the City of Toronto to the Regional Municipality of Durham in the Province of Ontario.

THE FOREGOING SPECIAL RESOLUTION is hereby consented to by all of the directors of the Corporation, as evidenced by their respective signatures hereto in accordance with the provisions of section 129(1) of the *Business Corporations Act* (Ontario), this   day of November, 20--.

_____   _____
Christopher Flannagan   Jonathan Cooper

THE FOREGOING SPECIAL RESOLUTION is hereby consented to and passed by all of the shareholders of the Corporation entitled to vote thereon at a meeting of shareholders, as evidenced by their respective signatures hereto in accordance with the provisions of section 104(1) of the *Business Corporations Act* (Ontario), this   day of November, 20--.

_____   _____
Christopher Flannagan   Jonathan Cooper

RESOLUTION OF THE DIRECTORS

OF

A.B.C. LETTERS LIMITED

1.   CHANGE OF LOCATION OF REGISTERED OFFICE

BE IT RESOLVED THAT:

the location of the registered office of the Corporation be and the same is hereby changed from:

> 123 Alphabet Street
> Toronto, Ontario
> M5H 3P5

> in the City of Toronto

to:

> 123 Clover Avenue
> Oshawa, Ontario
> L1G 4R7

> in the City of Oshawa
> in the Regional Municipality of Durham

THE FOREGOING RESOLUTION is hereby consented to by all of the directors of the Corporation, as evidenced by their respective signatures hereto in accordance with the provisions of section 129(1) of the *Business Corporations Act* (Ontario), this   day of November, 20--.

_____   _____
Christopher Flannagan   Jonathan Cooper

SPECIAL RESOLUTION

OF

METALIKA INC.

1.   CHANGE OF CORPORATE NAME

BE IT RESOLVED AS A SPECIAL RESOLUTION OF THE CORPORATION THAT:

the name of the Corporation be changed to:

MINE COPPER CORP.

and the directors and proper officers of the Corporation be and they are hereby authorized to do all things and execute all instruments and documents necessary or desirable to carry out the foregoing.

THE FOREGOING SPECIAL RESOLUTION is hereby consented to and passed by all of the shareholders of the Corporation entitled to vote thereon at a meeting of shareholders, as evidenced by their respective signatures hereto in accordance with the provisions of section 104(1) of the *Business Corporations Act* (Ontario), this   day of November, (year).

_____   _____
James Hetfeeld   Randy Roads

For Ministry Use Only
À l'usage exclusif du ministère

Ontario Corporation Number
Numéro de la société en Ontario

2011021

ARTICLES OF AMENDMENT
STATUTS DE MODIFICATION

Form 3
Business Corporations Act

Formule 3
Loi sur les sociétés par actions

1. The name of the corporation is: (Set out in BLOCK CAPITAL LETTERS)
   Dénomination sociale actuelle de la société (écrire en LETTRES MAJUSCULES SEULEMENT) :

M	E	T	A	L	I	K	A		I	N	C	.										

2. The name of the corporation is changed to (if applicable): (Set out in BLOCK CAPITAL LETTERS)
   Nouvelle dénomination sociale de la société (s'il y a lieu) (écrire en LETTRES MAJUSCULES SEULEMENT) :

M	I	N	E		C	O	P	P	E	R		C	O	R	P	.						

3. Date of incorporation/amalgamation:
   Date de la constitution ou de la fusion :
   20--, April, 21
   (Year, Month, Day)
   (année, mois, jour)

4. **Complete only if there is a change in the number of directors or the minimum / maximum number of directors.**
   Il faut remplir cette partie seulement si le nombre d'administrateurs ou si le nombre minimal ou maximal d'administrateurs a changé.

   Number of directors is/are: minimum and maximum number of directors is/are:
   Nombre d'administrateurs : nombres minimum et maximum d'administrateurs :

   | Number | minimum | and | maximum |
   | Nombre | minimum | et | maximum |

   [   ]   or / ou   [|]

5. The articles of the corporation are amended as follows:
   Les statuts de la société sont modifiés de la façon suivante :

   The name of the Corporation is hereby changed to Mine Copper Corp.

Document prepared using *Fast Company*, by Do Process Software Ltd., Toronto, Ontario
416.322.6111
866.367.7648

07119 (2008/06)

Page 1 of/de 2

6. The amendment has been duly authorized as required by sections 168 and 170 (as applicable) of the *Business Corporations Act*.
    La modification a été dûment autorisée conformément aux articles 168 et 170 (selon le cas) de la *Loi sur les sociétés par actions*.

7. The resolution authorizing the amendment was approved by the shareholders/directors (as applicable) of the corporation on
    Les actionnaires ou les administrateurs (selon le cas) de la société ont approuvé la résolution autorisant la modification le

20--, November, 08
_____
(Year, Month, Day)
(année, mois, jour)

These articles are signed in duplicate.
Les présents statuts sont signés en double exemplaire.

METALIKA INC.
_____
(Print name of corporation from Article 1 on page 1)
(Veuillez écrir le nom de la société de l'article un à la page une).

By/
Par:

_____   **President**
(Signature)   _____
(Signature)   (Description of Office)
                                        (Fonction)
"James Hetfeeld"

ocument prepared
ng *Fast Company*, by
Process Software Ltd.,
Toronto, Ontario
416.322.6111
866.367.7648

07119 (2008/06)

Page 2 of/de 2

RESOLUTIONS OF THE SHAREHOLDERS OF

RED LETTERS LIMITED

Amalgamation

RESOLVED, as special resolutions, THAT:

1. the Corporation is hereby authorized to amalgamate with 22 Numbers Limited upon the terms and conditions contained in an amalgamation agreement made as of the   day of August, 20--, between 22 Numbers Limited and the Corporation (the "Amalgamation Agreement");

2. any director or officer be and he is hereby authorized for and on behalf of the Corporation to execute the Amalgamation Agreement dated August   , 20--, and related Articles of Amalgamation with such alterations, additions, amendments or deletions as he may deem advisable, whose execution thereof shall be conclusive evidence of this and his approval to the Amalgamation Agreement and Articles of Amalgamation; and

3. any director or officer be and he is hereby authorized for and on behalf of the Corporation to execute and deliver all such other documents and to do all such other acts and things as may be necessary or desirable to give effect to the foregoing.

Pursuant to the provisions of the *Business Corporations Act* (Ontario), each and every of the foregoing resolutions are hereby signed by the shareholders of the Corporation.

DATED the   day of   , 20--.

_____   _____

_____   _____

Legal Office Procedures

THIS AMALGAMATION AGREEMENT entered into as of the   day of August, 20--.

BETWEEN:

RED LETTERS LIMITED,
a corporation incorporated under the laws of Ontario

(hereinafter called "RED")

OF THE FIRST PART

- and -

22 NUMBERS LIMITED,
a corporation incorporated under the laws of Ontario

(hereinafter called "22")

OF THE SECOND PART

WHEREAS RED and 22 are corporations to which the *Business Corporations Act* (Ontario) applies;

AND WHEREAS RED is authorized to issue an unlimited number of Class A Shares and an unlimited number of Class B Shares of which 100 Class A Shares are issued and outstanding;

AND WHEREAS 22 is authorized to issue an unlimited number of Class A Shares and an unlimited number of Class B Shares of which 100 Class A Shares are issued and outstanding;

AND WHEREAS the parties hereto, acting under the authority contained in the *Business Corporations Act* (Ontario), have agreed to amalgamate upon the terms and conditions set out hereunder.

NOW THEREFORE THIS AGREEMENT WITNESSETH as follows:

1)   **Definition**

In this agreement:

a)   **"Amalgamating Corporations"** means RED and 22;

b)   **"Amalgamation Agreement"** or **"Agreement"** means this amalgamation agreement;

c)   **"Act"** means the *Business Corporations Act* (Ontario);

d)   **"Corporation"** means the corporation continuing from the amalgamation of the Amalgamating Corporations;

e)   **"Effective Time"** means 12:01 a.m. on the Effective Date; and

f)   **"Effective Date"** means the date set out on the certificate endorsed by the Director appointed under the Act on the articles of amalgamation giving effect to the amalgamation herein provided for.

2)   **Agreement to Amalgamate**

The Amalgamating Corporations do hereby agree to amalgamate on the Effective Date under the provisions of the Act and to continue as one corporation upon the terms and conditions herein set out.

3)   **Name of Corporation**

The name of the Corporation shall be R2D2 Limited.

SCHEDULE A

The undersigned, Alexander Grate, being the President of Red Letters Limited, hereby states that:

1. There are reasonable grounds for believing that:

   (a) R2D2 Limited, the corporation continuing from the amalgamation of Red Letters Limited and 22 Numbers Limited (the "Amalgamated Corporation") will be able to pay its liabilities as they become due;

   (b) the realizable value of the Amalgamated Corporation's assets will not be less than the aggregate of its liabilities and stated capital of all classes;

   (c) no creditor will be prejudiced by the amalgamation; and

2. No creditor has notified RED that such creditor objects to the amalgamation.

   DATED this _____ day of _____, 20--.

   _____
   Alexander Grate

-4-

14) **Special Provisions**

(a) That the board of directors may from time to time, in such amounts and on such terms as it deems expedient:

   (i) borrow money on the credit of the Corporation;

(b) That subject to the provisions of the Business Corporations Act, the Corporation shall have a lien on the shares registered in the name of a shareholder who is indebted to the Corporation to the extent of such debt.

(c) That subject to the provisions of the Business Corporations Act, the Corporation may purchase any of its issued shares.

15) **Amalgamation**

   Upon the Effective Time:

a) the Amalgamating Corporations are amalgamated and continue as one corporation under the terms and conditions prescribed in the Amalgamation Agreement;

b) the Corporation possesses all the property, rights, privileges and franchises and is subject to all liabilities, including civil, criminal and quasi-criminal, and all contracts, disabilities and debts of each of the Amalgamating Corporations;

c) a conviction against, or ruling, order or judgment in favour or against either of the Amalgamating Corporations may be enforced by or against the Corporation;

d) the articles of amalgamation giving effect to the amalgamation herein provided for are deemed to be the articles of incorporation of the Corporation and, except for the purposes of subsection 117(1) of the Act, as may be amended from time to time, the certificate of amalgamation shall be deemed to be the certificate of incorporation of the Corporation;

e) the Corporation shall be deemed to be the party plaintiff or the party defendant, as the case may be, in any civil action commenced by or against either of the Amalgamating Corporations before the Effective Time.

16) **Termination**

   At any time before the Effective Time, this Amalgamation Agreement may be terminated by the directors of either of the Amalgamating Corporations, notwithstanding the approval of this Amalgamation Agreement by the shareholders of each of the Amalgamating Corporations.

   IN WITNESS WHEREOF this Agreement has been executed by the parties hereto as of the date and year first above written.

RED LETTERS LIMITED   **22 NUMBERS LIMITED**

Per: _____   Per: _____

I have authority to bind the Corporation.   I have authority to bind the Corporation.

1

For Ministry Use Only
À l'usage exclusif du ministère

Ontario Corporation Number
Numéro de la société en Ontario

1

Form 4
*Business
Corporations
Act*

*Formule 4
Loi sur les
sociétés par
actions*

ARTICLES OF AMALGAMATION
STATUTS DE FUSION

1. The name of the amalgamated corporation is: (Set out in BLOCK CAPITAL LETTERS)
Dénomination sociale de la société issue de la fusion: (Écrire en LETTRES MAJUSCULES SEULEMENT) :

R	2	D	2		L	I	M	I	T	E	D										

2. The address of the registered office is:
Adresse du siège social:

75 Wizards Road

Street & Number or R.R. Number & if Multi-Office Building give Room No. /
Rue et numéro ou numéro de la R.R. et, s'il s'agit d'un édifice à bureaux, numéro du bureau

Rainbow   ONTARIO | K | 5 | D | 2 | N | 3 |

Name of Municipality or Post Office /
Nom de la municipalité ou du bureau de poste   Postal Code/ *Code postal*

3. Number of directors is:
Nombre d'administrateurs :

Fixed number   **OR** minimum and maximum
Nombre fixe   **OU** *minimum et maximum* | 1 | 10 |

4. The director(s) is/are: / *Administrateur(s) :*

First name, middle names and surname *Prénom, autres prénoms et nom de famille*	Address for service, giving Street & No. or R.R. No., Municipality, Province, Country and Postal Code *Domicile élu, y compris la rue et le numéro ou le numéro de la R.R., le nom de la municipalité, la province, le pays et le code postal*	Resident Canadian State 'Yes' or 'No' *Résident canadien Oui/Non*
Alexander Grate	**57 Chevy Road** **Rainbow, Ontario K5T 9B6**	**Yes**
Melinda Melly	**90 Dahlia Road** **Rainbow, Ontario K5T 8B5**	**Yes**

Document prepared
using *Fast Company,* by
Do Process Software Ltd.,
Toronto, Ontario
416.322.6111
866.367.7648

07121E (05/2007)

3

6. Restrictions, if any, on business the corporation may carry on or on powers the corporation may exercise.
Limites, s'il y a lieu, imposées aux activités commerciales ou aux pouvoirs de la société.

None

7. The classes and any maximum number of shares that the corporation is authorized to issue:
Catégories et nombre maximal, s'il y a lieu, d'actions que la société est autorisée à émettre :

The Corporation is authorized to issue an unlimited number of Class A shares and an unlimited number of Class B shares.

Document prepared
using Fast Company, by
Do Process Software Ltd.
Toronto, Ontario
416.322.6111
866.367.7648

07121E (05/2007)

2

5. Method of amalgamation, check A or B
Méthode choisie pour la fusion - Cocher A ou B :

A - Amalgamation Agreement / *Convention de fusion :*

The amalgamation agreement has been duly adopted by the shareholders of each of the amalgamating corporations as required by subsection 176 (4) of the *Business Corporations Act* on the date set out below.
Les actionnaires de chaque société ont dûment adopté la convention de fusion conformément au paragraphe 176(4) de la Loi sur les sociétés par actions à la date mentionnée ci-dessous.

[X]

or
ou

B - Amalgamation of a holding corporation and one or more of its subsidiaries or amalgamation of subsidiaries / *Fusion d'une société mère avec une ou plusieurs de ses filiales ou fusion de filiales :*

[ ]

The amalgamation has been approved by the directors of each amalgamating corporation by a resolution as required by section 177 of the *Business Corporations Act* on the date set out below.
Les administrateurs de chaque société qui fusionne ont approuvé la fusion par voie de résolution conformément à l'article 177 de la Loi sur les sociétés par actions à la date mentionnée ci-dessous.

The articles of amalgamation in substance contain the provisions of the articles of incorporation of
Les statuts de fusion reprennent essentiellement les dispositions des statuts constitutifs de

Red Letters Limited

and are more particularly set out in these articles.
et sont énoncés textuellement aux présents statuts.

Names of amalgamating corporations *Dénomination sociale des sociétés qui fusionnent*	Ontario Corporation Number *Numéro de la société en Ontario*	Date of Adoption/Approval *Date d'adoption ou d'approbation*		
		Year *année*	Month *mois*	Day *jour*
Red Letters Limited	891011	*yyyy*/08/dd		
22 Numbers Limited	111098	*yyyy*/08/dd		

Document prepared
using Fast Company, by
Do Process Software Ltd.
Toronto, Ontario
416.322.6111
866.367.7648

07121E (05/2007)

5

9. The issue, transfer or ownership of shares is/is not restricted and the restrictions (if any) are as follows:
L'émission, le transfert ou la propriété d'actions est/n'est pas restreint. Les restrictions, s'il y a lieu, sont les suivantes :

The transfer of shares of the Corporation shall be restricted in that no shareholder shall be entitled to transfer any share or shares without either:

(a) The approval of the directors of the Corporation expressed by a resolution passed at a meeting of the board of directors or by an instrument or instruments in writing signed by a majority of the directors; or

(b) The approval of the holders of at least a majority of the shares of the Corporation entitling the holders thereof to vote in all circumstances (other than a separate class vote of the holders of another class of shares of the Corporation) for the time being outstanding expressed by a resolution passed at a meeting of the holders of such shares or by an instrument or instruments in writing signed by the holders of a majority of such shares.

10. Other provisions, (if any):
Autres dispositions, s'il y a lieu :

(a) That the board of directors may from time to time, in such amounts and on such terms as it deems expedient:

(i) borrow money on the credit of the Corporation;

(ii) issue, reissue, sell or pledge debt obligations (including bonds, debentures, notes or other evidences of indebtedness or guarantee, secured or unsecured) of the Corporation;

(iii) to the extent permitted by the Business Corporations Act (as from time to time amended) give directly or indirectly financial assistance to any person by means of a loan, a guarantee or otherwise on behalf of the Corporation to secure performance of any present or future indebtedness, liability or obligation of any person; and

(iv) charge, mortgage, hypothecate, pledge or otherwise create a security interest in all or any of the currently owned or subsequently acquired real or personal, movable or immovable property of the Corporation, franchises and undertaking, to secure any debt obligations or any money borrowed, or other debt or liability of the Corporation.

(b) To the extent permitted by the Business Corporations Act (as from time to time amended), that the board of directors may from time to time delegate to such one or more of the directors and officers of the Corporation as may be designated by the board

11. The statements required by subsection 178(2) of the Business Corporations Act are attached as Schedule "A".
Les déclarations exigées aux termes du paragraphe 178(2) de la Loi sur les sociétés par actions constituent l'annexe A.

12. A copy of the amalgamation agreement or directors' resolutions (as the case may be) is/are attached as Schedule "B".
Une copie de la convention de fusion ou les résolutions des administrateurs (selon le cas) constitue(nt) l'annexe B.

Document prepared
using Fast Company by
Do Process Software Ltd.,
Toronto, Ontario
416.322.6111
866.367.7648

07121E (05/2007)

4

8. Rights, privileges, restrictions and conditions (if any) attaching to each class of shares and directors authority with respect to any class of shares which may be issued in series:
Droits, privilèges, restrictions et conditions, s'il y a lieu, rattachés à chaque catégorie d'actions et pouvoirs des administrateurs relatifs à chaque catégorie d'actions qui peut être émise en série :

Not applicable.

Document prepared
using Fast Company by
Do Process Software Ltd.,
Toronto, Ontario
416.322.6111
866.367.7648

07121E (05/2007)

5A

10. continued

all or any of the powers conferred on the board above to such extent and in such manner as the board shall determine at the time of each such delegation.

(c) That the outstanding securities of the Corporation are beneficially owned, directly or indirectly, by not more than fifty persons or companies, exclusive of:

(i) persons or companies that are, or at the time they last acquired securities of the Corporation were, accredited investors (as defined under applicable Ontario securities laws, as may be amended from time to time); and

(ii) current or former directors, officers or employees of the Corporation or a corporation, company, syndicate, partnership, trust or unincorporated organization (each, an "Entity") affiliated (as defined under applicable Ontario securities laws, as may be amended from time to time) with the Corporation, or current or former consultants (as defined under applicable Ontario securities laws, as may be amended from time to time), who in each case beneficially own only securities of the Corporation that were issued as compensation by, or under an incentive plan of, the Corporation or an Entity affiliated with the Corporation;

provided that:

(A) two or more persons who are the joint registered holders of one or more securities of the Corporation shall be counted as one beneficial owner of those securities; and

(B) an Entity shall be counted as one beneficial owner of the securities of the Corporation unless such Entity has been created or is being used primarily for the purpose of acquiring or holding securities of the Corporation, in which event each beneficial owner of an equity interest in the Entity or each beneficiary of the Entity, as the case may be, shall be counted as a separate beneficial owner of those securities of the Corporation.

(d) That subject to the provisions of the Business Corporations Act, the Corporation shall have a lien on the shares registered in the name of a shareholder who is indebted to the Corporation to the extent of such debt.

(e) That subject to the provisions of the Business Corporations Act, the Corporation may purchase any of its issued shares.

Document prepared using *Fast Company*, by Do Process Software Ltd. Toronto, Ontario 416.322.6111 866.367.7648

0712IE (05/2007)

6

These articles are signed in duplicate.
Les présents statuts sont signés en double exemplaire.

Name and original signature of a director or authorized signing officer of each of the amalgamating corporations. Include the name of each corporation, the signatories name and description of office (e.g. president, secretary). Only a director or authorized signing officer can sign on behalf of the corporation. *Indiquer la dénomination sociale de chaque société, le nom du signataire et sa foction (p. ex. : président, secrétaire). Seul un administrateur ou un dirigeant habilité peut signer au nom de la société*

RED LETTERS LIMITED

Names of Corporations / *Dénomination sociale des sociétés*

By / *Par* _____

Signature / *Signature* _____
Print name of signatory / *Nom du signataire en lettres moulées*

Description of Office / *Fonction* _____

22 NUMBERS LIMITED

Names of Corporations / *Dénomination sociale des sociétés*

By / *Par* _____

Signature / *Signature* _____
Print name of signatory / *Nom du signataire en lettres moulées*

Description of Office / *Fonction* _____

Names of Corporations / *Dénomination sociale des sociétés*

By / *Par* _____

Signature / *Signature* _____
Print name of signatory / *Nom du signataire en lettres moulées*

Description of Office / *Fonction* _____

Names of Corporations / *Dénomination sociale des sociétés*

By / *Par* _____

Signature / *Signature* _____
Print name of signatory / *Nom du signataire en lettres moulées*

Description of Office / *Fonction* _____

Document prepared using *Fast Company*, by Do Process Software Ltd. Toronto, Ontario 416.322.6111 866.367.7648

0712IE (05/2007)

Legal Office Procedures

CHAPTER **29**

CORPORATE AND COMMERCIAL LAW

Buying a cup of coffee and borrowing money to pay for it are types of commercial activities. This chapter covers basic principles of corporate and commercial law, including security agreements under the *Personal Property Security Act* (PPSA) and liens under the *Repair and Storage Liens Act* (RSLA).

CORPORATE AND COMMERCIAL LAW

Corporate and commercial law is business law. It aims to protect businesses and consumers against losses and unfair business practices. Generally, corporate and commercial law deals with buying, selling, financing, and securing movable property known as **personal property**. The Companies and Personal Property Security Branch of the Ministry of Government and Consumer Services administers matters relating to personal property security.

What is personal property   Personal property is almost any property that is not real estate: for example, cars, businesses, and equipment. Personal property is also referred to as **chattels**. The key distinction between personal property and real estate, or real property, i.e. land, is that personal property is movable and real estate is not. The PPSA defines personal property thus:

> "personal property" means chattel paper, documents of title, goods, instruments, intangibles, money and investment property, and includes fixtures but does not include building materials that have affixed to real property.

The items included in the above definition may be categorized as tangible, intangible, and documents:

Tangible includes goods such as furniture, appliances, and automobiles. Because these goods are used for personal, family, or household purposes, they are referred to as "consumer goods" and are given special protection under the PPSA.

Intangible includes copyrights, trademarks, and goodwill.

Documents include chattel paper (basically, a document giving the seller the right to goods sold on credit), documents of title (e.g., transfers/deeds), instruments (e.g. IOU, letters of credit), securities (e.g. shares), leases, and charges/mortgages.

FINANCING PERSONAL PROPERTY

In addition to buying and selling personal property, corporate and commercial law deals extensively with borrowing to pay for the purchase of personal property. This is known as **financing**. There are two common methods of financing: (l) the buyer borrows money from a lending institution; (2) the buyer buys the goods on credit directly from the seller.

Buying by borrowing from lending institution When the seller requires payment in cash for the goods and the buyer does not have the money, the buyer borrows the money, usually from a bank, pays the seller, and then pays back the bank, usually by making monthly payments of a set amount, over a period of time.

Buying on credit from the seller When the buyer buys on credit from the seller, the seller does not require payment in cash from the buyer. Instead, the seller lets the buyer take possession of the goods and requires the buyer to pay back the purchase price directly to the seller, usually by making monthly payments of a set amount, over a period of time.

BASIC PRINCIPLES OF CONTRACT LAW

The following basic principles of contract law will help you understand how contracts work and why the law might interpret them the way it does. Business contracts, written or verbal, are business tools that enable people to legally rely on the business promises they make. If people breach their contracts, they may be sued and ordered to comply; however, the law offers this protection only if the contract is valid. To be valid, a contract must contain the following elements:

1. An offer and acceptance: "I would like to order a hot dog, please." (Offer) "OK." (Acceptance).
2. Consideration: Includes an exchange of goods (car), service (work done), and/or money, e.g. price of the hot dog.
3. Capacity: The parties must be of legal age and of clear mind.
4. Consent: There must be no misrepresentation, force (duress), or undue influence.
5. Legal purpose: There must be no criminal intent.

CONTRACTUAL RELATIONSHIPS

To protect businesses and consumers against unscrupulous dealings, the law deems buying and selling to be a commercial activity based on the above contract elements. The offer and acceptance may be verbal or written, and the contract is deemed to be in effect as of the moment the offer is accepted. Ownership of the goods purchased usually passes when the buyer is in possession of the goods. To dissuade frivolous cancellations, however, ownership technically passes when the goods are **ready for delivery**. The buyer must pay for the goods after receiving them, and this is consistent with the general business principle of "payment follows service." A breach of these contract elements entitles the wronged party to sue for damages. Once the contract is formed, certain standard terms known as **conditions** and **warranties** usually come into effect to protect the buyer.

Conditions and warranties Conditions are more serious terms than warranties in that, if the seller breaches them, the contract could be terminated. Examples of conditions include: the seller must have the right to sell the goods, e.g. the goods must not be stolen; the quality, quantity, date, and place of delivery must be as the buyer specifies. By contrast, if the seller breaches a warranty, the buyer may demand that the seller correct the breach and sue for any loss resulting from the breach, but the contract continues. An example of a warranty is the seller must sell debt-free goods, e.g. the buyer must not inherit the seller's debts on the goods.

COMMERCIAL CONTRACTS

Modern business activity has been described as "a bundle of contracts." The terms "contract" and "agreement" are interchangeable. There are endless types of contracts, including partnership agreements, employment contracts, shareholder agreements, and security agreements. Another frequently used commercial contract is a real estate lease agreement. A real estate lease agreement, also referred to as a commercial lease, is a contract that spells out the rights and obligations between a landlord and a tenant. In a lease, the lessee agrees to pay the lessor a certain amount of rent money on regular dates, usually monthly, in return for the right to exclusive use of the leased property for a specified length of time: for example, retailers, manufacturers, and lawyers often lease the premises on which they carry on business. Leases for offices, commercial buildings, and stores in shopping malls can be of considerable length– up to fifty or a hundred pages is not uncommon. See Precedent 29.1 for a partial sample of a commercial lease.

SECURITY AGREEMENTS

A security agreement is an agreement which pledges personal property, e.g. a car, as security (guarantee) for a loan. Personal property that is used as security for a loan is also referred to as **collateral**, or collateral security. In the event the borrower defaults in paying back the loan, the creditor, e. g. a bank, may take and sell the personal property e.g. a car, to recover payment. Following is a brief description of various types of security agreements, some of which are included in the **general security agreement**, Precedent 29.2:

Equipment   This type of security involves business equipment. A simple example of how a security agreement on business equipment would be created is as follows: Tom sells a business to Jerry for $500,000. Jerry can only pay $400,000 toward the purchase price and gives Tom a security agreement (a promise to pay) for the remaining $100,000, pledging the business equipment as security. Thus, if Jerry defaults in paying back the $100,000, Tom can seize Jerry's business equipment to recover the debt because, even though Jerry is in possession of the business equipment, the security agreement gives Tom the legal right to take the business equipment for non-payment.

Intangibles and book debts   Generally, this type of security involves pledging accounts receivable as security, which means a borrower transfers over to a lender, e.g. a bank, the borrower's rights to his or her accounts receivable. Accounts receivable are moneys that other business people owe to the borrower: for a simple example, if Jerry sold toys to Tom, the money Tom owes and has not yet paid on the invoices for the toys is Jerry's accounts receivable. If Jerry were to pledge the accounts receivable as security for a bank loan, Jerry would have to sign over his rights to his accounts receivable to the bank. Upon Jerry's default of payment to the bank, all of Jerry's accounts receivable moneys from Tom would go to the bank instead of Jerry.

Chattel paper   Generally, chattel paper is a contract prepared when goods are sold on credit. Chattel papers usually involve two transactions. The first transaction is where buyer A takes possession of the goods, and seller B retains a security interest in the goods in case buyer A defaults in payment. In this case, the **goods** are the collateral. The second transaction is one in which the **chattel paper** itself becomes the collateral. For example, after the chattel paper has been generated, seller B (the holder of the chattel paper) uses the chattel paper as security for obtaining a loan from the bank. Seller B assigns the chattel paper to the bank in return for the loan. The bank is then the secured party, and the chattel paper is security for the loan. Should seller B default in his payment obligation to the bank, the bank will usually look to the **buyer**, e.g. buyer A, to fulfill the payment obligation evidenced by the chattel paper. Therefore, before seller B's default to the bank, seller B has the right to the payments from buyer A. After seller B defaults in payment to the bank, the bank has the right to the payments from buyer A.

Security agreement on non-inventory purchase money (conditional sale contract)   Generally, this type of security is like a conditional sale contract where goods are purchased on credit, usually on an instalment plan. The buyer takes possession of the goods on the **condition** that the seller retain the legal title, or ownership, of the goods until the buyer pays the purchase price in full. Automobiles, furniture, appliances, and industrial equipment are often sold on the basis of conditional sale contracts. Upon default in payment, the seller is entitled to repossess and sell the goods to recover the amount owing.

PERSONAL PROPERTY SECURITY REGISTRATION (PPSR) SYSTEM

The Companies and Personal Property Security Branch of the Ontario Ministry of Government and Consumer Services operates a computer-based **personal property security registration (PPSR) system**. The PPSR system handles electronic filings under the *Personal Property Security Act* (PPSA) and the *Repair and Storage Liens Act* (RSLA).

The PPSR system is a public database and notice-filing system that records information concerning loans where goods and other personal property (not real estate) are pledged as security (guarantee) for loans. For example, if you buy a car and borrow money from a bank to pay for it, the bank will have you sign an agreement, known as a security agreement, which gives the bank rights to the car if you do not repay the loan. You would be known as a **debtor** and the bank as a **creditor**. The bank would register in the PPSR system a document known as **financing statement**. A financing statement is a notice to the public that you owe money to the bank and that the bank has priority in claiming payment from you over other creditors to whom you might owe money. The creditor registered first has first priority, followed by the creditor registered second, etc.

If you were to take your car in for repairs, the automobile repair shop has the right to retain possession of your car until you pay for the repair services provided. If the automobile repair shop gives up possession of the car before you pay for the repairs done, the automobile repair shop may register a **claim for lien** in the PPSR system to protect its interests in the car. Should you fail to pay the amount owing for the repair services, the registered claim for lien gives the automobile repair shop the right to have the sheriff seize the car in order to sell it to satisfy the lien.

Anyone can check in the system to see if there are any prior registrations on the personal property he or she is about to buy or lend money. For example, if you were to buy a pre-owned (used) car, or other used goods, you would want to do a PPSA search to see if the seller, or a previous owner, has pledged the car as security for a loan, or if an automobile repair shop has registered a claim for lien. If so, it means the car is indebted, and if you were to go through with purchasing it, you would be responsible for both of the debts (the loan and the lien) registered on it. You would be responsible for both debts even if you did not know before buying the car that it was indebted; since you did not know about the debts, you are not likely to make any payments toward the debts; thus, the bank and or the automobile repair shop could seize your car for non-payment.

ELECTRONIC REGISTRATION

The PPSR system is a fully electronic, paperless registration system. All PPSA and RSLA registrations are done only online via the ministry's **Access Now** website. To use the Access Now service, your firm must have a web account with the ministry. The ministry provides your firm with a user ID, password, and an account number which you require in order to access the online service. Electronic registration is accomplished by completing the following dual use electronic forms online only (paper forms of these forms are not available), as applicable:

- **financing statement/claim for lien, Form 1C**
- **financing change statement/change statement, Form 2C**

Private Service Providers   There are private service providers (PSPs) under contract with the ministry who can do PPSA electronic registrations for a fee: for example, the financing statement/claim for lien, Form 1C, in Precedent 29.3 has been prepared online through the website of OnCorp Direct Inc., a PSP, and the financing change statement/change statement, Form 2C, Precedent 29.4, has been prepared online through the website of Cyberbahn, a PSP. Once you enter the applicable data on, say, a financing statement/claim for lien, Form 1C, and submit the form online, you will almost instantly receive back a confirmation from the ministry containing a PPSA reference number which you must use when you file a financing change statement/change statement, Form 2C, on the same matter.

Here is a summary of how the electronic forms of the financing statement/claim for lien, Form 1C, and financing change statement/change statement, Form 2C, are used under the PPSA and the RSLA:

ELECTRONIC FORMS AND USES UNDER PPSA/RSLA			
Financing Statement/Claim for Lien, Form 1C		**Financing Change Statement/Change Statement, Form 2C**	
PPSA	RSLA	PPSA	RSLA
Financing Statement To register security interests	Claim for Lien To register claims for lien	Financing Change Statement To register • changes, renewals or discharges of previously registered financing statements	Change Statement To register • changes, renewals or discharges of previously registered claims for lien

FINANCING STATEMENT/CLAIM FOR LIEN, FORM 1C

The **financing statement/claim for lien, Form 1C,** is a dual purpose form. It is used as a **financing statement** when registering under the PPSA and as a **claim for lien** when registering under the RSLA.

FINANCING STATEMENT, FORM 1C

Security agreements almost always involve some form of financing, i.e. borrowing money, which is why the form used to register a security interest is called a **financing** statement, Precedent 29.3. The financing statement, when registered, serves as a public notice that the lender, say, a bank, holds a security agreement which the borrower has signed as a guarantee for a loan and that the bank has priority for payment over other creditors to whom the borrower might owe money. The financing statement is a public notice of the **existence** of the security agreement; it is not the security agreement itself. That is why the information required on a financing statement is only that which serves the purpose of a public notice: for example, in the case of a car loan, only the following information would be entered on the financing statement, and not the full details of the security agreement:

- borrower's name, address, and date of birth
- bank's name and address
- registration period
- classification of the collateral (the car) as consumer goods
- principal amount of the loan and date of maturity
- description of the car, including the motor vehicle identification number (VIN)

Valid period of registration   Every financing statement must indicate a registration period. The PPSA provides two registration period options--one for such period of years as is set out in the financing statement, and the other for a **perpetual** period indicated by the number **99**.

CLAIM FOR LIEN

What is a lien   A lien is a debt against a person's personal or real property for work or services done on either personal or real property. Individuals who provide labour or service may use liens as a means of securing payment for money owing to them. Generally, if the work or service is done on personal property, the individual or business providing the work or service may register a **claim for lien** under the *Repair and Storage Liens Act* in the Companies and Personal Property Security Branch of the Ministry of Government and Consumer Services.

Repair and Storage Liens Act   Under this act, there are **possessory** and **non-possessory** liens. A possessory lien is one where the person or business providing the repair or storage service is in possession of the article being repaired or stored, as for example, where an auto repair shop holds the owner's car until the owner pays for the repair costs. In this case, possession of the vehicle serves as security, and registration of a claim for lien would normally be unnecessary. A non-possessory lien means the person or business providing the repair or storage service has released the article, e.g. the car, on condition that the owner sign an acknowledgment of indebtedness, e.g. an invoice, and that he or she will pay the invoice. In addition to obtaining a signed acknowledgment, the non-possessory lien claimant must also register electronically a claim for lien in order to fully protect a lien interest in the article. Should the non-possessory lien claimant remain unpaid, the RSLA allows the non-possessory lien claimant to have the sheriff seize the article from the owner in order to sell it, or keep it, to satisfy the lien.

Construction Lien Act   Under this act, a right to a construction lien attaches as soon as the work begins, but the right ceases unless the individual or business doing the work registers a claim for lien, usually within forty-five days from the date the work is substantially completed.

Because the work was done on real property (as opposed to personal property), the individual or business doing the work must register the claim for lien on the **real property** on which the work was done, using a claim for lien under the *Construction Lien Act*.

CLAIM FOR LIEN, FORM 1C

Use the electronic form of the **financing statement/claim for lien, Form 1C,** as a **claim for lien** to register a repair or storage debt. Claims for lien are registered under the RSLA. There are no security agreements under the RSLA since the lien is for repair or storage services rendered and does not involve a loan. Proof of the debt is usually the invoice for the repair work done or for the storage services provided or a signed acknowledgment of indebtedness.

Valid period of registration The registration period for claims for lien is one to three years. The period restriction is for purposes of preventing unnecessarily lengthy registration periods against debtors. Registrations may be renewed only for a one-time total of three years; for example, if the original registration is for less than three years, the period may be renewed usually only until it reaches a total of three years.

FINANCING CHANGE STATEMENT/CHANGE STATEMENT, FORM 2C

Use this form as a **financing change statement, Form 2C**, Precedent 29.4, to make changes to a previously registered financing statement, Form 1C. Use it as a **change statement, Form 2C,** when making changes to a previously registered claim for lien, Form 1C. Thus, it is a financing change statement when registered under the PPSA and a change statement when registered under RSLA. Think of it as the document which corrects and updates an original registration.

CHANGES UNDER THE PPSA

Renewals Sometimes the debtor and the secured party renegotiate deals where they extend the original term of the debt, giving the debtor a longer than the original period to pay off the debt. To register a renewal under the PPSA, the secured party files a **financing change statement, Form 2C**. Generally, renewals add to the original period: for example, if the original registration period is ten years, and after eight years, the secured party registers a renewal of four years, the total registration period is fourteen years (10 original + 4 by renewal). The total unexpired period is six years.

Discharges When a consumer loan is repaid, the lender is required to register a discharge within thirty days by electronically filing a **financing change statement, Form 2C**. Generally, with registration periods other than perpetual registrations, if no discharge is registered, the registration will remain in the PPSR system until the end of the registration period. With the perpetual option, however, the secured party must register a discharge by filing electronically a **financing change statement, Form 2C,** once the debt has been repaid.

CHANGES UNDER THE RSLA

Discharge Register a discharge by use of a **change statement, Form 2C,** when the lien is paid in full. If no discharge is registered, the registration will remain in the PPSR system until the end of the registration period.

PPSA ENQUIRIES (SEARCHES)

A PPSA enquiry is commonly referred to as a **PPSA search**. It involves searching the system records to ensure the goods your client is buying, e.g. used car, or is accepting as security, are not subject to prior security interests: for example, if your lender client discovers prior security interests, the client might wish to reconsider lending because the previously registered secured party has priority for payment. Similarly, if there are prior security interests on the used car your client is buying, your client might lose the car because someone else owes money on it. Note, however, that a PPSA search is usually not required when buying a new car or other new goods from a dealer (as opposed to buying privately from an individual). Also, a PPSA search is not usually required when buying a used car from a registered motor vehicle dealer (as opposed to buying privately from an individual).

How to make the search Searches may be made online or by telephone. The PPSR system is indexed by debtor name; therefore, make enquiries against the debtor's name.

Debtor is a business If the debtor is a corporation, search the name of the corporation. If the debtor is a partnership, do a search against the registered partnership name. If the debtor carries on business under a trade name, also search against the trade name. A search against trade names catches any registrations that might have been made only in the trade name, as opposed to the official name, of the debtor. The search reports on the name of the business debtor you specified, as well as on any similar names: for example, XYZ LIMITED, XYZ LTD., and XYZ COMPANY LTD.

Debtor is an individual There are two types of individual name searches – an individual specific search or an individual non-specific search.

Specific search For a specific search against an individual, you must supply the first given name, initial of second given name, if any, and surname and date of birth. The results of this type of search will disclose only registrations against the exact name and date of birth.

Non-specific search For a non-specific search, give only the first given name and surname. The non-specific search is useful when you are not sure about the individual's second given name or birth date. The results of this type of search will also disclose only registrations against the exact name searched, but usually will also include the second name initial and birth date: for example, if you searched against JAMES BLOND, the report includes JAMES A. BLOND born OCT 31, 1975; JAMES B. BLOND born JAN 01, 1988, etc.

VIN Because motor vehicles are frequently pledged as collateral, the system also indexes by vehicle identification number (VIN). The vehicle identification number is the number the car manufacturer gives to the vehicle (usually found on a plate located on the dashboard). Thus, if the collateral includes a motor vehicle, make the enquiry against the debtor as well as against the VIN.

CHAPTER SUMMARY

Corporate and commercial law is business law. Business and commercial contracts form a large part of corporate and commercial law. To be valid, a contract must consist of an offer and an acceptance and an exchange of goods or money, and there must be no misrepresentation or force.

The buying, selling, or leasing of personal property often involves borrowing money which, in turn, involves security agreements. Security agreements pledge personal property as security for a loan. The lender may register his or her security interest in an electronic public database and notice filing system called **Personal Property Security Registration (PPSR) System** which the Companies and Personal Property Security Branch of the Ministry of Government and Consumer Services operates. The PPSR system also provides an electronic search mechanism for the purpose of checking whether or not the personal property in question has been already pledged as security.

Liens are debts which individuals or businesses can register electronically to secure payment for work or service that they provide. Liens for work or storage services are registered under the *Repair and Storage Liens Act;* liens for work done on real property are registered under the *Construction Lien Act*. All registrations are done electronically by filing an electronic form called a financing statement/claim for lien. It is a financing statement when filing under the PPSA and a claim for lien when filing under the RSLA.

REVIEW QUESTIONS

1. What is personal property?
2. What are the basic elements of a valid contract?
3. If you signed a security agreement with a bank pledging your Ford car as security for a loan,
   (a) which document would the bank register to ensure priority in payment against any other of your creditors?
   (b) where would such a document be registered?
   (c) under which statute would the document be registered?
   (d) which specific details would be included in the document to be registered?
4. How are changes to previous PPSA and RSLA registrations made?
5. What does the term **financing** mean?
6. What is the difference between claims under the PPSA and RSLA?
7. A VIN is an abbreviation for good wine.   Yes_____   No_____
8. What is the purpose of a PPSA search?
9. What is a PPSA non-specific search?
10. You bought a used BMW car from an individual, unaware of the existence of a registered debt on it:
    (a) would you or the seller be responsible for the debt on the car?
    (b) what would happen if the debt remained unpaid?
    (c) what could you have done prior to purchasing the car to discover the debt on it?

CONDOMINIUM UNIT LEASE AGREEMENT

THIS AGREEMENT made this   Day of   20–

In pursuance of the *Short Form of Leases Act*, the *Commercial Tenancies Act*, and the *Condominium Act of Ontario*

BETWEEN:

LAVENDER PROPERTIES LIMITED

(the "Lessor")

-and-

LIME LIGHTS INC.

(the "Lessee")

In consideration of the rents, covenants, and agreements hereinafter reserved and contained on the part of the Lessee to be paid, observed, and performed, the Lessor hereby leases unto the Lessee all those certain premises known as Unit 8, Level 1, York Region Condominium Plan No. 777, in the Town of Richmond Hill, Ontario, in the Regional Municipality of York, and its appurtenant common interests (hereinafter called the "unit"), comprising 2,025 square feet, more or less and known municipally as 77 Victory Avenue, #8, Richmond Hill, Ontario, forming part of a condominium building complex (hereinafter called the "building") upon the following terms and conditions:

1. TERM

The Lessee shall have and shall hold the unit for and during the terms of three (3) years, commencing from March 2, 20– to March 1, 20–.

2. DEPOSIT

The Lessee agrees to deposit with the Lessor the sum of $4,784.07 to be applied towards the first and last month's base and additional rent plus HST. If the Lessee abandons or vacates the premises, or this lease should be terminated or the Lessor should re-enter the unit by reason of the default of the Lessee, at any time prior to the expiration of the term of the lease, the Lessor shall be permitted to retain absolutely the aforesaid sum of money so deposited with the Lessor.

3. BASE RENTAL AND ADDITIONAL RENTAL

Rental Year	Base Rate Per Square Foot	Base Rent Per Annum	Monthly Net Rent Plus HST
Year 1	$8.00	$16,200.00	$1,350.00
Year 2	$8.25	$16,706.25	$1,392.19
Year 3	$8.50	$17,212.50	$1,343.38

The Lessee shall pay its proportionate share of realty taxes, outside maintenance, building insurance, and management fee, taxes maintenance & insurance (T.M.I.), currently estimated to be $5.25 per square foot per annum as per the following:

(a) All monthly common expenses as may be varied from time to time and as the same fall due levied by the Condominium Corporation and all extraordinary or special assessments levied or assessed by the Condominium Corporation. One twelfth (1/12) of this amount shall be paid to the Lessor monthly in advance at the same time as the rental payments. When the final tax and maintenance bill is received, there shall be an adjustment based upon the actual costs for the period.

-2-

(b) The cost of all utilities and other services, all insurance premiums and all other costs with respect to the maintenance, operation, repair, replacement and upkeep of the unit and its proportionate share of such cost with respect to the building and the common areas, including, without limiting the generality of the foregoing, the cost of outside maintenance, law, and shrubbery maintenance and snow removal, except to the extent that any such costs are included in the amounts paid by the Lessee under subsection (a) above.

The foregoing amounts shall be due and payable to the Lessor in the same manner and on the same days and times as base rental. The Lessor shall notify the Lessee of any changes in the monthly common expenses.

4. CHATTEL AND PERSONAL PROPERTY WITHIN THE UNIT

All chattels and personal property located or stored in the unit and/or the common elements shall be kept and stored at the Lessee's sole risk and expense and the Lessee shall indemnify and hold harmless the Lessor from and against any loss or damage to such property arising out of any cause whatsoever. The Lessor shall not be liable, for any injury, damage or loss resulting from any accident or occurrence in or upon the unit or the common elements or both sustained by the Lessee or any person through the Lessee.

5. ELECTRICAL AND MECHANICAL EQUIPMENT IN GOOD ORDER

The Lessor warrants that the existing fixtures, sprinklers, electrical systems, heating and air-conditioning equipment and all other utilities will be in good working order on the occupancy date. The Lessee agrees to maintain said fixtures systems heating and air-conditioning units during the lease term and agrees to the repairs only due to any damages caused by negligence of the tenant or its employees, trades or invitees are to be the Tenant's responsibility. The Lessee shall be allowed thirty (30) days after the date of commencement to report any deficiencies to the Lessor. The Lessor at its expense shall promptly arrange for those repairs.

31. OPTION TO RENEW

Provided the Lessee is not in default and is observing and performing all of the terms and conditions of this lease, and provided the Lessee has not been in material default of any obligations under this lease, the Lessee shall, upon written request, mailed to the Lessor at least four (4) months prior to the expiration of the term be entitled to renew for a further term of three (3) years, commencing...

IN WITNESS WHEREOF the parties have executed this agreement.

LAVENDER PROPERTIES LIMITED

Per:_____
      Lessor

LIME LIGHTS INC.

Per:_____
      Lessee

-3-

10. Upon any default under this security agreement, the secured party may declare any or all of the obligations to be immediately due and payable and may proceed to realize the security constituted under this security agreement and to enforce the debtor's rights by entry or by the appointment by instrument in writing of a receiver or receivers of the subject matter of such security or any part of such security and such receiver or receivers may be any person or persons. The secured party may remove any receiver or receivers so appointed and appoint another or others in the place and stead of such receiver or receivers; or by proceedings in any court of competent jurisdiction for the appointment of a receiver or receivers or for sale of the collateral or any part of it; or by any other action, suit, remedy, or proceeding authorized or permitted by this security agreement or by law or by equity. The secured party may file such proofs of claim and other documents as may be necessary or advisable in order to have its claim lodged in any bankruptcy, winding-up, or other judicial proceedings relative to the debtor. Any such receiver or receivers so appointed shall have power to take possession of the collateral or any part of it and to carry on the business of the debtor, and to borrow money required for the maintenance, preservation, or protection of the collateral or any part of it, or the carrying on of the business of the debtor, and to further charge the collateral in priority to the security constituted by this security agreement as security for money so borrowed, and to sell, lease, or otherwise dispose of the whole or any part of the collateral on such terms and conditions and in such manner as the receiver or receivers shall determine. In exercising any powers, any such receiver or receivers shall act as agent or agents for the debtor, and the secured party shall not be responsible for the actions of such receiver or receivers.

In addition, the secured party may enter upon and lease or sell the whole or any part or parts of the collateral. The debtor agrees that, considering the nature of that part of the collateral that is not perishable, it will be commercially reasonable to sell such part of the collateral as a whole or in various lots; and by a public sale or call for tenders or by private sale.

Any such sale shall be on such terms and conditions as to credit or otherwise and as to upset or reserve bid or price as to the secured party in the secured party's sole discretion may seem advantageous, and such sale may take place whether or not the secured party has taken possession of such property and assets.

No remedy for the realization of the security of this security agreement or for the enforcement of the rights of the secured party shall be exclusive of, or dependent on, any other such remedy, but any one or more of such remedies may, from time to time, be exercised independently or in combination. The term "receiver" as used in this security agreement includes a receiver and manager.

11. The debtor agrees to pay all reasonable expenses, including solicitor's fees and disbursements, and the remuneration of any receiver appointed under this security agreement, incurred by the secured party in the preparation, perfection, and enforcement of this security agreement, and the payment of such expenses shall be secured by this security agreement.

12. The secured party may waive any default referred to in this security agreement, provided always that no act or omission by the secured party in the premises shall extend to, or be taken in any manner whatsoever, to affect any subsequent default or the rights resulting from such default.

13. The debtor warrants and acknowledges that the debtor and the secured party intend each of the security interests in this security agreement to attach upon the execution of this security agreement and that value has been given and that the debtor has rights in the collateral.

14. The security under this agreement is in addition to and not in substitution for any other security now or in the future held by the secured party and shall be general and continuing security, notwithstanding that the obligations of the debtor shall, at any time, or from time to time, be fully satisfied or paid.

15. This security agreement shall enure to the benefit of and be binding upon the respective heirs, executors, administrators, successors, and assigns of the debtor and the secured party.

16. The debtor acknowledges receipt of a copy of this security agreement.

This security agreement has been executed by the debtor on the _____ day of _____ (year).

TERRIFIC BUSINESS LIMITED
Per:

SECURITY AGREEMENT

(In all underlying assets of a business as a going concern, under the PPSA)

TERRIFIC BUSINESS LIMITED of 57 Abby Road, Toronto, Ontario, M6K 3H3, (the "debtor") enters into this security agreement with DENNISON COMPANY INCORPORATED of 88 Beaver Street, Toronto, Ontario, M7P 4G5, (the "secured party") for valuable consideration and as security for the repayment of all present and future indebtedness of the debtor to the secured party and interest on such indebtedness, and for the payment and discharge of all other present and future liabilities and obligations, direct or indirect, absolute or contingent, of the debtor to the secured party. All of such indebtedness, interest, costs, liabilities, and obligations are collectively referred to as "obligations."

This security agreement is entered into pursuant to and is governed by the *Personal Property Security Act (Ontario)* insofar as it affects personal property located in Ontario.

1. The debtor represents and warrants to the secured party that the debtor has assets at the following locations in Ontario:

57 Abby Road, Toronto, Ontario.

2. The debtor:

(Where security is not granted on all four kinds of security in clauses (a) to (d), adapt to suit the new situation by deleting the inapplicable clauses and the references in the agreement. The rest of the agreement would be the same.)

Equipment (a) mortgages and charges to the secured party as and by way of a fixed and specific mortgage and charge, and grants to the secured party a security interest in all its present and future equipment and any proceeds from such equipment, including, without limiting the generality of the foregoing, all computer hardware and software, telephone system, all fixtures, machinery, tools, and all furniture now or in the future owned or acquired and any equipment specifically listed or otherwise described in any schedule to this security agreement;

Inventory (b) mortgages and charges to the secured party and grants to the secured party a security interest in all of the debtor's present and future inventory and any proceeds from such inventory, including, without limiting the generality of the foregoing, all raw materials, goods in process, finished goods and packaging material, and goods acquired or held for sale or furnished or to be furnished under contracts or rental or service;

Intangibles and Book Debts (c) assigns, transfers, and sets over to the secured party a security interest in all of the debtor's present and future intangibles and any proceeds from such intangibles, including, without limiting the generality of the foregoing, all of the debtor's present and future book debts and other accounts receivable, chattel paper, contract rights, and other choses in action of every kind or nature now due or in future to become due, including insurance rights arising from or out of the assets referred to in sub-clauses (a) and (b) above, and all goodwill, patents, trademarks, copyrights, trade names, and other industrial and intellectual property now or in the future owned by the debtor; and

Floating Charge (d) charges in favour of the secured party, as and by way of a floating charge, the debtor's undertaking and all of the debtor's property and assets, real and personal, moveable or immoveable, of whatsoever nature and kind, both present and future (other than property and assets that are in this security agreement validly assigned or subjected to a specific mortgage and charge and to the exceptions contained in this security agreement). For the purposes of this security agreement, the equipment, inventory, intangibles, undertaking, and all other property and assets of the debtor referred to in this clause 2 are from now on sometimes collectively called the "collateral."

3. The collateral is on the date of this security agreement primarily situate or located at the location(s) set out in clause 1 of this security agreement but may, from time to time, be located at other premises of the debtor. The collateral may also be located at other places while in transit to and from such locations and premises; and the collateral may, from time to time, be situate or located at any other place when on lease or consignment to any lessee or consignee from the debtor.

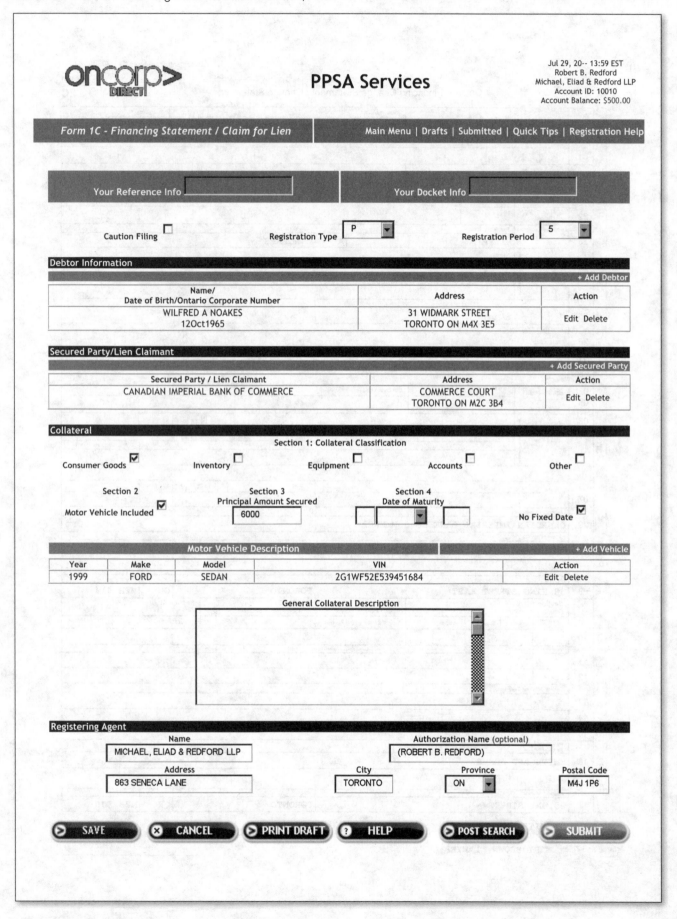

ONCORP DIRECT

PPSA Services

Jul 29, 20-- 13:59 EST
Robert B. Redford
Michael, Eliad & Redford LLP
Account ID: 10010
Account Balance: $500.00

Form 1C - Financing Statement / Claim for Lien

Main Menu | Drafts | Submitted | Quick Tips | Registration Help

Your Reference Info [ ]   Your Docket Info [ ]

☐ Caution Filing   Registration Type [P ▾]   Registration Period [5 ▾]

Debtor Information

+ Add Debtor

Name/ Date of Birth/Ontario Corporate Number	Address	Action
WILFRED A NOAKES 12Oct1965	31 WIDMARK STREET TORONTO ON M4X 3E5	Edit Delete

Secured Party/Lien Claimant

+ Add Secured Party

Secured Party / Lien Claimant	Address	Action
CANADIAN IMPERIAL BANK OF COMMERCE	COMMERCE COURT TORONTO ON M2C 3B4	Edit Delete

Collateral

Section 1: Collateral Classification

Consumer Goods ☑   Inventory ☐   Equipment ☐   Accounts ☐   Other ☐

Section 2   Section 3   Section 4
Motor Vehicle Included ☑   Principal Amount Secured [6000]   Date of Maturity [ ] [▾] [ ]   No Fixed Date ☑

Motor Vehicle Description				+ Add Vehicle
Year	Make	Model	VIN	Action
1999	FORD	SEDAN	2G1WF52E539451684	Edit Delete

General Collateral Description
[ ]

Registering Agent

Name
[MICHAEL, ELIAD & REDFORD LLP]

Authorization Name (optional)
[(ROBERT B. REDFORD)]

Address
[863 SENECA LANE]

City
[TORONTO]

Province
[ON ▾]

Postal Code
[M4J 1P6]

⊳ SAVE   ⊗ CANCEL   ⊳ PRINT DRAFT   ⊙ HELP   ⊳ POST SEARCH   ⊳ SUBMIT

Cyberbahn Transaction ID: 3703300

Ontario: Financing Change Statement / Change Statement

Form
2C

Part 1

	Registration No.		Expiry Date
	XXXXXXXXXXXXXXXXXXXXXXXXX		

01 | Caution Filing | Page | Total Page | Motor Vehicle Schedule | | | PPSA/RSLA |
1 of **1**

21 | Reference File No.
083890503

22 | Page No. of page to be amended | No Specific Page **X** | | Letter for Change **D** | Additional Years | Total Correct Registration Period

23 | Individual Debtor | First Given Name **WILFRED** | Initial **A** | Surname **NOAKES**

24 | Business Debtor | Name
| | Name cont'd

Part 2

25 | | Other Change

26 | Reasons for Amendment

27

28

Part 3

02/05 | Individual Debtor / Transferee | Date of Birth | First Given Name | Initial | Surname

03/06 | Business Debtor / Transferee | Name
| | Name cont'd | | Ontario Corporation No.

04/07 | Address | | City | Prov. | Postal Code

Part 4

29 | Assignor (as recorded)
CANADIAN IMPERIAL BANK OF COMMERCE

08 | Secured Party
GEORGE R. TULLOCH LTD.

09 | Address **38 KING STREET EAST** | City **TORONTO** | Prov. **ON** | Postal Code **M2B 4T4**

Part 5

Section 1: Collateral Classification					Section 2: Vehicle Included	Section 3: Principal Amount Secured	Section 4:	
Consumer Goods	Inventory	Equipment	Accounts	Other	Type 'X' if Motor Vehicle included		Date of Maturity	No Fixed Date of Maturity

10 | | | | | | | $ .00 | |

11 | Year | Make | | | Model | Vehicle Identification No.

12

13 | General Collateral Description

14

15

Part 6

16 | Registering Agent / Secured Party Name
SMITH AND JONES

17 | Address **95 BAY STREET** | City **TORONTO** | Prov. **ON** | Postal Code **M2B 5J6**

Company Name: **SMITH AND JONES**

Name and Title: **MARY BROWN, LAWYER**

CHAPTER 30
INTRODUCTION TO REAL ESTATE

This chapter covers an introduction to real property with a look at the most common types of land ownership.

REAL PROPERTY

Real property, or real estate, is said to be the "bread and butter"of lawyers. Real property is land and includes land that is vacant as well as land with permanent attachments such as buildings, trees, and fences. Real property is to be distinguished from personal property which consists of movable items such as mirrors, refrigerators, stoves, and electric light fixtures, which the owner may remove when selling. Real property may be bought, sold, leased, or financed for either residential or commercial use.

TYPES OF LAND OWNERSHIP

Whose land is it anyway Land in Canada belongs to the Crown, i.e. the government, until someone buys it from the Crown; then, it belongs to the person who bought it. Further, land **escheats** (reverts) to the Crown if an individual owner dies leaving no beneficiaries. Thus, the Crown is the ultimate owner of land. This is why the Crown has the power to expropriate land (take it away from its present owner), with or without compensation. This is also why individuals who own land are technically referred to as **tenants.**

Freehold estate This means the Crown permits people to own, or **hold**, land **free** from interference from others; hence, **freehold** estate (ownership). The most common types of freehold estates are **fee simple** and **life estate.**

FREEHOLD ESTATE	
Fee Simple Estate • Absolute ownership with right of survivorship	Life Estate • Lifetime ownership only, no right of survivorship

Fee simple estate Translated from old English, this phrase means permanent, or most absolute, ownership of land. It gives the right to pass the land to heirs, sell it, lease it, or dispose of it as the owner wishes. Most people own land in fee simple. The phrase has evolved from early invaders of England, thus:

Fe	Originally from Old Norse, prior to the year 500 A.D.
Feoh	Old English from 500 A.D. to 1100 A.D. and Middle English from 1180 A.D. to 1500 A.D.
Fee	Modern English from 1500 A.D. to present.
Sim(b)le	Old English, meant **permanent**.

Life estate   This type of land ownership gives one the right to own the land during one's lifetime. On the death of the life estate owner, the property passes to the fee simple owner. This type of land ownership is often used by family members where, for example, a father passes the property to a son or daughter, but the father retains the ownership and use of the land until he dies. The life estate owner, e.g. the father, may, except for selling it, do what he likes with it, including live on it, build on it, or lease it to someone else. If the life estate owner, the father, leases it to someone else and dies during the term of the lease, the property reverts to the fee simple owner, the son or daughter.

Leasehold estate   Leasehold ownership differs from a fee simple and life estate in that it requires a **lease** giving a right to possession of the land for a specified number of years (e.g. 99 years) in return for payment of rent.

TITLE

Basically, title tells who owns which land. Whoever holds title to a property is the owner of that property. Individuals, as well as corporations, may take title alone or together with others as follows:

Title by one individual or corporation   When title is registered in one individual's or corporation's name, it means only that individual or corporation owns the property. If an individual owner is married, the owner's spouse does not own any part of the property. If the property is used as a family home, however, the law gives as much right to the non-owner spouse to **live in it** as it does to the owner spouse. This is known as the non-owner spouse's **right of possession** of the matrimonial home.

Title as joint tenants   **Joint** means **together**; **tenants** is a historic reference to the Crown being the ultimate land owner. Title as **joint tenants** means two or more people own the property together with **right of survivorship**. If one joint tenant dies, the surviving joint tenant automatically receives the deceased's share of the property. Married couples often take title as joint tenants.

> **Equal and undivided ownership**   Joint tenancy gives equal and undivided ownership. **Equal** means all tenants own the same proportions; therefore, the title document cannot show unequal shares such as one-quarter by one tenant and three-quarters by another. Where there are two joint tenants, the ownership is 50/50; where there are four, the ownership is 25 percent each, etc. **Undivided** means the land must remain whole; the tenants cannot physically divide it in equal pieces. This is to prevent the tenants from indiscriminately dividing up and selling the land.

> **Joint tenancy and inheritance**   Only the last surviving joint tenant may pass property on to a beneficiary. This is because each surviving joint tenant receives the deceased's part of the property by right of survivorship. The last surviving joint tenant may will it to anyone, including to two or more people as joint tenants.

Joint tenancy and sale   None of the joint tenants can sell his or her share of the property without the consent of the others. Joint tenants may buy each other out, but the joint tenancy severs (breaks) where one joint tenant buys out the whole. The joint tenancy is intact only as long as the original joint tenants own the property. If a joint tenant conveys his interest to himself or herself, the joint tenancy between the original owners severs; for example, if A, B, and C are joint tenants, and A conveys his interest to himself, A becomes a tenant in common with B and C who remain as joint tenants. Thus, A could not still stand to inherit from B and C. If A conveys his interest to Y, B and C are still joint tenants with one another. Y holds his interest as tenant in common with B and C. If a joint tenant wishes to sell and the remaining joint tenants do not consent, that joint tenant may apply to the court for what is known as a **partition**. Partition means the court may order the land physically divided, usually only if it is vacant, or sold and the money divided among the joint tenants.

Title as tenants in common   This is a collective yet independent way of holding real property with no right of survivorship. Each tenant in common may sell his or her share to a stranger without the consent of the others, and the stranger becomes a tenant in common. If the entire property is sold, all tenants in common must consent. If one tenant in common dies, his or her share goes to his or her estate; it does not go to the surviving tenants in common. If a tenant in common wills it to a beneficiary, that beneficiary becomes a tenant in common. People who buy business properties use tenancy in common because it allows them to pool their money to buy collectively and sell individually.

Undivided interest   As with joint tenancy, tenancy in common gives an undivided interest, i.e. the land must remain whole, but unlike joint tenancy, it gives the right of unequal ownership. Thus, where the share is to be unequal, the title document must show who owns what proportion, the usual wording being: *John Smith as to an undivided one-quarter interest and James Brown as to the remaining undivided three-quarters interest.*

Title as partnership property   Title as partnership property may be in unequal interests, e.g. one partner may hold a one-third share and the other the remaining two-thirds. Title as partnership property is not in itself indicative of the legal rights of the owners because the partners may set out their various rights in their partnership agreement. Thus, partnership property is neither joint tenancy nor tenancy in common. No partner may sell his or her interest without the consent of the other partners or without following the terms of the partnership agreement.

OTHER INTERESTS IN LAND

Easements   These involve the right of one land owner to use part of the land belonging to another land owner for a special purpose. The most common types of easements are **rights of way** and **encroachments**.

Rights of way   A right of way gives one the right to cross another's land. Rights of way are common in rural areas: for example, Jones cannot get to his cottage unless he passes through Smith's land; also, if Jones were to install a telephone line or a gas pipe, it must go on or under Smith's land. To use Smith's property for this purpose, Jones must have the verbal or written permission of Smith, or Jones must buy the right of way strip of land from Smith.

Encroachments   An encroachment is where part of one owner's building rests on or over-hangs another's land: for example, eaves overhanging the other owner's land are an encroachment on that owner's property. The encroaching owner may obtain the right to encroach by verbal or written permission, by transfer from the other owner, or by prescription where applicable. If the encroachment is without permission, the owner encroached upon may demand that the offending portion of the building be torn down or that he or she be compensated for the encroachment.

 In a British Columbia case, a six inch eavestrough on the long-time residence of former NDP Attorney General Alex Macdonald hangs over Liberal Senator Jack Austin's property line on Vancouver's elegant Point Grey Road. Senator Austin insisted that his socialist neighbour either saw off the six inch encroachment or accept a limited easement from Senator Austin that would require him to tear down his entire house before selling it. Justice Ross Collver thought neither option feasible since the one would make Mr. Macdonald's house look absurd and the other would prevent him from dealing with his property. Justice Collver finally granted Mr. Macdonald an easement over Senator Austin's property for as long as Mr. Macdonald's house is standing. Justice Collver also ordered Mr. Macdonald to pay $10 to Senator Austin in compensation for the easement.

Mineral rights   In Ontario, the ownership of surface rights and mining rights varies from one parcel of land to the next. Generally, the landowner owns the surface of the land, and the Crown, i.e. the government, owns the minerals underlying the landowner's property and the mining rights. Under authority of the *Mining Act*, the Crown allows ownership of the mining rights to be staked by a person who has a valid prospecting license.

Water rights   The Crown, i.e. the government, owns the water. As a general rule, if water is in a natural watercourse, it must be permitted to flow. A natural watercourse is usually a stream of water which flows along a defined channel with a bed and banks, and may also include creeks and streams. The riparian landowner (landowner of the land through which the water flows) must allow the water to flow through all properties. The riparian owner can use the water for his or her own need, but cannot dam it, block it, or divert it from its natural watercourse so that a downstream neighbour is denied use of it. Nor can the riparian owner pollute or foul the water so that the neighbour is unable to use it. A landowner also does not own a body of water that is navigable water, e.g. lakes, bays, or navigable rivers, on which ships and boats can travel. Generally, the body of water ends at the first sign of permanent vegetation, e.g. a tree, and the land begins.

AGREEMENTS OF PURCHASE AND SALE

An agreement of purchase and sale is the well known **offer** used when buying real estate. Vendors usually list their properties for sale with a real estate agent. The listing may be either an exclusive listing, which generally means only the listing agent has a right to sell the property, or a multiple listing, which means any real estate agent may sell it. When a buyer is ready to make an offer, the real estate agency's sales representative usually prepares and presents it to the vendor for signing. The offer to purchase may go back and forth between the parties numerous times with price and term negotiations, but once both the buyer and the seller sign it, it becomes a binding contract known as an **agreement of purchase and sale**, Precedent 30.1. An agreement of purchase and sale begins the real estate transaction in the law office.

Reading the agreement of purchase and sale   Learn how to "read" the agreement of purchase and sale at a glance. This ability gives you a great deal of working freedom and your principal genuinely appreciates it. Here are some basic points you should be able to quickly "read": who is selling to whom; which property; who is the agent; what is the purchase price and what is included in it; what is the total cash paid (includes deposit); are there any charges/mortgages; what is the deadline for requisitions; what is the date of closing.

CHAPTER SUMMARY

Real estate deals with buying, selling, leasing, and financing real property as opposed to personal property. Real property consists of land and anything that is permanently attached to land, e.g. buildings, trees, etc.

There are three types of land ownership: (1) fee simple estate, which is the most common and the most permanent; (2) life estate, which is lifetime ownership; and (3) leasehold estate, which is land leased for a specified period of time. Once people or corporations buy land, they must decide how they want to take **title**; that is, they must decide in whose name to register the ownership of the land. There are three common ways of taking title: (1) title by one owner; this means ownership of the land is only in that one owner's name; (2) title as joint tenants; this means two or more people own the land with right of survivorship, i.e. a deceased's share of the property automatically passes to the survivor joint tenant/s; (3) title as tenants in common; this means two or more people own the land, without right of survivorship, and each tenant in common can deal with his or her share of the property as he or she wishes. There may be easements involved in property ownership which are almost always troublesome because they involve the right of one land owner to use part of the land belonging to another land owner.

Buying and selling real property begins with a document known as an offer to purchase. Once both the buyer and the seller sign the offer, it becomes a binding contract known as an agreement of purchase and sale. An agreement of purchase and sale begins the real estate transaction in the law office.

REVIEW QUESTIONS

1. Which term describes the most absolute ownership of land?
2. What is the difference between title as joint tenants and tenants in common?
3. Which term is used to describe rights of way and encroachments?
4. When does an offer become an agreement of purchase and sale?
5. What is meant by a life estate?
6. Explain why a freehold estate owner means the owner acquires land free of charge.
7. In "reading" the agreement of purchase and sale in this chapter:
   (a) who is selling to whom?
   (b) what is the address of the property being sold?
   (c) what is the purchase price?
   (d) how much is the deposit?
   (e) how is the total purchase price going to be paid?
   (f) what is the closing or completion date?

Precedent 30.1 Agreement of Purchase and Sale, Page 2

3. **NOTICES:** The Seller hereby appoints the Listing Brokerage as agent for the Seller for the purpose of giving and receiving notices pursuant to this Agreement. Where a Brokerage (Buyer's Brokerage) has entered into a representation agreement with the Buyer, the Buyer hereby appoints the Buyer's Brokerage as agent for the purpose of giving and receiving notices pursuant to this Agreement. **Where a Brokerage represents both the Seller and the Buyer (multiple representation), the Brokerage shall not be appointed or authorized to be agent for either the Buyer or the Seller for the purpose of giving and receiving notices.** Any notice relating hereto or provided for herein shall be in writing. In addition to any provision contained herein and in any Schedule hereto, this offer, any counter-offer, notice of acceptance thereof or any notice to be given or received pursuant to this Agreement or any Schedule hereto (any of them, "Document") shall be deemed given and received when delivered personally or hand delivered to the Address for Service provided in the Acknowledgement below, or where a facsimile number or email address is provided herein, when transmitted electronically to that facsimile number or email address, respectively, in which case, the signature(s) of the party (parties) shall be deemed to be original.

FAX No.: .... FAX No.: 416-363-2628
(For delivery of Documents to Seller) (For delivery of Documents to Buyer)

Email Address: raymond@castlessands.ca Email Address: rhrdfrd@mer.com
(For delivery of Documents to Seller) (For delivery of Documents to Buyer)

4. **CHATTELS INCLUDED:**

Nil

Unless otherwise stated in this Agreement or any Schedule hereto, Seller agrees to convey all fixtures and chattels included in the Purchase Price free from all liens, encumbrances or claims affecting the said fixtures and chattels.

5. **FIXTURES EXCLUDED:**

Nil

6. **RENTAL ITEMS (Including Lease, Lease to Own):** The following equipment is rented and **not** included in the Purchase Price. The Buyer agrees to assume the rental contract(s), if assumable.

hot water tank

The Buyer agrees to co-operate and execute such documentation as may be required to facilitate such assumption.

7. **HST:** If the sale of the property (Real Property as described above) is subject to Harmonized Sales Tax (HST), then such tax shall be .... the Purchase Price. If the sale of the property is not subject to HST,
included if/in addition to)
Seller agrees to certify on or before closing, that the sale of the property is not subject to HST.
Any HST on chattels, if applicable, is not included in the Purchase Price.

n/a

INITIALS OF BUYER(S): INITIALS OF SELLER(S):

Form 100 Revised 2015 **Page 2 of 6**
WEBForms® Jan/2015

Precedent 30.1 Agreement of Purchase and Sale, Page 1

Form 100 for use in the Province of Ontario

Agreement of Purchase and Sale

This Agreement of Purchase and Sale dated this ...... 8th ...... day of ...... January ......, 20 ......

BUYER, ... ARTHUR MELVILLE HOPE and PAMELA SUSAN HOPE ......, agrees to purchase from
(Full legal names of all Buyers)

SELLER: ...... VIRGINIA JONQUIL ......, the following
(Full legal names of all Sellers)

REAL PROPERTY:

Address ...... 77 Huntington Cres. ......

fronting on the ...... north ...... side of ...... Huntington ......

in the ...... City of Toronto ......

and having a frontage of ...... 35 Feet ...... more or less by a depth of ...... 173 Feet ...... more or less

and legally described as ...... Lot 2, Plan 363 ...... (the "property").
(Legal description of land including easements not described elsewhere)

PURCHASE PRICE: ...... Four Hundred Eighty-Eight Thousand ...... Dollars (CDN$) 488,000.00

DEPOSIT: Buyer submits ...... Herewith ......
(Herewith/Upon Acceptance/as otherwise described in this Agreement)

Forty-Eight Thousand ...... Dollars (CDN$) 48,000.00

by negotiable cheque payable to ...... TOMTIN REALTY ...... "Deposit Holder"
to be held in trust pending completion or other termination of this Agreement and to be credited toward the Purchase Price on completion. For the purposes of this Agreement, "Upon Acceptance" shall mean that the Buyer is required to deliver the deposit to the Deposit Holder within 24 hours of the acceptance of this Agreement. The parties to this Agreement hereby acknowledge that, unless otherwise provided for in this Agreement, the Deposit Holder shall place the deposit in trust in the Deposit Holder's non-interest bearing Real Estate Trust Account and no interest shall be earned, received or paid on the deposit.

Buyer agrees to pay the balance as more particularly set out in Schedule A attached.

SCHEDULE(S) A .... **attached hereto form(s) part of this Agreement.**

1. **IRREVOCABILITY:** This offer shall be irrevocable by ...... Buyer ...... until ...... 8:00 p.m. ...... on
(Seller/Buyer)
the ...... 15th ...... day of ...... January ......, 20 ......, after which time, if not accepted, this offer shall be null and void and the deposit shall be returned to the Buyer in full without interest.

2. **COMPLETION DATE:** This Agreement shall be completed by no later than 6:00 p.m. on the ...... 22nd ...... day
of ...... June ......, 20 .... Upon completion, vacant possession of the property shall be given to the
Buyer unless otherwise provided for in this Agreement.

INITIALS OF BUYER(S): INITIALS OF SELLER(S):

Form 100 Revised 2015 **Page 1 of 6**
WEBForms® Jan/2015

Precedent 30.1 Agreement of Purchase and Sale, Page 3

8. **TITLE SEARCH:** Buyer shall be allowed until 6:00 p.m. on the..........8th.......... day of..........February.........., 20--....., (Requisition Date) to examine the title to the property at Buyer's own expense and until the earlier of: (i) thirty days from the later of the Requisition Date or the date on which the conditions in this Agreement are fulfilled or otherwise waived or; (ii) five days prior to completion, to satisfy Buyer that there are no outstanding work orders or deficiency notices

affecting the property, and that its present use(..........single family residence..........) may be lawfully continued and that the principal building may be insured against risk of fire. Seller hereby consents to the municipality or other governmental agencies releasing to Buyer details of all outstanding work orders and deficiency notices affecting the property, and Seller agrees to execute and deliver such further authorizations in this regard as Buyer may reasonably require.

9. **FUTURE USE:** Seller and Buyer agree that there is no representation or warranty of any kind that the future intended use of the property by Buyer is or will be lawful except as may be specifically provided for in this Agreement.

10. **TITLE:** Provided that the title to the property is good and free from all registered restrictions, charges, liens, and encumbrances except as otherwise specifically provided in this Agreement and save and except for (a) any registered restrictions or covenants that run with the land providing that such are complied with; (b) any registered municipal agreements and registered agreements with publicly regulated utilities providing such have been complied with, or security has been posted to ensure compliance and completion, as evidenced by a letter from the relevant municipality or regulated utility; (c) any minor easements for the supply of domestic utility or telephone services to the property or adjacent properties; and (d) any easements for drainage, storm or sanitary sewers, public utility lines, telephone lines, cable television lines or other services which do not materially affect the use of the property. If within the specified times referred to in paragraph 8 any valid objection to title or to any outstanding work order or deficiency notice, or to the fact the said present use may not lawfully be continued, or that the principal building may not be insured against risk of fire is made in writing to Seller and which Seller is unable or unwilling to remove, remedy or satisfy or obtain insurance save and except against risk of fire (Title Insurance) in favour of the Buyer and any mortgagee, (with all related costs at the expense of the Seller), and which Buyer will not waive, this Agreement notwithstanding any intermediate acts or negotiations in respect of such objections, shall be at an end and all monies paid shall be returned without interest or deduction and Seller, Listing Brokerage and Co-operating Brokerage shall not be liable for any costs or damages. Save as to any valid objection so made by such day and except for any objection going to the root of the title, Buyer shall be conclusively deemed to have accepted Seller's title to the property.

11. **CLOSING ARRANGEMENTS:** Where each of the Seller and Buyer retain a lawyer to complete the Agreement of Purchase and Sale of the property, and where the transaction will be completed by electronic registration pursuant to Part III of the Land Registration Reform Act, R.S.O. 1990, Chapter L4 and the Electronic Registration Act, S.O. 1991, Chapter 44, and any amendments thereto, the Seller and Buyer acknowledge and agree that the exchange of closing funds, non-registrable documents and other items (the "Requisite Deliveries") and the release thereof to the Seller and Buyer will (a) not occur at the same time as the registration of the transfer/deed (and any other documents intended to be registered in connection with the completion of this transaction) and (b) be subject to conditions whereby the lawyer(s) receiving any of the Requisite Deliveries will be required to hold same in trust and not release same except in accordance with the terms of a document registration agreement between the said lawyers. The Seller and Buyer irrevocably instruct the said lawyers to be bound by the document registration agreement which is recommended from time to time by the Law Society of Upper Canada. Unless otherwise agreed to by the lawyers, such exchange of the Requisite Deliveries will occur in the applicable Land Titles Office or such other location agreeable to both lawyers.

12. **DOCUMENTS AND DISCHARGE:** Buyer shall not call for the production of any title deed, abstract, survey or other evidence of title to the property except such as are in the possession or control of Seller. If requested by Buyer, Seller will deliver any sketch or survey of the property within Seller's control to Buyer as soon as possible and prior to the Requisition Date. If a discharge of any Charge/Mortgage held by a corporation incorporated pursuant to the Trust And Loan Companies Act (Canada), Chartered Bank, Trust Company, Credit Union, Caisse Populaire or Insurance Company and which is not to be assumed by Buyer on completion, is not available in registrable form on completion, Buyer agrees to accept Seller's lawyer's personal undertaking to obtain, out of the closing funds, a discharge in registrable form and to register same, or cause same to be registered, on title within a reasonable period of time after completion, provided that on or before completion Seller shall provide to Buyer a mortgage statement prepared by the mortgagee setting out the balance required to obtain the discharge, and, where a real-time electronic cleared funds transfer system is not being used, a direction executed by Seller directing payment to the mortgagee of the amount required to obtain the discharge out of the balance due on completion.

13. **INSPECTION:** Buyer acknowledges having had the opportunity to inspect the property and understands that upon acceptance of this offer there shall be a binding agreement of purchase and sale between Buyer and Seller. **The Buyer acknowledges having the opportunity to include a requirement for a property inspection report in this Agreement and agrees that except as may be specifically provided for in this Agreement, the Buyer will not be obtaining a property inspection or property inspection report regarding the property.**

INITIALS OF BUYER(S): ( ) **INITIALS OF SELLER(S):** ( )

 Form 100 Revised 2015 **Page 3 of 6**

WEB*Forms*® Jan/2015

Precedent 30.1 Agreement of Purchase and Sale, Page 4

14. **INSURANCE:** All buildings on the property and all other things being purchased shall be and remain until completion at the risk of Seller. Pending completion, Seller shall hold all insurance policies, if any, and the proceeds thereof in trust for the parties as their interests may appear and in the event of substantial damage, Buyer may either terminate this Agreement and have all monies paid returned without interest or deduction or else take the proceeds of any insurance and complete the purchase. No insurance shall be transferred on completion. If Seller is taking back a Charge/Mortgage, or Buyer is assuming a Charge/Mortgage, Buyer shall supply Seller with reasonable evidence of adequate insurance to protect Seller's or other mortgagee's interest on completion.

15. **PLANNING ACT:** This Agreement shall be effective to create an interest in the property only if Seller complies with the subdivision control provisions of the Planning Act by completion and Seller covenants to proceed diligently at Seller's expense to obtain any necessary consent by completion.

16. **DOCUMENT PREPARATION:** The Transfer/Deed shall, save for the Land Transfer Tax Affidavit, be prepared in registrable form at the expense of Seller, and any Charge/Mortgage to be given back by the Buyer to Seller at the expense of the Buyer. If requested by Buyer, Seller covenants that the Transfer/Deed to be delivered on completion shall contain the statements contemplated by Section 50(22) of the Planning Act, R.S.O.1990.

17. **RESIDENCY:** (a) Subject to (b) below, the Seller represents and warrants that the Seller is not and on completion will not be a non-resident under the non-residency provisions of the Income Tax Act which representation and warranty shall survive and not merge upon the completion of this transaction and the Seller shall deliver to the Buyer a statutory declaration that Seller is not then a non-resident of Canada;
(b) provided that if the Seller is a non-resident under the non-residency provisions of the Income Tax Act, the Buyer shall be credited towards the Purchase Price with the amount, if any, necessary for Buyer to pay to the Minister of National Revenue to satisfy Buyer's liability in respect of tax payable by Seller under the non-residency provisions of the Income Tax Act by reason of this sale. Buyer shall not claim such credit if Seller delivers on completion the prescribed certificate.

18. **ADJUSTMENTS:** Any rents, mortgage interest, realty taxes including local improvement rates and unmetered public or private utility charges and unmetered cost of fuel, as applicable, shall be apportioned and allowed to the day of completion, the day of completion itself to be apportioned to Buyer.

19. **PROPERTY ASSESSMENT:** The Buyer and Seller hereby acknowledge that the Province of Ontario has implemented current value assessment and properties may be re-assessed on an annual basis. The Buyer and Seller agree that no claim will be made against the Buyer or Seller, or any Brokerage, Broker or Salesperson, for any changes in property tax as a result of a re-assessment of the property, save and except any property taxes that accrued prior to the completion of this transaction.

20. **TIME LIMITS:** Time shall in all respects be of the essence hereof provided that the time for doing or completing of any matter provided for herein may be extended or abridged by an agreement in writing signed by Seller and Buyer or by their respective lawyers who may be specifically authorized in that regard.

21. **TENDER:** Any tender of documents or money hereunder may be made upon Seller or Buyer or their respective lawyers on the day set for completion. Money shall be tendered with funds drawn on a lawyer's trust account in the form of a bank draft, certified cheque or wire transfer using the Large Value Transfer System.

22. **FAMILY LAW ACT:** Seller warrants that spousal consent is not necessary to this transaction under the provisions of the Family Law Act, R.S.O.1990 unless Seller's spouse has executed the consent hereinafter provided.

23. **UFFI:** Seller represents and warrants to Buyer that during the time Seller has owned the property, Seller has not caused any building on the property to be insulated with insulation containing ureaformaldehyde, and that to the best of Seller's knowledge no building on the property contains or has ever contained insulation that contains ureaformaldehyde. This warranty shall survive and not merge on the completion of this transaction, and if the building is part of a multiple unit building, this warranty shall only apply to that part of the building which is the subject of this transaction.

24. **LEGAL, ACCOUNTING AND ENVIRONMENTAL ADVICE**: The parties acknowledge that any information provided by the brokerage is not legal, tax or environmental advice.

25. **CONSUMER REPORTS: The Buyer is hereby notified that a consumer report containing credit and/or personal information may be referred to in connection with this transaction.**

26. **AGREEMENT IN WRITING:** If there is conflict or discrepancy between any provision added to this Agreement (including any Schedule attached hereto) and any provision in the standard pre-set portion hereof, the added provision shall supersede the standard pre-set provision to the extent of such conflict or discrepancy. This Agreement including any Schedule attached hereto, shall constitute the entire Agreement between Buyer and Seller. There is no representation, warranty, collateral agreement or condition, which affects this Agreement other than as expressed herein. For the purposes of this Agreement, Seller means vendor and Buyer means purchaser. This Agreement shall be read with all changes of gender or number required by the context.

27. **TIME AND DATE:** Any reference to a time and date in this Agreement shall mean the time and date where the property is located.

INITIALS OF BUYER(S): ( ) **INITIALS OF SELLER(S):** ( )

 Form 100 Revised 2015 **Page 4 of 6**

WEB*Forms*® Jan/2015

Page 6 — Schedule A

OREA Ontario Real Estate Association

Form 100 for use in the Province of Ontario

Schedule A
Agreement of Purchase and Sale

This Schedule is attached to and forms part of the Agreement of Purchase and Sale between:

BUYER: ARTHUR MELVILLE HOPE and PAMELA SUSAN HOPE ...., and

SELLER: VIRGINIA JONQUIL

for the purchase and sale of .... 77 Huntington Cres.

Toronto .... dated the .... 8th .... day of .... January ...., 20.--

Buyer agrees to pay the balance as follows:

The Buyer agrees to pay the balance of the purchase price, subject to the usual adjustments, to the Seller on the completion of this transaction, with funds drawn on a lawyer's trust account in the form of a bank draft, certified cheque or wire transfer.

The Buyer agrees to arrange and execute at the Buyer's own expense a new first charge/mortgage of not less than FORTY THOUSAND DOLLARS ($40,000.00) bearing interest at the rate of 11 1/4% per annum calculated semi-annually, not in advance, repayable in blended monthly payments of $403.69, including principal and interest, and to run for a term of five years.

This offer is conditional upon the Buyer arranging at the Buyer's own expense a new first charge/mortgage satisfactory to the Buyer in the Buyer's sole and absolute discretion. Unless the Buyer gives notice in writing delivered to the Seller not later than 8:00 p.m. on January 17, 20--, that this condition is fulfilled, this offer shall be null and void and the deposit shall be returned to the Buyer in full without deduction.

This offer is conditional upon the inspection of the subject property by a home inspector at the Buyer's own expense and the obtaining of a report satisfactory to the Buyer in the Buyer's sole and absolute discretion. Unless the Buyer gives notice in writing delivered to the Seller not later than 8:00 p.m. on January 17, 20--, that this condition is fulfilled, this offer shall be null and void and the deposit shall be returned to the Buyer in full without deduction.

The Seller agrees to leave the premises, including the floors, in a clean and broom-swept condition.

This form must be initialed by all parties to the Agreement of Purchase and Sale.

INITIALS OF BUYER(S): ( )   INITIALS OF SELLER(S): ( )

Form 100   Revised 2015   Page 6 of 6   WEBForms® Jan/2015

Page 5

28. SUCCESSORS AND ASSIGNS: The heirs, executors, administrators, successors and assigns of the undersigned are bound by the terms herein.

SIGNED, SEALED AND DELIVERED in the presence of: IN WITNESS whereof I have hereunto set my hand and seal:

.... (Witness)   .... (Buyer)   DATE.......... (Seal)
.... (Witness)   .... (Buyer)   DATE.......... (Seal)

I, the Undersigned Seller, agree to the above offer. I hereby irrevocably instruct my lawyer to pay directly to the brokerage(s) with whom I have agreed to pay commission, the unpaid balance of the commission together with applicable Harmonized Sales Tax (and any other taxes as may hereafter be applicable), from the proceeds of the sale prior to any payment to the undersigned on completion, as advised by the brokerage(s) to my lawyer.

SIGNED, SEALED AND DELIVERED in the presence of: IN WITNESS whereof I have hereunto set my hand and seal:

.... (Witness)   .... (Seller)   DATE.......... (Seal)
.... (Witness)   .... (Seller)   DATE.......... (Seal)

SPOUSAL CONSENT: The Undersigned Spouse of the Seller hereby consents to the disposition evidenced herein pursuant to the provisions of the Family Law Act, R.S.O.1990, and hereby agrees with the Buyer that he/she will execute all necessary or incidental documents to give full force and effect to the sale evidenced herein.

.... (Witness)   .... (Spouse)   DATE.......... (Seal)

CONFIRMATION OF ACCEPTANCE: Notwithstanding anything contained herein to the contrary, I confirm this Agreement with all changes both typed and written was finally accepted by all parties at.................. this................. day of.................. 20..........

.... (Signature of Seller or Buyer)

INFORMATION ON BROKERAGE(S)

Listing Brokerage... Tel.No...............
.... (Salesperson / Broker Name)

Co-op/Buyer Brokerage... Tel.No...............
.... (Salesperson / Broker Name)

ACKNOWLEDGEMENT

I acknowledge receipt of my signed copy of this accepted Agreement of Purchase and Sale and I authorize the Brokerage to forward a copy to my lawyer.

.... (Seller)   DATE...............
.... (Seller)   DATE...............
Address for Service... Tel.No...............
Seller's Lawyer.... Raymond G. Castles
Address. 205 Portage St., Markham, ON L3R 3G3
Email. raymond@castlesands.ca
905-495-2222   905-495-2223
Tel.No.   FAX No.

I acknowledge receipt of my signed copy of this accepted Agreement of Purchase and Sale and I authorize the Brokerage to forward a copy to my lawyer.

.... (Buyer)   DATE...............
.... (Buyer)   DATE...............
Address for Service... Tel.No...............
Buyer's Lawyer.... Robert B. Redford
Address. 863 Seneca Lane, Toronto, ON M4J 1P6
Email. rbrdfrd@amer.com
416-363-1079   416-363-2628
Tel.No.   FAX No.

FOR OFFICE USE ONLY   COMMISSION TRUST AGREEMENT

To: Cooperating Brokerage shown on the foregoing Agreement of Purchase and Sale:
In consideration for the Co-operating Brokerage procuring the foregoing Agreement of Purchase and Sale, I hereby declare that all moneys received or receivable by me in connection with the Transaction as contemplated in the MLS® Rules and Regulations of my Real Estate Board shall be receivable and held in trust. This agreement shall constitute a Commission Trust Agreement as defined in the MLS® Rules and shall be subject to and governed by the MLS® Rules pertaining to Commission Trust.

DATED as of the date and time of the acceptance of the foregoing Agreement of Purchase and Sale.   Acknowledged by:

.... (Authorized to bind the Listing Brokerage)   .... (Authorized to bind the Co-operating Brokerage)

Form 100   Revised 2015   Page 5 of 6   WEBForms® Jan/2015

CHAPTER 31

LAND REGISTRATION SYSTEMS

In most Canadian jurisdictions, land registration systems are similar in that land falls either within the land titles system and/or the registry system. As well, most Canadian provinces have automated their paper-based records and converted to electronic systems. The discussion in this chapter of the Ontario registry and land titles systems also applies to other provinces/territories, with appropriate modification.

LAND REGISTRATION SYSTEMS

The Ontario Ministry of Government and Consumer Services manages the system of land registration. Basically, the purpose of the land registry system is as follows:

(1) to provide a public record of land ownership;

(2) to give public notice of any debts or other encumbrances, e.g. charges/mortgages, liens, etc. on a property so as to protect lenders against lending money on properties that are already indebted; and

(3) to establish a priority of debts, the order of which is generally sequenced on a "first registered first paid" basis.

Two systems   There are two land registration systems operating concurrently in Ontario: the old Registry system and the newer Land Titles system. The reason the two co-exist is that when the new Land Titles system was originally introduced, it was too costly to convert the old Registry system records to the new system.

REGISTRY SYSTEM

The Registry system dates back to 1792 when the Crown originally registered in that system land that individuals could buy from the Crown. The Registry system is said to be a "registry of documents." Pursuant to s. 74 of the *Registry Act*, registration of a document constitutes notice of the document only and not necessarily of the legal effect of the document. The government, therefore, does not guarantee accuracy of title. Also, in the Registry system, a person can acquire title to land by virtue of having had uninterrupted use of someone else's land for ten years. This is known as **possessory title**, more commonly referred to as **squatter's rights**. A person cannot acquire possessory title under the Land Titles system.

Abstract book   The book in which the land registrar records documents registered in the Registry system is known as the **abstract book**, or **abstract index**. It is referred to as an abstract because it contains only a summary, or an abstract, of the documents registered on title, not the documents themselves. A sample page from an abstract book is in Precedent 31.3. It relates to Lot 2, Plan 363. Note that there are three "Grants" (deeds), three mortgages, and one discharge of mortgage, all abstracted, starting with the grant (deed) registered as No. 2265, giving title to John and Dorothy Bond as joint tenants, and ending with a mortgage registered as No. CT12809, between Virginia Jonquil and The Royal Trust Company. Now, take a look at Precedent 31.4, and see if you can locate Lot 2 on Plan No. 363. It is the second property in the sequence of Lots 1 through to 19 on Plan 363.

LAND TITLES SYSTEM

The Land Titles system is sometimes called the new system, or the Torrens system, so named after its Australian inventor in the 1850s. The Ontario government introduced it in 1885 under the *Land Titles Act* and placed all land located in northern Ontario in the Land Titles system. The act, however, did not make it compulsory at that time for any other land to be registered in the Land Titles system. Subsequently, the government placed land located in some parts of southern Ontario in the Land Titles system. In the Land Titles system, the government guarantees accuracy of title. Documents submitted for registration must be exactly as prescribed by law and completed correctly. No document is accepted for registration unless it is reviewed and approved by the land registrar. Each separately owned piece of land is called a "parcel" and the register in which it is recorded is called a parcel register, Precedent 31.2. All registers are electronic in the Land Titles system.

LAND REGISTRY OFFICES AND DIVISIONS

Land registry offices are central places where people submit title documents for registration. A land registry office is usually located in each county, district, or regional municipality and handles registrations of land located in that area. Each land registry office also represents a land registry division and, for easy identification, is given a number, e.g. Registry Division of the Toronto Land Registry Office (No. 66).

ELECTRONIC REGISTRATION

The *Land Registration Reform Act* (LRRA) has introduced many changes to the land registration system, including automation. Pursuant to the provisions of the LRRA, the Land Titles system is nearly completely automated, and the government has converted nearly all Registry system properties to the Land Titles system. Only properties with difficult problems on title remain in the Registry system and will continue to so remain until a transaction occurs which would cure the title problems, at which time, a conversion to the Land Titles system would occur.

Property Identifier Number (PIN)   For lands designated under Part II of the LRRA, each property has a property identification number, or PIN, for short. The PIN is a province-wide unique number which the land registrar assigns to each property for computerized searching. The PIN is made up of a block number consisting of five digits, and a property number consisting of four digits: for example, the PIN for the bolded property on the property index map, Precedent 31.1, is 07001-0004. Note that it is the same property as that described in the parcel register, Precedent 31.2. Where assigned, the PIN is the only number you need for accessing the computerized title records for electronic registration or electronic searching of title.

LEGAL DESCRIPTION OF LAND

Historically, lands were divided into counties which were subdivided into townships. Townships were divided into concessions and concessions were further divided into lots:

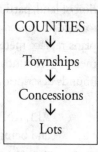

A legal description is not the street address of a property. It is the lot and plan number assigned to a property while still **vacant** because buildings and street names and numbers come later. A legal description, instead of a street address, is always used to formally describe land because that description remains constant even where street names, numbers, or buildings might change. In rural areas, the legal description usually consists of a lot and concession number and name of township; in urban areas a legal description usually consists of a lot and plan number and name of municipality:

Rural: Lot 14, Concession 10, Township of Neon, District of Oregon.

Urban, Registry system: Lot 52, Plan 444, City of Lester, Regional Municipality of Delmont.

Urban, Land Titles system: Parcel 6-1, Section 99M-789, being Lot 6, Plan 99M-789, City of Lough, County of Dent.

Registered plans of subdivision   See Precedent 31.4 for an example of a registered plan of subdivision in the Registry system and Precedent 31.5 for one in the Land Titles system. The government requires owners who **subdivide** large parcels of land into smaller groups of residential or commercial properties for sale to register a plan showing the measurements and boundaries of those properties; hence, registered plan **of subdivision**. The land registrar numbers the plans thus: Plan 345 in the Registry system and Plan M-345 in the Land Titles system. The M is a reference to **M**aster of titles, the former title for the land registrar in the Land Titles system.

Reference plans   A reference plan is like a survey; it is most frequently used to describe a single property that an owner severs (divides) to form two independent properties. Take a look at Lot 179, a corner lot on Plan M-1718 in Precedent 31.5. Now, see Precedent 31.6 for an example of the reference plan, No. 66R-9465, which describes the severance of Lot 179 into two parts.

Parts 1 and 4 refer to the land and buildings of the respective properties. Parts 2 and 3 refer to an easement (right-of-way) between the two properties; the parts divide into 2 and 3 because Part 2 is on one property and Part 3 is on the adjoining property. The "66" is usually the number of the land registry office; the "R" stands for reference to distinguish the reference plan from other types of plans. The government requires a reference plan from every owner who sells part of, or less than, the total lot he or she owns. The purpose of the reference plan is to provide a graphic "picture" of the description of the part being sold because severances often create irregular and complicated boundaries.   Reference plans are also drawn up to describe parcels of land granted to municipalities for municipal uses such as road allowances. The land registrar may also require a reference plan for any other legal description that he or she considers vague or complex or, if simple, grant an exemption. Reference plans eliminate the need for metes and bounds descriptions.

Metes and bounds description   This method of legal description gives the exact description of land, particularly land that is within a larger parcel, but is lengthy and cumbersome. It was formerly required in the same situations as those outlined above for reference plans. Reference plans replace metes and bounds descriptions except for properties that were already described in metes and bounds prior to the requirement of reference plans. Example wording of a metes and bounds description follows:

> ALL AND SINGULAR that certain parcel or tract of land and premises situate, lying and being in the Township of Almond, in the County of Raine and being composed of part of Lot 15, in Concession 6, more particularly described as follows:
>
> COMMENCING at the southwest angle of Lot 15;
>
> THENCE northerly along the westerly limit of the Lot a distance of twenty-seven point four three metres (90 ft.) to a point...

CHAPTER SUMMARY

A land registration system is a record of who owns which land and what debts are on it. There are two land registration systems, the Registry system and the Land Titles system. Under the *Land Registration Reform Act*, the government has converted nearly all Registry system properties to the Land Titles system and computerized the system so that almost all registrations are done electronically. For the purpose of electronic registration and electronic title searching, each property has been assigned a property identification number, or PIN, which enables the user to access the automated title records.

The Registry system is said to be a registry of documents basically because registration of a document constitutes notice of the document, not necessarily accuracy of title. The Land Titles system is a more accurate system than the Registry system because the land registrar checks all of the documents for form and legal effect, and the government guarantees accuracy of title.

Land is described by what is known as a legal description which in rural areas is usually by lot, concession number, and name of township, and in urban areas is by lot and plan number and name of municipality. Plans of subdivision show the size of each of many lots and, when registered, are given a plan number. There are also reference plans which are smaller scale plans than plans of subdivision, and the letter R precedes reference plan numbers to distinguish them from plans of subdivision.

REVIEW QUESTIONS

1. What is the most significant difference between the Registry and the Land Titles systems?
2. Which type of land description do reference plans eliminate?
3. How was land originally described?
4. What is legal description of land?
5. The legal description of a property is always its postal address because that is where all mail is being delivered. Explain.

6. What is the purpose of a PIN?
7. Highlight Lot 179 on Plan M-1718 (Plan of Subdivision of Part of Lot 33, Concession 4).
8. Examine Plan 66R-9465 and answer the following:
    (a) Which property lot does the reference plan describe?
    (b) How many properties has Lot 179 been divided into?
    (c) What is the number of the plan of subdivision in which Lot 179 was originally shown?
    (d) What part of the property does Part 1 on Plan 66R-9465 represent?
    (e) What do Parts 2 and 3 on the properties in Parts 1 and 4 together represent?
9. Highlight Lot 2 on Registered Plan 363.
10. Who is the owner of Lot 2, Plan 363?
11. (a) Who is the owner of Lot 15, Plan 966 in the parcel register?
    (b) When did the owner acquire the property?
    (c) How is title being held?

Precedent 31.1   Property Index Map

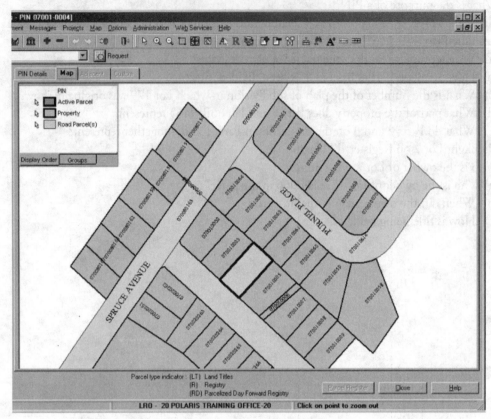

Precedent 31.2 Parcel Register

```
TRAINING
```

```
                LAND
              REGISTRY
              OFFICE #20        07001-0004 (LT)
```

* CERTIFIED BY LAND REGISTRAR IN ACCORDANCE WITH LAND TITLES ACT * SUBJECT TO RESERVATIONS IN CROWN GRANT *

PROPERTY DESCRIPTION: **** NOT VALID – TO BE USED FOR TRAINING PURPOSES ONLY **** LT 15 , PL 966 ; S/T 110069 BURLINGTON

PROPERTY REMARKS:
ESTATE/QUALIFIER: RECENTLY: PIN CREATION DATE:
FEE SIMPLE   FIRST CONVERSION FROM BOOK   1997/03/31
LT CONVERSION QUALIFIED
OWNERS' NAMES   CAPACITY SHARE
SZIVOS, CHRISTINE HAZEL   JTEN
SZIVOS, LASZLO JANOS   JTEN

REG. NUM.	DATE	INSTRUMENT TYPE	AMOUNT	PARTIES FROM	PARTIES TO	CERT/CHKD
				EFFECTIVE 2000/07/29 THE NOTATION OF THE "BLOCK IMPLEMENTATION DATE" OF 1997/03/31 ON THIS PIN		
				WAS REPLACED WITH THE "PIN CREATION DATE" OF 1997/03/31		
				** PRINTOUT INCLUDES ALL DOCUMENT TYPES (DELETED INSTRUMENTS NOT INCLUDED) **		
				**SUBJECT, ON FIRST REGISTRATION UNDER THE LAND TITLES ACT, TO:		
				** SUBSECTION 44(1) OF THE LAND TITLES ACT, EXCEPT PARAGRAPH 11, PARAGRAPH 14, PROVINCIAL SUCCESSION DUTIES *		
				** AND ESCHEATS OR FORFEITURE TO THE CROWN.		
				** THE RIGHTS OF ANY PERSON WHO WOULD, BUT FOR THE LAND TITLES ACT, BE ENTITLED TO THE LAND OR ANY PART OF		
				** IT THROUGH LENGTH OF ADVERSE POSSESSION, PRESCRIPTION, MISDESCRIPTION OR BOUNDARIES SETTLED BY		
				** CONVENTION.		
				** ANY LEASE TO WHICH THE SUBSECTION 70(2) OF THE REGISTRY ACT APPLIES.		
				**DATE OF CONVERSION TO LAND TITLES: 1997/04/01 **		
103707	1959/10/13	AGR SUBDIVISION				C
110069	1960/04/11	TRANSFER EASEMENT			THE CORPORATION OF THE TOWN OF BURLINGTON	C
119980	1961/01/25	BYLAW			THE PUBLIC UTILITIES COMMISSION OF THE TOWN OF BURLINGTON	C
813227	1993/10/29	TRANSFER	$144,000		SZIVOS, CHRISTINE HAZEL SZIVOS, LASZLO JANOS	C
813228	1993/10/29	CHARGE	$129,970		CANADA TRUSTCO MORTGAGE COMPANY	C
```

NOTE: ADJOINING PROPERTIES SHOULD BE INVESTIGATED TO ASCERTAIN DESCRIPTIVE INCONSISTENCIES, IF ANY, WITH DESCRIPTION REPRESENTED FOR THIS PROPERTY.
NOTE: ENSURE THAT YOUR PRINTOUT STATES THE TOTAL NUMBER OF PAGES AND THAT YOU HAVE PICKED THEM ALL UP.
```

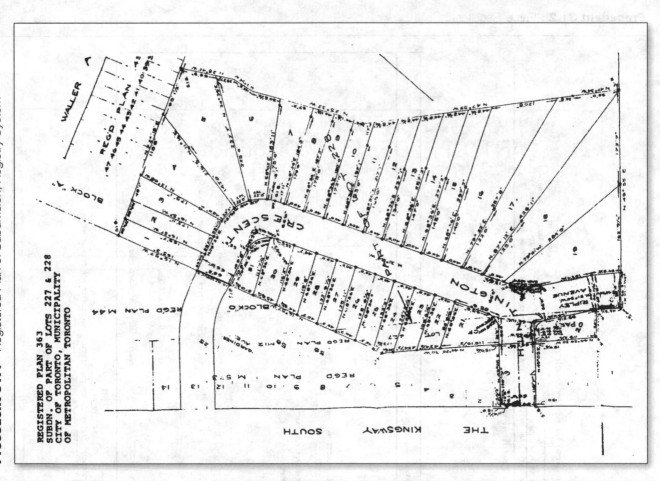

PAGE NO. 2

LOT **2** PLAN **363**

REGISTRATION NUMBER	INSTRUMENT	DATE OF INSTRUMENT	REGISTRATION DATE	GRANTOR	GRANTEE	CONSIDERATION ETC.	LAND AND REMARKS
2265	Grant	30 Apr 1959	28 May 1959	Joseph F. Mill / Jean Mill	John R. Bond / Dorothy S. Bond, Joint Tenants	$2. etc.	Lot 2
2266	Mtg	16 Apr 1959	28 May 1959	John R. Bond / Dorothy S. Bond	Prudential Insce Co. of America	7500.	Lot 2 DISCHARGED BY No. 15463 WT.
WT 15463	DISCHARGE OF MORTGAGE	21 June 1972	6 July 1972	The Prudential Insurance Company of America	John R. Bond / Dorothy S. Bond		Mort. 2266
WT 15786	Grant	19 June 1972	15 Aug 1972	John R. Bond / Dorothy S. Bond	Joseph A. Tuck / Donna E. Tuck his wife AS JOINT TENANTS	$2. etc.	Lot 2
WT 15787	MORTGAGE	26 June 1972	15 Aug 1972	Joseph A. Tuck / Donna E. Tuck	The Metropolitan Trust Company	$28 420	Lot 2
CT 12808	Grant	28 Feb 1975	1 Apr 1975	Joseph A. Tuck / Donna E. Tuck	Virginia Jonquil	$2. etc	Lot 2
CT 12809	MORTGAGE	18 Mar 1975	1 Apr 1975	Virginia Jonquil	The Royal Trust Company	9 350.	Lot 2

PLAN OF SUBDIVISION
OF PART OF LOT 33, CONCESSION 4
BOROUGH OF SCARBOROUGH
MUNICIPALITY OF METROPOLITAN TORONTO

M - 1718

APPROVED FOR REGISTRATION

29 Sept. 1976

Assistant Examiner of Surveys

PLAN M-1718 registered 4 Oer 1976
and entered on Parcel PLAN-1

Section M-1718

Land Registrar

CERTIFICATES, CONSENTS and DEDICATIONS are filed under No A-579-318 in the Office of Land Titles

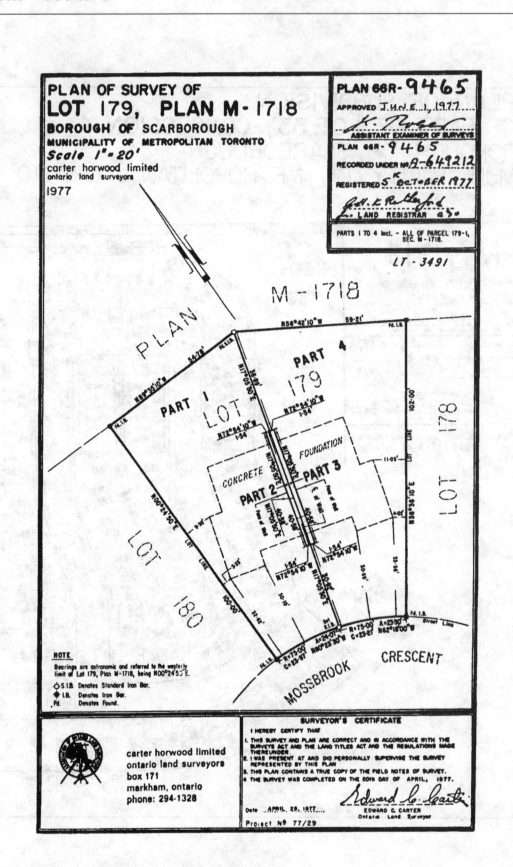

CHAPTER 32
TRANSFERS

This chapter discusses transfers of land and their role in conveying ownership of real property and also includes illustrated guidance on the electronic preparation and registration of transfers.

WHAT IS A TRANSFER

Title to real property **transfers** when real property changes hands; hence, **transfer** is the name of the document which accomplishes a transfer of title to a new owner. A transfer is commonly referred to as a **deed** or a **transfer/deed**, and we use transfer or transfer/deed interchangeably. Pursuant to the *Land Registration Reform Act*, however, the document which transfers title is a **transfer**.

ELECTRONIC TRANSFER

Pursuant to the *Land Registration Reform Act*, electronic registration is in force in nearly all parts of the province. Electronic registration, **e-reg** for short, is accomplished through the Teraview software by Teranet Inc., which is a government-approved software. Although the format of the e-reg transfer differs from that of the paper transfer/deed, Form 1, the substance of the information is the same for both forms. In both documents, the parties are referred to as **transferor** for the party selling, and **transferee** for the party buying. The lawyer for the vendor (transferor) usually prepares the transfer/deed (electronic or paper).

> **Legal TIP**
>
> The transferOR is the vendOR. Remember the identical OR ending to help you distinguish the transferor, who is selling, from the transferee, who is buying real property.

PREPARING THE ELECTRONIC TRANSFER

The following e-reg instructions assume that you are familiar with the Teraview e-reg software through either the law office or the Teraview Training System tutorial at your college. As a beginner in this chapter's introductory e-reg transfer, you may wish to use Precedent 32.1 for visual support and prepare that same transfer by applying the guided Teraview steps which follow and which relate to the same transfer. When done, your completed e-reg transfer should be the same as that in Precedent 32.1.

> **Legal TIP**
>
> The property map and the parcel register for this property are in Chapter 31.

Removable storage device Unless otherwise instructed, use the same valid removable storage device, account name, user name, and pass phrase (password) that you already use in your office or that you use/used in your Teraview Training System at the college.

Log in	**Exit Teraview**

⇨ Place storage device in removable device drive
   • Double click on Teraview folder on desktop
   • Double click on Training icon
   • Click Yes on Teraview Log in prompt
⇨   Enter:
     • Your training account, user name, pass phrase
     • Profile location: (removable storage device)
     • Click OK
‼ Do not remove your removable storage device until you have completed your Teraview session.
	⇨ Click on:
	   • Products in menu bar
	   • Exit Teraview
	   • Yes to confirm
	   • Yes to quit.
	
	‼ Keep your security device in the drive until the green light on the drive goes out after you log out.

Creating a new docket

Figure 32.1   New Docket

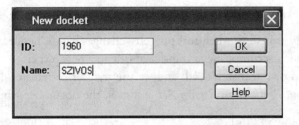

Create a New Docket	**Open Existing Docket**

⇨ Click on:
   • Administration from menu bar
   • Create Docket (dialog box opens)
   • Key in docket ID Number (client's file number e.g. 1960)
   • Key in docket name (client's name, e.g. SZIVOS)
   • OK
	⇨ Click on:
	   • Administration from menu bar
	   • Open Docket (dialog box opens)
	   • Key in docket ID number or
	   • Docket name (e.g. 1960;SZIVOS)
	   • Find
	   • OK

What is a new docket   Each new docket that you create in Teraview is used exclusively for doing all of the client's e-reg documents through Teraview, and it stores all of those electronic documents which are prepared through Teraview, e.g. transfer, charge/mortgage. Teraview deducts its charges from your firm's account with Teraview and charges them to the docket ID number, e.g. 1960. Your firm then recovers the charges from your client as disbursements at billing time. That is why law firms usually give the same ID number to a new e-reg docket as that of their clients' paper file number. For all other work on the file, you would use your regular software program/s.

Figure 32.2 Create a New Transfer

Create New Form - (Transfer)	Properties
⇨ Click on: • Instrument (on menu bar) • Create New (New Form window opens) • (+) (beside Transfer) • Transfer • Double click (Work in Progress window opens).	⇨ Key in consideration, e.g. $310,000.00 • Key in PIN, e.g. 07001 0004 (Legal description prepopulates in data fields) • Click on PIN in Properties branch • Property entry fields open; make any necessary changes to prepopulated information.

Figure 32.3 Properties

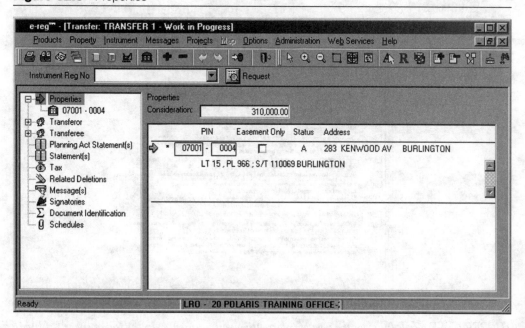

The **consideration** refers to the purchase price of the land and building only. If the purchase price, $100,000, includes chattels, e.g. stove, refrigerator, and the agreement of purchase and sale specifies the value of such chattels, e.g. $2,000, subtract the value from the purchase price, and key in the result, $98,000 ($100,000 - $2,000). If the purchase price does not specify the value of any chattels, key in $100,000.

Legal TIP

If you do not have a PIN, Search by Address from Property on menu bar, enter address, Area drop-down list, select city/town, OK. PIN and legal description should appear.

TRANSFERORS

The transferors are the vendors in a real estate transaction; they are the owners of the property they are selling. Among the statements which the transferors must include in the transfer are statements which the *Family Law Act* prescribes. These statements relate to the sale of the matrimonial home. The following information will help you understand the reasons why the *Family Law Act* requires such statements to be included in all electronic and paper transfers/deeds:

Legal TIP

The *Family Law Act* statements apply only to spouses who are legally married; they do not apply to common-law spouses.

Matrimonial home A matrimonial home may be any property that a married couple uses as a family home, and there may be more than one, e.g. a chalet in Florida for the winter, a summer cottage in Muskoka for the summer, and a house in Ottawa for the rest of the year. The matrimonial home belongs to the spouse in whose name it is registered. The *Family Law Act*, however, assures the non-owner spouse of shelter by giving that spouse as much right to **live** on the property as has the owner spouse. This is known as a **right of possession** (not ownership) of the matrimonial home. To protect this right, the *Family Law Act* requires the owner spouse to get consent from the non-owner spouse before the owner spouse can sell or charge/mortgage the matrimonial home. In practice, lawyers treat nearly every residential property as a potential matrimonial home and always include the applicable statements. When the transferor is an individual, Teraview prepopulates the *Family Law Act* and Age Statements as in Figure 32.4. You must select the age statement in every case, plus the applicable *Family Law Act* statement/s.

Figure 32.4 Transferor and Family Law Act and Age Statements

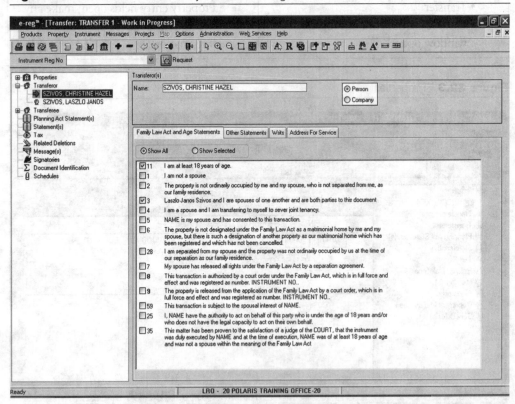

(UPPER CASE words indicate the type of information you must enter in the statement, e.g. NAME means key in name or person.)

Transferor(s)

A. *Family Law Act* and Age Statements tab: ⇨ Click on + in Transferor branch
- Select name of transferor (SZIVOS)
- Select Statement 11
- Select Statement 3 and key in name of other transferor

B. Other Statements tab: ⇨ Click on Other Statements tab
- Select box 2909 (Statement 2909 is mandatory in every case where the transaction is not made under a power of attorney.)
- (Omit Writs tab for now)

C. Address for Service tab: ⇨ Click on Address for Service tab
- Key in complete new address of transferor, 692 Garden Path, Toronto, Ontario M4K 1B2

Repeat steps in A, B and C for other transferor, LASZLO JANOS SZIVOS; key in "Christine Hazel Szivos" in Statement 3. If the address for service is different for the other transferor, key that address of that transferor.

NOTES:

If the transferor is a corporation, select the following statements:

☒10   I, (John Smith), have the authority to bind the corporation.
☒2909 or 2906   This document is not authorized under Power of Attorney by this party.
   (or Statement 2905 or 2908 if made under power of attorney).

If the transferor is a partnership, select the Transfer by Partnership form from the Transfer brach — the system prepopulates the names of the partners and the name of the partnership.

Select the applicable Family Law Act and Age Statements and the applicable power of attorney statement (2909/2906/2904/2907) for each partner, as for individual transferors, plus the following statements:

☒43   I am a partner.
☒54   This is the firm name of the partnership/limited partnership.

Figure 32.5

FAMILY LAW ACT STATEMENTS	
E-REG TRANSFERS	
Transferors are spouses; both on title as joint tenants	☒ box 3
Transferor's spouse is not on title	☒ box 5
Transferor/s is not a spouse	☒ box 1
Transferor's spouse has released all rights	☒ box 7 or 4, as applicable
Property is being sold under a court order	☒ box 8, 9 or 35, as applicable
Property is not a matrimonial home	☒ box 2, 6 or 28, as applicable

Change of name With e-reg, the system imports the name of the transferor. If the transferor's name has changed, e.g. by marriage, divorce, etc., since the old transfer was registered, you must register an **application to change name - owner**, Precedent 32.2, so that the new name will be registered on title. When you register an application to change name - owner, the system will automatically conduct an execution search against the former name of the transferor to ensure the change of name is not for the purpose of evading any executions. You may access the Application to change name - owner form through the Instruments menu, Create new, Change of name application.

TRANSFEREES

The transferee is the purchaser. With a paper transfer, the lawyer for the transferor usually prepares the transfer in its entirety from information which the transferee's lawyer provides to the transferor's lawyer. Practice varies with e-reg transfers. The lawyer for the transferor may either complete the parts relating to the transferee (on the basis of a letter or direction regarding title from the lawyer for the transferee) or message the e-reg transfer over to the lawyer for the transferee for that lawyer to complete the parts relating to the transferee. In this transfer, we will prepare the transferee's parts as follows:

Figure 32.6 Transferee

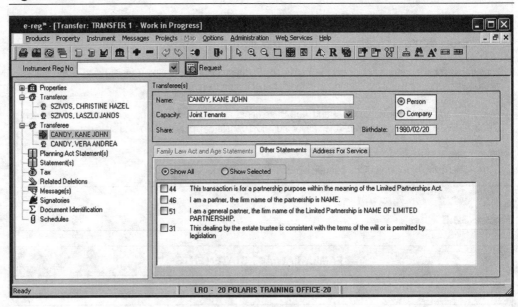

continued on next page

Transferee(s)

⇨ Click on:
- + beside Transferee in Transferee branch
- NEW PARTY
- **Name:** Enter Name of Transferee, LAST NAME(,) (space) FIRST NAME/S:
  >   CANDY, KANE JOHN
  >   Press tab
- ***Capacity:** Click on drop-down menu; select how transferee is taking title: Joint Tenants
- **Share:** (Applies only when two or more transferees will hold title by specified percentage)
- Enter date of birth yyyy/mm/dd: 1980/02/20
- **Other Statements tab:** select as applicable
- **Address For Service tab:** prepopulates address of property purchased; if purchaser is not moving into property purchased, key in address of purchaser, including postal code
- **Planning Act Statement(s):** These statements are optional; complete if so instructed
  >   Click on Planning Act Statements branch
  >   Check Boxes 21 and 22 (purchaser checks box 23)
- **Statements branch:** Check statement box/boxes, as applicable

⇨ Click on blue + (add a new party) on tool bar. Repeat the above steps for the other transferee, CANDY, VERA ANDREA.

NOTES:

*Other capacities from the drop-down menu:
If two or more transferees (who are not joint tenants), select <u>tenants in common</u>, for each transferee.
If one transferee, select <u>Beneficial owner</u>.
If transferee is a partnership, select <u>Partner</u> and the following statements for each partner:
☒46 I am a partner, the firm name of the partnership is NUMBERSRUS SERVICES.

Legal TIP

Teraview statements in **bolded** numbers mean the statements are law statements and therefore require a lawyer's signature.

LAND TRANSFER TAX STATEMENTS

The lawyer for the transferee usually completes the land transfer tax statements because it is the transferee who pays the land transfer tax; nevertheless, we will complete the land transfer tax statements so as to enable you to see the tax details that appear at the foot of the transfer printout. Full details of the land transfer tax statements, electronic and paper, are in Chapter 36.

Legal TIP

Party To is usually party who pays registration fees and land transfer tax.

Land Transfer Tax Statements

⇨ Click on:
- Tax branch
- ***All box from the Deponents tab.** (System prepopulates names of "all" transferees): CANDY, KANE JOHN; CANDY, VERA ANDREA.)
- Check (c)
- Consideration tab: enter in 1 (a) $310,000.00.
- Assessment Nos. tab: if there is no prepopulated assessment number, leave the field blank; if there is no Township name (township is mandatory), select from drop-down menu place where property is located, e.g. Burlington.

*Means all of the transferees will be signing the land transfer tax statements.

Legal TIP

You know it is an unregistered document form the "In preparation on..." note in the heading of the document.

Saving your document

➪ Click on:
- Options on Menu bar
- Save (document will save as Transfer 1)

If you wish to specify the name of your document:

➪ Click on:
- ∑ Document Identification in branch
- **Document Name** field: Enter name of document e.g. SZIVOS/TRANSFER
- **Acting For** field: Parties From – select from drop-down list (party you act for, Szivos)
- **Fee Payment** field: Party to – (Candy)
- **Transferor/Transferee client file number** field: Enter your client's file number in field
- Options on Menu bar
- Save

Printing an unregistered copy

Within the transfer Work in Progress window

➪ Click on:
- Instrument in menu bar
- Reports
- Arrow to right of Select Report field
- Select Document Preparation
- Include Attachments, if any (if you act for **purchaser**, also click Include Land Transfer Tax Statements Report)
- Print

OVER TO THE OTHER SIDE

Legal TIP

After the initial messaging between the vendor and the purchaser, either lawyer can access and work on the document without having to send it back and forth with any changes.

You are now ready to message the transfer over to the purchaser's lawyers to review the transfer and make any changes.

Messaging the transfer to the lawyers for the purchaser

➪ Click on:
- Messages
- Compose
- Account – if you know the account name of the law firm acting for the purchaser, enter it here; or
- User – enter name of lawyer acting for the purchaser, Raymond G. Castles (or select from drop-down list)
- Add User
- From the Re: Instrument list, select document you are sending, Szivos/Transfer

➪ Click on:
- Message area, type message, e.g. Please review the transfer.
- Send
- Products on menu bar
- Exit Teraview
- Yes to confirm

Legal TIP

With a Registry system property, search in Teraview by street address through the Property menu. If the resultant PIN has an LT (as opposed to R) ending, your property has been converted to Land Titles, and the new document would be more than likely prepared and registered electronically.

TRANSFER/DEED, FORM 1

The transfer/deed, Form 1, is the paper form used to transfer title from the current owner to the next in both the Registry and Land Titles systems. For your reference, Precedent 32.3 shows you an example of a paper transfer/deed, Form 1, as registered in the Registry system, and Precedent 32.4 shows you an example as prepared for registration in the Land Titles system. In the rare event of having to prepare a paper transfer/deed, Form 1, you may refer to these precedents for guidance.

Legal Office Procedures

CHAPTER SUMMARY

When real property changes hands, a transfer is electronically completed. In both the electronic transfer and the paper transfer/deed, Form 1, the party selling is referred to as the **transferor** and the party buying as the **transferee**, and the substance is the same in both forms. If the transferor is married, owns the property being sold alone and the property is a matrimonial home, the law requires the non-owner spouse to give up his or her right of **possession** (not ownership) of the property. Completing the *Planning Act* statements in the transfer is optional.

REVIEW QUESTIONS

1. What is a transfer?
2. In what situation would the spouse of a transferor be required to consent to a transaction?
3. Explain why a matrimonial home is a place where people go to get married.
4. Name the terms which describe the purchaser and the vendor in a transfer/deed.
5. Refer to the *Family Law Act* statements in this chapter, and write down the applicable statement in the following situations:
   (a) if you were married and held the property you are selling as joint tenants with your spouse;
   (b) if you were married and held the property you are selling in your name alone;
   (c) if you were not married and held the property you are selling in your name alone.

Precedent 32.1   Electronic Transfer, Joint Tenants

**** NOT VALID - TO BE USED FOR TRAINING PURPOSES ONLY ****

Properties

PIN	07001 - 0004 LT	Interest/Estate	Fee Simple
Description	LT 15 , PL 966 ; S/T 110069 BURLINGTON		
Address	283 KENWOOD AV BURLINGTON		

Consideration

Consideration	$ 310,000.00

Transferor(s)

The transferor(s) hereby transfers the land to the transferee(s).

Name	SZIVOS, CHRISTINE HAZEL Acting as an individual
Address for Service	692 Garden Path Toronto, Ontario M4K 1B2

I am at least 18 years of age.

Laszlo Janos Szivos and I are spouses of one another and are both parties to this document

This document is not authorized under Power of Attorney by this party.

Name	SZIVOS, LASZLO JANOS Acting as an individual
Address for Service	692 Garden Path Toronto, Ontario M4K 1B2

I am at least 18 years of age.

Christine Hazel Szivos and I are spouses of one another and are both parties to this document

This document is not authorized under Power of Attorney by this party.

Transferee(s)   Capacity   Share

		Capacity	Share
Name	CANDY, KANE JOHN Acting as an individual	Joint Tenants	
Date of Birth	1980 02 20		
Address for Service	283 Kenwood Avenue Burlington, Ontario L3B 4L6		
Name	CANDY, VERA ANDREA Acting as an individual	Joint Tenants	
Date of Birth	1981 06 27		
Address for Service	283 Kenwood Avenue Burlington, Ontario L3B 4L6		

STATEMENT OF THE TRANSFEROR (S): The transferor(s) verifies that to the best of the transferor's knowledge and belief, this transfer does not contravene the Planning Act.

Calculated Taxes

Provincial Land Transfer Tax	$3,125.00
Retail Sales Tax	$0.00

Precedent 32.2 Application to Change Name — Owners, Electronic

---

**** NOT VALID - TO BE USED FOR TRAINING PURPOSES ONLY ****

This document has not been submitted and may be incomplete.

LRO # 20   **Application To Change Name-Owners**

yyyy mm dd   Page 1 of 1

In preparation on 20– 08 15   at 11:46

Properties

PIN	24925 - 2000 LT
Description	LOT 80, PLAN 20M696, OAKVILLE ; S/T RIGHT H778324
Address	9 ROSEMARIE ROAD OAKVILLE

Party From(s)

Name	KOTA, MARIA BARBARA Acting as an individual
Address for Service	9 Rosemarie Road, Oakville, Ontario L4R 6D6

Applicant(s)   *Capacity*   *Share*

Name	CRUSH, MARIA BARBARA Acting as an individual
Address for Service	9 Rosemarie Road Oakville, Ontario L4R 6D6

This document is not authorized under Power of Attorney by this party.

Statements

The name has changed as a result of a marriage/dissolution of marriage and this statement is made for no improper purpose.

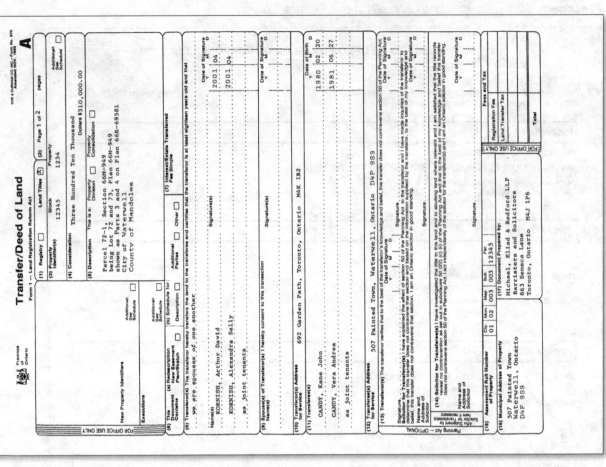

CHAPTER 33

CHARGES/ MORTGAGES AND REMEDIES

This chapter covers charges/mortgages and their role in purchasing real property and includes illustrated guidance on the electronic preparation and registration of charges/mortgages, and also discusses the various statutory remedies available to the lender.

WHAT IS A CHARGE

Pursuant to the *Land Registration Reform Act*, the term **charge** is the official name of the document. A charge is also referred to as a mortgage or a charge/mortgage, and we use **charge** and **charge/mortgage** interchangeably. A charge/mortgage is a debt on real property for the purpose of securing a loan. Thus, if the borrower were to default in repaying the loan, the lender, e.g. a bank, could force the sale of the borrower's property to recover its money. Since the bank is lending the borrower money for the borrower's own use, the bank will charge interest on the amount of the loan until the borrower repays the loan. The amount of the loan is known as the **principal.** In both the electronic system as well as the manual system, the party giving the charge/mortgage is referred to as the **chargor**, and the party who receives the charge/mortgage, e.g. the bank, as the **chargee**.

TYPES OF CHARGES/MORTGAGES

Charges/mortgages may or may not involve purchase and sale transactions. When they do, the purchaser places the property he or she is **purchasing** as security for a loan. When they do not, the party borrowing usually borrows for reasons other than purchasing a house, e.g. to pay off an IOU, and places the property he or she **already owns** as security for the loan. We focus here on charges/mortgages arising from purchasing real property because these help to also understand purchase and sale transactions. Generally, there are three types of charges/mortgages in purchase and sale transactions: new charges/mortgages, assumed charges/mortgages, and charges/mortgages taken back.

New charge/mortgage   Generally, a new charge/mortgage usually means the vendor wants his or her money in cash for the sale of his or her house, and the purchaser does not have it and has had to borrow it. A typical new charge/mortgage comes about when Smith sells his property for $300,000 in cash. Jones buys it, puts $100,000 cash of his own money toward the house and has had to borrow the remaining $200,000 from the bank, placing the property he is buying as security for the bank loan. Thus, Jones pays the $300,000 in cash to Smith ($100,000 of his own money, plus $200,000 borrowed from the bank) and owes $200,000 by way of a new charge/mortgage to the bank. Should Jones be unable to repay the charge/mortgage, the bank could seize his property and sell it to get its money. New charges/mortgages are the most frequently used charges/mortgages in purchase and sale transactions.

Assumed charge/mortgage   When the agreement of purchase and sale states that the purchaser will be assuming a charge/mortgage, it means there is an existing charge/mortgage on the property and the purchaser will be taking it over: for example, Smith sells the property for $200,000 but still owes $50,000 on his charge/mortgage to the bank. Jones buys the property, but has only $150,000 in cash of his own money, and for the remaining part of the purchase price, Jones **assumes** Smith's existing charge/mortgage of $50,000, which means Jones, instead of Smith, will be repaying it to the bank. This saves Jones the trouble of having to borrow from scratch, but the bank would have to approve Jones as the new chargor/mortgagor. A new charge/mortgage document is not prepared in this case because the assumed charge/mortgage already exists -- Smith has it and would usually hand it over to Jones on the closing of the transaction. Assumed charges/mortgages are used occasionally.

Charge/mortgage taken back   When the agreement of purchase and sale states that the vendor will take back, VTB for short, a charge/mortgage, it means this: Smith owes nothing on the property and sells it to Jones for $200,000. Jones pays $150,000 in cash of his own money and Smith "takes back" a charge/mortgage on the property for the remaining $50,000, i.e. Jones will be paying back the $50,000 to Smith gradually, instead of in cash, but with interest. A charge/mortgage document would be prepared with Jones as chargor/mortgagor and Smith as chargee/mortgagee. VTB charges/mortgages are used occasionally.

First, second, and third charges/mortgages   Pity the chargor/mortgagor of three or more charges/mortgages on the property. Although it is reasonable to assume from their numerical order that the chargor/mortgagor pays off the one before starting payments on the other, it is not so. The chargor/mortgagor makes payments on all three of them at the same time on each of their due dates. The ordinal order is a reference to the priority for payment in the event of default: for example, if the chargor/mortgagor defaults on any one of the charges/mortgages, the chargee/mortgagee on whose payments the chargor/mortgagor has defaulted may force the sale of the property, but payment from the sale money would go first to the first chargee/mortgagee, then to the second, and finally to the third. Proof of priority is the date and time of **registration** of each charge/mortgage. In effect, priority is on a "first registered, first paid" basis.

TYPES OF CHARGE/MORTGAGE REPAYMENTS

The repayment of charges/mortgages is done by the borrower making payments, usually monthly, to the lending institution, e.g. a bank, over the term of the charge/mortgage. The word **term** means the length of time before the charge/mortgage becomes due, or matures, e.g. three years. The term **matures** or **maturity** means time is up, e.g. the three-year term is up, at which time, the entire balance of the charge/mortgage must be paid in full. The payments during the term of the charge/mortgage are made up of principal and interest on either an amortized or a non-amortized basis.

Amortized payments   These are usually monthly payments, each of which includes principal and interest, and are therefore referred to as blended payments. They are called amortized because, even though the term of the charge/mortgage is fixed, e.g. for three years, the amount of the payments is usually calculated as if the term were twenty-five years so as to make the monthly payments more affordable. On the maturity date, however, the chargor must pay off the entire balance. If the chargor is not able to pay it off, the chargor must either borrow again, or if the charge/mortgage contains a renewal clause, the chargor may renew the charge/mortgage for a further period of time. Note the pattern and amounts of the amortized payments in the computerized amortization schedule in Figure 33.1. The chargor, for example, would make a monthly payment of $392.78 on January 1 made up of $163.72 principal and $229.06 interest. With each monthly payment made, the principal amount increases as the interest amount decreases. On the maturity date, payment 60, the entire balance is due and payable.

Figure 33.1 Amortization Schedule

Principal: $25,000.00
Interest rate: 11.25% per annum compounded 2 times per year
Monthly payment: $392.78
Payments Due: first day of each month

Pmt	mmm/yyyy	Payment	Interest	Principal	Balance
1	Jan/year	392.78	229.06	163.72	24,836.28
2	Feb/year	392.78	227.56	165.22	24,671.06
3	Mar/year	392.78	226.05	166.73	24,504.33
4	Apr/year	392.78	224.52	168.26	24,336.07
5	May/year	392.78	222.98	169.80	24,166.27
6	Jun/year	392.78	221.42	171.36	23,994.91
7	Jul/year	392.78	219.85	172.93	23,821.98
8	Aug/year	392.78	218.27	174.51	23,647.47
9	Sep/year	392.78	216.67	176.11	23,471.36
10	Oct/year	392.78	215.06	177.72	23,293.64
11	Nov/year	392.78	213.43	179.35	23,114.29
12	Dec/year	392.78	211.79	180.99	22,933.30
13	Jan/year	392.78	210.13	182.65	22,750.65
14	Feb/year	392.78	208.45	184.33	22,566.32
15	Mar/year	392.78	206.76	186.02	22,380.30
16	Apr/year	392.78	205.06	187.72	22,192.58
17	May/year	392.78	203.34	189.44	22,003.14
55	Jul/year	392.78	124.87	267.91	13,360.10
56	Aug/year	392.78	122.41	270.37	13,089.73
57	Sep/year	392.78	119.94	272.84	12,816.89
58	Oct/year	392.78	117.44	275.34	12,541.55
59	Nov/year	392.78	114.91	277.87	12,263.68
60	Dec/year	392.78	112.37	280.41	11,983.27

These calculations have been prepared using conventional compound interest principles. No liability is undertaken in regard to the interpretation or use which may be made of these calculations. It is your responsibility to ensure that the terms on which this schedule is based correspond to those in your mortgage.

E. & O. E.

Principal plus interest payments   These payments are usually quarter-yearly payments. The amount of principal is fixed, and the chargor must pay that amount in each payment, **plus** the amount of interest as calculated for each payment; hence, "principal plus interest." Principal plus interest payments ensure that the chargor will pay down a more substantial part of the principal by the maturity date. Note the pattern and amounts of the payments in the computerized quarterly payment schedule in Figure 33.2. On January 1, for example, the chargor would make a quarterly payment of $775 made up of principal in the amount of $400 and interest in the amount of $375. With each quarterly payment made, the principal amount remains constant and the amount of interest decreases. On the maturity date, payment 20, the entire balance is due and payable. Principal plus interest payments are used very occasionally in financing.

Figure 33.2 Charge/Mortgage Payment Schedule, Quarterly Payments, Principal plus Interest

Principal:	$15,000.00
Principal Payable at:	$400.00 quarterly, plus interest
20 payments	
Rate:	10.00% quarterly
Starting Date:	Oct. 1
First Payment:	Jan. 1

Payment No.	Date of Payment	Total Payment	Amout of Interest	Amount of Principal	Balance of Loan
1	Jan.1	775.00	375.00	400.00	14,600.00
2	Apr.1	765.00	365.00	400.00	14,200.00
3	Jul.1	755.00	355.00	400.00	13,800.00
4	Oct.1	745.00	345.00	400.00	13,400.00
5	Jan.1	735.00	335.00	400.00	13,000.00
6	Apr.1	725.00	325.00	400.00	12,600.00
19	Jul.1	595.00	195.00	400.00	7,400.00
20	Oct.1	- - -	185.00	7,400.00	7,585.00

PREPARING THE E-REG CHARGE/MORTGAGE

Although the e-reg charge/mortgage form differs from the paper one, the substance of information is the same for both forms. When preparing an e-reg (and paper) charge/mortgage, your firm usually acts for the chargor. In a purchase and sale transaction, your firm would usually also act for the chargee. Information for preparing the e-reg (and paper) charge/mortgage comes from the following sources, all of which should be in your client's file:

- the agreement of purchase and sale
- the charge/mortgage instructions to lawyer (which the bank/trust company supplied you with)
- if a private chargee (i.e. an individual), a letter from the chargee's lawyer about how the chargee would hold the charge/mortgage, and
- statement of adjustments.

The following e-reg instructions assume that you are familiar with the Teraview e-reg software through either the law office or the Teraview Training System tutorial at your college. As a beginner in this chapter's introductory e-reg charge/mortgage, you may wish to use Precedent 33.3 for visual support and prepare that same charge/mortgage by applying the guided Teraview steps which follow and which relate to the same charge/mortgage. When done, your completed e-reg charge/mortgage should be the same as that in Precedent 33.3. You prepared the transfer for the same property in Chapter 32. For instructions on how to log in, exit, create a new docket and open an existing docket in Teraview, see Chapter 32.

Figure 33.3 Properties, Charge/Mortgage

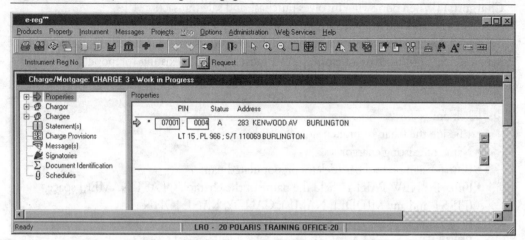

Create New Form — (Charge/Mortgage)	Properties
⇨ Click on: 　• Instrument (on menu bar) 　• Create New (New Form window opens) 　• (+) (beside Charge) 　• Charge/Mortgage 　• Double click/Create new 　• (Work in Progress window opens.)	⇨ Key in PIN, e.g. 07001 0004 (system prepopulates legal description) 　• Click on PIN in Properties branch 　• Property entry fields open 　• (Make any necessary changes to prepopulated information.)

Figure 33.4 Chargor

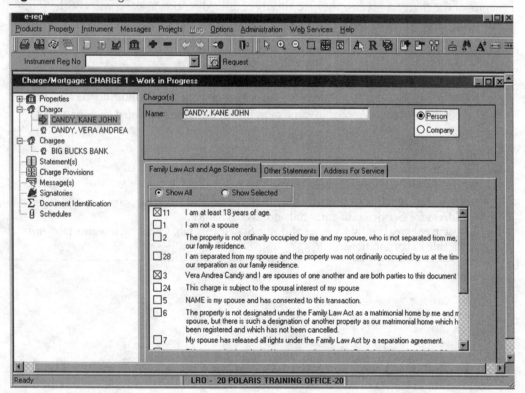

Chargor(s) (When borrowing involves purchase and sale transaction.)

In a purchase and sale transaction, the system will prepopulate the names of the **existing owners** of the property who are **not** the purchasers because the purchasers do not get registered on title until the date of closing. You must delete the existing (prepopulated) names and enter the names of the purchasers, i.e. the chargors, in the purchase and sale transaction.

⇨ Click on:
- \+ beside the Chargor branch
- Name of existing chargor/s
- **Blue (-)** sign on tool bar (deletes prepopulated name)
- Enter in *NEW PARTY* field the name of the chargor/s: LAST NAME(,) space (FIRST and any MIDDLE NAME), CANDY, KANE JOHN
- Press Enter key
- **Family Law Act and Age Statements tab**: check boxes 11 and 3
- Double click on NAME; enter full name of spouse: Vera Andrea Candy
- OK
- **Other Statements tab**: check box 2909
- **Address for Service tab**: key in complete address for service, e.g. 283 Kenwood Avenue, Burlington, Ontario L3B 4L6
- **Blue (+)** on tool bar; enter name of *NEW PARTY,* CANDY, VERA ANDREA Continue as for previous chargor, except enter Kane John Candy in name of spouse. (It is common practice to enter the address for the second chargor even if it is the same as that of the first chargor.)

Chargor(s) (When borrowing does not involve a purchase and sale transaction.)

A borrower may borrow money from a lending institution to pay off an IOU; this type of borrowing does not involve a purchase and sale transaction. Teraview prepopulates the names of the chargors because they are already registered on title as the owners of the property being charged/mortgaged.

⇨ Click on:
- (Prepopulated) Name of Chargor in Chargor branch
- Family Law Act and Age Statements tab, Other Statements tab and Address for Service tab same as above. Proceed in same steps for the other prepopulated chargor, if any.

Chargee

⇨ Click on:
- \+ beside Chargee in Chargee branch
- **Name**: Key in name of chargee, BIG BUCKS BANK
- **Address for Service tab:** enter full address of chargee.

(Capacity, Share, Family Law Act and Age Statements tab, Other Statements tab: not applicable to corporations.)

Figure 33.5 Charge Provisions

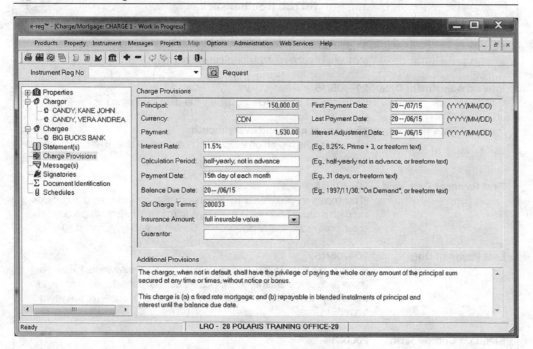

⇨ Click on:
  • Charge Provisions branch: click/tab to and complete each field. (See Notes, Figure 33.6.)
  • **Additional Provisions field:** Key in any additional provisions (provisions can also be imported from your files; see Precedent 33.1 for a list of special clauses). Any additional statements may also be entered in under Box 61 in the Statement(s) branch.

Figure 33.6

NOTES:	
Principal	**$ 150,000.00** (Enter the amount of the principal, which is the amount of money the chargor borrowed. If the charge is for the "balance of the purchase price," you must determine the amount of the principal by subtracting the following from the purchase price: the deposit, the further cash on closing, and the amounts of any new or assumed charges/mortgages. The result is usually the principal amount of the charge/mortgage.)
Calculation Period	**half-yearly, not in advance** (Enter how frequently interest is calculated.)
Balance Due Date	**20--/06/15** (This is the date (yyyy/mm/dd) on which the chargor must pay off the entire balance, i.e. the date of maturity.)
Interest Rate	**11.5%** (Rate of interest per year charged on the principal.)

figure continues on next page

Payments	**$1,530.00** (Amount of each monthly or quarterly payment.)
Interest Adjustment Date	**20--/06/15** (Date interest begins to run, usually the date of closing.)
Payment Date	**15th day of each and every month** (The day of the month on which each payment is due; if quarterly payments, enter 15th day quarter-yearly.)
First Payment Date	**20--/07/15** (If payments are monthly, enter one month after date of closing, e.g. if closing date is June 15, enter July 15 (yyyy/mm/dd); if payments are quarterly, enter three months after closing, e.g. September 15 (yyyy/mm/dd).)
Last Payment Date	**20--/06/15** (Enter same date as the date of closing, plus as many years forward as is the term of the charge, e.g. if closing date is June 15, this year, and the charge term is for five years, key (yyyy/mm/dd) June 15, five years from this year.)
Standard Charge Terms	**200033** (Lending institutions each file their own standard charge terms in the land registry office; the standard charge terms apply to every charge under that particular lending institution. A paper copy of the standard charge terms must be given to the borrower. See Precedent 33.2 for an excerpt from standard charge terms commonly used by private lenders.)
Insurance Amount	**full insurable value** (This entry is usually prepopulated. Obtain the insurable value from the chargee's instructions. Chargees require proof of insurance coverage for the full value of the property (building only, not contents) so that the chargee will recover its money in the event a fire destroys the property.)
Guarantors	(Complete this field usually when a chargor's income is inadequate to cover the repayment of the charge and the chargee requires an additional party to sign, guaranteeing that in the event the chargor is unable to pay, the guarantor will cover the charge payments.)

Note: The order of the above items differs between the system entry fields and the system printout.

Saving your document

➡ Click on:
- Options on Menu bar
- Save (system saves it as Charge 1)

If you wish to specify the name of your document:

➡ Click on:
- ∑ Document Identification in branch
- **Document Name field:** Enter name of document
  e.g. CANDY/CHARGE
- **Chargor/Chargee Client File Number** field:
- Enter your client's file number in field
- Options on Menu bar
- Save

Printing an unregistered copy

Within the transfer Work in Progress window

➡ Click on:
- Instrument in menu bar
- Reports on drop-down menu
- Select Report field
- Select Document Preparation
- Include Attachments, if any
- Print

CHARGE/MORTGAGE, FORM 2

The charge/mortgage, Form 2, is the paper form used in the manual system in both the Registry and Land Titles systems. The electronic charge/mortgage has replaced the paper charge/mortgage, Form 2; nevertheless, you are likely to encounter the charge/mortgage paper form from time to time. For your reference, Precedent 33.4 is an example of a paper charge/mortgage, Form 2, featuring monthly payments.

REMEDIES UNDER CHARGES/MORTGAGES

Things can go very wrong when the chargor is unable to pay down a charge/mortgage. A number of remedies are available to the chargee to recover payment on the charge/mortgage, including the following:

POWER OF SALE

The power of sale allows the chargee to sell the property charged/mortgaged without resorting to the courts. To exercise this power, the charge/mortgage or the standard charge terms must contain a clause permitting the chargee to sell, and the chargor must be in default of payment. The chargee may give written notice of default to the chargor and to any other chargees and notify the chargor that the chargor has a specified period of time to either bring the charge/mortgage in good standing or pay it off before the chargee sells the property. If, by the end of the specified period, the chargor is unable to either bring the payments up-to-date or pay off the charge/mortgage, the chargee proceeds with the sale. The chargee uses the sale money first toward its own debt and then toward that of any second and third chargees and execution creditors. The chargor is entitled to any surplus. The chargee may sue the chargor for any monetary deficiency. When the chargee sells, prepare a transfer: power of sale. See Precedent 33.5 for an electronic transfer: power of sale. To prepare a transfer: power of sale, you may access the form through the Teraview Instrument menu bar.

POSSESSION

Possession is a remedy that does not involve sale of the property; instead, it converts the chargee into a landlord and the chargor, i.e. the registered owner of the property, into a tenant. By virtue of the charge/mortgage and upon default of payment by the chargor, the chargee has a right of possession to the property. To obtain possession, however, the chargee, upon default by the chargor, must obtain a **writ of possession** from the court which, in effect, makes the chargee the landlord and the chargor the tenant. As a tenant, the owner pays rent to the chargee. If the property is vacant, the chargee may rent it out and collect the rent payments. The chargee deducts the expenses for maintaining the property from the rent payments, applies the balance toward the principal and interest of the charge/mortgage, and applies any remainder of the rent money to any other chargee and to the chargor.

FORECLOSURE

In a foreclosure, when the chargor is in default of payment, the chargee becomes the registered owner of the property. A foreclosure is a litigation procedure by which usually the first chargee obtains a final order of foreclosure from the court. The final order of foreclosure extinguishes all rights of the chargor as well as those of any second or third chargee and allows the first chargee to register itself on title as owner of the property. The foreclosure proceeding is similar to a regular litigation action. It begins with a **statement of claim—foreclosure** form. The first chargee is the plaintiff; the defendants are the chargor and all other chargees.

> ### Legal TIP
>
> With a Registry system property, search in Teraview by street address through the Property menu. If the resultant PIN has an LT (as opposed to R) ending, your property has been converted to Land Titles, and the new document would be more than likely prepared and registered electronically.

The defendant (chargor) or any one or more of the other defendants (chargees) may defend the foreclosure, or instead, request time to bring the charge/mortgage in good standing, or request a sale of the property under the court's supervision. If the chargor requests a sale, the chargor must pay a deposit toward the court costs. By requesting a sale, the chargor converts the foreclosure action into a normal sale transaction. That means the sale money is applied not only to the first chargee, but also to any second and subsequent chargees. Thus, the chargor releases himself or herself from the claims of all chargees to the extent that the sale money would cover. If the action had remained a foreclosure action, only the first chargee had a right to be paid.

If the chargor requests time to bring the charge/mortgage in good standing but fails to do so within the time the court permits, usually six months, or if the chargor requests a sale and a sale has not occurred, the chargee applies to the court for a final order of foreclosure. The chargee registers the final order of foreclosure on title, and by doing so, the chargee becomes the owner of the property and may sell it without court supervision.

JUDICIAL SALE

A judicial sale is the result of an unpaid judgment. It is also referred to as a sheriff's sale because the sheriff carries out the sale under the authority of a **writ of seizure and sale,** also known as a writ of execution. A judicial sale usually involves sale of the charged/mortgaged property by tender or public auction. The chargee applies to the court for possession, payment, and sale of the property. The money from the sale is applied first to the first chargee, then to the second and subsequent chargees, and finally, to the chargor.

CHAPTER SUMMARY

A charge/mortgage is the document you prepare to register a debt against real property. The lender is the chargee; the borrower is the chargor. There are three types of charges/mortgages: new charges/mortgages, assumed charges/mortgages, and charges/mortgages taken back. A new charge/mortgage is one where a purchaser borrows money pledging the property as security for the loan. An assumed charge/mortgage is one which already exists on a property and a purchaser is taking over as part of the purchase price. A charge/mortgage taken back is one where a vendor takes back a charge/mortgage from the purchaser as part of the purchase price.

A charge/mortgage may be repaid by way of amortized or non-amortized payments. Amortized payments are usually monthly payments of principal and interest. Non-amortized payments are usually quarter-yearly payments consisting of principal plus interest. A charge/mortgage is registered electronically. The paper charge/mortgage, Form 2, is prepared in both the registry system and the land titles system for properties not yet converted to Land Titles or automated. A number of remedies are available to a chargee when a chargor defaults on payment, including the following:

Power of sale. Generally, if the chargor is in default of payment, the chargee can sell the property without having to resort to the courts. Possession. This is a remedy which converts the chargee into a landlord and the registered owner of the property into a tenant who would pay rent to the chargee. Foreclosure. This remedy is usually available to a first chargee by taking measures to obtain a final order of foreclosure from the court, which court order allows the first chargee to register itself on title as the owner of the property. Judicial sale. This remedy usually involves the sale of the charged/mortgaged property by tender or public auction, which a sheriff carries out under the authority of a writ of seizure and sale.

REVIEW QUESTIONS

1. What is a charge/mortgage?
2. Does the purchaser or the vendor take back a charge/mortgage?
3. What is the usual frequency of amortized payments?
4. What is the term of a five-year charge/mortgage?
5. If the closing date is March 25, on what date would the first monthly payment be made?
6. If the closing date is March 25, on what date would the first quarterly payment be made?
7. The term **principal** in mortgages means the head of a particular school who borrows money to purchase supplies for the school classrooms. Explain.
8. What is a charge/mortgage foreclosure?
9. What is the authority which would give a chargee the right to a power of sale action?
10. What is the difference between the remedies of possession and foreclosure under a charge/mortgage?

SPECIAL CLAUSES FOR CHARGES/MORTGAGES

OPEN PAYMENT

The chargor, when not in default, shall have the privilege of paying the whole or any amount of the principal sum secured at any time or times without notice or bonus.

RENEWAL AT PREVAILING INTEREST RATE

The chargor, if not in default, shall have the privilege of renewing this charge at its maturity for a further period of five years at the interest rate prevailing at the time of maturity.

TEN PERCENT ON ANNIVERSARY DATE

The chargor, when not in default, shall have the privilege of paying, on any anniversary date, in addition to the regular monthly/quarter-yearly payments, an additional amount of principal not in excess of ten percent (10%) of the original amount of the charge, and such privilege shall not be cumulative, notwithstanding any such payment.

ONE-TWELFTH OF ANNUAL TAXES

The chargor, in addition to the monthly installments, shall pay one-twelfth (1/12) of the estimated annual taxes on the charged property.

GUARANTOR CLAUSE

The guarantor covenants and agrees with the chargee that the chargor will pay and satisfy all moneys at any time secured by this charge and duly perform and observe all covenants, agreements, and provisions in this charge and that the guarantor shall be considered as primarily liable to the chargee and shall not be released nor shall the liability of the guarantor be limited or lessened by any variation in or departure from the provisions of the charge.

MONTHLY POST-DATED CHEQUES

The chargor shall provide the chargee with a series of 12 post-dated cheques payable to the chargee at the commencement of this charge and subsequently on each yearly anniversary during the term of the charge, each cheque to be in the amount of the monthly instalment of principal and interest.

CONDOMINIUM CLAUSE

The chargor irrevocably assigns to the chargee and authorizes and empowers the chargee to exercise the right of the chargor as the owner of the said lands to vote or to consent to all matters relating to the affairs of the condominium corporation, provided, however, that:

(a) the chargee may at any time and from time to time give notice in writing to the chargor and to the condominium corporation that the chargee does not intend to exercise the said right to vote or consent, and in that event, until the chargee revokes the notice, the chargor may exercise the right to vote. Any such notice may be for an indeterminate period of time, or for a limited period of time, or for a specific meeting or matter;

(b) the chargee shall not by virtue of the assignment to the chargee of the right to vote or consent be under any obligation to vote or consent or to protect the interest of the chargor;

(c) the exercise of the right to vote or consent shall not constitute the chargee a chargee in possession.

Page 1

Land Registration Reform Act
SET OF STANDARD CHARGE TERMS
(Electronic Filing)

Filed by

Dye & Durham Co. Inc.

Filing Date: November 3, 2000

Filing Number: 200033

The following Set of Standard Charge Terms shall be applicable to documents registered in electronic format under Part III of the Land Registration Reform Act, R.S.O. 1990, c. L.44 as amended (the "Land Registration Reform Act") and shall be deemed to be included in every electronically registered charge in which this Set of standard Charge Terms is referred to by its filing number, as provided in section 9 of the Land Registration reform Act, except to the extent that the provisions of this Set of Standard Charge Terms are modified by additions, amendments or deletions in the schedule. Any charge in an electronic format of which this Set of Standard Charge Terms forms a part by reference to the above-noted filing number in such charge shall hereinafter be referred to as the "Charge".

Exclusion of Statutory Covenants

1. The implied covenants deemed to be included in a charge under subsection 7(1) of the *Land Registration Reform Act* as amended or re-enacted are excluded from the Charge.

Right to Charge the Land

2. The Chargor now has good right, full power and lawful and absolute authority to charge the land and to give the Charge to the Chargee upon the covenants contained in the Charge.

No Act to Encumber

3. The Chargor has not done, committed, executed or willfully or knowingly suffered any act, deed, matter or thing whatsoever whereby or by means whereof the land, or any part or parcel thereof, is or shall or may be in any way impeached, charged, affected or encumbered in title, estate or otherwise, except as the records of the land registry office disclose.

Good Title in Fee Simple

4. The Chargor, at the time of the delivery for registration of the Charge, is and stands solely, rightfully and lawfully seized of a good, sure, perfect, absolute and indefeasible estate of inheritance, in fee simple, of and in the land and the premises described in the Charge and in every part and parcel thereof without any manner of trusts, reservations, limitations, provisos, conditions or any other matter or thing to alter, charge, change, encumber or defeat the same, except those contained in the original grant thereof from the Crown.

Promise to Pay and Perform

5. The Chargor will pay or cause to be paid to the Chargee the full principal amount and interest secured by the Charge in the manner of payment provided by the Charge, without any deduction or abatement, and shall do, observe, perform, fulfill and keep all the provisions, covenants, agreements and stipulations contained in the Charge and shall pay as they fall due all taxes, rates, levies, charges, assessments, utility and heating charges, municipal, local, parliamentary and otherwise which now are or may hereafter be imposed, charged or levied upon the land and when required shall produce for the Chargee receipts evidencing payment of the same.

Interest After Default

6. In case default shall be made in payment of any sum to become due for interest at the time provided for payment in the Charge, compound interest shall be payable and the sum in arrears for interest from time to time, as well after as before maturity, and both before and after default and judgement, shall bear interest at the rate provided for in the Charge. In case the interest and compound interest are not paid within the interest calculation period provided in the charge from the time of default a rest shall be made, and compound interest at the rate provided for in the Charge shall be payable on the aggregate amount then due, as well after as before maturity, and so on from time to time, and all such interest and compound interest shall be a charge upon the land.

No Obligation to Advance

7. Neither the preparation, execution or registration of the Charge shall bind the Chargee to advance the principal amount secured, nor shall the advance of a part of the principal amount secured bind the Chargee to advance any unadvanced portion thereof, but nevertheless the security in the land shall take effect forthwith upon delivery for registration of the Charge by the Chargor. The expenses of the examination of the title and of the Charge and valuation are to be secured by the Charge in the event of the whole or any balance of the principal amount not being advanced, the same to be charged hereby upon the land, and shall be, without demand therefore, payable forthwith with interest at the rate provided for in the Charge, and in default the Chargee's power of sale hereby given, and all other remedies hereunder, shall be exercisable.

Costs Added to Principal

8. The Chargee may pay all premiums of insurance and all taxes, rates, levies, charges, assessments, utility and heating charges which shall from time to time fall due and be unpaid in respect of the land, and that such payments, together with all costs, charges, legal fees (as between solicitor and client) and expenses which may be incurred in taking, recovering and keeping possession of the land and of negotiating the Charge, investigating title, and registering the Charge and other necessary deeds, and generally in any other proceedings taken in connection with or to realize upon the security given in the Charge (including legal fees and real estate commissions and other costs incurred in leasing or selling the land or in exercising the power of entering, lease and sale contained in the Charge) shall be, with interest at the rate provided for in the Charge, a charge upon the land in favour of the Chargee pursuant to the terms of the Charge and the Chargee may pay or satisfy any lien, charge or encumbrance now existing or hereafter created or claimed upon the land, which payments with interest at the rate provided for in the Charge shall likewise be a charge upon the land in favour of the Chargee. Provided, and it is hereby further agreed, that all amounts paid by the Chargee as aforesaid shall be added to the principal amount secured by the Charge and shall be payable forthwith with interest at the rate provided for in the Charge, and on default all sums secured by the Charge shall immediately become due and payable at the option of the Chargee, and all powers in the Charge conferred shall become exercisable.

**** NOT VALID - TO BE USED FOR TRAINING PURPOSES ONLY ****

This document has not been submitted and may be incomplete.   yyyy mm dd   Page 1 of 2
LRO # 20   **Charge/Mortgage**   **In preparation** on 20-- 09 11   at 14:37

Properties

PIN	07001 - 0004 LT	*Interest/Estate*	Fee Simple
Description	LT 15 , PL 966 ; S/T 110069 BURLINGTON		
Address	283 KENWOOD AV BURLINGTON		

Chargor(s)

The chargor(s) hereby charges the land to the chargee(s). The chargor(s) acknowledges the receipt of the charge and the standard charge terms, if any.

Name	CANDY, KANE JOHN
	Acting as an individual
Address for Service	283 Kenwood Avenue Burlington, Ontario L3B 4L6

I am at least 18 years of age.

Vera Andrea Candy and I are spouses of one another and are both parties to this document

This document is not authorized under Power of Attorney by this party.

Name	CANDY, VERA ANDREA
	Acting as an individual
Address for Service	283 Kenwood Avenue Burlington, Ontario L3B 4L6

I am at least 18 years of age.

Kane John Candy and I are spouses of one another and are both parties to this document

This document is not authorized under Power of Attorney by this party.

Chargee(s)   Capacity   Share

Name	BIG BUCKS BANK
	Acting as a company
Address for Service	55 Fairweather Drive Waterwell, Ontario D4L 6N6

Provisions

Principal	$ 150,000.00	*Currency*	CDN
Calculation Period	half-yearly, not in advance		
Balance Due Date	20-- /06/15		
Interest Rate	11.5%		
Payments	$ 1,530.00		
Interest Adjustment Date	20-- 06 15		
Payment Date	15th day of each month		
First Payment Date	20-- 07 15		
Last Payment Date	20-- 06 15		
Standard Charge Terms	200033		
Insurance Amount	full insurable value		
Guarantor			

Precedent 33.3

Charge/Mortgage,
Monthly Payments,
Electronic, page 2

**** NOT VALID - TO BE USED FOR TRAINING PURPOSES ONLY ****

This document has not been submitted and may be incomplete.   yyyy mm dd   Page 2 of 2
LRO # 20   **Charge/Mortgage**   **In preparation** on 20-- 09 11   at 14:37

Additional Provisions

The chargor, when not in default, shall have the privilege of paying the whole or any amount of the principal sum secured at any time or times, without notice or bonus.

This charge is (a) a fixed rate mortgage; and (b) repayable in blended instalments of principal and interest until the balance due date.

Legal Office Procedures

Charge/Mortgage of Land
Form 2 — Land Registration Reform Act

Province of Ontario

Do Process Software Ltd. • (416) 322-6111

B

(1) Registry [X]   **Land Titles** [ ]   **(2) Page 1 of 1 pages**

(3) Property Identifier(s)   Block   Property   Additional: See Schedule [ ]

(4) Principal Amount

FIFTY TWO THOUSAND--------------------   Dollars $ **52,000.00**

(5) Description

Lot 732, Plan 9863
City of Toronto
Registry Division of the Toronto Land Registry Office (No. 66)

FOR OFFICE USE ONLY

New Property Identifiers   Additional: See Schedule [ ]

Executions   Additional: See Schedule [ ]

(6) This Document Contains (a) Redescription New Easement Plan/Sketch [ ]   (b) Schedule for: Description [ ] Additional Parties [ ] Other [ ]   **(7) Interest/Estate Charged** Fee Simple

(8) Standard Charge Terms — The parties agree to be bound by the provisions in Standard Charge Terms filed as number _____ and the Chargor(s) hereby acknowledge(s) receipt of a copy of these terms.

(9) Payment Provisions

(a) Principal Amount $ **52,000.00**	(b) Interest Rate **11.00** % per annum	(c) Calculation Period **half-yearly, not in advance**

** (d) Interest Adjustment Date Y 20 -- M 03 D 25	(e) Payment Date and Period **25th day of each month**	** (f) First Payment Date Y 20 -- M 04 D 25
** (g) Last Payment Date Y 20 -- M 03 D 25	(h) Amount of Each Payment Four Hundred Ninety-------------------------------- Dollars $ **490.00**	
** (i) Balance Due Date Y 20 -- M 03 D 25	(j) Insurance **Full replacement value** Dollars $	

(10) Additional Provisions

The chargor, when not in default, shall have the privilege of paying, on any anniversary date, in addition to the regular monthly payments, an additional amount of principal not in excess of ten percent (10%) of the original amount of the charge, and such privilege shall not be cumulative, notwithstanding any such payments.

Continued on Schedule [ ]

(11) Chargor(s) The chargor hereby charges the land to the chargee and certifies that the chargor is at least eighteen years old and that the person consenting below is my spouse.

The chargor(s) acknowledge(s) receipt of a true copy of this charge.

Name(s)	Signature(s)	Date of Signature Y M D
JOYCE, James		20 -- 03 25

(12) Spouse(s) of Chargor(s) I hereby consent to this transaction.

Name(s)	Signature(s)	Date of Signature Y M D
JOYCE, Francina		20 -- 03 25

(13) Chargor(s) Address for Service   12 Dubliners Drive, Toronto, Ontario M8P 4W6

(14) Chargee(s)

HUXLEY ALDOUS LOANS LIMITED

(15) Chargee(s) Address for Service   133 Brave New World Avenue, Toronto, Ontario M6W 4F6

(16) Assessment Roll Number of Property	Cty. 78	Mun. 99	Map 100	Sub. 200	Par. 50502	Fees

Registration Fee

(17) Municipal Address of Property

12 Dubliners Drive, Toronto, Ontario M8P 4W6

** (d) and (f) current year;
** (g) and (i) final year of term.

(18) Document Prepared by:

Michael, Eliad & Redford LLP
Barristers and Solicitors
863 Seneca Lane
Toronto, Ontario M4J 1P6

FOR OFFICE USE ONLY

Total

Document prepared using *The Conveyancer*

Precedent 33.5 Transfer: Power of Sale, Electronic

**** NOT VALID - TO BE USED FOR TRAINING PURPOSES ONLY ****

LRO # 20 **Transfer: Power Of Sale**

yyyy mm dd   Page 1 of 1
In preparation on 20-- 08 15   at 13:07

Properties

PIN	07001 - 0449 LT	Interest/Estate	Fee Simple
Description	LT 179 , PL 607 ; BURLINGTON		
Address	5464 RANDOLPH CR BURLINGTON		

Source Instruments

Registration No.	Date	Type of Instrument
H775207	1999 02 05	Charge/Mortgage

Consideration

Consideration $ 300,000.00

Transferor(s)

The transferor(s) hereby transfers the land to the transferee(s).

Name	BIG BUCKS BANK Acting as a company
Address for Service	55 Fairweather Drive Waterwell, Ontario D4L 6N6

I, James Johnston, have the authority to bind the corporation.

Transferee(s)   Capacity   Share

Name	BUYER, JACK Acting as an individual
Date of Birth	1965 04 27
Address for Service	5464 Randolph Court Burlington, Ontario L5B 6R6

Statements

The document is authorized under the charge and the Mortgages Act.

The sale proceedings and transfer comply with the charge, the Mortgages Act , and if applicable the Bankruptcy and Insolvency Act (Canada), the Condominium Act, the Construction Lien Act and the Farm Debt Mediation Act (Canada).

The charge was in default at the time notice of sale was given and continues to be in default and the money has been advanced under the charge.

There are no encumbrances to be deleted

This transaction is not subject to any writs of execution

Title to the land is not subject to spousal rights under the Family Law Act

Schedule: Notice of Sale was delivered on (date mm/dd/yyyy).

Calculated Taxes

Provincial Land Transfer Tax	$2,975.00
Retail Sales Tax	$0.00

CHAPTER 34

DISCHARGES AND RELATED DOCUMENTS

This chapter discusses documents that apply when there is no longer a debt over a property as well as documents that apply when changes in obligations under charges/mortgages become necessary.

DISCHARGE OF CHARGE

A discharge of charge (electronic or paper) is used when a charge has been paid either in full or in part. Once registered on title, it indicates that there is no longer a charge/mortgage outstanding on title against the chargor's property. The terms charge and charge/mortgage are used interchangeably. Although the forms of the electronic and paper discharge of charge differ, the substance is the same for both forms.

Who prepares and registers a discharge of charge   Either the lawyer for the chargee or the lawyer for the chargor may prepare and register a discharge of charge, but it is the chargee who must sign it. In the case of lending institutions, the lending institutions themselves usually prepare as well as register the discharge of charge electronically; they then forward a receipted (registered) copy of the discharge of charge, together with a letter releasing their interest in the chargor's insurance policy, to the lawyer for the chargor.

Who pays legal fees for a discharge of charge   The chargor pays a discharge fee for preparation of the discharge and also a registration fee for registration of the discharge. The general rule is that the chargee will do what the chargor requires in order to discharge the charge/mortgage, but at no cost to the chargee since giving the discharge of charge is in the interest of the chargor.

Documents required for preparing a discharge of charge   To prepare either an e-reg or paper discharge of charge, you require the following documents, as applicable:

1. A discharge statement setting out how much is still owing on the charge/mortgage being discharged. You get a discharge statement from the chargee after writing to the chargee for it. See, for example, how the discharge statement in Precedent 34.1 relates to the discharge of charge in Precedent 34.2.

2. The registered copy of the charge/mortgage being discharged (in possession of chargor).

*3. The registered copy of any transfer of charge, also referred to as assignment of charge/mortgage, (in possession of new chargee).

*4. The registered copy of any postponement of interest, also referred to as postponement of charge/mortgage, (in possession of chargee who should have been registered first).

* Where any of these documents relate to the charge/mortgage being discharged, you must refer to these documents, as applicable, in the discharge of charge (e-reg or paper) so that the land registry office can clear them off title.

THE E-REG DISCHARGE OF CHARGE

Following are Teraview instructions for preparing an e-reg discharge of charge, Precedent 37.1. See Chapter 32 for instructions on how to log in, create a new docket, and open an existing docket, and continue on as follows:

Figure 34.1   Source Instruments, Discharge of Charge

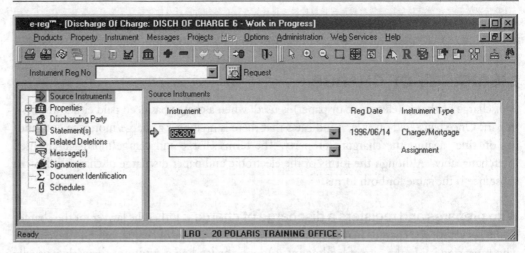

<table>
<tr><td rowspan="2">

Legal TIP

To save, click Options; click Save.

</td><td>

⇨ Click on:
  - Instrument (on menu bar)
  - Create New
  - +beside Discharge of Charge or Other Interests
  - Double click Discharge of Charge

</td><td>

⇨ Click on Source Instruments branch
  - Enter instrument number of charge/ mortgage being discharged
  - Assignment field — enter instrument number of any assignment of mort- gage/transfer of charge

</td></tr>
</table>

Figure 34.2   Properties, Discharge of Charge

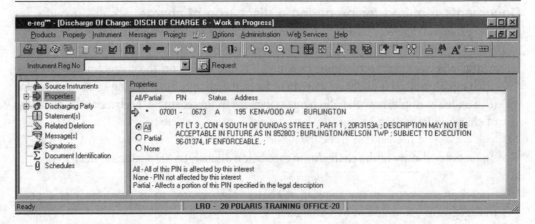

Properties

⇨ Click on Properties branch
  - *All or **Partial field
  - PIN on Properties branch; check/correct prepopulated property address

* All means the interest affects ALL of the PIN.

** Partial means the chargor is discharging one of several properties covered by the same charge/mortgage. This usually occurs with builders who "blanket-charge/mortgage" a whole subdivision and discharge the blanket charge/mortgage part-by-part (hence, **partial**) with each property they sell.

Legal TIP

The name of the chargor/mortgagor never appears on the e-reg discharge of charge nor in the preparation of it.

Figure 34.3 Discharging Party

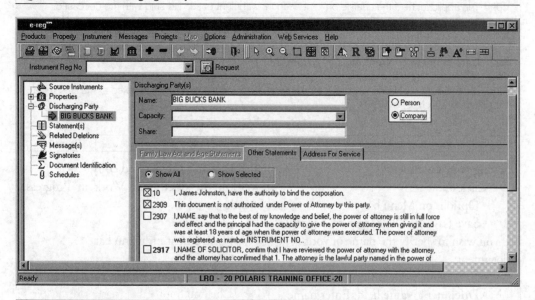

Discharging Party

⇨ Click on + Discharging Party branch. Click on Discharging Party Name
  - Other Statements tab: select box 10; double click on NAME, key in name of person who has authority to sign; select the following mandatory statements: 2909 and *3700 or *3710
  - **Address for Service tab**: key in chargee's complete address for service.

(Capacity, Share, *Family Law Act* and Age Statements apply to individuals.)

*3710 The party giving this discharge is the original chargee and is the party entitled to give an effective discharge. (Use this statement where the chargee is still the same chargee as on the originally registered charge/mortgage .)

*3700 The party giving this discharge is not the original chargee or is the original chargee and has changed its name but is the party entitled to give an effective discharge. (Use this statement where the chargee has changed its name or where there is a transfer of charge/ assignment of charge. Click Schedule 61 to provide details for the change.)

Chargee is deceased   The estate trustee would complete the discharge of charge and select the applicable one of the following statements as proof of death of the chargee (**bolding** means the statement requires the lawyer's signature and, therefore, the land registry office requires no further evidence):

3512   The applicant is appointed as Estate Trustee with a will by (name of court), under File No. NUMBER, dated yyyy/mm/dd and is still in full force and effect. (Use this statement where an estate trustee with a will has registered a certificate of appointment in the land registry office.)

3513   The applicant is appointed as Estate Trustee without a will by (name of court), under File No. NUMBER, dated yyyy/mm/dd and is still in full force and effect. (Use this statement where an estate trustee without a will has registered a certificate of appointment in the land registry office.)

609   The applicant held the charge on joint account with right of survivorship with the deceased. (Use this statement where one of the chargees on joint account is deceased and include one of the following statements):

622   Date of death of NAME was yyyy/mm/dd.
OR
623   Date of death of NAME was yyyy/mm/dd and the evidence of death is indexed at the land registry office as Index No. NUMBER.

Saving your document
⇨ Click on:
  • Options on Menu bar
  • Save (saves as Discharge of Charge 1)
If you wish to specify the name of your document:
    • Σ Document Identification in branch
    • **Document Name** field: Enter name of document
    • **Discharging Party Client File number** field:
    • Key in your client's file number
    • Options on Menu bar
    • Save

Printing an unregistered copy
Within the document Work in Progress window
⇨ Click on:
  • Instrument on menu bar
  • Reports
  • Arrow to right of Select Report field

  • Select Document Preparation
  • Include Attachments, if any
  • Print

THE DISCHARGE OF CHARGE/MORTGAGE, FORM 3

The discharge of charge/mortgage, Form 3, is the paper form used in the manual system in both the Registry and Land Titles systems. The electronic discharge of charge form replaces the paper discharge of charge/mortgage, Form 3. For your reference, Precedent 34.3 is an example of the paper form.

THE E-REG TRANSFER OF CHARGE

Prepare a transfer of charge, also referred to as assignment of charge/mortgage, Precedent 34.4, when a chargee sells the charge/mortgage he or she holds. The chargee selling the charge/mortgage is the **transferor**; the party buying it is the **transferee**. A transfer of charge might occur where the chargee needs immediate cash: for example, chargee X sells the charge/mortgage to Y, usually for the price of the principal amount of the charge/mortgage (sometimes for less to attract a buyer). Chargor Z makes future payments to Y, the new chargee/mortgagee. A transfer of charge may also occur where chargee X borrows money from the bank and uses the charge/mortgage itself as collateral for the loan. If X defaults on the bank loan, the bank becomes the recipient of the charge/mortgage payments which Z would have ordinarily made to X. To prepare an e-reg transfer of charge, you may access the form through the Teraview Instrument on the menu bar and proceed down the applicable branches. To print an unregistered copy of the transfer of charge, follow the instructions under the discharge of charge.

Acknowledgment   When you prepare a transfer of charge, also prepare an **acknowledgment**, Precedent 34.5. In the acknowledgment, the chargor confirms the rate of interest and principal amount of the charge/mortgage being transferred. Make three copies. Keep one in the file. Send two to the chargor, one to sign and return to you. Make a photocopy of the signed one for the file. Send the signed copy to the lawyer for the new chargee.

Notice of transfer of charge   After you register the transfer of charge, prepare a **notice of transfer of charge**, Precedent 34.6. The original chargee signs this notice to authorize the chargor to make future payments to the new chargee. Make three copies. Keep one in the file. Have the original chargee sign two. Make a photocopy of a signed one for the file. Send one signed copy to the chargor and the other to the lawyer for the new chargee.

THE E-REG POSTPONEMENT OF INTEREST

Use a postponement of interest, also referred to as postponement of charge/mortgage, Precedent 34.7, where a second charge/mortgage has been inadvertently, or otherwise, registered on title as a first charge/mortgage. The postponement of interest corrects the sequence by placing the first charge/mortgage first and the second charge/mortgage second. This correction places the first chargee in priority for payment in the event the chargor defaults and measures are taken for recovering payment. To prepare an e-reg postponement of interest, you may access the form through the Teraview Instrument on the menu bar and proceed down the applicable branches. To print an unregistered copy of the postponement of interest, follow the instructions under the discharge of charge.

CHAPTER SUMMARY

When a chargor pays off the entire balance due on a charge, the chargee signs a discharge of charge to acknowledge receipt of the money. Once registered on title, the discharge of charge indicates that there is no longer a debt on the property against which the charge/mortgage was registered. A transfer of charge is used when a chargee sells the charge to a new chargee. A postponement of interest is usually used where a second charge has been inadvertently, or otherwise, registered as a first charge on title. The postponement of interest reverses the order of priority in favour of the first chargee.

REVIEW QUESTIONS

1. Name the document used when a charge/mortgage has been paid off.
2. Is it the chargor or the chargee who signs a discharge of charge?
3. Why is the chargor always the party who signs a discharge of charge?
4. In what situation is a transfer of charge prepared?
5. In what situation is a postponement of charge prepared?
6. Who provides a discharge statement?

BIG BUCKS BANK
55 Fairweather Dr., Waterwell, Ontario   D4L 6N6

DISCHARGE STATEMENT

Charge/Mortgage No. 852804   Preparation date: November 11, (year)
Proposed settlement date: December 14, 20--   Conventional

Name: Frederick Flintstone   Interest Rate: 12.25000%
       Wilma Flintstone   Maturity date: April 1, 20--

Property address: 195 Kenwood Av. Burlington ON   L6W 1B1   Residential
Payment: (Principal + interest) Blended, Monthly, $965.47

THIS STATEMENT IS ONLY VALID FOR 30 DAYS FROM THE PROPOSED SETTLEMENT DATE.

THE TOTAL PAYABLE IS SUBJECT TO THE FOLLOWING:

1. Balances are projected on the assumption that all payments due up to and including
the instalment due on December 1, 20--, are paid on the due dates. This amount has
been calculated to be $4,992.35 and is included in the TOTAL PAYABLE below. If
any part or all of these payments have been made, deduct the amount paid from the
TOTAL PAYABLE. Regular payments include interest for the period <u>prior</u> to the
payment due date.

2. Total property taxes paid to date by the bank and charged to the charge/mortgage
account during the current year are $0.00. Taxes should be verified with the
appropriate municipality.

3. All amounts charged to the charge/mortgage account subsequent to the preparation
date of this statement, including property taxes, N.S.F. (dishonoured) payments, and
payments credited in error, are the responsibility of the borrower. These must be
added to the TOTAL PAYABLE and shall not merge in any discharge given.

Subject to the foregoing, the amount required to discharge your charge/mortgage on
the proposed settlement date is as follows:

Principal owing December 1, 20--	$ 91,206.49
Accrued interest to December 14, 20--	387.04
Prepayment charge - 3 months' interest	2,713.44
Property tax account balance	0.00
Discharge fee	90.00
Sub-total	94,396.97
Payments due	4,992.35
TOTAL PAYABLE TO BIG BUCKS BANK	$ 99,389.32

Per diem rate: $29.98

BIG BUCKS BANK

Per:_____

**** NOT VALID - TO BE USED FOR TRAINING PURPOSES ONLY ****

This document has not been submitted and may be incomplete.

LRO # 20   **Discharge Of Charge**

yyyy mm dd   Page 1 of 1

In preparation on 20-- 12 10   at 13:50

Properties

PIN	07001 - 0673 LT
Description	PT LT 3 , CON 4 SOUTH OF DUNDAS STREET , PART 1 , 20R3153A ; DESCRIPTION MAY NOT BE ACCEPTABLE IN FUTURE AS IN 852803 ; BURLINGTON/NELSON TWP ; SUBJECT TO EXECUTION 96-01374, IF ENFORCEABLE. ;
Address	195 KENWOOD AV BURLINGTON

Document to be Discharged

Registration No.	Date	Type of Instrument
852804	20-- 04 01	Charge/Mortgage

Discharging Party(s)

This discharge complies with the Planning Act. This discharge discharges the charge.

Name	BIG BUCKS BANK Acting as a company
Address for Service	55 Fairweather Drive Waterwell, Ontario D4L 6N6

I, James Johnston, have the authority to bind the corporation.

This document is not authorized under Power of Attorney by this party.

The party giving this discharge is the original chargee and is the party entitled to give an effective discharge.

DYE & DURHAM CO. INC.—Form No. 980
Amended NOV. 1992

🏛 Province of Ontario

Discharge of Charge/Mortgage

Form 3 — Land Registration Reform Act

C

(1) **Registry** ☐   **Land Titles** ☒   (2) Page 1 of 1 pages

(3) **Property Identifier(s)**   Block   Property   Additional: See Schedule ☐

(4) **Description**

Lot 7, Plan M-3021
City of Waterwell
County of Mandolee

FOR OFFICE USE ONLY

New Property Identifiers   Additional: See Schedule ☐

(5) Charge to be Discharged		(6) This is a
Registration Number	Date of Registration Y M D	
CT1375241	2000 01 02	Complete Discharge ☒ Partial Discharge ☐ Final Partial Discharge ☐

(7) **Description (cont'd.), Recitals, Assignments**

Agreement extending charge registered January 5, 2001, as No. 2345678.

Continued on Schedule ☐

(8) **Chargee(s)** I am the person entitled by law to grant the discharge and this charge is hereby discharged as to the land described herein.

Name(s)	Signature(s)	Date of Signature Y M D
LOCKSMITH LIMITED		20-- 12
	John Smith, president	
	I have authority to bind	
	the corporation.	

Additional: See Schedule ☐

(9) **Chargee(s) Address for Service**	(10) **Document Prepared by:**		Fees
72 Mitchell Drive Markham, Ontario L3G 4B9	Michael, Eliad & Redford LLP Barristers and Solicitors 863 Seneca Lane Toronto, Ontario M4J 1P6	Registration Fee	
		Total	

FOR OFFICE USE ONLY

**** NOT VALID - TO BE USED FOR TRAINING PURPOSES ONLY ****

This document has not been submitted and may be incomplete.		yyyy mm dd Page 1 of 1
LRO # 20 **Transfer Of Charge**	**In preparation** on 20-- 08 15	at 14:01

Properties

PIN	07001 - 0449 LT
Description	LT 179 , PL 607 ; BURLINGTON
Address	5464 RANDOLPH CR BURLINGTON

Source Instruments

Registration No.	Date	Type of Instrument
H775207	20-- 09 21	Charge/Mortgage

Transferor(s)

This transfer of charge affects all lands that the charge is against which are outstanding.

Name	STARBUG, BRUCE JACOB Acting as an individual
Address for Service	123 Brock Street Waterwell, Ontario D4L 6N6

This document is not authorized under Power of Attorney by this party.

Transferee(s)   Capacity   Share

Name	DRACO, MARIA MARGARET Acting as an individual
Address for Service	12 Baley Street Waterwell, Ontario D4L 6N6

Statements

The chargee transfers the selected charge for $75,000.00.

ACKNOWLEDGMENT

To: MARIA MARGARET DRACO *(transferee, new chargee)*

Re: Green Charge in Favour of Starbug, 5464 Randolph Cr., Burlington

We are the chargors in a charge registered September 21, 20--, which we made in favour of BRUCE JACOB STARBUG as chargee, charging the property known as 5464 Randolph Cr., Burlington, Ontario. We certify that there is now owing on this charge for principal $75,000.00 and interest on such principal at 11 ½ percent per year from September 21, 20-- *(last payment date)*. We also certify that such charge has not been discharged or invalidated in any way and is still in full force and effect.

Dated at Toronto on   , 20--.

_____
Nicholas Matthew Green *(chargor)*

_____
Penny Lisa Green *(chargor)*

NOTICE OF TRANSFER OF CHARGE

To: NICHOLAS MATTHEW GREEN and PENNY LISA GREEN *(chargors)*

Re: Green Charge in Favour of Starbug, 5464 Randolph Cr., Burlington

This is notice to you that the first charge on your property known municipally as 5464 Randolph Cr., Burlington, Ontario, has been transferred to MARIA MARGARET DRACO. Starting with and including the payment due on December 21, 20--, make all further payments on the charge to MARIA MARGARET DRACO at 12 Baley Street, Waterwell, Ontario D4L 6N6.

Dated at Toronto on   , 20--.

_____
Bruce Jacob Starbug *(original chargee/transferor)*

**** NOT VALID - TO BE USED FOR TRAINING PURPOSES ONLY ****

This document has not been submitted and may be incomplete.

LRO # 20   **Postponement Of Interest**

yyyy mm dd   Page 1 of 1

In preparation on 20-- 09 15   at 14:11

Properties

PIN	07001 - 0003 LT
Description	LT 16 , PL 966 ; S/T 110069 BURLINGTON
Address	289 KENWOOD AVENUE BURLINGTON

Source Instruments

Registration No.	Date	Type of Instrument
H762532	20-- 10 15	Charge/Mortgage

Party From(s)

Name	DIXIE, WENDY DIANA Acting as an individual
Address for Service	2 Stetson Street Waterwell, Ontario D4L 6N6

This document is not authorized under Power of Attorney by this party.

Party To(s)

             Capacity   *Share*

Name	BIG BUCKS BANK Acting as a company
Address for Service	55 Fairweather Drive Waterwell, Ontario D4L 6D6

Statements

The applicant postpones the rights under the selected instrument to the rights under an instrument registered as number H795369 registered on 20--/06/23

CHAPTER **35**

SALE TRANSACTIONS

This chapter sets out the process of completing residential real estate sale transactions and the role of those who may be involved in the transaction.

STANDARD DOCUMENTS PREPARED IN SALE TRANSACTIONS

- Verification of identity (individual or organization; see Chapter 2)
- Transfer/Deed (see Chapter 32 for preparation of electronic and paper transfer/deed)
- Statement of adjustments
- Direction regarding funds
- Affidavit re writ of execution (over $50,000)
- Statutory declaration re writ of execution (under $50,000)
- Direction re engrossing vendor-take-back charge/mortgage, if any
- Assumption letter (where a charge/mortgage is to be assumed)
- Acknowledgment of tenancy
- Re-Direction of funds
- Statutory declaration in support of compliance with law statements that are made by the vendor's lawyer
- Letter replying to requisitions
- Undertaking to re-adjust
- Warranty re UFFI/Bill of Sale/HST (purchaser usually forwards own version)
- Declaration of possession (purchaser usually forwards own version)
- Letter requesting discharge statement (where existing charge/mortgage is to be discharged)
- Discharge of charge/mortgage (where existing charge/mortgage is to be discharged)
- Lawyer's undertaking regarding discharge of institutional charge/mortgage and letter to financial institution enclosing certified funds necessary to discharge the charge/mortgage
- Acknowledgement and direction report (see Chapter 36 for precedent)
- Document registration agreement (see Chapter 36 for precedent)
- Letter for closing
- Reporting letter

JONES, Herbert Dennis and Mary Jane
Re: Sale to Smith
        146 Camelot Avenue, Toronto
        Closing Date: March 25, 20--

Mr. and Mrs. Jones have long since become empty-nesters. All three of their children have married and moved out, and the house on Camelot Avenue was just too big for them to maintain. They have sold it to John James Smith and Jill Smith, a young family with two kids and one on the way.

Castles & Sands will be preparing the charge/mortgage back to our clients. Assume that we have received an assumption statement from Trust Loans Limited showing the principal to be assumed in the amount of $30,321.53 plus interest. The second charge/mortgage back to the vendors is in the amount of $14,600. We have prepared all of the documents which relate to this transaction. We are ready to close.

THE SALE TRANSACTION

The sale transaction is commonly referred to as a real estate deal. It may involve the sale of a residential or commercial property. In a sale transaction, your firm acts for the **vendor**, the seller. The main job of the vendor's lawyer is to prepare the transfer/deed and the statement of adjustments and to see that the vendor receives the correct amount of money on closing. **Closing** means the date on which all title documents are registered, and the vendors get their sale money, and the purchasers get the keys to the property.

Agreement of purchase and sale   Your client or the real estate agent brings in the agreement of purchase and sale; it is the signed "offer." After reviewing it, the lawyer usually hands it to you to open a new file. Be sure you are able to readily "read" the agreement of purchase and sale as nearly all steps and documents in a purchase and sale transaction flow from the terms and conditions contained in the agreement of purchase and sale. See Chapter 30 for a sample of an agreement of purchase and sale.

Reminders   Make separate reminders for the closing and requisition dates, and monitor them carefully. These dates are in the agreement of purchase and sale.

Check for conflict of interest   Make sure your firm is not acting for both sides (vendor and purchaser). If so, bring it to the lawyer's attention. Here is an interesting case in point by the prolific and witty Mr. Justice John A. Scollin.

Mr. Justice John A. Scollin found a Dauphin, Manitoba, lawyer to have acted in conflict of interest and ordered him to pay $71,000 to the lawyer's own client. Mr. James D. Deans acted for both buyers and sellers in a land-flip scheme which artificially inflated land value by 300 to 400 percent in a few months. The scheme worked by transferring property back and forth to a small group of investors and collapsed when no new investors could be found. The purchaser, Mr. Roger Watson, sued his lawyer, Mr. Deans, for not advising him of the dangers of the scheme since Mr. Deans also acted for the promoter of the scheme, Mr. Douglas V. Barber. In the scheme's collapse, Mr. Watson discovered that the property he purchased for $50,000 was actually only worth $12,000 and would not price-balloon as the seller had led him to believe. In his decision, Mr. Justice Scollin found Mr. Watson "knowledgeable and greedy" but stated:

"Lawyers have too long danced at the Nit-Pickers' Ball" (relied on technicalities), and to reduce Mr. Deans's liability because of Mr. Watson's behaviour "would be somewhat like reducing the liability of a negligent brain surgeon because the patient had got his skull cracked in a gang war."

Obtain from client   Contact your client to bring in the following information and documents, all necessary for completing the sale transaction:

Information:
- How is the property heated (gas, oil, electric, or wood).
- Is the vendor discharging an existing charge/mortgage, or is the purchaser assuming it; if either, obtain the name and address of the chargee and the mortgage reference number.
- Is any part of the property rented out; if so, how much do the tenants pay, on what day, and have they paid a deposit for last month's rent.
- Is the property a matrimonial home; if so, spelling of full name of non-owner spouse.
- What will be the client's new address.
- Does client own any property abutting/adjoining the one he or she is selling.
- If client is a corporation, name and title of the person/s signing.

Documents:
Transfer/deed; fire insurance policy; latest regional assessment notice; last and this year's property tax bills and how much paid; existing/assuming charge/mortgage, if any; lease, if any; survey, if any, (unless the offer states otherwise, the vendor is obligated to supply a survey **only** if one is already in his or her possession).

Acting for builder   If the client is a builder, it usually means you will be dealing with the sale of all properties on a plan of subdivision. If the properties are new homes or condominiums, they must be enrolled in the government's home warranty program administered by the Tarion Program. This program offers varying lengths of structural and workmanship warranties on new homes. All builders must register with the program before they build. Are **you** expected to, or will the builder, enrol each home in the program; if the builder, obtain the enrolment number for each property before closing; is the enrolment fee to be credited back to the builder in the statement of adjustments; should you be ordering a survey for each property or is the builder providing it; are there any partial discharges to be registered as each deal closes. In most other respects, the purchase and sale transaction usually proceeds in the same manner as that in resale housing.

Manner of title   Write to the purchaser's lawyer asking how the purchasers will take title. You require this information to prepare the new transfer/deed. If you request it by phone, ask the purchaser's lawyer for a confirming letter and a direction regarding title. If your clients are individuals and are taking back a charge (check the agreement of purchase and sale), request a draft charge back, and state how your clients will hold the charge, e.g. on joint account with right of survivorship.

Transfer/deed-paper and e-reg   With the paper transfer/deed, the lawyer for the vendor usually prepares the entire transfer/deed and forwards a draft to the lawyer for the purchaser for review and return. Practice varies with the e-reg transfer. The lawyer for the vendor may prepare the entire e-reg transfer and message it over to the lawyer for the purchasers for review, or complete only the transferor's part of the transfer and message the transfer over to the transferee's lawyer for that lawyer to complete the transferee's part of the transfer. Refer to Chapter 32 for instructions on how to prepare an e-reg or paper transfer/deed and how to message the e-reg transfer to the lawyer for the purchaser.

STATEMENT OF ADJUSTMENTS

The purpose of the statement of adjustments is to show the purchasers how much money they must pay on the date of closing and how you arrived at that amount. Adjustments are made as of the day **before** the date of closing (generally expressed as **to** the date of closing). This requirement is in the standard adjustments Clause 18 in the agreement of purchase and sale. The statement of adjustments consists of two columns of credits: one for credits to the vendors, and the other, for credits to the purchasers. Basically, the vendor pays the old bills, and the purchaser pays the new bills; where the vendor has already paid the old bills, credit goes to the vendor; where the vendor has not paid the old bills, credit goes to the purchaser.

Basic calculation formula   To calculate the statement of adjustments, you must begin by finding the daily rate, also referred to as the **per diem** rate. To do this, divide annual bills by 365 days, half-yearly bills by 182 days, and monthly bills by the number of days in the specific month, e.g. a bill for March, divide by 31 days; a bill for April, divide by 30 days. The result is the daily rate. Multiply the daily rate by the number of days with which the vendor is to be credited or debited.

HST — Resale housing   A resale house, i.e. a used house, is not subject to HST, and therefore, the statement of adjustments usually makes no reference to HST on the sale price.

HST — New housing   A vendor of new housing is usually a builder or a developer. You can quickly determine this from the vendor's name; it is almost always a name of a company (instead of a name of a person). A purchaser of new housing pays HST of 13%: for example, on a sale price of $340,000 the HST would be $44,200 for a total sale price of $384,200. Where the sale price includes HST, you must deduct the amount of the HST for the purpose of preparing the statement of adjustments. The formula for doing this is as follows: gross sale price divided by 1.13, e.g $384,200 ÷ 1.13 = $340,000. To test the formula, multiply the sale price before HST by 1.13, e.g. $340,000 x 1.13 = $384,200.

HST Rebate — New housing   Where a purchaser is eligible for HST rebate, the Ontario and federal rebate percentages are as follows: The federal rebate is 36% of the federal HST for houses under $350,000 (excluding HST). The Ontario rebate is 75% of the Ontario HST for houses up to $400,000 (excluding HST) to a maximum of $24,000. For example, on a purchase price before HST of $340,000, the total HST would be $44,200 (federal $17,000 + Ontario $27,200). The federal and provincial rebate would be as follows:

Federal:	$340,000 × 5% = $17,000 × 36% =	$6,120
Ontario:	$340,000 × 8% = $27,200 × 75% =	<u>$20,400</u>
Total rebate:		$26,520

PREPARATION AND DISTRIBUTION OF STATEMENT OF ADJUSTMENTS

You require: The agreement of purchase and sale, tax bill(s), assumption statement, acknowledgment of tenancy, bills and receipts for any other adjustable items. Follow along in Precedent 35.4. Closing date is March 25.   Notes on items not self-explanatory follow:

> **Legal TIP**
>
> If the HST percentage changes, say, to 15%, the HST factor would be 1.15, e.g. $340,000 x 15% = $51,000 = total sale price including HST = $391,000. To find the price before HST, divide by 1.15, e.g $391,000 ÷ 1.15 = $340,000.

> **Legal TIP**
>
> With new housing, always look at the agreement of purchase and sale to determine whether or not the price includes HST and how any rebate is to be handled.

Vendor's Column

Sale price   Credit the vendors since the sale price represents money for the vendors.

Taxes   The annual estimated taxes are $2,500.00. The vendors paid $1,391.00. The vendors' share is $568.49 (see below for calculations). Since the vendors have paid past the time they will stay on the property, credit (reimburse) them in the amount they have overpaid, $822.51. Had the vendors not paid any taxes, you would have credited the purchaser $568.49 since the purchaser assumes the obligation of having to pay the taxes that the vendors should have paid. Further, had the vendors paid only, say $500.00 of the $568.49, you would have credited the purchaser $68.49 because that is the amount short of what the vendors should have paid to the date of closing. Here are some helpful ways in which you can calculate the taxes in various situations; tax amount and closing date are as in Precedent 35.4:

1. Find the daily rate of taxes: $2,500.00 divided by 365 = 6.849315 per day.
2. Find the number of days for which the vendor is responsible: January 1 to March 24 = 83 days.
3. Find the number of days for which the purchaser is responsible: March 25 to December 31 = 282 days.

Figure 35.1

When the vendor has paid part of the total taxes	When the vendor has paid the total taxes	When the vendor has paid none of the taxes
Taxes $2,500.00	Taxes $2,500.00	Taxes $2,500.00
Vendor paid $1,391.00	Vendor paid $2,500.00	Not paid $2,500.00
Vendor's share − 568.49	Vendor's share − 568.49	Purchaser's share − 1,931.51
$ 822.51	$1,931.51	Vendor's share 568.49
		Credit purchaser $568.49
(83 days x 6.849315=$568.49)	(83 days x 6.849315= $568.49)	(282 days x 6.849315=$1,931.51)
		Or
		Taxes not paid $2,500.00
Credit vendor $ 822.51	Credit vendor $1,931.51	Vendor's share 83 days $568.49
		Credit purchaser $568.49

Property tax bill, Precedent 35.1.   The local municipality collects taxes, also referred to as realty taxes or property taxes, to pay for such services as education, road maintenance, and garbage collection. The property tax department of the municipality where the property is located usually sends two tax bills each year to each property owner: an **interim** bill, which estimates taxes for the first half of the year, and a **final** bill, which shows the total taxes for the entire year. Taxes for transactions closing in the first half of the year are, therefore, usually adjusted on the basis of an **estimated** amount of the total year's taxes, using the previous year's total taxes as a guide. This is why you requested the current as well as last year's tax bills from your client. An estimated percentage increase, e.g. 5 percent, is often added to the interim tax bill.

Fuel oil   This applies only to properties heated with oil because oil is not metered. It usually involves filling up a standard size oil tank. To avoid conflict about how much oil is in the tank, the vendor's lawyer advises the vendor to leave a full tank on closing and be reimbursed for it in the adjustments. Obtain the price per litre from the client's receipt or from the oil company, multiply it by the number of litres, and credit that amount to the vendor and the amount of the HST charged.

The Purchaser's Column

Deposit   This is commonly referred to as down payment. It is the amount the purchaser paid at the time of presenting the offer, and it is a credit toward the purchase price. Obtain the amount from the agreement of purchase and sale.

First charge/mortgage assumed   Obtain from the assumption statement you requested from the chargee. Credit the purchaser because it represents money toward the purchase price. The amount of interest is what the vendor should have paid from March 16 to March 24; that is why the purchaser receives credit for it. The principal is not adjusted on a "per day" basis because unlike interest, which runs daily, the principal remains the same until the next payment is made. It then decreases by the amount of principal paid. There may be other items to be adjusted based upon the assumption statement, e.g. costs, tax account, etc. Assumed charges/mortgages are relatively rare. The adjustment has been purposely included in this transaction as help for that one time when you might come across it.

Second charge back   Credit the purchaser because it represents money toward the purchase price. Vendor-take-back charges/mortgages are relatively rare. This adjustment has been purposely included in this transaction as help for that one time when you might come across it.

Rent   If applicable, obtain from the acknowledgment of tenancy which you requested from the vendor's tenant. Residential rent is not subject to HST. Rent adjustment is rare. The adjustment has been purposely included here as help for that one time when you come across it.

Water account   Water is usually metered. It is adjusted only if it is on a flat rate basis, in which case, it is usually billed every six months. Metered items are not adjusted because either the purchaser or the vendor usually orders a meter reading to be carried out on the date of closing, and the vendor pays the old bill and the purchaser pays the new bill.

Fire insurance   The purchaser places his or her own fire insurance because fire insurance is usually not transferrable. Some lawyers make a note to this effect in the statement of adjustments.

Balance due on closing   This is the amount of cash on closing. To arrive at the balance due on closing, add up the vendor's column; add up the purchaser's column; deduct the purchaser's column from the vendor's column. E. & O.E. (errors and omissions excepted).

Number of copies, minimum 4:   Provide 2 to the purchaser's lawyers on closing; enclose 1 to vendor in reporting letter; keep 1 in client's file.

Assumption statement and discharge statement

If there is an existing charge/mortgage on the property, the vendor may pay it off, in which case, the charge/mortgage must be discharged. Occasionally, the purchaser assumes an existing charge/mortgage as part of the purchase price. Check the agreement of purchase and sale for information relating to a charge/mortgage to be assumed. Whether the charge/mortgage is to be discharged or assumed, you must write to the chargee, e.g. a bank, for a **discharge statement** or for an **assumption statement**, as the case may be, Precedent 35.3. If the vendors will pay it off, they need to know exactly how much is the balance owing. If the purchasers will assume it, you need to know exactly how much to credit the purchasers with in the statement of adjustments.

Vendor-take-back charge/mortgage (VTB)   Occasionally, a vendor may take back a charge/mortgage.   Check the agreement of purchase and sale for information relating to a VTB charge/mortgage.   Prepare a direction regarding a charge/mortgage back, Precedent 35.5, and have the vendor sign it.   Forward the signed copy to the purchaser's lawyer; it informs the purchaser's lawyer as to how to engross the VTB charge/mortgage.

Executions search   If the vendors are taking back a charge/mortgage, do an executions search against the chargor, i.e. the purchaser.   You want to ensure that the chargor is not already indebted and be therefore unable to pay back your client's charge/mortgage.   Executions searches play a more significant role in purchase transactions; see Chapter 36.

Acknowledgment of tenancy   If your client rents out any part or all of the property and the tenants will continue after closing, prepare an acknowledgment of tenancy, Precedent 35.2, and send it to the tenants to sign and return to you.   The acknowledgment confirms, among other matters, the rent figures which you will use to calculate the adjustments.

Reply to requisitions   Write a letter replying to the purchaser's letter of requisitions.   The purchaser's letter of requisitions usually requires documents and information which would clear up problems on title.   It is the vendor's responsibility to prepare those documents which affect the title to the property, e.g. documents relating to writs of execution.   Where there are writs of execution against a vendor (transferor), the vendor must pay them off.   If there are writs of execution against a person with the same last name and at least one same given name as that of the vendor, the lawyer for the vendor must select the applicable clearance statement/s from the drop-down list in Teraview:

⇨   Click on:
- + sign beside Transferor branch
- Instrument on menu bar
- Writs tab
- Retrieve writs
- Double click on transferor's name
- Click on writs tab
- Drop-down list; scroll to applicable clearance statement
- Select applicable clearance statement, e.g.
  I am not the party in the writ and the judgment is less than $50,000.
  (The vendor, not the lawyer, can make this statement when the writ is for an amount under $50,000.)

  The party is not one and the same as the party named in this writ.
  (The lawyer, not the vendor, must make this statement when the writ is for an amount over $50,000.)

- OK
- Repeat for each transferor.

In addition to the Teraview clearance statement/s, the purchaser's lawyer usually also requires of the vendor's lawyer the following paper documents to be prepared, signed and returned as evidence on file:

(a) **Affidavit as to writs of execution**, Precedent 35.7, when there are executions of less than $50,000 against a name similar to the name of the vendor. The vendor or the vendor's lawyer may sign it.

(b) **Statutory declaration**, Precedent 35.8, when there are executions of more than $50,000 against a name similar to the name of the vendor. The **lawyer** for the vendor must sign the statutory declaration. The intent is for the vendor's lawyer to absolutely establish that the vendor is not the same person as that against whom the execution is filed. The information about the execution number, etc. comes from the purchaser's letter of requisitions and enclosures.

Direction regarding funds   This direction authorizes the purchaser's lawyer to pay the balance due on closing to your firm instead of to the vendor. This enables you to pay out any bills on behalf of the vendor and also to pay your firm's fees and disbursements. Prepare it, Precedent 35.6, in triplicate; 2 signed copies to the purchaser's lawyer on closing; 1 file copy.

Re-direction of funds   This direction authorizes the purchaser's lawyers to make the balance due on closing payable to the parties set out in this re-direction, e.g. real estate commission. Prepare it, Precedent 35.10, in triplicate; 2 signed copies to the purchaser's lawyer on closing; 1 file copy.

Other closing documents   Note that if you are using the Conveyancer software, the program automatically generates the following closing documents: undertaking to re-adjust, warranty regarding UFFI/bill of sale/HST certificate, and declaration of possession. The program also generates these parallel documents for the purchaser, but with additional clauses. Although the lawyer for the vendor may choose either version, he or she usually accepts the purchaser's version of these closing documents which the purchaser's lawyer forwards to the vendor's lawyer for signature and return.

Acknowledgement and direction   This document, which the vendor signs, authorizes the vendor's lawyer to electronically sign the documents on behalf of the vendor. See Chapter 36 for details and precedent.

Document registration agreement   The lawyer for the party who will be registering electronic documents, usually the purchaser, prepares this document, signs it and sends it to the vendor's lawyer to sign and return. See Chapter 36 for details and precedent.

GETTING READY FOR CLOSING

Make an appointment for your client to come in one or two days before the date of closing to sign the closing documents. Ask your client to bring in the keys to the property. Prepare the letter for closing, Precedent 35.9, setting out the documents to be exchanged on closing. See Chapter 36 for details on e-reg and manual closings.

AFTER CLOSING

Final bills and notifications   Some of the items to be paid out from the moneys you received on closing include:

1. If, on closing, your client gave an undertaking to discharge a charge/mortgage, pay it off and register the discharge of charge. The amount to pay off the charge/mortgage would be shown in the discharge statement you earlier requested from the chargee/mortgagee.

2. Pay out any balance of the real estate commission, plus HST, as set out in the re-direction of funds. The percentage of commission is usually in the listing agreement and in a direction from the realtor which the realtor will send to you prior to closing. (Deduct any deposit already paid to the real estate agent.)   If the real estate agent is holding a deposit in excess of the amount of commission owing, request the agent to forward to your firm a cheque for the excess amount.

3. Pay your firm's legal fees and disbursements, as in the re-direction of funds.

4. Write to the tax department informing them of the sale and request that they update their records to reflect the purchaser's name as owner. Also request that they forward all future mailings and notices to the purchaser at the property address.

Reporting letter and account   Write a reporting letter and account to your client. The reporting letter, Precedent 35.11, summarizes the work done on behalf of the client during the transaction. Prepare the account and enclose it with the reporting letter.

CHAPTER SUMMARY

The sale transaction begins with the agreement of purchase and sale, which is the contract containing almost all of the terms on which the parties have agreed to buy and sell the real property. In a sale transaction, you act for the vendor. The vendor's most important job is to prepare the transfer/deed, prepare the statement of adjustments, and respond to any requisitions from the lawyer of the purchaser. A statement of adjustments is like a list of debits and credits belonging to either the purchaser or the vendor. Add the amounts credited to the purchaser and those credited to the vendor. Deduct the purchaser's total from the vendor's total. The result is the balance due on closing. On closing, the vendor's lawyers receive a cheque for the balance due on closing from the purchaser's lawyers and register any documents on behalf of the vendor. The vendor's lawyers write their reporting letter to the vendor.

REVIEW QUESTIONS

1. What is a transfer/deed?
2. In what situation would you require an assumption statement?
3. What is the purpose of a statement of adjustments?
4. What does a direction regarding funds authorize?
5. At what stage in the transaction are any necessary documents registered?
6. What are property taxes?
7. Closing date is the date on which the firm closes down for vacation. Yes___ No____
8. If the property taxes on the home you are selling were $2000/yr. and were all paid up for a closing of September 30, who would get credit for how many days and for how much in the statement of adjustments?
9. If the property taxes were $2000/yr. and you have paid $1,500 of the taxes for a closing of September 30, who would get credit for how many days and for how much in the statement of adjustments?
10. Examine the sample property tax bill in this chapter and answer the following questions:
    (a) What is the address of the property to which the property taxes apply?
    (b) Which municipality issued the property tax bill?
    (c) Is it an interim or a final property tax bill?
    (d) When was the property tax bill issued?
    (e) What is the total amount of the current billing?
    (f) What is the total annual amount of taxes?
    (g) What is the legal description of the property?
    (h) Who owns the property?
    (i) If the taxes for the year were paid in full for a closing date of December 20, who would get credit for how much in the statement of adjustments?
    (j) What is the amount of the interim taxes?
    (k) If only the interim amount of taxes were paid for a closing date of December 20, who would get credit for how much in the statement of adjustments?
    (l) If none of the taxes were paid for a closing date of August 15, who would get credit for how much in the statement of adjustments?
    (m) Is the property registered in the Registry or Land Titles system?

Precedent 35.1 Tax Bill

Jul. 28/--	**REALTY TAX BILL**		**CITY OF WATERWELL** MUNICIPAL OFFICE 678 9th STREET WATERWELL, ONTARIO D4P 2O2	
RESIDENTIAL & FARM		COMMERCIAL INDUSTRIAL OR BUSINESS		
Public School 310,000	Separate School	Public School	Separate School	Telephone: 905-123-4567	
Special Area Rates 155.93	Local & Other Charges 125.00	Total Taxes 3,260.11	Less Interim 1,422.56	Total Billing 1,837.55	Total Assessment 310,000

STATEMENT OF TAXES OUTSTANDING				
Total Billing 1,837.55	Current Year Unpaid Taxes	Current Year Realty Interest	Arrears	Roll Number Map Sub Parcel Prim/Sub 123 456 78910
HYLL, JACK HYLL, JILL 13 PAIL COURT WATERWELL, ONTARIO D4P 4U2		Account Number 007733456		13 Pail Court, Plan M-345, Lot 8 1234.00 SF 52.85 FR
		1st instalment due date Sept. 15/--$919.55		2nd instalment due date Nov. 17/-- $918.00

Precedent 35.2 Acknowledgment of Tenancy

ACKNOWLEDGMENT OF TENANCY

TO: John James Smith and Jill Smith

AND TO: Castles & Sands

RE: Jones sale to Smith, 146 Camelot Avenue, Toronto

I acknowledge and confirm that I am the tenant of the first floor of the above premises under a lease which expires on May 30, 20--, at a rental of $1,600.00 per month. My rent is paid to March 30, 20--.

I further acknowledge that there is a prepaid rental deposit in the amount of $1,600.00 as of January 1, 20--, and that interest on the prepaid rental deposit has not been paid to me.

Under the lease, I pay hydro rates with respect to the premises and have the option to renew the said lease for a further five years at a rental of $2,800.00 per month.

Dated at Toronto on January   , 20--.

———————————————
Jennifer O'Neelle, Tenant

Dear Sir or Madam:

Re: Jones and Trust Loans Limited
      Existing first mortgage
      146 Camelot Avenue, Toronto
      Charge No. 00000

I, Robert B. Redford, am the solicitor acting on behalf of Herbert Dennis Jones and Mary Jane Jones, being the vendors referred to above. Our clients are selling the above-noted property with a closing date scheduled for March 25, 20--, and according to the terms of the Agreement of Purchase and Sale, the above first mortgage on the property is to be assumed on closing.

Would you or your solicitor therefore provide our office with a mortgage statement for assumption purposes:

1.   confirming the essential terms of the mortgage;

2.   setting out all amounts outstanding under the mortgage as at such date on account of principal, interest and otherwise; and

3.   verifying that the mortgage is in current standing.

Kindly provide the statement to our office as soon as possible.

Yours very truly,

MICHAEL, ELIAD & REDFORD LLP

Robert B. Redford

RBR/yi

STATEMENT OF ADJUSTMENTS

Vendor: Herbert Dennis Jones and Mary Jane Jones

Purchaser: John James Smith and Jill Smith

Property: 146 Camelot Avenue, Toronto

Adjusted as of: March 25, (year)

		Credit Purchaser	Credit Vendor
SALE PRICE			$260,000.00
DEPOSIT		$13,000.00	
FIRST MORTGAGE ASSUMED			
Principal as at March 16, (year):	30,321.53		
Interest at 11.50% calculated			
from March 16, (year) to			
March 24, (year) (8 days):	76.43		
Credit Purchaser:		30,397.96	
SECOND MORTGAGE BACK TO VENDOR			
Credit Purchaser:		14,600.00	
REALTY TAXES			
(year) estimated total taxes:	2,500.00		
Vendor has paid:	1,391.00		
Vendor's share for 83 days:	568.49		
Credit Vendor:			822.51
TENANCY			
Monthly rent:	1,600.00		
Tenant has paid for rental period			
commencing March 1, (year)			
Vendor's share for 24 days:	1,238.71		
Credit Purchaser:		361.29	
PRE-PAID RENT			
Pre-paid rent amount:	1,600.00		
Interest at 6.00% calculated			
from January 1, (year) to			
March 24, (year) (83 days):	21.83		
Credit Purchaser:		1,621.83	
FLAT RATE WATER			
Billed semi-annually			
Current Bill:	147.36		
Vendor has paid:	0.00		
for period commencing October 1, (year)			
Vendor's share for 175 days:	141.30		
Credit Purchaser:		141.30	
HEAT - FUEL OIL			
900 litre oil tank			
at $0.3505 per litre	315.45		
HST calculated at 13.00%:	41.01		
Credit Vendor:			356.46
BALANCE DUE ON CLOSING			
payable to			
Michael, Eliad & Redford LLP, in trust			
or as further directed		201,056.59	
		$261,178.97	**$261,178.97**

E.&O.E.

Prepared using *The Conveyancer* by Do Process Software Ltd.

DIRECTION RE MORTGAGE BACK

TO: John James Smith and Jill Smith

AND TO: Castles & Sands

RE: Jones sale to Smith
146 Camelot Avenue, Toronto, Ontario

WE HEREBY AUTHORIZE AND DIRECT you to engross the Mortgage back with respect to the above transaction as follows:

JONES, Herbert Dennis
JONES, Mary Jane
on joint account with right of survivorship

Address for service: 58 Meandeep Drive, Toronto, Ontario, M9A 3P2

AND FOR SO DOING this shall be your good, sufficient and irrevocable authority.

DATED at Toronto, this   day of   , (year).

_____
Herbert Dennis Jones

_____
Mary Jane Jones

Precedent 35.6
Direction Regarding
Funds

DIRECTION

TO: John James Smith and Jill Smith

AND TO: Castles & Sands
Barristers and Solicitors

RE: Jones sale to Smith
146 Camelot Avenue, Toronto

This is to direct you and shall constitute your good and sufficient and irrevocable authority to make your cheque for the proceeds of sale in the above transaction payable in favour of our solicitors:

MICHAEL, ELIAD & REDFORD LLP, IN TRUST

or as they may otherwise direct.

DATED at Toronto, this   day of March, 20--.

_____
Herbert Dennis Jones

_____
Mary Jane Jones

<u>*THE LAND TITLES ACT*, Section 137</u>

<u>AFFIDAVIT AS TO WRITS OF EXECUTION</u>

IN THE MATTER OF: Parcel 5-1, Section M-342, City of Toronto

AND IN THE MATTER OF: certain writs of execution in the hands of the Sheriff of Toronto Region, copies of which have been filed in the Toronto Land Registry Office as Number(s): **-0004639

I, Herbert Dennis Jones, make oath and say as follows:

1.   I am the registered owner of the lands entered as Parcel 5-1, Section M-342.

2.   I am not the same person as Herbert D. Jones, the judgment debtor named in Writ of Execution Number **-0004639 wherein Walter Wonderful, as plaintiff, was awarded the sum of $9,950.00 plus costs of $850.00.

Sworn before me at the	}
City of Toronto	}
in the Province	}
of Ontario	}
this day of March, 20--.	} _____
	} Herbert Dennis Jones
	}

A COMMISSIONER, ETC.

<u>*THE LAND TITLES ACT*</u>, **Section 137**

STATUTORY DECLARATION AS TO WRITS OF EXECUTION

IN THE MATTER OF: Parcel 5-1

IN THE REGISTER FOR: Section M-342

AND IN THE MATTER OF: certain writs of execution in the hands of the Sheriff of Toronto Region, copies of which have been filed in the Toronto Land Registry Office as Number(s): **-0001111

I, Robert B. Redford, solemnly declare that:

1. I am the solicitor for Herbert Dennis Jones, a registered owner of the lands entered as Parcel 5-1, Section M-342, Lot 5-1, Plan M-342.

2. The said Herbert Dennis Jones is not the same person as Herbert D. Jones, the judgment debtor named in Writ of Execution Number **-0001111, wherein Grand Orchards Corporation, as plaintiff, was awarded the sum of $65,000.00 plus costs of $1,200.00.

AND I make this solemn declaration conscientiously believing it to be true, and knowing that it is of the same force and effect as if made under oath.

Declared before me at the	}
City of Toronto	}
in the Province	}
of Ontario	}
this day of March, 20--.	} _____
	} Robert B. Redford
	}

A COMMISSIONER, ETC.

Legal Office Procedures

<u>**Delivered by Courier**</u>   SALE

Re: Jones sale to Smith
        146 Camelot Avenue, Toronto
        Closing Date: March 25, 20--

In anticipation of the closing of the above-referenced transaction scheduled for March 25, 20–, please find enclosed the following:

1. Statement of Adjustments, in duplicate.
2. Direction re Funds, in duplicate.
3. Re-Direction of Funds, in duplicate.
4. Undertaking and Affidavit, in duplicate.
5. Warranties and Bill of Sale, in duplicate.
6. Declaration of Possession, in duplicate.
7. Statutory Declaration re Harmonized Sales Tax, in duplicate.
8. Undertaking to Discharge Mortgage, in duplicate.
9. Mortgage Discharge Statement, in duplicate.
10. Keys.

These documents are being exchanged with you to be held in escrow in accordance with the terms of the Document Registration Agreement pending receipt of the following from your office:

1. Direction re Title, in duplicate.
2. Certified cheques per Re-Direction of Funds.
3. Purchasers' Undertaking to Re-Adjust, in duplicate.

Upon receipt of these documents, we will sign and release the Transfer for registration. Please contact us upon registration in order that we may release the funds and provide confirmation that the keys maybe released to your clients.

Yours very truly,

MICHAEL, ELIAD & REDFORD LLP

Robert B. Redford

RBR/yi

Enc.

<u>**Delivered by Courier**</u>   PURCHASE

Re: Smith purchase from Jones
        146 Camelot Avenue, Toronto
        Closing Date: March 25, 20--

In anticipation of the closing of the above-referenced transaction scheduled for March 25, 20–, please find enclosed the following:

1. Direction re Title, in duplicate.
2. Certified cheques per Re-Direction of Funds.
3. Purchasers' Undertaking to Re-Adjust, in duplicate.

These documents are being provided to you in escrow in accordance with the terms of the Document Registration Agreement pending receipt and registration of a Transfer (and Charge) via electronic messaging together with the following:

1. Statement of Adjustments, in duplicate.
2. Direction re Funds, in duplicate.
3. Re-Direction of Funds, in duplicate.
4. Undertaking and Affidavit, in duplicate.
5. Warranties and Bill of Sale, in duplicate.
6. Declaration of Possession, in duplicate.
7. Statutory Declaration re Harmonized Sales Tax, in duplicate.
8. Undertaking to Discharge Mortgage, in duplicate.
9. Mortgage Discharge Statement, in duplicate.
10. Keys.

Please contact the undersigned to advise when the Transfer has been released for registration.

Yours truly,

CASTLES & SANDS LLP

Raymond G. Castles

RGC/yi

Enc.

DIRECTION RE FUNDS

TO: John James Smith and Jill Smith

AND TO: Castles & Sands
             Barristers and Solicitors

RE: Jones sale to Smith
             146 Camelot Avenue, Toronto

DATE: March 25, (year)

This is to direct you and shall constitute your good and sufficient authority to make certified cheques for the proceeds of sale in the above transaction payable as follows:

Coldwell Banker Case Realty	$910.00
Michael, Eliad & Redford LLP, in trust	1,650.00
Herbert Dennis Jones and Mary Jane Jones	198,496.59
TOTAL	**$201,056.59**

Michael, Eliad & Redford LLP

Per:

_____

Robert B. Redford

Prepared using *The Conveyancer* by Do Process Software Ltd.

Dear Mr. and Mrs. Jones:

Re: Your sale to Smith
           146 Camelot Avenue, Toronto

We are pleased to now submit our reporting letter in relation to your sale of the above property.

AGREEMENT OF PURCHASE AND SALE

This transaction was completed in accordance with the Agreement of Purchase and Sale executed by you and the purchasers. The sale price was $260,000.00 with $13,000.00 being paid as a deposit, the assumption of the first mortgage in the amount of $30,321.53 held by Trust Loans Limited, a second mortgage back to yourselves in the amount of $14,600.00 and the balance payable to you by certified cheque on closing subject to adjustments.

The transaction was completed on March 25, (year).

STATEMENT OF ADJUSTMENTS

The Statement of Adjustments sets out closing adjustments between you and the purchasers, calculated as at March 25, (year).

The Statement reflects a credit to you in the amount of $260,000.00, being the sale price of the property, and a credit to the purchasers for the deposit monies of $13,000.00.

FIRST MORTGAGE ASSUMED - The purchasers received credit with the sum of $30,321.53 on account of the principal outstanding under the first mortgage assumed as at March 16, (year), as well as with the sum of $76.43 representing interest thereon at 11.50% per annum calculated from March 16, (year), to March 25, (year).

SECOND MORTGAGE BACK TO VENDOR - The purchasers received credit in the Statement of Adjustments with the sum of $14,600.00, being the principal amount secured by the second mortgage which you took back.

REALTY TAXES - Taxes were adjusted based on the (year) estimated final tax bill of $2,500.00. Since your prorated share of the taxes, for the period from January 1, (year), to March 25, (year), amounted to $568.49 whereas you had paid $1,391.00 on this account, you received credit in the Statement of Adjustments with the sum of $822.51.

TENANCY - As you collected the rent of $1,600.00 for the monthly rental period commencing March 1, (year), and as your share thereof for the period from March 1, (year), to March 25, (year), amounted to $1,238.71, the purchasers received credit in the Statement of Adjustments with the sum of $361.29.

PRE-PAID RENT - The purchasers received credit in the Statement of Adjustments with the sum of $1,600.00 on account of the pre-paid rent which you had been holding (which amount now stands to the credit of the tenant in the purchasers' hands) as well as with the sum of $21.83 representing interest on the said sum of $1,600.00 at 6.00% per annum calculated from January 1, (year), to March 25, (year).

FLAT RATE WATER - Water for the property is billed semi-annually on a flat rate basis. Since you did not pay the bill for the period commencing October 1, (year), in the amount of $147.36 whereas your share thereof for the period from October 1, (year), to March 25, (year), amounted to $141.30, the purchasers received credit in the Statement of Adjustments with the sum of $141.30.

HEAT - FUEL OIL - You received credit in the Statement of Adjustments with the sum of $356.46 on account of the cost of filling to capacity a 900 litre fuel oil tank at the price of $0.3505 per litre plus HST.

BALANCE DUE ON CLOSING - After accounting for the foregoing adjustments, the purchasers were required to pay the balance due on closing in the amount of $201,056.59.

For details as to the disbursement of funds received by our office, please refer to our Trust Ledger Statement which is enclosed.

Mr. and Mrs. Herbert Jones   -2-   Date

FIRST MORTGAGE ASSUMED

In accordance with the Agreement of Purchase and Sale, the first mortgage in favour of Trust Loans Limited was to be assumed by the purchasers.

Prior to closing, we corresponded with the mortgagee and obtained a statement for assumption purposes confirming the precise balance outstanding under this mortgage. We are enclosing a copy of this Mortgage Statement for your reference.

You will see from the Statement of Adjustments that the purchasers received credit with the principal balance outstanding after application of your last payment together with interest accrued thereon to the date of closing.

SECOND MORTGAGE BACK TO VENDOR

Mortgagor:	John James Smith and Jill Smith
Mortgagee:	Herbert Dennis Jones and Mary Jane Jones
Principal:	$14,600.00
Interest Rate:	12.0% per annum
Interest Adjustment Date:	March 25, (year)
Maturity Date:	March 25, (year)

Regular Payments:

Payment Frequency:	Monthly
Principal and Interest:	$212.71
Payments Due:	25th day of each month
First Payment Date:	April 25, (year)

ENCLOSURES

We are enclosing the following documents:

1. Statement of Adjustments.
2. Direction Regarding Funds.
3. Re-direction of Funds.
4. Copy of First Mortgage Statement for assumption purposes.
5. Direction Regarding Mortgage Back.
6. Receipted Second Mortgage Back.
7. Second Mortgage Repayment Schedule.
8. Affidavit as to Writs of Execution.
9. Statutory Declaration as to Writs of Execution.
10. Our Statement of Account.
11. Our Trust Ledger Statement.

We trust that this transaction has been completed to your satisfaction and if you have any questions or comments, please do not hesitate to contact our office.

Yours very truly,

MICHAEL, ELIAD & REDFORD LLP

Robert B. Redford

RBR/yi

Enc.

CHAPTER 36

PURCHASE TRANSACTIONS

This chapter sets out the process of completing residential real estate purchase transactions and the role of those who may be involved in the transaction.

STANDARD DOCUMENTS PREPARED IN PURCHASE TRANSACTIONS

- Verification of identity (individual or organization; see Chapter 2)
- Consent to act re conflict
- Letter re title
- Utility letters: water/hydro/gas - when property is not title-insured
- Utility letters: water/hydro/gas - when property is title-insured
- Letter to Building Department - when property is not title-insured
- Letter to Tax Department
- Undertaking and affidavit as to residency
- Warranties and bill of sale
- Statutory declaration as to HST
- Declaration of possession
- Document registration agreement
- Letter of requisitions
- Direction re title
- Undertaking to re-adjust
- Acknowledgement and direction re electronic registration
- Acknowledgment and direction regarding title insurance
- Transfer/Deed (receipted sample)
- Land transfer tax statements, electronic
- Land transfer tax affidavit, paper
- Statutory declaration re compliance with law statements by purchaser's lawyer
- Charge/Mortgage, if applicable
- Standard charge/mortgage terms and acknowledgment
- Direction to lender re funds
- Reporting letter, purchase

BROWN, John Thomas and May June
Re: Purchase from Green
        5 Bundy Drive, Newmarket
        <u>Closing Date: November 11, 20--</u>

Mr. and Mrs. Brown have just bought a house from Graham Gerald Green. We are also acting for CIBC, the first chargee in this transaction. (Assume that we have already prepared the charge/mortgage in favour of CIBC.)

Our search of title revealed a charge/mortgage on title in favour of Super Trust Company and an execution against Graham Gerald Green. In our letter of requisitions, we have requested the vendor's lawyers, Castles & Sands, to solve these problems before closing.

THE PURCHASE TRANSACTION

The purchase transaction is commonly referred to as a real estate deal. It may involve the purchase of a residential or commercial property. In a purchase transaction, your firm acts for the purchaser. The job of the purchaser's lawyer is to check, check, and check to ensure that the purchaser will receive clear title. **Closing** means the date on which the purchaser obtains title to the property, i.e. the transfer is registered and the purchaser gets the keys to the property, and the deal is therefore completed, or **closed**. In a purchase transaction, the lawyer for the purchaser may also act for the chargee where the purchaser is taking out a new charge/mortgage. In that case, the lawyer for the purchaser usually requires the purchaser to sign a consent to act re conflict, Precedent 36.1. New file, agreement of purchase and sale, fees, HST, and conflict of interest as in Chapter 35.

Reminders   Make the necessary reminders, including the reminders for the closing and requisition dates, and monitor the dates carefully. These dates are in the agreement of purchase and sale. The due date for requisitions is the deadline by which you must write the letter of requisitions to the vendor's lawyer to fix anything that might be wrong on title. The vendor's lawyer is not obligated to comply with any requisitions that you make past that due date.

Letter regarding title   Write this letter, Precedent 36.2. It tells the lawyers for the vendors what names they should put on the transfer/deed. Instead of a separate letter, some law firms include the title information and the address for service in their letter of requisitions. Obtain the following information from the purchasers:

- How they wish to take title, e.g. one name alone, joint tenants, tenants in common, etc.
- Their full names and dates of birth.
- If they are arranging a charge/mortgage, who is the chargee/mortgagee (usually a lending institution). You might also be acting for the chargee/mortgagee, in which case, you will be preparing the charge/mortgage.

Search of title   Do the search of title well ahead of the deadline for making requisitions. Your letter of requisitions is based on what the title search reveals. Your search might also reveal such defects on title that might be best resolved by title insurance. Basically, if you have a PIN, a municipal address, and the owner's name, you can input the information in Teraview. You will get a printout of the parcel register (land titles) or the abstract index (registry). See Chapter 38 for complete details on how to do a search of title in Registry and Land Titles.

Legal TIP

Be sure you are able to "read" the agreement of purchase and sale as all steps and documents in a purchase and sale transaction flow from the terms and conditions in the agreement of purchase and sale.

Survey   If the lender requires an up-to-date survey, order it from an Ontario land surveyor (OLS). Inform your client of the cost before obtaining it because it is usually unexpectedly high. Standard agreements of purchase and sale usually require the vendor to produce a survey only if the vendor already has one.

Utilities   Water, hydro, and gas services are collectively known as utilities. Utilities inquiries are referred to as off-title searches or compliance search letters. In most municipalities, water is a public utility because it is a municipal government service. As a municipal service, any water arrears constitute a lien on the property, and the purchaser will inherit the debt if the vendor does not pay it. Hydro and gas services are not municipal utilities because the municipalities contract out the sale and distribution of hydro and gas to private companies. Any hydro or gas arrears, therefore, are a personal debt against the vendor, not a lien against the property, and it is up to the private utility companies to collect any arrears directly from the vendor. If the property will not be title-insured, lawyers usually write to these services (water, hydro, gas), Precedent 36.3, requesting a search of their records. The utilities services charge a fee for this information. If the property will be title-insured, lawyers usually write to these services (water, hydro, gas), Precedent 36.4, only to request a meter reading (no fee) because title insurance covers any water, hydro, and gas arrears.

Building Department   The Building Department is a municipal government department. Your purpose for writing, Precedent 36.5, is to ensure there are no building and zoning by-law violations or work orders against the property. If the property will not be title-insured, write to the Building Department of the municipality where the property is located requesting information as to any building and zoning by-laws violations or work orders against the property. If the property will be title-insured, many lawyers dispense with this inquiry as it does not involve money, and title insurance covers any building and zoning problems.

Tax Department   The Tax Department is a municipal government department which sets the **rate** of tax on properties that are within its own municipality and bills the property owners. It is to be distinguished from the Regional Assessment Office, which is a **provincial** government department that sets the **value** on which all properties in Ontario are taxed. Property owners pay property tax for such municipal services as garbage collection, education, etc. Your purpose for writing, Precedent 36.6, is to obtain a tax certificate so as to ensure there are no unpaid property taxes because unpaid taxes constitute a lien on the property. This information also enables you to ensure that the tax adjustment in the statement of adjustments is correct. See Precedent 36.7 for a sample tax certificate. Since title insurance covers any arrears of taxes, some lawyers dispense with this inquiry while others write for a tax certificate whether or not the property will be title-insured.

PPSA searches   If the purchase price includes chattels, conduct a PPSA (*Personal Property Security Act*) search through the Ministry of Government and Consumer Services against the vendor/s to make sure there are no debts registered against any chattels which the purchaser is buying from the vendor.

Corporate vendor searches   Where the vendor is a corporation, you should do **corporate name** and **status** searches through the Ministry of Government and Consumer Services. The searches usually establish the legal name of the vendor corporation and whether the corporation is still in business.

Legal TIP

Keep a handy list of addresses, telephone numbers, and any survey and fee requirements for municipalities you deal with. Address all off-title searches to the municipality where the property is located, e.g. if the property is located in Waterwell, write to Waterwell Hydro, Tax Department of the City of Waterwell, Building Department of the City of Waterwell, etc.

Legal TIP

Make all off-title searches before you write the letter of requisitions because if the responses show any problems, you must, in your letter of requisitions, require the vendor to correct them.

Executions search An execution search is not a title search. It is a search for debts against **names** of individuals, not against property. It works by matching the name of a registered owner on title with the name against which an execution is filed. Executions are unpaid judgments. The creditor (person or corporation who won the judgment) files in the sheriff's office and in the land registry office a document known as a **writ of seizure and sale**, also referred to as a **writ of execution**. It is referred to as an **execution** because it instructs the sheriff to **execute** (carry out) the seizure and sale of any personal property or real estate property which the debtor is found to own so as to pay out the judgment.

Figure 36.1 Writ of Execution Name Search

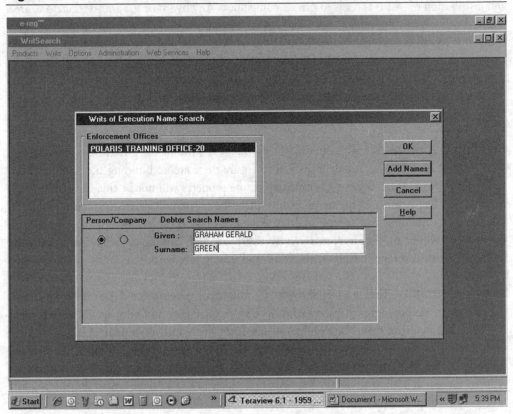

Searching for writs of execution through Teraview
⇨ Click on:
- Products
- Writs Search
- Click on Writs
- Click on Search by Name
- LRO (Land Registry Office where property is located)
- Key in name you wish searched, e.g. name of transferor/vendor
- Click OK

With Teraview, you search for executions electronically whether the property is in the Registry or Land Titles system. If there are any executions against any of the transferors, or against a person with the same last name and at least one same given name as the name of the transferor, the system will print to your local printer either a sheriff's certificate of executions clearance, Precedent 36.9, or a sheriff's certificate of executions, together with a report showing the details of the executions, Precedent 36.8. If there is a new charge/mortgage and you also act for the chargee, also search against the name of **your client**, the purchaser. The chargee requires it to ensure your client is not already indebted and be therefore unable to pay down the charge/mortgage.

Letter of requisitions   See Precedent 36.15 for a typical letter of requisitions. The vendor's lawyer is obliged to prepare and provide those requisitioned documents that clear up problems on title. The vendor's lawyer is not obliged to prepare documents which the purchaser's lawyer requires for precaution only. That is why it is common practice for the purchaser's lawyer to prepare such documents, known as closing documents, and to enclose them in the letter of requisitions. The following closing documents are almost always enclosed in the letter of requisitions for the vendor's signature and return:

1. **Undertaking and affidavit as to residency**   Lawyers require a variety of undertakings (promises), Precedent 36.10, from the vendor, usually for any unfinished business that is to be finished after closing. The **affidavit** is required as non-resident sellers of real estate in Ontario may be required to pay a non-residents tax. If the purchaser does not obtain confirmation that the vendor is a resident of Canada, it may become the purchaser's responsibility to pay the tax.

2. **Warranties and bill of sale**   This document, Precedent 36.11, provides for a variety of vendor's warranties about the condition of the property. The **bill of sale** part ensures that the vendor owns and has paid for any items (chattels), e.g. refrigerators, which the purchaser might be buying from the vendor in the transaction.

3. **Statutory declaration re HST**   This document, Precedent 36.12, ensures that the property is used housing and is therefore exempt from HST.

4. **Declaration of possession**   This document, Precedent 36.13, is a precaution against claims for possessory title, commonly referred to as squatter's rights. Because it contains clauses in addition to those relating to possessory title, it is used for all properties, including properties registered in the Land Titles system where there is no possessory title.

5. **Executions**   If there are any executions against the vendor, the lawyer for the purchaser usually sends a copy of the execution certificate and details of the writ of executions, Precedent 36.8, to the vendor's lawyer. The vendor must either pay off the executions or, if the executions are against a person with the same last name and at least one same given name as that of the vendor, prepare an affidavit as to writs of execution (for executions under $50,000) or a statutory declaration as to writs of execution (for executions over $50,000), as the case may be. See Chapter 35 for details and precedents.

6. **Document registration agreement**   This document, Precedent 36.14, is an agreement between the lawyer for the purchaser and the lawyer for the vendor which enables the two lawyers to work on documents electronically on behalf of their respective clients. The lawyer for the party who will be registering electronic documents, usually the lawyer for the purchaser, prepares this document, signs it and sends it to the vendor's lawyer for that lawyer's signature and return.

Direction regarding title   This direction, Precedent 36.16, instructs the lawyers for the vendor on how to engross the transfer/deed, i.e. how the purchasers wish to take title.

Transfer/Deed   Refer to Chapter 32 for precedents and instructions on how to prepare an electronic or a paper transfer/deed.   In the case of an e-reg transfer, if the vendor's lawyers have messaged over to you the e-reg transfer having completed only the transferor's part of the transfer, complete the transferee's part and the land transfer tax statements, including any required *Planning Act* statements.

The *Planning Act* statements   The *Planning Act* prohibits transferors from selling a part of a lot they own unless they obtain government approval in the form of a Committee of Adjustment (Land Division Committee in some areas) **consent**.   The reason for this restriction is to prevent transferors from chopping up their land and selling parts of it (e.g. the back half) to unsuspecting purchasers without allowing for such services as sewage, road allowances, etc.

The way to tell if transferors are selling only a part of a lot they own is to search if the transferors also own any remaining part abutting (sides are touching) the part they are selling.   To be considered abutting, the properties in question must share a common border.   In the sketch, for example, 1 abuts 2 and 3.   It does not abut 4, even though 1 and 4 meet at a point.

Since lawyers for every purchaser of a part lot property must search to ensure that the part lot property does not contravene the *Planning Act* requirements, the government introduced a three-signature scheme to save future purchasers from having to do the same search all over again.   Thus, when all three parties (the transferor, the transferor's lawyer, and the transferee's lawyer) sign the *Planning Act* statements, any *Planning Act* violations behind this transfer are deemed to have been cured; future purchasers of that part lot property need only check for *Planning Act* violations as of this transfer forward.   That is why selecting the *Planning Act* statements is optional; however, you must check the agreement of purchase and sale to see whether you are contractually obligated to select the statements.   As a general rule, unless you have specific instructions to select the statements, omit them.

Legal TIP

If there is an assumed charge/mortgage, you do not need to prepare it since it already exists.

Charge/Mortgage   See Chapter 33 for a precedent of an electronic and paper charge/mortgage, including instructions on how to prepare the electronic charge/mortgage.   Briefly, if the purchaser arranged a new charge/mortgage in the transaction, the purchaser's lawyer usually also acts for the lending institution, e.g. a bank.   This is partly so, to avoid duplication of work.   For example, the purchaser's lawyer searches title to ensure the property which the purchaser is buying is clear of problems on title; similarly, the chargee (bank) requires a problem-free title since the same property secures the new charge/mortgage; the one title search serves both purposes.   Thus, when the purchaser arranges a new charge/mortgage, there are technically two separate but simultaneous transactions: one transaction is on behalf of the purchaser, and the other transaction is on behalf of the lending institution, and the purchaser is responsible for the cost of both.   The purchaser's lawyer usually prepares the charge/mortgage upon instructions from the bank.   The bank sends instructions on preparing the charge/mortgage and any other documents they require, together with instructions stating that the lawyer is acting on behalf of the bank and the purchaser.   This is why the purchaser's lawyer has the purchaser sign a consent to act re conflict, Precedent 36.1.

Fire insurance   A chargee will not close without proof of fire insurance as the chargee could lose its money if fire were to destroy the property; therefore, if there are any charges/mortgages, instruct the purchaser as follows:

- to arrange for fire insurance coverage on the **building** in at least the total principal amount of all of the charges/mortgages (coverage of contents is up to the purchaser);
- to have the policy show loss payable to the chargee/mortgagee; and
- to have the insurance company send you prior to closing a binder letter or a certificate of insurance as proof of insurance.

Direction regarding funds   See Chapter 35 for a precedent. Prepare this direction usually if the purchaser arranges a new charge/mortgage. The signed copy goes to the chargee, e.g. bank; keep one file copy. The direction authorizes the chargee/mortgagee to send the loan money to your firm, instead of directly to the purchaser. Your receipt of the money enables you to pay out the balance due on closing and such items as land transfer tax and your firm's account.

Undertaking to re-adjust   This is a standard undertaking to re-adjust the statement of adjustments, after closing, if necessary, Precedent 36.17.

LAND TRANSFER TAX

Land transfer tax applies to all transfers of land in Ontario. The purchaser pays land transfer tax on the purchase price of the property basically for having the title transferred over to his or her name; hence, **land transfer** tax. Land transfer tax is payable on the land and building only; land transfer tax is not payable on any personal property items (chattels) which the purchaser might be purchasing from the vendor in the transaction, e.g. appliances, furniture, etc.

HST   HST is payable on the purchase of new housing. HST does not apply to resale housing. If it is a new housing transaction, be sure to calculate the land transfer tax on the purchase price before HST. See Chapter 35 for the calculation formula.

Ontario land transfer tax rate and formula   The rate of the Ontario land transfer tax and the formula for calculating it are as follows:

Figure 36.2

Ontario Land Transfer Tax Calculation Formula for a Single Family Residence on Purchase Price (before HST)	Example Calculation for Each of the Following Purchase Prices:	Total Ontario Land Transfer Tax Payable
Up to $55,000 x 0.5% = $275 $55,00 to $250,000 x 1.0%, less $275 $250,00 to $400,000 x 1.5%, less $1,525 Over $400,000 x 2.0%, less $3,525 (Anticipated rate change: Over $2,000,000 - 2.5%)	$50,000 x 0.5% = $150,000 x 1.0% = $1,500 less $275 = $300,000 x 1.5% = $4,500 less $1,525 = $450,000 x 2.0% = $9,000 less $3,525 = $500,000 x 2.0% = $10,000 less $3,525 =	$250 $1,225 $2,975 $5,475 $6,475

City of Toronto municipal land transfer tax (MLTT) The Toronto MLTT applies to all properties purchased in the city of Toronto. The Toronto MLTT is in addition to the provincial Ontario land transfer tax. Following is the rate of the Toronto MLTT for property containing at least one, and not more than two, single family residences and how it is calculated:

Figure 36.3

MLTT Calculation Formula for Single Family Residence on Purchase Price (before HST)	Example Calculation of MLTT on Purchase Price (before HST) over $400,000	Total MLTT Payable
Up to $55,000 x 0.5% $55,00 to $400,000 x 1.0% Over $400,000 x 2.0% 1.5% on commercial properties, including multi-residential units exceeding $400,000 up to $40 million 1.0% on commercial properties, including multi-residential units exceeding $40 million	$55,000 x 0.5% = $400,000 minus $55,000 = $345,000 x 1.0% = $500,000 minus $400,000=$100,000 x 2.0% = MLTT on $500,000 =	$275 $3,450 $2,000 $5,725
MLTT payable Plus Ontario LTT Total MLTT and Ontario LTT payable for a home of $500,000 in Toronto		$5,725 6,475 $12,200

First-time purchasers First-time purchasers are homebuyers who have never owned a home anywhere in the world. The Ministry of Finance provides a land transfer tax rebate (refund) on the provincial land transfer tax to first-time purchasers of a new or existing home. The City of Toronto also offers a rebate on the Toronto land transfer tax to first-time purchasers of a new or existing home. Eligible first-time homebuyers may claim a refund in one of two ways:

- in e-reg, by completing the required statements under the Explanation tab of the electronic affidavit.
- in manual system, by filing an **Ontario land transfer tax refund affidavit for first-time purchasers of eligible homes**, available through the Conveyancer software program. Fillable PDF forms are also available online on the Ministry of Finance and City of Toronto websites.

LAND TRANSFER TAX STATEMENTS/AFFIDAVIT

The e-reg land transfer tax statements, Precedent 36.21, replace the paper land transfer tax affidavit, Precedent 36.22. The transferor's lawyer may message the transfer over to you having the transferee's part either completed or not completed. If the transferee's part has been completed, continue as follows. If not completed, complete the transferee's part (details in Chapter 32), and continue as follows:

Legal Office Procedures

Figure 36.4 Land Transfer Tax Statements, Tax, Deponents

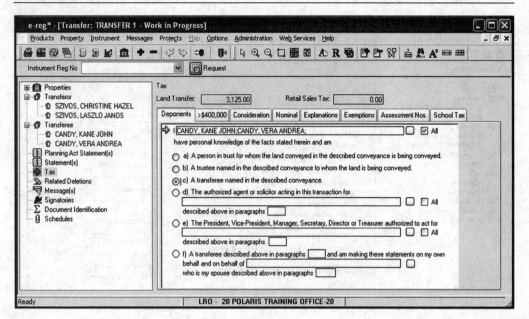

Land Transfer Tax Statements

⇨ Click on:

- Tax branch
- *All box from the Deponents tab. (System prepopulates names of "all" transferees: CANDY, KANE JOHN; CANDY, VERA ANDREA.)
- Check (c)
- Consideration tab: enter in 1 (a) $310,000.00
- Assessment Nos. tab: if there is no prepopulated assessment number, leave the field blank; if there is no Township name (township is mandatory), select from drop-down menu place where property is located, e.g. Burlington
- Unless otherwise instructed, omit School Tax statements

*Means all of the transferees will be signing the land transfer tax statements.

If two transferees are joint tenants and spouses of each other, and only one will be signing, make the statements in one transferee's name, mark box (f) or (g), and enter (c) in both blank brackets, plus the name of that transferee's spouse.

If the transferee is a corporation, mark box (e), enter (c) in the blank brackets, plus the name of the corporation.

Figure 36.5 Land Transfer Tax Statements, Consideration

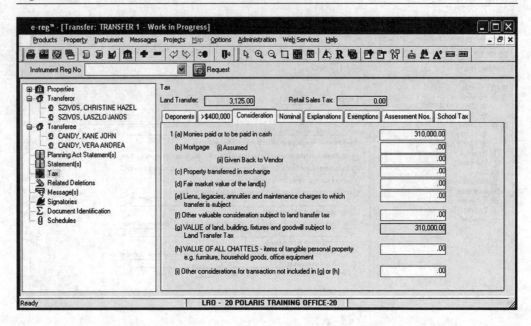

The e-reg version of the land transfer tax statements and the paper version of the land transfer tax affidavit are almost identical. Following is a typical example of how the **total consideration** in both versions would be completed on the basis of the following amounts. All of these amounts usually come from the agreement of purchase and sale and the statement of adjustments, and in the case of a mortgage assumed, they may also come from an assumption statement.

1. Total purchase price	**$350,000**
2. Deposit	25,000
3. Cash on closing	30,000
4. New charge/mortgage	250,000
5. Value of chattels (strove, fridge, etc. purchased with the house)	-5,000
Total cash	**300,000**
6. Mortgage assumed (principal 29,000 + $1,000 interest) =	30,000
7. Mortgage given back to vendor	15,000
8. Value of land	**$345,000**

Figure 36.6

3. The total consideration for this transaction is allocated as follows:	
(a) Monies paid or to be paid in cash	$300,000
(b) Mortgages (i) assumed (show principal and interest to be credited against purchase price)	30,000
(ii) given back to vendor	15,000
(c) Property transferred in exchange (detail below)	Nil
(d) Fair market value of the land(s)	Nil
(e) Liens, legacies, annuities and maintenance charges to which transfer is subject	Nil
(f) Other valuable consideration subject to land transfer tax (detail below)	Nil
(g) Value of land, building, fixtures and goodwill subject to land transfer tax (total of (a) to (f)	345,000
(h) VALUE OF ALL CHATTELS - items of tangible personal property	5,000
(i) Other considerations for transaction not included in (g) or (h) above	Nil
(j) Total consideration	350,000

Land transfer tax is payable on the value of the land only, e.g. $345,000. That is why the value of the chattels has been subtracted from the total purchase price which is the total consideration of $350,000. Where there are no chattels, the value of land should add up to the total purchase price, $350,000. With chattels, the value of land should add up to the total purchase price, minus the value of the chattels, $345,000. The total consideration should always add up to the total purchase price, $350,000, whether or not there are any chattels.

Nominal consideration or exemption from land transfer tax   This means no purchase price is payable. The property may be a gift from one member of a family to another (usually referred to as "natural love and affection") or the transfer may be made by a court order or by a separation agreement, e.g. one spouse taking over the property from the other because the spouses have separated. If so, check with the lawyer. If the consideration is nominal, enter Nil or 0.00, and select the appropriate land transfer tax statement from the list under the Nominal tab and/or the Explanations tab as to why the consideration is nominal. If the property is exempt from land transfer tax, select the appropriate statement/s in the Exemptions tab to explain the exemption.

Printing an acknowledgement and direction, Precedent 36.18.   Within the transfer Work in Progress window, click on Instrument in menu bar, click on Reports, click on Select Report arrow, select acknowledgement/direction, click the Select Party arrow, select your party, key your subject line in the Re text field, click Print. Have all of the purchasers sign the same acknowledgement and direction or print a separate one for each purchaser to sign, as your firm prefers. The signed acknowledgement and direction authorizes your firm to sign the electronic documents on behalf of your client. (If you are also acting for the purchaser on a charge/mortgage, you require a separate acknowledgement and direction for the purchaser to sign as the chargor, but the chargee need not sign one because you usually have the letter of authorization from the chargee to this effect.)

GETTING READY FOR CLOSING

Make an appointment for your client to come in one or two days before the date of closing to sign the documents. Contact the lending institution, if applicable, to have the funds (payable to your firm, in trust, according to the direction re funds) ready for your firm to pick up. Be sure that the money from any lending institution is sufficient to cover the following items:

- the balance due on closing (from statement of adjustments)
- the amount of land transfer tax (from transfer/deed or calculate)
- the amount of registration fees
- the amount of your firm's account, including HST, and any other amounts.

If the money from the lending institution is not enough to cover these items, ask the purchaser to bring in a certified cheque for the extra amount, payable to your firm, in trust. If the lending institution requires it, ask the purchaser to also bring in a series of post-dated cheques, usually in the amount of the charge/mortgage payments, plus 1/12 of the annual property taxes payable to the lending institution. Prepare a trust account cheque payable to the vendor's lawyers for the balance due on closing or as they may otherwise require.

Legal TIP

Chattels included in the sale of used residential housing are not subject to HST. HST on chattels is payable only where HST would be payable on the actual property, i.e. new house from a builder.

Legal TIP

Be sure to get a printout of an acknowledgement and direction **before** you register the transfer because you will be unable to print one out after registration.

THE E-REG CLOSING

The usual procedure in an e-reg closing is as follows:

The vendor   On the day of closing (or day before), the vendor's lawyers prepare a closing letter and package up the closing documents. They then courier these over to the purchaser's lawyers with a letter stating that the documents and keys are to be held in escrow, pending the terms of the document registration agreement until receipt of the closing funds. The package of closing documents usually includes, as applicable:

> statement of adjustments, direction re: funds, re-direction of funds, warranties and bill of sale, undertaking and affidavit, declaration of possession, statutory declaration re: HST, undertaking to discharge mortgage, mortgage discharge statement, and keys.

The purchaser   The purchaser's lawyer also prepares a letter for closing and packages up the closing documents, including the following, as applicable, and couriers them to the vendor's lawyer:

> certified funds as set out in the re-direction of funds, direction re: title, and purchaser's undertaking to re-adjust.

The vendor   When the vendor's lawyers receive the closing package, they compare the certified cheques to their re-direction of funds to ensure the cheques are correct, confirm they have received the signed documents, and then they log into Teraview and release (sign the transfer for completeness and release). The law clerk/assistant for the vendor's lawyer then calls the office of the purchaser's lawyer and tells them the transfer has been released for registration.

The purchaser   The purchaser's lawyer then logs on to Teraview (assuming they have received the closing package from the vendor's lawyer) and signs the transfer (and charge/mortgage but the charge/mortgage can be signed at any time since it is only a one party document and the vendor's lawyer doesn't have access to it) for completeness and release and then registers the transfer and mortgage. The law clerk/assistant for the purchaser's lawyer then calls the office of the vendor's lawyer and advises that the purchaser's lawyer has registered and the funds which the vendor's lawyer is holding in escrow can now be released. The law clerk/assistant for the purchaser's lawyer then calls their clients and tells them they can now pick up their keys to the property.

Sequence of registration   The correct sequence of registering the e-reg documents is very important. The vendor's lawyer must register any discharges of private mortgages first to effect clear title. Discharges of institutional mortgages are typically registered directly by the lender following closing. Then, the following registration sequence in the current transaction should occur by moving each document from the left over to the right in the Teraview Instruments for Registration:

1. Transfer
2. First charge/mortgage, if any
3. Second charge/mortgage, if any
4. Third charge/mortgage, if any, etc.

By registering the transfer first, the purchaser gets registered on title as the new owner of the property, and the charge/mortgage gets registered correctly as a charge/mortgage on the newly purchased property of the purchaser. If the electronic registration is successful, a dialogue box will state so and will display the registration number of each document registered. Teraview will automatically conduct an update search of executions when you electronically register a transfer. For charges, if any, the update search is not automatic; you must do the update search against the chargor through the Teraview Products, Writs search feature. The purpose of these update searches is to ensure that no executions slipped by on title since the last search. The correct sequence of any charges/mortgages is very important because it establishes priority of payment: for example, if the chargor cannot pay, any chargee/mortgagee who did not receive payment may force the property sold, but the chargee/mortgagee registered first has priority to be paid first out of the sale money.

Receipted copy of documents   After registering the transfer or the charge/mortgage, the land registry office will automatically send a receipted (registered) copy of the respective document to print to your office printer. You will know it is a registered copy by the "Receipted as" notation in the heading of the document and from the following standard parts which are added to nearly all e-reg documents after registration. See Precedent 36.20 for a receipted copy of a transfer.

Legal TIP

Registered copies of electronic documents are referred to as **receipted** copies

Signed by

Submitted by

Fees/Taxes/Payment

File Number

Manual closing   The manual closing involves a face-to-face meeting between the lawyers for the vendors and purchasers, or their respective representatives, in the land registry office where the property is located; all closing steps occur manually, including exchanging and registering the necessary closing documents.

AFTER CLOSING

Informing client   Call your client to say the deal is now closed and that you have the keys to the property for your client to pick up.

Reporting letter and account   For a precedent of a typical reporting letter in a purchase, see Precedent 36.23. Prepare the reporting letter and the account to the purchaser, reporting on the work done on the purchase transaction, including work done on any charge/mortgage transaction. Write a separate reporting letter to any lending institution, usually on the lending institution's own form, without an account, and forward the account for the charge/mortgage transaction to the purchaser, as it is the purchaser's responsibility.

TITLE INSURANCE

The *Rules of Professional Conduct* oblige lawyers to inform their clients of the following options that are available to the purchaser for obtaining good title. See Precedent 36.19 for a **direction and acknowledgment** regarding title insurance coverage.

Lawyer's certificate (opinion) on title   With this option, the lawyer does the traditional searches and provides the purchaser, usually in the reporting letter, with his or her opinion as to whether the title is "good and marketable." If the title is defective, the purchaser makes a claim against the lawyer's personal errors and omissions insurance.

TitlePLUS insurance   The Lawyers' Professional Indemnity Company (LPIC) provides this title insurance. It provides similar coverage as private title insurance companies and replaces the lawyer's opinion on title. The purchaser makes a claim, if any, against LPIC (not against the lawyer's personal errors and omissions insurance).

Title insurance by private companies   A title insurance policy from a private company replaces the lawyer's opinion on title. It covers, often without the need for an up-to-date survey, such title-related problems as conflicting ownership interests in the property, realty tax arrears, utility arrears, work orders, encroachments, and zoning by-laws. Any defects on title which title insurance companies cover over must have existed at the time of purchase. The purchaser makes a claim, if any, directly against the title insurance company.

When is title insurance necessary   Title insurance is most likely to be opted for either where there is no up-to-date survey, or where there is a title problem that would cost more to fix but that a title insurance company is willing to insure over the problem. Also, some lending institutions will insist on the purchaser obtaining title insurance before they will consider lending.

CHAPTER SUMMARY

The purchase transaction begins with the agreement of purchase and sale, and your firm acts for the purchaser. The lawyer for the purchaser usually makes various types of title-related and off-title inquiries to ensure that the purchaser inherits none of any debts of the vendor. Based on the findings of these inquiries, the lawyer for the purchaser prepares and sends a letter of requisitions to the vendor's lawyer requesting that lawyer to fix any problems before closing.

If there is a new charge/mortgage or a charge/mortgage that the vendor will be taking back, it is usually the purchaser's lawyer who prepares the charge/mortgage document. The lawyer for the purchaser also prepares the land transfer tax statements/affidavit, electronic or paper. The purchaser must pay the land transfer tax in order to have the title transferred in his or her name. On closing, after exchanging the closing documents, including the balance due on closing and keys to the property, in escrow, the purchaser's lawyer registers the transfer, including any charges/mortgages, and writes a reporting letter to the purchaser and to the chargee/mortgagee, if applicable.

REVIEW QUESTIONS

1. What is the purpose of utility inquiry letters?
2. What does an execution search reveal?
3. What is a direction regarding title?
4. Who pays land transfer tax?
5. What types of searches are updated on closing?
6. What is the purpose of a letter of requisitions?
7. Explain why the purchaser always prepares the statement of adjustments.
8. Calculate the total Ontario land transfer tax payable on a purchase price of $400,000.
9. a) Calculate the total Ontario land transfer tax payable on a purchase price of $345,000.
   b) Assume that the purchase price of $345,000 is for a property located in Toronto, and calculate the Ontario land transfer tax and the MLTT and show the total land transfer tax payable.
10. What is the amount of the arrears, if any, shown in the precedent of the tax certificate?

CONSENT TO ACT RE CONFLICT

TO: MICHAEL, ELIAD & REDFORD LLP

RE: John Thomas Brown and May June Brown
First mortgage to Canadian Imperial Bank of Commerce
Property: 5 Bundy Drive, Newmarket
Closing Date: November 11, 20--

The undersigned, John Thomas Brown and May June Brown, hereby acknowledge being advised by you that you are acting for both the undersigned as well as the Mortgagee, Canadian Imperial Bank of Commerce, in the above transaction, and notwithstanding being so advised, the undersigned hereby expressly consent to you acting in this capacity.

The undersigned further acknowledge being advised that all information received in connection with this transaction from either party cannot be treated as confidential insofar as the other party is concerned, and that the rules of the Law Society of Upper Canada require that when law firms act for both parties, this fact should be revealed to the other party with a recommendation that the other party obtain independent representation.

The undersigned further acknowledge having been advised that in the event of a material conflict between us and the Mortgagee, Canadian Imperial Bank of Commerce, which cannot be resolved, you will advise us thereof, and it may be necessary for you to discontinue acting for either party in this matter.

DATED at Toronto, this   day of   , 20--.

_____
John Thomas Brown

_____
May June Brown

Re: Brown purchase from Green
        5 Bundy Drive, Newmarket
        Closing Date: November 11, 20--
        Our File No.: 1511

Please be advised that we act for the purchasers in the above transaction and we understand that you represent the vendor.

Our clients will take title to the property as follows:

Full Name	**Birthdate**
BROWN, John Thomas	January 27, 1984
BROWN, May June	July 4, 1985
as joint tenants	

Kindly provide the following at your earliest convenience:

Draft Transfer.
Statement of Adjustments.
Plan of Survey.

We trust the foregoing to be satisfactory.

Yours very truly,

Precedent 36.3 Utility Letter, Water/Hydro/Gas - Without Title-Insurance

Dear Sir or Madam:

Re: Brown purchase from Green
       5 Bundy Drive, Newmarket
       Closing Date: November 11, 20--
       Our File No.: 1511

We are the solicitors for the purchasers in the above transaction which is scheduled to be completed on November 11, 20--. Please arrange for the water (*or* hydro/gas) meter to be read on the said closing date and also, kindly advise our office as to:

1.   whether or not the water account has been paid to date and, if not, the extent of the arrears; and

2.   whether you have installed equipment on the property pursuant to a sales or rental contract on which monies remain payable.

For your reference, the solicitors for the vendor are Castles & Sands, Suite 900, 205 Portage Street, Markham, Ontario, L3R 3G3.

In this regard, we are enclosing herewith our firm cheque in the amount of $ payable on account of your fee herein. Thank you for your co-operation.

Yours very truly,

Precedent 36.4 Letter to Water/Hydro/Gas - Title Insurance

Dear Sir or Madam:

Re: Brown purchase from Green
       5 Bundy Drive, Newmarket
       Closing Date: November 11, 20--
       Our File No.: 1511

We are the solicitors for John Thomas Brown and May June Brown, the purchasers in the above transaction which is scheduled to be completed on November 11, 20--.

Kindly arrange for the water (*or* hydro/gas) meter to be read on the said closing date.

For your reference, the solicitor for the vendor is:

       Castles & Sands
       Suite 900 - 205 Portage Street
       Markham, Ontario   L3R 3G3

Thank you for your co-operation.

Yours very truly,

Precedent 36.5   Letter to Building Department

Dear Sir or Madam:

Re: Brown purchase from Green
      5 Bundy Drive, Newmarket
      Closing Date: November 11, 20--
      Our File No.: 1511

We are the solicitors for the purchasers in the above transaction which is scheduled to be completed on November 11, 20--. Please advise as to the following:

1.   What is the zoning for the subject property?
2.   Are there any work orders or notices of violation outstanding pursuant to the applicable building or zoning by-laws or any other matters within your jurisdiction?
3.   Are the buildings or dwelling houses, as shown on the enclosed survey, in conformity with your zoning regulations for the subject property?
4.   Are there final inspections outstanding with respect to plumbing, heating, drainage, sewage or building permits?
5.   Are there any local improvements which have taken place or which are in process or planned in the near future?

In this regard, we are enclosing herewith our firm cheque in the amount of $ payable on account of your fee herein. Thank you for your co-operation.

Yours very truly,

Precedent 36.6   Letter to Tax Department

Dear Sir or Madam:

Re: Brown purchase from Green
      5 Bundy Drive, Newmarket
      Closing Date: November 11, 20--
      Our File No.: 1511

We are the solicitors for the purchasers in the above transaction which is scheduled to be completed on November 11, 20--.

Please provide our office with a tax certificate indicating whether there are any arrears of taxes affecting the property, and also setting out the amount of the current tax bill and the portion, if any, which has been paid to date.

In this regard, we are enclosing herewith our firm cheque in the amount of $ payable on account of your fee herein. Thank you for your co-operation.

Yours very truly,

CITY OF WATERWELL   <u>**TAX CERTIFICATE**</u>

MUNICIPAL OFFICE   678 9th STREET, WATERWELL, ONTARIO D4P 2O2   Telephone: 905-123-4567
                      (Under the *Municipal Act*, as amended)

Issued to: **Assessment Roll Number**

Michael, Eliad & Redford LLP   1234-56-2-890-11111
Barristers and Solicitors
863 Seneca Lane   DESCRIPTION OF PROPERTY
Toronto, ON M4J 1P6   23 Delaire Av., Pt. Lot 9, Plan 998
                                                 JILL DOE AND JOHN DOE

                                             TAX SUMMARY
                                                 (This year) Interim   3,432.50
                                                 (Last year) Total taxes   6,664.99

Statement showing taxes as at: February 17, (this year)
                             OUTSTANDING TAXES
Year   Description   Taxes   Interest   Fees   Total

(Last year)   Real estate tax (last year)   1,200.56   81.02   .00   1,281.58

<u>**Important notice:**</u> PLEASE ADVISE YOUR CLIENT OF TAXES NOT YET DUE
                             FUTURE PAYMENTS
Due Date   Amount Due   Description

March 1, (this year)   1,145.16   Real estate tax (this year)
April 1, (this year)   1,143.67   Real estate tax (this year)
May 1, (this year)   1,143.67   Real estate tax (this year)
              Total: 3,432.50

I hereby certify that the above statement shows all arrears of taxes (prior years) and unpaid current year's taxes against the above lands, and proceedings have not been commenced under the Municipal Tax Act as amended, unless otherwise indicated above.

THIS CERTIFICATE IS ISSUED SUBJECT TO CHEQUES TENDERED
IN PAYMENT OF TAXES BEING HONOURED BY THE BANK.
                                              N. O. Body
FEE PAID $ (current fee)   for each separate parcel.   Chief Financial Officer and Treasurer

<u>Important notes:</u>
1. This certificate covers levied tax arrears or current taxes.
2. There are a variety of services which may be added to the Collector's Roll and collected as taxes.   The most common are water services.
3. The amount of the levy does not include subsequent supplementary taxes that may be levied and added pursuant to sections 33 and 34 of the *Assessment Act*, as amended.

CERTIFICATE #:
NO DE CERTIFICAT:
07891011 - 1625366B

EXECUTION CERTIFICATE / CERTIFICAT

SHERIFF AT:
SHERIF A :

DATE OF CERTIFICATE: yyyy-mm-dd
DATE DU CERTIFICAT:

THIS CERTIFIES THAT LISTED BELOW ARE ALL WRITS OF EXECUTION, ORDERS
AND CERTIFICATES OF LIEN IN MY HANDS AT THE TIME OF SEARCHING AGAINST
THE REAL AND PERSONAL PROPERTY OF:

J'ATTESTE PAR LA PRESENTE QU'ENUMERES CI-APRES SONT TOUS LES BREFS
DE EXECUTION, LES PRIVILEDGE, ET LES ORDONNANCES DONT JE
DISPOSAIS AU MOMENT DE LA RECHERCHE FAITE SUR LES BIENS MEUBLES ET
IMMEUBLES DE:

	SURNAME / NOM	GIVEN NAMES / PRENOM (S)
(PERSON/PERSONNE)	GREEN,	GRAHAM
EXECUTION # ** - 6666*	GREEN,	GRAHAM GERALD

CAUTION TO PARTY REQUESTING SEARCH:
ENSURE THAT THE ABOVE INDICATED NAME IS THE SAME AS THE NAME SEARCHED.

CERTIFICATE #:
NO DE CERTIFICAT:
07891011 - 0040366B

WRIT DETAILS REPORT / RAPPORT DESDETAILSDUBREF

SHERIFF OF /
- - - - - - - - - - - - -

FILE NUMBER / NO DE DOSSIER   :   ** - 6666
ISSUE DATE / DATE DE DELIVRANCE: YYYY-11-05
DATE EFFECTIVE /   :   YYYY-11-05
DATE D'ENTREE EN VIGEUR   :
COURT FILE #   :   ** - CV-8910
DOSSIER DU TRIBUNAL NO.   :   SCJ - CIVIL
- - - - - - - - - - - -

DEBTOR SEARCH NAME(S) / NOM (S) DU (DES) DEBITEUR (S) RECHERCHE(S) :

(PERSON/PERSONNE)   GREEN, GRAHAM

DEFENDANT: GRAHAM GERALD GREEN
DEFENDEUR:

CREDITOR: BIG BUCKS BANK
CREANCIER: (complete address of creditor)

LAWYER: B. R. OKE
PROCUREUR: 92 ELM LANE, TORONTO, ONTARIO M4J 1P6

COMMENTS   PLAINTIFF BY ASSIGNMENT: (date of assignment)
REMARQUE:

ORIGINAL WRIT: BREF ORIGINAL:	AMOUNT MONTANT	INT RATE TAUX D'INT	START DATE DATE DU DEBUT
JUDGMENT/JUGEMENT:	17,300.00	12.4500	YYYY-10-05

CAUTION: ENSURE THAT THE NAME AND FILE NUMBER MATCH YOUR REQUEST.

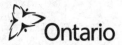 Ontario

CLEAR CERTIFICATE / CERTIFICAT LIBRE

SHERIFF OF / SHÉRIF DE :   *** NOT VALID - TO BE USED FOR TRAINING PURPOSES ONLY

CERTIFICATE # /
N° DE CERTIFICAT :   **** 12345678-1234567X

DATE OF CERTIFICATE /
DATE DU CERTIFICAT :   yyyy-mm-dd

SHERIFF'S STATEMENT

THIS CERTIFIES THAT THERE ARE NO ACTIVE WRITS OF EXECUTION, ORDERS OR CERTIFICATES OF LIEN FILED WITHIN THE ELECTRONIC DATABASE MAINTAINED BY THIS OFFICE IN ACCORDANCE WITH SECTION 10 OF THE *EXECUTION ACT* AT THE TIME OF SEARCHING AGAINST THE REAL AND PERSONAL PROPERTY OF:

DÉCLARATION DU SHÉRIF

CE CERTIFICAT ATTESTE QU'IL N'Y A AUCUNE ORDONNANCE ACTIVE OU AUCUN BREF D'EXÉCUTION FORCÉE OU CERTIFICAT DE PRIVILÈGE ACTIF DANS LA BASE DE DONNÉES ÉLECTRONIQUE MAINTENUE PAR CE BUREAU AUX TERMES DE L'ARTICLE 10 DE LA *LOI SUR L'EXÉCUTION FORCÉE* AU MOMENT DE LA RECHERCHE VISANT LES BIENS MEUBLES ET IMMEUBLES DE :

NAME SEARCHED / NOM RECHERCHÉ

#	PERSON OR COMPANY / PERSONNE OU SOCIÉTÉ	NAME OR SURNAME, GIVEN NAME(S) / NOM OU NOM DE FAMILLE, PRÉNOM(S)
1.	PERSON / PERSONNE	BROWN, JOHN THOMAS
2.	PERSON / PERSONNE	BROWN, MAY JUNE

CAUTION TO PARTY REQUESTING SEARCH:

1. IT IS THE RESPONSIBILITY OF THE REQUESTING PARTY TO ENSURE THAT THE NAME SEARCHED IS CORRECT.

2. BY VIRTUE OF THIS CERTIFICATE, THE SHERIFF IS ASSURING THAT THIS NAME WILL REMAIN CLEAR UNTIL THE END OF CLOSE OF THIS BUSINESS DATE, UNLESS THE SHERIFF IS DIRECTED OTHERWISE UNDER AN ORDER OF THE COURT.

AVERTISSEMENT À LA PARTIE QUI DEMANDE LA RECHERCHE :

1. IL INCOMBE À LA PARTIE QUI DEMANDE LA RECHERCHE DE S'ASSURER QUE LE NOM RECHERCHÉ EST EXACT.

2. EN VERTU DU PRÉSENT CERTIFICAT, LE SHÉRIF ASSURE QUE CE NOM DEMEURE LIBRE JUSQU' À LA FIN DE CETTE JOURNÉE DE TRAVAIL, À MOINS DE RECEVOIR DES DIRECTIVES CONTRAIRES AUX TERMES D'UNE ORDONNANCE DU TRIBUNAL.

CHARGE FOR THIS CERTIFICATE
/ FRAIS POUR CE CERTIFICAT : $ (Shows total fee charged for each name searched)

SEARCHER REFERENCE /
REFERENCE CONCERNANT
L'AUTEUR DE LA DEMANDE :   00-0000

CERTIFICATE # / N° DE CERTIFICAT: 12345678-1234567X   Page 1 of 1

UNDERTAKING

TO: John Thomas Brown and May June Brown

AND TO: MICHAEL, ELIAD & REDFORD LLP
              Barristers and Solicitors

RE: Brown purchase from Green
              5 Bundy Drive, Newmarket, Ontario

IN CONSIDERATION of and notwithstanding the closing of the above transaction, I hereby undertake as follows:

1.   TO deliver up vacant possession of the premises on closing;

2.   TO pay all arrears of taxes to the extent that an allowance has not been granted to the purchasers on account thereof and to pay the (year) taxes in accordance with the Statement of Adjustments;

3.   TO readjust, forthwith upon demand any item on the Statement of Adjustments, if necessary;

4.   TO pay all utilities accounts, including hydro-electric, water and gas charges, to the date of closing;

5.   TO supply and pay for fuel oil in accordance with the Statement of Adjustments, if applicable;

6.   TO make all payments on the mortgage to be assumed in accordance with the Statement of Adjustments and I hereby represent and warrant that there shall be no existing default under such mortgage as at the date of closing;

7.   TO pay off and discharge any existing mortgages, liens, executions and other encumbrances affecting the subject property which are not being assumed by the purchasers;

8.   TO leave on the premises all chattels and fixtures specified in the Agreement of Purchase and Sale, in good working order, free of encumbrances, liens and claims of any kind whatsoever.

DATED at Toronto this   day of November, 20--.

_____
Graham Gerald Green

AFFIDAVIT

I am not a non-resident of Canada within the meaning of Section 116 of the Income Tax Act (Canada) and nor will I be a non-resident of Canada at the time of closing.

DECLARED before me   }
at the City of Toronto   }
in the Province of Ontario   }
this   day of November   }   _____
20--.   }   Graham Gerald Green

A COMMISSIONER, ETC.

WARRANTIES AND BILL OF SALE

TO: John Thomas Brown and May June Brown

AND TO: MICHAEL, ELIAD & REDFORD LLP
Barristers and Solicitors

RE: Brown purchase from Green
5 Bundy Drive, Newmarket

W A R R A N T I E S

I, Graham Gerald Green, being the vendor in the above transaction, hereby warrant as follows:

1.   THAT during the time I have owned the property, I have not caused any building on the property to be insulated with insulation containing urea-formaldehyde, and that to the best of my knowledge, no building on the property contains or has ever contained insulation that contains urea-formaldehyde. If the building is part of a multiple unit building, this warranty shall only apply to that part of the building which is the subject of this transaction;

2.   THAT no damage has occurred to the property, including the buildings situate on the subject property as well as the chattels and fixtures included in the purchase price, since the same were inspected by the purchasers;

3.   THAT no work, construction or alterations have been done on the premises, or material supplied thereto, which could result in a lien being registered under the Construction Lien Act;

4.   THAT, as at the date of closing of this transaction, there are no work orders or deficiency notices outstanding and affecting the subject property and, if any should exist, they shall be rectified at my expense forthwith upon demand;

5.   THAT the warranties contained in the Agreement of Purchase and Sale, as well as those contained herein, shall survive closing;

6.   THAT any work to be done to the subject property by the vendor as stipulated in the Agreement of Purchase and Sale shall be completed prior to closing in a good and workmanlike manner.

B I L L   O F   S A L E

IN CONSIDERATION of the closing of the within transaction, the undersigned, being the vendor of the subject property, does hereby sell, transfer and convey to the purchasers the chattels and fixtures included in the purchase price as specified in the Agreement of Purchase and Sale; and I covenant that I am the lawful owner thereof and that I have the right to transfer and convey the same and that such chattels and fixtures are free of all encumbrances, liens and claims of any kind whatsoever.

DATED at Toronto this   day of November, 20--.

_____
Graham Gerald Green

IN THE MATTER OF Harmonized Sales Tax ("HST")
under the Excise Tax Act (Canada), as amended
(the "Act")

AND IN THE MATTER OF the sale of:
Lot 39, Plan 789
5 Bundy Drive, Newmarket, from Graham Gerald Green
to John Thomas Brown and May June Brown

I, Graham Gerald Green, SOLEMNLY DECLARE that:

1. The above property is occupied as a residential unit, and all parts of the property are reasonably necessary for the use and enjoyment of the property as a place of residence for individuals.

2. I did not acquire the property or carry on any construction or renovation of the property in the course of business or adventure or concern in the nature of trade.

3. I have not claimed an input tax credit under the Act in respect of the acquisition of the property or an improvement to it.

4. No part of the property is capital property used primarily in a business of mine.

5. The sale is not being made in the course of a business or adventure or concern in the nature of trade of mine in respect of which I have filed an election under the Act.

6. The property is a "used residential complex" and the sale of the property is exempt from HST under the Act, and I make this declaration to be delivered to the purchasers with intent that it be relied upon by the purchasers in claiming such exemption as a statement in writing or certificate delivered to the purchasers pursuant to Section 194 of the Act.

AND I make this solemn Declaration conscientiously believing it to be true, and knowing that it is of the same force and effect as if made under oath.

DECLARED before me   }
at the City of Toronto   }
in the Province of Ontario of   }
this   day of November   }   _____
20--.   }   Graham Gerald Green

A COMMISSIONER, ETC.

IN THE MATTER OF title to:
Lot 39, Plan 789
5 Bundy Drive, Newmarket

AND IN THE MATTER OF the sale thereof from
Graham Gerald Green to John Thomas Brown and May
June Brown

I, Graham Gerald Green, SOLEMNLY DECLARE that:

1.   I am the absolute owner of the above mentioned lands and either personally or by my tenants have been in actual, peaceable, continuous, exclusive, open, undisturbed and undisputed possession and occupation thereof, and of the houses and other buildings used in connection therewith throughout my period of ownership of the property.

2.   I am not aware of any person or corporation having any claim or interest in the said lands or any part thereof adverse to or inconsistent with registered title and am positive that none exists.

3.   Possession and occupation of the above lands by the vendor have been undisturbed throughout by any action, suit or other proceedings or adverse possession or otherwise on the part of any person whomsoever and during such possession and occupation, no payment has ever been made or acknowledgment of title given by the undersigned, or, so far as I know, by anyone else, to any person in respect of any right, title, interest or claim upon the said lands.

4.   To the best of my knowledge and belief, the buildings used in connection with the premises are situate wholly within the limits of the lands above described, and there is no dispute as to the boundaries of the said lands. Except as may be registered on title, I have never heard of any claim of easement affecting the lands, either for light, drainage, or right of way or otherwise.

5.   I do not retain the fee or the equity of redemption in, or a power or right to grant, assign or exercise a power of appointment with respect to any land abutting the lands being conveyed in the subject transaction.

6.   I am not a non-resident of Canada within the meaning of Section 116 of the Income Tax Act (Canada) and nor will I be a non-resident of Canada at the time of closing.

7.   I have carefully examined the survey prepared by   and dated   , a copy of which is attached hereto, and have compared my knowledge of the buildings situate on the subject property with those shown on the said survey. The survey accurately describes the property and buildings on the subject property as they exist today and there are no other buildings, additions, decks, swimming pools, outbuildings or any other structures not shown on such survey.

AND I make this solemn Declaration conscientiously believing it to be true, and knowing that it is of the same force and effect as if made under oath.

DECLARED before me   }
at the City of Toronto   }
in the Province of Ontario   }
this   day of November, 20--.   }
                                                          }   _____
                                                          }   Graham Gerald Green

A COMMISSIONER, ETC.

DOCUMENT REGISTRATION AGREEMENT

BETWEEN:

    ROBERT B. REDFORD

       (hereinafter referred to as the "**Purchaser's Solicitor**")

AND:

    RAYMOND G. CASTLES

       (hereinafter referred to as the "**Vendor's Solicitor**")

RE: John Thomas Brown and May June Brown (the "**Purchaser**") purchase from Graham Gerald Green (the "**Vendor**") of 5 Bundy Drive, Newmarket (the "**Property**") pursuant to an agreement of purchase and sale dated (date), as amended from time to time (the "**Purchase Agreement**"), scheduled to be completed on November 11, 20-- (the "**Closing Date**")

FOR GOOD AND VALUABLE CONSIDERATION (the receipt and sufficiency of which is hereby expressly acknowledged), the parties hereto hereby undertake and agree as follows:

Holding Deliveries
In Escrow

1.   The Vendor's Solicitor and the Purchaser's Solicitor shall hold all funds, keys and closing documentation exchanged between them (the "Requisite Deliveries") in escrow, and *shall* not release or otherwise deal with same except in accordance with the terms of this Agreement. Both the Vendor's Solicitor and the Purchaser's Solicitor have been authorized by their respective clients to enter into this Agreement. Once the Requisite Deliveries can be released in accordance with the terms of this Agreement, any monies representing payout funds for mortgages to be discharged shall be forwarded promptly to the appropriate mortgage lender. [1]

Advising of
Concerns with
Deliveries

2.   Each of the parties hereto shall notify the other as soon as reasonably possible following their respective receipt of the Requisite Deliveries (as applicable) of any defect(s) with respect to same.

Responsibility of
Non-Registering
Solicitor

and

Release of Requisite Deliveries
by Non-Registering Solicitor

3.   The Purchaser's Solicitor shall be responsible for the registration of the Electronic Documents (as hereinafter defined) unless the box set out below indicating that the Vendor's Solicitor will be responsible for such registration has been checked. For the purposes of this Agreement, the solicitor responsible for such registration shall be referred to as the "Registering Solicitor" and the other solicitor shall be referred to as the "Non-Registering Solicitor":

Vendor's Solicitor will be registering the Electronic Documents   ☐

4.   The Non-Registering Solicitor shall, upon his/her receipt and approval of the Requisite Deliveries (as applicable), electronically release for registration the Electronic Documents and shall thereafter be entitled to release the Requisite Deliveries from escrow forthwith following the earlier of:

    a)   the registration of the Electronic Documents;

    b)   the closing time specified in the Purchase Agreement unless a specific time has been inserted as follows [_____ a.m./p.m. on the Closing Date] (the "**Release Deadline**"), and provided that notice under paragraph 7 below has not been received; or

    c)   receipt of notification from the Registering Solicitor of the registration of the Electronic Documents.

If the Purchase Agreement does not specify a closing time and a Release Deadline has not been specifically inserted the Release Deadline shall be 6.00 p.m. on the Closing Date.

---

[1]Solicitors should continue to refer to the Law Society of Upper Canada practice guidelines relating to recommended procedures to follow for the discharge of mortgages.

Responsibility of Registering Solicitor	5. The Registering Solicitor shall, subject to paragraph 7 below, on the Closing Date, following his/her receipt and approval of the Requisite Deliveries (as applicable), register the documents listed in Schedule "A" annexed hereto (referred to in this agreement as the "**Electronic Documents**") in the stated order of priority therein set out, as soon as reasonably possible once same have been released for registration by the Non-Registering Solicitor, and immediately thereafter notify the Non-Registering Solicitor of the registration particulars thereof by telephone or telefax (or other method as agreed between the parties).
Release of Requisite Deliveries by Registering Solicitor	6. Upon registration of the Electronic Documents and notification of the Non-Registering solicitor in accordance with paragraph 5 above, the Registering Solicitor shall be entitled to forthwith release the Requisite Deliveries from escrow.
Returning Deliveries where Non-registration	7. Any of the parties hereto may notify the other party that he/she does not wish to proceed with the registration[2] of the Electronic Documents, and provided that such notice is received by the other party before the release of the Requisite Deliveries pursuant to this Agreement and before the registration of the Electronic Documents, then each of the parties hereto shall forthwith return to the other party their respective Requisite Deliveries.
Counterparts & Gender	8. This Agreement may be signed in counterparts, and shall be read with all changes of gender and/or number as may be required by the context.
Purchase Agreement Prevails if Conflict or Inconsistency	9. Nothing contained in this Agreement shall be read or construed as altering the respective rights and obligations of the Purchaser and the Vendor as more particularly set out in the Purchase Agreement, and in the event of any conflict or inconsistency between the provisions of this Agreement and the Purchase Agreement, then the latter shall prevail.
Telefaxing Deliveries & Providing Originals if Requested	10. This Agreement (or any counterpart hereof), and any of the closing documents hereinbefore contemplated, may be exchanged by telefax or similar system reproducing the original, provided that all such documents have been properly executed by the appropriate parties. The party transmitting any such document(s) shall also provide the original executed version(s) of same to the recipient within 2 business days after the Closing Date, unless the recipient has indicated that he/she does not require such original copies.

Dated this _____ day of <u>November, 20--.</u>

Name/Firm Name of Vendor's Solicitor   Name/Firm Name of Purchaser's Solicitor

<u>CASTLES & SANDS</u>   <u>MICHAEL, ELIAD & REDFORD LLP</u>

<u>Raymond G. Castles</u>   <u>Robert B. Redford</u>
Name of Person Signing   Name of Person Signing

_____   _____
(Signature)   (Signature)

Note: This version of the Document Registration Agreement was adopted by the Joint LSUC-CBAO Committee on Electronic Registration of Title Documents on _March 29, 2004_ and posted to the web site on _April 8, 2004_.

<u>SCHEDULE "A" TO THE DOCUMENT REGISTRATION AGREEMENT</u>

Electronic Documents to be registered on closing (in order of priority)

**Transfer/Deed of the Property from the Vendor in favour of the Purchaser.
Charge/Mortgage of the Property.**

_____

[2] For the purpose of this Agreement, the term "registration" shall mean the issuance of registration number(s) in respect of the Electronic Documents by the appropriate Land Registry Office.

Re: Brown purchase from Green
     5 Bundy Drive, Newmarket
     Closing Date: November 11, 20--
     Our File No.: 1511

Without prejudice to the rights of our clients under the Agreement of Purchase and Sale, and reserving the right to submit such further and other requisitions as may be deemed necessary from time to time as well as the right to waive any or all of them, we wish to raise the following requisitions:

1. REQUIRED: Draft Deed/Transfer of Land, engrossed as follows:

Full Name	Birthdate
BROWN, John Thomas	January 27, 1984
BROWN, May June	July 4, 1985
as joint tenants	

2. REQUIRED: An up-to-date survey of the subject lands. Please advise immediately if one is not available.

3. REQUIRED: Statement of Adjustments, in duplicate.

4. REQUIRED: On or before closing, satisfactory evidence of compliance with the following legislation:

    a) The Family Law Act, Ontario;
    b) Section 116 of the Income Tax Act, Canada;
    c) The Planning Act, Ontario, including completion of the Planning Act statements in the Deed/Transfer of Land;
    d) The Construction Lien Act, Ontario.

5. REQUIRED: On or before closing, satisfactory evidence that there are no executions affecting title to the subject property.

6. REQUIRED: On or before closing, production and delivery of evidence that all buildings situate on the lands herein are located entirely within the limits thereof, that possession has been consistent with registered title to the property and that there are no encumbrances, liens, rights of way, easements, encroachments, restrictions, or agreements of any kind affecting the property which are not disclosed by the registered title.

7. REQUIRED: On or before closing, evidence that there are no work orders outstanding and that the lands and premises and all structures erected thereon comply with all by-laws, standards and regulations enacted or passed by the Town of Newmarket and any other governmental body or department having jurisdiction thereover.

8. REQUIRED: On or before closing, evidence that:

    a) there are no arrears of municipal taxes or other municipal charges or assessments, including penalties, and that taxes have been paid in accordance with the Statement of Adjustments;

    b) payment of water, hydro, and gas are not in arrears and that each shall be paid to the date of closing;

Legal Office Procedures

- 2 -

9.   REQUIRED: On or before closing, satisfactory evidence that the property has not been insulated with urea-formaldehyde foam insulation.

10.   REQUIRED: On or before closing, satisfactory evidence that the fixtures affixed to the lands and buildings, and the chattel property included in the purchase price are the property of the vendor and are not subject to any conditional sales contract, chattel mortgage or lien note and that the vendor is the absolute owner of all such fixtures and chattels, free of any encumbrances.

11.   REQUIRED: An opportunity for our clients to perform a final inspection of the premises.

12.   REQUIRED: On closing, keys and vacant possession, subject to any tenancy which the purchasers has expressly agreed to assume pursuant to the Agreement of Purchase and Sale.

13.   REQUIRED: On or before closing, evidence that this transaction is not subject to Harmonized Sales Tax.

14.   REQUIRED: That the following documents which are enclosed herewith, be executed by the vendors and returned to our office, in duplicate, on or before closing:

   a)   Vendor's undertakings;
   b)   Warranties/Bill of Sale;
   c)   Declaration of Possession;
   d)   Statutory declaration re HST.

15.   REQUIRED: That the enclosed personal undertaking, having been prepared in the form required by our office, be executed by you and returned to us on closing.

16.   Instrument No. 21031 is a Charge registered July 7, (year) from Randolph Scott in favour of Super Trust Company securing the principal sum of $100,000.00.

   REQUIRED: On or before closing, production and registration of a good and valid discharge of this Mortgage.

17.   Our search of executions against the name Graham Gerald Green disclosed the existence of Execution No. 6666 against such person (or similar name), particulars of which have been enclosed herewith for your convenience.

   REQUIRED: On or before closing, satisfaction of the above execution(s) together with costs and the withdrawal thereof from the files of the Director of Titles. In the alternative, if the debtor is not one and the same person as Graham Gerald Green, at least 15 days prior to closing, production of a draft of documentation to be registered including the proper electronic statements to satisfy both the writer and the Director of Titles. Please note that an individual's statement will be acceptable if the principal amount of the writ is less than $50,000.00. If the principal amount is more, a solicitor's statement or a statement by the judgment creditor will be required.

Yours very truly,

DIRECTION RE TITLE

TO:	Graham Gerald Green
AND TO:	Castles & Sands Barristers and Solicitors
RE:	Brown purchase from Green 5 Bundy Drive, Newmarket

I HEREBY AUTHORIZE AND DIRECT you to engross the Deed or Transfer with respect to the above transaction as follows:

Full Name	**Birthdate**
BROWN, John Thomas	January 27, 1984
BROWN, May June as joint tenants	July 4, 1985

AND FOR SO DOING this shall be your good, sufficient and irrevocable authority.

DATED at Toronto, this   day of November, 20--.

_____
John Thomas Brown

_____
May June Brown

UNDERTAKING TO RE-ADJUST

TO: GRAHAM GERALD GREEN

AND TO: CASTLES & SANDS
                 Barristers and Solicitors

RE: BROWN purchase from GREEN
                 5 Bundy Drive, Newmarket, Ontario

IN CONSIDERATION of and notwithstanding the closing of the above transaction, the undersigned hereby undertake to readjust the Statement of Adjustments after closing should the same be found to contain any errors or omissions, forthwith upon written demand.

DATED at Toronto, this   day of November, 20--.

_____
John Thomas Brown

_____
May June Brown

<u>**ACKNOWLEDGEMENT AND DIRECTION**</u>

TO: Robert B. Redford

AND TO: MICHAEL, ELIAD & REDFORD LLP
            Barristers and Solicitors

RE: Brown purchase from Green
            5 Bundy Drive, Newmarket, Ontario
            Closing Date: November 11, 20--
            Our File No.: 1511

This will confirm that:

- We have reviewed the information set out in this Acknowledgement and Direction and in the documents described below (the "Documents"), and that this information is accurate.

- You, your agent or employee are authorized and directed to sign, deliver, and/or register electronically on behalf of us, the Documents in the form attached subject to minor changes or additions that may be necessary to complete the transaction described above.

- If required, the Document Registration Agreement shall designate the solicitor responsible for registering the electronic documents in clause 3 thereof and shall specify a "Release Deadline" in clause 4(b) thereof and such designation shall be as in Schedule "A" thereto.

- You are hereby authorized and directed to enter into an escrow closing arrangement substantially in the form attached hereto being a copy of the version of the Document Registration Agreement, which appears on the website of the Law Society of Upper Canada as of the date of the Agreement of Purchase and Sale herein. We hereby acknowledge the said Agreement has been reviewed by us and that we shall be bound by its terms.

- The effect of the Documents has been fully explained to us and we understood that we are parties to and bound by the terms and provisions of these electronic Documents to the same extent as if we had signed them.

- We are in fact the parties named in the Documents and we have not misrepresented our identities to you.

<u>**DESCRIPTION OF ELECTRONIC DOCUMENTS**</u>

The Documents described in the Acknowledgement and Direction are the documents selected below which are attached hereto as "Document in Preparation" and are:

☒   A Transfer of Land described above.

☐   A Charge of the land described above.

☐   Other documents set out in Schedule "B" attached hereto.

DATED at Toronto, this ____ day of _____, 20--.

WITNESS
(As to all signatures, if required)

_____   _____
                                 John Thomas Brown

                                 _____
                                 May June Brown

ACKNOWLEDGMENT AND DIRECTION FROM PURCHASER

TO: Robert B. Redford
MICHAEL, ELIAD & REDFORD LLP
Barristers and Solicitors

RE: Brown purchase from Green
5 Bundy Drive, Newmarket

This will confirm that you, as our lawyer, have reviewed and explained to us the various options available to protect our ownership interests arising from the purchase of the above property, and that, in particular, you have explained the advantages and disadvantages of protecting our interests through the purchase of title insurance as compared to a lawyer's opinion on title.

We hereby instruct you to proceed by way of the purchase of title insurance from Stewart Title Guaranty Company.

DATED at Toronto, this   day of   , 20--.

_____
John Thomas Brown

_____
May June Brown

LRO # 20   **Transfer**   **(SAMPLE)**   **Receipted as AT345678** on 20-- 01 01   at 16:12

The applicant(s) hereby applies to the Land Registrar.   yyyy mm dd   Page 1 of 2

Properties

PIN	07001 - 0004 LT	Estate/Qualifier	Fee Simple Lt Conversion Qualified
Description	LT 15, PL 966; S/T 110069 BURLINGTON		
Address	00283 KENWOOD AV BURLINGTON		

Consideration

Consideration $310,000.00

Transferor(s)

The transferor(s) hereby transfers the land to the transferee(s).

Name	SZIVOS, CHRISTINE HAZEL
Address for Service	692 Garden Path Toronto, Ontario M4K 1B2

I am at least 18 years of age.

Laszlo Janos Szivos is my spouse and has consented to this transaction.

This document is not authorized under Power of Attorney by this party.

Name	SZIVOS, LASZLO JANOS
Address for Service	692 Garden Path Toronto, Ontario M4K 1B2

I am at least 18 years of age.

Christine Hazel Szivos is my spouse and has consented to this transaction.

This document is not authorized under Power of Attorney by this party.

Transferee(s)

		Capacity	Share
Name	CANDY, KANE JOHN	Joint Tenants	
Date of Birth	1980 02 20		
Address for Service	283 Kenwood Avenue, Burlington, ON L3B 4L6		
Name	CANDY, VERA ANDREA	Joint Tenants	
Date of Birth	1981 06 27		
Address for Service	283 Kenwood Avenue, Burlington, ON L3B 4L6		

Legal Office Procedures

LRO # 20 **Transfer** *(SAMPLE)* **Receipted as AT345678** on 20-- 01 01 at 16:12

The applicant(s) hereby applies to the Land Registrar. yyyy mm dd Page 2 of 2

STATEMENT OF THE TRANSFEROR(S): The transferor(s) verifies that to the best of the transferor's knowledge and belief, this transfer does not contravene the Planning Act.

STATEMENT OF THE SOLICITOR FOR THE TRANSFEROR(S): I have explained the effect of the Planning Act to the transferor(s) and I have made inquiries of the transferor(s) to determine that this transfer does not contravene that Act, and based on the information supplied by the transferor(s), to the best of my knowledge and belief, this transfer does not contravene that Act. I am an Ontario solicitor in good standing.

STATEMENT OF THE SOLICITOR FOR THE TRANSFEREE(S): I have investigated the title to this land and to abutting land where relevant and I am satisfied that the title records reveal no contravention as set out in the Planning Act, and to the best of my knowledge and belief, this transfer does not contravene the Planning Act. I act independently of the solicitor for the transferor(s), and I am an Ontario solicitor in good standing.

Signed By

Robert B. Redford	863 Seneca Lane Toronto, Ontario M4J 1P6	acting for Transferor(s)	Signed yyyy mm dd (date)

Tel 416-363-1079
Fax 416-363-2628

I am the solicitor for the transferor(s) and I am not one and the same as the solicitor for the transferee(s).

I have the authority to sign and register the document on behalf of the Transferor(s).

Raymond G. Castles	900-205 Portage Street Markham, Ontario L3R 3G3	acting for Transferee(s)	Signed yyyy mm dd (date)

Tel 905-495-2222
Fax 905-495-2223

I am the solicitor for the transferee(s) and I am not one and the same as the solicitor for the transferor(s).

I have the authority to sign and register the document on behalf of the Transferee(s).

Submitted By

CASTLES & SANDS	900-205 Portage Street Markham, Ontario L3R 3G3	yyyy mm dd (date)

Tel 905-495-2222
Fax 905-495-2223

Fees/Taxes/Payment

Statutory Registration Fee	$ (current)
Land Transfer Tax	$ (current)
Total Paid	$ (total)

File Number

Transferor Client File Number:

**** NOT VALID - TO BE USED FOR TRAINING PURPOSES ONLY ****

LAND TRANSFER TAX STATEMENTS

In the matter of the conveyance of: 07001 - 0004   LT 15 , PL 966 ; S/T 110069 BURLINGTON

BY:	SZIVOS, CHRISTINE HAZEL		
	SZIVOS, LASZLO JANOS		
TO:	CANDY, KANE JOHN	Joint Tenants	%(all PINs)
	CANDY, VERA ANDREA	Joint Tenants	%(all PINs)

1. CANDY, KANE JOHN AND CANDY, VERA ANDREA

   I am

   ☐ (a) A person in trust for whom the land conveyed in the above-described conveyance is being conveyed;

   ☐ (b) A trustee named in the above-described conveyance to whom the land is being conveyed;

   ☑ (c) A transferee named in the above-described conveyance;

   ☐ (d) The authorized agent or solicitor acting in this transaction for _____ described in paragraph(s) (_) above.

   ☐ (e) The President, Vice-President, Manager, Secretary, Director, or Treasurer authorized to act for _____ described in paragraph(s) (_) above.

   ☐ (f) A transferee described in paragraph ( ) and am making these statements on my own behalf and on behalf of _____ who is my spouse described in paragraph (_) and as such, I have personal knowledge of the facts herein deposed to.

---

3. **The total consideration for this transaction is allocated as follows:**

(a) Monies paid or to be paid in cash	310,000.00
(b) Mortgages (i) assumed (show principal and interest to be credited against purchase price)	0.00
(ii) Given Back to Vendor	0.00
(c) Property transferred in exchange (detail below)	0.00
(d) Fair market value of the land(s)	0.00
(e) Liens, legacies, annuities and maintenance charges to which transfer is subject	0.00
(f) Other valuable consideration subject to land transfer tax (detail below)	0.00
(g) Value of land, building, fixtures and goodwill subject to land transfer tax (total of (a) to (f))	310,000.00
(h) VALUE OF ALL CHATTELS - items of tangible personal property	0.00
(i) Other considerations for transaction not included in (g) or (h) above	0.00
(j) Total consideration	310,000.00

PROPERTY Information Record

   A. Nature of Instrument: Transfer

   LRO 20   Registration No.   Date:

   B. Property(s):   PIN 07001 - 0004   Address 283 KENWOOD AV   Assessment   2402080 - 81908100
                                                    BURLINGTON   Roll No

   C. Address for Service: 283 Kenwood Avenue
                              Burlington, Ontario L3B 4L6

   D. (i) Last Conveyance(s): PIN 07001 - 0004   Registration No.

   (ii) Legal Description for Property Conveyed : Same as in last conveyance? Yes ☑ No ☐ Not known ☐

Ontario

Ministry of Revenue
Audit, Inspection and Resource Taxes Branch
Land and Resource Taxes
33 King Street West
PO Box 625
Oshawa ON L1H 8H9

Property Identifier(s) No.
54321 - 0104

Land Transfer Tax Affidavit
Land Transfer Tax Act

Ce formulaire est disponible en français
Refer to instructions on reverse side.

In the Matter of the Conveyance of *(insert brief description of land)*   Lot 39, Plan 789, Newmarket

BY *(print names of all transferors in full)*   GRAHAM GERALD GREEN

TO *(print names of all transferees in full)*   JOHN THOMAS BROWN AND MAY JUNE BROWN

I   JOHN THOMAS BROWN

have personal knowledge of the facts herein deposed to and Make Oath and Say that:

1. I am *(place a clear mark within the square opposite the following paragraph(s) that describe(s) the capacity of the deponents):*
   ☐ (a) the transferee named in the above-described conveyance;
   ☐ (b) the authorized agent or solicitor acting in this transaction for the transferee(s);
   ☐ (c) the President, Vice-President, Secretary, Treasurer, Director or Manager authorized to act for _____
   _____ (the transferee(s));
   ☒ (d) a transferee and am making this affidavit on my own behalf and on behalf of *(insert name of spouse)*   May June Brown
   _____ who is my spouse.
   ☐ (e) the transferor or an officer authorized to act on behalf of the transferor company and ☐ I am tendering this document for registration and
   ☐ no tax is payable on registration of this document.

2. **The total consideration for this transaction is allocated as follows:**

   (a) Monies paid or to be paid in cash .... $ _____300,000.00_____ ⎫
   (b) Mortgages   (i) Assumed *(principal and interest)* .... $ _____Nil_____ ⎟ *All blanks must*
   (ii) Given back to vendor .... $ _____Nil_____ ⎟ *be filled in. Insert*
   (c) Property transferred in exchange *(detail below in para. 5)* .... $ _____Nil_____ ⎬ *Nil*
   (d) Other consideration subject to tax *(detail below)* .... $ _____Nil_____ ⎟ *where*
   (e) Fair market value of the lands *(see Instruction 2(c))* .... $ _____Nil_____ ⎟ *applicable.*
   (f) Value of land, building, fixtures and goodwill subject to
   Land Transfer Tax *(Total of (a) to (e))* .... $ _____300,000.00_____ $ _____300,000.00_____ ⎭
   (g) Value of all chattels - items of tangible personal property .... $ _____Nil_____
   (h) Other consideration for transaction not included in (f) or (g) above .... $ _____Nil_____
   (i) Total Consideration .... $ _____300,000.00_____

3. To be completed where the value of the consideration for the conveyance exceeds $400,000.00.
   I have read and considered the definition of "single family residence" set out in subsection 1(1) of the Act. The land conveyed in the above-described conveyance:
   ☐ does not contain a single family residence or contains more than two single family residences;
   ☐ contains at least one and not more than two single family residences; or
   ☐ contains at least one and not more than two single family residences and the lands are used for other than just residential purposes. The transferee has
   accordingly apportioned the value of consideration on the basis that the consideration for the single family residence is $ _____ and the
   remainder of the lands are used for _____ purposes.

   Note: Subsection 2(1)(b) imposes an additional tax at the rate of one-half of one per cent upon the value of the consideration in excess of $400,000.00
   where the conveyance contains at least one and not more than two single family residences and 2(2) allows an apportionment of the consideration
   where the lands are used for other than just residential purposes.

4. If consideration is nominal, is the land subject to any encumbrance? ☐ Yes   ☐ No

5. Other remarks and explanations, if necessary. _____

Sworn/affirmed before me in the   City of Toronto,
in the Province of Ontario,
this _____ day of _____ November _____, 20 -- _____   ⎫ _____
⎬ Signature(s)
⎭

A Commissioner for taking Affidavits, etc.

Property Information Record

A. Describe nature of instrument: _____transfer_____

B. (i) Address of property being conveyed *(if available)*   5 Bundy Dr., Newmarket, Ontario

(ii) Assessment Roll No. *(if available)*   22 11 444 333 98765

C. Mailing address(es) for future Notices of Assessment under the *Assessment Act* for property being conveyed
5 Bundy Dr., Newmarket, ON L2D 6S6

D. (i) Registration number for last conveyance of property being conveyed *(if available)*   Y3456
(ii) Legal description of property conveyed: Same as in D (i) above.   ☒ Yes ☐ No ☐ Not Known

E. Name(s) and address(es) of each transferee's solicitor: Michael, Eliad & Redford LLP, 863 Seneca Lane, Toronto, ON M4J 1P6

For Land Registry Office Use Only
Registration No.

Registration Date *(Year/Month/Day)*

Land Registry Office No.

School Support (Voluntary Election) *(See reverse for explanation)*

		Yes	No
(a)	Are all individual transferees Roman Catholic?	☐	☐
(b)	If Yes, do all individual transferees wish to be Roman Catholic Separate School Supporters?	☐	☐
(c)	Do all individual transferees have French Language Education Rights?	☐	☐
(d)	If Yes, do all individual transferees wish to support the French Language School Board (where established)?	☐	☐

Note: As to (c) and (d) the land being transferred will receive French Public School Board Election unless otherwise directed in (a) and (b).

0449 (2010/05) © Queen's Printer for Ontario, 2010

Page 1 of 2

Date

Mr. and Mrs. Owen Khadra
22 Ever Avenue
Toronto, Ontario
M4C 4P2

Dear Mr. and Mrs. Khadra:

Re: Your purchase from Azar
          22 Ever Avenue, Toronto
          Part Lot 84, Plan 2285
          Our File No.: 22000

We are pleased to submit our reporting letter in relation to your purchase of the above Property, which transaction was completed on June 25, 20--.

AGREEMENT OF PURCHASE AND SALE

The transaction was completed in accordance with the Agreement of Purchase and Sale (the "Agreement") dated March 29, 20--, between Owen Khadra, as purchaser, and Stephen Azar and Denise Azar, as vendors (the "Vendor"). The Agreement provided for a purchase price of $650,000.00 and a deposit of $10,000.00. The balance of the purchase price was to be paid by cash or certified cheque on closing subject to the adjustments provided for in the Agreement.

TITLE

In accordance with your instructions, your title to the Property is protected under a title insurance policy issued by Stewart Title Guaranty Company as Policy No. W-000 100000. Schedules identifying the Property and the insured, and listing additional exceptions as well as affirmative assurances relating to matters not covered, excluded or excepted, are attached to the title insurance policy. Your copy of the policy, including Schedules, is enclosed with this report. Should you ever be required to file a claim, it is important that you follow the procedures set out in the policy.

Title to the Property was taken in the following manner:

Full Name	**Birthdate**
KHADRA, Owen	November 8, 1970
KHADRA, Wendy	July 25, 1976
as joint tenants	

We are enclosing herewith the duplicate registered Transfer/Deed, the original of which we registered on your behalf on June 25, 20--, as Instrument No. AT2425993.

Mr. and Mrs. Owen Khadra   -2-   Date

FIRST MORTGAGE ARRANGED

Mortgagee: ROYAL BANK OF CANADA

Address: 180 Wandar Street West
                                  1st Floor
                                  Toronto, Ontario
                                  M5J 1J1

Loan Number: SRF# 800-000-000

Principal: $600,000.00

Interest Rate: Variable- Prime Rate plus 7% calculated monthly, not in advance

The Standard Charge Terms filed as Number 200617 are incorporated by reference into this mortgage.

INSURANCE

It is of the utmost importance to maintain adequate fire and liability coverage on the Property, and we wish to confirm that you arranged fire insurance effective from the date of closing. Although it is recommended that the amount of coverage be for replacement cost, it is necessary to maintain, at the very least, coverage in an amount not less than the aggregate secured by any mortgages on the Property from time to time, and in addition, the interests of such mortgagees must be noted on the policy.

STATEMENT OF ADJUSTMENTS

We are enclosing herewith a copy of the Statement of Adjustments which contains details of the various adjustments to the purchase price. The statement is used so as to determine the cash balance which you were required to pay to the Vendor on closing. The figures on the right-hand side are credits to the Vendor (and, as such, are added onto the purchase price) while those on the left are credits to you.

You will see from the Statement of Adjustments that you were charged with the purchase price of $650,000.00, and you received credit with the deposit monies which you had already paid. With respect to realty taxes, the statement shows the Vendor's proportionate share of the annual tax bill for the period from January l, 20--, to the date of closing as well as the amount actually paid by the Vendor on this account. The difference between these two figures appears as an adjustment to the purchase price.

The balance due on closing was determined by adding to the sale price the credits to the Vendor, as shown in the right-hand column of the Statement of Adjustments, and deducting therefrom the credits to you as set out in the left-hand column.

LAND TRANSFER TAX

Land Transfer Tax in the amount of $**** and the required registration fees were paid on closing as set out in our Trust Ledger Statement enclosed.

Mr. and Mrs. Owen Khadra   -3-   Date

EXECUTIONS

We made a search of writs of execution and ensured that there were none outstanding which could form a lien against the subject Property in priority to your title.

UNDERTAKINGS TO READJUST

On closing we obtained an undertaking from the Vendor to readjust any of the items in the Statement of Adjustments, if necessary. You also provided the Vendor with an undertaking in this regard.

ENCLOSURES

We are enclosing the following documents:

1. Receipted Transfer No. AT2425993.
2. Statement of Adjustments.
3. Receipted Charge No. AT2425994.
4. First Mortgage Standard Charge Terms filed as No. 200617.
5. Undertaking and Affidavit.
6. Warranties and Bill of Sale.
7. Declaration of Possession.

8. Statutory Declaration re: HST.
9. Stewart Title Guaranty Company Title Insurance Policy No. W-000 100000.
10. Tax Bill.
11. Sheriff's Certificate of Executions Clearance.
12. Our Statement of Account.
13. Our Trust Ledger Statement.

We trust that this transaction has been completed to your satisfaction and if you have any questions or comments, please do not hesitate to contact our office.

Yours very truly,

MICHAEL, ELIAD & REDFORD LLP

Robert B. Redford

RBR/yi

Encls.

CHAPTER 37

CONDOMINIUMS

This chapter covers condominiums, including the unit, common elements, condominium corporations, occupancy agreements, and an overview of condominium resale transactions.

CONDOMINIUMS

Condominiums offer individual as well as collective real estate ownership. Generally, if you owned, instead of rented, the apartment you live in, you would own a condominium unit. Condominiums are multi-unit residential or commercial complexes, e.g. apartment buildings, plazas, and malls. Condominiums tend to make real estate more affordable since they require less land than traditional buildings. There are various types of condominiums, including the following:

Standard condominium The standard condominium is the traditional one where the condominium corporation owns the land and builds on it.

Vacant land condominiums This type of condominium allows people to buy their vacant lots and share in the common elements and later decide on the type of home they wish to build on their vacant unit.

Leasehold condominium This type of condominium leases the land on which the condominium corporation builds for a fixed number of years. Purchasers of a leasehold condominium unit have the right to sell, lease, and mortgage their unit without the consent of the landlord. The leasehold condominium corporation pays rent to the landlord, and the rent forms part of each unit owner's contribution to common expenses. When the term of the lease runs out, the land and buildings revert to the landlord, and the reserve fund is distributed to the landlord to repair any damage; the balance, if any, is distributed to the unit owners.

THE UNIT

The unit is the apartment you live in or the place in which you carry on business. The owner owns his or her unit in fee simple, much like a single-house owner. Each unit owner pays two sets of costs: one for personally maintaining the inside of his or her unit; and the other, for having the condominium corporation maintain those areas outside the unit that are used by all unit owners. Some of the major expenses that each unit owner pays for his or her own unit include the following:

Property tax The unit owner pays property tax on his or her unit. The amount of the property tax is based on unit size, and the unit owner pays it directly to the municipal tax department. Such property tax is separate and apart from that paid on the condominium complex.

Insurance   Each unit owner pays for fire insurance on the contents of his or her unit.

Utilities   Utilities such as water, hydro, and sometimes heating fuel, are usually individually metered, and each unit owner pays these directly to the respective municipal departments.

Ownership restrictions   The individual and collective ownership of condominiums necessitates some ownership restrictions: for example, the unit owner cannot make any internal structural changes to the unit or change the appearance of the exterior of the condominium complex without the consent of the board of directors of the condominium corporation.

COMMON ELEMENTS

Common elements are all of the areas outside of the unit. These areas are referred to as "common" because they are for use by all unit owners. They include places such as lobbies, hallways, parking lots, swimming pools, playgrounds, and elevators. Since it would be difficult for each unit owner to individually maintain the common elements, the *Condominium Act* requires the owners to create a condominium corporation to handle the maintenance of the common elements.

Common elements expenses fund   The law requires the condominium corporation to operate this fund and use it to pay for all maintenance of the common elements. Each unit owner pays monthly into the fund, usually in an amount equal to one-twelfth of the annual common elements budget. Common elements expenses include: repairs to the common elements, heating fuel for the common elements, fire insurance on the common elements, and property taxes on the common elements, as well as management fees.

Reserve fund   To ensure the condominium corporation can pay for major unexpected expenses, e.g. new heating system, the law requires the condominium corporation to also keep a reserve fund. Each unit owner usually pays a percentage of his or her common expenses into this fund for this purpose. The reserve fund is like an insurance policy for the unit owner and is non-refundable.

Reserve fund study and reserve fund plan   These plans involve a long-term analysis and budgeting for the long-term repair and maintenance obligations of the condominium corporation. Generally, the purpose is to determine whether the amount of money in the fund and the amount of contributions collected to date are adequate to cover forecasted maintenance and repairs.

Non-payment of common elements expenses   If a unit owner fails to pay into the common elements expenses fund or into the reserve fund, the condominium corporation can automatically place a lien against the owner's unit, or foreclose, or sell the unit. A condominium lien properly registered will take priority over a registered charge/mortgage.

CONDOMINIUM CORPORATIONS

Condominium corporations are corporations without share capital, created under the *Condominium Act* for the purpose of administering the operation, maintenance, and repair of the common elements and assets of the condominium. A condominium corporation is created as soon as the developer of the condominium building registers the following documents in the land registry office where the property is located, after which, the condominium developer must give a copy of each to each unit purchaser:

1. **Description** This is a plan giving the physical layout and legal description of the condominium complex.

2. **Declaration** This is the condominium corporation's charter or constitution. The declaration sets out the rights and voting requirements of individual owners to enable the corporation to make decisions on behalf of the unit owners.

3. **By-laws** These are rules governing the daily operations of the condominium corporation, e.g. how the condominium corporation will be organized, the roles of the officers, what a unit owner may or may not do, and how common expenses will be determined and collected.

Who owns the condominium corporation The unit owners own and control the condominium corporation. Each unit owner becomes a member of the corporation with the purchase of his or her unit. The condominium corporation has no share capital and operates in the same way as regular corporations.

The board of directors The unit owners elect from among themselves a board of directors, referred to as directors, to manage the condominium corporation.

Officers The directors of the condominium corporation elect from among themselves officers such as president, secretary, and treasurer. The president usually chairs the board meetings and is responsible for the affairs of the corporation. The secretary keeps the administrative records of the corporation. The treasurer is responsible for the financial records of the corporation.

Meetings The condominium corporation must hold annual meetings no more than fifteen months apart. All unit owners are entitled to vote at meetings and are eligible for election to the board of directors. There is one vote per unit, and if the unit is charged (mortgaged), the chargee has the right to vote instead of the owner. Most matters are voted on by a show of hands.

Management companies The board of directors of the condominium corporation is made up of unit owners who serve usually while holding down full-time jobs. For this reason, they frequently hire management companies to do the actual work of managing and maintaining the common elements. The key person contracted for the job is usually referred to as a property manager. The property manager reports to the board of directors and handles all maintenance of the common elements, collects the common expenses from the unit owners, pays all of the common elements bills, and usually prepares annual budgets and quarter-yearly financial statements for the approval of the board of directors.

OCCUPANCY AGREEMENTS

Since the developer (builder) of the condominium building cannot register the condominium until construction on the complex is almost completed, many of the earlier units are ready for occupancy; however, the unit buyers cannot move in as owners because they can only receive title after the condominium developer registers the condominium corporation. To defray their construction costs and make profitable use of the completed units, condominium developers require unit owners to sign an **occupancy agreement**, usually at the time of purchase. That agreement requires unit owners to move into their ready units as **tenants** and pay occupancy fees, i.e. rent, to the condominium developer until the condominium developer registers the condominium corporation. The monthly occupancy fee is not applied toward the purchase price of the unit. It goes to the condominium developer as payment for your interim use of your unit.

CONDOMINIUM RESIDENTIAL RESALE TRANSACTIONS

Condominium resale transactions follow the same procedure as ordinary purchase and sale transactions. Here are some of the more significant differences in condominium purchase and sale transactions:

Condominium plans Condominium plans are identified by a number, as well as by the name of the municipality where the condominium property is located, e.g. Peel Condominium Plan No. 456. The name of the plan is often also the name of the condominium corporation.

Status certificate The status certificate certifies that the unit owner has paid the common elements expenses and that the corporation has paid all bills concerning the common elements. In addition, the certificate will describe the status of the **reserve fund study** and the **reserve fund plan**. Usually, the purchaser's lawyer writes to the condominium corporation for a status certificate, along with the required fee, and either the condominium corporation or the property manager prepares and forwards the status certificate.

Executions search The purchaser's lawyer searches for executions against the condominium corporation as well as against the unit owner.

Statement of adjustments Those items peculiar to condominiums, such as common elements expenses, are adjusted, as in Precedent 37.1. There is usually no adjustment for the reserve fund since it represents money that is applied toward depreciating property; that is, property that requires repair, e.g. roof.

Charges/Mortgages Charge/Mortgage documents are the same as other charges/mortgages, except that some special condominium-related clauses are added; see chapter on charges/mortgages.

Reporting letter As in regular transactions, with appropriate modifications.

CHAPTER SUMMARY

A condominium consists of independent units within a large building complex, the common areas of which all individual unit owners collectively own and share. A condominium unit owner pays taxes, insurance, and utilities directly to the local municipality, just like any single-home owner.

The unit owners collectively form a condominium corporation for the purpose of maintaining the common elements, which include all of the areas outside of the individual units. The condominium unit owners elect a board of directors from among themselves to manage the condominium corporation. Often, the board of directors hires a management company to do the actual physical work of managing and maintaining the common elements. All condominium unit owners pay a certain amount of money to the condominium corporation toward common elements expenses.

A condominium resale transaction is much the same as a single home transaction, except that a would-be purchaser must check for executions against both the condominium unit owner and the condominium corporation.

REVIEW QUESTIONS

1. What areas are referred to as common elements?
2. For which areas of the condominium complex is the condominium corporation responsible?
3. What is the purpose of management companies?
4. What does a unit purchaser agree to do when he or she signs an occupancy agreement?
5. Which document certifies that the unit owner and the condominium corporation have paid their bills?
6. What type of share capital must condominium corporations have?
7. Who pays property taxes and utilities on the unit itself?
8. What is a reserve fund?

STATEMENT OF ADJUSTMENTS
Prince sale to Tyron
Unit 4, Level 7, York Condominium Plan No. 472
56 Oliver Crescent, Toronto
Closing date: June 28, (year)

	Credit Purchaser	Credit Vendor
SALE PRICE		$152,000.00
DEPOSIT	$ 15,200.00	

REALTY TAXES

Total (year) taxes	$1,730.00	
Vendor's share for 178 days	$843.72	
Vendor paid	-817.61	
Credit purchaser:	26.11	

COMMON EXPENSES
Paid to June 30, (year)
at $170.00 per month
Credit vendor: 17.01

UTILITIES
Metered - no adjustment

INSURANCE
Purchaser to arrange own - no adjustment

BALANCE DUE ON CLOSING
payable to
Castles & Sands, in trust   136,790.90
or as further directed

	Credit Purchaser	Credit Vendor
	$152,017.01	$152,017.01

E. & O. E.

CHAPTER 38

TITLE SEARCHING — A NEW PERSPECTIVE

This chapter covers steps in searching titles under the Registry and Land Titles systems, including searching under the *Planning Act* and searching writs of execution.

TITLE SEARCHING

Title searching is examining the past and present history of the ownership of a given property. It usually involves making notes and/or obtaining photocopies or printouts of land registry records that affect the property you are searching. A complete title search usually consists of four components, as applicable:

1. A title search.
2. A corporate status search.
3. An execution search.
4. An abutting lands search pursuant to the *Planning Act*.

When conducting a title search, you usually act for the purchaser in a purchase and sale transaction or for the chargee in a charge (or mortgage) transaction. In purchase and sale transactions, the purpose of searching title is to ensure the purchaser receives a good and valid title to the property he or she is purchasing. The purpose is the same in charge transactions since a good and valid title ensures the chargee's loan is secure. A lawyer or other person who reads your search should be able to determine the exact state of affairs of the title to the property in question, with a lawyer being able to readily give an opinion on title.

How land was originally divided   All land in Ontario was originally under the Registry system. Southern Ontario developed earlier and did so by first dividing the land into counties. These counties were divided into townships that were further divided into concessions and lots on the concessions. In certain areas of the province, however, mainly in northern Ontario, the Land Titles system is and always has been the only system available pursuant to the *Regulations* of the *Land Titles Act*. Northern Ontario's districts are equivalent to southern Ontario's counties.

Automation and conversion to Land Titles   Automation is the computerization of the original paper records of properties, enabling such work as land registrations and title searches to be conducted online. Nearly all Ontario properties have been automated and converted from the Registry system to the Land Titles system which is the system that guarantees good title.

> **Legal TIP**
>
> When a client purchases a title insurance policy (in purchase as well as in charge transactions), the lawyer is required to give an opinion on title to the title insurance company.

AUTOMATED TITLES IN REGISTRY SYSTEM

Non-converts   These are among a small percentage of properties that, although automated, have not been converted to Land Titles and continue to be governed by the *Registry Act*. The Province of Ontario has automated 40 years' worth of outstanding documents of these properties into a computerized format. The abstract index contains a Property Identification Number (PIN) followed by an "R" to indicate that these properties are still under the Registry system. These properties contain a serious flaw on title, such as a *Planning Act* violation, which prevented the conversion process of these lands from Registry to Land Titles, and ownership of the properties cannot be guaranteed; as a result, these properties remain subject to a 40-year title search.

AUTOMATED TITLES IN LAND TITLES SYSTEM

Land Titles Conversion Qualified (LTCQ)   These are Registry system properties that have been converted to the Land Titles system, subject to the qualifiers set out in the LTCQ parcel register. See Precedent 38.3 for an example of a parcel register of an LTCQ title. LTCQ properties are exempt from *Planning Act* and corporate status searches up to the date of conversion, but after the date of conversion, these searches are required. The LTCQ qualifiers, which usually include adverse possession, encroachments, and misdescriptions of boundaries, require searches whether before or after the date of conversion because such qualifiers existed at the time of conversion.

Land Titles Absolute Plus (LT Plus)   These titles have been upgraded from an LTCQ to LT Plus. An LT Plus title is said to be the best of all titles because the upgrade resolved any pre-existing title disputes or adverse possession claims. Corporate status and *Planning Act* searches need not extend behind the date of conversion into LTCQ.

Land Titles Absolute (LT Absolute)   These are all the original paper records of the Land Titles system that have been simply automated. See PIN 24916-0001 (LT), Precedent 38.9, for an example of an LT Absolute title. These lands are subject to the usual execution search against the registered owner of the land and remain subject to the usual corporate status search and abutting lands search.

TITLE SEARCHING — REGISTRY SYSTEM

A title search is done through a land registry office. There is a land registry office in each county and district for each property located in that county and district. You can find the land registry office of your property through ServiceOntario by the city or town where your property is located. A title search for a property registered in the Registry system that may not have been converted to the Land Titles system entails examining each registered document affecting a property because the Registry system does not guarantee a clear chain of title.

1. **The 40-year rule**   This rule refers to how far back you must go to establish what is referred to as a good root of title. The 40-year rule was firmly established by the *Fire v Longtin*, [1995] 4 SCR 3 case where the Supreme Court of Canada upheld the decision of the Ontario Court of Appeal that a title search need only go back as far as 40 years in order to establish a good root of title. This means going back 40 years in time from the date of closing of your current transaction to at least one conveyance, i.e. a transfer/deed; this is your **commencement point.** Then, proceed forward from your commencement point to the most current entry on your title. Note that it may be necessary at times to search behind the automated record, that is, look at the paper record that existed prior to automation, to find your point of commencement.

2. **Abstract book**   The abstract book contains a summary of every document registered against a particular property. See Precedent 31.3 for a sample page from a non-automated abstract book. An automated abstract book contains a PIN and a summary of only those documents registered against a property after the date of automation. Once you have found your property in the abstract book, the next step is to abstract (summarize) the instruments that appear in your full 40-year chain of ownership.

3. **Abstract for lawyer**   Copy all of the relevant details of the instruments as they appear in the computerized book or in the paper abstract book. Use one page for every instrument registered. See Precedent 38.1 for an example of what each page of your search might look like if you were abstracting the abstract book page shown in Precedent 31.3. Inquire from your employer as to whether you need to photocopy (non-automated) or print (automated) the documents in your 40-year search period, as this could be very costly for the client. As paper documents are being removed and destroyed due to automation, it is possible that some documents may only be verified or printed from microfilmed files.

4. **Registered plan of subdivision**   If your lands are on a registered plan of subdivision (as opposed to being on the original township map), purchase a copy of the registered plan of subdivision, sample in Precedent 31.4, that affects the lands being searched. Automated titles may be viewed using the property index mapping feature of the Teraview software. See Precedent 38.2 for an example of a property index map. These maps are useful for *Planning Act* searches because they show the abutting PIN numbers; they do not, however, show the boundaries of the properties.

5. **Reference plan**   Whether your lands continue to be described as a lot on a concession in a township, or a lot on a plan of subdivision, it is possible that the lands have been further divided by way of a reference plan. You will know this from the "R" designation which all reference plans have, e.g. Plan 66R-9465, Precedent 31.6. If the legal description refers to a reference plan, you should obtain a copy of this plan as well.

6. *Planning Act,* **execution, and corporate status searches**   These searches are required, as applicable. If your property is not a whole lot on a registered plan of subdivision, conduct a *Planning Act* **search** back forty years from the date of closing or until you come across a consent or the executed law statements. Conduct an **execution search** against all owners in your 40-year search period. If the purchaser or chargor is buying title insurance, an execution search against the current owner is all that is required. Conduct a **corporate status search** in your 40-year search period to make sure that any corporate owner did not cease to exist during its ownership of the land because if it did, the land would escheat (revert) to the Crown. Corporate searches are not required if your client is purchasing title insurance. Prepare a **title search summary** as described under the Land Titles searches, except also include the lawyer's abstract.

TITLE SEARCHING — LAND TITLES SYSTEM

Land titles properties are usually searched online in the land registry office where the lands are located. Because in the Land Titles system the government guarantees title, you need only go back to the last registered transfer to confirm who the registered owner of the property is and read your title carefully for any outstanding entries. Usually, you may ignore deleted entries. The guarantee of title means that you need not do a 40-year search, and you need not prepare a lawyer's abstract verifying the documents for validity.

1. **Find your computerized index** online (by PIN, municipal address, name, or instrument number) using the Teraview software and print a copy of the title. See Precedent 38.3, pages 1 and 2, for an example of an automated title to lands under the Land Titles system. Note that it is an LTCQ title and that the land is described as PIN 07001-0670 (LT), Part 4 on Plan 20R-3153A; it is the title to the lands that we are searching. (Note from the land description in the parcel register that this land stems from Part of Lot 3, Concession 4, but that it was further divided by way of a reference plan (Plan 20R-3153A)).

2. **Highlight the name of the current owners**, who are Ugo Felicetti and Luisa Felicetti, as joint tenants. Note that the title is currently subject to the following outstanding entries: a bylaw, Instrument No. 119980, and two agreements, Instruments No. 133037 and 409134, both in favour of the Corporation of the Town of Burlington. Verify with your employer whether you should print copies of these instruments for the purpose of determining their nature and effect on title.

3. **Obtain the property index map** and order a copy of the plan that the lands are on. See Precedent 38.2 for a copy of the property index map to our lands. Note that the PINs to all of the abutting lands are also given (see PINs in Precedents 38.4 to 38.7). These will be very useful should you be required to conduct a *Planning* Act search.

4. **Search executions** against the current owners only, e.g. Ugo Felicetti and Luisa Felicetti, in the land registry office where the property is located. There has not been a requirement to search executions against prior owners when dealing with any lands under the Land Titles system.

5. **Conduct a corporate status search** against any Ontario business corporation appearing on title as owner because any land owned by a business corporation escheats (reverts) to the Crown when the corporation ceases to exist. Be sure to check that the corporation did not cease to exist during its ownership of the land. Corporate status searches are not required if your client is purchasing title insurance because title insurance insures over escheats to the Crown.

6. **Determine whether the land being searched requires a section 50 *Planning Act* search** (part lot control). Our title requires such a search because the land is a part on a reference plan, and not the whole of a lot on a registered plan of subdivision, and is therefore not exempt. See Precedent 38.8, being the lands chart to the complete *Planning Act* search to our lands, PIN 07001-0670 (LT).

7. **Complete a title search summary**, Precedent 38.10, and staple it as a cover page to your search. Assemble your search in a logical order, e.g. title search summary, copy of title, sketch/plan, execution certificate, *Planning Act* search, if applicable, corporate status search, if applicable, followed by any other items your employer might require.

THE PLANNING ACT

Unless you are dealing with a condominium unit, the whole of a lot or the whole of a block on a registered plan of subdivision, you must, in addition to conducting a title search, also search the abutting (also referred to as adjoining) lands for compliance with section 50 of the *Planning Act*. In order to be considered as abutting lands, the properties in question must share a common border: for example, 1 abuts 2 and 3. It does not abut 4, even though Lots 1 and 4 meet at a point.

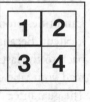

It is very important to conduct proper abutting land searches as any instrument registered in contravention of the *Planning Act* has been held to be of no value, as if it was never registered. Here are some *Planning Act* dates that play an important role in your *Planning Act* searches:

June 15, 1967: grandfather clause — legislation forgiving all contraventions prior to June 15, 1967. Search abutting lands from date of closing back to June 15, 1967.

May 2, 1968: ten-acre rule abolished — selling ten acres of land or more while retaining ten acres of land or more is no longer an exemption (useful answer on possible farmland contraventions).

June 27, 1970: mandatory subdivision and part lot control — for every part of a lot on registered plans of subdivision, search abutting lands from date of closing back to June 27, 1970, unless the municipality opted into the provisions of the act prior to this date.

December 15, 1978: retroactive legislation whereby all **consents** and/or registrations of **plans of subdivision** cure past *Planning Act* violations, whether such consents were obtained or such plans of subdivision were registered before or after December 15, 1978. Search from the date of closing back to the date of consent or the date of registration of the plan.

March 31, 1979: once a consent, always a consent — unrestrictive consents cure the past and take care of the future and therefore eliminate the requirement for an abutting lands search provided the same identical lands are being dealt with.

April 1, 1985: optional *Planning Act* law statements — search from date of closing back to the earliest of the three signature dates.

SEARCHING UNDER THE PLANNING ACT

You must conduct a *Planning Act* search if your lands are not the whole of a lot or block on a registered plan of subdivision. Your job is to see if any past or present owner of our lands has at any time in the past or present also owned abutting lands; if so, you must check to make sure that there has never been any division of lands without a **committee of adjustment** consent (government consent). Committees of adjustment are appointed by municipalities. Follow along in the following basic examples:

Part of Lot 1 Plan M-200	Part of Lot 2 Plan M-200

If X owns and is selling part of Lot 1, our lands, you want to make sure that X does not also own part of Lot 2 because part of Lot 2 is abutting land. If X also owns part of Lot 2, then X needs government consent in order to sell part of Lot 1 while still keeping part of Lot 2. Furthermore, you must apply this rule to all of the lands that abut part of the Lot 1 that X is selling.

Lot 1 on Concession A	Lot 2 on Concession A

X owns Lots 1 and 2 on Concession A. In selling one lot while keeping the other lot, X would need government consent because the lots are not on a registered plan of subdivision; you know

Legal TIP

Regardless of how your land is described, you can sell all of the abutting lands that you own, together, without the need for a consent because by doing so you are not dividing your lands.

this because there is no plan number. The lots are township lots on a concession. These lots are therefore not exempt from the act. On the other hand, if X was selling both lots together to Y, no consent would be required because X would not be retaining the fee in abutting lands.

Getting started   The first step in your *Planning Act* search is to obtain a copy of the property as shown on a plan or property index map showing our lands and the abutting lands together with any road access to the property. Precedent 38.2 is the property index map to the lands described in PIN 07001-0670 (LT). As you can see, the lands in question appear on Plan 20R-3153A. See Precedent 38.3, pages 1 and 2, being the printout for PIN 07001-0670 (LT) to which we will refer as our lands. Chances are that you would have already purchased the title at the time that you conducted your title search. You would then proceed to conduct the required *Planning Act* search.

1. Using an our lands chart, see Precedent 38.8, page 1, proceed to make notes on all conveyances (e.g. grants, deeds, transfers, powers of sale, foreclosures) that have occurred back in time. You begin your recording of information with the current owner, e.g. Ugo Felicetti and Luisa Felicetti, and work your way back (usually) forty years from the date of closing. If you come across a consent under the *Planning Act* or *Planning Act* law statements completed/executed, you need not search behind these dates because these items cure the past of any contraventions.

2. When you are searching lands under the *Land Titles Act*, remember to include survivorship applications as well as transmission applications because these documents amend title. This means that the ownership has changed to either delete an owner's name that has died (if lands were held as joint tenants) or to record the lands in the name of an estate trustee if the deceased held title alone or as a tenant in common. These documents are sometimes difficult to recognize as in recent years the land registrar simply stamps the title in the margin of the parcel register with a "name removed" comment/stamp. These documents are not used when dealing with lands under the *Registry Act*.

3. It is very important that you note whether the conveyances, i.e. transfers/deeds (you do not include mortgages, their postponements or their discharges or any other documents that do not transfer land) deal with all of the original lands over the years or whether part of the original lands have been severed off. If the original lands have been severed, you must point out that we are now dealing with a remainder. You must determine exactly what went out (usually through the registration of a reference plan) and whether the severed part(s) abut(s) our lands. If they do abut our lands, you must look for appropriate consents and document all of this information. Often lands are transferred out through an expropriation plan or a highway plan (whenever land is expropriated the registration of the plan of expropriation is deemed to convey (transfer) the land described i.e. no transfer/deed is required to be registered). These transactions are usually for the creation of roads or for road widening purposes. Such lands would usually have been transferred to the Crown and would be exempt from the *Planning Act*.

4. Using an abutting lands chart, see Precedent 38.8, page 2, begin recording the same information as above, starting with the current owner to each abutting property, back to either a consent, the optional *Planning Act* law statements, the registration date of a plan of subdivision (according to the *Planning Act*, the registration date of any plan of subdivision cures the past), or the grandfather clause. When relying on a consent or completion of the *Planning Act* law statements to shorten your search period, you should always provide a copy of these items and attach them to your search notes.

5. You must complete an abutting lands chart for all boundaries i.e. north, south, east, and west. It is not uncommon to have more than one parcel abut on one boundary. As well, one boundary is usually the property's access and should be shown as belonging to the Crown (e.g. City of Oshawa) on your chart. If there is no access, you should note on your sketch that the land is landlocked. For our purposes, we will be referring to the following abutting lands to our PIN 07001-0670 (LT):

   a.) Precedent 38.6 PIN 07001-0668 (LT) abuts our lands on the North boundary.
   b.) Precedent 38.7 PIN 07001-0671 (LT) abuts our lands on the South boundary
   c.) Precedent 38.8 PIN 07001-0669 (LT) abuts our lands on the East boundary.
   d.) Precedent 38.9 PIN 07001-0001 (LT) abuts our lands on the West boundary.

6. Once you have completed all of your charts, you must read through the chains of ownership to verify that no owner to our lands has sold any lands abutting without consent unless the transaction is exempt from the act. Precedent 38.8, pages 1 to 5, is the completed *Planning Act* search to PIN 07001-0670 (LT).

PLANNING ACT EXCEPTIONS, EXEMPTIONS AND RESTRICTIONS

Whole of a lot on a registered plan of subdivision The most common exemption is the whole of a lot on a registered plan of subdivision: for example, Greg may sell Lot 4 while retaining the fee in abutting Lot 5 or sell Lot 5 while retaining the fee in abutting Lot 4 because he is selling a whole of a lot on a registered plan of subdivision. Proper planning is deemed to have occurred upon registration of the plan of subdivision.

Lot 4, Plan M-100 Owner: Greg	Lot 5, Plan M-100 Owner: Greg

Abutting property is whole lot or whole block on a registered plan of subdivision An owner can deal with a part lot on a registered plan of subdivision while retaining the fee in abutting lands provided the abutting property is a whole lot or block on a registered plan of subdivision: for example, Danielle can sell her Lot 13 even though she owns the fee in abutting lands because Lot 13 is a whole lot on a registered plan of subdivision (Plan M-1414). If Danielle preferred, she could sell her part Lot 12 instead, even though it is not the whole of a lot on a registered plan of subdivision because even though she retains the fee in abutting lands, the abutting property is the whole of a lot on a registered plan of subdivision. However, if what Danielle owned were two part lots on Plan M-1414, she would require consent to sell one part without the other.

West ½ of Lot 12 Plan M-1414 Owner: Z	East 1/2 of Lot 12 Plan M-1414 Owner: Danielle	Whole of Lot 13, Plan M-1414 Owner: Danielle

Optional statements On April 1, 1985, the *Land Registration Reform Act* amended the *Planning Act* whereby under section 50(22) of the *Planning Act*, the vendor, the vendor's lawyer, and the purchaser's lawyer may sign law statements on behalf of their clients. The three signatures are deemed to cure the transfer at hand and all previous conveyances of any contraventions of

Legal TIP

Consent is government approval to divide (or sever) land by way other than a registered plan of subdivision. Such a government consent is usually made through a government agency known as a committee of adjustment (or a planning board) that ensures that the division of one's land is not an improper division.

section 50 of the *Planning Act*, effective from the date of registration of the transfer containing the three signatures. These statements are not, however, mandatory for registration purposes. This is why they are referred to as optional statements.

Municipal bylaws   Part lots on registered plans of subdivision are exempt if the municipality has passed a bylaw deeming that part lot control does not apply to certain properties. Subsection 50(7) gives municipalities the authority to pass such bylaws. This may occur when a developer of multiple part lot units on a registered plan of subdivision, instead of applying for a committee of adjustment consent for each individual unit, requests the municipality to pass a bylaw exempting from part lot control all of the part lot properties on the registered plan of subdivision. As well, changes in planning and development may necessitate that a municipality pass bylaws that **deregister** existing registered plans of subdivision so as to no longer be deemed as registered plans of subdivision for purposes of the act. Such a deregistration means that you will be unable to convey even a whole lot if you retain the fee in abutting lands because it will be as if the registered plan of subdivision does not exist at all as of the date of deregistration.

Government-related exemptions   Whole lots on plans of subdivision which have resulted into part lots due to expropriation remain exempt. Also, transactions that involve the government (municipal, provincial, and federal) are exempt, and acquisitions for conservation purposes and easements for transmission lines, e.g. pipelines, are also exempt from subdivision control.

Unrestrictive and restrictive consents   Lands that were the subject of a *Planning Act* unrestrictive consent are exempt. Unrestrictive consents came about on March 31, 1979, as a result of an amendment to the act. Unrestrictive consents are known as **once a consent, always a consent** because a new consent will not be required, regardless of whether the vendor retains the fee in any abutting lands. Such consent would bear the signature of the planning director certifying that the consent of a municipality was given and the date on which it was given. There are also restrictive consents that would bear the signature of the planning director and that would indicate that such consents apply only to a particular conveyance.

Simultaneous conveyances   Simultaneous conveyances are not allowed. If D owns two abutting non-exempt properties, D cannot sell one property to J while selling the other property, at the very same time, to G. In these circumstances D would be deemed to retain the fee in abutting lands.

TITLE SEARCHING USING TERAVIEW

With the Teraview software, you can conduct title searches electronically. It is possible to retrieve information about a property by searching by PIN, by municipal address, by name, and by instrument number. The following Teraview instructions assume that you are familiar with the Teraview software through either the law office or the Teraview Training System tutorial at your college. For instructions on how to log in, exit, create a new docket, open an existing docket and save a document in Teraview, see Chapter 32. The following step-by-step guidance relates to PIN 24916-0001(LT):

Legal TIP

References to the selling or mortgaging of land also include other transactions involving lands such as partial discharges, easements, foreclosures and powers of sale. Section 50 of the act basically affects most transactions involving land.

Legal TIP

Before June 27, 1970, municipalities could, by passing a bylaw, opt into the *Planning Act* in order to enforce subdivision control. After June 27, 1970, municipalities had to, by passing a bylaw, opt out of the *Planning Act* if they did not want part lot control to apply to certain lands.

⇨ **Click on:**
  • Property on menu bar.
  • Search by PIN; a search by PIN dialogue box will open - enter PIN, e.g. 24916-0001 (LT).
  • OK.
  • Parcel Register — Select All Active Instruments (it is best to Include Deleted Instruments).
  • OK. A Parcel Register for the property will open. It contains essential information that has been abstracted from the registered instruments, including the property description, estate qualifier, block implementation date, and other information. Remember that the category that your lands fall under will determine the searches that you must conduct and may very well shorten the length of your abutting lands search.
⇨ Open the owner(s) tab to confirm that the registered owner(s) is in fact the vendor in a purchase transaction or the chargor in a charge transaction.
⇨ Click on the green printer icon on the far left of the icon toolbar. The parcel register/ abstract index, Precedent 38.9, should print to your office printer.

Select the Most Recent Transfer to View
⇨ Return to your Parcel Register Screen.
  • Click on Instruments — Review list of instruments that appears.
  • Select the latest Transfer for viewing.
  • Right Click the instrument name and Click on Request Instrument button that will appear.
  • Instrument Options box will open — Check off the instrument you want to view, see Figure 38.1.
⇨ In the Range field to the right of the instrument, you can specify which pages you want to view.
  • Note that if an instrument has zero pages, it means that an image of the document is not available in the system. In a real office situation a hard copy of the document could be ordered by fax or courier or by attending the actual land registry office where the document is either stored as a paper document or on microfilm, but this cannot be done in the training System.
⇨ Click on the View button. You may get a message about the current default paper setting not being legal. Make a mental note of this.
  • OK. An image of the document will appear on the screen.
  • To print a hard copy,
⇨ Click on the Printer icon located just above the document.
  • OK. Close after printing the document.

Figure 38.1 Parcel Register

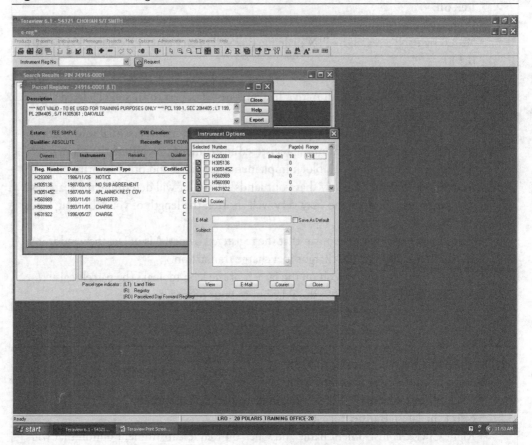

Viewing Map for Adjacent Properties

The original Search Results dialogue box should still be open.

➪ **Click on:**
- Map tab. A Confirm Message box will appear.
- Yes. A map of the area in which the property is located will appear. Note that you can zoom-in and zoom-out to change the scale of the map.
- Right Click on the map to get a list of options.
- Double click on the Adjacent branch of the Tree.

➪ Click Yes on the Confirmation Message that will appear. All adjacent properties are now highlighted in a different colour. Note that a list of adjacent properties now appears in the Tree.
- Click on the Adjacent tab on the right hand side of the window. Note that the PIN numbers and legal descriptions appear for all adjacent properties.
- If you want further details on any of the adjacent properties listed, click on the property you want to look at. Close the Search results window.

Writ Searching   The next step is to conduct a writ search. Writ searches are usually conducted by the law office acting on behalf of a purchaser or lender. The Ministry of the Attorney General Writs of Execution databases can be accessed through Teraview. You can undertake a Writ name search at any time during the completion of a document. If a writ search is done during the completion of a document through Teraview on the same day that the document is submitted for registration, the writ search is not completed a second time. This does not apply to a writ search conducted through the WritSearch product. Following are the steps for conducting a search through WritSearch when acting for a purchaser.

Using WritSearch while completing a transfer   If it is not already open, open the docket that you created for your purchaser. Open the Transfer document for your purchase file.

⇨   Click on the + icon next to Transferor branch to expand the branch. You will see a list of transferors. Select one of the transferors.

⇨   In the Work in Progress window, click on the Writs tab. Note that the status field indicates that no search has yet been performed.

⇨   Click on Instrument on the Menu Bar and then on Writs, and then on Retrieve Writs. A writ search will be undertaken. If there are no writs, you will soon see that the status is "Clear." Note that the system will retrieve writs for both transferors at the same time.

⇨   Click Options. Click Save.

Using WritSearch to conduct a writ search without completing a transfer. Open your ADMIN docket:

⇨   **Click on:**
   • Products on Menu Bar and then on WritSearch.
   • Writs on Menu Bar and then on Search by Name; ensure client/name is identified as a Person.
   • Enter name you would like to search.
   • Select the appropriate Enforcement Office (i.e. Toronto).
   • OK. A Print Writ Certificate dialogue box will open. Key your name into the Search performed by field. This is mandatory. (Your name will not be printed on the Certificate).

⇨   **Optional:**
   • Key in your student number in "Your reference" field. Your student number will print on the Certificate in the Searcher Reference number which helps you identify your printed document.
   • OK. The certificate will automatically be displayed on your computer and the Writs Execution Search list will open. Print the certificate. Review the information provided. If a Writ is found:

⇨   Click on the Details button. A writ Detail window will open. Review the information provided. Click on the Print button to print a detailed writ report. Complete the Print Writ Certificate dialogue box as discussed above; and
   • OK. The detailed writ report will be printed. Note that as long as the Writ Detail Box is open, you can make reprints of the Certificate without incurring additional charges. Once the Writ Details Box is closed, reprints are no longer free of charge.
   • Click on the DONE button to close the dialogue box.
   • Exit Teraview.

Conduct a Subsearch   Assume that you already conducted a full title search. At this time, you simply want to do a subsearch to ensure that the vendor still owns the property and has not encumbered it with any new mortgages or liens. If it is not already open, open the docket that you created for the purchaser.

⇨ **Click on:**
  - Property on Menu Bar.
  - Search by PIN. Key in the PIN for the subject property.
  - OK. A Search Results dialogue box will open.
  - Parcel register button at bottom of box - Parcel Register Options dialogue box will open.
  - Select All Active Instruments.
  - OK. The Parcel Register for the property will open. Review it carefully to ensure that the vendor still owns the property and has not registered a recent mortgage or otherwise encumbered title. Record the last registered document, print, and close the parcel register.

CHAPTER SUMMARY

Title searching involves searching the ownership history of a particular piece of land for the purpose of ensuring the purchaser (or lender) receives good and valid title to the property at hand. Searching can be done in person or on-line in the land registry office where the property is located or from your desktop using the Teraview software. Searching under the Registry system entails an examination of documents based on the 40-year rule of the *Registry Act*. In the Land Titles system, the government guarantees title (subject to some qualifications) and you are not required to verify documents for their validity.

Section 50 of the *Planning Act* places the onus on the lawyer for the purchaser (or lender) to satisfy himself or herself that no contravention of the act has occurred. For this reason, you must, when title searching, determine whether a *Planning Act* search of abutting lands is going to be required. It is important to remember that except for the electronic, instead of the manual, manner of obtaining your title searching information, the title searching work is in many respects done in the same manner as it has been prior to automation.

To search electronically, you need to have one of the following items: the PIN, the municipal address, the legal description or the owner's name, which you input into the computer. You then receive a printout showing the registrations against title to that property.

REVIEW QUESTIONS

1. What information do you require in your first step to searching title electronically?
2. What is the purpose of a *Planning Act* search?
3. What is the difference between these two plans: Plan 100 and Plan M-100?
4. Refer to the parcel register of our lands in Precedent 38.3 and answer the following questions:
   (a) What type of title is the property?
   (b) Who is/are the owner/s?
   (c) When was the property converted to the Land Titles system?
   (d) What is the legal description of the property?

(e) Is this property on a plan of subdivision, a reference plan, or a township map?

(f) Is a 40-year search required?

(g) Is a *Planning Act* search required?

(h) If a *Planning Act* search is required, how far back in time will you search?

(i) Are there any road accesses? If so, name the name/s of the road/s.

(j) List any outstanding encumbrances (e.g. charges, easements, bylaws) by instrument name and number.

(k) Assuming that no title insurance is being purchased, list the names against which you would search executions.

5. Draw a freehand side-by-side (abutting) sketch of the plots of land for each of the following questions and determine the answer to each scenario. Compare your answer to the answers given below.

(a) Your client Ryan Getslaugh owns abutting whole Lots 1 and 2, Concession A, in the township of NHL. Does Ryan require consent to sell his Lot 1 to Roberto Longago without being in contravention?

Ryan cannot sell his Lot 1 to Roberto without being in contravention because Lot 1 is not on a registered plan of subdivision and Ryan is retaining the fee in abutting lands to Lot 2. Ryan will require consent to sell one lot without the other.

(b) Your client Seednay Crosbie owns abutting whole Lots 3, 4 and 5 according to registered plan of subdivision No. 44. Can Seednay sell Lot 4 to Marten Brodoor without obtaining consent while retaining the fee in abutting lands to Lots 3 and 5?

Seednay can sell his Lot 4 to Marten without consent because Lot 4 is the whole of a lot on a registered plan of subdivision. It does not matter that Seednay is retaining the fee in abutting lands because whole lots on plans of subdivision are exempt.

(c) Your client Jason Shakeandblake owns abutting Parts 8, 9 and 10 according to Plan 36R-2233. Can Jason transfer his Part 8 to Todd Beartuzi without obtaining consent?

The land that Jason owns is on a reference plan and not on a registered plan of subdivision. These lands are not exempted from subdivision control and Jason will therefore require consent to sell his Part 8 to Todd because he will be retaining the fee in abutting lands.

Precedent 38.2 Property Index Map to PIN 07001-0670

Precedent 38.1 Sample, Lawyer's Abstract, pages 14 and 15

SERVICE ONTARIO

PRINTED ON 12 APR, 20XX AT 18:18:04
FOR RBREDFORD

SCALE
0 — 30 meters

PROPERTY INDEX MAP
HALTON (No. 20)

LEGEND
FREEHOLD PROPERTY
LEASEHOLD PROPERTY
LIMITED INTEREST PROPERTY
CONDOMINIUM PROPERTY
RETIRED PIN (MAP UPDATE PENDING) — 0449
PROPERTY NUMBER
BLOCK NUMBER — 08050
GEOGRAPHIC FABRIC
EASEMENT

THIS IS NOT A PLAN OF SURVEY

NOTES

REVIEW THE TITLE RECORDS FOR COMPLETE PROPERTY INFORMATION AS THIS MAP MAY NOT REFLECT RECENT REGISTRATIONS

THIS MAP WAS COMPILED FROM PLANS AND DOCUMENTS RECORDED IN THE LAND REGISTRATION SYSTEM AND HAS BEEN PREPARED FOR PROPERTY INDEXING PURPOSES ONLY

FOR DIMENSIONS OF PROPERTIES BOUNDARIES SEE RECORDED PLANS AND DOCUMENTS

ONLY MAJOR EASEMENTS ARE SHOWN

REFERENCE PLANS UNDERLYING MORE RECENT REFERENCE PLANS ARE NOT ILLUSTRATED

Ontario

Lot 2, Plan 363

Registration No.	Type of Instrument	Date of Instrument	Registration Date	Grantor 2 x ①	Grantee ②	Consideration	Land
CT12808	Grant	Feb.28/75	Apr.1/75	Tuck, Joseph A. Tuck, Donna E.	Jonquil, Virginia	$2 etc.	All

☒ SFCA   ☐ DEA   ☐ SFMA   ☒ GRANT   ☒ fee simple   ☐ joint tenant   ☐ ten. in com.   ☐ to uses   ☒ HAB   ☒ UC (4)   ☐ REL   ☐ B OF DWR   ☐ SP CONSENT   ☐ S & S ①   ☐ ONT.SUC.DUTY   ☐ A OF SEC.116   ☐ A OF LTT $25,000

☒ A OF SUB. WIT. ①   ☐ AFF PL ACT ①   ☐ STATE RE PL ACT   ☐ STATE OF AGE(1/4/85)   ☐ STATE OF SP.STATUS   ☐ Sp☒not asp☒sp of eaothr   ☐ not a mat. home   ☐ DT OF BRTH -TSFREE   1 ___ 2 ___   ☐ AFF OF PRTNR PROP   ☐ PUR AS PP   ☐ HELD AS PP   ☐ DOCUMENT GNRAL   ☐ SCHEDULE

Lot 2, Plan 363

Registration No.	Type of Instrument	Date of Instrument	Registration Date	Mortgagor ①	Mortgagee ②	Consideration	Land
CT12809	Mortgage	Mar.18/75	Apr.1/75	Jonquil, Virginia	The Royal Trust Company	$9,350	All

☒ SFCA   ☐ DEA   ☐ SFMA   ☐ GRANT   ☐ fee simple   ☐ joint tenant   ☐ ten. in com.   ☐ to uses   ☐ HAB   ☒ UC (4)   REL   ☐ B OF DWR   ☐ SP CONSENT   ☐ S & S ①   ☐ ONT.SUC.DUTY   ☐ A OF SEC.116   ☐ A OF LTT

☒ A OF SUB. WIT. ①   ☐ AFF PL ACT   ☐ STATE RE PL ACT   ☐ STATE OF AGE(1/4/85)   ☐ STATE OF SP.STATUS   ☐ Sp☒not asp☒sp of eaothr   ☐ not a mat. home   ☐ DT OF BRTH -TSFREE   1 ___ 2 ___   ☐ AFF OF PRTNR PROP   ☐ PUR AS PP   ☐ HELD AS PP   ☐ DOCUMENT GNRAL   ☐ SCHEDULE

TRAINING

LAND
REGISTRY
OFFICE #20

PARCEL REGISTER (ABBREVIATED) FOR PROPERTY IDENTIFIER

PAGE 1 OF 2
PREPARED FOR ANCanadore
ON 20xx/06/22 AT 12:44:50

| 07001-0670 (LT) |

* CERTIFIED BY LAND REGISTRAR IN ACCORDANCE WITH LAND TITLES ACT * SUBJECT TO RESERVATIONS IN CROWN GRANT *

**** NOT VALID - TO BE USED FOR TRAINING PURPOSES ONLY **** PT LT 3 , CON 4 SOUTH OF DUNDAS STREET , PART 4 , 20R3153A ; BURLINGTON/NELSON TWP

PROPERTY DESCRIPTION:

PROPERTY REMARKS:

ESTATE/QUALIFIER:
FEE SIMPLE
LT CONVERSION QUALIFIED

RECENTLY:
FIRST CONVERSION FROM BOOK

PIN CREATION DATE:
1997/03/31

OWNERS' NAMES   CAPACITY SHARE
FELICETTI, UGO   JTEN
FELICETTI, LUISA   JTEN

REG. NUM.	DATE	INSTRUMENT TYPE	AMOUNT	PARTIES FROM	PARTIES TO	CERT/ CHKD
				EFFECTIVE 2000/07/29 THE NOTATION OF THE "BLOCK IMPLEMENTATION DATE" OF 1997/03/31 ON THIS PIN		
				WAS REPLACED WITH THE "PIN CREATION DATE" OF 1997/03/31		
				**PRINTOUT INCLUDES ALL DOCUMENT TYPES AND DELETED INSTRUMENTS SINCE: 1997/03/27 **		
				**SUBJECT, ON FIRST REGISTRATION UNDER THE LAND TITLES ACT, TO:		
				** SUBSECTION 44(1) OF THE LAND TITLES ACT, EXCEPT PARAGRAPH 11, PARAGRAPH 14, PROVINCIAL SUCCESSION DUTIES *		
				** AND ESCHEATS OR FORFEITURE TO THE CROWN.		
				** THE RIGHTS OF ANY PERSON WHO WOULD, BUT FOR THE LAND TITLES ACT, BE ENTITLED TO THE LAND OR ANY PART OF		
				** IT THROUGH LENGTH OF ADVERSE POSSESSION, PRESCRIPTION, MISDESCRIPTION OR BOUNDARIES SETTLED BY		
				** CONVENTION.		
				** ANY LEASE TO WHICH THE SUBSECTION 70(2) OF THE REGISTRY ACT APPLIES.		
				**DATE OF CONVERSION TO LAND TITLES: 1997/04/01 **		
119980	1961/01/25	BYLAW				C
133037	1962/01/02	AGREEMENT				C
20R1957	1975/03/07	PLAN REFERENCE				C
409134	1975/04/11	AGREEMENT			THE CORPORATION OF THE TOWN OF BURLINGTON	C
		REMARKS: SKETCH ATTACHED				
20R3153A	1977/05/30	PLAN REFERENCE			THE CORPORATION OF THE TOWN OF BURLINGTON	C
505218	1979/07/03	TRANSFER	$2		FELICETTI, UGO	C

NOTE: ADJOINING PROPERTIES SHOULD BE INVESTIGATED TO ASCERTAIN DESCRIPTIVE INCONSISTENCIES, IF ANY, WITH DESCRIPTION REPRESENTED FOR THIS PROPERTY.
NOTE: ENSURE THAT YOUR PRINTOUT STATES THE TOTAL NUMBER OF PAGES AND THAT YOU HAVE PICKED THEM ALL UP.

Precedent 38.3   PIN 07001-0670 (LT) to Our Lands, page 2

TRAINING

LAND
REGISTRY
OFFICE #20

PARCEL REGISTER (ABBREVIATED) FOR PROPERTY IDENTIFIER

PAGE 2 OF 2
PREPARED FOR ANCanadore
ON 20xx/06/22 AT 12:44:50

| 07001-0670 (LT) |

* CERTIFIED BY LAND REGISTRAR IN ACCORDANCE WITH LAND TITLES ACT * SUBJECT TO RESERVATIONS IN CROWN GRANT *

REG. NUM.	DATE	INSTRUMENT TYPE	AMOUNT	PARTIES FROM	PARTIES TO	CERT/ CHKD
					FELICETTI, LUISA	

```
┌─────────────┐
│  TRAINING   │          PARCEL REGISTER (ABBREVIATED) FOR PROPERTY IDENTIFIER          PAGE 1 OF 1
└─────────────┘                                                                         PREPARED FOR ANCanadore
                    LAND                                                                 ON 20xx/06/22 AT 13:03:46
                    REGISTRY           07001-0668 (LT)
                    OFFICE #20
                              * CERTIFIED BY LAND REGISTRAR IN ACCORDANCE WITH LAND TITLES ACT * SUBJECT TO RESERVATIONS IN CROWN GRANT *
```

PROPERTY DESCRIPTION: **** NOT VALID - TO BE USED FOR TRAINING PURPOSES ONLY **** PT BROMLEY RD LYING BTN KENWOOD AV & HAMMERSMITH CT BEING ; PT LTS 2 & 3 , CON 4 SOUTH OF
                           DUNDAS STREET , AS IN 132330 & 170635 (SECONDLY); S/T 170635 ; PT BROMLELY RD , PL 607 ; PCL H, PL 607 ; BURLINGTON/NELSON TWP

PROPERTY REMARKS:
ESTATE/QUALIFIER: RECENTLY: PIN CREATION DATE:
FEE SIMPLE   FIRST CONVERSION FROM BOOK   1997/03/31
LT CONVERSION QUALIFIED
OWNERS' NAMES   CAPACITY SHARE
THE CORPORATION OF THE CITY OF BURLINGTON   BENO

REG. NUM.	DATE	INSTRUMENT TYPE	AMOUNT	PARTIES FROM	PARTIES TO	CERT/ CHKD
EFFECTIVE 2000/07/29 THE NOTATION OF THE "BLOCK IMPLEMENTATION DATE" OF 1997/03/31 ON THIS PIN						
WAS REPLACED WITH THE "PIN CREATION DATE" OF 1997/03/31						
** PRINTOUT INCLUDES ALL DOCUMENT TYPES AND DELETED INSTRUMENTS SINCE: 1997/03/27 **						
**SUBJECT, ON FIRST REGISTRATION UNDER THE LAND TITLES ACT, TO:						
** SUBSECTION 44(1) OF THE LAND TITLES ACT, EXCEPT PARAGRAPH 11, PARAGRAPH 14, PROVINCIAL SUCCESSION DUTIES *						
** AND ESCHEATS OR FORFEITURE TO THE CROWN.						
** THE RIGHTS OF ANY PERSON WHO WOULD, BUT FOR THE LAND TITLES ACT, BE ENTITLED TO THE LAND OR ANY PART OF						
** IT THROUGH LENGTH OF ADVERSE POSSESSION, PRESCRIPTION, MISDESCRIPTION OR BOUNDARIES SETTLED BY						
** CONVENTION.						
** ANY LEASE TO WHICH THE SUBSECTION 70(2) OF THE REGISTRY ACT APPLIES.						
**DATE OF CONVERSION TO LAND TITLES: 1997/04/01 **						
PL607	1955/06/15	PLAN SUBDIVISION				C
43063	1955/10/21	TRANSFER	$1			C
132330	1961/12/13	TRANSFER	$1		THE CORPORATION OF THE TOWNSHIP OF NELSON	C
170635	1964/07/29	TRANSFER	$1		THE CORPORATION OF THE TOWN OF BURLINGTON	C
185274	1965/06/23	BYLAW			THE CORPORATION OF THE TOWN OF BURLINGTON	C

NOTE: ADJOINING PROPERTIES SHOULD BE INVESTIGATED TO ASCERTAIN DESCRIPTIVE INCONSISTENCIES, IF ANY, WITH DESCRIPTION REPRESENTED FOR THIS PROPERTY.
NOTE: ENSURE THAT YOUR PRINTOUT STATES THE TOTAL NUMBER OF PAGES AND THAT YOU HAVE PICKED THEM ALL UP.

Precedent 38.5   PIN 07001-0671 (LT) South Boundary, page 1

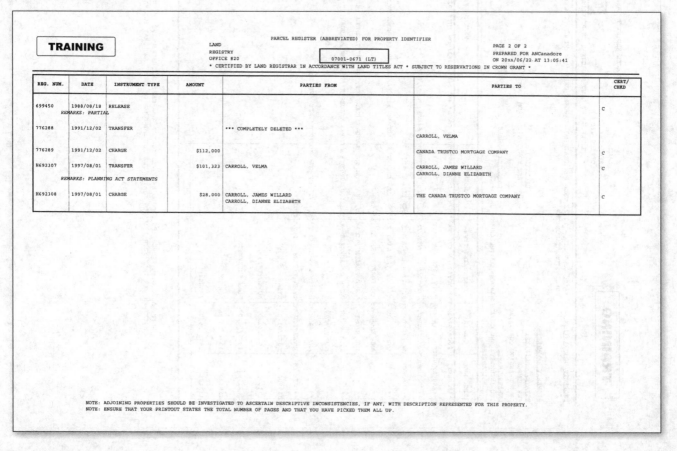

Precedent 38.5   PIN 07001-0671 (LT) South Boundary, page 2

TRAINING

```
                          PARCEL REGISTER (ABBREVIATED) FOR PROPERTY IDENTIFIER

                          LAND                                                              PAGE 1 OF 1
                          REGISTRY                                                          PREPARED FOR ANCanadore
                          OFFICE #20                                                        ON 20xx/06/22 AT 13:32:27
          07001-0669 (LT)    * CERTIFIED BY LAND REGISTRAR IN ACCORDANCE WITH LAND TITLES ACT * SUBJECT TO RESERVATIONS IN CROWN GRANT *
```

PROPERTY DESCRIPTION: **** NOT VALID - TO BE USED FOR TRAINING PURPOSES ONLY **** PT LTS 2 & 3 , CON 4 SOUTH OF DUNDAS STREET , PT 4, 20R1957; T/W 170635 ;
                        BURLINGTON/NELSON TWP

PROPERTY REMARKS:
ESTATE/QUALIFIER: RECENTLY: PIN CREATION DATE:
FEE SIMPLE   FIRST CONVERSION FROM BOOK   1997/03/31
LT CONVERSION QUALIFIED
OWNERS' NAMES   CAPACITY SHARE
THE INCUMBENT AND CHURCH WARDENS OF THE CHURCH OF   BENO
ST. ELIZABETH

REG. NUM.	DATE	INSTRUMENT TYPE	AMOUNT	PARTIES FROM	PARTIES TO	CERT/ CHKD
		**EFFECTIVE 2000/07/29	THE NOTATION OF THE "BLOCK IMPLEMENTATION DATE" OF 1997/03/31 ON THIS PIN**			
		WAS REPLACED WITH THE "PIN CREATION DATE" OF 1997/03/31				
		** PRINTOUT INCLUDES ALL DOCUMENT TYPES AND DELETED INSTRUMENTS SINCE: 1997/03/27 **				
		**SUBJECT, ON FIRST REGISTRATION UNDER THE LAND TITLES ACT, TO:				
		** SUBSECTION 44(1) OF THE LAND TITLES ACT, EXCEPT PARAGRAPH 11, PARAGRAPH 14, PROVINCIAL SUCCESSION DUTIES *				
		** AND ESCHEATS OR FORFEITURE TO THE CROWN.				
		** THE RIGHTS OF ANY PERSON WHO WOULD, BUT FOR THE LAND TITLES ACT, BE ENTITLED TO THE LAND OR ANY PART OF				
		** IT THROUGH LENGTH OF ADVERSE POSSESSION, PRESCRIPTION, MISDESCRIPTION OR BOUNDARIES SETTLED BY				
		** CONVENTION.				
		** ANY LEASE TO WHICH THE SUBSECTION 70(2) OF THE REGISTRY ACT APPLIES.				
		**DATE OF CONVERSION TO LAND TITLES: 1997/04/01 **				
119980	1961/01/25	BYLAW				C
133037	1962/01/02	AGREEMENT			THE CORPORATION OF THE TOWN OF BURLINGTON	C
20R1957	1975/03/07	PLAN REFERENCE				C
429420	1976/03/05	AGREEMENT			THE CORPORATION OF THE CITY OF BURLINGTON	C
432455	1976/05/05	TRANSFER	$2		THE INCUMBENT AND CHURCH WARDENS OF THE CHURCH OF ST. ELIZABETH	C

NOTE: ADJOINING PROPERTIES SHOULD BE INVESTIGATED TO ASCERTAIN DESCRIPTIVE INCONSISTENCIES, IF ANY, WITH DESCRIPTION REPRESENTED FOR THIS PROPERTY.
NOTE: ENSURE THAT YOUR PRINTOUT STATES THE TOTAL NUMBER OF PAGES AND THAT YOU HAVE PICKED THEM ALL UP.

TRAINING

PARCEL REGISTER (ABBREVIATED) FOR PROPERTY IDENTIFIER

PAGE 1 OF 1
PREPARED FOR ANCanadore
ON 20xx/06/22 AT 14:06:42

LAND
REGISTRY
OFFICE #20   07001-0001 (LT)

* CERTIFIED BY LAND REGISTRAR IN ACCORDANCE WITH LAND TITLES ACT * SUBJECT TO RESERVATIONS IN CROWN GRANT *

PROPERTY DESCRIPTION: **** NOT VALID - TO BE USED FOR TRAINING PURPOSES ONLY **** KENWOOD AV BEING ; KENWOOD AV , PL 966 ; BLK B , PL 1459 ; PT LT 3 , CON 4 SOUTH OF DUNDAS
STREET , AS IN 121807 ; SECONDLY ; 1 FOOT RESERVE SE KENWOOD AV , PL 966 ; BURLINGTON/NELSON TWP

PROPERTY REMARKS:

ESTATE/QUALIFIER: RECENTLY: PIN CREATION DATE:
FEE SIMPLE   FIRST CONVERSION FROM BOOK   1997/03/31
LT CONVERSION QUALIFIED

OWNERS' NAMES   CAPACITY SHARE
THE CORPORATION OF THE CITY OF BURLINGTON   BENO

REG. NUM.	DATE	INSTRUMENT TYPE	AMOUNT	PARTIES FROM	PARTIES TO	CERT/CHKD
EFFECTIVE 2000/07/29 THE NOTATION OF THE "BLOCK IMPLEMENTATION DATE" OF 1997/03/31 ON THIS PIN						
WAS REPLACED WITH THE "PIN CREATION DATE" OF 1997/03/31						
** PRINTOUT INCLUDES ALL DOCUMENT TYPES AND DELETED INSTRUMENTS SINCE: 1997/03/27 **						
**SUBJECT, ON FIRST REGISTRATION UNDER THE LAND TITLES ACT, TO:						
** SUBSECTION 44(1) OF THE LAND TITLES ACT, EXCEPT PARAGRAPH 11, PARAGRAPH 14, PROVINCIAL SUCCESSION DUTIES *						
** AND ESCHEATS OR FORFEITURE TO THE CROWN.						
** THE RIGHTS OF ANY PERSON WHO WOULD, BUT FOR THE LAND TITLES ACT, BE ENTITLED TO THE LAND OR ANY PART OF						
** IT THROUGH LENGTH OF ADVERSE POSSESSION, PRESCRIPTION, MISDESCRIPTION OR BOUNDARIES SETTLED BY						
** CONVENTION.						
** ANY LEASE TO WHICH THE SUBSECTION 70(2) OF THE REGISTRY ACT APPLIES.						
**DATE OF CONVERSION TO LAND TITLES: 1997/04/01 **						
PL966	1959/09/30	PLAN SUBDIVISION				C
104170	1959/10/22	TRANSFER	$1			C
121807	1961/03/23	BYLAM				C
		REMARKS: EXPROPRIATION				
PL1459	1971/03/16	PLAN SUBDIVISION			THE CORPORATION OF THE TOWN OF BURLINGTON	C
773828	1991/10/23	BYLAW			THE CORPORATION OF THE TOWN OF BURLINGTON	C

NOTE: ADJOINING PROPERTIES SHOULD BE INVESTIGATED TO ASCERTAIN DESCRIPTIVE INCONSISTENCIES, IF ANY, WITH DESCRIPTION REPRESENTED FOR THIS PROPERTY.
NOTE: ENSURE THAT YOUR PRINTOUT STATES THE TOTAL NUMBER OF PAGES AND THAT YOU HAVE PICKED THEM ALL UP.

Precedent 38.8 PIN 07001-0670 (LT) Our Lands Chart, page 1

OUR LANDS CHART

Known as: PIN 07001-0670 (LT) Legal Description: Part of Lot 3, Concession 4, South of Dundas Street, Part 4, Plan 29R-3153A, Burlington

DATE OF REGISTRATION	INSTRUMENT NAME AND NUMBER	REGISTERED OWNER(S)	HOW TITLE WAS HELD	WHAT HAD TRANSFERRED
1979/07/03*	Transfer 505218	Ugo Felicetti and Luisa Felicetti	Joint tenants	All of Part 4, 29R-3153A

*No need to search behind the automation date on an LTCQ title. Automation date is 1997/03/31. Lands have not been dealt with since automation.

Precedent 38.8 PIN 07001-0670 (LT) Abutting Lands Chart, page 2

ABUTTING LANDS CHART

Boundary on North side
Known as: PIN 07001-0668 (LT) Legal Description: Bromley Road

DATE OF REGISTRATION	INSTRUMENT NAME AND NUMBER	REGISTERED OWNER(S)	HOW TITLE WAS HELD	WHAT HAD TRANSFERRED
1964/07/29	Transfer 170635	The Corporation of the Town of Burlington – Exempt Land		Part of Bromley Road lying between Kenwood Avenue and Hammersmith Court

Precedent 38.8 PIN 07001-0670 (LT) Abutting Lands Chart, page 3

ABUTTING LAND CHART

Boundary on South side
Known as: PIN 07001-0671 (LT) Legal Description: Part of Lot 3, Concession 4, South of Dundas Street, Part 3, Plan 20R-3153A, Burlington

DATE OF REGISTRATION	INSTRUMENT NAME AND NUMBER	REGISTERED OWNER	HOW TITLE WAS HELD	WHAT HAD TRANSFERRED
1997/08/01*	Transfer H692307	James Willard Carroll and Dianne Elizabeth Carroll	Joint tenants	All of Part 3, 20R-3153A

*No need to search behind signed *Planning Act* statements in Transfer.

Precedent 38.8 PIN 07001-0670 (LT) Abutting Lands Chart, page 4

ABUTTING LANDS CHART

Boundary on East side
Known as: PIN 07001-0669 (LT) Legal Description: Part of Lots 2 and 3, Concession 4, South of Dundas St., Part 4, Plan 20R-1957, Burlington

DATE OF REGISTRATION	INSTRUMENT NAME AND NUMBER	REGISTERED OWNER(S)	HOW TITLE WAS HELD	WHAT HAD TRANSFERRED
1976/05/05*	Transfer 432455	The Incumbent and Church Wardens of the Church of St. Elizabeth	Beneficial	Part 4, 20R-1957

*No need to search behind automation date on an LTCQ title. Automation date is 1997/03/31. Lands have not been dealt with since automation.

Precedent 38.8 PIN 07001-0670 (LT) Abutting Lands Chart, page 5

ABUTTING LANDS CHART

Legal Description: Kenwood Avenue

Boundary on West side
Known as: PIN 07001-0001 (LT)

DATE OF REGISTRATION	INSTRUMENT NAME AND NUMBER	REGISTERED OWNER(S)	HOW TITLE WAS HELD	WHAT HAD TRANSFERRED
1959/10/22*	Transfer 104170	The Corporation of the Town of Burlington – Exempt Land		Plan 966; Block B, Plan 1459; Part of Lot 3, Concession 4, South of Dundas Street

*No need to search behind the automation date on an LTCQ title. Automation date is 1997/03/31. Lands have not been dealt with since automation.

TRAINING

PARCEL REGISTER (ABBREVIATED) FOR PROPERTY IDENTIFIER

PAGE 1 OF 1
PREPARED FOR AWCanadore
ON 20--/06/21 AT 10:22:30

LAND
REGISTRY
OFFICE #20

24916-0001 (LT)

SUBJECT TO RESERVATIONS IN CROWN GRANT

PROPERTY DESCRIPTION: **** NOT VALID – TO BE USED FOR TRAINING PURPOSES ONLY **** PCL 199-1, SEC 20M405 ; LT 199, PL 20M405 , S/T H305361 ; OAKVILLE

PROPERTY REMARKS:

ESTATE/QUALIFIER:
FEE SIMPLE
ABSOLUTE

RECENTLY:
FIRST CONVERSION FROM BOOK

PIN CREATION DATE:
1995/12/20

CAPACITY   SHARE

OWNERS' NAMES
CHOHAN, KULDIP SINGH   JTEN
CHOHAN, SURJIT   JTEN

REG. NUM.	DATE	INSTRUMENT TYPE	AMOUNT	PARTIES FROM	PARTIES TO	CERT/CHKD
EFFECTIVE 2000/07/29 THE NOTATION OF THE "BLOCK IMPLEMENTATION DATE" OF 1995/12/20 ON THIS PIN						
WAS REPLACED WITH THE "PIN CREATION DATE" OF 1995/12/20						
** PRINTOUT INCLUDES ALL DOCUMENT TYPES AND DELETED INSTRUMENTS SINCE: 1995/12/19 **						
H293081	1986/11/26	NOTICE			THE REGIONAL MUNICIPALITY OF HALTON	C
		REMARKS: AGREEMENT				
H305136	1987/03/16	NO SUB AGREEMENT			THE CORPORATION OF THE TOWN OF OAKVILLE	C
H305145Z	1987/03/16	APL ANNEX REST COV				C
H560989	1993/11/01	TRANSFER	$227,500		CHOHAN, KULDIP SINGH CHOHAN, SURJIT	C
H560990	1993/11/01	CHARGE	$150,000		CANADA TRUSTCO MORTGAGE COMPANY	C
H631922	1996/05/27	CHARGE	$25,000	CHOHAN, KULDIP SINGH CHOHAN, SURJIT	NATIONAL TRUST COMPANY	C

NOTE: ADJOINING PROPERTIES SHOULD BE INVESTIGATED TO ASCERTAIN DESCRIPTIVE INCONSISTENCIES, IF ANY, WITH DESCRIPTION REPRESENTED FOR THIS PROPERTY.
NOTE: ENSURE THAT YOUR PRINTOUT STATES THE TOTAL NUMBER OF PAGES AND THAT YOU HAVE PICKED THEM ALL UP.

TITLE SEARCH SUMMARY

LAND REGISTRY OFFICE: Halton
PROPERTY IDENTIFICATION NUMBER (PIN): 07001-0670 (LT)
LEGAL DESCRIPTION: Part 4, Plan 20R-3153A in the Town of Burlington
PROPERTY DIMENSIONS: 58.49 ft. x 107.01 ft. x 60.00 ft. x 107.01 ft.
ROAD ACCESS: Bromley Road and Kenwood Avenue
REGISTERED OWNER(S): Ugo Felicetti and Luisa Felicetti
LAST INSTRUMENT: Transfer 505218
TITLE INSURANCE: Not being purchased

PLANNING ACT SEARCH:	
Subdivision control bylaw (prior to June 27/70)	Not applicable
Post June 27/70 bylaw exempting land from part lot control	No
Post June 27/70 bylaw deregistering plan of subdivision	No
Full lot or block on a registered plan of subdivision	No
Prior to March 31/79 consent	No
Restrictive consent granted on or after March 31/79	No
Unrestrictive consent granted on or after March 31/79	No
Attached copy of consent	Not applicable
Attached Polaris optional scheme/statements	Not applicable
Attached abutting lands search	Yes
Section 50 contravention	No

EXECUTION SEARCH:	
Present registered owner(s)	Yes-Clear
OR	
Registered owners in 40-year chain	Not applicable
OR	
Chargor(s)	Not applicable

CORPORATE OWNER(S): None
BYLAW(S): Instrument number 119980 registered 1961/01/25
EASEMENT(S): None
SUBDIVISION AGREEMENT(S): None
CHARGE(S) or MORTGAGE(S): None
CONSTRUCTION LIEN(S): None
ANY OTHER ENCUMBRANCES OR COMMENTS: Title shows two Agreements registered in favour of the Corporation of the Town of Burlington
1) Agreement number 133037 registered 1962/01/02
2) Agreement number 409134 registered 1975/04/11

DATE:
SIGNATURE: "Tommie Titlesearcher"

CHAPTER **39**

WILLS AND POWERS OF ATTORNEY

This chapter covers legal documents that enable a person to provide instructions on how his or her money and property should be managed and distributed after his or her death and also includes documents that enable a person to appoint someone else to be in charge of his or her property and personal care during his or her lifetime.

THE WILL

All property belonging to a person at death is his or her **estate**. The law has for centuries provided that a person, by way of a legal device called a **will**, can say who should receive his or her estate after death and who should carry out the terms of his or her will. The person making the will is called a **testator** (feminine, **testatrix**). To ensure that the testator's wishes are carried out, the testator appoints in his or her will a personal representative known as an **estate trustee with a will** (also referred to as **executor**; feminine, **executrix**). Note that under the *Estates Act* and the *Succession Law Reform Act* the terms **testator** and **executor** are used to include both genders.

Who can make a will To make a valid will, a person must be over eighteen years of age. A person under the age of eighteen may also make a valid will if he or she is married, is a member on active service of the Canadian armed forces, or is a mariner at sea. The person making the will must be of sound mind and must not be coerced or unduly influenced by another person into signing the will. Here is a case in point:

In a St. Catharines, Ontario, case, Madam Justice Jean MacFarland ruled that Mr. Ralph Lewis Hoffmann used undue influence to obtain a gift, *inter vivos*, of guaranteed investment certificates (GICs) totalling $139,000 from 96-year-old Mr. Frederick Elmer Becker, just a month before Mr. Becker's death. Mr. Hoffmann, a non-relative, took Mr. Becker to a lawyer, Mr. C. H. Mahoney of St. Catharines, where Mr. Becker made a will naming Mr. Hoffmann as the major beneficiary. About six months later, Mr. Becker went back to the same lawyer where he made a new will, this time leaving only $15,000 to Mr. Hoffmann and making his niece the major beneficiary. Mr. Hoffmann learned of the new will when he noticed the hangers on Mr. Becker's coat rack were differently arranged, indicating Mr. Becker had gone out without Mr. Hoffmann's knowledge. Mr. Hoffmann then took Mr. Becker to another lawyer, Mr. L.R. Allen, of Beamsville, Ontario, who arranged the transfer of the GICs over to Mr. Hoffmann. Mr. Becker died a few days later. Madam Justice MacFarland ordered set aside (void) all GICs that Mr. Hoffmann had cashed to buy a new house; she also ordered all uncashed GICs transferred to Mr. Becker's estate, damages against Mr. Hoffmann of $54,000, and pre-judgment interest on $139,000 from the date of the GICs transfer.

Testator's domicile   Basically, domicile is where the testator lives permanently. If the testator lives in Ontario or has property in Ontario, his or her will, wherever executed, can be processed in Ontario if it is in the proper form. The testator may gift personal or real property located in or outside of Ontario, including property in another country. Under subsections 36(1) and (2) of the *Succession Law Reform Act*, a testator's gift of real property under a will is governed by the law of the place where the real property is located, and a testator's gift of personal property under a will is governed by the law of the place where the testator was domiciled (lived) at the time of his or her death.

Basic will provisions   The deceased's debts and death expenses must be paid before any beneficiary may receive the gifts under the will. The intent is that beneficiaries must not take the gifts under the will at the expense of the deceased's debtors. The following provisions, therefore, are included in every will, and if omitted, they are deemed to be included:

- Funeral expenses.
- Costs of administration (including the fees of the estate trustee with a will for settling the estate).
- Debts of the testator (including all bills and debts, other than charges/mortgages, the testator owed).
- Remaining assets. The rest of the estate goes to the beneficiaries named in the will.

Estate trustee with a will (executor)   The estate trustee with a will is the party whom the testator names in the will as the party responsible for gathering the assets of the testator, paying the testator's debts, and distributing the remainder of the testator's estate to the beneficiaries under the will. The testator should provide the estate trustee with a will with a copy of the will and advise the estate trustee with a will as to the location of the original will.

Trusts   In most wills, the testator's instructions to the estate trustee with a will (executor), e.g. "to pay," "to set aside," are referred to as **trusts**. This is why the estate trustee with a will is often referred to in a will as a **trustee**. The trusts may also include trust funds which testators often set up for their young children or grandchildren to be managed by the estate trustee with a will or by another named trustee until the children reach the age specified in the will.

Beneficiaries   The people or institutions named in the will to receive a gift under the will are collectively referred to as **beneficiaries**. Where the will reads: "I give **devise** and **bequeath**...," the word **devise** refers to a gift of real property, and the word **bequeath** refers to a gift of personal property, usually money, which gift is further known as a **legacy**. References to a **devisee**, therefore, usually mean a person who is named in a will to receive a gift of real estate; references to a **legatee** usually mean a person who is named in a will to receive a gift of personal property, usually money. Although the distinction between gifts of real estate and personal property is no longer recognized by the law, the terms "I give devise and bequeath..." are often found in wills. The term **issue** is often used in wills, and it generally means descendants such as children, grandchildren, great grandchildren.

Division of estate   The term **per capita** is often used in wills, and it generally means an estate gift to be divided equally among all of the testator's children, grandchildren, great grandchildren, etc. who are living at the time of the testator's death. The Latin term *per stirpes* is often used in wills, and it means "like the roots or branches of a (family) tree." Essentially, each "living branch" of the family tree gets an equal share, and the same applies within each branch or sub-branch. In other words, it means an estate gift is to be proportionally divided among the children of the testator and, if any of the children of the testator predecease the testator, then the share of the child who predeceased the testator is to be divided equally among the children of the child who predeceased the testator, for example:

> Ken has 3 children: Wendy, Adam, and Chris. Ken has provided in his will that upon his death, each child will receive 1/3 of his estate. Wendy dies before Ken. Wendy has 3 children. By *per stirpes* distribution, Adam would still receive 1/3, Chris would still receive 1/3, and Wendy's 1/3 would be divided equally among Wendy's 3 children, giving each of Wendy's children 1/9. If Ken had designated a per capita distribution, instead of *per stirpes*, Ken's estate would have been divided equally among Adam, Chris, and Wendy's 3 children, each receiving 1/5. (The gift of Adam and Chris would have been reduced from 1/3 to 1/5.)

Revoking a will   The testator may revoke (cancel) his or her will by intentionally destroying it by means of tearing, or burning, or by making a new will — a new will automatically revokes a previous will. A will made prior to marriage is automatically revoked by the marriage unless it is expressly made in contemplation of the marriage. Under section 17(2) of the *Succession Law Reform Act*, a termination of a marriage by divorce revokes only those provisions of a will that relate to the former spouse, and the will is construed as if the former spouse has predeceased the testator. Note, however, that a separation of married spouses does not revoke any provisions of a will, including any provisions that relate to a spouse.

Altering a will   Alterations such as minor corrections or word substitutions may be made to the will if the testator and two witnesses initial all such minor corrections or word substitutions at the time of executing (signing) the will. There must be no alterations made after the will is executed, except by codicil.

Losing a will   If on the death of the testator his or her will cannot be found, the will is presumed to have been revoked, unless evidence is produced to the contrary: for example, if a copy or a true copy of the will, or other proof of the testator's intention, can be produced to the satisfaction of the court, the court may treat the evidence as if it were a will.

Execution of will   The *Succession Law Reform Act* states that a will is not valid unless:

1. Three people are present together: the testator and two (or more) witnesses.
2. The testator signs the will while two (or more) witnesses watch.
3. The two (or more) witnesses sign the will while they watch each other sign and also while the testator watches them sign.

This cross-signing and witnessing of all three individuals aims to eliminate wills being executed under suspicious circumstances. The testator must sign the will personally, or if the testator is physically ill or illiterate, the testator may direct someone else to sign for the testator while the testator watches. The directed person writes the testator's name. If the testator is illiterate, the testator makes an "X" next to his or her name which the directed person wrote. If the testator is literate but is physically unable to write, the testator's fingerprint may be imprinted next to his or her name to confirm his or her intention to sign.

Witnesses must not be beneficiaries   The witnesses or their spouses must not be people to whom the testator leaves gifts in the will. If they are, the will is valid, but the witnesses cannot receive the gifts because the law presumes the witnesses had reason to influence the testator into signing the will.

Safekeeping of signed will   Most testators keep their wills in their safety deposit boxes. Many law firms also keep their clients' executed wills in vaults, usually at no charge, in anticipation that at the testator's death, the estate trustee with a will will retain the law firm to act for the estate. Firms should keep a strict record of the wills in their safekeeping, and if a testator decides at a later time to take the will into his or her own safekeeping, the firm must keep an equally strict record of having released the will. An executed will in the safekeeping of the firm must never be lost.

PREPARATION AND DISTRIBUTION OF WILL

You require: The client interview notes or checklist. The law prescribes no special form for wills. A commonly used form in practice is in Precedent 39.1. Notes on items not self-explanatory follow:

Wills must be extremely clear and precise and should be free of typographical errors and noticeable corrections and erasures since these might be construed as will tampering. This is why the testator and the witnesses must initial all noticeable corrections on the will. Most law firms prepare wills from their computerized will clauses and precedents. Key the will, usually in double spacing. The signature of the testator may be placed "at, after, following, under, or beside or opposite to the end of the will" (*Succession Law Reform Act*). Also, a will is not invalid if "the signature is on a side (or) page...on which no...paragraph...of the will is written" (*Succession Law Reform Act*). Some law firms also prepare a will cover, usually in blue or grey.

Number of copies, minimum 3: testator executes original; 1 executed photocopy. If the testator leaves the executed original will with the lawyer, the lawyer gives the executed photocopy to the testator. If the testator keeps the executed original will, the lawyer keeps the executed photocopy. Keep one unsigned copy in the file.

AFFIDAVIT OF EXECUTION OF WILL, FORM 74.8

Either one of the two witnesses must swear an affidavit stating that he or she saw the testator execute (sign) the will. The affidavit may be completed after the testator's death, at the time of submitting the testator's will to the court for approval. It may prove difficult to track down either of the witnesses at that time, however, as the testator's death may occur years after the testator executed the will. For this reason, lawyers usually prepare and have the affidavit of execution of will executed at the same time as the will.

PREPARATION AND DISTRIBUTION OF AFFIDAVIT OF EXECUTION OF WILL, FORM 74.8

You require: The will. See Precedent 39.2. The wording guides completion. The witness swears that he or she, the other witness, and the testator all signed the will. The affidavit is usually sworn at the place where the testator signs the will.

Number of copies, minimum 3: 1 witness executes; 1 executed photocopy. Attach the executed affidavit to the executed original will; attach 1 executed photocopy to the executed photocopy of the will; keep one unsigned copy in file.

HOLOGRAPH WILL

Holograph is from the Greek *olographo* and means entirely handwritten. A testator may handwrite his or her will and sign it without need for witnesses. A holograph will does not require witnessing because the testator's handwriting proves it is the testator's will. When applying for a certificate of appointment of estate trustee with a will, someone who knew the testator and could verify the testator's handwriting must sign an **affidavit proving execution of a holograph will**. The holograph will is submitted for a certificate of estate trustee with a will in the same manner as a witnessed will. The holograph will is not to be confused with commercially available pre-printed will forms. Here is a case in point:

In Saskatoon, Saskatchewan, Mr. Justice William Francis Gerein declared a pre-printed will invalid, even though the testatrix, Beatrice Edith Balfour, had completed it and signed it in her own handwriting. The testatrix had also added: "Whatever Brenda Goll my daughter decides is O.K. if anyone else doesn't like it too bad." Mr. Justice Gerein decided the will was not valid because it was not witnessed by two people, and it did not qualify as a holograph will because it was not entirely handwritten.

MULTIPLE WILLS

Lawyers may prepare multiple wills for their clients. The major purpose of multiple wills is to avoid paying estate administration taxes (formerly probate fees) on those assets of a deceased's estate that do not require a **certificate of appointment of estate trustee with a will**. Assets which require a certificate of appointment of estate trustee with a will before distribution to any beneficiaries are included in one will, referred to as the **primary will**. Assets which require no certificate of appointment of estate trustee with a will before distribution to any beneficiaries are included in another will, referred to as the **secondary will**. When a testator dies, only the primary will is submitted to the court for a certificate of appointment of estate trustee with a will, and taxes are paid only on the value of the assets under the primary will. It is important therefore that the signing of the secondary will does **not** revoke the primary will.

Examples of assets that require a certificate of appointment of estate trustee with a will include real estate, shares in a **public** corporation, government or corporate bonds, and substantial funds in a bank account. One reason that these types of assets require a certificate of appointment of estate trustee with a will is that the transfer agents for any securities and the bank will usually insist on a certificate of appointment of estate trustee with a will before they transfer or release such assets to the estate trustee. Examples of assets that require no certificate of appointment of estate trustee with a will include shares in a privately owned company, debts owing to the deceased from that company, and personal possessions. Here is the case that opened the doors to multiple wills:

In the *Granovky Estate v Ontario* (1998), 156 DLR (4th) 557, Mr. Philip Granovsky died leaving two separate wills dated the same date. The first included about $3.2 million in assets that required a certificate of appointment of estate trustee with a will (probate). The second included about $25 million in assets that did not require a certificate of appointment of estate trustee with a will. The assets in the second will consisted mainly of shares of a private company and debts owing to Mr. Granovsky from that company. The estate trustee submitted only the first will for a certificate of appointment of estate trustee with a will and paid taxes on the value of the assets that flowed under that will, which resulted in a savings of $375,000 in taxes. The Ontario government sued, making its case that taxes should have been calculated on the entire value of the estate. The court ruled in favour of the estate trustee, however, because the *Estates Act* provides for limited certificates of appointment of estate trustees with a will in certain circumstances. The Ontario government then appealed and later abandoned its appeal.

CODICIL

A codicil, Precedent 39.3, is a legal device for making a change to an executed will. It is used for making simple changes such as substituting one person as estate trustee with a will (executor) in the place of another. If the changes are major, most lawyers prefer to prepare a new will as the changes might render the original will ambiguous.

POWERS OF ATTORNEY

> **Legal TIP**
>
> In Canada, the term **attorney** means a substitute decision-maker; it does not mean lawyer as it does in the USA.

A power of attorney is a document that authorizes one person to act on behalf of another person when that person is incapable of doing so himself or herself. The difference between a will and a power of attorney is that in a will, the person making the will, John, appoints a representative, Mary, to represent John **after** John dies, whereas in a power of attorney, the person making the power of attorney, John, appoints a representative, Mary, to represent John during John's life.

Under the *Substitute Decisions Act*, there are two kinds of powers of attorney that people can use to appoint an attorney (a representative) in the event they become mentally or physically incapable: **continuing power of attorney for property** and **power of attorney for personal care**. A person is deemed mentally incapable if he or she cannot understand information that is relevant to making a decision or cannot appreciate what is likely to happen if a certain decision is made or if a decision is not made. The person making a power of attorney is usually referred to as **grantor** and the person appointed is referred to as **attorney** or substitute decision-maker.

Continuing power of attorney for property See Precedent 39.4. A person, John, may use this kind of power of attorney to appoint another person, Mary, to make decisions about John's property and manage his finances when John becomes mentally or physically incapable of making such decisions himself; areas may include signing documents, paying bills and taxes, looking after bank accounts, managing real estate and investments, or selling John's home. Except where John puts conditions or restrictions on Mary's authority in the power of attorney document, Mary has the power to do anything with John's property that John could do himself if he were mentally capable, except make a will for John. Both the grantor and the attorney must be at least eighteen years old. The continuing power of attorney for property is executed in a similar manner as a will. Two witnesses must be present while the grantor, John, signs, and John must be present while the witnesses sign. The witnesses must have no reason to believe that the grantor is mentally incapable of giving the power of attorney.

Power of attorney for personal care   See Precedent 39.5. A person, John, may use this kind of power of attorney to appoint another person, Mary, to make decisions about John's personal care when John becomes mentally or physically incapable of making such decisions himself. John may give instructions about where he would like to live, what kinds of foods he would like to eat, what he would like to wear, and what kind of medical treatment he would like to receive; for example, John may give Mary authority to allow or refuse medical treatment. John does not have to give such instructions, restrictions, or conditions; he may instead allow Mary to make decisions for him as best she can in the circumstances. Mary may not, however, make a will for John. Both the grantor and the attorney must be at least **sixteen** years of age. The grantor must be able to understand whether the attorney has a genuine concern for the grantor's welfare and appreciate that the attorney may need to make personal care decisions on behalf of the grantor. A person cannot be an attorney if he or she is getting paid for providing the grantor with health care or residential, social, or other support services, either in the grantor's home or in a long-term care facility, unless he or she is the grantor's spouse or relative; for example, a staff member who is paid to look after the grantor in a long-term care facility cannot be an attorney.

Witnesses   A witness (in both kinds of powers of attorney) must be at least eighteen years old. A witness must not be the **grantor's** child or spouse. A witness must not be the **attorney** or the **attorney's** spouse.

Responsibilities of attorneys   The *Substitute Decisions Act* spells out the attorney's responsibilities (for both kinds of powers of attorney), some of which include acting with honesty and in good faith, putting the grantor's financial needs and the needs of the grantor's dependants first, and keeping accounts of all transactions.

Compensation   An attorney (in both kinds of powers of attorney) may be compensated according to a scale set by regulation. The grantor may specify in the power of attorney an amount higher or lower than that provided by the scale or no amount. A higher quality of care is expected of an attorney who acts with compensation.

Revocation   A grantor may revoke either one or both types of powers of attorney at any time by making new power/s of attorney as long as the grantor is mentally capable of doing so.

Public Guardian and Trustee   The Public Guardian and Trustee has been granted certain powers to carry out, among other things, investigations of reports of abuse by attorneys and to replace them if necessary.

CHAPTER SUMMARY

A will is a document that instructs on how to distribute the property of a person after that person dies. Anybody over the age of 18 and of sound mind may make a will. By law, a will must provide for funeral expenses, administrative costs, and any debts of the deceased. The testator must sign the will before two witnesses who must not be beneficiaries under the will. If they are beneficiaries, the will is valid, but the witnesses cannot receive any gifts under the will. Either one of the witnesses may swear an affidavit of execution of will. The person that the testator names in the will to be his or her representative after death is called an estate trustee with a will (also referred to as executor). The testator may revoke a will by making a new will. If the testator wishes to make a change to a will that he or she has already executed, the testator may do so by way of a codicil which is similar to a will but contains only the changes. A holograph will is an entirely handwritten will. A holograph will needs no witnesses and is as effective as one that has been witnessed.

Two types of powers of attorney include a continuing power of attorney for property and a power of attorney for personal care. With a continuing power of attorney for property, the grantor gives power to the attorney to make decisions about the grantor's property in the event the grantor becomes mentally or physically incapable of doing so himself or herself. With a power of attorney for personal care, the grantor gives power to the attorney to make decisions about the grantor's personal care in the event the grantor becomes mentally or physically incapable of doing so himself or herself. The grantor can revoke both kinds of powers of attorney by making new ones. The Public Guardian and Trustee is empowered by law to investigate reports of abuse and replace attorneys if necessary.

REVIEW QUESTIONS

1. What is the role of an estate trustee with a will?
2. What happens when the witnesses are named in the will as beneficiaries?
3. What is a codicil?
4. What is a holograph will?
5. A testator is a witness who testifies in court. Yes_____ No_____
6. What is the difference between a continuing power of attorney for property and a power of attorney for personal care?

THIS IS THE LAST WILL AND TESTAMENT of me, **REBECCA TEALE SMYTHE**, of the Town of Whitchurch-Stouffville, in the Regional Municipality of York, and the Province of Ontario.

1.   I REVOKE all former wills, codicils, and other testamentary dispositions that I have at any time previously made and declare this only to be and contain my last Will and Testament.

2.   I DIRECT my Trustee to pay my just debts, funeral and testamentary expenses, and all succession duties and estate taxes, inheritance and death taxes, whether imposed by or pursuant to the laws of this or any province, state, country, or jurisdiction whatsoever that may be payable by any beneficiary of this my Will or any Codicil to it in connection with any insurance and/or annuities, pension plans, funds, superannuation, or other similar benefits on my life, or any gift or benefit given by me to any such beneficiary, either in my lifetime or by survivorship or by this my Will or any Codicil to it, and whether such duties and taxes be payable in respect of estates or interests which fall into possession at my death or any subsequent time. I authorize my Trustee to commute or prepay such duties or taxes. Any duties or taxes so paid shall be treated as an ordinary debt and paid out of the capital of my general estate.

3.   Provided he survives me for a period of thirty days, I NOMINATE, CONSTITUTE, AND APPOINT my husband, **THOMAS ARTHUR SMYTHE**, to be the Executor and Trustee of this my Will, and I refer to him as my "Trustee." I GIVE, DEVISE, AND BEQUEATH the whole of my property of every nature and kind and wheresoever situate, including any property over which I may have a general power of appointment, to my husband.

-2-

4.   If my husband, **THOMAS ARTHUR SMYTHE**, fails to survive me by at least thirty days, I NOMINATE, CONSTITUTE, AND APPOINT my son, **ANDREW JAMES SMYTHE**, to be the Executor and Trustee, and I refer to him as my "Trustee." I GIVE, DEVISE, AND BEQUEATH the whole of my property of every nature and kind and wheresoever situate, including any property over which I may have a general power of appointment, to my said Trustee upon the following trust:

(a)   To divide the whole of my estate equally among my children, **ANDREW JAMES SMYTHE, DONALD PETER SMYTHE**, and **MARY JANE SMYTHE**, provided that if any of them should have predeceased me leaving issue surviving, such issue shall take their deceased parent's share per stirpes.

5.   If any person should become entitled to any share in my estate before attaining the age of majority, the share of such person shall be held and kept invested by my Trustee. The income and capital, or so much of it as my Trustee in his absolute discretion considers advisable, shall be used for the benefit of such person until he or she attains the age of majority.

6.   I AUTHORIZE my Trustee to make any payment for any person under the age of majority to a parent or guardian of such person or to anyone to whom my Trustee in his discretion deems it advisable to make such payments, whose receipt shall be a sufficient discharge to my said Trustee.

7.   I GIVE my Trustee full power to sell the assets of my estate at such time and on such terms as he may deem advisable. I empower my Trustee to hold any or all of the assets of my estate in the form in which they may be at the time of my death for as long as my Trustee considers advisable, without being responsible for any waste or loss.

LAST WILL AND TESTAMENT OF

REBECCA TEALE SMYTHE

Michael, Eliad & Redford LLP
Barristers and Solicitors
863 Seneca Lane
Toronto, Ontario
M4J 1P6

-3-

8.   I AUTHORIZE my Trustee to make any such determinations, designations, and elections under the *Income Tax Act* or any relevant statute in connection with any of the assets of my estate as he in his discretion considers to be to the advantage of my estate.

9.   I GIVE my Trustee full power to make any division of my estate or set aside or pay any share or interest in my estate, either wholly or in part, in the assets forming my estate at the time of my death or at the time of such division, setting aside, or payment. I expressly Will and declare that my Trustee shall in his absolute discretion fix the value of my estate or any part of it for the purpose of making any such division, setting aside, or payment. The decision of my Trustee shall be final and binding upon all persons concerned, notwithstanding my Trustee may be beneficially interested in the property appropriated or partitioned.

IN TESTIMONY WHEREOF I have to this my last Will and Testament, written upon this and two preceding pages of paper, subscribed my name this   day of   October   20--.

SIGNED, PUBLISHED AND DECLARED
by the said REBECCA TEALE SMYTHE
as and for her last Will and Testament, in
the presence of us, both present at the same
time, who at her request, in her presence and
in the presence of each other, have subscribed
our names as witnesses.

)
)
)   Rebecca Teale Smythe
)
)

Signature of witness _____
Print name _____
Address _____
Occupation _____

Signature of witness _____
Print name _____
Address _____
Occupation _____

AFFIDAVIT OF EXECUTION OF WILL OR CODICIL
(Form 74.8 under the Rules)

ONTARIO

SUPERIOR COURT OF JUSTICE

In the matter of the execution of a will or codicil of **Arthur William Gold**.

AFFIDAVIT OF EXECUTION OF WILL

I, Stephen Walter Stans, of the   Town of Richmond Hill, in the Regional Municipality of York, MAKE OATH AND SAY/AFFIRM:

1.   On March 10, (year), I was present and saw the document marked as Exhibit "A" to this affidavit executed by Arthur William Gold.

2.   Arthur William Gold executed the document in the presence of myself and Mary Ellen Simmons, of the City of Markham, in the Regional Municipality of York.   We were both present at the same time, and signed the document in the testator's presence as attesting witnesses.

Sworn or Affirmed before me at the   )
City of Toronto   )
in the Province of Ontario   )
on   , (year).   )
)
)_____
) Stephen Walter Stans
_____   )
A Commissioner for Taking Affidavits   )

NOTE: If the testator was blind or signed by making his or her mark, add the following paragraph:
3. Before its execution, the document was read over to the testator, who (was blind)(signed by marking his or her mark). The testator appeared to understand the contents.

WARNING: A beneficiary or the spouse of a beneficiary should not be a witness.

THIS IS A FIRST CODICIL to the Will of me, PAUL GREEN, of the City of Waterwell, in the County of Mandolee, and the Province of Ontario, which Will is dated the 5th day of January, 20--.

1. I hereby add the following to my said Will as Clause II.

II. If my wife should predecease me, it is my wish that my wife's parents, JOHN WISE and JANE WISE, or the survivor of them, be the guardians of my infant children, or if both the persons so designated should predecease me, or if neither should be able or willing to act, then I wish my wife's cousin, RALPH GLEASON, and his wife, EMILY GLEASON, to be the guardians of my infant children.

2. In all other respects, I confirm my said Will.

IN WITNESS WHEREOF I have to this first Codicil to my Will which is written upon this page subscribed my name on the   day of April, 20--.

SIGNED by PAUL GREEN as a first Codicil	)
to his Will, in the presence of us, both present	)
at the same time, who at his request, in his	) _____
presence and in the presence of each other,	) Paul Green
have subscribed our names as witnesses:	)
	)
	)
Signature of witness_____	)
Print name_____	)
Address_____	)
_____	)
Occupation_____	)
	)
Signature of witness_____	)
Print name_____	)
Address_____	)
_____	)
Occupation_____	)

Continuing Power of
Attorney for Property

(Made in accordance with the Substitute Decisions Act, 1992)

1. I, RALPH WALDO HARRISON,   revoke any previous continuing power of attorney
   (Print or type your full name here.)
   for property made by me and **APPOINT**: ALBERT SCOTT HARRISON

   _____ to be my attorney(s) for property.
   (Print or type the name of the person or persons you appoint here.)

2. If you have named more than one attorney and you want them to have the authority to act
   separately, insert the words "jointly and severally" here:_____
   (This may be left blank.)

3. If the person(s) I have appointed, or any one of them, cannot or will not be my attorney because
   of refusal, resignation, death, mental incapacity, or removal by the court, **I SUBSTITUTE**:
   (This may be left blank.)

   _____
   to act as my attorney for property with the same authority as the person he or she is replacing.

4. I AUTHORIZE my attorney(s) for property to do on my behalf anything in respect of property
   that I could do if capable of managing property, except make a will, subject to the law and to
   any conditions or restrictions contained in this document. I confirm that he/she may do so even
   if I am mentally incapable.

5. **CONDITIONS AND RESTRICTIONS**
   Attach, sign, and date additional pages if required. *(This part may be left blank.)*

   None.
   _____

   _____

   _____

   _____

   _____

6. DATE OF EFFECTIVENESS

Unless otherwise stated in this document, this continuing power of attorney will come into effect on the date it is signed and witnessed.

7. COMPENSATION

Unless otherwise stated in this document, I authorize my attorney(s) to take annual compensation from my property in accordance with the fee scale prescribed by regulation for the compensation of attorneys for property made pursuant to Section 90 of the *Substitute Decisions Act, 1992.*

8. SIGNATURE:_____DATE:_____
(Sign your name in the presence of two witnesses.)

ADDRESS:_____
(Insert your full current address here.)

9. WITNESS SIGNATURE

[Note: The following people cannot be witnesses: the attorney or his or her spouse or partner; the spouse, partner, or child of the person making the document, or someone that the person treats as his or her child; a person whose property is under guardianship or who has a guardian of the person; a person under the age of 18.]

Witness #1: *Signature:* _____*Print Name:*_____

*Address:*_____

_____*Date:*_____

Witness #2: *Signature:* _____*Print Name:*_____

*Address:*_____

_____*Date:*_____

Power of Attorney for Personal Care

(Made in accordance with the Substitute Decisions Act, 1992)

1. I, __RALPH WALDO HARRISON,__ revoke any previous power of attorney for personal
   (Print or type your full name here)

   care made by me and APPOINT: __ALBERT SCOTT HARRISON__
   (Print or type the name of the person or persons you appoint here)

   to be my attorney(s) for personal care in accordance with the *Substitute Decisions Act, 1992.*

   [**Note:** *A person who provides health care, residential, social, training, or support services to the person giving this power of attorney for compensation may not act as his or her attorney unless that person is also his or her spouse, partner, or relative.*]

2. If you have named more than one attorney and you want them to have the authority to act separately, insert the words "jointly and severally" here: _____

   (This may be left blank)

3. If the person(s) I have appointed, or any one of them, cannot or will not be my attorney because of refusal, resignation, death, mental incapacity, or removal by the Court, I SUBSTITUTE: __JESSICA McLINTOCK__

   (This may be left blank)

   to act as my attorney for personal care in the same manner and subject to the same authority as the person he or she is replacing.

4. I give my attorney(s) the **AUTHORITY** to make any personal care decision for me that I am mentally incapable of making for myself, including the giving or refusing of consent to any matter to which the *Health Care Consent Act, 1996* applies, subject to the *Substitute Decisions Act, 1992*, and any instructions, conditions or restrictions contained in this form.

---

5. **INSTRUCTIONS, CONDITIONS and RESTRICTIONS**
   Attach, sign, and date additional pages if required. *(This part may be left blank.)*

   None. _____

   _____

   _____

   _____

6. **SIGNATURE:** _____ DATE: _____
   (Sign your name here, in the presence of two witnesses.)

   ADDRESS: _____
   (Insert your current address here.)

7. **WITNESS SIGNATURES**

   [**Note:** *The following people cannot be witnesses: the attorney or his or her spouse or partner; the spouse, partner, or child of the person making the document, or someone that the person treats as his or her child; a person whose property is under guardianship or who has a guardian of the person; a person under the age of 18.*]

   Witness #1: *Signature:* _____ *Print Name:* _____

   Address: _____ *Date:* _____

   Witness #2: *Signature:* _____ *Print Name:* _____

   Address: _____ *Date:* _____

CHAPTER 40

INHERITANCE

This chapter discusses the distribution of a person's property when that person dies with or without a will.

THE SUCCESSION LAW REFORM ACT

We may inherit by will, or if there is no will, we may inherit by law. The law which governs inheritance in Ontario is the *Succession Law Reform Act* (SLRA).

When there is no will   If a person dies without a will, he or she is said to have died **intestate**. The intestacy provisions of Part II of the SLRA set out who may inherit the deceased's estate. The line of inheritance is based on nearest blood relatives, generally referred to as **heirs** or **next of kin** (except for a spouse who is not a blood relative but who is given priority), as shown in the following simplified summary:

Figure 40.1

SUMMARY OF LINE OF INHERITANCE IN INTESTATE ESTATES	
Survivors	**Distribution of Estate**
Spouse but no children	All to the spouse (i.e. legally married spouse, not common-law spouse)
Spouse and one child	Preferential share $200,000 to the spouse; remainder split equally between spouse and the child
Spouse and two or more children	Preferential share $200,000 to spouse, plus one third of remainder; balance is split equally between the children
No spouse but one or more children alive	Children share equally: if one child is deceased but has children, those children get their deceased parent's share equally
No spouse, no children, but grandchildren	Grandchildren share equally
Only parents of deceased are alive	Parents share equally; if only one parent, that parent gets estate
No spouse, no children, no grandchildren, no parents, but brothers and sisters	To brothers and sisters equally; if one brother or sister is deceased, to children of deceased brother or sister equally
No spouse, no children, no grandchildren, no parents, no brothers, no sisters, but nieces and nephews	To nieces and nephews equally (children of deceased nephew/niece take no share; instead, share of deceased niece/nephew goes equally to surviving niece/s or nephew/s)
No spouse, no children, no grandchildren, no parents, no brothers, no sisters, no nieces, no nephews	To next of kin equally; if no next of kin, to the Crown
An adopted child shares equally with natural children of the intestate. An adopted child may not also inherit from his or her natural parents. A stepchild, having no blood relationship with the intestate, may not inherit by law, but may inherit by will.	

When a will exists   If a person dies leaving a will, he or she is said to have died **testate**. The people who inherit the deceased's estate are those who are named in the will; they are referred to collectively as **beneficiaries**. Under certain provisions of the SLRA, the testator should make provisions in his will for the surviving spouse and for relatives who may be dependent on the testator. Other SLRA provisions allow dependent children, and in some cases other dependants who are either left out of a will or who believe they have been inadequately provided for in a will, to challenge the will and claim part of the estate.

Survivorship in common disasters   Too often disasters such as automobile accidents or plane crashes occur that kill both spouses. Determining survivorship is often not possible. In Ontario, the law assumes that each spouse survived the other. The separate property of the spouses passes to the beneficiaries under their respective wills or, if there are no wills and no children, to their respective next of kin as set out in the *Succession Law Reform Act*. Where both spouses die owning property as joint tenants, each is deemed to have held the property as tenants in common. If, of two people (not necessarily spouses) killed in a common disaster, one had his or her own life insured and the other was the beneficiary, the law assumes the beneficiary died first. Thus, unless the life insurance policy names other beneficiaries, the insurance money is payable to the estate of the person whose own life was insured.

THE FAMILY LAW ACT

Some of the provisions of the Ontario *Family Law Act* (FLA) which relate to inheritance follow:

> **5.** (2) When a spouse dies, if the net family property of the deceased spouse exceeds the net family property of the surviving spouse, the surviving spouse is entitled to one-half of the difference between them.
>
> **6.**(1) When a spouse dies leaving a will, the surviving spouse shall elect to take under the will or to receive the entitlement under section 5.
>
> (2) When a spouse dies intestate, the surviving spouse shall elect to receive the entitlement under Part II of the *Succession Law Reform Act* or to receive the entitlement under section 5.

What is equalization payment   Basically, it is half of that amount by which the deceased's net family property is higher than that of the surviving spouse. Net family property (NFP) is basically property, less debts, each spouse owned on the **valuation date**, which is the day **before** the date of death of the deceased spouse. This is why the calculation of the equalization payment is made in the same way as if the spouses were divorcing; see Chapter 20 for details. The aim is to divide 50/50 (hence, "equalization payment") the family property that the two spouses have together worked to acquire during their marriage, regardless of whether the will of a deceased spouse gives less to a surviving spouse and regardless of whether the deceased spouse died with or without a will. Thus, spouses may not use wills to get around the 50/50 split. For a simple example, assume that the surviving spouse is entitled to an equalization payment of $250,000 (one-half of the difference of NFP between the spouses) and that the deceased willed $100,000 to the surviving spouse. The surviving spouse may elect to take the equalization payment of $250,000 or the $100,000 under the deceased's will.

Election in testate estates   If there is a will, the surviving spouse may elect (choose) to take the benefits under the will or the equalization payment, usually whichever is higher. If the surviving spouse chooses the equalization payment, the gifts made under a will are revoked unless the will expressly states otherwise.

Election in intestate estates   If there is no will, the surviving spouse may elect to take the preferential share under the SLRA or the equalization payment under the FLA, usually whichever is higher. If the surviving spouse takes the equalization payment, he or she is deemed to have disclaimed the preferential share.

Making the election   Regardless of whether the estate is testate or intestate, the surviving spouse must elect as to which share he or she will take (i.e. will, FLA, or SLRA) within six months from the date of death of the deceased spouse. The estate trustee (with or without a will) may not distribute the deceased's assets before this six-month period is over without the consent of the surviving spouse.

Jointly-held assets   Since the valuation date is the day before death, any joint property belongs equally to the spouses as it does not pass to the surviving joint spouse until the date of death; therefore, include the net one-half of any joint property in the NFP of each spouse.

Property not included   Same as in Chapter 20.

CHAPTER SUMMARY

When a person dies intestate (without leaving a will), the deceased's estate is distributed according to the *Succession Law Reform Act* (SLRA). Inheritance under the SLRA is based on nearest blood relatives referred to as heirs or next of kin. The first $200,000, referred to as preferential share, goes to the surviving spouse and any excess is divided according to the number of children, e.g. if one child, ½ of the excess goes to the spouse and the remaining ½ to the child; if two children, ⅓ of the excess goes to the spouse and the remaining ⅔ is divided between the two children.

In the case of an intestate estate, the surviving spouse may elect to take either the preferential share under the SLRA or the equalization payment provided for under the *Family Law Act*, usually whichever is higher. In the case of a testate estate, the surviving spouse may elect to take either the benefits under the will or the equalization payment, usually whichever is higher, but if the surviving spouse chooses the equalization payment, the surviving spouse forfeits any gifts under a will. The provisions under the FLA and the succession provisions under the SLRA extend only to spouses who are married to each other and exclude common-law spouses.

REVIEW QUESTIONS

1. Who inherits under a will?
2. Which act sets out the line of inheritance in intestate estates?
3. Why would a surviving spouse elect to take an equalization payment?
4. Explain why the preferential share applies only to common-law spouses.
5. Where a spouse dies intestate leaving a surviving spouse and one child, how would the estate of the deceased spouse be divided?
6. Where a spouse dies intestate leaving only brothers and sisters surviving, how would the estate of the deceased be divided?

CHAPTER 41

APPLICATION FOR CERTIFICATE WITH A WILL

This chapter discusses the steps and documents required when applying to the court for obtaining a certificate of appointment of estate trustee after a person dies leaving a will.

APPLICATION FOR CERTIFICATE OF APPOINTMENT OF ESTATE TRUSTEE WITH A WILL (INDIVIDUAL APPLICANT), FORM 74.4

Your firm files an application for certificate of appointment of estate trustee with a will, Form 74.4, on behalf of the estate trustee with a will (executor) to obtain a certificate of appointment of estate trustee with a will (formerly, letters probate). The certificate enables the estate trustee with a will to deal with the deceased's estate. Filing an application for certificate of appointment of estate trustee with a will is not necessary with small estates, usually ones which contain no real estate or stocks and bonds.

When your firm acts for an estate trustee with a will, the estate of the deceased is said to be a **testate** estate. Prior to preparing the application for certificate of appointment of estate trustee with a will, the lawyer usually has the estate trustee complete a checklist of all property and debts and liabilities of the deceased, as at the date of death, and often also a checklist of all of the property of a surviving spouse. This information may come from a variety of sources, including the estate trustee with a will, surviving spouse, relatives, and any safety deposit boxes of the deceased. The lawyer usually advises the estate trustee with a will to keep careful records of any out-of-pocket expenses and of all money received in the estate. Estate trustees are entitled to be paid a fee out of the deceased's estate in an amount based on the size of the estate and to also be reimbursed for any out-of-pocket expenses.

WILL

The estate trustee usually brings to the lawyer the deceased's executed will.

Affidavit of execution of will or codicil, Form 74.8   Either one of the two witnesses who witnessed the testator sign the will may sign this affidavit. In many cases, however, one of the witnesses may have already signed this affidavit at the time the testator signed the will. If not done then, track down one of the two witnesses, and call him or her in to sign the affidavit of execution of will, Form 74.8. See Chapter 39 for a precedent. Note that the same form is used for execution of codicil.

Will as exhibit   On the back of the executed page of the original will, key or rubber-stamp two Exhibit "A" marks, Precedent 41.1, one pertaining to the witness of the will and the other pertaining to the estate trustee with a will. The will is referred to as Exhibit "A" in the various documents to ensure all references to the will identify the same will. A commissioner, usually the lawyer, signs the exhibit marks. If the will or a codicil is in holograph form, prepare a Form 74.9 affidavit attesting to the handwriting and signature of a holograph will or codicil. If the will or a codicil is not in holograph form but contains an alteration, erasure, obliteration, or interlineation that has not been initialled, prepare a Form 74.10 affidavit of condition of will or codicil attesting that the will or codicil is now in the same condition as when it was executed.

Codicil as exhibit   The codicil as exhibit is made on the back of the executed page of the original codicil in the same manner as a will except that it is Exhibit "B"; if there is a second codicil, it is Exhibit "C," etc.

GOLD, Arthur William
Re: Estate

Mr. Gold, a retired bricklayer, died on June 13, leaving only his wife, Mrs. Ruth Gold, and a brother surviving him. See Chapter 39 for the affidavit of execution of Mr. Gold's will. We have Mr. Gold's proof of death certificate, Precedent 41.1a.

Mr. Gold appointed Mr. Randolph James Murphy, a close friend, as his estate trustee.   In his will, Precedent 41.1, Mr. Gold left his entire estate to Mrs. Gold, and were she to die within 60 days after him, Mr. Murphy is to transfer Mr. Gold's estate to Mr. Gold's brother, George James Gold, who lives in Newfoundland. We have prepared the application for certificate of appointment of estate trustee with a will, Precedent 41.2, the notice of an application for a certificate of appointment of estate trustee with a will, Precedent 41.3, Mr. Murphy's affidavit of service of notice, Precedent 41.4, and the certificate of appointment of estate trustee with a will, Precedent 41.7. We have also prepared the estate information return, Precedent 41.10. Once we receive the approved certificate from the court, Mr. Murphy may distribute Mr. Gold's estate according to the terms of Mr. Gold's will.

VALUE OF ESTATE

Estate means real and personal property that the deceased owns. One purpose for establishing the value of a deceased's estate is to determine the estate administration taxes, formerly probate fees, payable to the court. Under the *Estate Administration Tax Act*, estate administration taxes are based on the value of the deceased's estate. The value of a deceased's estate must be the fair market value at the date of death, i.e. the price a buyer will pay and a seller will accept for a property under reasonable and ordinary conditions. The information for calculating the value of the estate comes mainly from the estate trustee. To calculate the value of the estate, divide the assets which the deceased owned on the date of death in two categories: **personal property** and **real estate.**

PERSONAL PROPERTY

Include in this category the fair market value of all property that is not real estate and that is in the name of the deceased, including: bank accounts, bonds, shares, charges (mortgages), automobiles, business assets, furniture, jewellery, paintings, personal items, and life insurance policy payable to the deceased's estate. If the deceased's life insurance policy does not name a specific individual as beneficiary, the insurance money is payable to the estate; therefore, it must be included in the assets of the deceased's estate. See the court's decision about life insurance in the murder case below.

In a Toronto, Ontario, case, Mr. Justice George Finlayson, on appeal, ruled that the estate of a wife, who was murdered by her husband, cannot collect on the joint life insurance policies the spouses held. Gerald and Mary Brissette held two joint life insurance policies (i.e. each policy was in both their names as owners) on each other's lives, with benefits payable on the death of one spouse to "the survivor." Ms. Brissette died of a gunshot wound to the head in Detroit, Michigan. Later, Mr. Brissette was convicted of her murder. The insurance company refused to pay out under the policies. The executor, Mr. Bernard Bezaire, sued arguing that in both policies Ms. Brissette had insured **her own life**, with her husband as beneficiary. When her husband disentitled himself by murder, he argued, Ms. Brissette's estate became entitled to the insurance money. Mr. Justice Finlayson ruled, however, that according to the terms of the jointly-held policies, Ms. Brissette was the owner only of that part of the policies that insured the life of her **husband** and was not the owner of the part that insured her own life; therefore, Ms. Brissette's estate could not receive the insurance money, "not because of the crime committed by [her husband], but because the event she insured against did not occur. Her husband, whose life she insured, is still very much alive."

REAL ESTATE

Generally, include the fair market value of all real estate, including the matrimonial home if it is registered in the name of the deceased.

Property not included: Property that is not included in the value of a deceased's estate includes: personal property or real estate property that the deceased held jointly (with right of survivorship) with his or her spouse or with another party on the date of death. Such jointly-held property automatically passes to the surviving joint owner and does not, therefore, form part of the deceased's estate; real estate that is outside of Ontario since estate taxes are not collected in Ontario on that property; generally, assets such as life insurance, RRSPs, RRIFs, TFSAs payable to a named beneficiary, instead of to the estate of the deceased, do not form part of the deceased's estate and are therefore not included.

1. Add up the personal property to get the total value of that category. Enter this total in the application for certificate of appointment of estate trustee with a will. Do not deduct debts owing on personal property or other debts, e.g. car loans or credit card debts.

2. Add up the real estate. Deduct from each real estate property any charges/mortgages owing on it, as at the date of death, to arrive at the net value of each piece of real estate. Add up the net value of all real estate properties. Enter the resulting total in the application for certificate of appointment of estate trustee with a will.

Here is an example of a list of assets and how the estate administration tax is calculated:

Personal property:

Car in name of deceased valued at $8,000.00, $3,000.00 still owing on it	$ 8,000.00
RRSP $70,000.00, bank deposit $5,000.00, IBM shares $10,000.00, Canada savings bonds $15,000, all in deceased's name	100,000.00

Bank account held jointly with spouse, $10,000.00; not included

Clothing and personal effects belonging to deceased — $1,250.00

Insurance policy payable to the estate (does not name any beneficiary) — $50,000.00

Insurance policy payable to beneficiary $10,000.00; not included

Business assets in deceased's name valued at $150,000.00, $20,000.00 debt owing on assets — $150,000.00

Total personal property to be entered in application for certificate of estate trustee with a will — $309,250.00

Real estate:

Condominium, inherited, in deceased's name valued at $200,000.00, no charge/mortgage owing on it — $200,000.00

Family home held jointly with spouse $300,000.00, $50,000.00 charge/mortgage owing on it; not included

Cottage in deceased's name valued at $100,000.00, $10,000.00 charge/mortgage owing on it — $90,000.00

House in Florida, U.S.A, in deceased's name valued at $250,000.00, no charge/mortgage owing on it; not included

Business property in deceased's name valued at $400,000.00, $104,000.00 charge/mortgage owing on it — $296,000.00

Total real estate to be entered in the application for certificate of estate trustee with a will — $586,000.00

Total value of the deceased's estate to be entered in the application for certificate of estate trustee with a will ($309,250.00 + $586,000.00) = — $895,250.00

Total estate administration tax payable (as per the following tax formula) — $12,940.00

Tax formula as set out in the *Estate Administration Tax Act*:

$5 (or 0.5%) per $1,000.00 on the first $50,000.00 (50 × 5) = — $250.00

$15 (or 1.5%) per $1,000.00 on amounts over $50,000.00, rounded off to next $1,000.00, e.g. $895,250.00 = $896,000.00; ($896,000.00 − $50,000.00 = $846,000.00) (846 × 15) = — 12,690.00

$12,940.00

PREPARATION AND DISTRIBUTION OF APPLICATION FOR CERTIFICATE OF APPOINTMENT OF ESTATE TRUSTEE WITH A WILL (INDIVIDUAL APPLICANT), FORM 74.4

You require: The will and any codicils; the affidavit of execution of will and of codicil; proof of death certificate, Precedent 41.1a; calculations of the value of the deceased's estate. Follow along in Precedent 41.2. Most entries are self-explanatory. Notes on items not self-explanatory follow:

Details of Deceased: Key the name of the deceased exactly as it appears in the will. If the deceased was commonly known by another name, also key in that name, e.g. John Smith, also known as Babe Arnold. Type the county, district, or regional municipality where the deceased resided--this is what indicates in which court location you will file the application documents. If the deceased married after the date of the will, attach a schedule explaining why the applicant is applying for the certificate, since a marriage after the will revokes the will, unless the will was made in contemplation of the marriage. If the deceased divorced after the date of the will, attach a schedule giving details, since a divorce after the date of the will, in most cases, revokes the former spouse's right to act as estate trustee, if so named in the will, and also voids any gifts made to the former spouse in the will. This is so because usually the division of property between the spouses will have already occurred at the time of the divorce. If any witnesses or their spouses are also beneficiaries, attach a schedule giving details, since witnesses or their spouses cannot receive gifts under a will.

Value of Estate: Key the total value of personal property, total net value of real estate, and the total of the two values.

If the applicants in any way differ from the estate trustees (executors) named in the will, explain the reason for this in the space provided. One reason for this may be that one of the named estate trustees with a will (executors) has died or has renounced the right to be estate trustee with a will (executor). In the latter case, a **renunciation**, Precedent 41.5, signed by that estate trustee with a will (executor) must be filed with the application.

If an applicant is not named in the will as an estate trustee with a will, explain the reason for this in the space provided. One reason for this may be that the estate trustee with a will (executor) named in the will has predeceased the deceased or that the only named estate trustee with a will (executor) has renounced. In that case, attach a **consent**, Precedent 41.6, to the applicant's appointment by persons who are entitled to share in the distribution of the estate and who together represent a majority interest in the estate.

Affidavit of applicant: Key name, occupation, and address of estate trustee with a will. Complete the jurat to be sworn in the office of your firm.

Corporate estate trustee with a will: If the estate trustee with a will is a trust corporation, the application for certificate form is slightly different, and the corporation's authorized officer signs it, Precedent 41.9.

Preparation of schedules: Use plain paper to carry over or add any information to the application. Key a heading, e.g. "Schedule to the Application for Certificate of Appointment of Estate Trustee with a Will in the Estate of John Smith," and key the necessary information. Attach the schedule to the application.

Number of copies, minimum 2: Have estate trustee sign 1, which you send to court; keep 1 in client's file.

NOTICE OF AN APPLICATION FOR A CERTIFICATE OF APPOINTMENT OF ESTATE TRUSTEE WITH A WILL, FORM 74.7

Before filing the application for appointment of estate trustee with a will, you must serve a notice of an application for a certificate of appointment of estate trustee with a will, Form 74.7, Precedent 41.3, on all persons entitled to share in the estate, including any charities and contingent beneficiaries (those who will receive something only if some event happens, e.g. if another beneficiary dies before such a beneficiary receives his or her share of the estate). This notice is mailed out by regular mail. Almost all of the information to be entered relating to beneficiaries would come from the will. Note from Precedent 41.3 the specific parties to whom the notice is to be sent: for example, if there are any beneficiaries under the age of eighteen years (minors), the notice is to be sent to the parent or guardian of each minor as well as to the Children's Lawyer.

Copy of will   In addition to serving all of the beneficiaries under the will with a notice of an application for a certificate of appointment of estate trustee with a will, the estate trustee with a will must also include a copy of the entire will. The Children's Lawyer and the Public Guardian and Trustee are also entitled to receive a copy of the entire will, together with an indication of the estimated value of the interest of the person whom they represent. Note, however, that where a beneficiary is only entitled to a specific item or a set amount of money under a will, that beneficiary is entitled to receive a copy of only those provisions of the will that relate to his or her particular gift.

AFFIDAVIT OF SERVICE OF NOTICE (WITH A WILL), FORM 74.6

This affidavit proves service of the notice of an application for a certificate of appointment of estate trustee with a will. The affidavit, Precedent 41.4, must be filed with the application for certificate of appointment of estate trustee with a will.

CERTIFICATE OF APPOINTMENT OF ESTATE TRUSTEE WITH A WILL, FORM 74.13

The traditional term **probate,** from the Latin *probare,* means **to prove** the authenticity of a will. The certificate of appointment of estate trustee with a will (formerly, letters probate), Form 74.13, Precedent 41.7, is usually deemed to prove the authenticity of the will and to also confirm the appointment of the estate trustee with a will (executor). Once the court grants it, the certificate of appointment of estate trustee with a will permits the estate trustee with a will to deal with the deceased's estate and distribute it to the beneficiaries named in the will.

RENUNCIATION OF RIGHT TO A CERTIFICATE OF APPOINTMENT OF ESTATE TRUSTEE (OR SUCCEEDING ESTATE TRUSTEE) WITH A WILL, FORM 74.11

The court requires a **renunciation** from every living person who is named in the will or codicil as estate trustee, but who has not joined in the application and is entitled to do so. This applies where the estate trustee named in the will renounces the right to act. Prepare a renunciation of right to a certificate of appointment of estate trustee with a will, Precedent 41.5, where there is an estate trustee with a will (executor) named in the will who renounces (gives up) the right to act; hence **renunciation**.

CONSENT TO APPLICANT'S APPOINTMENT AS ESTATE TRUSTEE WITH A WILL, FORM 74.12

If the applicant is not named as an estate trustee in the will or codicil, prepare a consent to applicant's appointment as estate trustee with a will, Precedent 41.6, by persons who are entitled to share in the distribution of the estate and who together have a majority interest in the value of the assets of the estate at the date of death. This applies where there is a will but no estate trustee, either because the estate trustee (executor) named in the will has predeceased the deceased or because the only named estate trustee (executor) has renounced. Those consenting usually agree to dispensing with any requirement for a bond.

Majority interest   Generally, majority interest constitutes 50 percent plus $1 of the total value of the assets of the estate. A simple example calculation follows:

	Beneficiary 1	$ 21,000.00
	Beneficiary 2	30,000.00
	Beneficiary 3	30,000.00
	Beneficiary 4	19,000.00
	Total value of the estate	$100,000.00
Majority interest:	Beneficiaries 1 and 2 or 1 and 3	$51,000.00
	or	
	Beneficiaries 2 and 3	$60,000.00
	Consent required of Beneficiaries 1 and 2, 1 and 3, or 2 and 3	
Not majority interest:	Beneficiaries 1 and 4	$40,000.00
	or	
	Beneficiaries 4 and 2 or 4 and 3	$49,000.00
	Consent not required of Beneficiaries 1 and 4, 4 and 2, or 4 and 3	

Administration bond   This refers to a security bond which serves as a guarantee that the estate trustee will lawfully process the estate. It applies where the estate trustee with a will (executor) is either not named in the will or is not a resident of Canada or of any other country in the British Commonwealth.

Execution of application documents   Arrange an appointment for the estate trustee with a will (executor) to come in and sign the application for certificate of appointment of estate trustee with a will and any other necessary documents to be submitted to the court. If the estate administration tax is substantial, you may ask the estate trustee to bring in a certified cheque payable to the **Minister of Finance** in the amount of the estate administration tax. This can often be drawn on the deceased's estate bank account. Also arrange an appointment for the witness to sign the affidavit of execution of will, if it was not already signed when the testator signed the will. Arrange a similar appointment for the witness of any codicils. The lawyer usually serves as commissioner for all affidavits and exhibit marks.

Submission of application documents to court   Write a letter, Precedent 41.8, and send it by registered mail or courier to the Estates Office of the Superior Court of Justice in the place where the deceased resided, enclosing the applicable executed documents. The court retains the original will and any codicils and sends you a certified copy of the will and any codicils, to which the court attaches the **certificate of appointment of estate trustee with a will**, Form 74.13. The documents submitted to the court, including any renunciations and consents, where applicable, are usually as follows:

- Original will, Precedent 41.1 (plus a photocopy of the will, required by some court offices, including Toronto).
- Proof of death, Precedent 41.1a.
- Affidavit of execution of will.
- Application for certificate of appointment of estate trustee with a will, Precedent 41.2.
- Affidavit of service of notice (with a will), Precedent 41.4.
- Renunciation of right to a certificate of appointment of estate trustee with a will, if any, Precedent 41.5.
- Consent to applicant's appointment as estate trustee with a will, if any, Precedent 41.6.
- Bond, if any.
- Certificate of appointment of estate trustee with a will, Precedent 41.7.
- Cheque payable to the Minister of Finance in the amount of the estate administration tax.

APPLICATION FOR CERTIFICATE OF APPOINTMENT AS SUCCEEDING ESTATE TRUSTEE WITH A WILL, FORM 74.21

Use this application form when the estate trustee with a will (executor) dies **after** the court grants him a certificate of appointment of estate trustee with a will (letters probate) and **before** he completes the distribution of the deceased's estate **and** the testator has named an alternate estate trustee (executor) in his will: for example, the testator names A as estate trustee (executor), and if A should predecease him, he names B as his alternate estate trustee (executor). B applies for certificate of appointment as succeeding estate trustee with a will (formerly, double probate) to continue that part of the distribution of the estate which A left unfinished.

MEDIATION

Mandatory mediation is in place in some parts of the province. Mandatory mediation applies only in **contentious** litigation proceedings in estates, including virtually all disputes arising from wills, trusts, powers of attorney (both property and personal care), trustee accounting, and statutory claims against estates. The court may order the parties to attend mediation even where mediation is not mandatory. The mediation system is the same as that in civil litigation proceedings.

ESTATE INFORMATION RETURN

An **estate information return**, Precedent 41.10, sets out the assets of a deceased that were included in the application for certificate of appointment of estate trustee with a will, Precedent 41.2. Basically, the estate information return is for the purpose of showing to the Ministry of Finance how the value of a deceased's estate was arrived at and whether the correct amount of estate administration tax was paid. The estate information return must be filed with the Ministry of Finance, in testate or intestate estates, within **90 days** after a certificate of appointment of estate trustee (with or without a will) is **issued**. The estate information return form is available online through the Ministry of Finance and may be filed by fax, mail, courier, or at select ServiceOntario locations.

CHAPTER SUMMARY

When a person dies having left a will, nothing happens with the deceased's estate until the estate trustee with a will applies for, and receives, a certificate of appointment of estate trustee with a will from the court. The procedure to obtain a certificate of appointment of estate trustee with a will includes notifying all persons entitled to share in the distribution of the estate and applying to the court for the certificate.

The original will forms an exhibit to the application for a certificate of appointment of estate trustee with a will. If a named estate trustee is unwilling to act, that estate trustee must sign a renunciation of right to a certificate of appointment of estate trustee with a will. Where the named estate trustee has died or is incapable of acting, the court requires a consent to applicant's appointment as estate trustee with a will by those beneficiaries who together have a majority interest in the value of the assets of the estate.

The government, through the court, collects estate administration taxes from the estate of the deceased based on the total value of the estate. The total value is arrived at by including all real estate and personal property that is in the name of the deceased, excluding any jointly held real or personal property and any insurance policy that is payable to a named beneficiary. Deduct any debts from the value of real estate but not from any personal property. The total estate administration taxes are payable at the time of submitting the application to the court.

REVIEW QUESTIONS

1. Who applies for a certificate of appointment of estate trustee with a will?
2. In whose name must be the property that makes up the deceased's estate?
3. If a life insurance policy is not payable to a named beneficiary, to whom is it payable?
4. Why is jointly-held property excluded from the value of the deceased's estate?
5. No estate administration tax is payable if the deceased died testate. Explain.
6. Why is life insurance that is payable to the estate included in the value of the deceased's estate?
7. If the total value of a deceased's estate is $500,000, what would be the total estate administration tax payable?

-3-

(g) if RUTH GOLD does not survive me for a period of sixty days, my Trustee shall give and pay the entire residue of my estate to my elder brother, GEORGE JAMES GOLD, of St. John's, Newfoundland, for his sole use and benefit.

IN TESTIMONY WHEREOF I have to this my last Will and Testament written upon this and the two preceding pages, subscribed my name this _10th_ day of March, (year).

SIGNED, PUBLISHED AND DECLARED)	
by the said Arthur William Gold as)	
and for his last Will and Testament, in the)	_Arthur William Gold_
presence of us, both present at the same)	Arthur William Gold
time, who at his request, in his presence)	
and in the presence of each other have)	
subscribed our names as witnesses.)	

Signature of witness _Stephen Walter Stans_
Print name   Stephen Walter Stans
Address   46 Major Road
Richmond Hill, Ontario, L4C 1M1
Occupation   Software Developer

Signature of witness _Mary Ellen Simmons_
Print name Mary Ellen Simmons
Address   39 Minor Road
Markham, Ontario, L6P 1M2
Occupation   Law Clerk

(REVERSE SIDE OF THE LAST PAGE OF THE ABOVE WILL)

This is Exhibit "A" referred to in the
Affidavit of Stephen Walter Stans
sworn .... (year).

This is Exhibit "A" referred to in the
Affidavit of Randolph James Murphy
sworn ...., (year).

....
Commissioner for Taking Affidavits (or as may be)

....
Commissioner for Taking Affidavits (or as may be)

PROOF OF DEATH CERTIFICATE

DECEASED:

Gold
Last Name at Time of Death

Arthur William
Given Name(s)

February 7, 19xx
Date of Birth

June 13, 20xx
Date of Death

PLACE OF DEATH:

Toronto
City/Town

Ontario, Canada
Province/Country

Given under my hand at Toronto in the Province of Ontario, June 16, 20xx

Certified as per our records.

Tanner & Palmer
FUNERAL DIRECTORS

Per: *Robert Palmer*
Robert Palmer

ONTARIO

SUPERIOR COURT OF JUSTICE

APPLICATION FOR CERTIFICATE OF APPOINTMENT OF ESTATE TRUSTEE WITH A WILL (INDIVIDUAL APPLICANT)
(Form 74.4 Under the Rules (Page 1 of 3))
Courts of Justice Act

at **Toronto**

This application is filed by *(insert name and address)*
Robert B. Redford, Michael, Eliad & Redford LLP
863 Seneca Lane
Toronto, Ontario, M4J 1P6   Tel: 416-363-1079   Fax: 416-363-2628

DETAILS ABOUT THE DECEASED PERSON

Complete in full as applicable

First given name	Second given name	Third given name	Surname
Arthur	**William**		**Gold**

And if the deceased was known by any other name(s), state below the full name(s) used including surname.

First given name	Second given name	Third given name	Surname

Date of birth of the deceased person, if known: *(day, month, year)*
07 Feb 19xx

Address of fixed place of abode *(street or postal address) (city or town)*
123 Marble Street
Toronto, Ontario, M4V 6H6

(county or district)
City of Toronto

If the deceased person had no fixed place of abode in Ontario, did he or she have property in Ontario?   **N/A** ☐   No ☐   Yes ☐

Last occupation of deceased person
Bricklayer

Place of death *(city or town; county or district)*	**Date of death** *(day, month, year)*	**Date of last will** (marked as Exhibit "A") *(day, month, year)*
City of Toronto in the Province of Ontario	**13 Jun 20xx**	**10 Mar 20xx**

Was the deceased person 18 years of age or older at the date of the will (or 21 years of age or older if the will is dated earlier than September 1, 1971)? ☐ No   ☒ Yes
If not, explain why certificate is being sought. Give details in an attached schedule.

Date of codicil (marked as Exhibit "B") *(day, month, year)*	**Date of codicil** (marked as Exhibit "C") *(day, month, year)*
N/A	**N/A**

Marital Status ☐ Unmarried   ☒ Married   ☐ Widowed   ☐ Divorced

Did the deceased person marry after the date of the will?   ☒ No   ☐ Yes
If yes, explain why certificate is being sought. Give details in an attached schedule.

Was a marriage of the deceased person terminated by a judgment absolute of divorce, or declared a nullity, after the date of the will?   ☒ No   ☐ Yes
If yes, give details in an attached schedule.

Is any person who signed the will or a codicil as witness or for the testator, or the spouse of such person, a beneficiary under the will?   ☒ No   ☐ Yes
If yes, give details in an attached schedule.

RCP-E 74.4 (February 1, 2015)

APPLICATION FOR CERTIFICATE OF APPOINTMENT OF ESTATE TRUSTEE WITH A WILL (INDIVIDUAL APPLICANT)
(Form 74.4 Under the Rules (Page 2 of 3))

VALUE OF ASSETS OF ESTATE

Do not include in the total amount: insurance payable to a named beneficiary or assigned for value, property held jointly and passing by survivorship, or real estate outside Ontario.

Personal Property	Real estate, net of encumbrances	Total
$ 27,980.00	$ 204,000.00	$ 231,980.00

Is there any person entitled to an interest in the estate who is not an applicant? ☐ No   ☒ Yes

If a person named in the will or a codicil as estate trustee is not an applicant, explain.

N/A

If a person not named in the will or a codicil as estate trustee is an applicant, explain why that person is entitled to apply.

N/A

If the spouse of the deceased is an applicant, has the spouse elected to receive the entitlement under section 5 of the *Family Law Act?*   ☐ No   ☐ Yes
If yes, explain why the spouse is entitled to apply.

N/A

RCP-E 74.4 (February 1, 2015)

Document prepared using *Estate-a-Base* by Do Process LP, Toronto, Ontario 416.322.6111 or 1.866.367.7648

APPLICATION FOR CERTIFICATE OF APPOINTMENT OF ESTATE TRUSTEE WITH A WILL (INDIVIDUAL APPLICANT)
(Form 74.4 Under the Rules (Page 3 of 3))

AFFIDAVIT(S) OF APPLICANT(S)
(Attach a separate sheet for additional affidavits, if necessary)

I, an applicant named in this application, make oath and say/affirm:

1. I am 18 years of age or older.

2. The exhibit(s) referred to in this application are the last will and each codicil (where applicable) of the deceased person and I do not know of any later will or codicil.

3. I will faithfully administer the deceased person's property according to law and render a complete and true account of my administration when lawfully required.

4. If I am not named as estate trustee in the will or codicil, consents of persons who together have a majority interest in the value of the assets of the estate at the date of death are attached.

5. The information contained in this application and in any attached schedules is true, to the best of my knowledge and belief.

Name *(surname and forename(s))*	**Occupation**		
Murphy, Randolph James	Foreman		
Address *(street or postal address)*	*(city or town)*	*(province)*	*(postal code)*
46 Original Street	Aurora	Ontario	L2C 4T4

Sworn/Affirmed before me at the .....City......................

of .....Toronto..

in the .....Province..

of .....Ontario..

this ....day of ...., 20 ....

_____

Signature of applicant
Randolph James Murphy

_____
A Commissioner for taking Affidavits *(or as may be)*

Notice to applicant: Information provided on this form related to the payment of estate administration tax may be forwarded to the Ministry of Finance pursuant to clause 39(1)(b) and 42(1)(c) of *the Freedom of Information and Protection of Privacy Act*. This includes the name of the deceased, name and address of estate trustee(s), value of the estate and any undertakings and tax payments made or refunded. This information will be used by the Ministry of Finance to determine the value of estates and the amount of estate administration tax payable. Questions about the collection of this information should be directed to the Senior Manager – Audit, Advisory and Compliance Branch, 33 King Street West, PO Box 625, Oshawa ON L1H 8H9, 1-866-668-8297.

RCP-E 74.4 (February 1, 2015)

Document prepared using *Estate-a-Base* by Do Process LP, Toronto, Ontario 416.322.6111 or 1.866.367.7648

NOTICE OF AN APPLICATION
FOR A CERTIFICATE OF APPOINTMENT
OF ESTATE TRUSTEE WITH A WILL
Form 74.7
Courts of Justice Act

Ontario
Superior Court of Justice

(Page 1)

(insert name) IN THE ESTATE OF **Arthur William Gold**, deceased.

NOTICE OF AN APPLICATION FOR A
CERTIFICATE OF APPOINTMENT OF ESTATE
TRUSTEE WITH A WILL

(insert date) 1.   The deceased died on **June 13, 20xx**.

2.   Attached to this notice are:

(A)   If the notice is sent to or in respect of a person entitled only to a specified item of property or stated amount of money, an extract of the part or parts of the will or codicil relating to the gift, or a copy of the will (and codicil(s), if any).

(B)   If the notice is sent to or in respect of any other beneficiary, a copy of the will (and codicil(s), if any).

(C)   If the notice is sent to the Children's Lawyer or the Public Guardian and Trustee, a copy of the will (and codicil(s), if any), and if it is not included in the notice, a statement of the estimated value of the interest of the person represented.

3.   The applicant named in this notice is applying for a certificate of appointment of estate trustee with a will.

APPLICANT

Name	Address
Randolph James Murphy	**46 Original Street** **Aurora, Ontario, L2C 4T4**

4.   The following persons who are less than 18 years of age are entitled, whether their interest is contingent or vested, to share in the distribution of the estate:

Name	Date of Birth *(day, month, year)*	Name and Address of Parent or Guardian	Estimated Value of Interest in Estate*
Not Applicable			

* Note: *The Estimated Value of Interest in Estate may be omitted in the form if it is included in a separate schedule attached to the notice sent to the Children's Lawyer.*

RCP-E 74.7 (February 1, 2015)

NOTICE OF AN APPLICATION
FOR A CERTIFICATE OF APPOINTMENT
OF ESTATE TRUSTEE WITH A WILL
Form 74.7
Courts of Justice Act

(Page 2)

(insert name) IN THE ESTATE OF **Arthur William Gold**, deceased.

5.   The following persons who are mentally incapable within the meaning of section 6 of the *Substitute Decisions Act, 1992* in respect of an issue in the proceeding, and who have guardians or attorneys acting under powers of attorney with authority to act in the proceeding, are entitled, whether their interest is contingent or vested, to share in the distribution of the estate:

Name and Address of Person   **Name and Address of Guardian or Attorney***

Not Applicable

*Specify whether guardian or attorney

6.   The following persons who are mentally incapable within the meaning of section 6 of the *Substitute Decisions Act, 1992* in respect of an issue in the proceeding, and who do not have guardians or attorneys acting under powers of attorney with authority to act in the proceeding, are entitled, whether their interest is contingent or vested, to share in the distribution of the estate:

Name and Address of Person   **Estimated Value of
                                                                  Interest in Estate***

Not Applicable

* Note: *The Estimated Value of Interest in Estate may be omitted in the form if it is included in a separate schedule attached to the notice sent to the Public Guardian and Trustee.*

(Delete if not applicable) 7.   ~~Unborn or unascertained persons may be entitled to share in the distribution of the estate.~~

8.   All other persons and charities entitled, whether their interest is contingent or vested, to share in the distribution of the estate are as follows:

Name	**Address**
Ruth Gold **(wife)**	**123 Marble Street** **Toronto, Ontario, M4V 6H6**
George James Gold **(brother)**	**28 June Avenue** **St. John's, Newfoundland, A1A 2B6**

9.   This notice is being sent, by regular lettermail, to all adult persons and charities named above in this notice (except to an applicant who is entitled to share in the distribution of the estate), to the Public Guardian and Trustee if paragraph 6 applies, to a parent or guardian of the minor and to the Children's Lawyer if paragraph 4 applies, to the guardian or attorney if paragraph 5 applies, and to the Children's Lawyer if paragraph 7 applies.

RCP-E 74.7 (February 1, 2015)

Document prepared using *Estate-a-Base* by Do Process LP, Toronto, Ontario 416.322.6111 or 1.866.367.7648

NOTICE OF AN APPLICATION
FOR A CERTIFICATE OF APPOINTMENT
OF ESTATE TRUSTEE WITH A WILL
Form 74.7
Courts of Justice Act

(Page 3)

(insert name)   IN THE ESTATE OF **Arthur William Gold**, deceased.

If paragraph 10 does not apply insert "Not Applicable."   10.   The following persons named in the Will or being a member of a class of beneficiaries under the Will may be entitled to be served but have not been served for the reasons shown below:

Name of person (as it appears in will, if applicable)   Reason not served

Not Applicable

DATE: **June 30, (year)**

RCP-E 74.7 (February 1, 2015)

AFFIDAVIT OF SERVICE OF NOTICE
Form 74.6
Courts of Justice Act   *Ontario*
Superior Court of Justice

(insert name) IN THE ESTATE OF **Arthur William Gold**, deceased.

AFFIDAVIT OF SERVICE OF NOTICE

(insert name) I, **Randolph James Murphy**,

(insert city or town and country or district of residence) of **the Town of Aurora in the Regional Municipality of York**,

make oath and say/affirm:

1. I am **an applicant** for a certificate of appointment of estate trustee with a will in the estate.

2. I have sent or caused to be sent a notice in Form 74.7, a copy of which is marked as Exhibit "A" to this affidavit, to all adult persons and charities named in the notice (except to an applicant who is entitled to share in the distribution of the estate), to the Public Guardian and Trustee if paragraph 6 of the notice applies, to a parent or guardian of the minor and to the Children's Lawyer if paragraph 4 applies, to the guardian or attorney if paragraph 5 applies, and to the Children's Lawyer if paragraph 7 applies, all by regular lettermail sent to the person's last known address.

3. I have attached or caused to be attached to each notice the following:

    (A) In the case of a notice sent to or in respect of a person entitled only to a specified item of property or stated amount of money, an extract of the part or parts of the will or codicil relating to the gift, or a copy of the will (and codicil(s), if any).

    (B) In the case of a notice sent to or in respect of any other beneficiary, a copy of the will (and codicil(s), if any).

    (C) In the case of a notice sent to the Children's Lawyer or the Public Guardian and Trustee, a copy of the will (and codicil(s), if any) and a statement of the estimated value of the interest of the person represented.

If paragraph 4 does not apply insert "Not Applicable." 4. The following persons and charities specifically named in the Will are not entitled to be served for the reasons shown:

Name of person (as it appears in will, if applicable) Reason not served

Not Applicable

If paragraph 5 does not apply insert "Not Applicable." 5. The following persons named in the Will or being a member of a class of beneficiaries under the Will may be entitled to be served but have not been served for the reasons shown below:

Name of person (as it appears in will, if applicable) Reason not served

Not Applicable

AFFIDAVIT OF SERVICE OF NOTICE
Form 74.6
Courts of Justice Act

(Page 2)

(insert name) IN THE ESTATE OF **Arthur William Gold**, deceased.

6. To the best of my knowledge and belief, subject to paragraph 5 (if applicable), the persons named in the notice are all the persons who are entitled to share in the distribution of the estate.

Sworn/Affirmed before me at the **City**

of **Toronto**

in the **Province**

of **Ontario**

this .... day of ...., 20 ....

_____
Signature of applicant
Randolph James Murphy

_____
A Commissioner for taking Affidavits *(or as may be)*

RENUNCIATION OF RIGHT TO A
CERTIFICATE OF APPOINTMENT OF ESTATE TRUSTEE
(OR SUCCEEDING ESTATE TRUSTEE) WITH A WILL
Form 74.11
Courts of Justice Act   *Ontario*
Superior Court of Justice

(insert name)   IN THE ESTATE OF **Mary Jane Smith, deceased.**

RENUNCIATION OF RIGHT TO A
CERTIFICATE OF APPOINTMENT OF ESTATE TRUSTEE
(OR SUCCEEDING ESTATE TRUSTEE) WITH A WILL

(insert date)   The deceased died on **April 11, (year).**

(insert date)   In that person's testamentary document dated **October 13, (year),**

(insert name)   I, **Mark James Smithers,**

was named an estate trustee.

I renounce my right to a certificate of appointment of estate trustee with a will.

DATE: **April 28, (year)**

_____   _____
Signature of witness   *Signature of person renouncing*
                                                Mark James Smithers

RCP-E 74.11 (November 1, 2005)

CONSENT TO APPLICANT'S APPOINTMENT AS
ESTATE TRUSTEE WITH A WILL
Form 74.12
Courts of Justice Act

Ontario

Superior Court of Justice

(insert name) IN THE ESTATE OF **Mary Jane Smith, deceased.**

CONSENT TO APPLICANT'S APPOINTMENT AS ESTATE TRUSTEE WITH A WILL

(insert date) The deceased died on **April 11, (year).**

No estate trustee named in a testamentary document of that person is applying for a certificate of appointment of estate trustee with a will.

(insert name) I, **Helena Rubenstein,**

am entitled to share in the distribution of the estate.

(insert name) I consent to the application by **John William Davis**
for a certificate of appointment of estate trustee with a will.

(Delete if inapplicable) I consent to an order dispensing with the filing of a bond by the applicant.

DATE: **April 28, (year)**

_____
Signature of witness

_____
Signature of person consenting
Helena Rubenstein

RCP-E 74.12 (November 1, 2005)

Document prepared using *estate-a-base,* by Do Process Software Ltd., Toronto, Ontario (416) 322-6111 or (866) 367-7648

CERTIFICATE OF APPOINTMENT
OF ESTATE TRUSTEE WITH A WILL
Form 74.13
Courts of Justice Act

Court file no.

Ontario
Superior Court of Justice

(insert name)   IN THE ESTATE OF   **Arthur William Gold, deceased,**

late of   **the City of Toronto in the Province of Ontario,**

occupation   **Bricklayer,**

who died on   **June 13, 20xx.**

CERTIFICATE OF APPOINTMENT
OF ESTATE TRUSTEE WITH A WILL

Applicant	Address	Occupation
Randolph James Murphy	**46 Original Street** **Aurora, Ontario** **L2C 4T4**	**Foreman**

This CERTIFICATE OF APPOINTMENT OF ESTATE TRUSTEE WITH A WILL is hereby issued under the seal of the court to the applicant named above. Attached to this certificate is a copy of the deceased's last will dated <u>March 10, 20xx</u> (and codicil(s) dated <u>   n/a   </u>).

DATE: _____

_____
Registrar

Address of court office:

393 University Avenue
10th Floor
Toronto, Ontario
M5G 1E6

RCP-E 74.13 (February 1, 2015)

Court file no.

Ontario
Superior Court of Justice
at Toronto

**CERTIFICATE OF APPOINTMENT
OF ESTATE TRUSTEE WITH A WILL**

*Name, address, telephone number and fax number
of lawyer or party:*

**Robert B. Redford
Michael, Eliad & Redford LLP
Barristers and Solicitors
863 Seneca Lane
Toronto, Ontario
M4J 1P6**

**LSUC Registration No.: 48000R
Tel: 416-363-1079
Fax: 416-363-2628**

Document prepared using *Estate-a-Base* by Do Process LP. Toronto, Ontario   416.322.6111 or 1.866.367.7648
Form 74.13
RCP-E 4C (February 1, 2015)

IN THE ESTATE OF **Arthur William Gold**, deceased.

TELEPHONE NO. (416) 363-1079
FACSIMILE NO. (416) 363-2628
www.mer.ca
E-mail rbrdfrd@mer.com

MICHAEL, ELIAD & REDFORD LLP
BARRISTERS AND SOLICITORS
863 SENECA LANE
TORONTO, ONTARIO M4J 1P6

June 30, 20--

DELIVERED BY COURIER

Superior Court of Justice
Estates Office, 10th Floor
393 University Avenue
Toronto, Ontario
M5G 1E6

Dear Sirs and Madams:

Re: Estate of Arthur William Gold

We are the lawyers for the above estate and enclose the following documents in order to apply for a Certificate of Appointment of Estate Trustee with a Will:

1. Original Will of Arthur William Gold dated March 10, (year), together with a copy.
2. Proof of death of Arthur William Gold.
3. Affidavit of Execution of Will.
4. Application for Certificate of Appointment of Estate Trustee with a Will.
5. Affidavit of Service of Notice.
6. Certificate of Appointment of Estate Trustee with a Will.
7. Cheque in the amount of   for the estate administration taxes payable to the Minister of Finance.

We would appreciate receiving the Certificate as soon as possible.

Yours very truly,

MICHAEL, ELIAD & REDFORD LLP

Robert B. Redford

RBR/yi

Enc.

ONTARIO

SUPERIOR COURT OF JUSTICE

at **Waterwell**

APPLICATION FOR CERTIFICATE OF APPOINTMENT OF ESTATE TRUSTEE WITH A WILL (CORPORATE APPLICANT)
(Form 74.5 Under the Rules (Page 1 of 3))
Courts of Justice Act

This application is filed by *(insert name and address)*
Robert B. Redford, Michael, Eliad & Redford LLP
863 Seneca Lane,
Toronto, Ontario, M4J 1P6   Tel: 416-363-1079   Fax: 416-363-2628

DETAILS ABOUT THE DECEASED PERSON

Complete in full as applicable

First given name	Second given name	Third given name	Surname
James	David		Page

And if the deceased was known by any other name(s), state below the full name(s) used including surname.

First given name	Second given name	Third given name	Surname

Date of birth of the deceased person, if known: *(day, month, year)*
21 Apr 19xx

Address of fixed place of abode *(street or postal address) (city or town)*
18 Stairway Avenue
Waterwell, Ontario, D6A 4E6

(county or district)
County of Mandolee

If the deceased person had no fixed place of abode in Ontario, did he or she have property in Ontario?   **N/A** ☐ No   ☐ Yes

Last occupation of deceased person
Salesman

Place of death *(city or town; county or district)*
City of Waterwell in the County of Mandolee

Date of death
(day, month, year)
05 Nov 20xx

Date of last will
(marked as Exhibit "A")
(day, month, year)
25 Sep 20xx

Was the deceased person 18 years of age or older at the date of the will (or 21 years of age or older if the will is dated earlier than September 1, 1971)?   ☐ No   ☒ Yes
If not, explain why certificate is being sought. Give details in an attached schedule.

Date of codicil (marked as Exhibit "B")
(day, month, year)
N/A

Date of codicil (marked as Exhibit "C")
(day, month, year)
N/A

Marital Status ☐ Unmarried   ☒ Married   ☐ Widowed   ☐ Divorced

Did the deceased person marry after the date of the will?   ☒ No   ☐ Yes
If yes, explain why certificate is being sought. Give details in an attached schedule.

Was a marriage of the deceased person terminated by a judgment absolute of divorce, or declared a nullity, after the date of the will?   ☒ No   ☐ Yes
If yes, give details in an attached schedule.

Is any person who signed the will or a codicil as witness or for the testator, or the spouse of such person, a beneficiary under the will?   ☒ No   ☐ Yes
If yes, give details in an attached schedule.

RCP-E 74.5 (February 1, 2015)

APPLICATION FOR CERTIFICATE OF APPOINTMENT OF ESTATE TRUSTEE WITH A WILL (CORPORATE APPLICANT)
(Form 74.5 Under the Rules (Page 3 of 3))

AFFIDAVIT(S) OF APPLICANT(S)

(Attach a separate sheet for additional affidavits, if necessary)

I, a trust officer named in this application, make oath and say/affirm:

1. I am a trust officer of the corporate applicant.

2. I am 18 years of age or older.

3. The exhibit(s) referred to in this application are the last will and each codicil (where applicable) of the deceased person and I do not know of any later will or codicil.

4. The corporate applicant will faithfully administer the deceased person's property according to law and render a complete and true account of its administration when lawfully required.

5. If the corporate applicant is not named as estate trustee in the will or codicil, consents of persons who together have a majority interest in the value of the assets of the estate at the date of death are attached.

6. The information contained in this application and in any attached schedules is true, to the best of my knowledge and belief.

Name of corporate applicant
General Trust Company

Name of trust officer
John Paul Jones

Address of corporate applicant *(street or postal address)* *(city or town)* *(province)* *(postal code)*
925 Heather Road   Toronto   Ontario   M2W 6J6

Sworn/Affirmed before me at the City

of Toronto

in the Province

of Ontario

this .... day of .... 20 ....

Signature of trust officer
John Paul Jones

A Commissioner for taking Affidavits *(or as may be)*

Notice to applicant: Information provided on this form related to the payment of estate administration tax may be forwarded to the Ministry of Finance pursuant to clause 39(1)(b) and 42(1)(c) of the *Freedom of Information and Protection of Privacy Act.* This includes the name of the deceased, name and address of estate trustee(s), value of the estate and any undertakings and tax payments made or refunded. This information will be used by the Ministry of Finance to determine the value of estates and the amount of estate administration tax payable. Questions about the collection of this information should be directed to the Senior Manager – Audit, Advisory and Compliance Branch, 33 King Street West, PO Box 625, Oshawa ON L1H 8H9, 1-866-668-8297.

Document prepared using *Estate*●*Base* by Do Process LP, Toronto, Ontario. 416.322.6111 or 1.866.367.7648

RCP-E 74.5 (February 1, 2015)

APPLICATION FOR CERTIFICATE OF APPOINTMENT OF ESTATE TRUSTEE WITH A WILL (CORPORATE APPLICANT)
(Form 74.5 Under the Rules (Page 2 of 3))

VALUE OF ASSETS OF ESTATE

Do not include in the total amount: insurance payable to a named beneficiary or assigned for value, property held jointly and passing by survivorship, or real estate outside Ontario.

Personal property	Real estate, net of encumbrances	Total
$ 300,000.00	$ 128,000.00	$ 428,000.00

Is there any person interested in the estate who is not an applicant? ☐ No ☒ Yes

If a person named in the will or a codicil as estate trustee is not an applicant, explain.
N/A

If a person not named in the will or a codicil as estate trustee is an applicant, explain why that person is entitled to apply.
N/A

If the spouse of the deceased is an applicant, has the spouse elected to receive the entitlement under section 5 of the *Family Law Act?* ☐ No ☐ Yes
If yes, explain why the spouse is entitled to apply
N/A

Document prepared using *Estate*●*Base* by Do Process LP, Toronto, Ontario. 416.322.6111 or 1.866.367.7648

RCP-E 74.5 (February 1, 2015)

Ontario

Ministry of Finance

33 King St W
PO Box 625
Oshawa ON L1H 8H9

Enquiries: 1 866 ONT-TAXS (1 866 668-8297)
1 800 263-7776 Teletypewriter (TTY)
1 866 888-3850 (Fax)

Estate Information Return

Estate Administration Tax Act, 1998

Page 1 of 7

Ministry Use Only - Date Received

If you received a certificate of appointment of estate trustee from the Ontario Superior Court of Justice, this return **must** be completed and **received by the Ministry of Finance within 90 calendar days** after the certificate of appointment of estate trustee is issued. It will be used by the Ministry of Finance to administer the *Estate Administration Tax Act, 1998*.

If after submitting this return, you discover information was incorrect or incomplete, an amended return must be received by the Ministry of Finance **within 30 calendar days** from when the error or additional information about the property of the estate is known. See guide for additional information.

Is this an Amended Return?
(if yes, check ✓ box) . . . . ☐   Please explain below why this return is being amended ▼

Reason: (Note: If the return is amended due to a fulfillment of an undertaking, include particulars and amounts of additional tax paid.)

A   Information about the Certificate of Appointment of Estate Trustee

Indicate which type of certificate of appointment of estate trustee was granted by the Court (please choose one)

Form No.

☑ 74.13   Certificate of Appointment of Estate Trustee with a Will

☐ 74.13.1   Certificate of Appointment of Estate Trustee with a Will Limited to the Assets Referred to in the Will

☐ 74.20   Certificate of Appointment of Estate Trustee without a Will

☐ 74.20.3   Certificate of Appointment of Foreign Estate Trustee's Nominee as Estate Trustee without a Will

☐ 74.28   Confirmation by Resealing of Appointment of Estate Trustee

☐ 74.29   Certificate of Ancillary Appointment of Estate Trustee with a Will

Date (yyyy/mm/dd)

Enter the date above Certificate/Confirmation was issued 20xx/08/15

Enter the Court File No. assigned . . . .   0 - 2 9 6 4 / X X

Which Superior Court of Justice in Ontario was used to file your application? (please specify location)

Toronto

Was the deposit amount submitted based on an estimated value of the estate?
If yes, please attach a copy of the undertaking submitted to the court. . . . . . .
Yes ☐ No ☑   Date of Undertaking (yyyy/mm/dd)

Was the certificate of appointment of estate trustee issued without payment
of deposit equal to tax? . . . .
Yes ☐ No ☑
(subsections 4(1) and (2) of the *Estate Administration Tax Act, 1998*)

If yes, please attach a copy of the court order and details about the security provided to the court.

9955E (2015/07)   © Queen's Printer for Ontario, 2015   Disponible en français

---

Precedent 41.10   Estate Information Return, page 3

Page 3 of 7

Court File No.
0 - 2 9 6 4 / X X

Details of Estate Assets

List the fair market value of all assets and the balance of all bank accounts of the deceased at the date of death. If the court issued a Certificate of Appointment of Estate Trustee with a Will Limited to the Assets Referred to in the Will, only those assets included in such will are to be listed. If the court issued a Confirmation by Resealing of Appointment of Estate Trustee, a Certificate of Ancillary Appointment of an Estate Trustee with a Will, or a Certificate of Appointment of Foreign Estate Trustee's Nominee as Estate Trustee without a Will, only those assets located in Ontario are to be included. Only the value of encumbrances that are registered against real estate should be subtracted. Enter dollar amounts only (no cents).

D Real Estate in Ontario

Please also include assets/properties in which the deceased had an equitable interest, even though legal title was held by a person other than the deceased. (refer to guide)

Property 1 - Assessment Roll No.
19-04-123-456-78900-000

Property Identifier No. (PIN)
12457-6162

$ Fair Market Value (at date of death)
344,000.00

Percentage of Ownership
X 100 %

Address - Unit/Apt/Suite, Street Number and Name, Postal Str/Rural Route
123 Marble Street

Value of Percentage Owned
344,000.00

Subtract: Encumbrances (see guide)
140,000.00

City/Town
Toronto

Province ON

Postal Code M4V 6H6

$ Net Value
204,000.00

Property 2 - Assessment Roll No.

Property Identifier No. (PIN)

$ Fair Market Value (at date of death)

Percentage of Ownership
X %

Address - Unit/Apt/Suite, Street Number and Name, Postal Str/Rural Route

Value of Percentage Owned

Subtract: Encumbrances (see guide)

City/Town

Province ON

Postal Code

$ Net Value

Property 3 - Assessment Roll No.

Property Identifier No. (PIN)

$ Fair Market Value (at date of death)

Percentage of Ownership
X %

Address - Unit/Apt/Suite, Street Number and Name, Postal Str/Rural Route

Value of Percentage Owned

Subtract: Encumbrances (see guide)

City/Town

Province ON

Postal Code

$ Net Value

Attach separate list(s) if required.

Total Net Value of all Ontario Real Estate
- for percentage owned by the deceased at date of death
  Include amounts from separate list(s).
► $ 204,000.00   1

9955E (2015/07)

Precedent 41.10   Estate Information Return, page 2

Page 2 of 7

Court File No.
0 - 2 9 6 4 / X X

B Deceased Person Information

First Name
Arthur

Middle Name (s)
William

Last Name
Gold

If the deceased was known by any other name(s), please enter

Date of Birth (yyyy/mm/dd)
19xx/02/07

Date of Death (yyyy/mm/dd)
20xx/06/13

Address - Last Place of Residence (do NOT use post office box)

Unit/Apt/Suite   Street Number and Name (Postal Str/Rural Route)
123 Marble Street

City/Town
Toronto

Province/State ON

Postal/Zip Code M4V 6H6

Country
CANADA

C Estate Representative Information (For additional representatives, attach a separate list.)

First Name
Randolph

Middle Name
James

Last Name
Murphy

Business Name (if applicable)

Title

Telephone Number
(905) 752-2817

Extension

Fax Number

Email Address
rjmurphy@hotmail.com

Mailing Address

Unit/Apt/Suite   Street Number and Name (Postal Str/Rural Route)
46 Original Street

City/Town
Aurora

Province/State ON

Postal/Zip Code L2C 4T4

Country
CANADA

9955E (2015/07)

Court File No.

0 | - | 2 | 9 | 6 | 4 | / | X | X | | |

Details of Estate Assets continued   Page 5 of 7

F   Investments (list type and details of all shares, stocks, bonds, other investments, etc.)

Investment 1 - Name of Issuer
General Trust Company

Number of Units

Type and Details of Instrument or Account No.
GIC No. 25895-62586

Name of Broker/Agent
General Trust Company

Telephone No.

Address of Broker/Agent - Unit/Apt/Suite, Street Number and Name, Postal Stn/Rural Route
925 Heather Road

$ Fair Market Value (at date of death)
15,150.00

City/Town
Toronto

Province/State	Postal/Zip Code	Country
ON	M2W 6J6	CANADA

Percentage of Ownership   X | 100 | %

$ Value of Percentage Owned
15,150.00

Investment 2 - Name of Issuer

Number of Units

Type and Details of Instrument or Account No.

Name of Broker/Agent

Telephone No.

Address of Broker/Agent - Unit/Apt/Suite, Street Number and Name, Postal Stn/Rural Route

$ Fair Market Value (at date of death)

City/Town

Percentage of Ownership   X | | %

Province/State	Postal/Zip Code	Country

$ Value of Percentage Owned

Investment 3 - Name of Issuer

Number of Units

Type and Details of Instrument or Account No.

Name of Broker/Agent

Telephone No.

Address of Broker/Agent - Unit/Apt/Suite, Street Number and Name, Postal Stn/Rural Route

$ Fair Market Value (at date of death)

City/Town

Percentage of Ownership   X | | %

Province/State	Postal/Zip Code	Country

$ Value of Percentage Owned

Attach separate list(s) if required.

Total Value of all Investments
- for percentage owned by the deceased at date of death
  Include amounts from separate list(s).

▲ $ 15,150.00

3

9965E (2015/07)

Court File No.

0 | - | 2 | 9 | 6 | 4 | / | X | X | | |

Details of Estate Assets continued   Page 4 of 7

E   Bank Accounts (list details from all financial institutions in Canadian Funds - include credit unions and caisses populaires)

Bank Account 1 - Name of Financial Institution
Canadian Imperial Bank of Commerce

Account Number
79658-003

Address - Unit/Apt/Suite, Street Number and Name, Postal Stn/Rural Route
1216 Front Street East

$ Balance (at date of death)
$4,125.00

City/Town
Toronto

Province/State	Postal/Zip Code	Country
ON	M5M 1G1	CANADA

Percentage of Ownership   X | 100 | %

$ Value of Percentage Owned
$4,125.00

Bank Account 2 - Name of Financial Institution

Account Number

Address - Unit/Apt/Suite, Street Number and Name, Postal Stn/Rural Route

$ Balance (at date of death)

City/Town

Percentage of Ownership   X | | %

Province/State	Postal/Zip Code	Country

$ Value of Percentage Owned

Bank Account 3 - Name of Financial Institution

Account Number

Address - Unit/Apt/Suite, Street Number and Name, Postal Stn/Rural Route

$ Balance (at date of death)

City/Town

Percentage of Ownership   X | | %

Province/State	Postal/Zip Code	Country

$ Value of Percentage Owned

Bank Account 4 - Name of Financial Institution

Account Number

Address - Unit/Apt/Suite, Street Number and Name, Postal Stn/Rural Route

$ Balance (at date of death)

City/Town

Percentage of Ownership   X | | %

Province/State	Postal/Zip Code	Country

$ Value of Percentage Owned

Attach separate list(s) if required.

Total Value of all Bank Accounts
- for percentage owned by the deceased at date of death
  Include amounts from separate list(s).

▲ $ 4,125.00

2

9965E (2015/07)

Court File No.   0 | - | 2 | 9 | 6 | 4 | / | X | X |

Page 7 of 7

I   Summary of All Estate Assets (includes any amounts shown on separate lists)

Enter Dollars only

Total Net Value of all Real Estate in Ontario   1   204,000.00

Total Value of all: Bank Accounts ....   +   2   4,125.00

   Investment ....   +   3   15,150.00

   Vehicles and Vessels ....   +   4   5,875.00

   Other Assets ....   +   5   2,830.00

Total Value of all Estate Assets
- owned by the deceased at date of death (sum of Lines 1 to 5)   =   6   231,980.00

Total Amount of Estate Administration Tax Payable

Enter Total Estate Assets from Line 6   7   ▲   232,000.00
(round up this amount to the nearest $1,000)

The calculation should be:
a) $5 for each $1,000 of estate assets
   up to $50,000, plus   8   250.00
b) $15 for each $1,000 of estate assets
   over $50,000 ....   +   9   2,730.00

   =   10   2,980.00

Subtract: **Total Amount of Deposit Paid
with the Application for Estate Certificate** ...   –   11   2,980.00

Net Amount of Tax Owing (or Refund) ....   =   12   0
Make your cheque or money order in Canadian funds payable to the **Minister of Finance**.
Submit your payment to the Courthouse where the **certificate for appointment of estate** trustee was issued together with an affidavit attesting to the new total value of the estate.

J   Certification

I certify that the information I have given in this return, and in the documents I have provided, is true, correct and complete. Attach additional page(s) to include the signature of any other estate representative(s).

First Name   Randolph   Middle Name   James

Last Name   Murphy

Business Name (if applicable)   Title

Signature of Estate Representative   Date (yyyy/mm/dd)   20xx/08/

X

**It is an offence to make a false or misleading statement in a return as required under the *Estate Administration Tax Act, 1998*
and its Regulation.**

The personal information on the Estate Information Return is collected under the authority of the *Estate Administration Tax Act, 1998* and will be used to determine the value of estates and the amount of estate administration tax payable. This information may be used to develop and/ or evaluate tax or benefit policy. It may also be used in the administration or enforcement of an Act that imposes a tax or confers a benefit. Questions about the collection of this information should be directed to the Senior Manager-Audit, Advisory and Compliance Branch, 33 King Street West, PO Box 625, Oshawa ON L1H 8H9, 1 866 668-8297

9955E (2015/07)

Details of Estate Assets continued   Page 6 of 7   Court File No.   0 | - | 2 | 9 | 6 | 4 | / | X | X |

G   Vehicles and Vessels (include motorcycles, boats, all-terrain vehicles, bicycles, snowmobiles, etc.)

Vehicle/Vessel 1 - Vehicle Identification No. (VIN) or Hull Serial No. (HIN)
1FTRW12W14KC92815

$ Fair Market Value (at date of death)
$11,750.00

Make   Volkswagen

Percentage of Ownership
X   50   %

Model   Jetta   Year   20xx

$ Value of Percentage Owned
$5,875.00

Vehicle/Vessel 2 - Vehicle Identification No. (VIN) or Hull Serial No. (HIN)

$ Fair Market Value (at date of death)

Make

Percentage of Ownership
X   %

Model   Year

$ Value of Percentage Owned

Vehicle/Vessel 3 - Vehicle Identification No. (VIN) or Hull Serial No. (HIN)

$ Fair Market Value (at date of death)

Make

Percentage of Ownership
X   %

Model   Year

$ Value of Percentage Owned

Total Value of all Vehicles and Vessels
- for percentage owned by the deceased at date of death
Include amounts from separate list(s).

▲ $ 5,875.00   4

Attach separate list(s) if required.

H   Other Assets (include all other assets not listed in previous sections, e.g., business interests, copyrights, patents,
trademarks, household contents, art, jewelry, loans receivable, etc.)

Item 1 - Description
Household contents, art, jewellery, personal effects
Deceased's Interest: 50%

$ Fair Market Value (at date of death)
5,660.00

Percentage of Ownership
X   50   %

$ Value of Percentage Owned
2,830.00

Item 2 - Description

$ Fair Market Value (at date of death)

Percentage of Ownership
X   %

$ Value of Percentage Owned

Total Value of all Other Assets
- for percentage owned by the deceased at date of death
Include amounts from separate list(s).

▲ $ 2,830.00   5

Attach separate list(s) if required.

9955E (2015/07)

CHAPTER 42

APPLICATION FOR CERTIFICATE WITHOUT A WILL

This chapter discusses the steps and documents required when applying to the court for obtaining a certificate of appointment of estate trustee after a person dies without leaving a will.

APPLICATION FOR CERTIFICATE OF APPOINTMENT OF ESTATE TRUSTEE WITHOUT A WILL (INDIVIDUAL APPLICANT), FORM 74.14

When your firm acts for an estate trustee without a will, the estate of the deceased is said to be an **intestate** estate. Your firm files an application for certificate of appointment of estate trustee without a will, Form 74.14, on behalf of the estate trustee without a will (formerly, administrator) to obtain a certificate of appointment of estate trustee without a will (formerly, letters of administration). The certificate enables the estate trustee without a will to deal with the deceased's estate. Filing an application for certificate of appointment of estate trustee without a will is not necessary with small estates, usually ones which contain no real estate or stocks and bonds. Note the absence of references to a will or codicil. The information provided in Chapter 41 as to obtaining information from the estate trustee, record-keeping for any out-of-pocket expenses, estate trustee fee entitlement, value of estate, and instructions on how to calculate the value of an estate applies equally to intestate estates.

CHAMBERS, Joyce Marie
Re: Estate _____

Mrs. Chambers died intestate on April 30; she is survived by her husband, Mr. George Chambers; her son, Mr. William Chambers; and her daughter, Mrs. Grace Wilson. Although Mr. George Chambers is first in line to apply for a certificate of appointment of estate trustee without a will, he has renounced his right, Precedent 42.4, and has consented, Precedent 42.5, to appointing his daughter, Grace Wilson.

We have prepared the application for certificate of appointment of estate trustee without a will, Precedent 42.1. We have also prepared the notice of an application for a certificate of appointment of estate trustee without a will, Precedent 42.2, and the affidavit of service of notice, Precedent 42.3. Since the value of the estate is under $100,000.00, only one surety

> will suffice, and Mr. James Russell Killeen, a personal friend of Mrs. Wilson, has agreed to sign a bond, Precedent 42.6. We have also prepared the certificate of appointment of estate trustee without a will, Precedent 42.7. Once the court approves the certificate, Mrs. Wilson will have authority to distribute the estate according to the provisions of the *Succession Law Reform Act.*

PREPARATION AND DISTRIBUTION OF APPLICATION FOR CERTIFICATE OF APPOINTMENT OF ESTATE TRUSTEE WITHOUT A WILL (INDIVIDUAL APPLICANT), FORM 74.14

You require: The proof of death certificate and the calculations for the value of the deceased's estate. Follow along in Precedent 42.1. Most entries are self-explanatory. Notes on items not self-explanatory follow:

Key the name of the deceased: If the deceased was commonly known by another name, also key that name, e.g. John Smith, also known as Babe Arnold. Key the county, district, or regional municipality where the deceased resided--this is what indicates in which court location you will file the application documents. There are some additional questions dealing with uncertainty about the deceased's marital status and whether the deceased was living in a conjugal (common law) relationship. You will require this information to answer these questions.

Affidavit of applicant: Key name, occupation, and address of estate trustee without a will (administrator). Complete the jurat to be sworn in the office of your firm.

Corporate estate trustee without a will: If the estate trustee without a will is a trust corporation, the form is slightly different, and the corporation's authorized officer signs it; see precedent in Chapter 41.

Preparation of schedules: As in Chapter 41.

Number of copies, minimum 2: Have estate trustee sign 1, which you send to court; keep 1 in client's file.

NOTICE OF AN APPLICATION FOR A CERTIFICATE OF APPOINTMENT OF ESTATE TRUSTEE WITHOUT A WILL, FORM 74.17

Before filing the application for appointment of estate trustee without a will, you must serve a notice of an application for a certificate of appointment of estate trustee without a will, Form 74.17, Precedent 42.2, on all persons entitled to share in the estate. Such persons are determined by the provisions of the *Succession Law Reform Act*, as set out in the **summary of line of inheritance** in Chapter 40. The notice is mailed out by regular mail. Note from Precedent 42.2 the specific parties to whom the notice is to be sent: for example, if there are any heirs under the age of eighteen years (minors), the notice is to be sent to the parent or guardian of each minor as well as to the Children's Lawyer.

AFFIDAVIT OF SERVICE OF NOTICE (WITHOUT A WILL), FORM 74.16

This affidavit, Precedent 42.3, proves service of the notice of an application for a certificate of appointment of estate trustee without a will. It must be filed with each application for certificate of appointment of estate trustee without a will.

CERTIFICATE OF APPOINTMENT OF ESTATE TRUSTEE WITHOUT A WILL, FORM 74.20

When a person dies intestate, there is no will naming the person who is to act as the deceased's personal representative, i.e. estate trustee; therefore, someone, usually a relative, applies to the court for permission to act as one. The appointed personal representative is referred to as the **estate trustee without a will** (administrator). The capacity and duties of an estate trustee without a will are parallel to those of an estate trustee with a will in testate estates. The document the court signs to authorize the estate trustee without a will to deal with the deceased's estate is known as a **certificate of appointment of estate trustee without a will** (letters of administration), Precedent 42.7. Since there is no will naming the beneficiaries, the estate trustee without a will distributes the estate to the heirs, or next of kin, described in the *Succession Law Reform Act* (SLRA). See the **summary of line of inheritance** in Chapter 40.

Who may act as estate trustee without a will   Under the SLRA, persons entitled to act as estate trustee without a will (administrator), in order of priority, are as follows:

1. Spouse
2. Child or children
3. Grandchild or grandchildren
4. Great grandchildren or other descendants
5. Father
6. Mother
7. Brothers and sisters.

The estate trustee without a will must be an Ontario resident. If the family of the deceased prefer, they may nominate a trust company or another person to act as estate trustee without a will.

RENUNCIATION OF PRIOR RIGHT TO A CERTIFICATE OF APPOINTMENT OF ESTATE TRUSTEE WITHOUT A WILL, FORM 74.18

A **renunciation of prior right to a certificate of appointment of estate trustee without a will, Form 74.18,** Precedent 42.4, is required from any individuals who have priority to act as estate trustees without a will, but who renounce their right. Individuals with lower priority than the applicant need not sign one of these forms. The renouncing individual names the person who will be applying for a certificate of appointment of estate trustee without a will. The court requires a renunciation in the following situations:

1. When the surviving spouse does not wish to act. Prepare the form for the signature of the surviving spouse.

2. When there is no surviving spouse but there are children, only one or some of whom will act. Prepare the form for the signature of each child who renounces.

3. When the surviving spouse and the children wish to have a trust company act. Prepare one form for the surviving spouse and one for each of the children.

Make a minimum of two copies. Send a signed copy to the court, together with the application for certificate of appointment of estate trustee without a will; keep one copy in the file.

CONSENT TO APPLICANT'S APPOINTMENT AS ESTATE TRUSTEE WITHOUT A WILL, FORM 74.19

A **consent to applicant's appointment as estate trustee without a will, Form 74.19**, Precedent 42.5, is required from those individuals who have signed a renunciation of prior right to a certificate of appointment of estate trustee without a will. The consent serves as approval of the individual who will apply for a certificate of appointment of estate trustee without a will. The consenting individual may indicate, and usually does, that the applicant act without security, i.e. without posting a bond. Make a minimum of two copies. Send a signed copy to the court, together with the application for certificate of appointment of estate trustee without a will; keep one copy in the file.

BOND, FORM 74.33

In intestate estates, a bond is required under the *Estates Act* and the *Rules of Civil Procedure*, unless the court orders otherwise. The bond is a **guarantee** of money to be paid to the court if the estate trustee without a will fails to faithfully administer the estate. The bond must be posted by **sureties** who may be one or more individuals or an insurance company. Where the sureties are individuals, one individual is sufficient if the estate value does not exceed $100,000.00; otherwise, two individuals are usually required. The estate trustee without a will cannot act as a surety, nor can lawyers or court registrars. A bond is not required if the estate trustee without a will is a trust company or if the estate trustee without a will is the surviving spouse of the deceased and the value of the estate is less than $200,000.00 (preferential share).

PREPARATION AND DISTRIBUTION OF BOND, FORM 74.33

You require: The application for certificate of appointment of estate trustee without a will. Follow along in Precedent 42.6. Most entries are self-explanatory. Notes on items not self-explanatory follow:

There are two bond forms: **bond—personal sureties** and **bond—insurance or guarantee company**. These bond forms are almost identical, except that the **bond—personal sureties** contains two affidavits of surety; the **bond—insurance or guarantee company** contains none as none is required of corporations. The term **principal** in the bond means the estate trustee without a will. Where the surety is an insurer, the amount of the bond must be equal to the amount or the value of the estate. Where one personal surety is required, the amount in the affidavit of surety should be double the total value of the estate. Where two personal sureties are required, the amount in the affidavit of each surety should be the total value of the estate so that the two sureties together equal double the total value of the estate: for example, if the total value of the estate is $400,000.00, the amount of the bond would be doubled to $800,000.00; each surety's amount would be $400,000.00.

Number of copies, minimum 5: Submit 1, which the sureties sign, to the court with the application for certificate of appointment of estate trustee without a will; give 1 each to estate trustee without a will and sureties; keep 1 in client's file.

Cancellation of bond When the distribution of the estate is done, cancel the bond by filing (with the court) documents which include:

- A draft order cancelling the bond for the judge to sign and return to you.
- An affidavit proving the completion of the distribution of the estate.

- Releases from all of the heirs who were entitled to receive from the estate.
- An affidavit regarding the publishing of a notice to creditors.

The court signs the draft order and returns it to you, together with the bond, indicating the bond is cancelled.

Execution of application documents   Arrange an appointment for the estate trustee without a will (administrator) to come in and sign the application for certificate of appointment of estate trustee without a will and any other necessary documents to be submitted to the court. If the estate administration tax is substantial, you may ask the estate trustee to bring in a certified cheque payable to the **Minister of Finance** for the amount of the estate administration tax. This can often be drawn on the deceased's estate bank account.

Submission of application documents to court   Write a cover letter (see precedent in Chapter 41) to the Estates Office of the Superior Court of Justice in the county, district, or regional municipality where the deceased resided. Enclose the applicable documents. The court will sign and return the certificate of appointment of estate trustee without a will (letters of administration). The most common documents submitted to the court are as follows:

- Proof of death.
- Application for certificate of appointment of estate trustee without a will, Precedent 42.1.
- Affidavit of service of notice (without a will), Precedent 42.3.
- Renunciation of prior rights to a certificate of appointment of estate trustee without a will, Precedent 42.4.
- Consent to applicant's appointment as estate trustee without a will, Precedent 42.5.
- Bond, Precedent 42.6.
- Certificate of appointment of estate trustee without a will (letters of administration), Precedent 42.7.
- Cheque payable to the Minister of Finance in the amount of the estate administration tax.

APPLICATION FOR CERTIFICATE OF APPOINTMENT AS SUCCEEDING ESTATE TRUSTEE WITHOUT A WILL, FORM 74.24

If the appointed estate trustee without a will (administrator) dies before the estate is finished, the application to appoint a new estate trustee without a will is called **application for certificate of appointment as succeeding estate trustee without a will, Form 74.24,** (formerly, application for administration *de bonis non administratis*).

MEDIATION

See Chapter 41 for details.

ESTATE INFORMATION RETURN

See Chapter 41 for details and completed precedent.

CHAPTER SUMMARY

When a person dies intestate, an heir may apply to be the estate trustee without a will. The estate trustee without a will must notify all persons entitled to share in the distribution of the estate and submit to the court an application for certificate of appointment of estate trustee without a will.

If someone other than the surviving spouse is applying for a certificate of appointment of estate trustee without a will, you must prepare a renunciation of prior right to a certificate of appointment of estate trustee without a will and a consent to applicant's appointment as estate trustee without a will for the signature of all of those who have a prior right to apply for a certificate of appointment. In intestate estates, the court also requires a bond either by individuals or an insurance company as a guarantee for the faithful administration of the estate. Estate administration tax is payable on the value of the estate. Calculating the value of intestate estates is the same as that for testate estates.

REVIEW QUESTIONS

1. What is the role of an estate trustee without a will?
2. Who has the highest right to act as estate trustee without a will?
3. When is a renunciation of prior right to a certificate of appointment of estate trustee without a will required?
4. Estate administration taxes are not applicable in intestate estates. Explain.
5. What is a consent to applicant's appointment as estate trustee without a will?
6. What is the purpose of a bond?
7. What is a surety?
8. If the total value of a deceased's estate is $250,000, what would be the amount of the estate administration tax payable?

ONTARIO

SUPERIOR COURT OF JUSTICE

**APPLICATION FOR CERTIFICATE
OF APPOINTMENT OF ESTATE TRUSTEE
WITHOUT A WILL (INDIVIDUAL APPLICANT)**
(Form 74.14 Under the Rules (Page 1 of 3))
Courts of Justice Act

at **Waterwell**

This application is filed by *(insert name and address)*
Robert B. Redford, Michael, Eliad & Redford LLP
863 Seneca Lane
Toronto, Ontario M4J 1P6   Tel: 416-363-1079   Fax: 416-363-2628

DETAILS ABOUT THE DECEASED PERSON

Complete in full as applicable

First given name	Second given name	Third given name	Surname
Joyce	**Marie**		**Chambers**

And if the deceased was known by any other name(s), state below the full name(s) used including surname.

First given name	Second given name	Third given name	Surname
GIGI			

Date of birth of the deceased person, if known: *(day, month, year)*

Address of fixed place of abode *(street or postal address) (city or town)*	*(county or district)*
389 Bacon Street **Waterwell, Ontario, D6A 4R6**	**County of Mandolee**
If the deceased person had no fixed place of abode in Ontario, did he or she have property in Ontario? **N/A** ☐ **No** ☐ **Yes** ☐	**Last occupation of deceased person** **Executive**

Place of death *(city or town; county or district)*	**Date of death** *(day, month, year* **30 Apr 20xx**
City of Waterwell in the County of Mandolee	

Marital Status ☐ Unmarried   ☒ Married   ☐ Widowed   ☐ Divorced

Was the deceased person's marriage terminated by a judgment absolute of divorce, or declared a nullity? If yes, give details in an attached schedule.	☒ No ☐ Yes
Did the deceased person go through a form of marriage with a person where it appears uncertain whether an earlier marriage of the deceased person had been terminated by divorce or declared a nullity? If yes, give the person's name and address, and the names and addresses of any children (including deceased children) of the marriage, in an attached schedule.	☒ No ☐ Yes
Was any earlier marriage of a person with whom the deceased person went through a form of marriage terminated by divorce or declared a nullity? If yes, give details in an attached schedule.	☒ No ☐ Yes
Was the deceased person immediately before his or her death living with a person in a conjugal relationship outside marriage? If yes, give the person's name and address in an attached schedule.	☒ No ☐ Yes

RCP-E 74.14 (February 1, 2015)

Document prepared using *Estate-a-Base* by Do Process LP, Toronto, Ontario 416.322.6111 or 1.866.367.7648

APPLICATION FOR CERTIFICATE OF APPOINTMENT OF ESTATE TRUSTEE WITHOUT A WILL (INDIVIDUAL APPLICANT)
(Form 74.14 Under the Rules (Page 2 of 3))

PERSONS ENTITLED TO SHARE IN THE ESTATE

(Attach a schedule if more space is needed. If a person entitled to share in the estate is not a spouse, child, parent, brother or sister of the deceased person, show how the relationship is traced.)

Name	Address	Relationship to deceased person	Age (if under 18)
George Chambers	389 Bacon Street Waterwell, Ontario, D6A 4R6	husband	
William Chambers	389 Bacon Street Waterwell, Ontario, D6A 4R6	son	
Grace Wilson	24 Sumac Drive Ottawa, Ontario, K1N 6E4	daughter	

VALUE OF ASSETS OF ESTATE

Do not include in the total amount: insurance payable to a named beneficiary or assigned for value, property held jointly and passing by survivorship, or real estate outside Ontario.

Personal property	Real estate, net of encumbrances	Total
$ 25,480.00	$ 73,000.00	$ 98,480.00

Explain why the applicant is entitled to apply.

The applicant is the daughter of the deceased and the nominee of George Chambers, the spouse of the deceased.

RCP-E 74.14 (February 1, 2015)

APPLICATION FOR CERTIFICATE OF APPOINTMENT OF ESTATE TRUSTEE WITHOUT A WILL (INDIVIDUAL APPLICANT)
(Form 74.14 Under the Rules (Page 3 of 3))

AFFIDAVIT(S) OF APPLICANT(S)
(Attach a separate sheet for additional affidavits, if necessary)

I, an applicant named in this application, make oath and say/affirm:

1. I am 18 years of age or older and a resident of Ontario.

2. I have made a careful search and inquiry for a will or other testamentary document of the deceased person, but none has been found. I believe that the person did not leave a will or other testamentary document.

3. I will faithfully administer the deceased person's property according to law and render a complete and true account of my administration when lawfully required.

4. Consents of persons who together have a majority interest in the value of the assets of the estate at the date of death are attached.

5. The information contained in this application and in any attached schedules is true, to the best of my knowledge and belief.

Name *(surname and forename(s))*	Occupation		
Wilson, Grace	Bookkeeper		
Address *(street or postal address)*	*(city or town)*	*(province)*	*(postal code)*
24 Sumac Drive	Ottawa	Ontario	K1N 6E4

Sworn/Affirmed before me at the **City**

of **Toronto**

in the **Province**

of **Ontario**

this .... day of ...., 20 ....

Signature of applicant
Grace Wilson

_____
A Commissioner for taking Affidavits *(or as may be)*

Notice to applicant: Information provided on this form related to the payment of estate administration tax may be forwarded to the Ministry of Finance pursuant to clause 39(1)(b) and 42(1)(c) of *the Freedom of Information and Protection of Privacy Act*. This includes the name of the deceased, name and address of estate trustee(s), value of the estate and any undertakings and tax payments made or refunded. This information will be used by the Ministry of Finance to determine the value of estates and the amount of estate administration tax payable. Questions about the collection of this information should be directed to the Senior Manager – Audit, Advisory and Compliance Branch, 33 King Street West, PO Box 625, Oshawa ON L1H 8H9, 1-866-668-8297.

RCP-E 74.14 (February 1, 2015)

Document prepared using *Estate-a-Base* by Do Process LP, Toronto, Ontario 416.322.6111 or 1.866.367.7648

NOTICE OF AN APPLICATION
FOR A CERTIFICATE OF APPOINTMENT
OF ESTATE TRUSTEE WITHOUT A WILL
Form 74.17

Courts of Justice Act

Ontario
Superior Court of Justice

(Page 1)

(insert name) IN THE ESTATE OF **Joyce Marie Chambers (also known as GIGI)**, deceased.

NOTICE OF AN APPLICATION FOR A
CERTIFICATE OF APPOINTMENT OF ESTATE TRUSTEE WITHOUT A WILL

(insert date) 1. The deceased died on **April 30, 20xx**, without a will.

2. The applicant named in this notice is applying for a certificate of appointment of estate trustee without a will.

APPLICANT

Name	**Address**
Grace Wilson	**24 Sumac Drive** **Ottawa, Ontario, K1N 6E4**

3. The following persons who are less than 18 years of age are entitled to share in the distribution of the estate:

Name	**Date of Birth** (day, month, year)	**Name and Address of Parent or Guardian**	**Estimated Value of Interest in Estate***
Not Applicable			

* Note: *The Estimated Value of Interest in Estate may be omitted in the form if it is included in a separate schedule attached to the notice sent to the Children's Lawyer.*

4. The following persons who are mentally incapable within the meaning of section 6 of the *Substitute Decisions Act, 1992* in respect of an issue in the proceeding, and who have guardians or attorneys acting under powers of attorney with authority to act in the proceeding, are entitled to share in the distribution of the estate:

Name and Address of Person	**Name and Address of Guardian or Attorney***
Not Applicable	

*Specify whether guardian or attorney.

5. The following persons who are mentally incapable within the meaning of section 6 of the *Substitute Decisions Act, 1992* in respect of an issue in the proceeding, and who do not have guardians or attorneys acting under powers of attorney with authority to act in the proceeding, are entitled to share in the distribution of the estate:

Name and Address of Person	**Estimated Value of Interest in Estate***
Not Applicable	

* Note: *The Estimated Value of Interest in Estate may be omitted in the form if it is included in a separate schedule attached to the notice sent to the Public Guardian and Trustee.*

RCP-E 74.17 (November 1, 2005)

Document prepared using *estate-a-base*, by Do Process Software Ltd., Toronto, Ontario (416) 322-6111 or (866) 367-7648

NOTICE OF AN APPLICATION
FOR A CERTIFICATE OF APPOINTMENT
OF ESTATE TRUSTEE WITHOUT A WILL
Form 74.17
Courts of Justice Act

(Page 2)

(insert name) IN THE ESTATE OF **Joyce Marie Chambers (also known as GIGI)**, deceased.

6. All other persons entitled to share in the distribution of the estate are as follows:

Name	**Address**
George Chambers (husband)	**389 Bacon Street** **Waterwell, Ontario, D6A 4R6**
William Chambers (son)	**389 Bacon Street** **Waterwell, Ontario, D6A 4R6**
Grace Wilson (daughter)	**24 Sumac Drive** **Ottawa, Ontario, K1N 6E4**

7. This notice is being sent, by regular lettermail, to all adult persons named above in this notice (except to an applicant who is entitled to share in the distribution of the estate), to a parent or guardian of the minor and to the Children's Lawyer if paragraph 3 applies, to the guardian or attorney if paragraph 4 applies, and to the Public Guardian and Trustee if paragraph 5 applies.

If paragraph 8 does not apply insert "Not Applicable."

8. The following persons may be entitled to be served but have not been served for the reasons shown below:

Name of person	**Reason not served**
Not Applicable	

DATE:

RCP-E 74.17 (November 1, 2005)

Document prepared using **estate-a-base**, by Do Process Software Ltd., Toronto, Ontario (416) 322-6111 or (866) 367-7648

AFFIDAVIT OF SERVICE OF NOTICE
Form 74.16
Courts of Justice Act

Ontario
Superior Court of Justice

(insert name)   IN THE ESTATE OF **Joyce Marie Chambers (also known as GIGI)**, deceased.

AFFIDAVIT OF SERVICE OF NOTICE

(insert name)   I, **Grace Wilson**,

(insert city or town and country or district of residence)   **of the City of Ottawa in the Regional Municipality of Ottawa-Carleton**,

make oath and say/affirm:

1. I am **an applicant** for a certificate of appointment of estate trustee without a will in the estate.

2. I have sent or caused to be sent a notice in Form 74.17, a copy of which is marked as Exhibit "A" to this affidavit, to all adult persons named in the notice (except to an applicant who is entitled to share in the distribution of the estate), to a parent or guardian of the minor and to the Children's Lawyer if paragraph 3 of the notice applies, to the guardian or attorney if paragraph 4 applies and to the Public Guardian and Trustee if paragraph 5 applies, all by regular lettermail sent to the person's last known address.

If paragraph 3 does not apply insert "Not Applicable."   3. The following persons may be entitled to be served but have not been served for the reasons shown below:

Name of person (if applicable)	Reason not served
Not Applicable	

4. To the best of my knowledge and belief, subject to paragraph 3 (if applicable), the persons named in the notice are all the persons who are entitled to share in the distribution of the estate.

Sworn/Affirmed before me at the **City**

of **Toronto**

in the **Province**

of **Ontario**

this .... day of ...., 20 ....

_____
Signature of applicant
Grace Wilson

_____
A Commissioner for taking Affidavits *(or as may be)*

RCP-E 74.16 (November 1, 2005)

Precedent 42.5 Consent to Applicant's Appointment as Estate Trustee without a Will

CONSENT TO APPLICANT'S APPOINTMENT AS
ESTATE TRUSTEE WITHOUT A WILL
Form 74.19
Courts of Justice Act

Ontario
Superior Court of Justice

(Insert name) IN THE ESTATE OF **Joyce Marie Chambers (also known as GIGI), deceased.**

**CONSENT TO APPLICANT'S APPOINTMENT AS
ESTATE TRUSTEE WITHOUT A WILL**

(Insert date) The deceased died on **April 30, (year)**, without a will.

(Insert name) I, **George Chambers,**
am entitled to share in the distribution of the estate.

(Insert name) I consent to the application by **Grace Wilson**
for a certificate of appointment of estate trustee without a will.

(Delete if inapplicable) I consent to an order dispensing with the filing of a bond by the applicant.

DATE: **June 29, (year)**

_____
Signature of witness

_____
Signature of person consenting
George Chambers

Document prepared using **estate-a-base**, by Do Process Software Ltd., Toronto, Ontario (416) 322-6111 or (866) 367-7648

RCP-E 74.19 (November 1, 2005)

Precedent 42.4 Renunciation of Prior Right to a Certificate of Appointment of Estate Trustee without a Will

RENUNCIATION OF PRIOR RIGHT TO A
CERTIFICATE OF APPOINTMENT OF ESTATE TRUSTEE
WITHOUT A WILL
Form 74.18
Courts of Justice Act

Ontario
Superior Court of Justice

(Insert name) IN THE ESTATE OF **Joyce Marie Chambers (also known as GIGI), deceased.**

**RENUNCIATION OF PRIOR RIGHT TO A
CERTIFICATE OF APPOINTMENT OF ESTATE TRUSTEE
WITHOUT A WILL**

(Insert date) The deceased died on **April 30, (year)**, without a will.

(Insert name) I, **George Chambers,**
am entitled to apply for a certificate of appointment of estate trustee without a will in priority
to **Grace Wilson.**

(Insert name) I renounce my right to a certificate of appointment of estate trustee without a will in priority
to **Grace Wilson.**

DATE: **June 29, (year)**

_____
Signature of witness

_____
Signature of person renouncing
George Chambers

Document prepared using **estate-a-base**, by Do Process Software Ltd., Toronto, Ontario (416) 322-6111 or (866) 367-7648

RCP-E 74.18 (November 1, 2005)

BOND - PERSONAL SURETIES
Form 74.33
Courts of Justice Act

Court file no.

Ontario
Superior Court of Justice

BOND NO.   AMOUNT $ **196,960.00**

(insert name) IN THE ESTATE OF **Joyce Marie Chambers (also known as GIGI), deceased.**

BOND - PERSONAL SURETIES

(insert name) The principal in this bond is **Grace Wilson.**

(insert name) The sureties in this bond are **James Russell Killeen.**

The obligee in this bond is the Accountant of the Superior Court of Justice acting for the benefit of creditors and persons entitled to share in the estate of the deceased.

The principal and the sureties bind themselves, their heirs, executors, successors and assigns jointly and severally to the Accountant of the Superior Court of Justice in the amount of **One Hundred Ninety Six Thousand Nine Hundred Sixty** Dollars (**$ 196,960.00**).

The principal as an estate trustee is required to prepare a complete and true inventory of all the property of the deceased, collect the assets of the estate, pay the debts of the estate, distribute the property of the deceased according to law, and render a complete and true accounting of these activities when lawfully required.

The primary obligation under this bond belongs to the principal. The principal is liable under this bond for any amount found by the court to be owing to any creditors of the estate and persons entitled to share in the estate to whom proper payment has not been made.

The sureties, provided they have been given reasonable notice of any proceeding in which judgment may be given against the principal for failure to perform the obligations of this bond shall, on order of the court, and on default of the principal to pay any final judgment made against the principal in the proceeding, pay to the obligee the amount of any deficiency in the payment by the principal, but the sureties shall not be liable to pay more than the amount of the bond.

RCP-E 74.33 (November 1, 2005)

Document prepared using *estate-a-base,* by Do Process Software Ltd., Toronto, Ontario (416) 322-6111 or (866) 367-7648

Page 3

BOND - PERSONAL SURETIES
Form 74.33

AFFIDAVIT OF SURETY

I, **James Russell Killeen**
of the City of Windsor in the County of Essex

MAKE OATH AND SAY/AFFIRM:

I am a proposed surety on behalf of the intended estate trustees of the property of **Joyce Marie Chambers (also known as GIGI)** deceased, named in the attached bond.

I am eighteen years of age or over and own property worth **$ 196,960.00** over and above all encumbrances, and over and above what will pay my just debts and every sum for which I am now bail or for which I am liable as surety or endorser or otherwise.

SWORN / AFFIRMED BEFORE ME

at the **City**
of **Toronto**
in the **Province**
of **Ontario**
this   day of

_____   **James Russell Killeen**
A Commissioner for Taking Affidavits
(or as may be)

Page 2

BOND - PERSONAL SURETIES
Form 74.33
Courts of Justice Act

(insert name)

IN THE ESTATE OF   **Joyce Marie Chambers (also known as GIGI), deceased.**

The amount of this bond shall be reduced by and to the extent of any payment made under the bond pursuant to an order of the court.

The sureties are entitled to an assignment of the rights of any person who receives payment or benefit from the proceeds of this bond, to the extent of such payment or benefit received.

DATE: **June 29, (year)**

SIGNED, SEALED AND DELIVERED
in the presence of:

_____   _____
                                     Principal

_____   _____
                                     Surety
                                     James Russell Killeen

_____   _____
                                     Surety

CERTIFICATE OF APPOINTMENT
OF ESTATE TRUSTEE WITHOUT A WILL
Form 74.20
Courts of Justice Act

Court file no.

Ontario
Superior Court of Justice

(insert name) IN THE ESTATE OF **Joyce Marie Chambers (also known as GIGI), deceased,**

late of **the County of Mandolee,**

occupation **Executive,**

who died on **April 30, 20xx.**

**CERTIFICATE OF APPOINTMENT
OF ESTATE TRUSTEE WITHOUT A WILL**

Applicant	Address	Occupation
Grace Wilson	**24 Sumac Drive** **Ottawa, Ontario** **K1N 6E4**	**Bookkeeper**

This CERTIFICATE OF APPOINTMENT OF ESTATE TRUSTEE WITHOUT A WILL is hereby issued under the seal of the court to the applicant named above.

DATE: _____

_____
Registrar

Address of court office:

245 Windsor Avenue
Waterwell, Ontario
D9A 1J2

RCP-E 74.20 (November 1, 2005)

Document prepared using *estate-a-base*, by Do Process Software Ltd., Toronto, Ontario (416) 322-6111 or (866) 367-7648

(prepare backsheet)

CHAPTER 43

DISTRIBUTION OF ESTATES

This chapter covers the distribution of testate and intestate estates.

DISTRIBUTION OF ESTATES

Once the estate trustee, with or without a will, (executor or administrator) receives the certificate of appointment of estate trustee (letters probate or letters of administration), he or she may proceed to pay the deceased's debts and ultimately distribute the assets of the estate to those entitled to receive it. For clarity, in this chapter, the term **beneficiaries** describes persons benefiting under a will. Generally, the terms **heir** and **next of kin** describe persons benefiting under the *Succession Law Reform Act* since there is no will.

Testate estates   If there is a will, the estate trustee with a will (executor) deals with the estate as the will directs. A will may direct that a particular piece of property, or all of the estate, be transferred to one **beneficiary** or to a number of beneficiaries or, in many cases, to the **trustee** of the estate, who is usually the same person or corporation as the estate trustee with a will, to deal with as the will directs: for example, the testator may direct the trustee to manage the testator's estate until his children become of age, during which time, the estate must be held in the name of the trustee to enable the trustee to deal with it. The estate trustee with a will signs all of the transfer documents on behalf of the deceased. In testate estates, those beneficiaries receiving a gift of real estate under a will may sometimes be referred to as **devisees,** and those receiving a gift of personal property such as money, also referred to as a **legacy**, may sometimes be referred to as **legatees.**

Intestate estates   If there is no will, the estate trustee without a will (administrator) distributes the estate among the heirs as set out in the *Succession Law Reform Act*. See the **summary of line of inheritance** in Chapter 40. The heirs may decide among themselves who should receive which property, and the estate trustee without a will signs all of the transfer documents on behalf of the deceased.

Distribution of intestate estate   Pursuant to the provisions of the *Estates Administration Act* and the *Trustee Act*, no distribution is to take place on an intestacy for the period of one year.

> **Legal TIP**
>
> An estate trustee with a will (executor) or without a will (administrator) may be the same person as a beneficiary or heir, respectively.

NOTARIAL COPIES

Certificate of appointment of estate trustee (with or without a will) Once you receive from the court the certificate of appointment of estate trustee (with or without a will), prepare several notarial copies of it. The notarial copies serve in place of the original as proof that the estate trustee (with or without a will) has the authority to deal with the estate. Almost all agencies require a notarial copy of the certificate before they transfer property from the deceased to any beneficiaries or heirs.

To make a notarial copy of a certificate of appointment of estate trustee (with or without a will), key a notarial certificate, Precedent 43.1, for a notary (usually, the lawyer) to sign. Attach to the notarial certificate a copy of the certificate of appointment of estate trustee (with or without a will). Keep the original certificate of appointment of estate trustee (with or without a will) in the file for preparing any additional notarial copies.

Proof of death Have the estate trustee (with or without a will) bring in the death certificate (the funeral home usually provides it), and prepare notarial copies of the death certificate to submit to various agencies who might request it.

NOTICE TO CREDITORS

Generally, if the deceased operated a business or was likely to have creditors, you should publish a **notice to creditors** in a newspaper where the deceased resided. Creditors are individuals and corporations to whom the deceased owed money. Prepare the notice, Precedent 43.2, and send it to the newspaper, giving instructions as to the number of times the notice should appear in the newspaper, usually three times, and requesting proof of publishing. The newspaper usually forwards you an affidavit by one of its employees swearing to the publishing of the notice and attaching a copy of the published notice. Any unpaid creditors who do not respond are deemed to have no claim after the estate is distributed. If an estate trustee (with or without a will) fails to give notice of the death and the distribution of the estate, the estate trustee (with or without a will) could be held personally liable for any claim of a creditor of the estate.

There are also online platforms for posting legal notices such as notices to creditors. The online notices are discoverable and accessible for a period of time to any person conducting an internet search against the name of the deceased. The legal notices websites also provide notarized affidavits of publication as proof of publication, usually at an additional cost.

FINAL INCOME TAX RETURNS

If the death occurred between January 1 and October 31, the estate trustee (with or without a will) must file the final income tax return for the deceased, which an accountant usually prepares, by April 30 of the following year. If the death occurred between November 1 and December 31, the final income tax return must be filed within six months of the date of death. The estate trustee (with or without a will) should distribute the estate only after he or she receives a clearance certificate from the federal government showing no income tax owing.

DISTRIBUTION OF REAL ESTATE

Following are some commonly used documents relating to distribution of real estate. Note that the electronic precedents contain law statements (identified by **bold** lettering) which only lawyers may sign. Electronic estate documents relating to distribution of real estate are referred to as "one-party" documents because they require a signature on behalf of only the estate trustee (with or without a will). For instructions on how to log in, create a new docket, and create a new electronic (e-reg) document in Teraview, see Chapter 32.

Surviving joint tenant   Where the deceased owned real estate as a joint tenant, the surviving joint tenant (not the personal representative, unless both are the same person) must file a **survivorship application-land**, Precedent 43.3, to transfer the property to the name of the surviving joint tenant. Upon registering the survivorship application-land, the system automatically conducts an execution search against the name of the deceased. The Teraview writs tab provides the appropriate statements to either clear any outstanding writs or make the parcel register subject to any writs.

Figure 43.1   Survivorship Application — Land, Teraview

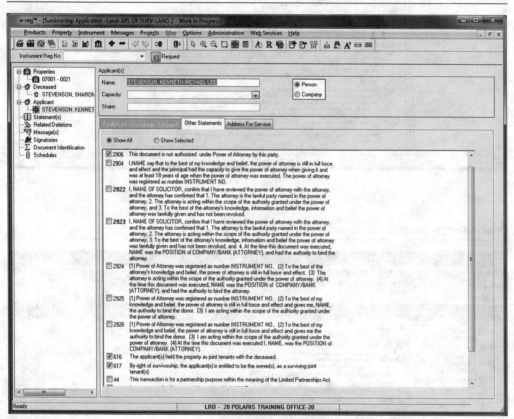

Transmission by personal representative-land   The procedure for transferring real estate involves two steps: first, the personal representative (estate trustee, with or without a will) registers himself or herself as owner of the property of the deceased by way of a **transmission by personal representative-land**, Precedent 43.4; second, the personal representative, as owner, either sells the property or transfers it to a beneficiary (devisee) or heir, as the case may be, by registering a **transfer by personal representative**, Precedent 43.5, in the same land registry office where the old transfer of land was registered. The land transfer tax statements form part of the transfer by personal representative:

Figure 43.2 Transmission by Personal Representative, Teraview

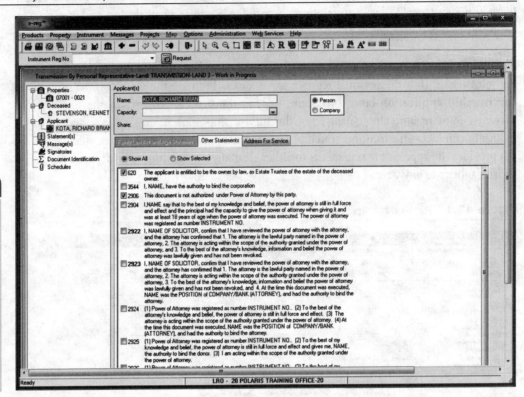

Figure 43.3 Transfer by Personal Representative, Teraview

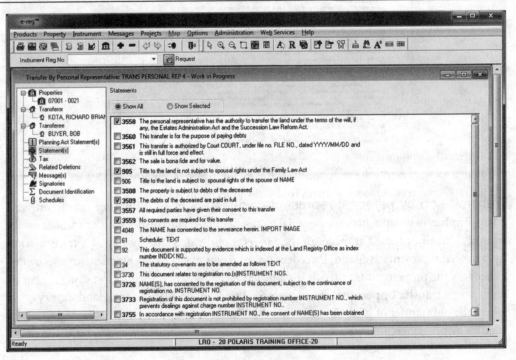

DISTRIBUTION OF PERSONAL PROPERTY

Personal property is all property that is not real estate. Personal property in the name of the deceased is usually transferred directly to the name of a beneficiary or heir, or to the name of the estate trustee (with or without a will) if the estate trustee is also a beneficiary or heir. An agency's requirement of a **declaration of transmission** is your clue that the distribution of that personal property requires a two-step process: first, the personal property is transferred to the name of the estate trustee (with or without a will); second, the estate trustee (with or without a will) as owner transfers the personal property to a beneficiary or heir. Some personal property commonly dealt with follows:

Government of Canada savings bonds To transfer government of Canada savings bonds to a beneficiary or heir, the Bank of Canada requires the following documents:

- Notarial copy of the certificate of appointment of estate trustee (with a copy of the will attached) or notarial copy of the certificate of appointment of estate trustee without a will.

- Completed Transfer Form, ETRF 2351, signed by the estate trustee (with or without a will). The signature of the estate trustee (with or without a will) must be guaranteed by the bank or the ETRF 2351 form must have been signed in front of a notary public, and the notary public must also sign and seal the form. The ETRF 2351 form is available in PDF format on the website of the Bank of Canada.

Corporate bonds and shares Generally, public corporations (corporations that trade their shares in a recognized stock exchange) have their own transfer agents who look after transferring the shares they issue. Private corporations (corporations not selling shares on the stock market) usually do not have their own transfer agents and, instead, have their corporate secretary look after the transfers. Thus, in the case of shares in a public corporation, send the transfer documents to that corporation's transfer agent. In the case of shares in a private corporation, send them to the secretary of that corporation. In the case of bonds, enquire with the corporation that issued the bonds as to where you should send the transfer documents because some corporations use independent transfer agents and others keep their own bond registers. Following is a list of some of the types of documents that transfer agents of public corporations might require in order to issue new share or bond certificates in the name of a beneficiary or heir:

- The deceased's original stock or bond certificate.
- Notarial copy of certificate of appointment of estate trustee (with or without a will).
- Declaration of transmission of shares (or bonds), Precedent 43.6.
- Power of attorney to transfer bonds-shares, Precedent 43.7.

Guaranteed investment certificates (GICs) Enquire with the trust company or bank that issued the GICs as to their own transfer requirements. Have them instruct you on the use of their own forms because the forms usually vary widely. Among the documents they are likely to require is a declaration of transmission, Precedent 43.6.

Bank and credit union accounts   The bank or credit union will require a notarial copy of the certificate of appointment of estate trustee (with or without a will). Usually, with this document, they will either close out the deceased's account and issue a bank draft payable to the estate, or convert the account to an estate account. If the estate trustee (with or without a will) transfers the account to a beneficiary or heir, enquire as to which forms the bank or credit union requires because the forms vary widely.

Joint bank accounts   If the deceased's joint bank accounts are with right of survivorship, provide the bank with the death certificate and request transfer to the surviving joint account holder.

Charges/Mortgages   Charges/mortgages are considered personal, instead of real, property because they are movable property, even though they are registered against real estate. The chargee is the deceased, i.e. the lender. A transfer of a charge/mortgage to a beneficiary (legatee) or heir enables the beneficiary or heir to receive the charge/mortgage payments that the deceased was receiving before death. Follow the same two-step procedure as for transferring land: that is, first prepare and register in the Land Titles office where the charge was registered a **transmission by personal representative-charge** (registering the estate trustee (with or without a will) as owner of the charge/mortgage), and second, a **transfer of charge** (see Chapter 34) from the estate trustee (with or without a will) to a beneficiary or heir.

RELEASE OF ESTATE TRUSTEE (WITH OR WITHOUT A WILL)

After the estate trustee (with or without a will) pays out the deceased's debts and distributes the estate, prepare a **release of estate trustee** (with or without a will), Precedent 43.8, for each beneficiary or heir to sign. The release releases the estate trustee (with or without a will) from further obligation to the beneficiaries or heirs.

WINDING UP THE ESTATE

An estate is said to be wound up when the estate trustee (with or without a will) completes the processing and distribution of the assets of the deceased's estate, obtains releases from all of the beneficiaries or heirs, receives his or her fees for having satisfactorily completed the estate, and closes out the estate bank account.

PASSING OF ACCOUNTS

Passing of accounts means the court examines the original assets of the estate, the debts paid, all moneys received and disbursed, the amounts paid to the beneficiaries or heirs, and the fees the estate trustee (with or without a will) is claiming. An estate trustee (with or without a will) must apply to the court to pass the estate accounts if:

> (a) any beneficiary or heir refuses to release the estate trustee (with or without a will) or challenges the actions of, or the handling of the estate accounts by, the estate trustee (with or without a will);

(b) there are minor or mentally incapable beneficiaries; or

(c) an estate trustee (with or without a will) voluntarily decides to pass accounts (usually because the estate is complex and the estate trustee wants court approval of the accounts).

In applying to the court to pass the accounts, the estate trustee (with or without a will) must file the following documents in court with proof of service of the * documents on each person who has an interest in the estate. If there are minor or mentally incapable beneficiaries, the * documents must also be served on the Children's Lawyer or the Public Guardian and Trustee, as the case may be, along with a copy of the will and a copy of the certificate of appointment of estate trustee:

- Accounts in accordance with rule 74.17. There is no prescribed form for accounts; see Precedent 43.9 for a simple example.

- Affidavit of the estate trustee verifying estate accounts, Form 74.43, Precedent 43.10.

- Copy of the certificate of appointment of estate trustee (with or without a will).

- *Notice of application to pass accounts, Form 74.44.

- *A blank notice of objection to accounts, Form 74.45.

- *A draft judgment the estate trustee is seeking, usually Form 74.50 or Form 74.51.

- Filing fee.

REPORTING LETTER AND ACCOUNT

It is customary to write reporting letters from time to time to the estate trustee (with or without a will) during the processing of the estate and to also enclose interim accounts so that lawyers receive payment of their fees gradually instead of waiting until the estate is completed. Lawyers write the final report and account to the estate trustee (with or without a will) when the estate is wound up and often to the beneficiaries or heirs (without an account) after the beneficiaries or heirs have received their respective shares of the deceased's estate and have signed releases.

CHAPTER SUMMARY

Once the estate trustee (with or without a will) receives from the court the certificate of appointment of estate trustee (with or without a will), the estate trustee is authorized to distribute the estate, either according to the terms of the will in testate estates, or according to the *Succession Law Reform Act* in intestate estates. Notarial copies of the certificate of appointment of estate trustee (with or without a will) are often required as evidence when distributing the estate of the deceased.

The procedure for transferring land electronically involves the estate trustee (with or without a will) registering a transmission application to transfer the land to the estate trustee as the **owner** before the estate trustee can transfer the property to a beneficiary or heir. The procedure to transfer personal property, e.g. savings bonds, shares, to a beneficiary or heir varies and depends on the policies of the individual corporation that issued the personal property. The one document they all might require, however, is a notarial copy of the certificate of appointment of estate trustee (with or without a will).

Once the estate trustee (with or without a will) has completed the distribution of the deceased's estate, the estate is said to be wound up. Generally, if any of the beneficiaries or heirs object to the amount of the estate trustee's fees or to the estate trustee's handling of the estate, the estate trustee (with or without a will) must file with the court a notice of application to pass accounts and have the court solve the outstanding issues.

REVIEW QUESTIONS

1. What are notarial copies of a certificate of appointment of estate trustee used for?
2. Which title document is used to transfer real estate to a beneficiary?
3. A transmission application is when you take your car in for transmission repairs. Explain.
4. What is the purpose of a transmission application?
5. What does a declaration of transmission accomplish?
6. In what situation would you usually prepare a power of attorney to transfer bonds/shares?
7. Who releases whom in a release of estate trustee (with or without a will)?
8. What is a survivorship application?
9. In what situation would an estate trustee be required to pass accounts?

Precedent 43.1 Notarial Certificate

NOTARIAL CERTIFICATE
OF TRUE COPY

CANADA
PROVINCE OF ONTARIO

(insert name)   I, **Robert B. Redford,**

a duly appointed notary public for the Province of Ontario, residing at the

(insert city or town and county or district, metropolitan or regional municipality of residence)   **City of Toronto,**

in the Province of Ontario, certify as follows:

1.   I have compared the attached document with a document produced and shown to me and purporting to be the original

(Applicable document)   **Certificate of Appointment of Estate Trustee With a Will in the estate of Arthur William Gold issued out of the Superior Court of Justice at Toronto dated August 15, 20xx and numbered 0-2964/xx.**

2.   The attached document is a true copy of the original.

DATE: _____

_____
Notarial Seal

_____
A Notary Public for the Province of Ontario
Robert B. Redford

Precedent 43.2 Notice to Creditors

NOTICE TO CREDITORS AND OTHERS

All claims against the estate of RUSSELL JOHN KING, late of the City of Waterwell, in the County of Mandolee, who died on or about the 9th day of June, (year), must be filed with the undersigned Personal Representative on or before the 15th day of August, (year), after which date the estate will be distributed having regard only to the claims of which the Estate Trustee then shall have notice.

DATED at Toronto, this   day of   , (year).

George Grant Orwell
Estate Trustee with a Will, by his solicitors
MICHAEL, ELIAD & REDFORD LLP
863 Seneca Lane
Toronto, ON   M4J 1P6

Precedent 43.3 Survivorship Application-Land, Electronic

**** NOT VALID - TO BE USED FOR TRAINING PURPOSES ONLY ****

This document has not been submitted and may be incomplete.
LRO # 20   **Survivorship Application -Land**

yyyy mm dd   Page 1 of 1
In preparation on 20xx 10 15   at 17:22

Properties

PIN   07001 - 0021   LT
Description LT 10 , PL 1459 ; BURLINGTON
Address   5321 BROMLEY RD
              BURLINGTON

Deceased(s)

	Capacity	Share

Name   STEVENSON, SHARON ELIZABETH ANN
                    Acting as an individual
Address for Service 5321 Bromley Road
                    Burlington, Ontario
                    L7L 3G3

Date of death was YYYY/MM/DD

The deceased and Kenneth Michael Lee Stevenson, a/the surviving joint tenant, were spouses of each other when the deceased died.

Applicant(s)

	Capacity	Share

Name   STEVENSON, KENNETH MICHAEL LEE
                    Acting as an individual
Address for Service 5321 Bromley Road
                    Burlington, Ontario
                    L7L 3G3

This document is not authorized under Power of Attorney by this party.

The applicant(s) held the property as joint tenants with the deceased.

By right of survivorship, the applicant(s) is entitled to be the owner(s), as a surviving joint tenant(s).

Precedent 43.4 Transmission by Personal Representative-Land, Electronic

**** NOT VALID - TO BE USED FOR TRAINING PURPOSES ONLY ****

This document has not been submitted and may be incomplete.
LRO # 20   **Transmission By Personal Representative-Land**

yyyy mm dd   Page 1 of 1
In preparation on 20xx 10 19   at 17:23

Properties

PIN   07001 - 0021   LT
Description LT 10 , PL 1459 ; BURLINGTON
Address   5321 BROMLEY RD
              BURLINGTON

Deceased(s)

	Capacity	Share

Name   STEVENSON, KENNETH MICHAEL LEE
                    Acting as an individual
Address for Service 5321 Bromley Road
                    Burlington, Ontario
                    L7L 3G3

Date of death was YYYY/MM/DD

Applicant(s)

	Capacity	Share

Name   KOTA, RICHARD BRIAN
                    Acting as an individual
Address for Service 36 Oakwood Avenue
                    Waterwell, Ontario
                    D4R 6D6

The applicant is entitled to be the owner by law, as Estate Trustee of the estate of the deceased owner.

This document is not authorized under Power of Attorney by this party.

Statements

The debts of the deceased are paid in full

The applicant is appointed as Estate Trustee with a will by the Ontario Superior Court of Justice Court, under file no. 05-CV-9999999, dated YYYY/MM/DD and is still in full force and effect.

**** NOT VALID - TO BE USED FOR TRAINING PURPOSES ONLY ****

This document has not been submitted and may be incomplete.   yyyy mm dd   Page 1 of 1
LRO # 20 **Transfer By Personal Representative**   **In preparation** on 20xx 04 12   at 16:49

Properties

		Interest/Estate	Fee Simple

PIN   07001 - 0021 LT
Description LT 10 , PL 1459 ; BURLINGTON
Address   5321 BROMLEY RD
             BURLINGTON

Consideration

Consideration $ 300,000.00

Transferor(s)

The transferor(s) hereby transfers the land to the transferee(s).

Name   KOTA, RICHARD BRIAN

                  Acting as an individual

Address for Service   36 Oakwood Avenue
                      Waterwell, Ontario
                      D4R 6D6

This document is not authorized under Power of Attorney by this party.

This transaction is not subject to any writs of execution. Execution search(s) completed on YYYY/MM/DD. Clear execution No(s)
28031270-1459803B against the deceased, Kenneth Michael Lee Stevenson. I Robert B. Redford confirm the appropriate party(ies)
were searched.

Transferee(s)

	Capacity	Share
	Registered Owner	

Name   BUYER, BOB

                  Acting as an individual

Date of Birth   19xx 12 25
Address for Service 5321 Bromley Road
                     Burlington, Ontario
                     L7L 3G3

Statements

The personal representative has the authority to transfer the land under the terms of the will, if any, the Estates Administration Act and
the Succession Law Reform Act.

Title to the land is not subject to spousal rights under the Family Law Act

The debts of the deceased are paid in full

No consents are required for this transfer

Calculated Taxes

Provincial Land Transfer Tax $2,975.00

**** NOT VALID - TO BE USED FOR TRAINING PURPOSES ONLY ****

LAND TRANSFER TAX STATEMENTS

In the matter of the conveyance of: 07001 - 0021 LT 10 , PL 1459 ; BURLINGTON

BY: KOTA, RICHARD BRIAN
TO: BUYER, BOB
                                          Registered Owner   %(all PINs)

1. BUYER, BOB

    I am

    ☐ (a) A person in trust for whom the land conveyed in the above-described conveyance is being conveyed;

    ☐ (b) A trustee named in the above-described conveyance to whom the land is being conveyed;

    ☑ (c) A transferee named in the above-described conveyance;

    ☐ (d) The authorized agent or solicitor acting in this transaction for ____ described in paragraph(s) (_) above.

    ☐ (e) The President, Vice-President, Manager, Secretary, Director, or Treasurer authorized to act for ____
          described in paragraph(s) (_) above.

    ☐ (f) A transferee described in paragraph ( ) and am making these statements on my own behalf and on behalf of
          who is my spouse described in paragraph (_) and as such, I have personal knowledge of the facts herein
          deposed to.

3. The total consideration for this transaction is allocated as follows:

(a) Monies paid or to be paid in cash	300,000.00
(b) Mortgages (i) assumed (show principal and interest to be credited against purchase price)	0.00
(ii) Given Back to Vendor	0.00
(c) Property transferred in exchange (detail below)	0.00
(d) Fair market value of the land(s)	0.00
(e) Liens, legacies, annuities and maintenance charges to which transfer is subject	0.00
(f) Other valuable consideration subject to land transfer tax (detail below)	0.00
(g) Value of land, building, fixtures and goodwill subject to land transfer tax (total of (a) to (f))	300,000.00
(h) VALUE OF ALL CHATTELS - items of tangible personal property	0.00
(i) Other considerations for transaction not included in (g) or (h) above	0.00
(j) Total consideration	300,000.00

PROPERTY Information Record

A. Nature of Instrument: Transfer By Personal Representative

                              LRO 20   Registration No.   Date:

B. Property(s):   PIN 07001 - 0021   Registration No.   Assessment   2402080 - 81911300
                                                                               Roll No

C. Address for Service: 5321 Bromley Road
                              Burlington, Ontario
                              L7L 3G3

D. (i) Last Conveyance(s):   PIN 07001 - 0021   Registration No.

   (ii) Legal Description for Property Conveyed : Same as in last conveyance? Yes ☑ No ☐ Not known ☐

DECLARATION OF TRANSMISSION

IN THE MATTER OF THE ESTATE OF JULIA CRAWFORD, late, of the City of Waterwell, in the County of Mandolee, in the Province of Ontario, Deceased.

I, DONALD WALLACE SHORTHILL, of 9 Francine Drive, Waterwell, Ontario, D5E 9E5

hereinafter referred to as the "Estate Trustee,"

DO SOLEMNLY DECLARE THAT:

1. The Deceased died at the City of Waterwell, in the County of Mandolee, on the 10th day of March, (year), testate, and at the date of death was resident and domiciled in the Province of Ontario.

2. A Certificate of Appointment of Estate Trustee With a Will was granted to the Estate Trustee on the 5th day of May, (year), by the Superior Court of Justice at Waterwell.

3. There are registered in the name of the Deceased on the books of Great Oke Enterprises Ltd. (hereinafter referred to as "the Company") the following shares of its capital stock:

Class of Shares	Number of Shares	Certificate Number
Preference	50	A-301-9876

4. At the date of death of the Deceased, the said certificates were physically situate in the Province of Ontario.

5. The Deceased and J. Crawford named in the certificate described above were one and the same person.

6. At the date of death of the Deceased, none of the beneficiaries of the estate of the Deceased was resident or domiciled in the Province of Quebec.

7. By virtue of the foregoing the said shares have devolved upon and become vested in the undersigned, being the sole personal representative of the Deceased, who desires to have the same recorded in the name of the Estate Trustee, Donald Wallace Shorthill, upon the register of the Company.

AND I make this solemn Declaration conscientiously believing it to be true, and knowing that it is of the same force and effect as if made under oath.

SWORN/AFFIRMED before me at the   }
City of Toronto   }
in the Province of Ontario   } _____
this   day of May, (year)   } Donald Wallace Shorthill

A Commissioner, etc.

POWER OF ATTORNEY TO TRANSFER BONDS & SHARES

KNOW ALL MEN BY THESE PRESENTS that for value received,

I, DONALD WALLACE SHORTHILL, of 9 Francine Drive, Waterwell, Ontario, D5E 9E5

the Estate Trustee of the Estate of Julia Crawford

have bargained, sold, assigned and transferred unto:

HUGH EDWARD CRAWFORD

the following shares of Great Oke Enterprises Ltd.:

Class of Shares	No. of Shares	Certificate Number	Registration
Preference	50	A-301-9876	J. Crawford

AND I DO HEREBY CONSTITUTE AND APPOINT INTERNATIONAL TRUST COMPANY

true and lawful Attorney, irrevocably, for the undersigned and in our name and stead, to transfer the said Shares, and for that purpose, to make and execute all necessary acts of assignment and transfer thereof and to substitue one or more persons with like full power, hereby ratifying and confirming all that the said Attorney or substitutes shall lawfully do by virtue hereof.

Dated at Toronto this   day of May, (year).

_____   _____
Witness to signature of Transferor   Donald Wallace Shorthill

Signature of Transferor is hereby guaranteed

RELEASE AND INDEMNITY

TO: **DONALD WALLACE SHORTHILL** (the "**Estate Trustee**")

The undersigned, HUGH EDWARD CRAWFORD, hereby irrevocably and unconditionally releases and forever discharges the Estate Trustee, including his heirs, executors and legal representatives (all such persons and entities being called the "**Releasees**"), of and from all manner of actions, causes of action, suits, demands, debts, accounts, covenants, contracts, damages and all other claims whatsoever which the undersigned, his heirs, executors and legal personal representatives (the "**Releasors**") ever had, now has or may in the future have against any of the Releasees for or by reason of any cause, matter or thing existing up to the date of this Release relating to the administration by the Estate Trustee of the Estate of JULIA CRAWFORD (the "**Estate**") as Estate Trustee and the distribution of the assets remaining in the Estate including the payment to the undersigned as a beneficiary of the sum of $50,000.00 (the "**Distribution Payment**") in the final distribution to be made by the Estate Trustee on the wind-up of the Estate, to be made upon receipt of this Release and Indemnity.

The undersigned hereby represents, warrants and covenants that he has not assigned and will not assign to any other person or entity any of the actions, causes of action, suits, demands, debts, accounts, covenants, contracts, damages and other claims which he is releasing herein.

The undersigned hereby agrees to indemnify and save harmless the Estate Trustee, in his capacity as Estate Trustee of the Estate, from and against any claim, to the extent of the percentage of the undersigned's interest in the estate, that may be made against the Estate Trustee personally with respect to any reassessment of income tax by the Canada Revenue Agency in which additional taxes are assessed as owing by the Estate from and after this date (the "**Indemnifiable Losses**"), provided that the amount of the Indemnifiable Losses, in the aggregate, shall not exceed the amount of the Distribution Payment, and such reassessment did not result from any fraud committed or misrepresentation made by the Estate Trustee.

DATED the   day of   , 20xx.

SIGNED in the presence of:)
)
)
)
_____) _____
) **Hugh Edward Crawford**

ACCOUNTS
Estate of **Wendy Joanne Zagginy**
Date of Death: November 11, 20–

Inventory of Assets as at November 11, 20–

100,000 Canada Savings Bond, Certificate #6	$100,000.00
3,000 Shares XYZ, Certificate #10	150,000.00
Bank Account 123-45678	50,000.00
	300,000.00

Capital Receipts

1. 03/12/-- Bank Account	50,000.00
2. 03/12/-- Bank Account accrued interest	100.00
3. 02/01/-- 100,000 CSB redeemed	100,000.00
4. 02/01/-- 100,000 CSB accrued interest	2,000.00
5. 15/01/-- 3,000 Shares XYZ sold	160,000.00
Total Capital Receipts	312,100.00

Capital Disbursements

1. 15/11/-- Funeral Account	10,000.00
2. 15/11/-- Cemetery Inscription	100.00
3. 18/11/-- Minister of Finance Estate Administration Tax	4,000.00
4. 13/12/-- Notice to Creditors	150.00
5. 14/12/-- Receiver General, Income Tax	13,903.83
6. 15/01/– Interim Distribution	250,000.00
7. 18/01/-- Lawyer's Fees	1,200.00
Total Disbursements	279,353.83

Estate Trustee's Compensation

Capital

Total Receipts	$312,100.00 at 2.5%	7,802.50
Total Disbursements	$279,353.85 at 2.5%	6,983.85
Total Compensation Claimed		14,786.35

Care and management fees: none claimed

Money on Hand at End of Period

Capital Receipts	$312,100.00	
Total Disbursements $279,353.83 + $14,786.35	- 294,140.18	17,959.82

No outstanding liabilities

AFFIDAVIT VERIFYING ESTATE ACCOUNTS
Form 74.43
Courts of Justice Act

Ontario
Superior Court of Justice

(insert name) IN THE ESTATE OF **Wendy Joanne Zagginy**, deceased.

AFFIDAVIT VERIFYING ESTATE ACCOUNTS

(insert name) I, **David Daniel Eagle,**

(insert city or town and county or district, metropolitan or regional municipality of residence) of **the City of Toronto, in the Province of Ontario,**

make oath and say / affirm:

1.   I am an estate trustee for this estate.

2.   The accounts marked as Exhibit "A" to this affidavit are complete and correct.

3.   The information contained in the notice of application to pass accounts with respect to this estate is true.

4.   All person having a financial interest in the estate are named as respondents in the notice of application to pass accounts.

5.   For any party with a disability, a representative has been identified in the notice of application.

SWORN / AFFIRMED BEFORE ME

at the **City**
of **Toronto**
in the **Province**
of **Ontario**
this   day of

_____   _____
A Commissioner for Taking Affidavits
(or as may be)   **David Daniel Eagle**
                                                                RCP-E 74.43 (November 1, 2005)

Document prepared using *estate-a-base,* by Do Process Software Ltd., Toronto, Ontario (416) 322-6111 or (866) 367-7648

Glossary

A

abstract book a book in which the land registry office keeps land ownership records, under the registry system.

abode place of residence.

abutting touching along a boundary of land.

acceptance of service a lawyer's personal acknowledgment of receipt of a document on behalf of a client, as well as confirmation that the lawyer represents that client in the action.

access a parent's right to visit his or her child.

account a lawyer's bill to a client.

act a written law; a statute; legislation.

action a civil lawsuit.

ad hoc for this purpose.

ADR alternative dispute resolution; a mediation process for settling issues out of court.

administration *de bonis non administratis* see succeeding estate trustee without a will.

admission of service a lawyer's acknowledgment of receipt of a document on behalf of a client.

adverse party an opposite party to an action.

adverse possession see possessory title.

adverse witness a witness giving testimony in favour of an opposite party.

affidavit a document stating facts which a person swears to be true.

age of majority legal age or the age at which a person is deemed to be an adult under the law. In Ontario it is 18 years.

agenda a list of issues to be discussed at a meeting.

a.m. before noon; Latin: *ante meridiem*.

amalgamation the merging or joining together of two or more companies to form one company.

amortize provisions for payment of a debt by fixed periodic payments, calculated to repay the debt, plus interest, over a stated period of time.

annex to attach.

application a civil lawsuit commenced by a notice of application or a court document which begins a family law case.

appurtenant inseparably connected, e.g. an easement or a covenant attached to a piece of land.

articles of amalgamation a document which joins together two or more companies.

articles of amendment a document which revises the articles of incorporation.

articles of incorporation a document which creates a business corporation.

assessment of costs a court officer's examining of a lawyer's fees and disbursements in a bill of costs to ensure the amounts comply with the tariff.

assessment officer a court officer who determines that the fees and disbursements in a bill of costs or in a lawyer's account to the client are correct.

assignee a person who receives rights from an assignor and who can enforce those rights against another.

assignment of mortgage see transfer of charge.

assignor a person who gives rights to an assignee and who can no longer enforce those rights against another.

assumption statement a statement indicating how much principal and interest is outstanding on a charge or mortgage to be assumed.

at arm's length a transaction between two unrelated people or strangers.

ats. at the suit of.

attendance money money paid to a witness for attending to testify.

auditor a public accountant authorized by law to examine the accounts of a corporation on behalf of the shareholders.

B

bail money or other security given as guarantee that an accused will appear in court at all stages of a proceeding.

bar of dower formerly, the relinquishing of a widow's right to a one-third life interest in her husband's real property.

barrister and solicitor a Canadian lawyer; as a barrister, the lawyer argues cases in court; as a solicitor, the lawyer practises in all other areas of law.

beneficiary a person to whom something is given in a will.

bequeath to give personal property by will (archaic).

bequest a gift of property by will.

bigamy marrying while being already married.

bill of costs a court document itemizing a lawyer's fees and disbursements for a party who won judgment and costs.

board of directors persons that a corporation's shareholders elect to manage the affairs of the corporation.

bona fide in good faith.

bond a document by which the estate trustee without a will and another person(s) or companies called sureties pledge to pay a sum of money to the court if the estate trustee fails to lawfully administer the estate.

breach of contract a failure to perform obligations under the terms of a contract.

bulk sale a sale of all, or a large part of, the assets of a business.

by-laws rules and regulations of a corporation.

C

call to the bar   the formal admission to the practice of law.

capital   the total amount of money or property which owners invest in their business.

case citation   a formal way of writing a decided case.

case law   a law based on judicial precedent rather than on legislation; also, common law.

case management   involves automation of the courts for faster processing of cases. Also, the court assigns a judge to a case. The judge manages the case all the way to trial, but a different judge must try it.

caveat emptor   let the buyer beware.

certificate of appointment of estate trustee with a will   a court document appointing an estate trustee in testate estates.

certificate of appointment of estate trustee without a will   a court document appointing an estate trustee in intestate estates.

certificate of divorce   a document indicating a divorce has become final.

certificate of incorporation   a document which certifies that a corporation is duly incorporated.

charge   a debt using real property as security.

chargee   in a charge, the lender.

chargor   in a charge, the borrower.

chattels   personal property that is movable, e.g. a car.

Children's Lawyer   a government-appointed lawyer for the purpose of protecting the rights of minors in legal proceedings.

citation   the correct written expression of statutes and and case law.

closing date   the date on which a real estate transaction is completed.

codicil   a legal document amending a will.

cohabitation agreement   a contract between spouses who agree to live together but who are not married to each other.

cohabitation   living together as spouses in common law.

collateral   something a borrower pledges to a lender as security for a loan. If the loan is not paid, the lender has rights against the collateral.

collusion   in divorce, an agreement between the spouses that one of them will commit an act in order that the other will have grounds for a divorce action.

commercial law   the area of law which deals with business transactions.

commissioner   a person authorized by law to place people under oath when they wish to swear to the truth of statements they have made in an affidavit. Lawyers are automatically commissioners. Non-lawyers may apply to the Attorney General to become commissioners for a specified period of time.

committee of adjustment   a committee which a municipality appoints under the Planning Act to rule on applications for severance of real property and other planning matters; also, land division committee.

common elements   in a condominium, those parts of the condominium owned in common by all the unit owners, e.g. land, elevators.

common elements expenses   in a condominium, payments that unit owners make toward the cost of maintaining the common elements.

common law   see case law.

common law spouses   spouses who live together as husband and wife, but who are not married.

common shares   shares of a corporation having voting rights but no special privileges.

condominium   a system of land ownership of individual units within a multi-unit structure, e.g. an apartment.

conflict of interest   a lawyer representing parties of opposing interests.

connivance   in divorce, one spouse willfully permitting the other spouse to commit adultery.

consideration   value given by one person to another for the purpose of forming a contract.

consumer goods   goods purchased for family or domestic use, as opposed to goods purchased for re-sale.

contingency fee   a legal fee charged only upon winning the case.

contingency fund   in condominiums, part of the common elements expense moneys are placed in this fund to pay for future large capital expenses such as major repairs; also, reserve fund.

contract   a legally binding agreement between two people.

conveyance   in real estate, transfer of title from one person to another.

corollary relief   in divorce, a claim for relief in addition to divorce, e.g. support and custody.

costs   a sum of money the court awards in a judgment to the successful party toward payment of legal expenses.

counsel   a lawyer who deals with court matters; a barrister; see lawyer.

counterclaim   a pleading in which a defendant makes a claim against the plaintiff or another person, within the same action.

covenant   an agreement or promise made in a legal document.

creditor   a person to whom money is owed.

cross-examination   a questioning of a witness under oath by a lawyer for the opposite party.

crossclaim   a pleading in which one defendant makes a claim against another defendant.

custody   the legal right of a parent to keep his or her children.

D

damages   monetary compensation which a court awards for loss suffered as a result of negligence or breach of contract.

date of closing   see closing date.

day book   in the land registry system, a book in which brief details are entered of documents that have not yet been abstracted.

debenture   a document which a corporation gives to a lender for security of a loan of money.

debtor   one who owes a debt.

declaration of possession   a document stating the vendor has been in possession of the property being sold so as to eliminate claims of possessory title by others.

declaration of transmission   a document which transfers bonds and shares from a deceased person to a beneficiary.

deed   see transfer.

default judgment   a judgment the court gives in favour of a plaintiff when the defendant fails to defend the action.

defendant   the party who is being sued.

deliver   to serve and file a pleading.

deponent   a person who makes (swears) an affidavit.

devise   a gift of real property by will.

direction   a document authorizing someone to do something.

direction regarding funds   a document authorizing money to be paid to a person's lawyer instead of to the person himself or herself.

direction regarding title   a document telling the vendor how to describe the purchaser in a transfer of land.

directors   see board of directors.

disbursements   expenses lawyers pay on behalf of their clients.

discharge statement   a document setting out the balance outstanding to pay off a charge/mortgage.

discharge   to pay off a charge/mortgage.

discovery   the stage in a civil law suit where the parties reveal to each other the relevant evidence in the case.

dividends   the profits of a corporation paid to its shareholders.

divorce   the permanent dissolution of a marriage.

docket   a form on which lawyers record the time spent on behalf of a client.

documentary evidence   evidence given by way of documents, e.g. affidavits.

domestic contract   contracts between spouses, e.g. marriage, cohabitation, and separation agreements.

domicile   place of a person's permanent residence.

donor   a person who makes a gift to another.

double probate   see succeeding estate trustee with a will.

dower   see bar of dower.

E

E. & O. E.   abbreviation for errors and omissions excepted, usually typed at the foot of accounts.

easement   a right over the land of another, such as a right of way.

e.g.   for example. Latin: *exempli gratia.*

encroachment   one person's unauthorized taking or adding to his or her own land an adjoining part of another person's land.

encumbrance   a liability charged against real property, e.g. a charge/mortgage.

enure   see inure.

enter   in litigation, submitting documents such as judgments and orders to the court for microfilming.

equalization payment   the net family property of spouses, at dissolution of their marriage, divided in half.

equity   a concept of justice and fairness applied to a case where the application of strict rules of common law would be unjust.

escheat   land reverting to the Crown.

escrow   to hold something in trust for another until the happening of an agreed event.

esquire or Esq.   The degree below a knight. Today, used as equivalent of Mr. and is placed following a lawyer's name.

estate   in estates, all real and personal property the deceased owned at the date of his or her death.

estate trustee with a will   a person named in a will to represent the estate of a deceased person; also executor/trix.

estate trustee without a will   a court appointed person to administer the estate of a person who died without a will.

et al   and others.

ex officio   by reason of office.

ex parte   a motion or an application having no opposing party.

examination for discovery   in litigation, an oral questioning of the opposite party.

examination in aid of execution   a questioning of a person against whom the court gave judgment to determine how that person should pay the judgment.

execution   the formal signing and witnessing of a legal document. Also, a writ of seizure and sale.

execution search   a search for any writs of seizure and sale filed with the sheriff.

executor   a male person named in a will to represent the estate of a deceased person; see estate trustee with a will.

executrix   feminine gender of executor.

F

factum a court document setting out the main facts and the statute and case law which support the case at hand.

fee simple the most absolute type of land ownership.

fiduciary a person who holds something in trust.

final order a court order which disposes of the entire proceeding, as opposed to an interlocutory order.

financial statement in family law, a court document showing the value of a spouse's property and debts.

financing change statement a document used to register a change in a financing statement.

financing statement a document used to register a security interest.

foreclosure a litigation action by which a chargee or mortgagee becomes the legal owner of real property after the chargor or mortgagor has defaulted in payment.

G

garnishment a procedure by which money owing by another person is applied to payment of the first person's debt to a third person.

general account the bank account of a law firm in which it keeps its own money.

general partnership a partnership in which there are no limited partners.

H

hearing the trial in applications and motions; also used to mean trial.

heir/heir at law a blood relative entitled to inherit under an intestate estate.

holograph will an entirely handwritten will.

I

i.e. that is; that is to say. Latin: *id est.*

indictable offence a more serious crime than a summary offence.

injunction a court order requiring a party to do or to stop doing something.

instrument a legal document.

inter alia among other things.

inter vivos in estates, a gift made while the parties are living, and not upon death, as in a will.

interim relief in family law, an order for support or custody until the proceeding is heard.

interlocutory order a court order, usually sought by way of a motion, that decides on a problem within a proceeding, but not on the entire proceeding.

intestate a person who dies having left no will.

inure to vest; to take effect for the benefit of another.

issue in estates, children or descendants; in litigation, a point in dispute; also, a court officer's signing of an originating process.

issued share in corporations, a sold share.

J

JD or **J.D.** Juris Doctor degree; it is a United States designation that is equivalent to LLB. It is used by Canadian lawyers who, like United States lawyers, usually have completed an undergraduate degree before entering law school to distinguish their degree from that of lawyers in Britain where students can attend law school straight out of high school.

joint custody an order giving custody to both parents; usually, this gives both parents input into decisions concerning the health, education, and welfare of the children, but the children may ordinarily reside with one parent.

joint tenants two or more persons owning real property together, with right of survivorship. Upon the death of one joint tenant, the property automatically passes to the surviving joint tenant(s).

jointly and severally rights and obligations shared collectively, as well as individually, as in partnerships.

judgment a final decision of the court handed down after trial.

jurat that part of an affidavit which begins with "Sworn before me..."

jurisprudence judicial decisions.

L

LL.B or **LLB** bachelor of laws degree.

land transfer tax tax payable on the purchase of real estate.

lawyer in Ontario litigation lawyers are referred to as lawyers (as opposed to counsel, solicitor, or barrister).

lawyer of record a lawyer acting in a case; also lawyer with carriage.

lease a document by which a landlord allows a tenant to use the landlord's property for a specified period of time, in return for the tenant's payment of rent.

leave court permission.

legislation see statute.

lessee a person who rents real property from the owner; a tenant.

lessor an owner of land who leases it to a lessee; a landlord.

letters of administration see certificate of appointment of estate trustee without a will.

letters probate see certificate of appointment of estate trustee with a will.

lien a legal right over the property, real or personal, of another, for a debt which the owner of the property owes.

life estate ownership of land extending only during the lifetime of the owner of the life estate (the "life tenant").

limitation period a period of time after which an individual loses his or her right to sue.

limited liability in corporate law, the fact that a shareholder is not liable for the debts of the corporation; his or her obligations are limited to the amount paid for the shares.

limited liability partnership a partnership where a partner is not liable for wrongdoings by other partners.

limited partnership a partnership which consists of a partner who has agreed to limit his or her obligation for the partnership's debts to the amount of money he or she has invested in the partnership.

liquidated damages a claim for monetary compensation for a debt owing, the amount of which can be clearly calculated, as in a loan.

litigation administrator a person whom the court appoints for the purpose of defending a deceased's estate in a lawsuit.

litigation guardian a person who represents a litigant under disability, e.g. a minor.

local registrar the administrative officer in a court office.

M

master a judicial officer with less jurisdiction than a judge.

master business licence a business licence which the government issues after a person registers a business name.

matrimonial home in family law, a real property the spouses use as their family home; the non-owner spouse has a right to possession of it, i.e. to live in it.

metes and bounds a land description which describes the parcel of land by stating the length and compass bearing of each boundary line.

minor a person who has not reached the age of majority.

mortgage see charge.

mortgagee see chargee.

mortgagor see chargor.

motion a request for a court decision on a problem within a proceeding.

municipality a county, district, regional municipality, city, town, borough, or township. It has an elected council and enacts by-laws.

N

N.B. note or mark well. Latin: *nota bene*.

natural person in corporate law, a corporation is deemed to be a natural person, as opposed to a human individual.

net family property the net value of property that married spouses accumulate during marriage.

next of kin a blood relative of a person who is deceased.

notarial certificate a certificate which a notary public signs and attaches to a copy of a document to certify that the copy is identical to the original.

notarial copy a copy of a document to which a notarial certificate is attached.

notary public a person empowered to authenticate documents and place people under oath. Lawyers and non-lawyers may become notaries public by applying to the Attorney General.

notice of application an originating process which begins an application, as opposed to an action.

notice of motion a court document requesting a court order to solve a problem during a proceeding.

noting pleadings closed instructing the local registrar to note in the court file that the time for serving pleadings is passed and that those parties who have not already delivered a pleading may no longer do so.

O

official examiner a person whom the Crown appoints to hold examinations for discovery and other examinations.

official guardian an officer of the provincial government who protects the interests of children involved in legal proceedings.

order a court decision resulting from a motion; also used to mean judgment.

originating process a document that begins a proceeding, e.g. statement of claim, petition for divorce, notice of application.

outstanding share in corporations, a sold share.

P

paralegal in Ontario, a licensed person authorized to provide legal services in specified areas of law; in most other provinces/territories, a person trained in legal work who may work under the supervision of a lawyer.

parcel register a land registry record/book which summarizes the history of ownership of properties registered under the land titles system.

partial indemnity a lower scale of fees and disbursements which a judge awards to a winning party.

partition a court ordering the division of real property held in joint tenancy, resulting in distinct portions.

partnership a joint enterprise which people undertake with the intention of making profit.

party in litigation, a person named in a title of proceeding.

passing of accounts court review of estate accounts.

per by or on behalf of a law firm.

per annum per year.

per capita equal division of an estate among beneficiaries on the basis of head count.

per diem per day.

perfection registration of a security agreement.

per se in or of itself.

personal property property that is not real estate, e.g. a car, equipment.

personalty personal property.

per stirpes division of an estate on the basis of representation of the same lineal stock, or the same family. The beneficiary takes the share to which his or her deceased ancestor would have been entitled.

petition for divorce a court document that begins a divorce action; now, application.

petitioner the person who sues for divorce; now, applicant.

plaintiff the person who begins a lawsuit.

pleadings in actions, documents which state a party's case, e.g. statement of claim, statement of defence.

p.m. after noon; Latin: *post meridiem*.

possessory title the "title" acquired to real property by virtue of continuous, open, undisturbed possession of such property, in the registry system, not in the land titles system.

postjudgment interest interest payable on an amount awarded after a judgment is given.

power of attorney a document authorizing one person to act for another as agent in a specific matter or in general.

power of sale a clause in a charge (or mortgage) which empowers the chargee, upon the chargor's default in payment, to sell the property to satisfy the debt.

preamble the opening paragraph of certain legal documents and statutes.

prebilling report a printout of an account before billing the client.

precedent a court decision which other judges may follow in deciding on a similar case; an example of a legal document followed in preparing another similar document.

preference shares a class of shares which usually gives its owners a right to payment of dividends before the owners of another class of shares and a right to share in the assets of the corporation when the corporation is dissolved, before the owners of another class of shares; also, special shares.

prejudgment interest interest payable on an amount before judgment is given.

preliminary hearing a hearing, not a trial, to determine whether there is sufficient evidence to try the accused in a higher court.

premises land, including the building and other structures on it.

prescription in real estate, a person becoming an owner of another's property, e.g. an easement, after a certain period of open and uninterrupted use.

prima facie on the face of it; at first glance.

principal the original amount of a loan.

privileged communication that cannot be disclosed in evidence because the law considers it to be confidential, e.g. communication between lawyer and client.

privy council the cabinet of the federal government.

probate the procedure by which the court determines the validity of a will.

pro bono for the good of the public.

procedural law the law which prescribes the practice and procedure (steps) to follow in putting the substantive law into practice.

proceeding a civil lawsuit.

pro forma made or done for form in advance, as an invoice.

property taxes taxes that a municipal government levies against owners of real property.

proprietorship an unincorporated business which one person owns.

proxy a document that empowers another person to vote in the place of the former person in a shareholders' meeting.

Public Guardian and Trustee a person the government appoints to oversee the administration of trusts for persons who are incapable of managing their own affairs.

public utilities such services as hydro, water, and gas supplied to homes and businesses.

Q

Q.C. Queen's Counsel. In England, a special title the government awards to lawyers considered to be worthy to argue cases for the Crown. In Canada, the title is often also awarded to lawyers who have never argued cases in court and who are often favoured by the government of the day. In 1985, the government of Ontario discontinued new awards.

quasi-criminal an offence which resembles a crime; a provincial offence.

quit claim deed a deed that serves as a release of any interest, title, or claim a person may have on a real property.

quorum the minimum number of persons required to be present at a corporate meeting to give validity to the decisions of the meeting.

R

realty taxes see property taxes.

registrar the head administrative officer of the court; supervisor of all local registrars.

relief some form of compensation a party seeks the court to award.

requisitions a lawyer's demand requiring a vendor's lawyer to correct any defects on title before the purchaser will accept title.

reserve fund see contingency fund.

resolutions formal decisions of directors and of shareholders.

respondent a person defending an application or a divorce action.

retainer a document a client signs to indicate the terms of hiring of a lawyer to act on his or her behalf in some legal matter.

right of way the right of a person to pass over another person's land.

right to possession of matrimonial home   the right of a non-owner spouse to live in the matrimonial (family) home which the other spouse owns.

riparian owner   owner of land which contains a spring or body of water.

S

secured party   generally, a lender whose loan is secured by personal or real property as guarantee of payment.

security agreement   a contract under which a creditor receives security (guarantee) on personal property as collateral for a loan.

security interest   the right of a creditor over personal property of a debtor.

separation agreement   a contract between spouses setting out the terms under which they wish to live separate and apart from each other.

severance   in real estate, the dividing of one parcel of land into two or more parcels.

sheriff   an officer of the Crown having various duties, including execution of writs of seizure and sale.

sole proprietorship   see proprietorship.

special damages   damages that can be calculated exactly.

special resolution   a resolution of the shareholders requiring a two-thirds majority vote to pass.

special shares   see preference shares.

specific performance   a court order requiring a party who has breached a contract to perform or to finish his or her obligations under the contract.

spousal consent   the consent, by way of signature, of a non-owner spouse to the sale or charging (mortgaging) of the matrimonial home.

squatter's rights   see possessory title.

stare decisis   rule of precedent. A previous court decision which the court must follow in similar cases.

statement of adjustments   in real estate, a statement listing the amounts of money credited to each of the purchaser and the vendor to be applied toward the purchase price of real property.

statement of claim   an originating process that begins an action.

statement of defence   a pleading setting out the defendant's case.

status certificate   a certificate which a condominium corporation gives to a purchaser, showing whether or not the owner of the unit being purchased has paid all common elements expenses.

statute   a law; an act; legislation.

statute citation   the formal written name of an act.

statutory declaration   a document parallel to an affidavit by which a party declares, as opposed to swears, the facts in it are true.

subpoena   a document requiring a person to attend and give testimony in court.

substantial indemnity   a higher scale of fees and disbursements which a judge awards to a winning party.

substantive law   the theory of law.

succeeding estate trustee with a will   an alternate estate trustee named in the will who is appointed to settle the rest of the deceased's estate left unfinished because of the death of the estate trustee who was originally named in the will.

succeeding estate trustee without a will   an estate trustee appointed to settle the rest of a deceased intestate estate because of the death of the original estate trustee.

summary offence   a less serious crime than an indictable offence; also, summary conviction offence.

summons   a call to appear in court.

summons to a witness   see subpoena.

support   in family law, money one spouse pays for living expenses of the other spouse and/or of children.

surety   a person who has signed a bond.

survivorship application   a document a surviving joint tenant registers in the land titles system to transfer the deceased's share of the property to his or her name only.

T

tariff   in civil litigation, a schedule of fees which the provincial government establishes for use in bills of costs; in non-litigation matters, a schedule of fees established by agreement among lawyers through law associations.

task reminder   an online system reminding of due dates.

tax certificate   a certificate which a municipality issues stating the amount of realty taxes owing on a property.

tenants in common   in real estate, a manner of holding title, giving each owner no right of survivorship.

testate   having left a will.

testator   a male person who makes a will.

testatrix   a female person who makes a will.

testimonium clause   a clause at a place in a document where a party signs.

third party claim   a defendant's claim against a new party within the same action.

tickler system   see task reminder.

title   ownership of real estate.

title insurance   a policy of insurance which insures over some problems on title in real estate.

title of proceeding   that part of a court document which names the parties to a law suit.

title search   a search made through land registry records to establish the history of ownership of real property.

tort   a wrongful or negligent act causing harm or injury.

trade name   another name by which a corporation transacts business.

transaction   in real estate, the purchase and sale of property.

transfer   in real estate, the document used to transfer title to a new owner.

transfer of charge   a document used when the chargee sells the charge; also, assignment of mortgage.

transferee   the person who receives title to real property, e.g. a purchaser.

transferor   the person who transfers title to real property to a new owner, e.g. a vendor.

transmission application   a document filed in the land titles office to have title transferred to the name of the personal representative of a deceased owner to enable the personal representative to deal with the property.

true copy   a copy that is identical to the original.

trust account   a bank account in which lawyers must keep money in trust for clients.

trustee   in estates, the executor.

U

unanimous shareholder agreement   an agreement by which all of the shareholders of a corporation agree to take away all or part of the powers of the directors.

unconscionable   terms of a contract so unreasonable as to render the contract invalid.

undertaking   a written promise to do something.

undue influence   pressure put on a person to benefit the person who pressures.

unliquidated damages   estimated damages that require the court to determine.

utilities   see public utilities.

V

v. or **v**   versus or against.

valuation date   date of separation in family law or death in estates, for purposes of calculating net family property.

vendor   in real estate, a person who is selling real property.

venue   the place of trial.

verification of identity   a process by which lawyers must verify the identity of their clients.

W

waiver   a document by which a person surrenders a legal right.

warrant   a court order for the arrest of a person.

warranty   an assurance or guarantee.

will   a legal document outlining how a person wishes his or her property to be dealt with after his or her death.

winding up   the process of completing and settling a deceased's estate.

without prejudice   a letter or document that cannot be used as evidence in court.

work order   an order which a building department gives to an owner of real property to do repair work to a building. It is a lien upon the land.

writ of execution   see writ of seizure and sale.

writ of seizure and sale   a court document ordering the sheriff to attempt to recover money from a judgment debtor on an unpaid judgment; also, writ of execution.

Z

zoning   a municipality's regulating of areas for certain purposes.

Index to Precedents

A

Abstract Book Registry System 578
Acceptance of Offer to Settle 222
Acceptance of Service Endorsement 117
Account and Trust Statement, Manually Prepared 39
Accounts, Sample (Passing of Accounts) 789
Acknowledgement and Direction re Electronic Registration 672
Acknowledgment and Direction re Title Insurance 673
Acknowledgment of charge 619
Acknowledgment of Tenancy 631
Admission of Service Endorsement 117
Affidavit 113
Affidavit as to Writs of Execution 635
Affidavit (General), (in Support of Motion), Family Law 362
Affidavit in Support of a Motion 269
Affidavit in Support of Application 246
Affidavit of Documents (Individual) 198
Affidavit of Execution of Will 720
Affidavit of Service by Facsimile Stamp 117
Affidavit of Service by Mail (on Lawyer of Record) 116
Affidavit of Service by Mail Stamp 117
Affidavit of Service by Personal Service - Originating Process 115
Affidavit of Service of Notice (with a Will) 746
Affidavit of Service of Notice (without a Will) 770
Affidavit Verifying Estate Accounts (Passing of Accounts) 790
Agreement of Purchase and Sale 568
Amalgamation Agreement 543
Answers on Written Examination for Discovery 202
Applicant's Notice, Mandatory Information Program 364
Application for Certificate of Appointment of Estate Trustee with a Will (Corporate Applicant) 753
Application for Certificate of Appointment of Estate Trustee with a Will (Individual Applicant) 740
Application for Certificate of Appointment of Estate Trustee without a Will (Individual Applicant) 765
Application Record 249
Application to Change Name — Owners, Electronic 591
Articles of Amalgamation 545
Articles of Amendment, Change of Corporate Name 540
Articles of Incorporation 468
Articles of Incorporation, Electronic 474
Assumption Letter 632

B

Bill of Costs 233
Bill of Costs, in Default Judgment 291
Block Letter Style 63
Bond, Personal Sureties 772
Brief of Authorities 230
By-law No. 1 486
By-law No. 2 489

C

Certificate of Appointment of Estate Trustee with a Will 750
Certificate of Estate Trustee without a Will 774
Certificate of Financial Disclosure 349
Certificate of Incorporation, Electronic 476
Certified Copy of Special Resolution 506
Charge/Mortgage, Monthly Payments, Electronic 606
Charge/Mortgage, Monthly Payments, Paper 607
Client Identification and Verification, Corporation 26
Client Identification and Verification, Individual 25
Codicil 721
Cohabitation Agreement, Modern Style 310
Commercial Lease 558
Confirmation of Application 254
Confirmation of Motion 274
Consent to Act as Director 503, 504
Consent to Act as First Director 476
Consent to Act re Conflict 655
Consent to Applicant's Appointment as Estate Trustee with a Will 749
Consent to Applicant's Appointment as Estate Trustee without a Will 771
Consent to Exemption from Audit 527
Continuing Record 381
Costs Outline 275

D

Declaration of Possession 665
Declaration of Transmission 786
Defence, Small Claims Court 96
Defence to Counterclaim 179
Direction Regarding Charge/Mortgage Back 634
Direction Regarding Funds 634
Direction Regarding Title 670
Direction to Enforce Writ 297
Directors' Register 496, 529
Discharge of Charge, Electronic 616
Discharge of Charge/Mortgage, Form 3, Paper 617
Discharge Statement 615
Discovery Plan 195
Document Registration Agreement 666

E

Electronically Generated Account 38
Electronic Client List of Law Firm, Excerpt, PCLaw 24
Electronic Client List of Lawyer, Excerpt, PCLaw 24
Electronic Transfer, Joint Tenants 590
Employee Confidentiality Agreement 9
Estate Information Return 755
Excerpt from the Dominion Law Reports, the Chantal Daigle Abortion Case 76

F

Factum 250
Financial Statement (Support Claims) 353
Financing Change Statement/Change Statement, Form 2C 562
Financing Statement/Claim for Lien, Form 1C 561
Form 6B: Affidavit of Service 406
Form 8A: Application (Divorce), Simple 432
Form 8: Application (General) 384
Form 10: Answer (Divorce) 416
Form 10A: Reply (Divorce) 420
Form 13.1: Financial Statement (Property and Support Claims) 389
Form 13B: Net Family Property Statement (Divorce) 426
Form 14C: Confirmation (Divorce) 429
Form 17A: Case Conference Brief - General (Divorce) 423
Form 17: Conference Notice, Family Law 422
Form 25A: Divorce Order 430
Form 35.1: Affidavit in Support of Claim for Custody or Access 399
Form 36: Affidavit for Divorce 435
Form 36B: Certificate of Divorce 431
Full and Final Release 278
Full Block Letter Style 62

G

General Security Agreement 560

I

Information for Court Use 149
Initial Return, Mandamo 507
Interoffice Memorandum, Block Style 77

J

Judgment 231
Judgment, Default 292
Judgment (in Applications) 255
Jury Notice 168

L

Land Transfer Tax Affidavit, Paper 677
Land Transfer Tax Statements, Electronic 676
Lawyer's Expense Sheet 34
Letter for Closing 637
Letter of Requisitions 668
Letter Regarding Title 656
Letter to Building Department 658
Letter to Court Enclosing Application for Certificate of Appointment Documents 752
Letter to Tax Department 658
Letter to Water/Hydro/Gas - Title Insurance 657

M

Marriage Certificate, Havisham 380
Marriage Contract, Traditional Style 307
Master Business Licence, General Partnership 449
Medical Authorization 156
Memorandum of Law 78
Minute Book and Corporate Seals 485
Minutes of a Meeting of Directors (Post annual) 524
Minutes of Annual Meeting of Shareholders 522
Minutes of Meeting of Directors (Pre-annual) 519
Motion Record 272

N

Notarial Certificate 783
Notarial Copy of Articles of Incorporation 505
Notice of Action (General) 150

Notice of an Application for a Certificate of Appointment of Estate Trustee with a Will 743
Notice of an Application for a Certificate of Appointment of Estate Trustee without a Will 768
Notice of Annual Meeting (of Shareholders) 520
Notice of Appearance 248
Notice of Application 243
Notice of Change, Mandamo Properties Ltd. 533
Notice of Examination (for Discovery) 201
Notice of Intent to Defend 162
Notice of Motion 265
Notice of Motion, Temporary Order, Family Law 360
Notice of Readiness for Pre-trial Conference, Simplified Procedure 133
Notice of Transfer of Charge 619
Notice to Creditors 783
NUANS Search 475

O

Offence Notice 98
Offer to Settle 221
Officers' Register 497
One-Client Template Docket 36
One-Day Template Docket 36
Ontario Child Support Guidelines 333
Order 271
Order 277
Order (General), Temporary, Family Law 363

P

Parcel Register 577
Partnership Agreement, Modern Style 447
Partnership Agreement, Traditional Style 445
PIN 07001-0001 (LT) West Boundary 705
PIN 07001-0668 (LT) North Boundary 702
PIN 07001-0669 (LT) East Boundary 704
PIN 07001-0670 (LT) Our Lands Chart 706
PIN 07001-0670 (LT) to Our Lands 701
PIN 07001-0670 (LT) Abutting Lands Chart 706
PIN 07001-0671 (LT) South Boundary 703
PIN 24916-0001 (LT) LT Absolute Title 707
Plaintiff's Claim, Small Claims Court 94
Postponement of Interest, Electronic 620
Power of Attorney for Personal Care 724
Power of Attorney for Property 722

Power of Attorney to Transfer Bonds-Shares 787
Pre-Billing Report 37
Pre-trial Conference Brief/Memorandum, Toronto Region 216
Proof of Death Certificate 739
Property Index Map 576
Property Index Map to PIN 07001-0670 700
Proxy 521

Q

Questions on Written Examination for Discovery 202

R

Record of Service 118
Re-Direction of Funds 638
Reference Plan 580
Registered Plan of Subdivision, Land Titles System 579
Registered Plan of Subdivision, Registry System 578
Registration, Ontario Limited Liability Partnership 450
Registration, Sole Proprietorship/General Partnership 448
Release of Estate Trustee 788
Renunciation of Prior Right to a Certificate of Appointment of Estate Trustee without a Will 771
Renunciation of Right to a Certificate of Appointment of Estate Trustee (or Succeeding Estate Trustee) with a Will 748
Reply 166
Reporting Letter, Purchase 678
Reporting Letter, Sale 639
Requisition for Default Judgment 287
Requisition for Garnishment 298
Requisition for Writ of Seizure and Sale 296
Resolution of Directors (Fixing New Address, New Municipality) 538
Resolution of Directors (Fixing New Address, same Municipality) 536
Resolution of Directors re Allotment and Issue of Shares 493
Resolutions of Directors 490
Resolutions of Directors in Writing (Post-annual), Camelot 528
Resolutions of Directors (Pre-annual), Camelot 525
Resolutions of Shareholders 500
Resolutions of Shareholders (Annual), Camelot 526

Resolutions of Shareholders - Exemption from Audit 501
Retainer Letter or Agreement 35

S

Sample, Lawyer's Abstract 700
Schedule A, Statement of Director re Amalgamation 544
Semiblock Letter Style 64
Separation Agreement, Modern Style 313
Share Certificate Front, Robert Roberts 531
Share Certificate (Stephen Thomas Brown) 495
Share Certificate (Thomas David Brown) 494
Shareholder's Ledger 498, 499, 530
Shareholders' Register 497, 529
Sheriff's Certificate of Execution Clearance 661
Sheriff's Execution Certificate and Writ Details 660
Special Clauses for Charges/Mortgages 604
Special Resolution of Shareholders (Approving Amalgamation Agreement) 542
Special Resolution of Shareholders, Change of Corporate Name 539
Special Resolution of Shareholders (New Municipality) 537
Special Resolution of Shareholders - Number and Election of Directors 502
Standard Charge Terms, Excerpt, Electronic 605
Standard Format for Court Documents - Statement of Defence 111
Statement of Adjustments 633
Statement of Adjustments, Condominium 686
Statement of Claim (Action Commenced by Notice of Action) 152
Statement of Claim (for Money Only) 154
Statement of Claim (General) 145
Statement of Claim (General), Simplified Procedure 128
Statement of Defence 163
Statement of Defence and Counterclaim (Against Parties to Main Action Only) 173
Statement of Defence and Counterclaim (Against Plaintiff and Person Not Already Party to Main Action) 175
Statement of Defence and Crossclaim, (Excerpt) 182
Statement of Issues, Simplified Procedure 132
Statutory Declaration as to HST 664
Statutory Declaration as to Writs of Execution 636

Stock Transfer Register 530
Subscriptions for Shares 492
Summons (Provincial Offences) 97
Summons to Witness (at Hearing) 220
Support Deduction Order 334
Support Deduction Order Information Form 335
Survivorship Application-Land, Electronic 784

T

Tax Bill 631
Tax Certificate 659
Third Party Claim 184
Title Search Summary to PIN 07001-0670, Our Lands 708
Transfer by Personal Representative-Land, Electronic 785
Transfer, Electronic (Receipted Sample) 674
Transfer/Deed, Joint Tenant Transferees 592
Transfer/Deed, Sample Registration Stamp, Registry 592
Transfer of Charge, Electronic 618
Transfer: Power of Sale, Electronic 608
Transmission by Personal Representative-Land, Electronic 784
Trial Brief 229
Trial Management Checklist, Simplified Procedure 134
Trial Record 209
Trial Record, Certificate of Lawyer 211
Trial Record, Certificate of Lawyer re Mediation, Toronto Region 214
Trial Record, Notice of Name of Mediator & Date of Session 215

U

Undertaking and Affidavit as to Residency 662
Undertaking to Re-Adjust 671
Utility Letter, Water/Hydro/Gas - Without Title-Insurance 657

W

Warranties and Bill of Sale 663
Will 717, 738
Writ of Seizure and Sale 293

Index

Symbols

20/40/60 rule 120, 158
40-year rule 688, 689

A

Abbreviations 71
Abstract book 572, 689
Abstract index. *See* Abstract book
Acceptance of offer to settle 207
Accounts
  Bank 27
  Disbursements 28
  Electronically generated 32
  Fees 28
  General 27
  Harmonized sales tax (HST) 31
  Pre-billing reports 32
  Trust 27
  Trust statement 32
Acknowledgment 613
Acknowledgement and direction re electronic registration 628, 641, 651
Acknowledgment and direction regarding title insurance 641
Acknowledgment of charge 613
Acknowledgment of receipt card 106
Acknowledgment of tenancy 627
ACL 3
Actions 135
Active voice 41
Activity list 29
Address for service 598
Addressing government and judicial officials 60
Administration bond 735
Administrative officers 83
Administrator 775
Admission of service 107
Adultery 366
Adverse party 191
Adverse witness 239
Affidavit 101, 102
Affidavit as to writs of execution 628
Affidavit in opposition 238, 261
Affidavit in reply 238, 261
Affidavit in support of claim for custody or access 371, 374-376
Affidavit of documents 189-190
Affidavit of execution of will 712
Affidavit of execution of will or codicil 729
Affidavit of service 105, 376
  Acknowledgment of receipt card 106
  By courier 108
  By document exchange 108
  By e-mail 108

  By facsimile 108
  By mail 108
  Leaving a copy with an adult person 105
  Personal service 105
  Service refused 107
  Stamp 104
Affidavit of service of notice 730
Affidavit of service of notice (without a will) 759
Age Statements 598, 611
Agreement of purchase and sale 566, 622
Alphabetical filing system 18
  Applicable to all names 18
  Applicable to business names 18
  Applicable to educational institution names 19
  Applicable to Personal Names 18
Amalgamation 516
  Articles of 516
  Long-form 516
  Short-form 517
Amendment to pleadings 158
Amortized payments 594
Annual meetings 511
Answers on written examination for discovery 193
Appeal courts 82
Appeal routes 82
Applicant's application record and factum 235, 240
Application for certificate of appointment of estate trustee with a will (individual applicant) 729, 730, 733
Application for certificate of appointment of estate trustee without a will (individual applicant) 759, 760
Application for certificate of authorization 461
Application (general) 371
Application of rule 125
Application to change name - owner 586
Applications 235
  Factum 240, 241
  Judgment 241
  Long 236
  Notice of 237
  On notice 236
  Record 240, 241
  Short 236
  Steps in 235
  When used 236
  Who hears 236
  Without notice 236
Appointment 21
Article 459
Articles of amalgamation 516
  Long-form 516

  Short-form 517
Articles of amendment 516
Articles of incorporation 453, 461, 462
  Preparation of 462
Articling student 1, 2
Assessment of costs 228, 242
Assets of a corporation 454
Assignment of charge 609
Associate 1, 2
Assumed charge 594
Assumed charge/mortgage 594
Assumption statement 626
Attendance money 207
Attention line 57
Attitude 6
Automated Civil Litigation (ACL) 102
Automated Land Titles Absolute (LT Absolute) 688
Automated reminder systems 20

B

Backsheet 102, 143
Balance due on closing 626
Balance of probabilities 90
Bank accounts 27
  General 27
  Trust 27
Barristers and solicitors 56
Beneficiaries 710, 726, 775
Bequeath 710
Beyond a reasonable doubt 84
Bill of costs 227, 280, 281
  Preparation and distribution of 227, 281
Bill of sale 645
Bills of Exchange Act 68
Blind copy notations 58
Block letter 55
Block quotations 66
Board of directors 453, 683
Bond—insurance or guarantee company 762
Bond—personal sureties 762
Book debts 551
Borrowing 455, 457
Brief of authorities 224
Builder, acting for 623
Building Department 643
  Letter to 643
Business Corporations Act 452, 459
Business licensing 440
Business names 18, 441
Business Names Act 441
Business name registration 441
Business name search 441
By-laws 478
  1 and 2 478

C

Calculation period 599
Calendars 20
  Appointments 21
Canada Business Corporations Act 452, 460
Canadian Bar Association 3
Canadian citizenship card 300
Canadian statute citations 68
Capital 462
  Authorized 462
  Clause 462
Capitals 53
Case citations 70
Case conference 410
  Brief, general 410
Case management 124, 340
Central Registry of Divorce Proceedings 369
Certificate of appointment of estate trustee
       776
Certificate of appointment of estate trustee
       with a will 734, 736
Certificate of appointment of estate trustee
       without a will 761, 763
Certificate of authorization 461
Certificate of financial disclosure 343, 372
Certificate of incorporation 459, 466
Certificate of independent legal advice 302
Certificate of non-attendance 192
Certified copy of a corporate document 482
Chair 510
Change of name 301, 586
Chargee 593, 609
Charge/mortgage 593, 646, 780
  Assumed 594
  E-reg 596
  New 593
  Special clauses 599
  Taken back 594
Charges/mortgages, condominium 684
Chargor 593, 609
Chattel paper 549, 551
Chattels 549, 583
Cheque requisitions 28
Chief Justice 80
Child support guidelines 328
Children's Lawyer 138, 369
Citation 67-72
City of Toronto municipal land transfer tax
       (MLTT) 648
Civil law 83, 90
Civil litigation 119, 120
Civil litigation actions 135, 136
Civil Marriage Act 299
Claim for lien 553, 554, 555
Class actions 125
Class Proceedings Act 126
Clerk 90
Client identification and verification 17
Client list 17
Close of pleadings 120, 121, 157,160

Closing 621, 628, 651, 652, 653
Closing files 20
Closing submissions 88, 92
Codicil 714, 729, 730
Cohabitation agreement 304
Collateral 551
Collecting on the judgment 92
Commercial contracts 551
Commercial law 549
Commercial lease 551
Common elements 682
Common elements expenses fund 682
Common-law 304
Companies and Personal Property Security
       Branch 549
Comparison of net family property 411
Compensation 715
Complimentary closing 58
Concessions 573
Conditional sale contract. See Security
       agreement on non-inventory pur-
       chase money
Conditions and warranties 550
Condominium Act 682
Condominium corporation 682
  Board of directors 683
  By-laws 683
  Declaration 683
  Description 683
  Management companies 683
  Officers 683
Condominium plans 684
Condominium units 681
Conference notice 410
Confidentiality 5
Confidentiality agreement 5
Confirmation of motion 262
Conflict of interest 12, 510, 622
Consent 733
  to applicant's appointment as estate trustee
       with a will 735
  to applicant's appointment as estate trustee
       without a will 762
Consent to act as director 482
Consent to act as first director 465
Consent to act re conflict 642
Consent to exemption from audit 513
Consent to motion to change 348
Consideration 583
Constitution Act 79
Construction Lien Act 554
Constructive trust 319
Consumer goods 549
Contemplation of litigation 189
Contentious 736
Contingency fees 28, 126
Continuing power of attorney for property
       714
Continuing record 377
Contract law 550

Contractual relationships 550
Conveyancer software 628
Copy notations 58
Corporate bonds and shares 779
Corporate name 460, 643
Corporate searches 643, 689
Corporate Supplies 478
Corporations 139, 451, 452, 459
  Articles of incorporation 461
  Assets 454
  Borrowing 455, 457
  Certificate of incorporation 459, 466
  Directors 453
  Incorporating 459
  Income and taxation 456
  Jurisdiction of 452, 459
  Limited liability 451
  Losses 457
  Name 460, 461
  Net worth 455
  Non-offering 452
  Number name 460
  Offering 452
  Officers 453
  Proportion of ownership 454
  Shareholders 453
  Taxation 457
  Trade name 460
  Types of 452
Corporations Information Act 482, 514
Correspondence 55. See Legal Writing;
       Letters
Costs 225, 242
Costs outline 262
Counterclaims 169
Court documents 99. See Documents
Court fees 337
Court of Appeal for Ontario 83
Court offices 83
Court officers 83
Court system of Canada 79
Courtroom etiquette 88, 91
Courts of Justice Act 53, 80, 142, 160
Criminal and civil law 83
Criminal Code 84, 86, 87
Criminal law 84
Crossclaim 171
  Defence to 171
  Reply to defence to 171
Cross-examination 88, 92, 239
Crown 563, 566
Crown prosecutor 85
Cruelty 366
Custody 367
  Joint 368
  Shared 368
  Sole 368
  Split 368

D

Damages 135
  General, liquidated, unliquidated, special
    141
Date line 56
De bonis non administratis 763
Death certificate 736
Debtor 552
  a business 556
  an individual 556
Debts 325
Declaration of possession 645
Declaration of transmission 779
Deed. *See* Transfer/deed
Default judgment 279
  In liquidated damages 280
  In unliquidated damages 281
  Preparation and distribution of 281
  Preparation and distribution of requisition
    for 280
Defence to counterclaim 170
Deponent 102
Deregistration 694
Developer 683
Devise 710
Devisee 710
Devisees 775
Direction and acknowledgment 653
Direction regarding funds 621, 628
Direction regarding title 645
Direction to enforce writ of seizure and sale
    284
Directors 453
Directors' meeting 480
Directors' register 481, 510
Disability 138
  Defendant under 138
  Individuals not under 138
  Individuals under 138
  Plaintiff under 138
Disbursements 28, 226
Discharge of charge 609
Discharge of charge/mortgage 612
Discharge statement 609, 626
Discontinuance 282
Discoveries 187
  Methods of 187
Discovery of documents 188
Discovery plan 187
  Form of 188
Dispensing with service 109
Distinctive name first 19
Divisional Court 82
Division of estate 710
Divorce 365
  Access 369
  Affidavit for 414
  Certificate of 413
  Collusion 367
  Contested 409

Final terms 413
Grounds for 366
Joint 368
Order 413
Physical or mental cruelty 366
Registry of 369
Separation 366
Simple/sole 414
Divorce Act (Canada) 366
DIVORCEmate 3, 345
Dockets 29, 30, 31, 582
Docket ID number 582
Document registration agreement 628, 645
Documentary evidence 236
Documents 99. *See* also Court Documents
  Delivery of 103
  Issuing 103
  Serving 103
  Preparation of 99
Domestic contracts 299, 301
  Preliminary considerations in preparing
    302
  Validity of 302
Dominion Law Reports 73
Donoghue v Stevenson 90
Duty counsel panel 33

E

Easements 565
E-discovery 188
Educational institution names 19
Effective date of service 105-109
Election to change surname form 301
Electronic document exchange 109
Electronic document identification
    footers 16
Electronic files 15
Electronic transfer 581
Electronically generated accounts 32
Email 12
Enclosure notations 58
Encroachments 565
Enforcement of orders 279
English law report series 75
English statutes 70
Envelopes 59
Equal and undivided ownership 564
Equalization of net family property 323
Equalization payment 324, 327, 412, 726
E-reg closing 652
Escheats 563, 689, 690
Essential requirements 299
Estate Administration Tax Act 732
Estate information return 736, 763
Estates Administration Act 775
Estates Office of the Superior Court of
    Justice 763
Estate taxes 730, 731, 763
Estate trustee 140, 709, 710, 759

Estate trustee without a will 761
Examination for discovery 187, 191, 193
Examination of witness 235, 239, 261
Examinations in aid of execution 285
Execution of will 711
Executions search 627, 644, 684, 687, 689,
    690, 696
Executor 709, 710, 775
Executrix 709
Exemption from land transfer tax 651
Exhibit 730
Existing owners 598
Expert witnesses 206

F

Factum 240, 262
  Form 240
Family Court 81, 337, 338, 366
  Clerk 338
Family Court of the Superior Court of
    Justice 81, 337
Family law 319-320, 341
  Motion 346
Family Law Rules 53, 337
Family Responsibility and Support Arrears
    Enforcement Act 331
Family Responsibility Office 331
  Federal Child Support Guidelines 328,
    330
  Simplified Tables for Ontario 328
Federal statutes 68
Fee simple estate 563, 564
Fees 28
  Contingency 28
  Hourly 28, 29, 33, 226, 227
  Law clerk and paralegals 28, 226
Files
  Client number 14
  Closing 20
  Electronic 15
  Electronic document identification
    footers 16
  Filing system 18
  Labels 15
  Matter numbers 14
  Opening 14
  Paper 15
Financial statement brief 346
Financial statement (property and support
    claims) 343, 344, 372
Financial statement (support claims) 343,
    344
Financing change statement 553, 555
Financing statement 553, 554
Fire insurance 626, 647
First appeals 83
First instance 83
Foreclosure 601, 602
Form 8A: application (divorce) 414

Form 10 answer 409
Form 10A reply 410
Form 14C confirmation (divorce) 410
Formal meetings 509
Formal requirements 300
Franchises 443
Free consent 300
Freehold estate 563
Fuel oil 625
Full and final release 260
Full block letter 55
Funeral expenses 710

G

Garnishments 285
    Notice of 285
General and special damages 141
General security agreement 551
Getting started 7
Government of Canada savings bonds 779
Government-related exemptions 693
Grammar 41
Grandfather clause 691
Grantor 714
Grounds for privilege 189
Guarantee 762
Guaranteed investment certificates
        (GICs) 779
Guarantors 600

H

Hearing 241
Heir 775
Heirs 725
Holograph will 713
Hourly rates 226, 227
HST 31, 624, 647
Hybrid offences 85

I

In contemplation of litigation 189
Incorporation 459-467
Incorporators 465
Indictable offences 84, 85, 86
    Steps to trial 88
Information for court use 143
Informing client 653
Inheritance 564, 725
Initial organization 477, 478, 479
Initial return 482
Inside address 56
Intangibles 551
Interest adjustment date 600
Interest 141, 142, 594, 595, 596
Interest rate 595, 599
Interim bill 625

Interoffice memorandums 65
Intestate 725, 759
Intestate estates 775

J

Joint tenants 564, 565
    Inheritance 564
    Sale 565
Jointly-held assets 727
Joint ventures 443
Judgment 135, 224, 241, 280, 281
    Issuing and entering 224
    Preparation and distribution of 224
    Reasons for 224
Judicial sale 602
Jurat 102
Jurisdiction 452, 459
Jury 81, 82, 85, 90, 160
Jury notice 160

K

KYC (know your client) 17

L

Land registration systems 571
Land registry office 572, 688, 689
Land Titles Conversion Qualified (LTCQ)
        688, 690
Land Titles Plus (LT Plus) 688
Land titles system 572, 688
Land transfer tax 647, 648
Land transfer tax statements 587, 648
Last name first 18
Last payment date 600
Law associations 3
Law clerks 3
    Practice and procedure 5
    Skills 3, 5
Law reports 70, 73, 75
Law Societies 3, 4
Lawyer of record 103, 107
Lawyers 1, 2
    Barristers and solicitors 2
    Criminal lawyers 84
    Education 1
    Lawyer of record 103
    Litigation lawyers 2
Lawyer's certificate (opinion) on title 653,
        687
Lawyer's expense sheet 28
Lawyers' Professional Indemnity Company
        (LPIC) 654
Leasehold condominium 681
Leasehold estate 564
Ledger statements 32
Legacy 710, 775

Legal accounts department 33
Legal administrative assistants. See legal
        assistants
Legal Aid Ontario 32
Legal assistants 3
    Practice and procedure 5
    Professionality 5
    Skills 3
Legal capitalization 53
Legal correspondence 43, 55
Legal description of land 573
Legal memorandum 65
Legal writing 41
    Active voice 41
    Basic principles of 41
    Grammar 41
    Misplaced modifiers 41
    Three-part structure 43
Legatees 775
Letter endings 57
Letter of requisitions 645
Letter regarding title 642
Letter to court enclosing application for
        certificate of appointment docu-
        ments 736
Letters 55
    Parts of legal letters 56
Licensed paralegals. See Paralegals
Lien 554
    Claim for 554, 555
    Non-possessory 554
    Possessory 554
Life estate 564
Limitation period 86, 137, 321, 369
Limited liability 1, 451, 455, 457
Limited Partnerships Act 438
Liquidated 279
Liquidated damages 141, 280
List of assets and liabilities 303
Litigation 119, 120, 135, 136
Litigation administrator 140
Litigation guardian 138
Litigation privilege. See Contemplation of
        litigation
Local registrar 83
Long-form amalgamation 516
LT Absolute 688

M

Majority interest 735
Mandatory Information Program 339
Mandatory mediation 122, 124, 204
    Failure to select a mediator 124
    How 124
Manner of title 623
Manual closing 653
Marriage 299
    Age 300
    Annulment of 301

Ceremony 300
Certificate 301, 370
Close relationships 299
Contract 302
Education and moral training of children 303
Essential requirements 299
Exceptions 303
Formal requirements 300
Marriage licence 300
Mental capacity 299
Property 303
Right of possession 303
Sexual capacity 300
Support obligations 303
Unmarried status 299
Marriage certificate 301, 370
Master business licence (MBL) 442
Matrimonial home 322, 584
Right of possession 322
Matures/Maturity 594
McEarlean v Sarel and the City of Brampton 83
Mediation 122, 124, 736, 763
Mediation co-ordinator 124
Medical authorization 136
Medical examination 193
Meeting of directors 512
Meeting of shareholders 512
Memo of law 65
Metes 574
Mineral rights 566
Minister of Finance 735, 736, 763
Minute book 478, 481
Minutes of meeting 509, 512
Motion hearing 263
Motion on consent 259
Motions 257, 258
Confirmation of 262
Costs 262
Hearing 263
In writing 259
Long 259
Notice of 260
On notice 258
Record 261
Short 259
Steps in 257
Without notice 258
Moving Party 258
Multi-unit commercial complex 681
Multi-unit residential complex 681

N

Name search 461
Natural watercourse 566
Nervousness 45
Net family property 321-327
Calculation formula 324, 326
Net family property (NFP) 324, 726

Net family property statement 344, 412
Net worth 455
Neutral citations 67, 72
New housing 624
Next of kin 725, 775
Nominal consideration 651
Non-Converts 688
Notarial certificate 776
Notarial copy 482, 776
Notice of action 135, 143
Notice of an application for a certificate of appointment of estate trustee without a will 760
Notice of annual meeting (of shareholders) 511
Notice of appearance 238
Notice of Application and Supporting Affidavit 235
Notice of discontinuance 282
Notice of election to proceed with counterclaim 282
Notice of examination 192
Notice of garnishment 285
Notice of intent to defend 159
Notice of meeting of directors 510
Notice of motion 260, 346
Preparation and distribution of 260
Notice of name of mediator and date of session 122, 204
Notice of readiness for pre-trial conference 122
Notice of transfer of charge 613
Notice to alleged partner 139
Notice to creditors 776
Noting pleadings closed 160
NUANS 461
Number name 460

O

OBCA. *See* Ontario Business Corporations Act
Objection to accounts 781
Occupancy agreement 683
Occupancy fee 684
Offer 566
Offer to settle 207
Defendant's offer 207
Plaintiff's offer 207
Office of the Children's Lawyer 369
Officers 453, 683
Officers' register 480
Online appointments 21
Ontario Business Corporations Act 459, 509
Ontario Business Corporations Act (OBCA) 459
Ontario Child Support Guidelines Regulation Tables 328
Ontario Children's Law Reform Act (CLRA) 338, 339, 367, 371
Ontario Court of Justice 80, 81, 340

Ontario Family Law Act (FLA) 320, 367, 726
Ontario land surveyor (OLS) 643
Ontario land transfer tax rate 647
Ontario Rules of Civil Procedure 119
Ontario Succession Law Reform Act 725
Oral examinations 191
Oral examinations for discovery 122
Oral presentations. *See* Presentations
Order 263, 413
In motions in writing 263
In opposed motions 263
Preparation and distribution of 263
Ordinary procedure 120
Ordinary service 107
Originating process 103, 136, 258

P

Paper files 15
Paper mail 12
Paralegals 3
Authorized Practice 7
Licensed 6, 439, 461
Representation 87
Rules of Conduct 7
Scope of practice 7, 87
Parallel construction 42
Parcel register 572
Partial indemnity 225
Partition 565
Partnership 437
Dissolution of 443
General 437
Liability 439
Limited 438
Limited liability 438
Name 441
Partnership agreement 442
Partnership declaration 438
Partnerships 139, 437
Partnerships Act 437
Par value 464
Passing of accounts 780
Paternity agreement 306
Paternity tests 327
Per 58
Per capita 710
Per diem 624
Perpetual existence 457
Perpetual period 554
Personal Names 18
Personal property 549, 552, 563, 730
Documents 549
Intangible 549
Tangible 549
Personal Property Security Act (PPSA) 549, 643
Personal property security registration (PPSR) 552
Personal representative 140

Personal service 105
Per stirpes 710
Pinpoint references 73
Placing action on trial list 205
Planning Act statements 587, 646, 689, 691, 692, 693
Plans of subdivision 573, 689, 690, 691
Plea bargaining 88
Pleadings 120, 158, 169
Positive form 42
Possession 601
Possessory title 571
Postjudgment interest 142
Postponement of interest 613
Postscript 58
Power of attorney 714, 715
Power of attorney for personal care 715
Power of attorney for property 714
Power of attorney to transfer bonds-shares 779
Power of sale 601
PPSA searches 552, 556, 643
Practice directions 125, 237, 259
Pre-annual meetings 512
Pre-billing report 32
Precedents 7
Prejudgment interest 141, 142, 280, 281
Prejudice
    without 56, 189, 190
Preliminary inquiry 89
Presentations 45
    Deductive reasoning 45
    Extemporaneous 46
    Impromptu 46
    Inductive reasoning 45
    Informative 45
    Manuscript 46
    Memorized 46
    Nervousness 45
    Persuasive 45
    Types of 45
Presumption of paternity 327
Pre-trial 120, 203
    Conference 121, 122, 205
    Conference brief 205
Primary will 713
Principal 593-596, 599
Principal plus interest payments 595
Principal sum 280
Private Service Providers (PSPs) 553
Probate 729
Pro bono 29
Professional corporation 461, 462
Proof of death 730, 733, 736, 760, 763, 776
Proof of service 103, 104-109
Property Identifier Number (PIN) 572, 688
Property index map 572, 689
Property tax 681
Property tax bill 625
Provincial and territorial courts 79, 80, 85, 87

Provincial offences 81, 85-88
    Prosecution of 85
Provincial offence notices 85, 86, 88
Provincial Offences Act 85, 86, 87
Provincial statutes 82, 85
Proxy 512
Public Guardian and Trustee 138, 715
Public record 441
Punctuation 43, 48, 52
    Apostrophe 51
    Colon 51
    Comma 48-50
    Ellipsis 66
    Mixed 55
    Open 55
    Quotation marks 52
    Round brackets 69, 71, 73, 75
    Semicolon 51
    Square brackets 67, 71
Purchase and sale transaction 593, 596, 598
Purchase transaction 641, 642, 653

Q

Questions on written examination for discovery 187, 193
Quorum 510, 512
Quotations 52, 65
    Long 66
    Short 66

R

R v Dudley and Stephens 83
Reader-centred 42
Reader-centred statements 42
Reading case citations 71
Ready for delivery 550
Real estate 563, 729-733, 775-777
Real property 563
    Fee simple 563
    Freehold estate 563
Receipted copy 609, 653
Record. See Trial record
Re-direction of funds 621, 628, 629
Reference initials 58
Reference plan 573, 574, 689, 690, 692
Registered plan of subdivision. See Plans of subdivision
Registrar 83
Registration, business name 441
Registration of divorce proceeding form 369, 370
Registration, Ontario Limited Liability Partnership 442
Registration, Sole Proprietorship/Partnership 442
Registry system 571-573, 588, 601, 687, 688
Release of estate trustee 780
Reminder systems 20, 21

Removable storage device 581, 582
Rent 626, 627
Renunciation 733, 734, 736, 761-763
Renunciation of prior right to a certificate of appointment of estate trustee without a will 761
Repair and Storage Liens Act 549, 552, 554
Repair and Storage Liens Act (RSLA) 549
Reply 157, 160, 409, 410
Reply to requisitions 627
Reporting letter 483, 629, 653, 684
Representative defendant 125
Representative plaintiff 125
Request to renew 284
Requisition for default judgment 280, 281
Requisition for garnishment 285
Requisition for writ of seizure and sale 284
Resale housing 624
Reserve fund 682
Reserve fund plan 682
Reserve fund study 682
Resolutions 478, 479, 480, 482
    In writing 480
    Methods of passing 479
    Ordinary 514
    Special 482, 511, 513, 516, 517
Resolutions of directors 479, 480
Resolutions of shareholders 479
Responding Party 257, 258, 261
Response to motion to change 348
Restrictive consents 694
Retainer 29
Revocation 715
Revoke 711, 715
Rhetoric 43
Right of possession 564, 584
Right of survivorship 563, 564
Rights of way 565
Root of title 688
Round brackets 69, 71, 73, 75
Rules of Civil Procedure 119, 121, 124, 125, 279, 282, 283, 285
Rules of Professional Conduct 3, 4, 12, 20, 653

S

Safeguards 84
Safekeeping 712
Sale price 624, 625
Sale transaction 621, 622, 623
Salutation 57
Schedule A, statement of director 517
Seal 478
Search, executions 627, 644, 653
Search of title. See Title searching
Second appeals 83
Secondary will 713
Secretary 509, 510
Security 551, 552-556, 593
Security agreement 551, 552, 554, 555

Security agreement on non-inventory pur-
  chase money 552
Semiblock letter 55
Separate property 320
Separation agreement 304, 305
Sequence of registration 652
Service
  Acceptance of service 106
  Acknowledgment of receipt card 106
  Admission of service 107
  Alternative to personal service 105
  By courier 108
  By e-mail 108
  By facsimile 108
  By leaving a copy 105
  By mail 108
  Document exchange 108
  Electronic document exchange 109
  Originating process 103, 104, 105, 106,
      107, 109
  Personal 105, 106, 109
  Proof of 103-110
  Refused 109, 117
  Substituted service 109
ServiceOntario 301, 442, 461, 465
Setting down for trial 203, 204
Settlement conference 92, 411, 412
  Brief, general 411
Sexual capacity 300
Share capital 452, 454
Stated capital 454
Share Certificate 478, 480, 481, 514
  Transferring 481
Shared custody 368
Shareholders 451, 453
Shareholder's ledger 481, 514
Shareholders' meetings 511, 512
Shareholders' register 481, 514
Shares 455, 462, 463
  Class A 463
  Class B 463
  Common 463
  Preference 463
  Value of 455
Sheriff's certificate of executions 644
Short-form amalgamation 517
Short quotations 66
Signature block 58
Silent partner 438
Simplified procedure 121,123
Simplified Tables 328, 329
Simultaneous conveyances 694
Small Claims Court 80, 90
  Defence, Form 9A 91
  Plaintiff's claim, Form 7A 91
  Steps to trial 90-92
Sole proprietorship 140, 437, 439
  Liability 440
Speakers' list 509
Special meetings 511
Special resolutions 482, 513

Split custody 368
Square brackets 71
Squatter's rights 571
Standard charge terms 600
Standard condominium 681
Stated capital 454
Statement of adjustments 624
  Preparation of 624
Statement of adjustments, condominium
      684
Statement of claim 119,121,140,141,142
Statement of claim—foreclosure form 601
Statement of defence 121, 159, 169
  And crossclaim 171
  To counterclaim 170
Statement of Defence 100, 121, 159
Statement of issues 122
Status certificate 684
Statutes 68, 70
Statutory declaration 628, 645
Stock transfer register 481, 514
Student-at-law 226, 227
Student, articling 1
Subdivide 573
Subdivision control 694
Subject line 57
Subordinates 6
Subscriptions for shares 480
Substantial indemnity 207, 225
Substantive law 3
Substitute Decisions Act 714
Substituted service 109
Succession Law Reform Act 725, 775
Succession Law Reform Act (SLRA) 725
Summary conviction offences 84, 85
  Steps to trial 87
Summary judgment 282
Summary of line of inheritance 725, 775
Summary trial 124
Summons to witness 239
Summons to witness (at hearing) 206
  Attendance money 207
Superior Court of Justice 80
Supplemental trial record 205
Support deduction order 331
  Information form 331
Support, arranging online 330
Supporting affidavit 238, 261
Supporting affidavit, Form 14A 347
Supreme Court of Canada 80
Sureties 762
Survey 643
Surviving joint tenant 777
Survivorship 726
Survivorship application-land 777

T

Tarion Program 623
Task manager 20
Taxation 456, 457

Tax certificate 643
Tax Department 643
  Letter to 643
Tax formula 732
Template docket 31
Temporary order 346, 347
Ten-acre rule 691
Tenants 563, 564, 684
Tenants in common 565
Teraview 3, 582
Teraview Training System 581
Testate 726, 729
Testate estates 775
Testator 709
Testator's domicile 710
Testatrix 709
The 20/40/60 rule 120, 158, 171
Third party claims 169
  File number 172
Third party defence 172
Ticklers 20
Time for service 103
Timer 31
Title 564, 565, 581, 623, 642, 645
Title insurance 653, 689, 690
Title of proceeding 99, 100, 137
TitlePLUS insurance 654
Title searching 642, 687
  40-year rule 688
  Abstract book 689
  Land titles system 689
  Planning Act 691
  Registry system 688
  Using Teraview 694
Torrens system 572
Torts 90
Total consideration 650
Township 573
Tracks 340
Trade name 460
Transcripts 192, 239
Transfer 581
Transfer by personal representative 777
Transfer/deed 622
Transfer of charge 610
Transferee 581, 586, 613
Transferor 581, 613
Transmission by personal representative-land
      777
Trial 87, 88, 90, 92, 223, 224
Trial brief 223
Trial courts 80
Trial management checklist 123
Trial management conference 412
Trial record 123, 204, 413
  Assembly of 205
  Certificate of lawyer 204
  Notice of name of mediator and date of
      session 204
  Preparation and distribution of 204
Trial stage 223

Trustee 709, 775
Trusts 710

U

UFFI/bill of sale 628
Unanimous approval resolutions 513
Undertaking and affidavit as to
    residency 645
Undertaking to re-adjust 647
Undivided interest 565
Unit 681
Unity of legal personality 320
Unliquidated 279, 281
Unliquidated damages 141, 281
Unrestrictive consents 691, 694
Utilities 643, 682
    Letter to 643

V

Vacant 573
Vacant land condominiums 681
Valuation date 321, 412
Vehicle identification number (VIN) 554,
    556

Vendor-take-back charge/mortgage (VTB)
    594
Verifying estate accounts 781
Voice mail 12
Voting rights 511, 512

W

Warranties 550
Warranties and bill of sale 645
Water account 626
Water rights 566
Will 709, 713, 729
    Preparation of 712
Without prejudice 56, 189
Witnesses 206, 711
Workmanship warranties 623
Writ of execution 644, 645
Writ of seizure and sale 283, 602, 644
    Direction to enforce 284
    Preparation and distribution of 284
    Requisition for 284
Writ searching 696
Writing. *See* Legal Writing

Y

Youth Criminal Justice Act 81, 82

Z

Zoning authorities 441
Zoning by-laws 643, 654